CONSTITUTIONAL DEMOCRACY IN CRISIS?

Praise for
Constitutional Democracy in Crisis?

"Constitutional democracies around the world are suffering assaults from within. Globally, political freedoms are becoming weaker. Democracy does not necessarily guarantee prosperity. This book provides a superb appraisal of democracy's current crisis. Those who wish to learn about what is happening to constitutional democracies around the world should read this groundbreaking, multiperspective, and transdisciplinary book."

SABINO CASSESE, Emeritus Justice, Italian Constitutional Court;
Emeritus Professor, University of Rome

"To question the current health of constitutional democracy is implicitly to affirm that there are more chapters to be written before we arrive at the end of history. Fortunately, we now have the exquisitely crafted chapters in this unique collection of essays to help us make sense of our current predicament. Written against the backdrop of a multitude of ominous developments that have shaken confidence in the stability and endurance of liberal democratic institutions, the contributors to this timely volume explore this portentous moment from all angles, leaving the reader richly informed, if not sanguine, about future prospects. A careful reading of *Constitutional Democracy in Crisis?* will, however, not end in despair, for as the most disturbing threats to political freedom and economic justice emanate from within, the challenge that they represent can also be met from within. Addressing it wisely will profit from the innumerable insights in this book."

GARY JEFFREY JACOBSOHN, H. Malcolm Macdonald Professor of Constitutional and
Comparative Law, The University of Texas at Austin

"This book is an indispensable resource for understanding the rise of illiberal populisms and the possibilities for sustaining constitutionalism and democracy. Contributors include leading global scholars of comparative constitutional law, whose chapters provide a diverse empirical base from countries around the world with which to evaluate constitutional democracy and its contemporary challenges and competitors. Theories are tested, data provided, and new concepts advanced—addressing, among other topics, the role of political parties, political leaders, religion, economic inequality, race, ethnicity, and immigration—in a set of readable and relatively short chapters that, as much as any edited scholarly collection could be, is a true 'page-turner,' hard to stop reading once one starts."

VICKI C. JACKSON, Thurgood Marshall Professor of Constitutional Law,
Harvard Law School

"This rigorous, wide-ranging, and engaging volume is an indispensable guide to the current crisis of constitutional democracy. The volume's theoretical essays raise profound new questions about the relationship between constitutionalism and democracy. Its high quality empirical chapters help us understand the global reach and historical roots of the current crisis. This is a landmark book for our troubled times."

PRATAP B. MEHTA, Vice-Chancellor, Ashoka University;
past President, Centre for Policy Research

"At the end of the 20th century, constitutional democracy had gained almost universal acceptance. At least, so it seemed. A decade later, we see constitutional democracy declining or mutating into more authoritarian forms of government in a number of countries. In this timely book, more than forty outstanding authors from many parts of the world offer a comprehensive analysis of this development and its causes, which should be of paramount interest not only to scholars and students of law and politics, but to everyone concerned about public affairs."

DIETER GRIMM, former Justice, Federal Constitutional Court of Germany;
Professor of Law, Humboldt University Berlin

"Many are convinced that liberal constitutional democracy is in the midst of a severe crisis, and is being replaced by illiberal constitutional democracy. This important book analyses the reasons for this development, both at the global level and at the national level. It presents original and illuminating answers to the question, 'Why is this shift occurring?' This scholarly foundation is necessary for finding answers to the question of how this trend can be reversed. The time is right for this book to be published by its first-class authors, and it provides the intellectual foundations necessary for each of us to cope with the changes that are occurring in our own constitutional democracies, and to try to turn the tide. For me, as a retired judge, the book provides food for thought about where we went wrong, and what we can do to take us in a new direction."

AHARON BARAK, former President of the Supreme Court of Israel;
Professor of Law, IDC Herzliya

Constitutional Democracy in Crisis?

Edited by
Mark A. Graber
Sanford Levinson
Mark Tushnet

OXFORD
UNIVERSITY PRESS

OXFORD
UNIVERSITY PRESS

Oxford University Press is a department of the University of Oxford. It furthers the University's objective of excellence in research, scholarship, and education by publishing worldwide. Oxford is a registered trademark of Oxford University Press in the UK and certain other countries.

Published in the United States of America by Oxford University Press
198 Madison Avenue, New York, NY 10016, United States of America.

Library of Congress Cataloging-in-Publication Data
Names: Graber, Mark A., editor. | Levinson, Sanford, 1941– editor. | Tushnet, Mark V.,
    1945– editor.
Title: Constitutional democracy in crisis? / edited by Mark A. Graber,
    Sanford Levinson, Mark Tushnet.
Description: New York, NY : Oxford University Press, 2018. | Includes index. |
    Includes bibliographical references.
Identifiers: LCCN 2018012359 | ISBN 9780190888985 (hardback : alk. paper) |
    ISBN 9780190919719 (pbk. : alk. paper).
Subjects: LCSH: Comparative government. | Democracy. | Constitutional history.
Classification: LCC JF51 .C626 2018 | DDC 321.8—dc23
LC record available at https://lccn.loc.gov/2018012359

9 8 7 6 5 4 3 2 1

Paperback printed by WebCom, Inc., Canada
Hardback printed by Bridgeport National Bindery, Inc., United States of America

To those around the world resisting the slide away from constitutional democracy

Contents

1   Constitutional Democracy in Crisis?

Introduction

Mark A. Graber, Sanford Levinson, and Mark Tushnet

CONSTITUTIONAL DEMOCRACIES AND constitutional democracy appear in trouble throughout the world. The United States, Israel, Turkey, South Africa, Hungary, Poland, and Venezuela seem particular problem children, but the Catalonian secession in Spain, Brexit in the United Kingdom, the rise of authoritarian constitutionalism in South Asia, the overthrow of the Morsi government in Egypt, and the continued weakness of constitutional democracy throughout Africa and Latin American suggest that no earthly haven is immune to whatever is ailing regimes that purport to be constitutional and democratic. As this volume was being completed, new challenges to constitutional democracy emerged in Italy and Brazil, with right-wing populist forces gaining strength in Germany and in the Netherlands. Scholars speak of "Democracy in Retreat,"[1] a "democratic recession,"[2] "democratic backsliding,"[3] "democratic deconsolidation,"[4] "constitutional retrogression,"[5] "constitutional failure,"[6]

---

[1] Joshua Kurlantzick, *Democracy in Retreat: The Revolt of the Middle Class and the Worldwide Decline of Representative Government* (New Haven: Yale University Press, 2014).

[2] Larry Diamond, "Facing Up to the Democratic Recession," *Journal of Democracy* 26 (2015): 141.

[3] Nancy Bermeo, "On Democratic Backsliding," *Journal of Democracy* 27 (2016): 5–19.

[4] Roberto Stefan Foa and Yascha Mounk, "The Signs of Deconsolidation," *Journal of Democracy* 28 (2017): 5.

[5] Aziz Z. Huq and Tom Ginsburg, "How to Lose a Constitutional Democracy," *UCLA Law Review* 65 (2018): 78, 83.

[6] Sotirios A. Barber, *Constitutional Failure* (Lawrence: University Press of Kansas, 2014). See also Ellen Kennedy, *Constitutional Failure: Carl Schmitt in Weimar* (Durham, NC: Duke University Press, 2004).

and "constitutional rot."[7] "Liberal democracy," Aziz Huq and Tom Ginsburg write, "is today subject to a plural array of corroding crosscurrents arising both from specific partisan formations and actors, and from cultural, socioeconomic or geopolitical dynamics of a structural nature."[8]

This global concern with the health of constitutional democracy has many causes. During the second decade of the twenty-first century, the global momentum toward constitutional democracy stalled and perhaps has begun to reverse. Across the universe of constitutional democracies, such conventional foundations of constitutional democracy as a strong middle class are weakening. Many past models of post-transition constitutional democracies, most notably Hungary and South Africa, are experiencing severe constitutional problems, with no new models of constitutional democracy emerging. Globalization, the Great Recession, terrorism, and other global phenomena create common afflictions for constitutional democracies around the world. Constitutional democracy has more difficult tasks than at any time in history and the cost of mistakes is higher, potentially catastrophic. For the first time since the Great Depression, when proto-fascist movements gained some traction, if not the Civil War, constitutional democracy in the United States appears to be weakening.

(1) TRENDS TOWARD CONSTITUTIONAL DEMOCRACY HAVE STALLED AND MAY BE REVERSING. Throughout most of the twentieth and early twenty-first centuries, the world witnessed an increase in the number of constitutional democracies and an increase in the percentage of regimes committed to some version of constitutional democracy. No such increase took place in the last decade or is on the horizon. Diminishing returns might explain a global slowdown. Fewer and fewer regimes are available for conversion to constitutional democracy, and the barriers to constitutional democracy in those regimes are particularly strong. Nevertheless, as both the Tom Ginsburg and Aziz Huq essay and the Zachary Elkins essay detail, even as the absolute number of constitutional democracies remains fairly constant, basic democratic and constitutional practices in many established and new constitutional democracies are weakening, and they are weakening at much faster rates than they strengthened in previous years.[9] This backsliding is a new trend. The end-of-ideology era appears to have ended. Constitutional democracy no longer seems the only game in town. David Law and Chien-Chin Lin point out that bureaucratic authoritarianism is gaining traction, particularly in East Asia, where crucial publics prefer autocrats who produce economic growth to a more chaotic democratic order.[10]

---

[7] Jack M. Balkin, "Constitutional Crisis and Constitutional Rot," *Constitutional Democracy in Crisis?*, in ed. Mark A. Graber, Sanford Levinson, and Mark Tushnet (Oxford University Press: New York, 2018).

[8] Huq and Ginsburg, "How to Lose a Constitutional Democracy," 82.

[9] Tom Ginsburg and Aziz Z. Huq, "Defining and Tracking the Trajectory of Liberal Constitutional Democracy," in *Constitutional Democracy in Crisis?*; Zachary Elkins, "Is the Sky Falling? Constitutional Crises in Historical Perspective," in *Constitutional Democracy in Crisis?*.

[10] See David Law and Chien-Chih Lin, "Constitutional Inertia in Asia," in *Constitutional Democracy in Crisis?*

(2) THE CONVENTIONAL FOUNDATIONS OF CONSTITUTIONAL DEMOC-
RACY ARE WEAKENING. Robert Dahl suggested that democratic orders are most
likely to thrive in a modern, pluralistic, dynamic society. In constitutional democracies
from Poland to Japan to the United States to South Africa, each element of the cultural
order underlying constitutional democracy seems under stress. Sectarian movements in
the global north and global south have challenged the scientific outlook associated with
modernity and liberalism. Right-wing populist movements insisting that national identity be based in ascriptive characteristics, such as race, ethnicity, and religion, are on the
rise across the globe as regimes respond to international immigration and refugee crises.
Globalism has produced unparalleled wealth for the investor class, while leaving many
persons in both established democracies and poorer nations with increasingly limited
chances of improving their circumstances. Surveys find that the young persons likely to
form the leadership class in many constitutional democracies have less and less allegiance
to constitutional democracy or the foundations of constitutional democracy.[11]

(3) SEVERAL REGIMES HELD UP AS ROLE MODELS OF NEW TRANSFORMA-
TIVE CONSTITUTIONAL DEMOCRACIES IN THE RECENT PAST ARE NOW
FACING SEVERE TENSIONS, WHILE NO NEW MODEL CONSTITUTIONAL
REGIME HAS EMERGED DURING THE PAST TEN YEARS. While the trend
toward constitutional democracy in all regimes is rarely consistently upward, as all constitutional democracies experience cycles of surges and backsliding, for most of post-
World War II history, success stories outpaced or at least kept pace with apparent failures
to launch. Some constitutional regimes collapsed in the 1990s, but Hungary and South
Africa served as models of transformative constitutional democracies that many hoped
would inspire existing and new regimes. At present, by contrast, the constitutional universe consists of constitutional democracies that are failing, constitutional democracies
that are backsliding, and constitutional democracies that are holding their own (or not
backsliding significantly). No prominent regime has emerged in the second decade of
the twenty-first century whose commitment to constitutional democracy is strengthening.[12] No polity is developing a new and exciting model of constitutional democracy that
future regimes might emulate.

(4) THREATS TO CONSTITUTIONAL DEMOCRACY ARE INCREASINGLY GLOBAL
RATHER THAN DISTINCTIVE TO PARTICULAR REGIMES. Constitutional democracies for the past hundred years have faced global challenges, threats that simultaneously
impact many if not all constitutional democracies. The Great Depression weakened
numerous constitutional democracies and played an important role in the downfall of

---

[11] Foa and Mounk, "Signs of Deconsolidation."

[12] Elkins points out that constitutional democracy has been gaining traction over the last decade in several
nations that have largely gone under the radar, most notably Georgia and Tunisia. Elkins, "Is the Sky Falling?."

the Weimar Republic. Hitler ended democratic regimes in Norway, Denmark, France, Belgium, and the Netherlands. Still, the American Civil War and the fall of the Fourth French Republic may be more typical instances of constitutional democracies in the nineteenth or mid-twentieth century threatening to fail or failing for largely internal reasons. Global threats to constitutional democracy now seem the norm. The Great Recession posed challenges to more constitutional democracies than the Great Depression, in part because more constitutional democracies existed at the turn of the twenty-first century than during the 1930s, but also because more regimes depend on the health of the global economic order in the present than was the case several generations ago. The contemporary constitutional universe now influences and is influenced by numerous international governmental and nongovernmental organizations. All countries are faced with the threat of terrorism and most with the threat of environmental catastrophe. The internet and other new modes of communication allow coordinated action both from those who would buttress and those who would destroy constitutional democracies around the globe.

(5) CONSTITUTIONAL DEMOCRACIES MUST PERFORM MORE TASKS THAN EVER BEFORE, WITH HIGHER, POTENTIALLY CATASTROPHIC COSTS FOR POLICY ERRORS. A twenty-first century constitutional democracy that had the same capacity to make intelligent policy as constitutional democracies in previous centuries would likely be a dismal failure. Contemporary constitutional democracies must successfully perform more tasks. No constitutional executive at present can emulate President Grover Cleveland, who blithely claimed that responding to the Panic of 1893 was not the business of national authorities. Constitutions ratified after World War II routinely require government officials to guarantee certain positive rights, such as rights to basic necessities, as well as protect such negative rights as the free exercise of religion. Some include such third-generation rights as guarantees to a healthy environment.[13] Reversion to the nightwatchman state will not substantially simplify governing tasks. A regime committed only to preserving the peace at home and preventing invasion would still have to find means to forestall cyberattacks and other threats that the founders of constitutional democracies in the mid-twentieth century could barely imagine. The costs of many policy mistakes are increasing exponentially. Mistaken policies on climate change, nuclear proliferation, the war on terror, and public health threaten global catastrophe if not human extinction. Constitutional democracies suffer from the gap between the skills necessary to be elected and the skills necessary to govern.[14] Even if that gap is not widening, as appears to be the case in the United States, the same sort of military heroes and

---

[13] For a discussion of the different generations of constitutional rights, see Peter E. Quint, "What Is a Twentieth-Century Constitution?," *Maryland Law Review* 67 (2007): 238.

[14] See George C. Edwards III, *Predicting the Presidency: The Path to Successful Leadership* (Princeton, NJ: Princeton University Press, 2016), 1.

celebrities who stumbled through governance in previous generations may through inexperience, inadvertence, or incompetence set in motion global environmental, nuclear, or public health disasters.

(6) CONSTITUTIONAL PROBLEMS IN THE UNITED STATES MAY BE FUELING CONCERNS THAT CONSTITUTIONAL DEMOCRACY IS IN TROUBLE. Even if the Constitution of the United States is no longer the model for the vast majority of constitutional regimes,[15] the United States was the model of a stable constitutional democracy during the twentieth century. The United States was the only regime that historically claimed a mission to advance the cause of constitutional democracy throughout the world, to make the world "safe for democracy," even as that commitment was always contested and often a perverse expression of the actual foreign policy of the United States. Given both the long-standing stability of the constitutional order in the United States as well as the long-standing role of the United States as a leader among constitutional democracies, if the United States is stricken by the constitutional democratic virus, this suggests that the virus is particularly virulent and that other stricken regimes seeking assistance may be on their own.

The constitutional adventures of Donald Trump, the Trump administration and the Republican majority in the Congress of the United States may nevertheless suggest that perceptions of a global constitutional crisis reflect nothing more than American parochialism and the exaggerated role the United States plays in comparative constitutionalism. All constitutional democracies experience long-standing ebbs and flows, the only difference between the present and recent past being that the United States is now clearly in the ebb column. That the contemporary ebb column is more populated than the contemporary flow column may reflect little more than the unsustainable growth of constitutional democracy in the recent past.

Constitutional democracies are constantly in crisis. The average constitution has a life span of less than twenty years.[16] Too obsessive a focus on the contemporary plight of such regimes as United States, Hungary, South Africa, Israel, Poland, and Venezuela risks imagining a golden age in which the vast majority of the world's constitutional democracies were stable. A quick glance at the Comparative Constitutions Project website,[17] which collects the text of all national constitutions, should abuse anyone of that notion. Both constitutions and constitutional democracies are more often than not ephemeral phenomenon that come and go, if not with the changing of the seasons, then more often than not with the changing of generations. Every decade after World War II provides the

---

[15] See David S. Law and Mila Versteeg, "The Declining Influence of the United States Constitution," *New York University Law Review* 87 (2012): 762.

[16] Zachary Elkins, Tom Ginsburg, and James Melton, *The Endurance of National Constitutions* (New York: Cambridge University Press, 2009).

[17] http://comparativeconstitutionsproject.org/.

material for a volume on constitutional democracies in crisis, differing only in the particular regimes emphasized and the distinctive causes of constitutional instability.

What many liberals and progressives regard as weakening the constitutional foundations of constitutional democracy may merely be the success of political rivals who are making fair use of the levers of constitutional democracy to implement their notions of desirable religious, immigration, and economic policies. Even if we concede that the democratic processes in the United States and other regimes that facilitated the rise of right-wing populism are badly flawed, the success of such movements globally demonstrates that a substantial and increasingly number of people in constitutional democracies are rejecting the dominant version of liberal constitutional democracy and successfully using existing constitutional forms to secure anti-liberal visions. Religious fundamentalists are pulling constitutional politics to the right in countries as diverse as the United States, Israel, Turkey, and India. Economic inequality is on the rise throughout the universe of constitutional democracies, with attendant gains by both the populist right and populist left, each with a grudge against the liberal constitutional regimes of the past. The racist backlash that propelled Trump to power in the United States helped propel Viktor Orbán to power in Hungary and is improving the fortune of white Christian supremacists in other regimes. Trump, Orban, and allied executive officials in other countries acknowledge they are rejecting liberal constitutional democracy but insist they are maintaining constitutional democracy, properly understood.

Past elite behavior, often celebrated by constitutional democrats, provoked many of these populist responses. Ran Hirschl in 2004 suggested that the new constitutionalism was in practice more devoted to making the world safe for globalization and secular elite values than to securing the rule of law.[18] The rise of anti-immigrant sentiment, religious fundamentalism, and increased tribalism is part of a backlash against liberal constitutional orders that have not improved the life chances for many citizens for more than a generation, while threatening what many right-wing populists regard as basic cultural norms. Contemporary populist efforts to transfer power from courts to executives, from this perspective, are no more an anathema to constitutional democracy then the previous liberal efforts to transfer power from legislatures to courts. All parties are engaged in the normal politics of constitutional democracy, as they empower the institutions they are must likely to control while weakening institutions controlled by their political rivals.

This volume explores whether constitutional democracies around the world are experiencing a global crisis—that is, a crisis of democracy in the large—or whether the apparent weakening of many constitutional democracies around the world is simply part of the normal ebb and flow of constitutional democracy that has been ongoing since the rise of constitutional democracy after World War II, or whether complaints about the present

---

[18] Ran Hirschl, *Toward Juristocracy: The Origins and Consequences of the New Constitutionalism* (Cambridge, MA: Harvard University Press, 2004).

status of constitutional democracy are largely from political actors and scholars on the political left upset to learn that many of their compatriots do not share their values on such matters as immigration, globalization, and the environment. Part I is devoted to background material on the nature of constitutional crises (Jack Balkin), general trends in constitutional democracy over the past decades (Tom Ginsburg/Aziz Huq, Zachary Elkins) and the fall of the Weimar Republic (Ellen Kennedy), the most important event during the last moment of perceived global constitutional crisis. Part II focuses on the state of constitutional democracy in specific regimes or regions. We have included essays on such contemporary problem children of constitutional democracy as the United States (Eric Posner; Jennifer Hochschild), Hungary (Gabor Halmai), Turkey (Ozan Varol), Venezuela (David Landau), Israel (Yaniv Roznai), Poland (Wojciech Sadurski), Spain (Victor Ferreres Comella), South Africa (Heinz Klug), and the European Union (Michaela Hailbronner; J.H.H. Weiler), constitutional democracies that appear to be stable such as Canada (Richard Albert/ Michael Pal) and Australia (Rosalind Dixon/Anika Gauja), and constitutional democracies that appear to be experiencing some turbulence that may or may not amount to a weakened commitment to constitutional democracy such as Mexico (Ana Micaela Alterio/Roberto Niembro), India (Manoj Mate), the United Kingdom (Erin Delaney), and France (Nicolas Roussellier). Part II also includes essays on the state of constitutional democracy in Africa (James Thuo Gathii) and in South America (Roberto Gargarella), regions that suffer from chronic constitutional problems, as well as an essay on constitutional democracy in South Asia (David Law/ Chien-Chih Lin), where alternatives to constitutional democracy are rapidly gaining public support. Part III examines the influence on constitutional democracy of such global forces as climate change (Robert Percival), religious fundamentalism (Ran Hirschl and Ayelet Shachar), terrorism (Oren Gross), economic inequality (Ganesh Sitaraman), globalization (David Schneiderman), immigration (T. Alexander Aleinikoff), populism (Samuel Issacharoff) and racism/ethnocentrism (Desmond King/Rogers Smith), as well as studies on the increasing weakness of political parties across the universe of constitutional democracy (Kim Lane Scheppele) and the role of constitutional design in maintaining or subverting constitutional democracy (Sujit Choudhry). Finally, in Part IV, we separately offer our thoughts on the contemporary state of constitutional democracy.

This collection serves three purposes. The essays that follow provide a general guide to the state of constitutional democracy during the second decade of the twenty-first century that should be useful for scholars, students, and general readers. The essays provide frameworks and information for assessing the contemporary state of constitutional democracy. Our concern is whether a global crisis of constitutional democracy is taking place, or whether the recent afflictions suffered by many constitutional democracies reflect only the success of constitutional democracy in the past, chronic problems with particular constitutional democracies, or problems distinctive to particular democratic regimes; or whether many commentators are confusing attacks on political liberalism or transformative constitutionalism with a weakening of constitutional democracy. The essays diagnose the causes of the present afflictions of constitutional democracies in particular regimes, regions, and across the globe. We do not, however, spend much energy offering cures, believing at this stage diagnosis is far more important, and not having any ready-made cures to offer. As Abraham Lincoln said in his "House Divided Speech," "If we could first know *where* we are, and *whither* we are tending, we could then better judge *what* to do, and *how* to do it."[19]

We did not insist that each chapter author conform to a standardized definition of "democracy," "constitutional," or "constitutional democracy." Some essays discuss regimes (United Kingdom, Israel) that are considered democracies, but may not be constitutional democracies. Others consider regimes (Burundi, Togo) that have constitutions but may not be democracies. This failure to standardize strikes us as more problematic in a quantitative than, as almost all essays are, qualitative studies. Insisting on conformity might well be fruitless and unproductive for our purposes. While the concluding essays attempt to discern some patterns in the information presented, that is largely a task for the reader. To the extent authors or readers discern that some kinds of regimes are experiencing more turbulence than others, or that some safeguards function better than others, this seems far more important than the label we stick on the regime. Knowing, for example, that Westminster systems that lack a judicially enforceable constitution seem vulnerable to some problems and not others seems more important than determining whether the United Kingdom and Israel are constitutional democracies.

For similar reasons we did not insist that authors conform to a standardized definition of "crisis" or "constitutional crisis." Jack Balkin in his essay elaborates an important distinction between "constitutional crisis" and "constitutional rot." Other essays explore alternative approaches to thinking about what constitutes a constitutional crisis. Some authors speak of constitutional crisis; others insist that particular regimes or constitutional democracies are experiencing "decline," "erosion," "retrogression," or "backsliding." Again, imposing standardized definitions would likely be both futile and unproductive. This volume is entitled *Constitutional Democracy in Crisis?* rather than *Constitutional Democracy in Crisis* in part because, as the essays below indicate, the nature of a constitutional crisis is as contestable as most other features of constitutionalism. Still, the whole may be greater than the parts. If many regimes are experiencing constitutional rot or constitutional regression, including long-standing constitutional democracies and those only a few years previously thought to be constitutional democracies, the conclusion may well be that a global constitutional crisis is occurring, even if only a few particular constitutional regimes have reached the crisis stage.

The ruminations on the following pages are more pessimistic than those that might have appeared in volumes on the state of constitutional democracy throughout the world written in prior decades (or, we hope, in subsequent ones). The past decade has witnessed

---

[19] Abraham Lincoln, *The Collected Works of Abraham Lincoln*, ed. Roy P. Basler (New Brunswick, NJ: Rutgers University Press, 1953), 461.

numerous instances of constitutional backsliding among established and new constitutional democracies as well as a fair share of failures to launch. The most successful constitutional entrepreneurs of the recent past offered models of transformative constitutional democracies that engaged and excited the constitutional imagination. The most successful constitutional entrepreneurs at present offer more authoritarian constitutional visions that often combine appeals to racial, ethnic, and religious identities with economic bounties to a small investor class. More so than any time after World War II, constitutional developments bring to the fore the fundamental question asked by the first founders of constitutional democracy, "whether societies of men are really capable or not of establishing good government from reflection and choice, or whether they are forever destined to depend for their political constitutions on accident and force."[20]

---

[20] Alexander Hamilton, James Madison, and John Jay, *The Federalist Papers*, ed. Clinton Rossiter (New York: New American Library, 1961), 33.

I Background

2 Constitutional Crisis and Constitutional Rot
Jack M. Balkin

NO ONE COULD accuse Donald Trump's presidency of being boring. His first year in office has careened wildly through scandals, revelations, outrages, and fracturing of political norms. Because Donald Trump is very unpopular, and because he regularly does things that his opponents consider outrageous, his critics have begun to describe his actions as creating or precipitating a "constitutional crisis," especially following his first executive order limiting entry into the United States,[1] and again after his firing of FBI director James Comey.[2]

---

[1] See, e.g., Jessica Schulberg and Sam Levine, "Trump Inches the U.S. Closer to Constitutional Crisis," *HuffPost*, February 5, 2017, http://www.huffingtonpost.com/entry/trump-constitutional-crisis-judge-robart_us_58964292e4b09bd304bba74f (quoting Senator Patrick Leahy's statement that President Trump "seems intent on precipitating a constitutional crisis").

[2] See, e.g., David Cole, "Trump's Constitutional Crisis," *New York Review of Books*, May 10, 2017, http://www.nybooks.com/daily/2017/05/10/trumps-constitutional-crisis-james-comey/ ("This is a constitutional crisis."); Alexandra Wilts, "Comey Fired: America Is Witnessing a Constitutional Crisis, Says Leading Democrat," *Independent*, May 10, 2017, http://www.independent.co.uk/news/world/americas/us-politics/james-comey-fired-donald-trump-constitutional-crisis-fbi-director-russian-investigation-latest-news-a7727341.html (quoting Representative Keith Ellison's remark that "[w]e are witnessing a constitutional crisis unfold before our very eyes").

In 2009, Sandy Levinson and I wrote an article about constitutional crises.[3] We argued that the term is overused; people apply it to many situations that are worrisome but that are not really constitutional crises at all. In this essay, I offer a brief explanation of the term and why it is so likely to be misused. I also introduce a second idea, "constitutional rot," and explain how it relates to Levinson's and my theory of constitutional crisis. Many claims of constitutional crisis about Trump's presidency, I argue, reflect a growing recognition of the constitutional rot in our nation's political institutions. Indeed, constitutional rot has been going on for some time in the United States, and Trump's rise to power is merely the latest symptom.

What Is a Constitutional Crisis?

A constitutional crisis occurs when there is a serious danger that a constitution is about to fail at its central task. The central task of constitutions is to keep disagreement within the boundaries of ordinary politics rather than breaking down into anarchy, violence, or civil war.[4] To be sure, constitutions are also valuable because they protect civil liberties and divide and restrain power, but their first job is to keep the peace and make people struggle with each other within politics rather than outside of it.

Constitutional crises come in three types. In Type One crises, politicians (or military officials) publicly announce that they won't obey the constitution.[5] In our system of government, government officials are supposed to obey judicial orders specifically directed to them. (This is true even if they believe that the judge has interpreted the law incorrectly.) Therefore defying a direct judicial order would also be tantamount to precipitating a constitutional crisis. When government officials (or the military) publicly announce that they will no longer play by the rules of the constitution, the constitution has failed. Constitutional crises of this type are very rare in American history.

Second, the constitution might fail because it keeps political actors from preventing a looming disaster.[6] We call these Type Two Crises.[7] These situations are even rarer because political actors (and the courts) usually conclude that the constitution allows them to escape disaster.[8]

Third, a constitution might fail because lots of people refuse to obey it—there are riots in the streets, states secede from the Union, the army refuses to obey civilian control,

---

[3] Sanford Levinson and Jack M. Balkin, "Constitutional Crises," *University of Pennsylvania Law Review* 157 (2009): 707–754.

[4] Ibid., 711, 714–715.

[5] Ibid., 714, 721–729 (describing Type One crises).

[6] Ibid., 714.

[7] Ibid., 729–738 (describing Type Two crises).

[8] Ibid., 729–731 (giving the example of President Abraham Lincoln taking a different view of the power to respond to rebellion than his predecessor, President James Buchanan).

and so on.[9] Type Three crises involve "situations where publicly articulated disagreements about the constitution lead political actors to engage in extraordinary forms of protest beyond mere legal disagreements and political protests: people take to the streets, armies mobilize, and brute force is used or threatened in order to prevail."[10]

When people are upset at what government officials have done, they often call these actions constitutional crises. However, most of these situations aren't really constitutional crises, because there is no real danger that the constitution is about to break down. The vast majority of uses of the term "constitutional crisis" are hyperbole.[11]

Sometimes when people call something a constitutional crisis, they really mean that there is a heated dispute about the best interpretation of the law or the Constitution, and that their political opponents are interpreting the law or the Constitution in the wrong way. That in itself, however, is not a constitutional crisis, because disputes about the best interpretation of the law and of the Constitution are a normal feature of American politics. Many, but not all, of those disputes are eventually settled in the courts. Others are settled through politics. Settlement of serious disputes through the courts or politics is not a constitutional crisis. On the contrary, it is how a constitution is supposed to work.[12]

Sometimes what people call constitutional crises are really what Mark Tushnet has called "constitutional hardball."[13] Constitutional hardball occurs when political actors stretch or defy political conventions that were previously considered unspoken rules of fair play in politics but were not clearly legally required.[14] People who engage in hardball tactics deliberately violate old norms in order to create new ones and gain a political advantage.[15] This often causes outrage and leads to reprisals in politics. The Republican-controlled Senate's refusal to hold a hearing for anyone President Obama nominated to the Supreme Court in his last year in office was an example of constitutional hardball.[16]

---

[9] Ibid., 714, 738–746 (describing Type Three crises).

[10] Ibid., 714.

[11] Cf. Jack M. Balkin, "Constitutional Hardball and Constitutional Crises," *Quinnipiac Law Review* 26 (2008): 579, 590 ("[M]any so-called 'constitutional crises' are not real crises at all, but rather heated disagreements about the Constitution in which people fear (whether reasonably or unreasonably) that the system will spin out of control. . . .").

[12] Levinson and Balkin, "Constitutional Crises," 714 ("Disagreement and conflict are natural features of politics. The goal of constitutions is to manage them within acceptable boundaries.").

[13] Mark Tushnet, "Constitutional Hardball," *John Marshall Law Review* 37 (2004): 523, 523.

[14] Ibid.

[15] See ibid., 523 ("[P]ractitioners [of constitutional hardball] see themselves as playing for keeps in a special kind of way; they believe the stakes of the political controversy their actions provoke are quite high. . . .").

[16] Michael Dorf, "Hardball, Structural Forces, Ineptitude, and Chaos on the Road to Trump and Beyond," *Dorf on Law*, November 15, 2016, 11:34 AM, http://www.dorfonlaw.org/2016/11/hardball-structural-forces-ineptitude.html (offering "the Republican Senate's successful intransigence in denying Judge Merrick Garland confirmation hearings or a vote" as an example of constitutional hardball); Paul Rosenberg, "The Year Democracy Broke—and How We Got Here," *Salon*, November 8, 2016, 7:00 PM, http://www.salon.com/2016/11/08/the-year-democracy-broke-and-how-we-got-here/ ("[W]hen Republican senators staunchly refused to let President Barack Obama appoint a new justice to the Supreme Court . . . [t]his was an example of . . . 'constitutional hardball' . . . .").

The Republican strategy violated what Democrats believed were unspoken norms of political fair play, and it will likely shape how Democrats behave in the future. What happened was not, however, a constitutional crisis.

A more accurate use of the term "constitutional crisis" involves situations in which people reasonably fear that the Constitution will fail in one of the three ways I've just described, even though the breaking point hasn't yet occurred. A constitution that is on the brink of failure is a constitution in crisis.[17]

If President Richard Nixon had refused to obey the Supreme Court's order to surrender the Watergate tapes in 1974, he would have precipitated a constitutional crisis of the first type.[18] People feared that Nixon wouldn't obey, and so one could say that this was a moment of potential constitutional crisis. Ultimately, however, he did obey the judicial order, and the potential crisis was averted.

Probably the most important constitutional crisis in the nation's history was the secession of the southern states and the resulting Civil War. This was a crisis of the first type and the third type.[19] Politicians and military officials openly stated that they would refuse to play by the rules of the Constitution; states seceded from the Union, and then they resisted through violence. That constitutional crisis resulted in enormous bloodshed and suffering, and required the Constitution to be reconstructed with three new amendments.

A constitutional crisis is a very serious thing, because if we were in the middle of a genuine constitutional crisis, there would be a real and serious danger that the Constitution would fail at its central task. But, as noted above, most things that people call constitutional crises don't involve serious threats of constitutional failure. In general, one should not confuse heated constitutional disputes with constitutional crises. Similarly, one should not confuse political crises—in which people struggle for power within the limits of the Constitution—with constitutional crises, in which the Constitution itself fails or is on the verge of failing.

Constitutional Rot

We should distinguish constitutional crises from another, related phenomenon, which we might call "constitutional rot."[20] Constitutional crisis could, in theory, happen to any

---

[17] See Levinson and Balkin, "Constitutional Crises," 745 ("People may have regarded Watergate, the 2000 election, and the Steel Seizure Case as crises not because they were crises in the sense we describe, but because they feared that they would become that sort of crisis.").

[18] Ibid., 742 (arguing that failure to comply with an order from the Supreme Court would have precipitated a Type One crisis).

[19] Ibid., 740 (noting that secession was a Type Three crisis). Because the rebel states publicly stated that they were no longer bound by the 1787 Constitution, it was also a Type One crisis.

[20] Jack M. Balkin, "Constitutional Rot," in *Can It Happen Here?: Authoritarianism in America*, ed. Cass R. Sunstein (New York: Dey Street Books 2018), at 19.

constitution; constitutional rot is a specific malady of constitutions of representative democracies—that is, republics. Constitutional crisis occurs during relatively brief periods of time; constitutional rot is a degradation of constitutional norms that may operate over long periods of time.

What is constitutional rot? Democratic constitutions depend on more than obedience to law. They depend on well-functioning institutions that balance and check power and ambition. They depend on the public's trust that government officials will exercise power in the public interest and not for their own personal benefit or for the benefit of private interests and cronies. Democracies also depend on forbearance on the part of public officials in their assertions of power and obedience to norms of fair political competition. These norms prevent ambitious politicians from overreaching, entrenching themselves and their ideological allies, and undermining public trust. These norms help to promote cooperation between political opponents and factions even when they disagree strongly about how to govern the country. Finally, these norms prevent politicians from privileging short-term political gains over long-term injuries to the health of the constitutional system.[21]

When politicians disregard norms of fair political competition, undermine public trust, and repeatedly overreach by using constitutional hardball to rig the system in their favor and keep themselves (or their allies) in power, they cause the system of democratic (and republican) constitutionalism to decay. This is an example of constitutional rot.

More generally, constitutional rot is a process of decay in the features of our system of government that maintain it as a healthy democratic republic.[22] As constitutional rot occurs, our system becomes simultaneously less democratic and less republican. The political system becomes less democratic because the power of the state becomes less responsive to popular opinion and popular will. The political system becomes less republican because representatives are no longer devoted to promoting the public good; instead, they seek to maintain themselves in power and please a relatively small set of powerful individuals and groups. When this happens, the republican system of representation fails—even if the system remains formally representative in the sense that we still have elections—and the result is oligarchy.[23]

Governments become oligarchical when political leaders become increasingly beholden to relatively small groups of backers who keep them in power. Because members of the public feel that their leaders are not responsive to them—and indeed, feel abandoned by the very people who are supposed to serve their interests—they lose faith in the political system.[24]

---

[21] For an excellent discussion of the importance of these norms in preserving democratic government, see Steven Levitsky and Daniel Ziblatt, *How Democracies Die* (New York: Crown 2018).

[22] Balkin, "Constitutional Rot," 19–20.

[23] Ibid., 20–21.

[24] Ibid., 21.

When constitutional rot becomes advanced, and the public's trust in government is thoroughly undermined, people turn to demagogues, who flatter the public, and who stoke division, anger, and resentment.[25] Demagogues promise that they will restore lost glories and make everything right again. They divert the public's attention to enemies and scapegoats within and without the republic. They divide the public in order to conquer it. They play on people's fears of loss of status. They use divisive rhetoric to distract attention, maintain a loyal set of supporters, and keep themselves in power. There are always potential demagogues in a republic, but healthy republics restrain their emergence and ascension. When demagogues manage to take power and lead the nation, however, constitutional rot has become serious indeed.

Four factors may hasten constitutional decay; I call them the "four horsemen" of constitutional rot.[26] The first factor is loss of trust, both in government and in one's fellow citizens.[27] The second factor is polarization, which causes members of the public to regard their fellow citizens as implacable enemies rather than members of a common enterprise; it also leads members of the public to waste their attention and energies on symbolic conflicts and zero-sum conflicts over social status.[28]

A third factor is increasing economic inequality, which creates anger and resentment, and leads the public to look for scapegoats and enemies who are the cause of its misfortunes.[29] The fourth factor is policy disasters, a term coined by Stephen Griffin.[30] Policy disasters are serious failures in decision-making by the public's representatives, which cause the public to lose faith in government. Examples of policy disasters in recent American history include the Iraq War and the 2008 financial crisis.[31] Policy disasters lead people to feel that their leaders are incompetent, untrustworthy, and unrepresentative. People increasingly feel that they have been abandoned by their leaders, who care only for themselves and not for the public they represent.

These four factors often exacerbate each other.[32] Rising economic inequality can increase polarization. Polarization diverts public attention to symbolic conflicts and zero-sum conflicts over status; this allows powerful interests to pursue policies that enhance inequality and entrench oligarchy. Increasing economic inequality and lack of responsiveness to the public's needs, in turn, undermine public confidence in the system and faith in one's fellow citizens, which may increase polarization. Polarization and

---

[25] Ibid., 21.

[26] Ibid., 22 (describing the "Four Horsemen of Constitutional Rot").

[27] Ibid., 22, 26–27.

[28] Ibid., 22, 26–27.

[29] Ibid., 22–23.

[30] Ibid., 22; Stephen M. Griffin, *Broken Trust: Dysfunctional Government and Constitutional Reform* (Lawrence: University Press of Kansas, 2015), 20–21 (defining policy disasters as "government outcomes that are in no one's interests").

[31] Griffin, *Broken Trust*, 20–21; Balkin, "Constitutional Rot," 22.

[32] Balkin, "Constitutional Rot," 22–23.

oligarchy insulate representatives from the public, produce overconfidence, and insulate decision-makers from criticism, which leads to policy disasters. Policy disasters, in turn, undermine trust in government, and so on.[33]

The idea of constitutional rot is very old. The political theory of republicanism familiar to the Constitution's founders asserted that republics were delicate institutions that were always susceptible to decay and corruption over time.[34] Time was the great enemy of republics, because ever-changing circumstances, and the driving force of people's ambitions and desire for power would open the door to—if not encourage—multiple forms of institutional corruption.[35] In modern democratic republics, this institutional corruption is constitutional rot.

Constitutional rot creates two serious risks to democratic politics. First, by playing too much hardball, enhancing political polarization, demonizing their opposition, and attempting to crush those who stand in their way, political actors risk increasing and widening cycles of retribution from their opponents. This may lead to deadlock and a political system that is increasingly unable to govern effectively. This, in turn, can cause even greater loss of confidence in government, distrust, and polarization, hastening constitutional rot.

Second, undermining or destroying norms of political fair play and using hardball tactics to preempt political competition may produce a gradual descent into authoritarian or autocratic politics.[36] Such states may preserve the empty form of representative

---

[33] Ibid.

[34] See Philip Pettit, *Republicanism: A Theory of Freedom and Government* (New York: Oxford University Press, 1997), 210 (explaining that in the republican tradition corruption occurs when people "make their decisions by reference not to considerations of the common good but rather to more sectional or private concerns"); J.G.A. Pocock, *The Machiavellian Moment: Florentine Political Thought and the Atlantic Republican Tradition* (Princeton, NJ: Princeton University Press, 1975), 527 ("Virtue can develop only in time, but is always threatened with corruption by time."); Gordon S. Wood, *The Radicalism of the American Revolution* (New York: A.A. Knopf, 1991), 105 ("Precisely because republics required civic virtue and disinterestedness among their citizens, they were very fragile polities, extremely liable to corruption.").

The founding generation also believed that a republic required a certain kind of political economy to prevent it from descending into oligarchy: a broad-based, stable, and economically secure middle class to create the right incentives for government officials to pursue the public good. For a modern version of this argument, see Ganesh Sitaraman, *The Crisis of the Middle Class Constitution* (New York: Alfred A. Knopf, 2017).

[35] Pettit, *Republicanism*, 210–211 (arguing that the basic problem of republics is to promote resilience and stability in the face of continual sources of temptation and corruption); Jack M. Balkin, "Republicanism and the Constitution of Opportunity," *Texas Law Review* 94 (2016): 1427, 1444 ("[T]ime is the great enemy of republics, because as time goes on and circumstances change, corruption finds ever-new ways of entering the system, weakening the institutions and practices that ensure republican government.").

[36] See Nancy Bermeo, "On Democratic Backsliding," *Journal of Democracy* 27 (2016): 5–19 (explaining democratic backsliding as "the state-led debilitation or elimination of any of the political institutions that sustain an existing democracy"). "Competitive authoritarianism" is another way of describing the general phenomenon. See Steven Levitsky and Lucan A. Way, *Competitive Authoritarianism: Hybrid Regimes after the Cold War* (New York: Cambridge University Press, 2010), 5 (defining competitive authoritarian regimes as "civil regimes in which formal democratic institutions exist ... but in which incumbents' abuse of the state places them at a significant advantage"). Competitive authoritarianism applies to regimes that never fully transitioned

democracy—they may have written constitutions and regular elections, and they may adhere for the most part to the rule of law formalities. But power is increasingly concentrated and unaccountable; the press, civil society, political opponents, civil servants, and the judiciary no longer serve as independent checks on the power of the people in charge. Indeed, political leaders may systematically seek to weaken or co-opt each of these possible sources of opposition.

These features of constitutional rot are likely to lead to increasing corruption, overreaching, and suppression of basic liberties. Regimes that slide into autocracy or authoritarianism may not suffer constitutional crises to the extent that they remain politically stable and successfully avoid civil unrest or civil war, but they have failed as *democratic* constitutional systems. Increasingly they are democracies in name only.

Obviously, these two risks—deadlock and descent into autocracy—are related. A system that has become so deadlocked that politics seems futile may lead to the election of demagogues and authoritarian-minded politicians who undermine democratic norms and lead a nation toward autocracy.

What is the relationship between constitutional crisis and constitutional rot? The two phenomena are not identical. As noted above, the question of constitutional crisis concerns whether the constitutional system can perform its central function of making politics possible—keeping struggles for power within politics and preventing violence, insurrection, and civil war. The three types of constitutional crises listed above can occur in many different kinds of systems, whether democratic or not. Constitutional rot, by contrast, is a feature of constitutional democracies and republics—it concerns how these systems degrade into deadlock and despair on the one hand, or into authoritarianism and autocracy on the other.[37]

There is another important distinction. The idea of "crisis" refers to a crucial moment in time—usually rather brief in duration—in which the constitutional system will adequately respond to a challenge, be undermined, or be successfully reconstituted. Constitutional rot, by contrast, is often a long and slow process of change and debilitation, which may be the work of many hands over many years. Crisis seems to come upon us suddenly—it focuses everyone's attention on the spectacle. Rot develops slowly and gradually and may be imperceptible in its earliest stages; sometimes features of constitutional rot are obvious, but sometimes they operate quietly in the background.

---

to democracy, as well as to fully democratic regimes in which democracy gradually decays into autocracy or authoritarianism.

[37] To be sure, one can speak of any form of government—for example a monarchy—as subject to decay. Imagine, for example, a regime—whether a monarchy or a dictatorship—that gradually becomes ripe for overthrow because it can no longer maintain its legitimacy. As I use the term, however, constitutional rot is a feature of representative government. That is because corruption and decay have historically been viewed as characteristic and central problems of republican government.

Even so, the two phenomena are connected. Continued constitutional rot in a democratic system may be the harbinger of a constitutional crisis years later. Stephen Griffin has argued that the most important source of constitutional dysfunction in the United States is increasing loss of public trust among citizens.[38] This loss of trust did not occur overnight; it is the result of decades of fateful decisions by political actors seeking short-term political success, stoking political polarization to win elections, and playing political hardball to lock in greater power and reduced accountability.[39] Griffin regards this as a sort of "slow-motion" constitutional crisis.[40] I would say that it is a description of constitutional rot.

Constitutional rot in a democracy need not always lead to constitutional crisis. It might simply lead to a less just and less democratic system of government. This is what happens when a democracy effectively becomes an oligarchy, or when a political system slides into autocracy. Nevertheless, constitutional rot, if unchecked, can lead to a constitutional crisis, just as placing increasing weight on a rotten tree branch can eventually cause it to snap. Indeed, constitutional rot can lead to any one of the three types of constitutional crisis that Levinson and I described.

Politicians may publicly reject constitutional obligations (Type One). The system may suffer severe crises of governance in which the state is unable to perform basic functions (Type Two). Finally, loss of public trust, combined with the rise of political opportunists and demagogues who stoke anger and resentment in their followers (or in their opponents), may produce cycles of political violence, or even insurrection (Type Three).

Constitutional rot, in other words, can eventually cause a democratic constitution to fail both as a *democratic* constitution—because the system degenerates into an oligarchy or autocracy; and as a democratic *constitution*—because the constitution no longer can keep political disagreement within the bounds of law and peaceful political dispute.

Are We in a Period of Constitutional Crisis?

The United States is not currently in a period of constitutional crisis. But for some time—at least since the 1990s—it has been in a period of increasing constitutional rot. The election of a demagogue such as Trump is further evidence that our institutions have decayed, and judging by his presidential campaign and his first year in office, Trump promises to accelerate the corruption.

---

[38] Griffin, *Broken Trust*, 31, 38–39.

[39] See Thomas E. Mann and Norman J. Ornstein, "How the Republicans Broke Congress," *New York Times*, December 2, 2017, https://www.nytimes.com/2017/12/02/opinion/sunday/republicans-broke-congress-politics.html ("beginning in the 1990s, the Republicans strategically demonized Congress and government more broadly and flouted the norms of lawmaking, fueling a significant decline of trust in government that began well before the financial collapse in 2008.").

[40] Personal communication with author, March 22, 2017.

When people talk about constitutional crisis in the Trump administration, they might point to the executive orders on immigration that began Trump's presidency, or the decision to fire FBI director James Comey, who had been investigating possible collusion between the Trump campaign and Russia.

Trump's first two executive orders on immigration were very unjust, and there are plausible arguments that both versions were unconstitutional.[41] (The courts are currently grappling with the third version.). But the orders did not precipitate a constitutional crisis. The courts often find that the executive branch of the United States government has violated the law or the Constitution, but that doesn't make each of these situations a constitutional crisis.

On the other hand, if President Trump ordered executive branch officials to defy judicial orders, and they did so, not merely in isolated instances out of confusion, but deliberately and consistently, that could precipitate a constitutional crisis. Isolated acts of recalcitrance by a few low-level DHS officials, however, do not constitute a genuine constitutional crisis. On the other hand, if President Trump announced that he would not follow the Constitution, if he arrested members of the Supreme Court, or if he defied a direct judicial order, that would mark a constitutional crisis.

Similarly, Trump's firing of James Comey was not in itself a constitutional crisis, because the president legally has the authority to fire the FBI director.[42] It happened once before, when Bill Clinton fired Director William Sessions because of ethics violations. Comey's firing had none of the features of a constitutional crisis. Trump did not assert, for example, that he was deliberately acting outside the Constitution. Rather, Comey's firing is a symptom of constitutional rot, as I will explain momentarily.

Now suppose that investigators discover that President Trump fired Comey from a corrupt motive—for example, to end any investigation into Trump's businesses and his

---

[41] Federal courts issued injunctions against the two executive orders, which the Supreme Court modified pending a hearing on the merits. These orders expired before the Court could hold a hearing. Washington v. Trump, 847 F.3d 1151, 1166 (9th Cir. 2017) (upholding preliminary injunction against first executive order); Int'l Refugee Assistance Project v. Trump, No. TOC-17-0361, 2017 WL 1018235, at *18 (D. Md. Mar. 16, 2017), aff'd, 857 F.3d 554 (4th Cir. 2017), cert. granted 137 S. Ct. 2080 (2017) (upholding preliminary injunction against second executive order), vacated, No. 16-1436, 2017 WL 4518553 (Oct. 10, 2017) (vacating and remanding after order expired); Hawaii v. Trump, No. 17-00050 DKW-KSC, 2017 WL 1167383, at *9 (D. Haw. Mar. 29, 2017), aff'd, 859 F.3d 741 (9th Cir. 2017), cert granted sub nom. Trump v. Int'l Refugee Assistance Project, 137 S. Ct. 2080 (2017) (upholding preliminary injunction against second executive order), vacated, No. 16-1436, 2017 WL 4518553 (Oct. 10, 2017) (vacating and remanding after order expired). Trump subsequently issued a third executive order, which is currently being litigated.

[42] See, e.g., Memorandum on the Constitutionality of Legislation Extending the Term of the FBI Director, Caroline D. Krass, Principal Deputy Assistant Attorney Gen., to Office of Legal Counsel (June 20, 2011), https://www.justice.gov/sites/default/files/olc/opinions/2011/06/31/fbi-director-term_0.pdf ("[T]he FBI Director is removable at the will of the President . . . . No statute purports to restrict the President's power to remove the Director."); Robert Chesney, "Backgrounder: The Power to Appoint & Remove the FBI Director," Lawfare, May 10, 2017, 11:55 AM, https://www.lawfareblog.com/backgrounder-power-appoint-remove-fbi-director ("Congress at no point has attempted to constrain the president's removal power.").

dealings with Russia—and the House of Representatives impeaches Trump for obstruction of justice. This would still not constitute a constitutional crisis. Impeachment is the Constitution's authorized method for deciding whether to remove government officials. Following this process keeps the struggle for power within the boundaries of politics. On the other hand, if Congress, following constitutional procedures, impeached and removed Trump from office, and Trump refused to give up power and called on the military to support him, the country would be in a constitutional crisis.

As Sandy Levinson and I pointed out in our original 2009 article on constitutional crises, American politicians almost never announce that they will go outside the Constitution or the law. Instead, they argue that they are complying with the law based on their interpretation of it.[43] One might object that this allows politicians to violate the Constitution if they just lie about their motivations or if their legal positions are objectively unreasonable. But there is a reason why forcing politicians to state their positions in terms of legality and constitutionality is important to constitutional government. This means that they are still publicly adhering to a political norm that everyone must obey the law and the Constitution. When politicians obey this norm, it drives controversies back into the courts or into ordinary politics for resolution. Achieving this result is what constitutions are supposed to do. To be sure, when people argue about what the law means or what the Constitution means, it is often very upsetting, because politicians often have incentives to make specious or disingenuous claims to justify their actions. But as long as the courts are open and are obeyed, this by itself does not produce a constitutional crisis.

Crisis is not the same thing as injustice. There are a lot of unjust things that happen in a constitutional system without precipitating a constitutional crisis. Constitutions make politics possible, and politics is often unjust. You can tell if you are in a constitutional crisis when politicians stop saying that they will comply with the law, with judicial orders, or with the Constitution. Or you can tell that you are in a constitutional crisis when there is widespread civil unrest or rebellion. Until that happens, you are not in a constitutional crisis, and for that, at least, you can be grateful.

Are We Experiencing Constitutional Rot?

Although America is not currently in the middle of a constitutional crisis, the country is experiencing constitutional rot, and people have been employing the language of constitutional crisis to describe it. This problem, I think, is what Griffin meant when he suggested that we are in a "slow motion" constitutional crisis caused by lack of public trust in government.[44]

---

[43] Levinson and Balkin, "Constitutional Crises," 722–723 (noting that American presidents have never asserted prerogative powers to act outside the Constitution; instead they offer controversial interpretations that justify their actions).

[44] See note 39.

Many Americans no longer trust government to act in the public interest, and many politicians act in ways that encourage their lack of trust.[45] We have also experienced severe political polarization, unwise policies have exacerbated economic inequality, and American politicians have produced a series of policy disasters—including, most recently, the global financial crisis of 2008. Thus, each of the "four horsemen" of constitutional rot[46]—loss of trust, political polarization, economic inequality and policy disaster—has been on the march for some time.

President Trump has only made matters worse; he has violated many preexisting political norms and governed through strategies of exacerbating division and polarization.[47] Meanwhile, the congressional wing of his party has cast aside customary legislative practices as it has tried to push through major legislation—first on healthcare, where it failed, and then on taxation, where it succeeded—with only Republican votes.[48]

The recent 1.5 trillion dollar tax bill is an especially worrisome sign of constitutional rot in the United States. The contemporary Republican Party is largely controlled by its wealthiest donors. To stay in power, congressional Republicans must please these donors, regardless of any promises made to their actual constituents. Some of the ways that one pleases donors involve ideological symbolism and low-profile deregulation, but others are essentially cash transfers. Measured from the baseline of then-existing law, the 2016 Republican tax bill was a stunning upward redistribution of income. Moreover, the

---

[45] See Pew Research Center, "Public Trust in Government: 1958–2017," May 3, 2017, http://www.people-press.org/2017/05/03/public-trust-in-government-1958-2017/ ("Public trust in the government remains near historic lows.").

[46] Balkin, "Constitutional Rot," 22.

[47] Ibid., 28–29 (describing Trump's strategy of deliberate polarization and division in order to maintain the loyalty of his supporters); Peter Baker, "A Divider, Not a Uniter, Trump Widens the Breach," *New York Times*, September 24, 2017, https://www.nytimes.com/2017/09/24/us/politics/trump-divisiveness.html ("Relentlessly pugnacious, energized by a fight, unwilling to let any slight go unanswered, Mr. Trump has made himself America's apostle of anger, its deacon of divisiveness."); Cathleen Decker, "Back into the Trump Vortex America Goes, Where the President Fuels a Divisive Debate," *Los Angeles Times*, September 26, 2017, http://www.latimes.com/politics/la-na-pol-trump-strategy-20170926-story.html ("America once again finds itself . . . pulled into the vortex of partisanship as a master publicist plays notes of division and dispute."); see also Levitsky and Ziblatt, *How Democracies Die*, 65-67, 195-201 (arguing that Trump has violated a wide range of democratic norms and displayed several key warning signs of authoritarian behavior).

[48] Congressional attempts to repeal and replace Obamacare are exemplary. See, e.g., Seung Min Kim, "Frustrated Republicans Try to Rewrite Congress' Rules," *Politico*, May 22, 2017, http://www.politico.com/story/2017/05/22/republicans-rewrite-congress-rules-agenda-238336 ("Long-standing norms are being swept aside in the GOP's haste to enact its agenda."); Elise Viebeck, "Seven Ways the Latest Republican Health-Care Effort Is Impulsive and Chaotic," *Washington Post*, September 25, 2017, https://www.washingtonpost.com/powerpost/seven-ways-the-latest-republican-health-care-effort-is-impulsive-and-chaotic/2017/09/24/4451aaf4-9fa1-11e7-8ea1-ed975285475e_story.html (describing how Congress has abandoned traditional legislative practices to pass health care reform).

deficits it produces will likely be used to justify cuts in social insurance programs, continuing the upward redistribution from poor to rich.[49]

Using the apparatus of government to pay off a small group of people who keep you in power is pretty much the whole point of oligarchy. The overarching need to reward wealthy donors is why congressional Republicans disregarded the collective judgment of economists and budget analysts about what the tax bill actually did; it is also why they repeatedly misrepresented the bill's effects to their constituents. The public justification of the bill had relatively little connection to the point of the bill, which was to please the relatively small class of powerful and wealthy people who keep the Republican Party in power. The public would not support a bill designed on these terms; hence Republicans had to rush the bill through with no hearings, and dissemble publicly about the nature and effects of their legislation.[50]

Nor is this all. Trump's administration has generated repeated accusations of corruption and conflict of interest,[51] and Trump himself seems to regard political office as a

---

[49] See, e.g., John Cassidy, "The Final G.O.P. Tax Bill Is a Recipe for Even More Inequality," *The New Yorker*, December 14, 2017, https://www.newyorker.com/news/our-columnists/the-final-gop-tax-bill-is-a-recipe-for-even-more-inequality ("As virtually every independent study has shown, the G.O.P. plan showers most of its goodies (tax cuts) on the richest people in the country while doing little for poor and middle-income households."); Facundo Alvaredo, Lucas Chancel, Thomas Piketty, Emmanuel Saez and Gabriel Zucman, "Inequality Is Not Inevitable—But the US 'Experiment' Is a Recipe for Divergence," *The Guardian*, December 14, 2017, https://www.theguardian.com/inequality/2017/dec/14/inequality-is-not-inevitable-but-the-us-experiment-is-a-recipe-for-divergence?CMP=share_btn_tw ("The tax bill . . . will turbocharge inequality in America. Presented as a tax cut for workers and job-creating entrepreneurs, it is instead a giant cut for those with capital and inherited wealth. It's a bill that rewards the past, not the future.").

[50] See, e.g., Derek Thompson, "Why the GOP Tax Bill Is So Unpopular," *The Atlantic*, November 25, 2017, https://www.theatlantic.com/business/archive/2017/11/gop-tax-bill-unpopular/546668/ ("Republican politicians, whose campaigns are often financed by wealthy conservative donors like Sheldon Adelson and the Koch family, are worried that a failure to cut taxes on corporations will have a detrimental effect on contributions from the party's corporate-libertarian wing."); John Cassidy, "The Passage of the Senate Republican Tax Bill Was a Travesty," *The New Yorker*, December 2, 2017, https://www.newyorker.com/sections/news/the-passage-of-the-senate-republican-tax-bill-was-a-travesty ("there have been no public hearings, and the measure is being rushed through in a few weeks, with virtually no transparency."); Tara Golshan, "How Republicans Misled the American Public on Their Tax Bill," *Vox*, December 22, 2017, https://www.vox.com/policy-and-politics/2017/12/19/16791552/republicans-tax-bill-promises-lies (explaining that Republicans falsely claimed that "their bill will simplify the tax code by having American taxpayers file their taxes on a postcard, . . . and that the tax cuts will pay for themselves," while President Trump promised that he "and America's highest earners won't benefit from the tax bill at all.").

[51] Patrick Radden Keefe, "Carl Icahn's Failed Raid on Washington," *The New Yorker*, August 28, 2017, https://www.newyorker.com/magazine/2017/08/28/carl-icahns-failed-raid-on-washington ("Conflicts of interest have been a defining trait of the Trump Administration."); Citizens for Responsibility & Ethics in Washington, "Trump Inc: A Chronicle of Presidential Conflicts," accessed February 19, 2018, https://www.citizensforethics.org/trump-timeline/ (cataloguing presidential conflicts of interest); Eric Lipton, Ben Protess, and Andrew W. Lehren, "With Trump Appointees, a Raft of Potential Conflicts and 'No Transparency,'" *New York Times*, April 15, 2017, https://www.nytimes.com/2017/04/15/us/politics/trump-appointees-potential-conflicts.html (describing the Trump administration's ethics problems).

device for enriching himself and his family.[52] When people in power no longer hesitate to use their power to enrich themselves, and when norms of fair political competition are pushed aside, the viability of our democratic constitutional system is threatened.

The real concern about James Comey's firing as FBI director is best understood in terms of constitutional rot. The FBI director serves for a ten-year term that is designed to span across presidential terms in office. The goal is to insulate the head of the nation's investigative service from political pressure by politicians—and especially the president, who always retains the power to remove the director. Thus, the technical legal rule that the president can fire the director is accompanied by more amorphous democratic norms: First, the president should hesitate to remove a director except for very good reasons; second, personal and political advantage are not good reasons to fire a director; and third, presidents should avoid any appearance that for personal or political reasons they are pressuring the FBI to compromise its investigative authority.

The Comey firing violates these democratic norms. The circumstances of the firing, as well as Trump's own shifting explanations for it, suggest that Trump acted out of corrupt motives. The concern is that Trump fired Comey because Trump sought to hinder ongoing investigations into connections between the 2016 Trump presidential campaign and the Russian government,[53] or between criminal enterprises (such as money laundering) involving Russian oligarchs and Trump's businesses.[54] Democratic norms exist to prevent even the appearance of political corruption. The worry is that Trump violated democratic norms in circumstances that scream conflict of interest and create the appearance of corrupt motivations—that Trump used his powers as president to obstruct an

---

[52] "How Donald Trump Is Monetising His Presidency," *Economist*, July 20, 2017, https://www.economist.com/news/business/21725303-six-months-mr-trumps-conflicts-interest-look-even-worse-how-donald-trump-monetising ("Mr Trump already appears to be monetising the presidency."); Kate Brannen, "Trump Family's Endless Conflicts of Interest: Chapter and Verse," *Newsweek*, July 3, 2017, http://www.newsweek.com/trump-familys-endless-conflicts-interest-chapter-and-verse-631216 (offering a list of a examples "of the vast number of issues that require oversight and scrutiny during this presidency."); Jeremy Venook, "Trump's Interests vs. America's, Dubai Edition," *Atlantic*, August 9, 2017, https://www.theatlantic.com/business/archive/2017/08/donald-trump-conflicts-of-interests/508382/ (offering "an attempt to catalogue the more clear-cut examples of conflicts of interest that have emerged so far").

[53] President Trump explained in a May 11, 2017, interview with Lester Holt of NBC News that he was determined to fire Comey even before receiving advice from Attorney General Jeffrey Sessions and Deputy Attorney General Rod Rosenstein, because he was angry with Comey's continued investigative focus on Russia. James Griffiths, "Trump Says He Considered 'This Russia Thing' before Firing FBI Director Comey," *CNN*, May 12, 2017, http://www.cnn.com/2017/05/12/politics/trump-comey-russia-thing/ ("And in fact when I decided to just do it, I said to myself, I said 'you know, this Russia thing with Trump and Russia is a made-up story.'"). Immediately after the firing, however, the White House's official explanation had been that Trump acted on the advice of Deputy Attorney General Rosenstein, "who sharply criticized the handling of the investigation into Hillary Clinton's use of a private email server as secretary of state." Ibid.

[54] See Matthew Rosenberg and Matt Apuzzo, "Days before Firing, Comey Asked for More Resources for Russia Inquiry," *New York Times*, May 10, 2017, https://www.nytimes.com/2017/05/10/us/politics/comey-russia-investigation-fbi.html?_r=0 (noting a recent shift in the Senate investigation to focus on illegal money-laundering operations).

ongoing criminal investigation. If one could prove Trump's intent to obstruct the FBI's investigations, this would constitute a violation of federal obstruction of justice laws, and very likely would constitute an impeachable offense to boot.[55]

Trump and his political allies well understand this. Hence his political surrogates— and his enthusiasts in conservative media—have floated multiple smears and conspiracy theories in an attempt to undermine the public's confidence in federal law enforcement officials and the intelligence services. Trump and his allies have flooded the American public sphere with propaganda attempting to divert attention from Trump's corruption and displace it onto almost anyone and anything else.[56] In particular, Trump has argued that the real scandal is the corruption of Hillary Clinton, whom he defeated in the 2016 presidential election; he and his supporters have repeatedly called for the FBI to drop its investigation of him and begin prosecuting his political adversary, Clinton.[57] These techniques, characteristic of autocratic regimes, used to be unheard of in the United States. Their appearance suggests that Trump and his allies are quite willing to undermine democratic norms to stay in power. Indeed, all of their incentives now point in one direction: to exacerbate constitutional rot.

Constitutional rot does not occur all at once; it is a gradual process. The constitutional system in the United States may well be able to survive even Donald Trump's misadventures. But Trump's demagogic rise to power, his conduct of the presidency, and the inability (or unwillingness) of members of Congress to stop him, are signs that all is not well

---

[55] See, e.g., David G. Savage, "Trump's Statements Linking Russia Investigation to Comey Firing Could Lead to Legal Problems," *Los Angeles Times*, May 12, 2017, http://www.latimes.com/politics/la-na-pol-trump-obstruction-legal-20170512-story.html (noting potential legal dangers for President Trump as a result of his interview with Lester Holt); Laurence H. Tribe, "Trump Must Be Impeached. Here's Why," *Washington Post*, May 13, 2017, https://www.washingtonpost.com/opinions/trump-must-be-impeached-heres-why/2017/05/13/82ce2ea4-374d-11e7-b4ee-434b6d506b37_story.html?utm_term=.fbfb7cd7c931 (arguing that there is sufficient evidence in the public record "for Congress to launch an impeachment investigation of President Trump for obstruction of justice").

[56] See, e.g., Jason Schwartz, "Fox News Hosts Ramp Up 'Deep State' Conspiracies," *Politico*, January 28, 2018, https://www.politico.com/story/2018/01/26/fox-news-deep-state-conspiracies-372856 ("Fox News opinion hosts have seized on claims by some Republican lawmakers about a 'secret society' at the FBI and 'deep state actors' to fashion unproven narratives designed to protect Trump and delegitimize [Special Counsel Robert] Mueller."); Philip Bump, "Your Guide to the Anti-FBI Conspiracy Theories Rippling through Conservative Media," *Washington Post*, January 24, 2018, https://www.washingtonpost.com/news/politics/wp/2018/01/24/your-guide-to-the-anti-fbi-conspiracy-theories-rippling-through-conservative-media/ ("this tactic has become pervasive: defending Trump by arguing that it's actually the president who is the victim of a conspiracy and whipping up whatever evidence is at hand to bolster that claim.").

[57] See, e.g., David A. Graham, "Using the Justice Department to Investigate Trump's Enemies," *The Atlantic*, January 5, 2018, https://www.theatlantic.com/politics/archive/2018/01/the-push-for-investigations-of-the-clinton-foundation-and-christopher-steele/549860/ ("The Clinton investigations are especially unusual. As a candidate, Donald Trump promised to investigate his opponent if elected—a form of retribution behavior common in failed states with weak rule of law. . . . [A]s the Russia investigation has become more threatening to him, he has become more and more agitated about it, and has publicly demanded to know why the Justice Department hasn't acted.").

in American constitutional democracy. To paraphrase Shakespeare, something is rotten in the state of America. The limbs of the great tree of state are decaying. At some point, if we put too much weight on our democratic institutions, they will snap. Then we really will be in a constitutional crisis.

The language of constitutional rot is a better way to understand people's recurrent use of "constitutional crisis" in describing the Trump administration. There is currently no actual constitutional crisis in the United States. But if constitutional rot continues, we are living on borrowed time.

3 Defining and Tracking the Trajectory of Liberal Constitutional Democracy

Tom Ginsburg and Aziz Z. Huq

Introduction

Tahrir Square, in the center of Cairo, was first called Ismail Square after an ambitious ruler who sought to develop a "Paris on the Nile" in the 1870s. Ismail's schemes for refashioning Cairo into a modern metropolis backfired. Laden with debt, Egypt succumbed to British occupation in 1882, and then stumbled into a long postcolonial twilight of autocracy. Almost 130 years later, on Tuesday January 25, 2011, activists inspired by pro-democracy protests in Tunisia filtered into Tahrir Square—now a rather scruffy traffic circle with a patch of green in its center—blocking cars, dodging riot police, and shouting "Irhal Mubarak!" (Leave Mubarak!) and "Yasqut al-Nizam" ("Down with the Regime"). In an echo of scenes that would not have been out of place in the Paris of 1789 or 1848, thousands more joined them, or else flocked to protest before public buildings in Cairo and Alexandria. On February 2011, Vice President Omar Suleiman announced that Hosni Mubarak, president since 1981, would resign, turning power over to a transitional military regime.[1] The day after, people wandered through the rubble of protest in

---

[1] These paragraphs draw upon Nezar Al-Sayyad, "A History of Tahrir Square," *Harvard University Press Blog*, April 1, 2011, http://harvardpress.typepad.com/hup_publicity/2011/04/a-history-of-tahrir-square.html; Tarek Osman, *Egypt on the Brink: From Nasser to Mubarak* (New Haven: Yale University Press, 2010); Malise Ruthven, "The Islamic Road to the Modern World," *New York Review of Books*, June 22, 2017. On the protests: Robert

Tahrir "with dazed smiles, as if they still couldn't quite believe it."[2] A complex process of political transition toward democracy began in March with a referendum on constitutional change, leading to a two-round presidential election in June 2012.

But at the end of June 2013, Tahrir Square was once more filled with protests, now demanding the removal of a democratically elected president, Mohammed Morsi of the Muslim Brotherhood. Since being elected, Morsi had sought to reverse a Supreme Court ruling dissolving an earlier parliament, had assumed sweeping decree-making power once wielded by the military, and pushed through a new constitution in a referendum process boycotted by most of the opposition. Echoing the authoritarian 1971 constitution, this new constitution gave short shrift to rights, democratic or otherwise, installed the Sunni version of sharia as a major source of law, and vested the president with sweeping new authorities. From the moment of constitution-making in late 2012, protests had been bubbling away again in Tahrir Square. These reached fever pitch in June, with an estimated half million marching in the Square, calling for Morsi's removal.

On July 3, the military forcibly deposed Morsi and proscribed the Muslim Brotherhood and Islamist broadcasters. The forcible cleansing of the Islamists' remaining street encampments in August 2013 left hundreds dead. Notwithstanding its promise to maintain the democratic transition, the Egyptian military assumed power once more. General Abdel Fattah al-Sisi pressed through a new constitution and assumed the presidency.[3] Within three years of the brief moment in which its citizens' passion for democracy had illuminated televisions and newsfeeds around the world, Egypt was once again "a police state more vigorous than anything . . . seen since" the 1960s.[4]

The drama of democratic rise and fall that played out in Tahrir Square is hardly unique. Consider another Middle Eastern urban space, also an undersized traffic island with a halfhearted sprout of greenery in its center. Gezi Park is one of the few remaining green spaces in the geographic heart of Istanbul's Beyoğlu neighborhood. Starting on May 28, 2013, protesters assembled in the park to protest plans by the then-decade-old government of Recep Tayyip Erdoğan to demolish the iconic green space in favor of a shopping mall, thus beginning a wave of public protests that diffused across Turkey. Although invoking primarily environmental concerns, the protests also embodied and channeled

---

F. Worth, *A Rage for Order: The Middle East in Turmoil: From Tahrir Square to ISIS* (New York: Farrar, Strauss and Giroux, 2016); Charles Tripp, *The Power and the People: Paths of Resistance in the Middle East* (New York: Cambridge University Press, 2013).

[2] Worth, *Rage for Order*, 33.

[3] On the transitional process, see Nathan J. Brown, "Egypt's Failed Transition," *Journal of Democracy* 24, no. 4 (2013): 45–58; Yasmine El-Rashid, "Egypt: Whose Constitution?" *New York Review of Books*, January 3, 2013. On the June-July protests and their aftermath, see Patrick Kingsley, "Protesters across Egypt Call for Morsi to Go," *Guardian*, June 30, 2013; Yasmine El-Rashid, "Scenes from a Crackdown: What Really Happened in Cairo?," *New York Review of Books*, September 22, 2013; Hazem Kandil, "Sisi's Turn," *London Review of Books*, February 20, 2014.

[4] Kandil, *Sisi's Turn*.

growing frustration among a segment of Turkey's population about Erdoğan's perceived authoritarian tendencies. While Erdoğan claimed broad public support, and had indeed legitimately won election after election, protesters saw his rhetoric and behavior as increasingly intolerant and exclusionary. In their view, Erdoğan claimed to speak for the nation as a whole. In so doing, he used nationalist and religious tropes to justify attacks on the democratic system in general and his own opponents in particular. As one Turkish academic told the *Guardian* newspaper, "The real problem is not Taksim, and not the park, but the lack of any form of democratic decision-making process and the utter lack of consensus."[5]

Yet, as in Egypt, so in Turkey there was to be no opening of democratic space in the wake of public protest. Three years later the first Gezi Park protests, Turkey suffered what seemed like an attempted military coup against Erdoğan's government. The latter, having survived the coup, embarked on an extensive crackdown on bureaucrats, civil society, academics, and journalists perceived as anything other than aligned with the regime. In the weeks after the coup, the government purged or detained some 9,000 police officers, 21,000 private school teachers, 10,000 soldiers, 2,745 judges, 1,700 university deans, and 21,700 Ministry of Education officials.[6] What progress had been made in integrating Kurdish citizens of Turkey into the political mainstream also ground to a halt, casting the shadow of renewed internecine conflict within the country, as well as intimating the prospect of conflict beyond its southern border.[7]

Tahrir Square and Gezi Park are snapshots from what has been called, among other things, a global democratic recession, decline, or full-blown retreat. They exemplify the heterogeneity of the moment. One is a story of democracy's failure to launch. The other is an instance of institutional erosion and collapse in a polity that, many hoped, had firmly turned its face away from an autocratic past. Egypt and Turkey are not the only instances of democratic repudiation. Hungary, Poland, and other countries in Eastern Europe, much like Turkey, have embraced populist leaders who promise to end the gridlock that is sometimes democracy's consequence. In the Philippines, the strongman Rodrigo Duterte was elected in 2016, after bragging of having personally carried out extrajudicial killings while serving as a mayor.[8] Even in seemingly well-established democracies, the quality of governance seems to be eroding. In Israel, for example, the government has proposed a series of laws limiting critical speech, while nongovernmental opponents of

[5] Christopher Letsch, "Turkey Protests Spread after Violence in Istanbul over Park Demolition," *The Guardian*, May 31, 2013; see also Kasi Genç, "In Gezi Park," *London Review of Books*, June 3, 2013; Coskun Tastan, "The Gezi Park Protests in Turkey: A Qualitative Field Research," *Turkey* 15, no. 3 (2013): 27–38.

[6] Josh Keller, Iaryna Mykhyalyshyn, and Safak Timur, "The Scale of Turkey's Purge Is Nearly Unprecedented," *New York Times*, August 2, 2016.

[7] Patrick Kingsley, "Amid Turkey's Purge, a Renewed Attack on Kurdish Culture," *New York Times*, June 29, 2017.

[8] Russell Goldman, "Rodrigo Duterte on Killing Criminal Suspects: 'I Used to Do It Personally,'" *New York Times*, December 14, 2016.

current policies are having funding scrutinized.[9] The Japanese government has pushed for tight new internal security legislation that imperils free debate on many issues of national importance.[10] And, of course, in the country that has devoted the most effort to promoting democracy abroad, the president of the United States has made a spectacle of breaking norms concerning transparency, corruption, respect for the media and political opponents, antidiscrimination values. and truth-telling.

Our aim in this chapter is to provide some definitional and empirical scaffolding for thinking about whether the Egyptian and Turkish cases are outliers or exemplars of the current state of democracy. This means first considering how "democracy" should be defined and analyzed. We argue that in thinking about democratic decline, it is most useful to focus on "liberal constitutional democracy" as a distinct species of democracy, one that has enjoyed a hegemonic status at least as an ideal since the mid-1990s. Our analysis complements other ongoing work of ours in a book and a number of articles. There, we have broken down liberal constitutional democracy into its consistent parts, and explained how each part can fail or persevere.[11] Turning back to this chapter, we more modestly analyze the present trajectory of democracy across the globe, roughly defined in these terms, in light of the available comparative data. Parsing competing claims about global trends, we suggest that it is normatively appropriate to consider both the Egyptian and the Turkish case in the evaluation of democracy's current trajectory, and that the two cases tell us something about the different risks that democracy faces in our current moment.

Defining Liberal Constitutional Democracy

In a paper delivered to the Aristotelian Society of London in March 1956, the philosopher Walter Bryce Gallie introduced the idea of an "essentially contested concept." Gallie drew attention to the fact that there is often agreement that there are certain concepts "the proper use of which inevitably involves endless disputes about their proper uses on the part of their users," disputes that "cannot be settled by appeal to empirical evidence, linguistic usage, or the canons of logic alone." One of the very first examples Gallie gave of an essentially contested concept "par excellence" was democracy itself. In his view, there was simply no way of offering an uncontroversial definition of that concept.[12]

---

[9] Peter Beaumont, "Israel Passes Law to Force NGOs to Reveal Foreign Funding," *The Guardian*, July 12, 2016.

[10] Mina Pollman, "Japan's New State Secrets Law: One Year Later," *The Diplomat*, December 9, 2015, http://thediplomat.com/2015/12/japans-controversial-state-secrets-law-one-year-later/.

[11] Tom Ginsburg and Aziz Z. Huq, "How to Lose a Constitutional Democracy," *UCLA Law Review* 65 (2018): 78–169.

[12] W.B. Gallie, "Essentially Contested Concepts," *Proceedings of the Aristotelian Society* 56 (1956): 167–198; W.B. Gallie, "Art as an Essentially Contested Concept," *Philosophical Quarterly* 6, no. 23 (April 1956): 97–114.

Gallie was right. The word "democracy" has moral force. But precisely because of that, it is easily and often diluted through reckless and profligate use. In the international sphere, the rhetorical currency of democracy has become universal—a reflection of the powerful grip that the ideal of democracy, however loosely understood, once exercised. So it is perhaps unsurprising that the most totalitarian state on earth is the *Democratic People's Republic* of Korea. North Korea is not alone in its hypocrisy. As an empirical matter, there is a *negative* correlation between the number of mentions of "democracy" in a country's constitution and the presence of commonly used markers of democratic practice.[13] Looking at the text of a country's fundamental law is not just unhelpful—it may even mislead as a guide to actual practice.

Philosophers and political scientists alike have intensely debated the core of democracy without converging on one view. A sole point of consensus seems to be there is no real consensus on that pivotal definitional question.[14] Still, some generalizations are possible, and worthwhile just to get some traction on events in the world. In the fields of economics and political science, the idea of democracy has been closely associated with the simple fact of elections. Most famously, in the early part of the twentieth century, the economist Joseph Schumpeter described democracy as an "institutional arrangement for arriving at political decisions in which individuals acquire the power to decide by means of a competitive struggle for the people's vote."[15] Similarly, the political scientist Adam Przeworski pithily stated that democracy is "a system in which parties lose elections,"[16] or (in another work) "a regime in which those who govern are selected through contested elections."[17] Other political scientists have preserved the focus on elections, but added caveats about the scope of suffrage or the number of contested elections.[18] Yet other scholars have defined democracy in terms of an abstract idea of "accountability" to the public without focusing on the specific institutional instantiation of that ideal.[19]

---

[13] The correlations range from −.21 for Van Hannens democracy index, −.17 for the Przeworski et al. measure; −.08 for the Unified Democracy Score measure, and −.05 for the Polity index. Data on file with the authors.

[14] Michael Coppedge, John Gerring, David Altman, Michael Bernhard, Steven Fish, Allen Hicken, Matthew Kroenig et al., "Conceptualizing and Measuring Democracy: A New Approach," *Perspectives on Politics,* 9, no. 2 (2011): 247–267.

[15] Joseph Schumpeter, *Capitalism, Socialism and Democracy* (New York: Harper & Row, 1942), 269.

[16] Adam Przeworski, *Democracy and the Market: Political and Economic Reforms in Eastern Europe and Latin America* (New York: Cambridge University Press, 1991), 10.

[17] Adam Przeworski, Michael E. Alvarez, Jose Antonio Cheibub, and Fernando Limongi, *Democracy and Development; Political Institutions and Well-Being in the World, 1950–1990* (New York: Cambridge University Press, 2000), 15.

[18] Carles Boix, *Democracy and Redistribution* (New York: Cambridge University Press, 2003), 61; Samuel P. Huntington, *The Third Wave: Democratization in the Late Twentieth Century* (Tulsa: University of Oklahoma Press, 1991), 266–267 (articulating now famous "two-turnover" test for democratic consolidation).

[19] Philippe C. Schmitter and Terry Lynn Karl, "What Democracy Is . . . and Is Not," *Journal of Democracy* 2, no. 3 (1991): 75–88.

While a focus on elections initially seems both usefully parsimonious and undemanding, unraveling complexity quickly emerges. Consider the elections to China's people's congresses, last held in November 2016 with ballots cast by 2.5 million people. Given the strict control maintained over candidate selection by the Chinese Communist Party and the tight regulation of election-related speech, it would be silly to say that the mere fact of these elections proved that China was appropriately classified as a democracy. Elections with only one feasible winner, either because only one entity competes, because the ability to stand for election is limited, or because only one entity will be allowed to exercise power, are clearly insufficient. Similarly, elections that happen once, never to be repeated, do not a democracy make. The slogan "one person, one vote, one time" is used to describe an election that leads to the end of democracy.[20] Instead, democratic elections must be ex ante uncertain, irreversible, and also ex post repeatable.[21]

What then more might be required beyond the fact of elections? Critics of the minimalist approach have argued persuasively that competitive elections do not by themselves act as a guarantee of inclusion of the public voice in politics, and have instead argued for a "realistic" definition of democracy.[22] But what such realism requires is itself contested, and there are several thicker definitions on offer. Perhaps unsurprisingly, many political scientists have focused on elements of the institutions that manage democracy. In one of the leading treatments of democracy, the political scientist Robert Dahl defined "polyarchy" (i.e., the rule of the many) to rest upon six "minimal" requirements, including free and fair elections, empowered election officials, freedom of association and autonomy, and inclusive citizenship.[23] Perhaps our generation's foremost student of democracy, Larry Diamond, focuses by contrast on the existence of institutions that create standing relationships of accountability within government and also between government and the electorate.[24] Yet other scholars focus on participation: systems are more democratic, they would say, to the degree they involve the public in meaningful ways.

These different approaches have different implications for how democracy might disappear or come under threat. Some see risks from the growth of the state itself: as bureaucracy expands and technocrats make more and more decisions, the exercise of a democratic franchise becomes less meaningful. Citizens can no longer comprehend, let alone evaluate, the thousands of varied policy and implementation decisions taken by a government. Others see the chief prerequisites as economic, believing that democracy

[20] Amb. Edward Djerejian, *The U.S. and the Mideast in a Changing World*, speech at Meridian House International, Washington, DC, June 2, 1992, http://www.disam.dsca.mil/pubs/vol%2014_4/djerejian.pdf (coining the expression "one man, one vote, one time").

[21] Adam Przeworski et al., "What Makes Democracies Endure?" *Journal of Democracy* 7, no. 1 (1996): 39–55.

[22] Guillermo O'Donnell, "Illusions about Consolidation," *Journal of Democracy* 7, no. 2 (1996): 34–51.

[23] Robert Dahl, *On Democracy* (New Haven: Yale University Press, 1999), 85–86.

[24] Larry Diamond, *Developing Democracy: Toward Consolidation* (1999): 10–12 (including vertical and horizontal accountability in a definition of democracy).

requires a minimal level of resources on the part of its individual citizens.[25] Without adequate economic or educational resources, citizens in democracy cannot adequately exercise judgment about potential office-holders necessary to make the franchise meaningful. Without economic vitality, democracy might not succeed. As a former Ghanaian coup leader once said, "one man, one vote is meaningless unless accompanied by the principle of one man, one bread."[26]

Some commentators start from the premise that democracy is an exercise in self-determination, and that self-determination can only occur among a people or a nation that is relatively homogenous. In the absence of feeling of mutual sympathy and solidarity, the ultimate rationale of democracy falls apart.[27] From this perspective, immigration might threaten democracy. Finally, and relatedly, one might focus on another sort of culture: one might say that a democracy cannot arise without a shared public culture in which meaningful deliberation can occur.[28] Absent a shared public sphere characterized by a single language and common values, which might indeed be shared across racial and ethnic lines, the deliberation at the heart of democratic practice cannot emerge. These positions suggest that economic, cultural, or discursive conditions are inseverable from the definition of democracy.

But each of these prerequisites rests on deeply contestable empirical and normative judgments. Consider, for instance, the materialist argument, which presumes that in the absence of sufficient resources, men and women are not able to assimilate information about their polity, or make judgments about what is likely to advance their own well-being. Comparative experience of elections across many different socioeconomic contexts does not suggest that there is a lower bound of material resources below which democratic participation is impossible. Mali, one of the poorest countries in the world, held free and fair elections for two decades after 1991, and voters in largely illiterate rural Afghanistan and Nepal are enthusiastic about exercising the franchise. Our own personal experience of electoral contestation in these contexts makes us leery of any contemptuous dismissal of their relevance as exemplars of democracy in action. Equally, it is hardly clear that ethnic or cultural homogeneity is in practice a necessary predicate for the successful practice of democracy. Our own city of Chicago, for example, is a mosaic of different races and ethnicities who do not share each other's languages, cultures, or temperaments. And yet democracy seems to emerge from the cacophony (at least some of the time!). More generally, the demand for homogeneity or cultural cohesion presumes the absence of the very disagreements that democratic institutions are, at their best, capable of resolving.

---

[25] Joshua Cohen, "Democratic Equality," *Ethics* 99, no. 4 (1989): 727–751.

[26] Rhoda E. Howard-Hassmann, "The Full-Belly Thesis: Should Economic Rights Take Priority over Civil and Political Rights? Evidence from Sub-Saharan Africa," *Human Rights Quarterly*, 5 (1983): 467–490.

[27] Jeremy Waldron, "Democracy," in *The Oxford Handbook of Political Philosophy*, ed. David Estlund (Oxford: Oxford University Press, 2012).

[28] Gabriel Almond and Sidney Verba, *The Civic Culture* (Beverly Hills, CA: Sage Publications, 1963).

Disagreement, rather than harmonious accord, is the natural condition and perhaps even a necessary predicate for democracy.[29] A truly homogenous society, in contrast, would not need to have democratic institutions to reach decisions in the first instance.

The range and variance in definitional approaches to democracy reflects foundational disagreements about the role of collective choice mechanisms in a democracy. It also suggests that a definition of democracy will in part reflect the needs and interests of the scholar offering it. The utility of an essentially contested term such as democracy arises from its ability to provide a starting point for many different lines of inquiry, whether institutional, social psychological, or normative in nature.

* * *

For the purpose of tracking contemporary democratic decline, we think a more parsimonious definition of democracy is preferable, one that does not rely excessively on controversial normative premises. We prefer the label "liberal constitutional democracy," to make clear the extent to which normative judgments enter into our delineation of democracy. Our definition integrates three system-level properties of national institutions that, in our view, intertwine and interact closely. It is only when they are all present together that a country warrants the label of liberal constitutional democracy. The term is meant to capture three conceptually separate but functionally intertwined institutional elements. These are, first, a democratic electoral system, most important periodic free-and-fair elections in which the modal adult can vote, and after which a losing side concedes power to the winning side. The second prong of our definition comprises the particular liberal rights to speech and association that are closely linked to democracy in practice. Finally, our definition looks for a level of integrity of law and legal institutions—that is, the rule of law—sufficient to allow democratic engagement without fear or coercion. Each word in the term "liberal constitutional democracy" hence corresponds to one of the three elements needed for a system of self-government to get off the ground.[30]

Let us say a bit more about each of these subcomponents. The electoral component does not require much explanation, given its centrality to the literature since Schumpeter. But it is less often appreciated that elections depend on a supporting structure of legal entitlements and institutions. Only if there are robust rights to speech and association can electoral choice be meaningful. Free speech is required to criticize and to make alternative policy proposals, as well as to facilitate a vigorous press. Without open and critical speech, in short, there is no possibility of accountability. (We set to one side, however, the complex problems raised by monopoly control over the channels by which information spreads, or the use of false or libelous means to impede the dissemination of truthful information. These are hard problems, but not necessarily symptomatic of all

---

[29] Jeremy Waldron, *Law and Disagreement* (Oxford: Clarendon Press, 1999).

[30] For more development of the concept, see our "How to Lose Constitutional Democracy,"

contestation over democracy). Free association is necessary, most obviously, for political parties to form, but it is also essential for the thick network of organizations and institutions that translate people's individual preferences into policy demands. Civil society plays a critical mediating role between citizens and the state, in part because it facilitates self-organizing groups that can serve as a counterweight against overbearing state actors. Associations, as has been noted since Tocqueville, help make democracy work.[31]

The rule of law, too, underpins any functional democracy in practice. Most obviously, a neutral administration is essential for electoral choice to function properly. When boundary-drawing, ballot preparation, and vote-counting becomes a partisan activity, free choice is at risk. The rule of law is also essential for robust protection of the key rights of speech and association that make democracy work. But it is also the case that a neutral bureaucracy, committed to upholding the law, is critical for implementing the policies that are adopted by elected leaders, especially after they leave office. Without neutral administration, elected leaders may never *want* to leave office, for to do so might put their policies and even their persons at risk.

As a system-level characteristic resting on three somewhat abstract and general institutional traits, our definition of democracy is not amenable to precise quantification. Part of the difficulty of quantification flows from the fact that none of the three institutional predicates that we describe is ever likely to be perfectly achieved. All democracies, however generally well-functioning, are likely to fall short in some ways in respect to one, or likely more, of the three institutional building blocks we have described. The United States, for example, is well known for robust free speech, but features a system of partisan gerrymandering that compromises our electoral quality to some extent. Other countries may score better on neutral electoral administration, but more vigorously regulate freedom of association.

Liberal constitutional democracy, as we have defined it, is an ideal type, but even if it is never perfectly achieved in practice, it remains useful as a way to orient our normative assessment.[32] We recognize that it is thus vulnerable to criticism for its imprecision and lack of empirical tractability. There are existing measures of "democracy," such as the Polity, Varieties of Democracy, and Freedom House scores that capture several elements of the definition.[33] We readily concede that existing metrics of the kind employed below are only partial measures. They are, nevertheless, sufficiently close to our core concept that they provide a useful platform for empirical analysis of the kind we present below.

---

[31] Robert Putnam, *Making Democracy Work: Civic Traditions in Modern Italy* (Princeton: Princeton University Press, 1993).

[32] Max Weber, *The Methodology of the Social Sciences*, ed. and trans. Edward Shils and Henry Finch (Glencoe, IL: Free Press of Glencoe, 1997), https://archive.org/stream/maxweberonmethod00webe/maxweberonmethod00webe_djvu.txt.

[33] Seva Gunitsky, "How Do You Measure 'Democracy'?" *Washington Post*, June 23, 2015, https://www.washingtonpost.com/news/monkey-cage/wp/2015/06/23/how-do-you-measure-democracy/?utm_term=.2cb5edf51c17.

Tracking the Current Arc of Liberal Constitutional Democracy

A large literature has emerged of late forecasting rough seas for constitutional democracy. In order to determine what to make of the resulting range of forecasts, we turn first to the question whether those forecasts are well-founded in methodological terms.

Writing in 2015, political scientists Steven Levitsky and Lucan Way offer perhaps the most compelling case for comfort rather than concern.[34] They evaluate the state of global democracy by looking at the mean national scores of several measures of democracy or liberal democracy, including the Freedom House, Polity, Economist Intelligence Unit, and Bertelsmann Indexes. These average scores reveal no downtick in democratic practice, they note, after examining data from 1990 to 2013. Moreover, they show that as of their writing, only seven countries—Bolivia, Ecuador, Honduras, Mali, the Philippines, Thailand, and Venezuela—have gone from being classified as "Free" to "Unfree" by Freedom House. Comparing Turkey to its pre-2002 state, Levitsky and Way characterize it as a polity that has transitioned from one form of imperfect democracy (or competitive authoritarianism) to another, echoing other studies that have looked at the distribution of regime types globally and declared democracy to have been at "a historical high water mark."[35] Perceptions of a decline, Levitsky and Way argue, are an artifact of "an excessively optimistic mindset" during the 1990s.[36]

On the other side of the debate are scholars who look at the same top-line global data, and perceive more cause for concern. In the most careful of these analyses, Larry Diamond looks at a slightly shorter period than Levitsky and Way do (2000 to 2015), and looks not at averages but rather searches for evidence of decline. He finds democratic breakdowns in twenty-seven countries. He further observes that in nearly half of the world's "swing states," that is, countries that are large enough to influence the general direction of global democracy, political liberties have eroded. The trend line in authoritarian regimes is similar. Less transparency, less openness, and less responsiveness to citizens are becoming the rule.[37] Diamond also contrasts a period of rapid expansion in the number and quality of democracies between the mid-1990s and the mid-2000s, and notes that since 2006, the world has experienced a prolonged stagnation in the rate of democratization.[38]

Joshua Kurlantzick echoes Diamond's analysis. He describes democracy as "in retreat" based on his view that the sheer number of democracies has ceased rising, and the number of notionally democratic countries in which the autocratic practices are pervasive

---

[34] Steven Levitsky and Lucan Way, "The Myth of Democratic Recession," *Journal of Democracy* 26, no. 1 (2015): 45.

[35] Wolfgang Merkel, "Are Dictatorships Returning? Revisiting the 'Democratic Rollback' Hypothesis," *Contemporary Politics* 16, no. 1 (2010): 17–31, 23.

[36] Levitsky and Way, "The Myth of Democratic Recession," 49.

[37] Larry Diamond, "Democracy in Decline: How Washington Can Reverse the Tide," *Foreign Affairs*, July–August 2016, 151.

[38] Larry Diamond, "Facing Up to the Democratic Recession," *Journal of Democracy* 26, no. 1 (2015): 141–155.

is on the rise. Writing in 2013, he estimated that nearly 53 of the 128 countries assessed by the Bertelsmann index were "defective democracies." Like Diamond, Kurlantzick is especially careful to look at polities that because of size or historical legacies may have an outsize role in shaping transnational trends. Like Diamond, he flags democratic declines in these polities, and cautions that because of their influence, these instances of erosion may be especially significant.[39] It is striking, however, that their lists of troubling swing states diverge with almost no ensuing overlap. Kurlantzick flags Russia and Kenya.[40] But Diamond identifies twelve worrying cases, including Taiwan, South Africa, Columbia, Indonesia, Mexico, and Thailand.[41] This suggests that different methods of looking for democratic decline can generate complementary sets of evidence.

Who then is correct? In important part, the debate is conceptual rather than empirical. Levitsky and Way, tellingly, reject sixteen of Diamond's cases of democratic breakdown on the ground that these involved no more than ephemeral "democratic moments" rather than the collapse of "actual democratic regimes."[42] In light of this approach, they would presumably not count the unwinding of Egypt's democratic order in 2013 because it was not an "actual" democracy, having only been partly democratic for less than two years. Turkey might be a closer case. But we can imagine arguments that it too should not "count" because it lacks a sufficiently entrenched history of democratic rule.

As our introduction intimated, we think that Diamond has the better of this argument. In our view, both Egypt and Turkey rightly belong in the deficit column when tallying democracy's status today. From the perspective of a polity's citizens, the closure of even a brief democratic opening and a relapse into authoritarian brutality may be just as tragic—perhaps even more tragic—than the erosion of a long-standing democracy. The Egyptian blogger Alaa Ad El Fattah captures this when he wrote the following about the Arab Spring's failure: "Despair prevails . . . Now tomorrow will be exactly like today and yesterday and all the days preceding and all the days following, I have no influence over anything."[43] Starkly put, an Egyptian is just as entitled to mourn the loss of her democracy future as an American, a Venezuelan, or a Turk.

More generally, we think that national failures can be as important as successes in determining the global trajectory of democracy and authoritarianism. In every case, the present members of a polity lose the anticipation of self-determination; how settled that expectation is as a historical matter seems of quite secondary importance. Moreover, it is not at all clear whether the sudden demise of a new democracy will be more or less

---

[39] Joshua Kurlantzick, *Democracy in Retreat: The Revolt of the Middle Class and the Worldwide Decline of Representative Government* (New Haven: Yale University Press, 2013).

[40] In other words, he describes worrying trends away from democratic norms in the Asian context. Joshua Kurlantzick, "Asia's Democracy Backlash," *Current History* 107, no. 712 (2008): 375.

[41] Diamond, "Facing Up to the Democratic Recession," 150.

[42] Levitsky and Way, "The Myth of Democratic Recession," 53.

[43] Alaa Ad El Fattah, "The Only Words I Can Write Are about Losing Our Words," *The Guardian*, January 23, 2016, https://www.theguardian.com/books/2016/jan/23/arab-spring-five-years-on-writers-look-back.

consequential than the erosion of an old one. Hannah Arendt famously observed that "the French Revolution, which ended in disaster, has made world history."[44] So it is also for the strangling of democracy in its cradle in, say, a China or an Egypt. The idea that the failure of a new democracy, or the thwarting of a democratic opening, is less important than the collapse of a more storied regime is untenable whether one looks at only the immediate human costs or at the possible long-term effects of the event.

The events of Egypt and Turkey are relevant to thinking about democracy's trajectory for another reason: despite the enlargement of what Samuel Huntington called the "third wave" of democratization between 1974 and 1990,[45] the consolidation of liberal democracy as global ideal has simply not come to pass. Rather, one of the most important features of the current democratic recession is the growing perception that liberal constitutional democracy is not the only game in town, and that it might not even be the *best* game in town. This is a perception that can be discerned with gathering strength not just in Egypt and Turkey, but across so-called established democracies in the United States and Western Europe. It is a perception shared by politicians seeking renewed office under democratic rule, parties that embrace with increasing frankness an "anti-system" posture, voters increasingly disillusioned with the justifications and results of democracy, and would-be autocrats looking simply for cover. In a way that was not the case even a decade ago, the force of constitutional liberal democracy as an aspirational benchmark—as the only morally acceptable form of government to embrace—is waning.

We turn next to a comprehensive look at the country-level data, including not just the top-line evidence of movements in and out of democracy but also trends within established democracies, the outcomes of potential transitions from democracy, and survey evidence about the continuing appeal of democracy as a system. Together, this pool of data provides reason for concern but not panic: democracy is not about to collapse around the world, but it does seem fair to say with Kurlantzick that it is in retreat as a practice and as an ideal.

COUNTRY-LEVEL TRENDS

Since the strongest evidence against the recession thesis turns on an examination of aggregated data of democracy's global trends, we start there. Two graphics provide summary snapshots of global trends, and starting points for analysis.

To begin, Figure 3.1 draws on data on democratic quality produced by Freedom House, which roughly matches our definition of liberal constitutional democracy, to show how the sheer number of democracies, autocracies, and hybrid regimes of various sorts has changed since 1980. In so doing, we can step back in time in order to see whether the

---

[44] Hannah Arendt, *On Revolution* (London: Penguin Books, 1990), 56.
[45] Huntington, *The Third Wave*, 266–267.

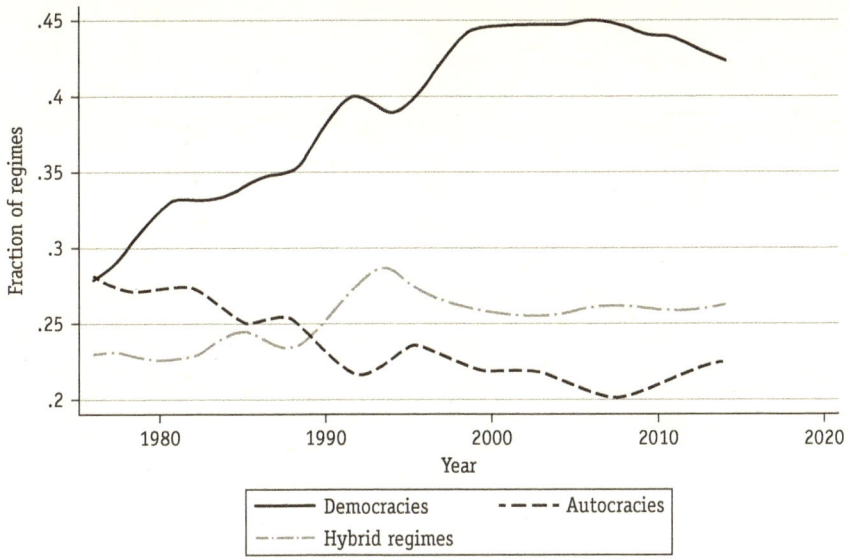

FIGURE 3.1 Regime types in the Third Wave.
Source: Adapted from Freedom House data 2016.

perception of global decline is indeed an artifact of the 1990s' high water-mark, as Levitsky and Way suggest.

This simple numerical counting exercise shows why Diamond, Kurlantzick, and others have reason to be concerned. On the one hand, there was been a dip, although not a collapse, in the sheer number of democracies. Indeed, Freedom House reports that 2016 marked the eleventh consecutive year of decline in the number of democracies.[46] On the other hand, there was been a gentle uptick in the number of autocracies (and perhaps in hybrid regimes). It seems clear, as Levitsky and Way argue, that in comparison to the pre-1990 period, democracy remains a relatively prevalent form of governance. At the same time, this sort of absolute tally is informative above and beyond the average democracy scores that Levitsky and Way focus upon. Annualized averages can obscure offsetting trends. Moreover, if we take their data at face value, Levitsky and Way analyze a period in which instances of democratization occurred in relatively small countries such as Liberia, Malawi, and Sierra Leone.[47] An unweighted mean score of the kind they use (and of the kind presented in Figure 3.1) treats all countries as equivalent. But it is hardly clear that the presence of democratic decay in populous, large, and strategically influential nations should be equated with gains in smaller and less influential contexts.

Moreover, the absolute number of transitions between democracy and its alternatives is not likely to tell the whole story, in part because the quality of democracy can

---

[46] Freedom House, *Freedom in the World 2017: Populists and Autocrats* (Washington, DC: Freedom House, 2017).

[47] Diamond, "Facing Up to the Democratic Recession," 142.

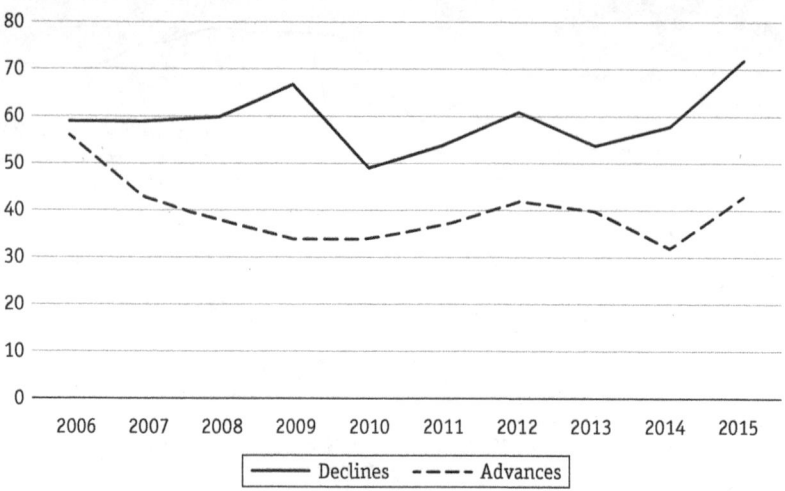

FIGURE 3.2 Democratic declines and advances.
Source: Freedom House data from Freedom in the World 2016.

be deteriorating even if there is no absolute change in regime type as captured in the political science measures. To evaluate that possibility, Figure 3.2 reports the number of jurisdictions that have seen advances rather than declines in the quality of democracy. We look at a narrower time frame here between 2006 and 2016 here to understand better what in practice global democratic "stagnation" looks like.

Figure 3.2 demonstrates that, while some countries have deepened their democracy, others have regressed in the past decade in comparison to what was the case in the 1990s. In recent years, there has been an uptick in both phenomena, suggesting that some kind of democratic decay is at work in some countries, but not all. Countries are thus growing further apart. This is consistent with Freedom House's own report, which notes that sixty-seven countries declined in 2016, while only thirty-six registered gains.[48]

We can also examine more fine-grained measures that purport to capture the subcomponents of our definition of liberal constitutional democracy. The Varieties of Democracy (V-DEM) Project has produced, for all countries since 1900, a set of annual scores that recognizes the multidimensional nature of democracy.[49] Since analysts often have particular conceptualizations in mind when they are discussing democracy, it is argued, any measure of democracy must reflect the underlying conceptualization. V-DEM purports to be an improvement on prior measures in this regard. One of their measures purports to measure

---

[48] *Freedom House 2017*, at 1. To some degree this is an artifact of the scale. As more countries approach the higher end of the measurement scale because of the Third Wave of democratization, the only place to go is down. For example, in the twenty-one-point Polity scale, roughly one-sixth of countries are at the maximum score of 10. Such countries cannot advance but can only decline. Regardless, the main point is that declines are in fact occurring.

[49] Varieties of Democracy, accessed February 26, 2017, https://www.v-dem.net/en/.

TABLE 3.1

Change in Varieties of Democracy Index 2007–2016

	Overall liberal democracy score	Freedom of association	Freedom of expression
No. of advances	77	66	67
Top 5 gains	Tunisia .56	Tunisia .66	Tunisia .66
	Bhutan .28	Libya .60	Libya .59
	Myanmar .25	Myanmar .43	Myanmar .43
	Sri Lanka .24	Bhutan .35	Bhutan .35
	Nepal .19	Guinea .24	Guinea .24
No. of declines	96	106	105
Top 5 declines	Turkey −.35	Thailand −.54	Turkey −.54
	Ukraine −.27	Burundi −.43	Ukraine −.36
	Poland −.25	Ukraine −.31	Burundi −.34
	Macedonia −.21	Nicaragua −.29	Yemen −.28
	Brazil −.19	Mauritania −.27	Thailand −.25

Source: V-DEM data 2016.

liberal democracy, and they also have subcomponents that measure freedom of expression and freedom of association. Each of these measures is normalized from 0 to 1. Comparing in Table 3.1 the 2016 scores with those of a decade earlier, we can evaluate how many countries have advanced and how many have declined on each of these dimensions.

These data, too, indicate diverging paths. Most gainers and losers had only slight shifts over the decade, but of those countries with large changes on the normalized index, losers outnumbered gainers for each variable. (Because the data is normalized, it is not as susceptible to problems of scale as are the other indices, which have absolute upward and lower bounds.)

A final set of data would be that on the rule of law. The World Justice Project has, since 2011, measured perceptions of the rule of law in different countries. Many countries have been surveyed at least three times since the beginning of the project. More countries improved their scores from the first to last assessment, but many in sub-Saharan Africa did not. Four countries suffered sharp declines: Hungary, Lebanon, Turkey, and Venezuela.[50]

In part, all these data also reflect the failure of a hoped-for "fourth wave" of democracy, which might have crested with the Arab Spring had events gone differently. That is, to observe not only that the budding Egyptian democracy failed, but that Libya, Yemen, and Syria descended into bloody internal conflict, while the Gulf states deepened their repression of political opposition, helps us to understand the tally of democracy's fortunes today. In only one country in the region, Tunisia, can we say there was a measure of

---

[50] Data on file with authors, from the World Justice Project, www.worldjusticeproject.org.

significant democratic advance. That high levels of social mobilization elsewhere in the region did not produce reform counts as evidence of democracy's lack of momentum.[51] It demonstrates the strength of the authoritarian form of government, manifested in local security forces' willingness to repress and international actors' unwillingness to withdraw support for repressive regimes.

Similarly, in the late 1990s in China, the process of economic liberalization seemed to be generating a measure of political reform, such that newly appointed prime minister Zhu Rongji could pronounce in 1998 that "Of course I am in favor of democratic elections." But twenty years later, any optimism for democracy seems far-fetched in light of Xi Jinping's aggressive crackdowns on lawyers and intellectuals, the announcement in 2018 that he would not be subject to the constitution's previously honored presidential term limits, China's close scrutiny of social media and other vectors for dissent, its increasingly heavy-handed approach to protests and dissent, and the severe management of even limited elections in Hong Kong.[52] This stalling of democratic progress and the entrenchment of violent authoritarian rule for another generation or two—as has happened across the Middle East with the exception of Tunisia—must count as a *defeat* for democracy, not merely a matter of indifference.

In short, even if Levitsky and Way are correct that the *average* quality of democracy across the world has not changed over time, there are other measures that do show stagnation, and even some reversal at the global level. At the same time, Levitsky and Way are correct in pointing out that once the lens is expanded beyond the 1990s, that decay starts to look more like reversion to a mean.

SURVEY DATA

Perhaps the best available data about public attitudes toward democracy comes from the World Values Survey (WVS). The breadth and the historical pedigree of the WVS instrument make it an invaluable tool for understanding how public attitudes have changed over time and across space, at least in the context of established democracies.

The WVS data about the United States and Europe suggest an uneven but growing level of disaffection with democracy. Drawing on the work of Roberto Stepfan Foa and Yascha Mounk, we start with the American data because we think it is especially illuminating to see shifting popular attitudes in what many view as democracy's current heartland.[53] Over the past three decades, the proportion of US citizens who believe it would

[51] Eva Bellin, "Reconsidering the Robustness of Authoritarianism in the Middle East: Lessons from the Arab Spring," *Politics* 44, no. 2 (2012): 127–149.

[52] "What Hong Kong Can Teach Xi Jinping," *The Economist*, July 1, 2017.

[53] Roberto Stefan Foa and Yascha Mounk, "The Democratic Disconnect," *Journal of Democracy* 27, no. 3 (2016): 5–17; Roberto Stefan Foa and Yascha Mounk, "The Signs of Deconsolidation," *Journal of Democracy* 28, no. 1 (2017): 5–15; Roberto Stefan Foa and Yascha Mounk, "The End of the Consolidation Paradigm: A

be a "good" or a "very good" thing for the "army to rule" has spiked from one in sixteen to one in six. Among the cohort of rich young Americans, moreover, the proportion of those who look favorably on military rule is more than one in three. The WVS instrument also asks about a strong leader who does not bother with elections. In the 2010–2014 wave of surveys, 35 percent of Americans thought this is a very good or fairly good idea (and nearly half of Americans also think that it would be fairly good or very good for technocrats to make decisions). This contrasts with the 1995–1997 wave, when just over one-fifth of Americans approved of a strong leader. The same pattern of increasing tolerance of, and even approval of, autocratic forms of government can be identified in the same period in countries such as Japan, Argentina, and South Korea.[54]

The WVS data also reveals a difference between different age cohorts, although the significance of this gap has been sharply contested. In the 2014 survey, almost four-fifths of Americans thought democratic governance was fairly good or very good for the country. That figure drops to 72 percent, however, for those under thirty. In addition, Americans are less intense in their attachment to democracy in the abstract than are citizens of other countries: only 37.8 percent (26.8 percent for thirty and under) rated democratic governance as "very good." This was a drop from findings of 43.2 percent in 2006 and 50.5 percent in 1999. (By way of comparison, the comparable figure in Germany was 64.8 percent). In response to the question of how important it is to live in a democratic country, 46.5 percent of Americans now assert that it is "absolutely" so—but that number drops to 29.2 percent for those under thirty. Finally, Americans' belief in the legitimacy of democratic outputs, measured in terms of both satisfaction and perceptions of corruption, have eroded dramatically over the past decade.

Not all scholars are convinced that these datapoints provide cause for concern. Looking at the same WVS data as Foa and Mounck, Pippa Norris finds that the decay in democratic affinities to be limited to a class of Anglophonic countries, but absent in Spain, Norway, the Netherlands, Chile, Germany, Hungary, and France. She further observes that the cohort effect identified in the 2014 WVS data also appears in the 1991 and 1995 data. The young, that is, have been consistently being more skeptical (and perhaps more demanding) of democracy. In a similarly vein, Eric Voeten finds no evidence that democracy is declining in popularity in comparison to autocratic or hybrid regimes. Both Norris and Voeten also exploit voting and survey data from the United States beyond the WVS to suggest that in practice older rather than younger citizens are more cynical about democratic institutions, as an "age-cycle" theory of democratic attitudes might suggest. As a result, both are less pessimistic about the long-term psychological

---

Response to Our Critics," *Journal of Democracy*, April 2017, updated June 26, 2017, http://journalofdemocracy.org/online-exchange-%E2%80%9Cdemocratic-deconsolidation%E2%80%9D.

[54] Amy C. Alexander and Christian C. Welzel, "The Myth of Deconsolidation: Rising Liberalism and the Populist Reaction," *Journal of Democracy* (online), April 2017, http://journalofdemocracy.org/online-exchange-%E2%80%9Cdemocratic-deconsolidation%E2%80%9D.

foundations of democracy on the theory that those candidates who are most likely to pursue policy agendas that undermine democracy obtain their support from aging segments of the population.[55]

The evidence of diminishing psychological affinity for democracy, in sum, must be understood in context. As a threshold matter, this evidence is more important in cases such as Turkey (where the threat to democracy emerges from elected incumbents) than in cases such as Egypt (where the threat materializes from non-elected actors such as the military). It points toward a distinct, populist threat to democracy. It is not a measure of the whole bundle of current pressures on democratic practice. Moreover, the evidence is hardly equivocal, and, as Norris suggests, not even uniform across national contexts. Rather, the data suggests that in certain national contexts, the stability of the democratic system rests on an increasingly fragile basis of popular support. Depending on the measure of democracy one uses, this fragility can seem either minor or cataclysmic in scale. Whether democracies will age out of it as young citizens come to adopt more tempered views, moreover, is a question that remains to be answered.

Whither the Global Democratic Recession?

The evidence of a global democratic recession, in short, is substantial but hardly suggestive of an immediate paradigm shift. The data we have canvassed suggests that the democratic recession of the early twentieth-first century takes many forms in widely disparate economic, social, and political circumstances. It is far too early to say with confidence that there is any one cause. For it would be striking indeed if the same underlying force explained the collapse of the Muslim Brotherhood in Egypt in 2013, the rise of elected officials with authoritarian tendencies in Turkey in 2002, the intervention of the Thai military to end elections in 2014, and the general shift in vote share toward parties or candidates with a loose or even adversarial relationship to democracy in 2016–2017. We have speculated elsewhere on the causes of the democratic recession. These include, in our view, structural changes to the global macroeconomy, and the long-term failure of economic policy to generate a sustainable pattern of returns to labor rather than capital; long-term demographic changes, in Europe and America, with regard to ethnic and racial heterogeneity; the demonstration effect from autocracies such as Russia that are able to maintain a democratic façade; and transnational networks of populist intellectuals and lawyers, who are able to diffuse antidemocratic instruments across borders. There is no scholarly consensus on the relative weight of all these factors.

---

[55] Pippa Norris, "Is Western Democracy Backsliding? Diagnosing the Risks," and Eric Voeten, "Are People Really Turning Away from Democracy?," *Journal of Democracy* (online), April 2017, http://journalofdemocracy.org/online-exchange-%E2%80%9Cdemocratic-deconsolidation%E2%80%9D.

So long as these factors continue to exist, the seemingly moderate nature of the democratic recession to date is hardly a reason for complacency. The historical record contains at least one other instance in which democratic hopes were pitched high, but then dashed, with global catastrophe following in short order. In the wake of World War I, seventeen new democracies were established around the world. In the first decades of last century, the British historian James Bryce could posit that democracy was "a natural trend, due to a general law of social progress." But by 1933, democracy was on the back foot around the world, with Estonia, Latvia, Lithuania, Italy, Portugal, Poland, Brazil, Argentina, Uruguay, Japan, and Germany all moving from democracy of a sort to authoritarianism of a sort.[56] And this was not the end of the democratic recession of the 1920s and 1930s. The democratic Spanish Republic lasted just five years before General Franco came to power in 1938, crushed opposition on both the Left and Right, and installed an authoritarian regime that was to endure until the mid-1970s.[57] The general failure of post-World War I democratization, coupled with the collapse of the overarching liberal project of international reordering under the League of Nations, was rapidly to lead to the horrors surrounding and unfolding of the Second World War.

Some of the gravest moral catastrophes of the twentieth century, then, emerged from the ruins of a failed democracy wave. Surveying their legacy—and thinking about the mounting human toll of authoritarian rule in countries such as Egypt and Turkey after the events of Tahrir Square and Gazi Park—the worry about crying wolf about democracy's withering seems overblown. To the contrary, it seems those who belittle the risks of democracy's retreat that seem morally negligent. For even if democratic failure is a low-probability risk, perhaps a surfeit of vigilance is well warranted given its enormous downstream costs.

We close with a note on the United States, a topic we have addressed at greater length in our book-length treatment on democratic erosion. Notwithstanding a long discourse on American exceptionalism, our view is that the country is not immune from trends in the rest of the world. To the extent that the United States has for several decades until the election of Donald Trump sought to promote democracy as a central prong of its foreign policy, it has provided moral and material support for the Third Wave. But more importantly, the United States is not immune from the trends that have buffeted the rest of the world: populism, economic stagnation, rising inequality, and massive immigration flows have challenged many established democracies in recent years. We view the current risk to be one of erosion and neglect rather than imminent collapse. But that is hardly a basis for complacency.

---

[56] Bryce is quoted in Robert Kagan, "The Weight of Geopolitics," *Journal of Democracy* 26, no. 1 (2015): 21–31.
[57] Antony Beevor, *The Spanish Civil War* (London: Penguin Books, 2001), 340–341.

4 Is the Sky Falling? Constitutional Crises in Historical Perspective

Zachary Elkins*

ANY PROFESSOR OF comparative politics who teaches democracy—and that qualifier may well be redundant—spends *some* time periodizing the concept's march through history. Inevitably, this historicization means describing *waves* of democracy. And if there is one law—something like Newton's third law—that one might convey to students, it's that these waves are followed by counter-waves of non-democracy. Democracy since 1900, in a sparkline, looks something like ⌄⌄⁄ . So here we are, standing on the crest of the third wave, waiting for Godot. And the signs do not look good. We bear witness to real unpleasantness in the form of executive hubris, intolerance, distrust, partyism, and constrained liberty in places as diverse as Hungary, Venezuela, India, and Turkey—countries that had always shown democratic promise. Add to that the phenomenon of Donald Trump, whom to many seems to embody, almost completely, the decline of Western civilization. Godot may well be on our doorstep.

Of course, we may be overreacting. Still, it is intellectually rewarding—and maybe even instructive and prudent—to entertain such fatalism. Dystopic and apocalyptic stories and films sell well for a reason. And the ups and downs of political and economic history suggest that we are by no means in the realm of fantasy. Market failures are littered

* I would not have written any of this if left to my own devices. Thanks to Mark Graber, Mark Tushnet, and Sandy Levinson for urging me to explore this question.

with Pollyannas who cannot distinguish a bubble from a sure thing. A skeptical observer would note that democracy has had a good run, but that some of its inherent tensions are showing: tensions that inevitably lead to frustration and experimentation with alternatives. What is more, there is no shortage of external challenges and crises—either natural or human-made—that threaten the stability of any institution.

Of course, most of us cannot help thinking that Bolivar and Churchill were right that democracy is indeed the worst system, except for all of its alternatives. Following that logic, we might hope that experiencing its alternatives will, once again, send us running back to the welcome shores of free and fair elections. In that sense, I am always reminded of a panel discussion at the *Latin American Studies Association* meetings some time in the 1990s (the height of the "End of History.")[1] The panel, as I recall, featured a series of scholarly critics of democracy, full of discontent. It was in the midst of some particularly strident democracy-bashing that Guillermo O'Donnell, having lived through the Argentine dirty war, slowly rose from his seat. With apparent frustration, he reminded us that a system that condoned the throwing of dissidents from airplanes was worse, much worse. Part of what is going on with democracy's critics must be nostalgia. Politics—even the unscrupulous kind—pretty much always looks better in the rear-view mirror. All of this to say that we may well be standing on the top of a democracy bubble and we should read the signs to see whether we're ready to burst. But any market correction may well be just that: a bump on the long march of liberty and equality.

Come Graber, Levinson, and Tushnet—no conspiracy theorists—who inquire about the extent of "constitutional crises."[2] That term is general enough that I will equate it with the crisis in democracy. Constitutional crises are usually democratic crises, since constitutions are almost always democratic in form.[3] My charge here is to don the hat of an epidemiologist. And with that hat on, I start with the observation that a set of countries seems to have presented with some real and virulent symptoms of non-democracy. But how serious are these, really? Are we on the cusp of a slide toward authoritarian rule? If so, where do we see such, and what does it look like? Attending physicians in this book will examine the patients themselves—I won't tread on their territory, though it will prove tempting to speak of cases. Instead, mine is an ostensibly simple task of applying the well-developed tools of comparative democratization, with its rich sets of historical data. I prod and probe the world's jurisdictions to understand where we stand in comparative historical perspective. Digging into data unearths new questions, which I attend to in passing. One question upon which I dwell and conclude is a troubling one. It is evident that part of the decline in democracy involves a failure of deliberation among elites

---

[1] Francis Fukuyama, *The End of History and the Last Man*. (New York: Simon and Schuster, 2006).

[2] Mark A. Graber, Sanford Levinson, and Mark Tushnet, *Constitutional Democracy in Crisis?* (New York: Oxford University Press, 2018).

[3] Zachary Elkins. "Diffusion and the Constitutionalization of Europe," *Comparative Political Studies* 43 (2010): 969–999.

and masses. Partisans are at each other's throats, which has led to an impasse in some of the basic functions of government. This dysfunction should be at the top of the agenda in comparative politics in ways that I describe below.

We've Been Here Before

Before we continue, let us recall that the democracy metaphor is one of waves. Remember where we are: ⌢⌣⌣╱. And so, we should shrug off any mock indignation at our current crisis. *Plus ça change, plus c'est la même chose*, as the French expression goes. And yes, we've been here before, and will likely be here again. But why? And how? Surely, it makes no sense to think about any non-democratic turn without understanding larger historical dynamics, if only to understand how we arrived.

In some sense, the idea of a periodic "crisis," whether democratic or constitutional, is hardwired. Those of us who live in "democracies," such as they are, understand exactly where they go wrong; in fact, the challenges are built into the very idea of dispersing power. One way to conceptualize these challenges is in terms of inherent tensions. The tensions are etched in my mind by four paradoxes described thirty years ago by Larry Diamond, but one finds them expressed in different forms throughout democratic theory.[4] Following Diamond, one tension is between *conflict* and *consensus*. All democrats enjoy a healthy battle of ideas, and we relish an active, participatory culture. This battle can come at the expense of a functioning government, which we also enjoy. And face it, these days the operative word in *loyal opposition* is, or should be, "loyal." System (not party) loyalty requires some ideological flexibility, tolerance, and trust among litigants in order to reach decisions (much more on this below). For that matter, *representation* also cuts against *consensus* sometimes. Think of a multiparty system that represents multiple and diverse segments of society, but at the same time decreases the probability of coalition building. A third tension has to do with *consent* and *effectiveness*, or what we might think of as the dynamic inconsistency problem. The idea is that it is very hard to make good long-term decisions in the face of short-term election perspectives. The classic case is austerity budgets; leaders facing re-election routinely find it hard to cut spending popular programs, even if the cuts are helpful to long-term prosperity and solvency. Fourth and finally, consider the tradeoffs between *liberty* and *equality*. Democracies (let's say market democracies) liberate ideas (and markets) at the cost of equality. Here, of course, social democracies and market democracies differ in their emphases of these two desiderata. Think of the lack of any campaign finance restrictions in US elections as a preference for liberty over equality (of voice).

Those four tensions help us understand something critical about democracy: that it is *not* an unmitigated good. We sometimes lose this balanced perspective, in part because

---

[4] Larry Jay Diamond, "Three Paradoxes of Democracy," *Journal of Democracy* 1(3) (1990): 48–60.

the word has become hopelessly positive, both at the folk and expert level. It is in part for that reason that the concept is the paradigmatic "essentially contested concept," in that it is both normatively charged *and* multidimensional—many things to many people, and all of them positive. We can admit that democracy is subject to these tensions—and therefore, some volatility—and we can evaluate its components in this light.

A Crisis of What, Exactly?

Here we need to do some very light conceptual work in order to unpack democracy, if we are to run tests on its components. Or at least I *think* that we need to disaggregate. For although I have quoted the opening lines of *Anna Karenina* enough by now that I feel that they are my words, I'm no longer sure if "an unhappy family is unhappy in its *own* [my italics] way." With respect to democracy, when things go wrong, they seem to go wrong in many of the *same*—if multiple—ways.[5]

What ways? Let's review, if only roughly and briefly. (And here follows a string of concepts in italics that I will assess in the fourth Section of this chapter, using data from the third Section). Many of us are trained—channeling Dahl—to think of democracy along two principle dimensions: *competition (contestation)* and *participation*.[6] Those are high-level dimensions, whose systemitized variants amount to competitive and participatory elections. But Dahl's dimensions—while arguably central—imply a set of other elective (accidental) elements. For example, any real election *must* be set against a backdrop of *civil rights* and *civil liberties*, if we are to have a free market of ideas. And if citizens are to review incumbent candidates for office, they must be afforded some system of *transparency* and *accountability* in order to carry out their evaluation.

Most of us would prefer not to contaminate the measure of democracy with something such as *corruption*, with the argument that—analytically at least—it doesn't make sense to mix in an element of political malfeasance that might crop up in *any* regime type. Still, many of the complaints about "democracy" are deeply rooted in the difficult relationship of money and politics. And corruption, depending upon its variant, almost surely compromises the equality of citizen voices.

For the same analytic reasons that I would set aside corruption, I might also set aside issues of *social* and *economic justice*, which may well be causes or consequences of political democracy, but arguably not part of it. Still, I recognize that others have a more expansive view of democracy. I am in the business here of detecting shifts across a range of phenomena, and I therefore include these concepts below in some macro tests.

Then we must understand that most, if not all, of the concerns regarding constitutional democracy have to do with an executive who insists upon transgressing

---

[5] Leo Tolstoy, *Anna Karenina* (New York: Lulu, 1966).
[6] Robert Dahl *Polyarchy: Participation and Opposition* (New Haven, CT: Yale University Press, 1971).

the limits of higher law. As such, we need to appreciate that meaningful democracy includes some element of *executive constraint* (i.e., a real legislature). But a balanced executive-legislative relationship is not the only relationship to consider. Many have come to view the courts as critical players in adjudicating the Constitution and signaling the transgression of its limits. So, add a strong *independent judiciary* to the mix.

Another element, which seems particularly relevant these days is *polarization*. Indeed, I might view divided publics as the single most important factor that threatens and undermines democracy, at least in modern presidential systems. I'm not alone. Dahl, in his early writing, as well as Rustow, Linz, Stepan, and other theorists of democracy have been clear that one of the most basic building blocks of democracy is that its citizens can reach agreement about some very basic existential assumptions, the most important of these being the rightfulness of the state unit.[7] Call this "stateness," following Linz and Stepan.[8] If ethnic minorities, or other identity groups, cannot agree on the frontiers of the state (as increasingly seems to be the case in Catalonia, for example), then the nuances of democratic quality seem almost irrelevant.

Partisan polarization may be less menacing to "stateness" than is ethnic division, but it is related and important. The rightfulness of the state unit may not be threatened under partyism, but certainly, the idea of democracy is in jeopardy if partisan strife is such that groups cannot abide an opposing party in power. Again, the operative term in loyal opposition is "loyal." Przeworski put this most memorably.[9] Democracy, in his formulation, is a system in which parties lose elections. That is, they lose elections and agree to abide by the results. For many of us, the most troubling element of US politics over the last ten years or so has been the strident partisanship and the idea, which seems increasingly possible, that partisans are unwilling to lose elections. Party polarization threatens the most basic objectives of governance.

Issues of state identity and polarization venture into the area of mass political culture, which are no doubt reflections—if not factors—of democratic quality. Political behaviorists over the last sixty years have identified a suite of attitudes—notably *trust* and *tolerance*—that are conducive to democracy; many of the relevant public opinion questions have been asked repeatedly across national samples. One might add other mass attitudes and behavior, such as *associationalism, political knowledge*, and *political interest*. A thorough examination of the decline of democracy would track national aggregates

---

[7] Robert Dahl *Polyarchy: Participation and Opposition* (New Haven, CT: Yale University Press, 1971). Juan Linz and Alfred Stepan. *Problems of Democratic Transition and Consolidation* (Baltimore, MD: Johns Hopkins University Press, 1996)., Dankwart A. Rustow "Transitions to democracy: Toward a dynamic model." *Comparative Politics* 2, no. 3 (1970): 337–363.

[8] Juan Linz and Alfred Stepan, "Stateness, Nationalism and Democratization," *Polis. Political Studies* 5.5 (1997).

[9] Adam Przeworski, *Democracy and the Market: Political and Economic Reforms in Eastern Europe and Latin America* (New York: Cambridge University Press, 1991).

of these concepts across time. I leave the analysis of such individual-level analysis for the sequel to this volume, assuming that the "troubles" continue.

Thus ends our tour d'horizon across the conceptual terrain of democracy. The tour had very specific ends: the idea is now to interrogate most of the concepts that appear in *italics* here with the idea of understanding where and how democracy has broken down, if it has at all. Disaggregating democracy is critical. Arguably, the most interesting question lurking behind this study has to do with what *part* of democracy, exactly, is foundering.

Measuring Democracy's Components

It is fortunate that we are in a position to evaluate each of the sub-concepts of democracy that I identify in the previous section. We live in a rather rich world of political data. Standard measures of the elements of democracy have been proliferating since at least 1970. I think here of Polity, Freedom House, Vanhanen, along with a set of more idiosyncratic measures. More recently, a major study—the Varieties of Democracy (V-DEM)—has emerged, which adds an even wider set of scores, measured by reports by country scholars. Add to this a set of cross-national *survey* measures (such as the World Values Survey, and other regional barometers) that have now established a rather long time series. Suffice it to say that an epidemiologist concerned with democratic downturn has some clear empirical reference points from which to work.

These data sets are promising, but we should not lose sight of threats to their validity in measuring the kind of crises that we have in mind. One threat has to do with the rather vast differences in time frame. Obviously, many of the events that are the subject of this volume are ongoing, dynamic, and in many cases, highly volatile. There is, admittedly, some disconnect between macro, yearly data and the daily ups and downs of "democracy." The news cycle in the early twenty-first century has grown exceedingly short. Tweets may allow us to stay relevant; a book chapter will not. It would be nice to have the equivalent of daily or hourly stock prices for democracy in these states (sovereign bond data might be close, actually). But our yearly snapshots are revealing, especially since there is some inertia in democratic culture, which I turn to below.

Another threat has to do with regression-to-the mean effects. We tend to view democracy as the hopeful investor might the market—expecting steady yearly increases in the Dow Jones average, only to take umbrage at the slightest correction. A more realistic view might see any of the retrenchments, and indeed this one, as a natural correction in the market.

None of these validity threats is enough to detain us, and we now proceed *cum grano salis*. Each of the concepts articulated above is associated with at least one measure from these data sets. Some of these measures deal with individual components; others are composite indices.

A Step Change in Democracy and Its Components?

We can start, then, with some over-time plots of measures of these various measures. The relevant questions are: (1) To what degree can we identify a step change, or structural break, in the mean of democracy in recent years?; (2) How does any break in democratic trends compare with prior breaks? That is, are these structural breaks reminiscent of the counter-waves of either the interwar years, or the 1960s?; and (3) Which aspects of democracy exhibit any sign of a structural break, or counter-wave?

Figure 4.1 provides an historical snapshot of democracy in the twentieth and early-twenty-first century across the world for sixteen indicators of democracy, either as an index or in its various components. It appears that the counter-wave that we may be anticipating—and witnessing—is real. Half of the curves have an unmistakable southern hook on their right tail, suggesting either a real regression to non-democracy or, at least, some stabilization/stalling of the third wave. For most of the indicators, the dip is fairly subtle. For some, it is quite pronounced. So, for example, measures of executive corruption have shifted so dramatically that they have dropped back to the level of the 1960s' counter-wave. Fifty years of improvement wiped out in a few years' time! Another sizable dip of particular interest to constitutional scholars is the judicial constraints measure. This composite measure, from V-DEM, captures aspects of judicial independence and authority. Another substantial decline is that in deliberation, understood as

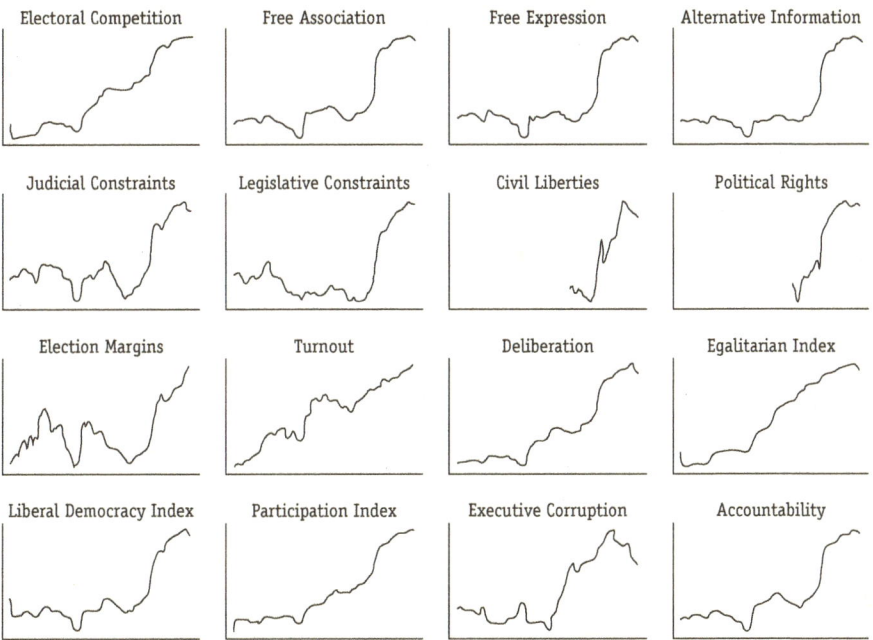

FIGURE 4.1 Signs of a counterwave? Sixteen indicators of democracy from 1900–2017.
Source: Varieties of Democracy 2017.

rational, consensus-seeking discourse. Of course, it remains to be seen whether these dips in democracy will continue to slide, rebound, or re-equilibrate. But prediction is not our concern here.

Some of these shifts hit one between the eyes—Tukey's famed interocular test—but we can assess these changes more formally by running a structural break analysis: that is, an analysis that identifies step changes—or change-points—in a time series for specific parameters, such as the mean, of a variable, in this case democracy.[10] The analysis confirms that the noticeable declines are significant breaks in the time series starting in the late oughts.

Democracies: Slow to Build, Quick to Break?

I return here to issues of timing, which I raise above in the context of measurement. If we are to look for structural breaks in the mean of democracy, we would also profit by measuring rates of change on either side of a transition (to and from democracy). Let me explain. Consider the aphorism, which I believe to be attributed to a former university president, that it takes a generation to build a great university, but only a few days to destroy it. It sounds right. Is such a thing true of democratic institutions as well, if it ever was of universities?

Upon reflection, I'm not sure why one direction of change would have more inertia than another. True, building something up *would* seem more complicated than would tearing it down. My colleagues Bob Duke and Art Markman tell the vivid story of a visit to the beach, where a group of children painstakingly build an elaborate sandcastle only to have a peer storm the castle and make quick work of three hours of construction.[11] But institutions are not buildings, much less sandcastles. And some institutions seem to come together quickly, only to endure mysteriously for years to come. The extreme case might be the Japanese constitution, which went up in two weeks in 1946 and has not been altered once—not once! We should also recall the summer of 1787, when a group of statesmen in Philadelphia wrote a constitution that also sometimes seems immutable to change, despite our best efforts. How is *that* for a summer project? Also, inertial forces in institutionalism and culture are strong. As such, national reputations for rule of law and democracy—like other national reputations—die hard. What is more, citizens seem to adapt to these stereotypes—whether positive or negative—quite readily and willingly, in some national version of the psychologists' *stereotype threat*. Will we ever be rid of quips about German rectitude and punctuality and Italian slothfulness? Suffice it to say that inertia can be strong on either side of a transition.

---

[10] I carry this out with a cumulative sum control chart procedure, which detects step changes in the mean of a time series.

[11] Bob Duke and Art Markman, "Two Guys on Your Head," March 2, 2018, http://kut.org/term/two-guys-your-head.

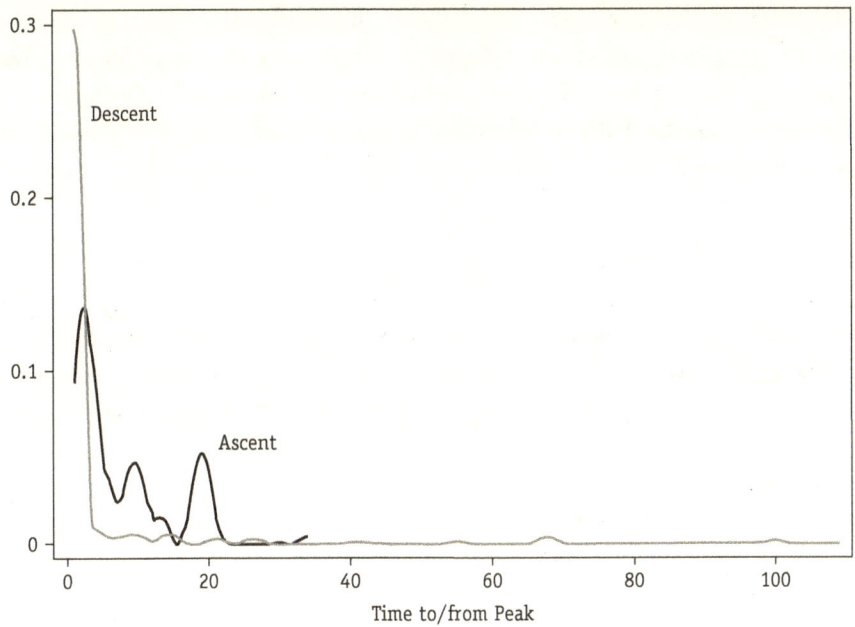

FIGURE 4.2 Democracies take more time to build than to destroy.
Source: Varieties of Democracy 2017.

Why worry about this issue of building/dismantling speeds? Precisely because if we are going to worry about constitutional crisis, we have to worry about relative resiliency (that is, recovery rates). If it takes significant time to build toward democracy, but a short time to destroy it, we should be *particularly* worried about constitutional crisis. Since this question of relative resiliency has not been tested (as far as I know), and since it is interesting and relevant, I will answer it here—albeit in G.K. Chesterton style.[12] The question is, basically, whether the slope toward an absolute maximum in democracy is steeper on the left side of the peak than it is on the right. So, something like —————⟍ as opposed to ⟋—————. But how to measure and analyze such? We will have to select a set of cases that enter the analysis at some relatively low level of democracy, achieve some relatively high level of democracy, and then regress to a low level. The simple question will be: How long does it take to ascend to the peak as against the time to descend? The answer lies in Figure 4.2. There, I have plotted the distribution of time *to* and time *from* the first democratic peak. (The peak is defined as the maximum level of democracy for a given country (its global maximum). The ascent begins the year the country reaches half of one standard deviation below the global maximum, and the descent ends when the country reaches the same point following the peak.)

---

[12] "If a thing is worth doing, it is worth doing badly." G.K. Chesterton. *What's Wrong with the World* (London, UK: Cassell and Company, 1912): p. 254.

The results are clear. For those countries that reach a zenith of democracy, and then sink to the abyss, the ascent takes twice as long as does the descent, on average. So, the university adage appears to be borne out in the case of democracy. Democracies are slow to build, but when they fall, they fall quickly.[13] Following prior imagery, it may now be hard not to imagine today's populists as demolition specialists in a beach of hard-won sand castles.

Trouble Spots (and Some Not-So-Troubled Spots)

Most of the aggregate indicators that we analyze above show only moderate—though notable—signs of weakness. Those who worry about a stock market bubble would not be much alarmed, I suspect. But some of the stocks (democracies) are clearly not doing well, and have experienced significant downswings. So which are they?

Again, I analyzed historical trends—this time at the country level—and tested for any significant step changes in the level of democracy (using the V-DEM measure, liberal democracy). Nine countries exhibited significant downward shifts since 2010, compared to their historical means. They are depicted here in Figure 4.3.

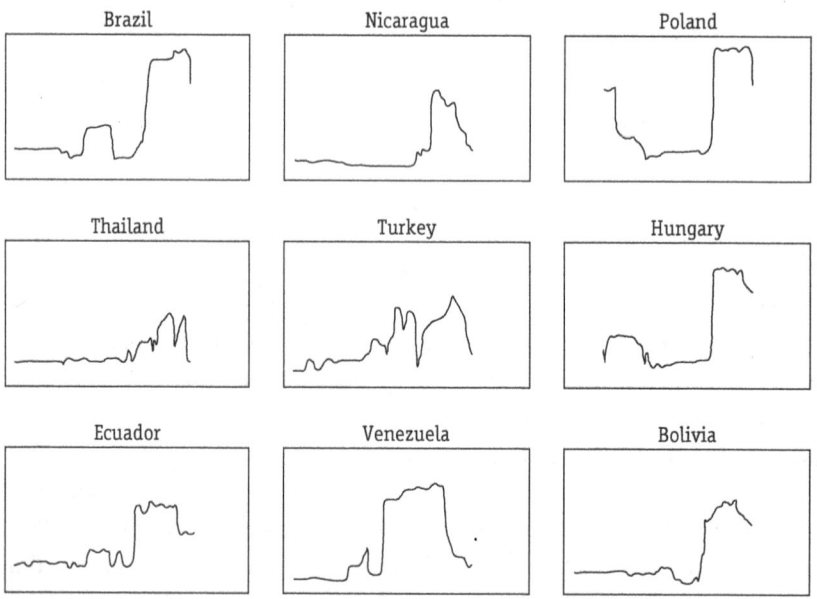

FIGURE 4.3 Nine countries in trouble.
Source: Varieties of Democracy 2017.

---

[13] I suppose that we should assume that some of this is a measurement artifact. That is, democracy coders are quicker to recognize one change than they are another. However, I confess that I don't know which direction this bias would go, though I suppose it depends whether democracy coders are optimists or pessimists.

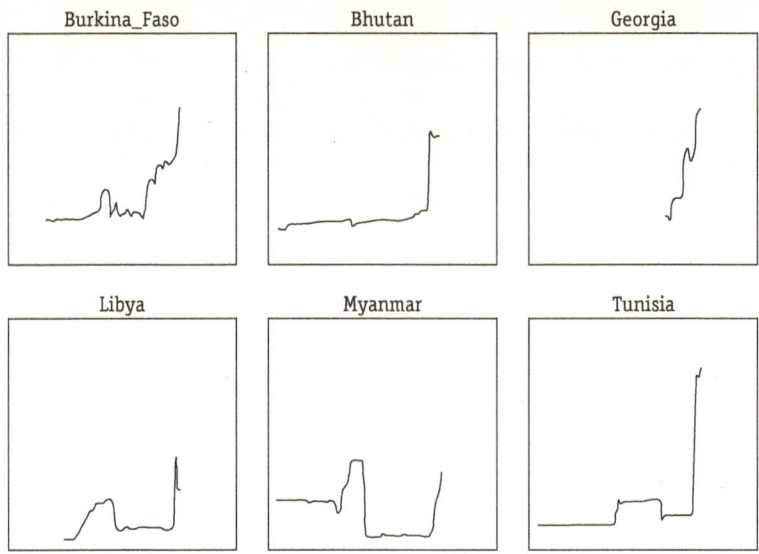

FIGURE 4.4 Six pleasant surprises.
Source: Varieties of Democracy 2017.

Though we are waiting patiently to ride out a counter-wave, it bears noting that several countries have showed marked advances in democracy during this same time, at least according to
V-DEM's Liberal Democracy measure. See Figure 4.4. Tunisia, and maybe Libya (it is much
too early to tell there), may have risen from the Arab Spring with real some democratic hopes.

Facing Up to the Heart of the Problem: Polarization

The ABCs of essay writing are simple: **A**cknowledge the question, **B**ridge to what you
really want to say, and **C**ommunicate that message. Well, here's **C**. My sense is that the
most troubling sign in modern democracies has to do with alarming levels of polarization. We saw some of that in the declines of deliberative democracy above. If democracy
is a system in which parties lose elections, we are at a moment in which partisans are not
willing to lose. We are seeing too many political contests, in too many polities, in which
partisans are taking their ball and going home. That much is not only clear from our
global assessment of democracy above but also to anyone who has been paying attention
to US politics over the last ten years.

But enough of impressions. Readers should demand proof—and comparative
evidence—of such widespread polarization. Indeed, understanding polarization comparatively should be at the top of the agenda for comparative political scientists, and
this Section advances the ball toward that goal. It is hard to conceive of variation in
polarization comparatively without an adequate conceptualization of the phenomenon. And, because abstract notions alone can cloud a grounded discussion of the

concept (not to mention any empirical inquiry), it is useful also to identify, and organize, concrete manifestations (indicators) of the relevant concepts. Since I have not yet encountered a comprehensive scheme for the conceptualization and measurement of polarization (at least with a comparative focus), I introduce one here (Table 4.1) in order to fix ideas.

I understand "Political Polarization," in a very general sense, to suggest simply a highly divided society—divided presumably by party, but potentially by some other political grouping. Clearly, polarization operates at both the elite and mass levels, each with its

TABLE 4.1

Components and Measures of Political Participation Relevant for Comparative Analysis		
Level	N[a]	Reference or Data Source[b]
Concept	(est.)	(e.g.)
Indicator		
Elite		
Legislative Gridlock		
Scope of Legislation	Small	Baumgartner and Jones (2010)
Success of Executive Proposals	Large	Saiegh (2009)
Roll Rate	Small	Cox and McCubbins (2005)
Ideological Distance		
Distribution of Legislative Votes, by Party	Small	Morgenstern (2003); Poole and Rosenthal (1997)
Distribution of Judicial Opinions, by Party	Small	Jessee and Malhotra (2013)
Extremity of Campaign Rhetoric	Small	Volkens et al. (2006)
Social and Political Interaction		
Inter-party Friendships	Small	Mann and Ornstein (2006)
Inter-party Bill Co-sponsorship	Small	Theriault (2013)
Homogeneity of Governing Coalition	Small	Power et al. (n.p.)
Mass		
Partyism		
Inter-party Marriage Rates	Small	Stoker and Jennings (1995)
Social Distance Score	Small	Iyengar and Westwood (2015)
Trust Games	Small	Westwood et al. (2015)
Ideological Distance		
Party Attributions	Small	Datafolha
Executive Approval, by Party	Large	LAPOP
Distribution of ideology, by Party	Large	Dimaggio et al. (1996)

[a] N is author's estimate of country coverage of a given variable. Small[<5]; medium[5–20];large[>20].

[b] References are US studies, comparative, or both.

behavioral and attitudinal dimensions. In Table 4.1, I identify dimensions at each level, which seem to represent a reasonable (though by no means authoritative) conceptual architecture. While this conceptualization should be considered a preliminary one, it helps us move forward. For each of these dimensions, I have identified indicators that have *some potential* for comparative analysis, across some number of countries. We might think of this table as a working guide or map for further comparative research. The estimated sample in the second column indicates the country-level coverage of existing, or easily harvested data. The intent is to provoke thinking about certain research designs as opposed to others.

Undoubtedly, these dimensions are highly interrelated *somehow*, and any research agenda on political polarization should consider the dimensions comprehensively. For example, the rich measures of "partyism" (think "racism") at the mass level that Iyengar and Westwood and others have begun to re-explore are no doubt related somehow to campaign rhetoric and legislative behavior at the elite level.[14] Nevertheless, each of these dimensions and measures are substantively thick and interesting enough to warrant more focused comparative analysis on their own. Partyism, as it manifests in the social relationships of both elites and masses, would seem to be a fascinating and highly textured area of inquiry.

One of the more tractable areas of study has to do with the ideological distance of legislators, something typically measured with roll-call data. Certainly, some comparability issues arise (as they do with any measure), but the degree of party discipline (unity) in these votes would seem to be a useful stock measure of whether a party has "separated" itself from others. Morgenstern's book on a small set of Latin American countries represents an exemplary study of this kind of data across contexts.[15] In the case of the United States, there seems to be little doubt that Republican and Democratic members of Congress are operating with two very different views of the world. Roll-call data shows this, but so too do the scores that interest groups give. Witness the average ideology scores produced by the interest group, Americans for Democratic Action (ADA), for the two parties since 1950 (Figure 4.5). It is hard to imagine the parties further apart or more ideologically constrained (note the thin "spread" of party scores).

This sort of ideological polarization is noticeable at the mass level as well. Consider Figure 4.6, in which Pew researchers have plotted the distribution of Republican and Democratic attitudes on a basket of ten policies. With something almost like a plate tectonic shift, the two publics have moved to their poles, leaving very little overlap in the middle. Of course, one could do something similar to this with comparative public opinion data.

---

[14] Shanto Iyengar and Sean J. Westwood, "Fear and Loathing across Party Lines: New Evidence on Group Polarization," *American Journal of Political Science* 59.3 (2015): 690–707.

[15] Scott Morgenstern, *Patterns of Legislative Politics: Roll-Call Voting in Latin America and the United States* (New York: Cambridge University Press, 2005).

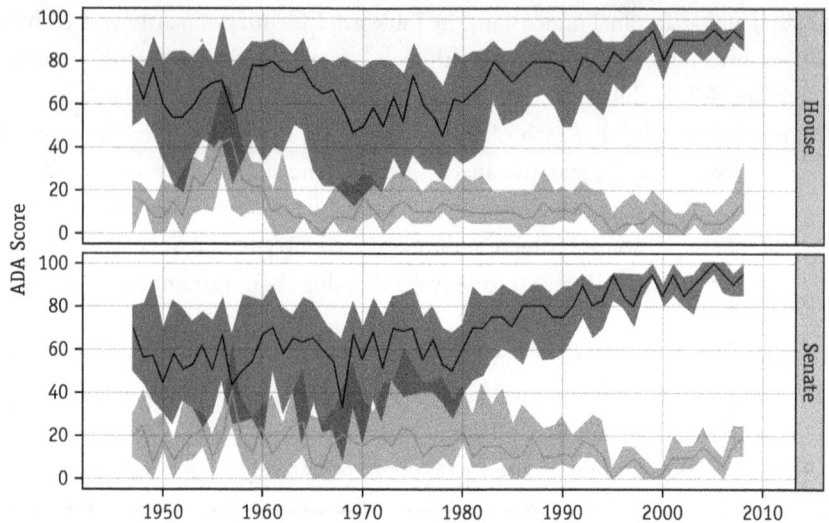

FIGURE 4.5 Legislative voting is more divided than ever.

Source: Americans for Democratic Action, Voting Records. Chart: Sharad Goel (2012).

Note: Goel, Sharad. "The Polarization of Political Parties." Messy Matters, January 31, 2012. http://messymatters.com/polarized/.

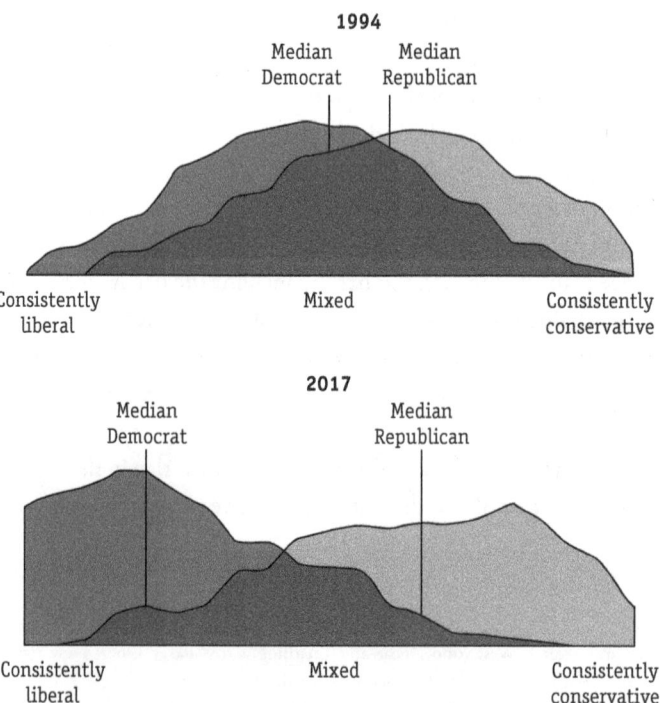

FIGURE 4.6 Attitudes of Democrats and Republicans, 1994 versus 2017.

Source: Pew Research Center 2017.

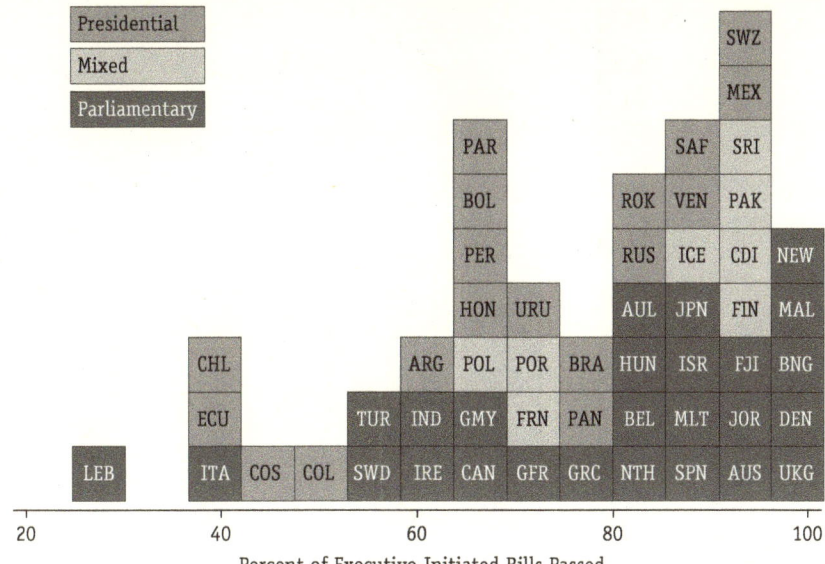

FIGURE 4.7 Executive success varies—even over constitutional systems.
Source: Saiegh (2009).

But, we would be right to be concerned about government outputs (brass tacks) over the rhetoric. Consider, in that sense, *legislative gridlock*, which is perhaps less of a *component* of polarization than it is its *consequence* (or even source—clearly, there is feedback). Even if the two ideas are analytically and conceptually separable, they are likely so tightly connected (causally and descriptively) that it might make sense here to think of them as parts of the same overarching construct. I am not alone, or original, in thinking so, by the way.[16] My focus on gridlock also stems from my assumption that the phenomenon represents the principal frustration for those living in polarized polities. At the very least, gridlock is the manifestation of polarization that concerns and interests me most.

There is some comparative legislative data that help us assess gridlock. One has to do with the degree that the executive is able to pass his or her legislative proposals. In a noteworthy contribution, Sebastian Saiegh has assembled data on both the number of executive proposals and the number of passed proposals for some forty-three countries across as many as forty-eight years for each, yielding what he refers to as the executive's batting average.[17] I've plotted the distribution in Figure 4.7, for parliamentary, presidential, and mixed systems. Note that the United States is not included in Saiegh's data since the US president cannot formally propose legislation. Nevertheless, given congressional dysfunction, many of us can probably imagine a "USA" block somewhere on the far left.

---

[16] Marc J. Hetherington, "Review Article: Putting Polarization in Perspective," *British Journal of Political Science* 39.2 (2009): 413–448.

[17] Sebastian Saiegh, "Political Prowess of Lady Luck? Evaluating Chief Executives' Legislative Success Rates," *Journal of Politics* 71 (2009): 1342–1356.

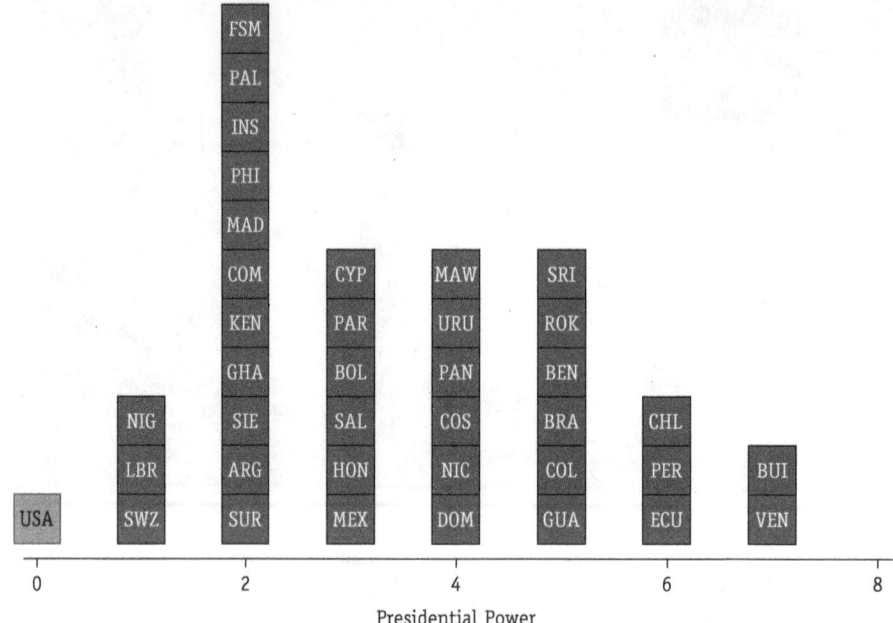

FIGURE 4.8 Executive lawmaking power (presidential systems).
Source: Comparative Constitutions Project (Elkins, Ginsburg, Melton).

Also, it won't be surprisingly to see that executives in parliamentary systems seem more effective than those in presidential system, but we also see some real variation in presidential systems. Not all are as paralyzed as the United States.

Why is that? During the Obama era, some astute observers began to decry the seemingly legislative weakness of the US president, an office that some had begun to vest with imperial power.[18] In a recent book, Terry Moe and William Howell have developed a set of proposals that would significantly increase executive power to legislate.[19] Of course, one wonders how such proposals would be viewed in the Trump years by those who may have been sympathetic to them during the Obama years. Nevertheless, after cycles of both Democratic and Republican gridlock, it seems very clear that US presidents are straining at the institutional bit to advance their agendas. I have turned to some data from our Comparative Constitutions Project in order to understand this a bit better.[20] If we consider an index of executive lawmaking power from a set of seven legislating powers, the US president appears utterly powerless.[21] The office lacks (formally) any of these seven powers. Meanwhile, as Figure 4.8 suggests, even other presidential systems in Latin

---

[18] Arthur M. Schlesinger, *The Imperial Presidency* (New York: Houghton Mifflin, 2004).

[19] William G. Howell and Terry Moe, *Relic: How Our Constitution Undermines Effective Government—And Why We Need a More Powerful Presidency* (New York: Basic Books, 2016).

[20] Zachary Elkins, Tom Ginsburg, and James Melton. *The Comparative Constitutions Project.* Data online at comparativeconstitutionsproject.org.

[21] Specifically, the power to (1) initiate bills, (2) issue decrees, (3) declare emergencies, (4) propose amendments, (5) propose referenda, (6) challenge the constitutionality of a law, (7) dissolve the legislature.

America, built originally in the image of the US Constitution, have adopted these more muscular attributes (to say nothing of parliamentary systems, many of whose executives have *all* of these powers).

Some of this talk will lead readers to think about institutional reform, which I suspect would be refreshing and probably long overdue in some polities. I mention these empirical opportunities mostly in order to whet appetites for comparative research on polarization, which should be at the top of political scientists' agenda these days—at least for those concerned about democratic decline.

Conclusions

So, is the sky falling? Evidently it is slipping a bit, yes. Democracy is, in fact, descending from a local and global maximum that it hit in 2011. Something like this, depending upon one's measure: ⌁⌁ . Importantly, some countries—such as Tunisia and Burkina Faso—seem to be making democratic advances in the face of this market downturn. Still, from a historical perspective, we might have expected some sky falling. Macro-democracy famously experiences cyclic setbacks. Many of us may have hoped that earlier counter-waves were unique historical moments. But if three of anything makes a pattern, it may well be time to think more systematically about counter-waves. I offer a simple explanation here, in which these regressions are hardwired into the very idea of dispersing power. We can think of democracy as an imperfect set of institutions subject to a set of inherent tensions. These tensions periodically lay bare what appear to be suboptimal institutional elements, which may be replaced by power-concentrating ones. But the process is something like a market "correction." With non-democracy as a reference point, it seems likely that democracy will once again look attractive by comparison, and march on. The problem with such cycling has to do with recovery rates. Evidently, democracy takes much longer to build than it does to destroy. Or so the data I show suggest. Clearly, analysts will want to take up that question more systematically.

What do the data say about the elements of democracy that are in danger? One casualty of the last five to ten years, which will surprise nobody, has been deliberative democracy. That is, according to the data, democratic publics and elites seem to be considerably less congenial and consensual. Indeed, this finding accords with what many observe in the United States, Venezuela, Hungary, and Turkey, to name a few settings. One implication of this finding is that polarization is even more of a "thing" than we may have thought. Indeed, the comparative study of polarization may be the key to understanding the health of democracy more generally. I map the conceptual and empirical domain, which suggests an analytic way forward.

5 Constitutional Failure Revisited
Ellen Kennedy

IN THE WAKE of the 9/11 attacks on the United States, then-president George W. Bush made expansive use of "executive prerogative," a practice that constitutional lawyers Eric A. Posner and Adrian Vermeule characterized as an "executive unbound." The modern administrative state, they argued, suffers from a severe case of liberalism, "which holds that representative legislatures govern and should govern, subject to constitutional constraints, while executive and judicial officials carry out the law."[1] Because liberals are afraid of executive powers, especially those unchecked by representative institutions, they neither see the reality of government in the twentieth century nor do they understand the institutional and political changes that have reduced legislative bodies to one function: carrying out the will of the executive. As a result, the practices of making and interpreting law have largely shifted to the judiciary and the executive. Whatever constraints might or should exist in regard to the executive branch are "shaky in normal times and weak or nonexistent in times of crisis."[2]

---

[1] Eric A. Posner and Adrian Vermeule, *The Executive Unbound: After the Madisonian Republic* (New York: Oxford University Press, 2010).

[2] Ibid., 2.

A classic case of the executive unbound, Posner and Vermeule argue, is exemplified by the arguments of the political theorist and constitutional lawyer, Carl Schmitt[3]. In the first years of the Weimar Republic, there were a series of attempted coups, which created an environment of latent civil war, but the economy was healthy and the political environment relatively stable, during its the middle years (1924–1929) despite a "waltz of portfolios" and governments.[4] Schmitt understood Article 48 WRV as a grant of broad executive discretion to act in emergency circumstances, legitimating practices that we call "executive prerogative" today. When the legislative branch cannot act, Schmitt argued, then the executive *must act*. But this argument, however imperative it might seem, gradually eroded participatory engagement in government and governing, to the extent that the legislative branch ceased to exist as a functional part of the state during the Weimar Republic. The narrative of this shift from participatory and representative government to government by decree is not unique to Weimar. We must confront an uncomfortable question: Why and how has America's constitutional process taken on attributes similar to those of the German 1920s?

Leading scholars of Weimar have described it as the "surrender of democracy" and characterized it as morally corrupt and cowardly; inflation and depression shadowed and disrupted the first republican constitution.[5] In great part these were consequences of the Treaty of Versailles, which demanded unconditional acceptance of the articles of peace, and imposed heavy monetary penalties on the Germans. Backed into a corner, they accepted the terms of peace. Almost simultaneously, the new and first German republic came into constitutional existence.[6]

Many questions familiar from the political-legal literature of the Weimar Republic came to the fore as a result of the Bush administration's foreign policies after the 9/11 attacks, and as a result many constitutional scholars took up the "emergency" capacities of the U.S. Constitution.[7] As practices of surveillance, "extraordinary rendition," the

---

[3] Schmitt was educated at the Humboldt University in Berlin. He taught at Greifswald, Bonn, the Handelshochschule (Munich), and finally returned to the Humboldt. He died in 1985 at the age of ninety-seven. A prolific theorist of law and constitutions, after 1933 Schmitt became editor of the most prestigious law journal in its day, the *Deutsche Juristenzeitung*. Excused from active service in World War I for health reasons, Schmitt served in the Munich office of the Reich military administration.

[4] The young Republic had twenty governments during the period before Hitler came to power. Ironically, the Weimar constitution was never repealed. Ernst Troeltsch commented that "as long as the Union of Constitutionalists (i.e., those loyal to the Republic) does not have an impressive majority of the nation behind it, and is not able to incorporate its opponents, there can be no sound foundation nor can the people heal." Hagen Schulze, *Weimar. Deutschland 1917–1933* (Berlin: Sieder, 1998), 221.

[5] Karl Dietrich Erdmann and Hagen Schultze, eds., *Weimar. Selbstpreisgabe einer Demokratie. Eine Bilanz heute* (Düsseldorf: Drost, 1980). More recently, Anthony McElligott considered that it might have been "a republic without authority." *Rethinking the Weimar Republic: Authority and Authoritarianism 1916–1936* (New York: Bloomsbury, 2014).

[6] Hans Mommsen, *The Rise and Fall of Weimar Democracy* (Chapel Hill: University of North Carolina Press, 1989).

[7] Bruce Ackerman, "The Emergency Constitution," *Yale Law Review* 113 (2004): 1029–1092; Kim Lane Scheppele, "Law in Time of Emergency: State of Exception and the Temptations of 9/11," *University of Pennsylvania Journal*

use of torture and indefinite confinement, practices in violation of fundamental rights and guarantees that are long and well established in common law and statute proliferated, Sanford Levinson described this regime as one in which legal norms have been suspended.[8]

As for Germany a century ago, so now for us a political crisis descended with the 2016 presidential election, and our constitutional life seems at this moment to have entered a crisis of disorder and confusion, something akin to the "Weimar moment." The expression means many different things, but it must certainly include the mark of a degenerate and violent public space.[9] Inflation and depression marked the political and legal theory of Germany's first Republic, but its greatest burdens grew from the 1914–1918 war that was halted by the Armistice of November 11, 1918. Revolt and violence continued within the Empire.[10] Right- and left-wing parties and activists fought in the streets as German representatives arrived at Versailles to negotiate a peace treaty. Instead President Woodrow Wilson issued an ultimatum: articles of peace must be accepted unconditionally. After the Reichstag ratified those, a Peace Treaty was signed in the Hall of Mirrors at Versailles Palace on June 28, 1919. Violence in Berlin caused the government's removal to Weimar, a small university town in Thüringen, where "The Constitution of the German Empire of August 11, 1919" (better known as the Weimar constitution) was drafted. Its second part contained a bill of rights, which was in reality a series of demands, many of them quite contradictory. This new constitution immediately confronted three stages of political and economic crisis.[11]

---

of International Law 6 (2004): 1001–1083; Kim Lane Scheppele, "North American Emergencies," *International Journal of Constitutional Law* 4 (2006): 213–242; Laurence H. Tribe and Patrick O. Gudridge, "The Antiemergency Constitution," *Yale Law Review* 113 (2004): 1801–1870; Oren Gross and Fionnuala Ní Aoláin, *Law in Times of Crisis: Emergency Powers in Theory and Practice* (Cambridge: Cambridge University Press, 2006); Oren Gross & Ni Aoláin, "Executive Emergency Powers and Constitutional Necessity" (LAPA "Executive Power," Princeton University, 2007); Mark V. Tushnet, "Emergencies and the Idea of Constitutionalism," in *The Constitution in Wartime: Beyond Alarmism and Complacency*, ed. Mark Tushnet (Durham, NC: Duke University Press, 2005), 39.

[8] After reviewing Madison and Hamilton on peace and war, Sanford Levinson found in Carl Schmitt a more appropriate analysis: "Now consider the following maxim: 'There exists no norm that is applicable to chaos.' (...) Schmitt contended that legal norms were only applicable in stable and peaceful situations—and not in times of war, when the state confronted 'a mortal enemy, with the threat of violent death at the hands of a hostile group.' It follows that conventional legal norms are no longer applicable in a state of emergency, when war and chaos pose a standing threat to public safety. To adopt the language of American constitutional law, every norm is subject to limitation when a compelling interest is successfully asserted, and it is hard to think of a more compelling interest than the prevention of violent death at the hands of a hostile group." Sanford Levinson, "Torture in Iraq and the Rule of Law in America," *Daedalus* 133 (2004): 5–9.

[9] Thomas Nevin, *Ernst Jünger and Germany. Into the Abyss, 1914–1945* (Durham, NC: Duke University Press, 1996).

[10] Arthur J. Jacobson and Bernhard Schlink, *Weimar. A Jurisprudence of Crisis* (Berkeley: University of California Press, 2002).

[11] Mommsen, *Weimar Democracy*.

Successive regimes in Germany from 1914 to 1945 relied on extraordinary measures in security and economic emergencies. The Weimar constitution specifically provided for presidential emergency power. Emphasis on the use of military and police forces in the article, and the history of civil disorder in 1918–1924 underline the article's security aspect. In instances where a member state could not enforce federal law or fulfill its constitutional duty to the federation, the Reich president could force it to do so "with the help of armed forces"; when "public safety and order are significantly disturbed or threatened" the president could "take all necessary measures" including the use of armed forces, and the president could also "suspend" (*ausser Kraft setzen*) seven fundamental rights enumerated in the constitution.[12] These dictatorial powers were limited by the requirement that the president notify the Reichstag and that such measures and actions be rescinded upon its demand (section 3). Governments of the member states were also authorized to take comparable steps with the limitation that the president or Reichstag could demand they be rescinded (section 4). The text foresaw that these quite general grants of authority in Article 48, which were agreed at the National Assembly in Weimar, would eventually be further defined in law (section 5).

As elsewhere in Europe, Germany recognized the legal institutions of martial law and the states of siege and emergency that emerged in the course of the nineteenth century. Like governments in the Empire and the Weimar Republic also relied on enabling laws, expansive legislative delegations of authority during periods of crisis.[13] During the period of inflation (1921–1924) four separate enabling laws were enacted by the Reichstag as governments tried to stabilize the mark and preserve the real economy. These were of limited duration. On October 13, 1923, as the mark became utterly worthless and as dozens of competing currency substitutes circulated throughout Germany,[14] an enabling act authorized the government to take "any measure in the financial economic and social

---

[12] These are all contained in Article 48, chapter 3 of the Weimar constitution "The Reich President and Reich Government," *The Reich Constitution of August 11, 1919.*

[13] There were ten enabling laws (Ermächtigungsgesetze) between 1914 and 1945 beginning with the Enabling Law of August 4, 1914 at the beginning of World War I (it remained in effect four years and three months), and finally Hitler's Gesetz zur Behebung der Not von Volk und Reich vom 24. März 1933 (in effect until the German defeat (twelve years, one month). In both periods these laws could be regarded as the actual constitution of German. See also Clinton Rossiter, *Constitutional Dictatorship—Crisis Government in the Modern Democracies* (Princeton, NJ: Princeton University Press, 1948). President Trump's frequent references to the possibility of nuclear warfare might be contrasted to Rossiter's "Constitutional Dictatorship in the Atomic Age," *Review of Politics* 11 (1949): 395–418 and "What of Congress in Atomic War," *Western Political Quarterly* 3 (1950): 602.

[14] The Hamburg Bank; "German dollar," October 25, 1923. Gerald D. Feldman, *The Great Disorder: Politics, Economics and Society in the German Inflation 1914–1924* (Oxford: Oxford University Press, 1993), 787ff. See also Milton Friedman's account of similar phenomena in the United States a few years later. Milton Friedman and Anna Schwartz, *The Great Contraction 1929–1933* (Princeton: Princeton University Press, 1965). During the financial crisis of 2008-2009 local script functioned in regions of North Carolina (the "Plenty") and the Berkshires (the Berk "Share"). It may be assumed that barter also accompanies such indicators of the value lost by central bank money.

spheres" necessary to stop inflation. The goal of stabilizing Germany's currency and preserving the real economy was achieved only when Hjalmar Schacht was appointed Currency Commissioner (*Währungskommissar*) on November 13, 1923 to oversee the new *Rentenmark* and its bank of issue.[15] Before that extraordinary step, other stabilization efforts failed for reasons familiar to us in the 2008 financial crisis when American markets collapsed and major investment banks failed: the "value" of nothing was certain, and the currency (in the American case, certain investment instruments and market derivatives) could not perform its notational function. The *Rentenmark* worked but at the cost of the political and civil law crisis of revalued debt (*Aufwertung*) that led to deep resentment across classes and created a massive culture of "moral hazard." Savers lost the value of their savings; debtors got off scot free. The cultural and moral effects of the great inflation are vividly described by Hans Ostwald in *Sittengeschichte der Inflation* and also documented by Joseph Roth, who wandered through the night-clubs and whorehouses of Berlin to report on the city's culture of decadence: "a race of courageous women setting foot on the stage as a battlefield, armored in corsets, in long skirts under which peep out—flirtatiously, seductively, sinfully—snow white or pink salmon stockings and tightly laced dancing shoes, Boadiceas with bare throats and powerful shoulders and with abundant hair piled up on their heads, such that a little nodding double-entendre can't have been an easy matter; and finally the dancers with round, shapely legs, sewn, one would think, into the whirling expanse of ruffled and lacy underskirts, loose girls of sweet harmlessness and easy virtue."[16] Still today, Germans abhor "easy money" as a platform for inflation.[17] In the ensuing legal turmoil German judges turned to equity and good faith (*Treu und Glauben*) rather than statute law to sort through property and other debt-associated claims in court.[18] Although this period of economic insecurity ended with monetary success, with four years of stability and prosperity following, debate and disagreement over basic concepts in law and jurisprudence deepened.

---

[15] The Rentenbank was "conveniently and appropriately located," Feldman remarks, "in offices belonging to the Reich Debt Administration and across the street from the Reich Printing Office and near the Reichsbank." Feldman, *The Great Disorder*, 793.

[16] Hans Ostwald, *Sittengeschichte der Inflation* (Berlin: Neufeld & Henius, 1931). Joseph Roth, *What I Saw. Reports from Berlin* (New York: Norton & Co, 2003), ch. 38 "The Berlin Pleasure Industry." Robert Gellately, *The Politics of Economic Despair* (Beverly Hills: Sage Publications, 1974) covers the period up to 1914, arguing that economic hardship more than illiberal ideology fed political resentment before the Great War.

[17] This culturally and historically received fear of inflation keeps the Euro a hard currency, a fact welcomed by Germans, but resented by other members of the EU. The British, although receiving the same trade terms and accepting freedom of movement all across the EU, never accepted the common currency and are now in the midst of withdrawing from the European Union.

[18] Michael Hughes, "Private Equity, Social Inequity: German Judges React to Inflation, 1914–1924," *Central European History* 41 (1983): 76–94. A mass political movement also formed around the issue demanding legislative action to revalue savings and debt obligations.

Law and Disorder: Article 48

The extent to which "the great disorder"[19] of the 1920s found its way into constitutional law was apparent when the association of German professors of state law met at Jena in spring 1924. Its chairman, Heinrich Triepel, remarked that "articles of the constitution were being chased around like a spooked horse at a fun fair."[20] Article 48 had been invoked repeatedly from the beginning of the Republic, and the great inflation was a period of economic turmoil—the price of bread rose to 140 billion Reichsmarks on November 5, 1923—and this carried over into street violence, plundering, and often explicitly anti-Semitic attacks.[21] In those circumstances, Article 48 was seen and used as one instrument in the toolbox of executive powers including enabling acts (which required parliamentary action): against currency speculation (October 7, 1923), to control exchange rates (June 22, 1923; June 29, 1923), and to ban trading in currency and commodities (July 3, 1923). As an alternative to the Enabling Act of October 13, 1923, Article 48 was held in reserve should the Reichstag fail to act (as it had).[22]

All this posed immediate questions of theory and practice for constitutional-state lawyers. Two papers on "The Dictatorship of the Reich President according to Article 48" were presented to them at Jena. The principal speaker was Carl Schmitt with another paper on the topic by Erwin Jacobi.[23] The established position on Article 48 understood the list of fundamental rights enumerated in paragraph 2 as a limitation on presidential emergency power. It contained, according to that reading, no expansive delegation of power to the president. This meant that all other articles in the constitutional text except 114, 115, 117, 118, 123, 124, and 153 were "dictator-proof" (*diktaturfest*). A robust version of this position was offered by Richard Grau in a book published two years earlier, in which he argued for a general constitutional theory and more specific rules. Grau's general theory assumed that the logic of having a constitution at all—limitations on the government's freedom to act, specifically on executive prerogative—necessarily implies that it is "inviolable."[24] A list of articles that may be suspended, secondly, must be understood

[19] Feldman, *The Great Disorder*.

[20] "Eröffnungsansprache," *Verhandlungen der Tagung der deutschen Staatsrechtslehrer zu Jena am 14. und 15. April 1924* (10). Triepel was a prominent constitutional lawyer during the Republic. Among his works are *Völkerrecht und Landesrecht* (1899), *Die Staatsverfassung und die politischen Parteien* (1927), and *Die Hegemonie. Ein Buch für führenden Staaten* (1938).

[21] On November 5 and 6, 1923 mobs roamed the Scheunenviertel in Berlin, looting and wrecking shops and looking for Jews, especially, Feldman writes, the easily identifiable Galician Jews. Feldman, *The Great Disorder*, 780.

[22] On October 7, 1923.

[23] Carl Schmitt, "Die Diktatur des Reichspräsidenten nach Art. 48 der Reichsverfassung," (63–10); Erwin Jacobi, "Die Diktatur des Reichspräsidenten nach Art. 48 der Reichsverfassung," *Verhandlungen der deutsche Staatsrechtslehrer*, Berlin: Walter de Gruyter Verlag, 1924 105–136.

[24] The German *unantastbar* also carries the connotation of "taboo," "sacrosanct," and thus points to a certain irrational moment of power and belief. It appears prominently in the Basic Law of the Federal Republic, which

to limit emergency power. *Enumerativ ergo limitativ.* Further, Article 76 WRV specified that the constitution can be changed through legislation, and the logic of that provision, Grau argued, closes other avenues to constitutional revision, specifically dictatorial revisions.[25] Finally on his reading of the constitutional debates at Weimar, members of the National Assembly had intended such limitations. They had, in fact, taken its ultimate statutory limitation by the Reichstag "for granted."[26] A limited construction had two advantages: the enumerations clause appears on that reading to constitute a logical constraint, and this construction conforms to the expectation that in a *Rechtsstaat* all power—especially any emergency powers that may be granted to an executive or, more generally to government—must be legal. They must, that is, have the form of law.

Schmitt argued at Jena against that reading of section two, and thus against a limited interpretation of Article 48, on the grounds of recent practice, government's stated policy, and the debates at Weimar. Unsurprisingly Schmitt's meta-jurisprudential perspective on the question of dictatorship found its way into his argument. As he had done in a series of other publications beginning with *Politische Romatik* (1918), Schmitt drew on the history of Western political thought about dictatorship, and specifically the Roman legal distinction between a "commissarial" and "sovereign" dictator.[27] In *Die Diktatur* (1921), Schmitt defended commissarial dictatorship as a temporary institution intended to preserve the fundamental constitutional order, a position that has been described as "an appropriate use of functional rationality, where a rule-bound constitutional order is presented as something worth defending and restoring."[28] I shall return to this dimension of the paper below. For now it suffices to say that these terms had not found their way into general discussions of Article 48 at this time. There was in fact considerable resistance to them among leading constitutional scholars who thought such distinctions an illegitimate expansion and who wanted to constrain, not expand, the reading of Article 48.

Schmitt found three reasons to doubt the adequacy of established interpretation. Its practice in the years from 1919 to 1924 meant that Article 48 was recognized as "valid law" independent of the provision foreseen (in paragraph 5) for legislation by the Reichstag.

---

declares that "human dignity is inviolable." Grundgesetz [GG] [Basic Law], Art.1, para.1., *translation at* http://www.gesetze-im-internet.de/englisch_gg/index.html.

[25] Richard Grau, *Die Diktaturgewalt des Reichspräsidenten und der Landesregierungen auf Grund des Artikels 48 der Reichsverfassung* (Berlin: Otto Liebmann, 1922), 53. Grau was Triepel's student and later a lawyer in Berlin.

[26] Ibid., 57. The declaration that a future statute would provide more substantial regulation of emergency powers in paragraph three, on which Grau draws here, never came to pass. Practice and usage had, by the last years of the Republic, made that provision a dead letter and resulted in the general acceptance of far-reaching dictatorial powers, limited only by the political will to use them or the political will to demand their suspension.

[27] Schmitt's major publications during the Weimar Republic were: *Dictatorship* (1921), *Political Theology* (1922), *Roman Catholicism & Political Form* (1923), *The Crisis of Parliamentary Democracy* (1923), *Political Romanticism* (1925), *Constitutional Theory* (1928), *The Concept of the Political* (1928), *The Defender of the Constitution* (1931), and *Legality and Legitimacy* (1932).

[28] John P. McCormick, "Dilemmas of Dictatorship," *Law as Politics,* ed. David Dyzenhaus (Durham, NC: Duke University Press, 1998), 218.

Whatever the normative weight of such considerations, they had not constrained emergency power and, Schmitt contended, effective restoration of public safety and order trumps the norm embodied in the enumerations paragraph. There had been general acceptance of this practice. To claim that such actions were illegal (invalid) amounts to saying, "the exceptions which the state of exception brings with itself, should never be exceptions from constitutional provisions unless they are [exceptions from] those seven fundamental rights." The established interpretation ignores "interventions in the organizational structure of the constitution that come with every exceptional circumstance (*Ausnahmezustand*)."[29]

Schmitt cites the use of military states of exception (*militärische Ausnahmezustand*) in which "all instruments of power are concentrated in the hands of the Reich" to support a broader interpretation of Article 48.[30] In the course of exercising emergency power the central government simply set aside the normal relationship of the member states (*Länder*) and the federal government, removed local officials of those states, took over their police forces, intervened expansively in the schools, and carried out confiscation of private property. The practice of emergency power in these cases demonstrates a pattern of presidential dictatorship going well beyond suspension of the enumerated seven fundamental rights. Finally the limited interpretation of Article 48 does not take into account divisions within the Reich government concerning its legal-constitutional meaning and scope. Beyond the general agreement that Article 48 is valid law the various ministries and branches of government held differing views on its use. The enumeration in paragraph two, however logical, fails to specify exactly what can be done to secure public order and civil peace (the stated purpose of dictatorial power) in a concrete instance.[31] Although paragraph two explicitly authorizes the president to suspend ("*ausser Kraft setzen*") the enumerated rights in part or whole, its silence on the means by which those rights can be suspended permits broad interpretation.

As a consequence, Schmitt argued, and until further specification by the Reichstag, the president may "take any measure necessary for the restoration of public safety and order;" presidential prerogative is limited neither by the enumeration clause nor by "any other article in the constitution."[32] The enumerations clause granted additional power (to suspend the specified rights) beyond the extensive grant contained by paragraph 1. In the National Assembly Schmitt saw a "sovereign dictator" whose power was completely unlimited by the rule of law but which should cease when its constitution came into effect. The fact that necessary legislation (section 4) had not been passed by parliament confirms that the delegation of power to the president was in principle unlimited. Only

---

[29] Schmitt, "Die Diktatur des Reichspräsidenten," 66–67.

[30] Schmitt here quotes the chancellor and minister of the Interior speaking before the Reichstag on December 4, 1923 and March 5, 1924.

[31] Schmitt, "Die Diktatur des Reichspräsidenten," 74.

[32] Ibid., 103.

the following considerations constrain the decision about when and how to use those extraordinary and exceptional powers:

1. Determination of what threatens public safety and order cannot be made independently of the constitution;
2. Article 48 cannot be used to abolish "an organizational minimum" (presidency, government, parliament) of the constitution; and
3. Article 48 contains temporary authority; it authorizes measures (*Maßnahmen*)—actions or arrangements necessary to overcome the circumstances at hand—which are not expected to persist indefinitely; actions and measures taken on the grounds of Article 48 should not make sovereign changes in the institutions which those measures are intended to protect.

Schmitt's argument at Jena drew on a larger reading of European political history to set the law and constitution within the frame of political institutions. "It might be politically possible," Schmitt argued, "to use Article 48 to destroy the Weimar constitution, as in France in 1851 the position of the French president was exploited and by coup d'etat a new constitution was introduced." In a distinction that would be drawn out more carefully in *Der Begriff des Politischen* and the *Verfassungslehre,* such changes belong to a political moment that by definition is tamed in a constitution. When the political moment emerges it can mark, depending on its severity, the end of an existing constitution. From that Schmitt developed a theory of constitutional defense as the purpose and end of dictatorial power. "It is not possible constitutionally, using Article 48, to transform the German Reich from a republic to a monarchy. [...] To break though (*durchbrechen*) the constitution is not to change it, to suspend it, to remove it. Those are the typical instruments of dictatorship: preservation of the constitution as a whole is the purpose of an exception to its provisions."[33] *Der Hüter der Verfassung* further expanded that theory with specific attention to the threats inherent in pluralism and polyarchy to constitutional government. If the paper at Jena contained the core of Schmitt's later constitutional theory, it also provided a quite different perspective on the famous first sentence of the *Politische Theologie*: "He is sovereign who decides on the state of exception."[34] In "Die Diktatur des Reichspräsident nach Art. 48" the perspective of "exception" is practical politics. The crucial difference between normal legal practice and actions in an exception is drawn, not by reference to theology, but from government statements in the Reichstag. Schmitt quotes the Interior minister speaking on March 5, 1924 to make this point: "'Obviously the exception in conformity to its name remains an exception and ceases as soon as the circumstances permit.'" The question, Schmitt comments further,

[33] Ibid., 91.
[34] "Souverän ist, wer über den Ausnahmezustand entscheidet."

which brings the argument of *Politische Theologie* immediately to mind is "who decides what the circumstances permit."[35]

The accompanying paper by Erwin Jacobi agreed in all significant points with Schmitt's. The National Assembly intended "without doubt" a broad grant of authority to the Reich president, Jacobi wrote, that gave the executive the possibility at least of all those powers typical of the Empire during the war. Rather than a list of legal delegation and their possible use, the National Assembly opted for a *Generalklausel* that "at least until the passage of a bill by the Reichstag further specifying such powers, was *plein pouvoir*."[36] No representative of the established interpretation denied such power to the president, Jacobi continued, because it had been "the core of what we learned about the law of exception" and unthinkable that at Weimar the assembled delegates intended to preclude their use. Nevertheless, Jacobi continued, "The established interpretation is here in insoluble contradiction with itself." Only one scholar had ventured to deny that Article 48 transferred executive power to the office of the president.[37] The resulting institution did "break through" the constitution in a manner similar to Bismarck's practice in the Empire. In order to find an invalid use (*ungültige*) of dictatorial power, one would have go back to the practices of the Länder[38]

Jacobi's argument in general agreed with Schmitt's. He denied, however, the Article 48 provided legitimate grounds for judicial review of action declared necessary to restore public safety and order. Jacobi also rejected claims that suits regarding the facts (of whether such disturbances had taken place) could be brought to a court for review. Jacobi concluded by urging the early passage of additional legislation by the Reichstag to clarify the whole complex of legal questions regarding the implementation of Article 48 by the president and further the development of federal regulation and oversight of Länder use of emergency powers.[39]

Jacobi's analysis of the self-contradictions within the established interpretation of Article 48 and Schmitt's theory of it as a "commissarial dictatorship" provoked what must have been a heated debate among the participants, whose temper is scarcely conveyed by the official report. Among those participants were Stier-Somo, Piloty, Nawiasky, Thoma, Anschütz, and Jellinek—leading representatives of the constitutional establishment and proponents of the limited interpretation. Some of the "young Turks" in constitutional law were also present and participated in the discussion, including Triepel and Hermann Heller. Details in each paper received less attention than the broad theory of presidential dictatorship as a commissarial institution that had been offered by Carl Schmitt.

---

[35] Schmitt, "Die Diktatur des Reichspräsidenten," 101.

[36] Jacobi, "Die Diktatur des Reichspräsidenten," 115.

[37] Fritz Stier-Somlo, "Die neuesten Entwicklungen des Gemeindeverfassungsrechts in Deutschland," *Veröffentlichungen der Vereinigung des Deutschen Staatsrechtslehrer* (Leipzig, Germany: Verein, 1925), 122–178.

[38] Jacobi, "Die Diktatur des Reichspräsidenten," 121.

[39] Ibid., 136.

The participants, we are told by the conference reporter, while rejecting Schmitt's view, agreed on some of the problems that continued to surround Article 48 as text and practice until the end of the Republic. Although dictatorial powers had been used frequently, that practice had led to no clear definition. Uncertainty remained about which actions were constitutional and which were unconstitutional, but participants tended to regard the practice of dictatorial powers as legally nonconforming—it should not persist until the Reichstag passed a bill. No one understood what it might mean for constitutional-state law to accept the "suspension" of laws through executive decrees and measures (*Maßnahme*). That discord did not lead to revision of the established interpretation, but to its reiteration. The enumerations clause *did* limit presidential power.

Article 48 at Weimar's End

The discussion of Article 48 at Jena divided participants along the two leading strands in contemporary jurisprudence: statute positivism and a political theory of law and constitution.[40] Lacking statutory definition of the powers available in Article 48, the majority of state-lawyers sought definition in the enumerations clause, even when its practice and thus the existing institution evidenced much wider use. Those who shared Schmitt's critique of that approach—but not necessarily his political preferences—sought, like him, to widen the sources of constitutional law by taking into account many aspects that doctrine excluded at the time. Most of these would, today, be considered normal reference points in American constitutional interpretation, and they were then too. Schmitt's radical conceptualization of the constitution, however, was remarkable in Weimar's context because it deliberately incorporated political history and political thought, and because it raised first order questions about matters that in positivist terms were presuppositions.[41] It also offered a political science of law and constitutions that could be used on the political Left and Right. That alone was an important change in German legal traditions, which until this point separated law from the political and specifically political claims.[42]

Many factors lead to "presidential dictatorship" after 1930. Anti-democratic political movements, party fragmentation, the erosion of the parliamentary system, a "legitimacy deficit"—any or perhaps all of these might have been mastered were it not for the financial and economic disaster that befell Germany and the world in 1929. Scarce credit and unemployment hardened the class conflicts of the Republic and increased the political stakes after the Great Coalition collapsed. Its demise in March of that year was a symptom

---

[40] I have explored this at length. Ellen Kennedy, *Constitutional Failure: Carl Schmitt in Weimar* (Durham: Duke University Press, 2004). esp. ch. 3, "Norm and Exception."

[41] See David Dyzenhaus, *Law as Politics. Carl Schmitt's Critique of Liberalism* (Duke University Press, 1998).

[42] That was already clear after the publication of *Begriff des Politischen* and *Verfassungslehre*. Kirchheimer and Neumann were the most prominent on the Left; on the Right were associates of President Hindenburg, notably Otto Meissner.

of deepening political conflicts over social programs, taxes, and funding. The proximate fall of the Müller cabinet was caused by disagreement among the parties in government over how to fund the workers' unemployment fund, but behind the scenes maneuvering focused on the use of Article 48 and "the collapse of the Müller cabinet had been very carefully scripted."[43] According to that narrative, reactionary interests wanted its end for their economic-financial reasons and also to enable the shift to a purely presidential government. Heinrich Brüning (Centrum) followed that course after becoming chancellor, and when Paul Moldenhauer (DVP) replaced Rudolf Hiferding (SPD) the fiscal course was set against the broad policy Hilferding called "economic democracy." From Brüning on, government by parliamentary majority became impossible. Brüning relied on presidential power and the "toleration" of that policy by the SPD.[44] Government continued only on that basis, and the practice of presidential authority went far beyond a limited interpretation of Article 48.

Gerhard Anschütz, the leading proponent of statutory positivism and author of an authoritative commentary on the Weimar constitution, viewed it as a national democracy based on "unity for the common good"—where unity was paramount. On those grounds, Peter Caldwell has argued, Anschütz "condemned the unions and employers' organizations that sought to realize their special interests over the supposed general interests of the democratic state."[45] According to that scheme, if the German people were the source of the constitution, the Reichstag was its central institution. As sovereign, the people's position was unlimited. In Anschütz and Thoma's commentary on the Weimar constitution they drew the conclusion that nothing in the document and no aspect of the constitution was above revision or revocation. According to the rules in Article 76 any provision could be revised if two-thirds of the Reichstag so voted, and should the Reichsrat object, the Reich president could ask for a referendum on the changes. "The constitution does not stand above the Reichstag," Anschütz wrote, "but rather at its disposal."[46] What Caldwell calls "the restraint and deference" to the legislative body reflected in the Anschütz-Thoma commentary gave way among even staunch statutory positivists as negative majorities in the Reichstag transformed parliamentary government.

Anschütz and Schmitt disagreed fundamentally on the sources and theory of the constitution, but agreed on "unity" and the destructive potential in the pluralism of vested economic interests. Both lawyers agreed that Germany after 1919 was a democracy, but they differed on which institution served as the repository of that democracy. Schmitt argued that it was the president. Anschütz argued that it was the Reichstag. Much of the

---

[43] Mommsen, *Weimar Democracy*, 287ff.

[44] Mommsen, *Weimar Democracy*. McElligott, *Rethinking the Weimar Republic*.

[45] Peter C. Caldwell, *Popular Sovereignty and the Crisis of German Constitutional Law: The Theory and Practice of Weimar Constitutionalism* (Durham, NC: Duke University Press, 1997), 66.

[46] Gerhard Anschütz, *Verfassung des Deutschen Reiches*, 14th ed. (Berlin, Germany: G. Silke, 1930), 401, 403. Quoted at Caldwell, *Popular Sovereignty*, 69.

statute positivists' resistance to Schmitt's argument for broad executive power in 1924 turned on the precedence given statutes over discretion, and the belief that representative assemblies best articulated and organized popular opinion and the people's will. It would have been expected, therefore, that if the constitution were completely open to any revision "at the disposal" of the Reichstag (Anschutz) then no executive power could or should "defend" it. On a legal positivist basis, there was Anschutz argued, nothing real to defend.

In June 1932 Anschütz prepared a legal brief for the ministers of Finance Paul Moldenhauer (DVP) and the Interior Joseph Wirth (Centrum) on whether Article 48 could be used instead of Article 87 to authorize credit.[47] The core question turned on statute versus prerogative, but the creation of credit by governmental fiat was also at stake. Over the previous two years, numerous executive orders had been issued using the authority of Article 48 in order to fund government expenditure when the Reichstag was not willing or able to pass a budget. Anschütz's argument moved "security" as a legal question from its location within established war powers to a place within the economy, and quite specifically, the president's prerogative in budgetary matters. Max Kühnemann, vice-chairman of the Reich Debt Administration, contended that Article 48 did not extend to Reich finances, specifically power over the budget and credit issued by the Reich.[48] Echoing the debate at Jena in opposition to Schmitt and Jacobi, Kühnemann insisted that only a statute could authorize the budget and the creation of credit through the issue of debt. Anschütz defended an expansive reading of Article 48 on the grounds of fiscal and economic security. There was no contradiction between the democratic basis of the constitution acknowledged and institutionalized by the National Assembly at Weimar, and the necessity of the moment.[49] This expansive reading by Anschütz and elsewhere by Richard Thoma[50] claimed that "in times of emergency, [...] such decrees are necessary for the existence of the state."[51] Ironically, given their methodological opposition in past years, Anschütz concluded his brief in support of bypassing the Reichstag in budgetary and fiscal matters with a long citation from Carl Schmitt's *Der Hüter der Verfassung*,

---

[47] "Only in case of extraordinary demand, and normally only for the purpose of paying for advertisement, may funds be acquired by the means of credits. Such acquisition, as well as reliability at the Reich's expense, may only be undertaken if based on a Reich law."

[48] Max Kühnemann, "Können Reichsetat und Reichskredite dikatorisch geregelt werden?" *Reichsverwaltungsblatt*, September 19, 1931.

[49] Gerhard Anschütz, *Reichskredite und Diktatur: zwei Rechtsgutachten* (Tübingen: J.C.B.Mohr, 1932), 10ff. Here the Reich president appears as a democratically elected official whose signature gave formal authority for government decrees in the financial and economic sphere.

[50] Richard Thoma, "Die Notstandsverordnung des Reichsprasidenten," *Zeitschrift für öffentliches Recht* 11 (1931), 17.

[51] The broad basis for this position had been stated by Anschütz some years earlier during the first constitutional crisis when he declared three principles to be the "leading ideas" of the Weimar constitution: (1) the Reich, (2) the unitary state, (3) a democratic-republican state form. Gerhard Anschütz, *Drei Leitgedanken der Weimarer Reichsverfassung* (Tübingen: J.C.B. Mohr, 1923).

saying "[this] dictatorship is not a sovereign but a constitutionally regulated and limited power that is [nonetheless] definitely and reliably guaranteed against the predominance of the Reichstag."[52] At any time the Reichstag could suspend the authority of Article 48 by a vote. That it does not do so, Anschütz concluded in citing Schmitt, underscores its incapacity to act. In that case, "it has no right to demand that all other responsible offices of government render themselves incapable."[53]

The "internal consolidation" of the presidential system between 1930 and 1932 meant that "there was increased willingness to use emergency degrees in areas hitherto considered exempt from emergency legislation [. . .] Whereas emergency decrees were originally limited to a specific period of time, this restriction was discarded along with the principle that the budgetary powers of the Reichstag was inviolable."[54] Mommsen is correct to conclude that "the dictatorial authority of the Reich president was now seen as an independent legislative right," which met little resistance.

A year earlier Schmitt reviewed and summarized the German practice of government by emergency decree for state law. With a glance at the old concepts of siege and martial law, he noted their inadequacy to the contemporary realities in which military threats were not immediate; rather, it was economic, fiscal, and financial crisis that opened the way to commissarial dictatorship in Germany under circumstances in which the normal lawmaker was rendered incapable. One may still question the extent to which the very existence of such a provision in the Weimar constitution was a wise and foresighted provision (as Max Weber and Hugo Pruss thought), or a dangerous temptation. In the context of American debates on similar matters that question is somewhat beside the point. The more imperative question was put in 1957: "the specific method with which a regime conducts itself [in the exception] reveals its constitutional organization. [. . .] Institutionalization is one way to evade the terrible problems of the state of exception. There is another, different from the legal, namely to exclude it. A definite time or sphere of action can be specified in order to free it up for the unrestrained action of a commissar. In a certain sense that is the general sense of *beyond the line*. The Statue of Liberty will be for a time covered up. When the drapery falls, the Normal steps forward—practically speaking, through a declaration of indemnity—with all its guaranteed rights."[55] What must be taken into account from our perspective, however, is the possibility that actors in such circumstances might ultimately, even deliberately, move the line between norm and exception, leaving little sense of the living thing that is liberty and constitutional government.

---

[52] Anschütz, *Drei Leitgedanken*, 22.

[53] Carl Schmitt, *Der Hüter der Verfassung*, (Tübingen: J.C.B. Mohr, 1931) 131, quoted by Anschütz, *Drei Leitgedanken* 22.

[54] Mommsen, *Weimar Democracy*, 362.

[55] Schmitt, "Die staatsrechtliche Bedeutung der Notverordnung" 1931 in *Verfassungsrechtliche Aufsätze* (Berlin: Duncker & Humblot, 1958), 260.

Conclusion

It has been suggested that the 2016 election revealed the shadow of Weimar's failure over the United States.

Constitutions fail in various ways. There were ten major parties in the Weimar Reichstag but dozens of smaller ones such as the "Beer Drinkers Party" or the "Bicyclist Party," a history that led to the Federal Republic's current law regarding political representation. Weimar was "an experiment in modernity."[56] Government by decree, based on Article 48, and the not insignificant influence of constitutional lawyers, such as Schmitt, reinforced the pattern of irregularity, justified by executive orders.[57] But has the American constitution failed—is it likely to fail—because Donald Trump now occupies the presidency? Although his behavior is irregular, his comments vulgar ("shithole" countries), and his preferred communication with citizens and foreign representatives carried out on Twitter, nothing he has done is moving this country to the state of constitutional failure. If we are traveling in that direction, it has been the policies enacted by the Bush administration in reaction to the attacks on major American cities on September 11, 2001. All three branches of the American government responded with care after those attacks, but the initial declaration of an emergency gradually became permanent, adding to the legal-institution structure a Department of Homeland Security, intended to guard against other attacks on the United States, that now employs 230,000 people in a variety of functions, from border control and aviation to cybersecurity.

But constitutional failure is more than questions of borders and hijacked planes. If a constitution is said to have failed or to be failing then we must look to its essential institutions, those branches of the national government, and the activities of state and local governments. If "all powerful concepts of modern state theory are secularized theological concepts" then we must *believe* in the modern *Rechtsstaat*, in the modern rule-of-law state.[58] Do we believe in the United States of America? Or have we, over the last decades become, if not disbelievers, at least agnostics on the crucial matter?

---

[56] Detlev J.K. Peukert, *The Weimar Republic* (London: Alan Lane, 1991), 276.

[57] The constitution of the Weimar Republic was never revoked. The emergency decree "for the Protection of the People and the State" (February 28, 1933) in reaction to the Reichstag fire suspended all constitutional rights, and was followed on March 23 by an Enabling Law. Normal legislation ceased. The Reichstag became an audience for Hitler's proclamations. Ironically, neither the Weimar constitution nor Hitler's decrees were ever revoked. As Allied troops occupied the former Third Reich, Germany ceased to exist and became simply a geographical expression.

[58] Carl Schmitt, *Politische Theologie. Vier Kapitel zur Lehre von der Souveränität* (Münich and Leipzig: Duncker & Humblot, 1922) 49.

II Countries and Regions

America's political dysfunction looks forbiddingly irreparable, its
government implacably hostile to expertise.... There is a risk that America's
institutional rot is too far advanced for mere deliberation to help.

THE ECONOMIST, December 2, 2017[1]

"Do you think the United States is basically okay after this year's presidential election,
or do you think the election has done real damage to the country?"

"Real damage" + "Unsure:" 55%

WASHINGTON POST/SCHAR POLL[2]

2017 was probably the very best year in the long history of humanity.

NICHOLAS KRISTOF, 2018[3]

6 What's New? What's Next? Threats to the American Constitutional Order
Jennifer Hochschild*

IT IS EASY to find claims by public intellectuals that the Trump presidency—or the
conditions that impelled Donald Trump into the presidency—are irrevocably damaging the United States' political system: "America died on Nov. 8, 2016, not with a bang
or a whimper, but at its own hand via electoral suicide.... We have destroyed the values
that have bound us.... Democracy can't cope with extremism."[4] Or more simply, "*we are
headed off a cliff.*"[5] Pundits have incentives to exaggerate, but in this case they have plenty
of support. As the first epigraph shows, even the sober, neoliberal *Economist* fears that
America's institutional rot is too far advanced; as the second shows, fewer than half of
Americans agree that the United States is basically okay after staggering out of the 2016
election.[6] Are they right? We are unlikely to really know for years or even decades—but

* Deep thanks for very helpful comments from Deborah Baumgold, Paul DiMaggio, Edwin Dorn, Mark Graber, Peter Hall, Sanford Levinson, David Mayhew, Kristin Monroe, and Mark Tushnet.

[1] "How to Get It Back," *The Economist*, December 2, 2017.

[2] Washington Post/Schar School Poll, November 11–14, 2016, https://www.washingtonpost.com/politics/polling/united-states-presidential-basically/2016/11/16/68774126-abf7-11e6-8f19-21a1c65d2043_page.html.

[3] Nicholas Kristof, "Why 2017 Was the Best Year in Human History," *New York Times*, January 6, 2018.

[4] Neal Gabler, "Farewell, America," *Moyers and Company*, November 10, 2016, http://billmoyers.com/story/farewell-america/.

[5] Publius Decius Mus, "The Flight 93 Election," *Claremont Review of Books*, September 5, 2016, https://www.claremont.org/crb/basicpage/the-flight-93-election/.

[6] Eight similar survey items show roughly the same results, although most include reference to a specific presidential candidate or to President Obama. Tellingly, the question was not asked before 2013.

fourteen months into Donald Trump's presidency, we can discern what might turn out to be early indicators.

In my view, America has not died and has not fallen off a cliff, but it is not basically okay. Some features of the American political system are strong and resilient, despite or perhaps even because of Trump's victory. But both democratic and liberal elements of the constitutional system are under considerable stress and might break.

Why Now?

An initial puzzle that both sets the context and provides evidence for evaluating America's political strength is why the United States is in such a political uproar at present. After all, by many important criteria, the country is thriving.[7] Nicholas Kristof's provocation about 2017, in the third epigraph, contains an element of truth.

First, in comparison to the past century, the United States is at relative peace. One must not overlook violence in the rest of the world—the horrors of the Syrian civil war, the genocide of Myanmar's Rohingya, or the savagery of Nigeria's Boko Haram. But these disasters have not led to the millions of deaths and international upheavals of two world wars, the "bloodlands" of the 1930s, the massacres of the Cultural Revolution, or even the Korean and Vietnamese wars—and relatively speaking, the United States has been lightly touched. Fewer than 1 percent of Americans serve in the military and reserves, and few—though too many—have been killed in armed combat over the past few decades.

Second, violence within the United States is at a similarly low level. In 1993, the Department of Justice reported an annual rate of 80 "violent victimizations" per 1,000 persons age twelve or older. That number has steadily declined; except for one year, the rate has been below 25 since 2008. The years 2014 through 2016 show a further slight decline.[8] Groups of Americans—most prominently, young urban African Americans and undocumented immigrants—feel as though they are under siege. But with these crucial exceptions, the United States is a more peaceful country, domestically as well as internationally, than it has been for decades.

Third, the American economy is growing. Median household income was higher in 2016 than at any previous point since the data have been collected, and has fully recovered from the 2008–2012 recession. Median incomes for black and Hispanic households

---

[7] A complete analysis requires comparison of the United States with the electoral and constitutional disruptions of comparable countries such as Great Britain, France, or Germany. This chapter cannot take on those comparisons; the rest of this book is invaluable for that purpose.

[8] Jennifer L. Truman and Rachel E. Morgan, "Criminal Victimization, 2015," *Bureau of Justice Statistics* (2015), https://www.bjs.gov/content/pub/pdf/cv15.pdf; Rachel E. Morgan and Grace Kena, "Criminal Victimization, 2016," *Bureau of Justice Statistics* (2016), https://www.bjs.gov/index.cfm?ty=pbdetail&iid=6166.

rose almost three times, and more than twice as much, respectively, as the incomes of non-Hispanic white households in 2016. The official poverty level declined in 2016 for the second consecutive year, and has recovered since the recession, although it remains higher than its lowest point in the early 1970s.[9] The number of Americans without health insurance is roughly half of what it had been in 2008, when these data were first collected.[10]

Other indicators show stable and reasonably high levels of success, or declines in failure. For example, nonmarital birth rates in the United States have dropped since a 2007 peak, especially among black and Hispanic women, and especially under age thirty.[11] Sales of new single-family homes are at their highest level since July 2007.[12] Educational attainment is at a historical high—for high school and college, for those under age thirty and those over, for men and women, and for non-Hispanic whites, blacks, Asians, and Hispanics (of any race).[13] Civilian employment has risen steadily since the sickening descent of 2008 to 2010. The civilian unemployment rate is at its lowest point since 2000, and the number of people suffering from long-term unemployment is at its lowest point since 2007. Unemployment has declined among all age groups, both genders, people with all levels of education, and in all four major racial and ethnic groups since the peak in 2010.[14] The gender pay gap is edging downward and is lower than ever before.[15] The right to marry is no longer constrained by sex.

And one must not forget that Americans twice elected a black man to be the most powerful individual in the world. That was due partly to the growing political strength of black and Latino/a citizens, and partly to the fact that white voters supported Barack Obama at higher levels in 2008 than they had done for any Democratic presidential candidate since Lyndon Johnson.

In sum, the United States is doing reasonably well, and better than at key moments in the recent past, on crucial measures of death, economic well-being, social capacity, and even racial or gender equity. Those are not the patterns we would expect for a nation that

[9] U.S. Census Bureau, "Income and Poverty in the United States: 2016," September 12, 2017, https://www.census.gov/library/publications/2017/demo/p60-259.html.

[10] U.S. Census Bureau, "Health Insurance Coverage in the United States: 2016," September 12, 2017, https://www.census.gov/library/publications/2017/demo/p60-260.html.

[11] National Center for Health Statistics, "Births and Birth Rates to Unmarried Women in the United States, Selected Years 1940-2015," *Data Visualization Gallery*, accessed February 27, 2018, https://www.cdc.gov/nchs/data-visualization/births-to-unmarried-women/index.htm.

[12] Trading Economics, "United States New Home Sales," accessed February 27, 2018, https://tradingeconomics.com/united-states/new-home-sales.

[13] U.S. Census Bureau, "CPS Historical Time Series Tables," 2017, https://www.census.gov/data/tables/time-series/demo/educational-attainment/cps-historical-time-series.html.

[14] U.S. Bureau of Labor Statistics, "Charting the Labor Market: Data from the Current Population Survey," https://www.bls.gov/web/empsit/cps_charts.pdf.

[15] U.S. Bureau of the Census, "Income, Poverty and Health Insurance Coverage in the United States: 2016," September 12, 2017, https://www.census.gov/newsroom/press-releases/2017/income-poverty.html.

is irreparably dysfunctional and dying by its own hand. As Kristof says, "we need some perspective as we watch the circus in Washington, hands over our mouths in horror. . . . Let's not miss what's going right."[16]

Mostly Sound and Fury?

Why, if so many things are going right, does no one (including Kristof) depict the American political system as buoyant, mutually beneficent, effective? An answer to that question starts with more systematic analysis of how much, why, or even whether, the American constitutional structure is threatened by our unusual level of political rancor.

At one end of the spectrum of anxiety, one can argue that the United States is simply going through a normal, perhaps unusually heightened, process of political contestation. As Larry Bartels wrote, "an extraordinary campaign [in 2016] has produced a remarkably ordinary election outcome, primarily reflecting partisan patterns familiar from previous election cycles. . . . The national election outcome was consistent with forecasts based on 'fundamental' factors like incumbency and the state of the economy."[17] Americans are closely divided between liberals and conservatives; at present, the Right is winning and the Left is losing, just as the reverse is sometimes the case. In a more stringent version of this view, the strength of American politics lies in precisely this capacity to recalibrate in both directions. When political actors move too far to the Left (Right) for the taste of a majority of voters, electoral dynamics bring the system back into equilibrium or even push it too far in the opposite direction, in which case the pendulum once again reverses course.[18]

Jack Balkin also perceives a normal process of political contestation. Using Stephen Skowronek's logic of the cycles of political time,[19] Balkin describes the Trump presidency as "disjunctive." Disjunctive presidents have the task of trying to hold together an aging coalition or party whose components increasingly oppose one another, cannot address new problems, are irrelevant to constituents, or are out of tune with demographic changes. Reagan's Republican regime is now almost exhausted; Trump's mission is to "take unorthodox positions designed to repair increasingly serious breaches within the party." Unfortunately for his supporters, however, "this mission is close to impossible. . . . His party will probably lose to the opposition party (most likely the Democrats)

[16] Kristof, "Why 2017 Was the Best Year."

[17] Larry Bartels, "2016 Was an Ordinary Election, Not a Realignment," *Washington Post*, November 10, 2016.

[18] Robert Erikson, Michael B. Mackuen, and James A. Stinson, *The Macro Polity* (New York: Cambridge University Press, 2002). The fact that Donald Trump did not actually receive majority support in the 2016 election complicates this argument. The American political system has, however, survived the distortions induced by the Electoral College in the past without a constitutional crisis.

[19] Stephen Skowronek, *The Politics Presidents Make: Leadership from John Adams to George Bush* (Cambridge MA: Harvard University Press, 1993).

in the 2020 presidential election."[20] To add to Trump's woes, half or more of Americans—sometimes including Republicans—reject many of his policy stances. Presidents "who fail to ... assess accurately the potential for obtaining public support ... are prone to overreach and political disaster."[21]

By another logic, norms and laws, rather than electoral dynamics, are functioning to preserve the American political system, at least so far. Perhaps the Trump administration's strenuous efforts to be disjunctive will merely drown in the Washington swamp, known to supporters as the "rule of law. Every penny spent on an 'incompetent bureaucrat' or a stupid program is spent according to a law that has been passed and that you [President Trump] would need to undo." In her epistolary essay, Elaine Kamarck points to federal civil service protections, entitlements, and interest payments that absorb almost two-thirds of the federal budget; legal prohibitions against agencies' shifting funds from their original purposes; courts' rejection of executive orders opposed by Congress; and other brakes on dramatic, or even substantial, change from politics as usual in Washington.[22]

And even if the Republican regime does succeed in draining some of what it understands to be the Washington swamp—for example, by not filling federal offices—it will still run up against the protective barrier of other governmental and quasi-governmental units. "The federal government relies on cooperation by the states in enforcing federal policy. If states and localities exercise their right to not cooperate with unconstitutional policies, this will very much impede the capacity of the federal government." Ironically to those who associate "states' rights" with segregation and racist violence, "states' rights federalism ... is the key to protecting our liberties."[23] States and localities are challenging the Trump administration on environmental policy, immigrant and immigration policy, tax policy, and numerous other initiatives.

The very messiness of local governance may be another brake on disjunctive ambitions. Political scientists and activists sometimes complain about the plethora of elections in the United States—too frequently they occur off cycle; turnout is embarrassingly low and voters are inexcusably ignorant; elections of judges and district attorneys may corrupt the rule of law. But elections "are remarkable shock absorbers."[24] More generally,

---

[20] Jack Balkin, "What Kind of President Will Trump Become? Part II—Donald Trump and the Politics of Disjunction," *Balkinization* (blog), November 14, 2016, https://balkin.blogspot.com/2016/11/what-kind-of-president-will-trump.html.

[21] George C. Edwards, III, "Can Donald Trump Persuade Americans to Support His Agenda? Its Not Likely," *The Washington Post*, December 27, 2016. Several paragraphs in this section appeared first in Jennifer Hochschild, "What Happens Next? A Tour of Social Scientists' Predictions for the Trump Presidency," *Brookings FIXGOV* (blog), January 6, 2017, https://www.brookings.edu/blog/fixgov/2017/01/06/tour-of-trump-predictions/.

[22] Elaine C. Kamarck, "Dear President-Elect, Here Are a Few Things You Need to Know about Washington," *Boston Globe*, November 11, 2016.

[23] Corey Brettschneider, "Local and State Government Can Protect the Constitution from Trump," *Time Magazine*, November 30, 2016.

[24] Personal communication from David Mayhew, January 1, 2018.

resistance to Trump and the sweeping Republican victories of 2016 may generate more robust electoral and civic engagement, as women, African Americans, young adults, veterans, Latinos and Latinas, and democratic socialists all vow to organize, mobilize, vote, and run for office in order to halt the spread of nativism, racism, sexism, elitism, or merely conservatism. (The multiplicity of terms in that sentence hint at the energy, although not yet the success, of electorally-focused opponents of the Trump regime.) One could add the norm-reinforcing forces of a constitutional court system,[25] what many understand to be the military obligation to disobey illegal orders, the ease of convening a substantial protest, the technological difficulty of silencing the press and social media, the self-limiting elements of populism,[26] and other features of the American political order, to argue that the United States' liberal democratic system is more likely to defeat any totalitarian or disruptive ambitions of President Trump than the reverse.[27]

One can even argue that the election and presidency of Donald Trump might strengthen rather than undermine American liberal democracy. The message from no less a sage than C. Vann Woodward is that "one must expect and even hope that there will be future upheavals to shock the seats of power and privilege and furnish the periodic therapy that seems necessary to the health of our democracy."[28] More particularly, American self-styled progressives and the Democratic party are at fault for not realizing the breadth and depth of anger and despair among Trump voters, and for not having offered effective policy and symbolic responses to their loss of jobs, prospects, status, and hope. However one tries to explain it away, for the party supposedly on the Left to relinquish the support of working class men and women (of the majority race, at least) is a grievous political failing—and the Democratic Party deserved Woodward's shock to the seats of power that they received in 2016. Democratic Party efforts to win back voters in "fly-over country" without relinquishing the Party's progressive principles or current supporters, and substantively serious responses from conservative Republicans, could benefit both liberalism and democracy.

Constitutional Dangers?

At the other end of the spectrum of anxiety, I see two reasons for grave concern about the American constitutional order as a result of the Trump presidency. Perhaps ironically, the fact that many conservatives also fear for the American constitutional order reinforces my

---

[25] Samuel Issacharoff, *Fragile Democracies: Contested Power in the Era of Constitutional Courts* (New York: Cambridge University Press, 2015).

[26] Rogers Brubaker, "Why Populism?" *Theoretical Sociology* 46 (2017): 357–385, 379–380.

[27] Christopher R. Browning, "Lessons from Hitler's Rise," *New York Review of Books*, April 20, 2017 (offering an especially thoughtful analysis of the barriers to a totalitarian presidency).

[28] C. Vann Woodward, *The Burden of Southern History*, 3rd ed. (Baton Rouge, LA: Louisiana State University Press, 1993), 166.

concern. Their language can be as apocalyptic as that of those on the Left: "If . . . Western governments can't, or won't, discharge the basic duties of providing physical safety and domestic tranquility, the question becomes whether democracies' citizens will come to regard the attributes that define their societies, such as pluralism, tolerance, and civil liberties, as unaffordable luxuries. The resulting democratic repudiation of democratic government and social norms will be . . . capable of generating a political crisis."[29] Tea Party protesters showed that "corruption had eaten deeply into constitutional foundations, and that government was slipping beyond the control of the governed." Only drastic action can "halt, much less reverse, the constitutional decay. . . . Has the national culture, popular and elite, deteriorated so much that the virtues necessary to sustain republican government are no longer viable? America is not there yet, though when 40% of children are born out of wedlock it is not too early to wonder."[30] To these analysts, a Trump presidency is a last-ditch heroic effort to save the republic—not evidence that America died on November 8, 2016.[31]

COSMOPOLITAN VERSUS LOCAL: UNDERMINING DEMOCRATIC GOVERNANCE. In my view, the conservatives are rightly anxious about threats to the American constitutional order but for the wrong reasons. I see two constitutional problems. The first is a problem of functioning democracy, understood in simple terms as the combination of representation of many public views *and* the capacity to govern responsively and effectively despite deep differences brought into the public arena by representatives. The core of the problem of democracy is Brexit-like: economic and social opportunities, societal institutions, individual behaviors, and political attitudes are all lining up to reinforce one another such that literal and metaphorical cosmopolitan areas are moving farther and farther away from literal and metaphorical localist areas. At some point, differences risk hardening into a belief that your group's win is ineluctably my group's loss, a situation that the geographically based American electoral order is poorly equipped to manage.[32]

Let us unpack this argument. Public opinion surveys provide a profile of the type of voters who preferred candidate Trump and continue to support the Trump presidency.

---

[29] William Voegeli, "What's at Stake," *Claremont Review of Books* 16 (2016): 26–34, 26.

[30] Charles Kesler, "Trump and the Conservative Cause," *Claremont Review of Books* 16 (2016): 10–16, 11, 12. See also Andrew Sullivan, "The Reactionary Temptation," *New York Magazine*, April 30, 2017, http://nymag.com/daily/intelligencer/2017/04/andrew-sullivan-why-the-reactionary-right-must-be-taken-seriously.html.

[31] Publius Decius Mus, "The Flight 93 Election," *Claremont Review of Books*, September 4, 2016, https://www.claremont.org/crb/basicpage/the-flight-93-election/. "2016 is the Flight 93 election: charge the cockpit or you die. You may die anyway. . . . There are no guarantees. Except one: if you don't try, death is certain."

[32] "Cosmopolitan" and "localist" are partly metaphorical terms in my usage; in this sense, they represent people for whom the United States as a whole, or even the world, is the appropriate moral and personal touchstone, as compared with people for whom a particular nation, state, community, or group is the appropriate moral and personal touchstone. But they are also literal terms—a distinction between people who live in metropolitan areas and people who live in small towns or rural communities. The metaphorical distinction can become

They are disproportionately white, middle-aged, Protestant, of middle income, with moderate education, living in towns or rural areas in the interior of the country, and employed in traditional jobs. They are disproportionately conservative religiously and culturally, mistrustful of elites, hostile to intellectuals, reliant on nonmainstream media, economically insecure, and fearful of downward mobility.[33] They tend to hold traditional gender views, to express pride in white identity and American nationalism—and perhaps to hold authoritarian, racially resentful, or nativist attitudes. Trump's supporters, in short, are "alienated, aggrieved, and profoundly distrustful,"[34] suffering from well-warranted status anxiety,[35] and disillusioned about public officials purporting to help them.[36]

Trump supporters' contexts reinforce these views, just as Trump opponents' environment strengthens *their* opinions. The all-too-evident fracturing of the electorate in the 2016 presidential election rests on a steady growth of geographically-based partisan division. In 1992, just over a third of voters lived in "landslide counties," defined as those in which one presidential candidate won by 20 percentage points or more. By 2016, "a whopping 60 percent" of voters lived in landslide counties. Republican landslide counties had more whites, more workers in "old economy" jobs, and more culturally traditional residents than did Democratic landslide counties; conversely, the latter had wealthier whites, more "new economy" workers, and more educated residents.[37] "America's political fabric, geographically, is tearing apart."[38]

Counties with many Trump supporters are disproportionately unhealthy, a pattern that both describes and causes growing economic and behavioral divides. "An index of public health statistics [life expectancy, obesity, diabetes, heavy drinking, exercise levels] . . . explain 43% of Mr. Trump's gains over Mr. Romney, just edging out the 41% accounted for by the share of non-college whites";[39] even with controls, the health index remains explanatory. Even more dramatically, "death predicts whether people vote for

---

politically dangerous, I am arguing, if it turns into a zero-sum dynamic that is tightly aligned with geographic location in a geographically determined electoral system.

[33] Neil Irwin and Josh Katz, "The Geography of Trumpism," *New York Times*, March 12, 2016.

[34] Institute for Policy Research Newsletter, "'Alienated, Aggrieved, and Profoundly Distrustful': Sociologist Andrew Cherlin Explores White, Working-Class Discontent," Northwestern University, Summer 2017, http://www.ipr.northwestern.edu/about/news/2016/cherlin-economy-family-workingclassdiscontent.html.

[35] Noam Gidron and Peter Hall, "The Politics of Social Status: Economic and Cultural Roots of the Populist Right," *British Journal of Sociology* 68 (2017): 557–584.

[36] Arlie Hochschild, *Strangers in Their Own Land: Anger and Mourning on the American Right* (New York: New Press, 2016); Katherine Cramer, *The Politics of Resentment: Rural Consciousness in Wisconsin and the Rise of Scott Walker* (Chicago: University of Chicago Press, 2016).

[37] Gregor Aisch, Adam Pearce, and Karen Yourish, "The Divide between Red and Blue America Grew Even Deeper in 2016," *New York Times*, November 10, 2016.

[38] David Wasserman, "Purple America Has All but Disappeared," *FiveThirtyEight*, March 8, 2017, https://fivethirtyeight.com/features/purple-america-has-all-but-disappeared/; see also Emily Badger and Quoctrung Bui, "Why Republicans Don't Try to Win Cities," *New York Times*, November 3, 2016.

[39] "Illness as Indicator," *The Economist*, November 19, 2016.

Donald Trump." In eight of nine states studied, "the counties with high rates of white mortality were the same counties that turned out to vote for Trump" in the 1916 Super Tuesday primary elections. Here too, the statistical and substantive significance of the white death rate persisted even with controls.[40]

Like partisan differences, health disparities are widening across communities. For example, although mortality rates from cardiovascular disease declined in all counties from 1980 to 2014, the counties with the highest rates in 2014 were also those with "particularly slow rates of improvement." Mortality rates from substance abuse "increased by more than 1000%" over those fifteen years in Appalachia and the lower Midwest—Trump country. Deaths from cirrhosis of the liver declined along the West and East coasts but rose in Appalachia, Texas, and the upper Midwest.[41] "During the period 1999–2015, and especially since 2007, the gap in [suicide] rates between less urban and more urban areas widened over time." Not only is suicide devastating to surviving family and friends, but also "the potential cumulative burden of suicide risk factors in less urban areas might affect . . . communities as well."[42]

Most shockingly, low status whites' life expectancy has declined over the past few years—a reversal of almost a century of progress. "Mortality among white non-Hispanics (males and females) [is] *rising* for those without a college degree, and *falling* for those with a college degree." That change is arguably occurring because poorly educated whites are experiencing a new phenomenon for them: "cumulative disadvantage from one birth cohort to the next—in the labor market, in marriage and child outcomes, and in health."[43] Most important for my political analysis, expected age of death for the poor correlates, especially in the Midwest and South, with not only smoking, obesity, and lack of exercise, but also community-level characteristics: income segregation, income inequality, low social capital, unemployment, population declines, and low labor force participation rate.[44] Life expectancy for blacks and Hispanics, conversely, is lengthening.[45]

---

[40] Jeff Guo, "Death Predicts Whether People Vote for Donald Trump," *Washington Post Wonkblog*, March 4, 2016, https://www.washingtonpost.com/news/wonk/wp/2016/03/04/death-predicts-whether-people-vote-for-donald-trump/?utm_term=.116dad3eb1fd.

[41] Laura Dwyer-Lindgren et al., "US County-Level Trends in Mortality Rates for Major Causes of Death, 1980–2014," *Journal of the American Medical Association* 316 (2016): 2385-2401, 2392, 2398.

[42] Scott Kegler, Deborah M. Stone, and Kristin M. Holland, "Trends in Suicide by Level of Urbanization—United States, 1999–2015," *Morbidity and Mortality Weekly Report* 66 (2017): 270-273.

[43] Anne Case and Angus Deaton, "Mortality and Morbidity in the 21st Century," *Brookings Papers on Economic Activity*, BPEA Conference Drafts, March 23–24, 2017, https://www.brookings.edu/wp-content/uploads/2017/03/6_casedeaton.pdf.

[44] David Cutler, "Comments on 'Mortality and Morbidity in the 21st Century' by Anne Case and Angus Deaton," *Brookings*, March 2017, https://www.brookings.edu/wp-content/uploads/2017/03/6b_cutler.pdf, slides 22, 23.

[45] Case and Deaton, "Mortality and Morbidity"; see Noah Smith, "The Blogs vs. Case-Deaton," *Noahpinion* (blog), March 29, 2017, http://noahpinionblog.blogspot.com/2017/03/the-blogs-vs-case-deaton.html for a summary and evaluation of critiques.

Finally and unsurprisingly, residence in a commuting zone with relatively low inter-generational mobility has a "small" but "robust" relationship with support for Trump.[46] Inequality and lack of opportunity cumulate across generations as well as within a community.

Like partisan division and health disparities, geographically-based economic inequality is growing. *The Economist* provides a measure of changes in regional inequality of income per person from 1980 to 2015 in the United States. The first fifteen years showed little difference in income inequality between metropolitan and other areas. Regional income inequality rose steeply after 1995, however, and reached its high point in 2015, when the analysis ended.[47] There seems to be little prospect of broad-based reversal of this trend: as of 2015, the San Francisco Bay area, New York City, and the Boston area accounted for 60 percent of venture capital investments. Overall, only twenty-eight counties, virtually all in or near cities, receive four-fifths of investments from venture capitalists.[48] The counties in which a majority of voters supported Trump in 2016 account for only 36 percent of the nation's economic activity.[49] The correlations between Democratic vote share and "metros with larger concentrations of startups, venture capital investment, and high-tech industry ... are all stronger for 2016 than they were in 2012."[50] Despite the aggregate and nonwhite increases in median income and in employment reported in the first Section, median household incomes in non-metro areas fell 2 percent in 2016, and employment remained 2 percent lower than in 2008.[51]

Attitudinal chasms reinforce and are strongly associated with demographic and structural divides. In congressional districts most exposed to import competition, moderate members of Congress have been replaced by more extreme members, to both Left and Right.[52] Even something as basic as what it means to be an American varies dramatically by location; people who define national identity as adherence to a set of values or who have little investment in the question are disproportionately urban; "ardent nationalists"

---

[46] Jonathan Rothwell, "Financial Insecurity Higher for Those Who Favor Trump," *Gallup*, October 10, 2016, http://news.gallup.com/poll/196220/financial-insecurity-higher-favor-trump.aspx.

[47] "Rage against the Dying of the Light," *The Economist*, December 12, 2016.

[48] Olav Sorenson, "Where Is the Money in Venture Capital?," *Yale Insights*, October 22, 2015, https://insights.som.yale.edu/insights/where-is-the-money-in-venture-capital; for a map, see Adley Bowden, "The Geography of U.S. Venture Investments," *PitchBook*, June 27, 2014, https://pitchbook.com/news/articles/thegeographyofu-s-ventureinvestments.

[49] Eduardo Porter, "President-Elect Found Votes Where the Jobs Weren't," *New York Times*, December 14, 2016.

[50] Richard Florida, "How America's Metro Areas Voted," *CityLab*, November 29, 2016, https://www.citylab.com/equity/2016/11/how-americas-metro-areas-voted/508355/.

[51] Porter, "President-Elect Found Votes."

[52] David Autor, David Dorn, Gordon Hanson, and Kaveh Majlesi, "Importing Political Polarization? The Electoral Consequences of Rising Trade Exposure," NBER Working Paper No. 22637, revised December 2017, http://www.nber.org/papers/w22637.

and "restrictive nationalists" are overrepresented in rural areas and small towns. That pattern holds even more strongly when the sample is restricted to whites.[53]

Qualitative studies show rural conservatives to be as bitterly scornful of urban cosmopolites as the reverse.[54] Survey and experimental evidence concur: "Both Republicans and Democrats increasingly dislike, even loathe, their opponents. . . . Affective polarization has permeated judgments about interpersonal relations, [and] exceeds polarization based on other prominent social cleavages."[55] That conclusion rests on data from the first decade of the twenty-first century; since then, "polarization of the American electorate has dramatically increased" and remains greater than division by race. Perhaps most important for an analysis of threats to liberal democratic governance, Americans "face no social repercussions for the open expression of these attitudes"; in fact, "increased partisan affect provides an incentive for elites to engage in confrontation rather than cooperation."[56]

By this point, Americans not only mistrust one another, but also deeply mistrust the American national government. Trust has never been close to unanimous; in 1972, 22 percent of Gallup respondents had little or no trust in the federal government to handle international problems, and 29 percent said the same about domestic problems. By September 2017, those figures had risen to 47 percent and 54 percent respectively. Mistrust of both president and Congress, though not of the Supreme Court, rose; by now almost two-thirds do not think Congress is worthy of their trust. Even several months after Trump assumed the presidency, barely a quarter of Republicans (and only a seventh of Democrats) trusted the government "to do the right thing" always or most of the time.[57]

I am not arguing that mistrust of government is a mistake; I do not trust the federal government at present. But when a majority, or large majority, of Americans of both major parties have no confidence, especially in the branch of government where their own representative resides, that can make democratic deliberation, negotiation, and even logrolling very difficult.

---

[53] Thanks to Bart Bonikowski and Paul DiMaggio for this analysis; it extends their argument in Bart Bonikowski and Paul DiMaggio, "Varieties of American Popular Nationalism," *American Sociological Review* 81 (2016): 949–980.

[54] Hochschild, *Strangers in Their Own Land*; Theda Skocpol and Vanessa Williamson, *The Tea Party and the Remaking of Republican Conservatism* (New York: Oxford University Press, 2012); Cramer, *The Politics of Resentment*.

[55] Shanto Iyengar, Gaurav Sood, and Yphtach Lelkes, "Affect, Not Ideology: A Social Identity Perspective on Polarization," *Public Opinion Quarterly* 76 (2012): 405–431, 405.

[56] Shanto Iyengar and Sean Westwood, "Fear and Loathing across Party Lines: New Evidence on Group Polarization," *American Journal of Political Science* 59 (2015): 690–707.

[57] Pew Research Center, "Public Trust in Government Remains near Historic Lows as Partisan Attitudes Shift," Pew Research Center, May 3, 2017, http://www.people-press.org/2017/05/03/public-trust-in-government-remains-near-historic-lows-as-partisan-attitudes-shift/.

Few of these disparities are new, and none by itself rises to the level of a constitutional crisis. James Madison recognized the centrality of political factions, Thomas Jefferson articulated the division between city and country, and John Maynard Keynes worried about the political impact of economic stagnation. Mark Twain pointed to the corruption of a gilded age of stark inequality. What *is* new, however, and what might be rising to the level of constitutional crisis, is the deepening associations among individual and community characteristics, partisan antagonism, and a geographically-based electoral system.

Scholars and constitutional designers have long worried about tight alignment along multiple dimensions. A near-canonical claim among observers of highly-divided societies is that the degree to which disagreements or cleavages are "crosscutting" constitutes a critical stabilizing feature of those political systems. When adversaries on one dimension are allies on another, political polarization and disaffection are reduced and stability enhanced, other things being equal.[58] As Donald Horowitz argued in his constitutional design for South Africa, even in conditions of intense group conflict, political institutions that "foster cooperation across group lines" can sustain a democratic polity.[59] "By contrast, when enmity persists across dimensions, disaffection and instability are likely to follow."[60]

If this claim is correct, the fact that race, income, education, health, mortality, economic prospects, cultural and religious commitments, partisanship, policy views, and values are all lining up along one dimension—like scattered iron filings coming into the presence of a powerful magnet—can make political negotiation and decision-making extremely difficult. Mistrust accumulates and builds on itself. The difficulty is worsened by the geographic basis of the American electoral system. "It has been a good decade for metropolitan America," reports the policy director of the Brookings Institution's Metropolitan Policy Program. But "you can't underestimate the economic and social pain across the rural tier."[61] As cosmopolites and localists come to see the other side as the cause of their pain and of their inability to alleviate it, their elected representatives are drawn into the same views—or at least into acting as though they hold the same views—if they want to remain representatives. Electoral incentives—responsiveness to voters in one's own district—have to come first for elected officials.[62] At that point the dictum that "all politics is local" shifts from being quaint folk wisdom to being a directive for aggressive or obstructive actions among people who are always facing the next election. Congress functions poorly; administrative agencies can be

[58] Sanford Gordon, Dimitri Landa, and Patrick LeBihan, "Crosscutting Cleavages and Political Conflict," Working Paper, June 23, 2015, http://patricklebihan.com/crosscutting_cleavages.pdf. These authors provide an excellent review of the literature supporting this claim, although they challenge at least its simple version.

[59] Donald Horowitz, *A Democratic South Africa? Constitutional Engineering in a Divided Society* (Berkeley: University of California Press, 1991), xii.

[60] Gordon, Landa, LeBihan, "Crosscutting."

[61] Porter, "President-Elect Found Votes."

[62] David Mayhew, *Congress: The Electoral Connection* (New Haven CT: Yale University Press, 1974).

directionless or self-contradictory; citizens become disgusted with government and perhaps with democratic governance; the old racial hierarchy roars back to life. The great risk is of a tipping point, as in 1860, after which representatives and constituents cannot find their way back to mutual engagement. The underlying health of the nation with which I began this analysis suggests that we may never reach it again; the political rot is not so far advanced. Nonetheless, the logic of a constitutional system of democratic representation through geographically defined communities offers few countervailing forces once the country coalesces into a contest between two factions that see the other as the enemy.

Trump and his supporters are not responsible for the growing split between cosmopolitan areas or sentiments and small town or rural communities or sentiments. In fact, the Republican strategy of making clear the depth of the divide could in the long run strengthen the American democratic order if political actors can find ways to bridge and eventually diminish the split. But Trump is partly responsible for the beliefs, and political strategies predicated on those beliefs, that the divide is a zero-sum game, that his opponents are "treasonous,"[63] and that the cultivation of cross-cutting cleavages are only for the weak. His inaugural speech, to cite only one example, proclaimed that "their ["a small group in our nation's Capital"] victories have not been your victories; their triumphs have not been your triumphs; and while they celebrated . . . , there was little to celebrate for struggling families all across our land." By invoking the populist trope of the "real people" versus the "aristocratic sores," as Andrew Jackson put it, Trump is making a hazardous political dynamic potentially untenable. As Indianapolis's Republican mayor Stephen Goldsmith lamented, this dynamic is "unimaginably distressing. . . . We had the opportunity [in the 2016 presidential race] to reach broadly across the country to have an inspiring voice of opportunity, and there's a set of Republican policies that would amplify that opportunity. We're doing the opposite."[64] The Madison of *Federalist #10* would have heartily agreed.

HOSTILITY AND DEGRADATION: CHALLENGING LIBERAL GOVERNANCE. The conflict between cosmopolitan and localist is about democracy—whether our electoral system still enables Americans to engage across battle lines, seek common interests, and resolve problems. The phenomenon of hostility and degradation, my other reason for fearing a constitutional crisis despite the United States' relatively favorable circumstances, addresses the issue of liberalism, understood as a cluster of rights, norms, and

---

[63] James Hohmann, "Why Trump Flippantly Accusing Democrats of 'Treason' Is Not a Laughing Matter," *Washington Post: The Daily 202*, February 6, 2018, https://www.washingtonpost.com/news/powerpost/paloma/daily-202/2018/02/06/daily-202-why-trump-flippantly-accusing-democrats-of-treason-is-not-a-laughing-matter/5a792a2130fb041c3c7d7657/?utm_term=.406978aef1c4.

[64] Badger and Bui, "Why Republicans Don't Try to Win Cities."

values. Are Americans willing and able to grant one another dignity, respect, political equality, forbearance, constitutional rights, and freedom of political action?

Of course, the Constitution's liberalism, mainly instantiated in its amendments, has always been compromised. Americans have never been good liberals with regard to all residents of the United States, and politicians and their ardent supporters have always attacked groups or institutions that challenge their dominance. But liberal norms, practices, and institutions are arguably under greater threat in the Trump presidency than they have been at any point in the past few decades.

Like that of cosmopolitans versus localists, my analysis of hostility to and degradation of liberalism revolves around a central empirical claim. A liberal democratic polity can work reasonably well only when a critical mass of political actors and the public share, or at least act as though they share, liberal norms and commitments, and trust (or act as though they trust) other Americans to do the same.[65] That is, private sentiments of racism or intolerance may be reprehensible, but as a general rule they become politically problematic only when expressed and acted upon, and politically dangerous only when endorsed and strengthened by social and political leaders or organizations. Similarly, individuals may perceive the media to be biased, intellectuals to be self-indulgent, and electoral politics to be corrupted, but the liberal values of free press, free speech, and fair electoral contestation are seriously threatened only when leaders undermine the institutions charged with promoting them.

These are situations now confronting Americans as a result of the Trump presidency. They come in several clusters. Consider first attacks on individuals or groups. Trump and some members of his administration consistently depict immigrants as criminals, and Muslims as actual or would-be terrorists. The administration has banned residents of specific countries, with congressional compliance if not approval. Trump portrays other American public officials as incompetent or biased because of their ethnic or racial background. He and other elected officials challenged the constitutionality of Barack Obama's presidency because of his putatively foreign birth.[66] Trump has been offensive and scatological about particular countries and their residents, again with lame support or awkward silence from allies. Trump and his supporters have hinted at anti-Semitism and support for white supremacist groups. He has boasted of sexual assault, and high-ranking members of his staff have protected others accused of sexual assault. Most prominent were his equivocal, perhaps even favorable, responses to the murderous march of neo-Confederates, anti-Semites, and neo-Nazis in Charlottesville, Virginia, in August 2017.

---

[65] Robert Dahl, *Who Governs? Democracy and Power in an American City*, 2nd ed. (New Haven, CT: Yale University Press, 2005); Danielle Allen, *Talking to Strangers: Anxieties of Citizenship since* Brown v. Board of Education (Chicago: University of Chicago Press, 2006).

[66] Jennifer Hochschild and Katherine Levine Einstein, *Do Facts Matter? Information and Misinformation in American Politics* (Norman: University of Oklahoma Press, 2015), 108–119.

Each of these actions undermines the essential but difficult practice of civic nationalism, the claim that American identity includes respect for or at least toleration of individuals and groups regardless of their racial, religious, national, or ethnic heritage.[67] Each action assaults the vague but crucial norm of human dignity, or respect for all persons with regard to, if nothing else, their essential personhood.

Next, consider attacks on organizations or institutions essential to a liberal polity. Trump has tolerated or encouraged violence against protesters and threatened prosecution of his electoral opponent. He persistently challenges the integrity of the electoral system and voting outcomes. Both before and during his leadership, the Republican party has sought to disfranchise millions of potential voters. Trump does all he can to undermine trust in the press, has excluded media outlets from press briefings, and suggested direct challenges to the First Amendment.[68] He has attacked the FBI, Department of Justice, federal prosecutors, the federal judiciary, and other agencies of the law. He has suggested that Democrats or the Democratic party are treasonous. Trump or his staff may have colluded with the Russian government to tamper with the 2016 election and to disseminate false information. The Trump administration constrains or censors federal agency reports. His steady stream of public lies undermines the legitimacy of the presidency itself and the legitimacy of all who work for or with him.[69] Trump claims to be above the law and legally incapable of obstructing justice. In these and other ways, he and his supporters move beyond challenges to civic nationalism into challenges to core constitutional institutions, practices, and restraints.

A final threat to liberal constitutionalism is even more amorphous than derogation of individuals, groups, or nations, and the undermining of liberal constitutional structures and practices. I refer here to disdain for norms of public discourse. As Peter Hall puts it, "by radically discounting the value once attached to the honesty of politicians ("Honest Abe"), they make it more difficult for the electorate to hold them accountable, and it increases cynicism about politicians and government in general."[70] Strictly speaking, lying, ignoring unpalatable truths, and propounding obviously double standards do not challenge the liberal rights and freedom of action championed by Thomas Jefferson or John Stuart Mill[71]—but reinforcing cynicism and disgust can only make democracy and liberalism harder to sustain.

---

[67] Gary Gerstle, *American Crucible: Race and Nation in the Twentieth Century* (Princeton, NJ: Princeton University Press, 2001); E.J. Dionne, Norman Ornstein, and Thomas E. Mann, *One Nation after Trump: A Guide for the Perplexed, the Disillusioned, the Desperate, and the Not-Yet Deported* (New York: St. Martin's Press, 2017).

[68] By one count, 89 of Trump's 167 post-inaugural Twitter attacks have been aimed at news organizations or specific journalists. Josh Delk, "Trump Attacks the Media More than Anything Else on Twitter: Report," *The Hill*, October 14, 2017, http://thehill.com/blogs/blog-briefing-room/355448-trump-attacks-the-media-more-than-anyone-else-on-twitter-report. On October 11, 2017, he tweeted, "With all of the Fake News coming out of NBC and the Networks, at what point is it appropriate to challenge their License? Bad for country!"

[69] David Leonhardt, Ian Prasad Philbrick, and Stuart A. Thompson, "Trump's Lies vs. Obama's," *New York Times*, December 14, 2017.

[70] Personal communication to author, December 29, 2017.

[71] And we can learn a lot about double standards from Jefferson.

This analysis reveals an asymmetry between the ability to monitor threats to democracy and the ability to monitor threats to liberalism. On the one hand, we can specify with reasonable clarity some indicators of representative institutions' level of dysfunction. If the standoff between cosmopolitan and localist forces is so intractable that members of Congress cannot pass a budget to prevent the government from shutting down, or cannot enable public agencies to help American citizens after a terrible natural disaster, or choose to ignore another country's efforts to subvert American elections, we can judge democratic dysfunction to be severe.

On the other hand, I can specify no clear indicators with which to judge the degree of liberal fragility. Is the murder of one black man running from armed police, or the murder of one counter-protester to a Nazi march, or one challenge to a legitimacy of a judge or the constitutional rights of the free press, or even a stream of vulgar and racist comments from the chief executive sufficient to declare liberalism in crisis? Probably not. And in any case, a numerical measure is probably not the right conceptual tool for evaluating the depth of threat to a Dahlian polyarchy. Since "agreement on rules and norms . . . tends to be incomplete, and typically it decays," it must constantly be renewed, sometimes through "deadly, heated battle."[72] Our inability to judge just how much the Trump administration threatens liberalism, inadvertently or intentionally, and how dire is the need for renewal, is a central part of the threat.

I have described threats to democracy and to liberalism separately, but they are entwined. And Americans are not abandoning liberal democracy in a wholesale fashion. There was not, for example, a notable increase in hate crimes in 2016 compared to the previous decade; people are still paying taxes and obeying court summonses. Nazi marchers are met with larger groups of counter-marchers. But the assaults could cumulate. Like belief in the ideology of the American dream, liberal democratic norms and practices can discipline political behavior only if people believe in their worth and trust that others are also abiding by them. At some point, people may relinquish that trust and its accompanying discipline. That point is likely to be reached sooner when the president sets an example of and promotes arguably authoritarian or racist behavior, speech, and laws.

What Next?

I conclude with two, contradictory, cautions. On the one hand, we should beware of false nostalgia. When was the United States ever a robustly liberal, democratic, constitutional polity? Before the 1860s? Enslavement and extermination were hardly

---

[72] Dahl, *Who Governs?*, 316, 321.

liberal.[73] At the end of the nineteenth century? It would have been difficult to persuade immigrants, laborers, Asians, women, and African Americans of the United States' democratic governance. In the 1930s? Present-day political nastiness pales before the very real threat of domestic fascism. In the 1940s and 1950s? Congressional committees charged left-wing activists with treason. In the 1960s? Many people thought the United States was falling apart. And so on. Democracy is never complete; liberalism is always under challenge; blinders and self-interest on the part of the dominant race or class are perennial; politicians are often venal. The fact that I and, I expect, most readers are dismayed by Trump's behavior and Trump administration policies is not in itself evidence that the United States is facing more of a constitutional challenge now than in the past.

On the other hand, we should beware false security. A normal election, a country mostly at peace, a growing economy, increasing equality in some domains, general adherence to the rule of law—all of these can be undermined by a talented demagogue, a citizenry afraid of the future and furious about the present, incompetent institutions, a narrowly self-regarding elite, the temptations of racism and nativism. The organizer and provocateur Stephen Bannon exhorted Alabamians to vote for Roy Moore for the Senate on the grounds that "if they can destroy Roy Moore, they can destroy you."[74] "Destroy" is a strong word. Democracies can die; liberal democracies can become illiberal democracies.[75] The United States' Constitution is ill-equipped to handle the electoral imperatives that can result from the united forces of intransigent opinions, intense passions, and mutually opposed interests. Madison warned us, and we could do worse than reread *Federalist #10*.

---

[73] Although they were arguably constitutional. Mark Graber, *Dred Scott and the Problem of Constitutional Evil* (New York: Cambridge University Press, 2006).

[74] Jeremy Peters, "Bannon Finds New Fight Backing Roy Moore, but Risks Are High," *New York Times*, December 5, 2017.

[75] Steven Levitsky and Daniel Ziblatt, *How Democracies Die* (New York: Crown, 2018).

7   The Trump Presidency
A Constitutional Crisis in the United States?
Eric A. Posner*

DONALD TRUMP'S ELECTION to the presidency of the United States, and his conduct in office during his first year, have sparked a constitutional crisis. Or so say many commentators.[1] But the claim that we are living through a constitutional crisis—or similar claims, such as a president is a "dictator"—is hardly unusual.[2] For decades, maybe longer, alleged constitutional crises have popped up every year or so. Is our constitutional order always in crisis, or has overuse of the word drained the meaning out of it? Or does Trump's presidency create a real crisis, and if so, what should we make of it?

To start, we need to get clear about what a constitutional crisis is, and why it matters. The second question is easier than the first. If Trump's election has created a constitutional crisis, then we will probably need to change the Constitution. If not, and if his election is just normal politics, then constitutional reform is not needed, or at least not urgently needed.

* Thanks to Mark Graber, Daniel Hemel, Aziz Huq, Daryl Levinson, Sandy Levinson, and workshop participants at Tel Aviv University and Hebrew University, for comments, and to Jill Rogowski and Kyle Trevett for research assistance.

1 See, e.g., David Leonhardt, "G.O.P. Support for Trump is Starting to Crack," *New York Times*, July 24, 2017; Paul Krugman, "Fascism, American Style," *New York Times*, August 28, 2017; "That Crazy Talk about Robert Mueller," *New York Times*, October 31, 2017.

2 On "tyrannophobia," see Eric A. Posner and Adrian Vermeule, *The Executive Unbound* (New York: Oxford University Press, 2010).

But what is a constitutional crisis? Unfortunately, the term is hardly self-defining, and it is easy to imagine a range of definitions, all plausible.[3] The normal meaning of the word "crisis" implies a point at which a system that has in the past operated in a normal fashion will collapse if it is not repaired or reformed. As applied to a constitutional order, the term implies that normal governance is on the verge of collapse because of an impasse or other problem. The crisis could result because of good-faith but profound disagreement about what the constitution requires or allows, leading to conflict among political agents that cannot be resolved through constitutional means. Or it could result because a significant group rejects the constitutional order, or elements of it. If the disagreement or rejection is profound enough, the crisis occurs because the normal methods for resolving political disputes break down.

Yet despite its connotation of a single point in time, in political discourse the word "crisis" can reflect different degrees; it is a continuous variable. The most important constitutional crisis in American history was, by a very wide margin, the Civil War, which lasted four years. Without straining the word too much, one could argue that the constitutional crisis caused by the slavery question began in the years leading up to the Civil War, perhaps as early as 1819, and was not resolved until the end of Reconstruction in 1876, before which the president continued to use the war power and the legal status of the southern states remained unsettled. Or, one might argue that a series of crises, each separated by periods of normalcy, took place over this period. There have been numerous lesser crises, where the constitutional disagreement was resolved in a relatively short period of time and with little damage to public well-being. The clearest such examples were the impasses over the secretary of war during the Johnson administration and over executive privilege and related matters during the Nixon administration. Both disputes interfered with governance, but for a relatively short period, and the interference was relatively limited. Moreover, the dispute about the secretary of war was resolved through impeachment and normal political bargaining, while the Watergate crisis was resolved by courts along with executive-branch acquiescence.

Thus, the idea of crisis as disruption in governance quickly bleeds into a more general notion of persistent disorder. A constitutional crisis might be said to exist whenever there is deep and persistent dissatisfaction with a constitutional system. The term "crisis" may underline the seriousness of the stakes rather than be used to imply a period of normalcy from which deviation is a matter of special interest. An interesting datum, discussed below, is that people are more inclined to refer to constitutional crises today than in the past. Is that because constitutional crises are more common, or that there is less confidence that our constitutional system remains functional? An argument could

---

[3] For two valuable discussions, see Keith E. Whittington, "Yet Another Constitutional Crisis," *William and Mary Law Review* 43 (2002): 2093–2150; Sanford Levinson and Jack M. Balkin, "Constitutional Crises," *University of Pennsylvania Law Review* 157 (2009): 707–754.

be made that a constitution is in crisis if enough people think it is in crisis, or say that it is, regardless of whether government is disrupted relative to some normal baseline. But if the constitutional order is in crisis, or nearly always in crisis, what analytical work does the concept do?

In this chapter, I explore claims that a constitutional crisis has erupted in the United States. I distinguish two types of crises. A "crisis-as-disruption" exists when government ceases to function, or is significantly hampered, because of profound disagreement about what the constitution requires: people take to the streets, the military is called out, states secede, fistfights break out in the legislature. A "crisis-as-dissatisfaction" exists whenever a substantial portion of the public expresses dissatisfaction with the constitutional order, or opposing political forces appear deadlocked and unable to implement policy that is broadly needed. I argue that, one year into the Trump administration, a crisis-as-disruption has not begun but a crisis-as-dissatisfaction has.[4] Government (and I mean national government) continues to function against a baseline of normal activity—the military conducts operations, the police keep order, taxes are collected, Medicaid payments are made, courts resolve disputes. Yet we seem constantly on the verge of disruption in normal governance, and the sense of multiplying near-crises by itself creates a kind of crisis atmosphere of the sort that the second definition tries to capture. But this crisis-as-dissatisfaction predates the Trump administration by many years: Trump is the culmination of a long-term trend.

Constitutional Crises: Definitions and Examples

CRISIS-AS-DISRUPTION

We can get some leverage on the meaning of a "constitutional crisis" by distinguishing it from other kinds of crises. A financial crisis, such as the mortgage crisis, of 2008, occurs when the financial system freezes up. Creditors stop making loans, assets lose value rapidly, and firms topple into bankruptcy. "Crisis" is the natural word because the system will collapse quickly unless the government intervenes. An economic crisis occurs when large-scale unemployment persists beyond a normal range, raising questions about whether the economy has been permanently damaged and whether the government can pull the economy out of its downturn. The Great Depression remains the paradigm. A military crisis, such as the Japanese attack on Pearl Harbor, exists when a surprising turn of events pushes the nation from peace to war or near-war, generating uncertainty about the nation's capacity and possible consequences.

---

[4] Crisis-as-disruption is similar to what Whittington calls a "crisis of constitutional operation," and what Levinson and Balkin call a "type three crisis." Whittington also identifies what he calls a "crisis of constitutional fidelity" (for Levinson and Balkin, "type one," more or less), which, as I discuss below, is not a useful concept for American constitutional history. Levinson and Balkin's "type two" is similar to what I call crisis-as-dissatisfaction.

The idea closest to a constitutional crisis is a political crisis, which occurs when normal political bargaining and compromise are replaced with an impasse with no obvious end. The deadlocked election of 1800 provides a good example. Because of the peculiarity of the electoral college system at the time, the Republicans' preferred president, Thomas Jefferson, and their preferred vice president, Aaron Burr, were technically tied. The Federalist-controlled House was therefore required to select among the two candidates. Many Federalists voted for Burr because of their dislike of Jefferson and disinclination to respect the wishes of their political opponents. The House deadlocked for seven days before finally choosing Jefferson in an atmosphere of barely suppressed violence.

The 1800 election might be interpreted as a constitutional crisis because the constitutional rules were defective, enabling the outgoing party to engage in strategic behavior that was inconsistent with the underlying constitutional norm of popular sovereignty. Those rules would be later corrected through the Twelfth Amendment—an event that itself could be interpreted as contemporary evidence that people believed that a constitutional crisis had occurred. What added to the sense of crisis was that the election was the first in which power was transferred to a political opponent of the incumbent president, and that most members of the House were Federalists hostile to both Jefferson and Burr. On the other hand, the 1800 election could be seen as merely a political crisis; or if the 1800 election was a constitutional crisis, it was a relatively minor one. The leading political agents took for granted that the constitutionally prescribed procedures were to be used, with the major uncertainty concerning how the political agents would act within those parameters. Moreover, the impasse did not last long enough to interfere with governance—it did not delay inauguration of the new president, or seriously impair the operations of Congress (and at a time when national business was limited and Congress met episodically).

The major implication of the "crisis-as-disruption" definition is that there is an acceptable baseline during which the government operates normally. Just as the human body is hardly noticeable to the person who possesses it except when illness flares up, the political constitution is hardly noticed most of the time, as officials act within its parameters or constitutional disputes occur only along the margin. But from time to time, a constitutional crisis, like a medical crisis, intrudes and grabs attention that would otherwise be paid to other things. While the constitutional crisis prevails, normal politics is pushed into the background. In extreme cases, government officials may not be able to take routine actions or make ordinary decisions because of uncertainty about lines of authority and government powers.

The greatest constitutional crisis in American history was, of course, the impasse over slavery, which flowered into a civil war. Slavery was a political problem from the founding era, but political and government officials were able to prevent a constitutional crisis over slavery through a series of compromises that limited the spread of slavery but did not eliminate it. As it became clear to southern states that compromise with the North was no longer sustainable, they seceded, while the national government and northern states denied that the Constitution permitted secession. When the states seceded, government was thrown into disarray since it was no longer clear as a legal matter, for example, whether a federal agent could enter the territory of a southern state. Ordinary governance by the national government became impossible—first in the southern states, and then nationally, as martial law was imposed over large areas and a full-scale state of war prevailed.

A few other examples will round out the discussion. Johnson's impeachment in 1868 was at most a minor constitutional crisis. Johnson and Congress disagreed about Johnson's powers, and hence whether he had violated the law by trying to fire the secretary of war, Edwin Stanton. But they resolved their disagreement with the constitutionally prescribed procedure of impeachment. Congress was paralyzed for a few months, but the government as a whole was not—not even the War Department, which managed to function despite the constitutional ambiguity about Stanton's status. Franklin Roosevelt's inaugural address—in which he made a veiled threat to act unilaterally if Congress failed to give him authority to respond to the banking crisis and Depression—and his court-packing plan both posed serious threats to the constitutional order, but did not cause a constitutional crisis. Congress gave him the powers he sought in the first case, and blocked the court-packing plan, and Roosevelt acquiesced. Watergate seems (at least, in hindsight) like a minor constitutional crisis. The president and Congress disagreed about the contours of presidential authority, including executive privilege, but all the disagreements were resolved—by the Supreme Court's ruling on executive privilege, and by Nixon's resignation under threat of impeachment. The presidency was hampered by the impeachment proceedings, though most of the operations of the executive branch were unaffected.

With these examples as background, we can see that the Trump administration has not sparked a crisis-as-disruption, at least not yet. In the first year, Trump's most consequential actions and accomplishments have followed the constitutional rulebook. The tax cut was duly enacted by majorities in both houses of Congress. Deregulation has taken place through executive orders and administrative actions that have been made pursuant to congressional delegations or recognized constitutional authority. Trump has appointed numerous judges, and one Supreme Court justice, using constitutional procedures laid out by the founders in 1787. Trump's withdrawal from the Paris climate agreement, and use of military force in Syria, also have the sanction of law and custom. Meanwhile, the government has operated normally—collecting taxes, servicing debt, making expenditures, keeping order.

The constitutional-crisis claims arise from different events. One source is the allegation that Trump and his aides "colluded" with Russia, exchanging promises to lift sanctions in return for help in defeating Hillary Clinton, which Russia supplied by hacking the Democratic National Committee and spewing propaganda through the internet. The allegation has led to an investigation, which will likely grind on for many months and may never implicate Trump personally. Even if it does, it is possible that the conflict will be resolved through constitutional means—via impeachment. By firing FBI director James Comey after Comey refused to assure Trump that the investigation would be terminated, Trump arguably engaged in obstruction of justice, but since the investigation remains in place, and Trump did have the authority to remove the director, there is no political will to remove Trump from office. Trump seems committed to engaging in constitutional brinksmanship but, as of this writing, has not started a crisis-as-disruption.

The other source of the constitutional-crisis allegation is Trump's rhetoric. Trump has frequently attacked, with violent language, constitutionally protected institutions—the press and the judiciary, above all—and showed contempt for constitutionally protected norms of equal citizenship and political competition. But the gap between words and actions is enormous. Trump has not ordered subordinates to jail journalists or disobey judicial rulings. Even when he calls for the Justice Department to prosecute Hillary Clinton, he does not seem to be willing to actually order the attorney general to act, or to threaten to fire him if he does not. Trump has not made any serious effort to put into play authoritarian methods. However, because people are accustomed to take a president's words seriously, these attacks have given rise to a widespread sense that these institutions are in serious danger. A crisis-as-disruption, then, may seem imminent even if it has not yet materialized.

CRISIS-AS-DISSATISFACTION

A constitutional crisis-as-dissatisfaction exists when a substantial portion of the public expresses dissatisfaction with the constitutional order, or opposing political forces appear deadlocked and unable to implement policy that is broadly needed. The major problem with this definition, which the crisis-as-disruption definition avoids, is that dissatisfaction may be in the eye of the beholder—deadlock even more. Many people believe that the national government should do very little, and admire the founders for designing so many veto gates. Inactivity, then, is not deadlock but the appropriate outcome when a political consensus for change has not yet appeared. Dissatisfaction, too, may simply be the price we pay for living in a large and diverse country in which policy disagreement is deep.

Still, the crisis-as-dissatisfaction definition cannot be ruled out because of these methodological difficulties. In principle, deadlock can be identified—when political agents take extreme positions that cannot realistically lead to compromise, resulting in government paralysis in areas not immediately concerned with the disagreement.

The Civil War can be seen as a culmination of a long-running constitutional crisis over slavery. From the crisis-as-disruption standpoint, the period leading up to 1861 was normal because the government was able to operate—it passed laws, annexed territory, collected taxes, and so on. But from another perspective, that period was not normal because the slavery controversy prevented the government from doing much more that needed to be done. Because southerners worried that a powerful national government would

TABLE 7.1

Confidence in Government Institutions and the Press

Institution	Great Deal/Quite a Lot of Confidence—1973	Great Deal/ Quite a Lot of Confidence—1995	Great Deal/ Quite a Lot of Confidence—2017
Supreme Court	45	44	40
Congress	42	21	12
Newspapers	39	30	27
Military	58 (1975)	64	72
Presidency	52 (1975)	45	32

Source: See "Confidence in Institutions," *Gallup*, accessed February 28, 2018, http://news.gallup.com/poll/1597/confidence-institutions.aspx.

eventually be used against slavery, they opposed a strong national government, almost from the beginning. As a result, the national government was weak for most of the nineteenth century, and hence unable to provide the services that other national governments of advanced counties at the time did supply—including a central bank, for example, as well as national regulation, poor relief, a professional civil service, or even a consistent foreign policy. All of this would have to wait until the late nineteenth or twentieth century, causing the United States to lag behind the political developments of countries like Great Britain, France, and even Germany, which unified only in the second half of the nineteenth century.

In trying to identify a crisis-as-dissatisfaction, we might consider surveys. Table 7.1 shows the results of a survey that suggests a steady loss of public confidence in American political institutions, which began in the 1960s.

The most serious decline is, of course, in Congress. The story of the presidency and the Supreme Court is more complex—with more variation over time—but the overall trend appears to be downward. Decline in confidence in the press is also fairly clear though not as dramatic as the case with Congress. Meanwhile, the rise in public confidence in the military—despite unsuccessful and inconclusive military action throughout the last two decades—gives further reason for worry, since it may suggest a growing hunger for authoritarian rule, while military involvement in politics has been a source of instability in other countries.

An even more dramatic picture of loss of confidence in government comes from a Pew study that aggregates surveys from different sources. Figure 7.1 shows the percentage of respondents who trust the government over time.

The data suggest that the turmoil of the 1960s caused a significant, long-term decline in public confidence in government—the most likely source the Vietnam War and the mendacity of the Johnson and Nixon administrations.[5] Interestingly, recovery in public

---

[5] See Stephen Griffin, *Broken Trust* (Lawrence: University Press of Kansas, 2015).

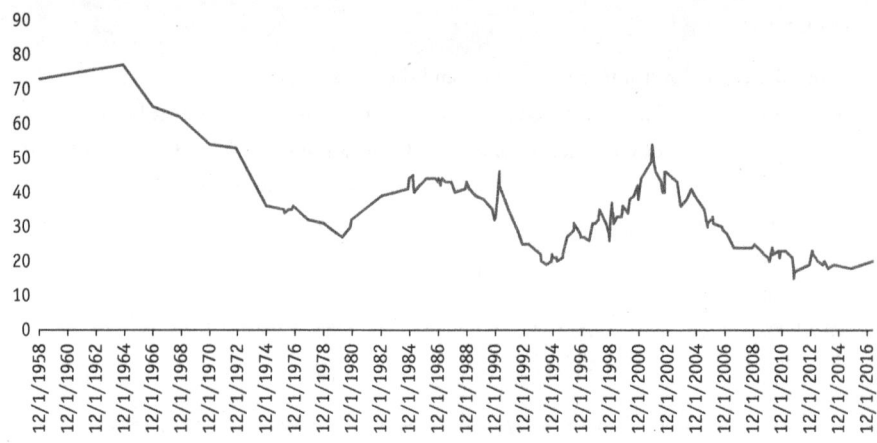

FIGURE 7.1 Public trust in government.

Source: "Public Trust in Government," *Pew Research Center*, May 3, 2017, http://www.people-press.org/2017/ 05/03/public-trust-in-government-1958–2017/ ("% who trust the government in Washington always or most of the time").

confidence in the early 1980s and early 2000s was likely the result of contingent events—the brief period of optimism ushered in by Reagan's election, and the rally-round-the-flag effect of the 9/11 attacks—and so did not last beyond a few years.

Another angle on the question is provided by the frequency with which people invoke "constitutional crisis" in public discussion. Figure 7.2 shows the number of newspaper or magazine articles that use this term per year since 1980, adjusted for the changes in the size of the data set.[6]

The data make intuitive sense, showing spikes for the Clinton impeachment and the 2000 election, and possibly for the Iran-Contra scandal in 1987. The term rarely appears in newspaper articles before the 1980s, and while this might reflect differences in political discourse, overall the data suggest a slight but meaningful increase in the frequency with which the term is used over time, suggesting—consistent with Table 7.1 and Figure 7.1—that the public is losing confidence in the constitutional order.

The final spike in 2016 and 2017, sure to continue through 2018, shows that the public, or at least the media, are again as consumed with worry about constitutional crisis, to the greatest extent since the 2000 election, and exceeding the Clinton impeachment. What

---

[6] The index equals the number of hits in a Lexis search for "constitutional crisis" divided by the number of hits for the word "Congress" alone. I tried other deflators as well, which tell a similar story. In terms of absolute numbers, the number of articles mentioning constitutional crisis has increased enormously, reflecting in part the growth in publications, but it can scarcely be denied that talk of constitutional crisis is far more prevalent today (4,252 articles in 2017; 1,206 in 2016) than during the Obama administration (ranging from 231 in 2009 to 828 in 2014) or the Bush administration (ranging from 144 in 2001 to 334 in 2007). In the 1990s, articles mentioning the term were in the hundreds except during the years surrounding Clinton's impeachment. In the 1980s, they were in the dozens; before then, in the single digits; in the 1960s, zero. I exclude earlier years from the chart because the difference in publication practices renders comparison difficult.

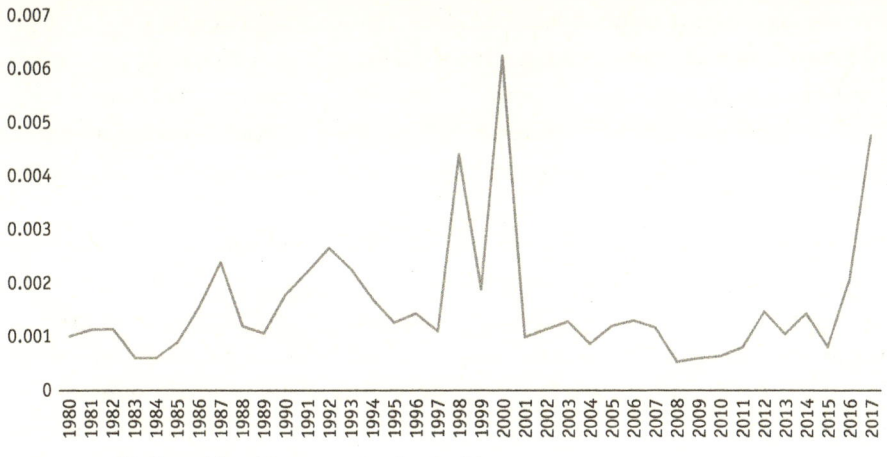

FIGURE 7.2 Media articles citing a constitutional crisis.

are we to make of it? At a minimum, a great number of people believe either that Trump's election and actions in his office have created a constitutional crisis or the heightened risk of one. On this interpretation, the graph suggests an imminent constitution-as-disruption, as discussed earlier.

The time trend does not prove that a constitutional crisis is in existence or in the making. The trend is relatively weak, and it could also reflect a cheapening of political discourse—maybe people use the word "crisis" more frequently in order to gain attention in a crowded public square. But the data do caution against the complacent assumption—possibly implied by the constitution-as-disruption definition—that a constitutional crisis cannot exist without a disruption in government operations.

CAUSES

The overall picture is a gloomy one. We might say that we have entered a period of constitutional crisis, or—my preference—a period of constitutional turmoil or dissatisfaction. This period began in the 1960s and has continued to the present day, with a few episodes of real crisis—Watergate above all, and possibly Iran-Contra, the Clinton impeachment, and maybe the stalemated election of 2000 that was resolved by the Supreme Court in *Bush v. Gore*.

Trump himself seems to be both a symptom of this long-term trend and (likely) a cause that will ensure that it continues. Trump's election has exacerbated the crisis-as-dissatisfaction by bringing to the surface long-standing concerns about many features of the US Constitution, including the role of the Electoral College, funding of political campaigns, the quality of public debate, gerrymandering in the election of public officials and the determination of the ideological composition of the government, and the powers of the president. Trump won the election despite losing the popular vote, an outcome that is hard to justify under the principle of popular sovereignty. The role of money in national elections is greater than ever—exemplified by the Clinton Foundation, which gave the impression of granting political influence to donors. Public debate was poisoned by foreign influence working through social media. And gerrymandering has damaged the democratic accountability of Congress, contributing to the polarized atmosphere.

A long-term trend must have a long-term cause. And the cause—or causes—are not hard to see. The United States has gone through tremendous disruption and change since the 1950s—the civil rights movement, the revolution in gender roles, the end of the Cold War, extreme economic turmoil in the 1970s and the 2000s, significant wars, an influx of immigration, polarization caused by geographic self-segregation that has reverberated through the geographic system of political representation, and on and on. Normally, we would expect a country that undergoes such convulsions to seek constitutional revisions in order to update governance structures. Yet because of the extremely high threshold for constitutional change in Article V, the formal document has been modified hardly at all. In contrast to virtually all other countries, as well as the American states, it is nearly impossible to update the constitutional order through the means provided in the constitutional document.

The Supreme Court initially led the way in updating the Constitution through judicial revision albeit within the limits set by some of the more rigid constraints of the founding document, but in doing so it has drawn itself into partisan conflicts, and in recent years it has acted as a break on constitutional change initiated by the other branches. It now seems imaginable that the next constitutional crisis will be a deadlock over appointments to the Court. But however the Court acts, it takes the risk that it will be the target of those who disagree with its rulings. And because its rulings lack the democratic legitimacy of a constitutional amendment, the Court is politically vulnerable. The combination of an archaic, unamendable Constitution and disruptive social changes is likely the source of the current constitutional turmoil or unhappiness—and this was before Trump won the election.

The Trump Administration

Donald Trump's presidency is both the result of, and a further contribution to, the crisis-as-dissatisfaction. A major factor in his electoral victory was his attack on the political establishment, an attack that resonated with millions of Americans. There is much truth to the now-commonplace idea that the election represented a right-wing populist revolt against establishment politicians, Republicans as well as Democrats. This interpretation is consistent with the evidence presented above of long-term public dissatisfaction with the major institutions of our constitutional democracy. The revolt can also be traced back to a more recent event—the financial crisis, which was simultaneously interpreted as a failure of liberal interventionism (federal housing policy before the crisis, the unpopular bailouts during it) and a failure of conservative economic policy (deregulation of the financial industry). Whichever it was, the establishment elites were blamed for the crisis and the aftermath, the bailouts that rewarded the wrongdoers and the recession that harmed virtuous workers and homeowners. Taking a longer view, we can see that economic stagnation and growing wealth inequality have also done their part in persuading the public that political and economic elites are corrupt. Believing with some justification that rule by experts and the established parties has failed, many voters supported an outsider, Trump, who tapped into their rage and helplessness.

Trump's assault on the establishment was not merely rhetorical. Trump's hardline nationalist positions on immigration, trade, cultural issues, and foreign intervention distinguished him from mainstream Republicans and Democrats, and appealed to citizens who felt that their views had been ignored by both parties.

But the populist tenor of the candidacy has set up Trump's supporters for disappointment. Governance requires establishment support, and so Trump has had to work with the elites he attacked. His appointees have mostly come from the world of business and finance, and his administration has mostly advanced a conservative business agenda, while providing some crumbs for evangelicals. Trump's rhetorical sallies on Twitter seem to keep him popular among his strongest supporters but also interfere with his efforts to implement policy.

Trump's first year in office illustrated the weakness of American political institutions, while possibly weakening them further. Because of political divisions caused by gerrymandering and the antiquated structure of the Senate, not even a unified Congress seems to be able to pass much legislation, leaving Trump unable to keep most of his campaign promises. Even the tax law, while a nominal legislative victory, was a betrayal of Trump's populist promises on the campaign trail. Trump has fallen back on his unilateral powers, which have enabled him to conduct foreign policy and some regulatory policy. But the weakness of unilateral action is that it can be sustained only for the duration of the presidency. Because of Trump's reversals of the Obama's administration's policies, including immigration, climate change, and trade, government policy has become unstable, disrupting expectations of citizens and relationships with allies.

Trump's election and presidency revealed deep ideological divisions that had been perceived by some experts but not fully recognized in public debate. His hostility to foreigners and (to all appearances) American minorities has energized the alt-right movement and coarsened public debate, while appalling liberals and the minorities he disdains. A notable feature of the election's aftermath was the bewilderment of the political establishment, as well as of many ordinary people, on both the Left and Right. They did not think that anyone would vote for Trump before Trump entered the election, that he could win the primaries after he launched his campaign, and that he could win the general election after he won the primaries. Their surprise showed that they fundamentally misinterpreted the values and beliefs of a huge portion of the public, and this has raised questions about whether our constitutional order can survive or remain functional when there is such a polarization. Reasonable ideological disagreement has poisoned and politicized empirical debate on a range of issues from climate change to the economic effects of immigration. On this interpretation, a crisis exists not only because of Trump's divisive rhetoric and policies but because of what his election reveals about ideological divisions in the country.

Lurking in the background are the allegations that Trump or his aides colluded with the Russians or engaged in other illegal activity during the campaign, and that he obstructed investigations into the allegations of illegal activity. To Trump's detractors, Trump's behavior raises questions about whether our constitutional order will hold. During Watergate, the crisis atmosphere developed in part because no one knew how far Nixon might go to stay in power. To Trump's supporters, the investigation further proves that the elites will stop at nothing to prevent an outsider from taking power. The investigation itself has fallen victim to doubts about whether polarized attitudes can be bridged by government institutions that enjoy the confidence of the public as a whole.

Implications: Three Futures

If the United States has entered a constitutional crisis, or is on the verge of one, what should be done? Crisis always calls for action, and in this case action would be constitutional reform. But what sort of reform? And is reform possible in the midst of crisis?

As Jon Elster has pointed out, many constitutions, including many successful constitutions, were motivated by, and negotiated and ratified in, a crisis atmosphere.[7] However, rather than predict or advocate constitutional reform, I will confine myself to the more modest (but still all-but-impossible task) of sketching out possible near-term futures.

STAGNATION. It is possible to argue that the current constitutional crisis—under the latitudinarian crisis-as-dissatisfaction definition—began in the 1960s or 1970s. A constitutional crisis that has lasted forty years could surely last another ten, twenty, or thirty years. On this view, we are trapped with an outdated constitution that interferes with government functioning, but reform does not occur because of the polarization of the public and the difficulty of amendment. This view seems to entail that the government is not *too* dysfunctional; at some point, even a polarized public will consent to reform. But we are condemned to a weak national government that is unable to address many of the country's most serious problems.

REASONABLE REFORM. It is imaginable that crisis will lead to reform. This could happen, for example, if the Trump presidency is catastrophic. The precedent here is Watergate, which led to a series of small but meaningful and reasonable reforms that enhanced the integrity of the executive branch. None of these reforms took place through

---

[7] Jon Elster, "Forces and Mechanisms in the Constitution-Making Process," *Duke Law Journal* 45 (1995): 364–396.

constitutional amendment; they involved statutes, as well as the emergence of political norms in favor of executive-branch restraint. One could also imagine, in a truly catastrophic case, a constitutional amendment that puts restrictions on the type of person who may be elected president (for example, requiring greater transparency of financial records, or government experience).

However, these types of reforms would not go to the heart of the constitutional disabilities identified above, which would require a full-scale constitutional convention. Nor is it clear what sort of constitutional order would emerge from a constitutional convention if one were held. Perhaps, people could reach a consensus that the national government should be shrunk (as conservatives hope) but that it should be put more firmly on democratic principles, with restraints on funding and gerrymandering, and with a better system of representation (as liberals hope). If ideological polarization in the national electorate is the source of our problems, the logical reform is devolution to the states, where a greater degree of homogeneity exists.

DEGENERATION. The third possibility is that the present crisis-as-dissatisfaction transforms itself into a full-scale crisis-as-disruption or a series of crises-as-disruption. The best American precedent would be the decades leading to the Civil War, when the slavery question paralyzed the national government. Yet the country does not seem nearly as polarized now as it was then, and civil war or any level of political violence seems quite distant. A more likely scenario is a serious failure at the national level, such as default on the national debt or a costly and unsuccessful war with a foreign country such as North Korea.

AMEND THE CONSTITUTION OR THE COUNTRY? A cross-cutting issue is whether a constitutional crisis exists if constitutional reform cannot resolve it. A possible view of the constitutional crisis that led to the Civil War was that the differences between North and South were irreconcilable. Constitutional reform (unless secession was deemed constitutional reform) could not have solved the crisis-as-dissatisfaction or stopped episodic crisis-as-disruptions. Today, it is possible that political preferences, interests, values, and beliefs among the public have diverged to such an extent that the crisis-as-dissatisfaction cannot be resolved through constitutional reform. If this is the case, the problem is not the Constitution, and it is not solvable; it just needs to be endured.

Conclusion

The election of Donald Trump has created a period of heightened political and constitutional tension, for which the term "constitutional crisis" is not unreasonable. If a crisis exists, it is a crisis-as-dissatisfaction rather than a crisis-as-disruption. But a crisis-as-dissatisfaction could produce a crisis-as-disruption at any moment, and in any event our constitutional system seems to have reached a point where constitutional reform is urgent.

Yet it is not clear that constitutional reform is possible, or that it will make much difference, or improve our system of national government. Everything depends on the nature and degree of polarization in the electorate, which can be glimpsed but remains poorly understood.

8

The Democratic Resilience of the Canadian Constitution
Richard Albert and Michael Pal

Introduction—Institutional Design or Constitutional Values?

A defining preoccupation of our time is how to respond to attacks on the integrity of constitutional democracies around the world. From Hungary to Venezuela, from Poland to Turkey, several countries that were once celebrated for their successful democratic transition and consolidation are now leading examples of the fragility of constitutional democracy.

Whether defined as democratic "decline,"[1] "backsliding,"[2] "recession,"[3] "retrogression,"[4] "decay,"[5] "degeneration,"[6] "breakdown"[7] or otherwise, this increasingly global

---

[1] Ian Marsh, "The Decline of Democratic Governance: An Analysis and a Modest Proposal," *Politics Quarterly* 228 no. 84 (2013): 228–237; Ian Marsh and Raymond Miller, *Democratic Decline and Democratic Renewal: Political Change in Britain, Australia, and New Zealand* (Cambridge: Cambridge University Press, 2012).

[2] Nancy Bermeo, "On Democratic Backsliding," *Journal of Democracy* 27 (2016): 5–19; David Waldner and Ellen Lust, "Unwelcome Change: Coming to Terms with Democratic Backsliding," *Annual Review of Political Science* 21 (2018): 5.1–5.21.

[3] Larry Diamond, "Facing Up to Democratic Recession," *Journal of Democracy* 26 (2015): 141–155, 147.

[4] Aziz Huq and Tom Ginsburg, "How to Lose a Constitutional Democracy," *UCLA Law Review* (forthcoming 2018).

[5] Tom Gerald Daly, "Contemplating the Future in the Era of Democratic Decay," *International Journal of Constitutional Law Blog* (September 15, 2017), http://www.iconnectblog.com/2017/09/contemplating-the-future-in-the-era-of-democratic-decay.

[6] See Richard Albert, "Constitutional Amendment and Dismemberment," *Yale Journal of International Law* 43 (2018): 1–84.

[7] Michael Pal, "Breakdowns in the Democratic Process and the Law of Canadian Democracy," *McGill Law Journal* 57 (2011): 299–350.

phenomenon is crying out for diagnosis and understanding. Why does democratic decline occur? Does this moment in history map onto the usual push and pull of politics? Or are we living a true moment of democratic failure? As this volume demonstrates by the breadth of its country studies and the depth of its transnational analyses, these are urgent questions in comparative constitutional studies.

In our view, it is not possible to fully understand the phenomenon of democratic decline without studying how successful constitutional democracies have resisted it. We refer to this countervailing phenomenon as *democratic resilience*, meaning the capacity of the regime to sustain competitive democratic politics and to withstand efforts from within to undermine its democratic foundations. We exclude resilience from external threats, such as war, from the concept so as to focus on democratic sustainability in the face of internal threats. We distinguish our concept of *democratic* resilience from a recently theorized idea of *constitutional* resilience,[8] which is similar in cause but different in outcome.

Both democratic and constitutional resilience refer to how well a constitutional order is equipped to survive serious shocks while retaining its core purpose.[9] Both go beyond what has been characterized as constitutional endurance, a measure of how long a constitution lasts, whether it has been changed by amendment or interpretation, transformed unrecognizably by a major reform brought on by an emergency period, or remained unchanged throughout.[10] What matters to both democratic and constitutional resilience is not simply the survival of the existing constitution over time; it is more importantly directed to how the constitution continues to operate. The critical difference between the two rests on their normative aspirations: constitutional resilience is concerned with ensuring the constitution can continue to function consistent with its primary values, whether or not those values are democratic.[11] It is decidedly a non-normative concept that takes no view on what makes a good constitution. What matters for constitutional resilience is principally that the constitution be capable of surviving shocks.

We are instead concerned with the resilience of a constitution's *democratic* institutions and their rules of political competition in the face of threats to the regime that risk weakening their strength. Democratic resilience is therefore rooted in a normative judgment about what in the constitution is worth preserving. For our present purposes, we focus on what makes it possible for a constitution's democratic character to resist pressures that could otherwise deteriorate the conditions for democracy in the regime and lead to its decline or its outright extinguishment.

---

[8] See Xenophon Contiades and Alkmene Fotiadou, "On Resilience of Constitutions: What Makes Constitutions Resistant to External Shocks?," *Vienna Journal on International Constitutional Law* 9 (2015): 3–26.
[9] Ibid., 22.
[10] Zack Elkins, Tom Ginsburg, and Tom Melton, *The Endurance of National Constitutions* (New York: Cambridge University Press, 2009), 12–64.
[11] Contiades and Fotiadou, "On Resilience of Constitutions," 22.

While alternative models to liberal democracy certainly exist,[12] what is common across the concepts attempting to capture democratic decline or breakdown is not the sense that democracy will be abandoned entirely, but something else. They seek to understand the phenomenon of long-standing or new democracies shifting to a quasi-democratic model that has the superficial veneer of democratic constitutionalism, but without actual, meaningful political competition or commitment to democratic norms. Hungary, Poland, and Turkey all continue to hold elections and will continue to do so, despite legitimate concerns about the robustness of democracy in these countries. Our concept of democratic resilience seeks primarily to address the hollowing out of democracy from within, rather than attempts to replace it outright.

In this chapter, we examine Canada as a case study in democratic resilience.[13] We are not the first to identify Canada as a refuge in the storm raging in constitutional democracies.[14] Yet what distinguishes our inquiry from others is our focus on the factors that have bred resilience and what lessons can be drawn for global constitutionalism. The Canadian portrait is not without its blemishes, however. We highlight some fault lines that rest below the surface but that could one day reveal themselves as imminent threats to the stability that Canada today enjoys.

We advance exclusively institutional explanations for the resilience of Canadian constitutional democracy in this chapter, though we certainly acknowledge the role of norms and Canada's enviable position, when viewed globally, of an imperfect but entrenched commitment to democratic values. No set of democratic institutions can persevere for long in the absence of elite and societal support. The idea of constitutional values certainly possesses some explanatory power, and the study of "political cultures" is rooted in a venerable scholarly tradition in Canada.[15] Yet we believe that a focus on institutional protections against democratic decline is more useful for this global comparative project in the decline of constitutional democracy.

Institutional flourishing or backsliding goes to the core of concerns about democratic decline. Nancy Bermeo's influential definition of democratic backsliding proceeds in largely institutional terms; it refers, she explains, to the "state-led debilitation or elimination of any of the political institutions that sustain an existing democracy."[16]

---

[12] David S. Law, "Alternatives to Liberal Constitutional Democracy," *Maryland Law Review* 77 (2017): 223–243.

[13] A useful discussion of this term may be found in International IDEA, *The Global State of Democracy: Exploring Democracy's Resilience*, 1st ed. (Stockholm: International Institute for Democracy and Electoral Assistance, 2017).

[14] See Sujit Choudhry, "Does the World Need More Canada? The Politics of the Canadian Model in Constitutional Politics and Political Theory," *International Journal of Constitutional Law* 5 (2007): 606–638; see also David S. Law and Mila Versteeg, "The Declining Influence of the United States Constitution," *NYU Law Review* 87 (2012): 762–858 (detailing the growing global influence of the Canadian Constitution).

[15] See Gregory S. Mahler, "Canada: Two Nations, One State?," in *Political Culture and Constitutionalism: A Comparative Approach*, ed. Daniel P. Franklin and Michael J. Baun (Armonk, NY: M.E. Sharpe, 1995). For a useful overview of the scholarly literature in this field, see Nelson Wiseman, *In Search of Canadian Political Culture* (Vancouver: UBC Press, 2007).

[16] Bermeo, "On Democratic Backsliding."

This definition is institutional in two ways. Its definition of the *driver* of decline is institutional, namely, the state and the political parties that capture state power in periodic elections. It also identifies the *targets* of would-be authoritarians as the institutions that support and sustain constitutional democracy. Other influential understandings of decline are similarly institutionally focused, particularly around the behavior of political parties.[17] Institutional explanations also have greater comparative purchase than those tied to political or national culture, or to constitutional values anchored in specific histories that cannot be easily transferred to other contexts. Institutional accounts therefore have a great deal to offer in terms of potential solutions to the growing problem of democratic decline.

Before proceeding, we must above all acknowledge that Canadian constitutional democracy is beset by a series of domestic challenges that dominate much of our internal debate. Most notable among these challenges is reconciliation with Indigenous peoples,[18] the balance between religious accommodation and other constitutional goods,[19] and the continuing possibility of Quebec secession that is never more than one provincial election away from once again approaching on the horizon. Other challenges will inevitably emerge. The basics of Canada's constitutional democracy are admittedly also not the most easily exportable. The Constitution is a strange brew of written text codified across multiple documents along with uncodified conventions and principles. No one would posit that a new democracy birthed in 2018 should have a head of government, in our case the prime minister, whose powers are not written down in any statute or constitutional text.[20] Nonetheless, the robustness of Canada's institutions has real relevance for other constitutional democracies.

We begin, in the second Section, with a first-order question in constitutional design: whether a democracy should adopt a presidential or parliamentary system. We argue that Canada's successful constitutional arrangements suggests that the answer may be neither. We show that Canada constitutes an example of Bruce Ackerman's "constrained parliamentarism" in action, and that this design has limited some threats that have manifested themselves in other democracies. The third Section identifies the presence of a robust

---

[17] Marsh, "The Decline of Democratic Governance"; Samuel Issacharoff, "Outsourcing Politics: The Hostile Takeover of Our Hollowed-Out Political Parties," *Houston Law Review* 54 (2017): 845–880; Samuel Issacharoff, "Democracy's Deficits," *University of Chicago Law Review* (forthcoming 2018).

[18] Truth and Reconciliation Commission, *Honouring the Truth, Reconciling for the Future: Final Report of the Truth and Reconciliation Commission* (Toronto: James Lorimer & Company Ltd., 2015).

[19] See Gérard Bouchard and Charles Taylor, *Building the Future: A Time for Reconciliation* (Québec: Commission de consultation sur les pratiques d'accommodement reliées aus différences culturelles, 2008).

[20] There are only two references to the prime minister in any of Canada's major Constitution Acts. One is an obscure requirement, since elapsed, that she or he convene an intergovernmental meeting to review the country's constitutional amendment rules within fifteen years of their coming into force. See Constitution Act, 1982, s. 49, being Schedule B to the Canada Act 1982 (UK), 1982, c. 11 ["Constitution Act, 1982"]. The other, still applicable today, is the obligation that she or he invite "representatives of the aboriginal peoples of Canada to participate in the discussions" on any amendment to relevant parts of the Constitution. See Constitution Act, s. 35.1.

"democracy branch" in Canada as both a source and driver of democratic resilience. The fourth Section situates the Supreme Court of Canada in the debate about the judicialization of mega-politics. We argue that the Court can be understood as highly *political* but as less *politicized* than in some comparator case studies of democratic decline. We identify with reference to specific cases how the Court has managed to issue highly political and quite controversial decisions without becoming perceived as being a partisan institution. We conclude by acknowledging the unfinished or "agonistic" nature of Canadian constitutionalism.[21] We also set out some longer-term challenges that we view as significant, despite Canada's relatively enviable position among the countries of the world in our present time.

Constrained Parliamentarism

In one of his field-shifting articles on constitutional design, Bruce Ackerman argued quite controversially at the time that new democracies should not adopt the American model of presidentialism with its strict separation of powers.[22] The peculiar design of presidential systems, he explained, makes more likely unhealthy concentrations of power that are particularly unwelcome in new democracies seeking to find their footing. A strict separation of powers is at odds, he continued, with the partly fused executive-legislative branches whose constitutional arrangements were seen as performing well around the world. The superior model, in his view, was not a pure parliamentary system, which allowed for relatively untrammeled concentrations of power as in pure presidentialism, but rather what he defined as "constrained parliamentarism." We show in this Section that Canada has provided some evidence to support Ackerman's argument in favor of constrained parliamentarism as a source and driver of democratic resilience.

FEATURES OF CONSTRAINED PARLIAMENTARY SYSTEMS

Ackerman draws from the political science literature on the failure of presidentialism in South America and Eastern Europe to build his case against American-style presidentialism.[23] He sets out in search of a more durable model for new or transitional democracies than the rigid separation that commonly by political practice results in elevating the executive branch dominated by the president over the legislature.

---

[21] Jeremy Webber, *The Constitution of Canada: A Contextual Analysis* (Portland, OR: Hart Publishing, 2015).

[22] Bruce Ackerman, "The New Separation of Powers," *Harvard Law Review* 113 (2000): 633–729.

[23] The major works in this long-standing debate include Juan J. Linz and Arturo Valenzuela, eds., *The Failure of Presidential Democracy: Comparative Perspectives* (Baltimore: Johns Hopkins University Press, 1994); Juan J. Linz and Alfred Stepan, *Problems of Democratic Transition and Consolidation* (Baltimore: Johns Hopkins University Press, 1996); Jose Antonio Cheibub, *Presidentialism, Parliamentarism and Democracy* (New York: Cambridge University Press, 2006). For a study suggesting that presidentialism and parliamentarism function similarly despite their differences in form, see Richard Albert, "The Fusion of Presidentialism and Parliamentarism," *American Journal of Comparative Law* 57 (2009): 531–578.

Ackerman argues that the American design of separated powers is less stabilizing than variations on the Westminster model that have proliferated in constitutional systems as diverse as Germany, India, and South Africa. These countries are examples of "constrained parliamentarism," a hybrid model of separated powers that features some of the standard facets of the Westminster system, including a prime minister and a cabinet accountable to the legislature. Yet constrained parliamentarism frustrates traditionally unfettered parliamentary sovereignty in meaningful ways with a written constitution that includes an enforceable bill of rights. Constrained parliamentary systems also entail a supreme or constitutional court empowered institutionally to check legislative and executive action. An additional important aspect of constrained parliamentarism involves what Ackerman labels the "one-and-a-half house solution,"[24] a bicameral national legislature with a dominant lower house and an inferior upper house, whether by constitutional design or evolution of institutional practice or, indeed, both.

CONSTRAINED PARLIAMENTARISM IN CANADA

Ackerman himself suggests without expanding in detail that Canada is an exemplar of his model of constrained parliamentarism.[25] We think Canada fits this model well. More important for our present purposes, we believe that some of the features Ackerman identified as key to constraining the political branches have contributed to Canada's democratic resilience. In this Section, we consider Canada in light of each of Ackerman's principal criteria for constrained parliamentarism and comment on how each of these features has contributed to democratic resilience. Our basic insight for other constitutional democracies around the world, especially those under attack from within, is that the Canadian Constitution and its institutional design of separated powers constrain the legislative and executive branches from committing intentional abuses or unintended oversteps of legal authority that drive democratic decline.

Executive Accountability to the Legislature

Canada has a bicameral legislative system composed of an elected House of Commons and an unelected Senate, with the cabinet drawn nearly exclusively from the lower house. The prime minister and cabinet ministers are therefore also members of Parliament sitting in the House. Canada's tradition of "responsible government" requires the executive, primarily the prime minister and cabinet, to be accountable to the House of Commons.[26] Canada is far from a pure Westminster model in this respect, however, as the executive has assumed a more robust role than initially envisioned in relation to the

---

[24] Ackerman, "New Separation," 635.

[25] Ibid., 640, 670 n.84, 672.

[26] Andrew Heard, *Canadian Constitutional Conventions: The Marriage of Law and Politics*, 2nd ed. (Ontario: Oxford University Press, 2014).

House. Academic,[27] journalistic,[28] and insider accounts[29] all confirm that the executive clearly dominates the legislative branch. Party discipline moreover blunts the possibility of frequent backbench rebellions against the government. This shift toward greater executive power has been a common feature across Westminster variants. The prime minister and his unelected advisors are more powerful in Canada perhaps even than in other Westminster democracies.[30]

Parliament, however, continues to exert considerable authority, particularly in minority government scenarios. Confidence votes can also be held at any time, and ministers are called to account in Question Period, the political equivalent of a prize fight, only it occurs every weekday Parliament is in session. The Conservative government of Stephen Harper knew well the measure of Parliament's power. The Harper government received minority mandates from the electorate in 2006 and 2008, and came close on several occasions to losing the confidence of the House.[31] Even under majority governments, the executive can find it difficult to retain the support of the House and the governing caucus. Not even party discipline could foreclose the intra-party conflicts that afflicted the Liberal government from 1993 to 2006, the last three years under a new prime minister who had pressured his intra-party predecessor to cede the reins.

In short, Parliament, not the prime minister, is the gatekeeper to the exercise of power in Canada, even if the executive remains the star of the show. True, the executive has a larger role today than it did in 1867. But Parliament retains the authority to constrain executive action and this power has had a disciplining effect in recent political history.

The Constraint of a Codified Constitution

Ackerman concludes that a codified constitution is a welcome change to the Westminster tradition of uncodified or common law constitutionalism—because of the additional and express limits it places on the exercise of authority. Canada departs from the classic Westminster model of uncodified constitutionalism, though the Canadian Constitution is an unusual mix of codified and uncodified sources.

Significant elements of the Canadian Constitution are unwritten, including the constitutional conventions that define much of the structure of government and the interactions among the branches. The role of the prime minister in the constitutional order,

---

[27] Donald Savoie, *Governing from the Center: Concentration of Power in the Canadian Politic* (Toronto: University of Toronto Press, 1999).

[28] Jeff Simpson, *The Friendly Dictatorship* (Toronto: McClelland & Stewart, 2001).

[29] Brent Rathgeber, *Irresponsible Government: The Decline of Parliamentary Democracy in Canada* (Toronto: Dundurn A.J. Patrick Boyer, 2014).

[30] See Peter Aucoin, Lori Turnbull, and Mark Jarvis, *Democratizing the Constitution: Reforming Responsible Government* (Toronto: Emond Montgomery Publications, 2011).

[31] Lorne Sossin and Peter Russell, eds., *Parliamentary Democracy in Crisis* (Buffalo, NY: University of Toronto Press, 2009).

for example, is not written down in a constitutional text or, for that matter, in an ordinary statute.[32] Also falling into this category are the unwritten principles on which the Supreme Court draws and which it develops to guide its interpretation of the text[33]— principles that have the force of law.[34]

The written portions of the Canadian Constitution can be divided into older documents and those forming part of the patriation package of 1982 that brought the Constitution home to Canada from the United Kingdom. The *Constitution Act, 1867*, previously known as the *British North America Act, 1867*, was a statute of the Parliament of the United Kingdom. The *Constitution Act, 1867* created what we know today as Canada and in the constitutional text detailed the division of powers. The provinces and the federal government have always been constrained by the principle of federalism through judicial interpretation of the powers assigned to them in sections 91–92 of the *Constitution Act, 1867*. Treaties between the Crown and Indigenous peoples entered into either pre- or post-Confederation were sometimes oral, but were often written down, and have the status of constitutional law.[35] The Constitution of Canada also includes a variety of other documents with constitutional status, some inherited from the United Kingdom, and many of which relate to the admission of provinces into the federation at various points as the country expanded.[36] These documents, often containing rights for minority language and education, are of course still relevant today.[37]

The 1982 package shifted the balance toward the written components of the Constitution and further constrained the actions of the political branches. The *Constitution Act, 1982* introduced the *Canadian Charter of Rights and Freedoms* to protect individual rights and freedoms where there had previously been no constitutional bill of rights, an elaborate set of amendment rules where there had previously been no written procedures, and Aboriginal and Treaty rights in section 35. The recognition of Aboriginal and Treaty rights constrained both federal and provincial governments,[38] which had earlier been legally permitted to "extinguish" the rights of Indigenous peoples. By its language, the written text guarantees federalism, protects rights and freedoms, enshrines the requirement of substantial consent among the federal and provincial– legislatures to change the text of the

---

[32] For the two exceptions to this rule, see note 20.

[33] See Reference re Secession of Quebec [1998] 2 S.C.R. 217.

[34] Trial Lawyers' Association of B.C. v B.C. (Attorney General) [2014] 3 S.C.R. 31.

[35] Sebastian Grammond, "Treaties as Constitutional Agreements," in *The Oxford Handbook of the Canadian Constitution*, ed. Peter Oliver, Patrick MacLen, and Nathalie DesRosiers (New York: Oxford University Press, 2017), 305. "Treaty rights" are recognized in section 35 of the Constitution Act, 1982. Section 35 also includes constitutional recognition for the fiduciary relationship between the Crown and Indigenous peoples. See Constitution Act, 1982, s. 35.

[36] See Schedule to the Constitution Act, 1982, s. 53.

[37] Caron v. Alberta [2015] 3 S.C.R. 511.

[38] See Tsilhqot'in Nation v. British Columbia [2014] 2 S.C.R. 257, paras. 133–134 (stating that s. 35 constrains federal and provincial governments and therefore the doctrine of interjurisdictional immunity should not be applied with respect to Parliament's authority to legislate pursuant to s. 91(24)).

Constitution, and recognizes treaties between the Crown and Indigenous peoples as well as rights flowing from the preexisting sovereignty of Indigenous nations. These textual rules create barriers to the abuse of state authority. Of course words alone cannot halt a country's slide into authoritarianism.[39] Still the textual referent that codification provides can at the very least put a speed bump in the road toward democratic decline.

The intricate amending procedures in the Constitution of Canada may be the most stringent in the world.[40] They are exceedingly difficult to meet for any government seeking meaningful amendment. Even a national government elected with a huge majority in the House of Commons would be frustrated in its quest to reshape the constitutional order, as the amendment rules require support across component units of the federation, rather than allowing transformative amendments by a supermajority in Parliament alone. An executive seeking to entrench itself through rewriting the constitutional text, as has occurred recently in Turkey, for example, would be frustrated by the amending formula contained in Part V of the *Constitution Act, 1982*.

The Primacy of the Lower House

Consistent with Ackerman's formulation, the Canadian House of Commons is politically dominant over the unelected Senate, and this arrangement has contributed to democratic legitimacy. The Senate has formal powers nearly equal to the House. The one notable exception is that money bills must be introduced in the House, on the principle that the House is directly accountable to voters for public spending. The House is also the nearly exclusive source of the cabinet. Senators have at times had a seat in the cabinet, but this has become exceedingly rare.

Despite its formally equal status and plenary legislative powers, the Senate rarely exercises its authority. This reticence is due to two perceived gaps in the legitimacy of the Senate's powers, which have been consistent in Canadian political discourse since 1867. First, the Senate is seen as anti-democratic. It remains an unelected body, which is a clear anomaly among major liberal democracies, with the notable exception of the House of Lords in the United Kingdom. Even the House of Lords, however, has undergone significant reforms in relation to its appointment process and membership. The same cannot be said of the Canadian Senate.

Second, the Constitution authorizes the governor general to appoint senators,[41] which in practice means on the advice of the prime minister. The political executive dictates

---

[39] See Walter Murphy, "Constitutions, Constitutionalism, and Democracy," in *Constitutionalism and Democracy: Transitions in the Contemporary World*, ed. Douglas Greenberg (New York: Oxford University Press, 1993), 3, 7.

[40] Richard Albert, "The Conventions of Constitutional Amendment in Canada," *Osgoode Hall Law Journal* 53 (2016): 399–441; Richard Albert, "The Difficulty of Constitutional Amendment in Canada," *Alberta Law Review* 53 (2015): 85–114.

[41] Constitution Act, 1867, 30 & 31 Victoria, c. 3 (U.K.), Pt. IV, s. 24.

appointments. Federal attempts to introduce Senate elections hit a dead end when the Supreme Court ruled that significant provincial consent would be required to do so under the amendment procedures.[42] The practice of the current Liberal government to appoint independent senators and cut ties between the governing caucus and the former Liberal Senate caucus has shifted dynamics somewhat in the Senate. Yet the custom that the Senate will make only minor modifications to bills sent to it from the House has remained unchanged.

The assignment of seats in the Senate also contributes to its legitimacy gap. The distribution of seats among regions deliberately deviates from the principle of representation by population, as is common in upper houses designed to accommodate subnational interests. The regional distribution, however, undermines the influence of western parts of Canada, to the benefit of Quebec and Atlantic Canada, and this has been the source of intense interprovincial grievances. "Western alienation" became a well-known phrase in the Canadian political lexicon in large part because of the failure of the Senate to adequately represent the regions.[43]

The dominance of the House over the Senate in nearly all matters has helped to foster democratic legitimacy. The political system locates power primarily in the body that is most closely connected to the electorate. This model incentivizes responsiveness in a manner that would not be true if the unelected Senate exercised greater influence.

The Judicial Constraint

Ackerman also suggests that a supreme or constitutional court is an important constraint on political actors that helps promote a healthy constitutional order. We discuss the role of Canada's apex court more fully below in the fourth Section. The Supreme Court of Canada has been in place since 1877 but it became the final court of appeal for Canada only in 1949, after appeals to the Privy Council in London were abolished.

For our purposes in this Section, it is worth noting only that the Court has played an increasingly important role in the federation.[44] The Court has always had the authority to strike down federal and provincial laws that violated the division of federal powers set out in Sections 91–92 of the *Constitution Act, 1867*. The package of major constitutional changes in 1982, however, empowered the Court to interpret the *Charter* as well as *Section* 35 regarding Aboriginal and Treaty rights in addition to the amendment procedures themselves. The Court now occupies an undeniably fundamental role in the constitutional order. It has frequently constrained legislative and executive action of all sorts, even on the most politically charged topics.

---

[42] Reference Re Senate Reform, [2014] 1 S.C.R. 704.

[43] Robert Lawson, "Understanding Alienation in Western Canada: Is 'Western Alienation' the Problem? Is Senate Reform the Cure?," *Journal of Canadian Studies* 39 (2005): 127–155.

[44] See Reference re Supreme Court Act, ss. 5 and 6, [2014] 1 S.C.R. 433.

The Democracy Branch

Ackerman posited that a parliamentary system is preferable to presidentialism if it is refined with some appendages and modifications to constrain the relatively untrammeled legislative and executive authority characteristic of a pure Westminster parliamentary model. He also argued, however, that the concept of a tripartite separation of powers was both an inadequate empirical understanding of how constitutional orders operate and a less-than-optimal standard for how they should. For Ackerman, constitutional democracies could benefit from a new branch of government focused on limiting abuses of state power. He noted that many existing democracies already had such a branch of government in full operation. Separation-of-powers theory, therefore, should be updated to reflect this need and reality, in his view.

Whether called a "democracy branch"[45] in Ackerman's framing or a "fourth branch"[46] of government, Canada's democratic resilience has been furthered by institutions outside of the traditional three branches of government. These institutions oversee misuses of legislative and executive authority. The federal electoral commission known as Elections Canada has been the central actor in Canada's fourth branch. On the strength of statutory and case law regulating political competition, Elections Canada has carved out for itself wide latitude to check abuses of authority in the electoral sphere.

FOURTH BRANCH IN THEORY AND PRACTICE

If, to use Bermeo's definition, democratic decline stems from interference by the executive or legislative branches with the institutions that sustain democracy, then election commissions must be at the center of the discussion. Election commissions, or electoral management bodies (EMBs) as they are often called, have largely been ignored in classic accounts of democratic resilience and development, though they have received more attention as of late. EMBs are relatively new creations but they have dramatically changed the way constitutional politics are played. Therefore only a partial account at best of constitutional democracy is possible if we interrogate it through the traditional three-part separation of powers.

Many constitutional texts constitute and empower EMBs as coequal actors with the three traditional branches. South Africa and India are the most well-known examples, but African, Asian, and Latin American democracies have in great numbers constitutionalized the status and role of their election commissions.[47] There is a powerful functional

---

[45] Ackerman, "New Separation," 699.

[46] See Michael Pal, "Electoral Management Bodies as a Fourth Branch of Government," *Review of Constitutional Studies* 21 (2016): 85–114.

[47] Pal, "Electoral Management Bodies"; Rafael Lopez-Pintor, *Electoral Management Bodies as Institutions of Governance* (New York: United Nations Development Programme, Bureau for Development Policy, 2000); Alan Wall, *Electoral Management Design: The International IDEA Handbook* (Stockholm: International IDEA, 2006).

rationale for doing so: the rules and procedures that structure elections are potentially outcome-determinative. Leaving election administration in the hands of the executive, or even the legislative branch, raises serious risks of partisan manipulation of electoral processes and, therefore, outcomes.

The gold standard in promoting electoral integrity is ensuring that elections are administered by arms-length, independent, and nonpartisan bodies.[48] Notable election failures in recent years, most recently in Kenya, have often been at least partially facilitated by partisan or executive capture of the formally independent and nonpartisan commission.[49] Indeed, partisan capture of election commissions has been on the "menu of manipulation"[50] in many notable jurisdictions in democratic decline.[51] Electoral malpractice is not limited to new, transitional, or developing democracies.[52] Even established democracies can be targeted in attempts to undermine the proper functioning of election commissions as a strategy of self-entrenchment.

CANADA'S FOURTH BRANCH OF GOVERNMENT

Attempts at partisan manipulation of electoral rules have been obstructed in Canada because of the signature strengths of our EMB. Part of the robustness of Canadian democracy can be attributed to the role played by Elections Canada and the other watchdog institutions that form the democracy branch, including the Offices of the Auditor General, the Commissioner of Lobbying, the Conflict of Interest and Ethics Commissioner, and the Public Sector Integrity Commissioner. Elections Canada is, by statute, an independent and nonpartisan institution, headed by a Chief Electoral Officer (CEO) who must reflect those characteristics.[53] Unlike the United States Federal Election Commission or EMBs in Mexico, the United Kingdom, and many other constitutional democracies, political parties have no representation on the Commission. Elections Canada interacts with parties through periodic meetings with a committee of all registered parties,[54] and responds to questions about its interpretation of provisions

---

[48] See Pippa Norris, Richard W. Frank and Ferran Martínez i Coma, *Advancing Electoral Integrity* (New York: Oxford University Press, 2014).

[49] Jason Burke, "Kenya Election Official Flees Country and Claims Presidential Vote Will Not Be Free," *The Guardian* (October 18, 2017), https://www.theguardian.com/world/2017/oct/18/kenya-election-official-flees-country-and-claims-presidential-vote-will-not-be-free.

[50] Andreas Schedler, "Elections without Democracy: The Menu of Manipulation," *Journal of Politics* 13 (2002): 36–50.

[51] Clava Brodsky, "Hungary's Dangerous Constitution," *Columbia Journal of Transnational Law Bulletin*, accessed February 10, 2018, http://jtl.columbia.edu/hungarys-dangerous-constitution; Miklós Bánkuti, Gábor Halmai, and Kim Lane Scheppele, "Hungary's Illiberal Turn: Disabling the Constitution," *Journal of Democracy* 23 (2012): 138–146; Jacques Rupnik, "Hungary's Illiberal Turn: How Things Went Wrong," *Journal of Democracy* 23 (2012): 132–137.

[52] Norris et al., *Advancing Electoral Integrity*.

[53] Canada Elections Act, SC 2000, c. 9, s. 16(b) ("Canada Elections Act").

[54] Canada Elections Act, s. 21.1(1)-(4).

in the *Canada Elections Act* to help parties comply with the law,[55] and the CEO appears before parliamentary committees to report on the institution's actions and to make recommendations for legislative reform. The institution otherwise operates at arms-length from the political actors it regulates.

In Canada the governing party cannot entrench itself through election administration because it does not control that lever of power. This approach has likely helped to build democratic resilience by hedging against the "one election" problem.[56] A party that wins power faces institutional barriers in its attempt to manipulate electoral rules in order to entrench itself from political competition. Another way of putting it is that we must acknowledge that it is not only courts, but also EMBs that "hedge" to protect democracy.[57]

Elections Canada has been lauded as an exemplary EMB in comparison to others around the globe, largely because of its impartiality.[58] It is an administrative body created by statute to be independent of Parliament. The appointment of a CEO must be approved by a resolution of the House of Commons.[59] On the surface this is a weak constraint, as the executive nominates the CEO and exercises control over the House through party discipline, especially in situations of majority government. The norm that the CEO must be nonpartisan, however, has prevailed and the individuals who have held the office have all been free from partisan entanglements. The CEO has the rank of a Deputy Minister, the highest level of nonpartisan civil servant other than the Clerk of the Privy Council, who is the head of the bureaucracy. From the CEO on down, professional career bureaucrats staff the agency, not political appointees. It is one of the few federal institutions that has a right to draw funds as needed to carry out its work without requiring parliamentary approval.

Preserving its legitimacy has admittedly been a challenge, given its near-constant entanglement with partisan politics. Disputes about voter identification rules as applying to veiled Muslim women,[60] allegedly vote-suppressing robocalls,[61] investigations for potential electoral malfeasance,[62] and other incidents have been pressure points in the

---

[55] Canada Elections Act, ss. 16.1–16.5.

[56] See Samuel Issacharoff, "The Democratic Risk to Democratic Transitions," *Constitutional Court Review* 5 (2013): 1–31.

[57] See Samuel Issacharoff, "Constitutional Courts and Democratic Hedging," *Georgetown Law Journal* 99 (2011): 961–1012.

[58] Jean-Pierre Kingsley, "The Administration of Canada's Independent, Non-partisan Approach," *Election Law Journal* 3 (2004): 406–411; Diane R. Davidson, "Enforcing Campaign Finance Laws: What Others Can Learn from Canada," *Election Law Journal* 3 (2004): 537–544.

[59] Canada Elections Act, s. 13(1).

[60] Lorne Sossin, "The Ambivalence of Administrative Justice in Canada: Does Canada Need a Fourth Branch?," *Supreme Court Law Review* 46 (2009): 51–76.

[61] Michael Pal, "Canadian Election Administration on Trial: Robocalls, *Opitz*, and Disputed Elections in the Courts," *King's Law Journal* 28 (2017): 324–342; McEwing and Kerr v. Canada (Attorney General) [2013] F.C. 525.

[62] Callaghan et al. v. Canada (Chief Electoral Officer), [2011] 2 F.C.R. 80. This matter is also known as the "in and out" case for the nature of the financial transactions at issue.

relationship between the EMB and the government of the day or political parties as a whole. Serious charges were made from within and outside of Canada that the EMB's independence was being undermined, perhaps deliberately, by the *Fair Elections Act* passed in amended form in 2011.[63] The *Fair Elections Act* reduced the term of the CEO from life (which means seventy-five years in Canada) to ten years, reduced Election Canada's mandate in some areas, restricted the outreach activities of the CEO, carved out some jurisdictional no-go zones, and split the independent investigatory arm of the agency from the rest of the EMB.[64] The risk of partisan capture or interference in independent election administration that led South Africa, India, and others to entrench their EMBs in the constitution is therefore a live concern in Canada. Yet Elections Canada has weathered recent storms and remains a formidable guardian of fair and neutral election administration. Some of this resilience is undoubtedly because of a normative commitment to fair electoral processes. The *Fair Elections Act* was widely criticized by the media, academics, and the Opposition parties. The government amended some of its most objectionable features. Institutional structures and rules are also a key part of the story.

Elections Canada plays a vital role in checking political authority within the structures set out by election law and the electoral system. It is also worth noting that Elections Canada is not alone. While it is perhaps the most obvious example of a fourth branch institution that we would regard as essential to constitutional democracy, there are other similar institutions in Canada that fit in the category to varying degrees. There are currently nine independent Officers of Parliament.[65] Some have relatively minor functions. Others, though, approach Elections Canada in their importance or at least have the potential to do so. Collectively, they are watchdogs over the political branches, and they may also check them indirectly by freely publicizing their errors and abuses. These Officers of Parliament have been criticized for doing too much, and also for doing too little.[66] They oversee the ethical behavior of elected representatives, the proper functioning of the public service, and financial accountability of public bodies, among other tasks. They do not at the moment possess the constitutional status that other countries have conferred upon their own functional and formal equivalents. Yet it is clear that the Canadian independent Officers aspire to fulfill, and in many cases do more than satisfy, the functions of a democracy branch as Ackerman envisioned two decades ago. Part of Elections Canada's success can be attributed to the tools it has at its disposal. The Canadian law of democracy in the hands of an independent and impartial EMB has proven to be a formidable model to promote democratic resilience. There are two main features here worthy of greater elaboration.

---

[63] Fair Elections Act, S.C. 2014, c. 12 ("Fair Elections Act").

[64] Pal, "Electoral Management Bodies."

[65] Anne Chaplin, *Officers of Parliament: Accountability, Virtue, and the Constitution* (Cowansville, Québec: Éditions Y. Blais, 2011).

[66] Chaplin, *Officers of Parliament.*

First, on campaign finance, the constitutional case law of the Supreme Court permitting limits on political spending, in combination with the *Fair Elections Act* and its interpretation by Elections Canada, have together created a level playing field for political participation. This approach is far from perfect,[67] but we would not be surprised to know that it is appreciated with envy by those in systems that permit unlimited political spending that distorts electoral outcomes. As a result, there is far less money in the Canadian political system than in many other democracies. The goal of ensuring a level playing field permeates Elections Canada's approach to election administration and its interpretation of its mandate under the *Fair Elections Act*. Undoubtedly, a more progressive redistribution of income than in the United States, for example, shapes the egalitarian contours of election law. Which is the chicken and which is the egg is an inquiry beyond the scope of this chapter. Whatever the cause, the egalitarian values within the campaign finance system have cemented a more level electoral playing field.

Elections Canada also oversees a mixed public/private funding regime that has offered some stability. Political parties receive significant state funding. A per-vote subsidy based on the number of votes the party received in the last election was recently cut to great controversy,[68] but parties continue to receive direct subsidies in the form of reimbursement of large portions of their election expenses, and indirect ones in the form of a generous tax rebate provided to their donors that exceeds what applies to charitable donations.[69] These generous public dollars accompany private donations, though the latter are capped at modest amounts.[70] This mix of public and private funding means that parties do not need to cater to the interests of the ultra-wealthy in order to fund their activities. They are incentivized to remain close to the people, by virtue of the need to solicit limited private donations.

Second, the political party system has proven to be relatively immune from the forces of extremism and populism when viewed in global context, at least to date. Canada's democratic resilience in this respect has roots in multiple factors. The first-past-the-post, single-member plurality electoral system encourages two-party competition generally, though Canada has bucked that trend with its long-standing multiparty system.[71] The

---

[67] See Lisa Young and Harold Jansen, eds., *Money, Politics and Democracy: Canada's Party Finance Reforms* (Vancouver: UBC Press, 2011); Michael Pal, "Is the Permanent Campaign the End of the Egalitarian Model of Elections?," in *The Canadian Constitution in Transition*, ed. Richard Albert, Paul Daly, and Vanessa MacDonnell (forthcoming 2018).

[68] Keeping Canada's Economy and Jobs Growing Act, 60 Elizabeth II, c. 24.

[69] See Leslie F. Seidle, "Public Funding for Political Parties: The Case for Further Reform," in *Money, Politics and Democracy*, 37.

[70] Individual donations are capped at $1,550 in 2017. This amount increases by $25 per year. Canada Elections Act, s. 367(1) and (1.1).

[71] For the most recent addition in a vast body of literature, see Richard Johnston, *The Canadian Party System: An Analytic History* (Vancouver, BC: UBC Press, 2017).

Liberal Party of Canada and Conservative Party of Canada have been the most electorally successful since the country's founding. The left New Democratic Party and the separatist Bloq Quebecois have each formed the Official Opposition in recent years. It has now three parties competing nationally, with a fourth seeking only votes in the second largest province, Quebec. Still, only two parties have ever formed a government at the federal level. The electoral system encourages large, brokerage parties that mediate and reconcile competing interests across a plurinational democracy, existing over an immense geography with regional cleavages and multiple competing identities.

The weakening of political parties in many established democracies has been a primary contributing factor to democratic decline, according to many well-informed observers.[72] Their studies largely conclude that parties have been "hollowed out."[73] Political parties are no longer, if they ever were, reflective of mass movements with large memberships and relevance to the daily lives of citizens. On this account, political parties are instead machines designed to fundraise, spend money on advertising, gather data, and activate their volunteers at election time.

Political parties in Canada are not immune to these broader trends. Membership has decreased, and their policy role has been reduced. Yet parties in Canada are incentivized to hue to the middle of the political spectrum. There are more votes to be found there under the current electoral system. There are multiple examples of populist or protest parties in Canada that eventually chose a more moderate course in order to occupy more fertile electoral ground.

The Political but Not Politicized Court

As we signaled earlier in the third Section, the Supreme Court of Canada has been a primary contributor to the country's democratic resilience. The Court has been a key player in checking legislative and executive authority, particularly after the enactment of the *Constitution Act, 1982.*

THE JUDICIALIZATION OF MEGA-POLITICS

Ran Hirschl identifies the judicialization of mega-politics as a defining trend in comparative constitutional politics.[74] Courts are increasingly called upon to adjudicate legal disputes over matters that previously would have remained within the realm of pure politics, or at least within the ambit of democratically elected legislatures. This trend is

---

[72] See Marsh, "The Decline of Democratic Governance"; Issacharoff, "Outsourcing Politics."

[73] Issacharoff, "Outsourcing Politics."

[74] Ran Hirschl, *Towards Juristocracy: The Origins and Consequences of the New Constitutionalism* (Cambridge, MA: Harvard University Press, 2004).

notable for its durability and global reach. Disputes about secession, the rightful winner of presidential elections, issues of fundamental moral disagreement, and other matters of existential importance to contemporary democracies are now routinely resolved by courts. For instance, the Supreme Court of Kenya recently invalidated the results of its presidential election, marking the first time a high court in Africa has done so, and one of the few times globally that a court has overturned an outcome that returned an incumbent.[75]

Given the range of deeply "political" subjects that they now routinely address, supreme or constitutional courts must walk a careful line. Courts risk being perceived as partisan or political actors, or as institutions with a stake in the game rather than neutral arbiters applying pre-established legal rules. They must make political decisions that at times constrain powerful actors, and they must do so without appearing politicized. In other words, their challenge is to protect constitutional democracy without losing legitimacy. The Supreme Court of Canada has had to walk this line, and in our view it has done so ably, fairly and in a way that has allowed it remarkably to grow in legitimacy.

THE ROLE OF THE SUPREME COURT OF CANADA

The Supreme Court of Canada has strengthened the country's democratic resilience by limiting abuses of legislative and executive authority. The Court has achieved the rare feat of regularly deciding highly political cases without, by international standards, becoming either in appearance or indeed in reality unduly politicized. In the last few years, the Court has heard controversial matters including physician-assisted dying,[76] constitutional reform of the upper house,[77] disputed election results,[78] and parliamentary authority to amend the legislation empowering the Court itself.[79] These cases have struck at the core of *Charter* rights and also at the foundations of the bargains that made Confederation possible.

There have been serious academic debates as to whether the Court has exceeded the bounds of its proper role within the separation of powers since the coming-into-force of the *Charter*. These academic conversations, largely centered on the concepts of "judicial

---

[75] Odinga v. Independent Electoral and Boundaries Commission, Presidential Petition No. 1 of 2017, Supreme Court of Kenya (2017), http://www.judiciary.go.ke/portal/assets/filemanager_uploads/A%20-%20 Decisions/Majority%20Full%20Judgment.pdf. The Kenyan Supreme Court later upheld the re-run presidential election that saw President Kenyatta elected after a boycott by the main opposition candidate, Raila Odinga.

[76] Carter v. Canada [2015] 1 S.C.R. 331.

[77] Reference re Senate Reform, [2014] 1 S.C.R. 704.

[78] Opitz v. Wrzesnewskyj [2012] 3 S.C.R. 76. See Pal, "Canadian Election Administration on Trial."

[79] Reference re Supreme Court Act, ss. 5 and 6, [2014] 1 S.C.R. 433.

activism"[80] and "dialogue,"[81] were relevant enough to the Court that they made their way into several decisions.[82] The most public conflict in recent years between the courts and the elected branches was "l'affaire Nadon," as it has come to be known.[83] In the *Reference re Supreme Court Act,* the Supreme Court ruled that the federal government's nominee to the Court itself, Justice Marc Nadon of the Federal Court of Appeal, was ineligible to fill one of the three seats reserved by section 6 of the *Supreme Court Act* for appointees from the province of Quebec. The *Reference* was punctuated by a virtually unprecedented public dispute pitting the chief justice at the time versus the minister of justice as well as the prime minister.[84]

Even still, the Court has managed to avoid the perception of inappropriate political or partisan conduct. The empirical research supports this view. While the empirical studies of judicial behavior in the Canadian context indicate that individual justices may have consistent ideological predispositions that at times manifest themselves in decision-making, the link between the party in government appointing the justice and judicial outcomes is not nearly as strong as it is in the United States.[85]

One structural cause for the stability and relative depoliticization of the Court may be the reference power, pursuant to which the Court may issue an advisory opinion on a matter of public interest. The federal cabinet is authorized by law to refer to the Court legal questions regarding the interpretation of the Constitution and the powers of Parliament and of the provincial legislatures, the constitutionality of federal or provincial

---

[80] Ian Brodie, *Friends of the Court: The Privileging of Interest Group Litigants in Canada* (Albany: State University of New York Press, 2002); Rainer Knopff and Ted Morton, *The Charter Revolution and the Court Party* (Peterborough, Ontario: Broadview Press, 2000); Emmett MacFarlane, "'You Can't Always Get What You Want'; Regime Politics, the Harper Government and the Supreme Court of Canada," *Canadian Journal of Political Science* (forthcoming 2018).

[81] Kent Roach, *The Supreme Court on Trial: Judicial Activism or Democratic Dialogue* (Toronto: Irwin Law, 2001); Peter Hogg, Allison Bushell Thornton, and Wade Wright, "Charter Dialogue Revisited—Or 'Much Ado about Metaphors,'" *Osgoode Hall Law Journal* 45 (2007): 1–66; Luc Tremblay, "The Legitimacy of Judicial Review: The Limits of Dialogue between Courts and Legislatures," *International Journal of Constitutional Law* 3 (2005): 617–648; Kent Roach, "Dialogic Judicial Review and Its Critics," *Supreme Court Law Review (2d)* 23 (2004): 49–104; Peter Hogg and Allison Bushell, "The Charter Dialogue between Courts and Legislatures," *Osgoode Hall Law Journal* 35 (1997): 75–124.

[82] See, e.g., Vriend v. Alberta [1998] 1 S.C.R. 493, paras. 137–139; Harper v. Canada [2004] 1 S.C.R. 827, para. 37. The full set of cases is available in Peter Hogg, *Constitutional Law of Canada* (Toronto: Carswell, 2012).

[83] Sebastian Grammond, "La Fonction Protectrice de la Formule de Modification de la Constitution," *Revue General de Droit* 47 (2017): 119–164.

[84] Canadian Press, "Nadon Spat between Harper, Chief Justice McLachlin Called 'Disturbing,'" *CBC.ca,* May 3, 2014, http://www.cbc.ca/news/politics/nadon-spat-between-harper-chief-justice-mclachlin-called-disturbing-1.2630896.

[85] Benjamin Alarie and Andrew Green, "Policy Preference Change and Appointments to the Supreme Court of Canada," *Osgoode Hall Law Journal* 47 (2009): 1–46; Benjamin Alarie and Andrew Green, "Charter Decisions in the McLachlin Era: Consensus and Ideology at the Supreme Court of Canada," *Supreme Court Law Review (2d)* 47 (2009): 475–511.

legislation, or indeed any matter deemed "important."[86] The *Supreme Court Act* empowers the executive to ask the Court about the constitutionality of any contemplated action, including the status of bills not yet passed by Parliament. Perhaps the most globally well-known instance of the use of the reference power in the last generation is the *Reference re the Secession of Quebec.*[87] The federal government has availed itself of the reference option on many other prominent occasions, including in connection with the patriation of the Canadian Constitution from the United Kingdom,[88] and the constitutionality of legislation on assisted human reproduction.[89]

The reference power is a clear violation of any strict theory of the separation of powers.[90] It does, however, arguably defuse conflicts between the branches by decreasing the costs of legislative failure. The government can refer bills to the Court before they become law, which therefore reduces the impact of the Court declaring some action to be unconstitutional. References have also been used strategically by governments on matters of high moral or political contention that divide the population, including marriage.[91] They are a useful vehicle for governments to avoid blame for unpopular outcomes dictated by the constitution in some instances. The existence of this reference power mitigates and reduces occasions of open conflict between branches, which we believe likewise contributes to democratic resilience.

The Court's recent reference jurisprudence has also arguably contributed to democratic stability. The Court's opinions in the *Nadon Reference* and also in the *Senate Reform Reference* curtailed the discretion of Parliament to make changes to the Supreme Court and Senate, respectively, without obtaining significant consent from among the ten provinces. Such consent is theoretically possible but, in practice, it has so far proven impossible to obtain. Richard Albert has labeled this the problem of the Constitution's "constructive unamendability."[92]

These two references can rightly be said to reduce the flexibility of the constitutional order and to impede the possibility of reform. The "fundamental nature and role" of the unelected Senate is locked-in indefinitely, despite its powers nearly coequal to those of the House of Commons.[93] The Supreme Court has moreover insulated itself from any changes to its "essential features" including its jurisdiction.[94] This line of judgments

---

[86] Supreme Court Act, R.S.C. 1985, c. S-26, s. 53(1).

[87] Reference re Secession of Quebec, [1998] 2 S.C.R. 217.

[88] Reference re Resolution to Amend the Constitution [1981] 1 S.C.R. 753.

[89] Reference re Assisted Human Reproduction Act [2010] 3 S.C.R. 457.

[90] Carissima Mathen, "The Question Calls for an Answer and I Propose to Answer It: The Patriation Reference as Constitutional Method," *Supreme Court Law Review (2d)* 54 (2011): 143–166.

[91] Reference re Same-Sex Marriage [2004] 3 S.C.R. 698.

[92] Richard Albert, "Constructive Unamendability in Canada and the United States," *Supreme Court Law Review (2d)* 67 (2014): 181–219.

[93] Reference re Senate Reform, [2014] 1 S.C.R. 704, para 48.

[94] Reference re Supreme Court Act, [2014]] 1 S.C.R. 433, para 74.

prevents potentially beneficial constitutional reforms, but it also hedges against any authoritarian impulses by a government seeking to weaken the Court's independence or to eliminate the long-standing check on the House of Commons provided (even if admittedly imperfectly) by the Senate.[95] As a result of the Court's reference judgments, two institutions core to the functioning of Canadian constitutionalism have been shielded from future governments inclined to undermine democracy.

Conclusion—Challenges to Democratic Resilience

It would be unwise for us to tell only a "good news" story about the resilience of Canada's constitutional democracy. The truth is that the rigid five-part amendment formula entails the consequence that the constitutional order is exceedingly difficult to update in order to better reflect the modern composition, aspirations, and values of our ever-diversifying country.

Reconciliation between the sovereignty of the Canadian Crown and the preexisting presence of sovereign Indigenous political communities with their own laws and governance structures is today the central political and constitutional challenge for the state. Reconciliation has great merit as an urgent matter of justice. How reconciliation will proceed and what the implications will be for the Canadian constitutional order are both matters of great contestation. The ultimate outcome of the process of reconciliation is unknown, most notably what changes will be required to the constitutional order. Canada's Constitution has always been an unfinished project that reflects multiple and often competing conceptions of the country. Jeremy Webber has labeled ours an "agonistic" constitutional order for these reasons. How these competing conceptions meet in the course of the reconciliation project will shape the future of our constitutional order.

Provincial secession may not appear imminent, but it always remains possible. Triumphalism from federalists about the death of Quebec separatism is never prudent. The experience with the violence-marred referendum in Catalonia, the jailing of Catalonian political leaders, and Catalonia's unilateral declaration of independence show how quickly conflict can escalate between the center and a region.[96] Canada has taken a legal approach that is different and perhaps wiser than the path Spain has chosen for managing separatist impulses. The *Clarity Act*,[97] the *Secession Reference,* and the legally permitted long-standing presence of separatist parties sitting in both Parliament and the Quebec National Assembly have, for now, helped reinforce Canada's democratic resilience, not to undermine it.

---

[95] Grammond, "La Fonction Protectrice."

[96] Thomson Reuters, "Catalan Independence Leaders Jailed in Spain," *CBC.ca*, October 16, 2017, http://www.cbc.ca/news/world/catalonia-independence-jailed-1.4357462.

[97] An Act to give effect to the requirement for clarity as set out in the opinion of the Supreme Court of Canada in the Quebec Secession Reference, SC 2000, c. 26 ("Clarity Act").

We nonetheless believe, from our vantage point as scholars of comparative constitutional studies around the world, that Canada is well prepared to withstand the pressures that no doubt will come. The present configuration of political actors may change, and the political center may well shift in the years ahead, but this is to be expected. Although Canada has so far shown itself to be a model for democratic resilience, the reality is that the blueprint for successful constitutional democracy in Canada remains as ever a continuing work in progress.

9   Constitutional Culture and Democracy in Mexico

A Critical View of the 100-Year-Old Mexican Constitution
Ana Micaela Alterio and Roberto Niembro

Introduction

Last year the Mexican Constitution turned 100 years old. The centenary could make us think that in Mexico we have a strong constitutional culture. However, this assumption is wrong, since the strength of a constitutional culture does not depend on the longevity of the Constitution. Constitutional culture is an open and incomplete project of learning, understanding, and interpreting the constitution by the people in a non-legalistic way.[1] From this perspective, Mexican constitutional culture is very weak. Constitutionalism in Mexico may not be in a crisis, understood as an acute period of serious difficulty, but it is suffering from a chronic illness of long standing.

The 1917 Mexican Constitution marked the end of the Mexican Revolution and the beginning of a new era. In the aftermath, a continuous confrontation between revolutionary leaders took place, leading in 1929 to the foundation of the *Partido Nacional Revolucionario*, predecessor of the Partido Revolucionario Institucional (PRI). Afterward came the stabilization of the regime and predominance of one political party for the next seventy years. Since 1977, electoral competition has slowly opened to opposition by legal and constitutional amendments to include representatives elected by proportional

---

[1] Jan-Werner Müller, *Constitutional Patriotism* (Princeton, NJ: Princeton University Press, 2007), 57, 61.

representation. With this legal change, Mexico moved to a pluri-party system. In 1989 the right-wing party Partido Acción Nacional (PAN) won its first gubernatorial election, and in 1997 PRI lost control of Congress. Three years later, PAN won the presidency. After twelve years of PAN's government, the PRI returned to Los Pinos, the presidential palace. With the return of the PRI to the presidency, there has been an authoritarian backlash in the country.

In 2006, Zamora and Cossío argued that with the rotation of the presidency in 2000, Mexico turned to a new constitutional order with a true separation of powers. They further argued that Congress and the Supreme Court began to make binding decisions and were not subordinated by the president. Mexico, they believed, was in a new era of constitutionalism in which an authoritarian government, or "Presidentialism," was unlikely to reappear any time soon.[2] They pointed to two important characteristics. On the one hand, the PRI's lack of ideological focus produced a flexible authoritarianism that allowed it to respond opportunistically to political forces without undermining the basic power structure. On the other hand, the Mexican president had become the supreme coalition builder.[3] Unfortunately, they didn't envisage what would develop from these two characteristics, and disregarded constitutional culture.

In our opinion, these authors' trust that an authoritarian government is unlikely to reappear was misguided. In another work, Niembro has described the sophisticated way in which Mexican ruling elites with an authoritarian mentality exercise power as a form of authoritarian constitutionalism.[4] Authoritarian constitutionalism's reliance on the constitution as a discourse explains why it is so important for Mexican political elites to have a written constitution and establish almost every public policy in it, while disregarding liberal democratic ideology.[5]

As the Mexican Constitution was amended more than seven hundred times, it became a large and opaque text. Moreover, political elites abandoned the conception of the Constitution as a nonbinding and aspirational document that expresses the promises of the Revolution and began talking about it as a binding document, at least when doing so was to their advantage. In this way, the Constitution helped them sustain a rule of law and democratic discourse with no serious commitment to democracy itself. Furthermore, theorists and practitioners guided the process with a minimalist conception of democracy

---

[2] Stephen Zamora and José Ramón Cossío, "Mexican Constitutionalism after presidencialismo," *International Journal of Constitutional Law* 4, no. 2 (2006): 411–412; *Contra* Jesús Silva Herzog Márquez, *El antiguo régimen y la transición en México*, 3rd ed. (Mexico City: Planeta, 2004), 150.

[3] Zamora and Cossío, "Mexican Constitutionalism," 415–416.

[4] Roberto Niembro Ortega, "Conceptualizing Authoritarian Constitutionalism," *VRÜ* 49, no. 4 (2016): 339–367.

[5] Octavio Paz, *El Laberinto de la Soledad, Postdata, Vuelta al Laberinto de la Soledad* (Mexico City: FCE, 1994), 133–134; José Antonio Aguilar Rivera, *La geometría y el mito: un ensayo sobre la libertad y el liberalismo en México, 1821–1970* (Mexico City: FCE, 2010), 12.

that focused only on electoral rules.[6] In fact, Mexico has invested a huge amount of resources in its electoral regime, including a specialized supreme electoral court and lower level courts, federal and local. Moreover, there is a high level of public financing for political parties.

According to the Third National Poll on Constitutional Culture made by the Universidad Nacional Autónoma de México (2017),[7] in contrast to political elites, 90.5 percent of Mexicans say they know a little bit or nothing at all of the Constitution. This situation is disturbing because it implies alienation from constitutional values, procedures, and structures. For example, according to the same poll, only 56.5 percent of the people think they should obey the law, 62.2 percent think gay couples should have the same rights as non-gays, 47 percent think it is permissible to torture someone to make him confess that he raped a women, 27.8 percent would not obey a majority rule if they do not agree with it, 25.8 percent think in some circumstances it is better to have a non-democratic government, and for 18.8 percent it does not matter if it is democratic or not.[8]

This high level of ignorance of the Constitution and alienation from the values, structures, and procedures it establishes for democracy give us a clue to the weakness of Mexican constitutional culture. Of course, a poll is not enough to support a robust conclusion, but it gives us a snapshot of what people actually think. If we take into account the poll results, it is urgent to think what is a constitutional culture, how can it be promoted, and what are the goals of having it.[9] This is especially true if a constitutional culture, among other things, is fundamental for a constitution to work properly.[10] In this chapter, we explain several relations between culture and a constitution and define constitutional culture as the active popular process of learning, understanding, and interpreting the values, structures, and procedures established in the Constitution in a non-legalistic way, with the goal of forming a popular habit and custom of demanding justification of governmental acts by political participation.

---

[6] See Ricardo Becerra, Pedro Salazar, and José Woldenberg, *La mecánica del cambio político en México. Elecciones, partidos y reformas* (Mexico City: Cal y Arena, 2005), 19.

[7] Héctor Fix Fierro, Julia Isabel Flores, and Diego Valadés, *Los mexicanos y su Constitución. Tercera Encuesta Nacional de Cultura Constitucional (Third National Poll on Constitutional Culture)* (Mexico City: IIJ-UNAM, 2017), 60. This high percentage of ignorance of the Constitution has decreased somewhat since the first poll made in 2003. In 2003, 92.6 percent of the people said they know a little bit or nothing at all.

[8] Ibid., 87, 127, 195, 198.

[9] On the culture of legality, see Pedro Salazar Ugarte, *Democracia y cultura de la legalidad* (Mexico City: INE, 2016), 33.

[10] John Ferejohn, Jack N. Rakove, Jonathan Riley, eds., "Editors' Introduction," in *Constitutional Culture and Democratic Rule* (Cambridge: Cambridge University Press, 2011), 2; Jason Mazzone, "The Creation of a Constitutional Culture," *Tulsa Law Review* 40 (2005): 671–672; Hans Vorländer, "What Is a Constitutional Culture?," in *Constitutional Cultures: On the Concept and Representation of Constitutions in the Atlantic World*, ed. Silke Hensel, Ulrike Bock, Katrin Dircksen, and Hans-Ulirhc Thamer (Cambridge: Cambridge Scholars Publishing, 2012), 21, 27; Manuel Aragón, "La constitución como paradigma," in *Teoría de la Constitución. Ensayos Escogidos*, ed. Miguel Carbonell (Mexico City: Porrúa, 2000), 118.

According to the classic Tylorian definition, culture is "that complex whole which includes knowledge, belief, arts, morals, law, custom and any other capabilities and habits acquired by man as a member a society."[11] In this way, culture includes knowledge, customs, and acquired habits. As we will explain, constitutional culture is a process of learning, understanding, and interpreting the constitution, with the goal of forming a habit and custom of limiting the power of the state by political participation.

This chapter is divided into four parts. In the first part, we reflect on the goals of shaping a constitutional culture. In the second part, we develop a narrative of what the Constitution tells us about the culture of Mexican political elites. It is necessary to understand Mexican political elites' culture and how they use the Constitution to figure out how to hinder popular constitutional culture. As we have said, throughout Mexico's independent history political elites have been worried about having a written constitution, while the majority of people know nothing about it. Moreover, we explain the last threat to constitutional culture. In the third part, we defend popular participation in constitutional amendment procedures and popular interpretation of the Constitution in the public sphere as necessary means to shape a constitutional culture. Finally, we reflect on the lessons we can learn from the new Latin-American constitutionalism that incorporates mechanisms of political participation at the heart of the institutional political system.

In this sense, constitutional culture is necessarily linked with popular political participation. Constitutions of democratic states are instruments for democracy in which government requires the consent of the people. Further, as Tocqueville says, participation is the means by which citizens learn their laws and rules of administration, which are their rights and means to protect them, and shape their habits and customs.[12] In other words, we learn and understand our Constitution through communication and social interaction.[13]

Finally, we have to keep in mind that shaping a constitutional culture is an open and incomplete dialectical process, with a strong tendency to preserve the status quo. Everywhere, citizens' conformity is promoted[14] and change is constrained by previous understandings.[15] And, these processes are necessarily related to a particular context.[16] In this sense, what we would say is closely connected with the Mexican context. Yet, though Mexico is not completely comparable to other countries, we hope our discussion will be valuable for readers elsewhere.

---

[11] Edward Burnett Tylor, *Primitive Culture* (London: Bradbury, Evans, and Co., 1871), 1.

[12] Alexis de Tocqueville, *Democracy in America* (Indianapolis, IN: Liberty Fund, 1835), 448–449.

[13] J.M. Balkin, *Cultural Software: A Theory of Ideology* (New Haven, CT: Yale University Press, 1998), 5, 14.

[14] Anthony G. Amsterdam and Jerome Brune, *Minding the Law* (Cambridge, MA: Harvard University Press, 2002), 231–233.

[15] See Balkin, *Cultural Software*, 41.

[16] See Müller, *Constitutional Patriotism*, 59. See Ferejohn, Rakove, and Riley, "Editors' Introduction," 10.

Constitutional Culture

Relations between culture and the constitution can be studied from different perspectives. Culture may be the object of regulation of a constitution, what some call cultural constitutional law.[17] For example, article 2 of the Mexican Constitution points to culture as one of the criteria to identify Indigenous peoples, and article 4 grants all persons the right to culture.

A constitution may be regarded as a cultural product, which means that it is an expression of a culture.[18] However, in plural societies there is more than one culture, so the constitution reflects the culture of several elites, different groups of civil society, communities, and more.[19] Moreover, a constitution may work as a limit on cultural values[20] and help shape a constitutional culture, furthering mentalities according to its values.[21] Finally, a constitution may be the object for a constitutional culture.

As a normative ideal, the object of a constitutional culture is the values, structures, and procedures established in the constitution. Even though we can distinguish groups of subcultures of citizens, of professionals and of authorities,[22] in a democracy, constitutional culture is citizens' culture.

Among the theorists that consider the constitution the object of constitutional culture, we may distinguish those interested in the opinions, perceptions, or attitudes of the people toward the content or the function of the constitution[23] from those that define it as the *dialectic* between "extrajudicial beliefs about the substance of the constitution" and the judiciary,[24] or "the understandings of role and practices of argument that guide *interactions* among citizens and officials in matters concerning the constitution's meaning."[25]

---

[17] Miguel Ángel Herrera, "Consideraciones sobre constitución y cultura," in *Derecho Constitucional y Cultura*, ed. Francisco Balaguer Callejón (Madrid: Tecnos, 2004), 121.

[18] Herrera, "Consideraciones," 124; Peter Häberle, "La Constitución como cultura," *Anuario Iberoamericano de Justicia Constitucional* 6 (2002): 178, 194; Roger Cotterrell, *The Sociology of Law: An Introduction* (New York: Oxford University Press, 1984), 24.

[19] Cotterrell, *Sociology of Law*, 23; Rainer Arnold, "La contribución de los países de Europa Central y Oriental al desarrollo de una cultura constitucional europea," in *Derecho Constitucional y Cultura*, ed. Francisco Balaguer Callejón (Madrid: Tecnos, 2004), 58.

[20] Modesto Saavedra López, "La constitución como objeto y como límite de la cultura," in *Derecho Constitucional y Cultura*, ed. Francisco Balaguer Callejón (Madrid: Tecnos, 2004), 151.

[21] Juan Fernando López, "Cultura y Derecho. Las dimensiones constitucionalmente relevantes de la cultura," in *Derecho Constitucional y Cultura*, ed. Francisco Balaguer Callejón (Madrid: Tecnos, 2004), 215; see Herrera, "Consideraciones," 125.

[22] Gabriel A. Almond and Sidney Verba, *The Civic Culture: Political Attitudes and Democracy in Five Nations* (Thousand Oaks, CA: Sage, 1989), 26; Ferejohn, Rakove, and Riley, "Editors' Introduction," 10.

[23] See Fierro, Flores, and Valadés, *Los mexicanos y su Constitución*, 17, 18.

[24] Robert C. Post, "Foreword: Fashioning the Legal Constitution: Culture, Courts, and Law," *Harvard Law Review* 117 (2003): 4, 8.

[25] Reva Siegel, "Constitutional Culture, Social Movement Conflict and Constitutional Change: The Case of the de facto ERA," *California Law Review* 94 (2006): 1323, 1325; Reva Siegel, "Community in Conflict: Same-Sex Marriage and Backlash," *UCLA Law Review* 64 (2017): 5–7.

Moreover, constitutional culture is a process of learning, understanding, and interpreting. Learning about, understanding, and interpreting the constitution are important but difficult tasks. They are important because only when we know, understand and interpret the constitution may we rationally evaluate attitudes such as attachment,[26] apathy, or alienation toward it. Furthermore, if we know and understand the constitution we can use its processes and structures for our political struggles. It is a difficult task because our Constitution is opaque, very long, and disorganized. However, learning, understanding, and interpreting it is one of the best resources to change its encryption. In fact, to refuse to learn and understand it means we leave it in the hands of experts.[27]

There is a different perspective on constitutional culture, according to which its object is the ideology of constitutionalism.[28] In accordance with a democratic conception, constitutionalism means limiting the power of the state and empowering those who would otherwise be powerless.[29] Furthermore, it is an ideology that helps us critique the status quo and present a transformative proposal.[30] Accordingly, constitutional culture looks for citizens' internalization of constitutionalism.[31]

Why Constitutional Culture Matters

Shaping a constitutional culture is not just a heuristic goal, but also a means to empower citizens, a tool of action.[32] To know, understand, and interpret the constitution allows citizens to use human rights and constitutional processes for their political and social struggles. Only by learning, understanding, and interpreting them can citizens use constitutional processes and structures. At the same time, participation generates new understandings and ways of thinking about the constitution. Through communication, citizens produce and spread culture that influences public officials.[33]

In other words, shaping a constitutional culture through popular participation is an activity oriented to democratize power. To think about constitutional culture is to

---

[26] In our opinion, a constitutional culture does not seek an alliance to the constitution or to constitutionalism. If we speak of alliance, then we should talk about constitutional patriotism, see Müller, *Constitutional Patriotism*.

[27] Gabriel Méndez Hincapíe and Ricardo Sanín Restrepo, "La constitución encriptada. Nuevas formas de emancipación del poder global," *Revista de Derechos Humanos y Estudios Sociales* 8 (2012): 113.

[28] See Ferejohn, Rakove, and Riley, "Editors' Introduction," 2, 4.

[29] Jeremy Waldron, "Constitutionalism: A Skeptical View," *NYU School of Law, Public Law Research Paper*, No. 10-87 (2012): 12–16, 25.

[30] Carlos de Cabo Martín, "El elemento utópico, ingrediente cultural del constitucionalismo," in *Derecho Constitucional y Cultura*, ed. Francisco Balaguer Callejón (Madrid: Tecnos, 2004), 55.

[31] See Arnold, "La contribución de los países," 59.

[32] See Balkin, *Cultural Software*, 16.

[33] Ibid., 270, 280–281. See Post, "Fashioning the Legal Constitution," 8.

think how to empower the people against the government. In an authoritarian constitutionalism regime, public officials prefer to keep people ignorant about constitutional processes and structures, so they can use the constitution according to their wishes and convenience.

Moreover, constitutional culture prepares citizens to question the political function that a constitution fulfills in a particular context.[34] That is, constitutional culture is a citizens' tool to criticize and reflect about the defects, lack of efficacy, or fraudulent application of the constitution, such as when a liberal democratic constitution is used as a façade of democracy just to legitimize or stabilize an authoritarian regime. In this sense, constitutional culture develops a critical approach of self-reflection and self-discovery.[35]

Furthermore, constitutional culture has the goal of forming a popular habit and custom of demanding justification of governmental acts by political participation.[36] This is the process of internalizing the ideology of constitutionalism. However, the important question is how to internalize the ideology of constitutionalism. This question is very relevant to Mexico, in which constitutionalism has been considered an issue for lawyers with focus on the higher/lower-level distinction,[37] disregarding the idea that a constitution becomes normative only with a specific kind of popular participation that demands justification of officials acts. Only in this way can the people internalize constitutionalism.[38]

In a constitutional culture people live constitutionalism.[39] They are accustomed to limiting the power of the state, and they are empowered by political participation. Peoples' experience of constitutionalism is more important than knowing the content of the constitution.[40] The constitution is a tool to achieve constitutionalism.[41] In this sense, for example, if a liberal democratic type of constitution is used for practical and authoritarian ideological functions, the people should be guided by the idea of constitutionalism to critique authoritarian practices or the constitution itself.

---

[34] Juan Carlos Velasco, "Patriotismo Constitucional y Republicanismo," *Claves de la Razón Práctica* 125 (2002): 33, 34.

[35] See Balkin, *Cultural Software*, 130.

[36] See Juan Carlos Velasco, "La fuerza pública de la razón. El papel de la deliberación en los procesos democráticos," in *Filosofía Política: entre la religión y la democracia*, ed. Guillermo Hoyos y Eduardo A. Rueda (Bogotá: Pontificia Universidad Javeriana, 2011), 78.

[37] José Ramón Cossío, *Dogmática Constitucional y Régimen Autoritario* (Mexico City: Fontamara, 2000); Alejandro Madrazo, "Estado de Derecho y Cultura Jurídica en México," *Isonomía* 17 (2002): 203–223.

[38] Jürgen Habermas, *Facticidad y validez: Sobre el derecho y el Estado democrático en términos de teoría del discurso* (Madrid: Trotta, 2000), 466.

[39] See Häberle, "La Constitución como cultura," 198; Akhil Reed Amar, "Popular Sovereignty and Constitutional Amendment," in *Responding to Imperfection: The Theory and Practice of Constitutional Amendment*, ed. Sanford Levinson (Princeton, NJ: Princeton University Press, 1995), 112.

[40] See Mazzone, "The Creation of a Constitutional Culture," 694; Velasco, "Patriotismo Constitucional," 38.

[41] J.M. Balkin, "The Declaration and the Promise of a Democratic Culture," *Widener Law Symposium Journal* 4 (1999): 167, 169.

The daily experience of constitutionalism is not only a commitment to abstract ideas but requires institutions, procedures, and practices.[42] The experience of using these institutions, procedures, and practices shapes a constitutional culture.[43] In this way, a constitutional culture is an ongoing process shaped by political participation and not a one-time decision.[44] It is by political participation that citizens limit the power of the state,[45] and, therefore, become interested and learn about constitutionalism.[46]

The habit and custom of political participation has a specific quality. It is the daily experience of exercising the right to justification,[47] demanding it for any official act. In this sense, a constitutional culture is a kind of a culture of justification: "a culture in which every exercise of power is expected to be justified; in which the leadership given by government rests on the cogency of the case offered in defense of its decisions, not the fear inspired by the force at its command. The new order must be a community built on persuasion, not coercion."[48]

The culture of justification is opposed to a culture of authority. A culture of justification bases legitimacy of law on the quality of reason. Citizens are empowered to demand justification, and public officials are compelled to give reasons for their actions. These actions could be amending the constitution, passing a law, a judge's ruling, or a momentary detention by a public official. However, a culture of justification becomes relevant in the everyday relationship between the administrative branch and citizens. In this sense, a culture of justification demands both, popular participation and public officials' commitment to the rule of law, in accordance with the principles of an internal morality of law. In this sense, they are obliged to support their decisions by legal reasons.[49]

On the contrary, in a culture of authority legitimacy is based on who issues the decision and because of fear of being coerced. In a culture of authority "the legitimacy and legality of governmental action is derived from the fact the actor is authorized to act," while in a

---

[42] See Velasco, "Patriotismo Constitucional," 35; Andrew M. Siegel, "Constitutional Theory, Constitutional Culture," *University of Pennsylvania Journal of Constitutional Law* 18 (2016): 1067, 1122; Kaarlo Tuori, "Democracy, Constitution and Culture," in *Teoría Política II* (Madrid: Marcial Pons, 2012), 223, 229.

[43] Habermas, *Facticidad y validez*, 627, 628.

[44] Ibid., 466; J.M. Balkin, "The Declaration and the Promise," 175; Carole Pateman, "Participation and Democratic Theory," in *The Democracy Sourcebook*, ed. Robert A. Dahl, Ian Shapiro, and José Antonio Cheibub (Cambridge, MA: MIT Press, 2003), 41–43.

[45] Adam Tomkins, *Our Republican Constitution* (Portland, OR: Hart Publishing, 2005), 10.

[46] James S. Fishkin, "The Voice of the People," in *The Democracy Sourcebook*.

[47] Rainer Forst, *The Right to Justification. Elements of a Constructivist Theory of Justice* (New York: Columbia University Press, 2012).

[48] Ettiene Mureinik, "A Bridge to Where? Introducing the Interim Bill of Rights," *South African Journal on Human Rights* 10 (1994): 31, 32.

[49] David Dyzenhaus, *Hard Cases in Wicked Legal Systems* (Oxford: Oxford University Press, 2010), 278–288; David Dyzenhaus, "Proportionality and Deference in a Culture of Justification," in *Proportionality and the Rule of Law*, ed. Grant Huscroft, Bradley W. Miller, and Grégorie Webber (Cambridge: Cambridge University Press, 2014), 234–258.

culture of justification it is not enough. A culture of justification requires rationality and reasonableness.[50]

The Mexican Constitution as the Expression of Political Elites' Culture

We started this essay saying that Mexican constitutional culture is very weak. Instead we find that the Mexican Constitution is an expression of political elites' culture. In this understanding it is possible to get two different impressions. If we look superficially into the content of the Constitution, we can conclude that it is designed for a liberal, social, and democratic culture. It establishes a high number of fundamental rights, including social, economic, and cultural rights, separation of powers and federalism, regulation of electoral processes, representative institutions, and popular participatory mechanisms.[51]

But, if we look at the details of those mechanisms or to the constitutional practice, we get a different picture, not compatible with the first.[52] The main example of the aforementioned is constitutional amendment practice. Amendments are made by federal and state political elites because they have the power to present initiatives, carry out the legislative processes, and vote. Ordinary citizens are not part of the constitutional amendment process established in article 135 of the Constitution and usually do not get involved with them.[53] In its one hundred years, article 135 of the Mexican Constitution has not been amended to include any participatory mechanism,[54] even as the majority ignores how often the Constitution is amended.[55] This fact is striking if we take into account that with more than seven hundred constitutional amendments and its wide scope, the 1917 Constitution is something very different today. The actual amendment practice shows that there is a great distrust of majorities and citizens.[56]

---

[50] Moshe Cohen-Eliya and Iddo Porat, *Proportionality and Constitutional Culture* (Cambridge, Cambridge University Press, 2013) 112, 113.

[51] See Salazar Ugarte, *Democracia y cultura*, 37.

[52] See Almond and Verba, *The Civic Culture*, 33.

[53] Article 135. The present Constitution may be added to or amended, but to become a part of it, such additions or amendments require the approval of the Congress of the Union through the vote of two-thirds of the congressmen present, and the approval, thereafter, of the majority of the state legislatures. The Congress of the Union or the Permanent Commission, as the case may be, shall count the votes of the legislatures and shall make the declaration to announce that the additions or amendments in question have been approved.

[54] A participatory mechanism does not exclude every deliberative filter in a parliamentary procedure; see Sanford Levinson, "Designing an Amendment Process," in *Constitutional Culture and Democratic Rule*, 278.

[55] According to the Third National Poll on Constitutional Culture made by *Universidad Nacional Autónoma de México* (2017), 31.0 percent of the people thinks the constitution is amended rarely, and 23.4 percent with some frequency. See Fierro, Flores, and Valadés, *Los mexicanos y su Constitución*, 54.

[56] Héctor Fix-Fierro, "¿Por qué se reforma tanto la Constitución mexicana de 1917? Hacia la renovación del texto y la cultura de la Constitución," in *Cien Ensayos para el Centenario*, ed. Gerardo Esquivel, Francisco Ibarra Palafox, and Pedro Salazar Ugarte (Mexico City: Instituto Belisario Domínguez del Senado de la República, 2017), 151.

A prominent example of this constitutional practice is the approval of an amendment to the Mexican Constitution regarding private investment in oil and hydrocarbons. A sensitive issue considering article 27 of the Constitution established public ownership of oil and hydrocarbons, and was considered one of the Mexican Revolution greatest achievements. This amendment was negotiated by a small group of congressmen, government leaders, and party leaders outside Congress in what has been called the Pact for Mexico (*Pacto por México*). The *Pacto por México* was a political agenda set by the three major political parties when Enrique Peña Nieto came to office. They put in place a board that negotiated and wrote up the proposed laws. There was no transparency in these discussions; the participants simply submitted the proposal to Congress to be approved.

According to article 135 of the Constitution, the amendment required the approval of a supermajority in both Houses and a majority of state legislatures. Even though this procedure is theoretically rigid, the constitutional amendment was approved by the House of Representatives the next day after receiving it from the Senate, and the state legislatures approved it in just a few days.[57] Moreover, according to the members of the left opposition, there were some irregularities in the committees of the House.[58] And some state legislatures approved the amendment within hours after receiving it without any further proceeding.[59]

After it passed the state legislatures, Congress made a public declaration of its constitutionality. Some days later, the president, congressmen from PRI, and members of the right-wing party defended the constitutional amendment in a big TV presentation, arguing that it would further the development of the country and make electricity and combustibles cheaper. The ruling elite argued that the amendment was inevitable under current conditions and highlighted that the amendment respected all the rules established by the Constitution, so it was constitutional.

Another example of this constitutional practice is the incorporation of the right to public consultation and the right to run as an independent candidate. In the case of public consultation, the amendment established several restrictions that severely limited the importance of public consultations. Article 35 of the Constitution requires public consultation to be requested by at least 2 percent of the citizens, but limits the object of the consultation in the following way: public consultation cannot deal with limiting human

---

[57] Animal Político Editorial Staff, "Reforma energética rompe récord en tiempo de aprobación constitucional," *Animal Político*, December 16, 2013, http://www.animalpolitico.com/2013/12/en-83-horasla-reforma-energetica-es-constitucional-17-congresos-la-avalan/#axzz2r5KR9aMK.

[58] Radio Fórmula Editorial Staff, "Violaciones a reglamento sustenta amparo reforma energética: PRD," *Noticias Radio Fórmula*, January 8, 2014, http://www.radioformula.com.mx/notas.asp?Idn=381947.

[59] It is worth noting that this fast-track processing of constitutional amendments has become a trait of the current government; see CNN México Editorial Staff, "La reforma energética avanza en los Congresos estatales," *CNN México*, December 13, 2013, http://mexico.cnn.com/nacional/2013/12/13/reforma-energetica-aprobacion-congresos-estatales; La Jornada Editorial Staff, "Entre protestas, seis congresos estatales refrendaron la reforma energética," *La Jornada*, December 14, 2013, http://www.jornada.unam.mx/2013/12/14/politica/009n1pol.

rights, the principles of article 40, electoral procedures, revenues and expenditures, and national security and the armed forces. The Supreme Court is in charge of reviewing the constitutionality of the consultation beforehand. Because these excluded topics are related to almost every public policy, there has not been a single consultation considered constitutional. The most striking consultation denial was the one massively required after the approval of the aforementioned amendment establishing private investment in oil and hydrocarbons. In the case of the right to run as an independent candidate, article 116 delegates regulation of independent candidates to state legislatures that have, in practice, narrowly restricted them.

A third, and more recent, example is the creation of a national anticorruption system in 2015. The system was introduced by a constitutional amendment some months after the widely publicized corruption scandal of President Peña Nieto. A prominent journalist published a detailed report of the very expensive "white house" of the president built by one of the main construction companies hired by the government.[60] Even though civil society pushed for this constitutional amendment, the timing of its approval was no coincidence. The political purpose of the publication was clear in the transitional articles. These articles established that the amendment would be in force 180 days after its publication, once the laws are passed. In other words, the constitutional amendment was an immediate response to the crisis derived from the scandal, without any real intention to implement it. The anticorruption public prosecutor has not yet been appointed. Moreover, the journalist who published the report was fired some months after the publication with no reason.

Also independent institutions such as the Electoral Court are being attacked. The last electoral judges' designation was full of constitutional challenges. Once the Supreme Court and the Senate made the appointments fulfilling a constitutional process, Congress amended the legal provision that established a judge's tenure by granting the judges a longer term in office. This change was seen as a threat to their judicial independence. The case arrived to the Supreme Court alleging a violation to judges' independence, and the Court in a 6-to-5 ruling declared the provision constitutional.

In our opinion, the normative and practical exclusion of citizens from the amendment procedure shows the distrust that political elites have of the people,[61] and the lack of interest in making the Constitution known to them. What matters to political elites is the Constitution being effective for *their* purposes,[62] making people into objects of control or governance.[63] In other words, the continuous amendments to the Mexican Constitution

---

[60] Aristegui Noticias Editorial Staff, "La casa blanca de Enrique Peña Nieto (investigación especial)," *Aristegui Noticias*, November 9, 2014, http://aristeguinoticias.com/0911/mexico/la-casa-blanca-de-enrique-pena-nieto/.

[61] See Levinson, "Designing an Amendment Process," 276.

[62] Robert M. Cover, "Foreword: Nomos and Narrative," *Harvard Law Review* 97 (1983): 4, 12–17.

[63] See Balkin, *Cultural Software*, 27.

exemplify that constitutional rigidity, in this case, is not a mechanism to limit the power of partisan majorities, but an obstacle for people to know the Constitution. Additionally, the multiplicity of amendments and their fast approval forbid robust social deliberation about their necessity and merits, and in that way, they hinder constitutional culture.[64] Furthermore, the lack of formal and informal popular participation indicates that this process is not a democratic mechanism.[65]

Finally, we should note the wide scope and excessive details established in the Constitution,[66] its lack of systematization, and some contradictory rules.[67] The Mexican Constitution regulates a huge number of institutions: for example, judicial review processes, autonomous municipalities, electoral regime, indigenous rights, agrarian rights, transparency regime, budget and accountability institutions, relations between the state and church, judicial careers, ombudsperson, oil and hydrocarbon production, and many more. These features make the Constitution an opaque text very difficult for the average Mexican to understand.

In fact, one of the duties of the Supreme Court is to systematize the Constitution by interpreting it. Sometimes this task is very difficult because some amendments that are already part of the Constitution have not come into force according to the transitory articles. For example, the penal reform of 2008 required an eight-year period before coming into force. However, all rights and duties are already in the text. Moreover, the delay of the coming into force of constitutional amendments has become a common practice. In this way, the Mexican Constitution is an encrypted text for a few experts in constitutional law, who have an unjustified power over other people.[68] In a few words, the Mexican Constitution and the practice of amending it has been used by Mexican political elites to hinder popular constitutional culture.

The Last Threat to Constitutional Culture

Unfortunately, after one hundred years of the Mexican Constitution, we still live between a culture of authority and a culture of authoritarianism. Nowadays, in most Mexican

---

[64] See Ana Micaela Alterio, "La relación entre rigidez y supremacía constitucional. Un análisis a la luz de las reformas constitucionales en México," *Revista del Centro de Estudios Constitucionales* 4 (2017): 209–231.

[65] Xenophon Contiades and Alkmene Fotiadou, "Models of Constitutional Change," in *Engineering Constitutional Change: A Comparative Perspective on Europe, Canada and the USA*, ed. Xenophon Contiades (New York: Routledge, 2013), 432–433.

[66] See Tom Ginsburg, "Constitutional Specificity, Unwritten Understandings and Constitutional Agreement," *Public Law and Legal Theory Working Papers*, No. 330, (2010): 69, 77, http://chicagounbound.uchicago.edu/cgi/viewcontent.cgi?article=1074&context=public_law_and_legal_theory.

[67] For example, article 73, XXI, a) and article 116, IV, o) of the Constitution grant to federal and state officials, at the same time, the power to establish electoral crimes.

[68] Carlos María Cárcova, *La opacidad del derecho* (Madrid: Trotta, 2006), 160.

cities it is common to have a high number of military "enforcing" the law. This, against articles 21 and 129 of the Constitution—while at the same time, police officers commonly torture many of those arrested in a context of general impunity.[69] For most Mexican citizens, law is imposed by force, and many times entails violating their fundamental rights, the latter a clear case of a culture of authoritarianism.[70]

In fact, the last threat for a constitutional culture, which may be the starting point of the consolidation of an authoritarian order, is the recently approved Law of Internal Security in December of 2017. This law completely militarizes the public safety in Mexico. It authorizes the executive branch to use the military as a regular force for public safety instead of the police—this, after ten years of a "war on drugs" that left thousands of people killed and missing.[71] As it is well known, the Mexican police are poorly equipped and not well-trained. They have been accused of massive violations on human rights, and many authors consider them part of the highly-corrupted system. In this sense, the police are incompetent to deal with regular security, and even less capable of dealing with the drug cartels emergency.

As a response to the security crisis in 2006, President Felipe Calderon, using a Supreme Court ruling of 1996 as the legal source, issued an administrative order to use the armed forces as law enforcement forces. Since then, military corps began to substitute police officers as the regular law enforcement officers. In 2010, President Calderon urged passage of a law regulating the military corps as a public safety institution. Even without such law, during 2016, there were 3,386 soldiers in the streets taking care permanently of the public safety.[72]

The constitutional debate regarding the possibility of using the armed forces as public safety forces began with the popular movement "Movimiento por la paz con Justicia y Dignidad." According to this social movement, articles 21 and 129 of the Mexican Constitution prohibit armed forces to substitute for the police. Article 21 establishes that public safety is a civil duty, and article 129 establishes that armed forces in times of peace should be limited to disciplinary duties. In fact, the original understanding of article 129 indicates it intended to allow the use of armed forces

---

[69] See J.A. Le Clercq Ortega and Gerardo Rodríguez Sánchez. (coord.), "IGI Índice global de impunidad 2017. Dimensiones de la Impunidad Global," *Centro de Estudios sobre impunidad y justicia (CESIJ), Universidad de las Américas Puebla y UDLAP Jenkins Graduate School,* http://www.udlap.mx/cesij/files/IGI-2017.pdf (last accessed May 15, 2018).

[70] See Cohen-Eliya and Porat, *Proportionality and Constitutional Culture,* 112.

[71] See "Situación de Derechos Humanos en México," Comisión Interamericana de Derechos Humanos, OEA, Doc 44/15, December 31, 2015. See also Centro PRODH: Centro de derechos humanos Miguel Agustín Pro Juárez A.C., *Perpetuar el modelo fallido de seguridad. La ley de seguridad interior y el legado de una década de políticas de seguridad en México contrarias a los derechos humanos* (Mexico City: Centro Prodh, 2017), http://www.centroprodh.org.mx/index.php?option=com_docman&task=doc_details&gid=226&Itemid=28&lang=es.

[72] "Situación de Derechos Humanos en México": Ibid.

only under very limited circumstances. However, the Supreme Court ruling of 1996 interpreted article 129 to allow armed forces to help civil authorities if requested by the latter.

As many NGOs documented during these years, the army is not prepared to justify its actions, as a well-trained police should do. So, after ten years of the armed forces being accused of human rights violations, in 2017 the secretary of defense publicly declared that if there is no law that protects them the army will go back to their barracks. After several protest and public declarations against the law by the UN High Commissioner for Human Rights, the ombudsperson, and human rights advocates, in December 2017 Congress approved the law. Two days after its approval, the secretary of defense thanked Congress for passing the law and said he will respect the final decision of the Supreme Court on its constitutionality.

Several NGOs, constitutional scholars, and civil society argued against the law, focusing on articles 21 and 129, which, as we already mentioned, establish that public safety is a duty of civilians.[73] In this public discussion, articles 21 and 129 are interpreted as a prohibition of militarizing public safety. There is no doubt this is one of the purposes of these articles. However, they have another unnoticed feature. The Constitution puts civilians in charge of public safety duties because it is the bridge for a culture of justification as opposed to a culture of authority. In this sense, the discussion about the constitutionality of the Law of Internal Security begs the question of what type of culture we want to pursue. It is not just an interpretative discussion about articles 21 and 129; it is a discussion about the culture we want for our country.

We want to clarify we are not arguing in favor of leaving the police in charge of public safety with no change in their practices and structures. Of course, the Mexican police has failed to prevent and persecute crimes effectively while respecting human rights. They urgently need a profound reform. However, at this critical moment in Mexico, after ten years of a failed strategy that involved thousands of people killed and missing, we are deciding which path we want to pursue: a culture of authority and probably authoritarian, or a change to a culture of justification. For sure, the latter will take time, money, and great effort to reform the police. However, we already have let ten years pass, and the former has been a complete failure. Moreover, the Law of Internal Security poses a real threat to political participation necessary to shape a constitutional culture. The presence of military forces in the street is a way of intimidation that hinders public protest. In short, it is an effective mechanism to dissuade political participation.[74]

---

[73] See a complete report at www.seguridadsinguerra.org.

[74] "We still miss 43" is one of the social mobilizations' slogans regarding forty-three students that disappeared during a protest, presumably taken by the army.

Amendment Procedure, Popular Interpretation, and Constitutional Culture

In shaping a constitutional culture, educational institutions have an important role.[75] As we know, education and schools are one of the main means to spread an ideology and democratic culture.[76] But the most effective means for shaping a constitutional culture is popular participation through institutions and in the public sphere.

One of these fundamental mechanisms to shape a constitutional culture is deliberative participation in constitutional amendment procedures,[77] such as open meetings, participatory forums, public hearings, popular initiatives, referenda,[78] or deliberative polling.[79] Participatory constitutional amendments would allow the citizenry to learn and understand the content of the Constitution, and it is a way of interaction between public opinion and institutions.[80] Participatory constitutional amendments have similar qualities to the ones Tocqueville found in juries as a republican institution that "places the real direction of society in the hands of the governed or of a portion of them, and not in the hands of those governing."[81] For Tocqueville, a jury had the following qualities: it serves to give the mind of all citizens a part of the habits of mind of the judge. It spreads in all classes respect for the thing judged and for the idea of right, teaches men the practice of equity and not to retreat from a responsibility for their own actions, and makes citizens feel they have duties to fulfill toward society and that they belong in their government. It serves to form the judgment and to augment the natural enlightenment of the people. It is a free school, where each juror comes to be instructed about his rights and enters into daily communication.[82] In our opinion, participatory constitutional amendments could turn into a free school if they were designed correctly.

Education through participation needs deliberation.[83] Deliberation can be achieved by different institutional mechanisms, such as two votes with time between them for

---

[75] See Häberle, "La Constitución como cultura," 198; see also Cover, "Nomos and Narrative," 66; Jack Crittenden and Peter Levine, "Civic Education," in *The Stanford Encyclopedia of Philosophy,* ed. Edward N. Zalta (Winter 2016 Edition), https://plato.stanford.edu/archives/win2016/entries/civic-education/.

[76] Hugh Collins, *Marxism and Law* (New York: Oxford University Press, 1982), 50; Axel Honneth, "La educación y el espacio público democrático. Un capítulo descuidado en la Filosofía Política," *Isegoría* 49 (2013): 377–395.

[77] Siegel, "Constitutional Culture, Social Movement Conflict," 1339.

[78] Gabriel Negretto, "Constitution-Making in Comparative Perspective," *Oxford Research Encyclopedia of Politics* (July 2017): 17–19.

[79] James Fishkin and Gombojav Zandanshatar, "Deliberative Polling for Constitutional Change in Mongolia: An Unprecedented Experiment," *Constitution Net,* September 20, 2017, http://www.constitutionnet.org/news/deliberative-polling-constitutional-change-mongolia-unprecedented-experiment.

[80] See Habermas, *Facticidad y validez,* 374, 375; Pateman, "Participation and Democratic Theory," 46.

[81] See Tocqueville, *Democracy in America,* 445.

[82] Ibid., 448, 449; Alexandra D. Lahav, "The Jury and Participatory Democracy," *William and Mary Law Review* 55 (2014): 1036–1038.

[83] The Ireland constitutional convention in 2012–2014 is a good example. See David M. Farrel, Clodagh Harris, and Jane Suiter, "Bringing People into the Heart of Constitutional Design: The Irish Constitutional

deliberation, or the requirement of electing a new decision-maker to approve the amend-ment.[84] The idea is to incorporate popular participation provided with information and time to deliberate.[85] In comparative constitutional law there are very useful examples of how to design a participative and deliberative mechanism. For example, design of referendums need to avoid an elite's manipulation and write the question precisely. To incentivize mobilization, it is necessary to avoid a high percentage for approval, and there should be enough time to deliberate.[86]

Beyond participation in constitutional amendment procedures, Mexico needs a new narrative that supports popular interpretation of the Constitution in the public sphere.[87] In Mexico popular interpretation of the Constitution has been disregarded or openly opposed. There is the idea that the Constitution is a body of laws interpretable only by experts and from which citizens are excluded. In shaping this belief legal academia has played an important role. In our tradition, there are two influential strands regarding popular interpretation of the Constitution. Some theorists are indifferent to popular interpretation of the Constitution while others are opposed to it. In fact, it is very difficult to find any defense of popular constitutionalism by Mexican scholars. In the last years, we have argued in favor of popular constitutionalism.[88] However, our constitutional law discussions are mostly court-centered.

Popular interpretation of the Constitution is an open and incomplete process that requires active participation of the citizens. Conflict and disagreement about its content and function is foreseeable,[89] but conflict and disagreement generate deliberation, social mobilization, and the creation of civil associations.

Convention for 2012–14," in *Participatory Constitutional Change: The People as Amenders of the Constitution*, ed. Xenophon Contiades and Alkmene Fotiadou (New York: Routledge, 2017), 131.

[84] Amar, "Popular Sovereignty and Constitutional Amendment," 111; Francisco J. Laporta, *El imperio de la ley. Una visión actual* (Lugar: Trotta, 2007), 225; Xenophon Contiades and Alkmene Fotiadou, eds., "The People as Amenders of the Constitution," in *Participatory Constitutional Change, The People as Amenders of the Constitution*, ed. Xenophon Contiades and Alkmene Fotiadou (New York: Routledge, 2017), 14.

[85] Contiades and Fotiadou, "The People as Amenders of the Constitution," 19; Alterio, "La relación entre rigidez y supremacía constitucional."

[86] Contiades and Fotiadou, "The People as Amenders of the Constitution," 16, 25, 26. On Greece experience, see Alkmene Fotiadou, "The Role of the People in Constitutional Amendment in Greece: Between Narratives and Practice," in *Participatory Constitutional Change, The People as Amenders of the Constitution*, ed. Xenophon Contiades and Alkmene Fotiadou (New York: Routledge, 2017), 131.

[87] As Contiades and Fotiadou explain, to understand models of constitutional change we need to understand correlations between the amending process, political system, constitutional ethos, and legal culture, see Xenophon Contiades and Alkmene Fotiadou, "Models of Constitutional Change," in *Engineering Constitutional Change, A Comparative Perspective on Europe, Canada and the USA*, ed. Xenophon Contiades (New York: Routledge, 2013), 441.

[88] Ana Micaela Alterio and Roberto Niembro Ortega, *Constitucionalismo popular en Latinoamérica* (Mexico City: Porrúa, 2013); Roberto Niembro, "Una mirada al constitucionalismo popular," *Isonomía* 38 (2013): 191–224.

[89] Ferejohn, Rakove, and Riley, "Editors' Introduction," 14. Siegel, "Constitutional Culture, Social Movement Conflict," 1329.

Through deliberation, it is possible to learn and understand a constitution with ambiguous and vague terms, as well as the structures and processes it establishes. In fact, constitutional clauses do not have only one meaning, and they relate in complex ways. In other words, learning and understanding the constitution is done by a reflective process of deliberation.[90] Through deliberation, we learn the origin of constitutional clauses, possible interpretations, how they relate to each other, and what purposes they are established for. In our opinion, before any processes of deliberation, not even the best constitutional law professor could say she found the right answer. It is by a deliberative process that the interpreter gathers information, classifies it, and elaborates on it; for example, we learn how it is applied in specific cases and what the public opinion is.[91] Moreover, through deliberation the people help establish what the constitution means,[92] accomplishing a rational, and not only emotional, respect for the constitution. In democracy, the constitution motivates us because it is ours, interpreted through a rational debate.[93]

This does not mean constitutional interpretation is limited to the constitutional text.[94] The language of the constitution is a point of departure that in some degree constrains constitutional debates, but it is not an unchangeable text, and its interpretation is disputable.[95] In this way, popular interpretation of the constitution goes beyond the constitutional text. Otherwise, political struggles are formalized and reduced to the terms established by legal experts.[96] If this were to be the case, power would remain on the ones who participate in constitutional amendment procedures and with the judicial branch being the only authority to establish and interpret the constitution.[97]

We want to stress the importance of the complementarity between participatory constitutional amendments and participation in the public sphere at shaping public opinion. Shaping a constitutional culture requires both. On the one hand, even in countries such as Mexico with a high rate of constitutional amendments, habits of discussing and interpreting the constitution are acquired by daily participation. Only a constant communication and participation can foster a constitutional culture.[98] On the other hand, participation in the public sphere is not enough, if there are no institutional mechanisms that oblige public officials to dialogue with the people[99] and that guarantee safe

---

[90] Habermas, *Facticidad y validez*, 399.

[91] Bernard Manin, "On Legitimacy and Political Deliberation," *Political Theory* 15, no. 3 (August 1987): 349–350; Habermas, *Facticidad y validez*, 372, 420.

[92] Siegel, "Constitutional Culture, Social Movement Conflict," 1341.

[93] J.M. Balkin, "The Declaration and the Promise of a Constitutional Culture," 167, 179.

[94] Ferejohn, Rakove, and Riley, "Editors' Introduction," 8, 9, 24.

[95] Müller, *Constitutional Patriotism*, 57.

[96] Jeremy Waldron, "A Right-Based Critique of Constitutional Rights," *Oxford Journal of Legal Studies* 13 (1993): 18, 26–27.

[97] See Méndez Hincapíe and Sanín Restrepo, "La constitución encriptada," 110, 111.

[98] Balkin, *Cultural Software*, 90.

[99] *See* Robert Post, *Citizens Divided* (Cambridge, MA: Harvard University Press, 2014), 34–36.

conditions of participation. The existence of institutional mechanisms allows people to forge constitutional interpretation, and empowers citizens to have an impact on the final decision, promoting the belief that they should participate in constitutional amendments and in the public sphere.

Lessons from Latin-American Constitutionalism

We have argued for deliberative participation as a necessary means to shape a constitutional culture. We conclude by reflecting on what lessons we can learn from the new Latin-American constitutionalism (NLC), which incorporates mechanisms of political participation at the heart of the institutional political system.[100] The NLC is an example of both reaction and response to deep constitutional and democratic crises. Facing exclusive and illegitimate political systems, the constitutional processes of Venezuela (1999), Ecuador (2008), and Bolivia (2009)[101] were enacted with the stated purpose of solving the political and social marginalization of certain groups (especially Indigenous people groups[102]), as well as social inequality resulting from the application of neoliberal policies, particularly during the 1980s and 1990s.[103] Likewise, their purpose was to overcome the concept of a constitution as power limiting and to conceive it as a democratic formula where the constituent power expresses its will.[104]

As for its constitutional model, we can point to some commonalities, especially because they all are based on the idea of citizen participation, which is the heart of their institutional political system. Participation goes far beyond the constituent act or the election of representatives, since it perpetuates along the constitutional texts in areas such as the popular, legislative, and constitutional initiatives or the approving, consultative, recall,

[100] See Francisco Palacios Romeo, "La reivindicación de la polis: crisis de la representación y nuevas estructuras constitucionales de deliberación y participación en Latinoamérica," in *Materiales sobre neoconstitucionalismo y nuevo constitucionalismo latinoamericano*, ed. Claudia Storini and José Francisco Alenza García (Navarra, Spain: Thomson Reuters Aranzadi, 2012), 147, 177.

[101] We will refer to these constitutions as part of the NLC as long as their creation processes have been described as "ground-breaking," "transformative," or "re-foundational." See Roberto Viciano Pastor and Rubén Martínez Dalmau, "Fundamento teórico del nuevo constitucionalismo latinoamericano," in *Estudios sobre el nuevo Constitucionalismo Latinoamericano*, ed. Roberto Viciano Pastor (Valencia: Tirant lo Blanch, 2012), 11, 30; Boaventura de Sousa Santos, *Refundación del Estado en América Latina. Perspectivas desde una epistemología del Sur* (Lima: Siglo del Hombre Editores, 2010), 85.

[102] Roberto Gargarella and Christian Courtis, *El nuevo constitucionalismo latinoamericano: promesas e interrogantes* (Santiago: United Nations ECLAC, 2009), http://www.palermo.edu/Archivos_content/derecho/pdf/Constitucionalismo_atinoamericano.pdf.

[103] Viciano Pastor and Martínez Dalmau, "Fundamento teórico del nuevo constitucionalismo latinoamericano," 21–22.

[104] Ibid., 15.

and abrogative referendums.[105] It is also reflected in public administration citizen control mechanisms[106] and in the recognition of forms of communitarian democracy developed by Indigenous peoples.[107] Finally, it is not limited to formal institutions, but also arises from provision of informal participation mechanisms such as the right of resistance.[108] In short, we find in the NLC an express willingness to "transcend elite constitutionalism towards a popular constitutionalism."[109]

However, other views of the same constitutions cast doubt on the effectiveness of the one stated above. Some scholars emphasize that it is difficult to expect development of wide citizen participation with an organization of power that is politically concentrated and territorially centralized.[110] These remarks, plus the political practice that has developed in these countries in recent years, are what have led scholars to describe Venezuela, Ecuador, and Bolivia as cases of populism in a context of lack of constitutional culture.[111]

Thus, the instrumental use of legislation, the concentration of power in the executive, the destruction of institutions that generated some control, and the restrictions on certain fundamental freedoms (in particular freedom of speech)[112] have forced even the original advocates of the model to become critics.[113] In the cases of Venezuela and Ecuador,

---

[105] For example, art. 70 of the Venezuelan Constitution. In Ecuador, articles 103–113; Article 11 of Bolivian Constitution; see Gerardo Pisarello, "El nuevo constitucionalismo latinoamericano y la constitución venezolana de 1999: balance de una década," *Sin Permiso* 1 (November 2009): 10.

[106] Like the creation of the "Citizen Power" in the constitution of Venezuela (Title V, Chapter IV), the "Power of Transparency and Social Control" in the 2008 Ecuadorian (Fifth Chapter, Title IV), and the function of "Participation and social control" in the 2009 Bolivian (articles 241 and 242). Only the last one is outside the institutions of the state and recognized as a communitarian and circumstantial organization of the people. See Albert Noguera Fernández, *El Sujeto Constituyente. Entre Lo Viejo y Lo Nuevo* (Madrid: Trotta, 2017) 144–145.

[107] See Rodrigo Uprimny, "The Recent Transformation of Constitutional Law in Latin America: Trends and Challenges," *Texas Law Review* 89 (2011): 1595; see also Sousa Santos, *Refundación del Estado en América Latina*, 118–122, in what is referred as intercultural democracy.

[108] Considered expressly in article 98 of the Ecuadorian constitution.

[109] Viciano Pastor and Martínez Dalmau, "Fundamento teórico del nuevo constitucionalismo latinoamericano," 42; *as expressed by* Detlef Nolte and Almut Schilling-Vacaflor, eds., "Introduction: The Times They Are a Changin': Constitutional Transformations in Latin America since the 1990s," in *New Constitutionalism in Latin America. Promises and Practices* (London: Ashgate Publishing, 2012), 3, 19: "the adoption of the new constitutions was part of bottom-up process, including legal mobilization, and was among the central demands of social movements and citizens that were discontent with the previous social and political order."

[110] See Roberto Gargarella, *Latin American Constitutionalism 1810–2010. The Engine Room of the Constitution* (New York: Oxford University Press, 2013), 172–177.

[111] See Ana Micaela Alterio, "El constitucionalismo popular y el populismo constitucional como categorías constitucionales," in *Constitucionalismo Progresista: Retos y Perspectivas. Un homenaje a Mark Tushnet*, coords. Roberto Gargarella and Roberto Niembro Ortega (Mexico City: IIJ-UNAM, 2016).

[112] Carlos de la Torre and Cynthia J. Arnson, eds., "Introduction: The Evolution of Latin American Populism and the Debates over Its Meaning," in *Latin American Populism in the Twenty-First Century* (Washington, DC: Woodrow Wilson Center Press/Johns Hopkins University Press, 2013), 1, 4.

[113] See César Rodriguez-Garavito, "Los derechos humanos y la 'nueva' izquierda latinoamericana," *Open Democracy*, March 12, 2014, https://www.opendemocracy.net/openglobalrights-blog/césar-rodr%C3%ADguez-garavito/los-derechos-humanos-y-la-"nueva"-izquierda-latinoame; Boaventura de Sousa Santos, "¿La Revolución

"people power tends to be invoked or cited, as an accompaniment or as acclamation, but not as autonomous power ..."[114] In this sense, Negretto explains that amongst all mechanisms of citizen participation, the only ones that have become effective are those that have a purely plebiscitary and anti-deliberative impact, such as the referendum.[115]

In the case of Venezuela, the 1999 Constitution had two effects: it weakened the legislative branch and transferred decision-making power to the executive, and it established direct ratification power in the people, without any intermediation. As a result, participation was considered within a centralistic perspective,[116] wherein the leader is the architect of the people's unity, with whom there is a hierarchical relation. In this approach, the source of the people is external and its unity fragile,[117] which makes it difficult to talk about empowerment of people and limitation of power.

In this sense, the NLC experience teaches us that it is not enough to argue for participatory democracy, but for bottom-up democratic participation. It urges us to think about the possibility of political participation that goes beyond the functions of expression and political legitimization; rather participation should focus on the aspects of deliberation, shaping power, and control.[118] In fact, without bottom-up participatory mechanisms of a deliberative kind and intermediate institutions, participation would not further a constitutional culture and would help to legitimize an antipopular, authoritarian constitutionalist regime. The challenge is open.

Conclusion

Unfortunately, after one hundred years of the Mexican Constitution, we have not been able to shape a constitutional culture. In fact, we lack a clear understanding of what this means or what direction we should pursue. However, it is a good moment to reflect collectively on what has been done wrong and what we need to do in the immediate future.

---

ciudadana tiene quién la defienda?" *Diario Público España*, May 9, 2014, http://blogs.publico.es/espejos-extranos/2014/05/09/la-revolucion-ciudadana-tiene-quien-la-defienda/.

[114] Roberto Gargarella, "El 'nuevo constitucionalismo latinoamericano': Un constitucionalismo que no termina de irse" (working paper, ITAM's faculty seminar, February 4, 2015), 25.

[115] Gabriel Negretto, "El populismo constitucional en América Latina. Análisis crítico de la Constitución Argentina de 1949," in *De Cádiz al siglo XXI. Doscientos años de constitucionalismo en México e Hispanoamérica (1812–2012)*, coords. Adriana Luna-Fabritius, Pablo Mijangos y Gonzalez, and Rafael Rojas Gutierrez (Mexico City: Taurus, 2012), 345, 370.

[116] In this sense, the issues to discuss are the ones that government is interested in; all broadcasting and media are dominated by the government; participation mechanisms are activated in order to prove popular support to the leader, independently of the issue in question. In other words, participation has an instrumental character that pretends to legitimize an act of government.

[117] Noguera, *El Sujeto Constituyente* 101–109.

[118] Claudia Zilla, "El acceso al poder, procesos electorales y partidos políticos," *Ius Constitutionale Commune en América Latina y las Estructuras del Estado* (Annual Seminar, Max Planck Institute for Comparative Public Law and International Law, December 6, 2016).

This chapter contributes to this collective enterprise, proposing a clear understanding of constitutional culture and a participatory path to achieve it.

Some legal scholars have focused on legal elites as motors of change disregarding popular communication and social learning; however, this path has not achieved any overall improvement. The good news is that there are alternative models that may stop the tendency of authoritarianism, but we need to take responsibility to carry out them. We need to work for a constitutional culture in which we are the agents and not its puppets.[119]

---

[119] See Balkin, *Cultural Software*, XI.

10 Constitution-Making and Authoritarianism in Venezuela
The First Time as Tragedy, the Second as Farce
David Landau

KARL MARX'S FAMOUS phrase holds that history repeats itself, "the first time as tragedy, the second as farce."[1] The phrase seems apt for the two Constituent Assemblies in Venezuela over the past twenty years: Hugo Chávez's in 1999 and Nicolas Maduro's in 2017. While constitution-making moments are sometimes romanticized as the high point of democratic constitutionalism, in Venezuela each of these two assemblies has helped—in first a tragic and then a farcical way—to construct or deepen Venezuela's slide toward authoritarianism.

In 1999, Hugo Chávez rapidly rewrote the Venezuelan constitution after winning election as an outsider to a delegitimized two-party system. Without negotiating with the opposition-controlled Congress, he unilaterally triggered a constituent process, and a constituent assembly dominated by his supporters rewrote Venezuela's constitution in the span of a few months. The new constitution, although innovative in key respects, greatly strengthened Chávez's presidential powers, and the Assembly wielded its own "constituent power" to shut down and reconstitute a range of institutions still controlled by the opposition. The 1999 process thus laid the groundwork for a competitive authoritarian regime in which elections continued to be held, but Chávez held immense advantages over his opponents and held power until his death in 2013.

---

[1] Karl Marx, *The Eighteenth Brumaire of Louis Bonaparte* (1852; New York: International Pub. Co., 1898).

Chávez's hand-picked successor, Nicolas Maduro, has relied on increasingly overt forms of authoritarianism to hold power in the face of a massive economic and political crisis. As the culmination of a series of dubious legal maneuvers to retain power and nullify the now opposition-controlled legislature, Maduro in 2017 called a new constituent assembly. The Assembly in its form and symbolism was modeled explicitly on its 1999 predecessor: it was unilaterally triggered by Maduro, completely controlled by Maduro, and immediately asserted sovereignty over all other state institutions by removing hostile officials and taking on legislative powers. The difference is that the 2017 Assembly enjoys none of the popular legitimacy of its predecessor. It is clearly designed as a last-ditch device to perpetuate the power of an embattled authoritarian regime.

Venezuela is not currently a democratic constitutional order and has not been one at least in its recent history. Nonetheless, its experience holds valuable lessons in a book on the crisis of democratic constitutionalism. First, it demonstrates a worst-case scenario for the global crisis of liberal democratic constitutionalism. The concentration of power and decline of horizontal accountability led by a classically populist figure such as Chávez may not end with a reinvigoration of democracy, but instead a slide deeper into authoritarianism. The reality of the Venezuelan present is a repressive state coupled with high levels of corruption, violence, and economic catastrophe. Reaching this worse-case scenario was due not only to the calculations of the regime and a dose of bad luck, but also to missteps by the opposition (most important a failed coup attempt against Chávez), which plausibly helped to deepen the slide into authoritarianism.

Additionally, Venezuela vividly demonstrates how the forms of liberal democratic constitutionalism can be used not to reinvigorate democracy but instead to undermine it. As applied to mechanisms of constitutional change, I have elsewhere referred to this phenomenon as "abusive constitutionalism."[2] Constitution-making, under certain conditions, can be a powerful tool for leaders to perpetuate power and cripple the opposition. But Venezuela may also demonstrate the limits of this strategy: the empty forms of democratic constitutionalism may fail to bolster an authoritarian legal order when, as with Maduro's 2017 Assembly, they no longer enjoy even a minimal level of popular legitimacy. Evidence suggests a near-term transition in Venezuela; the question is the form that transition will take and the terrible suffering the Venezuelan population will face in the meantime.

The Constituent Assembly of Hugo Chávez: The First Time as Tragedy

In 1998, President Chávez won election in Venezuela as an outsider to the existing constitutional system.[3] Indeed, he was the most obvious outsider imaginable—not

---

[2] See David Landau, "Abusive Constitutionalism," *University of California Davis Law Review* 47 (2013): 189–260.
[3] For more detailed recountings of the events examined in this Section, see Allan R. Brewer-Carias, *Dismantling Democracy in Venezuela: The Chávez Authoritarian Experiment* (New York: Cambridge University Press, 2010); David Landau, "Constitution-Making Gone Wrong," *Alabama Law Review* 64 (2013): 923–980.

only a mid-ranking military officer who had not previously held political office, and not only someone who ran on an anti-system platform, but in fact the leader of a prior attempted military coup against the regime. Chávez ran, in fact, as the paradigmatic populist—he adopted a discourse that differentiated between the "people" that he represented and that was virulently opposed to the elites that he stated previously ran the country.[4]

The political and economic situation of Venezuela at that time made this pitch an appealing one. The prior regime had been based on the 1958 Pact of Puntofijo signed between the two major parties, Democratic Action (AD) and COPEI, after the downfall of an authoritarian regime. It committed the winners of elections from these two parties to include the losers in their coalitions, thereby helping to stabilize the emerging regime. The pact was successful in preventing further interludes of military dictatorship; furthermore, the 1961 constitution of Venezuela became the country's most durable. At the same time, the two parties came to almost exclusively dominate Venezuelan public life. This over time created what has been called a "partyarchy"—the parties controlled a massive amount of resources because of state power over oil revenue, and the dominance of the parties extended deep into civil society, including labor unions and business organizations.[5]

Increasing perceptions of endemic corruption sharply reduced the legitimacy of the regime over time; in addition, drops in oil prices in the 1980s caused a significant economic crisis. In 1989, austerity measures including the end of oil subsidies caused large-scale rioting in Caracas; in 1992, Chávez (then a military colonel) led a failed military coup, an act for which he was imprisoned until being pardoned in 1994, but which also gained him public notoriety. By the time Chávez ran for president in 1998, the two-party partyarchy was already collapsing; Chávez's leading opponent in fact also ran as an independent. Chávez won handily, with 56 percent of the vote, but he still faced opposition from the vestiges of the old regime (and from other insurgent political forces) in virtually all other institutions: for example, his forces held only about one-third of Congress, most state governorships remained in the hands of AD and COPEI, and the judiciary was still dominated by judges affiliated with the partyarchy.

The existing Venezuela constitution of 1961 had a mechanism for "general reform" as well as "amendment," but this procedure required action by the Congress.[6] Instead of negotiating with the Congress over a constitutional overhaul, Chávez sought to work

---

[4] See Kirk A. Hawkins, *Venezuela's Chavismo and Populism in Comparative Perspective* (New York: Cambridge University Press, 2010).

[5] See Michael Coppedge, *Strong Parties and Lame Ducks: Presidential Partyarchy and Factionalism in Venezuela* (Stanford, CA: Stanford University Press, 1997).

[6] See Ven. Const., art. 246.

around it by holding a referendum on whether to convene a constituent assembly, a mechanism that was not recognized in the text of the 1961 constitution. The Supreme Court, operating under political pressure but as yet uncontrolled by the Chávez regime, allowed this maneuver in a key decision. In its ruling, the Court invoked aspects of the theory of constituent power: it held that the "people" had the right to remake their constitution, and could do so via an extra-textual constitutional mechanism such as a referendum and a constituent assembly.[7] The Court would subsequently try to hedge on this issue by holding in several decisions that the constitution-making process was nonetheless subject to basic principles found in the existing constitutional order. None of these decisions, however, placed significant constraints on Chávez.[8] Constitutional change was plausibly an important need in Venezuela in 1999, but Chavez's decision to proceed without activating the constitutional "general reform" mechanism, and the Supreme Court's approval of that decision, allowed him to replace the existing constitution without giving the opposition any input over the constitution-making process. Even if constitutional replacement was an important social goal in 1999, it is less clear whether it should have happened without any negotiation with members of the old "partyarchy."

The Venezuelan public approved the referendum by a wide margin, and Chávez's forces dominated the ensuing elections to the Assembly. This was partly due to political context and choices made by the opposition. The major opposition parties did not participate in the vote, and while many of their affiliates did participate, they did so as independent candidates rather than on party lists. This choice, which helped give the *chavista* forces significant organizational advantages, were magnified by electoral rules picked by Chávez and calculated to maximize his support. The rules, coupled with the dispersion of the opposition vote, allowed the Chávez coalition to win about 93 percent of seats with 65 percent of the votes. Thus, Chávez's forces held nearly all seats in the Assembly; independent candidates allied with the opposition won only about 6 of 131 seats.[9]

The ensuing constituent assembly was not devoid of debate: the constitution-making process involved significant popular participation, and the Chávez coalition was diverse. But the constitution nonetheless was imposed without any real input from the opposition, and was written quickly in only a few months. Some provisions tended to reduce checks and centralize power in the hands of the president. For example, the Congress was altered from a bicameral to a unicameral body, presidential terms were lengthened from five to six years with the president now being able to run for two consecutive terms, and

---

[7] See Caso: Junta Directiva de la Fundacion para los Derechos Humanos (Supreme Court of Justice, Political Administrative Chamber), Revista del Derecho Publico, nos. 77–80, 1999, at 56 (allowing referendum to proceed).

[8] See, e.g., Caso: Gerardo Blyde, contra la Resolucion No. 990217-32 (Supreme Court of Justice, Political Administrative Chamber), Revista del Derecho Publico, nos. 77–80, 1999, at 73 (requiring that referendum include a proposed electoral rule for election of Assembly).

[9] See Renata Segura and Ana Maria Bejarano, "Ni una asamblea mas sin nosotros! Exclusion. Inclusion, and the Politics of Constitution-Making in the Andes," *Constellations* 11 (2004): 217, 224 tbl.3.

presidential powers were strengthened considerably. These changes produced stronger formal powers in the president, although the overall package of formal powers was still within the regional and global mainstream.[10] At the same time, the new constitution was innovative in replacing or supplementing some traditional horizontal checks with other mechanisms of direct popular participation: it allowed for recall of the president, increased mechanisms for popular initiative and referendum, and envisioned a civil society commission as a key institution for selecting justices. In some ways, the philosophy of the new constitution was a reaction against the prior "partyarchy" and an embodiment of Chávez's populism: its text replaced some elite control over the state with more popular control.

Arguably more important than the constitutional text was the Assembly's role in rapidly reshaping the composition of other state institutions. Chávez and his allies in the Assembly declared it to be sovereign over other all other state institutions because it was the embodiment of the popular will. Thus, the Assembly asserted that it had the power not only to draft a new constitution, but also to close other institutions, replace their officials, and arrogate to itself their powers. Symbolically, this extended to the president himself; Chávez came before the Assembly and laid his mandate before it, and in one of the Assembly's first sessions, it confirmed Chávez as president and he was resworn in as president in front of it.[11] The Assembly would use these powers to carry out a number of key actions. Early in the Assembly's deliberations, it established a commission that replaced many members of the judiciary and sharply limited the powers and composition of the Congress. After the constitution had been approved in a referendum in December 1999, the Assembly closed down the Congress entirely and replaced it with a commission chosen by the Assembly (which in turn gave substantial decree powers to the executive), shut down state legislative assemblies, replaced key local executive and legislative officials, and even reconstituted union leadership (which again, had been a key component of the partyarchy).

The Assembly became a "despotic and all powerful actor" for about a year between the time it was constituted and the first set of elections under the new constitution.[12] The end result was a radically reshaped government at the national, state, and local levels: Chávez began his presidency facing opposition control of nearly every institution, but by the time the Assembly had finished his work, it had reshaped the landscape so that the old regime had been purged and Chávez's allies controlled virtually all key institutions. In

---

[10] The Venezuelan president under the 1961 constitution in fact had weak formal powers by Latin American standards, although his practical powers were much broader because he was the head of one of the two disciplined parties that made up the "partyarchy." See Brian F. Crisp, "Presidential Behavior in a System with Strong Parties: Venezuela, 1958–1995," in *Presidentialism and Democracy in Latin America*, ed. Scott Mainwaring and Matthew Soberg Shugart (New York: Cambridge University Press, 1997), 160.

[11] See Landau, "Abusive Constitutionalism."

[12] See Joshua Braver, "Hannah Arendt in Venezuela: The Supreme Court Battles Hugo Chávez over the Creation of the 1999 Constitution," *International Journal of Constitutional Law* 14 (2016): 555–583.

essence, the Assembly allowed Chávez to consolidate power unusually quickly, and without having to win as many intervening elections as he otherwise would have needed. This was a lesson that Maduro would remember nearly twenty years later when he called a new constituent assembly.

The Chávez Regime and Competitive Authoritarianism

The result of this process was that Chávez was able to construct what scholars have called a "hybrid" or "competitive authoritarian" regime, which lay somewhere between democracy and dictatorship. As Levitsky and Way define it, competitive authoritarian regimes continue to hold elections, and those elections are meaningful rather than illusory; at the same time, incumbents force challengers to compete on a highly tilted electoral playing field.[13] Institutions such as courts, electoral commissions, and the media in these regimes are often used to advantage incumbents and harass the opposition, rather than to act as mechanisms that hold the government accountable.

The Chávez regime fit this description in some respects from its inception, but moved closer after a failed coup attempt against Chávez in April 2002. The coup attempt occurred in a context of opposition concern with Chávez's legislative actions, populist discourse, and reshaping of institutions such as the national oil company. It occurred during an opposition-led general strike that was designed to cripple the national economy, and widespread popular mobilization that was violently repressed by the government. As in Turkey in 2017, the failed coup attempt was a significant moment—and a major opposition miscalculation—because it created a context in which Chávez could accelerate his efforts to establish control over institutions such as the media and the judiciary.[14]

For example, the Supreme Tribunal of Justice (TSJ) created by the 1999 Constitution initially retained some independence from the president as the original *chavista* coalition fractured, and was able to issue rulings against the regime in some cases (although usually not the most important ones). But a set of reforms to the organic law governing the judiciary in 2004 (after the coup attempt) ended this era: it allowed Chávez to pack the Court by greatly expanding its size, and it increased the regime's ability to remove non-pliant judges.[15] The result was a Court that became a reliable partner of the regime in tilting the playing field: the Court for example upheld actions manipulating the electoral rules and pulling opposition-held broadcast licenses, both of which harmed the

---

[13] See Steven R. Levitsky and Lucan A. Way, *Competitive Authoritarianism: Hybrid Regimes after the Cold War* (New York: Cambridge University Press, 2010).

[14] Chávez blamed elements of the private media for promoting the coup. In addition to the changes to the judiciary, the Law for Social Responsibility in Radio, Television, and Electronic Media was passed in 2004, and the new law gave the administration more power to limit and retaliate against media outlets.

[15] See Raul A. Sanchez Urribarri, "Courts between Democracy and Hybrid Authoritarianism: Evidence from the Venezuelan Supreme Court," *Law and Social Inquiry* 36 (2011): 854–884.

opposition. Other state institutions, such as the electoral authorities, played a similar role. Further, Chávez dominated the media, effectively monopolizing political attention. His charismatic personality and control over the media allowed him to drown out opposition voices, and he used his constant television presence to promote his agenda and pillory his enemies.

At the same time, elections and electoral support remained important in Chávez's Venezuela even after the 2002 coup attempt. A complete evaluation of Chávez's public policies is outside the scope of this brief chapter. But he clearly deployed programs in ways that were designed to enhance his electoral support. He used oil revenues derived from increasing oil prices, for example, to fund innovative social spending programs, and he may have directed some of this spending in order to maximize its electoral impact and punish opponents.[16] Furthermore, he created some new mechanisms for popular participation at the local level, although this development was uneven and often subject to interference by the regime.

Furthermore, the opposition continued to compete in elections and was able to win sometimes. In 2004, the country used the new recall mechanism to hold a vote on whether Chávez should continue as president; he won fairly easily with 58 percent of the vote. But he did not always prevail in key votes. In 2007, for example, Chávez narrowly lost a referendum that he presented as a deepening of the socialist project begun with the 1999 constitution, and that would have further increased presidential power and abolished all presidential term limits. Chávez accepted the vote but vowed to try again: echoing a statement he had made after his failed coup against the old regime, he said "for now, we could not" [*por ahora no pudimos*]. Many of the measures in the referendum were subsequently carried out through alternative formal and informal routes.

The presidential term limit itself was abolished in a subsequent 2009 referendum that Chávez won; the measure potentially allowed him to continue winning presidential re-election for life.[17] And indeed, he did serve as president for the rest of his life—after winning re-election to a fourth term in 2012, he died of cancer in 2013, creating a situation of great uncertainty. Many predicted Chávez's death would result in a transition away from competitive authoritarianism and toward democracy in Venezuela. As explained

---

[16] See Hawkins, *Venezuela's Chavismo*.

[17] The legitimacy of this second vote was contested for several reasons. First, the constitution provides that a failed proposal cannot be brought up again in the same legislative session, and the term limit proposal had already been raised in 2007. Furthermore, the constitution creates a three-tiered system of constitutional change, which differentiates an amendment, a constitutional reform, and a constitutional replacement. See generally Rosalind Dixon and David Landau, "Tiered Constitutional Design," *George Washington Law Review* 86 (forthcoming 2018). The Chávez regime used the intermediate constitutional reform procedure in 2007, but the least-demanding amendment procedure to abolish term limits in 2009, which critics of the reform argued was inappropriate. The procedure was challenged but the Chávez-dominated TSJ rejected the arguments. See, e.g., Decision 49 of 2009 (TSJ, Constitutional Chamber); 53 of 2009 (TSJ, Constitutional Chamber).

below, transition has occurred, but in the opposite direction: toward full authoritarianism under the watch of Chávez's handpicked successor, Nicolas Maduro.

Maduro and the Slide toward Full Authoritarianism

Following the constitutional line of succession, then-vice president Maduro assumed the presidency immediately after Chávez's death in March 2013. The constitution provided that a new election had to be held within thirty days of the death of the old president; this rapid calendar had the effect of giving the opposition an uphill battle because they had little time to organize. Nonetheless, Maduro won a close presidential election by only 1.5 percentage points.

Competitive authoritarianism proved to be highly unstable under Maduro, for several reasons. First, the economic environment deteriorated sharply, for a number of reasons including policy choices such as price controls, brain drain, and the sharp decline in oil prices associated with the global economic downturn. Venezuela has remained dependent on oil revenue, which constitutes more than half of its GDP and nearly all of its exports. This became a remarkably severe economic crisis after Maduro took power. Not only has the economy contracted substantially, but there has been massive hyperinflation and pervasive shortages of basic necessities including food and medicine. Second, problems with the regime itself, including an inability to deal with an extremely high crime rate and increasing perceptions of pervasive corruption, undermined its legitimacy over time. Finally, Maduro is clearly a far less charismatic and capable politician than Chávez. He lacks, for example, Chávez's mastery of television and other media. And he had more trouble holding together the *chavista* coalition at the elite level. In short, a number of factors put together made it difficult for the *chavista* coalition to win elections after Chávez's death, even with a tilted playing field.

The regime has responded in two major ways. The first is to increase its use of raw force as a substitute for subtler moves to rig the game. The second is to use the repressive apparatus of law to nullify, in an increasingly obvious way, the electoral victories or likely electoral victories of the opposition. Throughout this process, though, it has often used the forms of liberal democratic constitutionalism to carry out these maneuvers.

In terms of force, the regime in the past several years had relied on armed militants to carry out attacks and threats against political opponents and journalists, and the government itself has increasingly resorted to violence against protestors. Large-scale, chaotic, and sometimes violent street protests by opponents began in 2014 and have continued until the present. Supporters of the regime have at times held counter-protests. There have been many causes of these protests, including economic conditions and shortages of food and other necessities, corruption, and dubious legal maneuvers of the Maduro administration and its allies to weaken the opposition and perpetuate the regime. The government has responded to the protests with violence that observers have alleged has gone well beyond necessary crowd-control and has included lethal force.[18] Furthermore, the regime has arrested large numbers of protestors and others seen as opponents of Maduro. Human rights organizations have alleged a wide array of mistreatment, up to and including torture, of those being held.[19]

The Maduro administration's repressive use of law to prevent the opposition from gaining political power is also noteworthy. Of course, the Chávez administration, characteristic of competitive authoritarian regimes, relied on friendly interpretations and decisions of courts to perpetuate its power and weaken the opposition since its inception, and especially since the failed 2002 coup. But the Maduro administration has taken this to another level, wielding law as an increasingly inelegant and transparent club against opponents.

The legislative elections of December 2015 were a key moment: a broad coalition of the opposition won a decisive victory in the National Assembly (AN), gaining about two-thirds of the 167 seats in the unicameral chamber with about 58 percent of the votes. The Maduro regime argued that the results were tainted by fraud, and filed a series of complaints in the TSJ. Thus began a set of events in which the regime has used the judiciary, especially the TSJ, to neutralize the AN. The TSJ accepted one of these demands in Amazonas state and issued a decision suspending the electoral process for several deputies.[20] The AN refused to comply with this decision, arguing that the swearing in had legally occurred and could not be reversed. The opposition leaders may have done so in part because the deputies at issue were ones that the opposition may have needed for a two-thirds supermajority that allowed it to exercise certain constitutional powers such as modifying organic laws, calling a constituent assembly, or impeaching justices on the TSJ. In turn, the TSJ held the Assembly and its leadership in contempt, a decision that has had important subsequent effects.

After winning power the opposition explicitly sought routes to carry out a change of power in Venezuela. They settled on a multipronged strategy for legally removing Maduro from power: (1) a constitutional amendment to cut the presidential term, which could be carried out by a majority of the AN followed by a referendum, and which would apply to the current Maduro term; and (2) the trigger of a recall vote against Maduro. The Constitutional Chamber of the TSJ issued an interpretive decision holding that the amendment procedure could not be used to cut the term of the president in a way that would apply to the current term. It held that such a use would be a "fraud on the constitution" because it would run against the fundamental principle of non-retroactivity of the

---

[18] See Human Rights Watch, "Crackdown on Dissent: Brutality, Torture, and Political Persecution in Venezuela," Nov. 29, 2017, https://www.hrw.org/report/2017/11/29/crackdown-dissent/brutality-torture-and-political-persecution-venezuela.

[19] See ibid.

[20] See Decision 260 of 2015 (TSJ, Electoral Chamber).

law.[21] In other words, such an amendment would be an unconstitutional constitutional amendment.[22]

The recall attempt was also blocked. In 2016, opponents attempted to use the constitutional procedure to trigger a recall vote against Maduro, the same procedure that had been triggered against Chávez, and which Chávez had won comfortably in 2004. Given Maduro's low popularity and the country's state of crisis, of course, he would have been in much greater jeopardy of losing a fair recall election. Opposition leaders appeared to have abided by the initial stage of the process by gathering the signatures of 1 percent of voters, although the Maduro-controlled National Electoral Council (CNE) managed to delay this process considerably. The CNE then set the conditions for the second stage (the gathering of 20 percent of signatures, or about 4 million people), both delaying the process and setting extremely restrictive conditions for it to be carried out. For example, the CNE required that the 20 percent quota be met in every state, instead of nationally as in the 2004 referendum, and it offered a period of only three days for signatures to be collected. The opposition plausibly pointed out that meeting the quota under such restrictive rules would be impossible. Moreover, the CNE in October 2016 suspended the recall drive altogether, holding that it was required to do so because of lower court rulings that there had been fraud in the prior stage of the process.[23]

The TSJ also undertook a series of decisions strengthening the president and gravely weakening the Assembly. Some of these interpreted the president's emergency powers broadly. Others used the contempt ruling against the Assembly to declare laws unconstitutional and to transfer legislative powers to the executive. The TSJ held repeatedly that all of the acts of the legislature were void while the contempt order against it subsisted. Furthermore, a 2016 ruling gave the president the power to have the government budget issued via decree approved by the TSJ itself rather than the AN.[24] It stated as grounds the need to maintain order and the existence of a state of emergency following the contempt order, which it alleged made all of the legislature's acts null.

The most dramatic ruling occurred in March 2017, when the TSJ stripped the AN of all of its powers, arrogated those powers to itself, and gave itself the power to transfer those powers to any institution it wished (such as the executive).[25] It also weakened parliamentary immunity.[26] The decision again referred to the situation of contempt in which

---

[21] See Decision 274 of 2016 (TSJ, Constitutional Chamber).

[22] Rosalind Dixon and I have argued that this doctrine should aim in large part at protecting a minimum core of a democratic constitutional order, which this change would not threaten and in context might indeed reinforce. See Rosalind Dixon and David Landau, "Transnational Constitutionalism and a Limited Doctrine of Unconstitutional Constitutional Amendment," *International Journal of Constitutional Law* 13 (2015): 606.

[23] See Albinson Linares, "Autoridades Electorales Paralizan el Proceso Revocatorio Contra Maduro," *New York Times*, October 21, 2016, https://www.nytimes.com/es/2016/10/21/autoridades-electorales-de-venezuela-paralizan-el-proceso-revocatorio-contra-maduro/.

[24] See Decision 810 of 2016 and its "amplification" (TSJ, Constitutional Chamber).

[25] See Decision 156 of 2017 (TSJ, Constitutional Chamber).

[26] See Decision 155 of 2017 (TSJ, Constitutional Chamber).

the Court had held the AN because of its noncompliance with the electoral decision. It held that this created a "legislative omission" because there was no institution that was capable of legislating within the country. The doctrine of "legislative omission" is common in Latin America, but is usually used for different ends—to define the circumstances under which the court can interpret a law to fill a void within a defined statutory scheme, and thus to act as a regulator of the boundary between the judicial and legislative power.[27] Here, the doctrine was used to radically alter the separation of powers.

This decision caused an outcry both internationally and domestically. It was denounced by the Prosecutor General, who had previously been an ally of the regime. The outcry was loud enough that the Court several weeks later issued a "clarification" of the decision backtracking on some of its extreme effects.[28] The clarification suppressed the part of the decision allowing the Court or the institution of its choosing to exercise legislative powers. However, it is important to note that the new decision did nothing to alter the earlier rulings of the TSJ holding the AN in contempt and its actions void, or giving the president expansive emergency powers to bypass the legislature.

The Constituent Assembly of Nicolas Maduro: The Second Time as Farce

This is the context in which President Maduro activated a new constituent process beginning in May 2017. The overriding goal has been to perpetuate the regime and punish its opponents. The "constituent" process is ongoing, but thus far it has proceeded as a kind of farcical version of Chávez's 1999 constituent assembly. The context of course was radically different. In 1999, there was widespread popular opinion that the old two-party regime was spent and that constitutional replacement needed to occur. In 2017, opinion polls generally showed no such popular will, and indeed the Maduro regime was now widely seen as corrupt and in need of replacement. The new process therefore was aimed at extending the life of the old regime rather than sweeping it away.

First, like the 1999 process, the 2017 process was activated unilaterally by the president, without any negotiation with the opposition. Whereas Chávez relied on the theory of original constituent power to evade textual mechanisms that would have required him to negotiate with an opposition-controlled Congress, Maduro relied on textual provisions of the 1999 constitution that arguably had the same effect. The irony may be that the 2017 constitution-making process is on stronger legal ground than the 1999 process. The 1999 constitution allows a number of actors to trigger elections for a constituent assembly, including two-thirds of the national legislature, two-thirds of municipal councils, 15 percent of voters, or the president acting alone.[29] Thus, whether as a maneuver to

---

[27] See, e.g., Francisco Fernandez Segado, "El Control de Constitucionalidad de las Omisiones Legislativas. Algunas Cuestiones Dogmaticas," *Estudios Constitucionales* 7 (2009): 13.

[28] See Decisions 157 of 2017; 158 of 2017 (TSJ, Constitutional Chamber).

[29] See Venez. Const., art. 348.

increase presidential power or simply as an echo of the way the 1999 process proceeded, the constitution arguably allowed Maduro to call elections for a new assembly directly, completely ignoring opposition-held institutions. Indeed, in the 1999 process Chávez at least obtained approval in a referendum, which Maduro stated the text did not require him to do. The legality of the current process remains contested on a number of grounds, perhaps most important the argument that the constitution vests the "original constituent power" in the "people," and therefore that the process must originate with a demonstration of true popular will, rather than from the top-down, or that the process must include a referendum.[30] But it can at least be said that Maduro's unilateral move had some plausible constitutional support.

Second, the elections themselves produced results that were similar to that in 1999, but in a much more extreme context. Maduro like Chávez unilaterally wrote the electoral rules, this time combining direct election of about two-thirds of representatives in badly malapportioned territorial districts, with about one-third who were selected in a corporatist fashion from poorly-defined groups such as labor unions, business organizations, peasants and fishermen, students, persons with disabilities, and the elderly.[31] These rules gave Maduro even more power than Chávez to manipulate the composition of the new National Constituent Assembly (ANC). Opponents criticized these rules as well for being contrary to the constitution,[32] but their petition was rejected by the TSJ.[33]

The opposition completely boycotted the ANC elections, allowing the government to win all 545 seats. Opposition groups instead held a nonbinding vote in July 2017, which they alleged produced results that were overwhelmingly opposed to the holding of a constituent assembly (opinion polls suggested the same). Despite having no real opposition and acting in a context where the playing field was very tilted, the regime appears to have resorted to outright fraud, in order to goose what would otherwise have been extremely low vote totals. The company that provided the voting machines

[30] See José Ignacio Hernández G., "'Symposium on Venezuela's 2017 (Authoritarian) National Constituent Assembly'—Pursuing Constitutional Authoritarianism," *International Journal of Constitutional Law Blog*, September 1, 2017, http://www.iconnectblog.com/2017/09/symposium-on-venezuelas-2017-authoritarian-national-constituent-assemblyjose-ignacio-hernandez-g/. The Constitutional Chamber of the Supreme Court rejected the interpretation that a referendum was required before elections could be held in Decision 378 of 2017.

[31] See Decree 2878, May 23, 2017.

[32] See, e.g., Juan Alberto Barrios Ortigoza, "'Symposium on Venezuela's 2017 (Authoritarian) National Constituent Assembly'—(Mis)representing the People: Notes about the Electoral Bases of the 2017 National Constituent Assembly in Venezuela," *International Journal of Constitutional Law Blog*, August 31, 2017, http://www.iconnectblog.com/2017/08/symposium-on-venezuelas-2017-authoritarian-national-constituent-assemblyjuan-alberto-berrios-ortigoza/. For a more comprehensive set of arguments against the constitutionality of the Assembly, see the essays collected in *Estudios Sobre la Asamblea Nacional Constituyente y su Inconstitucional Convocatoria en 2017*, ed. Allan R. Brewer-Carias and Carlos Garcia Soto (Caracas: Fundacion Editorial Juridica Venezolana, 2017).

[33] See Decision 455 of 2017 (TSJ, Constitutional Chamber).

alleged that they were tampered with, and independent estimates of the vote estimated numbers of voters of far less than half of the eight million voters that Maduro claimed voted.[34]

Third, and most important, the 2017 ANC like the 1999 Constituent Assembly has relied heavily on its original constituent power to shut down and substitute for other institutions. In the 1999 process, the constituent assembly spent a considerable amount of time replacing and curbing other institutions while also legislating, although it was clear the constitution-making process was also a significant one; in 2017, at least to date, it is clear that the main purpose is deck-clearing rather than constitution-making. In other words, the 2017 ANC is primarily interested in its supposed role as supreme power of state and only secondarily (at best) interested in carrying out constitutional reforms. The ANC quickly began issuing "constituent decrees," which stated that it had "original constituent power." Its decrees have stated repeatedly that all other institutions are "subordinated to the National Constituent Assembly" and that it "has the power to adopt measures on the jurisdiction, functioning, and organization of the organs of state."[35] And as Chávez had done years before, Maduro laid his mandate down in front of the ANC and was reconfirmed in the position of national president, a demonstration of the ANC's constituent power.[36]

The ANC convened in August 2017 in the capitol building that normally houses the national legislature and issued an initial decree declaring that it would sit for two years. The day after it convened, it replaced the Prosecutor General who had criticized the earlier judicial decision regarding the AN, and who had become a major locus of dissent within the state, and it created a commission with the power to restructure the Public Ministry she had previously led.[37] It also stated in August that it now held the power to make laws on all topics, although it did not dissolve the AN. It has since used its power by discussing and passing significant laws on a variety of issues. One of these laws, for example, "The Constitutional Law Against Hate, For Peaceful Coexistence and Tolerance" allows the government to criminalize broad swaths of speech that may incite discrimination or hatred on a number of vague grounds, and impose severe criminal penalties (ten to twenty years) on individuals and extremely heavy fines on media companies who have violated the law.[38]

---

[34] See, e.g., "What Has Venezuela's Constituent Assembly Achieved?," *BBC News*, August 30, 2017, http://www.bbc.com/news/world-latin-america-41094889.

[35] See, e.g., Decreto Constituyente de ratificacion en el ejericio de sus funciones constitucionales a los magistrados y magistradas principales del Tribunal Supremo de Justicia, in Gaceta Oficial 41.214, August 15, 2017.

[36] See "ANC Ratificaa Maduro como Presidente de Venezuela," *El Espectador*, August 10, 2017, https://www.elespectador.com/noticias/el-mundo/anc-ratifica-maduro-como-presidente-de-venezuela-articulo-707489.

[37] See Decreto Oficial 6.322 extraordinario, August 5, 2017 (containing decrees removing the prosecutor, replacing the prosecutor, and declaring an emergency restructuring of the Public Ministry).

[38] See "Ley constitucional contra el odio, por la convivencia pacifica y la tolerencia," Gaceta Oficial 41.274, Nov. 8, 2017.

The ANC has also issued a number of significant decrees on electoral matters. It called new gubernatorial and mayoral elections, both then marred by irregularities, and required the winners of those elections to be sworn in in front of it on pain of being prevented from taking their posts.[39] Furthermore, it issued a decree stating that parties boycotting the mayoral elections (as the largest opposition parties did) would lose their electoral accreditation and would need to reapply to the Electoral Commission, an obvious threat against opposition movements.[40] In January 2018, it issued a decree calling new presidential elections for April or May 2018, which both the opposition and the international community has argued would lack both sufficient time and guarantees to ensure basic electoral fairness.[41]

The foregoing is not a complete record of the activities of the ANC since its inception, but it is sufficient to demonstrate its core purpose within the Maduro regime. One presumed goal would be to reset the institutional order as Chávez did in 1999, sweeping away most opposition power over the legislature and over local governments. Another would be to allow Maduro to stay in power for longer by winning a new election under dubious circumstances. Finally, the "Constitutional Law Against Hate" and other measures of the ANC suggest that it aims to give the president even greater powers to harass the opposition and control the media.

Conclusion

Recent Venezuelan experience is a paradigmatic example of how leaders can use legal devices normally associated with democratic constitutionalism to destroy a democratic constitutional order. The Constituent Assemblies and constitution-making processes of Chávez and Maduro are obvious examples. Beyond those moments, the TSJ has increasingly relied on doctrines such as the unconstitutional constitutional amendment doctrine and the legislative omission doctrine to frustrate political power that the opposition won in elections and to prevent attempts to check Maduro's power. The 2017 Constituent

---

[39] See, e.g., Gaceta Oficial 41.259, Oct. 20, 2017 (requiring governors to be sworn in by the assembly instead of regional councils); Gaceta Oficial 41.265, October 26, 2017 (setting elections for mayors).

[40] See "ANC aprobó un decreto para la validación de los partidos politicos," *El Nacional*, December 20, 2017, http://www.el-nacional.com/noticias/gobierno/anc-aprobo-decreto-para-validacion-los-partidos-politicos_216253.

[41] See, e.g., Statement of the Fourth Meeting of the Lima Group on the Situation in Venezuela, January 23, 2018, http://international.gc.ca/world-monde/international_relations-relations_internationales/latin_america-amerique_latine/2018-01-23-lima_group-groupe_lima.aspx?lang=eng&_ga=2.44345316.176855676 6.1516985732-1318292470.1516985732 (statement of Argentina, Brazil, Canada, Chile, Colombia, Costa Rica, Guatemala, Guyana, Honduras, Mexico, Panama, Paraguay, Peru, and Saint Lucia that the "decision renders it impossible to hold democratic, transparent and credible elections, in accordance with international standards, and contradicts democratic principles and principles of good faith in the context of the dialogue between the Government and the opposition").

Assembly, in this sense, is the culmination of an effort to use the forms of liberal democratic constitutionalism as a way to deepen authoritarianism. At a few points, problematic choices by the opposition (especially the failed 2002 coup) may also have played some causal role in the deepening of authoritarianism.

Whether Maduro's new Assembly will be successful is quite doubtful. The 2017 ANC enjoys none of the legitimacy of its 1999 predecessor. Most opinion polls have suggested before and after the election of the ANC that large majorities disapprove of its convocation and see no need for it.[42] Internationally, many countries and organizations, including not only hostile countries such as the United States but also important regional organizations such as the Organization of American States and regional powers such as Brazil, Chile, Colombia, Peru, and Mexico have denounced the ANC and called it illegitimate. The economic situation continues to be extremely dire, for example with a rate of inflation above 1000 percent in 2017. The ultimate fate of the Maduro regime remains unclear, although it seems likely to fall sometime in the near future. If negotiations are successful, that exit may be peaceful. If not, it could be quite violent. The question then will become whether and how Venezuela can establish a new democracy.

---

[42] See, e.g., "Una encuesta "raspa" a la ANC," *2001.com.ve*, September 3, 2017, http://www.2001.com.ve/en-la-agenda/168807/una-encuesta--raspa--a-la-anc.html.

11 Latin America
Constitutions in Trouble
Roberto Gargarella

Introduction

Are Latin American constitutions in crisis? The answer, I shall suggest, is no, if we are thinking about situations of "constitutional breakdowns," such as those that prevailed during the 1970s, when most Latin American countries were ruled by authoritarian governments, responsible for massive human rights violations. However, Latin American constitutionalism can be considered to be in trouble if we refer instead to the constitutional structure that gradually became dominant in the region after more than two hundred years of practice. The constitutional model that still prevails in Latin America concentrates political authority in the hands of the executive, seems ineffective from the viewpoint of political stability, is based on an unattractive approach to democracy, and does not contribute to the enforcement of the numerous social, economic, and cultural rights that it generously consecrates. The changes that, in most cases, were introduced into the original constitutional model in recent decades (i.e., in Colombia 1991, Argentina 1994, Bolivia 2009, Ecuador 2008, Venezuela 1999) were sometimes attractive and sometimes not, but the fact is that they did not challenge or significantly modify the traditional basic structure of Latin American constitutionalism.[1]

---

[1] For instance, Colombia's 1991 Constitution created its remarkable Constitutional Court and introduced important changes concerning legal standing; Bolivia's Constitution made a significant effort on behalf of the

In what follows, I shall critically examine the gradual development of Latin American constitutionalism and focus on the problems that characterize it. First, I will study the two main stages of constitutional creation in Latin America, namely the initial "founding period" that took place in the nineteenth century, and the second period of "social constitutionalism," which emerged in the twentieth century. I will then explore some of the most important difficulties generated by the still-prevailing model of Latin American constitutionalism.

Writing Constitutions in the Context of Plural Societies: Latin America's "Accumulation" Strategy in the Nineteenth Century

During Latin America's "founding period," most countries in the region gave shape to the basic structure of their constitutions (basically, the organization of powers, the declaration of rights), and they did so by following a very peculiar and problematic strategy, which I shall name the "accumulation strategy." In order to explain this strategy, I will distinguish it from alternative ones, which were also tried in the region during the nineteenth century.

Since the time of independence (around 1810), and trying to establish a constitution that was capable of working in the context of plural and divided societies, Latin Americans explored four main routes, namely "imposition," "silence," "synthesis," and "accumulation." The last alternative—"accumulation"—became the most common regional response to "the fact of pluralism." Let me briefly describe each of these alternatives.

IMPOSITION. Sometimes one of the factions simply imposed its own view—its comprehensive political or philosophical view—upon the others. Imposition was a common choice during the early years after independence, and was typically advanced by authoritarian governments. Ecuadorian president Gabriel García Moreno made this constitutional approach apparent in his inaugural speech at the Constitutional Convention of 1869 in Ecuador, when he claimed: "the first [goal of my power] will be that of harmonizing our political institutions with our religious beliefs; and the second will be that of investing our public authorities with the forces required to resist the assaults of anarchy." Not surprisingly, the 1869 Ecuadorian Constitution prevented the public exercise of religions other than Catholicism. A similar example of imposition appears in article 5 of Chile's 1833 Constitution, which read as follows: "The religion of the Republic of Chile is the Apostolic, Roman, Catholic; to the exclusion of the public exercise of any other." Likewise, the Colombian Constitution of 1886 (one of

---

legal and political integration of Indigenous groups. Also, and through its new Constitution, Ecuador began to recognize itself as a "plurinational" and "intercultural state," etc.

the last strongly conservative constitutions in Latin America's nineteenth Century) included article 38, which stated: "The Catholic, Apostolic, Roman religion, is that of the nation . . . public authorities shall protect it . . . as an essential element of the social order. . . ." In a similar vein, article 41 of the Constitution stated: "public education shall be organized and conducted in accordance with the Catholic Religion." All these cases simply illustrate what was a common move (particularly) during the early decades of the nineteenth century.

SILENCE. Another significant alternative among constitution-makers was the choice of saying nothing or remaining silent about divisive social issues. As Cass Sunstein once put it, sometimes people decide to "decide very little," to "leave things open," making "deliberate decisions about what should be left unsaid." This seems to be "a pervasive practice: doing and saying as little as is necessary in order to justify an outcome."[2] Silence seems to have been preferred when the different factions found it difficult to establish common points of agreement. The Mexican delegates at the 1857 Convention chose silence when they had to decide about the issue of Catholic religion. In fact, there was no other issue that mattered more to the delegates than the issue of religion. Liberals favored religious toleration, while conservatives wanted to give the Catholic religion a privileged status in the constitution. However, their differences were so profound that they finally decided to remain silent concerning the issue that they found most relevant. The delegates to the US Federal Convention decided to remain silent with regard to the issue of slavery, which was also of utmost importance at the time. Similarly, in his important book *Constitutional Theory*, Carl Schmitt explored this kind of strategy as applied to the Weimar 1919 Constitution. This document for instance included formulations "that satisfie[d] all contradictory demands and [left] in an ambiguous turn or phrase the actual points of controversy undecided. So the constitution contains only an external, semantic jumble of substantively irreconcilable matters."[3]

SYNTHESIS. A more interesting choice was the one we could call synthesis. This alternative appeared, for instance, when US delegates discussed the issue of religion at the Federal Assembly. The American "founders" agreed to look for a common ground on the matter, and managed to find a constitutional formulation that they could all fully subscribe from their own particular perspectives. This was the great achievement of the First Amendment, which reads as follows: "Congress shall make no law respecting an establishment of religion, or prohibiting the free exercise thereof; or abridging the freedom of speech, or of the press; or the right of the people peaceably to assemble, and to petition the government for a redress of grievances." This kind of solution is precisely the one that

---

[2] Cass R. Sunstein, *One Case at a Time* (Cambridge, MA: Harvard University Press, 2001), 3.
[3] Carl Schmitt, *Constitutional Theory* (Durham, NC: Duke University Press, 2008), 84.

John Rawls favored in his defense of an *overlapping consensus* (not surprisingly, the First Amendment became the main constitutional example of his view, in his work on *Political Liberalism*). For Rawls, "This political conception needs to be such that there is some hope of its gaining the support of an overlapping consensus, that is, a consensus in which it is affirmed by the opposing religious, philosophical and moral doctrines likely to thrive over generations in a more or less just constitutional democracy, where the criterion of justice is that political conception itself."[4]

ACCUMULATION. The most common strategy tried in Latin America was accumulation, the tendency to simply aggregate the different proposals, frequently in tension, preferred by the rival factions. In this way, the opposite groups obtain what they originally demanded, or something very close to it, advancing—rather than putting between brackets—their comprehensive views.[5] In Latin America, this alternative became popular at the mid-nineteenth century, when liberals and conservatives signed a quite unexpected political compact. The two factions had been violently confronting each other for decades. The liberal-conservative compact, which in most cases appeared as a barrier against the threat that was then posed by radical groups, became soon reflected in the texts of the new constitutions. Most of these constitutions combined the conflictive demands of the two factions. For example, they combined the liberals' concern with state neutrality on religion with the conservatives' defense of an official religion, or the liberals' model of checks and balances with the conservatives' proposal for a monarchical or quasi-monarchical government. Rather than finding a common point of agreement, liberals and conservatives decided not to renounce their fundamental demands and to instead create institutional structures that "added" both their contrasting demands. Remarkably—as we shall explore below—these arrangements came to define the basic structure of Latin American constitutionalism, since then and until today.

Social Constitutionalism in the Twentieth Century

Most Latin American countries advanced profound constitutional reforms during the twentieth century. Notably, the organization of powers of these modified constitutions remained basically unchanged: what those documents mainly changed, instead, was their declaration of rights. We can classify these reforms in two groups: (1) the changes that were adopted at the beginning of the twentieth century, and (2) the reforms that were introduced at the end of the same century.

---

[4] John Rawls, "The Idea of an Overlapping Consensus," *Oxford Journal of Legal Studies* 7, no. 1 (1987): 1–25, 1.
[5] Carl Schmitt, for example, explored the numerous "compromises," "ambiguities," and "contradictions" included in the Weimar 1919 Constitution, particularly in what regards "religious and class-based" issues. Schmitt, *Constitutional Theory*, 82–83.

The starting point of the first wave of constitutional reforms was the 1917 Mexican Constitution. The Mexican Constitution emerged after a revolutionary period that marked the end of the old system of "order and progress." The old, exclusive, and authoritarian political system that prevailed in most countries by the end of the nineteenth century seemed totally exhausted. All over the region, the political, social, and economic crisis of the time demanded the adoption of radical changes in the organization of society. Typically, these changes implied the introduction of welfarist policies and higher levels of state intervention in the economy. In the constitutional sphere, these changes resulted in the incorporation of a long list of social rights into the Constitution. Now, social, economic, and cultural rights were added on the top of the traditional list of liberal rights. In such a way, the original list of rights remained in place, basically unchanged. This was, in the end, a new exercise of the traditional "accumulation" strategy. Constitutions such as those of Brazil 1937, Bolivia 1938, Cuba 1940, Ecuador 1945, Argentina 1949, or Costa Rica 1949 illustrate this move toward what has usually been called *social constitutionalism*.

By the end of the twentieth century, Latin America experienced a new wave of constitutional reforms. These reforms brought with them some significant novelties. Most of the constitutions that were then enacted incorporated, usually for the first time, long lists of human rights, Indigenous rights, and the rights of minority groups. Constitutions such as those of Colombia 1991, Venezuela 1999, Ecuador 2008, or Bolivia 2009 illustrate the achievements of this new wave of constitutional changes. These reforms have frequently been described as the bases of the so-called *New Latin American Constitutionalism*.[6] Again, what we find here are new expressions of the "accumulation strategy," through which a new list of multicultural and human rights was added on top of the old (already expanded) list of rights, which remained still unchanged.

In sum, during the twentieth century, the original, liberal-conservative constitutional compact changed (the original compact was significantly expanded), but the method of constitutional creation—the "accumulation strategy"—continued. The liberal-conservative compact was first expanded as a result of the pressures of socially marginalized groups (from Indigenous groups to a growing working class), and then again out of renewed concerns that originated after the massive violation of human rights that took place in the 1970s. Remarkably, however, both these expansions of the original compact preserved, rather than modified, the main basis of the original pact, which resided in its organization of powers. In what follows, I shall examine the limits and fragilities that characterized these institutional developments.

---

[6] Roberto Viciano Pastor and Rubén Martínez Dalmau, "El nuevo constitucionalismo latinoamericano: Fundamentos para una construcción doctrinal," *Revista General de Derecho Público Comparado* 9 (2011): 1–24; Gerardo Pisarello, "El nuevo constitucionalismo latinoamericano y la constitución venezolana de 1999: balance de una década," *SinPermiso*, November 29, 2009, http://www.sinpermiso.info/textos/el-nuevo-constitucionalismo-latinoamericano-y-la-constitucin-venezolana-de-1999-balance-de-una-dcada.

Tensions between Rights

Latin Americans developed their constitutional systems through the "accumulation" of different, sometimes contradictory, institutional initiatives. In the area of rights, the inclusion of conflictive institutions has generated numerous difficulties. These include serious problems of constitutional interpretation. Clearly, if the Constitution says one thing, but at the same time denies or puts that same claim into question, then it improperly complicates the task of legal interpreters. Also, citizens may rightly feel mistreated by the presence of contradictory or ambiguous clauses. They may reasonably wonder: What is, in the end, the proper constitutional behavior? Take, for example, the conflictive clauses incorporated into the 1853 Constitution of Argentina (clauses that are still present in the Constitution, after the 1994 reform). Following the demands of conservative groups, the Constitution originally incorporated article 2, which states: "The Federal Government supports the Roman Catholic Apostolic religion," thus providing a privileged status to the Catholic Church. However, and following the demands of liberal groups, article 14 was adopted, which (still) reads as follows: "All the inhabitants of the Nation are entitled to the following rights, in accordance with the laws that regulate their exercise, namely: to publish their ideas through the press without previous censorship; ... to profess freely their religion; to teach and to learn." In the face of those contradictory commitments, a reasonable citizen may rightly ask herself: "What does the Constitution actually require from me, concerning my religious convictions?" "What does it require from the state in all those affairs related to religion?" "Does the Constitution ban or support religious education in public schools?"[7] By including both liberal and conservative conflictive commitments, the Constitution has strengthened rather than softened or dissolved a divisive social problem, in this case related to the relationship between the state and the Church.

Article 19 of the same Argentinean Constitution offers another illustration. In its original formulation, article 19 included a kind of Millean *harm principle*. It stated: "The private actions of men which do not injure a third party, are only reserved to God and are exempted from the authority of judges." However, during the constitutional debates, and as a result of the pressure of conservative groups, the first line of the article was modified, and a conservative proviso was added. Article 19 now reads: "The private actions of men which in no way offend public order or morality, nor injure a third party, are only reserved to God and are exempted from the authority of judges." Not surprisingly, the article has since then been a source of constitutional problems. Discussions about homosexual

---

[7] Two hundred years later, and while I am writing this chapter, the Argentine Court made a decision about this issue, on a cause related to the teaching of (Catholic) religion in public schools, in the province of Salta (December 12, 2017). The majority of the Court considered the teaching of religion in public schools as an initiative that run against the Constitution, while—based on similar textual citations—the minority vote affirmed the opposite view.

rights, same-sex marriage, and personal consumption of drugs have been the object of opposite legal approaches, always based on different readings of the same constitutional document. Within the span of a few years, for example, the Argentine Court adopted a very liberal approach concerning the personal use of drugs (in the *Bazterrica* case, from 1986), then changed it for a very conservative one (in the *Montalvo* case, from 1990), and more recently changed it again, now in favor of a liberal approach (in the *Arriola* case, from 2009). In all those cases, judges found textual support in the Constitution in favor of their opposite, contradictory views.

Other Latin American constitutions show similar tensions concerning fundamental rights. Typically, twentieth century regional constitutions exhibit tensions between the newly adopted social and economic clauses, and the more traditional (liberal-conservative) clauses that established strong protections to property rights. Think, for example, about the Brazilian 1988 Constitution. Title VIII, chapter VIII of the Constitution is entirely dedicated to the rights of Indigenous groups; and Title II, Chapter II of the same Constitution incorporates an impressive list of social rights. These social, cultural, and multicultural commitments do not fit well with the robust protections that Brazilian constitutionalism traditionally offered to private property and market liberties (for the 1988 Constitution see, for instance, what it establishes in Title VII of the Constitution, dedicated to the economic and financial order). A similar phenomenon appears in constitutions enacted during the last decades (during the period of the so-called "New Latin American Constitutionalism"). One crucial characteristic of these new constitutions was the effort they made to recognize and protect the rights of Indigenous communities. Typically, those constitutions consecrated new types of "property rights"—collective, communal—to honor the traditional ways of life of ancient aboriginal communities. Those constitutions introduced such novelties without paying much attention to the way in which the newly incorporated collective rights could collide with previously recognized rights to private property, which remained basically untouched. The failure to anticipate these conflicts suggests that constitution-makers did not notice the emerging tensions between the "old" constitution and the reforms that they themselves promoted.

Tensions in the Organization of Powers

This Section explores some of the problems created by the way in which Latin Americans structured the organization of powers within the text of their constitutions. In the mid-nineteenth century liberals and conservatives modeled systems of organization of powers that combined their conflictive political ambitions. Liberals favored a system of "checks and balances" like the one adopted in the United States, while conservatives preferred a model of concentration of powers, like the one that prevailed during the colonial period. Because of their compact, liberals and conservatives drafted constitutions that preserved the essence of both those (opposite) ideals: equilibrium of powers (liberals) and concentration of powers (conservatives). They thus created an imperfect system that we could (re)name an *unbalanced system of checks and balances*.

The 1891 Republican Constitution of Brazil provides an illustration. In its liberal side, the 1891 Brazilian Constitution favored federalism (in a way that many considered exaggerated), granted powers of judicial review to the Superior Tribunal, created the mechanism of impeachment, and prohibited all those constitutional reforms that affected the republican and federal character of the national organization.[8] Meanwhile, in its conservative side, the Constitution granted ample powers to the executive branch, established the power of federal intervention, and regulated the institution of the state of siege. So, this Constitution finally promoted political equilibrium *and* executive predominance—two contradictory goals.

Argentina's main constitutional ideologue Juan Bautista Alberdi explicitly defended this liberal-conservative approach to the organization of powers in his most influential book, namely, *Bases y puntos de partida para la organización política de la República Argentina* (the book would soon become the ideological foundation of Argentina's 1853 Constitution). In chapter 25 of *Bases*, Alberdi claimed that the US Constitution, which so far had represented the main influence within his own constitutional project, had to be set aside when designing the executive branch: at that stage, the model to be followed was going to be—he declared—the authoritarian Chilean Constitution of 1833.[9] In this way, Alberdi openly acknowledged the value of combining the US liberal structure of checks and balances with authoritarian features derived from the Chilean example. What we have here is, again, an internally contradictory project, which Alberdi openly defended.

This particular combination between liberal and conservative constitutional features (the search for both political equilibrium and a quite unrestrained executive authority) became a salient characteristic of Latin American constitutions. In spite of all the changes that have been incorporated since then in the different regional documents, no constitution significantly changed the old schema of powers that resulted from the nineteenth century liberal-conservative compact. In other words, even today, Latin American constitutions offer organization of powers that have been modeled according to goals, principles, and assumptions that were dominant in the region during the nineteenth century. Not surprisingly, such a structure became inefficient and, what is more significant for our present purposes, also normatively unattractive, in the light of our presently shared understandings about democracy.

---

[8] Boris Fausto, *Historia do Brasil* (Sao Paulo: Universidade de Sao Paulo, 2006).

[9] Juan Bautista Alberdi, *Bases y puntos de partida para la organización política de la República Argentina* (Buenos Aires: Ediciones Estrada, 1943), ch. 25.

Unbalanced Constitutions and Hyper-presidentialism

Latin America's "unbalanced system of checks and balances" announced (or worse, promised), from the very moment in which it was adopted, future situations of political instability. In fact, the presence of a (hyper) strong executive power puts into question, if not directly undermines, the very logic of the system of check and balances. That logic requires each branch of government to get an equivalent share of power, which—as the founders assumed—would prevent the problem of mutual encroachments. As James Madison put it, "the great security against a gradual concentration of the several powers in the same department, consists in giving to those who administer each department the necessary constitutional means and personal motives to resist encroachments of the others." Now, if—in contradiction with the original strategy—one branch of power, say the executive branch, is endowed with more capacities than the rest, then the very logic of the system of checks and balances becomes subverted. This is what tends to happen when the executive branch gains more powers, and thus more threatening capacities than the other branches.

Latin America's history of political instability seems to confirm those risks. In the long term, one could claim, the working of the system has been extremely poor. The schema of mutual checks did not contribute to the achievement of political equilibrium—rather, it appears to be at least partly responsible for the region's recurrent cycles of political crises and democratic breakdowns. Let me briefly summarize Latin America's history of political instability, with the help of a long paragraph written by Scott Mainwaring summarizing Latin America's cycle of democratic breakdowns between 1940 and the end of the twentieth century. According to Mainwaring:

In 1940 only one [out of 19 Latin American] countries (Chile) was a democracy, and only four others (Colombia, Costa Rica, Ecuador, and Peru) were semidemocratic. This situation improved slightly as the latter phases of World War II gave rise to a brief period of political liberalization and democratization in several countries. . . . As the Cold War set in, the US government and militaries, oligarchies, and conservatives in Latin America proved intolerant of progressive-leaning reformist regimes. . . . Democracy broke down in Venezuela in 1948 and in Guatemala in 1954. It quickly eroded in Argentina as Juan Perón (1946–55) became the first democratically elected leader of an authoritarian regime in the twentieth century. The number of authoritarian regimes, which had decreased from 14 in 1940–1 to 10 by 1946–7, increased back to 13 by 1951. After the 1954 coup in Guatemala, only Chile, Costa Rica, and Uruguay remained in the democratic camp, and only three others (Bolivia, Brazil, and Ecuador) were semidemocratic. In 1958 a new wave of democratization began as Venezuela switched back to democracy. . . . As had occurred with the brief wave of democratization in 1942–8, this one proved fragile. In the aftermath of the Cuban revolution, politics became deeply polarized in much of the region. The 1960s and 1970s witnessed a succession of democratic breakdowns. Military coups toppled elected governments in Peru in 1962, Bolivia and Brazil in 1964, Argentina in 1966, and Peru again in 1968. The two oldest democracies in the region, Chile and Uruguay, succumbed to breakdowns in 1973, leading to highly repressive military regimes. Another coup occurred in Argentina in 1976, spawning an even more brutal military dictatorship. By 1977 only Colombia, Costa Rica, and Venezuela were democratic. The other 16 countries were ruled by patently authoritarian governments ... Then the cycle of military regimes in the southern cone began to exhaust itself, starting with the Argentine generals' bellicose misadventure in the Falklands/Malvinas in 1982, which paved the way to a transition to democracy the following year. By 1994 no authoritarian governments except Cuba and Haiti remained.[10]

I do not want to suggest that Latin America's dramatic history of political instability is directly, only, or mainly linked to the nature of the prevailing constitutions. It seems obvious that the main roots of those crises reside in other areas of the social organization—be it the economic structure, the profound social inequalities that prevail in the region, and more. It also seems apparent that Latin American constitutions have not helped to prevent those crises and are at least in part responsible for their emergence. In fact—and in spite of the existence of different approaches and different and changing views on the matter—the literature seems to be quite pacific in this regard. Academics tend to agree on the fact that Latin Americas' hyper-presidentialist system is at least in part responsible for the frequent democratic breakdowns that occurred in the region during the twentieth century.[11]

---

[10] Scott Mainwaring, "Democratic Survivability in Latin America," in *Democracy and Its Limits*, ed. Howard Handelman and Mark A. Tessler (Notre Dame, IN: University of Notre Dame Press, 1999), 9–11.

[11] During the early 1980s, most academics seemed to agree on the existence of a strong connection between so-called hyper-presidentialism and democratic breakdown. Some years later, however, numerous academics began to challenge what had seemed to be "revealed truths" of the anti-presidentialist movement. In particular, many of them challenged the alleged link between hyper-presidentialism and democratic instability. Some of these new studies maintained that the then-common assertions that presidentialism tended to suffer cyclical crisis that provoked the breakdown of democracy were not empirically sound (i.e., Matthew Shugart and John M. Carey, *Presidents and Assemblies: Constitutional Design and Electoral Dynamics* (New York: Cambridge University Press, 1992)), or that the real causes of the instability of presidentialism resided in some other place (Matthew Shugart and Scott Mainwaring, "Presidentialism and Democracy in Latin America: Rethinking the Terms of the Debate," in *Presidentialism and Democracy in Latin America*, ed. Matthew Shugart and Scott Mainwaring (Cambridge: Cambridge University Press, 1997)); discussing some of this literature see, for example, Marcelo Alegre, "Democracia sin Presidentes," in *Teoría y crítica del derecho constitucional*, ed. Roberto Gargarella, Lucas Arrimada, Federico Orlando, and Nadia Rzonscinsky (Buenos Aires: Abeledo-Perrot, 2009).

Tensions between the Organization of Powers and the Declaration of Rights

Most Latin American constitutions became divided into two very different parts. First, they shaped their organization of powers according to the needs, ideals, and presumptions that prevailed during the mid-nineteenth century. Those prevailing assumptions mainly included an elitist political view, related to a narrow approach to democracy. The most influential liberal-conservative jurists of the time—including Alberdi (Argentina), Bello (Chile), Rui Barbosa (Brazil), or Samper (Colombia)—shared a restrictive view of democracy, and they all tried to organize the constitutional system in agreement with those elitist ideas. We can see examples of these views in the constitutions of Argentina 1853, Brazil 1891, and Colombia 1886.[12] Those constitutions proposed the adoption of organizations of powers that limited rather than encouraged political participation, favored the inclusion of endogenous rather than exogenous (or popular) controls or accountability systems, and conceived of political representatives as completely independent from their voters, rather than dependent upon the people's will.[13] In sum, in what concerns the system of organizing powers that they established, Latin American constitutions came to reflect, as they still do, a rather elitist approach to democracy.[14]

By the beginning of the twentieth century, the old, authoritarian model of "order and progress" came into crisis. Since then, Latin Americans began to demand the political rights that had been denied to them, assumed a more active participation in politics (usually through mass mobilizations in the streets), and asked for the adoption of substantive changes in the economic, political, and constitutional spheres. The constitutions that were enacted during the period of "social constitutionalism," introduced substantial changes in the old declarations of rights, while maintaining the old system of organizing powers basically unchanged. More significant for our present purposes, those constitutional texts appealed to a renewed and much more robust understanding of democracy.

In this way, Latin American constitutions became committed to two different and conflicting understandings of democracy and rights—since then, one could claim, they appeared to have two different and conflictive souls. Their organization of powers still reflect an old, elitist, nineteenth century-style conception of democracy, while their declarations of rights became strongly committed to a new, progressive, and thicker notion

---

[12] Roberto Gargarella, *The Legal Foundations of Inequality: Constitutionalism in the Americas* (Cambridge: Cambridge University Press, 2010).

[13] For instance, article 22 of Argentina's Constitution reads: "The people neither deliberate nor govern except through their representatives and authorities established by this Constitution. Any armed force or meeting of persons assuming the rights of the people and petitioning in their name, commits the crime of sedition."

[14] Gargarella, *The Legal Foundations of Inequality.*

of democracy. The decision to carelessly combine those different understandings of constitutionalism and democracy seems unattractive—and dangerous. The new declarations of rights promise to deliver things that the rest of the constitution—the one related to the organization of powers—is prepared to deny. Political institutions thus became like a straitjacket, unable to express the views of the majority, channel their political demands, and satisfy the social expectations that the new declarations of rights encouraged. The new constitutions incorporate in that way internal tensions that unnecessarily damage their actual functioning.[15]

In previous work, I summarized some of these difficulties by referring to the problem of the *engine room* of the constitution.[16] The idea is that, since the twentieth century, constitution-makers have concentrated most of their energies in renovating the declarations of rights of the old constitutions, while preserving the organization of powers (the "engine room" of the constitution) untouched. Latin American constitution-makers did so as if their reformist mission could not reach beyond the rights-section of the Constitution—as if the "engine room" could not be the object of any significant modification.[17]

Conclusion

As a conclusion of the previous analysis, we can say that Latin America's prevailing constitutional model is—if not in crisis—seriously in trouble. Most regional constitutions emerged after negotiations that created notoriously imperfect national documents, by which I mean constitutions that generated unnecessary internal tensions. These constitutions include rights that are in conflict with each other, an organization of powers that is

---

[15] In other works, I have provided numerous illustrations regarding how the "old" structure of powers blocked, rather than favored, the enforcement of the new social rights incorporated in those constitutions. Roberto Gargarella, *Latin American Constitutionalism* (Oxford: Oxford University Press, 2013). Ecuadorian professor Julio Echeverría arrives at a similar conclusion, which is also consistent with the main point that I have presented here. For him, the new Ecuadorian Constitution has to be seen as one "advanced from the perspective of the rights it includes, but at the same time retarded with regard to its organic part." Julio Echeverría, "Plenos poderes y democracia en el proceso constituyente ecuatoriano," in *Plenos poderes y transformación constitucional*, ed. Julio Echeverría and César Montúfar (Quito: Ediciones Abya-Yala, 2008), 33. For him, "the constitutional improvements" that the text presents come hand in hand with different problems and dis-functions included in what regards the organization of powers. These problems, he claims, affect in the end the institutional structure in charge of putting in motion the "public policies required" for the implementation of the new rights. Echeverría, 34; see also Ramiro Ávila Santamaría, *El neoconstitucionalismo transformador: El estado y el derecho en la Constitución de 2008* (Quito: Universidad Andina Simón Bolívar, 2011), 305.

[16] Gargarella, *Latin American Constitutionalism*.

[17] If they introduced any changes in the organization of powers, these were changes directed at allowing presidential re-election, or changes of the kind.

based on contradictory principles, and tensions between the organization of powers that they establish and the declarations of rights that they incorporate in their texts. These features have created unbalanced constitutions, which are at the same time rather conservative regarding their organization of powers, and social-democratic in what concerns their declarations of rights.

12 Brexit Optimism and British Constitutional Renewal
Erin F. Delaney*

Introduction

The Introduction to this volume warns of an impending global collapse of constitutional democracy, with threats emerging along a number of axes, including weakening foundations of constitutionalism, terrorism and environmental stresses, and ever-increasing policy demands from national populations. Evidence for this pessimistic view is amply provided by my fellow contributors, but the magnetic pull of a unifying narrative can sweep too broadly, obscuring meaningful distinctions.

Brexit has been included in this story of global democratic decline.[1] In this chapter, however, I wish to resist the trope that links Brexit to this broader crisis of constitutionalism. Certainly, superficial similarities exist: a vein of extremist racialized politicking against immigrants and socioeconomic disparities among voters seem to mark Brexit as

---

* I am grateful for helpful comments from the co-editors of the volume, as well as from Emily Kadens, Travis Lenkner, Julie Smith, and the members of the Northwestern Pritzker Zodiac Group. Michael Gajewsky provided excellent research assistance. This chapter draws in part on work previously published in Erin F. Delaney, "Judiciary Rising: Constitutional Change in the United Kingdom," *Northwestern University Law Review* 108 (2014): 548–553, and Erin F. Delaney, "Stability in Flexibility: A British Lens on Constitutional Success," in *Assessing Constitutional Performance*, eds. Thomas Ginsburg and Aziz Huq (Cambridge: Cambridge University Press, 2016), 393, 397.
[1] Note, for example, the first paragraph of the Introduction to this volume. Mark A. Graber, Sanford Levinson, and Mark Tushnet, "Constitutional Democracy in Crisis? Introduction," in *Constitutional Democracy in Crisis?*, ed. Mark A. Graber, Sanford Levinson, and Mark Tushnet (New York, Oxford University Press, 2018), 1.

part of the global rise of populist nationalism. At bottom, however, Brexit is the ultimately unsurprising instantiation of two trends that have affected the United Kingdom for some time: a particular substantive ambivalence toward European integration and a specific malaise stemming from the challenges of Westminster-style parliamentary democracy.

Brexit does portend a constitutional moment in Britain, but it is one that exists in parallel to the global issues and is not of them. Brexit showcases the long-standing inconsistencies of the unusual and uniquely British version of "constitutional democracy"—a constitutional monarchy that operates without a written constitution under political expectations developed in the late nineteenth century. The historical constitution privileges parliamentary sovereignty over popular sovereignty, and the rise of referendum politics—of which Brexit is only the most recent example—has complicated and undermined that consensus, shining a bright light onto certain insufficiencies of the British system. But rather than serving as a harbinger of constitutional failure, Brexit might well usher in both democratic and constitutional renewal, providing the United Kingdom with an opportunity to clarify and concretize a new constitutional settlement for the twenty-first century.

To advance this more optimistic argument, the chapter first provides a brief outline of certain elements of the traditional British constitutional consensus, including the doctrine of parliamentary sovereignty, the concept of responsible government, and the role of the two-party political system. It then argues that these core principles have come under strain over the past few decades. Social, political, institutional, and structural changes within the United Kingdom have contributed to a new volatility in electoral politics leading to increased party fragmentation. In response, parties have relied on popular referendums to mediate internal divisions.[2]

The chapter next explores this turn to referendums and their surrounding political dynamics. It highlights how this use of direct democracy—heretofore unthinkable—has factored into a heightened sense of constitutional instability.[3] It demonstrates that referendum politics have been marked by expediency and manipulation, tied to obtaining contingent electoral benefits or avoiding party fracture. And it claims that Brexit is the apotheosis of this trend: a high-stakes example of short-term political maneuvering. Only on this occasion, David Cameron misplayed his hand. The chapter explains how the Brexit referendum unfolded, and how the evolution of referendum politics over the

---

[2] The use of the word "referendums" is preferred in the United Kingdom. "Referendum" is a Latin gerund and thus has no plural. "The Latin plural gerundive referenda, meaning 'things to be referred', necessarily connotes a plurality of issues." Referendums, therefore, is "logically preferable as a plural form meaning ballots on one issue." University of College London, Constitution Unit, "Report of the Commission on the Conduct of Referendums," 100 (n. 1) (1996), http://www.ucl.ac.uk/constitution-unit/research/electionsandreferendums/conduct-of-referendums [hereinafter Conduct of Referendums] (taking advice provided by the editors of the Oxford English Dictionary).

[3] See generally Delaney, "Stability in Flexibility," 393–420.

preceding decades constrained the Cameron Government's ability to manipulate and control the result. Cameron clearly did not anticipate the possibility of losing the vote or the serious constitutional problems that could ensue.[4] Direct democracy "challenges the indirect, representative democracy that has been the essence of UK democracy. If the people vote one way, their representatives another, who should prevail, who is sovereign?"[5] Prior to Brexit, this question had only been hypothetical, never tested. The Brexit vote and its aftermath are forcing a reckoning.

It is here that the chapter concludes, by arguing that Brexit is a moment of tremendous potential. Referendum politics have introduced the possibility of shifting from a system of parliamentary sovereignty to one of popular sovereignty. This transformation will require a written constitution, and Brexit may hasten its arrival. Of course, how precisely any new constitutional settlement would take shape is uncertain. Popular sovereignty does not require direct democracy; referendums themselves may not endure. But the transformation itself should be understood not as a constitutional rupture or failure, but as a new stage in the evolution of the deep-seated British commitment to constitutionalism, one that has been in development over the past eight hundred years.

The Constitution, Parliamentary Sovereignty, and British Democracy

Partially written in various Acts and statutes and partially constructed out of conventions, practices, and understandings, the British constitution defies easy identification. Even senior judges and politicians struggle, describing it as "hidden, and difficult to find,"[6] or having a certain "back of an envelope" quality.[7] Not only are the specific substantive elements that make up the constitution subject to debate,[8] but competing understandings of its terms—in Scotland and England, in particular—have coexisted for centuries.[9]

The flexibility and uncertainty at the core of the British constitution stems from both its uncodified nature and its interaction with the doctrine of parliamentary sovereignty, the "dominant characteristic" of the British political system.[10] As articulated by Albert

---

[4] See Adam Evans, "Planning for Brexit: The Case of the 1975 Referendum," *The Political Quarterly* 89 (2017): 127–133.

[5] House of Lords Select Committee on the Constitution, *Referendums in the United Kingdom*, 20 (¶ 58) (2010), 12th Report of Session 2009–10. [hereinafter Referendums Report] (quoting Referendums Report: Minutes of Evidence Taken Before the Select Committee on the Constitution, Session 2009–2010 (undated) ("Memorandum by Peter Browning") 112–113).

[6] Lord Scarman, "Why Britain Needs a Written Constitution," *Commonwealth Law Bulletin* 19, no. 1 (1993): 317, 319.

[7] Peter Hennessy, *The Hidden Wiring: Unearthing the British Constitution* (London: Victor Gollancz 1995), 6 (citing Lord Callaghan).

[8] David Feldman, "None, One or Several? Perspectives on the UK's Constitution(s)," *Cambridge Law Journal* 64, no. 2 (2005): 346.

[9] Feldman, "None, One or Several?," 347.

[10] A.V. Dicey, *Introduction to the Study of the Law of the Constitution*, 8th ed. (London: MacMillion, 1915), 37.

Venn Dicey in his 1885 *Introduction to the Study of the Law of the Constitution*, parliamentary sovereignty is "the right to make or unmake any law whatever; and, further, that no person or body is recognized by the law of England as having a right to override or set aside the legislation of Parliament."[11]

The doctrine encompasses three important ideas: First, there is no entrenchment of fundamental or "constitutional" laws. In other words, to the extent that there may be some distinction between fundamental and ordinary law (a distinction Dicey himself denied[12]), fundamental law does not achieve its importance by means of its creation or implementation but by political convention. Second, Parliament is supreme. No other institution "can pronounce void any enactment passed by the British Parliament on the ground of such enactment being opposed to the constitution."[13] And third, even Parliament cannot bind itself. No Parliament can bind successor Parliaments.[14]

The principle thus gives rise to the sense, as J.A.G. Griffith wrote in 1979, that "the constitution is no more and no less than what happens. Everything that happens is constitutional. And if nothing happened that would be constitutional also."[15] Griffith's statement suggests that there are no limits on Parliament. But there may be political or moral ramifications to unconstitutional action. Better is the explanation provided by Lord Reid, who acknowledged that certain actions might be considered unconstitutional—that for moral or political reasons "most people would regard [them] as highly improper"—but recognized that such unconstitutionality "does not mean that it is beyond the power of Parliament to do such things."[16] Those actions could not be held invalid by a court of law.

This distinction between "constitutionality" and "legality" reinforces that it is the electorate's ability to select a new Parliament, unconstrained by its former instantiation, that serves as the "regulating wheel" of the constitution.[17] The people, in some sense, are sovereign, but only through their relationship with Parliament. The evolution of Parliament as a representative forum presents a complicated and detailed history, but ultimately its authority is derived from the institution's ancient connection to the monarchy, rather than due to the actions of a constituent power resting in "the people."[18]

Parliamentary sovereignty thus permits an "obfuscation" of the democratic principle on which the British constitution rests.[19] The sleight of hand that parliamentary

---

[11] Dicey, *Introduction*, 38.

[12] Ibid., 85.

[13] Ibid., 87.

[14] Ibid., 84.

[15] J.A.G. Griffith, "The Political Constitution," *Modern Law Review* 42, no. 1 (1979): 19.

[16] Madzimbamuto v. Lardner-Burke, [1969] 1 A.C. 645, 723 (P.C.) (appeal taken from S. Rhodesia).

[17] Walter Bagehot, *The English Constitution*, 2nd ed. (London: Oxford University Press, 1872), 204–205.

[18] See Jeffrey Goldsworthy, *Parliamentary Sovereignty: Contemporary Debates* (Cambridge: Cambridge University Press, 2010), 18–47.

[19] Martin Loughlin, *The British Constitution: A Very Short Introduction* (Oxford: Oxford University Press, 2013), 28.

sovereignty works is to suggest that Parliament "embodies the people, so that, when Parliament is assembled, the people are there assembled."[20] Of course, "when expressed in this way, [it] has the further consequence of leaving no constitutional role for the real people. The people cannot be both embodied in Parliament and yet exist *constitutionally* outside Parliament."[21]

Notwithstanding the jurisprudential complications underlying the British constitutional scheme, scholars have argued that this political constitutionalism has great normative benefits. Richard Bellamy makes the claim that political institutions—including party membership, equal voting power, and majority rule—can better reflect core republican values, such as non-domination and political equality, thus avoiding the potential oppression/domination of a written constitution (as outside of politics) and the anti-majoritarian nature of the courts.[22] Others expand on the possibility of parliamentary decision-making as deliberative democracy, touting it (in the right circumstances) as a collective approach to decision-making that has benefits beyond mere preference aggregation.[23]

As the mechanism of ensuring good government, this rosy version of parliamentary democracy relies on the twin pillars of responsible government and a robust party system. Responsible government is the idea that "government is carried on by persons who are responsible to the representative house of the legislature, the House of Commons."[24] In effect, responsible government assures, through political pressure, that "government is in tune with popular opinion,"[25] as it is expressed through party politics in the House of Commons.[26] Thus, responsible government must rest in turn on a vibrant *party* system,[27] which can accurately reflect the interests, views, and values of the people.[28]

In describing party government in the United Kingdom, Dicey called it "not the accident or the corruption but, so to speak, the very foundation of our constitutional

[20] D.J. Galligan, "The Constitutional Future of the UK: 'Matters of High Concernment'," in *Constitution in Crisis*, ed. D.J. Galligan (London: I.B. Tauris, 2017), 161.

[21] Ibid.

[22] Richard Bellamy, *Political Constitutionalism* (Cambridge: Cambridge University Press 2007), 147–175.

[23] See Judith Bara, Albert Weale, and Aude Biquelet, "Deliberative Democracy and the Analysis of Parliamentary Debate," (paper, ECPR Joint Sessions, Helsinki, Finland, May 7–12, 2007). Cf. Ivor Jennings, *The British Constitution*, 3rd ed. (Cambridge: Cambridge University Press, 1954), 81–84 (discussing the important role of the opposition and parliamentary debate in informing policy).

[24] Jennings, *The British Constitution*, 146.

[25] Jennings, *The British Constitution*, 149–150.

[26] This simple statement contains more layers in practice: explicating individual ministerial responsibility raises questions about the role of the civil service and the interaction between individual responsibility and the collective cabinet responsibility for government decisions.

[27] See *Representing the People: A Survey among Members of Statewide and Sub-state Parliaments*, eds. Kris Deschouwer and Sam Depauw (Oxford: Oxford University Press, 2014).

[28] Some scholars argue that the development of the cabinet system itself (with "not only executive but also legislative predominance") fostered the growth in party cohesion in the nineteenth century. See Gary W Cox, *The Efficient Secret* (Cambridge: Cambridge University Press, 1987).

system."[29] Two-party rule has been the hallmark of British electoral politics,[30] sustained by the plurality voting system known as "first past the post" (FPTP). Plurality rules encourage broad "big-tent" parties and tend to limit the rise of third parties.[31] Of course, there have always been third parties competing for seats,[32] but "a 'virtuous circle' calculus of voting and activism" works in favor of the main parties, as voters learn that "third-party votes and activism tend to be wasted in terms of gaining parliamentary seats."[33]

The benefits to parliamentary politics of a two-party system are significant: centrism and decisive governing capacity. As Ivor Jennings wrote, "[t]he swing of the pendulum is a familiar feature of British politics. . . . Majorities are unstable, and the Opposition of to-day is the Government of tomorrow."[34] And thus, "an administration that does not encompass the median voter is fragile."[35] Extremist minority parties are usually shut out of government,[36] and the instability of multiparty coalition government is largely avoided. Indeed, as Iain McLean has demonstrated, using more than 150 years of data, there is only a 0.17 probability of a coalition administration being formed at a general election.[37] Of course, this claim of generalized centrism does not preclude policy swings from occurring when the majority shifts—particularly if parties are cohesive and distinct.[38] Because a majority party can enact policies without seeking broader consensus,[39] governance can be effective, efficient, and partisan. And historically,[40] the two British parties have been both cohesive and distinct due to rigidity in class-based voting and strongly differentiated overarching policy positions about the use of government recourses.

A functioning system of centrist and effective Westminster-style parliamentary democracy might be that elusive democratic political system that "leaves [one] free not to care about it."[41] But if that world ever existed, it is certainly not today's situation. These core

---

[29] Dicey, *Introduction*, ci.

[30] Jennings, *The British Constitution*, 56.

[31] See generally Maurice Duverger, *Political Parties* (London: Methuen, 1954).

[32] David Sanders, "The UK's Changing Party System: The Prospects for a Party Realignment at Westminster," *Journal of the British Academy* 5 (May 2017): 94.

[33] Ibid., 93.

[34] Jennings, *The British Constitution*, 32.

[35] Iain McLean, "'England Does Not Love Coalitions': The Most Misused Political Quotation in the Book," *Government and Opposition* 47 (2012): 6.

[36] Peter Leyland, *The Constitution of the United Kingdom* (Oxford: Hart Publishing 2012), 113.

[37] McLean, "England Does Not Love Coalitions," 6.

[38] The present system can cause rapid shifts in power and "lurches from the relatively extreme positions adopted by the Labour and Conservative Parties." Leyland, *The Constitution of the U.K.*, 113.

[39] Ibid., 112.

[40] Strong party discipline emerged in the late nineteenth century. Andrew C. Eggers and Arthur Spirling, "Party Cohesion in Westminster Systems: Inducements, Replacement and Discipline in the House of Commons, 1836–1910," *British Journal of Political Science* 46 (2016): 567–589.

[41] Clive James, "A Point of View," *BBC Radio 4*, broadcast April 12, 2009, http://www.bbc.co.uk/programmes/b006qng8. Paul Webb, Tim Bale, and Paul Taggart, "Deliberative versus Parliamentary Democracy in the UK: An Experimental Study," *Sussex European Institute Working Paper No. 118* (2010), http://www.sussex.ac.uk/sei/publications/seiworkingpapers. Cf. John Hibbing and Elizabeth Theiss-Morse, *Stealth*

elements of the consensus constitution are under strain—both from substantive shifts in the content and structure of governance and from an increasing dissatisfaction with political parties and the electoral system.

Accelerating Change and Party Fragmentation·

Britain is on a course of rapid change.[42] Many scholars have addressed the substantive elements of institutional and structural change: the UK's membership in the European Union;[43] the enactment of a quasi-constitutional bill of rights;[44] devolved legislative power to Scotland, Wales, and Northern Ireland;[45] and the creation of a new Supreme Court;[46] among other examples.[47] At the same time, there has been an increasing and generalized dissatisfaction with party governance. Of course, changes to the substance of governance and frustration with the process of governance may not be linked. The two-party system, as critical as it appears to British politics, has been showing signs of decline for some time.[48] Scholars have diagnosed the problem variously as a function of the electoral system itself,[49] or as a result of: the decline in class-based voting, the rise of "alternative

---

Democracy: Americans' Beliefs about How Government Should Work (Cambridge: Cambridge University Press, 2002).

[42] Anthony King, *Does the United Kingdom Still Have a Constitution?* (London: Sweet & Maxwell, 2001) 53 ("[T]he United Kingdom's constitution changed more between 1970 and 2000, and especially between 1997 and 2000, than during any comparable period since at least the middle of the 18th century."). See also Delaney, "Stability in Flexibility," 413–414.

[43] See, e.g., Elizabeth Wicks, *The Evolution of a Constitution: Eight Key Moments in British Constitutional History* (Oxford: Hart Publishing, 2006), 137–165; N.W. Barber, "The Afterlife of Parliamentary Sovereignty," *International Journal of Constitutional Law* 9, no. 1 (2011): 144–154; Adam Tucker, "Uncertainty in the Rule of Recognition and in the Doctrine of Parliamentary Sovereignty," *Oxford Journal of Legal Studies* 31 (2011): 61, 72–77.

[44] See, e.g., Vernon Bogdanor, *The New British Constitution* (Oxford: Hart Publishing, 2009), 68; Roger Masterman, *The Separation of Powers in the Contemporary Constitution* (Cambridge: Cambridge University Press, 2011), 48, 152.

[45] David Jenkins, "Both Ends against the Middle: European Integration, Devolution, and the Sites of Sovereignty in the United Kingdom," *Temple International and Comparative Law Journal* 16, no. 1 (Spring 2002): 17; Mitchell, *Devolution in the UK*, 15, 134–135; Johan Steyn, *Democracy through Law* (Burlington: Ashgate, 2004), xvi–xvii; Robert Hazell, "Reinventing the Constitution: Can the State Survive?" *Public Law* 1999 (1999): 86.

[46] See Delaney, "Judiciary Rising."

[47] For a discussion of other institutional changes, see Delaney, "Stability in Flexibility."

[48] S.E. Finer, "The Decline of Party?," in *Parties and Democracy in Britain and America*, ed. Vernon Bogdanor (New York: Praeger, 1984), 6; see also Peter Mair, "The Party System," in *The Oxford Handbook of British Politics*, ed. Matthew Flinders et al. (Oxford: Oxford University Press, 2009), 285. As with other aspects of British political life, some of the perception of decline may be the cost of a harder and closer look at the institution itself—the halcyon days of history were never as bright as remembered. See Webb, "Are British Political Parties in Decline?," 316.

[49] A public perception of a "democratic deficit" is more likely to occur in systems with plurality voting, because they "exhibit the highest disparities between parties' vote shares and parliamentary seat shares." Sanders, "The UK's Changing Party System," 94. In the United Kingdom, a "single party receiving between 40 per cent and

identities" that vie for primacy and encourage the creation of new parties to reflect those identities, and/or cultural changes, ranging from a modern lack of deference to hierarchy to increased media criticism of politics.[50] But this Section suggests that substantive change itself—including the scope and amount of transformative legislation—is also negatively affecting the two-party system.

Foundational structural and institutional issues often do not hew to left-right divides over resource distribution. These questions are thus more likely to cut across party lines and to lead to party fragmentation.[51] And indeed, debates over constitutional structure or purpose have divided the two main British parties internally, and in some cases given rise to single-issue or regional third parties.[52] For example, European integration has not had a unidirectional political valence over time,[53] making it an often divisive and cross-cutting issue. Other topics, such as regional devolution, have complicated parties' national electoral politics, caused internal division, and encouraged the rise of regional parties. The party system is "increasingly fragmented,"[54] with multiple third parties and viable regional parties,[55] and in 2010, the country saw the first peacetime coalition government since the 1930s.

This decline (or perception of decline) in political party allegiance and effectiveness has observable effects in governance. Taking a definitive position on an issue that cuts across party lines or highlights internal party divisions can jeopardize party coherence. Because party cohesiveness is essential for effective governance,[56] party divisions that result in "cross-voting" or "backbench revolts"[57] threaten party leadership. It is hardly

---

45 per cent of the national vote stands a good chance of gaining an overall majority of seats in the House of Commons and therefore of forming a government." Leyland, *The Constitution of the U.K.*, 110 (noting that Labour achieved an overall majority of 180 seats with just under 44 percent of the popular vote in 1997).

[50] See Sanders, "The UK's Changing Party System," 102–112. Note also that the percentage of people who have "no party identification" has risen to a high-water mark of 20 percent. Ibid., 107.

[51] Matters of moral disagreement might also present this problem. But conscience issues, which usually "arise as a result of private members' bills," are often treated as "matters for a free vote in parliament in part because opinions on how to resolve them cut across party lines and are of special significance to parliamentarians as individuals." Albert Weale, Aude Bicquelet, and Judith Bara, "Debating Abortion, Deliberative Reciprocity and Parliamentary Advocacy," *Political Studies* 60 (2012): 646.

[52] See Peter Mair, "The Party System," 292–294 (discussing cleavages and decline in electoral alignments). Cf. Webb, "Are British Political Parties in Decline?," 316.

[53] See Erin Delaney, "The Labour Party's Changing Relationship to Europe: The Expansion of European Social Policy," *Journal of European Integration History* 8, no. 1 (January 2002).

[54] Sanders, "The UK's Changing Party System," 92.

[55] By breaking "old habits," regional elections themselves are also weakening two-party politics at Westminster. Sanders, "The UK's Changing Party System," 102; Mair, "The Party System," 298.

[56] Leyland, *The Constitution of the U.K.*, 112.

[57] Adrian Blau, "Majoritarianism under Pressure: The Electoral and Party Systems," in *Constitutional Futures Revisited*, ed. Robert Hazell (New York: Palgrave Macmillan, 2008), 234; see also Philip Crowley and Mark Stuart, "Backbench Rebellion in the House of Commons, 1997–2010: Making a Policy Difference or Barking at the Moon?," 2012, http://webpages.dcu.ie/~leg/Cowley.pdf.

surprising, therefore, that political party leadership has sought ways to mitigate these threats.[58] If engaging cross-cutting political issues is unavoidable, or if politicians fail to predict accurately which issues will create divisions, the obvious solution for legislators focused on re-election is to abdicate responsibility for them by deferring to other competent actors in the constitutional scheme.

In the American context, Mark Graber has argued persuasively that cross-cutting issues facilitate congressional delegation to the judiciary. If the political dynamics surrounding a particular issue will ensure that neither party can gain electoral benefit from raising or championing that cause, it is to both parties' benefit to avoid legislating on the topic. Elected politicians thus will opt to defer to other unelected actors in the constitutional scheme, such as the court.[59] Deference to the judiciary has been of more limited use in the United Kingdom, given the historically circumscribed role of the courts in a system of parliamentary sovereignty. But opportunities for judicial intervention are increasing, due to the expanding role of the British judiciary in defining rights under the Human Rights Act.[60] And there are some indications that, when confronted with obvious political costs, parliamentarians have chosen to "delegate" decision-making to the courts by acquiescing in judicial determinations on some contentious issues.[61]

On the most threatening cross-cutting or internally divisive political issues, however, the British political parties have found another group better placed than the judiciary— at least as a matter of democratic rhetoric—to which to defer: the electorate itself. Of course, just as with deference to the judiciary, deference to the electorate through the mechanism of a referendum sits uneasily in a world of parliamentary sovereignty. As outlined above, referendums have no competing external claim to bind Parliament, because the people have no external or preexisting authority. Furthermore, without express authorization by Parliamentary Act, referendums can have only advisory relevance.

---

[58] Of course, when there is sufficient electoral churn, a broader party realignment may occur, recalibrating the system. The historical example in Britain is the replacement of the Liberal Party by the Labour Party in 1931, the culmination of a decade-long process. Chris Cook and John Stevenson, *A History of British Elections since 1689* (London: Routledge, 2014), 143–149. Given the current political landscape, it would appear that a major realignment could (and perhaps should) be in order, but it is unlikely. See generally Sanders, "The UK's Changing Party System." See also Peter Mair, "The Party System," 295–298. As David Sanders has said, "Conservatives do not have a history of splitting and Labour activists and MPs have a visceral fear (if not hatred) of it." Sanders, 118. And, in any event, the ability of a meaningful third party to challenge the hegemony does not happen overnight; it takes time. McLean, "England Does Not Love Coalitions," 9 ("During a Duvergerian tipping point, it is not clear to the average voter which party is the most effective challenge to the hegemon, and the strong two-party effect is not reinstated until the answer to that question is clear.").

[59] See generally Mark A. Graber, "The Nonmajoritarian Difficulty: Legislative Deference to the Judiciary," *Studies in American Political Development* 7, no. 1 (Spring 1993): 35.

[60] On the Constitutional Reform Act, 2005, c. 4 and the changes to the judiciary, see Roger Masterman, *The Separation of Powers*; see also Erin F. Delaney, "Searching for Constitutional Meaning in Institutional Design: The Debate over Judicial Appointments in the United Kingdom," *International Journal of Constitutional Law* 14, no. 3 (July 2016): 752.

[61] See Delaney, "Judiciary Rising," 590–594.

Nevertheless, by calling for the public's views in a referendum, a government may be able to "circumnavigate the veto capacity of other actors" (such as recalcitrant backbenchers) in Parliament and externalize the costs of policy formation.[62] And notwithstanding the complicated constitutional implications that referendums present, the ostensible benefits to party politics have driven this move to direct democracy.

The Rise of Referendum Politics

The referendum—a direct vote by the public on a particular issue—is anomalous in the British constitutional scheme. The only serious proposal to integrate referendums into legislative proceedings was roundly rejected in 1910. It came at a time of parliamentary constitutional crisis, after the House of Lords had asserted itself against the House of Commons on a budgetary matter (an area left, by convention, to the Commons). Politicians were advocating stripping the Lords of their veto power, and an inter-party constitutional conference sought to find ways to mediate. One suggestion was to recognize "a special category of 'constitutional' legislation," which would "require the approval of the people, as well as Parliament, in a referendum."[63] The prime minister, H.H. Asquith, did not agree. In addition to identifying the threat referendums posed to parliamentary sovereignty, his critique of the plan highlighted the difficulty of identifying "constitutional" legislation in a system with a flexible and uncodified constitution.[64] Given this unpropitious history, referendums were "commonly said to be unconstitutional."[65]

When referendums re-emerged as a political tool in the 1970s, the topics they addressed were of serious importance to the country—the United Kingdom's relationship with Europe and the devolution of power to the regions, specifically to Scotland and Wales. But the surrounding political discourse was decidedly not about legitimizing constitutional change through popular sovereignty; rather it was about managing internal party division and externalizing costs, or insulating the government from responsibility for certain of its policies.[66]

---

[62] Matthew Flinders, *Democratic Drift* (Oxford: Oxford University Press, 2010), 234.

[63] Vernon Bogdanor, "Conclusion," in *The British Constitution in the Twentieth Century*, ed. Vernon Bogdanor (Oxford: Oxford University Press, 2003), 691. Other suggestions included using the referendum "as a regular part of government, to be used on issues where the two Houses reached deadlock and when 200 MPs petitioned for one." Conduct of Referendums, 19 (¶ 21) (1996).

[64] Bogdanor, "Conclusion," 691.

[65] Conduct of Referendums, 14 (¶ 1). The Report notes that some proposals "resurfaced periodically, including the suggestion by Winston Churchill in May 1945 that [a referendum] be used to extend the term of the wartime coalition Government." Conduct of Referendums, 19 (¶ 21).

[66] Cf. Vernon Bogdanor, *The People and the Party System* (Cambridge: Cambridge University Press, 1981), 69 (regarding the referendum, "the urge towards popular participation or self-government has not played a very important part in its advocacy").

The country's first nationwide referendum was born out of the internal struggles in the Labour Party over Europe; it was, in the words of James Callaghan, "a rubber life raft into which the party may one day have to climb."[67] The Conservative Party had orchestrated Britain's successful entry to the European Economic Community in 1972, with an effective date of January 1, 1973. At the time, the Labour Party's formal position was opposition to entry, but the party was functionally divided.[68] In an attempt to maintain party cohesion, Labour Leader Harold Wilson launched the life raft, holding a referendum on joining the EEC in 1975. Skewed toward the status quo, the referendum question— Do you think that the United Kingdom should stay in the European Community (the Common Market)?—passed with 67.2 percent of the vote, on 64.0 percent turnout.[69]

Although the 1975 referendum was thought to be a "one-off departure from constitutional practice,"[70] necessitated by the highly unusual transfer of sovereignty that joining Europe required, "once the precedent of the referendum had been conceded, it was difficult to prevent it[s] being invoked again."[71] Other contentious and complicated issues required addressing, particularly the mechanisms of governance within the regions of United Kingdom. Advisory regional referendums were held in 1973 in Northern Ireland on the peace process,[72] and in 1979 in Scotland and Wales on devolution.

These later votes contributed to a developing micropolitics of referendums. The 1975 vote had showcased the advantages of a simple question reflecting the status quo, and the 1979 devolution referendums demonstrated that procedural mechanisms could be deployed to engineer the ultimate result. The ad hoc nature of the referendum process lent itself to manipulation; because any individual vote's governing procedures were outlined in the very Act authorizing the referendum, politicians could play with process to try to influence substance. For example, in the Scottish referendum, on a turnout of 63.6 percent, the Scots voted 51.6 percent in favor of devolution to 48.4 percent against. But the referendum failed.[73] The enabling Act had incorporated a threshold requirement, designed to be a poison pill: for devolution to occur, 40 percent of the *total electorate*

---

[67] David Butler and Uwe Kitzinger, *The 1975 Referendum* (London: Macmillan, 1976), 12 (quoting Callaghan).

[68] Delaney, "The Labour Party's Changing Relationship to Europe," 127–133.

[69] House of Lords Select Committee on the Constitution, *Referendums in the United Kingdom*, 9 (2010), 12th Report of Session 2009–10 [hereinafter Referendums Report].

[70] Conduct of Referendums, 22 (¶ 27).

[71] Bogdanor, "Conclusion," 696.

[72] The first regional referendum (the "Northern Ireland Border Poll") was held in Northern Ireland in 1973, during the heart of The Troubles and after the suspension of the Stormont Parliament. Northern Ireland (Border Poll) Act, 1972, c. 77 and Northern Ireland (Temporary Provisions) Act, 1972, c. 22. The question—whether Northern Ireland should remain a part of the United Kingdom or join the Irish Republic—passed overwhelmingly in favor of remaining in the United Kingdom. But the turnout was only 58.7 percent and the poll was boycotted by Irish nationalists. Conduct of Referendums, 20 (¶ 23).

[73] The Welsh referendum was a clearer case. On 58.8 percent turnout, an overwhelming 79.7 percent voted no. Richard Dewdney, House of Commons Library, Research Paper 97/113, Results of Devolution Referendums (1979 & 1997) 9–10 (1997).

had to vote yes. The Scottish referendum's majority did not meet the threshold requirement: only 32.8 percent of the total electorate voted yes.[74] Given the lower turnout expected in referendum voting, this overlay was intended to put a thumb on the scale in favor of the unitary state.

By the mid- to late-1990s, politicians and activists had identified a wider range of political uses for the referendum. For some, referendums served as a rallying cry for political mobilization and a way to force issues onto the national agenda. Backbencher frustration with the Conservative Government under John Major, which had implemented the Treaty on European Union (Maastricht Treaty), led to fissures within the Conservative Party. And in 1995, the short-lived Referendum Party was founded by Tory Sir James Goldsmith as a single-issue party dedicated to a referendum on European integration. The United Kingdom Independence Party (UKIP) eventually eclipsed the Referendum Party, co-opting its single-issue agenda. This pressure likely contributed to the Conservative Party's expedient decision, in 1996, to include an election manifesto commitment to a confirmation referendum on European monetary union—if a future Conservative Government should legislate to join.[75]

For others, the referendum was an attractive way of removing issues from party politics: triangulation with the added benefit of showcasing a commitment to democracy.[76] In its 1997 election manifesto, New Labour committed to referendums on an assortment of major constitutional issues,[77] making a vote for Labour a vote for direct democracy and allowing the party to seek (and win) the median voter by promising the electorate a second bite at the policy apple. Once in office, the Labour Party did hold referendums on those subjects that, for the most part, garnered clear majorities in line with Labour Party objectives, such as devolution to the regions and to the Greater London Authority,[78] but

---

[74] Referendums Report, 9.

[75] Conservative Party Manifesto, 1997 General Election.

[76] Cf. Michael Temple, "New Labour's Third Way: Pragmatism and Governance," *British Journal of Politics and International Relations* 2, no. 3 (2000): 302.

[77] Referendums Report, 7 (¶ 3) (including "the adoption of the European single currency; the adoption of a new electoral system for the House of Commons; the establishment of a devolved Scottish parliament; the establishment of a devolved Welsh Assembly; the establishment of a Greater London Authority; and the establishment of Elected Regional Assemblies").

[78] In 1997, Scotland and Wales voted on devolution, *prior* to the introduction of devolution legislation in Parliament, in regional referendums that sought a simple majority position with no threshold requirements. These referendums were not binding on Parliament, but the favorable results, particularly strong in Scotland, eased the way for devolution legislation in the Scotland Act (1998) and the Government of Wales Act (1998). With a turnout of 60.2 percent, 73.4 percent voted in favor of the establishment of a Scottish Parliament. In Wales, the voters were more evenly divided—on a 50.1 percent turnout, 50.3 percent voted for devolution and 49.7 percent voted against. Feargal McGuinness et al., House of Commons Library, Research Paper 12/43, UK Election Statistics: 1918–2012, at 51–53 (2012). Similarly, in May 1998, the Blair Government held the promised referendum in Northern Ireland on the Good Friday Agreement, a referendum that, in combination with one held in the Republic of Ireland, cemented the Agreement and allowed for the passage of the Northern Ireland Act (1998). And finally, Londoners were given a chance to weigh in on their local government, providing a

it did not give voters their promised say on changes to the electoral system or joining the single European currency.[79] Nor did Labour promise or hold referendums on other sweeping constitutional reforms, such as the Human Rights Act (1998), the major alterations made to the House of Lords in 1999 (curtailing the hereditary peerage), or the Constitutional Reform Act (2005) (creating a Supreme Court of the United Kingdom). All of these transformative Acts followed the usual parliamentary processes of party government.[80]

Perhaps because of the divergent rationales for engaging in referendum politics, the use of referendums did not regularize. No obvious or principled substantive standard existed for determining what subject matter should garner popular input. Thus, as one contemporaneous assessment of the British Constitution put it, with typical understatement, the constitutional role of the referendum was "uncertain."[81]

The Blair Government did introduce some measures for the procedural regulation of referendums. The Political Parties, Elections and Referendums Act (2000) (PPERA) created an Electoral Commission and authorized it to regulate referendums. For any bill that provides for a referendum and specifies the wording of the question to be posed to the electorate, the Electoral Commission must "consider the wording of the referendum question and publish a statement of any views of the Commission as to the intelligibility of that question."[82] There is no obligation to take the Commission's advice, but in practice, politicians have been willing to respond to the Commission's suggestions.[83] Beyond this advisory function, the Commission's authority lies in meting out public funding for referendum campaigns: It determines which participants in a referendum campaign can be designated to receive public funds and it administers those grants.[84] Although these

---

referendum on the creation of the Greater London Authority; 72 percent of the voters were in favor, but only on a paltry 34 percent turnout. Referendums Report, 10.

[79] Cf. Aileen McHarg, "Reforming the United Kingdom Constitution: Law, Convention, Soft Law," *Modern Law Review* 71, no. 6 (2008): 875.

[80] Some have questioned whether the Blair Government's choice to "programme" certain bills through standing committees breached the convention that first-class constitutional bills should not be sent to standing committees. See Paul Seaward and Paul Silk, "The House of Commons," in *The British Constitution in the Twentieth Century*, ed. Vernon Bogdanor (Oxford: Oxford University Press, 2003), 160.

[81] Geoffrey Marshall, "The Constitution: Its Theory and Interpretation," in *The British Constitution in the Twentieth Century*, ed. Vernon Bogdanor (Oxford: Oxford University Press, 2003), 62.

[82] Political Parties, Elections and Referendums Act, 2000, c. 41, § 104(2).

[83] See Electoral Commission, "The 2004 North East regional assembly and local government referendums," ¶¶ 2.13–2.17 (2005) ("The Commission's role is wholly advisory but the Government adopted many of the Commission's recommendations to make the questions more intelligible."); Electoral Commission, "Referendum on membership of the European Union: Assessment of the Electoral Commission on the proposed referendum question," at ¶¶ 2.2–2.10 (2015). The Electoral Commission's suggested wording was, in fact, the wording that appeared on the ballot for Brexit.

[84] Political Parties, Elections and Referendums Act, 2000, c. 41, §§ 108, 109, 110.

powers may have bite in certain circumstances, PPERA provides only weak limits on governments.[85]

By 2010, the referendum was a ready weapon to deploy to deflect a range of political problems. It is to no surprise, therefore, that the United Kingdom's second national referendum emerged out of the political morass that marked the 2010 coalition government negotiations. Although initially proposed by the Labour Party to woo the Liberal Democrats,[86] a commitment to a referendum on a new parliamentary electoral system to replace FPTP—the "Alternative Vote (AV) Referendum"[87]—became a plank of the eventual coalition agreement between the Conservative Party and the Liberal Democrats. The agreement did not require either party to commit to anything other than *calling* for the referendum[88]—a wise limitation for the Conservatives, given that a majority of that party was opposed. Whatever its benefits to cementing the coalition, the referendum did not interest the public. On only 42 percent turnout, 67.9 percent voted against changing FPTP. The whole affair was later described as a "bad-tempered and ill-advised public debate."[89]

Although a typical example of expediency, the AV referendum did mark an important shift in broader referendum politics. In proposing the Bill authorizing the referendum,[90] Nick Clegg explained: "There are members of the Government who hold contrasting views on these systems. Come the referendum, there will be those of us who campaign on different sides. We emphatically agree, however, that the final decision should be made not by us, but by the British people."[91] To that end, the Bill proposed that the referendum result be binding. This blatant abdication of parliamentary duty to make substantive policy decisions in the name of popular sovereignty failed to persuade the House of Lords. Members of that House argued against the use of binding referendums and (unsuccessfully) proposed amendments to make the AV referendum advisory or to add threshold requirements and other means of controlling the possible end result.[92]

---

[85] See Referendums Report, 36 (¶ 146) (noting that notwithstanding timing rules in the PPERA, "the overall timetable for the conduct of any referendum is in government hands").

[86] *BBC*, "MPs Back Referendum on Voting System," February 9, 2010, http://news.bbc.co.uk/2/hi/uk_news/politics/8505255.stm.

[87] Under the proposed alternative vote system, voters would rank the candidates in order of preference instead of selecting just one candidate. If a candidate received a majority of the number-one slot votes, that candidate was the winner. If no candidate received a majority of the votes, then the candidate with the fewest votes was eliminated. The votes of the voters who selected the candidate with the fewest votes as their first choice then had their second choice evaluated. This process continued until a candidate received a majority of the votes and was declared the winner.

[88] The Conservative-Liberal Democrat Coalition Agreement, May 12, 2010.

[89] McLean, "England Does Not Love Coalitions," 10.

[90] Parliamentary Voting System and Constituencies Act, 2011, c.1, § 8.

[91] 515 Parl. Deb. H.C. (6th ser.) (2010) col. 41.

[92] Lord Rooker, 722 Parl. Deb. H.L. (5th ser.) (2010) col. 1400–01 (against referendums); 725 Parl. Deb. H.L. (5th ser.) (2011) col. 16–34 (proposed amendment).

Parliament's decision to legislate for a binding AV referendum reflected some respect for the legal distinction between binding and advisory referendums. The practical or functional import of that distinction, however, was likely already eroding. No party leadership had ever called for a *nonbinding* referendum that it couldn't (or didn't) win; thus, no government had experience in handling a nonbinding referendum that went against it. A major regional referendum could have put the issue squarely in front of the Coalition Government: the 2014 Scottish Independence Referendum.[93] That referendum was not binding on Parliament, providing political flexibility (and legal cover) to the national government should the Scottish people vote to leave the United Kingdom. Ultimately, the vote was in favor of Union.[94] But what would have happened had Scotland voted for independence? How would Prime Minister Cameron have responded? Could a referendum alone be allowed to radically transform the constitutional system?[95]

The emergence of referendum politics in the late twentieth century can be seen as a shift away from parliamentary sovereignty, but expedient, haphazard, and untheorized direct democracy only obliquely hinted at true popular sovereignty. Crucial questions abounded and went unresolved: On what topics should referendums be called? When should they be called? How should they be called? What are the procedural mechanisms for calling referendums? Who can vote? Should there be numerical thresholds? Should there be regional thresholds? Will the result of a particular referendum be binding on Parliament? Can a referendum result be overturned? It may have been that, had answers to these questions been made clear, Cameron would not have agreed to a referendum on Europe or the result may have been different, in light of complicated constitutional trade-offs that would have required resolution. But no one (aside from academics) really wanted to lift the lid on that constitutional Pandora's box. Now, in the aftermath of Brexit, the questions are demanding answers, and the box is wide open.

---

[93] While Westminster had to authorize the referendum to take place, The Scotland Act 1998 (Modification of Schedule 5) Order 2013, it was the Scottish Parliament that ran the referendum and set its terms under the Scottish Independence Referendum Act, 2013, asp 14.

[94] In response to the ballot question, "Should Scotland be an independent country?," 2,001,926 (55.30 percent) voted no and 1,617,989 (44.70 percent) voted yes. "Scottish Referendum: Scotland Votes 'No' to Independence," *BBC News*, September 19, 2014, http://www.bbc.com/news/uk-scotland-29270441.

[95] Note that in California, for example, the initiative and referendum procedures to enact constitutional amendments cannot sidestep legislative approval if the amendment would be radically transformative. An amendment that is tantamount to a constitutional *revision* requires a two-thirds vote of both houses of the California legislature before it is submitted to voters. Cal. Const. art. XVIII, § 2. And in Canada, the Supreme Court of Canada was unwilling to allow Quebecois secession to go forward without a mechanism of national negotiation. Reference re Secession of Quebec, [1998] 2 S.C.R. 217, 220–222 ("[S]ecession of a province 'under the Constitution' could not be achieved unilaterally, that is, without principled negotiation with other participants in Confederation within the existing constitutional framework.").

Brexit

European integration has always been a subject of ambivalence in the United Kingdom.[96] Stephen George's 1990 book title, *An Awkward Partner*, nicely encapsulates the UK's relationship to Europe, then as now.[97] This uncertainty over Britain's place in Europe is reflected clearly in the history of referendum politics. Whether the seeds for Brexit were sown in 1975 during the first referendum on European membership, in 1995 with the rise of the single-issue parties advocating for a referendum on European membership, or during the Blair Government when referendums on dividing and sharing legislative power were provided in the devolution context, it had long been a strong possibility that there would be a referendum on continued membership in the EU.

At the close of the polls on June 23, 2016, 17.4 million voters (51.9 percent) supported Leave, and 16.1 million (48.1 percent) voted to Remain in the European Union. Since the vote, many commentators have sliced and diced that roughly 4 percent margin. There is a general consensus that long-standing British skepticism of European integration combined with economic anxiety and nativist fears to produce a convergence of interests resulting in Leave.[98] But this merger of interests does not make Brexit a mass populist movement. From the outset, David Cameron's decision to provide this in/out referendum had more to do with affluent Eurosceptics and sovereigntist parliamentary backbenchers threatening the cohesion of the Conservative Party than it did populist pressure. At most, Brexit was a populist moment, facilitated by party weakness and expedient referendum politics.

To support this point, this Section evaluates a selection of Cameron's choices and highlights the broader influences of referendum politics on Brexit political maneuvering.

CALLING THE REFERENDUM

The Coalition government of 2010–2015 faced the "most rebellious Parliament of the post-war era," with backbench dissents affecting roughly 35 percent of Commons

---

[96] See John Curtice, "Why Leave Won the UK's EU Referendum," *Journal of Common Market Studies* 52, no. S1 (2017): 20–24. Curtice surveys Eurobarometer polls from 1992 to 2016 asking how individuals from the UK identified. In spring 2016, 60 percent of those asked said they were British and denied being European— exactly in line with the average since 1992. British Social Attitudes polls found only one-eighth of British people pick "European" as an identity. Nowhere else in Europe do so few voters acknowledge some kind of European identity.

[97] Stephen George, *An Awkward Partner* (Oxford: Oxford University Press, 1990).

[98] Leave was supported by a core group of affluent Eurosceptics (roughly 23 percent of the population); they voted at high numbers. It is true that they would not have succeeded without the help of two other distinct social groups: those who are economically deprived/anti-immigrant and the older working classes (Labour). Kirby Swales, *Understanding the Leave Vote* (London: NatCen Social Research, 2016), 27.

divisions.[99] For Prime Minister David Cameron, the "running sore" was the issue of EU membership.[100] In a speech in January 2013, he announced that, should the Conservative Party gain a majority at the next election, he would commit to holding an in/out referendum on Europe no later than 2017, following a renegotiation of the terms of British membership. Cameron hoped this promised referendum would silence his own backbenchers and neutralize the threat to the party posed by UKIP.[101] The risk seemed limited: opinion polls showed the likelihood of another hung Parliament, and a coalition with the pro-Europe Liberal Democrats would prevent him from "delivering" on his promise.[102]

But the May 2015 election was one of surprises. Ostensibly, it appeared a return to normalcy, as the Conservatives regained single-party government with a slim majority. But the details of the vote showed political churn and demonstrated the serious weakness of the major parties.[103] The Conservative Party did win an overall majority of twelve seats, but with just 36.9 percent of the vote—a margin at the very edge of the usual percentages thought to secure leadership.[104] And notwithstanding Cameron's referendum ploy, the Conservatives did suffer at UKIP's hands; although it secured only one seat in Parliament, UKIP garnered a tremendous 12.6 percent of the vote. Cameron was hamstrung: his weak parliamentary position and the strong showing for UKIP in the national

---

[99] See Philip Cowley, "The Most Rebellious Parliament of the Post War Era," *Political Insight Blog* (Political Studies Association), March 28, 2015, https://www.psa.ac.uk/insight-plus/blog/most-rebellious-parliament-post-war-era. If after a voice vote in the House of Commons, the result is uncertain, a division of the House may be requested. During the division, the MPs will physically walk into different lobbies in the House to demonstrate whether they are voting "aye" or "no." Mark Sanford, *Divisions in the House of Commons: House of Commons Background Paper* (London: House of Commons Library, August 2013) SN/PC/06401, http://researchbriefings.parliament.uk/ResearchBriefing/Summary/SN06401, 5.

[100] Julie Smith, "David Cameron's EU Renegotiation and Referendum Pledge: A Case of Déjà Vu?," *British Politics* 11, no. 3 (2016): 328. For example, in 2014, a letter was sent to Cameron, "signed by 95 Conservative MPs (out of a total of 303), demanding a bill to give the Westminster Parliament a veto on European legislation. All signatories to the letter must have known that this was incompatible with remaining in the EU under the terms of the British 1972 European Communities Act." It was an act of grandstanding to send a message. Nathaniel Copsey and Tim Haughton, "Farewell Britannia?," *Journal of Common Market Studies* 52, no. S1 (2014): 78.

[101] See Smith, *Déjà Vu?*, 329 ("[I]t meant that the sceptics on his backbenches who had beleaguered his premiership until that time would mostly remain silent until after the general election."); see also Copsey and Haughton, "Farewell Britannia?," 75 (backbenchers); Curtice, "Why Leave Won," 25 (UKIP).

[102] Julie Smith, "Gambling on Europe: David Cameron and the 2016 Referendum," *British Politics* 13, no. 1 (2018): 4. ; see also Curtice, "Why Leave Won," 25.

[103] The Labour Party won only 30 percent of the vote, hurt by the success of the Scottish National Party (SNP), which took fifty-six of the fifty-nine Scottish seats, becoming the third largest party in Parliament on 4.7 percent of the vote. The Liberal Democrats were decimated, retaining only eight seats and wining roughly 8 percent of the vote.

[104] Arend Lijphart's formula suggests a 35 percent notional effective threshold for the United Kingdom. Arend Lijphart, "Democracies: Forms, Performance, and Constitutional Engineering," *European Journal of Political Research* 25, no. 1 (1994); Mair, "The Party System," 285.

vote reinforced the Eurosceptic Conservative backbenchers and forced a referendum that he (and the country at large) may not have wanted.[105]

PREPARING THE BILL

Shortly after the June 2015 election, Cameron introduced a bill calling for a referendum on EU membership, making good on his commitment to an in/out vote,[106] but doing so *before* he had gone to the EU to "renegotiate" British membership. That decision, coupled with Cameron's request to "his own party to reserve judgment on whether to support remaining in or leaving the Union until after he had completed the renegotiations,"[107] meant that those in favor of remaining in Europe were forced to bide their time waiting for details of the new terms of membership. For hardcore Eurosceptics, however, no amount of negotiations would change the calculus to leave, and thus "for many of them, there was no point in waiting" to begin campaigning to exit, which they did.[108]

The new Cameron Government also quickly confronted the challenges of navigating referendum politics in an interconnected scheme of parliamentary governance. Actions that would have secured advantageous procedures (and results) for the referendum were unavailable given their broader political consequences. Two such examples include providing vote thresholds for the regions and lowering the minimum voting age. Incorporating a Scottish threshold requirement for the EU referendum might well have ensured a Remain victory, and an ex ante rule incorporating a quasi-federal aspect to national referendums would make sense in a country with ongoing devolution and meaningful power at the regional level.[109] But the Conservative Party was opposed to further autonomy for Scotland, making any concession difficult,[110] and the concept of thresholds was redolent of the manipulative referendum policymaking that occurred in the 1970s. The strategic calculation would have been obvious and inflammatory to the backbenchers—voters in Scotland were known to be far more pro-European than those in other regions of Britain. Requiring Scottish support would have ensured a Remain victory.

Regarding the voting age, members of the House of Lords sought to amend the Bill to allow sixteen- and seventeen-year olds to vote.[111] Making up almost 2.9 percent of the

---

[105] Smith, "Gambling," 14 (arguing that there was no widespread popular demand for a referendum).

[106] See Smith, "Déjà Vu?," 333.

[107] Ibid., 330.

[108] Ibid., 337.

[109] Switzerland integrates local and regional governments in their many referendums. See Theo Shiller, *Local Direct Democracy in Europe* (Wiesbaden: VS Verlag für Sozialwissenschaften, 2011), 11.

[110] Cf. Katrine Bussey and Jon Stone, "David Cameron Says He Could Give Scotland More Powers after Meeting with Nicola Sturgeon," *The Independent*, May 15, 2015, http://www.independent.co.uk/news/uk/politics/david-cameron-considering-giving-scotland-more-powers-after-meeting-with-nicola-sturgeon-10253335.html.

[111] George Parker, "Cameron Defeated as Lords Vote to Extend Age Limit in EU Poll," *Financial Times*, November 18, 2015, https://www.ft.com/content/3b365be6-8e1d-11e5-a549-b89a1dfede9b; Patrick Wintour, "Lords Reject Attempt to Lower EU Referendum Voting Age to 16," *Guardian* (UK), December 14, 2015, https://www.theguardian.com/politics/2015/dec/14/lords-reject--lower-eu-referendum-voting-age-16.

population,[112] these younger voters were thought to favor Remain. But they were also likely Labour supporters. Once again, the Cameron Government was in a bind: "Agreeing to give the vote to 16- and 17-year-olds in the EU referendum [could] have meant it would be necessary to make the same concession in the general election."[113] The Cameron Government thus fought the effort by the Lords; the Commons rejected the extension of the franchise, and the House of Lords decided not to press the issue.[114] In the referendum vote, over 60 percent of people over sixty-five voted Leave; and roughly 70 percent of the eighteen- to twenty-four-year olds voted Remain.[115] The higher turnout of the older people amplified the Leave vote on generational grounds; it is uncertain how much of a shift adding the sixteen- and seventeen-year-olds would have made, but it clearly would have narrowed the gap.

Increased political savvy surrounding referendum politics certainly constrained government flexibility, and the procedures under PPERA ended up having a limiting effect. The status quo phrasing of the referendum question proposed by the government, similar to the 1975 wording and likely skewed in favor of Remain—Should the United Kingdom remain a member of the European Union?—was critiqued by the Electoral Commission, which concluded that the question was not sufficiently balanced.[116] The government deferred to the Commission, and the question became: "Should the United Kingdom remain a member of the European Union or leave the European Union?"[117] Polling conducted by Leave organizations in advance of the confirmed question indicated that shifting to an "either/or" question from a status quo "yes/no" could provide as much as a four-percentage-point swing toward Leave.[118]

RUNNING THE CAMPAIGN

Turning to the vote itself: as Labour had done in 1975, Cameron waived cabinet responsibility, allowing cabinet members to argue against the Government's position on Europe. Michael Gove, the Justice Secretary, was therefore unleashed to campaign for Leave, and he "gave the anti-EU campaign a breath of appeal and a credibility that its predecessor in 1975 had lacked and which could not be provided by the leader of UKIP on his own."[119]

---

[112] Parker, "Cameron Defeated"; Wintour, "Lords Reject."

[113] Wintour, "Lords Reject."

[114] Ibid.

[115] Tony Helm, "EU Referendum: Youth Turnout Almost Twice as High as First Thought," *The Observer*, July 10, 2016, https://www.theguardian.com/politics/2016/jul/09/young-people-referendum-turnout-brexit-twice-as-high.

[116] Electoral Commission, "Referendum on Membership of the European Union: Assessment of the Electoral Commission on the Proposed Referendum Question," ¶ 1.2, ¶¶ 2.6–2.7, ¶ 3.19, ¶ 3.35 (2015).

[117] Electoral Commission, ¶ 2.7.

[118] Jessica Elgot, "EU Referendum's Reworded Question Welcomed by Experts and Campaigners," *Guardian* (UK), September 1, 2015, https://www.theguardian.com/politics/2015/sep/01/eu-referendums-reworded-question-welcomed-by-experts-and-campaigners.

[119] Curtice, "Why Leave Won," 25.

He became a co-chairman of Vote Leave, and provided a "cogent case for leaving the EU,"[120] without resorting to the anti-immigrant bigotry or populist nationalism of the UKIP campaign. Along with Gove, charismatic Tory Boris Johnson also joined Leave, giving additional star wattage and political persuasiveness to the campaign.[121] These key defections contributed to the split in the party: in the eventual vote, Conservatives were 55 percent for Remain, and 45 percent for Leave.[122]

Given this divide within the Conservative Party, the Remain campaign affirmatively required cross-party collaboration. Labour Party engagement was essential.[123] But yet another choice by Cameron undermined the effectiveness of the Remain campaign on this score: the timing of the referendum itself. To avoid ongoing internal party divisions, Cameron wanted resolution on Europe before the fall 2016 Conservative Party Conference, and so he scheduled the referendum for June.[124] This decision not only complicated his own timing in concluding the negotiations with the European Member States but also fell afoul of party politics. Elections in the regions were scheduled for May 5, and the need to contest these elections along multiple party lines "constrained the willingness of politicians on both sides of the debate to appear together at events," in particular limiting the engagement of Labour Remain politicians.[125]

* * *

Perhaps because he did not think he (or Remain) would lose, Cameron did not propose, nor did Parliament pass, any legislation that would go into effect contingent on the result.[126] The Referendum Act itself treated the vote as merely advisory. Once the Leave vote was tallied, therefore, it was unclear as a practical matter *whether* or *how* the United Kingdom was to go about withdrawing from the European Union. The resignation of David Cameron and the selection of Theresa May as Leader committed the Conservative Government to carry through on "Leave." But the very next question—could the Conservative Government, on its own and without parliamentary legislation, trigger Article 50 of the Lisbon Treaty to effectuate Brexit?—led to its own mini-constitutional crisis, complete with litigation. The constitutional issue underlying the question—do the

---

[120] Smith, "Gambling," 7.

[121] Curtice, "Why Leave Won," 25 ("Polling certainly persistently suggested that voters were more inclined to believe what Mr. Johnson said about Brexit than they were the utterances of any other politician, including the Prime Minister.").

[122] Ibid., 25.

[123] The Labour Party itself shares responsibility for the result. Party leader Jeremy Corbyn was notoriously ambivalent on Europe, having voted against joining in 1975. And when Gisela Stuart, a Labour MP, became co-chair with Gove of Vote Leave, her high-profile position added to a skew in the impressions of the electorate. More than a quarter of voters believed the Labour Party to be divided on Europe, when, in fact, the Parliamentary Labour Party was 96 percent in favor of Remain. Swales, *Understanding the Leave Vote*, 21.

[124] Smith, "Gambling," 5.

[125] Curtice, "Why Leave Won," 26.

[126] R (Miller) v. Secretary of State for Exiting the European Union, [2017] UKSC 5 ¶¶ 119–120 (appeal taken from [2016] EWHC 2768 (Admin) and [2016] NIQB 85).

well-established prerogative powers of the Crown to enter into and to withdraw from treaties apply to Article 50, or does a formal notice require parliamentary legislation[127]— is one that might never have been asked absent the referendum. The UK Supreme Court concluded legislation was required, forcing a showdown between the people and Parliament. Notwithstanding the advisory nature of the referendum, there was tremendous political pressure on parliamentarians to treat the result as binding (thus answering the theoretical question posed at the outset of this chapter). The ultimate result was "an event without precedent" in parliamentary history, as Members of Parliament were "required [by party politics] to vote for a policy which most of them oppose."[128]

The Opportunity for Constitutional Renewal

The aftermath of Brexit has called national attention to the vagaries of referendum politics and is forcing a reckoning with the obfuscations, weaknesses, and uncertainties in British constitutionalism. The immediate concern is with Brexit itself. In the wake of the referendum, both major parties are now internally divided.[129] The cross-cutting nature of the issue means that neither the Conservatives nor the Labour Party wants to re-campaign on Europe; both parties sidelined the European issue for the 2017 elections by treating the 2016 referendum as binding and final. By avoiding Europe, this approach appeared to strengthen the two-party system: Single-issue UKIP voters reverted to their original party affiliations, and even the regional parties garnered fewer seats.[130] But this may be the calm before the storm. Recent polls suggest that half of voters are in favor of a second referendum, with 34 percent opposed and 16 percent uncertain.[131] How long will or can party politics prevent the accommodation of public demand for a second poll? Pressure for another vote will only increase the demand for clarity on long-standing issues. If the people are to be sovereign, on what questions? When and how?

A new independent commission examining the role and conduct of referendums is collecting evidence for a report due later in 2018.[132] The commission has its work cut out for it. What would referendum "reform" look like? Brexit and its aftermath present an obvious issue: if the "people" want a vote and the parties do not, what public threshold might trigger a vote? Could there be one? There are currently no mechanisms for popular

---

[127] *Miller,* ¶ 2.

[128] Vernon Bogdanor, "On 'Popular Sovereignty,'" in *Constitution in Crisis,* ed. D.J. Galligan (London: I.B. Tauris, 2017), 39.

[129] See Swales, *Understanding the Leave Vote,* 27; Smith, "Gambling," 4.

[130] Smith, "Gambling," 13.

[131] Dan Roberts, "Brexit: Britons Favour Second Referendum by 16-Point Margin—Poll," *Guardian* (UK), January 26, 2018, https://www.theguardian.com/politics/2018/jan/26/britons-favour-second-referendum-brexit-icm-poll.

[132] For more information, see Independent Commission on Referendums, http://www.ucl.ac.uk/constitution-unit/research/electionsandreferendums/icreferendums.

initiative. A procedural mechanism unconnected to substance might allow any number of things to be put to a popular vote; it is unclear how such a system would work, however. Referendums remain nonbinding under the principle of parliamentary sovereignty; on important issues, political parties take note and appear to feel constrained. But if referendums could be called on any number of topics not necessarily of "constitutional" importance,[133] would the parties continue to feel constrained, or would they perceive the votes as opinion polls to be appreciated but not always followed? If one Parliament cannot bind another, how can any of this institutionalization happen through parliamentary statute?[134]

If, as now, only the government can call referendums through an Act of Parliament, then how can governments be reined in to prevent the expedient politicking of the political parties? Are the parties likely to agree ex ante on the substantive areas that should require popular voice? To the extent that referendums are about preserving or gaining political power, parties will be unlikely to constrain themselves in advance, given uncertainty about which future issues might be cross-cutting or threatening to party cohesion.[135] Even if a limitation on "constitutional" issues were to be agreed upon, the constitution itself is far from clear. In 2010, the House of Lords Select Committee on the Constitution sought to identify substantive principles for future use of the referendum. But it found "no unanimity amongst witnesses about whether certain questions should require a referendum."[136] As Vernon Bogdanor summarized, "[a]n elastic constitution, so it seems, implies an elastic use of the referendum. But this gives rise to a problem. . . . if use of the referendum lies at the discretion of government, it can be used to augment the power of government rather than limit it, by allowing a government to bring the

---

[133] Popular initiatives in states in the United States have covered such topics as condom usage in adult films (California Proposition 60, 2016, https://oag.ca.gov/initiatives/search?populate=adult+films) and marijuana legalization (California Proposition 64, 2016, https://oag.ca.gov/system/files/initiatives/pdfs/15-0103%20%28Marijuana%29_1.pdf).

[134] Efforts to "constitutionalize" certain acts by fiat have not been respected. For example, the Fixed-term Parliaments Act 2011, c. 14, requires that elections shall occur every fifth year, § 1(3), unless the House of Commons passes a no-confidence motion or a motion, by a two-thirds majority, that early elections shall be held, § 2. Nevertheless, Theresa May unilaterally announced elections without seeking such a motion first. Peter Walker, Rowena Mason, and Jessica Elgot, "Snap Elections and the Fixed-Term Parliaments Act: What Happens Next?," *Guardian* (UK), April 18, 2017, https://www.theguardian.com/politics/2017/apr/18/what-is-the-fixed-term-parliaments-act. The House of Commons did pass such a motion after the fact. Heather Stewart and Anushka Asthana, "Theresa May Wins Commons Backing for 8 June General Election," *Guardian* (UK), April 19, 2017, https://www.theguardian.com/politics/2017/apr/19/theresa-may-wins-commons-backing-8-june-general-election.

[135] See Referendums Report: Minutes of Evidence Taken Before the Select Committee on the Constitution, Session 2009–2010 (February 10, 2010) ("Memorandum by the [Brown] Government"): 94 ("The decision as to whether or not a referendum should be held should be made on a case-by-case basis. We do not believe that an objective test could be established as to the circumstances in which a referendum should and should not be held.").

[136] Referendums Report, 23 (¶ 75).

people into play against Parliament. . . . [It becomes] a tactical device, 'the Pontius Pilate' of British politics."[137]

Regularizing referendums within the current constitutional landscape seems nearly impossible. An attempt to provide a principled rule has focused on regional devolution-related referendums,[138] perhaps reflecting the more generalized (and global) approach to holding referendums in instances where a "major reallocation of sovereign rights" is contemplated—in other words, when distributing (or redistributing) territorially bounded policy autonomy.[139] But British referendums have not heretofore been limited to this principle, and thus no constitutional convention yet exists for constraining future governments in this way.

Constitutional scholar Robert Hazell has declared that "referendums are now an established part of our democracy, and there is no going back."[140] But this declaration dramatically overstates the situation. Referendums have not been properly integrated into the current constitutional consensus, and it is unlikely that they will be able to be so absorbed. Perhaps it is more precise to argue that the people themselves, outside of Parliament, are now being trusted with occasional constitutional decision-making, and that this shift has staying power.

If popular sovereignty is becoming an established part of British democracy, securing the people's role will eventually require a written constitution. Once ratified by the people, a written constitution could later be amended through any number of possible mechanisms. Whether such amendment would incorporate direct democracy is uncertain; the populist undertones of Brexit may well dampen British enthusiasm for further unmediated demands for democratic input. But if referendums are contemplated,[141] a written constitution could create enforceable answers to the many procedural and substantive questions listed above.

---

[137] Referendums Report, Minutes of Evidence Taken Before the Select Committee on the Constitution, Session 2009–2010 (January 20, 2010) ("Memorandum by Professor Vernon Bogdanor"): 45.

[138] Six of the nine referendums analyzed by the Referendums Report concerned devolution and Northern Ireland. Referendums Report, 9–10. Since the compilation of that Report, an additional Welsh devolution referendum was called in 2011, National Assembly for Wales Referendum (Assembly Act Provisions) (Referendum Question, Date of Referendum Etc.) Order 2010, http://www.legislation.gov.uk/uksi/2010/2837/pdfs/uksi_20102837_en.pdf, and the Scottish Independence Referendum was called in 2014, which might be considered an extreme devolution measure. Scottish Independence Referendum Act 2014, asp 14, http://www.legislation.gov.uk/asp/2013/14/pdfs/asp_20130014_en.pdf.

[139] Micha Germann and Fernando Mendez, "Contested Sovereignty: Mapping Referendums on the Reallocation of Sovereign Authority over Time and Space," (paper, ECPR General Conference, Glasgow, UK, September 3–6, 2014), 7.

[140] Robert Hazell, "We Need Fewer Referendums, with Higher Thresholds," in *Constitution in Crisis*, ed. D.J. Galligan (London: I.B. Tauris, 2017), 67. See also Referendums Report, 25 (quoting Hazell).

[141] Lawrence LeDuc, *The Politics of Direct Democracy* (Ontario: Broadview Press, 2003).

In a recent inquiry, the House of Commons Political and Constitutional Reform Committee canvassed the public, politicians, lawyers, and scholars on the issue of a written constitution. Those advocating in favor claimed it had "become too easy for governments to implement political and constitutional reforms to suit their own political convenience."[142] But the committee report concluded that historical tradition outweighed these threats of expediency.[143] Brexit may have finally changed this calculus. History has not been kind to Pontius Pilate.

---

[142] House of Commons Political and Constitutional Reform Committee, *A New Magna Carta?*, 19 (¶ 58) (2014), 2nd Report of Session 2014–15 (summarizing the debate). See also Delaney, "Stability in Flexibility."
[143] *A New Magna Carta*, 24.

13 France and the Fifth Republic
Constitutional Crisis or Political Malaise?
Nicolas Roussellier

FRANCE IS A country of numerous and rich constitutional experiments. All the modern political regimes of different types have been tried one after another in France. Through the nineteenth century they all were ephemeral, none lasting more than one or two generations (at least until the advent of the Third Republic in 1870–1875). Since the Revolution of 1789, the country displays a long and erratic history of monarchies, empires, and republics. For that "performance," France certainly deserves the surname of a constitutional and political *laboratory*. Not only did France experience the two opposite models of monarchy ("absolute" prior to the Revolution of 1789 and "constitutional" between 1814/1815 and 1848) but it also has two forms of monarchical "empire" under Napoleon I (1804–1814/1815) and Napoleon III (1853–1870). One can grasp best the constitutional instability of the French political history by noting the five different Republics.[1] This record of constitutional change both in number and in diversity of models should not overlook the ill-famed Vichy's Regime (1940–1944), an example of a full authoritarian regime.

---

[1] First Republic from 1792 to 1799 (with different forms and constitutions), the short-lived Second Republic (1848–1851), the Third Republic sometimes considered as a model of a parliamentary republic (1870–1940), the Fourth Republic hampered by the succession of colonial wars (1946–1958) and the Fifth Republic since 1958. For the parliamentary model, I take the liberty to refer to my book, Nicolas Roussellier, *Le Parlement de l'éloquence. La souveraineté de la délibération au lendemain de la Grande guerre* (Paris: Presses de Sciences Po, 1997).

By contrast with this long series of changes and failures, the Fifth Republic founded by General de Gaulle in 1958 has been praised as the first solid and durable constitution.[2] The new Republic established the stability of the executive, illustrated by the duration of some prominent presidents[3] and the length of prime minister's tenures. Georges Pompidou, for example, was prime minister for six years, between 1962 and 1968 before succeeding de Gaulle in the presidency in 1969. This term presents a sharp contrast with the average duration of Third Republic's prime ministers (around one year) and of the Fourth Republic's (around six months!). This new governmental stability is certainly the most spectacular feature of the new Republic. That instantly gave a new image of the French polity both within the Hexagon and outside. It has decisively contributed to the decrease—but not the disappearance—of antiparliamentarian feelings in French public opinion. With the Republic of De Gaulle, the instability and the divisions within Parliament did not reflect any more on the life and duration of the executive: the National Assembly has gained the role of a stable supporter of the government and the president. A party (or a coalition of one dominant party with smaller parties) that has won the general election could keep the reins of power until the next general election. To give a recent example, when Nicolas Sarkozy won the presidential election in 2007, he nominated François Fillon as prime minister, and despite some usual political and personal tensions they both stayed in power for the whole duration of the presidential term (five years).

For the first time in the history of French republican regimes, the word "Republic" is compatible with the strength of the executive.[4] It is altogether a new paradigm and a new practice. The new republican mindset accepts a central authority, which is embodied by the prominent role of the president.[5] That transformation represents a dramatic change in the very meaning of the French republican tradition. Whereas the "republican tradition" used to be focused on the preeminence of the Parliament and the distrust of any form of "personal power" (from the time of the Revolution in 1792 up into the middle of the twentieth century[6]), it has now become the "Republic of the President" (since 1958–1962). It is a "republican monarchy," to use a political oxymoron forged by Michel Debré who was the other "Founding Father" of the New Republic along with De Gaulle

---

[2] The best introduction to the Constitution of the Fifth Republic is Guy Carcassonne, *La Constitution* (Paris: Seuil, 2011). A more recent essay is Philippe Raynaud, *L'esprit de la Ve République. L'histoire, le régime, le système* (Paris: Perrin, 2017). The text of the Constitution in English can be found at the website of the Constitutional Council, http://www.conseil-constitutionnel.fr.

[3] Eleven years for De Gaulle between 1958 and 1969, fourteen years for Mitterrand between 1981 and 1995, twelve years for Jacques Chirac between 1995 and 2007.

[4] Nicolas Roussellier, *La force de gouverner. Le pouvoir exécutif en France, XIXe–XXIe siècles* (Paris: Gallimard, NRF Essais, 2015).

[5] For a perspective of "longue durée": Bernard Lacroix et Jacques Lagroye, eds., *Le Président de la République. Usages et genèses d'une institution* (Paris: Presses de la FNSP, 1992).

[6] See the classic by Claude Nicolet, *L'idée républicaine en France: 1789–1924*, 1st ed. (Paris: Gallimard, 1982).

(Debré was also his first prime minister between 1959 and 1962).[7] On the other side of the political spectrum, it has been denounced as a form of "dictatorship" by De Gaulle's leading opponent François Mitterrand (in his essay "Le coup d'Etat permanent" published in 1964[8]). The central strength of the executive in the Constitution of 1958 rests on two main features. First, the executive can use unilateral powers bestowed on the president such as the nomination of the prime minister, the dissolution of the National Assembly, or the appeal to popular referendums. Second, the executive has become the leading manager of the legislative process. For such a task it can resort to an impressive series of constitutional and political weapons: for example, it can compel the National Assembly to pass a governmental bill even if there is no positive majority (this "parlementarisme rationalisé" is best embodied by the famous paragraph "49.3" of the Constitution).

The strength of the executive allowed the new Republic to overcome military, political, and economic crises that would have probably entailed the fall of the former political regimes. The Algerian War (1954–1962), which had strongly contributed to the end of the Fourth Republic, became on the contrary a source of presidential preeminence under De Gaulle. Not only had he taken the leadership in the overall decision-making concerning the war (notably using his constitutional statute of "Chef des Armées," paragraph 15), but he also enjoyed enough authority to impose the final cut in the negotiations with the Algerians and the decision for the independence. He did that against the preference of some other members of his government and against his predominantly conservative majority in the National Assembly. De Gaulle's "management" of the Algerian War and Algerian independence became not only a political process but a constitutional tool: it imposed the predominance of the president over the prime Minister.[9] It clarified what was still unclear in certain parts of the written Constitution. De Gaulle's practice of the Constitution became to some extent more decisive than the literal signification of the Constitution. For example, the use of the national referendum imposed the figure of the president on a national scale and in the new mass media (with the then-state monopoly of television). Beyond the Constitution, De Gaulle invented new political tools along with new public rites such as press conferences held in the grand room of the Elysée or regular TV interventions such as New Year's presidential wishes. The May 1968 crisis shook the basis of the familial and the social forms of personal authority but

---

[7] See his book published at the outset of World War II, Michel Debré (with Emmanuel Monick), *Refaire la France* (Paris: Plon, 1945). See also Archives Sciences Po (now in National Archives), fonds Michel Debré, 1 DE n°13: note « Institutions constitutionnelles de la France » (22 décembre 1945).

[8] François Mitterrand, *Le Coup d'Etat permanent* (Paris: Plon 1964). Recently republished in François Mitterrand, *Oeuvres II, Le Coup d'Etat permanent, Ma part de vérité, Un socialisme du possible* (Paris: Les Belles Lettres, 2016) (introductions by Pierre-Emmanuel Guigo, Georges Saunier, Jean Vigreux).

[9] Maurice Vaïsse, ed., *De Gaulle et l'Algérie: 1943–1969* (Paris: Armand Colin, 2012); Benjamin Stora, *De Gaulle et la guerre d'Algérie* (Paris: Fayard/Pluriel, 2012); Maurice Vaïsse, *La grandeur. Politique étrangère du général de Gaulle 1958–1969* (Paris: Fayard, 1998); Jean Doise and Maurice Vaïsse, *Diplomatie et outil militaire 1871–1991* (Paris: Seuil, 1992).

eventually resulted in the strengthening of the regime especially in favour of the president (under Pompidou between 1969 and 1974 and Giscard between 1974 and 1981). In the aftermath of the 1968 crisis, during the 1970s the Socialist Party led by François Mitterrand endorsed more and more explicitly the core principles of the Fifth Republic. In the perspective of an ambitious program of economic and social reforms, the Left needed even more than the Right a strong regime with a strong executive.[10] For the first time since 1958, the Left took power in 1981 thanks to the election of François Mitterrand as president: it was both the first victory of the Left (socialists and communists) since the Popular Front of 1936[11] and also the acceptance of the president-centred Republic by the majority of the leftist political tendencies (communist, socialist, radical), which all had a long attachment to the myth of a sovereign Parliament.

For all these reasons, the regime of the Fifth Republic has been seen as a success in constitutional and political terms.[12] The election of the president by direct universal suffrage (since 1965) has met popular success in terms of turnout (around 80 percent, and sometimes more as in 2007 with 84 percent). The stability of the president as chief of state and leader of governmental policies has enhanced the nation's place on the world stage. It has been crucial inside the European process. The strength of French presidents has often been in contrast with other governmental leaders inside the European Union such as "weak" prime ministers corresponding to traditional parliamentary regimes (Italy being the most illustrative). Finally, the strength of the French executive was also in tune with the necessity for a modern state to handle a very complex machinery of government. In that respect, one can make the distinction among at least three distinctive "hubs" in the machinery. (1) There is the decision-making "pool" with the president at the Elysée, which enjoys a quasi-monopoly on the military and diplomatic issues and holds the final cut in case of deadlocked decisions at inferior stages. (2) There is the central political and administrative pool with the prime minister at Matignon working as the principal manager of the different governmental sections (ministries, inter-ministries meetings, expert units, etc.). (3) There are strong ministries such as the Ministry of Finance at Bercy, which is able to play its own part in the global decision-making.[13] The strong and modern executive built by the Fifth Republic enabled the cohesion and the continuity of ambitious

---

[10] The classic study on the ideological shift of the Socialist Party concerning the Constitution is Olivier Duhamel, *La gauche et la Ve République* (Paris: PUF, 1980). See also Alain Bergounioux and Gérard Grunberg, *Le long remords du pouvoir. Le parti socialiste français (1905–1992)* (Paris: Fayard, 1992).

[11] In 1956, the Socialist Party led by Guy Mollet won the legislative election but not in coalition with the Communist Party: it was not seen as a clear victory of the "Left."

[12] And the positive commentaries of the new Constitution and the new regime given by prominent constitutionalists, high civil servants, and political scientists of the period played no minor part in the success. See on that issue Brigitte Gaïti, *De Gaulle, prophète de la Cinquième République (1946–1962)* (Paris: Presses de Sciences Po, 1998); and Bastien François, *Naissance d'une Constitution* (Paris: Presses de Sciences Po, 1996).

[13] A good documentary on that topic is *Une pieuvre nommée Bercy*, a film by Jean Crépu, co-written by Thomas Bronnec, Laurent Fargues, and Jean Crépu (Ladybirds Films, 2011).

public policies in crucial domains of the social welfare: they give a leading role to the high civil servants.[14] The attachment of the French public opinion to the "Social Model" characterized by the Public Health Service, the state-guaranteed system of pensions, public services in education (elementary, secondary schools, and state universities), or a "Jacobin" administrative state (despite the traditional criticisms against the weight of the bureaucracy) has something in common with the overall popularity of the political regime itself. The Fifth Republic has long been identified with the efficiency and generosity of the French welfare state[15] and it is no minor explanation of the support given by the public to the regime.

Nonetheless, beyond all those indisputable signs of success, the Fifth Republic has entered into a phase of changes, questioning, and doubts since the 1990s. First and foremost, the regime had undergone the dangers of the experiment known as "cohabitations."[16] The "cohabitations" were characterized by a dual leadership shared by a president and a prime minister of different political parties and with contradictory agendas.[17] In 1986, 1993, and 1997, after the election of a new National Assembly with a new majority, the president decided to stay in place while nominating in the office of the prime minister the leader of the new winning coalition. In the duration of a "cohabitation," the prime minister along with the members of his government takes the lead for all the domestic affairs. But, in the domain of foreign policy, the prime minister and the president share the responsibilities of decision-making. In that respect, the "cohabitations" have been viewed as a liberal progress in terms of capacity to deliver compromises within the sphere of the executive.[18] It was also a way to restore a certain centrality to Parliament since the prime minister should gain the support, more than ever, of a political majority in the National Assembly (and more secondarily in the Senate). Nevertheless, the "cohabitations" have come to be seen also as a serious disturbance of the constitutional order and of the efficiency of the government. That underlines the flaws of the original Constitution of 1958, which had maintained a potentially dangerous ambiguity between the role of the

---

[14] In the continuity of the last decade of the Third Republic, (partly) the Vichy's Regime and the Fourth Republic. See Brigitte Gaïti, "Les modernisateurs dans l'Administration d'après-guerre. L'écriture d'une histoire héroïque," *Revue française d'administration publique* 136 (2002): 295–306; Delphine Dulong, *Moderniser la politique. Aux origines de la Ve République* (Paris: L'Harmattan, 1997). For a broader study, see the classic by Pierre Rosanvallon, *L'Etat en France de 1789 à nos jours* (Paris: Seuil, 1990).

[15] Even if it should be noted that most of the pro-welfare reforms dated back from the 1920s and 1930s, the Provisional Government (1944–1946) and the Fourth Republic.

[16] There were three, one in 1986–1988 between President Mitterrand and Prime Minister Chirac, one in 1993–1995 between President Mitterrand and Prime Minister Balladur, and the last one in 1997–2002 between President Chirac and Prime Minister Jospin.

[17] The best account on the "cohabitation" is to be found in Marie-Anne Cohendet, *La cohabitation: leçons d'une expérience* (Paris: PUF, 1993).

[18] See the bestseller of the 1980s, François Furet, Jacques Julliard, and Pierre Rosanvallon, *La République du centre: la fin de l'exception française* (Paris: Calmann-Lévy, 1988).

president and the role of the prime minister ("bicephalism" of the French executive in the jargon of French constitutionalists).

The danger associated with the "cohabitations" was the first and official reason for the important amendment to the Constitution in 2000. There were two crucial decisions. First, there was the adoption of a five-year term for the president in the hope that the presidential terms will always coincide with the terms of the National Assembly in the future. Second and perhaps more important albeit less visible, there was the choice to place the presidential election prior to the legislative election. Since 2002, the election of the president (Chirac in 2002, Sarkozy in 2007, Hollande in 2012, Macron in 2017) has always been followed by the election of a new Assembly only one month later. Each time the legislative election has confirmed the presidential one. The voters have given a political (and normally disciplined) majority to the president and his prime minister. Such a dual system of electoral contest represents the exact opposite of the cohabitation situation. The voters choose the same platform when it is presented by a presidential candidate and when it is defended four or five weeks later by a legislative candidate. The personality of the legislative candidate tends to disappear behind the crushing weight of the new president. The local campaigns in the constituencies have lost their interest: the best asset for a candidate is not his or her own personality but to appear as a clear supporter of the new president to take advantage of the "presidential wave" and the fresh and almost immaculate popularity of the new president. This characteristic of the legislative elections was particularly remarkable in the June 2017 election. The candidates with the label of Macron in many constituencies were almost certain to win. They did not have to display a political campaign worthy of the name. Even unknown figures and inexperienced candidates were easily elected. With the whole army of deputies elected under the name of the president, the National Assembly and its "presidential majority" is a direct support of the presidential program with the same duration of five years. It has become more unlikely than ever that an individual deputy or a group of deputies elected under the presidential flag would defect. They have no personal legitimacy, no political consistency. Even in a case of a division within the majority at the National Assembly (there is one precedent under Hollande in 2013–2015), the government would still have the possibility of imposing its views with the weapons in the arsenal of the "parlementarisme rationalisé." Defectors from the majority have low chances to be re-elected in the next election whether because they will not receive the official support of their party or because they will be sanctioned by the voters and viewed as traitors.

The overall outcome is the strengthening of the executive and especially the reinforcement of presidential authority. The revision of 2000 has worked as a global confirmation of presidential preeminence, which was inscribed in the text of 1958 Constitution and which has steadily increased through the practice of the successive presidents, whether from the right (De Gaulle, Pompidou, Giscard, Chirac, Sarkozy) or from the Left (Mitterrand, Hollande). The modern French executive has more to fear from the expanding role of the Constitutional Council than the improbable rebellion of the parliamentary sphere. The Constitutional Council has gained since the beginning of the 1970s and since the Constitutional Amendment of 2008 an impressive range of judicial powers. It can declare unconstitutional a whole legislative text or parts and paragraphs of it either by referring to the provisions of the Constitution or to the Declaration of Human Rights. It can also be called upon for a decision by an opposition group within the assemblies or by a private individual (despite the complexity of the process called "QPC" for *question prioritaire de constitutionnalité*[19]). With a large range of tools and possibilities for intervention, the Constitutional Council is clearly a powerful actor within the decision-making process of the Fifth Republic. Nevertheless, it works more as a judicial and benevolent advisor to the executive than as a real source of revival for the checks and balances model: it more often helps the government to revise and rewrite its bills (with a more judicially correct version) than to block the global decision-making. Because the "QPC" was introduced only in 2008–2010, it is too soon to measure its impact and its social diffusion among French litigants (whether individual or collective persons).

But the confirmation of presidential domination has also woken up the ancient strife over the sense of the regime. As it functions, the French Fifth Republic has never ceased to strengthen the powers of the executive and to weaken the role or raison d'être of the legislature. It presents liberal and democratic shortcomings. Today, despite the endorsement of the "Republic of the President" made by Mitterrand and his heir François Hollande, a large part of the French Left advocates for a constitutional alternative.[20] The fact that this alternative does not have a clear shape in detail—depending on which leftist tendency we take into consideration—does not mean that the debate is confined to the academic world. Indeed, the debate has an echo in French society. The Constitution and its presidential practice had fueled many criticisms: about the excessive weight of the president whether at the expense of the other actors in the executive or at the expense of the assemblies. A long debate on the "weakness" of the Parliament had been the characteristic of the whole narrative of the Fifth Republic since the beginning.[21] Some measures do not seem successful. They have aimed at the strengthening of the opposition (construction of the agenda for instance) but without rethinking the system as a whole. It should be noted in that respect that some proposals made public by the new president of the National Assembly, François de Rugy, have for the first time envisioned the development of expertise in the Assembly. Probably the main issue in the unequal competition between the executive and the legislative under the Fifth Republic was the "technocratic gap." Up to now almost all the units and means of economic or social expertise are to be

---

[19] Guy Carcassonne, Olivier Duhamel, and Aurélie Duffy-Meunier, eds., *QPC: la question prioritaire de constitutionnalité* (Paris: Dalloz, 2015).

[20] That was the case of Jean-Luc Mélenchon (France Insoumise) and Benoît Hamon (Socialist) in the 2017 presidential election.

[21] See the final chapter in Jean Garrigues, ed., *Histoire du Parlement de 1789 à nos jours* (Paris: Armand Colin, 2007).

found in the executive sphere.[22] French deputies and senators are very poorly provided with expert support or competent advisors. The perspective of a new model of deputy (or senator) devoted only to her or his legislative task[23] might be a way for the modernization and the renaissance of the Parliament.

Nevertheless, the first year of Emmanuel Macron at the presidency overtly played on the "vertical" and unilateral dimension of the presidential authority. He has not closely associated the assemblies in the fabrication of crucial economic and social reforms such as reform of the job market in the fall of 2017. Instead he has resorted to the use of executive orders (*ordonnances*). Thus, even if the decline of the Parliament might be placed as a long and common phenomenon for many other postmodern democracies, the inability of the legislative to raise an opposition to an abusive executive is a permanent issue or risk in case of a national crisis. The Parliament can't be seen as a counterweight to the government and even if this role has been assumed by the Constitutional Council (*Conseil constitutionnel*), it impairs the image of the assemblies in the public's eyes. The president has strong powers at his disposal but he also could be isolated (the "solitude du pouvoir") with no support inside the constitutional polity: under certain circumstances, he can become a weak president.

If the strength of the executive is not in jeopardy, the same can't be stated for the political system, outside the realm of the central institutions. Both the existence of the old political parties mostly founded in the twentieth century and their relations to the society and the public are called into question. This disruption of the political parties could have radical consequences on the whole system. Indeed, the "recipe" that had made the success of the Fifth Republic was based on the majority voting system and the relative clarity and simplicity of the French party system. In the 1960s, De Gaulle had not only forged a new constitution and a new model of democracy, he also had promoted a new political tendency: Gaullism with a tangible political identity (modern nationalism) and with political and disciplined organizations. The main opponent of De Gaulle, François Mitterrand with his public image of a potential president (gained during the first presidential election of 1965) managed to place the Socialist Party first in a leading position on the Left (at the expense of the Communist Party) then in the leading position in different national elections against the Right (victories in 1981, 1988, 1997, and 2012). Under Chirac and Sarkozy, the inheritors of Gaullism were able to form a large and reunited party encompassing the conservative right and the centre-right (UMP renamed LR for

---

[22] François de Rugy has just announced his proposal to transfer a technocratic unit that is now under the control of the prime minister, "France Stratégie" (with its one hundred agents), to the Parliament. Alexandre Lemarié, "François de Rugy veut renforcer le pouvoir du Parlement face à l'exécutif," *Le Monde*, January 12, 2018, http://www.lemonde.fr/politique/article/2018/01/12/francois-de-rugy-veut-renforcer-le-pouvoir-du-parlement-face-a-l-executif_5240660_823448.html.

[23] This new legislator is in contrast with the traditional deputy or senator who had multiple elected posts such as deputy and mayor, deputy and president of a regional council or of a department council.

"Les Républicains"). Most elections, especially presidential ones, were therefore structured on the duel between the Gaullist Party and the Socialist Party.

However, the two-party system started to show various weaknesses in the 1990s. The two main parties were confronted by competition from the National Front of Jean-Marie Le Pen, a party of the far right using populist and extremist arguments. The access to the second round of the presidential election both in 2002 (for Jean-Marie Le Pen) and in 2017 (for Marine Le Pen, his daughter) showed that the party system was changing. One part of the former historical voters of the Left (industrial workers, lower-middle-class employees) has sometimes shifted from a Communist tradition to the vote in favor of the National Front.[24] In recent times, this wind of change presents signs of a more radical and destructive implosion of political parties or identities. In 2017, the two most successful candidates, Emmanuel Macron (for a new Centre-Left) and Jean-Luc Mélenchon (for a new Radical Left) were supported not by a traditional party but by a "movement" that has been founded for the election and tailored for the candidate (respectively "En Marche!" and "France Insoumise"). Other electoral phenomena in the recent past also worked as early signals of the party system's implosion. In 2002, for example, the failure of the Socialist candidate was due to the relative success of so-called "small candidates" (*petits candidats*), especially from the extreme left. In the election of 2007, the electoral score of François Bayrou, candidate of the Centre, can be interpreted as a forerunner of Emmanuel Macron. All these "accidents" underlined the fact that a majority of French citizens do not want to vote any longer for the former big political parties. Even the traditional notion of political tradition or ideological identity could be called into question. The political science of the new century will have to forge new concepts and accurate tools if it wants to interpret correctly the new phenomenon.

The Fifth Republic is not the same under a totally different party system. The instability of some political parties especially from the right and the centre with divisions, schisms, and personality strife (the actual Socialist Party or the post-Gaullist Party) has ruined the candidacy of traditional politician such as Fillon, Hamon, and Hollande. In that respect, the introduction and generalization of "primaries" for the choice of a party candidate has contradictory effects.[25] It has been a way to revivify and relegitimize the old parties by a process of open choice offered to the voters (not only the members of the parties). It has also been a cause of a final failure in the presidential election: the voters at the primaries have chosen an "authentic" socialist or an "authentic" Gaullist who was for

---

[24] Pascal Perrineau, a political scientist has scrutinized this rising phenomenon of the « leftist-lepenist ». His most recent account is Pascal Perrineau, *Cette France de gauche qui vote Front National* (Paris: Seuil, 2017).

[25] Open primaries (*primaires ouvertes*), which are elections open to all citizens, have been held for the Socialist Party in 2006 (for the 2007 election with Ségolène Royal), in 2011 (for the 2012 election with François Hollande), and in January 2017 (election/selection of Benoît Hamon), and for the republican right (LR) in 2016 (for the 2017 with the election/selection of François Fillon). These open primaries have been a popular success with a turnout of 4.4 million (LR) and 2 million (PS) during the campaign of the 2017 election.

that reason less likely to gather multiple segments of the national electorate in the "real" election. The primaries also have the consequence of reducing the power of rank and file activists (*militants*).[26] They deepen the inner divisions of the party that were subsumed in the old days by the partisan process of meetings, committees, and national congress (or inner co-optation of the presidential candidate). Ironically, French politics are more fluid and in many ways more democratic than in the time of Charles De Gaulle, François Mitterrand, or Jacques Chirac. But this characteristic of unpredictability tends to nourish the popular feeling of a national malaise.

The overall outcome is that the personal and political legitimacy drawn from the presidential election could not be the same: despite his final and impressive victory, Emmanuel Macron has gathered under his name only 19 percent of the French citizens in the election of May 2017 (in the first round). His large victory in the second round has only the political significance that a majority of the French voters rejected the populist and somewhat extremist candidate of the National Front (Marine Le Pen). It did not imply a direct support to Macron's platform let alone the details of the platform (the economic and social reforms he proposed). This "negative vote" can also be invoked to explain the victory of François Hollande in 2012 over the incumbent president Nicolas Sarkozy whose performance in the financial and economic realm had been harshly criticized.

The implosion of the old party system has also affected local, regional, and European elections. The traditional parties are less and less capable of attracting the mainstream of the voters, and more and more citizens prefer to stay at home on election day. If the turnout for the presidential election still maintains itself at a high level, it is not at all the case for the other elections. The abstainers have now the *majority* in almost all elections (for department councils and regional assemblies). It is between 55 percent and 60 percent for European elections (to be compared with 40 percent in 1979 and throughout the 1980s). The most spectacular decline in that respect concerns the election for the National Assembly, which used to be the only national election and the only track for a democratic unction under the Republic of the Parliament (Third and Fourth). The rate of abstention was often around 20 percent of the citizens during the first three decades of the Fifth Republic (1960s–1970s–1980s) and then around 30 percent in the 1990s. It rose to 40 percent and 50 percent after 2000 (57 percent in the first round of 2017). That dramatic evolution indicates that the dynamic and even the very meaning of the regime have changed. The raison d'être of the legislative election and therefore the role devoted to the National Assembly is now the central issue of the regime. Thereby the Fifth Republic appears to be called into question not only by the implosion of its party system or by the success of populist tendencies but also by the democratic deficit of some of its central institutions. The disillusion brought by the general evolution that started

---

[26] This argument of a crisis of the activist party (*parti de militants*) has been advocated by Rémi Lefebvre, *Les Primaires socialistes: La fin du parti militant* (Paris: Raisons d'agir, 2011).

after 2000 explains on the other side the development of alternative and radical aspirations dealing with the concept of direct and popular democracy (citizens' juries, direct popular consultations).

Eventually, the "malaise" of the French Fifth Republic is rooted in the lack of popular confidence in the efficacy of the governmental institutions. The common feeling is that one pivotal part of decision-making powers has shifted from the national arena to extra-national arenas such as the European Union or other international entities (for environmental policies for example). The weakness of France as a global power can lead to the conclusion that strong presidential leadership is essential. It is overtly the option taken by President Macron since the spring of 2017. Therefore and for the time being, it would be an exaggeration to speak of a constitutional crisis. In comparison with other democracies inside the EU, France still enjoys a favourable political regime characterized both by the stability of the executive and the popularity of the presidential election. There are no political obstructions for the formation of governments, due for instance to the complexity of party coalitions (as in Italy, Belgium, Spain, or even Germany). There is no likelihood of a parliamentary blockade or a shutdown of an American type. It is still a typical French asset when the question of a European leadership is on the table. But there is behind the apparent strength a sense of constitutional malaise. The Fifth Republic had coincided with the strength of the national state for the economy, the society, and the culture. In the recent period, many changes have called into question those characteristics. The French administration does not have the same grasp on the national economy with the growth of European responsibilities (currency, monetary policy, commercial policy). French society of today is very different from the society in the time of Charles and Yvonne De Gaulle: it is less coherent and it displays new sources of division (ethnicity or religions). Therefore, the general lack of confidence in the political institutions taken as a whole has characterized the "mood" of the French opinion during the last decade. The "Polity" both in its abstract meaning and its concrete avatars (for instance social progress, progress for more equality) is not seen as able as it used to be in confronting economic forces. Even with a strong president (and now with a young and charismatic one), with an efficient executive, and a tradition of a strong civil service, the sense of the aim and capacity of the democracy could be in jeopardy.

14 Constitutional Crisis in Spain

The Catalan Secessionist Challenge
Victor Ferreres Comella

Introduction

In the past few years, a strong secessionist movement has emerged in Catalonia, one of the most economically advanced regions in Spain. Its leaders have encouraged and actually performed acts of legal disobedience to reach their ultimate goal: separating Catalonia from the rest of the country. They have developed the argument that the Spanish Constitution (as interpreted by the Constitutional Court) is unfair to the extent that it does not permit Catalans to decide in a referendum whether to exit from Spain. Separatist leaders therefore think it justified for citizens and political representatives to take the necessary steps to guarantee the Catalan people's "right to decide" their future, and to implement secession if the majority of voters express their support for it.

The Spanish authorities have reacted in various ways to the political and institutional actions Catalan separatists have engaged in. There is no doubt that the situation reached a critical point in the fall of 2017, when Catalonia's regional parliament formally declared independence from Spain on October 27 and a Catalan Republic was proclaimed. The strength of the national Constitution has been put to a test by this extraordinary episode.

In this chapter, I will describe and comment on the key events that have led to the current state of affairs. I will then highlight some features that the Catalan secessionist movement exhibits, which make it a variety of political populism. And I will end

with a brief note on the difficulties of working out a constructive solution to overcome the constitutional crisis.

The Constitutional Framework

In order to understand the current political situation in Catalonia, it is first necessary
to say a few words about the Spanish Constitution and the quasi-federal order it has
established.[1]

After the end of Franco's dictatorship (1936–1975), free elections were held in Spain in
June 1977. The democratic parliament formed as a result of the elections decided to enact
a new constitution for the country. During the parliamentary deliberations, it was clear
in everyone's mind that one of the biggest issues on the constitutional table concerned
the distribution of power between the central government and the regions.

Two territories, in particular, had traditionally exhibited a strong nationalist sentiment: Catalonia and the Basque Country. Historically, nationalist groups in both
territories had struggled to secure regional autonomy. Under the Constitution of the
Second Republic (1931–1936), Catalonia in 1932 and the Basque Country in 1936 were
granted political powers through "Statutes of Autonomy," after popular referenda were
held in those regions. Franco's dictatorship put an end to regional self-government.
The political forces that worked for decades to undermine the dictatorship and bring
back democracy were in agreement that both individual liberties and regional autonomy were to be restored.[2] So it was uncontested that the new democratic order to be
set up after Franco's death would have to accommodate regional self-government. The
Catalan and Basque nationalist parties present in the Spanish parliament in 1977 certainly pressed for it.

As a result, the Constitution finally adopted in 1978 laid down the conditions under
which political power would be decentralized. Catalonia and the Basque Country were
the first territories to be awarded self-government in 1979. Other regions came later.
In the end, all the territory of Spain was divided into seventeen self-governing units
called "Autonomous Communities" (*Comunidades Autónomas*). Each Community has
its own parliament, government, and public administration, which exercise their competences in various spheres of social, economic, and political life. Not all the territories
enjoy the same degree of authority, however. Some Communities have greater powers

---

[1] For a general introduction to Spain's decentralized political structure, see Victor Ferreres Comella, *The Constitution of Spain. A Contextual Analysis* (Oxford: Hart Publishing, 2013), 161–199, and Eliseo Aja, *El Estado autonómico: federalismo y hechos diferenciales* (Madrid: Alianza Editorial, 2007). For a more detailed treatment, see Santiago Muñoz Machado, *Derecho Público de las Comunidades Autónomas*, Volume 1 (Madrid: Iustel, 2007).

[2] On the positions held by the different parties and groups in this regard, see Santos Juliá, *Transición. Historia de una política española (1937–2017)* (Barcelona: Galaxia Gutenberg, 2017), 453–496.

than others. Although reforms were introduced in the 1990s to reduce the differences among the Communities, Catalonia still enjoys a higher level of autonomy than most other territories (regarding, for example, private law, language, police, and prisons).

The Catalan regionalist parties, moreover, have often played a key role on the Spanish national stage. When general elections have been held in Spain and the dominant political party (either the Socialist Party or the Popular Party) has not obtained an absolute majority of the parliamentary seats in Congress, agreements have typically been negotiated with the Catalan (and the Basque) regionalist political forces to gather the necessary votes to appoint the prime minister and his cabinet. On many occasions, such forces used their seats in Congress to exercise considerable political influence, thus helping shape the public policies that the central government implemented for the country as a whole. The Catalan (and Basque) nationalist parties have also used their bargaining chips to safeguard regional self-government and to introduce reforms to increase its scope. This has been the case, for example, in connection with fiscal matters.

The 2006 Statute of Autonomy of Catalonia

A new period in the evolution of Spanish constitutional politics began in the early 2000s, when some political parties in Catalonia decided to enact a more ambitious Statute of Autonomy, after more than two decades of regional self-government.[3] There was also talk in many political and academic quarters on the need to amend the Spanish Constitution, in order to better articulate the distribution of competences and the relationships between the state and the regions, reform the Senate, strengthen the links between the constitutional legal order and the European Union, and eliminate a constitutional provision on succession to the Crown that discriminates on gender.

When the Socialist Party won the elections in 2004, the new government under José Luis Rodríguez Zapatero proposed some constitutional reforms along such lines. It failed, however, to obtain the necessary agreement of the Popular Party in the opposition. To amend the Constitution, the general rule is that a supermajority of three-fifths of both Congress and the Senate is required. So the plan to modify the Constitution had to be abandoned for lack of parliamentary support.

It was in that scenario that the Catalan government headed by Pasqual Maragall, with the support of the Socialist Party and the central government, started the procedures to reform the Catalan Statute of Autonomy. A draft of a completely new Statute was produced by the Catalan parliament in 2005. The draft was then sent to the Spanish legislative assembly, which introduced some relevant changes. The main party in the

---

[3] For an account of the recent historical period, see Jordi Amat, *La conjura de los irresponsables* (Barcelona: Anagrama, 2017).

opposition, the Popular Party, voted against the new Statute. Actually, it decided to launch a frontal attack against it. It organized a campaign throughout Spain, collecting signatures to petition the government to hold a nationwide referendum whose ultimate goal was to block the passage of the Catalan Statute. The Popular Party gathered 4 million signatures. (Spain had a total population of 45 million at that time). Many Catalans felt indignant about this political move. The speeches uttered during this campaign were sometimes full of prejudices against Catalan self-government. Prime Minister Rodríguez Zapatero refused to hold such a referendum. The final text of the Statute of Autonomy, after its approval by the Spanish Parliament, was submitted to the Catalan people in a referendum that took place on June 18, 2006. Although voter turnout in the referendum was low (around 49 percent), the vast majority of citizens who went to the polls voted yes (74 percent). So the Statute was finally enacted into law.

The Statute, however, was problematic from a constitutional perspective. To a large extent, it tried to introduce changes that only a constitutional amendment could bring about. The Popular Party thus decided to challenge the Statute before the Constitutional Court. Unfortunately, it took a long time (four years) for the Court to hand down its decision.[4] When it did, it declared that some parts of the Statute were unconstitutional, as most scholars had already warned they were. Other parts were saved through interpretive techniques, while others were found to be perfectly constitutional. It bears emphasizing that the Court was unanimous as to the unconstitutionality of the provisions that were declared invalid. Dissenting opinions were filed, but what the dissenting judges said was, while they agreed with the majority on the invalidity of the provisions that were annulled, they were of the view that other provisions should also have been struck down.

It is important to note that for the Statute of Autonomy to be reviewed by the Court, it was not necessary for the Popular Party to bring a constitutional challenge. Nonpolitical actors would have triggered the Court's jurisdiction anyway. In particular, ordinary judges handling specific controversies could have raised many questions to the Court. So there was no need for the Popular Party to bring an abstract review challenge, with all the political drama that such an action entails.[5]

The Court's decision, in any event, contributed to Catalan disappointment. Even if the decision was rather technical and did not deviate significantly from the existing case law, many citizens found it hard to accept that a Statute of Autonomy that had been approved in a popular referendum could be partially struck down by a judicial body. The Court, moreover, was rather clumsy when it refused to give its constitutional imprimatur to the idea that Catalonia is a nation, an idea that the Preamble of the Statute expressed. The Court could have found subtle ways to accommodate this notion within the Spanish

---

[4] STC 31/2010.

[5] For a discussion of the pros and cons of abstract-review constitutional challenges filed by political actors, see Victor Ferreres Comella, *Constitutional Courts and Democratic Values. A European Perspective* (New Haven: Yale University Press, 2009), 55–70.

constitutional order. When the Court's decision was announced in the summer of 2010, a huge demonstration was organized in Barcelona in protest. People shouted in the streets: "We are a nation. We decide."

The Rise of the Secessionist Movement: The Elections of November 2012, and the Popular Consultation of November 2014

It is against this background that one has to understand the rise of the secessionist movement in recent years. It is also important to bear in mind that Spain was gravely hit by the global economic crisis that started in 2008. Both the Catalan government and the Spanish government had to take drastic measures within their spheres of competences to confront the situation. Among other things, they had to raise taxes and cut public expenditures, which harmed many people. In addition, various corruption scandals affected the Popular Party, which was governing Spain since the 2011 elections with Mariano Rajoy as prime minister, as well as the main Catalan nationalist party at that time (*Convergència i Unió*), which had won the Catalan elections in 2010 and had placed Artur Mas in the presidency of the Catalan government. For all these reasons, many citizens in Catalonia were frustrated and angry at their political representatives. It is noteworthy that in June 2011, crowds surrounded the Catalan legislative assembly and made it difficult for the political representatives to enter the building. The Catalan president and the president of the Catalan Parliament had to use a helicopter to get there.

In such circumstances, two powerful associations in Catalonia (*Assemblea National Catalana* and *Omnium Cultural*) started to organize demonstrations in the streets to advance Catalonia's independence. They enjoyed the support of the Catalan government and public media (especially Catalan public television). The most impressive meetings and marches took place in the context of the festivity of the Catalan *Diada Nacional*, which is celebrated on September 11 every year. In 2012, the associations gathered many people in Barcelona under the banner, "Catalonia, the next European state." The following year, they organized a human chain in favor of independence, that ran from the north to the south of Catalonia. Similarly massive events were arranged the following years.

The Catalan parliament was soon sensitive to this popular current in favor of secession. The elections held on November 25, 2012 produced a parliamentary majority in favor of organizing a referendum on independence. The Catalan president, Artur Mas, was committed to this plan. In January 2013, a parliamentary resolution was passed proclaiming that the Catalan people were "sovereign" and had the "right to decide" their future. A referendum on secession was consequently to be called. (The Constitutional Court later invalidated the resolution in part, and reinterpreted the rest of it in light of constitutional principles).[6]

---

[6] STC 42/2014. For comments on this judgment, see Enric Fossas Espadaler, "Interpretar la política: Comentario a la STC 42/2014, de 25 de marzo, sobre la Declaración de soberanía y el derecho a decidir del pueblo de

The problem with such an initiative is that the Spanish Constitution provides that a referendum can only be authorized by the state, with the support of the absolute majority of Congress.[7] This being so, the Catalan Parliament approved a resolution to request the Spanish legislative assembly to transfer to the Catalan government the authority to organize a referendum on the future status of Catalonia. The vast majority of the members of the Spanish Congress voted against the proposal: 299 voted against, while only 47 voted in favor, with one abstention. The two big parties, the Popular Party and the Socialist Party, were in agreement in their opposition to the referendum. They were against it for political reasons. They argued that it is not possible under the existing Constitution, as interpreted by the Constitutional Court, to hold a referendum on secession. A constitutional amendment would have to be passed to eliminate this obstacle.

Indeed, the Court had ruled in the past on a similar issue, when Juan José Ibarretxe, then president of the Basque government, wanted to hold a referendum to decide the future status of the Basque Country. The regional parliament had enacted a law in 2008 fixing the date of the referendum and the questions to be posed to the Basque citizens. The Spanish government under Rodríguez Zapatero brought a constitutional challenge to the law. In its decision, the Court held that it is not possible to submit to a popular vote a question that affects the foundations of the constitutional order, so that a decision in a particular direction requires the amendment of the Constitution.[8] To modify the Constitution, the procedure established in articles 167 and 168 needs to be followed. According to these articles, a referendum is sometimes required, depending on the norms or institutions to be amended. But the referendum must take place at the end of the process, after a parliamentary supermajoritarian agreement has been reached. It is not possible to introduce an additional referendum at a preliminary stage, the Court reasoned.

As a reaction against the refusal by Congress to give its green light to the Catalan proposal to call a referendum on independence, the Catalan legislative assembly enacted a statute that regulated "popular consultations," which could be convoked by the Catalan government on its authority. Such consultations were actually the same thing as referenda, just under a different name. On the basis of that statute, President Artur Mas issued a decree for a popular consultation on independence to be held on November 9, 2014. The central government under President Mariano Rajoy requested that the Constitutional Court suspend the operation of the statute and the decree. The Court did so. It later ruled, unanimously, that both acts were unconstitutional, for

---

Cataluña," *Revista Española de Derecho Constitucional* 101 (2014): 273–300, and Victor Ferreres Comella, "The Spanish Constitutional Court Confronts Catalonia's 'Right to Decide'," *European Constitutional Law Review* 10 (2014): 571–590.

[7] See articles 92 and 149.1.32 of the Spanish Constitution.

[8] STC 103/2008.

no relevant differences could be observed between a referendum, on the one hand, and the popular consultation that the Catalan statute had designed, on the other.[9]

In spite of several judicial rulings against it, a so-called "participatory process" nevertheless took place on November 9, 2014, organized by private associations with the support of the Catalan public administration. This was an informal process, primarily conducted by volunteers, but "official results" were given by the Catalan government: 2,305,290 citizens participated, and 80.76 percent voted in favor of independence. (There are about 6.5 million citizens in Catalonia). Two-and-a-half years later, on March 13, 2017, the Superior Court of Justice of Catalonia (*Tribunal Superior de Justícia de Catalunya*) convicted the Catalan president Artur Mas and some members of his cabinet for having disobeyed the Constitutional Court's orders to stop the popular consultation and the participatory process. Artur Mas was sanctioned with a fine and was barred from holding public office for two years.

The Catalan Parliamentary Elections of September 2015 and the Referendum of October 2017

The next elections, held on September 27, 2015, were the turning point in this story. The political parties that advocated secession (*Junts pel Sí*, and *CUP*) were very explicit during the electoral campaign that a vote for them was to be counted as a vote in support of secession. So the elections were given a "plebiscitary" character: they served, indirectly, as a referendum on independence. In the end, the popular vote the separatist parties gathered was less than 50 percent: they obtained 47.74 percent. It was a good result, but not the victory they had expected. Because the electoral system is not purely proportional, however, the separatist groups managed to get a majority of the parliamentary seats. On this fragile basis, they argued that they had received a democratic mandate to break Catalonia's ties with Spain.

On November 9, 2015, the secessionists passed a parliamentary resolution triggering the process to build an independent Catalan Republic. From then onward, the resolution stated, the Catalan government was exclusively bound by Catalan laws. The resolution also declared that the Spanish Constitutional Court had lost its legal authority to invalidate any decisions made by the Catalan government. The Constitutional Court, of course, later held such a resolution to be unconstitutional.[10]

As soon as a Carles Puigdemont was installed as the new Catalan president, the secessionist strategy continued. Initially, the plan was to construct an independent Catalan Republic in one year and a half. The democratic legitimacy for doing so was said to derive from the secessionist parties obtaining a majority of the legislative seats.

---

[9] STC 31/2015, and STC 32/2015.
[10] STC 259/2015.

As the deadline approached, however, the plan was reconsidered. The idea of having a referendum on independence returned to the political agenda.

The climax was reached in September 2017, when the Catalan Parliament passed two important statutes through a fast-track legislative procedure that eliminated all the rights of participation that the parties in the opposition normally enjoy. One statute called for a referendum on independence to be held on October 1, 2017. The other stipulated the procedure to be followed when declaring Catalonia's independence and giving birth to a new Catalan Republic. According to these laws, if the referendum showed that the popular votes in favor of independence outnumbered those against, the Catalan Parliament would be under the duty to issue a declaration of independence two days after the official publication of the results. A provisional set of laws would then apply, until a new constitution for the new Catalan Republic was adopted.

These political moves obviously amounted to a grave attack on Spain's constitutional order. Under the Spanish Constitution (as is true of almost all democratic constitutions in the world), it is unlawful for a region to unilaterally secede from the rest of the country.[11] The Spanish Constitution does not recognize the right of Catalans to "choose secession." Nor does the principle of self-determination of peoples, that is part of public international law, extend such a right to Catalans. No situation where international law is generally regarded to cover a right to secession obtains.[12] Catalonia is not a colony. Its territory has not been occupied by a foreign country. And its citizens are not victims of systematic human rights violations by the Spanish state.

As expected, the Spanish government challenged those two statutes before the Constitutional Court. The Court quickly suspended their operation by way of interim measures.[13] The Catalan authorities decided to proceed according to their plans in spite of it all. The Spanish government, the prosecutors, and the judiciary adopted various measures to neutralize the logistics of the referendum. The technical infrastructure was their target. The judiciary, in particular, ordered the police to prevent the referendum from taking place. In the end, however, many people went to the polling stations on October 1 and managed to cast their ballots. Only a few stations were closed, affecting 770,000 citizens, according to the information provided by the Catalan government. The official results were these: 90.18 percent voted in favor of independence, while only 7.83 percent voted against. (Out of 5,313,564 citizens who were entitled to participate, 2,286,217 votes were counted). No procedural guarantees were in place, however, so the official results were unreliable, as international electoral observers concluded.

---

[11] For a thoughtful comparative-law discussion of what constitutions say and should say about secession, see Vicki C. Jackson, "Secession, Transnational Precedents, and Constitutional Silences," in *Nullification and Secession in Modern Constitutional Thought*, ed. Sanford Levinson (Lawrence: University Press of Kansas, 2016), 314–342.

[12] On this issue, the opinion of the Supreme Court of Canada concerning Quebec is instructive. See Opinion of August 20, 1998, "Reference re Secession of Quebec" [1998] 2.S.C.R 217.

[13] The Court later ruled that the two laws were unconstitutional: STC 114/2017, and STC 124/2017.

In various polling stations, there were clashes between the state police forces (*Policía Nacional* and *Guardia Civil*) and crowds that tried to prevent the seizure of the ballot boxes. Some people were injured. The evidence of police excesses generated a major scandal, both in Spain and internationally. Thousands of citizens took to the streets on October 3 to express their outrage against the police.

In spite of the unlawful character of the referendum, the Catalan government decided to regard it as valid. It published the results and argued that there was now, finally, an unquestionable democratic mandate to proclaim the independence of Catalonia.

Then, on October 4, in the middle of the political turmoil generated by the illegal referendum and the moves toward secession, King Felipe VI made a grave speech to the nation expressing his opposition to the illegal actions of the Catalan authorities, as well as his endorsement of the necessary measures to be taken to restore constitutional order. The king's words helped strengthen the unity of the two largest political parties (the Popular Party and the Socialist Party) in support of the extraordinary measures that Prime Minister Rajoy would employ.

The Proclamation of the Catalan Republic and the Spanish Government's Reaction

As already indicated, one of the statutes that the Catalan Parliament had passed in September 2017 established that the declaration of independence was to be issued within two days of the publication of the results of the referendum, in the event of a secessionist victory. This deadline was not observed.

A first meeting took place in Parliament on October 10, where President Puigdemont expressed the position of his government. He assumed the mandate to declare Catalonia's independence, but suspended the effects of a declaration of independence. No debate took place and no parliamentary resolution was adopted. It was not clear what the legal impact of Puigdemont's words were.

As a response, Prime Minister Mariano Rajoy announced that its government would use the extraordinary mechanism detailed in article 155 of the Spanish Constitution to stop the secessionists. This article (which is taken with some alterations from article 37 of the German Constitution) empowers the central government to issue measures to confront a regional government that fails to comply with its constitutional or legal obligations or that gravely attacks the general interest of Spain. The consent of the Senate is required for such measures to be implemented. This mechanism had never been employed before.[14]

---

[14] On this mechanism, see Alberto López-Basaguren, "Regional Defiance and Enforcement of Federal Law in Spain," in *The Enforcement of EU Law and Values: Ensuring Member States' Compliance*, ed. András Jakab and Dimitry Kochenov (Oxford: Oxford University Press, 2017), 309–311. For a more detailed analysis, see

After some days of great confusion and anxiety, the expectation in the morning of October 26 was that President Puigdemont would call early elections in Catalonia to neutralize the central government's announcement to resort to article 155. The press was informed that that was the plan. But some members of the secessionist parties had publicly criticized the idea in the previous hours. They regarded early elections as a betrayal of the promises made to the people as to the consequences of the referendum. In the end, President Puigdemont could not resist the internal pressures and chose to go ahead with a parliamentary declaration of independence. Thus, on October 27, an independent Catalan Republic was proclaimed by the Catalan legislative assembly. As knowledgeable observers expected, no government in the world recognized the new state and the European Union sided with the Spanish government.

That same day, the central government obtained the Senate's authorization to adopt the extraordinary measures that article 155 contemplates. Prime Minister Rajoy announced next day (a Saturday) the decision of his government to call early elections in Catalonia, to be held on December 21, 2017. He also announced the removal of the Catalan president and his cabinet. The Catalan public administration would therefore be subject to the supervision and the instructions of the central government.

After a quiet weekend, the following Monday brought a big surprise: Puigdemont and some members of his cabinet had fled to Belgium, while others remained in Spain. All of them were facing criminal charges. The highest courts in Spain (the *Audiencia Nacional* and the Supreme Court) were conducting the proceedings. (They still are at the time of writing). There is no reasonable doubt that organizing the illegal referendum of October 1, and coordinating all the actions that culminated in the proclamation of an independent Catalan Republic amounts to a breach of the law. There is also no serious doubt that the principal actors in this movement disobeyed judicial orders and used public money in an unlawful way. Such actions are defined as criminal by the Spanish Penal Code. There is room for controversy with regard to the crimes of sedition and rebellion the leaders are also being charged with.[15] In any event, it seems inevitable that criminal sanctions will be imposed on them after the trial takes place in a relatively near future. So the courts handling these cases had to decide whether it was necessary to adopt provisional measures. They concluded that there was a risk that the criminal activity secessionists were being accused of might continue in the future, and thus ordered some of the leaders to be sent to prison as a provisional measure.

Jesús García Torres, "El artículo 155 de la Constitución española y el principio constitucional de autonomía," in *Organización territorial del Estado (Comunidades Autónomas)*, Volume II (Madrid: Instituto de Estudios Fiscales, 1984), 1189–1303, and Pedro Cruz Villalón, "La protección extraordinaria del Estado," in *La Constitución española de 1978. Comentario sistemático*, ed. Eduardo García de Enterría and Alberto Predieri (Madrid: Civitas, 1980), 689–717.

[15] Alberto López-Basaguren, "Regional Defiance," 311–315.

As expected, demonstrations were organized in Catalonia to protest against the central government's measures under article 155 and the judicial incarceration of the secessionist leaders. In this highly charged political atmosphere, the elections were finally held on December 21, 2017. There was a very high level of political participation: 79.04 percent of the people turned to the polls. The secessionist parties (*Junts per Catalunya, ERC,* and *CUP*) maintained their popular support: they gathered around 47.5 percent of the votes, which is almost as much as they had obtained in the previous elections of 2015. Because the electoral system is not purely proportional, as already noted, these parties achieved a majority of the parliamentary seats. It is thus likely that the new president will be chosen by the secessionist parties. Things remain uncertain at the time of writing. It is extremely unlikely, however, that Catalan separatists will pursue the same strategy in the future. The fact of the matter is that they have utterly failed to bring about Catalonia's independence and they have caused great collective damage. No country in the world has recognized the independent Catalan Republic. The European Union has expressed its clear opposition to illegal secession. The Catalan economy has suffered as a result of the political instability that secessionists have caused. Catalan society is deeply divided on the issue. Massive demonstrations in defense of the unity of Spain have already taken place in Catalonia. In spite of the significant percentage of citizens who have voted for the separatist political parties, they amount to less than 50 percent. There is no democratic mandate to construct an independent Republic. The vast majority of citizens who endorse independence, moreover, are not ready to engage in illegal acts and face the applicable penalties. Their social and economic situation is not so desperate as to make revolution a rational course of action for them.

Catalan Secessionism as a Form of Populism

How should we characterize Catalan secessionism? The movement has its own distinctive features, but it exhibits family resemblances with other political phenomena we normally associate with populism.[16]

A first characteristic of Catalan secessionism is its tendency toward a very simplistic political discourse. For Catalan separatists, the political world does not present complex problems that call for sophisticated solutions. Simple answers are to be given, that citizens can easily grasp. If the majority of Catalan citizens seem to be of the opinion that it would be better for Catalonia to leave Spain, the obvious thing to do, according to the secessionists, is to organize a referendum to test whether this majoritarian sentiment exists. If the answer is yes, then Spain must permit Catalonia to become a

---

[16] For a discussion of several manifestations of populism in the United States and Europe, see John B. Judis, *The Populist Explosion* (New York: Columbia Global Reports, 2016).

new independent state. A different approach is a betrayal of democracy. Political communities have a "right to decide" whether to remain within the larger polities they find themselves in.

There is a well-known problem, however, that the specialized literature on secession has always discussed: How should we define the boundaries of the relevant group that is supposed to have a right to exit? And how should we deal with secessions within secessions? Historical experience shows that this is a real issue.[17] In the case of Catalonia, for example, at some point a majority of Catalans may favor secession from Spain, but within Catalonia there is a large group of citizens who are concentrated in vast parts of the provinces of Barcelona and Tarragona that are clearly against independence. A name has already been invented to refer to this territory: Tabarnia. Would it not be fair, then, for this section of Catalonia to remain in Spain, while the other chooses to secede? This important question is thought to be ridiculous by Catalan secessionists, who consider that the unity of Spain is open to question, but the unity of Catalonia is not. To support their position, they ultimately have to rely on a nationalist assumption, according to which Catalonia is a true nation while Spain is an artificial combination of nations. But this is too simple a doctrine.

A second aspect of the Catalan secessionist movement is its endorsement of the idea that there is such a thing as a homogeneous "Catalan people," and that the majority of the people want independence. We have already noted that the secessionist parties have never garnered more than 50 percent of the popular vote. In addition, it is critical to observe that the political preference for leaving Spain is strongly correlated to membership in particular social and cultural groups. As studies have revealed, someone whose parents were born in Catalonia is more likely to favor secession than someone whose parents come from the rest of Spain. A person who belongs to the middle class is more likely to support secession than a person from the lower classes. People who live in the rural areas are more prone to support secession than people who live in large cities. The complex composition of Catalan society and the significant cleavages that the issue of independence has already produced are suppressed by the prevailing rhetoric. Secessionists make a simple appeal to "the Catalan people" without any nuances. This helps them draw a contrast between the Catalan people and the Spanish establishment centered in Madrid—the state apparatus and the social and economic elite whose interests are served by it. The struggle for Catalan independence is thus presented as a populist struggle.

---

[17] Many examples could be given. During the American Civil War, for instance, the Free State of Winston, an upper-state county in Alabama that had no desire to leave the Union, tried to exit from Alabama. More recently, if Quebec had seceded from Canada, the question of what to do with the parts of Quebec where Anglophones are concentrated would certainly have arisen. On these cases, see Sanford Levinson, "The 21st Century Rediscovery of Nullification and Secession in American Political Rhetoric," in *Nullification and Secession in Modern Constitutional Thought*, ed. Sanford Levinson (Lawrence: University Press of Kansas, 2016), 43.

The denial of heterogeneity and pluralism goes so far that in many villages and towns in Catalonia the secessionist flag (the "estelada") is displayed in local public buildings, as if it were the official flag. During the elections in recent years, major controversies have arisen when the Spanish organs in charge of supervising the fairness of the elections have ordered those flags to be removed, out of neutrality considerations.

A similarly populist move can be observed when Catalan separatists refer to Franco's dictatorship as an example of Spanish authoritarianism, and they contrast the latter with the democratic spirit that—they claim—has historically animated the Catalan people. They neglect, however, that Catalonia was deeply divided during the Civil War and that significant sections of conservative public opinion in Catalonia were supportive of Franco. Again, the reference to an abstraction (the Catalan people) hides the inconvenient fact that Catalan society, like Spain in general, was tragically divided on many issues, leading to a civil war and a brutal dictatorship. It is instructive that on September 24, 2017, the president of the Catalan Parliament, Carme Forcadell, asserted in public that the Spanish executive and judicial authorities that were adopting measures against unilateral secession were acting "exactly in the same way as under Franco's dictatorship." Her words illustrate the extent to which the dichotomy between Catalan democracy and Spanish authoritarianism is deeply entrenched in secessionist discourse.

A third feature of Catalan political separatism that deserves emphasis is its pronounced tendency to lose all sense of proportion when assessing the defects and virtues of existing institutional structures. Catalan secessionists are ready to exaggerate the defects of current arrangements, and to minimize the achievements that past generations have made to improve collective life in Spain. Thus, secessionists portray Spain as a very centralized polity that shows no sensitivity toward the interests and the national identity of Catalan citizens. Some of their grievances may be justified to a certain degree, but they underestimate the progress that has been made.

They complain quite rightly, for example, that more visibility should be given to Catalan language and culture at the state level. This does not mean, however, that Spain has shown no respect for Catalan identity. In public schools in Catalonia, for instance, Catalan is the basic medium of instruction—Spanish plays only a minor role. The Spanish Constitutional Court has accepted this. It has held that parents have no right to insist on Spanish as the only working language for their kids in public schools. The Court has thus ruled that it is perfectly legitimate for the Catalan government to establish Catalan as the "center of gravity" of the educational system. The Court has also said, however, that the Spanish language cannot be totally excluded.[18]

It is also true that the way resources are distributed among the different regions in Spain is not fair enough, and that Catalonia (as well as some other wealthy regions) should receive more public goods than it currently gets. But this does not mean that

[18] STC 337/1994, and STC 31/2010.

"Spain robs us (Catalans)" of 16,000 million euros each year, as secessionists often say.[19] Actually, Catalan separatists often argue that if Catalonia becomes independent in the future, the European Union will not be in a position to close its doors to the new state, given the wealth and industrial development that Catalonia exhibits. This suggests that being part of Spain has not been so terrible after all. Indeed, the existence of a protected Spanish market has historically been crucial for the growth of the Catalan industrial sector.

Similarly, it is uncontroversial that the Spanish government often issues laws and regulations that are so detailed that they drastically reduce the space left for regional self-government. A better system should be designed to safeguard regional autonomy against the legislative excesses from Madrid. It is an exaggeration, however, to say that Catalan self-government is minimal.

Secessionists also underestimate the extent to which the democratic system built around the Constitution of 1978 has been quite decent in terms of protecting fundamental rights. Spain was one of the first countries in the world to recognize same-sex marriage. (It did so in 2005). Under the existing Constitution, moreover, Spain has never responded to terrorism through laws allowing for unlimited detention of suspects without trial, as other nations unfortunately have. A key manifestation of the Spanish Constitution's liberal openness is the absence of any substantive barrier to constitutional amendment, since no principles are entrenched. No restrictions exist in Spain, therefore, regarding the goals and programs that political parties can pursue. The Constitutional Court has insisted in its jurisprudence that the Spanish Constitution does not embrace a model of "militant democracy." Over the years, secessionists have freely fought for their ideas in the political sphere and they have fully enjoyed the constitutional protection of freedom of speech, association, and assembly.

A fourth remarkable trait of the secessionist movement is connected to this lack of a sense of proportion. While Catalan separatists paint a very defective Spanish political system, they promise a rosy Catalan Republic. An independent Catalonia, they say, will be a model for the world: it will be a country like Denmark (but with nicer weather). They also describe a rather easy path to get to the future they envisage. They completely underestimate the economic, social, and cultural damage that would be produced if Catalonia were to sever its strong links with the rest of Spain through unilateral actions, such as the damage we already witnessed in the fall of 2017 when the parliamentary declaration of independence was issued.

This connects with a fifth aspect of Catalan secessionism: its capacity to build epistemic shields to protect people from reality tests. Many citizens are led to ignore inconvenient facts or to interpret them in imaginative ways in order not to let the facts undermine

---

[19] For a critical view of secessionist claims on economic matters, see Josep Borrell and Joan Llorach, *Las cuentas y los cuentos de la independencia* (Madrid: La Catarata, 2015).

their beliefs. It was instructive, for example, how people in secessionist circles reacted to the news that thousands of companies had decided to move their headquarters from Barcelona to Madrid (or to other cities in Spain) when those companies learned about the secessionist laws that the Catalan Parliament had passed in September 2017. The false story that the secessionist leaders were able to sell to many audiences was that the Spanish government had forced all those companies to abandon Barcelona in order to discredit the Catalan government.

When reality sometimes finally emerges, secessionists easily change gears. For a long while, for example, they contended that the European Union will help the cause of Catalan independence. When events proved them wrong, they started to criticize the Union. Thus, former president Carles Puigdemont declared on November 26, 2017, that the European Union is a "club of decadent countries," where a few people govern to serve economic interests of questionable legitimacy. He suggested that a referendum should be called in Catalonia to ask citizens whether they want to be part of such a Union.

The Difficult Way Forward

So what is to be done? There is wide consensus among commentators that the key political figures should sit down and negotiate an agreement to confront the Catalan crisis.

According to some voices, the agreement should include the terms under which the Spanish government could permit Catalonia to hold a referendum on independence. The problem with this proposal, first of all, is that it is doubtful that such an authorization would be valid under the current Constitution, given the Constitutional Court's case law, as already noted. More important, an existential question about the independence of Catalonia would produce enormous polarization among the citizenry, undermining the social fabric.

Instead of organizing a referendum to register the existence of a tiny majority for or against independence, it is much better to work out a middle-ground solution that can be accepted by a larger, much more stable majority. A package of reforms should be agreed upon by the relevant political representatives and offered to the Catalan people for a vote in a referendum. In that referendum, the secessionist forces could argue their case against the proposed reforms and in favor of independence. If the majority of citizens voted in favor of the package, the necessary legislative and constitutional changes would be introduced at a later stage.

There is no hope for progress, however, if there is only negotiation. There must also be a deliberative moment, when diverse citizens and political representatives try to explain why they think the way they do, and why they have developed the preferences they have. Big misunderstandings and false information could be eliminated through a deliberative process of some quality. It is also critical to restore feelings of mutual loyalty.

It is hard for the Spanish leaders at the center to increase Catalan self-government, if this will only make it easier for Catalan authorities to create an institutional platform to achieve secession in the future. Conversely, secessionist sentiment will not tend to be reduced unless the higher level of political autonomy that may be granted to Catalonia is securely protected against future erosion by the central authorities. So the way forward to construct a political solution to the Catalan problem is not easy at all. Only time will tell whether a successful constitutional reform is finally agreed upon.

15 A Coup Against Constitutional Democracy
The Case of Hungary
Gábor Halmai

The "Rule of Law Revolution" of 1989 and the "Constitutional Counter-Revolution" after 2010

Hungary was one of the first and most thorough political transitions after 1989, which provided all the institutional elements of constitutionalism: checks and balances and guaranteed fundamental rights. Hungary also represents the first, and probably the model case, of constitutional backsliding from a full-fledged liberal democratic system to an illiberal one with strong authoritarian elements. The current Hungarian constitutional system was made possible by FIDESZ's anti-pluralist nationalist populism. To achieve this aim the populist government misuses the country's lack of constitutional culture, and violates the values of constitutional democracy in the name of its own understanding of "national constitutional identity."

The characteristic of system change that Hungary shared with other transitioning countries was that it had to establish an independent nation-state, a civil society, a private economy, and a democratic structure all at the same time.[1] Plans for transforming the Stalin-inspired 1949 Rákosi Constitution into a "rule of law" document were delineated

---

[1] The terms "single" and "dual" transitions are used by Przeworski. Adam Przeworski, *Democracy and the Market: Political and Economic Reforms in Eastern Europe and Latin America* (New York: Cambridge University Press, 1991). Later, Claus Offe broadened the scope of this debate by arguing that post-communist

in the National Roundtable Talks of 1989 by participants of the Opposition Roundtable and representatives of the state party. Afterward, the illegitimate Parliament only rubber-stamped the comprehensive amendment to the Constitution, which went into effect in October 1990, and which was the basic document of the "constitutional revolution." Similar "post-sovereign"[2] or "pacted constitution-making"[3] process happened in Spain in the end of the 1970s and in South Africa from the beginning through the middle of the 1990s.

Both the state-party and the opposition were motivated in not leaving the establishment of the transition's constitutional framework to a new constitution by the fear that they could lose the democratic elections. Thus the 1989 constitutional amendment inserted new content into the 1949 framework, which can be considered as a rule of law document, even if the Rákosist-Kádárist skeleton lolls out sometimes, especially concerning the unchanged structure of the chapters, starting with the state organization, followed by the fundamental rights parts. Apparently, the negotiations-based drafting explains that the old-new constitution principally follows the model of a consensual democracy widely accepted in the continental European systems. The system of government, which assumes the presence of more than two parties in the Parliament and coalition-governance, at the same time meant that the parties knowingly rejected both the semi- or full presidential regime that was preferred by the Communists and was applied in many post-communist countries, and also the English Westminster-type of two-party parliamentarism. If compared to the Western European solutions, the decision-making process set up in 1989–1990 has another distinctive characteristic that obviously could be explained by the legacy of the forty-year-long totalitarian regime: it is not only based on consensus among the coalition parties, but in some cases it requires the involvement of the opposition, and it significantly strengthens checks on governmental powers. As regards acts requiring a two-third majority, hence the support of the opposition, in their original form as "acts with the force of the Constitution," it practically called for a two-third quorum on all questions concerning the structure of the government and fundamental rights.

The other decisive element of the new constitutional system was a very strong judicial review power. The first Constitutional Court led by László Sólyom expressly followed an activist approach in the interpretation of the Constitution, which was laid down in the concept of the "invisible constitution" elaborated in his concurring opinion to the decision on the death penalty: "The Constitutional Court must continue its effort to explain

---

societies actually faced a triple transition, since many post-communist states were new or renewed nation-states. *See* Claus Offe, *Varieties of Transition: The East European and East German Experience* (New York: MIT Press, 1997).

[2] Andrew Arato, "Post-Sovereign Constitution-Making in Hungary: After Success, Partial Failure, and Now What?," *South African Journal of Human Rights* 26 (2010): 19–44.

[3] The term is used by Michel Rosenfeld, *The Identity of the Constitutional Subject* (New York: Routledge, 2010).

the theoretical bases of the Constitution and of the rights included in it and to form a coherent system with its decisions, which as an 'invisible Constitution' provides for a reliable standard of constitutionality beyond the Constitution, which nowadays is often amended out of current political interest; therefore, this coherent system will probably not conflict with the new Constitution to be adopted or with future Constitutions."[4] Therefore, Sólyom and many academics argued that the text of the 1989 constitution and the jurisprudence of the Constitutional Court made a new constitution unnecessary.

This constitutional system without the second step of a post-sovereign constitution-making process, namely a final liberal democratic constitution, seemed to work for more than twenty years, until FIDESZ's overwhelming electoral victory in 2010.

Before the 2010 elections the majority of voters were already dissatisfied not only with the government, but also with the transition itself—more than in any other East Central European country.[5] The center-right FIDESZ strengthened these feelings by claiming that there had been no real transition in 1989–1990; the previous nomenclatura had merely converted its lost political power into an economic one, exemplified by the two last prime ministers of the Socialist Party, who both became rich after the transition due to the privatization process. FIDESZ with its tiny Christian Democratic coalition partner received more than 50 percent of the actual votes, but due to the disproportional election system received two-thirds of the seats in the 2010 parliamentary elections. With this overwhelming majority they were able to enact a new constitution without the votes of the weak opposition parties.

The populism of FIDESZ was directed against all elites, including those who designed the 1989 constitutional system (in which FIDESZ also took part), claiming that it was time for a new revolution. That is why Viktor Orbán characterized the results of the 2010 elections as a "revolution of the ballot boxes." His intention with this revolution was to eliminate any kind of checks and balances, and even the parliamentary rotation of governing parties. In a September 2009 speech, Orbán predicted that there was "a real chance that politics in Hungary will no longer be defined by a dualist power space.... Instead, a large governing party will emerge in the center of the political stage [that] will be able [to] formulate national policy, not through constant debates but through a natural representation of interests." Orbán's vision for a new constitutional order—one in which his political party occupies the center stage of Hungarian political life and puts an end to debates over values—has now been entrenched in a new constitution, enacted in April 2011. The new constitutional order was built with the votes of his political bloc alone, and it aims to keep the opposition at bay for a long time. The new constitutional

---

[4] Decision 23/1990. (XII. 31.) AB.

[5] In 2009, 51 percent of Hungarians disagreed with the statement that they were better off since the transition, and only 30 percent claimed improvements. (In Poland 14 percent and in the Czech Republic 23 percent detected worsening, and 70 percent and 75 percent respectively perceived improvement.). European Commission, *Eurobarometer: Public Opinion in the European Union*, 2009.

order of the Fundamental Law and the cardinal laws perfectly fulfill this plan: they do not recognize the separation of powers, and do not guarantee fundamental rights. Therefore, the new Hungary (not even a Republic in its name anymore) cannot be considered a liberal constitutional democracy, but rather an illiberal state.[6]

Before January 1, 2012, when the new constitution became law, the Hungarian Parliament had been preparing a blizzard of so-called cardinal—or supermajority—laws, changing the shape of virtually every political institution in Hungary and making the guarantee of constitutional rights less secure. These laws affect the laws on freedom of information, prosecutions, nationalities, family protections, independence of the judiciary, status of churches, functioning of the Constitutional Court, and elections to Parliament. In the last days of 2011, Parliament also enacted the so-called Transitory Provision to the Fundamental Law, which claimed constitutional status and partly supplemented the new Constitution even before it went into effect. These new laws have been uniformly bad for the political independence of state institutions, for the transparency of lawmaking, and for the future of human rights in Hungary. The independence of the judiciary was dealt with the constitutional amendment, which changed the appointment and reassignment process for judges. The Transitory Provisions to the Fundamental Law reduced the retirement age for judges on ordinary courts from seventy to sixty-two, starting on the day the new constitution went into effect. This change forced somewhere around 274 judges into early retirement. Those judges include six of the twenty court presidents at the county level, four of the five appeals court presidents, and twenty of the eighty Supreme Court judges.

According to the cardinal law on the status of the churches the power to designate legally recognized churches is vested in Parliament itself. The law has listed fourteen legally recognized churches and required all other previously registered churches (some 330 religious organizations in total) to either re-register under considerably more demanding criteria or continue to operate as religious associations without the legal benefits offered to the recognized churches (such as tax exemptions and the ability to

---

[6] In an interview on Hungarian public radio on July 5, 2013, Orbán responded to European Parliament critics regarding the new constitutional order by admitting that his party did not aim to produce a liberal constitution. He said: "In Europe the trend is for every constitution to be liberal, this is not one. Liberal constitutions are based on the freedom of the individual and subdue welfare and the interest of the community to this goal. When we created the constitution, we posed questions to the people. The first question was the following: what would you like; should the constitution regulate the rights of the individual and create other rules in accordance with this principle or should it create a balance between the rights and duties of the individual. According to my recollection more than 80% of the people responded by saying that they wanted to live in a world, where freedom existed, but where welfare and the interest of the community could not be neglected and that these need to be balanced in the constitution. I received an order and mandate for this. For this reason the Hungarian constitution is a constitution of balance, and not a side-leaning constitution, which is the fashion in Europe, as there are plenty of problems there." See "A Tavares jelentés egy baloldali akció" (The Tavares report is a leftist action), Interview with PM Viktor Orbán, *Kossuth Rádió*, July 5, 2013, https://www.youtube.com/watch?v=zAgi4UVpKHw.

operate state-subsidized religious schools). As a result, the vast majority of previously registered churches have been deprived of their status as legal entities.

On March 11, 2013, the Hungarian Parliament added the Fourth Amendment to the country's 2011 constitution, re-enacting a number of controversial provisions that had been annulled by the Constitutional Court, and rebuffing requests by the European Union, the Council of Europe, and the US government that urged the government to seek the opinion of the Venice Commission before bringing the amendment into force. The most alarming change concerning the Constitutional Court annuls all Court decisions prior to when the Fundamental Law entered into force. At one level, this makes sense: old constitution = old decisions; new constitution = new decisions. But the Constitutional Court had already worked out a sensible new rule for the constitutional transition by deciding that in those cases where the language of the old and new constitutions were substantially the same, the opinions of the prior Court would still be valid and could still be applied. In cases in which the new constitution was substantially different from the old one, the previous decisions would no longer be used. Constitutional rights are key provisions that are the same in the old and new constitutions—which means that, practically speaking, the Fourth Amendment annuls primarily the cases that defined and protected constitutional rights and harmonized domestic rights protection to comply with European human rights law. This made it possible for Prime Minister Orbán to raise the possibility of the reintroduction of the death penalty, declared unconstitutional by the Constitutional Court in 1990, or threaten retroactive political justice despite a 1992 ban by the Court. With the removal of these fundamental Constitutional Court decisions, the government has undermined legal security with respect to the protection of constitutional rights in Hungary. These moves renewed serious doubts about the state of liberal constitutionalism in Hungary and Hungary's compliance with its international commitments under the Treaties of the European Union and the European Convention on Human Rights.

In April 2014, FIDESZ, with 44.5 percent of the party-list votes, won the elections again, and due to "undue advantages" for the governing party provided by the amendment to the electoral system, secured again a two-thirds majority.[7] In early 2015, FIDESZ lost its two-thirds majority as a consequence of mid-term elections in two constituencies, but the openly anti-Semitic, anti-Roma far-right Jobbik Party, which in 2007 established the paramilitary organization Magyar Gárda, received another 20.5 percent of the party-list votes. After the 2018 parliamentary elections, when FIDESZ regained a two-thirds

---

[7] In December 2011 the Parliament enacted a controversial election law with gerrymandered electoral districts, making the electoral system even more disproportional, which favored the governing party in the elections to come. The main changes in the system were as follows: shift to the majoritarian principle by increasing the proportion of single-member constituency mandates, eliminating the second round, introducing a relative majority (plurality-winner) system instead of the absolute majority, and introducing "winner-compensation."

majority, the enemies of liberal democracy still enjoy the support of the overwhelming majority of the voters, who are not concerned about the backsliding of constitutionalism. But, as Jan-Werner Müller argues, with reduced media pluralism and an intimidated civil society, the real "popularity" of the populist illiberal state has limited meaning. Therefore, we cannot really conclude that "illiberal democracy" became a genuinely popular idea in Hungary.[8]

What we do know is that since the 1989 democratic transition, the Hungarian people have not yet subscribed to "constitutional patriotism,"[9] which would have meant that the citizens had endorsed what John Rawls once called "constitutional essentials," and that they were attached to the idea of a constitution based on the country's historical experiences. The core of this kind of constitutional patriotism is a constitutional culture centered on universalist liberal-democratic norms and values, refracted and interpreted through particular historical experiences. Instead of this, the Hungarian people found themselves confronted with the populist government's unconstitutional patriotism, a kind of nationalism that violates constitutional essentials in the name of "national constitutional identity."[10]

The Hungarian system of governance became populist, illiberal, and undemocratic;[11] this was Prime Minister Orbán's openly stated intention.[12] The backsliding has happened

---

[8] J-W. Müller, "Taking 'Illiberal Democracy' Seriously," *Public Seminar*, July 21, 2017, http://www.publicseminar.org/2017/07/taking-illiberal-democracy-seriously/.

[9] After Dolf Sternberger's and Jürgen Habermas' conceptions of constitutional patriotism at the end of 1970s and 1980s respectively, both of which have been answers to particular German challenges, Jan-Werner Müller developed a new theory of the term, concentrating on universal norms and constitutional culture. See Jan-Werner Müller, *Constitutional Patriotism* (Princeton, NJ: Princeton University Press, 2007).

[10] In 2016 the Orbán government invoked Hungary's "national constitutional identity" to defy the resolution of the European Council to relocate asylum seekers within the Member States of the EU. See Gábor Halmai, "From a Pariah to a Model? Hungary's Rise to an Illiberal Member State of the EU," *European Yearbook of Human Rights*, ed. Wolfgang Benedek et al. (Vienna: NWV, 2017).

[11] As Jan-Werner Müller rightly argues, it is not just liberalism that is under attack in these two countries, but democracy itself. Hence, instead of calling them "illiberal democracies" we should describe them as illiberal and "undemocratic" regimes. See Jan-Werner Müller, "The Problem with 'Illiberal Democracy,'" *Project Syndicate*. January 21, 2016, https://www.project-syndicate.org/commentary/the-problem-with-illiberal-democracy-by-jan-werner-mueller-2016-01?barrier=accessreg.

[12] In a speech delivered on July 26, 2014, before an ethnic Hungarian audience in neighboring Romania, Orbán proclaimed his intention to turn Hungary into a state that "will undertake the odium of expressing that in character it is not of liberal nature." Citing as models he added: "We have abandoned liberal methods and principles of organizing society, as well as the liberal way to look at the world. . . . Today, the stars of international analyses are Singapore, China, India, Turkey, Russia. . . . and if we think back on what we did in the last four years, and what we are going to do in the following four years, than it really can be interpreted from this angle. We are . . . parting ways with Western European dogmas, making ourselves independent from them. . . . If we look at civil organizations in Hungary, . . . we have to deal with paid political activists here. . . . [T]hey would like to exercise influence . . . on Hungarian public life. It is vital, therefore, that if we would like to reorganize our nation state instead of it being a liberal state, that we should make it clear, that these are not civilians . . . opposing us, but political activists attempting to promote foreign interests. . . . This is about the

through the use of "abusive constitutional" tools: constitutional amendments and even replacements, because both the internal and the external democratic defense mechanisms against the abuse of constitutional tools failed.[13] The internal ones (constitutional courts, judiciary) failed because the new regime managed to abolish all checks on its power, and the international ones, such as the EU toolkits, failed mostly due to the lack of a joint political will to use them.

Causes of Democratic Backslash

The main reasons for the turn away from constitutionalism in Hungary are as follows:

(a) Historically, in the East-Central European countries, there were only some unexpected moments—quick flourishes of liberal democracy—followed by equally quick acts to delegitimize them. Examples include the short period after 1945, until the communist parties took over, and after 1989, when liberal democracy again seemed to be the "end of history."[14] Otherwise, in the national histories of the Central and Eastern European countries, authoritarianism, such as the pre-1939 authoritarian Hungarian state, has played a much more important role.[15]

---

ongoing reorganization of the Hungarian state. Contrary to the liberal state organization logic of the past twenty years, this is a state organization originating in national interests." See Viktor Orbán, "Full Text of Viktor Orbán's speech at Băile Tuşnad (Tusnádfürdő) of 26 July 2014," *Budapest Beacon*, July 29, 2014, http://budapestbeacon.com/public-policy/full-text-of-viktor-orbans-speech-at-baile-tusnad-tusnadfurdo-of-26-july-2014/.

[13] The category of "abusive constitutionalism" was introduced by David Landau using the cases of Colombia, Venezuela, and Hungary. See David Landau, "Abusive Constitutionalism," *UC Davis Law Review* 47 (2013): 189–260. Abusive constitutional tools are known from the very beginning of constitutionalism. The recent story of the Polish Constitutional Tribunal is reminiscent of the events in the years after the election of Jefferson, as the first anti-Federalist president of the United States. On March 2, 1801, the second-to-last day of his presidency, President Adams appointed judges, most of whom were Federalists. The Federalist Senate confirmed them the next day. As a response, Jefferson, after taking office, convinced the new anti-Federalist Congress to abolish the terms of the Supreme Court that were to take place in June and December of that year, and Congress repealed the law passed by the previous Congress creating new federal judgeships. In addition, the anti-Federalist Congress had begun impeachment proceedings against some Federalist judges. About the election of 1800 and its aftermath, see Bruce Ackerman, *The Failure of the Founding Fathers. Jefferson, Marshall, and the Rise of Presidential Democracy* (Cambridge, MA: Harvard University Press, 2007).

[14] See Balázs Trencsényi, Maciej Janowski, Monika Baar, Maria Falina, and Michal Kopecek, *A History of Modern Political Thought in East Central Europe, Volume I: Negotiating Modernity in the 'Long Nineteenth Century'* (Oxford University Press, 2016).

[15] Shlomo Avineri, "Two Decades after the Fall: Between Utopian Hopes and the Burdens of History," *Dissent*, September 30, 2009, https://www.dissentmagazine.org/online_articles/two-decades-after-the-fall-between-utopian-hopes-and-the-burdens-of-history.

As surveys on the links between modernization and democracy show, a society's historic and religious heritage leaves a lasting imprint.[16] According to these surveys, the publics of formerly agrarian societies, including Hungary, emphasize religion, national pride, obedience, and respect for authority, whereas the publics of industrial societies emphasize secularism, cosmopolitanism, autonomy, and rationality.[17] Even modernization's changes are not irreversible: economic collapse can reverse them, as happened during the early 1990s in most former communist states. These findings were confirmed by another international comparative study conducted by researchers at Jacobs University in Bremen and published by the German Bertelsmann Foundation.[18] The study of social cohesion examined thirty-four countries in the EU and the OECD. Social cohesion is defined as the special quality with which members of a community live and work together. Hungary was ranked twenty-seventh, between Poland and Slovakia.

(b) Even though the transition to democracy in Hungary was driven by the fact that a large share of the population gave high priority to freedom itself, people expected the new state to produce speedy economic growth, with which the country could attain the living standards of the West overnight, without painful reforms.[19] In other words, one can argue that the average Hungarian person looked to the West as a model in 1989, not so much in terms of its economic and political systems, but rather in terms of living standards. As Hannah Arendt argued, it is impossible to establish a republic based on freedom without liberation from poverty and misery.[20] Claus Offe predicted the possible backsliding effect of

---

[16] Ronald Inglehart and Christian Welzel, "Changing Mass Priorities: The Link between Modernization and Democracy," *Perspectives on Politics* 8 (2010): 551–567.

[17] Ibid., 553. Christian Welzel in his recent book argues that fading existential pressures open people's minds, making them prioritize freedom over security, autonomy over authority, diversity over uniformity and creativity over discipline, tolerance and solidarity over discrimination and hostility against out-groups. On the other hand, persistent existential pressures keep people's minds closed, in which case they emphasize the opposite priorities. This is the utility ladder of freedom. Cf. Christian Welzel, *Freedom Rising: Human Empowerment and the Quest for Emancipation* (New York: Cambridge University Press, 2013).

[18] David Schiefer, Jolanda van der Noll, Jan Delhey, and Klaus Boehnke, *Cohesion Radar: Measuring Cohesiveness* (Bertelsmann Foundation 2013), https://www.bertelsmann-stiftung.de/fileadmin/files/Projekte/Gesellschaftlicher_Zusammenhalt/englische_site/further-downloads/social-cohesion/Social_Cohesion_2012.pdf.

[19] As Ulrich Preuss argues, the satisfaction of the basic economic needs of the populace was so important for both the ordinary people and the new political elites that constitutions did not really make a difference. See Ulrich Preuss, *Constitutional Revolution: The Link between Constitutionalism and Progress* (Atlantic Highlands, NJ: Humanities Press, 1993), 3.

[20] Arendt quotes Sain-Just: "if you wish to found a republic, you first must pull the people out of a condition of misery, which corrupts them." Hannah Arendt, "What Freedom and Revolution Really Means, Thoughts on Poverty, Misery, and the Great Revolutions of History," *The New England Review*, Vol. 38, No. 2 (2017). https://lithub.com/never-before-published-hannah-arendt-on-what-freedom-and-revolution-really-mean/.

economic changes and declining living standards, warning that this could undermine the legitimacy of democratic institutions and turn back the process of democratization.[21] This failure, together with the emergence of an economically and politically independent bourgeoisie, the accumulation of wealth by some former members of the communist nomenclatura, unresolved issues in dealing with the communist past, the lack of retributive justice against perpetrators of grave human rights violations, and a mild vetting procedure and lack of restitution of confiscated properties, were reasons for disappointment.

Trying to explain the attitudes of voters who support authoritarian populist leaders such as Orbán, Ronald Inglehart and Pippa Norris suggest that it would be a mistake to attribute the rise of populism directly to economic inequality alone, as psychological factors seem to play an even more important role. Older and less-educated people tend to support populist parties and leaders that defend traditional cultural values and emphasize nationalistic and xenophobia agendas, reject outsiders, and uphold old-fashioned gender roles.[22]

(c) According to some authors, the prospects for democracy in the newly independent states of Central and Eastern Europe following the 1989–1990 transition were diminished by a technocratic, judicial control of politics, which blunted the development of civic constitutionalism, civil society, and participatory democratic government as necessary counterpoints to the technocratic machinery of legal constitutionalism.[23] Adherents to this viewpoint argue that the legalistic form of constitutionalism, while consistent with the purpose of creating the structure of the state and setting boundaries between the state and citizens, jeopardizes the development of participatory democracy.[24] In other words, legalistic constitutionalism falls short, reducing the Constitution to an elite instrument, especially in countries with weak civil societies and weak political party systems that

---

[21] Cf. Claus Offe, "Designing Institutions for East European Transitions," *Institut für Höhere Studies* (1994), 15, https://www.ihs.ac.at/publications/pol/pw_19.pdf.

[22] Ronald F. Inglehart and Pippa Norris, "Trump, Brexit, and the Rise of Populism: Economic Have-Nots and Cultural Backlash," *Harvard Faculty Research Working Paper Series*, August 2016, https://research.hks.harvard.edu/publications/getFile.aspx?Id=1401.

[23] See this argument in Paul Blokker, *New Democracies in Crises? A Comparative Constitutional Study of the Czech Republic, Hungary, Poland, Romania and Slovakia* (London: Routledge, Taylor & Francis Group, 2014). Also Wojciech Sadurski argued that legal constitutionalism might have a "negative effect" in new democracies and might lead to the perpetuation of the problem of both weak political parties and civil society. See Wojciech Sadurski, "Transitional Constitutionalism: Simplistic and Fancy Theories," in *Rethinking the Rule of Law after Communism*, ed. Adam W. Czarnota, Martin Krygier, and Wojciech Sadurski (Budapest: CEU Press 2005), 9–24.

[24] See Richard Albert, "Counterconstitutionalism," *Dalhousie Law Journal* 31 (2008): 1, 4.

undermine a robust constitutional democracy based on the idea of civic self-government.[25]

The concept of civic or participatory constitutionalism is based on "democratic constitutionalism" (James Tully), emphasizing that structural problems in new democracies include the relative absence of institutions for popular participation, which is also related to "counterdemocracy" (Pierre Rosenvallon), as well as a robust institutional linkage between civic associations and citizens and formal politics. Critics of this approach say that it does not sufficiently take into account the rise of populism and the lack of civic interest in constitutional matters. Moreover, the approach does not account for the increasing irrelevance of domestic constitutionalism resulting from the tendencies of Europeanization and globalization, especially the internationalization of domestic constitutional law through the use of foreign and international law in constitution-making and constitutional interpretation.[26]

(d) There was also a lack of consensus about liberal democratic values at the time of the transition. In the beginning of the democratic transitions in these new democracies, preference was given to general economic effectiveness over mass civic and political engagement.[27] The satisfaction of basic economic needs was so important for both ordinary people and the new political elites that constitutions did not really make a difference.[28] Between 1989 and 2004 all political forces accepted a certain minimalistic version of a "liberal consensus" understood as a set of rules and laws rather than values, according to which NATO and EU accession was the main political goal. But as soon as the main political goals were achieved, the liberal consensus died,[29] and full democratic consolidation was never achieved.[30]

A POPULIST ILLIBERAL SYSTEM

If from the large range of definitions of populism, we use the one provided by Mudde and Kaltwasser, who define "populism" as a "thin-centered ideology that considers society to

---

[25] See Sadurski, "Transitional Constitutionalism," 23.

[26] See the reviews of Blokker, *New Democracies in Crises?* by Jiri Priban and Bogusia Puchalska, *ICONnect*, September 2013, www.iconnectblog.com/2013/09/book-reviewresponse-paul-blokker-jiri-priban-and-bogusia-puchalska-on-civic-constitutionalism.

[27] Dorothee Bohle and Béla Greskovits state that East Central European democracies had a "hollow core" at their inception. See Dorothee Bohle and Béla Greskokovits, *Capitalist Diversity on Europe's Periphery* (Ithaca, NY: Cornell University Press, 2012).

[28] See Preuss, *Constitutional Revolution*, 3.

[29] Ivan Krastev, "Is East-Central Europe Backsliding? The Strange Death of the Liberal Consensus," *Journal of Democracy* 18 (2007): 56–63.

[30] James Dawson and Seán Hanley, "What's Wrong with East-Central Europe? The Fading Mirage of the Liberal Consensus," *Journal of Democracy* 7 (2016): 20–34.

be ultimately separated in two homogeneous and antagonistic camps, 'the pure people' and the 'corrupt elite,' and which argues that politics should be an expression of the 'volonté générale' (general will) of the people,"[31] the Hungarian constitutional system became a populist one. This populism rejects the basic principles of constitutional democracy,[32] understood as limited government, governed by the rule of law, and protecting fundamental rights.[33] In Hungary we can also detect the main characteristics of populism, described by Luigi Corrias's work on popular sovereignty, as well as its approach to constitutional identity.[34]

For popular sovereignty, as Corrias argues, populism holds the belief that "the people" is a unit, and that, as such, it is present in the polity often only through the means of direct democracy, such as referenda. Particularly while in opposition, for populists, such as Orbán, representation merely serves as a tool to give voice to the unity.[35] But as Pinelli rightly points out, contemporary populists, especially being in government, do not necessarily reject representation, nor do they necessarily favor the use of referenda.[36] For instance, Orbán's FIDESZ party tried to undermine the legitimacy of representation after losing the 2002 parliamentary elections. He refused to concede defeat, declaring that "the nation cannot be in opposition, only the government can be in opposition against its own people." After the 2010 electoral victory, he claimed that through the "revolution at the voting booths," the majority has delegated its power to the government representing it. This means that the populist government tried to interpret the result of the elections as the will of the people, viewed as a homogenous unit. Also, the Orbán government, which after overthrowing its predecessor in 2010 as a result of a popular referendum, made it more difficult to initiate a valid referendum for its own opposition. While the previous law required only 25 percent of the voters to cast a vote, the new law requires at least 50 percent of those eligible to vote to take part, otherwise the referendum is invalid.[37] The ambivalence of Orbán toward representation and referenda in government and in opposition applies to his attitude regarding established institutions. While he readily attacked the "establishment" while in opposition, he very much protects his own governmental institutions. The situation

---

[31] Cas Mudde and Rovira C. Kaltwasser, *Populism: A Very Short Introduction* (Oxford: Oxford University Press, 2017), 6.

[32] See Cesare Pinelli, "The Populist Challenge to Constitutional Democracy," *European Constitutional Law Review* 7 (2016): 5–16, 6.

[33] See these "essential characteristics" of constitutional democracy in Michel Rosenfeld, "The Rule of Law and the Legitimacy of Constitutional Democracy," *Southern California Law Review* 74 (2001): 1307–1352, 1307.

[34] Luigi Corrias, "Populism in a Constitutional Key: Constituent Power, Popular Power, Popular Sovereignty and Constitutional Identity," *European Constitutional Law Review* 12 (2016): 6–26, 12.

[35] Ibid., 18–19.

[36] See Pinelli, "Populist Challenge," 11.

[37] It is the irony of fate that due to these more stringent conditions, the only referendum that the Orbán government initiated—one against the EU's migration policy—failed. On October 2, 2016, Hungarian voters went to the polls to answer one referendum question: "Do you want to allow the European Union to mandate the

is different with transnational institutions, such as the EU, which are also attacked by the Hungarian populist governments as threats to their countries' sovereignty. A good example is the Hungarian Parliament's reaction to the European Parliament's critical report from July 2013 on the constitutional situation in Hungary. The Hungarian parliamentary resolution on equal treatment reads: "We, Hungarians, do not want a Europe any longer where freedom is limited and not widened. We do not want a Europe any longer where the Greater abuses his power, where national sovereignty is violated and where the Smaller has to respect the Greater. We have had enough of dictatorship after 40 years behind the iron curtain." These words very much reflect the Orbán government's view of "national freedom," the liberty of the state (or the nation) to determine its own laws: "This is why we are writing our own constitution. . . . And we don't want any unconsolidated help from strangers who are keen to guide us . . . Hungary must turn on its own axis."[38]

The other element of populist constitutional theory, according to Corrias, is constitutional identity as collective selfhood. Here populists have the tendency to reject what they perceive as threats to the constitutional identity of the people by immigrants, refugees, and minorities.[39] This is the reason that as early as May 2015, a few days after many hundreds of refugees had drowned in the Mediterranean Sea, Orbán announced that "We need no refugees," arguing that Europe does not need immigrants at all, that the European Union should be sealed off and defended against intruders by the army, and that it should not overreach its immigration and refugee policies. Rather, the Member States should formulate their own policies and deal with their unwanted immigrants as they see fit. In the summer of 2015, the Hungarian government left thousands of refugees to languish in fields and on the streets, forcibly herded others into squalid detention camps, and fired water cannons and teargas at refugees gathered against the razor fence it had erected, first on its border with Serbia, and later with Croatia, another EU Member State. Orbán, styling himself as the defender of Europe's "Christian civilization" against an Islamic invasion, managed to encourage other eastern European governments to follow his example.

To legitimate this policy against Hungary's unwanted immigrants, the government announced it would hold a "national consultation." The government sent out eight million questionnaires to the voting-age population, with questions such as these: "Do you agree that mistaken immigration policies contribute to the spread of terrorism? In your

---

relocation of non-Hungarian citizens to Hungary without the approval of the National Assembly?" Although 92 percent of those who cast votes and 98 percent of all the valid votes agreed with the government, answering no (6 percent were spoiled ballots), the referendum was invalid because the turnout was only around 40 percent, instead of the required 50 percent.

[38] For the original, Hungarian-language speech of Orbán, entitled Nem leszünk gyarmat! [We won't be a colony anymore!] see https://index.hu/video/2012/03/15/orban_nem_leszunk_gyarmat. For an English-language report on Orbán's speech see: https://euobserver.com/political/115613.

[39] See Corrias, "Populism in a Constitutional Key," 13.

opinion did Brussels' policies on immigration and terrorism fail? Would you support a new regulation that would allow the government to place immigrants who illegally entered the country into internment camps?"

The Hungarian government, after the above-mentioned failed referendum, introduced the Seventh Amendment to defend Hungary's constitutional identity and politically legitimize noncompliance with EU law in this area. Since the proposed amendment fell two votes short of the two-thirds majority required to approve amendments to the Fundamental Law, the Constitutional Court, loyal to the government, came to the rescue of Orbán's constitutional identity defense of its policies on migration. The Court revived an abandoned petition of the also loyal Commissioner for Fundamental Rights filed a year earlier, before the referendum was initiated, and ruled that "the constitutional self-identity of Hungary is a fundamental value not created by the Fundamental Law—it is merely acknowledged by the Fundamental Law, consequently constitutional identity cannot be waived by way of an international treaty." Therefore, the Court argued, "the protection of the constitutional identity shall remain the duty of the Constitutional Court as long as Hungary is a sovereign State." Because sovereignty and constitutional identity are in contact with each other in many points, "their control should be performed with due regard to each other in specific cases."[40]

In this populist, illiberal system the institutions of a constitutional state (the constitutional court, ombudsman, judicial, or media councils) still exist, but their power is very limited. Also, as in many illiberal regimes, fundamental rights are listed in the constitutions, but the institutional guarantees of these rights are endangered through the lack of an independent judiciary and constitutional court. To be clear, if the competences of the constitutional courts were very strong in the beginning of the transition, they can be weakened provided that they still are able to fulfill their function as a check on governmental power, or if other control mechanisms exist. But the curtailment of the Court's jurisdiction clearly serves to eliminate its control function altogether, and has nothing to do with political constitutionalism, or all of the concepts rejecting strong judicial review, or judicial review altogether.[41] Political constitutionalists, such as Richard Bellamy, Jeremy Waldron, Akhil Amar, Sandy Levinson, and Mark Tushnet, who themselves differ from each other significantly, emphasize the role of elected bodies instead of courts in implementing and protecting the constitution, but none of them reject the main principles of constitutional democracy, as populists in the Hungarian government do. Similarly, in contrast to those who describe a new model of constitutionalism, based on deliberation between courts and the legislators, with the latter retaining the final word, in

---

[40] For a detailed analysis of the decision see Gábor Halmai, "Nationa(ist) Constitutional Identity?: Hungary's Road to Abuse Constitutional Pluralism," EUI Working Papers, 2017/08, http://cadmus.eui.eu/handle/1814/46226.

[41] See the opposite view of Lucia Corso, "What Does Populism Have to Do with Constitutional Law? Discussing Populist Constitutionalism and Its Assumptions," *Rivista di filosofia del Diritto* (2014): 443–469.

the Hungarian constitutional system the parliamentary majority not only decides every single issue without any dialogue, but there is practically no partner for such a dialogue, as the independence of both the ordinary judiciary and the Constitutional Court has been silenced.

Conclusion

Although Hungary became a liberal democracy on an institutional level after 1989, on a behavioral level, the consolidation of the system has always been very fragile. If one considers liberalism as not merely a limit on the public power of the majority, but as also a concept that encompasses the constitutive precondition of democracy—the rule of law, checks and balances, and guaranteed fundamental rights—then Hungary is not a liberal democracy anymore. Since the 2010 victory of the current governing FIDESZ party, all of the public power is in the hands of the representatives of one party. Freedom of the media and religious rights, among others, are seriously curtailed. And before the 2014 parliamentary elections, the electoral system became unfair, ensuring again a two-thirds majority for FIDESZ in the Hungarian parliament.

The problem with the Hungarian populist and illiberal constitutional system is that the country is currently a member of the European Union, which considers itself to be a union based on the principles of liberal democratic constitutionalism. Of course, the citizens of Hungary, as any other citizens of a democratic nation-state, have the right to oppose joint European measures, for instance on immigration and refugees, or even the development of a liberal political system altogether. However, this conclusion must be reached through a democratic process. There are still a significant number of people who either consider themselves to be supporters of liberal democracy, or at least represent views that are in line with liberal democracy. But if Hungarians ultimately opt for a non-liberal system, they must accept certain consequences, including parting from the European Union and the wider community of liberal democracies.

16 Constitutional Crisis in Poland
Wojciech Sadurski*

Introduction

A dramatic change in Polish politics occurred in 2015 with the election of the PiS-supported Andrzej Duda as president in May,[1] and then, in October, with the parliamentary victory of the PiS that gave it the authority to govern single-handedly. What happened next is best described as (un)constitutional backsliding: a dramatic deterioration in the democratic and constitutional standards already attained: early in the twenty-first century, Poland was described by a prominent US political scientist as among "the leaders of the group" of countries that were "a route to becoming successful, well-functioning democracies" within a broader "transitional" category.[2] No more.

This is not the place to analyze the sources of the PiS victory, but at least one factor must be pointed out: the eccentricities of the Polish electoral system. PiS won an absolute parliamentary majority, allowing it to form a government independently, with only 38 percent of those voting (the turnout was just above 50 percent of authorized voters). This is a substantial plurality, but not a majority, of voters. Due to the inability

---

* I am grateful to Dr. Michał Marek Ziółkowski for his excellent research, and to Bojan Bugaric, Adam Czarnota, Mark Graber and Martin Krygier for their comments.
[1] PiS is a Polish acronym for the Law and Justice Party, led by Jarosław Kaczyński.
[2] Thomas Carothers, "The End of the Transition Paradigm," *Journal of Democracy* 13 (2002): 5–21, 9.

of smaller parties (mainly on the Left) to come to terms with the need to form effective and persuasive coalitions or party mergers, some 15 percent of all voters saw their votes "wasted." Their preferred parties did not make it into Parliament. This 15 percent segment of the electorate unrepresented in the parliament was decisive for the success of PiS leader Jarosław Kaczyński, who benefited greatly from the absence of the Left in the Parliament.

No time was wasted in 2015. The end of the year witnessed the beginning of a fundamental transformation: the abandonment of various dogmas of liberal democracy, constitutionalism, and the rule of law that had been taken for granted. The campaign first against the Constitutional Tribunal (CT) and then against the regular courts rested on the idea that any restraints on the political majority are by their nature anti-democratic. The sequence of the main "reforms" in Poland in many respects closely parallels those in Hungary a few years earlier: fast-tracking of legislative changes with total disregard for the parliamentary opposition, attacks on NGOs, new media legislation, disempowering and capturing the Constitutional Court, removal of the "old" judges (of ordinary courts) by lowering the retirement age, an attack specifically on the chief justice of the Supreme Court, restructuring of the National Judiciary Council through the politicization of its selection, altering the membership rules of the electoral commission with the effect of giving the ruling party control of the commission, and identifying the European Union as a foreign, hostile entity that illegitimately interferes in the internal affairs of its Member States.

It is difficult to identify a tipping point during these events; only ex post do we realize that the line dividing liberal democracy from a fake one has been crossed. Threshold moments are not seen as such when we live in them. Many changes that are part of democratic backsliding occur *without a formal change* of institutions and procedures. They are invisible to a purely legal account. Institutions and procedures remain the same, but their substance is radically changed by practice. The best (or the worst, if you prefer) example is provided by the fate of the Constitutional Tribunal (CT). Rather than acting as a constraint upon the government, the CT has become a constraint upon the opposition and an active government helper.

While particular individual aspects of Polish backsliding may have their counterpart in this or that democratic state, what makes Poland such a qualitatively different case is the *comprehensiveness and the cumulative effect* of how liberal democracy is being undone. A virus in a sick body reinforces pathologies in other parts of the body, while a virus in a healthy organism is likely to be disabled from having a nefarious effect. A single nonliberal change does not provoke a major backlash if it takes place in the environment of a general liberal constitutional context. In Poland, however, it is a populist offensive *tous azimuts*: an all-out assault on liberal constitutionalism. And it is systemic: individual elements are functionally connected with the others. The paralysis of the CT was a prerequisite for the adoption of illiberal laws made immune from effective constitutional scrutiny. These illiberal laws, for instance on the right to assembly, make more difficult efforts to protest against capture of the CT. In this way, the sum is more than its parts.[3] That some individual legal provisions may exist in isolation from other problematic arrangements and practices in some particular states that are unimpeachably democratic is a powerful rhetorical instrument for regimes such as in Poland, and also imposes constraints upon critics, including those abroad. Foreign political actors may be loath to condemn democratic backsliding "if such practices enforce laws that exist in their own legal systems, lest they be criticized as hypocritical."[4]

The institutional changes discussed below are a part of a broader populist syndrome in which the key role is played by a catastrophic drop in the norms of civility and discourse, with an accompanying loss of trust. When the opponents of the government are treated as traitors and haters of their own nation, they will reciprocate with accusations of similar intensity. As a result, there are no shreds of mutual respect, of recognition that while the government and the opposition differ in their interpretation of the public good, they are equally sincere in the quest for common interest. Both sides deny legitimacy to each other: the opposition is seen by the PiS as treacherous and non-patriotic, hence undeserving of ever returning to power, while the PiS is viewed by its opponents as transgressing the minimal conditions of democratic legitimacy (based on respecting constitutional constraints). Polish politics is polarized along lines so fundamental that loyal cooperation between the main parties for the higher good is unthinkable these days. As political scientists know all too well, a low level of interpersonal trust is a favorable background for anti-democratic backsliding.

The most striking feature of Polish backsliding is the fate of the Constitution, which came to be seen as an annoying obstacle to the plans of the ruling party. Not having the majority necessary for constitutional amendments, the governing party proceeded by outright breaches of the Constitution, or by "constitutional amendments" through statute. The takeover of the CT is one, though not the only, arena where breaches of the Constitution have been committed. The parliamentary resolution (voted with a PiS majority, of course) removing the "legal effects" of the election of judges at the end of previous parliamentary terms violates the Constitution because the Constitution provides for the instances when a term of a judge can be extinguished, and the Parliament has no such power. The refusal by the president to swear in correctly elected judges violates the Constitution, which does not give the president any such role in designing the composition of the CT. The governmental refusal to publish some CT judgments is another usurpation by the government of powers that it does not have.

The second dimension of the anti-constitutional character of PiS rule is a series of de facto "amendments" to the Constitution via statutes that significantly alter constitutional

---

[3] See similarly Mark Tushnet, who, describing Singapore's authoritarian constitutionalism, constructs a useful figure of "a fallacy of decomposition" where "the components *lack* a property but the aggregate might have it," Mark Tushnet, "Authoritarian Constitutionalism," *Cornell Law Review* 100 (2015): 391–462, 409–410.

[4] Ozan O. Varol, "Stealth Authoritarianism," *Iowa Law Review* 100 (2015): 1673–1742, 1734.

dispensations. The setting up, by statute, of the Council of National Media, was a way of disempowering a constitutional body, the National Broadcasting Board, by endowing the former with much of the tasks of the latter. Several statutory provisions concerning the CT were meant to circumvent other constitutional provisions. For instance, in order to sideline Professor Stanisław Biernat, the then vice president of the CT (a constitutionally designated office), a statute of December 13, 2015, invented the position of "acting President" who performed the actions normally falling upon the vice president, with the difference that they fully met the expectations of PiS.

The account that follows demonstrates that the main aim of PiS in the first two years of its rule was to dismantle institutional checks and balances, in particular the CT. But PiS also proceeded to enact laws that substantively alter the system of rights and liberties in Poland.

Paralyzing and Transforming the Constitutional Tribunal

The most striking aspect of the unconstitutional post-2015 developments in Poland is how the changes were preceded and facilitated by incapacitating the main institution for constitutional maintenance in Poland after the fall of communism, the Constitutional Tribunal. As David Law and Mila Versteeg note in their pioneering work on "sham constitutions," "abusive governments can be expected to combine sham constitutions with sham judicial review. Government disrespect for a right will therefore translate into cramped judicial interpretation or enforcement of the right."[5] The PiS saw disabling the CT as an effective and robust interpreter and enforcer of the Constitution as an *instrumental* step leading to a situation in which the Constitution, while formally valid, does not matter whenever it conflicts with the government's designs for rearranging the boundary between its own targets and the sphere protected by the constitutional principles and rights as previously interpreted. The Constitution stops being "self-executing" because it lacks an internal legal instrument of assuring its self-binding character; its domination is eliminated by a politically dominant force.

The Constitutional Tribunal had established itself as a strong protector of the democratic process and limits on the legislative and executive powers. While many of its judgments were controversial, and according to some observers (including this author) lacked the required vigor, nevertheless in the landscape of European constitutional review the CT was a leading judicial actor contributing to the defense of human rights, European integration, and democratic governance. That is why the CT became the main target of the PiS offensive. The capture of the CT by the ruling party after 2015 took place in two main stages. The first stage was "paralysis," and consisted mainly in several actions aimed at rendering the CT powerless to curb arbitrary power. Once this aim was achieved by the

---

[5] David S. Law and Mila Versteeg, "Sham Constitutions," *California Law Review* 101 (2013): 863–952, 877.

end of 2016, the second stage consisted of the positive use of the CT against the opposition and in support of the ruling party. In contrast to the traditional anti-majoritarian mission of constitutional courts, the Tribunal became an active helper of the parliamentary majority.

The paralysis was achieved by a successful court-packing that proceeded by appointing "quasi-judges" to the Tribunal ("quasi"—because appointed to already filled seats), and then by a natural attrition, that enabled party faithfuls to replace those "old" judges who stepped down at the end of their term. The story about "quasi-judges" is long and complex, and will be described only briefly. Shortly before the 2015 parliamentary elections, on October 8, 2015, the Parliament elected five new judges to positions that were to become vacant. The PiS-dominated new Parliament adopted an unusual and arguably unlawful resolution on November 25, 2015, which declared that process for electing the five judges on October 8th irregular, and the elections of all five null and void. On December 2, 2015, the Parliament proceeded to elect five new judges. In fact only two of the five judges elected in October were elected irregularly because their seats would become vacant only in December, during the new parliamentary term. The three remaining judges were elected properly, to seats that became vacant before the new parliamentary term began.

The gambit of "electing" three judges to the already filled seats and not recognizing the three judges properly elected before the PiS gained a parliamentary majority would not have succeeded except for the active collaboration of President Andrzej Duda. The president swore in the five PiS-elected judges hours after the election (in the middle of the night), including three "quasi-judges" elected to the already occupied judicial posts. The swearing-in took place hours before the CT determined on the morning of December 3rd that the Sejm, the lower chamber of Polish Parliament, had constitutionally elected three judges during its the former term of Sejm. The three quasi-judges, sworn in by President Duda, although assigned offices in the Tribunal building and put on the payroll immediately after the swearing-in, were initially not included on judging panels throughout 2016, until the retirement of Andrzej Rzepliński as the president of CT. Julia Przyłębska (one of the two correctly elected new judges) almost immediately upon taking office in December 2016 as "Acting President" (a position newly established by statute, not known to the Constitution, and admittedly contrary to it) included the three quasi-judges on panels and on the General Assembly of Judges of the CT, which immediately elected her as president of the CT. The court-packing achieved its purpose. All the new judges and quasi-judges elected by PiS parliamentary majority, with a single illustrious exception,[6] have so far behaved predictably, voting in lockstep for the government positions in all cases considered by the Tribunal.

---

[6] Judge Piotr Pszczółkowski.

Court-packing was not the only process employed by PiS to disable the Constitutional Tribunal from scrutinizing PiS legislation. Throughout 2016, the Parliament adopted no less than six statutes on the CT, in addition to many drafts officially announced but eventually not submitted to a vote. The CT, bombarded by these new rules and drafts, was compelled to deal mainly with laws about itself rather than substantive laws adopted at the same time. This relentless production of new laws on the CT contained many devices that may be grouped into three categories: (1) those that would effectively exempt the new laws just adopted by PiS from constitutional scrutiny by the CT (e.g., a requirement of strictly respecting the sequence of judgments according to the time the motion reached CT);[7] (2) those that would paralyze judicial decision-making, by making handing down any judgment more difficult, and often impossible (e.g., a requirement of a difficult-to-achieve qualified majority for the General Assembly of two-thirds for judgments of the CT); (3) those that would increase the control by the executive and the legislative over the CT (e.g., the rule that the president of the Republic must agree to extinguishing a judge's term of office on disciplinary grounds even if the CT-based disciplinary panel has so decided). With the interventions by Venice Commission and the European Commission, as well as subsequent governmental responses to the Opinions of the Venice Commission, those drafts and laws produced a mosaic of interlocking provisions, some of which the CT invalidated, with some of these invalidating judgments remaining unpublished. The final result was a picture totally obscure and incomprehensible to the general public, which probably was the purpose. However, by the end of December 2016 all these changes vanished. They turned out to be unnecessary when the PiS finally obtained a majority on the Tribunal (the majority included "quasi-judges") and returned to the legal status quo ante. The statutes of November–December 2016 in all main respects restored the older provisions on CT.

In addition to court-packing and paralyzing the Tribunal by subsequent new bills on the Tribunal, the government unconstitutionally refused to publish judgments of the CT that it deemed improperly handed down. This refusal to publish violated a clear and imperative constitutional requirement that demands that the government publish judgments "immediately," and does not give the government any power to control the judgments submitted to it by the CT for publication. Simply speaking, publication is an absolute and unconditional obligation of the government. The government here plays the role of a printing press, nothing more.

---

[7] The Venice Commission lucidly recognized the true reason for the sequence rule: "constitutional courts have to be able to quickly decide urgent matters also in cases concerning the functioning of constitutional bodies, for instance when there is a danger of a blockage of the political system, as is the case now in Poland," Opinion on Amendments to the Act of 25 June 2015 on the Constitutional Tribunal of Poland, adopted by the Venice Commission at its 106th Plenary Session (Venice, March 11–12, 2016), Opinion no. 833/2015, CDL-AD(2016)001 para 63.

Once the combination of court-packing, inclusion in the Constitutional Tribunal of three improperly elected judges, and natural attrition due to the end of terms of office of "old" judges (including the president and the vice president of the Court) produced a PiS majority on the CT, a fundamental transformation of the Tribunal occurred. Rather than a body incapable of making any decisions at all, the Tribunal was transformed into a positive, active aide of the government and the parliamentary majority. The government found the Tribunal a useful means for legitimizing its power, and at the same time legitimated the Tribunal by activating it with its own motions.

Consider a CT judgment of June 20, 2017. on the National Council of the Judiciary (Polish acronym: KRS). In this judgment, the "new" CT found the existing statute on KRS unconstitutional because it discriminated against judges of the lower courts by differentiating the procedures for appointing judges-members of KRS by the level of courts they represent. But the Constitution does not mandate any particular methods for selecting judicial representatives on the KRS: the specific design of elections was completely within legislative discretion. The CT also found unconstitutional the system of "individual" terms of office for particular judges-members of the KRS, claiming that the Constitution requires a "joint/collective" term of office. The Constitution does not imply any such thing. Moreover, nothing in the existing statute rendered judicial terms individual rather than collective. These constitutional objections were clearly pretextual, designed to pave the way for a new statute on the KRS. The usefulness of this judgment became apparent when the parliamentary majority, and then the president (having vetoed the initial PiS bill) brought their bills on the KRS in mid-2017. These measures included extinguishing the constitutionally guaranteed terms for the judicial members of KRS and changing the mode for recruiting the judicial members, from election by judges to parliamentary election. This gave majority politicians a decisive say in the composition of KRS. When defending the termination of the KRS members' terms of office halfway through their terms, notwithstanding the constitutional guarantee of a four-year term, parliamentary majority spokespersons and the president pointed at the CT judgment of June 20, 2017, that deemed unconstitutional the statute under which those judicial members were elected. (More on the election of KRS below).[8]

The constitutional designers of the "3rd Republic" (a term designating post-Communist Poland) saw the Constitutional Tribunal as the centerpiece for the protection of the rule of law and the constitutional checks upon majoritarian politics. That was when the Tribunal was largely peopled by liberal lawyers of the highest standards. Their judgments eventually created a canon of liberal constitutionalism in Poland. In contrast, constitutional designers in Poland despised the "dispersed" model of constitutional review because "ordinary" judges (many tainted by their service in the previous regime) were not to be trusted with the protection of new values. Or such was the near-consensus

---

[8] Remarks by President Andrzej Duda in a TV interview, November 26, 2017, at TVN24.

among liberal constitutionalists.[9] But if one places all one's trust in a small, fifteen-person body, to carry the enormous burden of the constitutional control of politics, one makes it easy for populists to quickly dismantle the system by hitting at its centerpiece. This is exactly what has happened. The incapacitation of the Constitutional Tribunal was one of the most spectacular and earliest actions by the PiS. With hindsight, it would have been much more difficult for them to succeed had a legal culture been generated under which all judges, low and high, could refuse to apply a statute they deemed unconstitutional. There is a textual basis for this "dispersed" control (Article 8 of the Constitution proclaims its "direct applicability") but there are no habits, culture, and skills among the judges to act accordingly. The years of hubris by the Constitutional Tribunal and its acolytes (granted, often for the best of reasons) made the "regular judiciary" less constitutionally empowered.

Subjecting the "Regular" Judiciary to the Ruling Party

The elimination of the CT as a device of constitutional review triggered a debate about a dispersed, or decentralized, constitutional review, performed by all courts, US-style. While under the "old" CT it has become generally accepted that the CT has a near-monopoly on constitutional adjudication, many Polish lawyers began considering a diffusion of constitutional authority in light of the Polish laws reducing the power of the CT. The specter of regular judges conducting, in the process of concrete adjudication, review of PiS laws provided a special incentive for PiS to fundamentally transform the common courts, including the Supreme Court (SC). That explains why the second main target of the populist assault, after the CT, has been the "regular" judiciary, which has been the subject of three new laws.

The first of those laws concerned the KRS, a constitutionally designated body with the key role in all judicial nominations. The new law of December 2017 transformed the composition of the KRS radically, by determining that the fifteen judges in KRS will be elected by the Sejm—thus, making them de facto the ruling party's nominees. While there is a provision allowing the opposition parties to select "their" members of the KRS, the majority of judges on KRS, and of the KRS as a whole, is safely under PiS control. The law also permits pre-term removal of all the judges currently sitting as members of the Council despite a constitutionally guaranteed term of office (of four years).[10] Based on

---

[9] For a description and critique, see Wojciech Sadurski, *Rights before Courts*, 2nd ed. (Dordrecht: Springer, 2014), 40–43.

[10] According to the Constitution the KRS consists of fifteen judges; the remaining members are: chief justices of the SC and Supreme Administrative Court, minister of justice, representative of the president, four MPs "elected by the Sejm" and two senators "elected by the Senate." The Constitution does not provide explicitly that the judges on KRS are elected by judiciary: it only says that fifteen members are "chosen from amongst the judges" (Art. 187), but so far it has always been understood that they are elected by the judiciary itself, and

the new statute (initially vetoed by president Duda but eventually repassed with minimal changes) a "new" KRS was reconstituted by March 2018. Some 80 percent of the judges elected to the KRS are either friends of the Minister of Justice, or his direct subordinates (so called "delegated judges" working in the Ministry), or beneficiaries of the "reforms" of the regular judiciary, having been only recently promoted to positions of presidents of courts. The whole process was shrouded in secrecy. At the time of writing this chapter, the names of judges who supported or seconded the members of the KRS were not publicly disclosed. So much for the transparency of the process that was presented as one of the main virtues of the new model.

The second law in the judicial package concerned the SC—a body whose members vocally critiqued the destruction of the rule of law under PiS. Under the new law, those judges of the SC (including the chief justice, notwithstanding her constitutionally guaranteed term of office of six years) who reach the newly lowered retirement age of sixty-five have to step down or request that the president grant them a right to continue in their office. (As of writing, no judge has formally applied to the president for this privilege). The new retirement age (formerly seventy) means that about 40 percent of judges of the SC, including the most experienced ones, found themselves in the retirement zone, or compelled to make a demeaning request to the president, who maintains discretionary power on the matter. The law mandates a substantial increase in the overall number of judges on the SC (from 82 to 120), including the judges who will sit in two new chambers created in the SC, that are to be fully staffed by the new SC judges elected by the "new" KRS (ominously, one of the new chambers will be in charge inter alia of electoral disputes). Combined with the forced stepping down of many judges over sixty-five, this, according to conservative assessments, created vacancies for about 60 percent of all judges on the SC, to be filled of course by a "new" KRS. In this ingenious way, the law produces a brand new composition of the top court, peopled largely by judges selected by the parliamentary majority.

The laws on the KRS and on the SC should be considered jointly: their cumulative effect is that the judges selected by judges-members of the KRS who are selected by the politicians will occupy majority of seats on the SC, including all the seats on the new chambers of the SC. This gives the parliamentary majority and the president (who obtained great discretionary powers over the composition of the SC, an enhanced power over the selection of the chief justice, and a power of adopting the rules of procedure of the SC) extraordinary new controls over the apex court of the Polish judicial system.

The third statute in the "judicial" package concerns the organization of the common courts. This statute (which, in contrast to two former statutes, was not initially vetoed by President Duda) put the court system under effective control of the minister of justice

---

accordingly the statute on KRS established a complex mode of elections within different branches and types of the judiciary.

(MJ) to an even higher degree by giving the MJ the power to appoint and dismiss the presidents of all courts within six months of the law's passage. The MJ exercised this power to extinguish the judges' previously set terms, without the need to give any reasons and without having to take into account the opinion of the general assembly of judges of the affected court. Minister Zbigniew Ziobro was happy to exercise this authority, replacing by the end of the transitional period (12 February 2018) some one-fifth of all the senior management of all courts (149 court presidents and vice-presidents, out of 730). After the transitional period, the MJ maintains this power to dismiss court presidents under vague standards of "serious or persistent failure to comply with the official duties" or "other reasons which render remaining in office incompatible with the sound dispensation of justice," grounds easily manipulable to suit the minister's wish.

The three judiciary-related statutes enacted by the PiS majority contain many questionable features, but their truly nefarious effect is produced by accumulation. The new laws create a system in which the threat to independence of the judiciary in one provision in one statute is amplified by another provision of another statute. The lowering of the age of retirement in the statute on the SC combined with the new composition of KRS allows for a large influx of politically dependent and vulnerable judges to the SC. The creation of two new chambers of the SC entrusted with politically highly sensitive matters is compounded by the participation of lay judges, elected by a simple majority of the Senate. A possible measure of control of the executive in one act is disarmed by a measure in another act. The power of KRS to control the ministerial dismissal of a court's president is weakened by the political composition of KRS and a requirement of a two-thirds majority of votes for such a decision, which is highly unlikely to be obtained. The "positive reinforcement" effect is even stronger given the blatant unconstitutional provision in these statutes that are unreviewable after the transformation of the CT.

The law of early 2016 on the Public's Prosecutor's Office further aggravates the politicization of the judiciary. The law merged the hitherto separate positions of MJ and Prosecutor General (PG), and endowed the newly merged position with enhanced, substantial prerogatives. The 2016 law put an end to the principle of independence of prosecutors that was the declared aim of the earlier law of 2009. The PG/MJ may now intervene in prosecutorial investigation at any stage, give orders regarding specific cases, transfer cases from one prosecutor to another, change and revoke a decision of any subordinate public prosecutor, inspect the materials collected in the course of any preparatory proceedings, and reveal details of non-final investigations to public authorities and to "other persons" (including media). This degree of interference by the MJ is unknown to any other European system. This merger of offices means that a party to the proceedings (qua the PG) will at the same time have huge control over the judges (qua the MJ). This merger of the PG and MJ violates the Constitution, which forbids public prosecutors (inter alia) to be MPs, the reason being an attempt to prevent overt politicization of the office. But the PG, qua MJ, *is* a political official and an MP.

Delegitimizing the Opposition

The opposition in any democracy is an important element of checks and balances, and the treatment of the opposition by the ruling parties is a test of how seriously they take the idea that alternation in power is a crucial criterion of democratic governance. In Poland under PiS the opposition parties have been treated as an alien body in politics, and in particular in the Parliament. In addition to many slurs and insults that have been inflicted on the three main opposition parties, Civic Platform (PO) and "Nowoczesna" and the Peasant Party (PSL), the main manner in which the opposition has been denied a meaningful political role has been the legislative process, which was turned into a voting machine by PiS, and the opposition parties have been reduced to a marginal role, as irritants treated with open hostility rather than vehicles of possibly helpful amendments to legislative drafts.

This has been mainly achieved by a simple device of legislative fast-tracking, and proposing some of the most significant items of PiS legislative changes as private members' bills rather than governmental initiatives, even if de facto they were very much elaborated and put forward by the government. In the first full year of the rule by PiS, 2016, over 40 percent (76 out of 181), including the most important ones, of PiS legislative proposals were submitted as private members' bills (in the two previous parliamentary terms, the percentages were respectively 15 and 13 percent). In addition, with regard to those bills that formally did go through the procedure of consultations, expert opinion, and impact statements, the requirement to publish on the parliamentary website all the opinions was dropped, so the general public has no way of knowing whether any negative opinions were supplied. As one example of fast-tracking consider the law on the Public Prosecutor's office, discussed above. Even though de facto it was prepared by the Ministry of Justice, it was formally presented as a private members' bill. Notwithstanding that a number of entities produced opinions about the bill, including the SC and the KRS, they were effectively disregarded during the legislative process.

The frantic pace with which some of the most important legislative acts have been pushed through the parliamentary commissions and in plenary debates of the Sejm and Senate resulted in a virtual silencing of the opposition through devices such as using gag rules during the "deliberations"; placing new items on the agenda without any notice and speeding the deliberation, often late into the night or early morning; ignoring critical expert opinions, etc.—the speed not being justified by any substantive urgency of the proposals. The NGO called "Civic Legislative Forum"[11] lists the following examples of reducing the voice of the opposition in the Sejm: limiting speeches to one minute, voting en bloc on the amendments, with bundling of all the amendments together not on the

---

[11] See "Civic Legislative Forum," Batory Foundation, accessed February 28, 2018, http://www.batory.org.pl/en/operational_programs/anti_corruption/civic_legislative_forum.

basis of their subject matter but on the basis of which party proposed them; failure to provide enough time to read some proposed amendments; working late into the night; and failure to respond to observations of legislative mistakes in the bills.[12] In addition, opposition MPs occasionally have been excluded from the parliamentary floor on disciplinary grounds; procedural tricks were used to sidestep the opposition—for example the 2017 budget was adopted not in the Sejm assembly hall, but in a smaller room where the so-called parliamentary session was held immediately as a follow-up to the meeting of the parliamentary caucus of PiS, where no reliable counting of votes was possible, and with many allegations that the opposition MPs were not allowed in.

Assault on Individual Rights

The disempowering of the Constitutional Tribunal and regular courts should be seen not as a phenomenon in itself, but as an important instrument of disabling judicial review of liberal rights such as freedom of assembly and speech. As Polish constitutional scholar Tomasz Tadeusz Koncewicz observed: "The Constitutional Court was targeted first because that would ensure that next phases would sail through without any scrutiny from its side. Who cares that the new legislation flies in the face of the constitution since there is no procedural and institutional avenue to enforce constitutional rules?"[13] Some observers initially asked a question: What is the purpose of eliminating effective checks and balances, implying that the PiS had plans for a more direct assault upon rights and freedoms of citizens? These fears turned out to be well-founded.

RIGHT OF ASSEMBLY

The statute of December 13, 2016, ensures a privileged position for assemblies devoted to patriotic, religious, and historic events, which in specific Polish circumstances single out in particular pro-governmental or government-supported assemblies, such as monthly events held to commemorate the Smoleńsk aircraft crash of April 10, 2010. These monthly manifestations, held in the center of Warsaw and culminating always with speeches by Jarosław Kaczyński in front of the Presidential Palace, have become a sort of hate rally against the opposition, and in time, have provoked peaceful counter-assemblies. The new law has, as its effect, made it illegal for counter-assemblies to take place in the direct

---

[12] Obywatelskie Forum Legislacji—Fundacja im. Stefana Batorego, "Jakość stanowienia prawa w drugim roku rządów Prawa i Sprawiedliwości: X Komunikat Obywatelskiego Forum Legislacji o jakości procesu legislacyjnego na podstawie obserwacji w okresie of 16 listopada 2016 do 15 listopada 2017 roku" (2017) at 2 and 11.

[13] Tomasz Tadeusz Koncewicz, "Farewell to the Separation of Powers—On the Judicial Purge and the Capture in the Heart of Europe," *VerfBlog*, July 19, 2017, http://verfassungsblog.de/farewell-to-the-separation-of-powers-on-the-judicial-purge-and-the-capture-in-the-heart-of-europe.

vicinity of these PiS monthly assemblies. Organizing a demonstration in the same location where a so-called "cyclical assembly" organized by public authorities or churches is to take place is now legally impossible. After the law was enacted, participants of counter-manifestations (relegated by the new law to the status of inferior assemblies) became subjected to increasingly harsh persecutions, with hundreds of persons interrogated by police, often treated quite brutally by the police and voluntary security teams of the PiS-sponsored assemblies.

FREEDOM OF SPEECH

The PiS has attempted to silence independent journalists and writers by threatening them with legal action, often disproportionate to alleged "offences." In a separate development, the Parliament enacted at the end of January 2018 a statute that amends the Law on the Institute of National Remembrance. The new law establishes an offense, punishable by up to three years in jail, of attributing publicly and falsely responsibility or co-responsibility to the Polish nation or the state for crimes against humanity committed by the Nazis during World War II. The same law provides civil sanctions for statements violating the reputation of Poland or the Polish nation. The chilling effect of such penal and civil laws upon scholarly or journalistic debates regarding the darker sides of Polish history is obvious. The laws clearly resonate with a highly nationalistic governmental rhetoric, under which Polish history is comprised entirely of heroic acts and undeserved victimhood, never of criminal actions. The proposed law is sometimes referred to as "lex Gross," referring to Polish-American scholar Professor Jan T. Gross whose books and articles depicting Polish crimes against Jews on German-occupied territories during the World War II have provoked heated public debates in Poland over recent decades. As of writing, the new law is pending before the CT. Whatever judgment the Tribunal hands down will be a reflection of a political decision by Jarosław Kaczyński about how to deal with this highly embarrassing piece of legislation.

COUNTERTERRORISM MEASURES AND POLICE ACT

The statute of June 10, 2016, established vast and vaguely defined powers for the Internal Security Agency (ISA) in order to protect the state against terrorism, as well as to control citizens and collect personal data without following "regular" statutory procedures. There is no clear definition of the term "terrorist act," even though the new law is one of the most important statutory criteria for action by the antiterrorist services. A new database will be created by the ISA in order to control persons associated with terrorist acts. The provisions do not guarantee any efficient judicial control over the database, nor do they allow an interested party to demand, correct, and delete false or incomplete data. The ISA may demand and shall have open (and in fact unlimited) access to data and information collected by all public agencies or bodies at the central as well as local level. A risk or an attempt to commit a terrorist act shall be a sufficient premise to apply for pretrial detention. The statute of January 15, 2016, gives police and its agencies access to internet data, including the communication's content, under court orders (up to three months but without a requirement of necessity or proportionality) or to metadata without the need for court orders.

ELECTORAL LAW

The PiS at the end of 2017 and in the beginning of 2018 brought about a massive change to the electoral law, introducing enhanced control by the parliamentary majority and by the executive over the mechanism for conducting elections, "de-judicialisating" electoral institutions, and entrusting the new-model "commissioners" (no longer judges) with full authority for redrawing electoral boundaries. Under the new law, adopted by the Sejm on December 14, 2017, the main body in charge of elections, the National Electoral Commission (Polish acronym: PKW) was completely restructured. Rather than, as had been the case being composed of nine judges, appointed in equal numbers by three presidents of the top courts, the CT, the SC, and the Supreme Administrative Court (from among the judges of those courts), the new PKW is composed only of two judges of the CT and SAC, accompanied by seven members appointed by the Sejm (who do not need to be judges). The head of the National Electoral Bureau (not to be confused with the Commission), which is an executive arm of the Commission, will be appointed by the new PKW from among three candidates submitted by the minister of the interior; he or she will be also able to be removed by PKW with consent of the minister of the interior. The responsibility in local electoral districts will fall upon one hundred "commissioners" who will be appointed by PKW, but again, from the candidates proposed by the minister of the interior. At the same time, electoral disputes will be considered by a new chamber of the SC, composed exclusively of judges appointed by a "new" KRS, with the majority of members elected by the parliamentary majority. The electoral process will be thus fully controllable by the ruling party, either by the parliamentary majority or by the minister of the Interior who is a member of a narrow party leadership.

CIVIL SOCIETY

There is a large network of NGOs, think tanks, and social organizations ranging from foreign policy to free soup for the homeless, from rights of refugees to protection over historical cemeteries. . . . It took PiS two years to come up with legislation that helps subordinate civil society to the political hegemon. Two new institutions were created for this purpose: the Committee for Public Benefit and an institution with an Orwellian title "The National Institute of Freedom: Centre for the Development of Civil Society," in order to centralize state control over government funds for NGOs.[14]

The former institution is composed mostly of members of the government (the President of the Committee, who is also a member of the Council of Ministers,[15] Secretary of State in the Chancellery of Prime Minister, ministers, and Director of the National Institute of Freedom). Statutory competences and membership render the Committee (on which no NGOs representatives sit) the highest political body on all matters concerning the financing, controlling, and development of civil society by the government.

The general avowed objective of the second of the above-mentioned institutions ("The National Institute of Freedom") is to support financing and development of civil society in accordance with governmental guidelines. The statute unfortunately does not guarantee a sufficient level of pluralism, legal certainty, or lack of arbitrariness. The Institute is charged with implementation of tasks defined on a case-by-case basis by the President of the Committee—giving this person (a member of the government) and the prime minister (to whom he or she reports) enormous power over dispensing grants to NGOs. The governance model of the Institute renders it fully subordinate to the government: the majority of members of the Institute's Council are appointed by the governmental Committee for Public Benefit, and so indirectly by the prime minister. Although there are to be some NGO representatives on the Council, they are in a minority (five out of eleven), and in any event the Council has only an advisory role. To make things worse, the "NGO representatives" are appointed by the President of the Committee (let us recall, a member of the government) who has full discretion over whom to appoint from among candidates proposed by NGOs. Considering great pluralism within Polish civil society, there is no obstacle toward appointing only or mainly representatives of right-wing or Christian organizations.

Importantly, a preamble to the new law mentions "Christian values," which may indicate a built-in bias in the system toward faith-based NGOs. But even before the new law, there was a clear shift in priorities: those with a Christian, conservative agenda have been privileged in reallocation of funds while those with more "liberal" or "left" agendas have been disfavored.

Conclusion

Over twenty years ago, Guillermo A. O'Donnell published an influential article that put forward a concept of "Delegative Democracy" (DD): a system under which

---

[14] Previously, decisions on allocation of funds were shared between different ministries, and this facilitated distribution to multiple beneficiaries.

[15] On December 11, 2017 the minister of culture (Piotr Gliński) was appointed by President Duda to be the Chairman of the Committee for Public Benefit (see Official Gazette of the Republic of Poland 2017, item 1152). Minister Gliński, who is also deputy prime minister, is known for his numerous restrictive actions against (what he sees as) left-liberal and nonpatriotic trends in theater, cinema, and museums.

"whoever wins election to the presidency is thereby entitled to govern as he or she sees fit, constrained only by the hard facts of existing power relations and by a constitutionally limited term of office."[16] While O'Donnell's discussion is modelled on Latin American post-authoritarian presidential systems, it can be adapted, mutatis mutandis, to Polish semi-presidentialism, with the leader of the winning party performing a function similar to that of a Latin American president. PiS uses a majority-based legitimacy as the basis of its title to represent the "high interests of the nation" as a whole, and those persons who are not captured by the interests represented by PiS, do not count.

What DD is missing, in contrast to a true *representative* democracy, is accountability during term of office, and what O'Donnell calls "horizontal accountability," exercised through "a network of relatively autonomous powers (i.e., other institutions) that can call into question, and eventually punish, improper ways of discharging the responsibilities of a given official."[17] Again, if we replace "delegative presidents" with "a leader of the ruling party," this is a good account of Poland under PiS. As this chapter has documented, the main fire of the parliamentary majority, the government and the president—all coordinated skilfully by the leader of the ruling party—is addressed against various institutions of horizontal accountability in Poland, including the constitutional court, ordinary courts, parliamentary opposition, NGOs, and the media.

Whether Poland under PiS will remain democratic at its core—in the moment when the electoral "delegation" is being decided by the electorate—remains to be seen at the next elections. While in the first electoral cycle, "illiberal democracy" may carry some genuine meaning (the free and fair elections give the illiberal leaders of the winning party a mandate to act within their electoral promises even if we dislike them), in the longer term "illiberal democracy" becomes an oxymoron. The very liberal rights that are part of the irreducible guarantees of democracy are eroded of substance and dispensed with.

Two veteran political scientists observe that free and fair elections are not a sufficient condition for a democratic political order. Political orders must not only be democratic in their pedigree, they actually must behave within the bounds of the democratic rules of the game as defined by the constitution and other laws: "[N]o regime should be called a democracy unless its rulers govern democratically. If freely elected executives (no matter what the magnitude of their majority) infringe the constitution, violate the rights of individuals and minorities, impinge upon the legitimate functions of the legislature, and thus fail to rule within the bounds of a state of law, their regimes are not democracies."[18] By rejecting effective checks and balances, populist parties such as the PiS undermine the subjection of democratic politics to the constitutional rules of the game. By denying

---

[16] Guillermo O'Donnell, "Delegative Democracy," *Journal of Democracy* 5 (1994): 55–69, 59.

[17] Ibid., 61.

[18] Juan J. Linz and Alfred Stepan, "Toward Consolidated Democracies," *Journal of Democracy* 7 (1996): 14–33, 15.

equal moral status to members of groups they despise, whether recent migrants, Islamists, atheists, or simply political rivals, they strike at the value of political equality that is at the core of democracy. Majority rule derives its weight precisely from the value of political equality it serves. Insofar as majority rule is inconsistent with that value, it loses its normative bearings. The widespread tendency to characterize contemporary populisms as fundamentally democratic, or at least as not non-democratic,[19] is therefore highly questionable, and assumes an arithmetical, purely majoritarian concept of democracy. It also ignores the right-wing populists' distaste for *representative* democracy, and their claim to communicate with the people as a whole, over the heads of representative institutions. They favor simple solutions, where alternatives are reduced to black-and-white stories, and quick solutions, as the frenzied pace of pushing through the main pieces of legislation in Poland under PiS exemplifies.

Perhaps the concept of "plebiscitary autocracy" is more adequate: there are by-and-large free and regular elections though not necessarily fair, due to some restraints upon democratic rights, such as restrictions on assembly and the media, various ways of delegitimizing the opposition, and the politicization of the institutions that manage the electoral process. With the government controlling all the levers of government, and suffocating the opposition and pluralism in the media, election days are a plebiscite in favor or against the ruling elite. However, there is no accountability and no subjection of the government to effective constitutional constraints *between* the elections; the plebiscites are about whether the electorate approves of the governmental disregard for the constitution in the period between elections.

How to explain the unconstitutional populist backsliding in Poland? No doubt, a crucial role in generating societal support was played by a new welfare policy. The program "500+" (providing each family a monthly stipend of PLN 500, or EUR 120, per month for each child over and above the first one) with 2 million families as its beneficiaries was ingenious in its simplicity. This is a typical instance of pork-barrel politics, employed with great shrewdness by PiS. While various benefits "in kind" may be economically much more rational (free preschool facilities, improvement of public schools, public transport and infrastructure aimed at disadvantaged regions, and in particular improvement in health services), their effects are delayed in time and less tangible. In contrast, giving cash to every family with more than one child, immediately and with no conditions attached, is instantly attractive; for example, in a low-income family of three children or more, it may translate into a doubling of the family income. These big social transfers are presented by PiS, and seen by its supporters, as a huge act of social justice and as a recognition of the legitimate claims of people who felt harmed and humiliated by the transformation—either in reality, or as an effect of skilful PiS anti-elite propaganda. The

---

[19] See, e.g., Sheri Berman, "Populism Is Not Fascism," *Foreign Affairs* 95 (November/December 2016): 39–45, 43 (stating that current right-wing extremisms, which she dubs populisms, "are certainly illiberal, but they are not antidemocratic").

early criticisms of the program by the opposition and the liberal media who represented it as a massive bribe only helped to strengthen the perception that it is only PiS that understands, empathizes with, and helps ordinary people.

By providing generous welfare provisions, as well as an elaborate system of patronage and spoils, and a sense of pride based on nationalistic rhetoric and a sense of protection based on fear of immigrants combined with anti-elite, anti-cosmopolitan and anti-European rhetorics, the PiS posits to the voters a Faustian bargain for the net benefit of confirming the government in power despite its constitutional non-compliance. A major part of the bargain is about dispensing with strong and independent courts that protect democratic rights minorities, because such courts are not vital for a party that confidently controls all the branches of government, and does not anticipate an imminent defeat, but in which case such courts would be helpful to it.

The picture drawn in this chapter is gloomy. But there is no inevitability in further backsliding for Polish democracy: as of the time of writing, no political movement in the history of human society carried with it inevitable outcomes. PiS is hopefully no exception. Poland has the strong societal and political resources necessary to arrest and reverse the trends described above, and then unravel all the nefarious institutional changes brought about by PiS rule. There is still a vibrant and resilient civil society; there are strong if rather episodic social protest movements; there is an independent body of commercial media, both electronic and print; and there are passionate debates in social media. Universities are free, and the only censorship, when it occurs in academia, is self-imposed. Cultural institutions—theaters, film industry, museums—articulate a rich diversity of political views, and although the state makes occasional and rather awkward attempts at control, both administrative and financial, Polish culture maintains an independent spirit. The opposition parties, while divided along many lines, have a combined electorate not far below the electorate of PiS. There are a number of iconic personalities with great historical credentials and impeccable liberal-democratic outlooks who constitute the symbolic capital that PiS lacks: Lech Wałęsa, Adam Michnik, Władysław Frasyniuk have authority that Kaczyński and his cronies lack. There is a courageous and intelligent Commissioner for Human Rights (Ombudsman), Dr. Adam Bodnar, who enjoys a degree of constitutional protection against dismissal, even though PiS media and individual politicians occasionally suggest revoking his tenure prior to the end of his term.

Populisms, such as PiS's, often carry a seed of self-destruction: they are, in the long run, ineffective and counterproductive, relying upon the knowledge (imperfect) and charisma (doubtful) of a single person. With its paranoid excesses and narrow epistemic base, populism has low capacity for effective governance. By disconnecting the real center of political power from constitutionally established institutions and procedures, the regime reduces the likelihood of self-correction facilitated by inter-institutional accountability. The main legitimating ground of populism—that it effectively delivers the goods to its electorate—seems to have a long-term tendency to decline. As Ben Stanley notes, populist parties "often fell victim to the same public scepticism they had sought to cultivate when attacking established parties."[20] There is no reason to believe that, in the longer run, PiS will escape the force of this "scepticism" espoused by its most faithful electorate which is, at the same time, the most conducible to anti-establishment attitudes.

---

[20] Ben Stanley, "Populism in Central and Eastern Europe," in Cristóbal Rovira Kaltwasser, Paul Taggart, Paulina Ochoa-Espejo & Pierre Ostiguy, eds., *The Oxford Handbook of Populism* (Oxford University Press: Oxford 2017): 140-160 at 157-58.

17 Beyond Legitimacy
Europe's Crisis of Constitutional Democracy
Michaela Hailbronner

FOR ANYONE UNDER the age of thirty-five, the European Union has been in a state of almost perpetual crisis. The Maastricht Treaty (1992) appeared to be a great leap forward, cementing the three big pillars of European integration: the common market, police and judicial cooperation, and foreign policy. Yet that decade also saw the rise of extreme right-wing political movements in European countries from Austria to the Netherlands and France, and a surge of neo-Nazi attacks on foreigners in Germany. From the mid-2000s onward, the European Union has been nearly permanently in trouble, starting with the failure of the constitutional treaty in the referenda in France and the Netherlands in 2005. Even the entry into force of the subsequent Lisbon treaty, which replaced the failed constitutional treaty and put in place a new decision-making structure for an enlarged Union, could not ultimately provide the pragmatic solution to European problems of governance and legitimacy it was meant to; it coincided with the beginning of the European financial crisis. Today, though those fortunate enough to live in the richer Northern Member States may think that those events lie in the past, those grappling with the effects of financial austerity in the South see things differently. The European Union's debt crisis management also marked the moment in which many Europeans fell out of love with the idea of Europe as a postnational community of solidarity. On the heels of the debt crisis came the migration crisis and thus another failure of European states to find a common solution to a common challenge. Alongside all of this, nationalist right-wing regimes have come to power in Hungary and Poland (and outside the EU, but close to it, in Turkey) whose commitments to key constitutional principles are doubtful, and similar movements are on the rise in the traditional core Member States, including Germany, France, the Netherlands, and Austria. And to cap it off, in 2016, for the first time, a Member State (Britain) voted to leave the Union.[1]

About all of these events, volumes can be and have been written. The task of this chapter cannot be to rehash that literature. Instead, I engage with the more particular question this volume suggests, namely whether there is currently a crisis of constitutional democracy in Europe, focusing mainly on the European Union rather than Europe more generally. Before taking on that issue, however, there are two preliminary questions we need to address: First, what counts as a crisis of constitutional democracy? Second, how does this apply to the European Union, given its supranational sui generis character? Drawing on the broader comparative literature on the crisis of constitutional democracy, I argue that it is important to distinguish between Europe's oft-lamented crisis of legitimacy and its more recent and worrying crisis of constitutional democracy, which I define in the following as a weakening of European democracy and of the normative force of important European constitutional principles. I suggest that the EU's crisis of constitutional democracy is related to but not identical with its existing legitimacy problems.

The three crises I deal with below—the debt crisis, the migration crisis, and the rise of right-wing nationalism—all affect the public legitimacy of the Union. This is perhaps particularly true for the debt crisis. Its management has impaired the Union's legitimacy by damaging its status in the eyes of the people of Europe as both a means to promote their well-being, above all economic, and as a promise of a better postnational future (in Weiler's terms, the "messianic" vision of the EU).[2] Whatever one's ultimate position on the EU, the economic benefits of joining the common market have not been much debated. Previous data demonstrated that membership typically came with a leveling up of standards of living of the poorer Southern Member States, thus decreasing inequality between richer and poorer countries. More recent research investigating the effects of the crisis and its financial austerity policies paints a distinctly more nuanced picture, even though there seems to be no consensus view yet as to the exact effects of those policies.[3] Whatever the final answer to that question, however, the crisis management has also laid bare the limitations of financial solidarity between Member States. In doing so, it has shattered the progressive vision of many elites of the European Union as a postnational

[1] For an excellent German summary of the Union's recent history see Ulrich Haltern, *Europarecht. Dogmatik im Kontext. Band I: Entwicklung, Institutionen, Prozesse* (Tübingen: Mohr Siebeck, 2017), 104–187.

[2] Joseph H.H. Weiler, "In the Face of Crisis: Input Legitimacy, Output Legitimacy and the Political Messianism of European Integration," *Journal of European Integration* 34, no. 7 (2012): 825–841.

[3] See Martin Heidenreich, ed., *Exploring Inequality in Europe: Diverging Income and Employment Opportunities in the Crisis* (Cheltenham, Northampton: Edward Elgar, 2016).

community based on solidarity and shared political values, with its "European Social Model"[4] more robust and cosmopolitan than that of the United States.[5]

But our three crises not only affect the Union's public legitimacy; they also affect European constitutional democracy, albeit in more subtle and varied ways as I explain in the following. Each places question marks against key constitutional values such as mutual trust and solidarity and, most important, Europe's commitment to human rights and democracy. The debt crisis and its management in particular have weakened European democracy. Together with the constitutional problems raised by the Union's and Member States' approach to migration and the rise of less democratic and less liberal governments in particular in Eastern Europe, these developments represent a crisis of constitutional democracy in Europe, as distinct from its long-standing existing problems of public acceptance and legitimacy.

Crisis of Constitutional Democracy

Clearly, not every violation of one or other right or principle indicates that constitutional democracy is in crisis. Several authors in this volume start from the definition provided by Jack Balkin: "A constitutional crisis occurs when there is a serious danger that the Constitution is about to fail at its central task."[6] That central task is understood to be "keep(ing) disagreement within the boundaries of ordinary politics rather than breaking down into anarchy, violence, or civil war."[7] For the broader global project this volume pursues, this definition strikes me as too narrow. How so? The project starts from the observation that, after the global rise of constitutional democracy in the 1990s and 2000s, there have more recently been a number of regime- and indeed constitutional changes in a range of countries that have systemically weakened the protection of individual rights, threatened important constitutional principles such as the separation of powers, and impaired the independence of the judiciary and democracy. The paradigm cases are countries such as Turkey or Hungary. The broader question is thus whether there is indeed global backlash against the principles of constitutionalism and democracy. Insofar as we are looking back in history and worry about whether events in the 1920s and 1930s in Europe are repeating themselves, we know from existing analyses by David Landau and

---

[4] Tony Judt, *Postwar. A History of Europe from 1945* (Penguin, 2006), 793.

[5] See, e.g., Isabel Feichtner's powerful statement that I, like many shared, Isabel Feichtner, "Nein!," EJIL Talk!, July 28, 2015, available at www.ejiltalk.org/nein/.

[6] Jack Balkin, "Constitutional Crisis and Constitutional Rot," *Constitutional Democracy in Crisis?*, ed. Mark A. Graber, Sanford Levinson, and Mark Tushnet (New York: Oxford University Press, 2018), 18. (referring to Sanford Levinson and Jack M. Balkin, "Constitutional Crises," *University of Pennsylvania Law Review* 157 (2008): 707); see similarly Eric Posner, "The Trump Presidency: A Constitutional Crisis in the United States?" *Constitutional Democracy in Crisis?*, 105–11. James T. Gathii, "Term Limits and Three Types of Constitutional Crisis in Africa," *Constitutional Democracy in Crisis?*, 313–14.

[7] Balkin, "Constitutional Crisis," 14.

Kim Lane Scheppele that the current changes take more constitutional and less violent forms—hence Landau's label of "abusive constitutionalism"[8] and Scheppele's convincing attempt to grasp Hungarian developments with the idea of a "Frankenstate."[9] We can add to this another widely discussed concept in the comparative literature today, namely populism, defined by Jan-Werner Müller as a form of anti-pluralism that entails a claim to the exclusive representation of the "real people."[10] Behind all of these terms stands an effort by authors to capture contemporary political trends that have weakened fundamental principles and ideas of constitutionalism and democracy, without amounting to an explicit rejection or overthrow of constitutionalism or democracy per se. Defining constitutional crisis in terms primarily of civil unrest and disorder therefore runs the risk of remaining stuck in the paradigms of nineteenth century United States or early twentieth century European developments and not being able to capture the new challenges adequately. There seems little risk of civil unrest in Hungary today, nor indeed do most Hungarians seem to be dissatisfied with the constitutional order (a "crisis as dissatisfaction" in Posner's terms) as Hungarians have just voted to confirm Viktor Orbán's government once again. Yet it makes sense to speak of a crisis of constitutional democracy, understood in a broader sense as a systemic weakening of the power of constitutional norms to provide direction for and constraints on the exercise of political power and/or a considerable decrease in the quality of democracy.

Or to make the point in German legal jargon: A crisis of democratic constitutionalism raises doubts with regard to the "normative Kraft" ("normative force")[11] of the constitution. It makes us wonder openly whether restoring it requires changing the constitution itself or changing whatever conditions led to the crisis. This is not miles away from Balkin's and other definitions employed in this volume, but it also includes developments such as systemic violations of human rights by the government or a significant weakening of democratic institutions that do not include explicit declarations by officials or amount to civil disorder.

Application to the European Union

The concepts of constitutionalism and democracy are of course rooted in the nation-state. Their transfer to the European Union, whose character as a "constitutional democracy" is contested at the best of times, may thus appear problematic. I use the terms "constitutionalism" and "democracy" in this chapter in a functional sense.

---

[8] David Landau, "Abusive Constitutionalism," *UC Davis Law Review* 47 (2013): 189.

[9] Kim Lane Scheppele, "The Rule of Law and the Frankenstate: Why Governance Checklists Do Not Work," *Governance* 26, no. 4 (2013): 559–562.

[10] Jan-Werner Müller, *What Is Populism?* (Philadelphia, PA: University of Pennsylvania Press, 2016).

[11] That term goes back to the famous German constitutional theorist Konrad Hesse, *Die normative Kraft der Verfassung: Freiburger Antrittsvorlesung* (Tübingen: Mohr Siebeck, 1959).

I understand constitutionalism as the establishment and constraint of political power by foundational laws (here, important principles and the institutional setup of common structures in the European treaties),[12] and democracy as a form of political organization where the people exercise political power directly or indirectly through elected representatives, leaving to one side the long-standing debates over the constitutional nature of the European Union[13] and its "democratic deficit."[14] What I am concerned with in what follows is thus whether there are new European developments that point toward a significant weakening of the normative force of European constitutional principles and democracy. The answer to that question is yes, and this, I argue, is something new.

Three Crises and Their Effects on European Constitutional Democracy

We would be much less likely to ask whether there is a crisis of constitutional democracy in the European Union if there had not recently been three particularly troubling developments: the debt crisis and its management, the challenges of mass migration to the Union and the lack of adequate responses, and the rise of populism, in particular in Eastern Europe. In the following, I take a look at each of these to see how, if at all, these developments have affected European constitutional democracy.

In contrast, I do not examine Brexit here in any detail, quite simply because it represents no crisis of European constitutional democracy by whatever standard we apply. It does not affect European constitutional principles or democracy (the option to exit the Union is explicitly provided for in the treaties).[15] Insofar as it represents a crisis of legitimacy that may have been prompted by similar Euroskeptic forces as those involved in the rise of right-wing populist movements in the Union, it is those general forces, and not the British manifestation of them alone, that merit discussion in terms of a crisis in the Union.

---

[12] Ingolf Pernice, "The Treaty of Lisbon: Multilevel Constitutionalism in Action," *Columbia Journal of European Law* 15 (2008): 349.

[13] For an introduction see the two most famous contributions by Dieter Grimm, "Does Europe Need a Constitution?," *European Law Journal* 1, no. 3 (1995): 282–302 and Jürgen Habermas, "Remarks on Dieter Grimm's 'Does Europe Need a Constitution?,'" *European Law Journal* 1, no. 3 (1995): 303–307.

[14] For many see the two key positions staked out by Giandomenico Majone, "Europe's 'Democratic Deficit': The Question of Standards," *European Law Journal* 4, no. 1 (1998): 5–28, and Andrew Moravcsik, "In Defense of the 'Democratic Deficit': Reassessing the Legitimacy of the European Union," *Journal of Common Market Studies* (2002): 603–624. For a very recent, more positive assessment see Athanasios Psygkas, *From the "Democratic Deficit" to a "Democratic Surplus": Constructing Administrative Democracy in Europe* (New York: Oxford University Press, 2017).

[15] See Art. 50 Treaty on European Union (TEU).

THE DEBT CRISIS

How is the debt crisis relevant to European constitutionalism and/or democracy? The answer must be that it has prompted the establishment of new European mechanisms of economic oversight that have shifted power to Member State governments and also, partly, to the Commission and thus to the executive branch[16] and away from national and European parliaments. As a result, it has arguably weakened national and European democracy.

To understand these arguments, some background is necessary (skip forward if you are familiar with the story):[17] The debt crisis arose out of the global financial crisis, which revealed that several governments, in particular in Southern European states, were unable to bail out involved banks and had generally amassed considerable debt that they would be unlikely to repay. The possibility of offering straightforward financial support to suffering Eurozone states was complicated by a prohibition of bailouts under the EU treaties, adopted in the interest of securing fiscal stability and preventing inflation. Instead, richer Member States offered some help within the IMF framework, the conditions of which were negotiated with Greece by the so-called Troika, the European Commission, the European Central Bank, and the IMF. Besides a host of temporary measures by various actors, the crisis led to the creation of a permanent framework to better address and prevent similar situations in the future. The new framework has prompted a communitarization of exchange rates and monetary and banking policy. New institutions have been created to provide financial assistance in future crisis, mainly through the European Stability Mechanism (ESM),[18] and a broader supervisory regime has been established over Member States' economic and budgetary policies, introduced through the so-called Six-Pack-[19] and the supplementing Two-Pack-Regulations.[20] The ESM establishes a structure outside of the European treaties and thus outside community methodology. It relies

---

[16] The term "executive branch" here refers not just to the Commission, but also to the executive branch within Member States, that is, the governments as they are represented in the EU in both the Council (of Ministers) and the European Council (of Heads of States) as well as in non-EU institutions that are run by Member State governments.

[17] For a good overview see, e.g., Matthias Ruffert, "European Debt Crisis and European Union Law," *Common Market Law Review* 48 (2011): 1777 or (in German) Haltern, *Europarecht*, 104 ff.

[18] The legality of the ESM has been sharply contested in the literature (see, e.g., for a critique Jonathan Tomkin, "Contradiction, Circumvention and Conceptual Gymnastics: The Impact of the Adoption of the ESM Treaty on the State of European Democracy," *German Law Journal* 14 (2013): 169), but was confirmed by the European Court of Justice in C-370/12—*Pringle*. I am not engaging with the debate over the ESM's legality here because even if its establishment contravened EU primary law, the provisions in question were of a more technical and not of a constitutional nature.

[19] The term encompasses the following six pieces of EU legislation: EU Regulation 1175/2011 of November 16, 2011 amending Regulation 1466/97, Regulation 1177/2011 of Nov. 8, 2011 amending Regulation 1467/97, Regulation 1173/2011 of November 16, 2011, Directive 2011/85/EU of November 8, 2011, Regulation 1176/2011 of November 16, 2011, Regulation 1174/2011 of November 16, 2011 amending Regulation 1466/97.

[20] These are Regulation 472/2013 of May 11, 2013 and Regulation 473/2013 of May 11, 2013.

instead directly on the Member State governments whose representatives unanimously take all key decisions concerning the provision of financial assistance (Art. 6 TESM).[21] The Six-Pack Regulations in contrast operate under the roof of the treaties and invest the Commission and the Council with supervisory powers over Member States' economic policies—including commenting on Member States' budgets—with the approval of the Council (of Ministers) whose role has greatly increased since the crisis. The debt crisis has also strengthened the authority of the European Central Bank (ECB). The ECB has assumed an enlarged mandate during the crisis by adopting the so-called OMT program (outright monetary transactions), under which it can buy Member State bonds to stabilize their economies, a highly contested measure triggering a renewal of the long-standing debate between the German Constitutional Court and the ECJ.[22] The ECB has subsequently been involved in several of the new post-crisis mechanisms.

A broad literature describes these developments in terms of constitutional change, as a "constitutional mutation"[23] or shift in the "constitutional balance" of the European Union.[24] Floris de Witte and Mark Dawson argue that the debt crisis prompted, first, a transfer of competences with regard to economic redistribution to the EU that had always been understood as fundamentally national competences, and second, a transfer of these competences to the executive. The European Parliament was almost entirely bypassed and the role of the Commission changed from a more gubernatorial role (initiating new legislation) toward a more traditional executive function of implementation. In this process, they argue, power was redistributed to the richer and more powerful Member States from the poorer and smaller ones.[25] Yet, their analysis is not uncontested. Bruno de Witte has argued that the new structures all lie within the realm of the European Monetary Union (a long-standing area of intergovernmental cooperation) and have thus increased institutional variation in the EU, but have not fundamentally altered its constitutional structure.[26] Indeed, it is useful to recall that there have been other projects such as the Schengen Agreement of 1985 that started from an intergovernmental basis and later became part of Community law.

---

[21] Treaty Establishing the ESM, signed on February 2, 2012, available at https://www.esm.europa.eu/legal-documents/esm-treaty.

[22] German Constitutional Court, Judgment of June 21, 2016, 2 BvR 2728/13, 2 BvE 13/13, 2 BvR 2731/13, 2 BvR 2730/13, 2 BvR 2729/13, available at https://www.bundesverfassungsgericht.de/SharedDocs/Entscheidungen/EN/2016/06/rs20160621_2bvr272813en.html.

[23] Kaarlo Tuori and Klaus Tuori, *The Eurozone Crisis—A Constitutional Analysis* (New York: Cambridge University Press, 2014), 137ff.

[24] Mark Dawson and Floris Witte, "Constitutional Balance in the EU after the Euro-Crisis," *The Modern Law Review* 76, no. 5 (2013): 817–844.

[25] Dawson and de Witte, "Constitutional Balance"; similarly Federico Fabbrini, "States' Equality v States' Power: the Euro-Crisis, Inter-State Relations and the Paradox of Domination," *Cambridge Yearbook of European Legal Studies* 17 (2015): 3–35.

[26] Bruno de Witte, "Euro Crisis Responses and the EU Legal Order: Increased Institutional Variation or Constitutional Mutation?" *European Constitutional Law Review* 11, no. 3 (2015): 434–457.

For our project here, the question is not whether there has been constitutional change as a result of the debt crisis but rather if it has prompted a crisis of constitutional democracy. The answer to that question must ultimately be yes, I believe, but it is a hard question. To begin with, the debt crisis certainly demonstrated that the existing institutional and legal setup for regulating the EMU was insufficient. On a formal level then, these flaws in the existing constitutional structure of the EMU could be seen as a constitutional crisis of the EU. On the other hand, given that the EMU had long operated on an intergovernmental footing and according to its own particular rules, it is not clear why a constitutional crisis of the EMU should without more qualify as a crisis of constitutional democracy of the European Union more broadly. Yet, both of these arguments are ultimately too formalistic. From a broader perspective, what matters cannot be the exact details of the new institutional arrangements and their compatibility with existing EU law, but how much the EMU matters to the enterprise of European integration. The answer to that question is that it matters a great deal. Moreover, there are signs that the shift toward a more executive and intergovernmental mode of decision-making, though most explicit in the debt crisis, is not confined to this area, as the following pages will demonstrate. This signals at the very least an interruption and indeed likely a partial reversal of long-standing trends and efforts toward democratization in the Union through the enhancement of the European Parliament's powers and through the Commission's efforts for public participation in its lawmaking processes.

Second, the management of the crisis has affected national democratic politics by forcing Member States applying for financial support into a corset of external requirements and reform. The effect of these requirements on national democracy has been sharply debated—ranging from the popular Twitter hashtag "#ThisIsACoup" to the defense of the measures as the price paid for the sovereign decision of the Greek government to apply for help. Doubtless, both sides make some sense. But what is perhaps more important is that Member States now coordinate their fiscal and economic policies with the objectives agreed at the EU level during the so-called European Semester (a newly established recurring policy cycle). The Commission and the Council are thus now involved in Member State's budgetary policy decisions, with all the risks, such as the domination of economically weaker states by more powerful and richer ones, that this entails, and the European Parliament has been relegated to an advisory role.[27]

Together, these domestic and European developments at the very least weaken democracy. In my view, they also indicate a crisis of democracy because they prompt the question if democracy as the fundamental organizing principle both in the Union and domestically may be losing some of its previously self-evident normative appeal.[28]

---

[27] *See* European Parliament resolution of February 25, 2016 on the European Semester for economic policy coordination: Annual Growth Survey 2016 (2015/2285(INI)), Nr. 36.

[28] For some early and moderate suggestions for a greater role of the European Parliament see Henrik Enderlein, and Jörg Haas, "Structural Policies for Growth and Jobs," Jacque Delors Institute Berlin Policy Paper Nr. 174, Nov. 8, 2016, available at http://www.delorsinstitut.de/2015/wp-content/uploads/2016/11/

THE "MIGRATION CRISIS"

The arrival of millions of new migrants in Greater Europe since 2014 has confronted the Union and the Member States with a new set of challenges. It has tested their commitment to key European values and human rights as expressed in numerous provisions in European law, but most prominently by Art. 2 TEU: "The Union is founded on the values of respect for human dignity, freedom, democracy, equality, the rule of law and respect for human rights, including the rights of persons belonging to minorities. These values are common to the member states in a society in which pluralism, non-discrimination, tolerance, justice, solidarity and equality between women and men prevail." Member States and the Union have arguably responded both badly and slowly to the arrival of migrants, many of them refugees from war-torn Syria, and have thus both allowed human rights violations to occur and, sometimes, become violators themselves. A crisis of trust among Member States accompanied the human tragedy and has found its judicial expression in the jurisprudence of the European Court of Justice (ECJ).

What happened? The arrival of large numbers of refugees in Europe beginning in 2014 was always going to pose administrative and social challenges to the Member States and the Union.[29] The recurring deaths of migrants drowning while seeking to cross the Mediterranean by boat and the EU's lack of a convincing response to this politically difficult but tragic situation did not help the Union's image as a "Fortress Europe" whose human rights seemed to apply only sometimes and partially to outsiders. Under the EU's so-called Dublin framework, the responsibility to process third country migrants lies with those Member States through whose territory they have first entered the Union (absent specific circumstances such as the presence of an existing entry visa to specific Member States, existing family ties, etc.).[30] Unsurprisingly, this arrangement heavily burdened those Member States bordering the Mediterranean such as Greece and Italy, leading to disastrous hygienic and physical conditions in camps for new arrivals and human rights violations by domestic and European authorities (e.g. Frontex, the European Border and Coast Guard Agency), in particular in Greece.[31] The European Court of Justice subsequently suspended the operation of the Dublin framework (following a judgment of the European Court of Human Rights),[32]

RoleEurogroup-EnderleinHaas-JDIB-Oct16-1.pdf (based on study on request of the European Parliament itself); for a much more grand proposal involving a new constitutional structure, see Mark Dawson and Floris Witte, "From Balance to Conflict: A New Constitution for the EU," *European Law Journal* 22, no. 2 (2016): 204–224.

[29] Daniel Thym, "The 'Refugee Crisis' as a Challenge of Legal Design and Institutional Legitimacy," *Common Market Law Review* 53, no. 6 (2016): 1545–1573.

[30] Art. 7 Regulation (EU) No 604/2013 of the European Parliament and the Council of June 26, 2013.

[31] See Human Rights Watch, "The EU's Dirty Hands: Frontex Involvement in Ill-Treatment of Migrant Detainees in Greece," September 2011, available at https://www.hrw.org/sites/default/files/reports/greece-0911webwcover_0.pdf.

[32] ECtHR, M.S.S. v Belgium and Greece [GC], Application No. 30696/09.

temporarily prohibiting any return of refugees to Greece. The situation in Greece has since improved as a result of a host of Greek and European measures, but this relief came at a high price.[33]

First, part of the reason for the improvement of the current situation is the problematic deal between the EU and Turkey. This agreement allows for a return of migrants to Turkey in exchange for increased efforts to resettle Syrian refugees in the European Union and significant financial support of Turkey by the Union. Turkey has ratified the Geneva Convention on the Rights of Refugees only with a geographical restriction excepting persons originating from non-European states from the Convention's ambit, and though it has a number of legal safeguards for refugee protection in place, it is contested whether its legal system offers sufficient guarantees to ensure non-refoulement, especially given its broader contemporary political situation.[34] Though the European position with regard to migration is in line with broader global practice (see, e.g., Australian and US policies), it is nevertheless particularly troubling for a legal system that has in the past two decades tried to frame its public legitimacy in particular in terms of shared values and high human rights standards. Of course, the scope of human rights protections for migrants trying to cross borders is among the more contested issues of global public law, with a wide range of positions, from traditional notions of strong state sovereignty to those advocating a human right to asylum.[35] Yet, part of Europe's professed lessons from the past has long been that there are no persons beyond the law—and this idea is now running into difficulties as European states seek to shut their borders, taking into account multiple deaths in the Mediterranean each year. Moreover, the migration crisis suggests the truth of the old saying that how we treat others always tells us something about ourselves. Perhaps not surprisingly, many of the states that are most strongly opposed to taking in any new migrants, such as Hungary or Poland, are those going through other problematic constitutional changes.

Conservatives might not agree with this assessment. From a conservative perspective, mass migration may have led to tragic events but is otherwise seen more in terms of an administrative failure[36] or in some cases—turning the matter on its head—as a violation of constitutional duties to safeguard the integrity of national borders by opening

---

[33] ECJ, N. S. - C-411/10 and M. E. C-493/10.

[34] See the debate on the legality of the EU-Turkey deal on the Verfassungsblog with contributions from March and December 2017, available at https://verfassungsblog.de/tag/eu-turkey-deal/. The first instance court (General Court) of the ECJ has recently dodged the issue by dismissing the case on grounds of jurisdiction, General Court, T-192/16, T-193/16 and T-257/16.

[35] See, e.g., the different positions of the European Court of Human Rights and the US Supreme Court on the extraterritorial application of the right against non-refoulement: ECtHR, Hirsi Jamaa v. Italy, App. No. 27765/09 and US Supreme Court, Sale v. Haitian Centers Council, 509 U.S. 155 (1993). For a strong pro-human-rights approach, see Itamar Mann, *Humanity at Sea: Maritime Migration and the Foundations of International Law* (New York: Cambridge University Press, 2016).

[36] In this direction Kay Hailbronner and Daniel Thym, "Grenzenloses Asylrecht? Die Flüchtlingskrise als Problem europäischer Rechtsintegration," *JuristenZeitung* 71, nos. 15–16 (2016): 753–763.

national borders to migrants (e.g., with respect to Germany's policy in summer 2015).[37] Deciding precisely what kind of crisis is the migration crisis is thus an ideologically fraught endeavor—to those emphasizing a traditional conception of state sovereignty it clearly denotes other things than it does to human rights advocates. The traditional state-centered perspective and its corresponding neglect for the human rights of migrants strikes me as hard to reconcile with broader legal European and global developments toward the expansion of human rights. At the very least it represents a retreat from past ideals and public rhetoric.[38]

The migration crisis has also laid bare another troubling development in the European Union, namely the increasing lack of a basis for mutual trust between Member States. This connects the migration crisis not merely with some of the analysis we see on the causes of the recent rise of right-wing populism in the United States as well as in Europe, but it also represents a particular constitutional issue for the European Union. How so? The principle of mutual recognition was originally developed by the ECJ in the context of the internal market, to ease cross-border trade. It made it harder for Member States to impose their own standards and rules on products that already complied with the rules of their home Member State, thus freeing producers from the requirement to comply with several different sets of standards when operating in multiple EU Member States.[39] As a principle of mutual trust, it also prohibited double-checking the fulfillment of European law standards in other Member States in the area of police and judicial cooperation. The migration crisis posed a challenge to this concept because it forced the ECJ to confront a situation where the basis for trust in the compliance with European legal standards by one Member State (Greece) had quite clearly been eroded. The ECJ reacted to this situation, as previously mentioned, by prohibiting the return of refugees under the Dublin system to their states of first entry into the Union where *structural failures* in those states were present.[40] In doing so, it handed the matter back to Member States to deal with rather than treating it as a task of the Union itself—suggesting that where trust is eroded,

---

[37] See, e.g., the advisory opinion of the German scholar and former Constitutional Court Justice di Fabio on behalf of the state government of Bavaria, Udo di Fabio, "Migrationskrise als föderales Verfassungsproblem," 2016, available at http://www.bayern.de/wp-content/uploads/2016/01/Gutachten_Bay_DiFabio_formatiert. pdf; I share the criticism of this view presented by Jürgern Bast and Christoph Möllers, "Dem Freistaat zum Gefallen: über Udo Di Fabios Gutachten zur staatsrechtlichen Beurteilung der Flüchtlingskrise," *Verfassungblog*, January 16, 2016, available at https://verfassungsblog.de/dem-freistaat-zum-gefallen-ueber-udo-di-fabios-gutachten-zur-staatsrechtlichen-beurteilung-der-fluechtlingskrise/.

[38] See, e.g., for an example of European rhetoric between idealism and managerialism Jean-Claude Juncker, President of the European Commission, "State of the Union 2015: Time for Honesty, Unity and Solidarity," September 9, 2015, available at http://europa.eu/rapid/press-release_SPEECH-15-5614_en.htm.

[39] Koen Lenaerts, "The Principle of Mutual Recognition in the Area of Freedom, Security and Justice," *Il diritto dell'Unione europea* (2015): 525–551. For a critical perspective see also Thomas Wischmeyer, "Generating Trust though Law: Judicial Cooperation in the European Union and the Principle of Mutual Trust," *German Law Journal* 17 (2016): 339–382.

[40] ECJ, Cases N. S. - C-411/10 and M. E. C-493/10.

the default authority lies with Member States.[41] This impression was reinforced by the perhaps laudable conscious suspension of the Dublin framework by some Member States during the height of the crisis in 2015, as well as by the contemporaneous refusal by Hungary, the Czech Republic, and Poland to accept a certain share of migrants as agreed to under the existing European frameworks, thus treating the "refugee question" as a vital concern of national sovereignty.[42]

Do these developments mark a crisis of constitutional democracy in the Union? On their own, perhaps not. The mere reclaiming of competences by Member States hardly qualifies as a crisis of constitutional democracy, nor does the suspension of the principle of mutual trust among Member States, in particular where it has a solid basis in fact. Nevertheless, the breakdown of trust and the problematic human rights issues raised in the context of mass migration have exacerbated other existing problems familiar from the debt crisis, in particular the failure of solidarity when it comes to burden-sharing among Member States. Solidarity represents another key constitutional principle of the Union—albeit one of a more transformative nature and perhaps one cherished less by the general public than by Europe's much traveled elites.[43] But even where not shared by everyone, aspirational constitutional principles, too, must at the very least represent aspirations for European policy in order to have some normative appeal. That this, too, seems unclear at the moment, points toward a crisis of European constitutionalism.[44]

RIGHT-WING POLITICS AND THE RETURN OF POPULISM

The rise of nationalist, less democratic, and less liberal governments in many Member States of the Union further contributes to the crisis of European constitutionalism. Unlike the debt or migration crises, it is much less clear that the Union bears responsibility for this development except in an indirect way, for example, insofar as they are reactions to the migration crisis, rising inequality, and more. But no one would deny that domestic events influence European constitutional democracy. It matters of course on a symbolic level that the European Union, with its important public commitments

---

[41] Ultimately skeptical toward approaches that emphasize borders and a return to national sovereignty in the context of migration, albeit from rather different political angles, see Hailbronner and Thym, "Grenzenloses Asylrecht?," supra note 36, and Anuscheh Farahat and Nora Markard, "Forced Migration Governance: In Search of Sovereignty," *German Law Journal* 17 (2016): 923–947.

[42] See also the ECJ decision upholding the relevant Council decision against challenges, ECJ, September 6, 2017, Judgment in Joined Cases C-643/15 and C-647/15.

[43] Jan Delhey, Katharina Richter, and Emanuel Deutschmann, "Transnational Sense of Community in Europe: An Exploration with Eurobarometer Data," *pre-prints of the DFG Research Unit Horizontal Europeanization* 5 (2014), available at https://horizontal-europeanization.eu/fileadmin/user_upload/proj/horizontal/downloads/pre-prints/PP_HoEu_2014-05_Delhey_Richter_Deutschmann_2014_SenseofCommunity_0.pdf.

[44] For a fuller exploration see Andreas Grimmel and Susanne My Giang, eds., *Solidarity in the European Union: A Fundamental Value in Crisis* (Heidelberg: Springer, 2017).

to constitutionalism and human rights, now encompasses states whose political lead-ers subscribe to concepts such as "illiberal democracy"[45] or are trying to control and manipulate previously independent judiciaries (Poland and Hungary). However, the European Union has only limited means to influence countries' internal political devel-opments once they have joined the Union, even though as a prerequisite for joining they must fulfill the so-called Copenhagen criteria encompassing rule-of-law and democracy standards.

This state of affairs is a disappointment to those who would like the European Union to play a more active role in combatting problematic developments in individual Member States, but does it represent a crisis of constitutional democracy on its own? There are two arguments that suggest it might: first, given that European law is depend-ent for its implementation on Member State legal systems, developments that threaten judicial independence or the application of rights in individual Member States are prob-lematic not just from an internal perspective, but also from a broader European one. Mutual trust, as previously mentioned, is an integral part of European law. Where that trust is threatened because independent judicial review or individual rights appear more broadly endangered, a key basis of the system breaks down, threatening in addition the equal application of laws and thus, ultimately, fairness. Where goods and people may cross borders without undergoing checks and without having to comply with a host country's particular requirements, trust in other Member States' administrative and legal apparatus is essential. If several Member States are becoming increasingly undemo-cratic, we will be more suspicious, and rightfully so, of being ruled by other Europeans rather than by our own domestic governments. If democracy or the legal system of a series of Member States is therefore significantly damaged, this affects not just national but European governance. This illustrates a recent reference to the ECJ by the Irish High Court questioning whether extraditions to Poland on the basis of a European Arrest Warrant are still permissible given the systemic threats to the rule of law present in Poland.[46]

Second, the rise of less democratic and illiberal governments might constitute a con-stitutional crisis insofar as the existing European constitutional regime may be failing to provide adequate tools to address this situation.[47] This supposes, however, that a more robust European approach would in fact be realistic, and this seems doubtful. Existing European law provides for both political and legal responses to the rise of right-wing politics in Eastern Europe. The political toolbox includes the Commission's Rule of Law

---

[45] Viktor Orbán, Speech at the 25th Bálványos Summer Free University and Student Camp, July 26, 2014, available at http://www.kormany.hu/en/the-prime-minister/the-prime-minister-s-speeches/prime-minister-viktor-orban-s-speech-at-the-25th-balvanyos-summer-free-university-and-student-camp.

[46] Irish High Court, The Minister of Justice and Education v. Celmer, [2018] IEHC 119, Decision of March 12, 2018.

[47] Carlos Closa and Dimitry Kochenov, eds., *Reinforcing Rule of Law Oversight in the European Union* (Cambridge: Cambridge University Press, 2016).

framework, which allows the Commission to engage in a dialogue with the concerned state.[48] More important, it also contains in Art. 7 TEU a preventive and a sanctions mechanism. Adopted after the participation of Austria's right-wing party in a coalition government in the early 2000s, Art. 7 TEU enables the Council to issue a warning to the concerned Member State (the preventive mechanism, Art. 7 (1) TEU) and to withdraw certain rights under the Treaties including voting rights (the sanctions mechanism, Art. 7 (2) and (3) TEU). The latter, it should be noted, requires unanimity in the European Council, making it difficult to deploy. The judicial toolbox primarily[49] offers the infringement procedure, which can be launched by individual Member States or the Commission bringing a matter before the European Court of Justice (Art. 259–260 TFEU). One legal problem with the use of that procedure is, however, that though Art. 2 TEU notes that values such as respect for human rights are common to all Member States, European fundamental rights as provided for in the European Charter only apply when Member States are implementing European law (Art. 51 Charter of Fundamental Rights). They do not apply in purely domestic situations, as a general rule. However, in a recent groundbreaking decision, the ECJ has transformed the requirement to provide sufficient remedies to "ensure effective legal protection in the fields covered by Union law" unter Art. 19 (1) TEU into a guarantee of judicial independence in individual Member States, whether or not Union law is being implemented in the concrete case at hand.[50] This judgment is widely understood to set the stage for future ECJ jurisprudence targeting other Member States such as in particular Poland with regard to the organization of the judiciary and the safeguarding of judicial independence—even though, as Joseph Weiler has recently pointed out[51], the European Union sits in something of a glass house when it comes to championing democracy or indeed, given the ECJ's own rules of appointment, judicial independence, but it will have to be seen how much this will matter in future conflicts.

In addition, the Commission has referred recent Polish developments to the Council, which will have to decide (by a four-fifths majority) whether to issue a warning under

---

[48] Dimitry Kochenov and Laurent Pech, "Better Late than Never? On the European Commission's Rule of Law Framework and Its First Activation," *Journal of Common Market Studies* 54, no. 5 (2016): 1062–1074.

[49] See for a more comprehensive discussion of judicial strategies Michael Blauberger and Daniel R. Kelemen, "Can Courts Rescue National Democracy? Judicial Safeguards against Democratic Backsliding in the EU," *Journal of European Public Policy* 24, no. 3 (2017): 321–336.

[50] European Court of Justice, Judgment of 27 February 2018, Associação Sindical dos Juízes Portugueses, C-64/16.

[51] Joseph H.H. Weiler, "Epilogue: Living in a Glass House: Europe, Democracy and the Rule of Law," in *Reinforcing Rule of Law Oversight* supra note 47; Joseph H.H. Weiler, "Editorial: Those Who Live in Glass Houses . . . ," *European Journal of International Law* 28, no.3 (2017): 665-668, available at https://www.ejiltalk.org/ejil-in-this-issue-vol-28-2017-no-3/.

Art. 7 (1) TEU against Poland.[52] How the Council reacts, whether it will issue a warning, and how much this will change matters on the ground, remains to be seen.[53] Poland has already ignored a series of rule-of-law recommendations, and given that members of the Visegrad-Group (Czech Republic, Hungary, Poland, and Slovakia) have already announced their opposition to any steps against Poland, making impossible any effective sanctions, a warning by the Council might not influence Polish developments very much. On the other hand, the Polish government does seem receptive to political and legal pressure from both the EU and internally, and shortly before the time of this writing completed a major reshuffle of its government to improve relations with Europe. Yet, the Polish government has given mixed signals with regard to its willingness to comply with judicial orders of the ECJ in the recent environmentalist dispute over logging in the forest of Bialowiza, where it ignored interim orders of the Court and sent mixed signals with regard to its compliance with the expected final order.[54] Yet, given all of this, it would be premature to consider the existing European mechanisms so toothless and deficient as to call the resulting problems a crisis of constitutional democracy in the Union. Moreover, it is far from obvious what a better mechanism would look like. Though there have been a series of reform proposals, it is not really that clear that the proposed mechanisms and institutions could achieve much more than is currently the case. As the time of writing, I would not describe the rise of right-wing populist politics on its own as a crisis of constitutional democracy in the Union. But this could change quickly, and as with the migration crisis, such events contribute to the undermining of key European values such as mutual trust, solidarity, key human rights, and not least democracy.

Legitimacy Crisis as a Crisis of Constitutional Democracy?

To focus on the state of European constitutional democracy, this chapter has largely left questions of legitimacy to one side. As I have said above, not every crisis of legitimacy represents a crisis of constitutional democracy. Of course, there is some overlap—for example when it comes to developments that weaken European democracy. Nevertheless, I find

[52] European Commission, Press Release, December 20, 1917, available at http://europa.eu/rapid/press-release_IP-17-5367_en.htm; see also Maciej Taborowski, *The Commission Takes a Step Back in the Fight for the Rule of Law*, Verfassungsblog, January 3, 2018, available at http://verfassungsblog.de/the-commission-takes-a-step-back-in-the-fight-for-the-rule-of-law/, DOI: https://dx.doi.org/10.17176/20180103-121110.

[53] For an early optimistic analysis see Dimitry Kochenov, Laurent Pech, and Kim Lane Scheppele, "*The European Commission's Activation of Article 7: Better Late than Never?*," Verfassungsblog, December 23, 2017, available at http://verfassungsblog.de/the-european-commissions-activation-of-article-7-better-late-than-never/.

[54] Agnieszka Barteczko, Pawel Sobczak, "*Poland says it should decide future of forest at center of EU dispute*," Reuters, March 28, 2018, at https://www.reuters.com/article/us-poland-environment/poland-says-it-should-decide-future-of-forest-at-center-of-eu-dispute-idUSKBN1H42ST. The ECJ's final judgment in that case was scheduled for April 17, 2018.

the frequent confusion of issues of legitimacy and constitutional problems in this context somewhat troubling. The constant focus on legitimacy in relation to the European Union is interestingly different from the writing we find on constitutional crises elsewhere: even in Hungary or Turkey, where clearly all is not well, we do not fear for and debate the survival of the Turkish or Hungarian state. With regard to the European Union, however, every crisis seems to threaten its very survival because there always seems to be a clear alternative: the return to national sovereignty.

This conclusion is, for one thing, chauvinist: it claims that only national governments can represent the people, and not European institutions (including the European Parliament), echoing what Müller has defined as the populists' characteristic claim to exclusive representation of the "true people" in a domestic context. Such arguments are, in other words, not merely nationalist but in a certain sense anti-pluralist.

Yet the deeper point is that the nation-state alternative is of course a smoke screen. It is no secret that nation-states have lost regulatory power as a result of social and economic changes during the second half of the nineteenth century. States that turn their backs on international cooperation risk a loss of regulatory power with regard to powerful private actors such as big corporations. The problems discussed in this chapter are not easy to describe or solve in domestic terms. And, conversely, the standard operating modes of "normal" international cooperation are not necessarily more democratic than the tighter EU arrangements: even though states have to consent to being bound by international agreements, such agreements bind them for long time periods into the future and even when governments change. International law, even in its most traditional operating mode, clearly has a democracy deficit. More important still, for some time the international trend has been toward the establishment of more permanent international regimes with decision-making powers that are often opaque, allow only limited room for judicial review and even less for political contestation, and are heavily expert-based. In short, one must either believe that the issues affecting Europe could be better addressed nationally—which seems questionable at best on many of these issues—or accept that, if we do need a supranational approach, the standard EU legitimacy concerns are less worrying than they are made out to be because other supranational arrangements are no better in this respect. This is not, of course, to deny the validity of all objections based on national sovereignty. Nor is it to deny that the European Union has many problems—it does—or to deny that it suffers from a crisis of legitimacy—it does. But it is not so clear to me that existing alternatives are any better, and thus it makes me wonder if our obsession with the legitimacy of the European Union has become part of the problem.

It sometimes helps to play the counterfactuals game and imagine what would have happened if there had not been a European Union in any of the recent crises. In that case, the debt crisis might have played out better for Greece and some other Member States, who might have managed to adjust their own currency to deal with some of the fallout from the financial crisis. Yet, there would still have been a recession. With regard to the migration crisis and the rise of populism, however, I cannot really imagine any better scenario in the absence of the Union. If anything, it seems to me, the European Union is making an overall positive contribution to the situation, even if it may have disappointed expectations.

For these reasons, it seems to me that the angle proposed by this volume, the focus on constitutional democracy, provides a sobering lens for viewing current developments. It helps us to see where work must be done rather than grieving over our lost ideals of Europe. As I have argued above, European constitutional democracy is indeed in crisis. Its ordinary governance framework with its existing democratic elements does not apply to the new instruments of budgetary oversight and crisis support created in the wake of the debt crisis. Its commitment to human rights is called in question as a matter of its current immigration policy—even if comparable and indeed stricter immigration policies elsewhere in the rich world do not usually trigger talk of a constitutional crisis. Key constitutional ideas such as the principle of mutual trust and solidarity have lost considerable normative force. All of these are important problems that need fixing. To those who wonder if things will ever get easier with the European Union, our answer must be the therapist's standard reply: No, but we can get better at it. It looks like we will need to.

18 State Capture or Institutional Resilience
Is There a Crisis of Constitutional Democracy in South Africa?
Heinz Klug

Introduction

Ever since Thuli Madonsela, South Africa's former Public Protector—a constitutional institution empowered to investigate government impropriety—released her final report entitled "State of Capture" in late 2016, there has been a growing sense of crisis at the heart of the country's constitutional order.[1] While corruption in post-apartheid South Africa has grown in political and economic significance, the question is: When does government malfeasance become a constitutional crisis? From the earliest days of democracy in the mid-1990s there have been episodes of corruption that have been exposed, investigated, and have even led to the fall and imprisonment of senior politicians and their corrupt enablers. From the "travelgate" saga and the "arms deal" that dated from Mandela's presidency to the claims of "State Capture" that embroiled President Jacob Zuma, the extent of corruption and consequent threat to the process of governance has continued to mount. Furthermore, the exposure of rampant corruption and self-dealing in South Africa's private sector has made it clear that the danger extends beyond government to all the key sectors of the political and economic life

---

[1] Public Protector, *State of Capture*, Report No: 6 of 2016/17, released October 14, 2016, saflii.org/images/329756472-State-of-Capture.pdf.

of South Africa.[2] But what exactly makes this a crisis for South Africa's constitutional democracy?

South Africa's constitutional democracy is based, like most constitutional democracies, on two core constitutional features: First, a constitutional structure designed to produce and protect democracy from elite capture or creeping authoritarianism through the separation of powers and allocation of government authority to different institutions and levels of government; and second a set of justiciable constitutional rights designed to protect political, social, and other minorities. The elaborate Bill of Rights in chapter two of the South African Constitution goes even further, protecting social, economic, and cultural rights in addition to political participation. While the actual capacity of the government to fulfill the promise of the social and economic rights provisions, including housing, remains in question, the drafters of the South African Constitution did not take the road of other constitution-makers, such as in India, Ireland, and Namibia, who chose to explicitly differentiate "aspirational" goals from those that are in fact justiciable. Thus, if our concern about a crisis in constitutional democracy were to focus on the government's policy and implementation failures, from the ailing education system to badly constructed houses for the poor and the failure to address chronic unemployment, then it may be argued that this is simply bad—or, at the very least, disappointing—governance, and we might anticipate that the democratic process will eventually punish the ruling party. In this context, the electorate's failure to punish the government might indicate either weaknesses in the democratic process or simply a political legacy in which the opposition political parties lack political legitimacy or do not offer a serious alternative to the governing party. In the case of South Africa, the unipolar nature of national politics since the democratic transition in 1994 has reflected the dominance of the African National Congress—the party of Mandela and national liberation—and the weakness of the political opposition whose major factions are split between parties that have either broken away from the ANC or evolved from formerly all-white political parties that served in the apartheid Parliament. Thus, so long as there is a functional government and periodic free and fair elections as prescribed by the constitution, there seems to be no basis for a claim of constitutional crisis.

Yet, over the last five years the extent of government malfunction, malfeasance, and contestation within political and government institutions, as well as among political and government leaders, has led to a sense of near permanent crisis. In addition to sagging investor confidence and downgrades by the international ratings agencies—adding to the country's continuing economic woes—and media revelations of high-level corruption and deep divisions within the ruling ANC, there has been a seemingly endless series of legal challenges to government decision-making. The resulting "lawfare" in which

---

[2] See, for example, Gay Davis, "Steinhoff Scandal Inquiry Set for End of January," *Eyewitness News*, January 11, 2018, ewn.co.za/2018/01/11/steinhoff-inquiry-set-for-end-of-january.

litigants, often rival state entities or officials, seek to use the courts to achieve their political goals or simply use the legal process as a means to gain access to state resources or frustrate attempts to check malfeasance, has brought nearly all institutions of governance and accountability created by the Constitution into the arena of politics and pulled the courts into a whirlwind of political contestation. The exposure of "state capture" by the Public Protector, in which it is claimed that appointments to the executive branch (the cabinet) as well as to the boards of major state-owned corporations were dictated by the private economic interests of a single family, the Guptas, dramatically escalated this political-legal conflict. It is the disarray and dispersal of political power that this "lawfare" generates and the undermining of institutional capacity that results, that does threaten to create a real crisis of constitutional democracy.

If government institutions are unable or unwilling to perform their constitutional functions, then we can truly say a country is facing a constitutional crisis. If corruption and "lawfare" undermine the capacity to govern—as resources are diverted and institutions become embroiled in conflict—then maladministration and the failure to deliver social and other government services may provoke civil and political strife. While vigorous political and social engagement is to be embraced in a dynamic constitutional democracy, when constitutional institutions become dysfunctional through capture or undermined by conflict, then the constitutional order itself may be threatened. While patronage and "ordinary" corruption as well as the employment of litigation strategies to delay legal accountability are not exceptional, the claim in South Africa is that these "normal" social and governance problems have reached a higher level of systemic dysfunction. If patronage and corruption involve specific acts of malfeasance in which individuals benefit from their relationship to state resources, state capture is "systemic and well-organized by people with established relations" and seeks to access and redirect "rents away from their intended targets and into private hands."[3] Unlike regular patronage or corruption, state capture sees the use and formal manipulation of state institutions to achieve the goals of redirecting state resources and protecting the culprits from being held accountable. Similarly, the idea of "lawfare" in this context goes beyond the normal use of litigation strategies and instead involves the deliberate use of legal process to protect malfeasance and to frustrate any attempts to obtain accountability through the state institutions designed to protect the public against such predation.[4]

---

[3] Haroon Borat et al., *Betrayal of the Promise: How South Africa Is Being Stolen* (State Capacity Research Project, May 2017), http://pari.org.za/wp-content/uploads/2017/05/Betrayal-of-the-Promise-25052017.pdf.

[4] While the term "lawfare" was initially coined by Colonel Charles J. Dunlap Jr., of the United States Air Force, to describe "the use of law as a weapon of war" (Law and Military Interventions: Preserving Humanitarian Values in 21st Conflicts, Prepared for the Humanitarian Challenges in Military Intervention Conference, Carr Center for Human Rights Policy, Kennedy School of Government, Harvard University, Washington, DC, November 29, 2001, p.2) it has been increasingly used to describe the use of law to achieve goals contrary to the norms of justice promised by the applicable legal or constitutional order. See also "Is Lawfare Worth Defining?

In order to explore whether these developments have produced a crisis in constitutional democracy in South Africa or whether the country's constitutional institutions are proving resilient in the face of widespread nepotism, corruption, and the undermining of state bodies, this chapter will first describe the history of corruption since the beginning of the democratic era in 1994 and how accusations of corruption became part of internal struggles within the ruling party and beyond. Second, the chapter will explore how legal challenges over maladministration and corruption became a feature of struggles to remove and replace senior state officials, including the president, and how these legal processes became a form of "lawfare." The third section explores whether these struggles and the emergence of "state capture" has undermined the constitutional institutions created to "ensure accountability, responsiveness and openness" as promised in the founding provisions of the Constitution.[5] Fourth, the chapter explores the response of the courts and the role they have played in the struggles to protect and maintain the constitutional democracy in the face of state capture and corruption at the highest levels of the state. The chapter concludes by arguing that processes of political change embedded within the constitutional order and political parties—such as regular democratic elections, the five-year elective conferences, and a tradition of limited terms for the president of the ANC— as well as the institutional resilience of various constitutional institutions, including the courts, provide a source of hope for constitutional renewal rather than crisis in South Africa's constitutional democracy.

Corruption and Constitutional "Lawfare"

Corruption in the "arms deal" had its roots in the early years of the democratic era when in 1996 Nelson Mandela's government embarked on the procurement of new military hardware. Mark Gevisser, a prominent author and journalist, suggests that the decision to modernize the military might have been based as much on concerns over a "disaffected military" and the threat of internal destabilization it posed, as on concern about external threats to national security. The "arms deal" involved a complex policy of military modernization and hoped-for economic investment for the country coupled with possible kickback funding for the ruling party and a plethora of secondary contracts providing ample opportunity for simple old-fashioned graft. Deputy-President Thabo Mbeki chaired the pertinent Cabinet subcommittee from 1996 to 1999, and headed the official procurement process that oversaw and "commissioned the purchase of R30 billion worth of armaments—specifically, submarines and frigates—from a French-German consortium and fighter-jets from a

Report of the Cleveland Experts Meeting, September 11, 2010," *Case Western Reserve Journal of International Law* 43 (2010): 11–28.
[5] Constitution of the Republic of South Africa, 1996, Section 1(d).

British-Swedish one."[6] The government justified such vast expenditures on armaments by arguing that they provided an opportunity for industrial investment and
job creation, since the bidders promised that the deal would lead to investments
in the South African economy worth approximately R104 billion and would create around 65,000 jobs. In the end, the arms deal cost twice the amount originally
agreed upon, produced only 13,000 jobs by 2006, and became what Gevisser has
described as the "poisoned well of post-apartheid South African politics."[7]

The scandal first hit the headlines when Member of Parliament Patricia de Lille (then
of the opposition Pan Africanist Congress) stood up in the National Assembly and
announced that she had in her possession a ten-page briefing authored by "concerned"
ANC MPs accusing senior ANC politicians of corruption and questioning whether the
promised "off-sets" would ever become a reality.[8] When the Auditor-General released
the first official report on the arms deal on August 15, 2000, questioning the "off-sets"
and arguing that the "practice of choosing the Hawk [aircraft] did not meet standard
regulations on acquisitions,"[9] the issue was formally placed in the hands of the National
Assembly's Standing Committee on Public Accounts (SCOPA). While there is no
constitutional duty to do so, the ANC's initial commitment to open government and
accountability led to the practice of giving the chair of SCOPA to an opposition member of the National Assembly. When the Auditor-General's report came before SCOPA
in late 2000, the chair, Gavin Woods of the Inkatha Freedom Party, together with the
other members of SCOPA, agreed that further investigation was necessary. When
Andrew Feinstein, the leading ANC member of SCOPA reported this decision to senior
ANC leaders in the legislature, he met with a mixed reaction. Jacob Zuma, then Deputy-
President and the leader of Government's Business in Parliament was at first supportive and insisted to Feinstein that the Committee continue with its constitutional role.
However, the ANC's Chief Whip in Parliament Tony Yengeni argued that a public hearing was not a good idea and that the matter be considered an internal one. The government turned defensive when SCOPA insisted on continuing its investigation. The ANC
leadership in Parliament then moved against SCOPA. First, Feinstein was removed from
his role as head of the ANC Study Group in SCOPA; then the Committee was stacked
with loyalists who would be sure to follow instructions. As ANC Chief Whip Tony
Yengeni, who would later be jailed for taking a bribe related to the arms deal, told a press
conference, "there was no committee in respect of the ANC which is above party political discipline."[10]

---

[6] Mark Gevisser, *A Legacy of Liberation: Thabo Mbeki and the Future of the South African Dream* (New York: Palgrave MacMillan, 2009), 256.

[7] Ibid., 258.

[8] Paul Holden, *The Arms Deal in Your Pocket* (Jeppestown, South Africa: Jonathan Ball, 2008) 38.

[9] Ibid., 40.

[10] Andrew Feinstein, *After the Party* (Jeppestown, South Africa: Jonathan Ball, 2007), 160–161.

If the "arms deal" was the "poisoned well" of South Africa's democracy, Jacob Zuma's political resurrection and assumption of the presidency of South Africa in 2009 saw the poison of corruption engulf the state. Zuma's rise to power on a populist platform within the ANC took place in the face of then-president Thabo Mbeki's repeated efforts to sideline him. After Mbeki succeeded Mandela as South Africa's second democratically-elected president in 1999 he continued Mandela's policies but failed to address the rising HIV/AIDS pandemic. Despite Mbeki's landslide election to a second term in 2004 governance became increasingly embroiled in the political struggles being waged between different political factions within the ANC, at every level of government. Most dramatic were the accusations of corruption—based on the arms deal—that led to Mbeki's dismissal of Deputy President Jacob Zuma and the counter-accusation that Mbeki improperly influenced the National Prosecuting Authority in that case, an accusation that ultimately led to his resignation as president. The fact that a High Court judge, on very little evidence, endorsed these claims of political interference hastened Mbeki's departure and thus had powerful political consequences despite the fact that the High Court's decision was subsequently overruled and severely criticized by the Supreme Court of Appeals. Aside from this rather dramatic example of the way in which law and legal process were used to wage and resolve political struggles for power within the ruling party, there are also myriad examples of cases in which government officials, high and low, are accused of corruption or other malfeasance. These accusations see different political factions and patronage networks assert legal and administrative process to gain access to positions of power and authority while those they accuse are "suspended" on full pay from their government positions.[11]

Factional struggles over political and bureaucratic control of the state from within the dominant party were driven both by patronage politics[12] and the use of legal process—including criminal, civil, and administrative or constitutional claims. Among the most notorious legal cases during this period were: the suspension, trial, and acquittal of Jacob Zuma for rape; the trial and conviction of Jackie Selebi, the National Commissioner of Police for corruption; the trial and acquittal of Billy Masetlha, the director-general of the National Intelligence Agency who was accused of fraud and withholding information from the inspector-general of intelligence. In addition, there was the removal of two consecutive national directors of public prosecutions—heads of the National Prosecuting Authority (NPA). In both cases the individuals were removed from their positions while official Commissions of Enquiry appointed by the president investigated the claims against them. In the case of Bulelani Ngcuka—who was the prosecutor involved in bringing the initial corruption charges against Zuma—he was accused and then exonerated of

---

[11] See Crispian Olver, *How to Steal a City: The Battle for Nelson Mandela Bay—An Inside Account* (Jeppestown, South Africa: Jonathan Ball, 2017).

[12] See Mcebisi Ndletyana, Pholoana Oupa Makhalemele, and Ralph Mathekga, *Patronage Politics Divides Us: A Study of Poverty, Patronage and Inequality in South Africa* (Johannesburg: Real African Publishers, 2013).

being an apartheid spy. His successor, Vusumzi "Vusi" Pikoli, was first fired by President Mbeki and then found by the Ginwala Commission of Enquiry to have in fact been fit to hold office. While at times based on real acts of malfeasance these legal processes had the effect of excluding different officials and factions from processes of procurement and authority that have become the lifeblood of patronage and power. In the case of suspensions, they continue to receive their government salaries and benefits, thus allowing them to continue to engage in the political struggles that led to their unmasking or possibly malicious denouement. Add to this the fact that the government has in many cases felt legally obliged to cover the legal costs of those accused of wrongdoing in their official capacities and the result is a process of political struggle through law within the executive branches of the post-apartheid state.

While the "arms deal," and the eight-year long controversy over the money spent on the construction and then upgrading of Zuma's rural homestead at Nkandla, may be characterized as "ordinary graft" even if they involved the highest official in the land, the form and extent of corruption that has been described as "state capture" is of a qualitatively different magnitude. Not only do the amounts involved in "normal corruption" pale in comparison to the "looting" revealed by the state capture revelations but the very nature of the network and system of patronage and corruption is unique. This is evident from revelations about the relationship of President Zuma to the Gupta family, three brothers who immigrated to South Africa from India in the early 1990s and who subsequently built a business empire based on getting access to procurement deals and the state-owned enterprises that form a key sector of the South African economy. It is now claimed that South Africa has lost over US$50 billion to corruption since the dawn of democracy in 1994,[13] and while only partially responsible, the Gupta family has become symbolic of the process in which politically connected individuals have used their influence to steer procurement decisions and even political appointments for the benefit of themselves and their collaborators. The media's acquisition of between 100,000 and 200,000 email records from within the Gupta business empire in June 2017 produced the direct evidence of corruption and political influence that had first been exposed by the Public Protector's "State of Capture" report, which she released only days before the end of her term of office in 2016.

While Public Protector Madonsela's report focused on her investigation into the relationship between state functionaries, including the president, and the Gupta family, the details uncovered in the Gupta emails reveal a pattern of corrupt influence that stretches further back in time and involves the close business relationship the family developed with Duduzane Zuma, the then-thirty-five-year-old son of the president. If even a portion of the allegations are true, the extent of corruption and private influence over public

---

[13] Al Jazeera, "How Corrupt Is South Africa?" *Inside Story*, September 30, 2015, http://www.aljazeera.com/programmes/insidestory/2015/09/south-africa-corruption-150930214450269.html (reporting on the anticorruption marches on September 30, 2015).

decision-making is massive. In a report entitled *Betrayal of the Promise: How South Africa Is Being Stolen* issued in May 2017 a group of academics working together as the "State Capacity Research Project" argued that South African politics today is all about "resistance and capture." The report describes how a Zuma-centered power elite has engaged in a political project "to repurpose state institutions to suit a constellation of rent-seeking networks that have been constructed and now span the symbiotic relationship between the constitutional and shadow state."[14] The publication of investigative journalist Jacques Pauw's book *The President's Keepers: Those Keeping Zuma in Power and Out of Prison* in late October 2017 added a further dimension to the Zuma saga. In this most recent expose, Pauw focuses on the struggles waged within state institutions, including the intelligence services, and the prosecuting and tax authorities, in which particular individuals and networks have worked to preserve and defend President Zuma despite the mounting evidence of corruption.[15] The picture that emerges is one of "lawfare" as a war of position within the state.

The Undermining of Democratic and Constitutional Institutions

Parliament's first major oversight challenge occurred in early 1996 when it was revealed in the press that the Department of Health was spending R14.2 million on a musical that was to tour the country providing education on the growing HIV/AIDS pandemic, an expenditure that represented a significant portion of the health department's HIV/AIDS prevention efforts. The musical itself was criticized for failing to impart a clear public health message. But the scandal focused on the high costs of production—including the salaries, luxurious facilities, and what was seen as the inappropriate grandeur of the production itself. When the Portfolio Committee first called on the minister of health to justify this expenditure, she purportedly refused to attend the hearing. After the government realized that the minster's refusal to attend would be politically embarrassing, her appearance before the committee merely demonstrated how new the concept of oversight was for the legislature. First, the MPs relied mainly on press reports to challenge the minister, instead of demanding access to the official documentation, which was their right. Second, the ANC members remained extraordinarily passive, caught between the exercise of their parliamentary duty and loyalty to the government. As one ANC member later admitted, "It was still early days. We did not know how to deal with something like this. Perhaps we should be condemned for it, perhaps we should be forgiven, but we were more concerned with damage control than we were with

---

[14] Borat et al., *Betrayal*, 2.

[15] See Jacques Pauw, *The President's Keepers: Those Keeping Zuma in Power and Out of Prison* (Cape Town: Tafelberg, 2017).

parliamentary accountability."[16] The Committee's failure was further highlighted when the Public Protector issued a report in June 1996 that documented the mismanagement of tender procedures and the "unauthorized expenditure of foreign aid" in this project.[17]

Parliament's ability to act as an effective watchdog was further undermined by its own dalliance in addressing a pattern of systematic abuse by Members of Parliament (MPs) from across the political spectrum. The first inklings of what would come to be known as "travelgate" surfaced in the year 2000 when Speaker of Parliament Frene Ginwala publicly rebuked two MPs for abusing travel vouchers, granted annually in a checkbook type format, so that MPs could travel between Parliament in Cape Town and their constituencies or homes around the country.[18] By the time the scandal unraveled in 2007 it embroiled more than a hundred MPs who were forced to resign, plead guilty, and enter into plea bargains to repay millions of rands to Parliament for fraudulent claims; or were brought to trial and convicted as a result of their misuse or even the sale of their parliamentary travel allocations for private benefit. Even more damaging has been the fact that "senior ANC leaders and Cabinet members involved have, in most instances, quietly paid back the money that was defrauded from Parliament."[19] As a result, the integrity of the institution was severely compromised since the toleration of corrupt practices within Parliament made it harder to claim the high ground when policing similar practices in the executive.

Apart from Parliament, there are a number of legal and constitutional institutions that have the duty and authority to provide accountability for individuals and government offices engaged in corruption and maladministration.[20] First among these is the criminal law, which aside from a range of anticorruption statutes includes specialized institutions whose task it is to address organized crime and corruption. It was the disbandment of the original Directorate of Special Operations (known as the "scorpions") that first led to a series of court cases challenging the government's anticorruption efforts and that saw the Constitutional Court recognize that the government has an obligation "arising out of the constitution . . . to establish effective mechanisms for battling corruption."[21] In addition to the criminal law, the post-apartheid constitutional order creates a number of "integrity institutions" including the offices of the Auditor-General and the Public Protector to insure transparency and public accountability for government spending and maladministration. It was after March 19, 2014, when the Public Protector

---

[16] Richard Calland, "The First 5 Years: A Review of South Africa's Democratic Parliament," *Political Information Monitoring Service*, IDASA (Cape Town 1999), 36.

[17] Ibid., 35.

[18] Feinstein, *After the Party*, 241–242.

[19] Ibid., 242.

[20] See Heinz Klug, "Accountability and the Role of Independent Constitutional Institutions in South Africa's Post-apartheid Constitutions," *New York Law School Law Review* 60 (2015–2016): 153–182.

[21] *Glenister v. President of the Republic of South Africa and Others* (Glenister II) [2011] ZACC 6, para. 84.

issued her report on the "security upgrade" at President Zuma's rural home at Nkandla, that the question of that institution's constitutional role and independence also headed to the courts.

As far as some in the ruling party were concerned the Public Protector was responsible to Parliament, which they felt had the right to both question the activities of the institution as well as decide whether the decisions of the Public Protector needed to be implemented. In support of their claim they pointed to section 181(5) of the Constitution which states that the Public Protector, along with the other chapter nine institutions, is "accountable to the National Assembly." In contrast to this broad claim of parliamentary authority the Public Protector has in each annual report since its founding pointed out that section 182(1) empowers the institution to investigate, report, and "take appropriate remedial action." Finally, the Public Protector pointed to section 181(2) of the Constitution, which states that "[t]hese institutions [the chapter 9 institutions] are independent, and subject only to the Constitution and the law, and they must be impartial and must exercise their powers and perform their functions without fear, favor or prejudice." The first opportunity the courts had to address these questions with respect to the Public Protector came when the official political opposition, the Democratic Alliance, brought a suit demanding that Hlaudi Motsoeneng, the Chief Operations Officer (COO) of the South African Broadcasting Corporation (SABC)—the government broadcaster—be immediately suspended. They based their suit on the Report of the Public Protector into allegations of maladministration, systemic corporate governance deficiencies, and abuse of power by the COO as well as a claim that his appointment by the Board of the SABC was irregular. While the Western Cape High Court ordered his suspension and that disciplinary proceedings be instituted against him, the Court's decision on the powers of the Public Protector led to some confusion. On the one hand the court ruled that the decisions of the SABC Board and the Minister of Communications to ignore the recommendations of the Public Protector were irrational and therefore unconstitutional. On the other hand, the judge, relying on earlier court decisions analogizing the Public Protector to the position of an ombudsman, held that the Public Protector's findings are not directly binding and enforceable since they do not have the same legal status as court orders. Nevertheless, the judge argued that while the recommendations of the Public Protector are not binding, the government officials to whom they are directed are not free to disregard them based on their own conclusion but rather need to either implement them or provide rational reasons for refusing to do so. This decision, an exercise of public power in its own right, would be subject to review by the courts as would any decision by the Public Protector that may be challenged by those affected by the Public Protectors' findings or recommendations.[22]

When the case reached the Supreme Court of Appeals (SCA) the Court upheld the decision of the High Court requiring the SABC to subject its COO to a disciplinary

---

[22] *Democratic Alliance v. South African Broadcasting Corporation*, 2015 (1) SA 551 (WCC), para. 71.

hearing and noted that "[i]n modern democratic constitutional States, in order to ensure governmental accountability, it has become necessary for the guards to require a guard. And in terms of our constitutional scheme, it is the Public Protector who guards the guards."[23] The SCA then rejected the High Court's analogizing of the Public Protector to the British Parliamentary ombudsperson, noting that "the powers conferred on the Public Protector in terms of s 182(1)(c) of the Constitution far exceeded those of similar institutions in comparable jurisdictions."[24] Responding to the government counsel's suggestion that the powers of the Public Protector are defined by legislation rather than the Constitution, the SCA argued that "[t]he problem with that suggestion is that the Constitution is the primary source and it stipulates and refers to 'additional' powers to be prescribed by national legislation,"[25] and thus the suggestion that the Public Protector's powers are legislatively defined is "contrary to the constitutional and legislative scheme outlined above and would have the effect of the tail wagging the dog."[26] Noting that all parties to the litigation found the metaphor of a watchdog "a useful metaphor for the Public Protector," the SCA concluded that "this watchdog should not be muzzled."[27]

The Role of the Courts in Defending Constitutional Institutions

As conflict over the role of President Zuma in the corrupt practices of the Gupta family has grown, different political parties, nongovernment organizations, and the president himself increasingly turned to the courts to address their claims. A representative sample of these cases reveals the scope of "lawfare" as well as the increasing willingness of the courts to intervene in the unfolding political and constitutional crisis. First, there was a series of cases challenging the authority of the Public Protector, particularly with respect to that institution's remedial powers. Second, there have been a set of cases in which the opposition parties in Parliament have approached the Constitutional Court in their attempt to force the ruling party in Parliament to hold the president accountable. Finally, there has been an increasing wave of legal challenges to the legitimacy of executive appointments and actions taken in the appointment, suspension, and buying-out of the leadership of those government institutions that have the responsibility of investigating corruption and official malfeasance.

Unlike the SABC case, which wound its way up through the lower courts, the conflict over the failure of President Zuma to "pay back the money" for his housing upgrade and Parliament's decision that he owed nothing brought the question of the Public

---

[23] *South African Broadcasting Corporation and Others v. Democratic Alliance and Others* [2015] ZASCA 156; [2015] 4 All SA 719 (SCA) (*SABC v. DA*), para. 3.

[24] Ibid. para. 43.

[25] Ibid.

[26] Ibid.

[27] Ibid.

Protector's powers directly to the Constitutional Court. In its dramatic decision—read out on national television by Chief Justice Mogoeng Mogoeng—the Constitutional Court linked the response to the Public Protector's report on the expenditure of public funds on the president's home at Nkandla to the Constitution's foundational commitment to the rule of law, arguing that "[o]ne of the crucial elements of our constitutional vision is to make a decisive break from the unchecked abuse of State power and resources that was virtually institutionalised during the apartheid era. To achieve this goal, we adopted accountability, the rule of law and the supremacy of the Constitution as values of our constitutional democracy."[28] As a result, he argued, "public office-bearers ignore their constitutional obligations at their peril."[29] Discussing the institution of the Public Protector the Court noted that the Constitution requires it "to be independent and subject only to the Constitution and the law," which would not be necessary if its decisions were to be "at the mercy of those against whom they are made."[30] Furthermore, the "constitutional safeguards in section 181 would also be meaningless if institutions purportedly established to strengthen our constitutional democracy lacked even the remotest possibility to do so."[31] Rooting its powers within the Constitution the Court made it clear that the legislature cannot "eviscerate" the powers provided by the Constitution as the "power to take remedial action is primarily sourced from the supreme law itself. And the powers and functions conferred on the Public Protector by the Act owe their very existence or significance to the Constitution."[32]

Recognizing that the Public Protector has wide but not unfettered power the Court noted that the "remedial action is always open to judicial scrutiny."[33] However, "[w]hen remedial action is binding, compliance is not optional, whatever reservations the affected party might have about its fairness, appropriateness or lawfulness" and therefore "cannot be ignored without any legal consequences."[34] In conclusion, the Court held that due to his manifest failure in disregarding the "remedial action taken against him by the Public Protector in terms of her constitutional powers" as well as his failure to "assist and protect the Public Protector so as to ensure her independence, impartiality, dignity and effectiveness by complying with her remedial action" the president has "failed to uphold, defend and respect the Constitution as the supreme law of the land."[35]

While challenges to the nature of the remedial powers of the Public Protector were thus resolved by the Constitutional Court in the *Nkandla* case, the most recent challenge

---

[28] *Economic Freedom Fighters v. Speaker of the National Assembly and Others; Democratic Alliance v. Speaker of the National Assembly and Others* [2016] ZACC 11, para. 1.

[29] Ibid.

[30] Ibid., para. 49.

[31] Ibid.

[32] Ibid., para. 64.

[33] Ibid., para. 71.

[34] Ibid.

[35] Ibid., para. 83.

saw President Zuma attempt to prevent the release of the Public Protector's report on state capture. Bringing an urgent application on October 13, 2016, the president argued that the Public Protector should be prevented "from finalizing and releasing that report."[36] After the president learned that the Report was in fact already finalized and would be released his lawyers continued to bring urgent applications to the courts; however once the court was ready to hear arguments the president's lawyers simply withdrew the application and offered to pay the costs of the other parties who had challenged the initial attempt to prevent the release of the Report. As a result, a number of the other parties brought an application demanding that the president pay for these legal costs himself since he had claimed his challenge to the Report was to protect his own dignity and interests. In an opinion on the same day, also written on behalf of a full bench by Judge President Mlambo, the head judge of the Gauteng Division of the Supreme Court of South Africa, the High Court found President Zuma personally responsible for all the legal costs from the day that he was informed that the Report had in fact been finalized.

In his substantive challenge to the Public Protector's Report on state capture the president objected to the decision by the Public Protector that called upon the president to establish a judicial Commission of Inquiry into state capture but required the head of the commission to be nominated by the Chief Justice of South Africa rather than the president as provided for in the Constitution. In its decision on this question the High Court argued that while the "power to appoint a commission of inquiry vests in the President alone and only he can exercise that power" it does not follow "that there are no constraints upon the exercise" of this power.[37] The High Court went on to argue that "even though the Constitution vests in the President the power to appoint a commission of inquiry, this power is not an untrammelled one; it must be exercised within the constraints that the Constitution imposes. The President's power to appoint a commission of inquiry will necessarily be curtailed where his ability to conduct himself without constraint brings him into conflict with his obligations under the Constitution."[38]

Faced with a refusal by the ANC majority in Parliament to hold President Zuma and his government accountable for a pattern of corruption that was being openly discussed in the country's print and electronic media, the opposition parties have also turned to the courts. The focus of these cases has been an attempt to force the leadership in Parliament, and particularly the Speaker of Parliament, to bring a vote of no confidence to the floor of the National Assembly for debate and vote. First the Constitutional Court issued a decision that required the dominant party to allow the opposition parties to bring a vote of no confidence to the floor,[39] and finally a year later the Court issued another ruling

---

[36] *President of the RSA v. The Office of the Public Protector (Economic Freedom Fighters & Others Intervening)* (79808/16) [2017] ZAGPPHC 748 [2018] 1 All SA 576 (GP), December 13, 2017, para. 1.

[37] *President of the RSA v. The Office of the Public Protector* (91139/2016) [2017] ZAGPPHC 747 (December 13, 2017) para. 62.

[38] Ibid., para. 71.

[39] *Mazibuko v. Sisulu and Another* (CCT 115/12) [2013] ZACC 28.

indicating that although the decision lay with the Speaker of Parliament, any decision made by the Speaker must be rational, and while it was not for the Court to decide, it would seem most rational if the Speaker decided to allow a secret vote on the motion.[40] Despite the Speaker of Parliament's subsequent decision to hold a vote of no confidence in secret as well as massive countrywide demonstrations calling for action against corruption, President Zuma survived his seventh no-confidence vote on August 8, 2017. The significance of this vote however was the fact that when the vote was tallied it became clear that members of the president's own party had for the first time voted against him, highlighting the growing rift in the ANC.[41]

In another case brought by the parliamentary opposition a majority on the Constitutional Court found that Parliament had failed in its constitutional duty to hold the president accountable for failing to implement the Nkandla Report.[42] Accountability in this context is separate from a motion of no confidence since the Constitution provides a separate standard and consequences for impeachment of the president. The opposition parties pointed out that Parliament had not established any procedures for an impeachment process, and a majority of the Court held that Parliament had a constitutional duty to create a regulatory structure for the implementation of section 89 of the Constitution, which provides for the impeachment of the president by two-thirds of the National Assembly if the president is in "serious violation of the Constitution," has engaged in "serious misconduct," or is unable to perform the functions of the office.

The final set of cases involve those challenging the hiring and firing of government officials, often involving very large settlements. Among these, an extraordinary decision, *Corruption Watch v. President of RSA*,[43] was handed down by a full bench of the High Court of South Africa (Gauteng Division) on December 8, 2017. In this case the High Court invalidated the termination of the appointment of yet another Director of Public Prosecutions, Mxolisi Nxasana, as well as the settlement reached among him, the president, and the minister of justice that awarded him R17.3 million while declaring that he was a fit and proper person to hold the office.[44] As a consequence of this holding the High Court also declared invalid the appointment of the existing Director of Public Prosecutions, Shaun Abrahams. Furthermore, given the sustained criticism of Abrahams for failing to bring charges of corruption against the president or even to investigate the claims against the Guptas, the Court held that the president had a conflict of interest and therefore a new Director of Public Prosecutions must be appointed by the

---

[40] *United Democratic Movement v. Speaker of the National Assembly and Others* (CCT89/17) [2017] ZACC 21.

[41] Niren Tolsi, "Zuma Survives No-Confidence Vote Despite ANC Dissenters," *Mail & Guardian*, August 8, 2017, https://mg.co.za/article/2017-08-08-no-confidence-vote-the-people-versus-jacob-zuma.

[42] *Economic Freedom Fighters and Others v. Speaker of the National Assembly and Another* (CCT76/17) [2017] ZACC 47 (December 29, 2017).

[43] *Corruption Watch (NFP) and Freedom under Law (NFP) v. President of the Republic of South Africa et al.*, Case No. 62470/2015, decided on December 8, 2017.

[44] Ibid., para. 77.

deputy president of the country—Cyril Ramaphosa—who was also given the constitutional authority, normally exercised by the president, to make all decisions involving the appointment, suspension, or removal of the Director of Public Prosecutions so long as the incumbent president remains in office.[45] This reallocation of the president's constitutional authority is an extraordinary remedy but one designed to preserve the integrity of the prosecuting authority, which many argued had been "captured" and was no longer performing its functions without fear or favor as required by the Constitution.

These decisions, announced within the same period as the ANC's National Elective Conference in which the party elected a new president, Cyril Ramaphosa, set the stage for the next round of political conflict. Now that Jacob Zuma is no longer the leader of the ANC and his own preferred candidate failed to be elected, the possibility of the ruling party "recalling" him from the presidency of the country is being repeatedly raised. Faced with this threat President Zuma finally complied with the remedy imposed by the Public Protector in her "State of Capture" report, announcing in January 2018 that he would appoint a Commission of Enquiry into State Capture to be headed by the deputy chief justice who was nominated by the chief justice as required by the Public Protector. However, the senior leadership of the ANC remained split, and the possibility of President Zuma resigning under threat of impeachment in Parliament—which would deny him all pension and other benefits—was floated as a possibility. Regardless of President Zuma's future,[46] the challenge facing the ANC is to rebuild public confidence before the 2019 elections in which the party faces the possibility of losing its electoral majority for the first time since the dawn of democracy in 1994.

Conclusion: Political Change and Constitutional Resilience ·

While the struggle for political power and against corruption continues in the ANC, the narrow defeat of Jacob Zuma's political faction by Cyril Ramaphosa's anticorruption platform at the end of 2017 raised the possibility of political change both within the dominant party and the state. The overarching importance of these internal party conflicts to South Africa's constitutional democracy reflects the unipolar structure of South African politics. So long as the ANC remains a dominant party at the national level—despite losing major metropolitan areas in the 2016 local government elections—there exists a form of dual state in which the party and state are deeply entwined. Under Jacob Zuma this relationship led to the emergence of a form of "shadow state" in which corrupt

---

[45] Ibid., para. 128.

[46] On February 14, 2018, President Jacob Zuma went on national television and resigned with immediate effect after the ANC National Executive Committee recalled him and Parliament scheduled a no-confidence vote for 14:00 hours on February 15, 2018. On February 15, 2018, Cyril Ramaphosa was sworn in to fill the remaining fourteen months of the president's term.

private interests seem to have gained ascendency over even formal party structures by attaching themselves to a network of corrupt regional and national government leaders within the party. While the existence of networks, corrupt or otherwise, within polities is not unique to South Africa or even dominant party democracies, the relative weakness of opposition parties, and the remote chance of electoral punishment makes combating these systems of political relations and patronage more difficult. It is however just such a network, including President Zuma himself, that has been increasingly challenged from both within the party and through constitutional means.

A marked feature of the struggle between different factions within the ruling party and South Africa's political-economy more generally has been the use of law and the impact on different constitutional and governmental institutions. While President Thabo Mbeki was forced to resign on the claim that he interfered in the corruption prosecution of Jacob Zuma, the ascendance of the Zuma faction led to the hollowing out of key state institutions—such as the elite police anticorruption unit, the prosecution authorities, and the widely respected tax authorities, as well as the intelligence services—and their increasing deployment to protect President Zuma from accusations of corruption. "State capture" added a further dimension as private interests began to directly dictate significant decisions, including cabinet positions and executive appointments to the boards of state-owned entities, producing grossly corrupt decisions that benefitted the first family and their private collaborators. Even as the executive used its appointment powers to undermine each constitutional institution—including the Public Protector—a political backlash gathered ground from civil society and the political opposition, as well as from within the ruling party itself. Resistance from within state and constitutional institutions received increasing support from the courts, and the dramatic decrease in electoral support for the ANC, which led to the loss of major metropolitan areas to opposition parties in the 2016 local government elections, fermented a political revolt from within the ruling party.

Given the degree with which corrupt networks have managed to penetrate the state and the resultant undermining of significant state institutions such as the national intelligence,[47] prosecution, and tax agencies,[48] we might be justified in arguing that South Africa's constitutional democracy is in crisis. Despite these developments however, there is ample evidence that a number of constitutional institutions, ranging from the Public Protector to the courts, and the Constitutional Court in particular, have been at times able to make significant interventions, exposing malfeasance and propelling various institutions, from Parliament to the executive, to fulfill their constitutional obligations. Even if some of these institutions, such as the Public Protector, were finally brought to heel through the end of one Public Protector's term in office and the appointment of a new

---

[47] See Pauw, *The President's Keepers*.

[48] See Johann Van Loggerenberg, *Rogue: The Inside Story of SARS's Elite Crime-Busting Unit* (Johannesburg: Jonathan Ball, 2016).

Public Protector from within Zuma's faction, it has been the existence of such a plethora of constitutional institutions and the protection of rights, particularly of the press, that has enabled the resistance and frustrated those intent on using the state to achieve their private goals. It is this resilience of the constitutional institutions and the constitutional order more generally that suggests the constitutional crisis—if the "lawfare," political conflict, and undermining of public institutions may be said to have reached crisis proportions—may yet be contained.

public... account from certain Roman sources... it has been because... of such... it is said of contemporaries, historians and... representatives of... the reporters that...

19 Term Limits and Three Types of Constitutional Crisis in Sub-Saharan Africa

James Thuo Gathii*

Introduction

Africa is replete with political conflicts that threaten the foundations of constitutional government or the establishment of such governments. This has been particularly so since African countries began holding regular elections in the 1990s, in a period marking the de jure end of one-party rule. Since then many countries have returned to power one-party or military incumbents who were not constitutionally eligible for re-election. This has in turn often triggered or produced political violence. Unsurprisingly, therefore, many of the constitutional crises discussed in this chapter deal with the political instability that arises when constitutional safeguards for the peaceful transfer of power are violated, or where a constitution is suspended; or where an incumbent government argues that it is required to adhere to the constitution even though doing so would result in a crisis.

For the purposes of this chapter, a constitutional crisis arises when "the basic functions of constitutionalism—to channel conflict into everyday politics and thus to provide for political stability—have failed."[1] This chapter focuses on three types

---

* The author would like to thank Yusuf Abdulkareem, Ala Salemeh, and Laurel Hattix for excellent research assistance.
[1] Sanford Levinson and Jack M. Balkin, "Constitutional Crises," *University of Pennsylvania Law Review* 157 (2009): 707, 721.

of constitutional crisis: First, "where publicly articulated disagreements about the Constitution leads political actors to engage in extraordinary forms of protest beyond mere legal disagreements and political protests: people take to the streets, armies mobilize, and brute force is used or threatened in order to prevail."[2] Second, a constitutional crisis can also occur when leaders suspend the constitution because it limits their ability to address the exigencies of a situation.[3] In those instances, addressing the crisis is justified as a higher goal that requires sacrificing constitutional fidelity. Third and finally, a constitutional crisis can arise in "situations where fidelity to constitutional forms leads to ruin or disaster."[4]

The uprisings of the Arab Spring in countries such as Tunisia that began in December 2010 and Egypt that began in early 2011 were examples of constitutional and political revolution rather than constitutional crisis. Similarly, the 2017 military-induced resignation of President Robert Mugabe of Zimbabwe that had overwhelming public support was not a constitutional crisis either. In these revolutionary instances, there was no constitution to be faithful to.[5] Constitutional crises are characterized by serious disruptions of ordinary government operations or the substantial threat thereof. This may include a coup d'etat, a crippling civil war, or a failure of the state. Countries under the control of a strong authoritarian ruler that have not experienced major disruptions in their polity, such as Uganda, are for purposes of this chapter regarded as experiencing constitutional malfunctions that have not yet ripened to a full-blown constitutional crisis. This chapter shows that violations of presidential term limits in Africa are highly correlated with constitutional and other types of crisis in Africa. To that extent, this chapter adds a different dimension to understanding constitutional crisis in countries that have not consolidated democracy. The existing literature on term limits and constitutional crisis has primarily focused on democracies and argues that term limit violations in democracies are rarely accompanied by constitutional crisis. Notably of course, many of the constitutional crises arising from abrogations of term limits arise in African countries that are not consolidated constitutional democracies.

While the challenges of institutionalizing constitutionalism date back to the immediate post-independence era, it is noteworthy that formal rules as a constraint on power have played an increasingly prominent role in some African countries.[6] As an example,

---

[2] Ibid., 714.

[3] Ibid.

[4] Ibid.

[5] In fact, the removal of Mugabe has been referred to as a type of democratic coup d'etat. See Ozan Varol, "Zimbabwe's Coup Could Provide an Opening for Democracy," *Wall Street Journal*, November 16, 2017.

[6] Daniel N. Posner and Daniel J. Young, "The Institutionalization of Political Power in Africa," *Journal of Democracy* 18 (2007): 126–140. Indeed, Kenya is not anywhere near what B.O. Nwabueze, *Constitutionalism in Emergent States* (Rutherford, NJ: Fairleigh Dickinson University Press, 1973) described as accounting for the demise of constitutionalism in Africa: coups, counter-coups, military governments, and permanent states of emergency. However, corruption and rigged elections are a feature of Kenyan politics notwithstanding a written constitution making both illegal.

there have been at least twenty peaceful alternations of presidencies since 1990, with several of these succeeded by candidates who run on opposition parties.[7] Thus in countries such as Ghana there have been three consecutive and four overall peaceful transitions of power between parties to date. Ghana certainly meets Samuel Huntington's two turnover test for a consolidated democracy. According to Huntington, if "the party or group that takes power in the initial election at the time of transition loses a subsequent election and turns over power to those election winners then peacefully turn over power to the winners of a later election,"[8] then this test has been met. Yet elections in and of themselves are only one part of what constitutes a democracy. In a democracy, we would also expect to have the rights of individuals protected, checks on arbitrary power particularly through independent institutions such as courts, legislatures, and civil society groups as well as civilian control of the military.[9]

Constitutional Crisis Arising from Fundamental Disagreements That Result in Extraordinary Forms of Protest

In Africa, election violence is a major source of crises arising from fundamental disagreement leading to extraordinary forms of protest. There are at least three reasons that account for this type of crisis. Incumbents seek to be re-elected even when constitutional rules do not permit them do so; or are unwilling to hold free, fair, and credible elections; or incumbents defeated at the polls are unwilling to concede defeat. In addition to using brute force to gain or maintain power, incumbents use constitutional and legal rules to undermine the impartiality and independence of election bodies, to tilt and control electoral processes including how electoral boundaries are drawn, to influence the registration of voters in their favor, to decide which parties and candidates are allowed to compete, to affect the regulation of campaigns, and to determine how ballots get counted after they are cast on election day. These structural advantages incumbents enjoy in many of Africa's authoritarian regimes illustrate the difficulties involved in democratizing them.[10] Although Burundi and indeed many of the countries discussed in this chapter are not fully-fledged constitutional democracies, the types of crisis situations discussed are not ordinary disagreements about constitutional

---

[7] These include Ghana (2001, 2009, and 2017); Sierra Leone (2007); Cape Verde (2001); Benin (2006); and Kenya (2002).

[8] S.P. Huntington, *The Third Wave: Democratisation in the Late Twentieth Century* (Norman: University of Oklahoma Press, 1993), 267.

[9] See Michael Bratton, "Second Elections in Africa," *Journal of Democracy* 9 (1998): 51.

[10] Authoritarianism here "refers to arbitrary governmental authority. The common feature of authoritarian states is the enforcement of obedience to a central authority at the expense of personal freedoms, rule of law and other constitutional values and principles"; see Gábor Attila Tóth, "Authoritarianism," *Max Planck Encyclopedia of Comparative Constitutional Law*, February 2017.

interpretation. This is particularly so because constitutional term limits have very high public approval as mechanisms for ending the legacy of long-tenured, often despotic presidents in Africa. For this reason, not to mention the high probability of military interventions, violations of term limits are often accompanied by constitutional and other types of crisis. In short, the first type of crisis is generated by constitutional and legal rules, particularly those relating to elections, being disabled as the vehicle for transfer of power. Burundi's 2015 electoral crisis and Cote d'Ivoire's 2010–11 electoral crisis offer good illustrations.

Burundi's 2015 crisis about whether the March 2005 Constitution and the Arusha Peace and Reconciliation Agreement of August 2000 allowed President Pierre Nkurunziza to be elected for a third term is a classic example of a constitutional crisis that went well beyond mere legal disagreement. President Nkurunziza was elected under the Arusha Peace and Reconciliation Agreement (hereinafter "Agreement") in 2005. This negotiated peace agreement is widely regarded as the "political and institutional road-map for post-conflict Burundi"[11] since it ended the country's twelve-year civil war. The Agreement introduced a power-sharing deal between the Hutu and Tutsi ethnic groups in Burundi.[12] Under the deal, the Tutsi, who comprise 14 percent of the population, were guaranteed 40 percent membership in the National Assembly and 50 percent in the Senate. Burundi also has a proportional representation system with a closed list under which political parties cannot nominate more than two-thirds of candidates from the same ethnic group.[13] President Nkurunziza was first elected by Burundi's two-chamber Parliament as required by the Agreement. In 2010, he was re-elected, this time through universal suffrage under the March 2005 Constitution. A coalition of opposition parties boycotted the second round in that election. While some in the opposition were really doing the government's bidding, those that did not, including civil society groups and protestors, were arrested and imprisoned. The 2005 Constitution provided for a two-term presidential limit. The constitutional and legal disagreement related to whether President Nkurunziza could run for another term. The opposition argued that he could not be elected for a third term because he had been elected twice, once under the Arusha Peace and Reconciliation Agreement, and then again under the March 2005 Constitution in 2010.

Arrests and imprisonments did not prevent thousands from protesting against his third term bid in 2015. There were even defections from his own party by politicians who believed that the Constitution did not allow him to pursue a third five-year term.

---

[11] Stef Vandeginste, "Briefing: Burundi's Electoral Crisis: Back to Power-Sharing Politics as Usual?" *African Affairs* 114 (2015): 623.

[12] The Twa minority group was incorporated in the deal in some respects as well. See Stef Vandeginste, "Political Representation of Minorities as Collateral Damage of Gain: The Batwa in Burundi and Rwanda," *Africa Spectrum* 49 (2014): 1.

[13] The Constitution also requires a fifty/fifty split in the military, and an 80 percent supermajority in the National Assembly and two-thirds in the Senate to amend the Constitution.

Indeed in March 2014, President Nkurunziza lost a parliamentary vote that would have allowed him to pursue a third term notwithstanding the fact that his party controlled Parliament. President Nkurunziza's supporters by contrast argued that he could run for a third term without amending or violating the Constitution because the Constitution did not apply to him as the first post-transition president. President Nkurunziza purged those within his ruling party who were opposed to a third term. He also prevailed on Burundi's Constitutional Court to rule in his favor, a move that resulted in the Court's vice president fleeing the country.

Street protests erupted against President Nkurunziza's third term bid and the crackdown brutally silenced his opponents. In May 2015, a section of the military opposed to the third bid staged a coup d'etat attempt while President Nkurunziza was in a neighboring country. Large crowds came out to celebrate the apparent end of his presidency. The fact that the coup plotters included both Tutu and Hutu officers and that those who supported the apparent fall of President Nkurunziza were from both the Hutu and Tutsi communities demonstrated that opposition to him transcended ethnic boundaries.[14] The failure of the coup attempt, primarily because the rest of the armed forces remained loyal, set the stage for repressing the coup plotters.

Although the main opposition parties boycotted the elections of June 29, 2015, held after the failed coup attempt, which were characterized by voter intimidation and bribery, the elections nevertheless legitimized President Nkurunziza's third term.

The constitutional crisis that Burundi faces is the desire of a dominant political party with a weak demographic (Hutu) ethnic majority having temporarily gained power through a power-sharing agreement, subsequently seeking to end the power-sharing agreement inconsistently with the concessions and guarantees the agreement gives to minority groups who comprise the political opposition. In so doing, President Nkurunziza has in effect ruled Burundi as a one-party state.[15] Ending such a power-sharing agreement could plunge the country into mass murders, or at worst genocide, between Burundi's Hutu and Tutsi communities—a prospect that has an unfortunate historical legacy in that country. What makes a constitutional crisis such as the one in Burundi particularly difficult is that those excluded from a power-sharing deal have an incentive to plunge the country into political violence again through armed force as a strategy of negotiating themselves back to power.[16] Stef Vandeginste pointedly identifies the heart of Burundi's constitutional crisis as lying in the prospect that elites excluded from power-sharing may come to see armed violence as a tool to "force the government to engage in political dialogue and 'cake-sharing.'"[17]

[14] Vandeginste, "Briefing: Burundi's Electoral Crisis," 632.

[15] Ibid.

[16] Stef Vandeginste, "Power-Sharing as a Fragile Safety Valve in Times of Electoral Turmoil: The Costs and Benefits of Burundi's 2010 Elections," *Journal of Modern African Studies* 49 (2011): 329.

[17] Ibid., 333.

Burundi's constitutional crisis is a reflection of how a power-sharing arrangement initially crafted as a conflict resolution framework has been transformed into a way for those contending for political power "share control of the state among elite actors and their networks."[18] For these elites, pursuing peace is about pursuing the "equilibrium in the allocation of power, state resources, and privilege" among themselves.[19] Since elections are seen as opportunities for making a claim to scarce national resources, they invariably come with the risk of upsetting the previous equilibrium. The instability that comes with elections in this context makes realizing the promise of constitutional guarantees of free, fair, and credible elections difficult.

This is because elections have an inbuilt potential to unsettle the existing allocation of power and state resources, a prospect that a party that controls the entire machinery of government, including the electoral system, the judiciary, and even Parliament is unwilling to give up. Under these circumstances, independent checks on the government are unable to perform their roles to hold an incumbent president accountable. Further, the lack of independent institutions means elections are unlikely to be free, fair, and credible or that an incumbent president would be willing to concede electoral defeat.

Burundi's constitutional crisis was characterized by the fact that a section of the military took advantage of the uncertainty that arose from an incumbent's third-term ambitions by attempting a coup d'etat, demonstrating its willingness to further paralyze peaceful change accomplished through constitutionally provided paths. The coup attempt in turn justified increasingly centralized power even when the Constitution requires it to be shared and dispersed. With increased centralization has come increased authoritarianism in Burundi. Those in the opposition have therefore come to see the government as a predatory one with the elites in power sharing the spoils of the state while rewarding their supporters. In the meantime, the underlying dynamics make it difficult to resolve the crisis in the near-term without a major external shock. Such a shock could be a unified regional and international opposition and rejection of an unconstitutional usurpation of power as happened in Cote d'Ivoire in 2010–11.

Public disagreements about what the Constitution required arose after Cote d'Ivoire's elections in October 2010. The Independent Electoral Commission declared opposition candidate Alassane Quattara the winner with 54.1 percent of the vote. The Constitutional Council, controlled by incumbent president Lauret Gbagbo, over-ruled the Independent Electoral Commission. It declared President Gbagbo as president by a 51 percent margin. President Gbagbo denied that the opposition had won the election and began unleashing a reign of terror to suppress widespread protests against his actions.[20] Both

---

[18] Vandeginste, "Briefing: Burundi's Electoral Crisis," 634.

[19] Ibid.

[20] Jennifer Cook, "The Election Crisis in Cote d'Ivoire," *CSIS Briefing Paper*, December 7, 2010, https://www.csis.org/analysis/election-crisis-c%C3%B4te-d%E2%80%99ivoire.

Quattara and Gbagbo proceeded to have themselves sworn in as president and appointed members of their cabinet. As the crisis unfolded, more than 3,000 people were killed and more than a million displaced to neighboring countries.[21] Global condemnation of the reversal of the results followed not least from the African Union.[22] Gbagbo perhaps miscalculated that the international community, and in particular, France, the European Union, and the United States, would quietly acquiesce to his refusal to concede electoral defeat. Further he may have thought that by firmly holding on to power and refusing to concede defeat and unleashing violence against the opposition and its supporters, subsequent mediation efforts would result in a power-sharing government as a concession to ending violence.[23] The violence that erupted did not play out in President Gbagbo's favor; rather it may very well have helped tip the balance in favor of regional and international support for the opposition's electoral victory. The uprising that dislodged President Gbagbo also rose again to defeat his presidential guard when it tried to remove the transitional government that replaced him in September 2015.

President Gbabgo was captured by Quattara's forces with the help of French troops in April 2011. He was subsequently transferred to The Hague to face charges of crimes against humanity in the International Criminal Court. His capture helped to avoid a return to the full-scale violence that Cote d'Ivoire had experienced between the north and the south in 2002–3. The opposition too was responsible for human rights violations during the crisis.[24] As a result of that earlier round of violence, UN peacekeepers and several French military soldiers helped to keep the peace. Regional and international support of Quattara's victory over President Gbagbo in 2010–11 was decisive in resolving the Ivoirian crisis created by an incumbent president's refusal to concede electoral defeat. Unlike in Zimbabwe in 2008 and Kenya in 2007 when incumbents who lost elections to the opposition forced power-sharing governments instead of conceding defeat, President

---

[21] Ibid.

[22] The African Union has often acquiesced to unconstitutional changes of government or failed to unconditionally condemn leaders who failed to concede electoral defeat in what many argued was some kind of authoritarian collaboration between dictators. In fact, the African Union's initial response was not a definitive condemnation of Gbabgo's refusal to concede. That eventually changed after the African Union not only condemned President Gbabgo but also demanded that he concede power. The African Union had recently suspended the voting rights of countries that experienced unconstitutional changes of government such as Egypt. On the inconsistency of state responses to unconstitutional change of government in Africa, see Erika de Wet, "The Modern Practice of Intervention by Invitation in Africa and Its Implications for the Prohibition of the Use of Force," *European Journal of International Law* 26 (2015): 979.

[23] In so doing, President Gbagbo may have sought to be in a "position to continue to exert and expand his own influence and that of his allies in government," Cook, "The Election Crisis in Cote d'Ivoire."

[24] UN Human Rights Council, "Report of the Independent, International Commission of Inquiry on Côte d'Ivoire," June 2011, http://www2.ohchr.org/english/bodies/hrcouncil/docs/17session/A.HRC.17.48_Extract.pdf and Human Rights Watch, "Côte d'Ivoire: Ouattara Forces Kill, Rape Civilians during Offensive," August 2011, https://www.hrw.org/news/2011/04/09/cote-divoire-ouattara-forces-kill-rape-civilians-during-offensive.

Gbabgo was not only unseated, but also charged with crimes against humanity in the International Criminal Court.[25]

Cote d'Ivoire and the removal of one of Africa's longest-serving presidents, Abdoulaye Wade of Senegal show how electoral crises in Africa have increasingly come to require external checks.[26] Because President Gbabgo controlled the military, it was unlikely that opposition electoral victory or violence would have tipped the scales against him without regional and international support. To be installed as president, Quattara was supported by his own opposition party together with its militias and civil society groups at home and abroad, but also by a united group of Western countries that had invested in democracy assistance to Cote d'Ivoire.[27] This transnational network of actors together with Quattara's forces eventually led to President Gbabgo's relinquishing power.[28] Manipulating elections breeds political violence and a zero-sum struggle for control of the state. In this context, electoral contests are likely to be accompanied by bloodshed, an outcome further exacerbated by ethnic and regional divisions that make elections a "life-and-death struggle."[29]

Another country that has experienced a constitutional crisis that has resulted in extraordinary forms of protest is the Democratic Republic of Congo (DRC). After serving the limit of two five-year terms as provided in Article 70 the 2006 Constitution, President Joseph Kabila was required to hand over the presidency in December 2016. However, more than two years after the expiration of his constitutionally mandated two five-year term limit, Kabila is still in power. His continued hold on power beyond his two five-year terms triggered widespread and violent protests and a repressive, often deadly,

[25] Open Justice Initiatives, "The Trial of Laurent Gbagbo and Charles Blé Goudé at the ICC," January 2016, https://www.opensocietyfoundations.org/sites/default/files/briefing-gbagbo-FINAL-20160121%20(1).pdf.

[26] Paul Collier, "The Lessons of Cote d'Ivoire," Global Policy Journal, December 17, 2010, http://www.globalpolicyjournal.com/blog/17/12/2010/lessons-cote-d%C3%A2%E2%82%AC%E2%84%A2ivoire. Another example where an incumbent was removed from power through collaborative action by domestic and external actors is Mali's Ahmadou Toumani Toure, who toppled in a coup in March 2012 and the coup plotters were forced to transfer power to an elected government in August 2013.

[27] For the argument about the role of international factors (in addition to domestic ones) in democratization or in consolidating authoritarianism see C. Von Soest, "Democracy Prevention: The International Collaboration of Authoritarian Regimes," European Journal of Political Research (2015), https://www.giga-hamburg.de/sites/default/files/publications/ejpr_12100_rev2.pdf. See also C. Von Soest and M. Wahman, "Not All Dictators Are Equal: Coups, Fraudulent Elections and the Selective Targeting of Democratic Sanctions," Journal of Peace Research 52 (2015): 17–31 (arguing that authoritarian elections might serve as a focal point for the opposition, popular protest, and external democracy promoters to impose pressure).

[28] For other cases where transnational activism led to the defeat of authoritarian incumbents, see Valerie Bunce and Sharon Wolchik, Defeating Authoritarian Leaders in Postcommunist Countries (Cambridge: Cambridge University Press, 2011). By contrast, rather than focusing on such transnational activism, Paul Collier has instead suggested that supporting opposition electoral victory may require international troops. See Paul Collier, "The Lessons of Cote d'Ivoire," Global Policy Journal, December 17, 2010, http://www.globalpolicy-journal.com/blog/17/12/2010/lessons-cote-d%C3%A2%E2%82%AC%E2%84%A2ivoire.

[29] Paul Collier, War, Guns, and Votes: Democracy in Dangerous Places (New York: HarperCollins Publishers, 2009).

response from his government. His overarching strategy for staying in power has been indefinitely delaying scheduled electoral preparatory timelines to prevent elections from being conducted within the constitutionally required time frames. This policy of letting election timelines slide by has come to be referred to as *glissment* in French.[30] Thus, unlike African presidents who have sought term extensions or abrogations through referenda and constitutional amendments, President Kabila chose to extend his term by doing nothing—ignoring the constitutional requirements of holding presidential elections that under the Constitution must be held every five years.[31]

Some of the reasons that President Kabila has advanced to justify his *glissment* strategy include the need for a new census as a precursor for registering voters so that the country has a credible voter roll that would satisfy all political actors. Kabila has also argued the Constitution requires the country to hold legislative elections ahead of presidential elections. He has also made the case about the need to ensure that there was peace in the entire country to guarantee civic education and so that election materials could be delivered safely, particularly in those experiencing civil war such as the Kasai Province. President Kabila further contributed to the crisis by starving the electoral body, the Commission Electorale Nationale Indépendante (CENI), of funds in addition to instigating the resignation of its widely respected and independent chairperson.[32] Like in the rest of the African continent, there is vast public support for term limits in the DRC.[33] This means that the violation of term limits in the DRC has triggered massive protests. By declining to give up the reigns of the presidency, Kabila therefore continued the legacy of denying the country a peaceful transition of power. The restiveness that has accompanied the delayed presidential elections has turned what on the surface seem to be ordinary disagreements on constitutional interpretation into a full-blown political and constitutional crisis.

Another strategy of delaying elections involved using a newly established constitutional court whose judges President Kabila and Parliament, which is dominated by his party, appoints.[34] Several months in advance of the elections scheduled at the end

---

[30] Stephanie Wolters, "DRC Slip-Slides into Electoral Delays," *Institute for Security Studies*, March 14, 2016, https://issafrica.org/iss-today/drc-slip-slides-into-electoral-delays and Aryn Baker, "Congo's President Is Refusing to Step Down, Raising Fears of Bloodshed," *TIME*, December 16, 2016, http://time.com/4604626/congo-kabila-protests-glissement-katumbi/.

[31] Perhaps President Kabila decided to pursue a different term-limit extension strategy because Section 220 of the Constitution of the Democratic Republic of Congo provides that presidential term limits are unamendable.

[32] Nick Long, "DRC Electoral Body Pleads Lack of Funds," *Voice of America News*, October 13, 2015, https://www.voanews.com/a/democratic-republic-congo-electoral-body-pleads-lack-funds/3004596.html.

[33] Baker, "Congo's President" (reporting a poll toward the end of 2016 indicating that 80 percent of the DRC population wanted him to step down at the end of his two terms). See also Boniface Dulani, "AD30: African Publics Strongly Support Term Limits, Resist Leaders' Efforts to Extend their Tenure," *Afrobarometer*, 2015, http://afrobarometer.org/publications/ad30-african-publics-strongly-support-term-limits-resist-leaders-efforts-extend-their.

[34] Three of its nine judges were selected by the Kabila-controlled Parliament, three by the president himself, and the last three by the Judicial Council, a body that is staffed by Kabila allies, including the powerful president of the Supreme Court.

of his second five-year term in November 2016, the Constitutional Court issued an advisory opinion on three constitutional provisions that his supporters argued were unclear. The questions posed to the Constitutional Court revealed President Kabila's strategy. In particular, the Constitutional Court was asked to opine on a constitutional provision that the requesters argued did not make it clear who would be president if an election scheduled at the end of the second term of a president was not held. Let me briefly summarize the three provisions of the Constitution that needed clarification to answer this question. First, Article 70 limits the president to two five-year terms. Second, Article 73 requires elections to be held ninety days before the expiration of the president's five-year term. The third provision is Article 75, which requires the president to hand over the reins of government to the Senate President during the election. Article 70, however, states that the president's term expires after the winner is declared and assumes office.

Kabila and his supporters argued that the requirement that the president hand over power during the election and the provision that elections must be held ninety days before the expiration of the president's five-year term were in conflict and therefore needed to be clarified. The opposition saw the request for an advisory opinion as a strategy to evade the two-term limit. They were right because the Constitutional Court ruled that an incumbent president could stay in office beyond the two five-year term limit if there is no president or president-elect when the incumbent's second term comes to an end.[35] The opposition disagreed, arguing that the Constitutional Court should instead have used another provision of the Constitution that requires the President of the Senate to step in as Interim President in the absence of a president.[36] That was not all. In yet another example of how the Constitutional Court has legitimized Kabila's policy of *glissment*, it held in an October 2016 decision that it was constitutional to postpone the November 2016 elections.[37]

When President Kabila failed to hold the November 2016 elections, an agreement, referred to as the New Year's Eve Agreement, was brokered by the Catholic bishops in the country between him and the opposition.[38] Under that agreement, which Kabila

---

[35] See Amedee Mwaraby Kiboko, "Top Congo Court Says Kabila Would Stay in Power if Election Delayed," *Reuters*, May 11, 2016, https://www.reuters.com/article/us-congodemocratic-politics/top-congo-court-says-kabila-would-stay-in-power-if-election-delayed-idUSKCN0Y21PL.

[36] John Mukum Mbaku, "The Postponed DRC Elections: What Does DRC's Situation Look Like Now?," *Brookings Institution*, November 22, 2016, https://www.brookings.edu/blog/africa-in-focus/2016/11/22/the-postponed-drc-elections-what-does-the-drcs-situation-look-like-now/.

[37] Article 76 of the Constitution of the DRC in part provides that "In the case of force majeure, this delay may be extended by the Constitutional Court on request by the Independent National Electoral Commission to one hundred and twenty days (120) at the maximum."

[38] This agreement has also been referred to as the Saint Sylvester Agreement. See Issa Sikiti da Silva, "Praying for Change in Congo: The Catholic Church Takes on Kabila," *IRIN News*, February 1, 2018, http://www.irin-news.org/analysis/2018/02/01/praying-change-congo-catholic-church-takes-kabila.

subsequently declined to sign, he was supposed to hand over power and hold elections in November 2017.[39] That agreement also included a power-sharing accord with the opposition. President Kabila strategically chose a prime minister who divided the burgeoning opposition alliance, making it more difficult for the opposition to ensure that President Kabila kept his word to hold the rescheduled election in November 2017. The death of Etienne Tshisekedi in early 2017, who had been leader of the opposition in the DRC over a period of four decades, further weakened the opposition. This was particularly the case since he was the designated prime minister under the power-sharing arrangement agreed to under the New Year's Eve Agreement. The one opposition candidate who was regarded as capable of mounting a competitive bid against President Kabila, former governor Moïse Katumbi, was sentenced to a three-year prison term on what were widely regarded as a trumped-up charges.

After failing to hold the rescheduled election in November 2017, President Kabila's government announced that elections would be held on December 23, 2018,[40] and a new president inaugurated in January 2019.[41] Opposition political parties and civil society groups have rejected this new timeline. On a visit to the DRC, the United States ambassador to the United Nations, Nikki Halley, told President Kabila that he must hold elections in 2018.[42] What is clear though is that President Kabila's strategy of *glissment* has succeeded in keeping him in power well beyond his two five year-term limit. Holding elections in December 2018 will require meeting the scheduled timelines, and the logistical arrangements that the President Kabila argues will have to be financed with donor support.[43] Civil society groups have come together under the umbrella Manifeste du Citoyen Congolais. They have invoked Article 64 of the Constitution, which provides for people to organize against those who violate the Constitution. Their goal is to forcibly depose Kabila and replace his government with a transitional one that would organize elections.[44] Thus citizens in the DRC are organizing to enforce term limits, indicating the popular support they enjoy. Indeed, under the Constitution of the DRC term limits are

---

[39] "Voici L'integralite de L'accord Signe le Mardi 18 Octobre a la Cite de L'oua," *7Sur7*, October 18, 2016, https://7sur7.cd/new/2016/10/voici-laccord-lintegralite-de-laccord-signe-le-mardi-18-octobre-a-la-cite-de-loua/.

[40] "Joint Communique—The African Union and the United Nations Welcome the Publication of the Electoral Calendar in the DRC and Urge for Consensus on the Electoral Process," *United Nations Organization Stablization Mission in the DR Congo*, November 9, 2017, https://monusco.unmissions.org/en/joint-communique-african-union-and-united-nations-welcome-publication-electoral-calendar-drc-and.

[41] "Décision N°065/CENI/BUR/17 du 5 Novembre 2017 portant publication du calendrier des élections présidentielle, législatives, provinciales, urbaines, municipales et locales," CENI, November 5, 2017.

[42] Michelle Nichols, "U.S. Says Congo Must Hold Long-Delayed Election by End of 2018," *Reuters*, October 27, 2017, https://www.reuters.com/article/us-congo-us-haley/u-s-says-congo-must-hold-long-delayed-election-by-end-of-2018-idUSKBN1CW1IG.

[43] RDC: "la CENI rappelle les conditions pour le respect du calendrier électoral," RFI, November 10, 2017.

[44] Ange Kasongo Adihe, "RDC: Tout Savoir Sur Le 'Manifeste Du Citoyen Congolais' Signe Vendredi a Paris," *Manifeste du Citoyen Congolais*, August 17, 2017, http://www.manifesterdc.com/tout-savoir-sur-le-manifeste-du-citoyen-congolais/.

unamendable. This explains in part why President Kabila has preferred a strategy of *gliss-ment* rather than seeking to amend the Constitution.

In the meantime, President Kabila and his government have continued to engage in massive corruption and plundering of the mineral riches of the country, while brutally repressing the opposition and civil society groups. His military and security forces have engaged in deliberately producing chaos in the country in a bid many believe have under-mined stability and security as a strategy to justify his continued hold on to power. The constitutional crisis in the DRC is further exacerbated by a civil war that has pitted gov-ernment troops against Kabila's opponents, particularly in the Kasai Province. Since 2016 over 2 million people have been displaced. In 2017, eighty mass graves where govern-ment forces are suspected to have buried political opponents were discovered. Violent clampdowns often resulting in death have been used on a regular basis against protestors, opposition leaders, and journalists opposed to President Kabila's unconstitutional exten-sion of his term of office, resulting in hundreds of deaths.[45] In addition thousands of protesters against President Kabila's bid to remain in office beyond his two terms have been arrested and imprisoned without charge and without being given access to their families or lawyers.

Constitutional Crisis Arising from Suspensions of the Constitution

This part of the chapter addresses constitutional crises that occur when leaders suspend the constitution because it limits their ability to address the exigencies of a situation. In those instances, addressing the crisis is justified as a higher goal that requires sacrificing constitutional fidelity. Several examples are discussed to illustrate this type of constitu-tional crisis. These are the suspension of the Constitution of Togo in early 2005 and the Constitution of Burkina Faso in October 2014. This part also discusses some chroni-cally unstable countries that have experienced constitutional suspensions. These are the Central African Republic in March 2013, in Mali in March 2012, and last in Guinea-Bissau in April 2012. These cases show how constitutional suspensions are used by incum-bents to defeat presidential term limits or as strategies by insurgent groups or the military to take over governments. This part therefore concludes by reflecting on term limits and constitutional crisis in Africa.

The first instance of suspension of the Constitution comes from Togo. This occurred after the sudden death of President Gnassingbe Eyadema in early February 2005. Under the Togolese Constitution, a presidential vacancy arising from a death was to be filled by the President of the National Assembly until a new election was held within

---

[45] "Time for Concerted Action in DR Congo," *International Crisis Group*, December 4, 2017, https://www.crisisgroup.org/africa/central-africa/democratic-republic-congo/257-time-concerted-action-dr-congo.

sixty days of the vacancy arising. Instead of immediately swearing in the President of the National Assembly, the military suspended the Constitution, dismissed the Speaker of the National Assembly, and swore in President Eyadema's son as the new president. The military claimed this subversion of the constitutionally-required transfer of power had been undertaken to "avoid a power vacuum."[46]

Opposition weakness in Togo exacerbated by years of President Eyadema's crackdown against it and civil society made it difficult for them to confront what was clearly an unconstitutional transfer of presidential authority. Opposition protests against this irregular transfer of power were met with police brutality by security forces.[47] The military's intervention ensured that President Eyadema's minority ethnic community, the Kabiye, continued to dominate not only the military, but also state power.[48] To the opposition's credit, and with the support of neighboring countries including the Economic Community of West African States (ECOWAS), the African Union, and Togo's Western donors, President Eyadema's son stepped aside and the Deputy Speaker was appointed interim president. However, the opposition objected to this appointment, calling for the return of the Speaker who was exiled in a neighboring country. The opposition argued that President Eyadema's son had stepped aside only temporarily to pave the way for an election that he could win.[49]

The irregular transfer of power and the subsequent election that legitimized President Eyadema's son as president was justified as necessary to ensure national security and stability.[50] The constitutional crisis reached a high point when the opposition rejected the results of the April 2005 election, and the opposition leader "declared himself President and called for an armed insurrection" against the government.[51] Tens of thousands fled from the heavy government repression across the border to Benin and Ghana in a crisis in which at least seven hundred people died.[52] However, unlike in Cote d'Ivoire in 2010–11, there was insufficient regional and international support to unseat President Eyadema's son from power.

Another example of a crisis that involved the suspension of the Constitution arose in late October 2014 in Burkina Faso when then-president Blaise Compaore sought to extend his twenty-seven-year rule. Compaore's plan to extend his rule prompted mass demonstrations and protests in Ouagadougou, the capital, which culminated in the protesters setting fire to Parliament and city hall, as well as homes of Members of Parliament. The protesters sought Campaore's resignation and for Parliament

---

[46] Adewale Banjo, "Constitutional and Succession Crisis in West Africa: The Case of Togo," *African Journal of Legal Studies* 2 (2005): 151.

[47] Ibid., 154.

[48] Ibid., 155.

[49] Ibid.

[50] Ibid., 158.

[51] Ibid., 159.

[52] Ibid., 160.

to abandon voting to allow Compaore to run for a third term inconsistently with the 2000 Constitution.[53] Campaore and his family were forced into exile in Cote d'Ivoire. Upon Campaore's departure, the military announced the suspension of the Constitution and set up a transitional body promising a return to constitutional rule within twelve months. The military's intervention was justified as necessary "given the power vacuum" created by Campaore's resignation and departure from the country. Further, the military argued that the army would prevent further violence, restore order, and prepare the country for a transition back to democracy. The general who took over from Campaore was Campaore's confidant, a fact that led the protesters and opposition parties to reject his seizure of power. The opposition and protesters argued that the Constitution had a succession procedure in the event of the resignation of the president.[54] As in Togo's case above, in Burkina Faso the suspension of the Constitution was triggered by a military takeover.

In some countries, guerilla groups are a threat to constitutional order. That was the case in my next case study, from the Central African Republic.

In March 2013, the leader of the Séléka rebel group, Michel Djotodia, deposed the president of the Central African Republic in a bloody coup accompanied by violence and looting.[55] Djotodia also suspended the Constitution. The Séléka group, a Muslim led rebel alliance, set up a transitional government in place of the institutions established under the previous Constitution. The coup had been preceded by a period of insecurity and political violence as the Séléka group advanced toward the capital. The Séléka group entrenched the divisions between the minority Muslim and majority Christian populations in the country. The atrocities committed by the Séléka group following the coup led to the formation of opposition militias. These groups, among others, were responsible for committing war crimes, including systematic rape and acts of sexual violence, and crimes against humanity between 2013 and 2015.[56] Notably, Michel Djotodia's post-coup government did not have territorial control of the country or the legitimacy in the eyes of a majority of its people.[57] As a result, the United Nations Security Council declared that

---

[53] "Burkina Faso Army Announces Emergency Measures," *BBC*, October 30, 2014, http://www.bbc.com/news/world-africa-29840100.

[54] Article 43 provided for the prime minister to take over the office of the president as a transitional head of government should the president be temporarily incapacitated and unable to undertake his or her duties. Elections should then be held between sixty and ninety days after a vacancy in the presidency.

[55] Benno Muchler, "In Post-Coup Central African Republic, Instability Remains," *National Public Radio*, April 5, 2013, https://www.npr.org/2013/04/05/176334015/in-post-coup-central-african-republic-instability-remains.

[56] "Populations in the Central African Republic Face an Imminent Risk of Mass Atrocity Crimes Committed by Various Armed Groups and Militias," *Global Centre for the Responsibility to Protect*, January 15, 2018, http://www.globalr2p.org/regions/central_african_republic.

[57] Freedom House, "Central African Republic: A Failed State," *Freedom House*, December 20, 2013, https://freedomhouse.org/blog/central-african-republic-failed-state.

law and order had completely broken down in the Central African Republic.[58] It was the fourth time that a Constitution had been suspended in the chronically unstable country. By December 2013, between 3,000 and 6,000 people had been killed in the crisis and nearly a million people had been displaced from their homes while tens of thousands had fled to neighboring countries.[59] The United Nations concluded that the instability that followed the March 2013 was a non-international armed conflict.[60] Peace-keeping forces from the African Union, as well as the United Nations, joined French forces who were already in country, and were mobilized to prevent the Central African Republic from descending into even greater war.[61]

As the constitutional suspension in the Central African Republic in March 2013 illustrates, such suspensions in Africa are often one part of what is usually a much larger conflict.[62] Thus the suspension of Mali's Constitution in March 2012 came after a coup led by military officers dissatisfied with the democratically elected government's inability to decisively defeat a secessionist rebellion led by Tuareg Islamists in the desert north of the country.[63] Promising to restore stability, the coup leaders decided not to wait for a new government that would have been formed following a presidential election that was less than a month away. The election had no clear front runner, and it seemed the coup leaders did not trust that a new government would be able to put down the rebellion in the north, and address drug trafficking and the needs of the military.[64] The Constitution suspended in March 2012 was the first post-authoritarian Constitution under which the deposed president was completing his second and final five-year term.[65] Therefore the coup and suspension of the Constitution frustrated a peaceful transfer of

---

[58] United Nations, Department of Meetings Coverage and Press Releases, *Security Council, Unanimously Adopting Resolution 2127 (2013), Mandates Mission in Central African Republic to Protect Civilians, Restore State Authority*. SC/11200, December 5, 2013, https://www.un.org/press/en/2013/sc11200.doc.htm.

[59] United Nations, Security Council, *The International Commission of Inquiry on the Central African Republic: Final Report*, S/2014/928 (December 22, 2014), http://www.securitycouncilreport.org/atf/cf/%7b65BFCF9B-6D27-4E9C-8CD3-CF6E4FF96FF9%7d/s_2014_928.pdf.

[60] Ibid.

[61] These forces were put together under the umbrella, Multidimensional Integrated Stabilization Mission in the Central African Republic; see "Violence in the Central African Republic," *Council on Foreign Relations*, February 12, 2018, https://www.cfr.org/interactives/global-conflict-tracker?marker=18#!/conflict/violence-in-the-central-african-republic.

[62] See Morten Boas, "Mali 2013: A Year of Elections and Further Challenges," *E-International Relations*, December 22, 2013, http://www.e-ir.info/2013/12/22/mali-2013-a-year-of-elections-and-further-challenges/ (arguing that the "Malian crisis was a crisis of multiple dimensions, with each feeding the others. It started in the north with a rebellion originally based on Tuareg grievances, but as the Malian army fled south, Islamist-inspired insurgents took control of large parts of northern Mali.").

[63] Bruce Whitehouse, "What Went Wrong in Mali?," *London Review of Books*, August 30, 2012, https://www.lrb.co.uk/v34/n16/bruce-whitehouse/what-went-wrong-in-mali.

[64] Ibid.

[65] "Freedom in the World 2016 Report: Mali," *Freedom House*, 2016, https://freedomhouse.org/report/freedom-world/2016/mali.

power through the ballot box. An immediate result of this frustration of a democratic transition through an election was a humanitarian emergency as thousands of people escaped from the Tuareg secessionists and Islamists into the southern parts of the country and into neighboring countries.[66] Thus the suspension of Mali's Constitution in 2012 was in part a reflection of the larger divide in the country between the relatively well-off southern part of the country, on the one hand, and the more isolated, desert and nomadic and Islamic northern part of the country, on the other. To raise money, some of the secessionist Islamist groups engage in kidnapping and the trafficking of narcotics, people, and weapons.[67]

Mali is not the only chronically unstable country in West Africa whose transition to multiparty politics has been undermined by a military not ready to be subjected to civilian control.[68] Between 1997 and 2012, Guinea-Bissau experienced five military coups. Like the coup in the Central African Republic in March 2013, the coup in Guinea-Bissau in April 2012 came right before a presidential election. Not only did the coup interrupt a runoff presidential election, it also resulted in the suspension of the prior Constitution. Corruption and impunity are endemic in the country where the Balanta, the country's largest ethnic community, dominates the military and institutions of governance.[69] The March 2013 coup in Guinea-Bissau was sparked by fears in the military that the government was preparing to take over the military with the assistance of troops from Angola that were stationed in the country to keep the peace.[70]

Mali and Guinea-Bissau, like other instances discussed in this chapter, illustrates how uncertainty and lack of consensus among those involved in post-authoritarian transitions are likely to result in the kind of political and social polarization that constitutes a constitutional crisis.[71] It also shows the difficulties posed to transitions when the military is not subject to civilian control, a difficult legacy to overcome when new civilian governments have yet to gain both legitimacy and control of day-to-day governance.[72] Constitutional suspensions in Africa are therefore characteristic of countries where opposition political parties have no meaningful democratic procedures available to them for transfer of power.

---

[66] Boas, "Mali 2013."

[67] "Mali Coup Highlights African Country's Divisions," *CBC News*, April 5, 2012, http://www.cbc.ca/news/world/mali-coup-highlights-african-country-s-divisions-1.1127767.

[68] Valerie Ramet, "Policy Briefing: Civil-Military Relations in Guinea-Bissau: An Unresolved Issue," Directorate-General for External Policies, European Parliament, http://www.europarl.europa.eu/RegData/etudes/briefing_note/join/2012/491437/EXPO-DEVE_SP(2012)491437_EN.pdf.

[69] "Freedom in the World 2013 Report: Guinea-Bissau," *Freedom House*, https://freedomhouse.org/report/freedom-world/2013/guinea-bissau.

[70] "Nouveau Coup D'Etat en Guinee-Bissau, L'armee Aux Comandes," *Jeune Afrique*, April 14, 2012, http://www.jeuneafrique.com/152346/politique/nouveau-coup-d-tat-en-guin-e-bissau-l-arm-e-aux-commandes/.

[71] Adewale Banjo, "Constitutional and Succession Crisis in West Africa: The Case of Togo," *African Journal of Legal Studies* 2 (2005): 154.

[72] Banjo, "Constitutional and Succession Crisis," 155.

Ultimately, the two types of crisis discussed in this chapter so far demonstrate that violations of term limits are highly correlated with constitutional and other types of crisis in Africa. This chapter therefore adds a different dimension to understanding constitutional crisis in countries that have not consolidated democracy. The existing literature on term limits and constitutional crisis has primarily focused on democracies. A primary finding in that literature is that on balance, in democracies "constitutional crisis induced through term limit violations is relatively rare."[73] This chapter by contrast shows that term limits abrogation in Africa, where democracies are few and far between, are highly correlated with constitutional crisis. Thus, while the introduction of term limits in African constitutions has reduced the number of presidents serving for particularly long periods of time, there have been several cases of upending term limits that directly result in constitutional and other types of conflicts. In these cases, term limits seem more consistent with legitimizing than constraining the power of incumbent presidents.[74]

It is noteworthy that since 1990 when term limits were first introduced in African constitutions, the number of presidents leaving office through elections has risen to thirty-five from a mere one in the pre-term limits period before 1990.[75] Thus although term limits have a propensity to result in crisis where a term-limited incumbent does not want to leave office, term limits have their utility. They play a role in neutralizing incumbent advantage and promote alternation of not just individuals holding office but also of the president's party.[76] However, there have been at least fifteen successful term-limit abrogations, as shown in Table 19.1, many of which led to a constitutional and political crisis of one form or the other as discussed in this chapter. In other words, to the extent term limits in Africa are a response to ending presidencies that last for decades and decades, countries that experience such long-tenured policies are likely to experience severe pushback, often resulting in a crisis, when incumbents signal their unwillingness to comply with term limits. This is the case even in countries without a long history of strong civil society organizations and opposition political parties such as the Democratic Republic of Congo.

---

[73] See Tom Ginsburg, Zachary Elkins, and James Melton, "Do Executive Term Limits Cause Constitutional Crisis," in *Comparative Constitutional Design*, ed. Tom Ginsburg (New York: Cambridge University Press, 2012), 374.

[74] Denis Tull and Claudia Simons, "The Institutionalization of Power Revisited: Presidential Term Limits in Africa," *Africa Spectrum* 52 (2017): 79–102, https://www.ssoar.info/ssoar/bitstream/handle/document/54845/ssoar-afrspe-2017-2-tull_et_al-The_Institutionalisation_of_Power_Revisited.pdf?sequence=2.

[75] Ibid. Note that twenty-one out of thirty-nine presidents stepped down after the expiration of their term limits since the limits were introduced.

[76] Nic Cheeseman, "African Elections as Vehicles for Change," *Journal of Democracy* 21 (2010): 139–153. For analysis that updates the statistics of term limit abrogations, see Tull and Simons, "The Institutionalization of Power Revisited."

TABLE 19.1

Attempted modification or elimination of term limits

Successful	Unsuccessful
Togo (Eyadema, 2002)	Zambia (Chiluba, 2001)
Gabon (Bongo, 2003)	Malawi (Muluzi, 2003)
Uganda (Museveni, 2005)	Nigeria (Obasanjo, 2006)
Chad (Deby, 2005)	Burkina Faso (Compaore, 2014)
Cameroon (Biya, 2008)	
Djibouti (Guellah, 2010)	
Rwanda (Kagame, 2015)	
Burundi (Nkurunziza, 2015)	
Republic of Congo (Nguesso, 2015)	
DRC (Kabila, 2016)	
Guinea (Conte, 2001)	
Sudan (al-Bashir, 2005)	
Niger (Tandja, 2009)	
Senegal (Wade, 2012)	
Namibia (Nujoma, 1999)	

Sources: "Constitutional Term Limits for Africa Leaders," *Africa Center for Strategic Studies*, September 2017, https://africacenter.org/spotlight/constitutional-term-limits-african-leaders/; Tull and Simons, "The Institutionalization of Power Revisited" and B. Dulani, Personal Rule and Presidential Term Limits in Africa (Doctoral Dissertation) 2011.

In addition, there have been four instances of unsuccessful term-limit change attempts, as shown in Table 19.1. The failure of efforts to overcome or abrogate presidential term limits by incumbents does suggest that at least in some cases, formal rules limiting term limits are playing a more prominent role in the politics in some African states.[77] Yet, it is also important to recognize that the failure to overcome or abrogate term limits does sometimes accompany a constitutional and political crisis as was the case in Burkina Faso in 2014. In addition, as noted above, there have been at least twenty peaceful alternations of presidencies since 1990, with several of these succeeded by candidates who ran on opposition parties.[78] So there is merit in the claim that when presidents step down when their constitutional term of office ends, it may very well be helping to

---

[77] Daniel N. Posner and Daniel J. Young, "The Institutionalization of Political Power in Africa," *Journal of Democracy* 18 (2007): 126–140. Indeed, Kenya is not anywhere near what Nwabueze, *Constitutionalism in Emergent States* decried accounted for the demise of constitutionalism in Africa: coups, counter-coups, military governmentsm, and permanent states of emergency. However, corruption and rigged elections are a feature of Kenyan politics notwithstanding a written constitution making both illegal.

[78] These include Ghana (2001, 2009 and 2017); Sierra Leone (2007); Cape Verde (2001); Benin (2006); and Kenya (2002).

instill a precedent of succession that makes it less likely for their successors to violate term limits.[79]

When Actors Believe Fidelity to the Constitution Requires Them to Act in Ways That Lead to Constitutional Crisis

This part of the chapter discusses constitutional crises that arise where actors believe that fidelity to the Constitution requires them to act in ways that lead to a crisis. This situation confronted Kenya in 2017 following the opposition boycott of a repeat presidential election. Under the 2010 Constitution, the election had to be held within sixty days following judicial nullification of a previous election. The opposition argued that sixty days was not long enough to prepare adequately to hold a free, fair, and credible election. They relied on statements of the chairman of the Independent Boundaries and Electoral Commission (IEBC) to that effect. Pursuant to the requirement of the Constitution and the order of the Supreme Court, the IEBC nevertheless proceeded with planning the election. Indeed, the constitutional rules were clear. Article 140(3) of the 2010 Constitution required that where the Supreme Court determines the election of a president-elect is invalid, "a fresh election shall be held within sixty days" after that determination. The Supreme Court had therefore ordered the repeat election to be conducted in "strict conformity" with the requirements of the "Constitution and the applicable election laws." The IEBC became "too invested in maintaining and exercising the powers" the Constitution gives them without taking into account that in so doing, they were exacerbating a political crisis. This was unsurprising for the opposition because the IEBC lacked legitimacy in their eyes and they regarded it as incapable of preparing for a free, fair, and credible election.

Had incumbent President Uhuru Kenyatta and opposition candidate Raila Odinga sat down to discuss if there was sufficient readiness on the part of the IEBC and a conducive environment to conduct a free, fair, and credible election in sixty days, many deaths and injuries, wanton destruction of property, and severe disruptions of the operations of government could have been avoided. By insisting the election be held within the constitutional time frame, a president was elected without the participation of a significant portion of the electorate who boycotted that repeat election, robbing the government of legitimacy.

---

[79] Gideon Maltz, "The Case for Presidential Term Limits," *Journal of Democracy* 18, no. 1 (2007): 128–142. Indeed, as two scholars have argued, leadership alternation generates shared levels of legitimacy between winners and losers in the general population, thus furthering democratic consolidation, Devra Moehler and Staffan Lindberg, "Narrowing the Legitimacy Gap: The Role of Turnovers in Africa's Emerging Democracies," *The Journal of Politics* 71 (2009): 1448–1466.

Rather than treating the constitutional requirement to hold the election within sixty days in the context of the preservation of the country to avoid further implosion, the IEBC and the government decided to stick to the sixty-day time limit even if it would have a self-destructive result. To preserve and defend the country and its Constitution, President Uhuru Kenyatta and opposition leader Raila Odinga could have led their elected party members into Parliament and together agreed to amend the 2010 Constitution by extending the timeline within which a repeat election under Article 140(3) of the Constitution must be held. This would also have given MPs from all political parties, including independents, an opportunity to consider the necessary amendments to various election laws that may be necessary to allow for a free, fair, and credible election and to vote on them.

Indeed, there was precedent for such a united response to changing the Constitution and election laws in a moment of crisis in Kenya. In 2008, after post-election violence, Parliament sat late into the night of March 18th as Members from all political parties debated and passed an amendment to the Constitution to create the position of prime minister, and the National Accord and Reconciliation Bill. Mwai Kibaki, the incumbent at the time attended the debate not as president, but as a Member of Parliament, in a gesture that suggested the thawing of relations with the opposition after he had refused to concede defeat. Also in attendance was Raila Odinga, in what was an atmosphere of reconciliation, as he and Kibaki in the nationally televised proceedings pleaded with Kenyans to rebuild the country. Members of Parliament on the government side crossed the floor to sit with their colleagues on the opposition side and vice versa. It was this unity of purpose together with pressure from Kenyans that eventually led to the enactment of the 2010 Constitution two years later.

A major hurdle that the National Accord and Reconciliation Bill faced was that it created the office of the prime minister, yet the Kenyan Constitution at the time did not recognize such an office. This office was therefore created notwithstanding its obvious constitutional inconsistency. In support of this temporary deviation from the Constitution, then Justice and Constitutional Affairs Minister Martha Karua cited Tanzanian legal scholar Paschal Miyho to the effect that "the law is an ass and an idiot. We have to flog it to make it work for us."[80] Karua acknowledged the bill was not a good legal precedent but that it was required by what she termed "absolute political necessity." In making the case to Parliament that evening, she argued that Kenya had a choice to overcome the civil unrest unleashed by post-election violence through the

[80] Kenya National Assembly Official Record (Hansard), March 18, 2008, https://books.google.com/books?id=G7K8uR4f2lMC&pg=PP1&lpg=PP1&dq=national+assembly+of+kenya+hansard+of+18+march+2008&source=bl&ots=qH4vF9_XxP&sig=EhZ6rxKdH-QMNFBOmF2mzBUOVcE&hl=en&sa=X&ved=0ahUKEwju4POnn5fZAhUERKoKHfgxATUQ6AEISzAJ#v=onepage&q=national%20assembly%20of%20kenya%20hansard%20of%2018%20march%202008&f=false.

use of force, but that such violence would hardly remove the "bitterness and hate from peoples' hearts."[81]

In early 2018, the constitutional crisis in Kenya continued with the opposition candidate who boycotted the repeat presidential elections of 2018 having sworn in himself as the "Peoples President," and the government embarked on a repressive streak reminiscent of the days of authoritarian one-party rule. In March 2018, the crisis seemed to abate following rapprochement between President Uhuru Kenyatta, and Raila Odinga, the opposition presidential candidate who had sworn in himself as President about two months before.

Another country that has experienced a constitutional crisis involving the continuity of constitutional government arising from long periods of absence of the president from the country is Nigeria. This crisis arose because the actors involved believed that adherence to a particular interpretation of the Constitution was necessary. The uncertainty created by the absence of a formal transfer of power to the vice president meant that "many crucial aspects of state power and national interest remain[ed] in abeyance."[82] In the latest crisis, current president Muhammadu Buhari was absent from the country for 103 days, raising questions of his fitness to rule when the country was experiencing the resurgence of militancy against oil installations in the Niger Delta, a struggling economy, and a humanitarian crisis caused by the destabilization caused by Boko Haram in the northeast of the country that has resulted in close to 1.8 million people being internally displaced. President Buhari's absence was not regarded as much a constitutional crisis as the absence just a few short years before had been, when President Umaru Yar'Adua was absent from the country for a seventy-nine-day period while seeking medical attention abroad.[83] His family and close associates denied access to the president and did not disclose truthful information about his health to the public. The resulting uncertainty about whether the vice president at the time, Jonathan Goodluck, was acting as president exacerbated the sense that there was a power-vacuum, that was thought likely to lead to a possible military takeover and instability. Yar'Adua's absence from the country was seen by some as setting up the country of 140 million people to be managed by proxy and telephone

---

[81] This dilemma of a strict constitutional timeline within which the repeat election must be held, reminds me of Justice Robert Jackson of the United States Supreme Court when in dissenting in a 1949 case, he noted that the Constitution is not a suicide pact. He called on his colleagues in the majority to temper their doctrinaire approach with some practical wisdom. For him, the choice was not simply or merely between liberty and order, but rather liberty with order, and anarchy without either.

[82] "What the Constitution Says on the Prolonged Absence of the President," *HG.org*, https://www.hg.org/ article.asp?id=18122 (last accessed, April 5, 2018).

[83] In the view of some commentators, the Twenty-Fifth Amendment to the United States Constitution attempts to acknowledge the possibility of long absences of the president from the country. Some scholars such as Charles Black once suggested that such absences of the president from Washington, DC, rather than outside the country as in the Nigeria case, would be an impeachable offense. See Charles L. Black, *Impeachment: A Handbook* (New Haven, CT: Yale University Press, 1974).

conversations from his hospital bed in Saudi Arabia.[84] The crisis was exacerbated by at least four factors. First, when the crisis arose, the Nigerian federal cabinet defied a judicial order[85] that they perform their duties under the Constitution to decide if the president was capable of discharging the functions of the office.[86]

Second, Section 145 of the Nigerian Constitution was regarded as requiring President Yar'Adua to formally write a letter to the president of the Senate and the speaker of the House of Representatives indicating his inability to discharge the functions of his office so that the National Assembly could then temporarily transfer power to the vice president, but Yar'Adua did not do so.[87] Third, the National Assembly together with all State governors in the country only declared Jonathan Goodluck as acting president after the United States, France, Britain, and the EU issued a joint statement encouraging Nigeria to "address the current situation through appropriate democratic institutions."[88]

The fourth reason is more complex. After Yar'Adua secretly returned from medical treatment, then United States Assistant Secretary of State for African Affairs Johnnie Carson noted that "Nigeria needs a strong, healthy, and effective leader to ensure the stability of the country and to manage Nigeria's many political, economic and security challenges." The United States argued that President Yar'Adua's health remained fragile and that he therefore would be "unable to fulfill the demands of his office."[89] Yar'Adua's absence contributed to the constitutional crisis not merely because of the United States's active involvement that suggested its preference for an acting president. Instead, it was the fact that someone from the south of Nigeria would become the acting president in place of the elected but ill president, from the north of Nigeria. The effect of having an acting president from the south was widely regarded as inconsistent with an understanding that it was the turn of a northerner to hold the presidency for eight years in the informal rotation of the presidency between the north and the south.[90]

---

[84] Reuben Abati, "Who Is in Charge of Nigeria?," *The Guardian*, November 29, 2009.

[85] Adam Nossiter, "Nigerian Parliament Names Acting President," *New York Times*, February 9, 2010, http://www.nytimes.com/2010/02/10/world/africa/10nigeria.html.

[86] "Nigeria Cabinet Told to Rule on Sick President Yar'Adua," *BBC News*, January 22, 2010, http://news.bbc.co.uk/2/hi/africa/8474669.stm.

[87] Section 145 of the Nigerian Constitution provides "Whenever the President transmits to the President of the Senate and the Speaker of the House of Representatives a written declaration that he is proceeding on vacation or that he is otherwise unable to discharge the functions of his office, until he transmits to them a written declaration to the contrary such functions shall be discharged by the Vice-President as Acting President."

[88] Funmi Fevide-John, "Nigeria's Constitutional Crisis and U.S. Interference," *Pambazuka News*, March 4, 2010, https://www.pambazuka.org/governance/nigerias-constitutional-crisis-and-us-interference.

[89] Ibid. Yar'Adua's return was not publicly announced in advance to prevent those opposed to his continued to be President an opportunity to make arrangements to prevent him from returning back into the country." See Sani Tukur, "Why dying Yar'Adua was sneaked into Nigeria without Jonathan's knowledge—Tanko Yakasai," *The Premium Times*, November 22, 2013 available at https://www.premiumtimesng.com/news/150148-exclusive-why-dying-yaradua-was-sneaked-into-nigeria-without-jonathans-knowledge-tanko-yakasai.html (last accessed, May 10, 2018).

[90] I use the term north and south here in general terms. Nigeria has six geopolitical regions or zones. These are the South–east; South–South; South–west; North–east; North–west and North–Central.

In short, Nigeria faced a question of governing authority as a result of the president's prolonged absence. The constitutional crisis arose because the Senate, the country's courts, and the attorney general did not believe that the absence of the president required them to formally notify the National Assembly of his absence or that his absence indicated he was incapable of running the affairs of the country. Leaders from northern Nigeria feared if Yar'Adua temporarily relinquished power, the acting President would decline to hand power back to him after he recovered and returned to the country. Unable to satisfactorily respond to their critics that there was a lacuna in the leadership of the country, the European Union and the United States prompted the government to signal that the vice president was in charge in the absence of the president. This in turn triggered concerns that Nigeria's external partners were tipping the balance of power in favor of the south and against the north.

Conclusion

A common thread through the examples of the first two types of constitutional crisis discussed in this chapter is that they all relate to mobilization of economically and politically disenfranchised and aggrieved individuals in riots, protests, and civil disturbances that challenge and rebel against authoritarian and repressive regimes. It is not surprising that "repression breeds rebellion, protests and organized movements"[91] against autocratic political systems in which elites loot and share public resources among themselves and their supporters. In addition, particularly in unstable countries, civilian governments remain vulnerable to military takeovers and sometimes to ragtag armies.

From this perspective, it is highly unlikely that political pluralism in itself is what has created unstable political formations in Africa. Since the 1990s constitutions have inaugurated competitive politics through elections. This has however not guaranteed the establishment of stable party politics and has often raised the question whether constitutional governance can withstand the resurgence of authoritarianism that accompanied the inauguration of competitive politics in Africa.[92] Three major observations arise from the constitutional crisis analyzed in this chapter.

First, it is difficult to conclude that the contentious politics unleashed by political pluralism are incapable of being managed through constitutional processes and mechanisms,

---

[91] Rollin F. Tusalem, "Democracies, Autocracies and Political Stability," *International Social Science Review* 90, no. 1 (2015): 1, also citing Mark Irving Lichbach, "Deterrence or Escalation? The Puzzle of Aggregate Studies of Repression and Dissent," *Journal of Conflict Resolution* 31 (1987): 266–297 to the effect that an "increase in a government's repression of non-violent activity may reduce the level of non-violent activities of opposition groups but it may increase the level of violent activities against the state. This results because the relative costs of non-violent activities to the opposition groups has been raised," Tusalem, 34. Also citing James Scott, *Weapons of the Weak: Everyday Forms of Peasant Resistance* (1987) (to the effect that "in societies where power is centralized in the hands of the few, the weak and disenfranchised will find a way to challenge or supplant the oppressiveness and exclusivity of the system," Tuaslem., 32.

[92] See for example, Richard Joseph, "Dilemmas of Democracy and State Power in Africa," *Brookings*, January 2016, https://www.brookings.edu/opinions/dilemmas-of-democracy-and-state-power-in-africa/.

when one considers the repressive practices of incumbents and their control of legislatures, judiciaries, and all the mechanisms of government. This control gives incumbents the ability to ignore or subvert constitutional rules and processes, particularly when these excesses are tolerated and even excused by regional or Western countries who have may have leverage to change the course of events, as happened quite exceptionally in Cote d'Ivoire in 2010–2011 where President Gbabgo was captured and sent to The Hague to face international criminal charges after refusing to concede electoral defeat. The subversion of constitutional rules and processes combined with repressive practices by authoritarian regimes exacerbates the likelihood of contentious politics becoming violent and significantly disrupting not only the political system set up by the Constitution, but the economy and society at large. Civil war and long periods of political unrest and uncertainty triggered by such protests in turn are used by authoritarian regimes and militaries to justify their continued control of the state. In particular, this chapter has shown that term-limit violations in Africa are highly correlated with constitutional and political crisis. Given the centrality of the presidency, term-limited incumbents and military leaders do not see the uncertainty that comes with elections as the way to decide who the next president will be.[93]

Second, given that many of the constitutional crises analyzed in this chapter involve authoritarian regimes seeking to remain in control, the protests that are generated in response are also directed at the manner in which those excluded from state power are disfranchised economically. While an authoritarian government engages in repressive practices to control the state and its resources, groups protest because they may be worse off if they "fail to collectively mobilize" and protest.[94] Not only therefore do protests target repressive state practices, they also target the kind of massive youth unemployment that characterizes many African countries, the pilfering of state resources by the elite connected to the state, the rising prices of food and other necessities of life, and the general exclusion of disfavored ethnic groups or regions from state resources by the government of the day. That economic exclusion in Africa is a source of instability is consistent with research showing that countries in which the bottom billion of the world's population live—such as those in sub-Saharan Africa—are much more prone to insurgency and civil war than the rest of the world.[95] Hence, although free, fair, and credible elections can provide a peaceful path to seeking political power and could lead those contesting for

---

[93] See Nic Cheeseman, "African Elections as Vehicles of Change," *Journal of Democracy* 21 (2010): 143, arguing that "decisions to extend tenure of an incumbent in Africa are motivated by the fear of going through the ... unsettling act of choosing a new leader.... this is a huge hurdle for parties in Africa, because the centrality of the executive to political life and the low institutionalization of political parties tend to magnify the stakes of succession politics ... moreover, many unregulated successions deteriorate into political crises and violence."

[94] Paul D. Almeida, "The Role of Threats in Popular Mobilization in Central America," in *Social Movement Dynamics: New Perspectives on Theory and Research from Latin America*, ed. Federico M. Rossi and Marisa Von Bülow (Burlington, VT: Ashgate, 2015), 119.

[95] Paul Collier, *The Bottom Billion* (New York: Oxford University Press, 2017).

power to refrain from violence between election cycles, elites unwilling to concede electoral defeat are likely to spark the types of political and constitutional crisis discussed in this chapter.[96]

Finally, the constitutional crises discussed in this chapter show the importance of domestic, regional, and international factors in their resolution. Cote D'Ivoire in 2010–11 provides the best example of how a transnational network of actors played a role in resolving the crisis in favor of an opposition candidate who had won an election but had been denied the victory by an intransigent incumbent. However, regional and international actors are often reluctant to get involved in resolving intractable conflicts generating the constitutional and political crisis that arise when constitutional commitments to channel conflict into everyday politics fail. Yet it is precisely these types of crisis that are least likely to be solved only through negotiation. For this reason, authoritarian regimes that do not want to give up power may opt to improve their military capabilities in order to settle things decisively on the battlefield where there is no prospect of outside help from the outside. This is the sobering reality when elites are not committed to constitutional rules and processes to resolve conflicts amongst themselves. The news from Africa is not all bad news. There are examples of recent peaceful transfers of power that also included party alternations in Ghana, Nigeria, and Liberia. These hopeful examples are however largely the exception to the rule.

---

[96] S.P. Harish and Andrew T. Little, "The Political Violence Cycle," *American Political Science Review* 111 (2017): 237–255.

20 Stealth Authoritarianism in Turkey
Ozan O. Varol

IT WAS 1996. I was fifteen years old, living in my native city of Istanbul and watching television. My ears perked up at a surprisingly frank remark by a politician. During a talk show, the mayor of Istanbul compared democracy to a streetcar: "You ride it until you get to your destination," he said, "and then you step off."

It took more than two decades, but the mayor himself would make good on this prediction. His name was Recep Tayyip Erdoğan. Today he is the president of Turkey—a country that has stepped off the streetcar of democracy under his leadership.

Turkey's plunge into dictatorship didn't happen overnight. There was no dramatic break from the democratic past, no military coup to enforce a violent transition to tyranny, no single measure significant enough to generate widespread domestic or global resistance. Erdoğan relied, not on an army of soldiers, but a cabal of legal consultants to create a well-oiled authoritarian machine.

In a prior article,[1] I used the phrase "stealth authoritarianism" to refer to the use by authoritarians or would-be authoritarians of seemingly legitimate legal mechanisms for anti-democratic ends. For example, instead of jailing journalists or shutting down media outlets, modern authoritarians sue them for libel, which raises the costs of critical commentary. Rather than imprisoning political opponents without due process, they prosecute them for violations of nonpolitical criminal laws. They employ seemingly legitimate

---

[1] Ozan O. Varol, "Stealth Authoritarianism," *Iowa Law Review* 100 (May 2015): 1673–1742.

and neutral electoral laws, frequently enacted for the purported purpose of eliminating electoral fraud or promoting political stability, to create systematic advantages for themselves and raise the costs to the opposition of dethroning them. Often with the backing of international organizations, they adopt surveillance laws and institutions with the purported purpose of combatting organized crime and terrorism, but use those laws to blackmail or discredit political opponents. They rely on judicial review, not as a check on their power, but to consolidate power. To shape perceptions and deflect attention from anti-democratic practices, they frequently enact democratic reforms and invoke rule-of-law rhetoric.

These practices permit the incumbents to retain their seats even in the face of changing political preferences by the electorate. That, in turn, undermines a core component of democracy: competitive, multiparty elections and the resulting alternation in government power.

These practices also create a significant discordance between appearance and reality by concealing anti-democratic practices under the mask of law. In the modern era, authoritarian wolves rarely appear as wolves. They are now clad, at least in part, in sheep's clothing.

This chapter analyzes how the current government of Turkey, under the leadership of Recep Tayyip Erdoğan, used stealth authoritarian practices to neutralize checks on government power and weaken the ability of political opponents to meaningfully challenge the regime.

The chapter begins with a brief background on Turkey. Following that background, I examine the various means used by Erdoğan to consolidate power and silence his opponents, including the use of the legal system to erode free speech, selective prosecution of dissidents for nonpolitical crimes, and the employment of democratic rhetoric to detract from an authoritarian agenda. The chapter then surveys the formal changes that have been made to Turkey's constitution that have brought institutions that were supposed to check the government within the government's control. The chapter concludes with a discussion of the 2016 coup attempt and its aftermath, an event that set the stage for the creation of an all-powerful executive branch with Erdoğan at its helm.

Background

Turkey, a sprawling country roughly twice the size of Germany, sits at the crossroads between Europe, Asia, and the Middle East. Although Turkey is not a member of the European Union (a bitter point for many Turks), it has been a NATO member since 1952 and a critical Western ally. Southern Turkey is home to the American airbase in Incirlik, from which combat operations in Afghanistan, Iraq, and beyond have been launched.

Turkey boasts the second largest military in NATO, after the United States. Mandatory for all men over the age of eighteen, military service is viewed as a rite of passage. Historically, many, but certainly not all, Turks have thought of themselves as "an army nation" (*asker millet*), reflecting the perception that the army and the nation are bound together in a symbiotic relationship.

According to official figures, Muslims make up 99 percent of Turkey's population. Unlike many other majority-Muslim countries, Turkey has espoused secularism since its establishment in 1923. The Turkish word for secularism (*laik*) and the Turkish conception of secularism were adopted from their French counterparts (*laïcité*). Historically, Turkish secularism, championed by the country's elite, demanded a strict exclusion of religion from the public domain and restrictions on religious freedom, including a now-lifted ban on the wearing of Islamic headscarves in educational institutions.

Before Erdoğan's rise to power, Turkey's democratic record was far from perfect. The Turkish Armed Forces had staged four coups, forced political leaders to resign, and acted as a de facto, if not de jure, fourth branch of the Turkish government.[2] The rights of ethnic and religious minorities were underenforced. The lack of rights enforcement was particularly acute with respect to the Kurds, who are Turkey's largest ethnic minority. Throughout Turkish history, they were marginalized and denied the right to education and media in their own language.[3] Kurdish political parties were also dissolved by the Constitutional Court almost as quickly as they were established. The primary ground for dissolution was supporting separatist activities contrary to "the State's territorial and national integrity," which is one of the grounds listed in the 1982 Constitution for party banning. Political parties with a religious orientation were also repeatedly banned by the Constitutional Court on the basis that they advocated a change in the secular character of the regime.

Despite these significant deficiencies in Turkish democracy, elections were free and fair. Press freedom was largely protected, as private media outlets freely criticized incumbent politicians with impunity. Government power rotated frequently between different political parties. Most prime ministers in modern Turkish history served only a handful of years before they were replaced. This frequent alternation of government power, indicative of a functioning democracy, also generated problems: fragile coalition governments struggled to maintain continuity and stability, creating frequent power vacuums, which in turn, prompted interventions by the military. The weakness of the governments in power also negatively affected the Turkish economy, culminating in a full-blown financial crisis in 2001.

---

[2] Ozan O. Varol, "The Turkish 'Model' of Civil-Military Relations," *International Journal of Constitutional Law* 11 (2013): 727–750, 730.

[3] Ozan O. Varol, "Alien Citizens: Kurds and Citizenship in the Turkish Constitution," *Virginia Journal of International Law* (forthcoming 2018).

The country's political and constitutional dynamics began to change with the ascension to power in 2002 of the Justice and Development Party (Adalet ve Kalkinma Partisi) (AKP).[4] Established in 2001 by the charismatic Recep Tayyip Erdoğan—the current president of Turkey—AKP was the antithesis of the Turkish secular elite.[5] The party was formed as an offshoot of the Welfare Party (Refah Partisi) and the Virtue Party (Fazilet Partisi), both of which had been dissolved by the Turkish Constitutional Court for advocating an Islamic change in the secular regime of the Turkish Republic.[6]

AKP touted itself as a mainstream conservative party that represented a rising rural, pious middle class that challenged the status quo and the secular elite that championed it. But unlike its predecessors, AKP claimed to support secularism. The party also stood for religious freedom, a liberal market economy, and Turkish membership in the European Union. AKP's mission to improve the ailing Turkish economy resonated with large segments of the public far beyond its core constituency. Shortly after AKP took office, the country experienced several years of rapid economic growth, which bolstered AKP's popularity.

AKP's message also initially appealed to segments of the population that considered themselves progressives. Many progressives got on board with AKP's mission to broaden political participation, bolster the rights of ethnic and religious minorities, and curb the power of the military.

It became clear relatively quickly that AKP's goal wasn't to eliminate or reform these institutions. Rather, it was to bring them under its control and consolidate power in AKP's leader, Erdoğan, who, over time, achieved a cult of personality that rivals that of the country's deeply revered founder, Mustafa Kemal Ataturk. The AKP achieved this outcome by implementing a number of legal and constitutional measures to curb individual rights, decrease dissent, and make it prohibitively difficult for the opposition to mount challenges against it.

Free Speech

With AKP in control of the government, free speech quickly came under attack. When Erdoğan first assumed power, simply shutting down media companies or jailing journalists would have been too crass and obvious. Instead, he lawyered up—and filed hundreds of libel lawsuits against his critics.

Libel lawsuits can raise the costs of criticism by exposing the speaker to expensive legal fees. Such exposure can create a "chilling effect" on speech, and thus lead to

---

[4] Varol, "Turkish 'Model,'" 744–745.
[5] Ibid.
[6] Ibid.

self-censorship of critical commentary,[7] undermining the public's ability to observe the incumbent politician's behavior and reward or punish incumbent behavior accordingly. As prime minister, Erdoğan sued "perhaps hundreds of private individuals for insulting him . . . [including] a student theater troupe that does skits wearing long black hippie wigs; unemployed siblings who posted a song about Mr. Erdoğan on the Internet; and a British teacher-cum-anti-Iraq war activist-cum-fortune teller, who made a collage showing Mr. Erdoğan's head on a dog."[8]

Erdoğan's enthusiasm for silencing his critics extended beyond satirists and activists to ensnare members of the media who did not toe the government line. For example, in July 2013, prominent journalist Ahmet Altan was fined 2,800 euros for insulting Erdoğan in an article.[9] In another case, Erdoğan sued columnist Mahir Zeynalov for his Twitter posts about a corruption investigation that targeted several high-ranking government officials in Turkey in December 2013.[10] In May 2014, another prominent journalist was sued for waging a "psychological campaign" to defame Erdoğan on Twitter.[11] The constant onslaught of litigation forced journalists to burn through funds they didn't have and promoted widespread self-censorship.

Turkey also deployed other existing laws against journalists with "disturbing frequency," including ones that prohibit "'breaching the confidentiality of an investigation' and 'influencing a fair trial'" through news coverage."[12] Although there are no official numbers, Turkish press groups report that thousands of criminal prosecutions against journalists were pending by the end of 2011.[13] Many of these laws were carefully constructed to comport with the free speech provisions in Article 10 of the European

---

[7] Dyuldin v. Russia, App. No. 25968/02 ¶ 43 (European Court of Human Rights July 31, 2007), http://hudoc.echr.coe.int/sites/eng/pages/search.aspx?i=001-82038. As the European Court of Human Rights has explained:

> If all State officials were allowed to sue in defamation in connection with any statement critical of administration of State affairs . . . journalists would be inundated with lawsuits. Not only would that result in an excessive and disproportionate burden being placed on the media, straining their resources and involving them in endless litigation, it would also inevitably have a chilling effect on the press in the performance of its task of purveyor of information and public watchdog.

Ibid.

[8] Marc Champion, "Call the Prime Minister a Turkey, Get Sued," *Wall Street Journal*, June 7, 2011, http://www.wsj.com/articles/SB10001424052702304563104576357411896226774.

[9] Ekin Karaca, "Journalist Ahmet Altan Receives 11 Months of Prison," *Bianet*, July 18, 2013, http://bianet.org/english/freedom-of-expression/148576-journalist-ahmet-altan-receives-11-months-of-prison.

[10] Tim Arango, "In Scandal, Turkey's Leaders May Be Losing Their Tight Grip on News Media," *New York Times*, January 11, 2014, http://www.nytimes.com/2014/01/12/world/europe/in-scandal-turkeys-leaders-may-be-losing-their-tight-grip-on-news-media.html.

[11] "Erdoğan Sues Journalist for Retweeting Critical Posts," *Today's Zaman* (May 13, 2014, 10:29 PM), http://www.todayszaman.com/news-347728-erdogan-sues-journalist-for-retweeting-critical-posts.html.

[12] Committee to Protect Journalists, "Turkey's Press Freedom Crisis," October 2012, http://cpj.org/reports/Turkey2012.English.pdf.

[13] Ibid.

Convention on Human Rights, which permits limitations on free speech "for the protection of the reputation or rights of others, for preventing the disclosure of information received in confidence, or for maintaining the authority and impartiality of the judiciary."[14]

In July 2012, in response to European pressure, the Turkish government made largely cosmetic changes to these laws but retains an extensive arsenal of libel laws to use as sticks against criticism and dissent.[15] That arsenal, and its effects on media coverage, were on full display during the widespread protests against the incumbent government in summer 2013. On June 7, 2013, at the height of the protests, six popular mainstream newspapers published identical headlines, all trumpeting Erdoğan's commitment to democracy.[16]

After Erdoğan relinquished the prime minister position and became president, civil suits became criminal ones. Prosecutors filed thousands of cases for the crime of insulting the president. In one infamous example, a doctor was charged with a criminal offense for depicting Erdoğan as Gollum from the *Lord of the Rings*. Although Gollum should have been the one to take offense, the judge took the allegations of defamation seriously, even ordering expert testimony on whether Gollum was good or evil.

Selective Prosecutions of Political Opponents for Nonpolitical Crimes

In addition to the decay of free speech, the ranks of Erdoğan's political opponents were decimated by seemingly legal measures. Erdoğan's rule can be summed by the motto attributed to various Latin American rulers: "For my friends, everything, for my enemies, the law." Throughout his term, Erdoğan showered his inner circle with gifts, promotions, and lavish government contracts. But his political enemies found themselves the target of criminal prosecutions for nonpolitical crimes.

These prosecutions involved selective, though often legally accurate, application of the existing criminal laws that didn't overtly concern political opposition, such as tax evasion, fraud, and money laundering. The prosecutions were often supported with sufficient evidence of guilt, which made it more difficult to detect whether the motive for the prosecution is political.

A nonpolitical prosecution of a dissident reduces the costs associated with overt repression, which might draw domestic and international opprobrium. It also allows the regime to portray the prosecution to domestic and global audiences as an application of the rule of law. The legitimacy provided by a nonpolitical prosecution increases

---

[14] "Convention for the Protection of Human Rights and Fundamental Freedoms," November 4, 1950. United Nations Treaty Series 213, 221: art. 10.2.

[15] Committee to Protect Journalists, "Turkey's Press Freedom Crisis."

[16] Sibel Utku Bila, "Young Turks Use 'Disproportionate Wit' to Shake Up Erdogan," *Al-Monitor*, June 9, 2013, http://www.al-monitor.com/pulse/originals/2013/06/turkey-protests-humor-resistance.html.

where the conviction is blessed by a supranational arbiter, such as the European Court of Human Rights.

A good example is the prosecution of Sevan Nişanyan, a vocal critic of Erdoğan. Nişanyan was sentenced to more than sixteen years in prison for violating various building codes. The convictions may have been legally accurate, but in Turkey, illegal construction is the norm, not the exception. Erdoğan's own thousand-room presidential palace was constructed in violation of numerous zoning laws and court decisions. Nişanyan's infractions would likely have escaped notice, were it not for his political activism.

Newspapers and television stations critical of the government also found themselves the target of tax audits and inspections, an increasingly potent tool for punishing political dissidents. Most media companies in Turkey are subsidiaries of larger corporations, which in turn allows the government to award government contracts to corporations with loyal media subsidiaries and to impose tax fines on corporations with dissident media subsidiaries.[17]

For example, a $2.5 billion tax fine was levied in 2009 against the largest media company, Dogan Media Group, a few months after Prime Minister Erdoğan asked the Turkish public to boycott its newspapers for publishing critical commentary.[18] Although the fine was reduced to approximately $600 million, the Group was forced to downsize by selling two of the country's largest newspapers and its main television station.[19]

Turkey's largest company, the Koc Group, also became the subject of tax audits after a hotel owned by the Koc Group offered refuge to protesters escaping from tear and pepper gas during protests in summer 2013.[20] In response, Prime Minister Erdoğan accused Koc Group of aiding and abetting unlawful activities.[21] A few weeks thereafter, the Ministry of Finance raided the three major energy-sector companies of Koc Group to conduct financial audits.[22] Although the Ministry of Finance branded the audits as "routine," investors were more skeptical.[23] The day after the raids, all three companies registered losses on the Istanbul stock market, and the Koc Group is estimated to have lost approximately $930 million in one day.[24]

---

[17] Mehul Srivastava et al., "Erdogan's Media Grab Stymies Expansion by Murdoch, Time Warner," *Bloomberg*, March 3, 2014, http://www.bloomberg.com/news/2014-03-03/erdogan-thwarts-murdoch-as-graft-probe-reveals-turkey-media-grab.html.

[18] Kadri Gursel, "Is Audit of Koc Companies Erdogan's Revenge for Gezi Park?," *Al-Monitor*, July 29, 2013, http://www.al-monitor.com/pulse/originals/2013/07/koc-audit-raid-turkey-interest-rate-lobby-gezi.html.

[19] Dexter Filkins, "The Deep State," *New Yorker*, March 12, 2012, www.newyorker.com/magazine/2012/03/12/the-deep-state.

[20] Gursel, "Audit of Koc Companies."

[21] Ibid.

[22] Ibid.

[23] Ibid.

[24] Ibid.

Democratic Reforms and Rhetoric

To distract observers from authoritarian practices, Erdoğan frequently reiterated his grand vision of creating an "advanced democracy" in Turkey.[25] He also rebutted criticisms levied at controversial government measures either by citing a constitutional or legal basis for the measure or invoking comparative law and pointing to a democratic country (usually in the West) that has implemented the same measure.

For example, Erdoğan's government instituted a widespread array of democratic reforms after assuming power in 2002. During Erdoğan's term, ethnic and religious minorities in Turkey obtained increased legal and constitutional protections.[26] Many of these measures, however, were cosmetic, and despite increased legal protections on paper, religious and ethnic minorities continue to experience discriminatory treatment by the government.[27] For example, under the AKP's reign, the pro-Kurdish party in the Parliament—called the People's Democratic Party (Halklarin Demokrasi Partisi) (HDP)—came under attack. In May 2016, the Parliament voted to temporarily lift the parliamentary immunity of its members who are under indictment for committing a criminal activity.[28] The joint leaders of HDP, along with numerous other HDP deputies, were then arrested for allegedly supporting the terrorist group PKK, the Kurdistan Workers' Party (Partiya Karkeran Kurdistan).[29] These arrests crippled the functioning of the party, eliminating a source of opposition against Erdoğan's rule.

To an unsuspecting observer, Erdoğan appeared like a Western democrat—and he managed to fool academics, think tanks, the IMF, and other politicians. To them, Erdoğan's Turkey was a miracle: a democracy in a majority-Muslim country. Perhaps it was wishful thinking on the part of the West as much as it was successful PR on Erdoğan's part, but whatever the source, Western politicians were fooled into believing that Turkey was a democratic dream come true.

---

[25] Ayla Albayrak, "Half of Turks Say Erdogan Is Becoming Authoritarian," *Wall Street Journal*, June 17, 2013, http://blogs.wsj.com/emergingeurope/2013/06/17/half-of-turks-say-erdogan-isbecoming-authoritarian/.

[26] Hugh Pope, "Erdoğan's Decade: Has the Justice and Development Party Changed Turkish Politics Forever?," *Cairo Review* (April 2012): 43, 44, http://www.aucegypt.edu/GAPP/CairoReview/Lists/Articles/Attachments/149/CR4-Pope.pdf.

[27] "World Report 2013: Turkey," Human Rights Watch, http://www.hrw.org/world-report/2013/country-chapters/turkey (last accessed on May 10, 2018).

[28] Giriş Tarihi, "'Kokunulmazlik kanunu' Resmi Gazete'de," *Sabah*, June 8, 2016, http://www.sabah.com.tr/gundem/2016/06/08/dokunulmazlik-kanunu-resmi-gazetede.

[29] Ceylan Yeginsu, "Turkish Parliament Approves Stripping Lawmakers of Their Immunity," *New York Times*, May 20, 2016, http://www.nytimes.com/2016/05/21/world/europe/turkey-parliament-immunity-kurds.html?_r=0.

Formal Constitutional Changes

With a focus on the illusion of democracy, Erdoğan's government made constitutional reform a centerpiece of its agenda, with the ultimate goal of replacing the existing constitution with a new civilian constitution. When Erdoğan came to power as prime minister in 2002, the then-existing Constitution was ratified in 1982 following a military coup. The 1982 Constitution was widely viewed as illiberal and a blemish on Turkey's democracy. Erdoğan used the unpopularity of the Constitution to implement numerous changes to curb the power of institutions standing in his way.

Many of the changes to the 1982 Constitution were directed at curbing the constitutional authorities of the military as part of Turkey's accession to the European Union. The 1982 Constitution had institutionalized the Turkish military's role in domestic politics. The National Security Council, established in Turkey's 1961 Constitution, obtained additional powers in the 1982 Constitution. The Council consisted of five military members and five civilians, with the Council's civilian president frequently voting with the military.[30] The Council's decisions covered an extensive array of internal policy matters, including, for example, determining school curricula, regulating broadcasting hours for television stations, outlining the substance of the laws on terror and capital punishment, and determining whether to offer Arabic as an elective in schools.[31] The 1982 Constitution also required the cabinet to give "priority consideration" to the Council's "decisions."

To establish effective civilian control of the military, the amendments to the 1982 Constitution curbed the military's influence on the National Security Council. The military had traditionally used the Council as an institutional avenue for asserting its weight on civilian politics. The amendments increased the number of civilians on the National Security Council, emphasized the Council's advisory role, deprived the Council of its executive powers, and replaced the Council's military Secretary-General with a civilian leader. Under the amendments, the government would no longer give "priority consideration" to the Council's views and would merely assess its "recommendations."

In addition, the military judges serving on the state security courts (Devlet Güvenlik Mahkemeleri)—which had jurisdiction over cases involving crimes against state security—were removed and the courts became entirely civilianized (and were later abolished). The armed forces were also brought under the jurisdiction of the Turkish Court of Accounts (Sayıştay), which is authorized to audit state departments.

In addition to these legal reforms that curbed the military's prerogatives, the military became a target of criminal investigations and charges. Under the Ergenekon and

---

[30] Ersel Aydinli, Nihat Aliz Ozcan, and Dogan Akyaz, "The Turkish Military's March toward Europe," *Foreign Affairs* 85, no. 1 (January 2006): 82.

[31] Umit Cizre Sakallioglu, "The Anatomy of the Turkish Military's Political Autonomy," *Comparative Politics* 29, no. 2 (January 1997): 158.

Sledgehammer prosecutions—which alleged a conspiracy to overthrow the AKP government by a coup—scores of high-ranking military officers were arrested and imprisoned. The clash between the AKP government and the military culminated in the mass resignation of Turkey's military high command in late July 2011. The resignations, according to Turkish columnist Yavuz Baydar, represented a "new phase, a sharp curve towards pushing the military to adapt to the current changes in Turkey" and "showed how toothless the military has become compared to the civilian authority."[32] Because the military leaders chose to resign rather than dig in, Henri Barkey described the resignations as "the day the military threw in the towel."[33]

In addition to amendments directed to curbing the power of the military, Erdoğan also implemented several constitutional amendment packages to bolster the powers of the presidency and curb those of other checking institutions, including the judiciary.

The first package was adopted by a referendum in 2007 and amended, among others, several provisions of the Constitution relating to the presidency. Although the 1982 Constitution had bolstered the powers of the president, the presidency remained a largely ceremonial, nonpolitical office. The president could not hold a party affiliation and was elected by the Parliament.

The 2007 amendments altered the election procedures for the presidency, authorizing the election of the president by popular vote, rather than by the Parliament. Then-prime minister Erdoğan himself advocated for this change, arguing that, as one holding a political position, the president should be elected by the public. This change elevated the status of the president, who could now claim a popular mandate to push his views of public policy.

A second set of amendments arrived in September 2010, in a referendum symbolically held exactly thirty years from the date of the 1980 coup. The amendments, according to the AKP, were intended to accelerate Turkey's accession process to the European Union and to democratize the anti-democratic 1982 Constitution. The amendments proposed a sweeping set of reforms. Among other things, the AKP proposed empowering Parliament to pass affirmative-action laws for women, children, veterans, and the elderly; expand the constitutional right to privacy; and prohibit military courts from trying civilians except during wartime.

The 2010 Amendments also presented Erdoğan with a way to target the judiciary in a seemingly legitimate way. Tucked into the broader 2010 amendment package were provisions that altered the structure of the Turkish Constitutional Court and the Supreme Council of Judges and Prosecutors, which is empowered to make judicial and prosecutorial appointments. The Turkish Constitutional Court had proved to be a formidable counter-majoritarian force against AKP's legal reform agenda. For example, in 2008,

---

[32] Gul Tuysuz and Liz Sly, "For Turkish Military, A Telling Change," *Washington Post*, July 31, 2011.
[33] Ibid.

the Constitutional Court voted for AKP's dissolution six to five—one vote short of the seven-vote supermajority required to dissolve a political party. Although AKP escaped dissolution by a slim margin, the Court stripped the party of half of its public funding and issued a "serious warning" to the party to conform its agenda to the Republic's secular principles. The Court also struck down a constitutional amendment—dubbed the "Headscarf Amendment"—that would have permitted the wearing of Islamic headscarves in educational institutions.[34]

The provisions in the 2010 amendment package would expand the size of the Constitutional Court and the Supreme Council of Judges and Prosecutors, permitting the government to pack them with members favorable to its ideology. The changes were purportedly proposed, however, to decrease the influence of what the incumbent government viewed as an activist constitutional court that served as a guardian of the old political order and secular elites.

The 2010 referendum exacerbated already existing divides within Turkish society. The supporters of the amendments underscored the importance of the reform package to Turkey's accession to the European Union. The supporters also argued that, with the amendments, both the Constitutional Court and the Supreme Council of Judges and Prosecutors would become more inclusive institutions.

In contrast, the opponents argued that the reforms were democratic window dressing. They contended that the reforms would not eradicate or weaken anti-democratic institutions, but simply bring them within the AKP's control. In a resounding victory for the AKP, the Turkish voters approved the amendment package by 58 percent of the vote. Although the amendment package included changes to twenty-six different provisions, the referendum required the voters to accept or reject the entire package, with no possibility of voting on individual amendments. In the name of democratizing and diversifying the Court, Erdoğan was thus able to pack it with ideologues. My coauthors and I demonstrated empirically that the changes to the Court's structure shifted the ideology of the Court in a conservative direction.[35] The shift is increasing in magnitude over time.

Toward a Presidential System

Riding on the coattails of the 2010 referendum victory, Erdoğan pushed forward with more extensive constitutional changes. The ultimate goal, made clear in campaign promises in the lead-up to the 2011 parliamentary elections, was to discard the existing Constitution and rewrite it from scratch. The Turkish Constitution, like most other constitutions, describes only how it may be amended, but contains no procedures for

---

[34] Anayasa Mahkemesi [Constitutional Court], Decision of October 22, 2008, Esas No. 2008/16, Karar No. 2008/116 (Turk.).

[35] Ozan Varol, Lucia Dallapellegrina, and Nuno M. Garoupa, "An Empirical Analysis of Judicial Transformation in Turkey," *American Journal of Comparative Law* 65 (2017): 187–216.

its total replacement. If a constitutional amendment is approved by two-thirds of the Parliament (367 votes), the amendment becomes effective immediately, without a popular referendum. Alternatively, if the amendment obtains approval only from three-fifths of the Parliament (330 votes), the amendment must be submitted to a popular referendum before it becomes effective.

The 2011 parliamentary elections landed the AKP a total of 326 seats in the 550-seat Parliament—four seats short of the supermajority that the party needed to submit a new Constitution to a referendum. The AKP thus enlisted the assistance of other political parties in the constitution-making process. In October 2011, the AKP-led Parliament authorized a Constitutional Conciliation Commission, comprising three members from each of the four major parties in the Parliament, to draft a new Constitution.

In the constitutional negotiations, a proposed transition to a presidential system assumed center stage. According to the AKP, a strong, "American-style" president was necessary to bring much-needed stability to Turkey and eliminate the problems that the political system suffered in the past from weak coalition governments.

The opposition argued that this asserted reason was a fig leaf. At the time, then-prime minister Erdoğan was serving his third, and under his party's rules, final term as prime minister. The opposition believed—correctly, it turned out—that Erdoğan would run for president, providing him a strong incentive to bolster the powers of the office he would soon occupy.

Although the Constitutional Conciliation Commission reached consensus on numerous provisions, the AKP's insistence on a presidential system was at least partially responsible for derailing the constitution-making process. The executive proposed by the AKP had sweeping powers and resembled the Russian, not the American, model. Under the AKP proposal, the president was empowered to veto legislation, issue executive orders that have the force of law on all "subjects necessary to execute the laws," unilaterally appoint and remove all cabinet members and heads of all administrative agencies, unilaterally appoint and remove all university rectors, and unilaterally appoint half of the members of the Constitutional Court, the Council of State (Turkey's highest administrative court), the Supreme Board of Judges and Prosecutors, and the Higher Education Council. The president was also authorized to declare martial law (*sıkıyönetim*) and "a state of exception" (*olağanüstü hâl*), allowing the curtailment of individual rights and liberties. Under the AKP's proposal, the executive could not be removed by the Parliament through a no-confidence motion, but could only be impeached upon the commission of a crime.

The proposal for a strong president without adequate checks and balances troubled many within Turkish society. Indeed, the provisions in the proposal allowing the president to declare a "state of exception" replicated the authoritarian components of the 1982 Constitution that the new draft ostensibly sought to transform. In addition, the problem of weak coalition governments—which the AKP's presidentialism proposal sought to rectify—had largely faded into the past under AKP's stable one-party rule since the early 2000s.

Calls for a new constitution following the November 2015 election once again brought the debate over presidentialism to the political fore. Selahattin Demirtaş, the Co-Chair of the Peoples' Democratic Party (Halkların Demokratik Partisi) (HDP), was quick to react. Although he acknowledged the need for a new, more liberal Constitution, he argued that the AKP's proposed system was not a presidential system, but a one-man system, impliedly referring to President Erdoğan.

Despite the attention it generated, the debates over the wisdom of a presidential system were largely a red herring because Turkey was already operating under a de facto presidential system. Though the office of the presidency had remained formally unaltered since Erdoğan became president, he had dramatically expanded his powers through informal means.

Yet Erdoğan continued to push for a formal consolidation of his powers in an all-powerful constitutional office of the president. The boost he needed came from an unlikely source: an attempted military coup that gave him a well-timed crisis.

The July 2016 Coup d'État Attempt

Despite the apparent ease with which Erdoğan had enacted drastic changes in Turkey, all was not well in paradise. While Erdoğan was vacationing in a resort in Marmaris, a tranquil town located on the coast of the Aegean Sea, hundreds of junior military officers took advantage of his absence and began to execute what turned out to be an ill-fated coup attempt. Beginning the evening of Friday, July 15, key bridges and media stations were seized, major roads were blocked, and two dozen F-16 fighters thundered over Istanbul, triggering sonic booms strong enough to shatter windows in nearby buildings. Tanks surrounded the Parliament building in Ankara and opened fire. A news anchor for Turkish Radio and Television was forced to read on live television a statement by the coup-makers. The statement declared, prematurely it turned out, that the government had been toppled, a "peace council" was running the country, and martial law was imposed. As the motive for the coup, the coup-makers cited government corruption, erosion of human rights, and the government's loss of credibility both domestically and globally. "The secular and democratic rule of law has been virtually eliminated," said the visibly anxious news anchor reading the statement under the watchful eye of armed soldiers.

Meanwhile, a defiant Erdoğan appeared on television using FaceTime—an ironic act for a president who has long sought to censor the internet—and called on his supporters to take to the streets and resist the military. The sounds of low-flying jets piloted by the coup-makers were soon met with unscheduled calls to prayer from mosques, beckoning the faithful to heed Erdoğan's call to action. Erdoğan's supporters were quick to respond. Thousands flooded the streets and overwhelmed the coup-makers, who were forced to decide between commencing a bloodbath against a large group of demonstrators and giving up their haphazard plan.

The coup failed with remarkable speed. By early Saturday morning, Erdoğan declared the coup attempt over, framing its failure as a triumph of democracy over anti-democratic factions within the military. The clashes prompted by the coup attempt left hundreds dead, and tens of thousands of people were arrested and detained during an ensuing state of emergency. The blame for the attempted coup fell on estranged military officers associated with Fetullah Gülen, an influential Islamist preacher living in self-exile halfway around the world in Pennsylvania, with a loyal following in Turkey. An alliance of convenience between Gülen and Erdoğan had broken down in recent years, as Erdoğan blamed Gülen's followers within the police and the military for a sweeping corruption investigation against Erdoğan and members of his cabinet in 2013. A clash of ideologies soon turned personal, locking the two men in an endless vendetta.

As coups go, the July 15 attempt will rank among the most incompetent in history. The coup plotters would all fail Coup-Making 101. Although the details remain a mystery, the plotters were among hundreds of officers expecting imminent expulsion from the military for their ties to Gülen. The coup was sloppily planned and executed, with no real direction or coordination. A coup against the sitting executive, by definition, requires coup-makers to neutralize that executive and other senior government officials. But the coup-makers were apparently confused about basic facts—including President Erdoğan's whereabouts—even though the location of his resort was publicized in the media before the coup began. The junior military officers who attempted the coup also failed to garner support from the military's top brass. After the coup was launched, senior officers denounced it and ordered all personnel to return to the barracks.

The plotters also severely miscalculated the effort required to topple a stable government. Coups are always fraught with hazard, but coups against stable popular governments are a fool's errand. Although Turkey had its share of turmoil in 2016 in the form of terrorist attacks and an influx of Syrian refugees in the millions, President Erdoğan was stronger than ever. The plotters hit one of the most stable governments in Turkish history. It would have taken nothing short of a civil war to oust Erdoğan from power.

What's more, having failed at their costly adventure, the coup-makers emboldened the very man they set out to destroy. Erdoğan, a firm believer in the adage that a good crisis should never go to waste, authorized an immediate crackdown against so-called Gülenists. The numbers are dizzying: in less than a week after the coup attempt, the government detained 6,823 soldiers, 2,777 judges and prosecutors (including two judges on the Turkish Constitutional Court), and dozens of governors. To top it off, 49,321 civil servants were removed from their positions, and the teaching licenses of 21,000 private school teachers were terminated. Nearly 1,600 university deans were asked to resign, and academics at Turkish universities were required to return home and refrain from traveling abroad. The massive scale of the purge extended well beyond those who might have been connected to the coup attempt. Many of my academic colleagues in Turkey lost their jobs or, worse, found themselves in indefinite detention.

In the end, the failed coup attempt turned out to be Erdoğan's finest hour. Having emerged unscathed from a full-frontal confrontation with a powerful nemesis, he solidified his already tight hold on Turkish politics.

The April 2017 Referendum

In April 2017, Erdoğan obtained the long-desired formal boost to his constitutional powers. In a referendum that took place under the looming shadow of a state of emergency, the voters narrowly approved a constitutional amendment package that created an all-powerful constitutional executive unencumbered by any real checks on his authority. The referendum was bitterly contested and fraught with credible evidence of ballot-box stuffing captured clearly on camera. (In what I recall now as a chilling moment, but at the time just seemed strange, it was Donald Trump who jumped in front of other Western leaders and congratulated Erdoğan on his referendum victory.).

The constitutional amendments adopted in the referendum abolish the role of the prime minister and consolidate all executive authority squarely in the hands of the president.[36] The president thus holds his government in a vise grip—capable of appointing sympathetic judges to the judiciary and ordering full disciplinary investigations on any of Turkey's 3.5 million governmental employees if he feels so inclined.[37] If Erdoğan emerges victorious in the first presidential elections under the new constitutional framework, he will be permitted to remain in power for two five-year terms, three if the second is cut short by early elections—meaning that Erdoğan could keep his stranglehold on Turkey until at least 2029.[38]

The three opposition parties in Turkey were complicit in Erdoğan's consolidation of control. The main secular opposition party CHP (Cumhuriyet Halk Partisi) remained paralyzed by internal squabbles and petty power politics. It embraced its role in the opposition, relying primarily on a criticism of Erdoğan's policies, rather than an alternative way forward. The leadership of another opposition party, MHP (Milliyetçi Hareket Partisi) abruptly changed course on its opposition to Erdoğan's agenda and backed the "yes" campaign for the April 2017 referendum. The third party, HDP, which represents Kurdish interests in Turkey, failed to adequately distance themselves from the separatist Kurdish rebels, PKK, and chart an autonomous political path. As a result, they made themselves easy targets for prosecution by the government for supporting terrorist activities.

---

[36] BBC News, "Turkey's President Erdogan Wins Power-Boosting Vote," *BBC News*, January 21, 2012, http://www.bbc.com/news/world-europe-38703704.

[37] Patrick Kingsley, "Erdogan Claims Vast Powers in Turkey after Narrow Victory in Referendum," *New York Times*, April 16, 2017, https://www.nytimes.com/2017/04/16/world/europe/turkey-referendum-polls-erdogan.html?_r=0.

[38] Ibid.

Conclusion

Many of Erdoğan's practices, standing alone, appeared insignificant. But their strength lay in their sustained accumulation. Over time, the pressure on democratic institutions built up, like increased hydraulic pressure on a water pipe. These measures slowly, but surely, corroded the already shaky foundations of Turkey's democracy—until the pipe eventually burst.

No country is immune to the election of leaders who ride the streetcar of democracy to their destinations and then step off. It can happen anywhere. In this century, the threat to democracy will come, not from military coups or openly repressive dictators, but from elected politicians in seemingly democratic countries who gradually roll out an authoritarian agenda.

Democracy-minded people must remain vigilant against the type of skillful authoritarian strategies employed by Erdoğan and resist even minor encroachments on democratic freedoms. Without early intervention, molehills can easily become mountains.

21 Israel: A Crisis of Liberal Democracy?
Yaniv Roznai*

Introduction

Liberal Democracies are now in crisis. Whether one terms the occurrence "democratic decay,"[1] "constitutional rot,"[2] "democratic decline,"[3] "Democratic Backsliding,"[4]

* I would like to thank Kim Lane Scheppele, Suzie Navot, and Ilan Saban for assistance and support, Maoz Rosenthal and Wojciech Sadurski for helpful discussions, and Lee Rozen for her excellent research assistance. The ideas reflected in this chapter were developed and discussed at earlier stages with my colleague Nadiv Mordechay. Some of our thoughts were presented at the Maryland Constitutional Law Schmooze (March 2–3, 2017), under the leadership of Mark Graber, and appeared in: Nadiv Mordechay and Yaniv Roznai, "A Jewish and (Declining) Democratic State? Constitutional Retrogression in Israel," *Maryland Law Review* 77 (2018): 101–127. I would like to express my deepest appreciation to the co-editors of the present volume for their remarks on an earlier draft and for organizing this important project.

[1] See, e.g., Tom Gerald Daly, "Democratic Decay in 'Keystone' Democracies: The Real Threat to Global Constitutionalism?" *International Journal of Constitutional Law Blog*, May 10, 2017, http://www.iconnect-blog.com/2017/05/democratic-decay-in-keystone-democracies-the-real-threat-to-global-constitutionalism-i-connect-column/.

[2] Jack M. Balkin, "Constitutional Crisis and Constitutional Rot," *Maryland Law Review* 77 (2017): 147–160.

[3] András L. Pap, *Democratic Decline in Hungary: Law and Society in an Illiberal Democracy* (New York: Routledge, 2017).

[4] Nancy Bermeo, "On Democratic Backsliding," *Journal of Democracy* 27 (2016): 5–19.

"constitutional capture,"[5] or "constitutional retrogression,"[6] each carrying different nuances, what seems to be clear—and bearing in mind the methodological and conceptual difficulties of defining and measuring democratic backsliding[7]—is that constitutional democracies around the world are facing major challenges.

While some argue that "the gloomy discourse on democracy dominating today is exaggerated,"[8] the global "democratic recession" seems to be real.[9] Since 2005, the global democratic wave suffered sustained reversals as the number of democracies worldwide declined, together with a gradual erosion of certain freedoms.[10]

The wave has not skipped Israel. Upon the release of the Israeli Democracy Index 2017, Yohanan Plesner, the president of the Israel Democracy Institute (IDI), stated that "the Index reveals that Israel's democracy is suffering an ongoing crisis with no imminent signs of a change of trend."[11] According to the index, 45 percent of the total sample (which included 1,024 interviewees—864 Jews and others, and 160 Arabs—who constitute a representative sample of the adult Israeli population) believe that "Israeli democracy is in grave danger."[12]

The threat to the democratic character of Israel, some claim, is a real existential danger to Israel.[13] American liberal political commentator Peter Beinart, for example, claims that there is a "very real prospect that Israeli democracy will die."[14] Mordechai Kremnitzer,

---

[5] Laurent Pech and Kim Lane Scheppele, "Illiberalism Within: Rule of Law Backsliding in the EU," *Cambridge Yearbook of European Legal Studies* 19 (2017): 3–47, 9.

[6] Aziz Z. Huq and Tom Ginsburg, "How to Lose a Constitutional Democracy," 65 *UCLA Law Review* (forthcoming 2018), https://ssrn.com/abstract=2901776.

[7] David Waldner and Ellen Lust, "Unwelcome Change: Coming to Terms with Democratic Backsliding," *Annual Review of Political Science* 21 (2018): 5.1–5.21.

[8] Mélida Jiménez, "Is Democracy in a Worldwide Decline? Nope. Here's Our Data," *Washington Post*, November 15, 2017, https://www.washingtonpost.com/news/monkey-cage/wp/2017/11/15/is-democracy-in-a-worldwide-decline-we-measured-it-heres-what-we-found/?utm_term=.e6edc520dbbd.

[9] See Zachary Elkins, "Is the Sky Falling? Constitutional Crises in Historical Perspective," in *Constitutional Democracy in Crisis*, ed. Mark A. Graber, Sandy Levinson, and Mark Tushnet (New York: Oxford University Press, 2018).

[10] See Amichai Magen, "The Democratic Entitlement in an Era of Democratic Recession," *Cambridge Journal of International and Comparative Law* 4 (2015): 368–387; Valeriya Mechkova, Anna Lührmann, and Staffan I. Lindberg, "How Much Democratic Backsliding?" *Journal of Democracy* 28 (2017): 162–169. In other work I have suggested that international law should take some progressive measures. See Amnon Rubinstein and Yaniv Roznai, "The Right to a Genuine Electoral Democracy," *Minnesota Journal of International Law* 27 (2018): 143–178.

[11] "Israel Democracy Index 2017," press release, *IDI*, December 12, 2017, https://en.idi.org.il/articles/20283l.

[12] A summary of Tamar Hermann, Chanan Cohen, Ella Heller, Tzipy Lazar-Shoef, and Fadi Omar, *The Israeli Democracy Index 2017* (Jerusalem: The Israel Democracy Institute, 2017), 2, https://en.idi.org.il/media/9837/israeli-democracy-index-2017-en-summary.pdf.

[13] Chemi Shalev, "The Great Betrayal: American Jews Stay Silent as Israeli Democracy Withers," *Haaretz*, January 4, 2016, https://www.haaretz.com/opinion/.premium-u-s-jews-stay-silent-as-israeli-democracy-withers-1.5385621; Gideon Levy, "Is 'the Only Democracy in ME' Becoming Undemocratic?," *Al Jazeera*, August 12, 2017, http://www.aljazeera.com/indepth/opinion/2017/08/democracy-undemocratic-170812115219016.html.

[14] Peter Beinart, *The Crisis of Zionism* (New York: Times Books, 2012).

until recently the vice president of the IDI, has repeatedly argued that Israeli democracy is under threat.[15]

Other prominent voices disagree. Discussing what he characterizes as "the never-ending impending collapse of Israeli democracy," Jonathan Greenberg, the senior vice president of the Haym Salomon Center and an expert in Middle East policy, claimed that "Israeli democracy is perfectly healthy."[16] Similarly, Michael Oren, an American émigré who became Israel's ambassador to the United States, responded to such critics that "to say Israel is undemocratic is just dead wrong"; "democracy in Israel," he emphasizes, "is today more robust and effervescent than ever."[17]

So which is it? Is liberal democracy in Israel in crisis, or have the reports of the death of Israeli democracy been greatly exaggerate? The conflicting answers to these questions can be understood considering different understandings of democracy, in itself a contested concept.[18] As I demonstrate in this chapter, the main problem is not that Israeli democracy is in danger but more accurately that *liberal and substantive notions of democracy are under attack in the name of a purely procedural or majoritarian version of democracy,* according to which the political majority represents the sovereign and is thus omnipotent.[19] The disputes are a version of the well-known tension between constitutionalism and democracy, as the political branches aim to undercut constitutional restrictions constraining the ruling power of the demos and their representatives.

In this chapter I review recent events that I characterize as a counterrevolution to the constitutional revolution. These include attempts to shift the balance between the Jewish and democratic characters of the state—two disharmonic values at the first place[20]—in favor of the former, and to reverse the judicialization processes that characterized the Israeli public sphere in the recent three decades, in an attempt to grant the political majority rather than the judiciary "the final word." I thereafter provide three different approaches for analyzing these events: first, recent events represent a fulfillment, not an undermining, of democracy; second, alarms concerning the danger to the Israeli democracy are greatly exaggerated; and third, Israel is undergoing, or is on a dangerous slope toward constitutional capture. I argue that while Israel is still a vibrant

---

[15] Tobias Buck, "Israel's Eroding Democracy: A Shadow Is Cast," *Financial Times*, December 9, 2011, https://www.ft.com/content/ca198710-20d6-11e1-8133-00144feabdco.

[16] Jonathan Greenberg, "The Never-Ending Impending Collapse of Israeli Democracy … or Not," *The Hill*, January 18, 2016, http://thehill.com/blogs/congress-blog/266109-the-never-ending-impending-collapse-of-israeli-democracyor-not.

[17] Michael Oren, "Israel's Resilient Democracy," *Foreign Policy*, April 5, 2012, http://foreignpolicy.com/2012/04/05/israels-resilient-democracy/.

[18] See, e.g., Milja Kurki, "Democracy and Conceptual Contestability: Reconsidering Conceptions of Democracy in Democracy Promotion," *International Studies Review* 12 (2010): 362–386.

[19] See, e.g., Yoseph M. Edrey, "The Knesset Is Not Omnipotent," *Haaretz*, January 25, 2018, https://www.haaretz.co.il/opinions/.premium-1.5766407 ("It appears that according to the Minister of Justice, democracy is fulfilled through elections and satisfying the majority's will.").

[20] See, e.g., Dan Avnon, "The Israeli Basic Laws (Potentially) Fatal Flaw," *Israel Law Review* 32 (1998): 535–566.

and strong democracy, there are troublesome processes that might lead Israel toward a dangerous constitutional retrogression.

The "Constitutional Revolution"

Israel's brief constitutional history can be divided into before and after the 1990s, what has come to be called Israel's "constitutional revolution," which includes two components: the enactment, without a wide public participation and awareness, of two basic laws on fundamental rights that for the first time imposed substantive limits on the legislative powers of the Knesset (the Israeli Parliament), coupled with a strong judicial enforcement of these basic laws through substantive judicial review.[21] An extensive interpretation of the rights protected in the basic law together with a broad right of standing before the court and minimal justiciability restrictions, have elevated the status and powers of the Israeli Supreme Court vis-à-vis the political branches.

The Declaration of Independence of May 14, 1948, explicitly stated that the Israeli regime would be based on a constitution. However, after deep political disagreements over the need to adopt a constitution at that stage, on June 13, 1950, the Knesset adopted the "Harari Decision" according to which instead of completing the constitutional project at once, the Knesset, which holds both legislative and constituent powers, would enact Basic Laws in stages, and those would eventually comprise the Israeli constitution.[22] Until the early 1990s, the Knesset enacted several Basic Laws that regulated governmental structure and institutions. Moreover, the High Court of Justice (HCJ) served as a legal defender of unwritten common law rights and freedoms even without an entrenched bill of rights. Yet the prevailing approach was that of legislative supremacy.[23]

In 1992, the Knesset enacted two significant Basic Laws on human rights: Basic Law: Human Dignity and Freedom, and Basic Law: Freedom of Occupation. These two Basic Laws provide substantive limits on the legislative powers of the Knesset by stipulating conditions for infringing protected constitutional rights. Three years later, in the pioneer judgment of *United Mizrahi Bank v. Migdal Cooperative Village*,[24] the Supreme Court held that the Basic Laws hold a normative constitutional status superior to ordinary laws and that the court has the power to conduct judicial review and invalidate unconstitutional legislation. The constitutional revolution then reached a peak.

---

[21] Much has been written on the Israeli constitutional revolution, so I shall keep this description to the minimum. See, e.g., Gideon Sapir, "Constitutional Revolutions: Israel as a Case-Study," *International Journal of Law in Context* 5 (2009): 355–378.

[22] See, e.g., Hanna Lerner, *Making Constitutions in Deeply Divided Societies* (New York: Cambridge University Press, 2011), ch. 3.

[23] See, e.g., Amos Shapira, "Judicial Review without a Constitution: The Israeli Paradox," *Temple Law Quarterly* 56 (1983): 405, 421–423.

[24] CA 6821/93 United Mizrahi Bank Ltd. v. Migdal Cooperative Village, 49(4) P.D. 221 (1995).

In addition to the constitutional revolution, the Court has extended its authority through the years by taking a broad notion of justiciability by declaring that "the world is filled with law; anything and everything is justiciable," thereby refusing to place political questions beyond the scope of judicial review. It also removed the traditional requirement of legal standing (locus standi) for petitioners before the HCJ, and allowed petitions brought by "public petitioners" as long as they concern significant rule of law or constitutional questions. It developed the "reasonableness" ground for reviewing and invalidating governmental decisions, and finally, in a series of judicial decisions that followed the *United Mizrahi Bank* case, the HCJ broadly interpreted "human dignity" so as to include certain aspects of the right to equality and freedom of expression, according them a constitutional status even though these rights were intentionally excluded from the Basic Laws on human rights.[25]

The Supreme Court has therefore emerged as a dominant branch of government with a central constitutive role in collective decision-making. Amnon Rubinstein, the "father" of the Basic Laws on human rights and a renowned professor of constitutional law, wrote that "in fact, in many senses, under Barak's leadership, the Court has turned itself into an alternative government."[26] Describing the Supreme Court under the leadership of President Barak, Richard Posner wrote that: "What Barak created out of whole cloth was a degree of judicial power undreamed of even by our most aggressive Supreme Court justices."[27] Accordingly, the Israeli judiciary has been regarded by many observers, in Israel and abroad, as one of the world's activist courts, perhaps even "the most activist in the world."[28]

The court's empowerment shifted the balance of powers toward the judiciary vis-à-vis the legislative and the executive branches. Ran Hirschl explained the motivation behind the empowerment of the court and the process of judicialization of politics in Israel as "a strong interest in preserving the political and cultural hegemony of the ruling elite and its secular bourgeois constituency, as well as entrenching Israel's contested western, relatively cosmopolitan identity."[29] Indeed, some politicians and members of the public have criticized the court as representing the "leftist elite" and promoting "universal values" in

---

[25] HCJ 6427/02 Movement for Government Quality in Israel v. The Knesset, ver 61(1), 619 (2006) (regarding equality); HCJ 10203/03 The National Census LtD v Attorney General, PD 62(4) 715 (2008) (regarding political expression). See Suzie Navot, *The Constitution of Israel—A Contextual Analysis* (Portland, OR: Hart Publishing, 2014), 235. See generally Daphne Barak-Erez, "Broadening the Scope of Judicial Review in Israel: Between Activism and Restraint," *Indiana Journal of Constitutional Law* 3 (2009): 118.

[26] Cited in Suzie Navot, "The Israeli Supreme Court," in *Comparative Constitutional Reasoning*, ed. András Jakab, Arthur Dyevre, and Giulio Itzcovich (New York: Cambridge University Press, 2017), 471.

[27] Richard A. Posner, "Enlightened Despot," *New Republic*, April 23, 2007, www.newrepublic.com/article/enlightened-despot.

[28] See Menachem Mautner, *Law and the Culture of Israel* (New York: Oxford University Press, 2011), ix.

[29] Ran Hirschl, *Towards Juristocracy: The Origins and Consequences of the New Constitutionalism* (Cambridge, MA: Harvard University Press, 2004), 74.

contrast with "the political will of the people." This point, as we shall see, has become central in the debate surrounding the current constitutional crisis.

Such criticism was intensified in light of the feeling, in some sections of the public, that the composition of the Supreme Court is homogeneous in its demographic characteristics, representing the historically influential elites, and that the candidacy of prominent figures to the Supreme Court is being intentionally blocked by the court's leadership due to different perspectives.[30] As Hirschl put it bluntly, "jurists who are Opera-goers and Ha'aretz subscribers, whose mothers knew Yiddish, and who own an apartment or two in an upscale neighborhood are much more likely to get appointed to the Supreme Court than those who celebrate the Mimoona (a Northern-African Jewish feast), wear Tefillin (phylacteries) every weekday morning, speak fluent Arabic, were born in the former Soviet Union, or have a close family relative under the poverty line. As it happens, over two-thirds of the Israeli electorate falls into at least one of these categories."[31]

So, the increase of judicial powers together with the growing involvement of the Court in political and security questions,[32] and the perceived homogenous character of the Court, attracted vast public and political criticism. Notwithstanding such criticism, for twenty years following the constitutional revolution, the Court remained strong and independent, earning an international reputation. Likewise, the Basic Laws on human rights remain in force, and both the government and the legislature take them seriously during the legislative process. It is important to mention that due to the Court's judicial activism and expansive interpretation of Basic Law: Human Dignity, the Knesset refrained from enacting new Basic Laws on Human Rights. This was clearly manifested by one of the leaders of the religious parties, MK Arie Deri, who claimed that "even if the Knesset should decide to add the Ten Commandments to the constitution, we would still oppose that because they would still be subject to the Supreme Court's interpretation."[33]

The Counterrevolution

Notwithstanding the constitutional revolution, recent years brought with them strong winds of change. From the judiciary's perspective, it was that President Barak—the most dominant figure in the process of Israel's judicialization and

---

[30] In 2005, President Barak objected to the appointment of law professor Ruth Gavison, a vocal critic of the Supreme Court's political orientation and judicial activism, to the Supreme Court because she has an "agenda." Yuval Yoaz, "Supreme Court Head Barak Explains Opposition to Gavison Appointment," *Haaretz*, November 13, 2005, https://www.haaretz.com/1.4881516.

[31] Ran Hirschl, "The Socio-political Origins of Israel's Juristocracy," *Constellations* 16 (2009): 476, 487.

[32] Yoav Dotan, "Judicial Accountability in Israel: The High Court of Justice and the Phenomenon of Judicial Hyperactivism," *Israel Affairs* 8 (2002): 87, 97.

[33] Cited in Navot, *The Constitution of Israel*, 42.

constitutionalization—retired in 2006, after twenty-eight years of sitting on the Supreme Court, due to the age limit on service on the Supreme Court. The retirement of such a heroic figure from the bench marked the beginning of a new era characterized by a political counterrevolution. This is what Mark Tushnet calls the backlash "after the heroes have left the scene": once a heroic court has exercised what is regarded as aggressive constitutional review, and by that positioned itself as a political actor, this creates a political backlash against judicial activism and a political assault to limit the court's jurisdiction or to change judicial selection.[34] Indeed, one may claim that the perceived strength of the Supreme Court and its activism is a contributing factor to the "Constitutional Backlash."[35] Furthermore, some argue that, perhaps due to the criticism of and the personnel changes to the Supreme Court, in recent years there has been a decline in judicial activism.[36] What seems clear is that in recent years the HCJ has developed and been increasingly using judicial tools such as the "suspension of declaration of invalidation" or "notice of validity" remedies, and the ripeness doctrine, which allow it to act in a more restrained manner.[37]

More importantly, recent years witnessed the rise of right-wing parties that support national, traditional, and religious agendas together with aspirations of a "greater Israel." As Arie Perliger and Ami Pedahzur demonstrate, political right discourse in Israel is characterized, inter alia, by *nativist ideas* that include "territorial nativism," which promotes Israeli control on the West Bank, the Golan Heights, and East Jerusalem, as well as "ethnic nativism," which is manifested through the aspiration for ethnic/religious homogeneity. Perliger and Pedahzur write that "both types of nativism, which initially were restricted to particular radical right parties and movements, eventually spread into larger segments of the Israeli party system. This is reflected both in the actual practices promoted by parties via their policy initiatives and legislative efforts and in their public rhetoric."[38] In addition to nativism, the authors emphasize the central role of *authoritarianism*, which is "reflected in attempts to emphasize the superiority of national values and practices over individual ones" to the extent that "sentiments that place Israel's interests above democratic principles and individual civil rights became more predominant and legitimate

---

[34] Mark Tushnet, "After the Heroes Have Left the Scene: Temporality in the Study of Constitutional Court Judges," paper presented at the Workshop: Understanding Constitutional Change: The State of the Field (Tulane Law School, October 14, 2017) (copy with author).

[35] Stephen Gardbaum, "Are Strong Constitutional Courts Always a Good Thing for New Democracies?," *Columbia Journal of Transnational Law* 53 (2015): 285, 320 ("where it is actively exercised, the power of judicial review can and has triggered political backlashes against the judiciary that threatens to reduce or eliminate its independence, a clearly counterproductive development and one that courts often have few powers or means to resist.")

[36] See in Navot, "The Israeli Supreme Court," 471.

[37] See, e.g., Suzie Navot, "The Constitutional Dialogue: A Debate through Institutional Mechanisms," *Mishpatim Online* (forthcoming 2018) (on file with authors) [Heb.].

[38] Arie Perliger and Ami Pedahzur, "The Radical Right in Israel," in *The Oxford Handbook of the Radical Right*, ed. Jens Rydgren (New York: Oxford University Press, 2018), 667, 672.

within Israeli political discourse.[39] Finally, "in recent years, far right discourse promotes populist worldviews arguing that the will of the people is being ignored or manipulated as a result of the control of certain left-wing elite groups in the media, in parts of civil society, in the higher education system, and in the judiciary."[40]

There are multiple reasons for the success of right-wing political parties and the push to counter the constitutional revolution with its liberal and universal values.[41] *First*, there is an identification in the public between "critical voices" and "disloyalty" to the state or its "delimitation." Accordingly, critical voices from the media, political opposition, or civil society are easily displayed as being disloyal. *Second*, there is an anti-elite sentiment in parts of the general public, which is being directed against the judiciary, the media, and academia. *Third*, the extreme right-wing is succeeding in creating a correlation of the left-wing with values such as liberalism and human rights. According to the 2017 Democracy Index, 72 percent of Jewish right-wing voters agree with the statement that "the leftist judiciary, media, and academia interfere with the elected right wing's ability to rule."[42] *Fourth*, the endless terrorism and security challenges coupled with the hopeless Israeli-Palestine conflict lead to public support of right-wing political parties.[43]

True, Benjamin Netanyahu has been prime minister for a cumulative term of twelve years (three from 1996 to 1999, and nine from 2009 to 2018), an extremely long period in Israeli politics. However, in contrast with the earlier coalitions led by Netanyahu, following the 2015 elections, Netanyahu is now leading a government dominated by right-wing parties with no moderating influences.[44] Netanyahu's political dominance, together with the most right-wing government in the nation's history pushing for national, traditional, and religious values, and the territorial integrity of Israel, carry implications for the fragile Israeli constitutional system, which some regard as under an "overall right-wing assault on the liberal democracy."[45] Accordingly, in

---

[39] Ibid., 674–75.

[40] Ibid., 676.

[41] See an interview of Professor Mordechai Kremnitzer in Hagar Buchbut, "Is There a Risk to Israeli Democracy?," *Ynetnews*, May 31, 2016, http://www.ynet.co.il/articles/0,7340,L-4803112,00.html. On political radicalization in Israel, see also Dani Filc, "Political Radicalization in Israel: From a Populist Habitus to Radical Right Populism in Government," in *Expressions of Radicalization: Global Politics, Processes, and Practices*, ed. Kristian Steiner and Andreas Önnerfor (Cham, Switzerland: Palgrave Macmillan 2018), 121.

[42] "Israel Democracy Index 2017," press release.

[43] See, e.g., Peter Lintl, "The Dynamics of a Right-Wing Coalition—How the Failure of the Peace Process Encourages Domestic Populism in Israel," *SWP Comments*, October 2016, 45, https://www.swp-berlin.org/fileadmin/contents/products/comments/2016C45_ltl.pdf; Tamar Mitts, "Terrorism and the Rise of Right-Wing Content in Israeli Books," August 24, 2017, http://tamarmitts.com/wp-content/uploads/2016/06/Terrorism_Books_v4_1.pdf.

[44] Joel Peters and Rob Pinfold, "Consolidating Right-Wing Hegemony: The Israeli Election 2015," *Mediterranean Politics* 20 (2015): 405.

[45] Chemi Shalev, "The Right-Wing Assault on Israeli Democracy," *Haaretz*, October 17, 2017, https://www.haaretz.com/opinion/.premium-the-right-wing-assault-on-israeli-democracy-1.5458440; see also Aluf Benn,

recent years, Israel has gone through an assault on the constitutional revolution—a counterrevolution.[46]

Various developments give rise to the claims that Israel's liberal democracy is in a "crisis."[47] One manifestation of the counterrevolution is the manifold legislative attempts to undermine "legal gatekeepers." One example is a private bill, supported by the government, to restrict the authority of the state comptroller.[48] Another example is a proposed bill designed to change the way in which legal advisors are appointed to government ministries. Instead of a professional tender, in which a minister is unable to influence the outcome of the nomination, candidates will be selected by a search committee in which the minister has a de-facto majority. The bill, which as of the time of writing had passed first reading, faced objections from various jurists, including the attorney general.[49] Notably, six former Supreme Court justices, who also had served as attorney general or state attorney, submitted to the minister of justice their objection to the bill, which, in Yitzhak Zamir's words, is a "bill against the rule of law."[50]

More importantly, there are multiple legislative attempts to limit the Court's competence to conduct judicial review, to limit locus standi, to change the voting method in the judicial selection committee, or the seniority principle for selecting the president of the Supreme Court. Such attempts join critical voices of coalition politicians against the Court, including the minister of justice, Ayelet Shaked, who warned against judicial activism and has pushed to nominate conservative judges.[51]

A clear example of such an attempt is the recently proposed Basic Law: Legislation.[52] On the one hand, this bill recognizes the constitutional revolution by explicitly authorizing the courts to conduct judicial review. On the other hand, it seeks to greatly restrict the courts' authority, compared to its existing authority; only the HCJ could strike down legislation (currently every court has judicial review power *inter partes*), and striking

---

"The End of the Old Israel: How Netanyahu Has Transformed the Nation," *Foreign Affairs*, July–August 2016, 16.

[46] Arguably, the counterrevolution began in 2007 with the appointment of Daniel Friedman as the minister of justice, who waged a campaign to curb the judiciary power. See Doron Navot and Yoav Peled, "Towards a Constitutional Counter-Revolution in Israel?," *Constellations* 16 (2009): 429. However, in recent years, this counterrevolution has had much greater momentum.

[47] See elaboration in Nadiv Mordechay and Yaniv Roznai, "A Jewish and (Declining) Democratic State? Constitutional Retrogression in Israel," *Maryland Law Review* 77 (2018): 101.

[48] Marissa Newman and Tamar Pileggi, "State Comptroller 'Regrets' MKs' Attempts to Curb His Powers," *Times of Israel*, November 21, 2017, https://www.timesofisrael.com/state-comptroller-regrets-mks-attempts-to-curb-his-powers/.

[49] Tova Tzimuki and Yael Friedson, "Shaked and AG Prepare to Lock Horns over Legal Advisor Bill," *Ynet*, October 24, 2017, https://www.ynetnews.com/articles/0,7340,L-5033267,00.html.

[50] Yitzhak Zamir, "The Legal Advisors Law: A Bill against the Rule of Law," *Haaretz*, February 1, 2018, [Heb.], https://www.haaretz.co.il/opinions/.premium-1.5785167.

[51] Mordechay and Roznai, "A Jewish and (Declining) Democratic State?," 253–254.

[52] Moran Azulay and Tova Tzimuki, "Basic Law Proposal Seeks to Limit Supreme Court's Ability to Strike Down Laws," *Ynet*, December 20, 2017, https://www.ynetnews.com/articles/0,7340,L-5059358,00.html.

down the Knesset's legislation would require a minimum of a nine-judge panel and a two-thirds majority. Moreover, the proposal includes an "override clause" that would allow a majority of 61 Knesset members (out of 120) to overcome HCJ decisions and to re-enact laws that were deemed as unconstitutional. Such laws would be valid for five years with an option of extension. Finally, the proposal includes a non-justiciability clause, according to which the court would lack the authority to invalidate legislation due to flaws in the legislative process or to conduct substantive review of basic laws.[53] When presenting the proposed Basic Law, Minister Shaked criticized judicial activism that has "harmed Israeli democracy," saying that "from the current judicial chaos there will be order and a balance will be achieved between the three branches of government." Education Minister Naftali Bennett added that "Today we tell the court . . . The government ought to govern and the judges ought to judge."[54] This rationale might be appealing to right-wing voters, among which, a small majority (53 percent) believes that the authority to overrule legislation should be taken away from the Supreme Court. However, as the 2017 Democracy Index reveals, the majority of the general public (58 percent) actually oppose the "override clause."[55]

In a comparative perspective, some arguments can be made in favor of this proposal. Proposing to transform from a diffuse system of judicial review to a centralized model in which only the HCJ can strike down legislation would turn Israel into something like most of the European countries. This is not the problematic aspect of the proposal, and it is supported by prominent jurists, Barak included.[56]

The main problems are with allowing a majority of sixty-one MKs to enact unconstitutional legislation and with providing the Knesset, exercising its "constituent power hat," limitless power regarding substance. What is the problem, one may claim? Arguably, the mechanism of override exists in Canada's constitutional law,[57] and in some perfectly democratic states, such as the UK or the Netherlands, the guiding principle is legislative supremacy.[58] Moreover, such a mechanism already exists in Basic Law: Freedom of Occupation.

---

[53] This non-justiciability clause was inserted after two recent contentious decisions of the HCJ invalidating legislation based upon flaws in the legislative process (HCJ 10042/16 Kventinsky v. Knesset, August 6, 2017), and issuing an invalidation notice to a temporary basic law that changed the annual budget rule to a biennial one, for the fifth time in a row (HCJ 8260/16 Academic Center of Law and Business v. Knesset, September 6, 2017). See Yaniv Roznai, "The Israeli Supreme Court as Guardian of the Knesset," *VRÜ* (forthcoming 2018).

[54] Cited in Azulay and Tzimuki, "Basic Law Proposal."

[55] "Israeli Democracy Index 2017," press release.

[56] See Aharon Barak, "Judicial Review of the Constitutionality of Statutes: Centralism v. Decentralism," *Mishpat Umimshal* 8 (2005): 13 [Heb.].

[57] Section 33 of the Canadian Charter of Rights and Freedoms.

[58] Article 120 of the Constitution of the Netherlands prohibits the judicial review of laws and treaties against the Constitution. In the UK, according to Section 4 of the Human Rights Act 1998, the Supreme Courte can only make a non-binding "declaration of incompatibility" with the European Human Rights Convention, which does not affect the validity of laws.

Without attempting to thoroughly analyze this here, several replies may be in order. *First*, in these two countries there is an effective mechanism of constitutional review within the legislative process. In the Netherlands, bills are presented to the Advisory Division of the Council of State that determines the constitutionality of the bill. True, its advice is not binding, but it plays an important role as the Council's advice cannot be freely deviated from, and such a deviation requires the support of sufficient grounds.[59] In the UK, the Joint Committee on Human Rights acts as a parliamentary legal advisory mechanism that plays an important and decisive role in better protecting human rights.[60] *Second*, there is a distinction between allowing overriding the freedom of occupation and overriding the right to life or dignity. *Third*, in contrast with members of the Council of Europe, Israel is not a party to the European Convention on Human Rights, so there is no supranational court above the Supreme Court, and there are no Strasburg judges to guard the fundamental rights of individuals. *Fourth*, it is clear that such examples of countries without judicial review, New Zealand included, are the exception rather than the rule.[61] *Fifth*, the Israeli legislature is composed of a single chamber, without a second chamber that can function as a restraint, and the legislative process is dominantly controlled by the executive. Waldron asked, in the New Zealand context, "a deserted chamber, Bills rushed through under urgency, members subservient to the executive, constant closure motions, no second chamber, no checks and balances—is that the sort of process that can reassure us that judicial scrutiny is not necessary?"[62] This is equally applicable to the Israeli scenario. *Finally*, Israel is a young democracy without a long and established democratic culture or tradition, and some sections of the Israeli public have no actual commitment to liberal democracy. This political culture makes the proposed override mechanism less appropriate than other countries, such as Canada. Especially, the proposed majority of sixty-one MKs is inadequate as it would in practice allow any coalition in the Knesset to enact unconstitutional legislation. A supermajority of at least eighty MKs, I believe, would be more appropriate. Accordingly, the proposed Basic Law carries the perilous implications of unlimited legislative powers being granted to the Knesset, risking cuffing the hands of the HCJ from defending against the tyranny of the majority. Indeed, the

---

[59] J.C.A. de Poorter, "Constitutional Review in the Netherlands: A Joint Responsibility," *Utrecht Law Review* 9 (2013): 89, 92–93.

[60] See, e.g., Janet L. Hiebert, "Parliament and the Human Rights Act: Can the JCHR Help Facilitate a Culture of Rights?," *International Journal of Constitutional Law* 4 (2006): 1–38.

[61] See David S. Law and Mila Versteeg, "The Evolution and Ideology of Global Constitutionalism," *California Law Review* 99 (2011): 1163, 1199 ("In 1946, only 35% of countries had either de jure or de facto judicial review; by 2006, about 87% did").

[62] Jeremy Waldron, "Compared to What? Judicial Activism and New Zealand's Parliament," *New Zealand Law Journal* 180 (2005): 441, 443.

attorney general, Avichai Mandelblit, warned that the proposed bill would "cause significant harm to Israeli democracy."[63] Barak stated that if the bill is enacted in its current form, it would "take back Israeli law 25 years."[64]

Speaking at the 2018 annual conference of the Israeli Association of Public Law, Minister Shaked said that by challenging the Knesset's legislation, the judiciary was "fleeing the people" and their choices, and that this derived from "a disconnect between some of the old elite from the realities of life." Referring to the original Greek meaning of "democracy"—"Demos" ("people") and "Kratos" ("rule")—Shaked argued that in the eyes of the court "the 'demos' has become a demon."[65] The minister of justice is portraying the Court as an elite group that treats the people as the enemy, which makes the Court, in its turn, the people's enemy. This anti-elitism and the claim to be the sole representatives of the people is clear populism.[66]

As already mentioned, apart from populism, Perliger and Pedahzur identify in the political discourse of the political right *ethnic nativism,* which aspires for ethnic/religious homogeneity, and *authoritarianism* that places national values above and superior to individual rights.[67] This is clearly manifested in the currently proposed "Basic Law: Israel as the Nation-State of the Jewish People," which concerns the state's identity as a "Jewish and Democratic" one, as the two Basic Laws of 1992 specify, and seeks to shift the balance between the democratic and the Jewish values of Israel in favor of the latter.[68]

While in the past there have been several recurring efforts to enact such a Basic Law, in this Knesset's term the bill has received strong governmental support. As of the time of writing, the bill is being negotiated in a special ministerial committee. Apparently, there is still disagreement on whether to specify that Israel is "a Jewish state with a democratic form of government," or to omit any reference to democracy.[69] Obviously, both options deviate from the formula of "Jewish and Democratic." This constitutional change of the dominant principles in Israel is reflected in the recent declaration of Justice Minister

---

[63] Cited in "Justice Minister, Chief Justice and A-G Clash Publicly over Court Authority," *Times of Israel,* December 21, 2017, https://www.timesofisrael.com/justice-minister-chief-justice-and-a-g-clash-publicly-over-court-authority/.

[64] Tova Tzimuki and Amira Lam, "Aharon's Laws," *Yediot,* January 31, 2018, https://www.yediot.co.il/articles/0,7340,L-5078841,00.html [Heb.]

[65] "Justice Minister, Chief Justice and A-G Clash."

[66] See Jan-Werner Müller, *What Is Populism?* (London: Penguin UK, 2017).

[67] Perliger and Pedahzur, "The Radical Right in Israel," 672–675.

[68] Joel Greenberg, "Israel Takes First Step Towards 'Jewish Nation-State' Law," *Financial Times,* May 10, 2017, https://www.ft.com/content/cod7bod2-35b6-11e7-bce4-9023f8cofd2e; Lahav Harkiv, "What Does the Jewish 'Nation-State' Bill Mean for Israel?," *JPost,* November 5, 2017, http://www.jpost.com/Israel-News/What-does-the-Jewish-nation-state-bill-mean-for-Israel-513405.

[69] Jonathan Lis, "New Nation-State Bill Will Not Define Israel as 'Jewish and Democratic' State," *Haaretz,* July 7, 2017, https://www.haaretz.com/israel-news/.premium-new-nation-state-bill-will-not-define-israel-as-jewish-and-democratic-state-1.5492404.

Shaked that: "Zionism should not continue, and it will not continue to bow down to the system of individual rights."[70]

True, many other constitutions entrench national symbols or protect the nationhood of a certain people and their right to self-determination. Yet, these constitutions also expressly include protection of equality, which is missing in the current proposal. As Minister Shaked expressly acknowledges, "Israel is a Jewish state. It isn't a state of all its nations. That is, equal rights to all citizens but not equal national rights ... There are places where the character of the State of Israel as a Jewish state must be maintained and this sometimes comes at the expense of equality."[71] Therefore, some scholars regard the proposal as "a radical change in the existing balance between 'Jewish' and 'democratic' and makes the democratic element subservient to the Jewish element. Let us not be naïve. This proposal is not intended to reflect the status quo but to alter it in a fundamental way—to puff up the state's Jewish-national character and diminish and curtail its democratic character."[72]

Consolidation of power within the government and the prime minister himself, is another sign for worry. At one point, Prime Minister Netanyahu held simultaneously the positions of the prime minister, foreign minister, communications minister, economy minister, and regional co-operation minister. The HCJ held that while this practice was technically legal it was not conducive to democracy.[73] In contrast with a healthy separation of powers, the government is increasing its powers over the legislature, reducing points of checks and balances. One example is the reform in the state budget. The established constitutional rule in Israel was that the government must submit the budget for the approval of the Knesset annually. Budget approval is an important supervision mechanism because the Knesset is dissolved if the budget is not approved. However, in 2009 the government established a biennial budget, as a temporary measure to handle the global economic crisis. This temporary measure was prolonged four additional times (until 2018).[74] Taken together with the limited constructive vote of no confidence, which has existed from 2014, the biennial budged further limited the oversight capacity of the legislature. At the end of 2017, the HCJ issued a notice of invalidity for any future temporary biennial budget.[75]

---

[70] Revital Hovel, "Justice Minister Slams Israel's Top Court, Says It Disregards Zionism and Upholding Jewish Majority," *Haaretz*, August 29, 2017, https://www.haaretz.com/israel-news/1.809617.

[71] Revital Hovel, "Justice Minister: Israel Must Keep Jewish Majority even at the Expense of Human Rights," *Haaretz*, February 13, 2018, https://www.haaretz.com/israel-news/justice-minister-israel-s-jewish-majority-trumps-than-human-rights-1.5811106.

[72] Amir Fuchs and Mordechay Kremnitzer, "Basic Law: Israel as the Nation State of the Jewish People—A Danger to the Zionist Enterprise," *IDI*, May 12, 2014, https://en.idi.org.il/articles/6443.

[73] HCJ 3132/15 Yesh Atid v. Prime Minister of Israel (April 13, 2016) (Isr.).

[74] On the increasing use of temporary legislation in Israel see Ittai Bar-Siman-Tov, "Temporary Legislation, Better Regulation and Experimentalist Governance: An Empirical Study," *Regulation and Governance* (2018), http://onlinelibrary.wiley.com/doi/10.1111/rego.12148/full.

[75] HCJ 8260/16 (n 53).

Coupled with this concentration of power is the weakening of political opposition powers and critical voices from civil society, such as: an amendment to Section 7(a) of Basic Law: The Knesset, which extends the standards for banning candidates for election, by clarifying that these include not only actions but also speeches; legislation raising the Knesset electoral threshold; legislation that allows a supermajority of MKs to dismiss MKs who support the struggle of a terrorist organization; legislation that denies state funding to institutions that view the establishment of the State of Israel as a tragedy ("Nakba Law"); the "anti-boycott law," according to which individuals or organizations who publicize a call for an economic, cultural, or academic boycott against a person or entity merely because of its affiliation to the State of Israel, to an Israeli institution or to a specific region under Israeli control, may be sued civilly, in tort, by a party claiming that it might be damaged by such a boycott;[76] and legislation that imposes various disclosure obligations on civil society organizations funded by foreign countries labeling them as "foreign agents."[77]

Civil society organizations, mainly those critical of the government's policies, that promote human rights and defend Palestinians' rights, have come under attack by the right-wing government and right-wing organizations, often describing them as "anti-patriotic" or "enemies of the public."[78] This attack can be contrasted with the clear rise in the power of conservative nationalist civil society organizations, supported by politicians in the government.[79]

Indeed, loyalty is a central theme in contemporary Israeli politics. Not only are human rights organization or philanthropic funds frequently accused of being disloyal, but the minister of culture, Miri Regev, also promotes a dependency between public funding and "cultural loyalty" to the Israeli State, its symbols or values, intended to effectively silence critical positions.[80] The prevailing rhetoric of

---

[76] See Lior A. Brinn, "The Israeli Anti-boycott Law: Balancing the Need for National Legitimacy against the Rights of Dissenting Individuals," *Brooklyn Journal of International Law* 38 (2012): 345–372. The constitutionality of the law was challenged before the HCJ. The Court held calls for boycotts do not comply with original objectives of freedom of expression and therefore will not be protected by the Court. However, the Court held that Article 2(c) of the Law, which allowed the imposition of unlimited damages without proof of actual harm, was disproportionate and therefore unconstitutional and void. See HCJ 5239/11 Uri Avnery et al v. Knesset (published on Nevo, April 15, 2015).

[77] See Mordechay and Roznai, "A Jewish and (Declining) Democratic State?."

[78] Yusuf Sarfati and Aviad Rubin, "Introduction: Israel and Turkey in Comparative Perspective," in *The Jarring Road to Democratic Inclusion*, ed. Aviad Rubin and Yusuf Sarfati (Lanham, MD: Lexington Books, 2016) 1, 6.

[79] Amal Jamal, "The Rise of 'Bad Civil Society' in Israel—Nationalist Civil Society Organizations and the Politics of Delegitimization," *SWP Comments*, January 2018, 2, https://www.swp-berlin.org/fileadmin/contents/products/comments/2018C02_jamal.pdf.

[80] See, e.g., Jessica Steinberg, "Miri Regev's Cultural War Heats Up," *Times of Israel*, January 29, 2016, https://www.timesofisrael.com/miri-regevs-cultural-war-heats-up/; Editorial, "Escalation in Israeli Minister's Culture War," *Haaretz*, September 8, 2017, https://www.haaretz.com/opinion/editorial/the-lawyer-didnt-like-the-show-1.5449270.

loyalty is part of the populist wave that undermines the pluralism that character-ized the Israeli society.[81]

The delegitimization of those opposing government's policies on the one hand and the promotion of a single state-vision on the other hand is also evident in the govern-ment's complicated relationship with the media: aiming to control statutory media authorities and excoriating media channels and reporters critical of the prime minister or the government. This aim to control the media was expressed in a question raised by Culture Minister Regev, during a cabinet debate over a new body meant to replace the Israel Broadcasting Authority. "It's inconceivable that we'll establish a corporation that we won't control. What's the point?"[82] Indeed, the Freedom House 2017 report states that "while Israel has historically enjoyed a vibrant and pluralistic media sector, these and other problems have caused press freedom in the country to decline in recent years."[83]

One can add to this list the increasing attempts to change the status of the occupied territories through domestic legislation, with the clear aim to unilaterally annex parts of them into Israel,[84] and the delegitimization of the Arab minority as expressed in the prime minister's 2015 Election Day speech where he called his supporters to go out and vote because "the rule of the right is in danger," since the Arab voters were being "bused to the polling stations by left-wing NGOs" and were turning out in vast numbers (both claims were false).[85]

The move to a populist right-wing political agenda and the gradual breakaway from the liberal model of democracy have shaken the constitutional revolution.

Is Democracy in Crisis?

Israelis dispute whether these policies and practices constitute a democratic backsliding. There are three main approaches for analyzing the situation.

---

[81] Alon Harel, "The Triumph of Israeli Populism," *I-CONnect*, August 22, 2017), http://www.iconnectblog.com/2017/08/the-triumph-of-israeli-populism; see also Naama Weiss Yaniv and Keren Tenenboim-Weinblatt, "Israel: Right-Wing Populism and Beyond," in *Populist Political Communication in Europe*, ed. Toril Aalberg et al. (London: Routledge, 2016), ch. 16.

[82] Barak Ravid, "Miri Regev: Why Set Up New Broadcasting Corporation if We Don't Control It?," *Haaretz*, July 31, 2016, https://www.haaretz.com/israel-news/miri-regev-why-set-up-new-broadcasting-corporation-if-we-dont-control-it-1.5418699.

[83] Freedom House, *Freedom of the Press 2017: Press Freedom's Dark Horizon* (Lanham, MD: Rowman and Littlefield, 2017), 9–10, https://freedomhouse.org/report/freedom-press/freedom-press-2017.

[84] See, e.g., Meron Rapoport, "Israel on the Fast Track for West Bank Annexation," *Middle East Eye*, December 16, 2016, http://www.middleeasteye.net/columns/israel-fast-track-west-bank-annexation-1895356809; Steven A. Cook, "Israel Moves to Annex the West Bank—This Is How the Two-State Solution Dies," *Council on Foreign Relations*, January 8, 2018, https://www.cfr.org/blog/israel-moves-annex-west-bank-how-two-state-solution-dies.

[85] "Netanyahu's 'Arab Droves' Warning May Have Been Decisive in His Victory," *Times of Israel*, March 25, 2015, https://www.timesofisrael.com/netanyahus-arab-droves-warning-may-have-been-decisive-in-his-victory/.

FULFILLMENT—NOT CRISIS—OF DEMOCRACY

Netanyahu's government and its supporters maintain that the constitutional revolution is a crack in Israeli democracy, which must be corrected. According to their perspective, the constitutional revolution is not a democratic success story, but rather an unwelcome restriction upon the people's representatives, who represent the majority opinion. According to this view, through the constitutional revolution, the judiciary has turned itself into the final arbitrator of society's values, and what is worse, the judiciary represents the old-elite left-wing, which prefers universal and liberal values over national particular ones. If this is indeed the case, then all the actions taken by the government to curtail judicial authority and to promote a single vision of Israel as the nation-state of Jewish People alone are vindication, not a crisis, of democracy.

A strong representative of this approach is the Minister of Justice Shaked, who believes that the judiciary is exceeding its jurisdiction and disturbing "the path to democracy and governance."[86] Minister Shaked criticizes the court for prioritizing individual rights while ignoring "Israeli uniqueness, our national tasks and our very identity, history and Zionist challenges," arguing that the Israeli judiciary adopts a "utopian and universal worldview sanctifying individual rights to an extreme degree and ceasing taking part in the struggle for Israel's very existence."[87] According to Shaked, the constitutional revolution, brought about through the judiciary, caused "Israeli democracy to run away from the nation," and that critiques of her counterrevolutionary actions derive from "a 'deep fear' by various 'detached old elites' that they would lose control of the system."[88]

Responding to critics Minister Shaked claims that not every change will be the end of democracy. Teasing her critics, she claimed: "they declared its death so many times, that it seems that not only cats have nine lives, but also our democracy." In Shaked's opinion, "Israeli democracy is as healthy as a bull," and the processes that are taking place correct past injustices and strengthen Israel's constitutional basis.[89]

---

[86] Ayelet Shaked, "The Path to Democracy and Governance," *Hashiloach*, May 25, 2017, https://hashiloach.org.il/path-democracy-governance/ [Heb.].

[87] Gilad Morag and Tova Tzimuki, "Shaked Denounces HCJ Illegal Aliens Ruling, Calls For New Constitutional Revolution," *Ynetnews*, August 29, 2017, https://www.ynetnews.com/articles/0,7340,L-5009369,00.html.

[88] Yonah Jeremy Bob, "Shaked: Judges Are Not the Sons of Light, Legislators Are Not Sons of Darkness," *Jerusalem Post*, December 22, 2017, http://www.jpost.com/Israel-News/Shaked-Judges-are-not-the-sons-of-light-legislators-are-not-sons-of-darkness-519767.

[89] Itamar Levin, "Naor against Shaked: It Is Forbidden to Examine the Positions of a Judge," *News1*, December 1, 2016, htt://www.news1.co.il/Archive/001-D-385614-00.html.

"CRY WOLF" OR A NATURAL BALANCE

Another approach claims that the pendulum is simply moving back after a long period of judicial activism; it is a way for the political branch to reclaim its supremacy. It is the legitimate manner by which the political right aims to fulfill its political agenda.

Iddo Porat, for example, regards the described developments as "a generally legitimate democratic response by one side of the political map in Israel—the Right—to its relative weakness in several public spheres and to the growing dominance of the Left in them."[90] The case is simply of one political side of the map competing for dominance in the legal system, the media, academia, education, and civil society. The promotion of conservative judges by the minister of justice, for example—an arena that has undergone clear politization—comes after more than two decades in which no conservative judges were appointed. Likewise, civil society associations are clearly conducting political activity mainly for one political side of the map—the Left. Promoting right-wing NGOs and regulating social society activities are legitimate responses by the Right. The elected government can legitimately manifest the citizens' preferences, as reflected in its election, and now that voters have given power to the right-wing parties, they are entitled to make changes that will lean toward strengthening Zionist values.

According to Barak Medina, it is true that there may be some risks in the recent processes, but it is too early to make statements about a "constitutional capture." According to Medina, some of the laws enacted by the Knesset in recent year may indeed be "morally wrong and possibly also constitutionally invalid," yet these laws and policies are "quite limited in their adverse effect on free speech and other human rights." The Basic-Law: Human Dignity and Liberty is, as a political matter, absolutely entrenched, the gatekeepers' powers were not curtailed, and the Supreme Court continues to conduct judicial review. So, while acknowledging the risk, Medina does not share the view that "Israel has already slid into a process of 'constitutional capture.'"[91]

As Ruth Gavison summarizes: "even if all the allegedly anti-democratic bills are passed (highly unlikely)—this in itself will not perpetuate the rule of one man or party or bloc." For Gavison, elections need a certain "populism" in the sense of identifying what the "people" want and need; this measure of populism is "a core of democracy" that should be celebrated "rather than condemn[ed] . . . outright as anti-democratic."[92]

---

[90] Iddo Porat, "Is There Constitutional Capture in Israel?," *I-CONnect*, August 25, 2017), http://www.iconnect-blog.com/2017/08/is-there-constitutional-capture-in-israel.

[91] Barak Medina, "The Israeli Liberal Democracy: A Critical Assessment," *I-CONnect*, August 24, 2017, http://www.iconnectblog.com/2017/08/the-israeli-liberal-democracy-a-critical-assessment.

[92] Ruth Gavison, "Some Concluding Comments: What Is the State of Democracy? How to Defend It?," *International Journal of Constitutional Law Blog*, August 26, 2017, http://www.iconnectblog.com/2017/08/some-concluding-comments-what-is-the-state-of-democracy-how-to-defend-it.

CONSTITUTIONAL RETROGRESSION OR CAPTURE

According to the third approach, there is a negative trend that seeks to undermine the basic principles of the liberal democracy. MK Tzipi Livni, former foreign minister and minister of justice, for example, criticizes the governmental leadership for pushing to a "greater Israel" and for weakening Israeli democracy and the judicial system that protects its values. Israeli democracy, Livni declared, "is crumbling."[93]

Such voices appear also from academia. Gila Stopler argues that Israel is in the developing stages of constitutional capture, a process that is far from completed. Analyzing some of the processes I outlined in this chapter, Stopler claims that these "indicate that Israel is in the midst of an intentional legislative and political process which aims to weaken and circumvent democratic checks and balances and liberal-democratic principles, in order to facilitate a process of constitutional capture."[94] For Stopler, this process is particularly risky in Israel because it is a deeply divided society and because Israeli constitutionalism is what she terms "Semi-Liberal" due to the continued occupation of the territories, some features of state-religion relations, and some treatment of the Arab citizens.

While the question of whether Israel is on the edge of a constitutional capture remains controversial, some external observers find this third view convincing.[95]

Concluding Remarks

Israel is a vibrant democracy with strong and effective judicial and democratic institutions. It is still "the only democracy in the Middle East."[96] Nonetheless, a strong leadership coupled with rising political elites are leading to an incremental erosion of Israel's democratic institutions through countless initiatives to prevent antigovernment criticism, to weaken the judiciary, to infringe minority rights, and to modify the democratic rules of the game. These should be regarded as warning signs to Israel's liberal democracy.[97]

However, many of the threats described in this chapter are mere legislative proposals, that have not, or have not yet, materialized to laws. Thus, one may arguably claim that

---

[93] "Livni Says Israeli Democracy Is Crumbling," *Arutz Sheva*, October 5, 2016, https://www.israelnationalnews.com/News/News.aspx/218623.

[94] Gila Stopler, "Constitutional Capture in Israel," *I-CONnect*, August 21, 2017), http://www.iconnectblog.com/2017/08/constitutional-capture-israel.

[95] See, e.g., Andrew Arato, "Populism, the Courts and Civil Society," December 4, 2017, https://ssrn.com/abstract=3082596.

[96] According to the Economist Intelligence Unit's 2016 Democracy Index, Israel is characterized as a flawed democracy, yet it is ranked first in the Middle East and North Africa region, and it is the best performer in the region, climbing five places and rising to twenty-ninth place globally. See The Economist Intelligence Unit, *Democracy Index 2016: Revenge of the "Deplorables,"* (2017), 44, http://felipesahagun.es/wp-content/uploads/2017/01/Democracy-Index-2016.pdf.

[97] Nahum Barnea, "The Future of Israeli Democracy Is in Our Hands," opinion, *Ynetnews*, April 4, 2017, http://www.ynetnews.com/articles/0,7340,L-4943757,00.html.

I give them "too much weight" in the discourse. To this, Ilan Saban provides a strong answer. Counter-reaction is not fulfilled in crystallizing an explicit and formal legal change. Condemnatory and threat expressions by powerful political elites carry great influence both on judges and the society and culture within which they act. Moreover, the influence of such maneuvers is strong because the threats become not only more frequent but more real. The explicit threat in a severe counter-political backlash toward the judiciary carries with it credibility, in light of the government's clear control over the legislative process, the various laws already adopted in recent years, and the lack of moderating actors in the coalition. Finally, an additional purpose of the various legislative proposals is not only to deter the court, but to carry symbolic and rhetorical weight in the struggle over the legitimacy of the judiciary in the political and cultural debate.[98]

Israel is by no means in a similar stage of democratic backsliding as states such as Turkey, Hungary, or others, but the resemblance of some of the processes is alarming. Take Poland, for example. As I have tried to demonstrate, many of the signs of democratic backsliding apply to various degrees in Israel. For instance, writing on "anti-constitutional populist backsliding" in Poland, Wojciech Sadurski describes various cumulative legal transformations such as weakening the judiciary, silencing and delegitimization of the opposition, transforming public media into a governmental propaganda machine and criticizing private media, attempting legislatively to subordinate civil society to the political hegemony, financially supporting projects concerning the national heritage and tradition, privileging organizations with a conservative agenda while disfavoring those with more "liberal" or "left" agendas, and manipulating electoral competition mechanisms, with the aim of entrenching the hegemony of the ruling party.[99] The resemblance, even if not identical and even if not at the same extent, is alarming.

And many of the processes in Israel correspond with what Sadurski describes as "populism's source of appeal":[100] "national, cultural and religious sentiment and distrust towards multiculturalism and liberalism"—expressed by the prioritization of nationalistic Jewish values over democratic ones; "encouragement of xenophobic attitudes toward 'others', particularly migrants and refugees"—expressed, for example, in MK Miri Regev's statement that African migrants are "a cancer in the body" of the nation (a statement that 52 percent of Jewish Israelis agree with[101]), and in the prime minister's warning that the "left" is busing Arabs to vote, in effect inciting against Arab citizens who exercise their democratic right to vote; "resentment towards universalism, globalisation

---

[98] Ilan Saban, "Israel: The Political Counter-Reaction to the Constitutional Revolution," *The Public Sphere* 13 (2017): 13, 21–23.

[99] Wojciech Sadurski, "How Democracy Dies (in Poland): A Case Study of Anti-constitutional Populist Backsliding," Sydney Law School Research Paper No. 18/01, January 17, 2018, https://ssrn.com/abstract=3103491.

[100] Ibid.

[101] "52% of Israeli Jews Agree: African Migrants Are 'a Cancer'," *Times of Israel*, June 7, 2012, https://www.timesofisrael.com/most-israeli-jews-agree-africans-are-a-cancer/.

or internationalism and a renewed support of nationalism"—manifested in the minister of justice's declaration that "Zionism should not continue, and . . . will not continue, to bow down to the system of individual rights"; "dissatisfaction with the remoted elites, insensitive to the needs of 'real people'"—clearly represented by Minister Shaked's criticism of the judiciary for being "detached old elites" that ignore the people's will; "cultural resentment, expressed in a distrust of multicultural tolerance"—clearly manifested in the Minister of Culture's push for "loyalty in culture"; and finally, "impatience with liberal constraints upon government powers and viewing checks and balances as an obstacle to governance and to the expression of the will of the People"—as clearly manifested by the argument that the majority represents the sovereign people's will and accordingly should not be limited.

In the Polish context, Sadurski explains that some of the actions are done "ostensibly in the name of a purely majoritarian democracy, and of the 'sovereign' having a right to rule as it wishes. The 'will of the sovereign' expressed allegedly through an electoral choice ('winner takes all') was declared a fundamental legitimation for a general transformation of the state . . . The campaign . . . rested upon the idea that any restraints upon the political majority are by their nature antidemocratic."[102]

This is clearly the rationale behind the proposed Basic Law: Legislation mentioned earlier, according to which laws enacted by more than sixty-one Members of Knesset should be allowed to violate protected rights and, likewise, when the Knesset enacts basic laws, there should not be any substantive limits on its constituent power. Legal and judicial limitations on the power of the majority are considered anti-democratic. However, this confuses democracy with pure majoritarianism. Of course, a condition sine qua non of democracy, as a system of self-government, is the ability of the citizens to make majority collective decisions. But this is not all. Democracy also includes protection of certain rights and principles.[103] This is why the first approach describing the events as fulfillment of democracy is to my mind mistaken.

What about the second approach? Aren't some of the laws or policies of the government legitimate? Isn't the shout-out of the end of democracy exaggerated? After all, Israel is not on the path to becoming a de-facto one party democracy.

Indeed, perhaps some of the laws and policies discussed here are justifiable. Yet *the incremental aggregation of events is leading to a wide-ranging risk to the Israeli liberal-constitutional order, to an erosion of its democratic institutions, and to a gradual democratic backslide.* As Sadurski writes, the "comprehensive assault upon liberal-democratic constitutionalism produces a cumulative effect, and the sum is greater than the totality of its parts."[104]

---

[102] Sadurski, "How Democracy Dies (in Poland)," 3.

[103] See, e.g., Ronald Dworkin, "Constitutionalism and Democracy," *European Journal of Philosophy* 3 (1995): 2–11.

[104] Sadurski, "How Democracy Dies (in Poland)."

That is why the approach of exaggeration or "cry wolf" is to my mind risky. Medina writes that "if I'm right in my assessment that the 'constitutional capture' has yet to come, we should avoid crying wolf, in part in preparation for the time it really arrives."[105] However, that is precisely the problem with democratic backsliding. The incremental element is crucial. Kim Lane Scheppele recently demonstrated how charismatic leaders use their electoral mandates to consolidate power and eliminate effective opposition, using subtle legal means, ultimately dismantling the constitutional system. "To the casual visitor who doesn't pay close attention," Scheppele remarks, "a country in the grip of an autocratic legalist looks perfectly normal. There are, after all, no tanks in the streets."[106]

Nowadays, democratic breakdowns occur not by an immediate break—a sudden suspension or destruction of the constitution following a coup d'état, but by elected governments using, abusing, and subverting the democratic institutions themselves. Since there is no single moment of constitutional breakdown that can mark the "crossing the red line" toward dictatorship or to an authoritarian regime, democratic backsliding is dangerously misleading. The erosion of democracy is virtually unnoticeable: "democracy's assassins use the very institutions of democracy—gradually, subtly, and even legally—to kill it," and those who criticize the government's abusive actions are dismissed as exaggerating or crying wolf.[107] Therefore, we must neither exaggerate in our warnings, nor give the warning signs short shrift.

When Aharon Barak was recently asked whether he thinks that Israeli democracy is in danger, he replied "danger is a too extreme expression. However, there is a trend, which if aggravated can lead to danger. We are on a slippery slope, and who knows where it will stop. It might not stop, and then there will be total deterioration. If the current trend continues or worsens, it could lead to 'tyranny of the majority'. . . I am not saying we are there, but if we continue to do so, we will get there."[108]

There is a famous (but seemingly untrue[109]) story that if you put a frog into a pot of boiling water it will jump right out, but if you put it in cool water and then heat it, the frog will tolerate the water until it is too weak to jump, and eventually would be boiled to death. Likewise, and in light of how democracies die, we should be aware of the incremental dismantlement of democracy in Israel and elsewhere. Otherwise, when we wake up against attacks upon the liberal democracy, it may very well be too late.[110]

---

[105] Medina, "The Israeli Liberal Democracy."

[106] Kim Lane Scheppele, "Autocratic Legalism," *The University of Chicago Law Review* 85 (2018): 545, 575.

[107] Steven Levitsky and Daniel Ziblatt, *How Democracies Die* (New York: Crown, 2018). This citation is from Steven Levitsky and Daniel Ziblatt, "This Is How Democracies Die," *Guardian* (UK), January 21, 2018, https://www.theguardian.com/us-news/commentisfree/2018/jan/21/this-is-how-democracies-die.

[108] Tzimuki and Lam, "Aharon's Laws."

[109] James Fallows, "The Boiled-Frog Myth: Stop the Lying Now!," *The Atlantic* September 16, 2006, https://www.theatlantic.com/technology/archive/2006/09/the-boiled-frog-myth-stop-the-lying-now/7446/.

[110] See, recently, Emanuel Gross, "Ayelet Shaked's Chutzpah," *Haaretz*, February 5, 2018, https://www.haaretz.co.il/opinions/.premium-1.5790249 [Heb.] ("I believe that we need to put an end to the silence of important sections in our public concerning what the current government is doing to the rule of law; and it is time to rise and defend the Israeli democracy because if we will not, it will not defend us" [translation by author]).

22 Constitutional Erosion and the Challenge to Secular Democracy in India
Manoj Mate

IN AUGUST 2017, India celebrated the seventieth anniversary of its independence from British colonial rule, and nearly seven decades of its experiment with constitutional democracy. The Indian Constitution has arguably functioned somewhat effectively in structuring the operations of national, state, and local governance; in managing India's complex religious, cultural, and ethnic pluralism; and in creating a constitutional and legal framework for effectuating the protection of fundamental rights.[1] However, assessing the current state of India's *constitutional democracy* requires an assessment not only of the resilience of India's constitutional framework, but also of the functioning and operation of constitutional governance and electoral democracy, and whether they are consistent with India's constitutional framework and foundational principles.

This chapter assesses and evaluates the current state of constitutional democracy in India. India's constitutional system has arguably proven to be resilient and successful in allowing for and accommodating constitutional change.[2] Its constitutional framework has allowed for important social and political transformation and changes through the

---

[1] See generally Granville Austin, *Working a Democratic Constitution: A History of the Indian Experience* (New York: Oxford University Press, 1999).

[2] In comparative constitutional studies, the functioning and stability of constitutional frameworks have been assessed by analyzing constitutions in terms of their resilience or success. For example, Tom Ginsburg and Zack Elkins have analyzed what factors help explain "constitutional endurance." See Zachary Elkins, Tom Ginsburg, and James Melton, *The Endurance of National Constitutions* (New York: Cambridge University Press, 2009);

amendment process, while its system of separation of powers and judicial review have provided important checks on this power. Although the Constitution has been amended frequently, the Supreme Court has successfully asserted limits on Parliament's constituent power of amendment through the assertion of the basic structure doctrine.[3] While the Supreme Court ultimately acceded to and upheld the Emergency Rule decrees of Indira Gandhi's regime (1975–1977), key decisions of the Indian judiciary also helped entrench a "constitutional guardian" role for the Court prior to and at the end of the Emergency, and the Court has continued to consolidate its role as a guardian in the ensuing decades.[4] Moreover, India's system of constitutional democracy has proven to be relatively resilient through various challenging and potentially destabilizing moments in its history.[5]

However, this account of constitutional performance and resilience becomes more complicated when examining India's recent trajectory of democratization, electoral politics, and governance. At one level, India's system of electoral democracy has been arguably successful in terms of an increasing trend toward multipartyism and electoral competitiveness as reflected in the emergence and success of opposition parties, and inclusion of new groups in politics and governance. From the 1950s to the late 1980s, India's national political system was mostly dominated and led by the Congress Party, though Congress as an organizational institution was weakened through Indira Gandhi's "deinstitutionalization" of the party.[6]

Tom Ginsburg, "Constitutional Endurance," in *Comparative Constitutional Law* ed. Tom Ginsburg and Rosalind Dixon (Northampton, MA: Edward Elgar, 2011), 112.

[3] See Pratap Bhanu Mehta, "The Inner Conflict of Constitutionalism: Judicial Review and the Basic Structure," in *India's Living Constitution: Ideas, Practices, Controversies*, ed. Zoya Hasan, Eswaran Sridharan, and R. Sudarshan (London: Anthem, 2002), 179–206; Sudhir Krishnaswamy, *Democracy and Constitutionalism in India: A Study of the Basic Structure Doctrine* (New Delhi: Oxford University Press, 2009).

[4] See Manoj Mate, "Two Paths to Judicial Power: The Basic Structure Doctrine and Public Interest Litigation in Comparative Perspective," *San Diego International Law Journal* 12 (2010): 175–222; Manoj Mate, "Judicial Supremacy in Comparative Constitutional Law," *Tulane Law Review* 92 (2017): 393–468. The Supreme Court's assertiveness has been bolstered by the high level of independence it enjoys as a result of the control it exercises over its own appointments processes. In the Second Judges' Case (1993), the Supreme Court asserted judicial primacy and control over its own appointments processes, and today the Chief Justice of India and a collegium of four senior justices now have primacy over the executive branch in appointments. See Supreme Court Advocates on Record Association v. Union of India (1993). The Court recently reaffirmed its supremacy in appointments in the NJAC decision (2015) in invalidating a constitutional amendment creating a National Judicial Appointments Commission that would have restored the primacy of the executive branch in appointments. See Supreme Court Advocates on Record Association v. Union of India (2015).

[5] This has included national level crises, including the India-Pakistan war over Bangladesh; Indira Gandhi's Emergency Rule regime (1975–1977); regional disputes, and internal state-level insurgencies; the assassinations of Indira Gandhi and later Rajiv Gandhi; the implementation of the Mandal Commission Report in 1989; India's balance of payments crisis in 1991; and the Hindu-Right-led campaign that destroyed the Babri Masjid in 1992, and resulted in violence and strife.

[6] Lloyd Rudolph and Susanne Hoeber Rudolph, *In Pursuit of Lakshmi: The Political Economy of the Indian State* (Chicago: University of Chicago Press, 1987), 134–140.

From the late 1980s to 2014, the Congress Party saw its dominance in politics continue to erode as India was governed by a series of multiparty coalition governments, including coalition governments led by the Hindu right Bharatiya Janata Party (BJP).[7] From the perspective of democratization and democratic development, India's current phase of electoral democracy has been characterized by the successful mobilization of new political parties and movements that have, at least in the short term, replaced the relatively weak Congress Party-left coalitions that were in power since the early 1990s. In 2014, India entered a new phase when the BJP, led by Narendra Modi, for the first time successfully won a decisive governing majority in Parliament and also won electoral majorities across many state governments.

Juxtaposed against this relatively sanguine assessment of India's constitutional resilience and record of democratization must be a sober assessment of current challenges to India's constitutional and political framework. In this chapter, I argue that one of the major challenges to the stability and integrity of India's constitutional democracy stems from another facet of India's evolution as a democracy—the rise of religiosity in politics, and the increasing success of the BJP and allied parties in Indian elections. The BJP's deployment of religion as a vehicle for political mobilization can be traced back to the 1990s, and in light of its victory in the 2014 elections, and recent victories in state elections, it appears that the BJP will continue to deploy majoritarian religiosity and religious rhetoric in its election campaigns.

In contrast to its earlier stints in power as a leader of coalition governments in the late 1990s and early 2000s, the BJP government today commands strong political majority support having won 274 out of the 545 seats in Parliament in the 2014 Lok Sabha elections. In 2014, the Congress Party suffered its worst electoral performance since the 1977 elections, winning less than 20 percent of the popular vote, and dropping from 206 seats to only 44 seats. Under Indian parliamentary rules, the Congress Party does not meet the minimum threshold seat share requirement (10 percent) for official recognition as the opposition party in Parliament. As a result, the BJP government is now poised to, and has already taken actions that undermine and erode secularism in unprecedented ways. Indeed, the BJP's relatively modest victory, and the surprisingly strong performance of the Congress Party in the 2017 Gujarat elections, suggests a new concern: that *both* the BJP and the Congress Party are now deploying religiosity as a strategy for electoral mobilization.[8]

---

[7] Yogendra Yadav, "Electoral Politics in the Time of Change: India's Third Electoral System, 1989–1999," *Economic and Political Weekly* 34 (1999): 2393–2399. Although it is not the focus of this chapter, corruption also remains an ongoing challenge to electoral democracy and governance in India. See generally Milan Vaishnav, *When Crime Pays: Money and Muscle in Indian Politics* (New Haven, CT: Yale University Press, 2017).

[8] "'Is it Wrong to Visit a Temple' Asks Rahul Gandhi," *Times of India*, December 12, 2017, https://timesofindia. indiatimes.com/elections/assembly-elections/gujarat/is-it-wrong-to-visit-a-temple-asks-rahul-gandhi/ articleshow/62035431.cms; "Rahul Gandhi's Temple Tour in Gujarat: A Congress Explanation," *NDTV*, December 12, 2017, https://www.ndtv.com/india-news/rahul-gandhis-temple-tour-in-gujarat-sponsors-a-congress-explanation-1756137.

This chapter examines how the ongoing drift toward continued and increasing religiosity in electoral politics and constitutional governance poses a significant threat to the ideal of a secular constitutional democracy enshrined in the Indian Constitution. I argue that India is in the midst of an intensifying process of "constitutional erosion" whereby the increasing resort to and use of religiosity in elections and governance are continuing to weaken and undermine secularism as a constitutional and governing principle.[9] The continuing invocation and deployment of religion and religious rhetoric in elections and government policies threatens other core constitutional values—including unity, communal harmony, and political stability—and as a result, poses a fundamental threat to the integrity of India's constitutional order. Since the 2014 elections, BJP policies, speeches, and rhetoric have inflamed communal tensions and have triggered an increase in anti-Muslim violence, and also led to significant attacks on intellectuals and critics of the government.

In particular, I suggest that India's current constitutional and legal framework, and its framework of electoral regulation, are failing to adequately restrict and contain the increased use of religion in electoral politics, and in governance. In particular, I argue that the Indian Supreme Court's decision in the *Hindutva* cases, along with relatively weak enforcement of criminal prohibitions on the use of religion in the Representation of People Act, have created "political space" for ongoing deployment of religious speech and rhetoric in elections. Through statutory interpretation of the RPA, the Supreme Court of India has arguably helped to facilitate a weakening and erosion of secularism in India's constitutional framework. India thus illustrates the need to explore how constitutional secularism is gradually eroded through the interrelated processes of increasing resort to religiosity in politics, and electoral corruption, which prevent other parties from challenging the drift toward majoritarian religiosity.

This chapter begins by providing a brief background and context on the nature of secularism in India's constitutional and political framework. It proceeds to evaluate the ongoing erosion of secularism dating back to the early 1990s coinciding with the ascendance of the BJP as a national political party and its first electoral victories at the national level, and the constitutional response in a series of Supreme Court decisions. It then concludes by analyzing current use of religious speech in elections, and the enactment of symbolic legislation and other government actions since the election of the BJP government in the 2014 elections that has led to increased violence against Muslims and critics of the government.

---

[9] This ongoing erosion of secularism is akin to what Aziz Huq and Tom Ginsburg call "constitutional retrogression." According to Huq and Ginsburg, constitutional retrogression refers to the "incremental (but ultimately substantial) decay in three basic predicates of democracy—competitive elections, liberal rights to speech and association, and the adjudicative and administrative rule of law necessary for democratic choice to thrive." Aziz Huq and Tom Ginsburg, "How to Lose a Constitutional Democracy," *UCLA Law Review* 65 (forthcoming 2018).

Secularism and the Indian Constitutional Framework

At its inception, the Indian Constitution did not contain a direct and explicit textual reference to secularism as a foundational principle, despite efforts by members of the Constituent Assembly to include the word "secular" in the preamble.[10] It was not until the Forty-Second Amendment that secularism was actually added into the preamble of the Indian Constitution.[11] Although the Constituent Assembly did not include the term "secular" or "secularism" in the Indian Constitution, the debates in the Constituent Assembly confirm that the leaders of the Assembly chose not to include secularism in the preamble because they did not want to adopt US or Western conceptions of secularism.[12] Instead, the framers of the Indian Constitution envisioned a broad, accommodationist conception of secularism, which balanced individual and religious freedom and liberty, with the concern about potential communal tensions and violence.[13]

India's constitutional framework entrenched a model of secularism that was primarily concerned with preventing and inhibiting religious and communal conflict and violence, and with reforming Hinduism, the dominant state religion, in order to protect fundamental rights and advance equality by addressing inequities, including caste-based discrimination and exclusion in Indian society.[14] Rajeev Bhargava, a leading scholar of Indian secularism, argues that the form of secularism entrenched in the Indian Constitution can be described as "contextual secularism," and that this particular model of secularism was informed and adopted in response to the deterioration of Hindu-Muslim relations.[15] Contextual secularism, for Bhargava, entails a model that allows for politics to maintain a "principled distance" from religious institutions, while allowing for political or state intervention in religion in order to "secure a dignified life for all, prevent discrimination on grounds of religion, check religious bigotry, and manage frenzied internecine

---

[10] See Suhrith Parthasarathy, "Understanding Secularism in the Hindu Context," Op-ed, *The Hindu*, January 2, 2018, http://www.thehindu.com/opinion/lead/the-secular-condition/article22347527.ece; Shefali Jha, "Secularism in the Constituent Assembly Debates," *Economic and Political Weekly* 37, no. 30 (July 27–August 2, 2002): 3175–3180.

[11] See Parthasarathy, "Understanding Secularism."

[12] Ibid.

[13] See Rajeev Bhargava, "India's Secular Constitution," in *India's Living Constitution*, 105; D.E. Smith, "India as a Secular State," in *Secularism and Its Critics*, ed. Rajeev Bhargava (New York: Oxford University Press, 1998).

[14] Rajeev Bhargava, "Secularism in India: The Recent Debate," in *Secularism and Its Critics*, 517. See Gary Jacobsohn, *The Wheel of Law: India's Secularism in Comparative Constitutional Context* (Princeton, NJ: Princeton University Press, 2003); Mark Galanter, *Competing Equalities: Law and the Backward Classes in India* (Berkeley: University of California Press, 1984).

[15] Bhargava, "Secularism in India," 517. In distinguishing the Indian model of secularism from American and Israeli constitutional models, Gary Jacobsohn uses the term "ameliorative secularism" to describe the Indian constitutional model of secularism as encompassing the commitment to social reform and advancing a vision of intergroup comity. See Jacobsohn, *The Wheel of Law*, 94.

conflicts that plunge societies into barbarism and into an escalating spiral of violence and cruelty."[16]

As Bhargava suggests, India's constitutional model of secularism was informed by the broader context of national communal violence and strife resulting from the partition of India, and the Constituent Assembly debates reveal that the Assembly and drafters of the Constitution were concerned about unity and preventing communal violence, informed by the broader context of national violence and strife resulting from the partition of India.[17] As a result, the Assembly rejected separate electorates and reserved seats in the national and state legislatures on the basis of religion, and also rejected adopting provisions aimed at reforming minority religions' personal laws.[18]

The "protective" conception of Indian secularism as instrumental to maintaining communal harmony, national unity, and equality is illustrated by the Supreme Court's decision in *S.R. Bommai v. Union of India* (1994). As discussed later, in *SR Bommai*, the Supreme Court upheld the declaration of President's Rule and the dismissal of three state governments that had been found to have aided or acquiesced in the campaign to destroy the Babri Masjid as part of the Ram Janmabhoomi agitation, on the grounds that secularism was part of the basic structure of the Constitution, and that the declaration of President's Rule was essential to preserve secularism and national integrity.[19] Since 2014, the BJP Government's policies, rhetoric, and actions at both the national and state level have arguably threatened not only national unity and integrity, but other constitutional values including fundamental rights protections for free speech, religious freedom, and equality.

Two primary institutions have played a central role in defining and enforcing the parameters of secularism through constitutional doctrine and India's statutory framework governing religious speech in elections. First, the actual legal and doctrinal contours of secularism have been articulated by the Supreme Court of India through key decisions, including SR Bommai.[20] Later, the Court in subsequent decisions would further delineate the meaning and understanding of secularism in the context of disputes involving federalism, and electoral speech. Second, the Election Commission of India has also played an important role as the constitutional authority charged with enforcing the Representation of People Act of 1951 (RPA), the statutory framework governing India's elections. The RPA specifically contains prohibitions on appeals to religion by candidates and parties in elections. However, the Election Commission has been heavily constrained

---

[16] Bhargava, "Secularism in India," 515–516.

[17] See Uday Mehta, "Constitutionalism," in *The Oxford Companion to Politics in India*, ed. N. Jayal and Pratap Bhanu Mehta (New Delhi: Oxford University Press, 2007), 16.

[18] Bhargava, "Secularism in India," 515–516.

[19] Ibid.

[20] In Kesavananda v. State of Kerala, the landmark decision that asserted the basic structure doctrine for the first time, multiple judges suggested that secularism was a basic feature of the Indian Constitution. See Kesavananda Bharati v. State of Kerala (1973).

by the Supreme Court's interpretation of the RPA in the *Hindutva* decisions, although in a recent decision, the Supreme Court adopted a broader interpretation of Section 123's prohibition on corrupt practices as covering a broader scope of religious speech.

The Rise of the BJP in National Politics and the Ayodhya Controversy

The origins of the BJP can be traced to the Bharitaya Jana Sangh (BJS) party, founded by Dr. Syama Prasad Mukherjee in 1951. The BJS party emerged from the broader Hindu nationalist movement that began in the 1920s under the British Raj in India, in part as a reaction to the Khilafat movement in the 1920s.[21] The Khilafat movement protested the end of the Caliphate in Istanbul, leading to a series of demonstrations that led to riots from 1921 to 1927.[22] Within this Hindu nationalist movement, two prominent groups, the Hindu Mahasabha, a radical Hindu nationalist party, and the Rashtriya Swayamsevak Sangh (RSS) ("National Volunteers Corps") emerged.[23] The RSS embraced the ideology of Hindutva, based on the writings of the Indian revolutionary V.D. Savarkar. According to this ideology, Indian identity is based on a broader conception and understanding of Hindu culture that extends beyond the Hindu religion, and includes common and universal Hindu values and traditions associated with the history of Indian civilization, including the Sanskrit language. Like the RSS, the ideology of the BJS was one of historical and religious nationalism, based on the ideology of Hindutva. In 1965, the BJS adopted the philosophy of integral humanism, formulated by RSS leader Deendayal Upadhyaya, and along with the core doctrine of Hindutva, integral humanism is the official philosophy of the BJP.[24]

The BJS party gradually increased its power base and share of seats in the Lok Sabha in the 1950s and 1960s, rising from two seats in the 1953 Lok Sabha to thirty-five seats in the 1967 elections. Following the end of Indira Gandhi's Emergency rule period, the BJS, along with several opposition parties, formed the Janata Party coalition, which won the 1977 elections with 295 seats. After the Janata party coalition was defeated by Congress in the 1980 elections, Atal Bihari Vajpayee formed the BJP Party.[25]

As the Congress Party continued to weaken in the 1980s, the BJP entered a period of radical politics aimed at expanding support among Hindu voters.[26] The BJP capitalized

[21] Christophe Jaffrelot, "Refining the 'Moderation Thesis' regarding 'Radical Parties': The Jana Sangh and the BJP between Hindu Nationalism and Coalition Politics in India," *Research in Question No. 34*, December 2010, https://hal.archives-ouvertes.fr/hal-01069458/document, 5.

[22] Ibid.

[23] Ibid.

[24] Ibid., 6–8.

[25] This electoral history draws from "History of the BJP," accessed February 22, 2018, http://www.bjp.org/about-the-party/history.

[26] Jaffrelot, "Refining the 'Moderation Thesis.'"

on the controversy surrounding the Supreme Court's decision in the *Shah Bano* case in 1984.[27] In that decision, the Court held that pursuant to Section 125 of the Criminal Procedure Code (CPC), a divorced Muslim wife was entitled to maintenance from her husband beyond the three-month period prescribed by Muslim family law. The Court held that the Muslim Personal Laws could not be interpreted to provide an exemption from the CPC's requirements, and went further in recommending that Parliament enact a Uniform Civil Code.[28] In an attempt to maintain the support of Muslim voters, the Congress government overrode *Shah Bano* by enacting the Muslim Women (Protection of Rights on Divorce) Act of 1985, which exempted Muslim men from Section 25 of the CPC and excluded a Muslim wife's right to maintenance beyond the three-month period under Muslim family law.[29] The BJP subsequently challenged and criticized this Act as providing special rights and protections for Muslims as part of its broader effort to build electoral support among Hindu voters.

The BJP sought to widen its base of political support among Hindus in North India and nationwide through invocation and deployment of religious rhetoric based on the ideology of Hindutva, and as a result, was able to increase its seat share in the Lok Sabha from two seats in 1984 to eighty-five seats in 1989.[30] After the Janata Dal-National Front implemented the Mandal Commission recommendations and expanded quotas in government jobs for members of the Other Backward Classes (OBCs), upper caste Hindus engaged in violent nationwide protests. In order to shift the focus and mobilize Hindu supporters, the BJP joined the Ram Janmabhoomi movement aimed at constructing a Rama mandir (temple) in the ancient city of Ayodhya at a site where the Babri Masjid was located.[31] Ultimately, the BJP withdrew its support for the coalition government, toppling the Janata Dal-National front government and triggering new elections.

The 1991 BJP manifesto was entitled "Toward Ram Rajya" and explicitly called for the building of the Rama Mandir in Ayodhya, along with other planks including deletion of Article 370 (which granted Jammu-Kashmir special autonomous status under the Indian Constitution), a uniform civil code, Hindutva, and the overall goal of building a "Hindu rashtra (nation).[32] The 1991 manifesto also called for integrated rural development measures, and policies aimed at liberating "the economy from the clutches of bureaucratic controls."[33] In 1992, the BJP, led by its president, L.K. Advani, initiated the

---

[27] Md. Ahmed Khan v. Shah Bano Begum (1984). See Seval Yildirim, "Expanding Secularism's Scope: An Indian Case Study," *American Journal of Comparative Law* 52 (2004): 901, 913.

[28] Yildirim, "Expanding Secularism's Scope," 913–915.

[29] Ibid., 914.

[30] Jaffrelot, "Refining the 'Moderation Thesis,'" 12–14.

[31] See Inder Malhotra, "Mandal v. Mandir," *Indian Express*, March 23, 2015, http://indianexpress.com/article/opinion/columns/mandal-vs-mandir/.

[32] Pratap Chandra Swain, *Bharatiya Janata Party: Profile and Performance* (New Delhi: A.P.H. Publication, 2001), 209–210.

[33] Ibid.

Rath Yatra movement to build national support for the construction of a Rama temple in Ayodhya.[34] On December 6, 1992, Hindu nationalists destroyed the Babri Masjid in Ayodhya, leading to widespread communal riots and violence across India.[35]

The Political and Constitutional Response: The Supreme Court and Secularism

In the mid-1990s, the Supreme Court of India defined the nature and scope of secularism in a series of landmark decisions involving federalism and electoral regulation involving the Hindu Right and BJP. While the Supreme Court did help entrench secularism as a basic feature of the Indian Constitution in these decisions, it also created greater *political space* for the deployment of religious speech and rhetoric in governance and electoral campaigns. The Court in *S.R. Bommai v. Union of India* (1994) reaffirmed that secularism was a basic feature, in the context of the central government's authority under Article 356 to declare "President's Rule" in displacing state governments in response to Hindu nationalist agitation in the mid-1990s. In *Bommai*, the Court adjudicated a challenge to the declaration of President's Rule in response to the Ram Janmabhoomi agitation and the destruction of the Babri Masjid.[36] Pursuant to Article 356, the president dismissed state governments and dissolved legislative assemblies in six states.[37] The Court ultimately upheld the dismissals and dissolution of three state governments, ruling that the declaration of President's Rule were necessary to preserve secularism and the rule of law as part of the basic structure of the Constitution.[38] The Court also expanded the scope of its review of central government political decisions relating to state elections and politics.[39]

Although the Court in Bommai helped further entrench secularism as a basic feature of the Indian Constitution, the *Hindutva* decisions would open political space for the increased deployment of religious rhetoric and speech in elections by the BJP and allied

---

[34] Jaffrelot, "Refining the 'Moderation Thesis,'" 13.

[35] Ibid., 13.

[36] S.R. Bommai v. Union of India, (1994) 3 S.C.C. 1 (India). See Jacobsohn, *The Wheel of Law* (analyzing the *S.R. Bommai* and *Hindutva* cases in comparative context).

[37] Krishnaswamy, *Democracy and Constitutionalism*, 50 (citing S.R. Bommai, (1994) 3 S.C.C. at 149).

[38] See S.P. Sathe, *Judicial Activism in India: Transgressing Borders and Enforcing Limits* (New York: Oxford University Press, 2002), 96–98; Jacobsohn, *The Wheel of Law*, 130–141, 146–156. Article 356 of the Indian Constitution authorizes the president to declare "President's Rule" in dissolving and temporarily asserting control over state governments.

[39] See Sathe, *Judicial Activism in India*, 152. The Court in *Bommai* examined the manifesto and political ideology of the BJP party in determining that the BJP governments would not act in accordance with "the principle of secularism." Sathe, 176; S.R. Bommai, (1994) 3 S.C.C. at 137–138, 147, 151–153, 172–175, 290–293. But see Justice Verma's opinion in S.R. Bommai, (1994) 3 S.C.C. at 85–87 (asserting that there are no "judicially manageable standards" for scrutinizing presidential actions under Article 356, and that such controversies "cannot be justiciable").

political parties and groups. The *Hindutva* judgments were a series of decisions of the Supreme Court of India in 1996 that involved challenges to the conviction of several prominent members of the BJP and Shiv Sena under Section 123 of the Representation of People Act, 1951.[40] In each of these cases, the Bombay High Court held that three politicians, Dr. Ramesh Prabhoo, Manohar Joshi, and Ramchandra Kapse had each committed corrupt practices under Section 123(3) of the RPA, and on that basis, invalidated all three candidates' elections to the state legislature.[41] On appeal, the Supreme Court of India upheld the Bombay High Court's decision *Prabhoo v. Kunte*, but overturned the High Court's decisions in the *Joshi* and *Kapse* decisions.[42]

Writing for the majority in *Kunte*, Justice J.S. Verma suggested that not all references to religion in elections would violate Section 123(3). While the Court acknowledged that candidates' direct appeal to voters on the basis of their own religion violated the RPA, Justice Verma's opinion held that the use of the term "Hindutva" or other references to the Hindu religion could not themselves be criminalized and prohibited under the RPA, as "Hindutva" referred to a "way of life or state of mind, and is not to be equated with or understood as religious Hindu fundamentalism."[43] However, the Court upheld the conviction in *Prabhoo v. Kunte* on the ground that Shiv Sena leader Bal Thackeray had made speeches advocating for the election of Prabhoo on the basis that Prabhoo was a Hindu, and in the same speeches attacked Muslims and the Muslim community.

In the *Joshi* case, the Bombay High Court had convicted Manohar Joshi, the leader of the BJP-Shiv Sena coalition in Maharashtra, for stating that if his party won the state elections, Maharashtra would become the "first Hindu state." The Supreme Court overturned Manohar Joshi's conviction on the ground that this mere reference to Hinduism did not constitute a corrupt practice. The Supreme Court's decision in *Kapse* also significantly widened political space for the use of and appeals to religion by political parties, by delinking candidate activities from their party manifestos that openly invoked and relied on appeals to religion. The Bombay High Court had found Kapse in violation of the RPA on the basis of the BJP party manifesto, which made direct and overt references to Hindutva and Hinduism. However, the Supreme Court overturned the conviction and held that a candidate could not be found to have committed a corrupt practice under Section 123(3) of the RPA if that candidate was not directly involved in the drafting of the election manifesto.[44]

---

[40] See Prabhoo v. Kunte (1996) 1 SCC 130; Joshi v. Patil (1996) 1 SCC 169; Kapse v. Singh (1996) 1 SCC 206.

[41] Sathe, *Judicial Activism in India*, 185–186; Jacobsohn, *The Wheel of Law*, 163–182, 191–207.

[42] See Sathe, *Judicial Activism in India*, at 185, citing Praboo v. Kunte (1996) 1 SCC 130 at 147–148.

[43] See Sathe, *Judicial Activism in India*, 185, citing Prabhu v. Kunte (1996) 1 SCC 130 at 159. While the Supreme Court overturned the conviction of Manohar Joshi under the RPA, it did uphold the conviction of Shiv Sena leader Bal Thackeray for speeches that directly appealed to Hinduism and attacked Muslims. See Brenda Cossman and Ratna Kapur, "Secularism's Last Sigh?: The Hindu Right, the Courts, and India's Struggle for Democracy," *Harvard International Law Journal* 38 (1997): 113–170.

[44] Sathe, *Judicial Activism in India*, 185, citing Kapse v. Singh (1996) 1 SCC 206.

Constitutional Erosion in Elections and Governance
in the Post-*Hindutva* Cases Era

Following the *Hindutva* decisions, the BJP began to hone its broader message of religious nationalism and its economic policy. Coupled with the decline of the Congress Party, the BJP's support for the Ram Janmabhoomi agitation and its broader Hindutva agenda allowed it to expand its level of electoral support, and for the first time, the BJP won more than 20 percent of the national vote in the 1991 elections. In 1996, the BJP for the first time in history won the most seats in the Lok Sabha. From 1996 to 1998, India was governed by a series of coalition governments as neither the Congress Party nor the BJP was able to win a majority of votes in Parliament. As a result, the BJP was forced to moderate its politics in order to maintain the support of coalition partners during this period.[45] As Suhas Palshikar argues, the BJP in the mid-1990s was forced to adopt some elements of centrist politics including a strong emphasis on economic policy and national security in order to broaden its electoral appeal.[46]

In its 1998 manifesto, the BJP reiterated its commitment to cultural nationalism, Hindutva, and the goal of building a Lord Rama temple in Ayodhya: "... *Hindutva* has immense potentiality to re-energize this nation and strengthen and discipline it to undertake the arduous task of nation-building. . . . It is with such integrative ideas in mind, the BJP joined the Ram Janmabhoomi movement for the construction of Shri Ram Mandir at Ayodhya. This greatest mass movement in post-Independence history reoriented the disoriented polity in India and strengthened the foundation of cultural nationalism."[47] The 1998 manifesto critiqued the Congress Party approach to external economic liberalization and globalization, and instead offered a "Swadeshi" approach to reform based on internal liberalization, deregulation, and reform.[48] It also called for the Central Government to play a significant role in economic policy, including the development of infrastructure, energy and power, and policies aimed at human development.[49] The 1998 manifesto also stated that a BJP government would "re-evaluate the country's nuclear policy and exercise the option to induct nuclear weapons," and "expedite the development of the Agni series of ballistic missiles with a view to increasing their range and accuracy."[50]

---

[45] See Thomas Blom Hansen and Christophe Jaffrelot, "Introduction: The BJP after the 1996 Elections," in *The BJP and the Compulsions of Politics in India*, ed. Thomas Blom Hansen and Christophe Jaffrelot (New York: Oxford University Press, 1998), 2–10.

[46] Suhas Palshikar, "The BJP and Hindu Nationalism: Centrist Politics and Majoritarian Impulses," *South Asia: Journal of South Asian Studies* 38 (2015): 719, 730–731.

[47] BJP Manifesto, 1998, http://www.bjp.org/documents/manifesto/bjp-election-manifesto-1998/chapter-4.

[48] Ibid.

[49] Ibid.

[50] Ibid.

During the 1998 campaign, the BJP adopted an assertive posture vis-à-vis Pakistan, and BJP leader A.B. Vajpayee stated that the BJP government, if elected, would "take back that part of Kashmir that is under Pakistan's occupation."[51] After winning the most seats in 1998, the BJP government officially tested a series of nuclear weapons in May 1998.[52] The BJP-NDA coalition won the 1998 elections, and following the withdrawal of support of a supporting party, the BJP again won the 1999 elections and formed a government that stayed in power until 2004. During this period, the imperatives of maintaining the support of allied coalition parties forced the BJP to moderate its agenda.[53] Still, although the government focused primarily on national security and economic issues, the BJP continued to expand its appeal to Hindu voters through selectively pursuing initiatives emphasizing the party's support for Hinduism, including a series of initiatives introducing the teaching of aspects of Hinduism in public schools.[54]

The BJP lost the next two national elections to the Congress Party in 2004 and 2009, but it continued to deploy and reference Hindutva and religious nationalist themes in its campaigns. In the 2004 elections, the BJP, led by A.B. Vajpayee, somewhat moderated its electoral agenda by de-emphasizing Hindutva and religious nationalism, and campaigned on a platform of economic reform, progress, and prosperity that it called "India Shining." However, the BJP's 2004 Vision Statement issued during the 2004 campaign also rooted the BJP's agenda within broader historical and cultural narratives about the greatness of India's ancient civilization.[55] In articulating an "inclusive" conception of Hindutva, the Vision Statement also drew on the Indian Supreme Court's Hindutva decision[56] in observing: "Contrary to what its detractors say, and as the Supreme Court itself has decreed, Hindutva is not a religious or exclusivist concept. It is inclusive, integrative, and abhors any kind of discrimination against any section of the people of India on the basis of their faith. . . . It accepts the multi-faith character and other diversities of India, considering them to be a source of strength and not weakness. It firmly upholds secularism, understood as Sarva Pantha Samabhav (treating all faiths with respect)."[57]

---

[51] "India's Nuclear Weapons Program—Operation Shakti 1998," March 30, 2001, http://nuclearweaponarchive. org/India/IndiaShakti.html.

[52] Ibid.

[53] Palshikar, "The BJP and Hindu Nationalism," 722.

[54] The Supreme Court of India upheld these new educational recommendations in the Aruna Roy decision in 2002, in holding that the study of religion in schools would not violate secularism and that religious teachings were essential to inculcating "human and spiritual values" in students. Aruna Roy v. Union of India (2002) 7 SCC 368; see Sathe, *Judicial Activism in India*, at xl–xli (discussing and critiquing the *Aruna Roy* decision).

[55] Sathe, *Judicial Activism in India*, at xl–xli.

[56] The Hindutva judgments refers to a series of decisions of the Supreme Court of India in 1996, involving the conviction of several prominent members of the BJP and Shiv Sena under Section 123 of the Representation of People Act, 1951. Ronojoy Sen, "Legalizing Religion: The Indian Supreme Court and Secularism," *Policy Studies 30* (Washington: East-West Center, 2007), http://www.eastwestcenter.org/fileadmin/stored/pdfs/ PS030.pdf.

[57] BJP Vision Statement, 2014.

In its 2009 national campaign, the BJP party emphasized Hindutva and religious nationalist themes more prominently. The 2009 BJP Manifesto was entitled Good Governance, Development, and Security, and continued many of the themes from the 2004 manifesto.[58] In its first section, "Fear Shall No Longer Stalk This Land," the manifesto highlights the series of terrorist attacks that occurred between 2005 and 2009, and criticized the Congress-UPA Government for dismantling the series of anti-terror laws enacted by the BJP-NDA government, including the Prevention of Terrorism Act (POTA).[59] Like the 2004 manifesto, the 2009 manifesto championed inclusive pro-growth policies. The introduction to the 2009 manifesto, authored by BJP president Murli Manohar Joshi, echoed themes from the 1996 and 1998 manifestos in advancing the core tenets of Hindutva, and praising the greatness of India's pre-colonial history as an advanced civilization, and the BJP party's leadership of the Ayodhya-Ram Temple movement.[60] Much of the manifesto's planks regarding Hindutva and cultural nationalism were placed within a broader historical narrative as part of a section called "Preserving Our Cultural Heritage" that also included references to the Ram Temple, the Ram Setu (Ram bridge), and the Ganga River.[61]

The Current Challenge to Secularism in the Post-2014 Era

In the 2014 Lok Sabha elections, Narendra Modi and the BJP defeated the Congress-NDA, winning 282 out of 543 seats in the Lok Sabha, and marking the first time since the 1980s that one party won a majority of seats in the Lok Sabha.[62] Remarkably, the BJP did not actually release its election manifesto until very late—April 7, 2014, on the first of the nine days of polling in the 2014 elections.[63] Prior to that date, the BJP official website listed a series of "core issues" on its website, led by the "ModiMantra," which articulated a concise vision of Modi's development and good governance agenda: "The India of tomorrow is looking at empowerment, faster connectivity, more jobs, better education and improved quality of life. The Good Governance model of Shri Narendra Modi, enrapturedly referred to as #ModiMantra encompasses these broad themes into simple takeaways which have the potential of transforming India in the near future."[64]

---

[58] President Murli Manohar Joshi's introduction to the manifesto, "To Build a Prosperous, Powerful Nation, Recall India's Past," places a strong emphasis on recalling the greatness of India's history in the precolonial, pre-British Raj era.

[59] BJP Manifesto, 2009.

[60] Ibid.; see N. Ram, "We Need to Talk about This Manifesto," *The Hindu*, April 7, 2014, http://www.thehindu.com/todays-paper/tp-opinion/we-need-to-talk-about-this-manifesto/article5880885.ece.

[61] BJP Manifesto, 2009.

[62] See Milan Vaishnav and Danielle Smogard, "A New Era in Indian Politics?," *Carnegie Endowment for International Peace*, June 10, 2014, http://carnegieendowment.org/2014/06/10/new-era-in-indian-politics-pub-55883.

[63] Ram, "We Need to Talk about This Manifesto."

[64] BJP, "BJP's Take on #ModiMantra," accessed February 22, 2018, http://www.bjp.org/en/core-issues/modimantra.

Modi was successful in rebranding the message and vision of the BJP in the 2014 elections, drawing on his own previous campaign messaging, rhetoric, and strategies from his own populist campaigns for chief minister in Gujarat.[65] As Jaffrelot argues, from 2002 onward, Modi increasingly distanced himself from the organizational cadres of the RSS in Gujarat, and by 2007, was relying on his own personalized campaign style and approach based on "high tech" populism using television (including his own "NaMo channel"), the use of projected holograms, and the use of "Yatra" (religious pilgrimage) politics championing the ideology of Hindutva.[66] Modi combined these appeals to Hindutva with a populist brand of development ideology, and in 2007 he focused his development vision on the emerging "neo middle class."[67]

In the 2014 campaign, Modi built on this earlier vision in articulating the core message of inclusive development and good governance—this message was captured in the title of the 2014 manifesto, "Sabka Saath, Sabka Vikas" (Together with All, Development for All) that harnesses India's advantages of "democracy, demography, and demand."[68] In contrast to earlier BJP manifestos, the 2014 manifesto did not overtly advocate for or use the term "Hindutva" and emphasized primarily a new development agenda.[69] However, the manifesto did still contain references to nationalism and the Hindu religion, and as Palshikar notes, although Modi himself de-emphasized Hindutva, other BJP leaders did invoke Hindutva in certain states and localities during the campaign.[70] The main references to cultural nationalism appeared in the preface, which hailed the achievements and advance progress of India's civilization prior to the British raj under the heading "Cultural Heritage," much like the 2009 manifesto.[71]

The Cultural Heritage section included several planks including the BJP's stance of exploring "all possibilities within the framework of the constitution to facilitate the construction of the Ram Temple in Ayodhya," affirmation that the "Ram Setu (bridge) is a part of our cultural heritage and also of strategic importance due to its vast thorium deposits," and a plan on the sacred status of the Ganga river and the need for cleaning and purifying that river of pollution.[72] The section also included planks that called for "Cow and its progeny to be protected and promoted" and for drafting and adopting a "uniform civil code, which protects the rights of all women . . . by drawing upon the best traditions and harmonizing them with the modern times."[73]

---

[65] Christophe Jaffrelot, "Gujarat Elections: The Sub-Text of Modi's 'Hattrick'—High Tech Populism and The 'Neo-Middle Class,'" *Studies in Indian Politics* 1 (2013): 79–95.

[66] Ibid., 80–83.

[67] Ibid., 83–84.

[68] BJP Election Manifesto, 2014.

[69] Ibid., 2014.

[70] See Palshikar, "The BJP and Hindu Nationalism," 731.

[71] BJP Election Manifesto, 2014, 41.

[72] Ibid., 41.

[73] Ibid.

The Erosion of Secularism in Governance

As a result of the BJP's landslide victory in 2014, and subsequent victories at the state level (the BJP and its allies now control twenty out of twenty-nine state governments), the BJP and its party allies at the state level have enacted a series of sweeping measures envisioned in their manifesto aimed at advancing an agenda of promoting Hindu nationalism. This in sharp contrast to earlier periods of BJP rule where the imperatives of coalition politics limited the BJP's push for such measures.[74] In particular, the BJP has seized on two key issues—a ban on cow slaughter for beef consumption, and reforming Muslim personal laws without input from Muslim religious communities. The BJP has sought to enact bans on cow slaughter for meat consumption as the majority of beef butchers in India are Muslims, and cows are considered a sacred animal in Hinduism. Since 2014, several BJP state governments have enacted bans on cow slaughter, and in July 2017 the national government enacted new rules introducing a ban on cow slaughter for consumption.[75] These new bans on cow slaughter have led to an increase in the lynchings of Muslims nationwide. In addition, following the Supreme Court of India's decision in August 2017 holding that triple talaq divorces were invalid, the Lok Sabha went further and enacted legislation that criminalized triple talaq, allowing Muslim men who attempt to invoke triple talaq divorce to be prosecuted and imprisoned.[76] The legislation is still pending consideration in the Rajya Sabha.

In the last year, the BJP has considerably increased its deployment of majoritarian religion and religious rhetoric. In order to further appeal to Hindu voters, the BJP selected a Hindu monk and religious leader, Yogi Adityanath, to serve as chief minister of the BJP government in the state of Uttar Pradesh, India's largest state.[77] As Chief Minister, Adityanath has made numerous speeches that directly appeal to Hindutva and Hinduism and are critical of Muslims, and has introduced controversial measures including "Romeo

---

[74] See Palshikar, "The BJP and Hindu Nationalism," 730–731.

[75] See Chetan Chauhan, "Centre Bans Sale of Cows for Slaughter at Animal Markets, Restricts Cattle Trade," *Hindustan Times*, July 19, 2017, http://www.hindustantimes.com/india-news/centre-bans-cow-slaughter-across-india-cows-can-be-sold-only-to-farmers/story-8sFXJxiNmZ8eD6NXDgbvnL.html; see Christophe Jaffrelot, "India's Democracy at 70: Toward a Hindu State?," *Journal of Democracy* 28 (2017), 52–63.

[76] Sandeep Phukan, "Lok Sabha Passes the Triple Talaq Bill," *The Hindu*, December 28, 2017, http://www.the-hindu.com/news/national/lok-sabha-passes-the-triple-talaq-bill/article22319663.ece. According to one interpretation of Muslim law, one of the ways in which a Muslim man may divorce his wife is by uttering "talaq" three times. See John L. Esposito (with Natana J. DeLong-Bas), *Women in Muslim Family Law* (Syracuse, NY: Syracuse University Press, 2001), 29–35.

[77] "BJP Springs Surprise: Yogi Adityanath to be the New Uttar Pradesh CM," *Economic Times*, March 18, 2017, https://economictimes.indiatimes.com/news/politics-and-nation/bjp-springs-surprise-yogi-adityanath-to-be-the-new-uttar-pradesh-cm/articleshow/57707752.cms. Prior to becoming Chief Minister, Adityanath was criticized for delivering several anti-Muslim speeches that led to violence, and for his founding of the Hindu youth militia, the Hindu Yuva Vahini. See Christophe Jaffrelot, "India's Democracy at 70: Toward a Hindu State?," *Journal of Democracy* 28 (2017), 52–63 at 58–59.

squads" that purport to police various areas in order to protect women from men, but have been used to target Muslim men.[78]

The Erosion of Secularism in Elections and Campaigns

In addition, India's legal and regulatory framework has proven incapable of restricting the ongoing and escalating invocation and deployment of religion in elections, as illustrated by the recent elections in Gujarat in 2017. In 2017, the Supreme Court of India in *Abhiram Singh and Ors. v. Commachen* did adopt a more expansive interpretation of Section 123 of the Representation of People Act.[79] The Court overturned its earlier interpretation of the Act in the *Hindutva* cases, which stated that only a candidates' appeals on the basis of the religion of the candidate, or on the basis of the religion of an opposing candidate, could be prohibited under Section 123 of the RPA. Instead, the Court in *Abhiram Singh* interpreted Section 123 as prohibiting any reference to religion, caste, race, or community of the candidate, the candidate's opponent, or of the voters in order to secure votes in an election or to discourage voters from voting for a candidate's opponent.[80]

At the same time, the Court refused to revisit its holding in the *Hindutva* decision that candidates' appeals to or references to Hindutva in election speeches do not constitute corrupt practices under Section 123 of the RPA. Despite the expansive interpretation adopted by the Court in *Abhiram Singh*, the BJP has continued to use and deploy religion, as illustrated by the recent campaign in the 2017 Gujarat state elections. Faced with weakening economic indicators, and a resurgent Congress Party campaign led by Rahul Gandhi that sought to build a broad-based coalition across different castes, Modi and the BJP returned to invoking religious rhetoric and attacks on Muslims. For example, in a speech on December 4, 2017, Modi stated that "Congress leaders have yet again proved they are no different from the Mughals when it comes to handing over power. We don't want their Aurangzeb rule," referring to Aurangzeb, a Mughal emperor in Indian history.[81] In addition, the BJP also invoked religious and communal overtones in releasing a

[78] Aman Sharma, "Uttar Pradesh: Over 7 Lakh Men 'Checked' by Anti-Romeo Squads, 538 Cases Lodged," *Economic Times*, https://economictimes.indiatimes.com/articleshow/58918514.cms?utm_source=contentofinterest&utm_medium=text&utm_campaign=cppst.

[79] Abhiram Singh and Ors. v. Commachen (2017) 2 SCC 629.

[80] Ameen Jauhar, "Supreme Court Ban on Religion in Politics: Court's Order Should Be Lauded for Filling in Loopholes Left by Gutless Legislature," *Financial Express*, January 6, 2017, http://www.financialexpress.com/opinion/supreme-court-ban-on-religion-in-politics-courts-order-should-be-lauded-for-filling-in-loopholes-left-by-gutless-legislature/498294/.

[81] Rutam Vora, "Gujarat Elections: Modi Congratulates Congress for Aurangzeb Rule," *Hindu Business Line*, December 4, 2017, http://www.thehindubusinessline.com/news/national/gujarat-elections-modi-congratulates-congress-for-aurangzeb-rule/article9981146.ece; see Christophe Jaffrelot, "India's Democracy at 70: Toward a Hindu State?," *Journal of Democracy* 28 (2017), 52–63 (discussing the BJP's deployment of Hindu nationalist rhetoric in state elections in Uttar Pradesh and Assam in 2016 and 2017).

poster during the campaign that framed that campaign as a battle between "RAM" (the name of the Hindu king and incarnation of the Hindu God, Vishnu), an acronym based on Gujarat chief minister Vijay Rupani, BJP president Amit Shah and Prime Minister Narendra Modi, and "HAJ," (the annual Muslim pilgrimage), an acronym of Congress leaders Hardik Patel, Alpesh Thakor, and Jignesh Mevani.[82] Indeed, in an attempt to compete with the BJP, even the Congress Party resorted to invoking religion in its campaign, as Rahul Gandhi himself conducted a tour of various Hindu temples during the Gujarat campaign.[83]

According to a 2017 report released by the Centre for Study of Society and Secularism (CSSS) and the UK-based Minority Rights Group International (MRG), there were over seven hundred outbreaks of communal violence in 2016 that killed 86 and injured 2,321 people, and the actual numbers could be significantly higher as many cases are not reported.[84] The report also concluded that the failure by government authorities to investigate or prevent attacks by right-wing religious groups (including cow protection and anti-Romeo squads) have "created a climate of impunity" that "might lead to continued attacks."[85] This climate of impunity has also seen a rise in attacks and violence targeting intellectuals, journalists, and other critics of the BJP and Hindu Right. In the past three years, three prominent intellectuals or journalists who have been publicly critical of the BJP have been murdered.[86]

Conclusion

Although India is arguably not in the midst of a constitutional crisis, the BJP's continued and accelerating use of religious speech in electoral campaigns, and the enactment of legislation and other policies targeting Muslims, threatens to further undermine the secular ethos of India's constitutional framework. Since the 1990s, the BJP and Hindu Right parties have continually sought to use and deploy religious nationalist speech and rhetoric in

---

[82] "BJP Calling Hardik, Alpesh, Jignesh 'HAJ' Divisive Politics: Chidambaram," *NDTV*, December 4, 2017, https://www.ndtv.com/india-news/bjp-calling-hardik-patel-alpesh-thakor-jignesh-mevani-haj-divisive-politics-chidambaram-1783283.

[83] " 'Is It Wrong to Visit a Temple' Asks Rahul Gandhi,"; "Rahul Gandhi's Temple Tour In Gujarat: A Congress Explanation."

[84] Nilanjana Bhowmick, "Modi's Party Stokes Anti-muslim Violence in India, Report Says," *South China Morning Post*, June 29, 2017, http://www.scmp.com/week-asia/politics/article/2100513/modis-party-stokes-anti-muslim-violence-india-report-says (citing to Center for Study of Society and Secularism and Minority Groups International, *A Narrowing Space: Violence and Discrimination against India's Religious Minorities*, June 2017, http://minorityrights.org/wp-content/uploads/2017/06/MRG_Rep_India_final.pdf).

[85] Center for Study of Society and Secularism and Minority Groups International, *A Narrowing Space*.

[86] Jeffrey Gettleman and Hari Kumar, "In India, Another Government Critic Is Silenced by Bullets," *New York Times*, September 6, 2017, https://www.nytimes.com/2017/09/06/world/asia/gauri-lankesh-india-dead.html.

order to build support and win elections, and in the process have effectively undermined core tenets of secular democracy in India. Unfortunately, India's Supreme Court has arguably failed to counter this process of constitutional erosion. Although the Supreme Court helped entrench a particular conception of secularism as constituting part of the basic structure of the Indian Constitution in *Bommai*, the Court in the *Hindutva* cases opened up "political space" for the continued use and invocation of religious rhetoric in Indian elections by the BJP and Hindu Right parties. Because the Court has refused to overturn its earlier decision in the *Hindutva* cases, the Election Commission has been constrained in being able to aggressively police and restrict the use and invocation of religion in election communications and campaign speeches.

At the same time, since its electoral victory in 2014, the BJP government and its party allies in various states have sought to enact and implement a series of legislative and other measures that are explicitly designed to appeal to Hindu voters by injecting religion into political discourse and debates. These measures have further inflamed tensions between Hindus and Muslims, and have led to violence and lynchings nationwide. More recently, prominent leaders of the BJP, including Minister of State for Employment and Skill Development Anantkumar Hegde, have openly called for fundamentally changing the secular character of the Indian Constitution.[87] Given the current weakness of the Congress party and other opposition parties, it is unclear that resort to political processes alone can counter the erosion of secularism in India. For reformers and advocates seeking to protect secularism, the Indian judiciary and Election Commission of India remain the last best hope. In the long term, reforming India's jurisprudential and statutory framework to restrict religion and religious speech in Indian politics must be an imperative, so as to allow other parties to be able to counter and serve as a check on India's continued majoritarian drift toward religious politics.

---

[87] "Union Minister Anantkumar Hegde Kicks Up Row with Remarks on Secularism," *The Hindu*, December 24, 2017, http://www.thehindu.com/news/national/karnataka/hegde-kicks-up-a-fresh-row-with-remarks-on-secularism/article22271584.ece; see Suhrith Parthasarathy, "Understanding Secularism in the Hindu Context," Op-ed, *The Hindu*, January 2, 2018, http://www.thehindu.com/opinion/lead/the-secular-condition/article22347527.ece.

23 Australia's Non-Populist Democracy?
The Role of Structure and Policy
Rosalind Dixon and Anika Gauja*

Introduction

From a comparative perspective, the state of democracy in Australia looks quite healthy. The two major parties that have historically dominated the political landscape, the Australian Labor Party (ALP) and the Liberal-National Coalition, continue to command more than three-quarters of the combined vote at national elections, and exert significant control over the selection of their own leadership.[1] There has been no major turn against the parties, nor hostile takeover of these parties from within.[2] Australians also continue to express relatively high levels of confidence in the democratic system: of a sample of twenty-five countries surveyed as part of the International Social Survey

* The authors thank Mark Graber, Richard Holden, Bert Huang, Paul Kildea, and Richard McHugh for helpful comments on previous versions of the chapter, and Melissa Vogt and Max Groemping for outstanding research assistance.

[1] See Richard Pildes and Stephen Gardbaum, "Populism and Democratic Institutional Design: Methods of Selecting Candidates for Chief Executive in the United States and Other Democracies," *NYU Law Review* (forthcoming).

[2] Compare Samuel Issacharoff, "Outsourcing Politics: The Hostile Takeovers of Our Hollowed Out Political Parties," *Houston Law Review* 54 (2017): 845–880.

Program, Australia ranked second (behind only Norway) in its level of satisfaction with democracy.[3]

This picture, however, also somewhat understates the potential threats to democracy—and liberal democratic values—in Australia. Perhaps the most significant single threat, and the focus of this chapter, has been the resurrection of the right-wing populist political party, One Nation. After a period of deep electoral unpopularity, the One Nation Party re-emerged as a significant electoral threat to the established major parties at the 2016 federal election, winning four seats in the Australian Senate. The party suffered a major defeat in the subsequent WA and Queensland state elections, but only after a period in which it was thought that it might gain enough votes to form a coalition government with the Liberal-National Party.[4] Since it was established in 1997, the party has consistently espoused values, and policies, that closely parallel many of the illiberal forms of populism surveyed elsewhere in this volume—that is, economic protectionism, opposition to immigration, especially Muslim immigration, and an attack on liberal institutions, such as the media, the arts, and universities.[5]

The fact that One Nation has largely been contained as a threat, therefore, is an important dimension to the recent Australian democratic experience that calls for explanation. The chapter suggests that it is best explained through the lens of two interconnected factors: first, it is the product of structural safeguards in the Australian political system that create a firewall against the risk of a full-scale populist takeover of the democratic system. Second, it is a product of a quite high degree of policy responsiveness on the part of both major parties in key policy areas that have intersected with One Nation's agenda, such as immigration, and energy and climate change policy, which have helped diffuse the threat of a full-scale populist takeover.

The two dynamics are also potentially interconnected: some of the core structural safeguards of non-populist democracy in Australia come from the country's system of mandatory, preferential voting. These features of the electoral, or small "c" constitutional system, reduce the effect of turnout as an influence on Australian electoral outcomes, and the impact of any small party—whether liberal or illiberal—in key electoral subunits. They also give the major parties strong incentives to appeal to the median voter, rather than a subsection of their base, or that of minor/third parties at either the far right- or left-tails of the political spectrum.[6]

---

[3] Pippa Norris, "Australian Democracy in Comparative Perspective," in *The People's Choice: Australia's Experiments in Democracy*, ed. Marian Sawer (Melbourne: Allen and Unwin 2000).

[4] Brendan Foster, "One Nation to Become New 'Kingmakers' in WA Politics: Political Expert," *WA Today*, November 1, 2016, http://www.watoday.com.au/wa-news/one-nation-to-become-new-kingmakers-in-wa-politics-political-expert-20161101-gsf9bf.html.

[5] *One Nation*, accessed February 23, 2018, http://www.onenation.com.au/; Michael Leach, Geoff Stokes, and Ian Ward, eds., *The Rise and Fall of One Nation* (St. Lucia: University of Queensland Press, 2000).

[6] See Benjamin Reilly, *Democracy in Divided Societies: Electoral Engineering for Conflict Management* (Cambridge: Cambridge University Press, 2001).

What are the lessons of this from a comparative perspective? One lesson, we suggest, concerns the value of a system of mandatory, preferential voting in containing the threat of populist illiberalism. Another concerns the value of policy responsiveness on the part of mainstream political parties. The two lessons, however, may translate quite differently in a comparative context: structural safeguards of this kind may be highly normatively desirable, but extremely difficult for other countries successfully to "borrow" in the face of rising illiberal populism. Conversely, greater policy responsiveness may be easier for other countries to achieve, but more ambivalent from a normative democratic perspective: the restrictive immigration and trade policies, and approach to pluralism generally, adopted by both major Australian parties in the last decade may have helped undercut the threat posed by One Nation, but at some real price to liberal democratic values. We therefore conclude by suggesting that the lessons of the Australian democratic constitutional experience in this context are distinctly mixed: Australia offers a promising, yet unlikely, model for borrowing at the level of basic democratic constitutional design; and a quite plausible, but normatively ambivalent model, at the level of basic political responsiveness.

The remainder of the chapter is divided into five sections following this introduction. The second section sets out the current electoral landscape in Australia, and the relatively high levels of support in Australia both for democracy itself, and the two major political parties. The third section explores the real but contained threat posed by One Nation to Australia's representative or non-populist democratic system. The fourth section outlines one of the key structural safeguards we suggest have contributed to the containment of this threat—that is, Australia's system of mandatory, preferential voting. The fifth section explores the potentially more contingent, policy-based factors underpinning the containment of One Nation, especially the quasi-populist policies of Liberal and Labor governments on free trade and immigration since the Tampa, and One Nation's approach to energy policy and Indigenous rights and recognition. Finally the last section offers a brief conclusion about the broader lessons to be gained from the Australian experience, about democracy and the threat of populism.

The Australian Political and Electoral Landscape

As we noted in the introduction, Australia is often categorized as a "healthy" political system. Perhaps most important, national surveys conducted since the 1960s have shown a long-standing pattern of satisfaction with democracy in Australia.[7] In fact, there have been only two clear "dips" in Australians' level of satisfaction with democracy as measured by the Australian Election Study (AES). As Figure 23.1 illustrates, the first of these

---

[7] *The Australian National Political Attitudes Survey*, https://www.ada.edu.au/social-science/browse/politics-and-elections/australian-national-political-attitudes-survey; *The Australian Election Study*, http://www.australianelectionstudy.org/; *The Australian Survey of Social Attitudes*, http://aussa.anu.edu.au/.

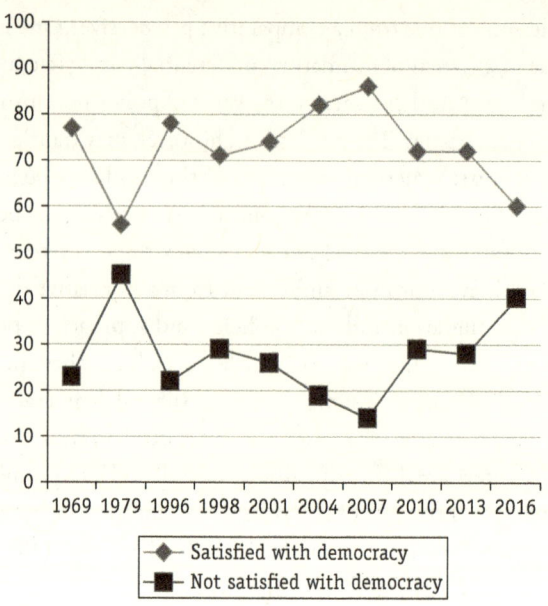

FIGURE 23.1 Australians' satisfaction with democracy 1969–2016 (percentage of respondents).
Source: Australian National Political Attitudes Survey (1969, 1979), Australian Election Study (1996–2016). Respondents were asked: "On the whole, are you very satisfied, fairly satisfied, not very satisfied or not at all satisfied with the way democracy works in Australia?"

occurred in 1979, when the proportion of respondents claiming satisfaction with democracy in Australia fell to 56 percent (down from 77 percent in 1969). This followed a major constitutional crisis, in 1975, when the then-Labor prime minister, Gough Whitlam, was dismissed from office by the governor general, John Kerr, in a contested use of his constitutional reserve powers. The second "dip" occurred in the most recent study, representing the culmination of a period of democratic satisfaction that has been tracking downward for the best part of a decade. In 2016, those claiming to be satisfied with democracy in Australia fell to 60 percent of all respondents, declining from an all-time high of 86 percent in 2007.[8]

In addition, there is a longstanding tradition of electoral competition between two relatively stable major parties, as well as a range of minor parties, in Australian politics.[9] Although it has been declining, the proportion of voters who identify with a particular political party remains high by international standards and, as Ian McAllister argues,

---

[8] Ian McAllister and Sarah Cameron, *Trends in Australian Political Opinion: Results from the Australian Election Study 1987–2016* (Canberra: The Australian National University, 2016), 74.

[9] On the importance of political competition to even the thinnest notions of democracy, see, e.g., Issacharoff, *Fragile Democracies*; Rosalind Dixon and David Landau, "Competitive Democracy and the Constitutional Minimum Core," in *Assessing Constitutional Performance*, ed. Tom Ginsburg and Aziz Huq (New York: Cambridge University Press, 2016), 268.

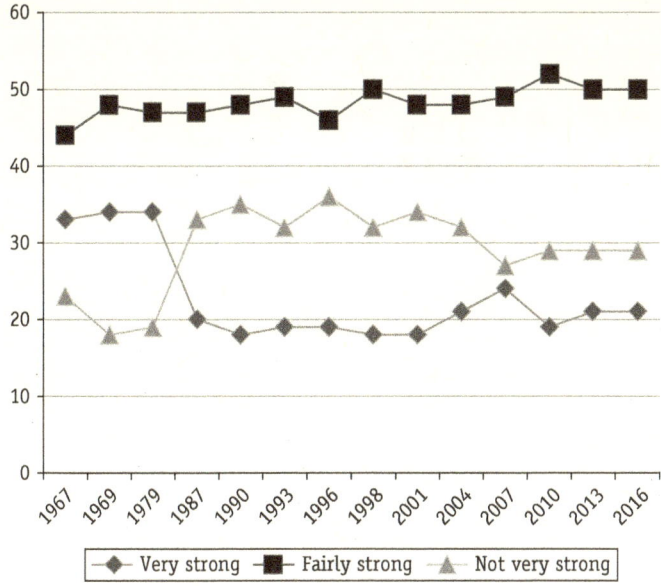

FIGURE 23.2 Australians' strength of political partisanship 1967–2016 (percentage of AES respondents).

Source: Australian National Political Attitudes Survey (1967, 1969, 1979), Australian Election Study (1996–2016). Respondents were asked: "Would you call yourself a very strong, fairly strong, or not very strong supporter of that party?"

there has been "surprisingly little criticism of parties as institutions."[10] In 2016, 71 percent of AES respondents claimed very or fairly strong identification with a political party (see Figure 23.2).

High levels of political partisanship are instrumental in preserving the stability of the political system and protecting the constitutional order in Australia, as elsewhere. Parties commit to the basic "rules of the political game," and in so doing, create and perpetuate norms of stable electoral competition, the general acceptance of representative institutions, and constitutional enforcement. In turn, partisanship, or a sense of attachment to the major parties, reinforces their importance by creating cues or shortcuts for voters and reducing the "information cost" of voting.

The role that Australian political parties play is also both highly institutionalized and routinized: parties monopolize political recruitment through the selection of candidates for public office, they structure electoral choices through the distribution of "how to vote" cards, and control the legislative agenda through the exertion of significant party discipline in parliamentary voting.[11] The role that the established parties play in creating

---

[10] Ian McAllister, *The Australian Voter: 50 Years of Change* (Kensington, NSW: UNSW Press, 2011), 37.

[11] McAllister, *The Australian Voter*, 11; Anika Gauja and Marian Sawer (eds.), *Party Rules* (Acton, ACT: Australian National University Press, 2015); Graeme Orr, *The Law of Politics: Elections, Parties and Money in Australia* (Annandale, NSW: Federation Press, 2010); Anika Gauja, Narelle Miragliotta, and Rodney Smith, "Australian

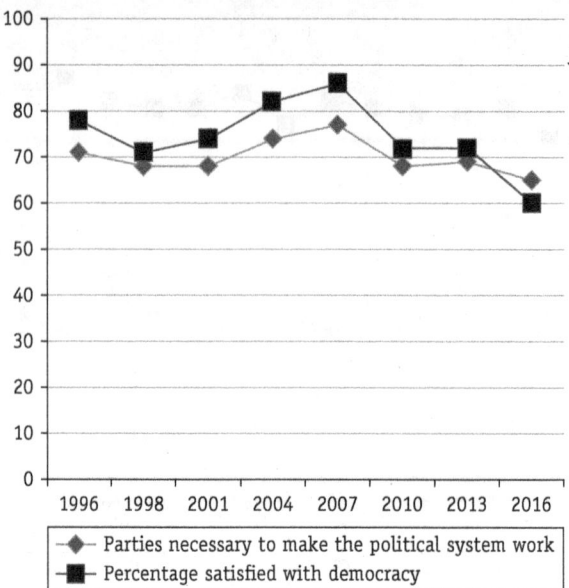

FIGURE 23.3 Australians' attitudes to parties and democracy (percentage of AES respondents).
Source: Australian Election Study (1996–2016). Respondents were asked: "On the whole, are you very satisfied, fairly satisfied, not very satisfied or not at all satisfied with the way democracy works in Australia? On a scale of 1–5, how necessary are political parties to make our political system work?"

faith in the political system is nicely illustrated by AES data, which shows that voters' attitudes toward the major parties generally track their overall satisfaction with democracy (Figure 23.3).

Democratic Non-Stability: The Rise of One Nation

This picture, however, potentially overstates the degree to which Australian democracy has been immune to "populist" shocks or challenges. Populism, as other contributors to this volume note, is hard to define precisely. There are a range of definitions used by scholars, many of which overlap, but which differ based on the context or purpose for which they are used.[12] We also cannot in this short chapter devote significant attention

Party Organisation: The State of the Field," in *Contemporary Australian Political Party Organisations*, ed. Narelle Miragliotta, Anika Gauja, and Rodney Smith (Clayton, Vic.: Monash University Press, 2015), xi; Dean Jaensch, *Power Politics: Australia's Party System* (St. Leonards, NSW: Allen and Unwin, 1994); Ian McAllister, "Political Parties in Australia: Party Stability in a Utilitarian Society," in *Political Parties in Advanced Industrial Democracies*, ed. Paul Webb, David Farrell, and Ian Holliday (Oxford: Oxford University Press, 2002), 379.

[12] "Public Law and the New Populism," *The Jean Monnet Center*, https://jeanmonnetprogram.org/activities-at-the-jean-monnet-center/event-highlights/public-law-and-the-new-populism/; Alison Young, "Populism, Sovereignty and Referendums" (unpublished manuscript 2017); Pippa Norris and Ronald Inglehart,

to debates over the best way of understanding the term: we thus focus simply on one plausible notion of populism—that is, the idea of "illiberal populism,"[13] or populist parties and movements that are directly opposed to core liberal commitments—to the rule of law, human rights, and the post-World War II global order, or the relatively free movement of goods and persons across national borders.[14]

Populism, in this sense, is close to the understanding of populism adopted by Jan-Werner Müller—that is, a movement that claims to speak for the people in order to criticize existing institutional arrangements and policies, in a way that is distinctly nationalistic, exclusionary, and anti-pluralistic in nature.[15]

On this definition, Australia has also seen the rise in recent decades of at least one distinctly populist party—that is, the One Nation Party. Despite the general acceptance of the established parties in everyday political life in Australia, the last few decades have seen something of a shift away from the two traditional major political parties, the ALP and the Liberal-National Coalition, toward greater support for a variety of minor party players. Figure 23.4, below, captures the scale of this trend.

As the Figure shows, minor (or third) parties have always been a feature of Australian electoral politics, attracting on average around 20 percent of the national vote. They have also played a significant role in Australian politics over the last few decades, often holding the balance of power in the Senate, and achieving representation in various state legislatures.[16] This influence has been especially notable in the Australian Senate: the upper house, in Australia, is elected according to a system of proportional representation, by single transferable vote (PR-STV). This gives minor parties a quite high chance of gaining representation in the Senate, and in recent decades, minor parties have consistently

---

Cultural Backlash and the Rise of Populist Authoritarianism (Cambridge University Press, forthcoming 2018); Robert Inglehart and Pippa Norris, "Trump and the Populist Authoritarian Parties: The *Silent Revolution* in Reverse," *Perspectives on Politics* 15 (2017): 443–454. See Michaela Hailbronner and David Landau, "Introduction: Constitutional Courts and Populism," *I-Connect*, April 22, 2017, http://www.iconnectblog.com/2017/04/introduction-constitutional-courts-and-populism/.

[13] Compare Norris and Inglehart, *Cultural Backlash.*

[14] For this as a plausible definition of liberalism, and its core commitments, see, e.g., Ed Sparer, "Fundamental Human Rights, Legal Entitlements, and the Social Struggle: A Friendly Critique of the Critical Legal Studies Movement," *Stanford Law Review* 36 (1984): 509–574; Fareed Zakaria, "The Rise of Illiberal Democracy," *Foreign Affairs* 76 (1997): 22.

[15] See, e.g., Jan-Werner Müller, "Populist Constitutions—A Contradiction in Terms?," *Verfassungsblog*, April 23, 2017, http://verfassungsblog.de/populist-constitutions-a-contradiction-in-terms. See also discussion in Hailbronner and Landau, "Introduction"; Rosalind Dixon, "Populist Constitutionalism and the Democratic Minimum Core," *Verfassungsblog*, April 26, 2017, http://verfassungsblog.de/populist-constitutionalism-and-the-democratic-minimum-core/. Compare also Daniele Albertazzi and Duncan McDonnell, "Introduction: The Sceptre and the Spectre," in *Twenty-First Century Populism: The Spectre of Western European Democracy*, ed. Daniele Albertazi and Duncan McDonnell (New York: Palgrave Macmillan, 2008), 3.

[16] The Australian Democrats held the balance of power in the Senate from 1983 to 1993, and more recently, the Greens from 2010 to 2013. The Democrats' strongest regional electoral performance was in South Australia, while the Greens have performed well in New South Wales, Victoria, West Australia, and Tasmania.

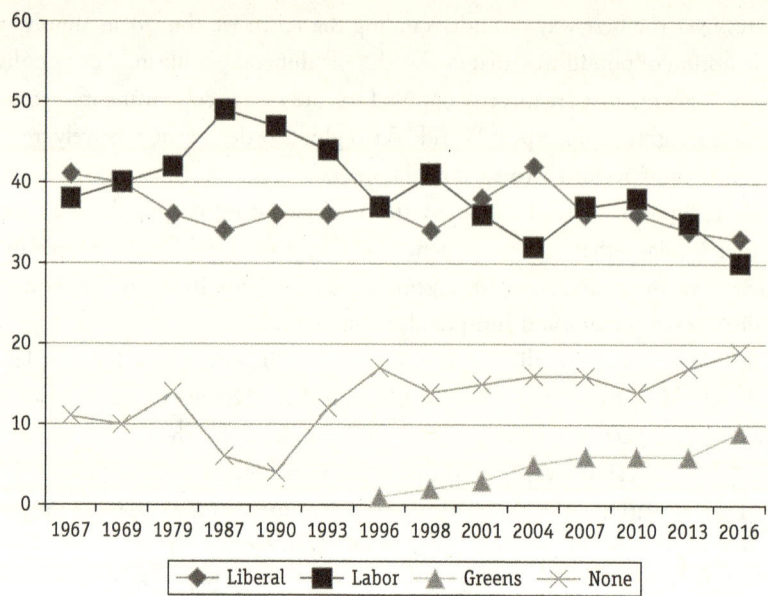

FIGURE 23.4 Direction of political partisanship 1967–2016 (percentage of AES respondents).
Source: Australian National Political Attitudes Survey (1967, 1969, 1979), Australian Election Study (1996–2016). Respondents were asked: "Generally speaking, do you usually think of yourself as Liberal, Labor, National or what?"

held the balance of power—and therefore also the power to block, and propose amendments, to the government's legislative policy agenda.[17]

While parties such as the Greens, and before them the Australian Democrats, have generally used this power to enhance rights-based democracy,[18] public support for minor parties has not been limited to the Left and non-populist players. The last decade has seen the rise (on the Right) of a series of populist politicians, including Bob Katter, Clive Palmer, and Jacqui Lambie,[19] and the re-emergence of at least one distinctly populist political party: One Nation. One Nation has at various times also posed a serious threat to several state governments, and to the balance of power in the Australian Senate.

The party's public profile peaked in 1998 when it secured almost a quarter of the vote in the Queensland state election on a platform of populist opposition to immigration from Asia and support for gun ownership.[20] In the 1998 federal election, One Nation secured 8.4 percent of the vote for the lower house of the Parliament (the House of

---

[17] Dean Jaensch and David Mathieson, *A Plague on Both Your Houses: Minor Parties in Australia* (St. Leonards, NSW: Allen and Unwin, 1998).

[18] See, for example, John Warhurst, ed., *Keeping the Bastards Honest: The Australian Democrat's First Twenty Years* (St. Leonards, NSW: Allen and Unwin, 1997); Stewart Jackson, *The Australian Greens: From Activism to Australia's Third Party* (Carlton, Vic: Melbourne University Press, 2016).

[19] See Benjamin Moffitt, "Populism in Australia and New Zealand," in *The Oxford Handbook of Populism*, ed. Christobal Rovira Kaltwasser et al. (Oxford: Oxford University Press, 2017), 121.

[20] McAllister, "Political Parties in Australia," 382.

Representatives), but failed to win any seats. In 2001, One Nation's vote halved to 4.3 percent and the party largely disappeared from the political landscape, at least at the federal level.[21] In 2016, One Nation returned to the federal Parliament, winning four seats in the Senate (two from Queensland and one each from New South Wales and Western Australia). The party polled 9.2 percent in Queensland and just over 4 percent in New South Wales and Western Australia.

One Nation has also adopted a distinctly *illiberal populist* stance. The statement that heads One Nation's policy document states: "One Nation is committed to Australian sovereignty, the Constitution and Government of the people by the people for the people."[22] One of the party's core policies also involves the establishment of citizen-initiated referenda (CIR):

> One Nation supports the CIR as a system that allows all members of society to have a direct say in Government decision-making. Representative Democracy only allows individuals or parties the right to decide for the rest of us. One Nation believes in not only upholding the right but the need for all Australians to effectively raise debate on issues of concern and have the mechanism to democratically pursue those issues to produce an outcome of legislative change that is actually the will of the people.[23]

In this sense, the One Nation party seeks to promote a direct voice for the people, in ways that are quite foreign to the Australian constitutional tradition. Section 128 of the Australian Constitution provides for the people to play a role in approving formal constitutional change via a national referendum process, but there have been only two other occasions in Australia in which democratic politics has involved other forms of direct democracy, or plebiscite: the 1916–1917 plebiscites on conscription, and the 2017 same-sex marriage postal survey.

The party also adopts strongly critical and nationalist rhetoric. Its policies are explicitly anti-pluralistic, and anti-globalization, and thus opposed to both Indigenous rights and recognition and most forms of immigration to Australia. This is reflective of the party's origins: One Nation was originally formed in April 1997 by Pauline Hanson, a Liberal candidate for the 1996 federal election who had subsequently lost her Liberal Party endorsement following controversial comments she made in a local newspaper concerning Indigenous Australians.[24] One Nation was established as a party to "preserve

---

[21] The party held one seat in the Queensland State Parliament from 2004 to 2008.

[22] *One Nation*, http://www.onenation.com.au/, accessed December 18, 2017.

[23] "Current Affairs: Citizens Initiated Referendum," *One Nation*, accessed February 22, 2018, http://www.onenation.com.au/current_affairs/citizens-initiated-referendum.

[24] See Zareh Ghazarian, *The Making of a Party System: Minor Parties in the Australian Senate* (Clayton, Victoria: Monash University Press, 2015), 114–15; Michael Leach, Geoff Stokes, and Ian Ward, eds., *The Rise and Fall of One Nation* (Brisbane: University of Queensland Press, 2000).

the Australian way of life, be strong against crime, treat all Australians equally with government assistance based on need not race and to bring about the necessary changes for fair and equal treatment of all Australians, within a system of government recognising and acting upon a need for Australia to be truly One Nation."[25]

The party further has a strong anti-immigration focus. In the 1990s, its policies focused on opposing immigration from Southeast and East Asia, whereas in the 2016 federal election, it called for a ban on all forms of Muslim immigration, including refugees.[26] The party platform also includes proposals to abolish Halal certification, and current Australian multiculturalism policy.

To date, however, Australian democracy remains relatively stable and non-populist due to what has ultimately been the only limited electoral success of One Nation in a range of contexts. Despite gaining representation in the Australian Senate, the party has never won a seat in the House of Representatives. [27] Recent results at state-level elections have also been mixed. While the party won three upper house seats in the West Australian state election (March 2017), it failed to win any lower house seats. The November 2017 Queensland state election also did not bring the results the party had hoped for: a state-wide vote of 13 percent resulted in just one parliamentary seat.

One reason for this undoubtedly relates to the leadership of the party, and the profile of individual candidates. As Kefford argues, One Nation's electoral performance "has been largely wedded to that of Hanson, and in the nearly 20 years since its formation most of the significant results have been achieved when Hanson has been leader of the party."[28] The years when One Nation performed poorly were characterized by intra-party division and poor organizational management.[29] In the next section, however, we suggest that a range of other structural and political factors have also been critical to the relative non-success of One Nation, and thus the stability of Australian non-populist democracy in this context.

Australian Electoral and Constitutional Safeguards

The rise of illiberal populism worldwide clearly has many complex causes—including a seeming loss in many countries of faith in mainstream democratic institutions and parties,

---

[25] Cited in Zareh Ghazarian, "Organisational Approaches of the Right-of-Centre Minor Parties," in *Contemporary Australian Political Party Organisations*, ed. Narelle Miragliotta, Anika Gauja, and Rodney Smith (Clayton, Vic.: Monash University Press, 2015), 53.

[26] See Sara Dehm and Max Walden, "Refugee Policy: A Troubling Bipartisanship," in *Double Disillusion: The 2016 Australian Federal Election*, ed. Anika Gauja et al. (Acton, ACT: Australian National University Press, 2018).

[27] See, however, Pauline Hanson's victory as an unendorsed Liberal candidate: Reilly, above n 7, at 55-6.

[28] Glenn Kefford, "The Minor Parties' Campaigns," in *Double Disillusion: The 2016 Australian Federal Election*, ed. Anika Gauja et al. (Acton, ACT: Australian National University Press, 2018).

[29] See Gahazarian, "Organisational Approaches," 50, 53.

rising economic inequality and stagnation in middle class wages and income, and a sense of crisis around national or cultural identity.[30] At a structural level, some countries' constitutional arrangements also seem to have amplified the effect of underlying pressures on constitutional democracy, where others seem to have constrained them.

In some countries, for example populist parties have succeeded in part due to historically low levels of popular turnout at elections: while the median voter in these countries may not support such parties, they seem sufficiently disaffected with more mainstream political parties not to turn out at key legislative elections.[31] Similarly, the rise of illiberal populism seems to have been aided in certain contexts by the rise of third parties, which have effectively undermined the electoral viability of previous liberal democratic parties. In some cases, this has been because minor parties on the political right have taken vote-share away from more mainstream conservative parties. In others, it has been because left-leaning—arguably quite liberal, democratic parties—have undermined electoral support for the moderate Left, and thereby contributed to the electoral success of more conservative parties, with a distinctly illiberal platform.[32] But in both cases, minor parties have arguably contributed to undermining the electoral viability of mainstream *non-populist* political parties.

Australia, we suggest in contrast, has an electoral system that makes it difficult for a party such as One Nation to exert major control of national political processes, at least in the House of Representatives: first, it has a system of compulsory voting, and second,

[30] See, e.g., Dylan Chambers, "The Threat of Illiberal Populism," *Policy Corner*, June 19, 2017, https://www.policy-corner.org/en/2017/06/19/the-threat-of-illiberal-populism/; Olga Oliker, "Putinism, Populism and the Defence of Liberal Democracy," *Survival* 59 (2017): 7; Dani Rodrik and Sharun Mukand, "Why Illiberal Democracies Are on the Rise," *Huffington Post*, accessed February 23, 2018, https://www.huffingtonpost.com/dani-rodrik/illiberal-democracies-on-the-rise_b_7302374.html; Bojan Bugaric, "The Populists at the Gate: Constitutional Democracy under Siege?," paper presented at the New York University School of Law, Public Law and the New Populism Conference, September 15–16, 2017; Andras Laszlo Pap and Anna Sledzinska-Simon, "The Rise of Illiberal Democracy and the Remedies of Multi-Level Constitutionalism," paper presented at the New York University School of Law, Public Law and the New Populism Conference, September 15–16, 2017; Silvia Suteu, "The Populist Turn in Central and Eastern Europe: Is Deliberative Democracy the Solution?," paper presented at the New York University School of Law, Public Law and the New Populism Conference, September 15–16, 2017.

[31] On the role of low electoral turnout in the election of illiberal populist governments in Hungary and Poland, see, e.g., Bugaric, "The Populists at the Gate." For the general role of electoral turnout in influencing the outcome of elections in countries with voluntary voting, such as the United States, see also William H. Frey, Ruy Teixeira, and Robert Griffin, *America's Electoral Future: How Changing Demographics Could Impact Presidential Elections from 2016 to 2032*, February 2016, https://www.brookings.edu/wp-content/uploads/2016/02/SOC2016report.pdf.

[32] In the United States, for example, several commentators suggest that President Trump's election to the presidency was at least in part due to the electoral support enjoyed by the Green Party candidate, Jill Stein, in key states such as Wisconsin, Michigan, and Pennsylvania, which might otherwise have voted for Hillary Clinton and the Democratic Party. Ben Schreckinger, "Jill Stein Isn't Sorry," *Politico*, June 20, 2017, https://www.politico.com/magazine/story/2017/06/20/jill-stein-green-party-no-regrets-2016-215281. The effect of this has also been undoubtedly to increase the degree of populist rhetoric and policy in US politics. Yeganeh Torbati, "U.S. Visas to Six Muslim Nations Drop after Supreme Court Backs Travel Ban," *Reuters*, September 29, 2017, https://www.reuters.com/article/us-trump-effect-visas-analysis/

a preferential electoral system in the federal lower house.[33] Taken together, these features create important safeguards against the risk of a full-scale populist takeover of Australian democratic politics: they help reduce the risk that low electoral turnout will give rise to illiberal populist governments, and the risk that small parties—on both the Left and Right—may indirectly help elect such a government.

In this sense, they are also safeguards that are arguably small "c" constitutional in nature: in some countries, the capital "C" constitution expressly sets out the rules governing elections, or the basic structure of the electoral system. In others, the constitution simply "defers" or delegates these questions, by authorizing the legislature to enact various "super-statutes" regulating the electoral system. In both cases, however, the design of the electoral system is a question of fundamental importance to the operation of government, and the distribution of political power, in ways that give the relevant laws a form of constitutional status.

Finally, these are features of the electoral system that make Australian democracy unique. While majoritarian electoral systems are reasonably common throughout liberal democracies (used by around a quarter of the world's democracies),[34] the variant that Australians would term "preferential voting" (or the alternate vote) is used at the national level only in Australia and Papua New Guinea.[35] Compulsory voting, likewise, exists only in a handful of other democracies, including Belgium, Brazil, Luxemburg, Peru, Liechtenstein, and Uruguay.[36] Taken together, the combination of compulsory, preferential voting is used only in Australia.

COMPULSORY VOTING

Compulsory voting is one of the most distinctive features of Australian elections.[37] Australian law makes voting compulsory in federal elections for anyone on the electoral

u-s-visas-to-six-muslim-nations-drop-after-supreme-court-backs-travel-ban-idUSKCN1C40FP; Ana Swanson and Kevin Ganville, "What Would Happen if the US Withdrew from NAFTA," *New York Times*, October 12, 2017, https://www.nytimes.com/2017/10/12/business/economy/what-would-happen-if-the-us-withdrew-from-nafta.html; Mireya Solid, "Trump Withdrawing from the Trans-Pacific Partnership," *Brookings*, March 24, 2017, https://www.brookings.edu/blog/unpacked/2017/03/24/trump-withdrawing-from-the-trans-pacific-partnership/.

[33] David M. Farrell and Ian McAllister, *The Australian Electoral System: Origins, Variations and Consequences* (Sydney: UNSW Press, 2006).

[34] Elisabeth Carter and David Farrell, "Electoral Systems and Election Management," in *Comparing Democracies 3*, ed. Lawrence LeDuc, Richard G. Niemi, and Pippa Norris (Thousand Oaks, CA: Sage, 2010) 25, 27. On the interaction between preferential and compulsory voting, see Benjamin Reilly and Michael Maley, "The Single Transferable Vote and the Alternative Vote Compared," in *Elections in Australia, Ireland and Malta Under the Single Transferable Vote: Reflections on an Embedded Institution*, ed. Sean Bowler and Bernard Grofman (Ann Arbor: University of Michigan Press, 2000).

[35] Although note previous use in Fiji.

[36] "Compulsory Voting," *International IDEA*, accessed February 23, 2018, https://www.idea.int/data-tools/data/voter-turnout/compulsory-voting.

[37] "Compulsory Voting in Australia," *Australian Electoral Commission*, February 14, 2011, http://www.aec.gov.au/About_AEC/Publications/voting/index.htm. For discussion, see, e.g., Lisa Hill, "Compulsory Voting in Australia: A Basis for a 'Best Practice' Regime," *Federal Law Review* 32 (2004): 479–498.

register, and provides for the Electoral Commission to impose (modest) fines on any-one who does not vote. Similar provisions also exist in almost all Australian states and territories.[38] A variety of sociocultural norms also support the understanding that voting is compulsory: elections are always held on a weekend (i.e., a traditionally non-working day), and there are a variety of options available for prepoll or absentee voting. Public schools also often serve as polling stations, and run popular events on voting day designed to increase the attractiveness—or decrease the inconvenience—of voting as a compulsory activity.[39]

As Figure 23.5 illustrates, compulsory voting also enjoys consistently high levels of support from Australian voters, with 70 percent of respondents in the 2016 AES indicating their support for the measure. Eighty percent would have voted even if voting had not been compulsory.[40] This sustained acceptance is particularly interesting, given the global trend toward disaffection with formal political institutions,[41] and the fact that there in an inherent contradiction between compulsion and the principles of freedom in Australian liberal democracy.[42]

Moreover, the system of compulsory voting in Australia operates to mitigate the challenge of populist politics in two ways. First, it reduces the capacity of populist parties to capture an increased vote-share by simply having a more mobilized political support base than more mainstream non-illiberal parties. Second, it helps ensure that the large number of voters who neither support illiberal populism, nor strongly oppose it, actually vote, and thereby continue to support more mainstream, non-illiberal parties.[43] High levels of political partisanship reinforce this trend by fostering voter loyalties toward the mainstream parties and creating shortcuts for voters based on established left/right policy positions.[44]

---

[38] *Commonwealth Electoral Act 1918* (Cth) s 245(1); *Parliamentary Electorates and Elections Act 1912* (NSW) div 13; *Electoral Act 2002* (Vic) div 2; *Electoral (Improving Representation and Other Legislation Amendment Act 2016* (Qld); *Electoral Act 1907* (WA) div 7; *Electoral Act 1985* (SA) s 85; *Electoral Act 1992* (ACT) s 129; *Electoral Act* (NT) s 279; *Electoral Act 2004* (Tas) s 152.

[39] See, e.g., "Australia Takes Its Democracy with a Side of Sausage," *BBC News*, July 2, 2016, http://www.bbc.com/news/world-australia-36692402. Admittedly, these events also aim to raise funds for local schools.

[40] McAllister and Cameron, *Trends in Australian Political Opinion*, 55.

[41] See, e.g., Colin Hay, *Why We Hate Politics* (Malden, MA: Polity Press, 2007); Peter Mair, "Ruling the Void: The Hollowing of Western Democracy," in *On Parties, Party Systems and Democracy: Selected Writings of Peter Mair*, ed. Peter Mair and Ingrid van Biezen (Colchester, UK: ECPR Press, 2006), 531.

[42] Some suggest that this may be due to a distinctly pragmatic, utilitarian strand in Australian political culture; see, e.g., McAllister, *The Australian Voter*, 20.

[43] Malcolm Mackerras and Ian McAllister, "Compulsory Voting, Party Stability and Electoral Advantage in Australia," *Electoral Studies* 18 (1999): 217–233.

[44] Russel Dalton, David Farrell, and Ian McAllister, *Political Parties and Democratic Linkage: How Parties Organize Democracy* (New York: Oxford University Press, 2011), 97–98.

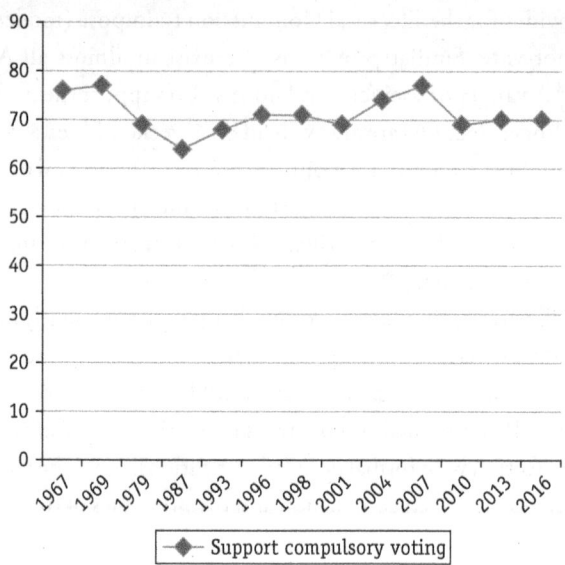

FIGURE 23.5 Percentage of AES respondents who support compulsory voting (1967–2016).
Source: Australian National Political Attitudes Survey (1967, 1969, 1979), Australian Election Study (1987–2016). Respondents were asked: "Do you think that voting at Federal elections should be compulsory, or do you think that people should only have to vote if they want to?"

To take a recent example, we can look at the effect of compulsory voting versus voluntary voting by examining the results of the recent "same-sex marriage" postal survey. The survey was requested by the Liberal-National Coalition government to honor its 2016 election commitment to conduct a popular poll on whether same-sex couples should be legally allowed to marry. The survey was administered by the Australian Bureau of Statistics between September 12 and November 17, 2017. The survey achieved a turnout rate of 80 percent, which was substantially lower than the 2016 Australian federal election in which voting was compulsory (91 percent). The majority of those participating in the survey (62 percent) thought that the law should be changed to allow same-sex couples to marry, while 38 percent voted no. While we do not suggest that opposition to same-sex marriage is necessarily illiberal, we do suggest that it reflects the views of a relatively small, but mobilized minority of voters in Australia.

We confirmed the disproportionate influence of this group by undertaking a statistical analysis of the correlation between turnout rates and the "no" vote across all 150 Australian electorates. While we did not find any association between turnout and deviation from the national mean, low turnout was positively correlated with a higher "no" vote. Assuming that a "no" vote could be influenced by an elector's religion, age, cultural background, and income, we controlled for these factors in a linear (OLS) regression analysis. Even when accounting for these factors, we found that a lower turnout is associated with a higher "no" vote (M5, see Table 23.1).

TABLE 23.1

Explaining postal survey outcomes

	Absolute deviation	'Extreme' deviation Yes/No	'Extreme' deviation (towards 'Yes') Yes/No	'Extreme' deviation (towards 'No') Yes/No	Percent 'No' vote
	logistic	*logistic*	*logistic*	*logistic*	*OLS*
	M1	M2	M3	M4	M5
Abstention rate	−3.965 (12.977)	−13.398** (6.833)	−82.705*** (25.503)	33.120** (12.953)	0.645*** (0.119)
% secular	−4.667 (7.052)	−5.487 (3.656)	45.075*** (14.222)	−27.742*** (6.544)	−0.584*** (0.067)
% language other than EN	0.786 (2.951)	0.452 (1.741)	−29.448*** (9.421)	10.845*** (3.630)	0.314*** (0.032)
Median weekly family income	0.0002 (0.001)	0.0003 (0.001)	0.003* (0.002)	−0.001 (0.001)	−0.00005*** (0.00001)
% young (<35yrs)	4.294 (9.137)	9.152 (6.211)	62.524*** (21.808)	−43.530*** (16.269)	−0.571*** (0.103)
% urban	0.656 (2.610)	−0.342 (1.458)	4.546 (3.802)	−0.270 (2.681)	−0.055** (0.027)
Constant	−1.975 (4.417)	2.136 (2.288)	−15.394* (8.056)	7.694** (3.389)	0.595*** (0.041)
Observations	149	149	149	149	149
R²					0.860
Adjusted R²					0.854
Pseudo R²		0.135	0.851	0.673	
Log Likelihood	−11.866	−94.795	−21.747	−39.774	
Akaike Inf. Crit.	37.732	203.590	57.494	93.547	
Residual Std. Error					0.039 (df = 142)
F Statistic					145.580*** (df = 6; 142)

Note: *p<0.1; **p<0.05; ***p<0.01

Using this same model, we also predicted the likely "no" vote (had voting been compulsory) and found (with 95 percent confidence) that had this been the case the national average of the "no" vote would have been between 21 and 31 percent (the actual vote was 38 percent).[45] In other words, under a system of voluntary voting, the "no" vote was significantly higher (7–17 percent) than it would have been had voting been compulsory.

PREFERENTIAL VOTING AND THE ELECTORAL SYSTEM

Second, Australia has a distinctive electoral system, which helps mitigate the threat posed by *any minor party* to the current major non-populist parties, and their electoral viability, in the House of Representatives. The House of Representatives in Australia is elected according to a distinctive "alternate vote" method, which aims to translate the aggregate majority of electors' preferences into legislative seats. This process also disadvantages smaller political parties that may receive a sizeable percentage of the vote in each electorate, but fail to gain a plurality of votes. In addition, the effects of this system are compounded by the system of preference allocation that operates in Australian elections, whereby the second and subsequent choices of the electors who voted for less popular parties are redistributed to the major contenders in the electoral contest. In contrast, the electoral system used for Senate elections, PR-STV, aims to distribute seats in proportion to the percentage of the vote that a party receives, leading to a much more "proportionate" outcome between votes and legislative seats.

Comparing the electoral results of One Nation in both the House of Representatives and the Senate illustrates the operation of these different systems. As Table 23.2 shows, the party has never won a seat in the federal lower house. In 2016, the party contested fifteen House of Representatives seats and polled over 10 percent of the vote in nine of them, yet this did not translate into any legislative gains in that chamber. By contrast, the party managed to win four seats in the Senate with a nationwide vote of just over 4 percent.

Of course, how a preferential voting system operates in practice will also depend in part on the behavior of the parties within a system—or the actual choices made by parties about the allocation of preferences. If major parties choose to preference each other, this can provide an important safeguard against the threat that minor parties will undermine the viability of existing, non-populist parties; whereas if any major party chooses to enter a preference deal with a populist minor party, this may end up contributing to the increased influence of such parties, within certain electoral subunits.

To date, however, Australian parties have generally chosen *not* to preference One Nation, so that the system of constituency-based, preferential voting in the Australian

---

[45] The intercept associated with the regression line is 0.26, putting the predicted mean no vote under compulsory voting at 26 percent, with an upper confidence limit of 31 percent and a lower limit of 21 percent.

TABLE 23.2

One Nation—primary vote and seats won in the Australian federal parliament, 1998–2016

Election	House of Representatives (%)	Seats	Senate (%)	Seats
1998	8.4	0	9.0	1
2001	4.3	0	5.5	0
2004	1.2	0	1.7	0
2007	0.3	0	0.4	0
2010	0.2	0	0.6	0
2013	0.2	0	0.6	0
2016	1.3	0	4.3	4

Source: Australian Electoral Commission.

lower house has tended consistently to contain—rather than amplify—the threat of illiberal populist influence in democratic policymaking. Where it has happened, the practice has attracted significant public criticism. For example, at the March 2017 West Australian state election the Liberal Party decided to preference One Nation in the upper house in return for One Nation's lower house preferences, citing political expediency in what was termed a "mathematical exercise" designed to "maximise the Liberal vote."[46] The move was heavily criticized not only by opposition parties, but by the Liberals' own support base who turned against the party. After eight-and-a-half years in power, the West Australian state Liberal government was defeated at the polls with a 16 percent swing against it. As a general norm, mainstream voters expect the major parties to eschew One Nation, and punish them when they do not.

Policy Responses

Another important factor in the successful "containment" of the populist threat posed by One Nation, in Australia, has been at the level of policy, rather than electoral system design. Both major parties in Australia, we suggest, have made a distinct shift in their policies over the last two decades toward a more populist approach to certain key issues—such as immigration, energy and climate change policy, and to a lesser extent, the recognition of Aboriginal and Torres Strait Islander peoples.

---

[46] Former Liberal state premier, Colin Barnett, cited in "Coalition Braces for Backlash over WA Libs," *Australian Financial Review*, March 10, 2007, http://www.afr.com/news/politics/coalition-braces-for-backlash-over-wa-libs-embrace-of- one-nation-20170309-guuyxc.

POLICY RESPONSIVENESS

The most notable populist shift in Australian politics over the last two decades has undoubtedly occurred in the context of refugee and migration policy. Both major parties in Australia since the late 1990s have taken a distinctly restrictive approach to laws and policies toward those seeking onshore asylum.

In the late 1990s, the then-Labor Government introduced a policy of mandatory detention for all asylum seekers entering Australia by boat.[47] It also began to limit the grounds of judicial review available to those denied asylum. In the early 2000s, the conservative Coalition government further extended these restrictions to progressively prevent almost any form of onshore asylum-claim by those reaching Australia by boat. In 2001, for example, then-prime minister John Howard launched the Liberal Party election campaign with a speech that famously pronounced: "we will decide who comes to this country and the circumstances in which they come."[48] Once in office, the Howard Government also cut the immigration intake for 1997–1998 by 13.5 percent, and implemented the "Pacific solution," introducing a system of offshore processing for all boat-arrivals to Australia, and excised Christmas and Melville Islands from Australia's immigration zone.[49] This was all in order to limit rights to judicial review under Australian law, and deter boat arrivals to Australia.[50]

In 2007, Labor was again elected to office, and debated changes to this policy. But in the final event, the Labor caucus decided to continue the previous government's policies of offshore processing, and simply increased the quota for refugee resettlement. Labor in 2001 had narrowly lost an election it expected to win, to the Howard Government, in large part because of the Tampa affair, and leading Labor figures decided as a result that the party needed to maintain a restrictive approach to onshore asylum seekers if it were ever to win national office.

These policies were also ultimately quite popular with a majority of the Australian electorate. Since 2001, a large proportion of AES respondents have supported the idea

---

[47] *Migration Act 1958 (Cth)* s 186/192. See discussion in *Chu Kheng Lim v Minister for Immigration* (1992) 176 CLR 1; *Al-Kateb v Godwin* (2004) 219 CLR 562; *Re Woolley; Ex parte Applicants M276/2003* (2004) 225 CLR 1; *Plaintiff M61/2010E v Commonwealth of Australia; Plaintiff M69 of 2010 v Commonwealth of Australia* [2010] HCA 41.

[48] John Howard, Speech delivered at Sydney, NSW, October 28, 2001, https://electionspeeches.moadoph.gov.au/speeches/2001-john-howard.

[49] Rae Wear, "Permanent Populism: The Howard Government 1996–2007," *Australian Journal of Political Science* 43 (2008): 617, 626.

[50] On whether deterrence in this context was aimed at people smugglers, or rather than asylum seekers themselves, see, e.g., Jane McAdam, "Australia and Asylum Seekers," *International Journal of Refugee Law* 25 (2013): 435–448; Janet Phillips, "A Comparison of Coalition and Labor Government Asylum Policies in Australia since 2001," *Parliament of Australia*, updated February 2, 2017, https://www.aph.gov.au/About_Parliament/Parliamentary_Departments/Parliamentary_Library/pubs/rp/rp1617/AsylumPolicies; Jessica Howard, "To Deter and Deny: Australia and the Interdiction of Asylum Seekers," *Refuge* 21, no. 4 (2003): 35–50.

of turning back boats seeking asylum (on average, 53 percent).[51] They also paralleled the policies of One Nation on this issue: they embraced many of One Nation's themes and elevated the version of Anglo-Australian identity that Pauline Hanson and her party defended, but also "made policy commitments consistent with One Nation's demands."[52] In 2001, Pauline Hanson in fact claimed that Howard and the Liberals had stolen her policies on the issue.[53]

The same pattern can be seen in more recent shifts to limit pathways for skilled migration. The Coalition Government, under Prime Minister Turnbull, in 2017 announced new policies restricting the availability of temporary skilled migration visas, and the category of jobs in which persons on these visas could be employed. It thus abolished the previous "457 visa" scheme, which allowed foreign workers to stay for four years in a broad range of occupations, and thereby become eligible to seek permanent residency, and replaced it with a two-year visa, and a narrow four-year visa category for high-skilled workers, with no pathway under either to longer-term residency.[54] In announcing this policy, the government also used strongly protectionist—and arguably populist—language. It suggested that the policy change aimed to ensure "that Australian jobs are filled by Australians."[55] The ALP, under the leadership of Bill Shorten, has also promised to go even further in this direction if elected to government.

There also again parallels between this kind of restrictive approach to skilled migration and the policies of One Nation in this area. One Nation has consistently opposed free trade and globalization and promised to "restore Australia's Constitution so that our economy is run for the benefit of Australians."[56] Therefore, despite criticism from a range of industries suggesting that the new visa policy will create real skills shortages and harm Australian competitiveness and productivity, populist immigration policies prevail.[57]

There are also other areas in which both major parties have adopted an increasingly populist—anti-global, anti-pluralist—stance. For instance, both major parties in the last few years have retreated from a commitment to global leadership in addressing climate change in favor of more nationalistic rhetoric about the best interests of Australians, and

---

[51] Cameron and McAllister, *Trends in Australian Political Opinion*, 98.

[52] Wear, "Permanent Populism," 617.

[53] Rae Wear, "Commonwealth of Australia," *Australian Journal of Politics and History* 48 (2002): 241, 243.

[54] See Karen Barlow, "Turnbull Government to Abolish and Replace Skilled Migration '457' Visas," *Huffington Post*, April 18, 2017, http://www.huffingtonpost.com.au/2017/04/18/turnbull-government-to-abolish-and-replace-skilled-migration-45_a_22043823/. Admittedly, the prime minister did acknowledge limits to this, and Australia's historical reliance on immigration.

[55] Ibid.

[56] "Economics and Tax Policy," *One Nation*, http://www.onenation.com.au/policies/economics, accessed December 18, 2017.

[57] "Malcolm Turnbull's 457 Visa Immigration Crackdown Disaster for Universities," *Australian Financial Review*, April 20, 2017, http://www.afr.com/opinion/columnists/malcolm-turnbulls-457-visa-immigration-crackdown-disaster-for-universities-20170420-gvoh6f.

the need to ensure energy security and affordability in Australia.[58] The Conservative government has also deployed a distinctly nationalist set of arguments for the priority of domestic energy users, over global energy markets, and existing global energy contracts.[59]

This again also parallels a range of One Nation policies and priorities on energy and the environment: One Nation has questioned the science of climate change,[60] argued for policies that promote "cheap, accessible [and] reliable energy" for both manufacturing and household consumption,[61] and criticized the UN's action plan for sustainable development, Agenda 21, as well as the support for it from both Labor and the Coalition, as an attempt to "control" Australians and "their way of life."[62]

Another area in which both major parties in Australia have arguably adopted a quasi-populist approach, at least at the federal level, is in relation to the rights of First Nations. In 2010, with the election of the ALP minority government under prime minister Julia Gillard, the government undertook seriously to consider proposals to amend the Australian Constitution to give greater rights and recognition to Aboriginal and Torres Strait Islanders peoples. It appointed an Expert Panel of eminent Indigenous and non-Indigenous Australians to advise on options for reform; in 2012, the Panel gave its report to the government calling for a new preamble, the removal of an outmoded clause on electoral disqualification, changes to the Commonwealth's power to regulate based on race, and a new guarantee of non-discrimination or equal protection based on race.[63] The government, however, lost its majority before acting on any of these recommendations.[64]

The new conservative Coalition Government also ruled out the possibility of any substantive change to the race power, or the introduction of a justiciable non-discrimination guarantee. But it suggested a willingness to consider alternative mechanisms for reform—including

[58] Australian Government Department of the Environment and Energy, *Powering Forward*, https://powering-forward.energy.gov.au/, accessed April 7, 2017.

[59] Luke Cooper, "Turnbull Government Strikes Deal with Gas Companies to Cover East Coast Shortfall," *Huffington Post*, September 27, 2017, http://www.huffingtonpost.com.au/2017/09/27/turnbull-government-strikes-deal-with-gas-companies-to-cover-east-coast-shortfall_a_23224138/.

[60] "Climate Change? You Decide," *One Nation*, July 25, 2013, http://www.onenation.com.au/current_affairs/climate-change-you-decide.

[61] "Economics & Tax Policy: Additional Information," *One Nation*, http://www.onenation.com.au/policies/economics/economics-4, accessed December 18, 2017.

[62] "Agenda 21/2030 (A.K.A. Sustainable Development," *One Nation*, http://www.onenation.com.au/policies/agenda21, accessed December 18, 2017 . . .

[63] *Final Report of the Expert Panel on Recognising Aboriginal and Torres Strait Islander Peoples in the Constitution* (2012), https://www.pmc.gov.au/resource-centre/indigenous-affairs/final-report-expert-panel-recognising-aboriginal-and-torres-strait-islander-peoples-constitution.

[64] Harry Hobbs, "Will Treaties with Indigenous Australians Overtake Constitutional Recognition?," *UNSW Law*, December 20, 2016, http://www.law.unsw.edu.au/news/2016/12/will-treaties-indigenous-australians-overtake-constitutional-recognition; "Recognise: The Debate That Is Failing and Dividing Black Australia," *New Matilda*, March 5, 2015, https://newmatilda.com/2015/03/05/recognise-debate-failing-and-dividing-black-australia/.

the possibility of a new First Nations Voice to Parliament. On this basis, Aboriginal and Torres and Strait Islander leaders also decided to conduct a nationwide process of regional "dialogues," to seek their views of First Nations on different proposed models for change. The process ended in support for the proposed model of parliamentary-based change—that is a Voice to Parliament, coupled with a process of statutory-based truth and reconciliation ("Makarrata"). The government, however, announced that it was unwilling to put the idea to the electorate at a national referendum.[65]

The current policy stalemate on this issue also again parallels the position of One Nation on Indigenous rights, and its populist attack on measures aimed at promoting pluralism and diversity, or recognizing historical injustices via differential treatment of Indigenous and non-Indigenous Australians: One Nation has opposed any change to the Constitution recognizing First Nations as the traditional owners of the land, including the most modest "symbolic" or preambular change.[66] The party has also emphasized a commitment to formal, over substantive, equality in the context of race,[67] and to broader notions of pluralism and diversity.[68]

The only potential difference from immigration and energy policy is that policies of this kind may be distinctly populist, without necessarily being broadly *popular* with the Australian electorate. While the government itself has suggested that it is unwilling to support constitutional change, out of a concern that it lacks popular support, many commentators attribute the government's position to the unwillingness of key conservative MPs to support, or at least *be seen to support*, constitutional change affirming commitments to pluralism and substantive over formal equality for Indigenous Australians.[69]

[65] See Dan Conifer et al., "Indigenous Advisory Body Rejected by PM in 'Kick in the Guts' for Advocates," *ABC News*, October 26, 2017, http://www.abc.net.au/news/2017-10-26/indigenous-advisory-body-proposal-rejected-by-cabinet/9087856; "Turnbull Government Says No to Indigenous 'Voice to Parliament'" *The Conversation*, October 26, 2017, https://theconversation.com/turnbull-government-says-no-to-indigenous-voice-to-parliament-86421; Calla Wahlquist, "Nigel Scullion Says Indigenous Voice to Parliament 'Would Not Fly' with Voters," *The Guardian*, October 27, 2017, https://www.theguardian.com/australia-news/2017/oct/27/nigel-scullion-says-indigenous-voice-to-parliament-would-not-fly-with-voters.

[66] "Our Aims," *One Nation*, http://www.onenation.com.au/aims, accessed December 18, 2017. (opposing "acknowledging Aboriginal and Torres Strait Islanders" in the Constitution on the basis that "One Nation believes that all Australians are owners and custodians of this land and should work toward unification, not segregation, under the one law for all").

[67] Ibid. (emphasizing a commitment to "fair and equal treatment of all Australians, within a system of government recognising and acting upon a need for Australia to be truly one nation," and to "treat all Australians equally and justly and with government assistance based on need, not race").

[68] Ibid. (emphasizing the unified, Christian character of Australia as a nation).

[69] See, e.g., Rosalind Dixon, "Let's Give Indigenous People a Voice in Parliament," *The Australian*, July 21, 2017, www.theaustralian.com.au/business/legal.../87aa6750f1f4ba5a29d9715ee115c781; Shalailah Medhora, "Indigenous Recognition Sticking Point Is Racial Discrimination in Constitution," *The Guardian*, July 6, 2015,

DEFEATING (OR ADVANCING) POPULISM?

We do not necessarily suggest that these policy shifts have been *causal to* or directly attributable to the role of One Nation. In some instances, it may simply reflect a decision on the part of both major parties to respond to what they perceive to be changes in the underlying preferences and attitudes of voters in Australia, and not any immediate electoral threat posed by parties such as One Nation.

Indeed, there is potentially an important connection between the system of mandatory, preferential voting we noted above, and policy responsiveness of this kind on the part of the major political parties in Australia: a system of mandatory voting reduces the payoff to parties appealing solely to their base, rather than the views of the median voter (or at least the median voter in competitive electorates or electoral districts). A system of preferential voting also reduces the pressure on major parties to court voters at the far-Left or far-Right of the political spectrum, who might otherwise vote for minor parties, and thus encourages greater responsiveness to the views of the median voter.

Whatever the proximate cause, however, the effect of these policy shifts has been the same from a liberal democratic perspective: by adopting a more populist approach to certain key policy areas, both major parties in Australia have effectively undermined the electoral appeal of One Nation in many parts of the country, and thereby contributed to stabilizing the broader democratic system in Australia. At the same time, in doing so they have arguably undermined certain aspects of the *liberal* democratic tradition in Australia.

Liberal democracy, many commentators suggest, involves at least some minimum commitment on a national level to judicial independence, the rule of law, and human rights, and to basic norms of dignity and respect for all systems. On a global level, it also arguably involves a commitment to at least forms of global cooperation aimed at ensuring common peace and security.[70] While arguably not threatening the "minimum core" of these commitments,[71] recent Australian policies have also clearly eroded the more

---

https://www.theguardian.com/australia-news/2015/jul/06/indigenous-recognition-sticking-point-racial-discrimination-in-constitution; Bridie Jabour, "Divisions over Indigenous Recognition Fuels Pressure for Meeting with PM," *The Guardian*, April 13, 2015, https://www.theguardian.com/australia-news/2015/apr/13/divisions-over-indigenous-recognition-fuels-pressure-for-meeting-with-pm.

[70] Otfried Hoffe, *Kant's Cosmopolitan Theory of Law and Peace*, trans. Alexandra Newton (New York: Cambridge University Press, 2006); John Rawls, *The Law of Peoples* (Cambridge, MA: Harvard University Press, 1999). See, e.g., Seyla Benhabib and David Alvarez, "Cosmopolitan Democracy," in *The Encyclopedia of Political Thought* (Malden, MA: John Wiley & Sons, 2014); Thomas W. Pogge, "Cosmopolitan and Sovereignty," *Ethics* 103 (1992): 48–75.

[71] Compare Rosalind Dixon and David Landau, "Transnational Constitutionalism and a Limited Doctrine of Unconstitutional Constitutional Amendment," *International Journal of Constitutional Law* 13 (2015): 606–638; David Landau and Rosalind Dixon, "Constraining Constitutional Change," *Wake Forest Law Review* 50 (2015): 859–890; Rosalind Dixon and David Landau, "Competitive Democracy and the Constitutional Minimum Core," in *Assessing Constitutional Performance*, ed. Tom Ginsburg and Aziz Huq (New York: Cambridge University Press, 2016), 268–292.

rights-respecting, global, and pluralist aspects of Australia's constitutional and political traditions.

Australia, for example, has a long history of immigration, especially post-World War II, and a tradition of embracing immigration and multiculturalism. The Australian national anthem in fact contains language expressly affirming Australia as a country that favors immigration: it suggests that "for those who've come across the seas, we've boundless plains to share."[72] This tradition, however, has arguably been replaced by a new, far less liberal discourse of deterrence, border control, and national security. Similarly, Australia has a history of openness to free trade, and leadership in a range of global spheres— including on climate change, but moved increasingly toward a language of national self-interest in the context of energy and environmental policy.

Thus while, on the one hand, various shifts in policy in Australia have muted the threat of populist parties such as One Nation, they have had important consequences for the strength of Australian representative democracy in other ways.

Conclusion: Comparative Lessons

The state of Australian democracy is relatively strong, but also under ongoing threat from Australia's One Nation party, a distinctly illiberal populist party with significant electoral support in certain parts of the country. The containment of that threat, to date, also depends on at least two interrelated dimensions to Australian democratic practice: first, a range of structural safeguards against the threat of a hostile populist takeover of the system; and second, a degree of *quasi-populist* political responsiveness on the part of both major parties in Australia.

We point, for example, to two key structural features of the Australian political system that have helped create a firewall against the danger of illiberal populism capturing core democratic institutions—that is, Australia's system of compulsory, mandatory preferential voting. In a comparative context, we suggest, populist strategies have succeeded in increasing electoral turnout from a mobilized base, while the success of populist parties often reflects historically low levels of turnout by ordinary voters. In Australia, in contrast, mandatory voting has consistently reduced turnout as a predictor of electoral outcomes, and thereby also the threat posed by the mobilized support enjoyed by One Nation.

Similarly, populism has thrived in certain countries because of the success of minor parties in quite a small number of electoral subunits, which have proven dispositive in the resolution of broader electoral contests. While these parties themselves may, or may not, have been illiberal populist, their capacity to win votes away from liberal democrats

---

[72] "The Australian National Anthem," *Australian Government*, accessed February 23, 2018, https://www.pmc.gov.au/government/australian-national-anthem.

has arguably contributed to the success of illiberal populists in certain key electoral contests.[73] In Australia, in contrast, the distinctive electoral system used in the House of Representatives and Senate reduces the capacity for any minor party radically to alter the composition of the legislative or executive branch of government—other than via negotiation with major parties to form a minority government, or guarantee supply. This has again also served to cabin the potential role of One Nation, in the lower house, as a decisive influence on the identity or composition of the government.[74]

Both major parties in Australia have also adopted a range of policies that are quasi-populist in nature: they have supported a more restrictive approach to immigration, and to policies that provide for a system of onshore asylum. They have emphasized energy supply and affordability, over long-term energy security or climate change goals, and rejected calls for a more formalist rights-based approach to the relationship with Australia's First Nations. Policies of this kind are also popular with a significant number of Australian voters. In this way they have arguably helped diffuse the electoral threat posed by One Nation, in most parts of the country, and thereby the direct threat to mainstream democratic governance. The price, however, has arguably been a significant erosion in the more liberal, pluralist, and rights-respecting aspects of Australia's constitutional traditions.

What are the lessons of this for a broader comparative perspective? One lesson, we suggest, concerns the advantages of the key features of the Australian democratic design we identify above—that is, a system of mandatory, preferential voting. These structural features of a democratic system will obviously play out differently in various contexts, and need to be adapted to the particularities of a nation's constitutional and electoral system. But they are a set of safeguards that, we suggest, have universal value, which it is plausible to think that other countries could adopt.[75]

Australia's own system of mandatory, preferential voting was not part of the original design of the 1901 Constitution. Rather it was the product of later legislative change,[76] and arguably, a concern about historically low levels of voter turnout in the 1919 and

---

[73] See, e.g., Tara Golshan, "Did Jill Stein Voters Deliver Donald Trump the Presidency?" *Vox*, November 11, 2016, https://www.vox.com/policy-and-politics/2016/11/11/13576798/jill-stein-third-party-donald-trump-win; "Jill Stein: Democratic Spoiler or Scapegoat?" *FiveThirtyEight*, December 7, 2017, https://fivethirtyeight.com/features/jill-stein-democratic-spoiler-or-scapegoat/; Emily C. Singer, "How Third-Party Voters Likely Helped Sink Hillary Clinton's Presidential Candidacy," *Mic*, November 9, 2016, https://mic.com/articles/158991/how-third-party-voters-likely-helped-sink-hillary-clinton-s-presidential-candidacy#.Txyr7bt2O.

[74] Note, however, the existence of a consistent push towards centrism: Benjamin Reilly, "Democratic Design and Democratic Reform: The Case of Australia," *Taiwan Journal of Democracy* 12(2) (2016): 1–16.

[75] Note, however, Benjamin Reilly's view that uses of the preferential voting system overseas so far have been driven by local factors, rather than the appeal of Australia's political model: Benjamin Reilly, "The Global Spread of Preferential Voting: Australian Institutional Imperialism?" *Australian Journal of Political Science* 39(2) (2004): 253–266.

[76] Federal law, for example, was changed in 1911 to make enrolment in federal elections compulsory, and voting was made compulsory in federal elections by legislation adopted in 1924. *Commonwealth Electoral Act 1918* (Cth) s 245(1). See Tim Evans, *Compulsory Voting in Australia* (Australian Electoral Commission, 2006).

1922 federal elections.[77] Similarly, twenty-four countries worldwide now have a system of mandatory voting in at least some elections,[78] and many of those countries adopted that system well after the adoption of their national constitution.[79]

Many free speech scholars also argue that a system of mandatory voting is compatible with commitments to freedom of expression: a system of this kind may *limit* the right to freedom of speech, but in ways that are generally reasonable and proportionate, given a concern to protect the integrity of the democratic system.[80] It is thus quite plausible to think that a range of other countries could adopt similar changes in their own system of voting.

The second key feature of Australia's electoral system is the majoritarian, alternative (preferential) vote. Like compulsory voting, this was introduced almost two decades after federation (1919), with the motivation that a candidate should be elected *only* if he or she has majority support within the electorate.[81] Unlike a first-past-the-post system, where a candidate can win with a minority of support, the preferential system counts down voters' preferences until one competitor reaches 51 percent of the vote. It remains unique to Australia, Papua New Guinea, and (previously) Fiji at the national political level, though it is used at the subnational level in the United States.

The difficulty, however, is that there will often be significant *sociopolitical* obstacles to quasi-constitutional change of this kind: many features of a constitution are quite "sticky," or immune to formal constitutional change.[82] The United Kingdom's rejection of the alternative vote in its 2011 parliamentary voting referendum is an example of this kind. Constitutional systems are far more likely to adopt *formal* change that is in some way familiar, or historically rooted, within that system, than if it is a wholly foreign or novel constitutional innovation.[83] Partisan political, and interest group dynamics, can also make change of this kind difficult to achieve: few major political parties will vote for change of this kind, unless they see an immediate electoral benefit to their own party.[84] A system of noncompulsory voting may also increase the influence within a party of

---

[77] Evans, *Compulsory Voting*.

[78] Mark See, "The Case for Compulsory Voting in the United States," *Harvard Law Review* 121 (2007): 591–612.

[79] Laura Santhanam, "22 Countries Where Voting Is Mandatory," *PBS*, November 3, 2014, https://www.pbs.org/newshour/politics/22-countries-voting-mandatory.

[80] See, e.g., See, "The Case for Compulsory Voting"; Bart Engelen, "Why Compulsory Voting Can Enhance Democracy," *Acta Politica* 42 (2007): 23–39; Justine Lacroix, "A Liberal Defence of Compulsory Voting," *Politics* 27 (2007): 190–195. This seems especially true if the law imposes only modest penalties, and/or allows some possibility of an informal or protest vote, as restrictions of this kind are arguably a reasonable and proportionate means of protecting democracy. But compare also Hans A. von Spakovsky, "Compulsory Voting Is Unconstitutional," *Heritage*, April 1, 2015, http://www.heritage.org/political-process/commentary/compulsory-voting-unconstitutional (taking the opposite position).

[81] Clive Bean, "Australia's Experience with the Alternative Vote," *Representation* 34 (1997): 103–110.

[82] Ozan O. Varol, "Constitutional Stickiness," *UC Davis Law Review* 49 (2016): 899–962.

[83] Ibid.

[84] In Australia, for example, compulsory voting was first introduced in Queensland in 1915, when the liberal government perceived that it was less effective in mobilizing its voters than the opposition Labor Party: see Evans, *Compulsory Voting*.

certain (interest) groups, and those groups may then oppose any change that threatens that influence.[85]

In this sense, the key difficulty to "learning" from the Australian experience in this context is simply what scholars such as Eric Posner and Adrian Vermeule have called the "inside-outside" problem,[86] or the problem of institutional path-dependence.[87] In most countries, existing democratic institutional arrangements create overwhelming obstacles to adopting democratic safeguards of this kind. While the same might be said for the responsiveness of major parties to broader preference shifts in the electorate, a key difference in this context is one of *time-horizon*.

Policy change of this kind can often occur gradually, through the actions of a range of individual candidates or party leaders proposing new policies and approaches, in ways that lead to a long-term shift in the overall identity and policies of a party.[88] The difficulty with other countries "borrowing" an approach of this kind, therefore, is not ultimately one of practicability. It is that borrowing of this kind has a distinctly ambivalent character from a liberal democratic perspective: in Australia, at least, the restrictive immigration, and economically protectionist, policies adopted by both major parties seem to have helped undercut the threat posed by One Nation, but at some real price to liberal democratic values. Whether this is a price worth paying is also one that is clearly open to reasonable disagreement.[89]

There is at least some reason to think that, at least in the form it has taken in Australia to date, a quasi-populist turn in mainstream democratic politics is a price worth paying for preserving the minimum core of a democratic system, in the face of a credible threat of illiberal populist takeover. But the erosion over the last two decades of broader liberal democratic commitments to liberal toleration, openness, and inclusion in Australia has also been far from trivial. There is also clearly the danger of a slippery slope from more minor to more major incursions on liberal democratic values.

---

[85] In Australia, it is notable that the 1924 federal legislative change was introduced by a private members bill and not by either major party. Ibid.

[86] See Eric A Posner and Adrian Vermeule, "Inside or Outside the System?" *University of Chicago Law Review* 80 (2013): 1743–1798.

[87] See Sanford Levinson, "How Many Times Has the United States Constitution Been Amended?: Accounting for Constitutional Change," in *Responding to Imperfection: The Theory and Practice of Constitutional Amendment*, ed. Sanford Levinson (Princeton, NJ: Princeton University Press, 1995), 13. Compare also Varol, "Constitutional Stickiness"; Rosalind Dixon and Julie Suk, "Liberal Constitutionalism and Economic Inequality," *University of Chicago Law Review* (forthcoming).

[88] Compare Cass R. Sunstein, "Social Norms and Social Roles," *Columbia Law Review* 96 (1996): 903–968.

[89] On reasonable disagreement and constitutional law generally, compare Jeremy Waldron, *Law and Disagreement* (New York: Oxford University Press, 1999); John Rawls, *Political Liberalism* (New York: Columbia University Press, 1993).

Whether the trade-off made in Australia is one worth making, for the preservation of democracy, is thus ultimately a question that can only be decided well after the publication of this book. Clearly, to combat illiberal populism democrats are required to fight fire with fire. The question, however, is how to do so without burning the whole democratic house down. At present, the Australian experience also offers only modest reason for optimism about our ability to succeed in this task.

24 Constitutional Inertia and Regime Pluralism in Asia
David S. Law and Chien-Chih Lin*

IS THIS THE best of times or the worst of times for constitutional democracy? Judging from recent experience in Asia, the answer might be a bit of both. As the existence of this volume attests, many are concerned that constitutional democracy is increasingly (or inherently) fragile, prone to backsliding, or vulnerable to the rise of illiberal tendencies.[1] By one measure, more than half of the world's countries became less democratic over the last year, with Asia experiencing a larger decline than any other region.[2] Others view such concerns as unwarranted or based upon unrealistic expectations.[3] Until recently, the arguments on both sides were fueled largely by the experience of Latin America and Central and Eastern Europe, but recent experience has given rise to fears on the part of American scholars that backsliding may be a problem closer to home as well.

* We are grateful to Mary Hui and Lorraine Wu for diligent research assistance, and to Tom Ginsburg, Po Jen Yap, and the editors of this volume for very helpful feedback. Portions of part 3 of this chapter are taken or adapted from David S. Law, "Alternatives to Liberal Constitutional Democracy," *Maryland Law Review* 76 (2017): 223–243.

[1] *See* Larry Diamond, "Facing Up to the Democratic Recession," *Journal of Democracy* 26 (2015): 141, 144.

[2] "Democracy Continues Its Disturbing Retreat," *Economist*, January 31, 2018, https://www.economist.com/blogs/graphicdetail/2018/01/daily-chart-21; Economist Intelligence Unit, *Democracy Index 2017: Free Speech under Attack*, at 25, accessed February 26, 2018, https://www.eiu.com/public/topical_report.aspx?campaignid=DemocracyIndex2017.

[3] See Steven Levitsky and Lucan Way, "The Myth of Democratic Recession," *Journal of Democracy* 26 (2015): 45–58.

If we are serious about understanding whether constitutional democracy is in crisis at the global level, however, it is essential to consider Asia. On the one hand, as home to the majority of humanity and the world economy, Asia has the heft to make or break global trends and demands more, not less, attention than other regions. On the other hand, Asia has long been a highly competitive environment for different regime types. Americans speak of "swing states," but Asia might well be described as a "swing region." Constitutional democracies coexist cheek by jowl with authoritarian regimes; politicians openly advocate alternatives to constitutional democracy and make controversial claims about so-called "Asian values" to justify illiberal rule.[4] The sheer variety of regime types on display in Asia holds an added benefit for scholars: it renders the region an ideal source of comparative data. Europe, North America, and even Latin America look downright homogenous compared to the vast expanses of East, Southeast, and South Asia. If we are to understand or explain the longevity of a particular type of regime— such as constitutional democracy—we must be able to make comparisons against other types of regimes.

For all of these reasons, Asia offers an appropriate test of several theories that might account for the longevity (or lack thereof) of constitutional democracies. Let us consider three hypotheses in particular, which we might call (1) the contagion hypothesis, (2) the constitutional inertia hypothesis, and (3) the regime performance hypothesis. The contagion hypothesis holds that constitutional democracy is vulnerable to regional and global trends. The constitutional inertia hypothesis, by contrast, holds that stable regimes are likely to remain stable, whereas unstable regimes are likely to remain unstable, regardless of whether they are constitutional democracies. The regime performance hypothesis holds that the key to longevity is not regime type, but rather regime performance, meaning a regime's ability to satisfy fundamental (and primarily material) needs.

Comparison of a few Asian jurisdictions—including South Korea, Taiwan, Singapore, Hong Kong, China, and Thailand—is sufficient to cast doubt on (1) but suggests that (2) and (3) are both plausible. If the experience of these jurisdictions is any indication, constitutional democracy is here to stay in Asia, and both inertia and regime performance may help to explain why. But constitutional democracy is probably also doomed to long-term coexistence with a variety of successful regimes that are more illiberal than liberal, and less democratic than bureaucratic. What the future holds for Asia, in other words, is more of the same—namely, regime pluralism.

---

[4] Tom Ginsburg, "East Asian Constitutionalism in Comparative Perspective," in *Constitutionalism in Asia in the Early Twenty-First Century*, ed. Albert H.Y. Chen (New York: Cambridge University Press, 2014), 32, 32–33; Jiunn-Rong Yeh and Wen-Chen Chang, "The Emergence of East Asian Constitutionalism: Features in Comparison," *American Journal of Comparative Law* (2011): 805, 809.

1. The Contagion Hypothesis

In an age of globalization, it is hard to shake the feeling of global constitutional interdependency. A contagion or domino effect may be at work, and it may be working to the disadvantage of constitutional democracy. Scholars frequently speak of waves of regime change: democratization, it is said, has occurred in several waves from the early nineteenth century through the late twentieth century.[5] But if waves of liberalization and democratization can emanate outward from the world's democracies, so too might waves of illiberalism and autocracy wash back in our faces from the world's non-democracies.

This hypothesis is entirely consistent with the literature on policy diffusion, which consistently finds that policy approaches do in fact spread from country to country, and seeks to identify the factors that predict and influence policy diffusion.[6] If specific policies can spread from one country to the next, so too can overall forms of government. In part, a learning effect may be at work: one regime sets an example that others may emulate if it seems successful and transferable. International politics and competitive dynamics may also be at work: like-minded regimes may lend each other support while undermining those that are different.[7]

The contagion hypothesis is not, however, well supported by recent experience in Asia. If there is such a thing as an international contagion afflicting constitutional democracies, it does not appear to have spread to, or within, Asia. The region as a whole exhibits no clear signs of tipping against constitutional democracy. Table 24.1 is a rough list of all regime changes in East, Southeast, and South Asia over the last thirty years, since South Korea and Taiwan transitioned to democracy in 1987.

As the data shows, the last thirty years have been a period of nearly complete regime stability in East Asia. There have been no full-blown changes in regime type anywhere in the region since 1990. And to the extent that there has been any movement in East Asia in recent decades, it has been toward rather than away from constitutional democracy. The closest thing to a wave would be the shift in the late 1980s in East Asia, with South Korea and Taiwan democratizing in 1987 and Mongolia democratizing in 1990. Those regimes have been stable ever since.

---

[5] See Samuel P. Huntington, *The Third Wave: Democratization in the Late Twentieth Century* (Norman: University of Oklahoma Press, 1991), 13–26, 290–293 (identifying three historical "waves of democratization").

[6] See, e.g., Everett M. Rogers, *The Diffusion of Innovations*, 5th ed. (New York: Free Press, 2003), 38–86; Zachary Elkins and Beth A. Simmons, "The Globalization of Liberalization: Policy Diffusion in the International Political Economy," *American Political Science Review* 98 (2004): 171–189.

[7] It is well documented that regimes of the same type tend not to go to war with each other. See, e.g., John R. Oneal and Bruce M. Russett, "The Classical Liberals Were Right: Democracy, Interdependence and Conflict, 1950–1985," *International Studies Quarterly* 41 (1997): 267, 288–289 (reporting that democracies are less likely to go to war with each other than with autocracies, and that autocracies likewise are less likely to fight each other than to fight democracies).

TABLE 24.1

Regime Transitions in Asia, 1988–2018

	Transition to constitutional democracy	Movement back and forth	Transition away from constitutional democracy
East Asia	Mongolia—1990 (communist regime to democracy)	None	None
Southeast Asia	Indonesia—1998 (hybrid regime to democracy) East Timor—2002 (newly independent state; constitutional democracy) Myanmar—2010 (partial transition from military to civilian rule)	Cambodia—1993, 1997 (socialist regime to democratic constitutional monarchy to authoritarian rule) Thailand—1991, 2006, 2014 (fluctuation between civilian and military rule, but consistently under royal authority)	None
South Asia	Bangladesh—1990 (military rule to multiparty democracy) Nepal—2006 (monarchy to parliamentary democracy) Bhutan—2008 (traditional monarchy to democratic constitutional monarchy) Maldives—2008 (single-party rule to multiparty system)	None, for now (but see Bangladesh and Maldives)	None

If we broaden the focus to include Southeast Asia, the prognosis for constitutional democracy looks better, not worse. Like East Asia, Southeast Asia is characterized more by regime stability than backsliding or a penchant for a particular type of regime. But to the extent that there have been changes, a clear majority of the transitions have been at least partly in the direction of constitutional democracy. For example, Myanmar has taken much-ballyhooed baby steps from military rule to democratic civilian rule, while

Indonesia transitioned from strongman rule to democracy with the fall of Suharto in 1998, much as the Philippines had transitioned in 1986 with the exile of Marcos.

As of this writing, the situation in South Asia is potentially more worrisome but remains highly fluid. In Bangladesh, the conviction of former prime minister Khaleda Zia calls into question the country's commitment to a genuinely multiparty system,[8] while in the Maldives, an increasingly autocratic president has declared a state of emergency in advance of upcoming elections.[9] In both cases, however, it is probably too soon to speak of regime change, much less anti-democratic contagion in South Asia (especially given the solidity of Bhutan's recent transition to constitutional democracy). As tempting as it is to make predictions that incorporate the very latest in current events, the only thing one can predict with much confidence is that such predictions will be obsolete by the time they see print.

No one wants to overlook the warning signs of democratic decay. But it is also important to keep the latest news in perspective. Some developments may push our buttons yet do not signify fundamental change. The Philippines is a case in point. The execution of suspected criminals without any semblance of legal process is exactly the kind of behavior that lawyers are trained to find utterly unacceptable, but the Philippines under Rodrigo Duterte has not relapsed into dictatorship; indeed, it is not even a straightforward case of democratic backsliding. For better or for worse, the extralegal killing of criminal suspects does not evidence a lack of electoral accountability or the onset of political oppression. On contrary, Duterte's pledge to kill drug dealers and users helped to get him elected,[10] and not even his staunchest critics think the crackdown is targeted at regime opponents. Nor does it seem accurate to describe Duterte as despotic or anti-constitutional, given his push for constitutional reforms that would strip the presidency of certain powers and introduce a decentralized system of government.[11] Reform of this variety elevates the role of the constitution rather than undermining it. And turning power over to other officials and other levels of government is exactly the opposite of what one would expect from a strongman ruler bent on usurping power and debilitating institutional safeguards.

The countries that have experienced the most conspicuous setbacks—meaning actual regime change—would be Cambodia and Thailand, yet even in these cases, the implications for the viability of constitutional democracy elsewhere in Asia appear limited. Both have obviously experienced backsliding—repeatedly, in the case of Thailand—but neither reflects the worst-case scenario of the failure of an established constitutional democracy. They are better described instead as situations of regime instability punctuated by brief periods of constitutional democracy. In Thailand, a civilian government was overthrown in 1991 by the military, as were the populist governments of Thaksin Shinawatra

---

[8] "In the Dock and on the Ropes," *Economist*, February 8, 2018, at 26, 27,

[9] "A Tropical Tempest," *Economist*, February 8, 2018, at 30.

[10] Aurora Almendral, "Scorned Abroad, Duterte Remains Popular in Philippines," *New York Times*, October 14, 2016, at A6.

[11] "Dancing the Cha-Cha," *Economist*, February 3, 2018, at 26.

and his sister Yingluck in 2006 and 2014, respectively. But it would not be accurate to describe Thailand as a constitutional democracy descending into authoritarianism. It would be more accurate to say that the country has been stuck for decades in a revolving door between military and civilian rule.

In Cambodia, the odds were stacked against constitutional democracy from the start. Cambodia transitioned from socialist dictatorship to multiparty democracy in 1993 before the equivalent of a coup d'état in 1997—a mere four years later—that consolidated strongman rule. It would thus be accurate to say that Cambodia merely reverted to its long-standing ways; indeed, any other result would have been surprising. Constitutional democracy would need to be robust indeed—a virtual miracle cure—to have taken hold quickly and permanently after the years of slaughter, genocide, occupation, and war that came before.[12] It is hard to imagine less favorable conditions for lasting democratization. And even the hybrid regime in place today constitutes a real improvement over most of what came before.

To be sure, the state of constitutional democracy in Asia could be better. But it could also be worse. Most regimes in Asia—democratic or otherwise—are stable, while the unstable regimes come as no surprise. The changes that do occur hardly suggest that a sea change is underway. For each backsliding Thailand, there is a Myanmar unsteadily inching forward, and vice versa. The glass is simultaneously half-empty and half-full.

2. The Constitutional Inertia Hypothesis

Newton's first of law of motion is that an object at rest tends to stay at rest, while an object in motion tends to stay in motion. Something similar could be said of governments: stable regimes tend to remain stable; unstable regimes tend to stay unstable. There is a rich body of theory to support the notion of constitutional inertia. Perhaps the single most important insight of game theory—expressed by the concept of equilibrium—is that certain patterns of political behavior, once established, tend to remain in place, even if many (or even most) people might prefer to settle upon a different pattern.[13] Equilibria exist because people behave strategically: that is to say, they behave in ways that make the most sense in light of how they expect others to behave. Once people expect certain behavior on the part of others (cars stop on red and go on green; court orders are obeyed), they act in anticipation of this behavior (they stop on red and go on green; they

---

[12] Sean Bergin, *The Khmer Rouge and the Cambodian Genocide* (Buffalo, NY: Rosen Publishing Group, 2008), 29–39; Joakim Öjendal and Mona Lilja, "Beyond Democracy in Cambodia: Political Reconstruction in a Post-Conflict Society" in *Beyond Democracy in Cambodia: Political Reconstruction in a Post-Conflict Society*, ed. Joakim Öjendal and Mona Lilja (Copenhagen: NIAS Press, 2009), 1–30.

[13] David S. Law, "A Theory of Judicial Power and Judicial Review," *Georgetown Law Journal* 97 (2008): 723, 766 (discussing the scenario of the unpopular king who remains in power even though everyone—including his own troops—would prefer to overthrow him).

obey court orders), and the behavior becomes self-reinforcing, even in the absence of external enforcement. The expectation of order generates order; the expectation of chaos generates chaos. Expectations become self-fulfilling prophecies.

Constitutions, in turn, are well suited to generating behavioral expectations. They are, in other words, coordinating devices, and once coordination has been achieved, it tends to be self-sustaining.[14] The fact that constitutions perform coordinating functions helps to explain why they remain stable even in the absence of external enforcement. It is also the case that constitutional systems generate path dependence and a variety of lock-in effects.[15] For all these reasons, equilibrium is difficult to dislodge once established. The longer that a regime is in place, the more it enjoys advantages that help it to remain in place.

But equilibrium is not to be confused with regime stability. Persistent instability is also an equilibrium that feeds on itself. Just as stability begets stability, instability begets instability. If past instability leads to widespread expectations of more instability, the result can be an equilibrium of chronic instability. If people expect the regime to be gone tomorrow, compliance with the regime will not be forthcoming; investments of loyalty and resources that might stabilize the regime will not be made. Expectations of regime instability can thus become self-fulfilling and self-reinforcing.

On this view, regime stability may have little to do with regime type. Instead, the best predictor of whether a regime will still be around next year is whether the regime was around last year, and the year before that. States at rest will stay at rest; states in flux will remain in flux.

The notion of constitutional inertia is certainly consistent with the high degree of regime stability seen throughout East Asia and much of South and Southeast Asia. Even the seemingly exceptional case of Thailand is, from this perspective, not exceptional at all. Rather than standing for the proposition that constitutional democracy is an inherently or especially vulnerable type of regime, it stands instead as an illustration of constitutional inertia. There are two contradictory ways of interpreting the Thai experience. Oddly enough, however, both interpretations support the constitutional inertia hypothesis.

The most obvious interpretation would be that Thailand has been highly unstable. But that does not necessarily mean that Thailand demonstrates any inherent vulnerability or weakness on the part of constitutional democracy as opposed to other regime types. Its instability cuts both ways. It is not simply the periods of democratic

---

[14] Russell Hardin, *Liberalism, Constitutionalism, and Democracy* (New York: Oxford University Press, 1999), 82–140; Russell Hardin, "Why a Constitution?," in *Social and Political Foundations of Constitutions*, ed. Denis J. Galligan and Mila Versteeg (New York: Cambridge University Press, 2013), 59–62.

[15] Daryl Levinson, "Parchment and Politics: The Positive Puzzle of Constitutional Commitment," *Harvard Law Review* 124 (2011): 657, 745–746; Ozan O. Varol, "Constitutional Stickiness," *UC at Davis Law Review* 49 (2016): 899, 912.

civilian rule that fail to last, but also the periods of military rule. For every coup that has moved Thailand from civilian to military rule, there has also necessarily been a corresponding movement in the opposite direction, from military to civilian rule. Instead of hitting the sweet spot between populism and oligarchy where constitutional democracy thrives, Thailand careens between the two extremes.[16] The Thai experience can be defined as a succession of constitutional democracies that succumb to a succession of military coups. Equivalently, however, it could also be described as an unstable military regime that suffers from periodic bouts of democratic civilian rule. Thailand's instability is not good evidence of the inherent fragility of constitutional democracy for the simple reason that, in Thailand, pretty much every regime—democratic or otherwise—has proven fragile.

A very different interpretation would be that, contrary to superficial appearances, the true Thai regime, if properly understood and defined, has in fact been highly stable for decades. For example, we might define the actual Thai regime as consisting of an alliance between the monarchy and the military, which tolerates constitutional democracy only if and to the extent that it does not undermine or infringe upon this alliance. From this perspective, the various coups could be characterized as having both the purpose and the effect of preserving this alliance.[17] What they shared in common was the removal of governments that lacked the support or confidence of the king.

Alternatively, we might follow the lead of Melkinsburg and define the Thai regime as one in which the king decides who is allowed to seize power, subject to the requirement that the transfer of power must occur free of substantial violence or bloodshed.[18] If we use this "king-as-kingmaker" definition of the Thai regime, then the Thai regime has been highly stable for decades: Rama IX was, at the time of his death, the world's longest-reigning monarch. At the risk of emphasizing the obvious, the defining constant throughout the decades-long reign of Rama IX was the reign of Rama IX. The other defining constant was his recognition and acceptance of the government. No government—military or civilian—held power without his approval, whether tacit or explicit.

Ultimately, however, it does not matter which interpretation one adopts because, under either interpretation, Thailand supports the constitutional inertia hypothesis. Either it is an example of an object in motion remaining in motion, or it is an example of an object at rest remaining at rest.

---

[16] Dan Slater, "Democratic Careening," *World Politics* 65 (2013): 729, 730, 733 (describing Thailand as a "paradigmatic case of democratic careening" between populism and oligarchy, rather than true "democratic breakdown").

[17] Steven Erlanger, "Coup in Thailand Follows Old Pattern," *New York Times*, February 24, 1991, http://www.nytimes.com/1991/02/24/world/coup-in-thailand-follows-old-pattern.html.

[18] Zachary Elkins, Tom Ginsburg, and James Melton, *The Endurance of National Constitutions* (New York: Cambridge University Press, 2009), 190–191.

3. The Regime Performance Hypothesis

Countless factors might be said to contribute to or undermine regime longevity. But it is questionable whether any of them matter as much as popular support. A regime that is deeply unpopular faces an uphill battle in the long run. In the short-to-medium term, regimes can hang onto power through oppression. In the long term, though, total oppression is hard to sustain. To paraphrase P.T. Barnum, you can oppress some of the people all of the time, or all of the people some of the time, but you cannot oppress all of the people all of the time.[19] Whether people will support the regime or yearn to overthrow it, in turn, will probably depend on the government's ability to deliver basic things that people most want and need from government. On this view, constitutional democracy is no different from any other form of government: it will last if and to the extent that it manages to perform successfully along whatever practical dimensions happen to drive popular support.

What we must avoid from the outset, however, is the mistake of equating democracy with popular support and thus greater longevity. Historically speaking, democracies have not enjoyed much of an advantage when it comes to longevity: on average, they have barely outlasted autocracies over the last two centuries (twenty-three years versus twenty-one years).[20] Logically speaking, it is wrong to think either that only democratic regimes can enjoy popular support, or that an unelected government must by definition lack popular support. Elections are not a necessary condition for popular support; indeed, they may not even be a sufficient condition. An election is simply a crude rank ordering of the options available to a particular electorate at a particular point in time—nothing more. (And the result, as Americans have discovered in two of their last five presidential elections, may not even reflect the majority's rank ordering.)

On the one hand, it is obvious from looking at Asia that a regime can fail to hold genuine elections yet still enjoy popular support. A government need not submit to elections to figure out what people care most about and provide it, then actually deliver it. Elections are a noisy, crude measure of public sentiment. They are, by design, mechanisms for choosing between candidates for office rather than eliciting information. Candidates bundle together a variety of positions on a variety of issues, and a simple thumbs-up or thumbs-down vote does little to signal agreement or disagreement with particular aspects of this policy bundle. There are other, possibly better ways of ascertaining the wishes of

---

[19] Cf. Bruce Bueno de Mesquita et al., *The Logic of Political Survival* (Cambridge, MA: MIT Press, 2003), 7–8 (arguing that leaders, both democratic and otherwise, must retain the support of a minimum "winning coalition" to remain in power, which is not necessarily the same as a majority).

[20] Carl Henrik Knutsen and Håvard Mokleiv Nygård, "Institutional Characteristics and Regime Survival: Why Are Semi-democracies Less Durable than Autocracies and Democracies?," *American Journal of Political Science* 59 (2015): 656, 659. The record shifts in favor of democracies if the analysis is limited to the twentieth century, especially from 1950 onward. See ibid.

the people. Opinion polling is a more targeted and precise form of information-gathering than an election. Indeed, simply talking to a cross section of citizens on a regular basis would probably be more informative than the results of an election, which are invariably open to endless and inconclusive interpretation and debate.

It should thus come as no surprise that some governments can and do keep most people reasonably happy without holding elections. Witness, for example, the odd spectacle of Bhutan, where a hereditary absolute monarch tried with mixed results to persuade his (very loyal) subjects of the need for an elected government that would operate within the limits of a formal constitution. The people of Bhutan were happy with the reign of the fourth king, Jigme Singye Wangchuck, and his three predecessors. They were so satisfied, in fact, that had the king himself not insisted on a transition to a "democratic constitutional monarchy," Bhutan would probably still be a traditional monarchy.[21] Likewise, notwithstanding the often brutal steps that the Chinese Communist Party (CCP) has taken to consolidate its grip on power and squelch dissent, it is far from clear that the Chinese people, given the choice, would in fact eject the CCP from power.[22]

On the other hand, the winner of an election may simply be the least despised of the options on offer (in the eyes of those whose votes are decisive according to the rules governing the specific electoral system in question). Elected governments routinely fail to deliver the things that people want and need. A country in which elections work well, but little else, is not necessarily a country in which people affirmatively support the government. It is merely a country in which people are free to choose, from among the available options, the option that they detest the least. In the face of widespread voter indifference (plausible) or dislike of the options on offer ("a pox on both your houses"—even more plausible), an election may reveal little more than which of two choices was less disliked by those who could be bothered to vote (subject, again, to potentially arcane and archaic electoral rules that may enable the loser of the vote to win the election).

So what is the difference between a popular and an unpopular regime? The difference probably lies in its ability to address the problems that most people care most about. In other words, the success of a regime is going to turn on its ability to deliver on the basics or fundamentals—what we might call first-order needs. A regime that fails to take care of first-order needs is going to be fragile and vulnerable. An analogy might be drawn

---

[21] See David S. Law, "Alternatives to Liberal Constitutional Democracy," *Maryland Law Review* 77 (2017): 223, 232–233.

[22] See, e.g., Teresa Wright, *Accepting Authoritarianism: State-Society Relations in China's Reform Era* (Stanford, CA: Stanford University Press, 2010), 19 (observing that "popular support for the CCP-led political regime is strong, and public interest in liberal democratic change appears weak"); Bruce J. Dickson, "No 'Jasmine' for China," in *The China Reader: Rising Power*, ed. David Shambaugh, 6th ed. (New York: Oxford University Press, 2016), 93, 97 ("The CCP is promoting the interests of Chinese in the middle class in order to maintain their support for, or at least acceptance of, the status quo. So far, the strategy is working.").

between the idea of first-order needs and Maslow's hierarchy of needs,[23] which posits that people do not pursue higher-level needs (such as esteem and self-actualization) until more basic needs (such as physical sustenance and safety) are first met. First-order needs are akin to Maslow's basic needs writ large. If Maslow is correct as a descriptive matter that there exists a hierarchy of needs at the individual level, it stands to reason that societies have a hierarchy of basic needs as well, and that a regime that fulfills the highest-priority (or first-order) needs is a regime that people will accept and support over a regime that might do a better job of satisfying second-order needs but bungles the basics.

What are these basics that most people care most about? The regime performance hypothesis holds that regime longevity depends on the satisfaction of a few basic criteria. Oppression, tribalism, lack of physical security, and lack of economic security are central and recurring problems for governments everywhere. To address these problems is to satisfy the first-order needs of the population and to stand an excellent chance of survival. Conversely, a regime that cannot lay serious claim to addressing any of them is unlikely to command much popular support and will have to struggle against its own people in order to survive.

If the regime performance hypothesis is correct, the implications for constitutional democracy in Asia are mixed. On the one hand, various constitutional democracies in the region have proven themselves capable of performing well along all plausibly relevant dimensions. On the other hand, the region is also home to a number of authoritarian regimes that boast considerable economic success and have been able to claim "performance legitimacy" as a result.[24] It is not self-evident that constitutional democracy enjoys an inherent advantage over other forms of government when it comes to the satisfaction of first-order needs.[25]

If, for example, people were to view constitutional democracy as a first-order need in and of itself, then its advantage would be obvious. But there is little sign that they do. The regime-type preferences of the average citizen are probably not as firm or as principled as constitutional scholars might like to think. Reflexive allegiance to constitutional democracy has been weakening across a number of Western democracies (including the United States),[26] is clearly not the case in Latin America,[27] and certainly cannot be assumed in

---

[23] See A. H. Maslow, "A Theory of Human Motivation," *Psychological Review* 50 (1943): 371, 372–385.

[24] Michael C. Davis, "Strengthening Constitutionalism in Asia," *Journal of Democracy* 28 (2017): 147, 149.

[25] Arguments about the inherent synergy between constitutional democracy and economic development can, of course, be made and may well be correct. See, e.g., Michael C. Davis, "East Asia after the Crisis: Human Rights, Constitutionalism, and State Reform," *Human Rights Quarterly* 26 (2004): 126, 138–140. Our point is simply that the correctness of such arguments clearly cannot be taken for granted.

[26] Roberto Stefan Foa and Yascha Mounk, "The Signs of Deconsolidation," *Journal of Democracy* 28 (2017): 5, 5–6. In 2011, a record 24 percent of young Americans described democracy as a "bad" or "very bad" way of running the country. The proportion of Americans expressing support for "army rule" has risen over the last two decades from one in sixteen to one in six. See ibid.

[27] See, e.g., Rodolfo Sarsfield and Fabián Echegaray, "Opening the Black Box: How Satisfaction with Democracy and Its Perceived Efficacy Affect Regime Preference in Latin America," *International Journal of Public Opinion Research* 18 (2005): 153, 156 fig. 1 (reporting, inter alia, that only 36 percent of Latin American respondents

Asia, where single-party regimes[28] and even full-blown monarchies have proven capable of commanding healthy levels of public support.[29] This is not to say that political ideals such as constitutionalism and democracy are never valued or desired for their own sake. But for most people—not legal or political elites, but ordinary folks—they are probably not at the top of the list.[30] They are not nonnegotiable needs that must be satisfied first and foremost if a regime is to survive. At the end of the day, no matter what its democratic bona fides, if Weimar Germany cannot put food on the table, Weimar Germany is going to be in trouble. Conversely, regular folks are often willing to overlook any number of constitutional and legal niceties in exchange for a government that does a better job of keeping them safe. Most Filipinos appear perfectly happy to trade away the rights of criminal suspects in exchange for a reduction in drug crime.

It is hard to think of anything about authoritarian or autocratic regimes that renders them inherently incapable of satisfying the masses. Consider, for example, the supposedly greater propensity of authoritarian regimes for corruption. Studies have found, on the whole, a negative relationship between democracy and corruption (but with a variety of important caveats[31]). In theory, we might expect kleptocracy and corruption to undermine regime longevity by sapping the nation's wealth and productivity and thus hurting the regime's ability to address first-order needs. In reality, however, corruption appears to have no such effect on the longevity of authoritarian regimes.[32] Moreover, at least in

---

described themselves as "very" or "fairly" satisfied with democracy, while only 55 percent expressed a preference for democracy over authoritarianism).

[28] Singapore and China are examples of single-party regimes that enjoy meaningful public support, as discussed below, 437–440.

[29] In Bhutan, the transition from monarchy to "Democratic Constitutional Monarchy," Bhutan Const. art. 1(2), was forced by the king himself upon a highly skeptical, if not resistant, population. See Lyonpo Sonam Tobgye, *The Constitution of Bhutan: Principles and Philosophies* (Thimphu, Bhutan: Bhutan National Legal Institute, 2008), 19–20; "Bhutan's Mock Election: Voting for the Thunder Dragon," *Economist*, April 26, 2007, at 50.

[30] Herbert McClosky, "Consensus and Ideology in American Politics," *American Political Science Review* 58 (1964): 361, 364–365 ("[Elites] exhibit stronger support for democratic values than does the electorate[.] The average citizen has greater difficulty appreciating the importance of certain procedural or juridical rights, especially when he believes the country's internal security is at stake.").

[31] See, e.g., Ivar Kolstad and Arne Wiig, "Does Democracy Reduce Corruption?" *Democratization* 23 (2016): 1198, 1211 (finding that democracy reduces corruption significantly, and that the magnitude of the effect increases when endogeneity is taken into account); Michael Jetter, Andres Ramírez, and Alejandra Montoya Delojado, "The Effect of Democracy on Corruption," *World Development* 74 (2015): 286, 286 (finding that democracy reduces corruption only in countries that have already crossed a GDP per capita level of approximately US$2,000, and that democratization may actually increase corruption in poorer countries); Michael T. Rock, "Corruption and Democracy," *Journal of Development Studies* 45 (2008): 55, 55–57 (finding an inverted-U relationship between the age of a democracy and the level of corruption, meaning that corruption initially increases in new democracies before reaching a turning point after ten to twelve years).

[32] See Hanne Fjelde and Håvard Hegre, "Political Corruption and Institutional Stability," *Studies in Comparative International Development* 49 (2014): 267, 279–280 (reporting that low-corruption democracies outlast high-corruption democracies, but high-corruption authoritarian regimes outlast low-corruption authoritarian regimes).

Asia, the supposed relationship between democracy and corruption seems rather weak. Singapore is authoritarian but also the cleanest country in the entire region;[33] its neighbor, Malaysia, is more democratic but also more kleptocratic.[34] China, a highly populous dictatorship, performs slightly better than India, a highly populous democracy, when it comes to corruption.[35]

Autocratic or authoritarian regimes may not satisfy second-order needs for a sense of autonomy or self-governance or a feeling of civic engagement, but these needs will take a back seat to the satisfaction of economic and physical needs. What matters first and foremost is getting the basics right. It is perfectly plausible that people might support an authoritarian regime that skims a bit off the top but nevertheless delivers the goods, for example, over a democratic and squeaky clean regime that fails to address basic needs. Things such as democracy and clean government are nice, but for many if not most, they may be valued mainly as a means to an end; they do not, in and of themselves, keep the lights on or put food on the table.

What we see in Asia is broadly consistent with the regime performance hypothesis: the regimes that have turned in strong economic performances have also tended to stick around. It is also clear, however, that constitutional democracy is not the only type of regime capable of performing well. The Asian countries that are currently delivering peace and prosperity are a motley mix of constitutional democracies, authoritarian states, and hybrid regimes. If the regime performance hypothesis is indeed correct, there are at least two regime types that we should expect to persist. One is constitutional democracy; the other is what we might call bureaucratic authoritarianism.[36]

CONSTITUTIONAL DEMOCRACY

In the 1970s, four countries were dubbed the Four Asian Tigers on account of their outsized economic performance: South Korea, Taiwan, Singapore, and Hong Kong.[37] All four remain prosperous and stable; none of the four appears likely to switch regime types in the foreseeable future. South Korea and Taiwan are unambiguously liberal

---

[33] "Corruption Perceptions Index 2017," *Transparency International*, February 21, 2018, https://www.transparency.org/_view/feature/8162 (ranking Singapore sixth in the world and Malaysia sixty-second).

[34] The Economist Intelligence Unit's 2016 Democracy Index gives Malaysia a score of 7.54 (out of 10) and Singapore a score of 6.38.

[35] "Corruption Perceptions Index 2017" (ranking China seventy-seventh and India eighty-first in the world for corruption).

[36] Guillermo O'Donnell is known for his elaboration of a concept of "bureaucratic authoritarianism" to describe certain Latin American regimes. Guillermo A. O'Donnell, *Bureaucratic Authoritarianism: Argentina, 1966–1973, in Comparative Perspective* (Berkeley: University of California Press, 1988). We use the term in a simpler, literal sense to describe authoritarian regimes that operate like bureaucracies.

[37] Gary Gereffi, "Rethinking Development Theory: Insights from East Asia and Latin America," *Sociological Forum* 4 (1989): 505, 505–506.

constitutional democracies; Hong Kong and Singapore are not. Are South Korea and Taiwan up to the challenge of meeting the basic needs of the citizenry? Clearly they are. Are they alone in doing so? Clearly they are not. Even highly skilled workers from advanced constitutional democracies seem satisfied with what Hong Kong and Singapore have to offer. Both are home to substantial numbers of workers from countries such as Australia, Canada, France, and the United Kingdom. These global elites make deliberate choices about where to live. They vote with their feet and with their capital, not at the ballot box. And whatever their nonnegotiable requirements may be, living in a constitutional democracy, in and of itself, is obviously not one of them.[38]

The fact that more than one form of government is capable of performing competitively should come as no surprise (unless one believes that constitutional democracy performs better along all relevant dimensions, under all conditions, over all other forms of government). At the risk of stating what should be obvious, every form of government has both advantages and disadvantages. And in some cases, constitutional democracy's advantages may matter less, while its disadvantages may matter more. Like any form of social or political organization, constitutional democracy is better suited to meeting certain challenges than others.

Among its strengths, constitutional democracy purports at least to directly address the problem of oppression. If the people (or at least a majority of them) get to choose their own leaders and participate directly in government, they cannot easily argue that they are being oppressed. But even democracy does not solve the problem of oppression entirely. Instead, it raises the specter of minority oppression. Mere democracy, in the form of unchecked majority rule, leaves the door open to oppression of minorities. This is a known and recognized weakness of constitutional democracy: it does not have a reputation for coping well with the challenges posed by divided societies.[39] Constitutional democracy is also not known for having a programmatic response to the problem of economic insecurity, other than placing faith in the ability of markets to generate so much wealth that basic needs are mostly met. Some scholars even contend that, as an empirical matter, authoritarian rule is more conducive to economic development than democracy.[40]

The rote solution of liberal democracy to the problem of minority oppression is constitutionalism: divide sovereignty among multiple actors so as to minimize the likelihood of dangerous concentration, and guarantee constitutional rights that place certain decisions beyond the reach of popular majorities. The same solution is supposed to work for the problem of tribalism as well: constitutionalism imposes limits on what any one tribe

---

[38] *See* Foa and Mounk, "Deconsolidation," 6 (reporting that only a minority of younger citizens in Great Britain, the Netherlands, Sweden, Australia, and New Zealand consider it "essential" to live in a democracy).

[39] See, e.g., Robert A. Dahl, *Dilemmas of Pluralist Democracy: Autonomy vs. Control* (New Haven, CT: Yale University Press, 1982), 56–57; Arend Lijphart, *Democracy in Plural Societies: A Comparative Exploration* (1977) (New Haven, CT: Yale University Press, 1977): Arend Lijphart, *Patterns of Democracy: Government Forms and Performance in Thirty-Six Countries* (New Haven, CT: Yale University Press, 2012), 31–32.

[40] For a survey of this debate, see Weitseng Chen, "Constitutionalism, Authoritarianism, and Economic Development," in *The Oxford Handbook of Constitutional Law in Asia*, ed. David S. Law et al. (forthcoming 2019).

can do to the others via the mechanism of the state, which in the liberal view is the only agglomeration of power that needs to be restrained.[41]

Neither South Korea nor Taiwan poses much of a test of constitutional democracy's inherent weaknesses. Indeed, if ever there was a best-case scenario for the success of constitutional democracy, it might arguably have been South Korea or Taiwan in the late 1980s: both were increasingly prosperous societies lacking the kinds of deep cleavages along ethnic, religious, and linguistic lines that doom many states. First, by the time that they democratized, economic insecurity was no longer much of a problem for either South Korea and Taiwan. One might argue that the credit for this prosperity belongs to the decades of authoritarian rule that preceded democratic rule. Neither country was democratic during the 1970s, when their economies boomed; both had already transformed for the better by the time that they democratized. Neither case tells us much about the ability of constitutional democracy to generate prosperity because, in both cases, constitutional democracy was born with a silver spoon in its mouth.

Second, neither South Korea nor Taiwan has much history of minority oppression or sectarian conflict. South Korea's political cleavages are more regional in character, while Taiwan inverts the story of majority-minority oppression: for years, the local majority (the Taiwanese, meaning speakers of the Taiwanese dialect) complained of oppression by a minority (expatriate mainland Mandarin-speaking Chinese who arrived with the Kuomintang Government following its defeat by the Communists). Thus, in both countries, constitutional democracy has succeeded and taken root, but that success must be viewed in context. What form of government is not capable of performing well when dealt a very good hand of cards from the outset?

BUREAUCRATIC AUTHORITARIANISM

A more demanding test of constitutional democracy, by contrast, would be Singapore. Its immutable characteristics play to the weaknesses of constitutional democracy. It was a majority-Chinese state in a majority-Malay country, which led to its ejection from Malaysia. It has a history of race riots, of which the government remains highly mindful. It has to contend with sizeable, well-established minorities. Moreover, its minorities are simultaneously ethnic and religious and thus not very susceptible to assimilation.[42]

---

[41] See Frank I. Michelman, "Constitutions and the Public/Private Divide," in *The Oxford Handbook of Comparative Constitutional Law*, ed. Michel Rosenfeld and András Sajó (New York: Oxford University Press, 2012), 298, 305–306 (observing that the "proto-liberal" ideas behind the rise of constitutionalism in eighteenth-century Europe included the notion that there must exist "constitutional" laws expressly designed for the purpose of controlling the state's unique powers).

[42] Seventy-five percent of the population is Chinese and Buddhist-leaning; 13 percent is Malay and Muslim; 9 percent is Indian and Hindu. Singapore Department of Statistics, *Population Trends 2017* (2017), 5, http://www.singstat.gov.sg/docs/default-source/default-document-library/publications/publications_and_papers/population_and_population_structure/population2017.pdf.

Might constitutional democracy nevertheless work in Singapore? Probably. Is constitutional democracy obviously the only workable system of government that Singapore could possibly adopt? Should we be shocked if some other approach proves capable of working reasonably well in Singapore? Perhaps not.

Singapore practices what might best be described as bureaucratic authoritarianism. It has the formal trappings of a constitutional democracy: a formal constitution, elections, courts that pride themselves on their independence. But it does not fit the mold of constitutional democracy. It has always been ruled by the same party, which takes a stingy approach to civil and political freedoms.[43] Censorship is routine; criticism of the government is fraught with peril.[44] The power of judicial review exists, but is not exercised in practice. Although the government respects constitutional limits and the rule of law in a formal sense, it is a thin version of constitutionalism and the rule of law that does little more than impose procedural requirements on the government. Provided that the government takes the time to dot its "i"s and cross its "t"s, there is little constraint on what it can do to political opponents and dissenters.

Elections are held, but pursuant to rules that ensure the ruling party is never actually at risk of losing power.[45] In place of competitive elections, Singapore offers paternalism writ large. The people are placed under the tutelage and micromanagement of technocrats groomed and promoted within a single-party regime that places a heavy premium on competence and rule-following. This is authoritarianism, but it is a type of authoritarianism that prides itself on technocratic competency and observance of formalities; it is authoritarianism with a bureaucratic and legalistic face.

The challenge for constitutional democracy lies in the fact that Singapore feels like a roaring success along a number of dimensions that most people deem very important. There are the sparkling shopping malls, the lush crime-free parks, the luxurious public "swimming pools" that resemble amusement parks.[46] The typical cab driver is genuinely happy with life

---

[43] Mark Tushnet, "Authoritarian Constitutionalism," *Cornell Law Review* 100 (2015): 391, 448–454; Gordon Silverstein, "Singapore: The Exception That Proves Rules Matter," in *Rule by Law: The Politics of Courts in Authoritarian Regimes*, ed. Tom Ginsburg and Tamir Moustafa (New York: Cambridge University Press, 2008), 73, 92–97.

[44] Silverstein, "Singapore: The Exception," 86–92; Adrienne Stone, Rishad Chowdhury, and Martin Clark, "The Comparative Constitutional Law of Freedom of Expression in Asia," in *Comparative Constitutional Law in Asia*, ed. Rosalind Dixon and Tom Ginsburg (Cheltenham: Edward Elgar, 2013), 227, 238 (observing that "no [ruling party] politician has ever lost a defamation suit" in Singapore, and that the damages awards in such suits are "crippling").

[45] See Tushnet, "Authoritarian Constitutionalism," 410–413.

[46] See Sport Singapore, "The Top 5 Public Swimming Pool for Families," *ActiveSG*, September 26, 2016, https://www.myactivesg.com/read/2016/9/top-5-public-swimming-pool-for-families (describing, inter alia, the "undeniably impressive and extensive range of water park facilities" available at the public Jurong East Swimming Complex, including "intertwining spiral water slides, stretching from 22 to 155 metres and 5.5 to 17.7 metres" and an "energetic wave pool").

in Singapore and with the government, and it is hard to say that this satisfaction is merely the product of false consciousness.[47] Certain freedoms are curtailed, but the large part of the population is satisfied with the trade-off or simply does not care that much about the freedoms in question. For the average Singaporean, crushing defamation suits against government critics are a small price to pay for lavish swimming pools and efficient, corruption-free public services.

Likewise, Hong Kong is difficult to square with the notion that only a constitutional democracy can satisfy first-order needs. Like Singapore, it is a constitutional regime, in the sense that government behavior complies with legal limits. But it is even less democratic than Singapore. There is not even a pretext that the executive or legislature is elected on the basis of a universal franchise: half of the legislature is reserved for "functional constituencies" stacked in favor of Beijing,[48] and widespread agitation for an elected chief executive has made no headway whatsoever.[49] But it is just as prosperous as Singapore,[50] and significantly more liberal in terms of the freedoms that people enjoy. Hong Kong is that rarest of rare birds: a liberal non-democracy.

The question one must confront in Hong Kong when it comes to the lack of democracy is: So what? How does Hong Kong's lack of democracy actually affect life for the worse? It depends on who you are and whether you matter. If Beijing fears that you might wield actual influence, then you are at risk. The space within which pro-democracy activists and opposition figures can operate keeps contracting.[51] For most people, however, there is little sense of oppression in the air, at least for now.[52] On the contrary, Hong Kong is

---

[47] See "Singapore Tops Asia in Safety, Quality of Living Survey," *Channel News Asia*, February 23, 2016, http://www.channelnewsasia.com/news/singapore/singapore-tops-asia-in-safety-quality-of-living-survey-8176190.

[48] See Po Jen Yap, *Constitutional Dialogue in Common Law Asia* (Oxford: Oxford University Press, 2015), 34–37; "How Hong Kong's Version of Democracy Works," *Economist* August 25, 2016, https://www.economist.com/blogs/economist-explains/2016/09/economist-explains-1.

[49] See Michael C. Davis, "The Basic Law, Universal Suffrage and the Rule of Law in Hong Kong," *Hastings International and Comparative Law Review* 38 (2015) 275, 294–296 (discussing the promise of universal suffrage in Hong Kong under the Basic Law and the subsequent moves by Beijing that have placed universal suffrage increasingly beyond reach).

[50] See Courtney Subramanian, "Hong Kong Edges Out Singapore in Millionaire Wealth," *Time*, June 24, 2013, http://newsfeed.time.com/2013/06/24/hong-kong-edges-out-singapore-in-millionaire-wealth.

[51] Opposition figures may be ousted from office, for example, or simply prevented from running for office in the first place. See Elson Tong, "4 More Elected Pro-democracy Lawmakers to Be Ousted following Hong Kong Court Ruling," *Hong Kong Free Press*, July 14, 2017, https://www.hongkongfp.com/2017/07/14/breaking-4-elected-pro-democracy-lawmakers-ousted-following-hong-kong-court-ruling (describing the judicial disqualification of opposition lawmakers for such reasons as reading the oath of office too slowly, or speaking the words "People's Republic of China" in the oath with a "rising intonation"); Kong Tsung-gan, "Disqualified: How the Gov't Compromised Hong Kong's Only Free and Fair Election," *Hong Kong Free Press*, January 31, 2018, https://www.hongkongfp.com/2018/01/31/disqualified-hong-kong-govt-compromised-citys-free-fair-elections.

[52] There is some question as to whether routine and inconsequential expressions of dissent will continue to be ignored. See Joanna Chiu, "China Mulls 3-Years' Jail for Anthem Disrespect in Hong Kong," *Yahoo! News*, October 31, 2017, https://sg.news.yahoo.com/china-disrespecting-national-anthem-could-mean-three-years-072127246.

not merely liberal, but laissez-faire.[53] Unlike in Singapore or mainland China, there are no great firewalls, and there is no censorship of the media. To turn on one's television or to walk into a shopping mall is to be spoiled for choice: hundreds of channels, thousands of shops. Physical security is not an issue either: crime rates are among the lowest in the world.[54] What, if anything, is talismanic about the combination of constitutionalism with democracy? Even if the laws lack democratic legitimacy, why is that troublesome for the average inhabitant as long as the reach of those laws remains within constitutional limits? Might it be that constitutionalism by itself, without democracy, can successfully deliver what most people care most about?

The more we look around Asia, the more examples we find of regimes that deliver material success and citizen satisfaction without practicing constitutional democracy. China, as mentioned previously, is one example. The Chinese Communist Party (CCP) has, as a practical matter, staked its legitimacy on delivering a rising standard of living, and it is not crazy for many if not most Chinese citizens to support the regime for this reason.[55] Plenty of Americans vote on the basis of pocketbook issues, and no one blames them for doing so.

Even the region's best known, longest-standing constitutional democracy turns out, upon closer inspection, to be more bureaucratic than democratic and to lack much of a rights culture. Japan is not an authoritarian state, but in a number of important respects, it resembles Singapore more than South Korea or Taiwan. Like Singapore, Japan is prosperous and stable and exhibits the formal trappings of a constitutional democracy—such as elections and judicial review—but it is not, in fact, a competitive multiparty democracy.[56] The Liberal Democratic Party has ruled Japan almost without interruption for the last seventy-plus years and is so entrenched that it has evolved mechanisms for controlling the bureaucracy that resemble those of the CCP.[57] And in Japan as in Singapore, the

---

html (noting that spectators at athletic events in Hong Kong have repeatedly booed the Chinese national anthem, and that the National People's Congress has responded by moving to make expressly applicable in Hong Kong a Chinese law that would entail sentences of up to three years imprisonment for behavior deemed "disrespectful" toward the anthem).

[53] The libertarian Cato Institute has for many years scored Hong Kong higher than the United States (or anywhere else) in terms of the freedom of its economy. See James A. Dorn, "Hong Kong: World's Freest Economy," *Cato Institute*, July 28, 2004, https://www.cato.org/publications/commentary/hong-kong-worlds-freest-economy.

[54] "Crime in Hong Kong," *Wikipedia*, accessed February 26, 2018, https://en.wikipedia.org/wiki/Crime_in_Hong_Kong.

[55] See text accompanying note 22.

[56] See Ethan Scheiner, *Democracy without Competition in Japan: Opposition Failure in a One-Party Dominant State* (New York: Cambridge University Press, 2006), 22–28.

[57] Mamoru Seki, "The Drafting Process for Cabinet Bills," *Law in Japan* 19 (1986): 168, 171, 185 (discussing the organization of the LDP's Policy Board or "seimu chosakai").

judiciary is notoriously averse to enforcing constitutional rights.[58] Recall what was said of Singapore: "The power of judicial review exists, but is not exercised in practice. . . . Elections are held, but pursuant to rules that ensure the ruling party is never actually at risk of losing power."[59] Between the world-leading passivity of the Japanese Supreme Court and an unconstitutional electoral malapportionment scheme that has never been fixed,[60] the same could be said of Japan.

If Asia is any indication—and what better indication could there be?—constitutional democracy performs well enough to be safe from extinction. The same could be said, however, of other regime types. Based on their performance, we would expect to see stable constitutional democracies coexisting with stable bureaucratic-authoritarian states. This is, in fact, precisely what we see in the region.

Constitutional democracy is here to stay. But so too are its competitors. Somewhere between triumphalist predictions of the end of history[61] and pessimistic projections of anti-democratic contagion lie the dull realities of constitutional inertia and regime pluralism. Stability begets stability; instability begets instability. Ideologies clash but cannot escape coexistence.

---

[58] See David S. Law, "The Anatomy of a Conservative Court: Judicial Review in Japan," *Texas Law Review* 87 (2009): 1545, 1546–1548.

[59] See text accompanying notes 44–45.

[60] See Law, "The Anatomy of a Conservative Court: Judicial Review in Japan," 1547–1548, 1586–1588.

[61] Francis Fukuyama, *The End of History and the Last Man* (New York: Free Press, 1992), xi–xii.

III Factors

25 Populism versus Democratic Governance
Samuel Issacharoff

THE CURRENT POPULIST wave presents an existential challenge to democracy. Populism claims to be the true expositor of the will of the people, enabled where it can through the electoral conquest of government office. An engaged electoral majority claiming its due appears as both the realization of democratic aspirations and its demise. It is a short step from the will of the people to the tyranny of the majority.

Undoubtedly, the rise of elected governments is the historic legacy of the period after the fall of the Soviet Union. Using a relatively austere metric of whether the head of state and legislature are elected, Freedom House captures the dramatic transformations at the end of the twentieth century. In 1987, there were only 66 countries that were considered electoral democracies. By 2003, there were 121 electoral democracies, a number that has remained more or less stable, with the most recent figure being 123 countries that can claim a head of state and legislature elected through substantially free and fair elections.[1]

The first cut inquiry is consistent with a parsimonious account of democracy as being governance by an elected head of government, chosen by at least a plurality of the population under stable rules of selection and broad eligibility for the franchise. Such a definition would embrace both parliamentary and presidential systems, it would allow for

---

[1] *Freedom in the World 2017* (Washington, DC: Freedom House, 2017), https://freedomhouse.org/sites/default/files/FH_FIW_2017_Report_Final.pdf.

plebiscitary powers as in Switzerland, it would tolerate requirements for plurality versus majority vote for officeholding, and it would accept a host of limitations of the franchise based on citizenship, age, incarceration, and so forth. Such a definition would even allow for a nominal head of state that is not elected, as with the Queen's authority in Australia.

For the most part, such a standard account of democracy is not necessarily incompatible with populism. There is an authoritarian streak to both left- and right-wing populist movements, which, with alarming frequency, threatens some of the preconditions of democratic governance. Populists tend not to tolerate opposition parties; they tend to use police and prosecutorial power against adversaries; they tend toward suppression of dissident speech, either through curtailment of access to the media or through legal retaliation; they tend to push the boundaries of executive unilateral authority.[2] Certainly, questions of intensity and degree may take the Venezuela of Nicolás Maduro or the Hungary of Viktor Orbán outside the boundaries of democracy. But elements of aggressive use of incumbent power are seen in many regimes that still function as democracies, even if beleaguered ones at times.

Thus, unfortunately, the formal processes of governmental selection tell only part of the story. While the number of electoral democracies has nominally remained high, the number of countries that afford relatively free political rights to opposition groups, rival political parties, minorities, and others seeking to dislodge the incumbent regime is much smaller. Only eighty-seven countries are deemed "Free" by Freedom House in affording the political rights associated with democracy and ensuring acceptable levels of transparency and noncorruption in government.

The Freedom House data present a simplified picture of elections as a matter of form in terms of elected heads of state and as a matter of substance in terms of the institutional attributes of democratic governance. The focus on political freedoms and transparency of government hearkens to the basic Schumpeterian notion of democracy as fundamentally a system of retrospective accountability by which an informed populace can remove from office those who have lost the confidence of the voters.[3] The measure of political freedom is an important point of demarcation for liberal democracy from illiberal regimes in which opposition electoral prospects are compromised, if not totally illusory.

But the populist challenge to democracy is not simply a matter of illiberalism. Certainly there are xenophobic streaks to current populism, together with overt antagonisms on racial and religious grounds. And there is a manifest lack of commitment to civil liberties, starting with freedom of the press and continuing on to freedom of expression and worship. The interplay of these factors is the subject of extensive definitional inquiry, as well addressed by Jan-Werner Müller and taken up in many current debates. But populism also responds to the perceived failure of democratic regimes to protect the laboring classes

---

[2] Jan-Werner Müller, *What Is Populism?* (Philadelphia: University of Pennsylvania Press, 2016), 41–49.

[3] Joseph A. Schumpeter, *Capitalism, Socialism, and Democracy*, 3rd ed. (1950; repr., New York: HarperCollins, 2008), 269–273.

from economic dislocation. The combination of the economic downturn after 2008 and the impact of globalized trade on wages in the advanced industrial countries tarnished the legitimacy of democratic regimes as an insider's game, a means of institutionalizing elite prerogatives.

Rather than attempt another comprehensive account of populism, I want to shift the focus to the engagement between populism and democratic governance as an institutional account of how democracies function. Post-2008 anti-elitism as a social commitment translated to a robust anti-institutionalism in terms of state authority. The aim is not so much to provide definitions of either populism or democracy as to call attention to the features of democratic rule that have commanded attention for the era of democratic ascendancy over the past two centuries and that now seem subject to deep challenge. Without claiming apocalyptically that this era of democratic ascendancy has come to a close, it is nonetheless worth examining how it operated to see the sources of contemporary disrepair. Here the suggestion is that there may be more inherent conflict with populism, turning not so much on the ultimate issue of an elected head of government but on the limits on the exercise of power.

* * *

With the rise of new democracies, much attention was given to the elements necessary for these new regimes to stabilize in oftentimes foreboding national settings. The necessary institutional arrangements, including the increasingly robust presence of constitutional courts restraining the political branches, was the focus of my monograph, *Fragile Democracies.*[4] What the current populist surge invites is applying the same tools of analysis in reverse. Rather than asking how the preconditions for democratic governance can be established, the question becomes the stability of established democracies in the face of populist challenges to these same institutional buttresses of democratic governance.

While the potential list is extensive, a few points are worth considering as key:

THE TEMPORAL DIMENSION OF DEMOCRACY. At the heart of any conception of democracy is the simple ability "to throw the bums out." Whether termed "rotation in office," as advanced by Adam Przeworski and his collaborators,[5] or as a renewal of consent, as framed by Bernard Manin,[6] there is a requirement of repeat play necessary for democratic governance. Indeed the central challenge in any new democracy is the ability to convince the losers of today that they might indeed be the winners of tomorrow, made critical by the fact that in any new democracy there will by definition have been no

---

[4] Samuel Issacharoff, *Fragile Democracies: Contested Power in the Era of Constitutional Courts* (New York: Cambridge University Press, 2015).

[5] Adam Przeworski et al., *Democracy and Development: Political Institutions and Well-Being in the World, 1950–1990* (Cambridge: Cambridge University Press, 2000), 18–27.

[6] Bernard Manin, *The Principles of Representative Government* (Cambridge: Cambridge University Press, 1997), 29.

evidence of a successful electoral surrender of power to future challengers. It is well worth recalling the lack of historical precedents for the American election of 1800, the first time an incumbent head of state was removed electorally by a challenger.

Stable democracies require an internalization of politics as repeat play. Populist elections claim a mandate from the people beyond choosing officeholders. The mandate does not hearken back to the successes in office of past partisan affiliates but to an indictment of a system that is claimed to be rigged or captured by enemies of the people. Elections over mandates risk the same repudiation of institutional accommodation of divisions as do plebiscites. It is not that populism is plebiscitary as such; rather, neither is well suited to institutionalized politics that presume deliberation, procedural order, and accommodation. For both plebiscites and populism, the election defines the agenda. Period.

In each case, there is an up/down choice as to policy outcomes, without intermediation of legislative trade-offs, measures of the intensity of preferences, negotiated accommodation, and all the mechanisms that elicit cooperation from those in dissent and moderation from those in power. Recognition of the temporal dimension of democratic governance draws back at least as far as Tocqueville's famous account of pre-Civil War America. Among his many observations, Tocqueville focused on the prospect of deep mistakes in elections that could promote men of unknown capacities or unproven temperament. The famous warning about the "tyranny of the majority" was penned in observations about America under President Andrew Jackson, a wealthy and rapacious real estate speculator, elected on the crest of popular hatred of the "elites" represented by John Quincy Adams and the established politics after the Revolution.[7] For Tocqueville, a central question in the survival of the republican experiment was the chance to make what he termed "retrievable mistakes," the capacity to allow time to correct missteps.[8]

The concept of intertemporal trade-offs is key to the design of many democratic institutions. One theory for the acceptance of judicial review is precisely the desire—in the face of uncertainty about future electoral prospects—of all parties to hedge their bets. In new democracies with strong constitutional courts this is the process that I have termed "democratic hedging"[9] and that Tom Ginsburg addresses as an "insurance" theory of limits on the exercise of political power.[10] Many of the institutional features of healthy democracies incorporate structures that serve as a check on the majority, ranging from the Shadow Cabinet in Britain to the use of the American filibuster to force supermajority legislation on issues of deep contestation.

---

[7] Everything old is, of course, new again. Steve Inskeep, "Donald Trump and the Legacy of Andrew Jackson," *The Atlantic*, November 30, 2016, https://www.theatlantic.com/politics/archive/2016/11/trump-and-andrew-jackson/508973/.

[8] Alexis de Tocqueville, *Democracy in America*, trans. George Lawrence (New York: Harper & Row, 1988), 232.

[9] Issacharoff, *Fragile Democracies*, 223–225.

[10] Tom Ginsburg, *Judicial Review in New Democracies: Constitutional Courts in Asian Cases* (Cambridge: Cambridge University Press, 2003), 22–30.

Impetuous populism rejects temporal restraints in the name of the will of the people. As a result there is an urgency to overcoming all such restraints so as to maximize the power of angry incumbency. The forms vary, but the need to unleash the power of the moment persists. If the Venezuelan Congress is an impediment to the increasingly tyrannical rule of President Nicolás Maduro, then the captive Supreme Court can declare the Congress disbanded and a new constituent assembly created.[11] At the other end of the spectrum, if the North Carolina Republicans lose the governorship, they too can rewrite the rules of government by neutering gubernatorial power and curtailing voter access to the polls.[12] In each case, the institutions that cool off politics prove vulnerable to a one-time power grab.

FRACTIONATED POWER. In *Fragile Democracies,* I devote considerable attention to the distinct frailties of new democracies as they emerge from conflict or an autocratic past. One of the defining characteristics is that the complete package of democratic institutions rarely mature together, or quickly. Democracy proves to be a complicated interaction among popular sovereignty, political competition, stable institutions of state, vibrant organs of civil society, meaningful political intermediaries, and a commitment to the idea that the losers of today have a credible chance to reorganize and perhaps emerge as the winners of tomorrow. Few if any of these criteria are likely to be satisfied amid the birth pangs of a new democratic order. In circumstances of duress and uncertainty, power gravitates to the first organized entity to consolidate. Almost invariably that will be the executive, and with it comes the pathologies associated with unilateral executive rule: corruption, cronyism, and clientelism. A hypertrophied executive in turn resists efforts to limit its authority and has every incentive not to allow other sources of constitutional authority to realize their mandate.

Populism runs this account in reverse. Populism takes issue with obstacles to immediate returns to electoral success, in which case all separation of powers fail a legitimacy test before the mandate of the national leader. What James Madison hailed as the virtues of "filtration" of popular sentiment through institutional intermediation[13] becomes the

---

[11] Rachelle Krygier and Anthony Faiola, "Venezuela's Pro-government Assembly Moves to Take Power from Elected Congress," *Washington Post*, August 18, 2017, https://www.washingtonpost.com/world/venezuelas-pro-government-assembly-moves-to-take-power-from-elected-congress/2017/08/18/9c6cd0a2-8416-11e7-9e7a-20fa8d7a0db6_story.html.

[12] Richard Fausset, "North Carolina Governor Signs Law Limiting Successor's Power," *New York Times*, December 16, 2016, https://www.nytimes.com/2016/12/16/us/pat-mccrory-roy-cooper-north-carolina.html. After courts blocked portions of the law, efforts redoubled. Mark Joseph Stern, "North Carolina GOP Votes to Dilute Governor's Power and Curtail Voting Rights—Again," *The Slatest* (blog), *Slate*, April 12, 2017, http://www.slate.com/blogs/the_slatest/2017/04/12/north_carolina_republicans_dilute_governor_s_power_and_curtail_voting_rights.html.

[13] Noah Feldman, *The Three Lives of James Madison: Genius, Partisan, President* (New York: Random House, 2017), 112–115.

frustration of the will of the people. The hostility to cross-institutional constraints flows from the same impulse as the narrowing of the time frame for political rewards. As Jan-Werner Müller addresses in his book on the subject, the new populism begins with hostility to pluralism.[14] There is a claim to speak for a unified people, fighting against elites whose illegitimacy is a source of great anger. The impulse toward what Nancy Rosenblum terms "holism"[15] challenges the concept of institutional accommodation that underlies constitutional democracy. A monist commitment to an abiding truth that captures the interests of all the people (save the unredeemable outliers) cannot commit to separation of powers any more than it can to rotation in office.

Part of this phenomenon is kicking in an open door; the dysfunctionality of the legislative branches is a plague upon almost all the houses of democracy. As I address more fully in an article on *Democracy's Deficits,*[16] the premise of modern constitutional democracies is the primacy of the legislative branch, denominated the Article I power in the US setting. Legislative weakness furthers the trend, as regulatory authority grows, for expanded executive authority. No one rises to the level of chief executive without a desire to act, and legislative inaction invites executive circumvention. But legislative inaction can result from sheer legislative dysfunction, political disagreement with the agenda of the executive, or the inability to cohere on a policy initiative in the face of internal political disagreement.[17] An executive riding a populist wave would not distinguish among the sources of legislative inaction, and would instead see each as a rejection of the electoral mandate.

Also vulnerable to populist attack is the judiciary. In the face of legislative lack of capacity to govern, a strong executive increasingly finds the judiciary to be a major obstacle to its immediate designs. Part of this is structural, especially in recent democracies that followed the German example of creating a powerful constitutional court. Such apex courts stand apart from the ordinary judiciary in being tasked with restraint of anti-democratic excesses of the state and frequently find themselves in pitched battles with consolidating political power. Part as well is that judicial appointment typically marches to a different beat than political election. Judicial terms do not dovetail with legislative or executive elections and thus serve to retard the immediate realization of the popular will—by design.

Around the world, populist regimes attempt to curtail any challenge to executive authority. In Poland the current form includes an attack on judicial independence, in Hungary it even includes the attempt to expel the entire Central European University, and in South Africa it includes President Zuma's efforts to handpick government officials

---

[14] Müller, *What Is Populism?*, 20.

[15] Nancy Rosenblum, *On the Side of the Angels: An Appreciation of Parties and Partisanship* (Princeton, NJ: Princeton University Press, 2008), 11.

[16] Samuel Issacharoff, "Democracy's Deficits," *University of Chicago Law Review* (2018) 85: 485–519.

[17] My thanks to Donald Verrilli for this helpful formulation.

ranging from ministers to chief justice of the Constitutional Court, to anticorruption enforcers.[18] In each case, the overweening executive appeals to the plebiscitary authority of his own election.

Not surprisingly, the courts are a frequent irritant to the populist agenda. No less surprising, the courts become the targets for political attack, most clearly in countries such as Poland and Hungary where curtailing the power of the courts is a central plank of the populist agenda. But in numerous other countries, such as Israel, South Africa, and Argentina, to name but a few, a plebiscitary executive tries to use his or her political wave of support to overwhelm the judiciary. When Donald Trump rails against "so-called judges" or the "Mexican judge" he joins a well-orchestrated chorus of attacks on judicial independence as a division of power that thwarts the demand for immediacy of the populist surge.

The institutional capacity for judicial resistance is limited. Depending on the form of judicial appointment, the executive is restrained for varying time periods in dismantling judicial frustration of a populist agenda. In Israel, for example, the self-selection of Supreme Court justices was overcome by nomination reforms. In Argentina, the Kirchner government repeatedly sought to make any federal judge removable by a majority vote in the Congress, a threat that only ended with the defeat of the Peronists in national elections.[19] In Poland, the government limited the ability of the Constitutional Tribunal to publish opinions and imposed lowered age limits to remove many from office—a tactic borrowed from the Orbán assaults on the Hungarian Constitutional Court.[20] And in the United States, the primary legislative success of the Trump administration has been the rapid appointment of young, ideologically-tinged judges who will alter the political valence of the federal judiciary.[21]

---

[18] Mfuneko Toyana, "South African Court Rules Zuma Appointment of State Prosecutor Invalid," *Reuters*, December 8, 2017, https://www.reuters.com/article/us-safrica-zuma/south-african-court-rules-zuma-appointment-of-state-prosecutor-invalid-idUSKBN1E2151; Daniel Boffey and Christian Davies, "Poland Cries Foul as EU Triggers 'Nuclear Option' over Judicial Independence," *The Guardian*, December 20, 2017, https://www.theguardian.com/world/2017/dec/20/eu-process-poland-voting-rights; Andrew Byrne, "Orban Goads Soros with Hungarian University Laws," *Financial Times*, March 29, 2017, https://www.ft.com/content/3a125962-148c-11e7-80f4-13e067d5072c.

[19] Daniel Politi, "Cristina and the Supremes," *Latitude* (blog), *New York Times*, July 5, 2013, https://latitude.blogs.nytimes.com/2013/07/05/cristina-and-the-supremes/.

[20] Poland's attacks have come in waves. In 2015, it imposed a supermajority vote requirement on its constitutional court. Reuters, "Poland: Law Altering Top Court Goes Into Effect Despite Criticism," *New York Times*, December 28, 2015, https://www.nytimes.com/2015/12/29/world/europe/poland-law-altering-top-court-goes-into-effect-despite-criticism.html. In December 2017, it targeted judges on the Supreme Court with age limits. Marc Santora and Joanna Berendt, "Poland Overhauls Courts, and Critics See Retreat from Democracy," *New York Times*, December 20, 2017, https://www.nytimes.com/2017/12/20/world/europe/eu-poland-law.html. Orbán pledged "solidarity" after the move, having led his own judicial purge in 2013. Andrew Byrne, "Hungary's Orban Vows to Defend Poland from EU Sanctions," *Financial Times*, July 22, 2017, https://www.ft.com/content/b1bd2424-6ed7-11e7-93ff-99f383b09ff9.

[21] "Full Court Press," *The Economist*, January 11, 2018, https://www.economist.com/news/united-states/21734409-everything-else-could-theory-be-reversed-his-effect-law-will-be-profound-donald.

INTERMEDIARY ORGANIZATIONS. In separate works, David Cole[22] and Jack Goldsmith[23] argue that the risk of executive unilateralism is held in check, even in an era of legislative dysfunction, by the soft power of civil society institutions. These take many forms, from the formal organizations of trade unions or churches, to the volunteer missions of groups such as the American Civil Liberties Union, to the systemic review offered by an independent media. By and large, modern populism eschews the hard edge of state repression as such. While there are some regimes—Recep Tayyip Erdoğan's Turkey comes immediately to mind—that have used the police power to jail journalists and selected political opponents, that is more the exception than the rule.[24] While these intermediary institutions play an invaluable checking function against anti-governance excess, they are also perceived to be the rearguard fighters for the established order against which the populist wave rebels.

The easiest example is the press. The parcelization of information is an increasing feature of the high-tech era. The loss of a common core of observed facts in face of social media networks facilitates polarized politics and fuels the paranoid streak that invariably accompanies populism. The desire to retrench amid the familiar is a commonplace reaction to social and economic insecurity, something that new information sources can nurture and insulate from challenge. Thus is born the cry of "fake news" as part of the rallying cry against the established order. And as Hollywood sets the cultural norms for the arts, Washington has inspired every tyrant in the making to accede to the fake news claim, invariably to obscure misdeeds ranging from corruption to human rights violations.

But the issue cuts deeper. Embedded within the populist impulse is, in Müller's words, the desire "to cut out the middleman ... and to rely as little as possible on complex party organizations as intermediaries between citizens and politicians."[25] The classic intermediary institutions of modern democracy are the political parties. Indeed, as famously formulated by E.E. Schattschneider, "political parties created democracy and modern democracy is unthinkable save in terms of the parties."[26] But as democratic governance is hollowed out by the failing legislative branch, the parties and the party leaders become perceived as what Robert Dahl in 1965 already identified as the "new democratic Leviathan," a self-perpetuating form of governance that is "welfare-oriented, centralized, bureaucratic, tamed and controlled by competition among highly

---

[22] David Cole, *Engines of Liberty: The Power of Citizen Activists to Make Constitutional Law* (New York: Basic Books, 2016).

[23] Jack Goldsmith, *Power and Constraint: The Accountable Presidency after 9/11* (New York: W.W. Norton, 2012).

[24] As of December 2017, Turkey was responsible for 73 of the 262 journalists jailed worldwide. Sewell Chan, "Number of Jailed Journalists Hits Record High, Advocacy Group Says," *New York Times*, December 13, 2017, https://www.nytimes.com/2017/12/13/world/europe/journalists-jailed-committee-to-protect-journalists.html.

[25] Müller, *What Is Populism?*, 35.

[26] E.E. Schattschneider, *Party Government* (New York: Holt Rinehart and Winston, 1942), 1.

organized elites, and in the perspective of the ordinary citizen, somewhat remote, distant and impersonal."[27]

The hollowing out of customary democratic politics, to borrow Peter Mair's formulation, is most vivid in Europe and results in part from the expansion of European-level bureaucratic command in which "there is little scope for input-oriented legitimacy and decision-makers can only rarely be mandated by voters."[28] In exaggerated form, this means that Belgium and Spain can withstand many months without a national government and yet continue most functions relatively unimpeded. The traditional political parties become not so much organized forms of policy debate as rival administrators of the same bureaucratic enterprise that largely exists outside the sphere of democratic accountability. Nor is this simply a European disorder. Substitute Beltway for Brussels and the demand for starving the beast for Brexit and the same phenomenon is observable in the United States as well.

Without intermediary institutions capable of transmitting interests into governance, the executive strongman appears as the only hope for the ill-defined populist agenda. Intermediary institutions cease serving as the glue that ties the population to the project of self-governance. Instead, like the press and political parties, their utility is only in fidelity to executive commands. The advent of social media and targeted broadcasting allows direct engagement to bypass the organizational structures formerly necessary for populism. Even a comparison of Donald Trump and Silvio Berlusconi shows the difference in impulse. Whereas Berlusconi carefully built a party apparatus of Forza Italia, with local committees adjacent to every parish in Italy, Trump used Twitter and other forms of direct outreach to communicate directly to disengaged partisans.[29]

TRANSPARENT GOVERNANCE. With few exceptions, where the full range of institutions of democratic governance fail to take hold, what emerges is executive rule. It is far easier to elect the national savior than it is to forge political parties and legislative competence. Such rulers have a propensity to identify themselves with the struggle of the people, often with justification when a despot has been toppled, and an unfortunate identification of their continued rule with the fruition of the popular will. Not for nothing the cynical British account of postcolonial rule: "one man, one vote, one time."[30] The engorged executive stands as the key to any claim to government benefits, contracts, or favors. In turn,

---

[27] Robert Dahl, "Reflections on Opposition in Western Democracies," *Government and Opposition* 1, no. 1 (October 1965): 21.

[28] Peter Mair, *Ruling the Void: The Hollowing of Western Democracy* (London: Verso, 2013), 138.

[29] Michael E. Shin and John A. Agnew, *Berlusconi's Italy: Mapping Contemporary Italian Politics* (Philadelphia: Temple University Press, 2008), 73–85.

[30] Issacharoff, *Fragile Democracies*, 3. The phrase is oft-attributed to former assistant secretary of state and US ambassador to Syria and Egypt Edward Djerejian. For further discussion, see Ali Khan, "A Theory of Universal Democracy," *Wisconsin International Law Journal* 16, no. 1 (1997–1998): 106.

much of economic life becomes impossible without increased engagement with state regulatory authority, further collapsing the prospect of democratic contestation.

In newly minted democracies, the risk is that the first party in office will use the soft forms of power to cement rule. Concentrated state authority means that prospects for employment and government contracts depend on contacts to the ruling elite, oftentimes the ruler himself. From the post-revolutionary PRI in Mexico to the legacy of Robert Mugabe in Zimbabwe, unfractionated power in the hands of a dominant leader or party translates to a kleptocratic network that reinforces the pivotal role of the central leader. South Africa's painful descent into corruption is an object lesson here. The South African constitution makes the president the head of state and head of government, and his selection is by the National Assembly, meaning that there is no separation of powers anywhere in the federal government except for the independent Constitutional Court.[31] No opposition party has matured in South Africa, and there is no experience of rotation in office post-apartheid. The dominance of the ANC beyond the political realm is captured in the derisive term of "tenderpreneurs" which denotes wealthy so-called business venturers whose primary capital is lucrative government contracts.[32]

As with the problem of fractionated power, the experience of new democracies illustrates the risk for the established ones. Populism tends to unwind internal norms of compliance that help keep self-interest within tolerable bounds. In some ideal fashion, government decision-making should be transparent, the rules should be well established ex ante, and there should be independent ombudsmen to check temptations to graft and a host of institutional practices that smooth transitions in governance. The problem is that no democracy ever satisfies all of these conditions all the time. Incumbents are always eager to do more than they should before ceding office. Partisans are always rewarded with an extra dollop of government jobs or contracts. There is always a temptation to alter the rules so as to stymie the prospects of the opposition. Even as a formal matter, rules may be bent; Britain still allows the government the power to call elections when it perceives it most suitable to its prospects for re-election.

What sets apart the populist regimes is the systematic assault on all of these structures of governance. One result is a propensity to govern through one-off arrangements that take on the forms of clientelism that plague despotic regimes. An obvious rhetorical example is President Trump, who champions himself as mastering the art of the deal. President Trump rejects institutional forms of doing business, with examples from NAFTA to every multilateral treaty in the international domain. This translates into attacks on the State Department, the intelligence services, and any institutional byway that dos not turn on idiosyncratic personal assessments. All new presidents resent the constraining role of the administrative state, which has all the dexterity of an overloaded cruise ship in changing direction. But

---

[31] Issacharoff, *Fragile Democracies*, 248–264.

[32] Andrew England, "South Africa Corruption Fear Grows," *Financial Times*, March 25, 2015, https://www.ft.com/content/b7564954-c896-11e4-b43b-00144feab7de.

that bureaucratic constraint allows government to function predictably across changes in administration and helps order the lives of the dependent citizenry. In populist times, however, those ordinary workings become a challenge to immediate returns.

Consider the most recent US tax bill, not so much for its paradoxical redistribution toward corporate earnings as for the process of its implementation. There were no committee hearings, no attempt to reconcile the likely impact on the deficit with the scoring of the fiscal impact of the congressional budget estimates, no attempt to cohere a policy that justified disparate treatment of similarly situated taxpayers. The previous institutional checks on budget impacts, the requirement of scoring spending and tax bills through the Congressional Budget Office and the Joint Committee on Taxation, were jettisoned. Indeed, when the Congressional Budget Office issued a caustic report on the proposed Trump repeal of Obamacare, the Republican response was a proposed dismantling of the office. Similarly, any mechanism of public debate was removed from adoption of the tax bill by the Senate, the so-called world's greatest deliberative body. Power not policy is the leitmotif of populist governance, even if few of the benefits are likely to benefit the populist electorate.

The dismantling of independent checks on command-center politics bears special attention. Again South Africa provides a cautionary note. As President Zuma consolidated power and plunged the country into the deeper and deeper recesses of cronyist corruption, there was little if any opposition from within government itself. The exceptional checking function came from the National Prosecuting Authority and its Directorate of Special Operations, an independent anticorruption watchdog agency. In 2009, at the instigation of President Zuma, the Congress abolished these organizations and placed their power within the national police, which were in turn accountable to the Security ministry and, by extension, to President Zuma himself. Only the intervention of the South African Constitutional Court in *Glenister v. President of the Republic of South Africa* saved this last bastion of independent accountability.

Using the history of fragile democracies as a warning for mature ones suggests a discomforting parallel to the United States. The corruption scandals that swirl around the Trump candidacy and presidency also sparked investigations by independent authorities. The response to date from the administration has been the firing of a non-subservient FBI director and the increasingly vitriolic attacks on the independent prosecutor Robert Mueller. The United States is not South Africa, but the warning signs are there.

NORMS OF GOVERNANCE. A constitutional democracy is defined by more than the formal allocations of power, the parchment barriers of last resort. As Steven Levitsky and Daniel Ziblatt note, "Democracies work best—and survive longer—when constitutions are reinforced by norms of mutual toleration and restraint in the exercise of power."[33]

---

[33] Steven Levitsky and Daniel Ziblatt, "How a Democracy Dies," *New Republic*, December 7, 2017, https://newrepublic.com/article/145916/democracy-dies-donald-trump-contempt-for-american-political-institutions. Adapted from Steven Levitsky and Daniel Ziblatt, *How Democracies Die* (New York: Crown, 2018).

English constitutionalism provides the great lesson in how institutional accommodations never reduced to writing can nonetheless provide a blueprint for democratic governance.[34] Whether in the unwritten British model, or in the norms that give life to the spare American text, constitutional governance requires fidelity to norms that are understood to constrain the exercise of power, even if never reduced to formal commands. American constitutional law tends to overvalue Supreme Court decisions, particularly on matters of contested definitions of individual rights, at the expense of the less celebrated and less litigated experienced-based forms of governance. Only rarely do such institutional matters present themselves for litigated resolution. And even then, as often as not, they are treated as political questions not proper for judicial resolution.

Two examples illustrate this point. The first grows out of the presumption of legitimacy of the political opposition in a system that accepts rotation in office as a historic norm. Invariably, the shift in power means that one side has control of the police power, which includes the power to prosecute. Successful democracies avoid criminalizing the opposition or, put another way, democracies that use the criminal law to retaliate politically do not long remain democracies. Despite arguable violations of law during the Bush War on Terror, the Obama administration wisely resisted calls for initiating criminal prosecutions of the prior administration. Similarly, despite the power of a Congress to initiate impeachment proceedings against an opposition party president, such examples are rare in American history. The three historic examples highlight the importance of restraint. The impeachment of Andrew Johnson was the highpoint of Republican congressional efforts to more aggressively prosecute the Civil War, and yet the particulars for which Johnson was impeached involved political choices of the executive, and Johnson was ultimately absolved in the Senate.[35] By contrast, Richard Nixon was charged with an offense against his office and was forced to resign. But the impeachment of Bill Clinton bore neither the historic decisiveness of the Civil War nor the clear criminality of the Nixon obstruction of justice. Rather, it signaled a descent from principle into the demonization of the opposition and tarnished politics.

No greater departure from the presumption of democratic legitimacy of the opposition can be found than the ongoing fixation of the current administration with "crooked Hillary." The crowd incitement to "lock her up" is unheard of in American history. History looks well upon the pardon of Richard Nixon by Gerald Ford, preferring the political repudiation of official misconduct to the criminal justice system. But populist impatience allows none of these niceties. To the campaign chorus of locking up Clinton is added the persistent berating of the Department of Justice for not turning on Trump's

---

[34] A.V. Dicey, *Introduction to the Study of the Law of the Constitution*, 8th ed. (London: Macmillan, 1915; Indianapolis, IN: Liberty/Classics, 1982).

[35] Cass Sunstein, "Impeaching the President," *University of Pennsylvania Law Review* 147 (1998): 295–316.

political opponents.[36] There is no constitutional principle that prohibits prosecution of the nominee of one major political party by her victorious opponent, assuming the norms of indictment and trial are followed. Nor is there any textual restraint on a president's efforts to direct the investigative powers of federal law enforcement authorities. But constitutional culture is to the contrary. Quite simply, there has never been anything like this in American history.

Similarly under attack is the presumed legitimacy of the civil service. The post-New Deal United States has functioned with a narrow strata of political appointees overseeing a large and cumbersome career bureaucracy. The sheer size of the federal government and its pervasive role in American society require no less. Yet there is no constitutional mandate for the civil service, which operates under a series of statutory restrictions on appointment and political engagements. Indeed, the Supreme Court has read into the First Amendment a constitutional protection of incumbent nonpolitical civil servants against politically-motivated removal and replacement.

Many are the presidents frustrated by an administrative life of its own. But none has acted to rid the federal government of the personnel needed to function. The first example came at the Department of State. The career focus on regional expertise and the demands of diplomacy fit poorly with the freewheeling style of government by decree. So State stands depleted of appointments not only at the agency level but also across crucial ambassadorial posts.[37] The historically accepted need for state-to-state relations proves also vulnerable.

More striking are the reported efforts at the Environmental Protection Agency to investigate and weed out employees deemed hostile to the political agenda of the agency administrator, Scott Pruitt.[38] One of the characteristic court interventions in new democracies in sharply divided countries is the prevention of wholesale removal of disfavored groups from public employment and public activity. State policies aimed at lustration are met with stringent constitutional review from skeptical courts. Certainly in the United States there have been periods of fear of antagonistic penetration of the government

---

[36] None bang the drum louder than the president himself. Donald J. Trump (@realDonaldTrump), "Everybody is asking why the Justice Department (and FBI) isn't looking into all of the dishonesty going on with Crooked Hillary & the Dems..," Twitter, November 3, 2017, https://twitter.com/realdonaldtrump/status/926403023861141504.

[37] As of this writing, 70 of 156 appointed positions in the Department of State (including political ambassadorships) lack even nominees. Only 61 positions at State have been filled. "Tracking How Many Key Positions Trump Has Filled So Far," *Washington Post,* updated January 11, 2018, https://www.washingtonpost.com/graphics/politics/trump-administration-appointee-tracker/database/.

[38] Eric Lipton and Lisa Friedman, "E.P.A. Employees Spoke Out. Then Came Scrutiny of Their Email," *New York Times,* December 17, 2017, https://www.nytimes.com/2017/12/17/us/politics/epa-pruitt-media-monitoring.html.

apparatus. But the general conclusion that the McCarthy period was a constitutional embarrassment has yielded strong efforts to avoid repetition. Until now.

* * *

Successful democratic governance has a soft underbelly. Success depends on an acceptance of both assumptions about power and institutional limitations with recognized boundaries, yet few hard constitutional walls for protection. In countries emerging from autocratic rule, the habits of incremental power and the legitimacy of the opposition are hard to inculcate. Populism puts these values as much at risk in mature democracies. From the beginning of the Madisonian experiment, the challenge has been how to allow the electoral victors to prevail, but not too much. That challenge persists.

26 Populism, Racism, and the Rule of Law in Constitutional Democracies Today

Desmond King and Rogers M. Smith

IN THE MID-1990S, scholarly works increasingly proclaimed the end of nation-state citizenship, washed away by rising tides of globalization and transnational political and economic organizations, even as many nation-states were adopting new "transformative" constitutions that promised greatly expanded sets of rights—social and economic rights; racial, ethnic, and religious minority rights; Indigenous rights; environmental rights; and more—shaped by globalist progressive agendas.[1] However, by the second half of the second decade of the twenty-first century, the global political landscape appeared strikingly different from merely a quarter century earlier. Older forms of nationalism and overt racism resurged in ways that posed fresh dangers to constitutional democracy in many polities. The destruction of a multinational Yugoslavia, including the declaration of an independent Kosovo from Serbia, certainly put the lie to the proposition that virulent nationalism was only a thing of the past. At the present moment, though, one need look no further than the dramatic headlines from Barcelona in October 2017—where the Catalan Parliament audaciously (and with dubious legality) proclaimed its independence from Spain—to see a revivified, separatist nationalism rooted far more in ethnic and

---

[1] Rogers M. Smith, "Citizenship and Membership Duties toward Quasi-citizens," in *The Oxford Handbook of Citizenship*, ed. Ayelet Shachar, Rainer Bauböck, Irene Bloemraad, and Maarten Vink (Oxford: Oxford University Press, 2017), 818–820.

political vexations than class or economic grievances.[2] Though it thereby precipitated a constitutional crisis, the Catalan case was, to be sure, unusual in one key respect: it was an affluent region seeking independence from the nation-state, Spain, of which it has been a core constitutional part. More typical were right-wing populist movements proclaiming concerns for national sovereignty based on opposition to immigration, particularly an immigrant population seen as ethnically or religiously different (or both), as well as economically burdensome. In countries such as Poland, Hungary, and others, these champions of narrow nationalism sought to curb the independence of judiciaries protective of human rights and minority rights, and sometimes to rewrite constitutions to preclude such protections.[3] Notions of allegiance to a cosmopolitan vision of the European Union often took second place to more parochial national loyalties.

A lively debate has emerged about whether economic or ethnocultural concerns are more central to this recent wave of populist nationalisms.[4] We have long stressed the persistence of racial concerns as factors shaping American politics.[5] Even so, we take no satisfaction in observing that in regard to both American and European politics; though most scholars see economic and ethnocultural grievances as present and intertwined, much recent work gives particular emphasis to the latter.[6] Even scholars such as Larry Bartels, who has tended to stress economic motivations for voting and who notes that anti-immigrant attitudes are not themselves surging, recognize that right-wing populist entrepreneurs are often succeeding by tapping into narrow ethnocultural nationalist views with greater efficacy.[7]

---

[2] Yasmeen Serhan, "Catalonia's Self-Defeating Independence Declaration," *The Atlantic*, October 27, 2017, https://www.theatlantic.com/international/archive/2017/10/catalonias-self-defeating-independence-declaration/544205/.

[3] Anne Applebaum, "The Rise of National Socialism: Why Austria's Revolution Is Not Over," *Washington Post*, May 23, 2016; Senni Salmi, "Democratic Backsliding in Poland and Hungary," 2017, https://www.researchgate.net/publication/320625158_Democratic_backsliding_in_Hungary_and_Poland; Zosia Wasik and Henry Foy, "Poland Uses Strict Catholic Criteria to Select Syrian Refugees," *Financial Times*, August, 22, 2015.

[4] Ronald Inglehart and Pippa Norris. "Trump and Populist-Authoritarian Parties: The Silent Revolution in Reverse." *Perspectives on Politics* 15(2) (2017): 443–454.

[5] E.g., Desmond King and Rogers M. Smith, "Racial Orders in American Political Development," *American Political Science Review* 99 (2005): 75–92; Desmond King and Rogers M. Smith, *Still a House Divided: Race and Politics in Obama's America* (Princeton, NJ: Princeton University Press, 2011).

[6] E.g., Democracy Fund, "Democracy Fund Voter Study Group: Executive Summary," June 2017, https://www.voterstudygroup.org/publications/2016-elections/executive-summary; Brams Spruyt, Gil Keppens, and Filip Van Droogenbroek, "Who Supports Populism and What Attracts People to It?," *Political Research Quarterly* 69 (2016): 335–346.

[7] Larry M. Bartels, "The 'Wave' of Right-Wing Populist Sentiment Is a Myth," *The Monkey Cage*, June 21, 2017, https://www.washingtonpost.com/news/monkey-cage/wp/2017/06/21/the-wave-of-right-wing-populist-sentiment-is-a-myth/?utm_term=.8739616d9b5a.

The importance of appeals to ethnic divisions is indeed powerfully demonstrated across European democracies. The French presidential election in 2017 pitched an extreme nationalist candidate (Marine Le Pen) against the eventually successful centrist, Macron (himself an "outsider" electoral novice who had never been elected to office and in effect built his own populist movement). While Le Pen faltered, the center-right Austrian People's Party success in the fall 2017 opened the door to a coalition government with the far-right, neo-Nazi-founded, anti-immigrant Freedom Party.[8] In Germany's federal elections, an until recently obscure extremist anti-immigrant party, the Alternative for Germany (AfD), surged to take close to a hundred seats by winning 12.6 percent of the votes cast and becoming in the process the third largest party in the Reichstag. Should Chancellor Angela Merkel prove successful in sustaining yet one more "grand coalition" of the Christian Democratic and Socialist Parties, the AfD would become the official opposition party within the Bundestag. In Hungary the populist-right party Fidesz led by Prime Minister Viktor Orban, which has passed a new constitution that critics allege dilutes judicial independence and weakens independent media, won a third electoral victory in spring 2018.[9]

The keenly anti-immigrant and anti-Muslim AfD was the leading party in Saxony. Ironically as in the United States, where Trump support was inversely related to the number of immigrants in a state, so in Germany the AfD did best in districts where the foreign-born population is lowest; similarly, in the UK, the strongest support for Brexit often correlated with the lowest number of immigrants despite the prominence of the theme to "control immigration" amongst Brexit agitators.[10] All these votes were in different ways expressions of anti-foreign and anti-immigrant exclusionary preferences, whether rooted in some authentic economic fear of labor market competition or in a nationalist mobilized definition of the nation, or in an ugly combination of both. Since most of these states were doing well economically at the time of their most recent election, it has to be at most fear of economic distress, rather than the experience of such difficulty, that adds to the power of ethnocultural aversions. Undoubtedly, however, right-wing populists have planted deeper roots in the economically hardest pressed regions of their respective countries.

---

[8] Anna Grzymala-Busse, "Austrian Election Proves Right-Wing Populism Is New Normal in Europe," *The Hill*, October 22, 2017, http://thehill.com/opinion/international/356575-austrian-election-proves-right-wing-populism-is-new-normal-in-europe.

[9] Neil Buckley and Andrew Byrne, "The Rise and Rise of Viktor Orban," *Financial Times Weekend Magazine*, January 27, 2018.

[10] Rafaela M. Dancygier and David D. Laitin, "Immigration in Europe: Discrimination, Violence and Public Policy," *Annual Review of Political Science* 17 (2014): 43–60; Ruud Koopmans, "Multiculturalism and Immigration: A Contested Field in Cross-National Comparison," *Annual Review of Sociology* 39 (2013): 147–169; Alexander Schmidt-Catran and Dennis Spies, "Immigration and Welfare Support in Germany," *American Sociological Review* 81 (2016): 242–261; Griff Witte, "Behind Sweden's Warm Welcome for Refugees, a Backlash Is Brewing," *Washington Post*, October 19, 2015.

Although recent right-wing movements in both the United States and Europe are commonly labeled as mobilizations of "populism," this term's generality and imprecision renders it of limited analytical value unless further specifications are provided. Rather in the way that Moliere's seventeenth-century *Bourgeois Gentleman*, Monsieur Jourdain, discovered he had been speaking prose all his life, so populist language has in recent years suddenly been embraced across the political spectrum—whether in economic or cultural terms—and exploited as much by Bernie Sanders and Jeremy Corbyn as by Donald Trump, Boris Johnson, and Viktor Orban. Most irksome from the standpoint of constitutional democracy are those forms of populism that blend both narrow ethnocultural conceptions of who "the people" are with convictions that constitutionalism and the rule of law are meant only to serve "the people's" will, without regard for other values or other persons. When populists slip comfortably into disparaging existing constitutional rules—such as the legitimacy of electoral processes or the independence of the judiciary—they weaken the legitimacy of their country's rule of law and constitutional framework.[11]

Definitions and Parameters

Populism is a notoriously slippery and broad term. There is, for example, within the United States a vigorous historiographical dispute about American populists. Admirers see them historically as an insurgency of oppressed farmers and workers against those who exploited them; critics tend to emphasize the extent to which some populists were overtly anti-Semitic or anti-immigrant (and anti-urban and anti-cosmopolitan more generally). Over time "populism" has proved capable of assuming comfortably the clothes of both the ideological Left and ideological Right—Latin American countries provide multiple examples of populist governments of the Left and Right.[12] Spain's Podemos party is left-wing whereas AfD and other populist parties are determinedly right-wing.

Scholars are increasingly converging on a minimalist definition of populism as any position that valorizes a "people" whose will deserves always to prevail against an "elite" that is hostile to the people's well-being.[13] Populist leaders assert a direct connection between "the people" and their own capacity to formulate and deliver policies designed to satisfy the needs of the people. Although "the people" can be defined in many terms, including class, religion, ideology, and region, and more or less expansively and heterogeneously, in

---

[11] Steven Levitsky and Daniel Ziblatt, *How Democracies Die* (New York: Penguin, 2018); Nancy Bermeo, "On Democratic Backsliding," *Journal of Democracy* 27 (2016): 5–19.

[12] Marco D'Eramo, "They, the People," *New Left Review* 103 (2017): 129–139.

[13] E.g., Cas Mudde and Cristóbal Rivera Kaltwasser, "Exclusionary vs. Inclusionary Populism: Comparing Contemporary Europe and Latin America," *Government and Opposition* 48 (2013): 147–174; Giorgos Katsambekis, "The Populist Surge in Post-democratic Times: Theoretical and Political Challenges," *Political Quarterly* 88 (2017): 202–210.

many instances today this category is narrowly circumscribed to accommodate a single identity, usually racial or ethnic, and lucidly to determine exclusions—that is, who does not fit into this identity.

What might be termed "inclusive populism" has, however, always been a standard trope in American politics. One can think of Barack Obama's rejection of a "red state" or "blue state" America in favor of a vision of a single America that stood united behind certain values that he articulated. A more "exclusive populism" was instead manifested in President Donald Trump's Inaugural Address in January 2017. He castigated the Washington elites arrayed behind him at the United States Capitol while he spoke to emphasize his connection to the "people" and his desire to put "America First"—an America he had promised throughout the campaign to protect against Mexican immigrants, Muslim terrorists, those who choose not to say "Merry Christmas," and also the nation's first black President, whose Americanness Trump persistently challenged. Similar narrowly conceived populist conceptions of nationhood fueled the AfD, France's FN, the British UKIP, Austria's Freedom Party, and other European right-wing, anti-immigrant parties, as well as Modi's Hindu nationalism in India and arguably the Chinese nationalism of Xi Jinping, along with Donald Trump's brand of Republican Party ideology.

TRANSFORMATIVE CONSTITUTIONALISM AND THE NEW POPULISMS

Though scholars of recent populist movements have been commendably attentive to populist attitudes toward constitutionalism and the rule of law,[14] few have explored the possibility that these movements are reactions against the dominant ideology revealed in the spate of drafting of new constitutions that occurred around the world in the last quarter century. In brief, the writing and adopting of new national constitutions became a ubiquitous feature of politics globally in that period, heightening especially in the decade after the fall of communism in 1989. Writing in 1998 about the already widely emulated 1996 South African Constitution, Karl Klare labeled many of these constitutions, often written under the watchful eye of international NGOs, "transformative." They sought to remake fundamentally, rather than to preserve, the existing social, economic, and political orders of their societies.[15] For a time, transformative constitutionalism appeared to be very much the path of, and toward, new forms of constitutionalism globally, and many still hope it will prove to be such a trajectory.[16] Rich details are available on the valuable Comparative Constitutions Project led by

---

[14] E.g., Jan-Werner Müller, *What Is Populism?* (Philadelphia: University of Pennsylvania Press, 2016).

[15] Karl E. Klare, "Legal Culture and Transformative Constitutionalism," *South African Journal on Human Rights* 14 (1998): 146–188.

[16] Michaela Hailbronner, "Transformative Constitutionalism: Not Only in the Global South," *American Journal of Comparative Law* 65 (2017): 527–565.

Zachary Elkins, Tom Ginsburg, and James Melton.[17] According to their site, from 1990 to 2015, the world's nations adopted a total of 105 new written constitutions, 41 between 1990 and 1996, when South Africa adopted what became one of the most influential modern constitutions. In most of these new constitutions, as in many other constitutions written after World War II, "negative" rights limiting governmental powers, which dominated in the 1787 United States Constitution, are increasingly accompanied by "positive" rights creating governmental duties to provide for many dimensions of their people's well-being. The 2008 Ecuador Constitution, for example, written by a left-populist coalition of labor groups, Indigenous peoples, and environmentalists, includes social welfare rights to education, food, water, health, social security (meaning income supports for those not able to work), and employment for workers. The Ecuadorian Constitution also includes extensive antidiscrimination rights: no discrimination on basis of ethnicity, place of birth, age, sex, gender, culture, civil status, language, religion, ideology, political affiliation, legal record, socioeconomic condition, migratory status, sexual orientation, health status, HIV carrier, disability, or physical difference. The Constitution also says, however, that the state *must* adopt affirmative action policies to address many forms of unjust inequality, and to insure representation of women equally with men. It makes international human rights directly enforceable in Ecuadorean courts. And, going well beyond early American doctrines of natural rights as well as later social democratic ideas, the Ecuadorian Constitution guarantees rights for nature herself, rights that anyone can raise on nature's behalf against public and private policies.[18]

But a decade after the adoption of its transformative constitution, Ecuador, like most of the left-leaning populist regimes in Latin America, was in severe economic, political, and social disarray, in part due to declining prices for oil and gas resources that had enabled much of Latin America to prosper when the United States and Europe were experiencing the Great Recession. Adopting a strong constitution had proven not to preclude a populist disregard of new rights. Conservatives there and in many other lands had become sharply critical of many of the social rights, minority rights, immigrant rights, internationally enforceable human rights, and other doctrines characteristic of transformative constitutions, and of judiciaries that sought to enforce such rights. In 2011, Hungary's right-wing Fidesz Party adopted a new constitution that repealed all the decisions of the nation's previously progressive Constitutional Court and established new provisions that gave both constitutional and electoral protection to its policy positions and partisans.[19]

---

[17] Comparative Constitutions Project, accessed February 27, 2018, http://comparativeconstitutionsproject.org/.

[18] Constitute Project, "Ecuador's Constitution of 2008," updated January 17, 2018, https://www.constituteproject.org/constitution/Ecuador_2008.pdf.

[19] Clava Brodsky, "Hungary's Dangerous Constitution," *Columbia Journal of Transnational Law Bulletin* (2016), http://jtl.columbia.edu/hungarys-dangerous-constitution/.

Under the right-wing populist Law and Justice Party, the Polish legislature adopted over thirteen laws from 2015 on that, in the eyes of the European Union, presented "systemic threats to the rule of law," as the ruling majority sought to bend the judiciary to its will.[20] The EU formally sanctioned Poland because of these new laws, the first such rebuke to a Member State ever.

In the United States, Donald Trump has repeatedly questioned the integrity and authority of those he terms "so-called" judges who have ruled against him. Moreover, the remarkable degree to which selection of federal judges in the United States is integrated into party politics has been demonstrated in his administration's attempts, largely successful, to place on federal benches and immigration courts distinctly right-wing judges who are thought to share Trump's basic ideological commitments. In some few cases, embarrassingly unqualified nominees chosen only on the basis of their ideologies and Trump loyalty have been rejected,[21] but in fact Trump has placed a significant number of judges on the federal bench in his first year.

What might be termed "judicial capture" is certainly not an aspect of "American exceptionalism," however. Many scholars perceive a link between populist nationalisms and threats to the rule of law in a number of parts of the world. The British *Daily Telegraph,* for example, castigated British judges via a headline "The Judges versus the People," when some of them appeared to have doubts about the evasion of Parliament instantiated in the referendum to exit from the European Union.[22] Proclaiming in 2017 that the "rise of populist and nationalist sentiment threatens to undermine the separation of powers, with judges being portrayed as elitist and 'enemies of the people', and governmental interference with judicial matters becoming routine," the British Academy organized an international conference on "Challenges to Judicial Independence in Times of Crisis" in spring 2018.[23]

---

[20] Sabrina McCubbin, "Summary: European Commission Addresses Judicial Independence in Poland," *Lawfare,* December 23, 2017, https://lawfareblog.com/summary-european-commission-addresses-judicial-independence-poland.

[21] Maria Sacchetti, "Immigration Judges Say Proposed Quotas from Justice Dept. Threaten Independence," *Washington Post,* October 12, 2017, https://www.washingtonpost.com/local/immigration/immigration-judges-say-proposed-quotas-from-justice-dept-threaten-independence/2017/10/12/3ed86992-aee1-11e7-be94-fabb0f1e9ffb_story.html?utm_term=.5e69f2d7b10c; Kyle Barry, "Trump Threatens Judicial Independence and the Rule of Law with 'Not Qualified' Nominees," *Medium,* November 9, 2017, https://medium.com/@NAACP_LDF/trump-threatens-judicial-independence-and-the-rule-of-law-with-not-qualified-nominees-e6472e27251c.

[22] See, e.g., Peter Walker, "Daily Mail Accused of 'Attack on the Rule of Law' amid Criticism of Tabloid Brexit Legal Challenge Coverage," *Independent,* November 4, 2016, http://www.independent.co.uk/news/uk/politics/brexit-legal-challenges-judges-daily-mail-express-sun-uk-newspapers-condemned-a7396961.html.

[23] "Challenges to Judicial Independence in Times of Crisis," British Academy Conference, March 8–9, 2018, https://www.britac.ac.uk/events/challenges-judicial-independence-times-crisis.

Populism and Constitutional Challenges: Some Mechanisms

Why have discontents developed in Western democracies in the last decade, and why have they passed thresholds facilitating profoundly anti-system candidates, often populist, to thrive? Though populist political entrepreneurs have pumped up xenophobic and racist scapegoats to blame for all their societies' ills, even as their policies have aided the already-advantaged, these populist leaders have been able to do so in part because many widespread and understandable grievances have been inadequately addressed. They have also been able to do so, however, because of increasingly successful efforts to reduce the social, economic, and political rights and opportunities of ethnic, racial, and religious minorities, limiting the power of those groups to defeat right-wing movements.

In making this case, we focus on the United States to identify some of the mechanisms promoting these tendencies because they have been overlaid upon entrenched racial divisions epitomized by the distinct race policy alliances salient in American politics that we have long studied. But comparable triggers exist in other advanced democracies.

DECLINING RESPONSIVENESS TO VOTERS' PREFERENCES

First, *weak policy representativeness* is a factor in most advanced democracies in the sense that while governments respond to some voters, the interests of many are neglected. Contentions that "the people" are being ignored often have real foundations. Larry Bartels has pursued this thesis especially in respect to the United State, concluding that the current level of partisan polarization results in little meaningful representation of many voters' preferences and views at the legislative level.[24] Politicians can rely on partisan turnout and mobilization to deliver votes rather than having to demonstrate policy representation. Because increased elite polarization makes partisan differences clearer to voters, it thereby contributes to additional ideological division as "increasing polarization on the elite level is driving the rise of vitriolic politics on the mass level."[25]

One leading political scientist notes that in the US case, legislators do respond to the voter preferences, "but . . . responsiveness is strongly tilted toward the most affluent citizens. Indeed, under most circumstances, the preferences of the vast majority of American appear to have essentially no impact on which policies the government does or doesn't adopt."[26] This critique is advanced further by Achen and Bartels in their account of the

---

[24] Larry M. Bartels, *Unequal Democracy* (Princeton, NJ: Princeton University Press, 2008).

[25] Joshua N. Zingher and Michael E. Flynn, "From on High: The Effect of Elite Polarization on Mass Attitudes and Behaviors, 1972–2012," *British Journal of Political Science* 48 (2018): 23–46, 43; and see also James N. Druckman, Erik Peterson, and Rune Slothuus, "How Elite Partisan Polarization Affects Public Opinion Formation," *American Political Science Review* 107 (2013): 57–79.

[26] Martin Gilens, *Affluence and Influence* (Princeton, NJ: Princeton University Press, 2012), 1.

limits of democratic institutions effectively to represent public opinion.[27] For these two scholars, received wisdom about medium voter theory and the efficacy of democratic institutions is part of a "folk theory" enjoying scant accuracy: "election outcomes turn out to be largely random events from the viewpoint of contemporary democratic theory."[28] Writing on his own about comparative patterns, Bartels worries about the consistent failure of policymakers to address the preferences of low income citizens: "insofar as policy-makers respond to public preferences, they seem to respond primarily or even entirely to the preferences of affluent people. Indeed, allowing for the effective political influence of citizens to vary with income, the influence attributed to poor citizens is not just less than that attributed to affluent citizens, but consistently *negative*."[29] The fact, for example, that the tax bill enacted by narrow margins in the House and Senate at the end of 2017 had significantly less than majority support in any polls taken during the period was irrelevant to its passage. Articles in the United States regularly referred to the necessity of the Republican Party to respond to its "donor base" rather than to the electorate.

BUILDING DIFFERENTIAL INFLUENCE AND ACCESS

Second, the influence of the "donor base" extends into a wider point. Not only are the views of many voters ignored by many elected politicians but concurrently *differential influence based on income* has gained an increasing saliency in analyses of advanced democracy. This mechanism is an extension of the first, and we differentiate them to underline the power of money. The rich do have particular influence and that influence has facilitated a stream of measurable benefits, especially in tax policy. Two political scientists, Jacob Hacker and Paul Pierson, have developed an influential argument principally about the United States as a "winner takes all society"; the framework has been applied to other advanced states such as Britain.[30] Thus, Hopkin and Shaw report a similar "winner take all" type of political outcomes in Britain to those in the United States but identify distinct mechanisms in addition to the organized combat described by Hacker and Pierson, namely a structural embeddedness of financial interests flowing from post-1980s deregulation and financialization.[31]

At least three factors help explain the differential influence enjoyed by society's elite and powerful. First, trade unions are largely deracinated in the United States, with union density in single figures. If public sector union membership is removed, the percentage of unionized workers is tiny, both in historical comparison and compared with other advanced democracies. Some unions retain influence, principally with the Democratic

[27] Christopher Achen and Larry Bartels, *Democracy for Realists* (Princeton, NJ: Princeton University Press, 2016).

[28] Ibid., 2.

[29] Larry M. Bartels, "Political Inequality in Affluent Democracies: The Social Welfare Deficit," CSDI Working Paper No. 5-2017, 47, https://www.vanderbilt.edu/csdi/includes/Working_Paper_5_2017.pdf.

[30] Jacob Hacker and Paul Pierson, *Winner Takes All Politics* (New York: Simon and Schuster, 2010).

[31] Jonathan Hopkin and Kate Alexander Shaw, "Organized Combat or Structural Advantage? The Politics of Inequality and the Winner-Take-All Economy in the United Kingdom," *Politics and Society* 44 (2016): 345–371.

Party, but as an institution organized to help middle and working class workers they have only meager power. Unions matter for lots of reasons. One important effect is to raise wages not only for those in a unionized plant or work place, but through their collective bargaining processes they help raise the wages of non-unionized workers in the same local labor market.[32] In Sweden trade union membership is just over 70 percent of the working population, and through reaching collective agreements unions regulate fair wages, annual leave, insurance, and pensions. They set both national standards and monitor enforcement in workplaces. The gap between incomes is lower and wage rates are flattened out across the course of working lives. German and Swiss trade unions are centrally involved in these two countries' successful apprenticeship and training schemes, maintaining common standards across different firms and ensuring that such workers receive the wage benefits of collective bargaining.

Second, business is increasingly organized and focused or targeted on key points of influence and policymakers.[33] Through contributions to electoral candidates of both parties, and focused lobbying efforts, employers have ensured direct access to policymakers and decisive influence on legislation. Money dominates US election campaigns.[34] Both traditional sectors such as manufacturing and new financial services have deployed their resources astutely;[35] furthermore, both parties have aggressively pursued these funding sources, with Democrats as likely to receive Wall Street largesse as Republicans. A pliant Supreme Court has steadily eroded regulation about the size of contributions to campaigns and the need to disclose a donor's identity. Foundations have played a key role shaping these favorable employer conditions through donations, the provision of model legislation at the state level, and the fostering of intellectual arguments by generously funding think tanks to promote conservative pro-business ideas.[36]

Third, tax rates have been falling since the Economic Recovery Act in 1981, rationalized by supply side logic which declared, with no empirical support, that lower tax rates would in fact generate higher tax revenues because of economic growth. Major subsequent tax reductions acts included the Tax Act (1986), Contract with America-driven changes in the 1990s, and the George W. Bush era reforms in 2001 and 2003. Tax rates have been on a downward path since the Reagan initiative. Seizing on this development, the anti-tax conservative lobbyist Grover Norquist mobilized his Americans

---

[32] Bruce Western and Jake Rosenfeld, "Unions, Norms, and the Rise in US Wage Inequality," *American Sociological Review* 76 (2011): 513–537.

[33] Alexander Hertel-Fernandez, "American Employers as Political Machines," *Journal of Politics* 79 (2017): 105–117.

[34] Robert G. Kaiser, *So Damned Much Money* (New York: Knopf, 2009); Jane Mayer, *Dark Money* (New York: Knopf, 2017).

[35] Nolan McCarty, "The Politics of the Pop: The U.S. Response to the Financial Crisis and the Great Recession," in *Coping with Crisis: Government Reactions to the Great Recession*, ed. Nancy Bermeo and Jonas Pontusson (New York: Russell Sage Foundation, 2012).

[36] Alexander Hertel-Fernandez and Theda Skocpol, "The Koch Network and Republican Party Extremism," *Perspectives on Politics* 14 (2016): 681–699.

for Tax Reform organization, founded in 1985. He persuaded virtually all Republican candidates for national offices to sign a pledge against tax increases. Adroit lobbying in this anti-tax atmosphere has generated numerous important changes in the federal tax code such as "carried interest." Diverting tax benefits into the less visible tax expenditure realm, Suzanne Mettler's "submerged state" has abetted this privileging of high taxpayers' interests.[37] (Unremarkably but contrary to his populist rhetoric, President Trump's tax reforms continued the long-term trend, a modification that may alienate some of his voters.) Assaulting tax revenues reduces the fiscal resources available to the federal government. This shrinkage in government capacity goes hand in hand with the delegation of more powers to private sector actors to deliver public services,[38] and the expansion of responsibilities by states. One consequence of the recent tax bill, though, is to make it considerably more difficult for states to raise tax revenues themselves, by reducing the deductibility of state property and income taxes.

In sum, the long march toward a neoliberalism of lower taxes, a rolling back of federal regulatory powers (including in respect to civil rights laws' enforcement), a more conservative judiciary, and a greater responsiveness to corporate interests initiated in the early 1980s under the Reagan administration set a trajectory largely uninterrupted since that significant shift to the right in American politics began.

RISING INEQUALITY

Third, though there may not be a demonstrable causal link between rising economic inequality and populist election outcomes and the spread of exclusionary ideologies of nationhood, the unaddressed and intensified pattern of income inequality animates post-2008 politics. It fosters a very real sense that government is in the hands of elites who care only for themselves, not "the people."

The well-documented growth in *income inequality* in several advanced democracies including the United States, the United Kingdom, and even Sweden is a grievance-generating mechanism. Hacker and Pierson document how wages stagnated from the 1990s for middle and working class Americans, while the top 1 percent of households raked in a hugely disproportionate amount of salary increases—between 1979 and 2008 they received "36 percent of all gains in household income." If we go more fine-grained within this group, we see that the top 0.1 percent "received over 20 percent of all after-tax income gains between 1979 and 2005, compared with the 13.5 per cent enjoyed by the bottom 60 percent of households."[39] This analysis has been replicated and refined by other scholars, notably French economist Thomas Piketty, who has demonstrated the

---

[37] Suzanne Mettler, *The Submerged State* (Chicago: University of Chicago Press, 2016).

[38] Andrea Louise Campbell and Kimberly J. Morgan, "The Delegated Warfare State," in *Health Politics and Policy*, ed. Jim Morone and Dan Ehlke, 5th ed. (Stamford, CT: Cengage Learning, 2013).

[39] Hacker and Pierson, *Winner Takes All Politics*, 3.

massive returns to capital enjoyed by small segments of US and French society. These trends have intensified since the Great Recession in 2008, as unemployment and home-ownership foreclosures rose, and central bank quantitative- easing measures facilitated a surge in stock market values and returns to the super wealthy.

REDIRECTION AND MISDIRECTION OF SENSES
OF POWERLESSNESS AND GRIEVANCE

Fourth, lack of political responsiveness to all but the privileged in systems of rising inequality has in many regions, with Latin America a partial exception, been at least as associated with right-wing, ethnoculturally-centered populisms as with economically-centered, often left-wing ones. Voters have, for good reason, seen most of the elites shaping government policies as favoring immigration and consequent cultural diversity, and as skeptical if not hostile toward religious and cultural traditionalists. As a result, and as Bartels suggests, political entrepreneurs appear to have frequently succeeded in shifting the focus of many voters on to perceived ethnocultural threats that are often also blamed for economic anxieties. John Sides reports that in the 2016 US election campaign, issues of race, ethnicity, and religion were more salient to voters than in most recent elections, though this pattern represented a culmination of growing trends.[40] White hostility to affirmative action and other race-conscious measures has grown steadily in the United States since the 1980s, with white support for most such programs now standing well below 10 percent.[41] But this focus on the racial dimensions of public policies was whipped up during the Obama presidency in several ways. The Tea Party movement, orchestrated against the Affordable Care Act, was an overwhelmingly white phenomenon that stirred up broader anxieties that "real Americans" were losing out to largely nonwhite undeserving Americans and foreigners.[42] The birther movement championed by candidate Trump had an unsubtle racially framed agenda and target. The level of white hostility to any sort of race-conscious programs soared to the extent that by 2016, close to 50 percent of Trump's voters complained that discrimination against whites in America was greater than that against African Americans. Whether mobilized in stories about disgruntled white rural voters in Wisconsin,[43] Appalachian hillbillies,[44] southern "strangers in their own land,"[45] or

[40] John Sides, "Race, Religion, and Immigration in 2016," *Democracy Fund Voter Study Group*, 2017, https://www.voterstudygroup.org/publications/2016-elections/race-religion-immigration-2016.

[41] Vincent Hutchings, "Change or More of the Same: Evaluating Racial Policy Preferences in the Obama Era," *Public Opinion Quarterly* 73 (2009): 917–942.

[42] Christopher S. Parker and Matthew A. Barreto, *Change They Can't Believe In: The Tea Party and Reactionary Politics in America* (Princeton, NJ: Princeton University Press, 2013).

[43] Kathleen Cramer, *The Politics of Resentment* (Chicago: University of Chicago Press, 2016).

[44] J.D. Vance, *Hillbilly Elegy* (New York: Harpercollins, 2016).

[45] Arlie Hochschild, *Strangers in Their Own Land* (New York: New Press, 2016).

"clueless" white class victims,[46] numerous scholarly and journalistic accounts showed that many Americans blamed their senses of powerlessness and loss of standing not on hostile economic policies but on measures hostile to native-born white Americans. And opinion poll after opinion poll has documented the profound deepening of racial polarization in the American electorate over time,[47] a gulf now almost identical with the partisan polarization that is itself deeply linked to the divides over color-blind (Republican) versus race-conscious (Democratic) policies that drive the politics of racial inequality in America today.[48]

PERSISTENT DISCRIMINATION LIMITING THE ECONOMIC RESOURCES OF ETHNOCULTURAL MINORITIES

This channeling of senses of political and economic displacement into ethnocultural grievances has fostered a fifth contributor to the current appeal of right-wing populism. Even as mounting economic inequalities have heightened the distance between the most advantaged, usually white in America, and the least advantaged, usually nonwhite, *compensatory schemes* such as affirmative action or antidiscrimination in labor or housing markets have been eroded. Hidden beneath the struggle over populist antagonism to policies perceived to benefit African Americans or other nonwhite groups in the United States are the persistence of multiple forms of discrimination against people of color in many of America's key markets, including housing, employment and voting. Scholars employing experimental methods or audit studies continue to expose robust and persistent patterns of discrimination toward African Americans and Latinos in employment and housing markets, in addition to the long-standing inequalities in such areas as household wealth, income, and health. Robust audit and experimental studies demonstrate for instance the difficulties facing job seekers with a criminal record.[49] These obstacles are widespread for minority citizens.

An experiment to test the responses of 5,300 local bureaucrats toward queries about voting rules in the United States found "causally identified evidence of bias" in how

---

[46] Joan Williams, *White Working Class* (Cambridge, MA: Harvard Business Review Press, 2017).

[47] Michael Tesler, *Most Racial, Post Racial* (Chicago: University of Chicago Press, 2016); Lawrence D. Bobo, "Racism in Trump's America: Reflections on Culture, Sociology, and the 2016 US Presidential Election," *British Journal of Sociology* 68 (2017): 87–104.

[48] King and Smith, *Still a House Divided*; Desmond King and Rogers M. Smith, "The Last Stand? *Shelby County v. Holder*, White Political Power, and America's Racial Policy Alliances," *Du Bois Review* 13 (2016): 25–44; Desmond King and Rogers M. Smith, "A New Era for Old Racial Policy Alliances: The Trump Coalition," Paper presented at the annual meetings of the APSA, San Francisco, 2017.

[49] Devah Pager, *Marked: Race, Crime and Finding Work in an Era of Mass Incarceration* (Chicago: University of Chicago Press, 2007); Devah Pager and Hana Shepherd, "The Sociology of Discrimination: Racial Discrimination in Employment, Housing, Credit and Consumer Markets," *Annual Review of Sociology* 34 (2008): 181–209.

they responded to Latino and non-Latino citizens. This bias was exposed when Latinos compared with non-Latinos wrote local voting officials with questions about upcoming elections. Not only were Latino questioners 5 percent less likely to get a response compared with non-Latino emailers, but any reply provided was "less likely to convey accurate information about ID requirements."[50] Such discretionary behavior by street-level bureaucrats is hardly limited to officials responding about voting rules. Researchers unearthed discriminatory patterns among administrators of a major welfare program, TANF, including higher sanction rates toward nonwhite recipients.[51] In nations such as the United States, where political leaders are far more responsive to the wealthy than to working class and poor populations, policies that heighten the economic hardships of already less advantaged communities, often ethnic and racial minorities, mean that those groups have even fewer weapons to defend their interests against hostile right-wing movements. Because right-wing populists tie their appeal to racial themes—implicitly or explicitly—they have a larger constituency to mobilize. Right-wing populists have benefitted immensely from the turn against globalization, which has gathered momentum since the Great Recession of 2008. Since global trade and integration is a key neoliberal imperative, it has been much harder for mainstream conservative politicians to criticize the harmful effects of globalization on jobs and wages. This has opened an opportunity for populists (left-wing in the Sanders mode too). They have seized it.

WEAKENING THE RIGHT TO VOTE, ESPECIALLY
FOR ETHNOCULTURAL MINORITIES

That is all the more true in the United States because, sixth, voting rights there have been under sustained pressure since 2000, particularly for less wealthy and nonwhite Americans who are likely Democratic voters. In one sense this is remarkable given the historical struggles to achieve voting rights;[52] on the other hand the very scale of those historical struggles conveys the fragility and vulnerability of many protections for voting rights. The decision in 2016 of Virginia's governor, Terry McAuliffe, to end the ban on former felons' voting rights (benefitting close to 200,000 ex-offenders) is a rare instance of enhancing rather than narrowing voter rights.

At least three issues have weighed heavily on these constitutional protections. Since the presidential election of 2000, many state legislatures controlled by Republicans have engaged in systematic efforts to limit poor and minority voters' access to registration and voting. Photo ID laws have been enacted, and although many of these have been

[50] Ariel R. White, Noah L. Nathan, and Julie K. Faller, "What Do I Need to Vote? Bureaucratic Discretion and Discrimination by Local Election Officials," *American Political Science Review* 109 (2015): 129, 130.
[51] Lael R. Keiser, Peter R. Mueser, and Seung-Whan Choi, "Race, Bureaucratic Discretion, and the Implementation of Welfare Reform," *American Journal of Political Science* 48 (2004): 314–327.
[52] Alexander Keyssar, *The Right to Vote* (New York: Knopf, 2000).

challenged in the courts, the overall impact has been to reduce the number of voters in several states. Photo ID requirements exclude potential voters who lack a driver's license and previous forms of acceptable identification—such as some government IDs without photos—have been excluded from the list of permissible IDs. States have shortened the period for postal voting, cut the hours of opening on voting day, and ended or reduced the number of early voting days. All these measures hit poor voters hardest. Complementing these state restrictions to voting rights is the Supreme Court's momentous decision in 2013, *Shelby County v. Holder*, significantly rolling back the oversight measures enshrined in the Voting Rights Act of 1965.[53] The 1965 Act identified a group of counties and states that were prohibited from making any further changes to their electoral laws without permission from the US Department of Justice or a federal appellate judge. Those identified included some of the most notorious abusers of African-American voting rights. Despite evidence that issues of voter suppression and county level discrimination persists, the Court ruled by 5-4 that it was no longer appropriate to require such executive or judicial scrutiny, and indeed that requiring it was unconstitutional. Another aspect of the voting system that poses significant constitutional issues is the electoral college used to elect presidents.[54] The system gained salience in the 2000 *Bush v. Gore* election when inconclusive results led to a Supreme Court ruling in favor of George W. Bush despite evidence that the popular vote favored Gore and that interference with voting rolls compilation in Florida undercounted the Democrat's support. In 2016 the gap between the electoral college vote achieved by the Republican and Democratic candidates and the national popular vote was vast, close to 3 million votes. Finally, as noted above the deregulation of both the size of contributions during the election campaign and the disclosure of donor identity have permitted extravagant sums of money to pour into presidential and congressional campaigns nationally and in individual states. So-called Super PACs, groups supposedly eschewing coordination with individual candidate's campaigns, can flood contested elections with focused advertisements and funding for their preferred candidate.

OPPOSITION TO JUDICIAL INDEPENDENCE IN THE SERVICE OF RIGHTS OF THE LESS ADVANTAGED

In the eyes of many right-wing populists in America and elsewhere, judges who advance some version of modern "transformative constitutionalism," or indeed the rights of immigrants, women, racial, ethnic, and cultural minorities, and the poor in any fashion, are serving the values of cosmopolitan cultural and economic elites, not of the ordinary people of their countries. Even though the US Supreme Court has had a majority

---

[53] King and Smith, "The Last Stand?."

[54] George C. Edwards, *Why the Electoral College Is Bad for America* (New Haven, CT: Yale University Press, 2004).

of Republican appointees since the early 1970s, and even though it has often ruled in favor of powerful wealthy interests as in its campaign finance decisions, still its occasional receptivity to international law and human rights doctrines, and its rulings in favor of LGBTQ rights, abortion, separation of church and state, rights of accused persons, takings of property without compensation, and much more, have made it a target of conservative populist attacks, reviving a long-standing pattern in American history.[55] To be sure, as Jan-Werner Müller and others have argued, conservative populists are not necessarily anti-judiciary or anti-constitutionalist.[56] But as in Poland and Hungary, they do insist that courts must be under their control, and that constitutions be interpreted in ways that support their agenda, which they equate with what is genuinely good and virtuous. They are often hostile, as President Trump clearly is, to judges who are instead genuinely independent, and to constitutions, like many of those enacted in the wave of new constitutions during the 1990s and early 2000s, that advance what they regard as anti-populist elite values. Many populist leaders feel their mandate from "the people" makes it legitimate for them to compel courts to conform to their preferred policies, as well as to insure that courts do not interfere with the sometimes dubiously conducted elections that they claim give them title to power.

Constitutional Crisis?

From a small-"d" democratic perspective, some might ask, what's wrong with that? On the analysis here, populists on the Right as well as the Left are responding, however sometimes misguidedly, to authentic senses of political and economic disempowerment and grievance. And in constitutional democracies, courts and the constitutions they interpret ultimately derive their authority from "the people." Why should not populist leaders and parties ensure that courts and constitutions actually serve what they regard as the people's rightful will, interests, and values?

Yet true as those points are, it also cannot be forgotten that in *constitutional* democracies, courts are supposed to uphold the rule of law to check abuses by authoritarian regimes—of which populist nationalist ones are the most rapidly spreading and dangerous current forms. Courts are, of course, imperfect governing institutions at best. But they are also ubiquitous, and for good reasons. They have gained legitimacy as bodies with governing authority in many societies over many centuries in part because of the conscientious efforts of many judges to conform to some degree to the norms of fairness

---

[55] Ed Kilgore, "Trump and the Right-Wing Populist Tradition of Judge-Bashing," *New York Magazine*, February 12, 2017, http://nymag.com/daily/intelligencer/2017/02/trump-and-the-right-wing-populist-tradition-of-judge-bashing.html; Eric A. Posner, "Liberal Internationalism and the Populist Backlash," University of Chicago, Public Law Working Paper No. 606, January 11, 2017, https://ssrn.com/abstract=2898357 or http://dx.doi.org/10.2139/ssrn.2898357.

[56] Müller, *What Is Populism?*, 60–63.

and consistency that have always been demanded of them.[57] Whenever that hard-won legitimacy is used to rationalize authoritarian and discriminatory actions that are in fact unfair, indeed often brutal, we lose something of great value in modern political life. The rise of right-wing populist nationalisms that translate understandable grievances into discriminatory scapegoating and policies that only augment existing systems of economic privilege, if extended through the capture of courts and constitutions in ways that make them instruments of the same agendas, thus does indeed pose the danger of a crisis for constitutional democracy in the modern world. It does so as a crucial symptom of an even deeper crisis of humane governance that threatens to make the twenty-first century a sobering rebuke to all who have wanted to believe in the inevitability of human progress. It is vital to attend to the grievances that drive modern populist nationalisms, in the United States and in many other parts of the world. But it is equally vital to attend to the threats those often authoritarian nationalisms can pose to the non-arbitrary rule of law and the concerns for human rights, especially for those long disadvantaged, that are central to constitutional democracy at its best.

---

[57] See Ezequiel A. Gonzalez-Ocantos, *Shifting Legal Visions: Judicial Change and Human Rights Trials in Latin America* (New York: Cambridge University Press, 2016), for a recent example from Latin American judges.

27 Inherent Instability
Immigration and Constitutional Democracies
T. Alexander Aleinikoff*

IN THIS CHAPTER, I adopt an understanding of a constitutional democracy as a bounded polity of equal citizens who choose leaders through free and fair elections and whose rights enshrined in a fundamental law are protected by an independent judiciary. On this account, immigration is a destabilizing force. The arrival of large numbers of non-citizens of the state undercuts the idea of a bounded polity; the residence of noncitizens challenges ideas of equality of those persons residing within state territory and subject to the laws of the state; enforcement measures undertaken to preserve state territorial and membership boundaries run up against fundamental values upon which constitutional democracies purport to be founded.

The conceptual challenge of immigration is ever-present. In times of constitutional crises, immigrants may be blamed for the ills of society that require measures that threaten fundamental democratic and constitutional norms, and they may be the first victims of such measures. But even in healthy constitutional democracies, migrants remain problematically positioned—in but not of the polity. The ambiguity of their status can open up profound and vituperative debates within the bounds of the normal politics of the

* This chapter has benefitted from the comments of the volume editors, David Abraham, and Linda Bosniak, and the research assistance of Emmanuel Guerisoli.

state. Anti-immigrant "populist" movements, and the politicians who fan the flames for electoral gain, may arise in both good times and bad.

In this chapter, I do not argue that immigration and controversies about immigration occasion or significantly contribute to constitutional crises. The adoption of intolerance toward immigrants in a democracy is more likely to be a symptom than a cause of crisis. So too such policies may also be the result of everyday politics, as democracies define and redefine understandings of membership and the benefits that attach thereto. In either case, the fact that immigrants are excluded from electoral politics weakens their ability to prevent harsh policies undertaken in the name of the demos. I will conclude by suggesting that immigration, somewhat paradoxically, has the potential for bringing about transformative change in constitutional democracies.

The Impact of Immigration on the State-Territory-Citizen Construct

Constitutional law scholarship tends to begin with an already existing state. Exactly how the constitutional order itself was constituted is rarely examined (except when the "original meaning" of a constitution is consulted as an interpretive strategy). The legitimacy of the order and its founding documents is not generally questioned, even though serious issues may arise as to the lawfulness of claims to state territory, the authority of the "founders" to act on behalf of persons included within the new order, and the exclusion of (often many) persons subject to the authority of the new order from decision-making about the establishment and scope of that order. The past is not prologue; constitutional time begins day one year one.

This unexamined hermetically sealed conceptual constitutionalism has obvious consequences for nonmembers. Constitutional democracies are understood to have been created for (and sometimes, by) a demos—a citizenry. There is generally assumed to be congruence between the two. As stated most boldly by the US Supreme Court: "Citizenship in this Nation is a part of a cooperative affair. Its citizenry is the country, and the country is its citizenry."[1] Noncitizens are, by definition, outside the constitutional compact and the demos. "We" founded a state—a democratic constitutional order—for "ourselves," bestowing on (most of) "us" the title of citizen. Such orders are defended in normatively appealing terms—popular sovereignty, the equality of citizens, fundamental rights—in which nonmembers generally figure not at all.

I am positing the state-territory-citizen construct as an ideal type. To be sure, as I discuss below, constitutional democracies often recognize certain rights on behalf of resident nonmembers, but such recognition, I will argue, represents an accommodation, a deviation from the traditional conceptual paradigm to which appeal always remains available.

---

[1] Afroyim v. Rusk, 387 U.S. 253, 268 (1967).

In the discussion that follows, I will identity a number of ways in which immigration can both put pressure on and strengthen the traditional paradigm.

At the Founding

As just noted, the legitimacy of constitutional democracies is established self-referentially. A state exists and exercises sovereignty over a territory and people because it has called itself into being. There may well be rules for establishing statehood (set down by some form of constituent assembly), but there is nothing prior to which appeal can be made to legitimate those rules. Thus, for example, the US Constitution provides its own rule for when it would be deemed ratified and the United States established as a state,[2] but no prior legal authority established that rule or, indeed, established who had the authority to make that rule.

Noncitizens lay bare the constitutional bootstrap. By what right, they may be seen as asserting, does a state purport to claim a piece of the earth and exclude all others from it? Surely the answer "because we say so" is not one that those excluded should be expected to respect. This challenge applies to all assertions of territorial sovereignty, but it is particularly poignant when applied to constitutional democracies—because then the answer comes back, "we the people, in an act of self-realizing popular sovereignty, do ordain . . ." It is one thing for a king to define his (inferior) subjects; it is quite another for a group of free and equal people to tell other human beings that they are something less. The construction of a demos, it turns out, is nasty work.

Who Can Participate?

Democratic theory generally assumes that persons should have the right to participate (directly or indirectly) in the making of the rules that rule them. This is a norm based on citizenship, not territorial location: resident noncitizens are not understood to have the right to vote, while citizens outside the country are generally subject to the authority of the home state and usually have some ability to participate in elections inside the country. Noncitizens put significant pressure on this widely held presupposition of constitutional democracies. Those inside the state are plainly subject to state power (tax, regulatory, criminal laws). It is sometimes asserted that noncitizens are not enough imbued with the "national culture" or knowledge of the political system of the state to make extension of the franchise to them sensible. But this is obviously questionable as an empirical matter

---

[2] Art. VII: "The Ratification of the Conventions of nine States, shall be sufficient for the Establishment of this Constitution between the States so ratifying the Same." More than four score years later a constitutional rule on citizenship was established.

(and as compared to the actual degree of knowledge possessed by many citizens), and is increasingly unpersuasive for long-term noncitizen residents.[3] National mythologies can be invoked—for example, that citizens "pledge to each other our Lives, our Fortunes, and our sacred Honor"[4]—to suggest something unique that citizens and only citizens share, but these are hard to sustain in large and diverse constitutional democracies (particularly where the children of recently arrived nonmembers are citizens at birth and where the descendants of those who were not present at the founding are full citizens).

Outside the territory of the state matters do not necessarily get easier. In today's world many constitutional democracies influence events and affect the lives of persons regionally and around the globe (bombs, greenhouse gases, trade policies, and much more). Political theorists have suggested an "all affected" test for political rights that would expand electorates beyond national boundaries.[5]

Values Intrinsic to the (Particular) Constitutional Order

Even if there were to be general agreement that constitutions are written by and for citizens and that noncitizens have no role to play or rights to assert, particular constitutional democracies may decide that noncitizens should be afforded constitutional protections. Thus, provisions in many national constitutions either expressly or implicitly apply to noncitizens as well as citizens.[6] Such norms may reflect a state's self-conception at a deep level—for example, that the constitution embodies human rights norms applicable to all persons, or that a country is a "nation of immigrants" and should extend rights to "citizens-in waiting."[7] Whatever the source of these commitments, they render the traditional paradigm an inadequate description of many constitutional democracies.

Workers or Human Beings?

In theory, constitutional democracies run their economies by and for their citizens; in practice, elites often have the power to dominate electoral and legislative processes to ensure continued rewards. On either account, it is fully expected that the polity will place the interests of members first in considering economic and social policy, both at home and abroad. But constitutional democracies are not autarkies; they are self-contained

---

[3] This is hardly a new argument. See Gerald M. Rosberg, "Aliens and Equal Protection: Why Not the Right to Vote?," *Michigan Law Review* 75 (1977): 1092–1136.

[4] U.S. Declaration of Independence.

[5] Discussed in Gustaf Arrhenius, "The Boundary Problem in Democratic Theory," in *Democracy Unbound: Basic Explorations I*, ed. Terman Folke (Stockholm: Stockholms Universitet, 2005), 14–29. Arash Abizadeh: "On the Demos and Its Kin: Nationalism, Democracy, and the Boundary Problem," *American Political Science Review* 106 (2012): 867–882.

[6] Examples are discussed below.

[7] Hiroshi Motomura, *Americans in Waiting: The Lost Story of Immigration and Citizenship in the United States* (New York: Oxford University Press, 2007).

neither as to the workforce nor the production and distribution of goods. In most such states, noncitizen workers are useful—even essential—to the healthy functioning of the economy and the welfare of citizens. This need not be a challenge to the state-territory-citizenry paradigm: members could decide, based on their own interests, whom they would like to admit and on what terms. Outsiders could accept or not as they choose, but they could assert no rights. But, in the oft-quoted words of Max Frisch, "We asked for workers and human beings came." These (noncitizen) human beings make claims that states are either obligated to respect due to constitutional norms or often choose to respect as a matter of the legal and political culture. It is thus not surprising that workers' rights are regularly understood to extend to resident noncitizens in constitutional democracies.[8]

Similarly, in most constitutional democracies settled immigrants are eligible for welfare state programs (including social security and health benefits, and free public education). These may be available either as a matter of constitutional right or through the discretion of the government. It is not easy to square these constitutional and legislative commitments with a tight interpretation of the traditional paradigm.

Refugees

Against the idea of the plenary authority of a constitutional democracy to regulate state borders and make admission decisions, one class of would-be entrants presses a particularly powerful normative claim: refugees. The moral strength of that claim is precisely a function of a world of states. As virtually all the territory of earth has been state-claimed, refugees—forced out of their home state—can seek safety only within the territory of another state. This is not to say that today all those seeking rescue are being adequately welcomed, not by a long shot. But the normative claim is widely understood even if it is not as widely respected.

HOW MIGRATION STRENGTHENS THE STATE-TERRITORY-CITIZEN CONSTRUCT

The preceding discussion suggested several bases upon which a claim by noncitizens for inclusion might be recognized. But migration can give rise to arguments that cut in precisely the opposite direction—supporting exclusionary policies to preserve principles deemed fundamental to constitutional democracies.

To preserve the state-territory-citizen construct, constitutional democracies need some degree of closure; they need to know the metes and bounds of their domain and

---

[8] E.g., Constitution of the Argentine Nation, Arts. 14 & 14bis; Constitution of the Italian Republic, Arts. 35–38 (using the word "workers" in contrast to other provisions that guarantee rights to "citizens"); Preamble to the [French] Constitution of 27 October 1946, paras. 5–8.

the people living thereon. Importantly, closure does not necessarily entail enforced borders: in a world of low migration, neither the state nor the make-up of its citizenry is likely to be deemed to be at risk by the arrival of noncitizens. But quantitative and qualitative impacts arising from migration may be perceived as creating threats to constitutional democracies, in both conceptual and practical terms, which in turn call for measures to reinforce the boundaries of both the paradigm and the state. In this way, it is migration—not the inherent nature of a state—that creates borders[9] and supports the exclusion of noncitizens.

Sometimes the very existence of the state is said to be at risk. It is just this reasoning that lay behind the nineteenth century cases in which the US Supreme Court affirmed Congress's "plenary power" to regulate immigration. In upholding the Chinese Exclusion laws, the Court stated:

> That the government of the United States . . . can exclude aliens from its territories is a proposition which we do not think open to controversy. Jurisdiction over its own territory to that extent is an incident of every independent nation. It is a part of its independence. If it could not exclude aliens, it would be to that extent subject to the control of another power.[10]

The Court has never backed away from these words, and I have located no dissenting views in the decisions of courts in other constitutional democracies.[11]

At a more symbolic but perhaps no less powerful level, immigration enforcement is justified in the name of preserving the "rule of law"—again, a core value of the traditional paradigm. To tolerate the entry of undocumented migrants or to fail to deport noncitizens with orders of removal is to undermine respect for the law usually thought necessary for the proper functioning of a constitutional democracy.

Perceived threats to the existence of the state or respect for the rule of law go to the state-territory aspects of the traditional paradigm. Migration may also be seen as a threat to the demographic constitution of the citizenry. The demos may have racial, religious,

---

[9] Nicholas De Genova, "Citizenship's Shadow: Obscene Inclusion, Abject Belonging, or the Regularities of Migrant 'Irregularity,'" in *Within and beyond Citizenship: Borders, Membership and Belonging*, ed. Roberto G. Gonzales and Nando Sigona (New York: Routledge, 2017), 17–35 ("without migrants, there would be no borders").

This is not always so: the United States existed as a constitutional democracy without much border enforcement until the end of the nineteenth century.

[10] Chae Chan Ping v. United States [The Chinese Exclusion Case], 130 U.S. 581 (1889).

[11] As David Abraham has noted, "[p]rinciples of sovereignty and nationhood were not easily or quickly established, and they will not be displaced or overcome anytime soon. . . . Notwithstanding the growth of a certain amount of universalism and humanitarianism in international law . . . immigration laws remain intensely sovereigntist." David Abraham, "Law and Migration: Many Constants, Few Changes," in *Migration Theory: Talking across Disciplines*, ed. Caroline Brettell and James Frank Hollifield, 3rd ed. (New York: Routledge, 2014), 292, 289, 305.

ethnic, or social characteristics deemed fundamental to their self-conception and the preservation of which is the basis of national policy. The National Origin Quota System adopted by the United States in the 1920s is a textbook example, as were the "White Australia" policies that held sway until the middle of the twentieth century. More recently, Hungarian anti-immigrant policies have been based primarily on ethnic and religious grounds,[12] and recent election results in Austria and in the UK on Brexit turned largely on immigration issues. The goal of maintaining Israel as a "Jewish state" is at the core of its immigration and citizenship policies.

A (Provisional) Constitutional Settlement

In the preceding section, I argued that the state-territory-citizen construct is open to serious claims for inclusion—claims that can be made in terms fully consistent with the postulates of the construct. At the same time, the construct can yield reasons for the power of democracies to exclude and distinguish.

Constitutional democracies tend to find ways—through constitutional provisions, court decisions, and state policies—to mediate these conflicting claims. The settlement arrived at by most constitutional democracies has been felicitously described by Linda Bosniak as "hard on the outside, soft on the inside."[13] That is, initial decisions as to whom and how many may enter a state are left to state discretion; but once admitted, migrants will generally benefit from constitutional and legal protections afforded to citizens.[14] This settlement gives the citizenry pretty firm command over the shape of the demos; as if the nation were a club, existing members decide which new members will be invited to join (except that they are generally unable to control births to noncitizens, who in many constitutional democracies will acquire full membership at birth). But constitutional norms and culture will then emphasize fair and equal treatment for those admitted.

In the US context, the courts have put weight on the fact that most constitutional rights are guaranteed to "persons" not "citizens."[15] This reading guarantees immigrants

---

[12] Viktor Orbán: "The most important danger is the debate between globalists and nations... Europe has decided that it can step into a post-Christian and post-nation world." Radoslav Tomek, "Immigration Will Dominate Hungary's 2018 Elections, Orban Says," *Bloomberg*, November 9, 2017, https://www.bloomberg.com/news/articles/2017-11-09/immigration-will-dominate-hungary-s-2018-elections-orban-says.

[13] Linda Bosniak, *The Citizen and the Alien: Dilemmas of Contemporary Membership* (Princeton, NJ: Princeton University Press, 2006), 34–35.

[14] Unauthorized arrivals destabilize the approach. On the one hand, they have not been invited to enter; on the other, they are human beings. The results here have been mixed. In the United States, for example, the Supreme Court has ruled that states may not exclude undocumented children from public schools. Plyler v. Doe, 457 U.S. 202 (1982). But the ineligibility of undocumented adults to participate in state programs has not been successfully challenged.

[15] See Alexander Bickel, "Citizenship in the American Constitution," *Arizona Law Review* 15 (1973): 369, 369. "Remarkably enough . . . the concept of citizenship plays only the most minimal role in the American constitutional scheme."

substantive rights as well as the protection of the general antidiscrimination norm in the Fourteenth Amendment. Similar interpretations are found in other constitutional democracies. For example, the South African Supreme Court has ruled that permanent resident aliens who have applied for old-age and child-support grants are protected by a constitutional provision guaranteeing "[e]veryone" the right to social assistance.[16]

These protections reflect political principles that are fundamental to liberal democracies: "arbitrary" distinctions cannot justify differential and discriminatory treatment. Arguably, nonmembership might—by definition—be deemed a non-arbitrary distinction.[17] But the crucial question is: Non-arbitrary in relation to what? For most purposes, most courts in most constitutional democracies have concluded that nonmembership is not an adequate ground for denying fundamental rights (other than political rights) enjoyed by citizens of that state.[18]

The pro-migrant aspects of the settlement are counter-balanced by a strong reading of the immigration power—one that permits an interpretation of the border as penetrating to the interior.[19] Thus enforcement officers operate inside the state as well as at its borders, and resident aliens may be deported on grounds of public safety and public policy. In the United States, the federal immigration power is understood to permit federal laws that render immigrants ineligible for benefits, even if similar state laws are condemned by the Fourteenth Amendment.[20] And norms of equality generally do not apply to migrant voting, or the holding of political office, at the national level.

The various norms variously applied do not always supply a coherent picture, and there is adequate space for recalibration of the settlement in times of normal politics. In times of constitutional crisis, the settlement (and migrants) could be fully at risk.

---

[16] Khosa and Others v Minister of Social Development and Others, Mahlaule and Another v Minister of Social Development (CCT 13/03, CCT 12/03) [2004] ZACC 11; 2004 (6) SA 505 (CC); 2004 (6) BCLR 569 (CC) (4 March 2004). See also, e.g., Constitution of Mexico, Art. 1 ("every person" is guaranteed the rights provided in the Constitution; provisions on political rights apply to "citizens").

[17] Sugarman v. Dougall, 413 U.S. 634, 651 (1973) (Rehnquist, C.J., dissenting): "[T]he Constitution itself recognizes a basic difference between citizens and aliens. That distinction is constitutionally important in no less than 11 instances in a political document noted for its brevity."

[18] France: E.g., Conseil Constitutionnel, décision n° 93-325 du 13 août 1993 (Constitutional council Decision N 93-325 August 13, 1993)—relying on the Constitution's incorporation of Article 16 of the 1789 Declaration of the Rights of Man and of the Citizen; Italy: Sentenza della Corte di Cassazione, Sezioni unite civili, n. 2515 del 21 febbraio 2002 ("citizens of a country other than the EU ones do not only enjoy the fundamental human rights as provided for by national law, international conventions and common principles of international law, but also the principle of equal treatment as Italian citizens with respect to judicial guarantees and due process of law").

[19] I thank Linda Bosniak for pressing this point in comments on a previous draft.

[20] Compare Mathews v. Diaz, 426 U.S. 67 (1976), with Graham v. Richardson, 403 U.S. 365 (1971).

The Current State of Play

The constitutional settlement just described holds when threat levels are perceived as low. It is interesting that the US Supreme Court declared aliens a "discrete and insular minority" meriting special judicial protection when the percentage of foreign-born persons in the United States was at an historic low.[21] But the challenges that immigration poses never disappear; at best they can be held in abeyance. They cannot disappear because they are a product of the state-territory-citizen construct.

When threat levels are perceived to rise, the strength of the normative claims for inclusion declines and demands for vigorous action against (always latent) threats come to the fore. The histories of many constitutional democracies reveal disturbing episodes of discrimination, repression, and forced removal. We are now in the midst of one of those historical moments. Political actors and parties, with an eye to electoral gain, have been effective in raising the threat level by characterizing migration as a clear and present danger to the physical, economic, and political survival of the state.

THE "CRISIS" OF IMMIGRATION

Appeals to a purported "immigration crisis" are used to justify harsh anti-immigrant policies in constitutional democracies. These claims of crisis should not be mistaken for evidence of a "constitutional crisis" (although states in crisis may be more likely to adopt harsh policies). Rather, such appeals are usually based on premises, and made with arguments, compatible with existing constitutional understandings and arrangements. Their ability to persuade are in part a function of their consonance with the state-territory-citizen construct.

Flipping Normative Claims for Inclusion

Trump's "America First" slogan (originally invoked by pre-World War II nativists) says it all pretty clearly. It finds echoes in other right-wing party platforms. Geert Wilder's Party for Freedom stated in its 2016 election literature that "instead of financing the entire world and people we don't want here, we'll spend the money on ordinary Dutch citizens."[22] On this line of reasoning, in democracies the demos means something and it means something special. Preferring citizens is what states should be about. The claims to common ownership of the earth's land, to free movement, to rights to participate in elections of states in which one is not a member, have little or no normative weight—and certainly no historical practice to support it. Even the Refugee Convention includes no

---

[21] Graham v. Richardson. In 1970, the foreign-born totaled 4.7 percent of the population of the United States.

[22] "Preliminary Election Program PVV 2017-2021," *Geert Wilders' Weblog*, August 26, 2016, https://www.geertwilders.nl/index.php/94-english/2007-preliminary-election-program-pvv-2017-2021.

right to enter another state to claim asylum; it simply protects against return to a state where one would face a risk of persecution.[23] For populists, there is no engagement with the normative claims of noncitizens. It is a stiff arm to the face of nonmembers (who are free to return to their home state where they can pursue self-governance).

Securitization

Movements of large numbers of migrants are regularly described in cataclysmic terms—as a "flood," an "invasion." Occasionally in the modern era, there is a claim that migrants are being sent by home states to destabilize receiving states. During the Mariel boatlift of 1980, it was asserted that Castro was emptying his prisons, sending criminals amidst the refugees. Donald Trump's campaign statements on immigration echoed these views in a particularly ugly way: "When Mexico sends its people, they're not sending their best. . . . They're sending people that have lots of problems, and they're bringing those problems with us. They're bringing drugs. They're bringing crime. They're rapists."[24] As president, he has (incorrectly) stated that the US diversity visa program permits foreign states to "give us their worst people."[25] Populist xenophobic parties in Italy and Germany have supported a total stop to refugee and migrant flows that they see as disguised foreign invasions.[26]

But the threat today is more likely to be perceived as arising from nonstate actors—terrorist groups, smugglers, and traffickers, and transnational criminal organizations—as well as from migrants themselves (who enter states without authorization). Politicians in constitutional democracies have repeatedly asserted that the very existence of the nation is at stake if borders cannot be better enforced. Donald Trump has repeatedly stated that a nation that does not enforce its borders will cease to be a nation.[27] In France, National Front presidential candidate, Marine Le Pen, has declared: "At some point in the 2000s, migrants and their children—not all, but a large majority— declared war on France. . . . They have intimidated and threatened France via a series of anti-French and terrorist

---

[23] Claims by refugees for protection are undermined by characterizing applicants as economic migrants who are abusing the asylum system.

[24] "Donald Trump Announces a Presidential Bid," *Washington Post*, June 16, 2015, https://www.washingtonpost.com/news/post-politics/wp/2015/06/16/full-text-donald-trump-announces-a-presidential-bid/?utm_term=.e040664cc5b8.

[25] Miriam Valverde, "Pick Them from a Bin? Donald Trump Mischaracterizes Diversity Visa Lottery," *Politifact*, December 20, 2017, http://www.politifact.com/truth-o-meter/statements/2017/dec/20/donald-trump/pick-them-bin-donald-trump-mischaracterizes-divers/.

[26] Joey Millar, "Milan 'CONTROLLED' by Migrants after 'INVASION' Claims Lega Nord Leader," *Express* (UK), August 18, 2016, https://www.express.co.uk/news/world/701638/milan-lega-nord-migrants-control-invasion-Matteo-Salvini; Riham Alkousaa, "Germany's Far Right AfD Calls for Repatriation of Syrian Refugees," *Reuters*, November 9, 2017, https://www.reuters.com/article/us-europe-migrants-germany-syria/germanys-far-right-afd-calls-for-repatriation-of-syrian-refugees-idUSKBN1D92QI.

[27] Donald Trump: "A nation without borders is not a nation." (December 18, 2017.)

attacks. Civil war is no longer a dream, but a real possibility."[28] Populist movements have called for—and those in power have implemented—a wide array of policies and practices, from walls and fences at borders to interdiction and "pushbacks" of migrants, as well as enhanced domestic security operations within states.

Demography as Destiny

Many constitutional democracies have witnessed a substantial increase in foreign-born populations in recent years. In the United States, the percentage of foreign-born residents (14 percent) is approaching levels not seen since the 1920s, when the National Origin Quota system was adopted. In Sweden and Austria, the percentage is above 18 percent; in Germany, 15 percent; and in France, the United Kingdom, and Spain it is over 12 percent. It is not clear what the "tipping point" is for generating populist reaction to demographic change, but there are now strong right-wing movements in all these countries seeking new restrictions on immigration.[29] The motivations are a mixture of racial, religious, ethnic, and economic concerns that may best be expressed in terms of "this is not our country anymore."[30] This is a threat to the demos' self-conception, and it sparks profound anxiety. The population groups that have seen themselves as core to the cultural and demographic definition of "the people" of the state believe that the ground underneath them is shifting. The metaphor is intentional: the demographic changes are perceived as destabilizing

---

[28] Romina McGuinness, "Le Pen Says Uncontrolled Immigration Has Pushed France to the Brink of "CIVIL WAR," *Express* (UK), March 14, 2017, https://www.express.co.uk/news/world/778995/marine-le-pen-french-election-president-civil-war-immigration. See also Uri Friedman, "'We Don't Like Islamic Invasion': The Leader of Germany's Rising Right Speaks Out," *The Atlantic*, October 2, 2017, https://www.theatlantic.com/international/archive/2017/10/gauland-afd-germany/541530/.

[29] The Freedom Party of Austria—now a part of the governing coalition—has called for the end of all immigration to Austria. The platform of the Netherland's Party for Freedom proposes to "[d]e-islamize the Netherlands" with the following policies:

- Zero asylum seekers and no immigrants anymore from Islamic countries: close the borders
- Withdraw all asylum residence permits which have already been granted for specific periods, close the asylum centers
- No Islamic headscarves in public functions
- Prohibition of other Islamic expressions which violate public order—Preventive detention of radical Muslims

Geert Wilders, "Preliminary Election Program."

[30] Orbán: "The question is whether the character of European nations will be determined by the same spirit, civilisation, culture and mentality as in our parents' and grandparents' time, or by something completely different." And: "We want to preserve the foundations of Europe. We do not want parallel societies, we do not want population exchanges, and we do not want to replace Christian civilisation with a different kind." Nicole Stinson, "'Europe Is Facing a BATTLEFIELD of Migration' Hungarian Prime Minister Viktor Orbán Claims," *Express* (UK), April 17, 2017, https://www.express.co.uk/news/world/792750/Europe-migration-battlefield-Hungary-prime-minister-Viktor-Orban-European-Union.

the state. Plainly such concerns lay at the foundation of the "leave" movement in Britain and support the new attacks on "chain migration" in the United States.[31]

Economic Considerations

Changing the size and characteristics of the supply of labor will affect economic conditions in a country. The size of the labor force will be affected by births, deaths, and migration (including births to migrants). In many constitutional democracies, migration is a significant factor in overall population growth (given low birth rates), and the foreign-born constitute a sizeable proportion of the labor force (20 percent in Canada, 17 percent in the United States, 12 percent in the United Kingdom, 10 percent in Germany, Italy, Denmark, Belgium, and South Africa[32]). The consensus view is that migration, on balance, contributes to economic growth, and that owners of capital and consumers are likely to benefit.[33] At the same time, specific sectors of the labor market are likely to be adversely affected, particularly low wage workers facing job competition from immigrant workers.

Politicians and political movements may overstate the impact of migration on domestic employment and wrongly claim that immigration is a primary cause of dimming prospects for native workers. For example, the anti-immigrant rhetoric of the Trump campaign is said to have appealed to "Rust Belt" workers despite the fact that there was no evidence that migration is a cause of reduced employment in the US mining sector.[34] But the demonstration of even a small impact can undercut the conception of the state as a construct to pursue first and foremost the interests of its citizens.

At the same time that migrants are portrayed as harming the job prospects of citizens, they are also described as abusers of generous welfare state programs. Heinz-Christian Strache, vice chancellor of the Austria and chairman of the far-right Freedom Party, has put it this way

---

[31] Such concerns are also reflected in proposals in the United States to amend birthright citizenship rules to exclude children of undocumented migrants.

[32] Canada: "Foreign-Born Participation Rates," OECD Data, 2018, https://data.oecd.org/migration/foreign-born-participation-rates.htm. European countries: Eurostat, "People in the EU: Statistics on Origin of Residents," accessed February 22, 2018, http://ec.europa.eu/eurostat/statisticsexplained/index.php/People_in_the_EU_%E2%80%93_statistics_on_origin_of_residents; South Africa: Bundeszentrale für politische Bildung, "Immigration," December 2, 2015, http://www.bpb.de/gesellschaft/migration/laenderprofile/200498/immigration; United States: "Immigration's Impact on Past and Future U.S. Population Change," *Pew Research Center*, September 28, 2015, http://www.pewhispanic.org/2015/09/28/chapter-2-immigrations-impact-on-past-and-future-u-s-population-change/.

The percentages are considerably lower in Japan (1.5 percent) and France (4 percent), and in Latin America generally, "Foreign-Born Participation Rates," OECD Data.

[33] E.g., Francine D. Blau and Chrisopher D. Mackie, *The Economic and Fiscal Consequences of Immigration* (Washington, DC: National Academies Press, 2017).

[34] The idea that immigrants are beneficial to national economies is not shared everywhere. In Hungary, immigrants constitute 5.8 percent of the population and just 0.6 percent of the workforce. At a 2016 press conference, Viktor Orbán declared: "Hungary does not need a single migrant for the economy to work, or the population to sustain itself, or for the country to have a future." Further, "[f]or us migration is not a solution but a problem[;] ... not medicine but a poison, we don't need it and won't swallow it." "Hungarian prime

in a Facebook post (approved by 10,000 people): "Never again will it happen that migrants, who have not worked a single day here and have never paid anything into the system, receive a thousand euros in social welfare!"[35] Again, the facts at the aggregate level tend to undermine claims that migrants are a drain on welfare states. Overall, public coffers of developed states benefit from migration—that is, they take in more in taxes from migrants than they give out in social benefits.[36] But the use of social welfare programs by noncitizens is always open to question for those who see the state-territory-citizen construct as ironclad.

COUNTERARGUMENTS

The claims of crisis merit a critical examination. First, it can be noted that the global north has already constructed pretty good walls that protect the homeland from large numbers of uninvited entrants. The Australian ban on boats, Fortress Europe (secured by the deal with Turkey on Syrian refugees), the dramatic reduction in illegal border crossing in the United States (which began years before Trump took office), Israeli border and detention policies, wide-spread visa requirements and carrier sanctions, to mention just a few of the control efforts now in place, have established a significant degree of border security for developed states. Trump's wall is wrong for many reasons, but a primary one is that, even on its own terms, it is simply unnecessary.[37] In short, migration poses no existential threat to global northern states.

Furthermore, a strong case can be made that the future sustainability of many constitutional democracies will require the continued contribution of immigration. In many developed states, migration is a major factor in population growth—responsible for 100 percent of population growth in Germany, Spain, Italy, Poland, Hungary, Finland, and Japan; and 70 percent of growth in the (pre-Brexit) Sweden and Denmark. A recent study by the Pew Research Center finds that 88 percent of population growth in the United States between now and 2065 will be due to migrants and their descendants.[38] And as already noted, the foreign-born constitute a substantial part of the workforces of these states.

To state these factual propositions is not to assert that they have much purchase in the current debates. But I believe that these kinds of arguments could make a difference in policy spaces not inflamed by the rhetoric of crisis. This is not where we are today. Crisis

---

minister says migrants are 'poison' and 'not needed,'" *Guardian* (UK), July 26, 2016, https://www.theguardian.com/world/2016/jul/26/hungarian-prime-minister-viktor-orban-praises-donald-trump.

[35] Melissa Eddy, "Austria's New Government: A Mix of Far-Right, Pro-Europe and Youth," *New York Times*, December 18, 2017, https://www.nytimes.com/2017/12/18/world/europe/austria-chancellor-kurz.html.

[36] Blau and Mackie, *The Economic and Fiscal Consequences of Immigration*. As with impacts on the labor market, there may be distributional differences (i.e., national governments may gain substantially, even as local governments experience a net deficit).

[37] Of course, many of these policies face strong claims that they violate human rights and international law guarantees—so the existence and efficacy of these policies may well not be pressed as an anti-populist argument.

[38] "Immigration's Impact," *Pew Research Center*.

talk will continue to dominate so long as substantial portions of citizens believe that their states are not able to effectively control their borders.

What's Next?

BLEAK MIRROR

It is apparent that the tilt in many constitutional democracies is toward policies less favorable to immigrants. The populist moment shows no sign of abating. Right- and far- right parties that have made anti-immigrant policies central to their platforms have shown new and surprising strength in a number of states, including, among others, Austria, Denmark, Germany, Hungary, Italy, and Poland.

Enforcement against illegal immigration has been stepped up at the border, in the interior of states, and beyond state borders.[39] The Trump administration has supported proposals to reduce legal immigration levels and to reconfigure the flow;[40] and US concerns about "chain migration" are now being repeated in Europe. Efforts to restrict welfare benefits for refugees and other migrants are gaining ground in Sweden, Demark, and elsewhere in Europe. Indeed, what cannot be ruled out is a return to virulent anti-immigrant programs of the past: mass deportations, roundups and internment policies, an expansion of summary removal procedures—projects that go considerably beyond current restrictive visa policies and the building of border barriers.

The arguments identified above—based on security, demographic, and economic concerns—have been ably mobilized by right-wing movements and politicians who seek their support. They play into an overall narrative of anxiety and of a loss of control—of the nation's borders (and respect for its laws), of the characteristics of the nation's people, of the scope and shape of the national labor market and the welfare state.[41] The ways in which immigration problematizes the traditional narrative of state-territory-citizen from the Left are now being used for precisely the opposite purposes: if immigration challenges assumptions about the nature of the state, then it is migrants that must yield, not the assumptions. (Timothy Garton Ash notes that a slogan used by some of the rightists in German—*Wir sind das Volk* (We are the People)—was taken from East German protesters in 1989 marching against communist rule.[42])

---

[39] On "externalization" of immigration controls, see James C. Hathaway and Thomas Gammeltoft-Hansen, "Non-refoulement in a World of Cooperative Deterrence," *Columbia Journal of Transnational Law* 53 (2015): 235–284.

[40] President Donald J. Trump Backs RAISE Act, Aug. 2, 2017, https://www.whitehouse.gov/briefings-statements/president-donald-j-trump-backs-raise-act/.

[41] They thus resonate with broader concerns about globalization.

[42] Timothy Garton Ash, "It's the Kultur, Stupid," *New York Review of Books*, December 7, 2017, http://www.nybooks.com/articles/2017/12/07/germany-alt-right-kultur-stupid/.

Part of the power of the demands of the right, then, is that they seek not to transform the state or the form of government or to radically change the population of the nation; rather they are made in the name of principles that are thought to undergird the idea of a constitutional democracy: security of territory, a self-governing demos, a rule of law. Viktor Orban's rejection of the EU's decision to allocate asylum seekers among EU states is made in terms of national security and popular sovereignty, even as the state lurches toward an authoritarianism antithetical to liberal and democratic values: "National governance in Hungary is under continuous pressure and attack ... the most important thing at stake is whether we will have a parliament and a government that will seek to serve the best interests of the Hungarian people, or a parliament and a government that will seek to serve foreign interests."[43]

All that has been described above can take place within "normal" politics, and would represent a recalibration of the settlement not its wholesale abandonment. That is, courts could develop constitutional norms that legitimate a right turn through reinterpretation (and perhaps selective abandonment) of precedents and commitments to fundamental rights.[44] The constitutional settlement is not written in stone, even if nominally secured by constitutional texts that grant rights to "persons" rather than "citizens." Laws disfavoring migrants could be upheld if citizenship status is now considered a legitimate ground for distinction. A new version of the settlement would be hard on the inside and even harder on the outside.

This charts a crucial role for courts—again, a vital element of a well-functioning constitutional democracy. There is some evidence that courts will continue to play this role in the current moment, striking down blatant acts of race or religious discrimination or crass violations of due process. Take, for example, the now thrice-rejected Trump executive orders banning visas to certain (mostly Muslim) countries.[45]

But political and public pressure can obviously have an impact on judicial behavior, as can appointments to courts made by elected leaders. Furthermore, the actions of enforcement officers can be removed from judicial scrutiny, as accomplished by the United States in sending interdiction migrants to Guantanamo, and by Australia in "excising" outlying territory from the country's "migration zone." And courts can be "reformed" through legislative action that shortens the length of terms, changes the number of judges, takes

---

[43] Stinson, "Europe Is Facing a BATTLEFIELD."

[44] In US constitutional law, the holding that immigrants are a "discrete and insular minority" warranting special judicial protection could be overturned without too much judicial angst. *Plyler v. Doe* is also potentially vulnerable.

[45] IRAP v. Trump, 4th Cir., Feb. 15, 2018; Hawai'i v. Trump, 878 F.3d 662, 673 (9th Cir. 2017). Other notable recent examples include *NF v. European Council*, General Court of the European Union, Order February 28, 2017, http://curia.europa.eu/juris/document/document.jsf?text=&docid=188483&pageIndex=0&doclang=EN&mode=lst&dir=&occ=first&part=1&cid=112059; *N.D. and N.T. v. Spain*, ECtHR, nos. 8675/15 and 8697/15, 3 October 2017, http://www.asylumlawdatabase.eu/en/content/ecthr-nd-and-nt-v-spain-application-nos-867515-and-869715-3-october-2017.

cases away from the judiciary, or otherwise reduces judicial authority, as has happened in recent years in Venezuela and Poland.[46] These policy shifts are made easier, of course, when the persons harmed by these actions (noncitizens) find themselves fully outside a "reinvigorated" interpretation of the constitutional democratic narrative.

OTHER FUTURES?

There are, however, other possible outcomes—largely, and somewhat ironically, due to prior immigration policies. As noted above, the foreign-born now constitute a fairly sizeable proportion of the populations of many constitutional democracies. Many of them naturalize and have children (and grandchildren) who are citizens.[47] This provides a potential source of political power that can push back against anti-immigrant policies. California became "deep blue" after and in response to adoption of Proposition 187 in 1994. Further evidence comes from strong support from the Democratic Party in the United States for legislation to regularize the status of the "Dreamers" (migrants brought as children to the United States by their undocumented parents) as well as robust opposition in Congress to large cuts in legal immigration.

In addition to electoral influence, migrants and their descendants have added significantly to the diversity of receiving states, and this in turn will influence how the demos' defines itself. United States history is a long story of changing narratives of "who" is an American. Narratives elsewhere have changed as well: in the 1970s, the public discourse among Germans was that Germany is not a country of immigration. Angela Merkel has more recently rejected that view, adding "[t]here is something enriching if someone wants to come to us."[48]

A moderate outcome for the immigration battles is further supported by other data. As previously noted, the contribution of immigration to population growth and the labor force plays a major role in a number of constitutional democracies. Furthermore, the net positive impact of immigration on the economy may come to be of increasing interest as states face increasing competition from around the world.

---

[46] Recent Polish legislation (1) lowers the mandatory retirement age for Supreme Court justices from seventy to sixty-five, which will immediately lead to the removal of 40 percent of the justices, and (2) adds a requirement that members of the National Judiciary Council (which selects judges) be approved by a 60 percent vote in the legislature (for the fifteen members of the Council selected by judges). Rick Lyman, "The Polish Parliament Reshapes Courts, Drawing Criticism," New York Times, December 8, 2017. In 2004, legislation in Venezuela expanded the number of Supreme Court judges from twenty to thirty-two in order to guarantee a chavista majority. Daniel Wilkinson, "Court-Packing Law Threatens Venezuelan Democracy," Human Rights Watch, June 21, 2004.

[47] In the United States, nearly 50 percent of the foreign-born are naturalized, and children born in the United States to non-naturalized foreign-born are citizens at birth.

[48] "Merkel: Germany Is Becoming a 'Country of Immigration,'" DW, June 1, 2015, http://www.dw.com/en/merkel-germany-is-becoming-a-country-of-immigration/a-18491165.

This can be taken one step further. All that has been said so far operates within the traditional understandings of a state and state sovereignty. It is conceivable, however, that in the long run migration will help transform those concepts. This would come about through the valorizing of the human rights claims of migrants (and citizens) made under international law, which implicitly moves toward narratives of state legitimacy not grounded in popular sovereignty.[49] Some of those claims are pressed in terms not likely to be recognized by domestic or international courts, such as a right to freedom of (international) travel,[50] but which could be the basis for political campaigns and movements. So too the traditional concept of state authority limited to a bounded territory is increasingly confounded by transnational networks of migrants and by home states that seek to assist their nationals in states of settlement.[51]

If these kinds of political claims succeed even modestly it will mean that policy changes in states, and the very concept of a constitutional state, will have come not from some outside power seeking to harm a state (as concerned the US Supreme Court in the cases establishing the "plenary power" doctrine). Rather it will come from the everyday actions and self-conscious political agitations of migrants themselves—whom states have invited in in the exercise of their sovereignty or who have arrived without authorization to work or to flee persecution in their home states.

I conclude with no prediction as to the outcome of these contestations. Repression may, at the moment, seem more likely than transformation. Or perhaps the center will hold. The political instability of the moment simply magnifies the conceptual instability of the immigrant's place in constitutional democracy.

---

[49] Yasemin Soysal, *Limits of Citizenship: Migrants and Postnational Membership in Europe* (Chicago: University of Chicago Press, 1995); Seyla Benhabib, *The Rights of Others: Aliens, Residents and Citizens* (New York: Cambridge University Press, 2004).

[50] Luis Cabrera, *The Practice of Global Citizenship* (New York: Cambridge University Press, 2010), ch. 5; Luis Fernandez and Joel Olson, "To Live, Love and Work Anywhere You Please: Critical Exchange on Arizona and the Struggle for Locomotion," *Contemporary Political Theory* 10 (2011): 412–419.

[51] Alexandra Delano, "Immigrant Integration vs. Transnational Ties? The Role of the Sending State," *Social Research* 77 (2010): 237–268; Alexandra Delano, "The Diffusion of Diaspora Engagement Policies: A Latin American Agenda," *Political Geography*, 41 (2014): 90–100.

28 The Party's Over
Kim Lane Scheppele

AS ONE CONSTITUTIONAL democracy after another has fallen on hard times, the "P word" has often been invoked. *Populism* has been blamed for many of the world's democratic failures, as the people have fallen for the promise of becoming the winners who take all. Analysts of democratic dysfunction are wringing their hands and quoting Brecht:

> ... [T]he people
> Had forfeited the confidence of the government
> And could win it back only
> By redoubled efforts. Would it not be easier
> In that case for the government
> To dissolve the people
> And elect another?[1]

In my view, however, the blame-the-populists camp is far too harsh on "the people" who, after all, were only choosing an option that they were offered. The populist explanation begs the prior question of why democratic publics are being served up destructive choices in the first place. When one more closely examines the choices—how options

---

[1] Bertold Brecht, "Die Lösung" [The Solution], in *Bertolt Brecht, Poems 1913–1956*, ed. John Willett and Ralph Manheim (London: Methuen 1976), 440.

that would lead to disaster came to be put on ballots around the world—another "P word" emerges as even more important: "*Parties*." Political parties.

In this chapter, I will argue that if one traces the failing and failed democracies, one will generally find that traditional parties in that country had first fallen victim to insidious infighting, ideological drift, or credibility collapse in a way that disrupted the ability of those mainstream parties to screen out toxic choices put to voters. And the voters, not realizing that the safety checks had disappeared when they were offered up seriously bad options, picked one of the options they were given—which in turn sent their countries down the rabbit hole of autocracy. Collapsing democracies follow on collapsing political parties. In short, democracy is in trouble when the party is over.

When this happens in one country, it's a national tragedy with a national explanation. But when it happens in many countries at once, something more general is going on. As we are seeing now, parties are failing in many different democratic systems at once, something that suggests that the cause is more general.

Why are parties collapsing? I will suggest in this chapter that traditional parties are being torn apart by a revolution in political sensibility that has become too powerful for them to handle. As democracies have emerged around the world over the last two centuries, a class-based political spectrum from Left to Right came to dominate most of them. The Left was grounded in support for the working class and favored a strong state and robust redistribution while the Right was grounded in support of the managerial and upper classes and was in favor of limited government and property rights. But as the economies that sustained traditional class divisions—classes that in turn underwrote Left/Right politics—have been replaced by economies that sustain a tiny globalized elite on the backs of a large, locally bound precariat,[2] Left/Right political divisions no longer reflect the social landscape and, as a result, they are struggling to continue to shape the political landscape. Political parties have therefore become increasingly hard to classify on a Left/Right scale.

The Left/Right political spectrum is now being undermined and overwritten by another major social division that is coming to underwrite a new political division. People with international passports and liberal education, with global horizons and universal values are in one political camp while those who stay close to home, speak one language, and see both their neighbors and their nations as the horizon of politics are in another. (That's too simple of course, but so was the description of traditional parties as being primarily Left or Right.) Cosmopolitans/globalists have a different set of political interests than the nationalists/localists—and the traditional parties are being torn apart by the fact that there are cosmopolitans and nationalists, globalists and localists *within* the mainstream parties of both Left and Right. Parties that have been built around a Left/Right continuum cannot cope with a shift to a global/local axis without fanning a civil war within their parties. Out of the wreckage of these failing parties come spectacularly bad electoral choices.

---

[2] Guy Standing, *The Precariat: The New Dangerous Class* (London: Bloomsbury Academic, 2011).

Across the world, one-party states are emerging out of the collapse of parties caused by this reorientation of the political space. In places where democracy has failed, it is often because strongmen backed by their own self-made political parties have come to power and pushed the last vestiges of traditional parties into the dustbin of history. By looking at concrete cases and their depressing trajectories, we can see precisely how dangers emerge from weakened and disoriented political parties.

If this is the problem that is causing democratic decline, what is to be done? A renewed commitment to constitutionalism is needed to shore up democratic states by ensuring that they have democratic parties. This is a delicate moment, when the old politics of Left and Right are being supplanted by a new politics of global and local. We need to think about parties not as the political black boxes out of which emerge candidates for our consideration but as spaces of governance within which aspirational leaders are trying out their styles. Unless constitutional regulation can reach into parties to check their constitutional and democratic health before those parties enter the general public sphere, intra-party civil wars and intra-party dictatorships can grow and spread beyond their boundaries, to the detriment of those who then get to vote on what the parties put forward as choices. Without having a constitutional account of the crucial role of parties and a constitutional strategy for ensuring their democratic health, a collapse of constitutional democracy as such becomes not only thinkable but perhaps even inevitable.

Parties and the Political Tsunami: A Tale of Two Countries

In collapsing democracies around the world, elected leaders have now become the primary agents of democratic destruction. Where once constitutional coups were launched without regard to electoral niceties as military coup-makers and other self-appointed strongmen pushed aside elected leaders, they are now more likely to be launched by elected leaders who have promised radical change in the name of the people but who instead create autocracies. Why do voters vote for leaders who become—either immediately or eventually—autocrats?

Closer looks at collapsing democracies make it clear that voters do not in general intend to give up their rights to make democratic choices in the future by openly electing an autocrat. At times of trouble, voters vote for new policies, for fresh faces, to get politics unstuck. They vote to "throw the bums out" by supporting the opposition after the governing party had been in power long enough to have worn out its welcome. But in altogether too many places, voters vote for what looks like a legitimate party and autocracy is the result.

This is not the usual story of voters being swept away by anti-constitutional parties threatening a democratic order. "Militant democracy" can defend itself against political parties whose platforms reject the basic rules of the game. In response to the great totalitarianisms of the twentieth century, many constitutions now incorporate provisions that allow anti-constitutional parties—communist and fascist parties lead among them—to be banned. As Samuel Issacharoff has shown,[3] these bans customarily require analyzing party programs to determine whether the goals that the party wants to achieve are permissible under the constitution. That is why he immediately assimilated these party bans in comparative law to the free speech provision of the American constitution, which permits only content-neutral restrictions on speech. Militant democratic tactics are thus foreign to American constitutional thinking. But, as Issacharoff shows, party bans are very common in other constitutional democracies.

But what if anti-constitutional *ideology* is not the terrain on which the new autocrats fight? In general, the new autocrats are not particularly ideological in the twentieth century totalitarian sense. Their parties do not generally announce a political program that threatens the supremacy of democracy or constitutional government as political forms. Even if "populism" poses an illiberal challenge to a liberal constitutional order, the face that the populist puts forward in an election is the face of a law-respecting democrat. The new autocrats may promise major change, but not in ways that immediately signal that the values underwriting the constitution are threatened. How can constitutions defend against parties that do not announce their leaders' autocratic ambitions? As the wave of faltering and collapsing democracies indicates, stealth autocracy that is more technocratic than ideological is a threat that has not yet been taken on board in constitutional design.

To illustrate this problem, I will examine in this Section two cases that might seem at first to be wholly different. Venezuela's democracy collapsed with a challenge from the Left and Hungary's democracy is threatened with a challenge from the Right. But during the campaigns that brought these countries' new autocrats to power, unconstitutional ideology was not the problem. In 1998, Hugo Chávez in Venezuela ran a fiery-in-style but ultimately conventional-in-content campaign. His central campaign promises pledged to improve the living standards of the poor and to eliminate corruption. In 2010, Viktor Orbán in Hungary spent much of his time attacking the dismal record of the Socialist party, which had already been in power for eight years. The short and unhelpful party platform of Orbán's Fidesz party listed unobjectionable goals such as "an ability for every man to look after his family" and "honest jobs and honest wages."[4] Orbán vaguely promised big change but did not appear to be out of the ideological mainstream. But, as I will argue below, both Chávez and Orbán were elected against the background of a collapsing party system that was no longer able to organize resistance to an autocratic drive for power.

---

[3] Samuel Issacharoff, *Fragile Democracies: Contested Power in the Era of Constitutional Courts* (New York: Cambridge University Press, 2015).

[4] Agnes Batory, Election Briefing No 51: Europe and the Hungarian Parliamentary Elections of April 2010, European Parties and Referendums Network, accessed February 28, 2018, https://www.sussex.ac.uk/webteam/gateway/file.php?name=epern-election-briefing-no-51.pdf&site=266.

Venezuela is now at the very bottom of democracy indices and very nearly a failed state.[5] When Hugo Chávez came to power in 1998, he won with 56.2 percent of the valid votes atop his Movimenieto V República (Fifth Republic Movement) party, which was on the ballot for the first time. His strongest competition came from a candidate who was also running with a brand new party. What happened to the parties that usually won Venezuelan elections before that time? They had been fatally weakened and had largely vanished in the run-up to the fateful 1998 election. But this collapse of the traditional parties did not happen overnight.

With the return of democracy in Venezuela in 1958 following the Pérez Jiménez dictatorship, a robust array of parties contested each election for two decades. Democratic Action (AD) was the largest traditional party of the center-Left and the Committee of Independent Political Organization (COPEI) was the largest political party of the center-Right. Other parties came and went over the years in a lively political competition so that in any given election, voters had a wide array of party choices. Starting in the 1970s, however, national elections for both the presidency and the Parliament started to converge on what was essentially a two-party system. By 1988, the AD and the COPEI together accounted for 93 percent of the presidential votes cast and 75 percent of parliamentary votes. As the political system narrowed to two parties, a "punishing vote" practice evolved. At each election throughout the 1970s and 1980s, with one exception, the party in power was voted out, and the other party voted in. In the meantime, the smaller parties that might have provided alternatives disappeared from the scene. As party choice narrowed, the abstention rate increased. Voters were clearly cycling between two well-known options in search of something else. And dissatisfied voters were leaving the system.

Then there was austerity. In 1989 after debt mounted to unsustainable levels, the AD (Left) government in power was forced to adopt austerity measures as a condition of being bailed out by the International Monetary Fund (IMF).[6] To fulfill its promises to the international financial institutions, the government raised mass transit fares and gasoline prices. The result was violence in the streets. A state of emergency was declared; the army was deployed across the capital and eight other cities across the country. The death toll climbed to at least three hundred (or one thousand) or more. Normal politics was badly shaken. Against this background, then-Lieutenant Colonel Hugo Chávez staged a coup d'état in 1992, a coup that failed. In the face of this coup attempt, large majorities of Venezuelans nonetheless insisted to pollsters that they preferred civilian government

[5] This account of parties and electoral results is drawn from the data-rich and detailed account provided in Daniel Eduardo Varnagy Rado and Herbert Koeneke, "The Role of Political Parties in Venezuela's Political Culture," *Politeja* 2 (2013): 81–105, https://www.researchgate.net/publication/272165777_The_Role_of_Political_Parties_in_Venezuela%27s_Political_Culture.

[6] "Dozens of Venezuelans Killed in Riots over Price Increases," *New York Times*, March 1, 1989, http://www.nytimes.com/1989/03/01/world/dozens-of-venezuelans-killed-in-riots-over-price-increases.html.

even as 85 percent of Venezuelans agreed that political parties did nothing to solve the country's problems.[7] The political system was not toppled, but all was not well.

At the next election in 1993, Venezuelans again threw the bums out, but not before then-president Carlos Andrés Pérez, whose popularity had already reached an all-time low, was impeached for embezzlement. The voters, unconvinced by the candidate put forward as the new face of the AD, failed to support the party at the next election. Following what had by then become the normal pattern, the voters should have migrated to COPEI, but COPEI was also in trouble. Its long-time leader, Rafael Caldera, had given well-received speeches promising an end to austerity, an end to corruption, and social provision for the poor. But instead of nominating him as the obvious candidate to stand for president, COPEI decided to have an open primary. Caldera chose not to participate, since he (probably accurately) interpreted the open primary as a snub. He went off and formed his own new party in alliance with fourteen other organizations. Running outside the two-party framework, Caldera received the largest share of the vote in 1993. But the largest share of the vote only amounted to 30 percent of the total in an election where nearly half of the voters stayed home.

Caldera's election in 1993 made clear that the traditional party system was in shambles. Both of the traditional parties had entered the presidential election campaign that year after having expelled their most well-known leaders, and both lost badly. Moreover, since the party of the center-Left had brought in the austerity program that gutted social benefits, the party of the center-Right promised a redistributive program. What, then, was Left and what was Right? Instead of trusting either of the traditional parties, the voters trusted an individual candidate whom they already knew. But they did not endorse Caldera by such an overwhelming vote that it would have counted as a true mandate to rebuild the party system. "Party dealignment" had occurred.

Caldera, already governing on shaky ground, also had economic bad luck. With inflation above 70 percent and a banking crisis that threatened to bring down the economy, he was forced to double down on austerity measures because the international financial institutions gave him no choice. He, too, became massively unpopular. By the 1998 presidential election, the former face of COPEI had been undone by economic policy in Venezuela was being dictated from abroad. The parties of both Left and Right had been discredited and, given that no leader could change economic policy, which was not made locally in any event, the party system as such collapsed.

In 1998, against this background, voters elected Hugo Chávez, the former coup plotter who was running atop a coalition of Leftist organizations, headed up by a new party of his own creation. Chávez ran against corruption and for equality, against the IMF and for social redistribution. Once elected, he began his assault on all the other political

---

[7] Anibal Romero, "Rearranging the Deck Chairs on the Titanic: The Agony of Democracy in Venezuela," *Latin American Research Review* 32 (1997): 7–36.

institutions until they came under his control. His victorious new party had little toehold in the other branches of government, so he launched a concerted attack on the constitutional system he inherited, summoning a new constituent assembly to write a constitution that better suited his new rule. He designed the rules for election of representatives to this constituent assembly in a way that gave his party 95 percent of the seats in the assembly with 60 percent of the popular vote.[8] The new constitution that resulted from a convention full of "chávistas" (as Chávez supporters were called) gave Chávez everything he wanted. Among other things, it established an even stronger presidency with a lengthened term of office (six years instead of four). It abolished the Senate, which had been an important constraint on executive power before that time.[9] Many checks on executive power were eliminated. Autocratic legalism had begun.

At first, however, it was hard to tell. Chávez was genuinely popular; his reforms were met with great enthusiasm by the part of the population that was politically mobilized. The other parties, with their declining number of supporters, were remarkably inert during this transformation. One might well have described the drive toward a new constitution and the political changes made by that constitution as a democratic transformation. The key to understanding the dangers lay in the precise nature of the changes. Despite many institutions remaining intact under the new constitution, their ability to check the president was diminished. The Chávez constitution concentrated power in the executive and buffered the executive from accountability to other political forces. The dangers only became evident to the Venezuelan public at large when they wanted to get rid of Chávez's handpicked successor and found that they could not.

Though Chávez had clearly planned to govern for an extended period without allowing himself to be displaced, nature had other ideas. Chávez died in 2013. Promising to carry on the Chávez legacy, his anointed successor Nicolás Maduro has proven to be far less competent and popular as a leader. When his party lost the parliamentary election in 2015 to a coalition of opposition parties, Maduro convened another constituent assembly to rewrite the constitution yet again. This constituent assembly displaced the opposition-dominated Parliament with the help of the Chávez-picked judiciary before backing down in the face of international criticism. But the opposition is still beleaguered as Maduro uses his power to fragment and disrupt it. Venezuela is no longer a constitutional democracy.[10] From a robust and pluralistic democracy widely thought to be one of the most stable in Latin America, Venezuela first saw its array of parties narrow, then settle into a two-party rotation, then collapse. Multiparty democracy was overthrown altogether as

---

[8] David Landau, "Constitution-Making Gone Wrong," *Alabama Law Review* 64 (2013): 923, 940–941.

[9] Javier Corrales, "Autocratic Legalism in Venezuela," *Journal of Democracy* 26 (2015): 37, 38, 51.

[10] As I write, a snap election has been called and the disorganized opposition has had no time to prepare. That said, the level of deprivation in the country and the falling popularity of Maduro may give even a disorganized opposition an opportunity to make electoral gains. The Election Commission, however, is firmly under control of the Maduro government, and began the campaign by disqualifying the most substantial opposition parties.

a new leader rode a wave of democratic discontent and established one-party rule that future democratic majorities could not displace.

Like Venezuela, Hungary has fallen the farthest out of the family of democratic states in its region of the world and is now at the bottom of the Freedom House rankings for countries in the European Union. Prime Minister Viktor Orbán has steered the country swiftly toward autocracy. He came to power in 2010 in an election that saw his Fidesz party win 53 percent of the vote and gain more than two-thirds of the seats in the unicameral Parliament. Though Orbán was a familiar face in 2010, having participated in every election since 1990, his opponents had been warning for more than a decade that he had autocratic tendencies. At the time of the 2010 election, however, Orbán's party looked like the only reasonable choice, given the other options on offer. Fidesz had led a coalition government from 1998 to 2002 that didn't crash the constitutional system. But in 2010, like Chávez in 1998, Orbán upon election immediately carried out a constitutional transformation of the country, concentrating all power in his hands without effective checks and turning what had been a robust if flawed democracy into a state in which the people can no longer remove their leader. How did Hungary get to this point? The story is surprisingly similar to Venezuela's.

The post-1989 landscape in Hungary initially featured many political parties, so the first democratic election law was written to ensure that elections could produce stable governments with a splintered array of parties. The new election law put its thumb on the scale to benefit the plurality party by giving that party bonus seats. As it turns out, that corrective was probably unnecessary because after the first election in 1990, Hungary settled into a stable pattern with no more than six parties in any given Parliament.

The first democratic government elected in 1990 was led by the Democratic Forum (MDF), a big umbrella party of former dissidents. The MDF was in coalition with a Christian Democratic party (KDNP) and a revived interwar conservative party, the Smallholders. In opposition were three parties: the old Communist Party now retooled under new management as the Hungarian Socialist Party (MSzP) and two liberal parties, the Free Democrats (SzDSz), heavy with Budapest intellectuals who had been dissidents in the communist time, and Fidesz, a libertarian party started by a young firebrand from the countryside whose name was Viktor Orbán. Almost as soon as the MDF was elected, however, it moved sharply away from its prior anti-communist liberal stand toward the nationalist right, losing the support of many of its initial voters.

Not surprisingly, in the second multiparty election in 1994, the voters threw out their government. In Hungary, as in many governments in post-communist Europe, the communist-legacy party made a comeback. The Socialists gained an absolute majority of the seats in the Parliament though they did not win a majority of the votes because the election law still threw bonus mandates to the plurality party. But even though its parliamentary majority meant that the Socialists didn't need a partner to govern, many—including many in the Socialist Party itself—thought that it would be alarming to a Hungarian public that had just emerged from fifty years of communism to have the now-ex-communists back in charge alone. So the Socialists formed a coalition government with the Free Democrats, the more Left-leaning of the two liberal parties, leaving Orbán's Fidesz party as the only one of the original six parties that had not yet been in government. Seeing an opportunity in the declining fortunes of the MDF and realizing that its electoral strategy needed refreshing, Fidesz gave up its liberal program and began its move toward the nationalist Right in search of voters who had once voted for the MDF.

Hungary emerged from the communist period with the largest per capital debt in the former Second World. Though it had been in the lead in liberalizing its economy during the communist time, it was slow engaging in further change after 1989 as the MDF government prioritized nationalist symbolic issues over economic restructuring. By 1995, when the Socialist/Liberal government was in power, the IMF notified Hungary that it would stop refinancing Hungary's debt unless Hungary engaged in a major structural adjustment designed to privatize state assets, cut state budgets, and slash social programs. Though it tried to hold out against IMF pressure, the government eventually had to accept austerity. The Constitutional Court softened the blow by declaring major parts of the austerity program unconstitutional. But though the Court decision slowed down the implementation of the IMF program, eventually neoliberal restructuring was forced on Hungary as both deficits and redistributive programs were slashed. A government of the Left had been forced to govern in substantive terms like a government of the Right, just as had occurred in Venezuela.

Not surprisingly, since the Socialist/Liberal government had broken almost all of its election promises with austerity measures, voters at the next opportunity in 1998 once again threw the bums out. Viktor Orbán's retooled conservative party Fidesz got the plurality bonus this time, but not enough seats to govern alone. He formed a coalition with the much diminished MDF and the even smaller Smallholders. Mired in scandals, the Christian Democratic Party disappeared from Parliament altogether that year but a new sixth party emerged: the Hungarian Justice and Life Party (MIÉP), the first party of the far Right to appear in the Parliament.

In 2002, despite polls initially showing that Fidesz would win re-election, Hungarians again threw out the incumbents for the fourth time in a row. In a surprise upset, the Socialists and Free Democrats each won enough seats to sustain a parliamentary majority together, though again without a majority of the popular vote.[11] This election continued the trend in which declining conservative parties disappeared from the Parliament entirely as their leaders fell victim to scandals. Both the Smallholders and MIÉP collapsed and vanished from the Parliament after the 2002 election, just as the Christian Democrats had done before them. The MDF only won seats because it ran candidates

---

[11] This account of the 2002 election is from Ken Benoit, "Like Déjà Vu All Over Again: The Hungarian Parliamentary Elections of 2002," *Journal of Communist Studies and Transition Politics* 18 (2002): 119–133.

on joint party lists with Fidesz. As a result, Fidesz occupied the right side of the political spectrum very nearly alone. On the left side of the political spectrum, the liberal Free Democrats also lost ground though they crept into the government. The 2002 election results revealed stark party concentration as two parties—Fidesz and the Socialists—between them won 90 percent of the seats. Just as we saw in Venezuela, the electorate first voted for a wide array of parties before entering a vote-punishing pattern in which the voters threw out each successive government. And then the system converged rather quickly on just two parties.

In the 2006 election, this pattern was broken when a government was re-elected for the first time since the democratic transformation of 1989. The Socialist/Liberal coalition was voted back into office, handing Fidesz a second defeat in a row. Much of the reason was the Socialists' replacement of an unpopular prime minister with a new and charismatic young leader, Ferenc Gyurcsány. During the campaign, Gyurcsány had trounced Viktor Orbán in a highly visible debate. But after the Socialist/Liberal coalition won re-election, trouble soon appeared—on two fronts.

For the first time since the end of communism, violence erupted in the streets when leaked tapes of a Socialist Party congress caught Gyurcsány admitting that, during the election campaign, the party had lied "morning, noon, and night" about the country's dire financial situation. The violent street protests were met with a police overreaction, and the ensuing chaos immediately discredited the government, which had in its re-election campaign hid the extent of financial trouble that the government faced. Debt once again shuffled the deck of politics. The first Orbán government from 1998 to 2002 had started running up the state debt to unsustainable levels, but the Socialists had made things much worse. Rather than deliver the promised milk and honey as many Hungarians imagined would flow upon accession to the European Union in 2004, the EU delivered austerity, which resulted in massive budget cuts. Debt also spooked the currency markets, which sent the Hungarian forint (the national currency) tumbling, making Hungary's financial woes even worse. Most Hungarian debt was held in foreign currencies, and a collapse of the forint against the euro and Swiss franc made the debt unpayable. This did not just affect government debt: middle-class Hungarians typically held their home mortgages in foreign currencies too. On the leading edge of the global financial crisis, both the Hungarian state and a wide swath of Hungarian homeowners suddenly found themselves underwater. Hungary was forced to seek a bailout from the IMF to keep itself from defaulting. The elected government stood down as a technocratic caretaker government was installed to bring in sweeping austerity measures. After four years of swingeing budget cuts with a population underwater, to say nothing of a series of corruption scandals that had come to light, the Socialists were bound to lose the next election.

But by the 2010 election, Hungarian voters had few choices. The Socialists had become the face of pain, misery, and scandal. The Free Democrats were so disorganized and unpopular by 2010 that they didn't even run a party list. The other repeat-player parliamentary parties since the 1990s—the Christian Democrats, Smallholders, and the

MDF—had collapsed in the preceding elections, leaving Fidesz as the only remaining major party. There were some new parties on offer in 2010, which some voters sampled, given the dearth of other choices. The far-right party Jobbik was the most popular of the new parties, claiming 16 percent of the vote in 2010 and receiving only eight fewer seats than the trounced Socialists, while the LMP, a tiny vaguely green (but mostly vague) party, just squeaked over the 5 percent threshold. Given the competition, it is not surprising that Fidesz won 53 percent of the popular vote, which, with the victor's bonus still part of Hungarian election law, gave the party more than two-thirds of the seats in the Parliament. In 2010, the voters didn't have much of a choice. By voting for Fidesz, Hungarian voters were not voting to end democracy; they were making what would have seemed like the sanest choice at the time. They voted for the one conventional party that remained standing, a party that was not implicated in the preceding years of pain. They did not know they were electing an autocrat.

Venezuela and Hungary are striking in their similarities. In both countries, an earlier dictatorship was immediately followed by a robust multiparty democratic government, featuring a vibrant array of parties. Observers found each country to be the most impressive and stable democracy in its region. But eventually, multiple parties collapsed into a two-party system and a punishing-vote practice emerged in which the electorate threw out the government at every opportunity save one. Joint crises involving violence in the streets and extreme austerity measures began a political death spiral in which all those associated with either problem—the violence or the austerity—were driven out of politics. Voters eventually voted for the one party leader left standing in a key election in which all other parties were weakened, discredited, or untried. And that person turned out to be someone who swiftly consolidated power in an autocratic manner under a new constitution while running on a substantively conventional party platform. The paths that led to Chávez and Orbán involved progressively narrowing party choices, ending eventually in an election in which the budding autocrat was the only reasonable-looking option among the available limited choices. In short, party collapse preceded democratic collapse.

Why did Venezuela and Hungary, otherwise quite different, meet the same fate around the same time? A global trend affected both. Traditional political parties, arrayed along a Left/Right spectrum, found themselves wrong-footed by a new political orienting scheme: globalist versus localist politics. Venezuela under Chávez (now Maduro) governed to the Left and Hungary under Orbán tilted to the Right. But Chávez and Orbán both governed as nationalists, appealing primarily to less-educated constituents outside the major cities who felt that the world was against them.[12] In both cases, their policies

---

[12] Unlike Orbán, Chávez originally had the support of urban intellectuals. But he lost this support when his autocratic ambitions became clearer. That said, Chávez long retained the support of many Leftist intellectuals outside Venezuela who apparently did not understand his progressive weakening of checks on the powers of the president and only supported his anti-capitalist agenda.

were aimed at curtailing foreign influence, railing against international bankers and international institutions, and trying to claw back domestic control over economic policy.

Chávez's nationalism had undeniable Left elements, since he fought capitalist globalization. But his nationalism was even stronger:

> Chávez's political movement, the new constitution and even Venezuela were renamed as "Bolivarian." The ideology of Bolivarianism portrayed Simón Bolívar as an anti-imperialist hero, and as the founding father of "Latin Americanism" vis-à-vis US-dominated "Pan-Americanism" . . . Bolivarianism advocated the self-determination of a Venezuela free from the interests of multinational corporations. It was also understood as a project to strengthen Venezuela's cultural identity . . . [13]

Orbán governs from the Right, but he governs primarily as a nationalist also, relying—as did Chávez, on constituents who themselves have a localist view of the world. Whenever he can, Orbán rails against the EU for its imperialism, against international banks for seeking to destroy Hungarians' way of life and against cosmopolitan "liberals" everywhere.

Both Chávez and Orbán have defined themselves against precisely the sort of globalization represented by multilateral financial and trade agreements, claiming that their domestic opponents are foreign puppets who are trying to overthrow what "the people" want. Only strong leaders can defend the people, they say. But soon the people lose the choice.

What lessons can we learn from the rise of Chávez and Orbán? In both cases, their ascents to power were preceded by economic crisis in each country that in turn required foreign-generated radical austerity programs. In both cases, the timing of the economic crises meant that Left governments in power at the time were the ones forced to slash budgets, which meant acting contrary to their political programs. But when voters voted for the other guys—the parties of the Right in what had become two-party systems—voters got more of the same, eventually destroying the ability of Right-leaning parties to carry out their promises as well. As voters in these two countries learned, in the cosmopolitan and interdependent world in which we all now live, the broad outlines of economic policy are largely beyond national control. As a result, when voters alternate between competing parties, they quickly learn that their votes cannot produce enough change to fix the insufficiency and maldistribution of economic resources. Voters then vote for the party or leader that promises to defend the country against foreign influences—the nationalists of either Left or Right. And that person governs as an autocrat. Whether the autocrat comes from the Left or the Right is a matter of local political culture.[14] But

---

[13] Carlos de la Torre, "Populism and Nationalism in Latin America," *Javnost—The Public* 24 (2017): 375–390, 379.

[14] Former MEP Rui Tavares has provocatively suggested that a country's new autocrat comes from the side of the Left/Right political spectrum opposite the last dictatorship—so former military and fascist dictatorships produce autocrats of the Left and former communist dictatorships produce autocrats of the Right.

the political dynamics that bring autocrats to power—decades of voters swinging from Left to Right parties only to find that neither party can make a difference—also change the ideological spectrum. Once voters realize that economic policy cannot be affected by national elections, they vote for the nationalists who pledge to take their countries out of the global economic order.

As we have seen from this close-up look at what may have seemed like very different examples, the stories of Hungary and Venezuela reveal a common script. Global interdependence has put key policy choices beyond the reach of national governments, and yet national governments are the sites where people have choices of leaders who promise to change policies that are no longer within their power. The end result has been first a convergence of party systems on fewer and fewer parties, followed by a collapse of the traditional parties, along with the conventional markers of what is Left and what is Right. If pre-globalization politics pitted workers against managers and arrayed redistributive programs against entrenched property rights, then political programs under globalization pit educated, urban, and cosmopolitan elites who defend economic globalization and all that comes with it against less-educated, rural, and localist masses who are economic globalization's victims. Party leaders who understand this new politics and pitch their campaigns to the more numerous, less-educated voters win—and then can use their power to entrench themselves for the long term.

Politics Has Failed the People, Not the Other Way Around

If this is the script that leads to the new autocracy, then we can see that the people have not failed democracy by becoming unreasonable populists eager to follow a Pied Piper into unfreedom. Instead, democratic publics are doing what they are supposed to do: voting to rotate power and to shake things up in systems in which the prior leaders have failed to keep their promises. But the people are betrayed by party systems that fail to put forward reasonable alternatives when the time comes to change leaders.

Political renewal is generally a good thing; it is one of the advantages of democratic systems over their alternatives that power can be rotated reliably and peacefully. A steady supply of new ideas and fresh faces in politics is necessary to disrupt both clientelism and corruption as well as to keep refreshing the cast of characters who steer the state. Newcomers entering politics or old-timers with new programs are supposed to offer novel options, fresh directions, *democratic* regeneration. That's how democracies keep up with their times and accommodate the shifting views of voters. By voting to throw the bums out over and over again, voters renew their democracies.

In order for democratic regeneration to occur, however, reliable institutions with the democracy's general health in mind must screen this steady supply of new entrants into politics. If new people and new ideas enter politics without being vetted effectively by strong and sensible political parties, then voters who vote to rotate power and to replace the current leaders—as voters *should* do frequently in a robust democracy—may be inadvertently voting to kill their democratic institutions instead. Preventing toxic choices from being put before the voters is an important role for parties, a role that is no longer performed when a party system is weakened or fails.

It would be easy to imagine that the story of declining democracies is confined to shaky new democracies that were not fully consolidated, rather than being a story about democracy as such. Perhaps the stories of Hungary and Venezuela seem too remote from problems in democracy's once-stable core. But the more one examines democracies that were once thought to be fully consolidated, the more one sees that the stories of Venezuela and Hungary are not so unusual. Civil wars within parties of both Left and Right as well as the collapse of traditional parties and the rise of new untested parties are the signs that party systems are failing.

Take the United States and the United Kingdom, core countries that have boasted solid democracies for centuries but that have recently seen voters cast caution to the wind and vote for untested and untried alternatives. The voters who supported Brexit in the UK and Republican candidate Donald Trump in the US were very similar. Many had moved from being reliable supporters of parties of the Left to vote in desperation for an option put forward by the extreme edge of parties on the Right. But their choices were less about Left and Right than about whether to stay the course with unresponsive parties or vote for a change. In both cases, this meant abandoning global engagement and choosing localism over cosmopolitanism.

The once-Left parties, the Democrats in the US and Labour in the UK, had taken working-class support for granted in an attempt to rebrand their parties. The decisive turn came in the 1990s when Bill Clinton's Democratic Leadership Council and Tony Blair's New Labour advocated for economic globalization with only minimal redistribution at home. Both parties practiced fiscal restraint when their constituents clamored for social protection and repeatedly sided with globalists on issues such as free trade and the deepening of globalized capitalism. Working-class voters may have gone along with this for a while, but their attachment to these parties weakened as engagement with the rest of the world seemed to wreak havoc on the lives and livelihoods of the working class in prosperous democracies. By the time a toxic choice was put before them when they wanted change, they had little loyalty left for the Left.

In the meantime, all was not well with conservative parties as they descended into civil war precisely over the local/global axis. A pitched battle had for decades arrayed the nationalist wings of the parties (the Brexiteers in the UK and the Tea Party/America Firsters in the US) against their parties' cosmopolitan wings (the free-traders and international-business-friendly globalists). Among UK Tories, whether to stay in or split from the European Union was tearing the party apart precisely along nationalist/cosmopolitan lines. In 2015, David Cameron's pledge to ask voters about Brexit brought him a surprisingly strong election victory, after which he felt he had to put the party's most divisive question before a general electorate. The Tory Nationalists won the day and took over the party, banishing the globalists to the sidelines. Among American Republicans, business-friendly conservatives had been battling social conservatives for decades even before they found themselves grappling with a pure nationalist in Donald Trump. In 2016, different wings of the party put up competing candidates who split their faction's vote at a time of weak party leadership, and so Donald Trump, who had no competition as a pure play for nationalism, won the Republican nomination. Splits within the Tories and Republicans put Brexit and Trump directly to the voters.

Once Brexit and Trump got onto the ballots in their respective countries, less-educated voters outside the major cities, fed up with politics as usual for other reasons, voted for change. Many were voters who used to favor the Left alternative over the Right. But enough alienated Labour voters voted for Brexit and alienated Democratic working-class voters in Rust-Belt states voted for Trump to make these options victorious. Voters of both Left and Right cast votes for nationalism, blaming international forces for their own economic misery. Left and Right had little to do with the outcome; voters were unified in their nationalism.

That Brexit and Trump were on the general ballot spoke to the weakness of parties, which should have found a way to screen out destructive choices that would bring on constitutional crises before those choices ever got to the voters. Had the Tories figured out what they thought about the EU, they could have teed up a referendum in which Brexit was an informed choice instead of a leap in the dark. Or prevented Brexit from being a referendum issue at all. Had the Republicans been able to put up a presidential candidate in 2016 who had come up through the Republican ranks and actually been screened by those who knew him/her, voters would not have been given the choice of Trump. But the mainstream parties were in complete disarray at the time that Brexit and Trump snuck through as serious alternatives. In fact, the options of Brexit and Trump were leading indicators that the conservative parties could no longer manage their internal fights. Alienated voters who were fed up with inequality and saw no sign of economic hope voted for change. Having a toxic choice on the ballot just when voters looked for a new alternative produced constitutional crises in both countries. But it's not clear that voters thought they were doing anything other than voting for something new.

We see signs of party weakness across wide swaths of the EU. In the multiparty systems of France, Austria, Germany, the Netherlands, and Italy, which have all gone through elections in 2017 and 2018, the weakness of the party system can be seen in the decline of traditional parties and the rise of extremist parties of both Left and Right. Voters increasingly see their choice as between centrist parties of Left and Right that are virtually indistinguishable in their support for cosmopolitan programs and parties of the extremes that offer nationalist support for beleaguered majorities at home. Voters have been expressing their frustration in European elections not by switching from Left-leaning to Right-leaning parties, but by switching from cosmopolitan centrist parties to parties that defend nationalism on both Left and Right. While some analysts describe European politics as divided between system and anti-system parties, a closer looks reveal that the anti-system parties are providing localist alternatives to the cosmopolitan defaults of the system parties. Left and Right as party orientations are nearly invisible to the average voter. "What passes for populism" is therefore a rejection of centrist parties that have tied their programs to cosmopolitanism.

Those who are worried about populism assume that voters have become intolerant, resistant to evidence, and ideologically committed to a political program in which their specific group becomes "the people" in whose exclusive name politicians should govern. But when we look up-close at the cases where populism seems to be on the rise, the story looks quite different. The vote for a new anti-system party—perhaps the democracy's final true choice given the number of new autocrats lurking in these anti-system parties— is preceded by party trouble, which has narrowed the options to a range of unattractive choices. Voters—left without screened and vetted decent alternatives—vote for something new. This can be seen as a bid for democratic renewal, not a suicide pact. But when parties too weak to ensure responsible choices are put to electorates, democratic death may well be what voters get.

What Is to Be Done?

Around the world, democracy is in trouble. And one of the key signs of this trouble is that party systems have become unstable and increasingly likely to offer bad choices to voters. Traditional politics have been destabilized by a political tsunami of economic crises and other regime-rattling events. In some democracies, traditional parties have descended into civil war, split into factions, or simply disappeared, offering voters fewer choices, and even fewer reasonable choices. In others, traditional parties have been supplemented or replaced by upstart parties that scramble the old Left/Right political spectrum.

We have seen in this chapter how important parties are to the maintenance of democracy. But surprisingly few democracies regulate parties constitutionally, apart from the party ban provisions that we canvassed at the start, and some (often weakly enforced) campaign finance rules. But if the dangerous parties of our time do not present themselves as unconstitutionally ideological—if instead, they present themselves as practical and moderate alternatives to a system that doesn't work—then banning parties for having the wrong ideology will not be effective. If autocrats learn to dress like sheep, they won't be spotted by those screening out wolves.

So perhaps we need to think about a different sort of party regulation. Among consolidated constitutional democracies, Germany has perhaps the most constitutionalized sense of the role of the parties in the democratic order. Parties are protected under the German Basic Law as core elements of the state and, as such, their internal affairs are subject to constitutional regulation. Article 21 of the Basic Law lays out both the importance of parties and the conditions that parties must meet to sustain the importance accorded them in the political order:

Article 21 [Political parties]

(1) Political parties shall participate in the formation of the political will of the people. They may be freely established. Their internal organisation must conform to democratic principles. They must publicly account for their assets and for the sources and use of their funds.

(2) Parties that, by reason of their aims or the behaviour of their adherents, seek to undermine or abolish the free democratic basic order or to endanger the existence of the Federal Republic of Germany shall be unconstitutional. The Federal Constitutional Court shall rule on the question of unconstitutionality. . . .

Many have commented on Germany's commitment to militant democracy expressed in Article 21(2) of the Basic Law, but fewer have noted that the permissibility of party bans is embedded in a larger conception of parties that make them a necessary part of the "formation of political will" as expressed in Article 21(1). In this constitutional conception of a "party state," parties must meet important conditions, including their own internal conformity to democratic principles and to the transparency of their funding. The party ban provision of Article 21(2) requires that parties publicly adhere to the German Basic Law in their political programs, but the internal organization provision of Article 21(1) requires that parties actually *be* democratic and transparent in their internal operations even before one begins to assess whether their party programs meet constitutional standards.

In the constitutional systems that we have considered in this chapter, however, the constitutional law of these states has left the internal structures of parties to each party's own devices, often protected constitutionally from external meddling by a particular conception of freedom of association. As a result, the internal organization, principles of self-governance, and even commitment to both the constitution and democratic order as principles of organizational structure (and not just ideology) are often left unregulated as an aspect of corporate freedom. But parties are not just any old form of organization. They are the building blocks of democratic contestation and, as such, must be treated differently than other associations for democracy to survive.

In Chávez's movement-turned-party and in Orbán's Fidesz, the internal organization of both parties was hierarchical and dictatorial. Both leaders governed their own party faithful with iron-fisted control and expelled those who fell out of line. Chávez, of course, had first tried to intervene in Venezuelan politics through a coup, hardly the sign of a faithful constitutionalist. But when he came back as an apparent democrat at the head of his own party, the newly created party was merely a vehicle for Chávez's drive for the presidency. It had no democratic internal structure, no system of regular rotation of leadership, no transparency about its own governance. Orbán's Fidesz party was similar. When Orbán's party came to power in 2010, he had already been the head of the party for twenty years and had repeatedly purged others who might threaten his grip on it. In the 2010 election he personally vetted each of the candidates who stood for a Fidesz parliamentary seat, and he has been widely rumored to have signed resignation letters already in his desk, waiting to be pulled out and put to use whenever any MP or cabinet minister crosses him. The new autocrats may put a democratic face forward in a general election, but in their own parties, the personal style that they will adopt as national leaders is already evident in the way that they govern their parties.

Democratic and constitutional governments can develop rules for determining whether a party has a democratic and constitutional character, not just in its political program (the usual reason for party bans), but in the way that the party is run. If we see the way a leader governs his party as a training ground for the way that a leader will govern his country, we might have a better sense for which candidates are dangerous to the constitutional order and which are not. Of course, specifying the precise rules (Must there be term limits on party leadership? How may the leadership be selected? How is the minority within the party treated?) will take some work. But the goal is clear.

In their new book *How Democracies Die*, Steven Levitsky and Daniel Ziblatt[15] demonstrate the importance of political norms for the maintenance of democracy. In particular, they argue that the willingness of those in power not to use all the power that they have and to respect the loyal opposition as legitimate is crucial for sustaining democratic norms and forms. They are clearly right. But by limiting their analysis to events and claims made on the general political stage without extending their analysis to the parties that bring forward alternative into politics, they miss the lessons of this chapter. Before autocrats appear before the general public as the danger that they will become, signs of trouble have often been evident backstage within their parties. In short, Levitsky and Ziblatt come to the party too late—when the political party that will generate dangerous options has already been captured through methods that would not pass constitutional muster if they were carried out on the general political stage itself.

In order to prevent constitutional collapse, then, non-partisan constitutional institutions like constitutional courts or neutral election commissions must be charged with checking the general health of parties and party systems. In failing democracies, we can see that party dysfunction is alarmingly common in this era of shifting political orientations as the political spectrum swings from a Left/Right orientation to a localist/globalist one. This disorientation in turn makes it easier for voters to steer their ships of states off constitutional course.

But we shouldn't blame the voters. Without constitutionalized processes in which parties can be assessed, the building blocks of a democratic state can become subject to

---

[15] Steven Levitsky and Daniel Ziblatt, *How Democracies Die* (New York: Crown Books, 2018).

internal corruption and eventually to a potentially anti-democratic turn. Once parties enter the political stage with anti-democratic and anti-constitutional methods of governance that are well-entrenched as party norms, then voters may be given toxic choices that masquerade as democratic options. Ordinary voters only see the democratic faces of candidates projected toward the public; they do not see the budding autocrats dominating their parties behind the scenes. People easily vote for change, but generally not for self-enslavement. But the new autocrats do not campaign on the basis of the program they plan to enact if elected.

If constitutional democracies can recognize the importance of parties to a democratic order and find ways to support and regulate them so that autocratic leaders can be spotted through the way that they take over or build their parties, then democracies may be saved from self-destruction. The secret to democratic self-preservation may rest in the realization that the party isn't over yet.

29 "Religious Talk" in Narratives of Membership
Ran Hirschl and Ayelet Shachar*

Introduction

Contrary to the predictions of secularization theory, religion is back with a vengeance. Following the tradition of the Enlightenment and adhering to theories of modernization and secularization, the canonical view across the human sciences in the second half of the twentieth century held that religion would fade away and lose its once-powerful, omnipresent hold on humanity. A perfect synopsis of this view is captured in C. Wright Mills's words (1959): "Once the world was filled with the sacred—in thought, practice, and institutional form. After the Reformation and the Renaissance, the forces of modernization swept across the globe and secularization, a corollary historical process, loosened the dominance of the sacred. In due course, the sacred shall disappear altogether except, possibly, in the private realm."[1]

These predictions have failed to materialize. From the surge in Christian fundamentalism to revivalist Islam to the spread of Catholicism and Pentecostalism in the global

---

* The authors thank the volume editors for their helpful comments on an earlier draft, as well as Jan Mertens for his effective research assistance.
[1] C. Wright Mills, *The Sociological Imagination* (New York, NY: Oxford University Press, 1959), 32–33. For an overview of the secularization debate, see Pippa Norris and Ronald Inglehart, *Sacred and Secular: Religion and Politics Worldwide* (Cambridge: Cambridge University Press, 2004).

south, and from the rise of Hindu and Buddhist nationalisms in Asia to heated debates about religion-infused morality, cultural heritage, and boundaries of membership in the Americas and in Europe, it is hard to overstate the significance of the religious revival in early twenty-first century politics. The numbers are striking. Across the world, two-thirds of the population defines itself as religious; it is estimated that 91 percent of sub-Saharan Africa's population, 70 percent of the Middle East's population, and 80 percent of Latin America's population identify as religious, with North America (a whopping 47 percent) and Europe (44 percent) as the least religious regions. Strikingly, the two largest democracies in the world, India and the United States—both of which adhere to a constitutional separation of religion and state—are frequently mentioned as the two most religious societies in the world, as measured by how significant religion is in public discourse and in private lives.[2] Meanwhile, virtually every major religious tradition has produced its own forms of extremism and growing disregard for the rights of "Others." In an increasing number of countries the alignment between religious identity and populist-nationalist politics seems stronger than ever. At the same time, religious communities have been thriving at the level of civil society, oftentimes offering forms of belonging that undercut territorial borders and forge transnational allegiances. The constitutional domain has been a means for and the target of much of this religious revival. Consequently, religion's challenge to constitutional democracy has once again come to the fore.

Despite these momentous trends, the common assumption in the legal literature is that religion is as an "outsider" to the constitutional order, a threat and a force that cannot coherently be related to the modern conception of a sovereign people in whose name the constitution is written and ordained. This familiar perspective itself relies on a set of dichotomies that valorize the liberal constitutional order as progressive and enlightened, as a force of light against a sea of darkness, as a public, political enterprise that exercises tolerance toward those who do not share the liberal idea, in part through drawing a distinction between the public sphere of reason and deliberation, and the private sphere of religion and emotion.[3] These dualities have been subject to extensive criticism, and we will not repeat these lines of argument here. Instead, we want to highlight an often-neglected angle that has proven vital in the recent surge in populist and anti-immigrant nativist social movements and political parties that increasingly pose a challenge to constitutional democratic orders that are committed to fundamental rights, human dignity, the protection of minorities, and the values of pluralism and equality. The focus of our analysis is on the growing importance of "religious talk," which operates not as a rigorous practice or set of beliefs, but as a marker of shared identity, performing

---

[2] See Religion Data From End of Year Survery 2016, 25 (WIN/Gallop, April 10, 2017).

[3] For a comprehensive account, see Susanna Mancini and Michel Rosenfeld, eds., *Constitutional Secularism in an Age of Religious Revival* (Oxford: Oxford University Press, 2014). See also Matthias Kumm et al., "Editorial: The End of the 'West' and Global Constitutionalism," *Global Constitutionalism* 6 (2017): 1–11.

a boundary-drawing function. It distinguishes between the "true" and "authentic" people that, according to these movements, have too long been suppressed and now deserve to raise their head, and those who hold, or aspire to hold, equal membership in the political community, but are forever relegated to second-class citizenship on account of "who they are" (or are perceived to be)—namely, their "incompatibility" with the shared identity markers of the dominant majority.[4] As we show in the following pages, religious talk is fueling division and tension in countries that at least de jure, although not necessarily de facto, are committed to basic constitutional principles of equality, fairness, and freedom to all.

In the context of today's populist backlash, harnessing religious talk to draw boundaries between insiders and outsiders takes two forms. First, insiders can be defined positively as belonging to the dominant religious or ethnonational community (e.g., Hindu nationals in India, Jews in Israel, Muslim Malay in Malaysia); and second, the us/them division may be sustained by what we might call "anti"-politics, that is, by negatively defining who does *not* belong. The anti-immigrant, anti-Muslim rhetoric that has propelled the far right across Europe in the ballot boxes—France, Germany, the Netherlands, Austria, Hungary, and Poland are merely a few key examples—has relied heavily on this "anti"-strategy, which in turn permits papering over divisions within the majority. In these examples, the inflated contrast with the feared "*autres*" helps construct a unified "*nous*."[5] These tensions and contradictions have allowed political leaders and parties that have benefitted from the renewed emphasis on identitarian-conflict and majority-under-threat narratives to alternate between, or strategically combine, these positive and negative methods of defining the collective "we" under an alleged civilizational attack by "them," eroding some of the core tenants of liberal democracy along the way.

Our discussion proceeds in two steps. In the second Section, we identify four frontiers of clash between religion and constitutionalism, in particular of the prevalent liberal breed: (1) the ideational friction between liberal constitutionalism and religious doctrine; (2) the "clash of orders" challenge; (3) the transnational nature of religious solidarity and affiliation, and the challenge it poses for the statist constitutionalist project; and (4) the increasingly common affinity between (majoritarian) religion-based affiliation and populist variants of nationalism, and the threat that affinity poses to more inclusive definitions of "who belongs" within the domain of constitutional democracy. In the third Section, we

---

[4] On the centrality of the concept of the true and authentic people to populist movements, see, e.g., Jan-Werner Müller, *What Is Populism?* (Philadelphia: University of Pennsylvania Press, 2016).

[5] Social scientists and legal scholars have long been fascinated with various techniques of boundary making. Of this vast literature, see, e.g., Rogers Brubaker, *Citizenship and Nationhood in France and Germany* (Cambridge, MA: Harvard University Press, 1992); Michéle Lamonte and Marcel Fournier eds., *Cultivating Differences: Symbolic Boundaries and the Making of Inequality* (Chicago: University of Chicago Press, 1992); Sanford Levinson, " 'Who Counts'; 'Sez Who?,' " *Saint Louis University Law Journal* 58 (2014): 937–987.

explore in some detail the strategic deployment of religious talk by populist movements, parties, and leaders to promote "us/them" sentiments and to drum up nationalist meta-narratives of collective identity under siege. We suggest that the rise of "religious talk" as a form of political discourse is real and persistent not only because it rides on sentiments of fear and anxiety in a globalizing world, but also because it builds on some inconsistencies and competing narratives that are *internal* to the constitutional order in discordant political settings.[6] Such religious talk revives latent ethnic and cultural tropes, bringing back nativist and illiberal visions of membership that have never ceased to exist but have until recently been kept in check under the lid of liberal constitutionalism.

Constitutionalism and Religion: Four Frontiers of Clash

The first and most obvious clash between religion and constitutionalism is their different substantive values, ideational platforms, and policy preferences. Increasingly, these value conflicts manifest themselves through high-profile legal clashes and court cases in which the stakes for the competing parties and the social groups they represent are both high and visible.[7] Protection of gender equality, reproductive freedoms, LGBTQ rights, or the right to die with dignity are considered some hallmarks of the current liberal constitutional rights jurisprudence. Not all religious circles resist this emerging canon, yet many of them do, and some quite vehemently. The stance of the traditional Catholic Church, conservative Evangelical movements, Wahhabist Islam, and Ultra-Orthodox Judaism on these issues is well known.[8] It is diametrically opposed to the liberal constitutional

---

[6] For a now-classic analysis, see Rogers M. Smith, *Civic Ideals: Conflicting Visions of Citizenship in U.S. History* (New Haven, CT: Yale University Press, 1997). See also Ran Hirschl, *Constitutional Theocracy* (Cambridge, MA: Harvard University Press, 2010); Gary Jeffrey Jacobson, *Constitutional Identity* (Cambridge, MA: Harvard University Press, 2010); Charles Taylor, *A Secular Age* (Cambridge, MA: Harvard University Press, 2007).

[7] For a concise overview of such clashes and the stakes they raise, see Douglas NeJamie and Reva Siegel, "Religious Accommodation, and Its Limits, in a Pluralist Society," in *Religious Freedom and LGBT Rights: Possibilities and Challenges for Finding Common Ground*, ed. Robin Fretwell Wilson and William N. Eskridge Jr. (Cambridge: Cambridge University Press, 2018).

[8] Whereas the classic European wars of religion were fought primarily between Catholics and Protestants, in today's cultural wars a new division has emerged between liberal and conservative branches of the very same religions, be it Christianity, Judaism, Islam, and so on. This leads to the creation of new coalitions, too, in relation to supporting or opposing topics such as gender equality or sexual orientation. For example, in the landmark *Reference re Same Sex Marriage* [2004] 3 S.C.R. 698 [Canada], brought before the Supreme Court of Canada by the attorney general of Canada, the amicus interveners included various branches of religious groups, such as the Canadian Coalition of Liberal Rabbis for same-sex marriage (supporting the legislation); the Metropolitan Community Church of Toronto, which was the first Church in Canada to marry same-sex couples; and the Canadian Unitarian Council, which advocated equal marriage to all regardless of sexual orientation, on the one hand, and the more conservative branches of the Islamic Society of North America, the Catholic Civil Rights League, and the Evangelical Fellowship of Canada, which collectively created the Interfaith Coalition on Marriage and Family to oppose the same-sex legislation, on the other. Similar patterns are prevalent in other jurisdictions as well.

view. Diverging worldviews also persist in broader areas such as general education versus denominational curricula, the legal status of religious entities (e.g., in the context of labor or tax law), and the general status of religion within a given polity's constitutional order. Constitutional clashes over these differing worldviews, ideational platforms, and their realization in various policy areas are countless and omnipresent in virtually all constitutional democracies. In polities with a history of religion-infused law and morality, issues such as blasphemy, proselytism, inheritance, and personal status often collide with constitutional provisions regarding equality, freedom of expression, and freedom of religion. Religious sectors' fierce reactions to landmark court rulings such as the *Obergefell v. Hodges* decision in the United States, the UKSC ruling in *R v. JFS*, the ECtHR's judgment in *SAS v. France*, or most recently the ECJ's ruling in *Achbita v. G4S* are merely a few recent examples.[9]

A second source of clash between religion and the constitutional domain is structural: both represent competing governance orders. In most constitutional democracies, the role formerly granted to religion is conspicuously supplanted; a polity's constitutional framework is often its "supreme law" and, as such, tends to infiltrate many facets of public and private life, just as religion has been traditionally wont to do.[10] In some settings—the United States immediately comes to mind—the Constitution may itself acquire near-numinous status; much like holy scripture, it is enshrined.[11] As Aharon Barak, former president of the Supreme Court of Israel, once suggested, "nothing falls beyond the purview of judicial review. The world is filled with law; anything and everything is justiciable."[12] Under such an all-encompassing outlook, the law systemically conceives of religion in terms cognizable within the legal or constitutional framework.[13] It thus "formats" or reconstructs religion in a way that subjects it to the constitutional order.[14] Although the

---

[9] *Obergefell v. Hodges*, 576 U.S. ___ (2015); *R (E) v Governing Body of JFS* [2009] UKSC 15 [UK] (subjecting admission criteria in a North London Jewish day school to general administrative law and constitutional law equality provisions); *SAS v France*, Application No 43835/11 (ECtHR Grand Chamber, Judgment of July 1, 2014) [Council of Europe] (holding that, in the context of France's so-called "burqa ban," state autonomy and regulatory powers over wearing religious attire in the public sphere trump faith-based freedoms); *Achbita v. G4S*, Case C-157/15 (decision released March 14, 2017) [European Court of Justice] (holding that under certain conditions, employers may dismiss employees who refuse to comply with company policy concerning wearing religious attire while on duty).

[10] Constitutions typically include a supremacy clause, defining them as "the supreme law of the land" (in the United States), or simply the "supreme law" (in Canada). See, respectively, U.S. Constitution, Article VI, Clause 2; The Canadian Charter of Rights and Freedoms, Part I (ss. 1–34) of the Constitution Act 1982, Schedule B of the Canada Act 1982, 1982, c. 11 (U.K), s. 52.

[11] See, e.g., Sanford Levinson, *Constitutional Faith* (Princeton, NJ: Princeton University Press, 1988).

[12] Ran Hirschl, *Towards Juristocracy: The Origins and Consequences of the New Constitutionalism* (Cambridge, MA: Harvard University Press, 2004), 169.

[13] See, e.g., Benjamin Berger, *Law's Religion: Religious Difference and the Claims of Constitutionalism* (Toronto: University of Toronto Press, 2015).

[14] See, e.g., Ran Hirschl, "Constitutional Courts as Bulwarks of Secularism," in Robert Kagan et al., eds. *Consequential Courts: Judicial Roles in Global Perspective*, ed. Diana Kapiszewski, Gordon Silverstein, and Robert Kagan (Cambridge: Cambridge University Press, 2013), 311–334.

sovereign state and its human-rather-than-divine-made constitution are historical new-comers in comparison to the centuries-old reign of religion, modern law has consistently aimed to establish "the final authority to delimit the boundary between the religious and the nonreligious, the public and the private, the right and the good."[15]

In some parts of the world, this division of labor has permitted secular constitution-alism to frame religion as secondary. However, as widespread constitutionalism and its reach may be, it still lags behind religion's omnipresence in people's lives. As Benjamin Berger astutely observes, "the religious conscience ascribes to life a divine dimension that infuses all aspects of being. The authority of the divine extends to all decisions, actions, times, and places in the life of the devout."[16] Precisely because of its wholeness, ubiqui-tous nature, and embedded authority, religion addresses the human need for "belonging," "meaning," or "guidance" in a manner that is often more wholesome and effective (from the perspective of the believer and the faith community) than a given polity's consti-tutional framework. In its abstract plentitude, spiritual power, and supra-territoriality, religion is a kingdom without end; sovereign in the eyes of its followers, past, present, and future; here, there, and everywhere. Religion therefore presents a challenge to the state's monopolist power in the Weberian sense[17] or to the "seeing like a state" logic for-mulated by James Scott.[18] It further blurs expectations concerning functional differentia-tion, moral authority, and legal hierarchy, in line with Niklas Luhmann's social systems theory, by offering a comprehensive alternative source of law- and identity-making for its adherents.[19]

A third source of tension between constitutional orders and religion stems from the transnational nature of religious solidarity and advocacy. Religion knows no borders, metaphysical or territorial. Its ambit of authority and influence is distinctly supranational. Its global spread, worldwide leadership (the Holy See is an obvious example) aided by an intricate multinational institutional apparatus of congregations, ministers, and mission-aries, and by new information and communication technology, position religion as a powerful force in world politics. In particular, Christianity, Islam, and Buddhism have followed patterns of migration and diasporic settlement to become truly world religions.

---

[15] Cécile Laborde, *Liberalism's Religion* (Cambridge, MA: Harvard University Press, 2017), 5.

[16] Berger, *Law's Religion,* 247.

[17] Max Weber defined the state as a "human community that (successfully) claims the *monopoly of the legitimate use of physical force* within a given territory" (emphasis in original). He continues, "[i]f the state is to exist, the dominated must obey the authority claimed by the powers that be." See Weber's lecture "Politics as a Vocation" (1919) for a discussion of this conception of statehood.

[18] James Scott, *Seeing Like a State: How Certain Schemes to Improve the Human Condition Have Failed* (New Haven, CT: Yale University Press, 1998), 4–8.

[19] On these tensions, see, e.g., Ayelet Shachar, "State, Religion, and the Family: The New Dilemmas of Multicultural Accommodation," in *Shari'a in the West*, ed. Rex Ahdar and Nicholas Aroney (Oxford: Oxford University Press, 2010), 115–130; Ran Hirschl and Ayelet Shachar, "The New Wall of Separation: Permitting Diversity, Restricting Competition," *Cardozo Law Review* 30 (2009): 2535–2560.

The Protestant Pentecostal and Evangelical movements have acquired significant influence among the local populations in Latin America, Africa, and Asia. These processes are perfectly aligned with globalization processes and what has been termed "the network society."[20] Taken as a whole, the challenge posed by the deterritorialized reach of religion to the current international order that still manifests many of the hallmarks of "Westphalian" constitutionalism, with its territorial-centered nation-building and "we the people" narrative, is obvious. The global reach of religion, with its cross-border transnational solidarity basis, offers a viable alternative to the territory-, nation-, or polity-based constitutional framework.

In some respects, the transnational religion challenge to constitutionalism resembles the challenge posed by global economic conglomerates to state regulatory powers. Interests and resources may be managed on a global scale that evades the grip of any single state-based constitutional order. In other important respects, the challenge of religion is mightier, as few corporate leaders (let alone constitutional thinkers) enjoy the visibility, clout, and popular following of a Catholic pope, Shia Grand Ayatollah, Mahayana Buddhist leader, or even various star "televangelists." The influence of such religious leaders in support of a cause or policy is likely to far outweigh the words or actions of any nonreligious leaders or stakeholders.[21]

An important aspect of religion's transnational nature and alternative basis for solidarity is its tremendous capacity to mobilize people across borders. The effect on the scope and reach of "cause-lawyering" religious litigation has been considerable. Christian and other faith-based civil society organizations in the United States have developed a "protecting religious liberty" agenda with legal aid, litigation-oriented strategies, case-based grassroots activism, cause-lawyering, and amicus briefs to advance religious interests in countries across the globe.[22] In recent years, the American experience alongside the more general take-home message of Charles Epp's "support structure for legal mobilization" thesis[23] have reached world religions. Increasingly, international religious groups have appropriated rights discourse, and have harnessed its power to advance their causes in a way characterized as "frame-jacking."[24] The zeitgeist of this phenomenon is captured by the words of a former director of the Center for Law and Religious Freedom (CLRF): "If my wife had a brain tumor and I said all we are doing is praying because my God is a mighty God and he can save and heal and he can take care of that tumor, you would say to

---

[20] See Peter van der Veer, "Religion after 1750," in *The Cambridge World History* (Cambridge: Cambridge University Press, 2015), 7:178.

[21] Such patterns are further manifested in those cases where religious groups serve as the main source of information for their adherents when it comes to forming an opinion about charged political topics.

[22] C-FAM: The Catholic Family and Human Rights Institute and the Christian Legal Society ["seeking justice with the love of God"] are merely two examples.

[23] Charles R. Epp, *The Rights Revolution: Lawyers, Activists, and Supreme Courts in Comparative Perspective* (Chicago: University of Chicago Press, 1998).

[24] Clifford Bob, *The Global Right Wing and the Clash of World Politics* (Cambridge: Cambridge University Press, 2012); Clifford Bob, "The Global Right Wing and Theories of Transnational Advocacy," *The International Spectator* 48 (2013): 71–85.

us 'We admire your faith, but go to the doctor.' So when it comes to religious liberty this idea of just praying without going to a lawyer is inadequate, superficial and unbiblical."[25]

Expanding its reach beyond Europe and North America, internationally-funded religious freedom litigation has now taken a global turn, advocating on behalf of the rights of religious minorities (notably Christian communities in non-Christian settings such as China, India, Vietnam, and Egypt), or, conversely, fueling litigation-oriented campaigns against expansion of reproductive freedoms (e.g., in Latin America and the Philippines) or against a similar expansion of protection of LGBTQ rights (e.g., in Africa).[26]

A fourth, emerging source of tension between constitutional democracy and religion is the strategic use of "religious talk" by populist-nationalist leaders to promote and exploit exclusionary divisions within the body politic. It is to that source of tension, arguably the most pertinent to the thematic framework of, and challenges identified by, this volume that we now turn.

Who Belongs? Religious Talk and the Surge of Populist Nationalism

No longer a "default design choice," liberal constitutionalism is under siege in many parts of the world.[27] One of the main characteristics of the current populist or illiberal trend in world politics is the increasing reliance on religious rhetoric and the heightened demarcation of "us/them." Religion-based boundaries (real or imagined) are reintroduced into politics or strategically deployed to advance exclusionary or nativist platforms. Much has been written about President Trump's persistent recourse to playing the anti-Muslim card, his portrayal of the United States as a Christian nation under siege, his repeated association of Islam with evil, and his countless allusions to Christian scripture and prophecy.[28]

---

[25] Cited in Kevin den Dulk, "In Legal Culture, But Not of It," in *Cause Lawyers and Social Movements*, ed. Austin Sarat and Stuart Scheingold (Stanford, CA: Stanford University Press, 2006), 197, 211.

[26] Kapya Kaoma, *Globalizing the Culture Wars: U.S. Conservatives, African Churches & Homophobia* (Political Research Associates, 2009); Kapya Kaoma, *American Culture Warriors in Africa: A Guide to the Exporters of Homophobia and Sexism* (Political Research Associates, 2014). See also Johanna Kalb, "Human Rights Proxy Wars," *Stanford Journal of Civil Rights and Civil Liberties* 13 (2017): 53–94.

[27] Tom Ginsburg, Aziz Hug, and Mila Versteeg, "Symposium Introduction: The Coming Demise of Liberal Constitutionalism," *University of Chicago Law Review* 85 (2018): 239–255.

[28] See, e.g., Phillip Gorski, "Why Evangelicals Voted for Trump: A Critical Cultural Sociology," *American Journal of Cultural Sociology* 5 (2017): 338–354; Nina Burleigh, "Does God Believe in Trump? White Evangelicals Are Sticking with Their 'Prince of Lies,'" *Newsweek*, October 5, 2017; Michelle Goldberg, "Donald Trump, the Religious Right's Trojan Horse," *New York Times*, January 27, 2017; Emma Green, "Donald Trump Declares a Vision of Religious Nationalism," *The Atlantic*, February 2, 2017. As Sanford Levinson has noted, debates about how to define the "American people" have in the past deployed certain homogenizing aspects of religious talk, as in the Federalist 2: "With equal pleasure I have as often taken notice that Providence has been pleased to give this one connected country to one united people—a people descended from the same ancestors, speaking the same language, professing the same religion, attached to the same principles of government, very similar in their manners and customs, and who, by their joint counsels, arms, and efforts, fighting side by side throughout a long and bloody war, have nobly established general liberty and independence." For critical analysis,

Recent sociological research further suggests that symbolic defense of the United States' perceived Christian heritage was a considerable factor in voters' support for Trump in the 2016 presidential elections.[29] In Russia under President Putin, observers note, the relations between the Kremlin and the Russian Orthodox Church have not been this close in over a century. The Russian Parliament adopted a series of laws that set out to protect majoritarian "religious feelings" and "traditional values," thereby explicitly targeting core tenets of constitutional democracy.[30] Meanwhile, in Turkey, President Recep Tayyip Erdoğan and the AKP party have been advancing an illiberal constitutional agenda that, among other things, brings back faith-based values into the national collective identity discourse after over eighty years of militant secularism guided by the Kemalist vision. In virtually all these settings, the wave of religion-infused political rhetoric has translated into the quest for greater political control of apex courts' composition and the accompanying appointment of conservative judges sympathetic to the religio-nationalist line; nationalist legislation on matters such as sovereignty, citizenship, and immigration; and rapidly diminishing respect for pluralism, minority rights, and civil liberties. These tendencies are often complemented, if not fueled, by an "us first" attitude and steadfast positions against global constitutionalist values viewed as an elitist, liberal project.[31]

The alliance between religious-infused markers of identity and the current populist-nationalist assault on constitutional democracy is also evident in less commonly traversed settings. In Poland, President Andrzej Duda and the right-wing, national conservative Law and Justice Party (PiS) rediscovered religion as a voter magnet in that country, and stress the close ties between Roman Catholicism and Polish national identity.[32] As in other places, women's rights were among the first causalities. One of the new government's initial actions was to support a proposed citizens' bill, known as the "Stop Abortion" legislation, which would have tightened an already restrictive law, making abortion punishable with a five-year prison term. Widespread protests and rallies around the country, most

---

see Sanford Levinson, *An Argument Open to All: Reading "The Federalist" in the 21st Century* (New Haven, CT: Yale University Press, 2015).

[29] See, e.g., Andrew L. Whitehead, Samuel L, Perry, and Joseph O. Baker, "'Make America Christian Again' Christian Nationalism and Voting for Donald Trump in the 2016 Presidential Elections," *Sociology of Religion* (forthcoming in 2018), https://doi.org/10.1093/socrel/srx070.

[30] Mikhail Antonov, "Religion, Sexual Minorities and the Rule of Law in Russia: Mutual Challenges," St. Petersburg National Research University, Higher School of Economics Research Paper No. WP BRP 45/PS/ 2017; Alicja Curanović, "The Guardians of Traditional Values Russia and the Russian Orthodox Church in the Quest for Status," *Transatlantic Academy Paper Series* (February 2015).

[31] For further discussion, see, e.g., Ran Hirschl, "Opting Out of 'Global Constitutionalism,'" *Law & Ethics of Human Rights* 12 (forthcoming 2018).

[32] The preamble of the Constitution of Poland (1997) refers to "We the Polish Nation—all citizens of the Republic, [B]oth those who believe in God as the source of truth, justice, good and beauty; [A]s well as those not sharing such faith but respecting those universal values as arising from other sources." It also includes this phrase: "Beholden to our ancestors for their labours, their struggle for independence achieved at great sacrifice, for our culture rooted in the Christian heritage of the Nation and in universal human values."

of them organized and led by women, have eventually led to a withdrawal of the government's support for the proposed bill, but not from its broader agenda.

Meanwhile, in Hungary a direct confrontation between the nationalist government led by Viktor Orbán, and the EU regarding centralized migrants relocation policies, has been brewing since the 2015 refugee crisis. Religious talk has been invoked by Orbán to defy EU policies on the matter. Orbán went on record stating that "[T]hose arriving have been raised in another religion, and represent a radically different culture. Most of them are not Christians, but Muslims. This is an important question, because Europe and European identity is rooted in Christianity. Is it not worrying in itself that European Christianity is now barely able to keep Europe Christian? There is no alternative, and we have no option but to defend our borders."[33] The level of such exclusionary rhetoric in Hungary, as well as in neighboring Poland, the Czech Republic, and Slovakia—the four members of the Visegrád Group—constituting a cultural and political alliance of Central European countries that have jointed the EU as part of its eastward expansion in 2004, has been elevated in recent months. These countries are now governed by Eurosceptic leaders who have adopted nationalist, anti-immigrant positions to bolster their standing. This has led to repeated clashes with the European Commission and other EU bodies concerned with a deepening gap between the West and East in the bloc in terms of respect for democracy and the rule of law. These tensions have further aggravated in the wake of a September 2017 European Court of Justice ruling that upheld the EU refugee relocation scheme aimed at spreading more evenly the burden of accommodating incoming refugees among the EU Member States, while flatly dismissing the claims to the contrary raised by Hungary and Slovakia, leading a growing number of commentators to portray the Hungarian and Slovakian stance as intolerant and illiberal.[34]

In India, the largest constitutional democracy in the world, Hindu-based exclusionary talk is thriving. Narendra Modi, prime minster of India, has appealed to Hinduism and Hindu nationalism (what is commonly known as *Hindutva*—the official ideology of the Bharatiya Janata Party (BJP) since 1989) to galvanize support for his party. The official BJP platform begins with these words: "The Hindu awakening of the late twentieth century will go down as one of the most monumental events in the history of the world. Never before has such demand for change come from so many people. Never before has Bharat, the ancient word for the motherland of Hindus—India, been confronted with such an impulse for change. This movement, Hindutva, is changing the very foundations of Bharat and Hindu society the world over." To put its money where its mouth is, the BJP-led government has since been promoting a new citizenship bill (2016) that once

[33] "Migration Crisis: Hungary PM Says Europe in Grip of Madness," *The Guardian*, September 3, 2015, https://www.theguardian.com/world/2015/sep/03/migration-crisis-hungary-pm-victor-orban-europe-response-madness.
[34] See Joined Cases C-643/15 and C-647/15 *Slovakia and Hungary v Council* (decision released September 6, 2017) [European Court of Justice]. See also Maria Skóra and Matthias Hasler, *The Future of the Visegrad Group*, Roundtable Report: Mapping the Interests with the V4 (Das Progressive Zentrum, October 9, 2017).

enacted would ease the path to citizenship for Hindus, Sikhs, Buddhists, and Christians fleeing persecution in Afghanistan, Pakistan, and Bangladesh (all Muslim countries). Seemingly welcoming, the proposed bill rekindles religious and ethnic tensions in India by omitting Muslims from its purview, despite the fact that India is home to approximately 170 million Muslim citizens—the largest Muslim minority in the world.

Several BJP-led Indian states have followed suit in adopting exclusionary, religion- and ethnicity-based policies. In 2017, to pick one example, the governments of Uttar Pradesh, Madhya Pradesh, Rajasthan, and Gujarat (all ruled by the BJP, with a combined population of approximately 400 million people) defied a string of Supreme Court of India rulings concerning freedom of expression and the nature of "public order" in the Indian constitution, and imposed statewide bans on screening the film *Padmavati*; Hindu nationalists claim that the film depicts the legendary Rajput queen Padmavati in a poor light, in particular in implying she was engaged in intimate relations with Alauddin Khalji, Sultan of Delhi (1296–1316). Exotic as the details may be, they reflect the ever-increasing political reliance on culturally-infused religion- and ethnicity-based talk to promote an enhanced Hindu-based version of Indian nationalism against a strong constitutionally-backed notion of secularism.[35]

In Israel, the right-wing nationalist coalition government led by Benjamin Netanyahu, and in particular the coalition party Ha'Bait Ha'Yehudi (Hebrew: the Jewish Home)— the party's name speaks for itself—are forcefully advancing the "Israel is a Jewish state" ticket, thereby threatening to alter the foundational two-tenet character of Israel as a Jewish *and* democratic state. Since 2014, Ha'Bait Ha'Yeudi has promoted the adoption of a new Basic Law: Israel as the Nation State of the Jewish People, dubbed the "nation-state bill" aimed at bolstering the country's Jewish-national character while limiting its democratic character; the proposed bill would instruct the Supreme Court to favor, in case of a conflict or lacuna, the "Jewish" (however difficult this term remains to define) over the "democratic" character of the state.[36] The draft law is also aimed at bolstering the status of Jewish law as an interpretive source. It proposes to prescribe Jewish law in the absence of legal precedent and instruct courts to interpret laws in the spirit of Israel as the homeland of the Jewish people.[37] These legislative attempts are backed by strong political rhetoric. In August 2017, to pick one example, the minister of justice (of the Ha'Bait Ha'Yehudi party) declared publicly in reaction to a moderately liberalizing ruling of the Supreme

---

[35] The 42nd Amendment (1976) to the Indian constitution inserted into the preamble to the constitution the words "socialist" and "secular" so that it reads: "We, the people of India, having solemnly resolved to constitute India into a sovereign, socialist, secular democratic republic." Thus "secularism" has formally been incorporated into the constitution. The Supreme Court of India has since held that secularism is indeed part of the basic structure of the constitution. See, e.g., *S. R. Bommai v. Union of India*, AIR 1994 SC 1918 [India].

[36] "Bill Would Force High Court Rulings to Favor Israel's Jewish Character over Democracy," *Ha'Aretz*, July 11, 2017, http://www.haaretz.com/israel-news/.premium-1.800834?=&ts=_1499855787280.

[37] "Israeli Bill Prescribes Jewish Law in Absence of Legal Precedent," *Ha'Aretz*, September 17, 2017, http://www.haaretz.com/israel-news/.premium-1.812648.

Court of Israel in the context of asylum-seeker rights that matters of demography and the Jewish majority have become a legal "blind spot" for the Court in as much as they carry no decisive weight in comparison to questions of individual rights. "Zionism should not continue, and I say here, it will not continue," the minister added, "to bow down to the system of individual rights interpreted in a universal way that divorces them from the history of the Knesset and the history of legislation that we all know."[38] To signal her seriousness, the minister of justice successfully orchestrated a campaign to appoint a new Jewish nationalist cohort of judges to the Supreme Court.

Attempts to prioritize Israel's Jewish nature over its democratic one are evident in other domains of public life. In order to "Judaise" mix-cities, a so-called "Muezzin bill" that muffles calls for prayers in Muslim neighborhoods was passed, formally on an excessive-noise prevention rationale (an exemption for Ultra-Orthodox Jewish end-of-Shabbat horn is included in the law). The exclusionary agenda is further promoted through a fear-mongering campaign against Arab citizens ("Arab voters are moving en masse to the voting polls; go to vote," tweeted Netanyahu to his millions of followers on election day in March 2015), alongside extensive "religification" of public discourse and popular culture as well as government support for enhanced Judaic studies in school curricula, promoted by the minister of education, who, since 2015, is the leader of the aforementioned Ha'Bait Ha'Yehudi party.

The central role of religious talk in the nationalist-populist turn in contemporary Israel is also manifested in the considerable retreat from attempts to break the monopoly of the Orthodox stream over the provision of religious services. In a direct blow to more liberal and progressive streams of Judaism, the government approved in 2017 a controversial bill enshrining the strictly Orthodox chief rabbinate's monopoly over conversions to Judaism, thereby providing the Ultra-Orthodox branch of Judaism with control over the perennial "who is a Jew?" question and its implications for the naturalization processes prescribed by Israel's Law of Return.[39] In adopting this law, the government overturned a string of Supreme Court decisions that recognized the pluralistic character of the world's Jewish community and upheld the legitimacy of conversion to Judaism according to different streams of Judaism. In contrast, the new legislation and the exclusionary rhetoric that surrounded it reject this pluralism. Instead, Israel—the only Jewish state in the world and a country that since its inception has seen itself as the homeland of the entire world's Jewry—has adopted a new set of policies that effectively render the better part of Jewish communities outside of Israel, most notably American Jews affiliated with the Reform and Conservative movements, inauthentic, "second class" Jews.

---

[38] "Justice Minister Slams Israel's Top Court, Says It Disregards Zionism and Upholding Jewish Majority," *Ha'Aretz*, August 29, 2017, http://www.haaretz.com/israel-news/1.809617.

[39] See Isabel Kershner, "Israel Faces Uproar Aboard as Netanyahu Yields to Ultra-Orthodox Jews," *New York Times*, July 3, 2017.

The "Women of the Wall" (Ne'shot Ha'Kotel) saga provides another telling illustration.[40] For the last fifteen years, an organization representing Reform, Conservative, and other non-Orthodox Jewish organizations has fought to secure the rights of women to pray at the Western Wall, traditionally reserved exclusively for Orthodox and Ultra-Orthodox stream prayers controlled by the Chief Rabbinate. In a series of rulings the Supreme Court of Israel, sitting as the High Court of Justice, sided with the Women of the Wall group on various gender equality, freedom of expression, and administrative law grounds, and ordered the government to accommodate the Western Wall prayer rights of non-Orthodox Jews. After an arduous process, a compromise was reached in early 2017. However, later that year, the Netanyahu government succumbed to pressure from Ultra-Orthodox parties upon which the governing coalition depends and suspended the plan, citing concerns about the "authentic Jewish tradition" of Reform and Conservative Jews. Ultra-Orthodox rabbis went on to declare members of these streams as "heretical" and as "worse than gentiles."

The process of "religification," which places non-Jews or non-Orthodox Jews under a cloud of suspicion, is corrosive to the inherently pluralistic fabric of Israeli society. The latest casualties in this ongoing battle for the constitutional identity and "soul" of the country are women's rights. The current round of challenge focuses on core mainstream public institutions, including the halls of study of higher education and the army, whereby an otherwise legitimate cause to encourage Ultra-Orthodox Jews to serve in the military and to enroll in colleges and universities has taken an exclusionary turn. Recent calls have been made to change the law so as to permit the establishment of sex-segregated military units and the provision of male-only educational programs. As the Association for Civil Rights in Israel observes in an official letter of objection to these proposed legislative encroachments on the values of equality, pluralism, and freedom of thought: "The universities and colleges in Israel are attended today by religious and secular Jews, Mizrahim and Ashkenazim, traditional Jews and Arabs, Druze, Israelis of Ethiopian origin, and immigrants from the Former Soviet Union. This is the most important civil arena in Israeli society, where everyone meets just before they go on to become part of the Israeli job market and economy. The proposed law permitting gender segregation in academic institutions will seriously damage this arena."[41] The matter is now before the legislature and the courts, reflecting the widening gaps among the different sectors of the Israeli society and the deepening patterns of discrimination, which, disturbingly, are endorsed by, rather than countered and dismantled, by the current governmental establishment.

---

[40] See, generally, Yuval Jobani and Nahshon Perez, *Women of the Wall: Navigating Religion in Sacred Sites* (New York: Oxford University Press, 2017).

[41] The Association for Civil Rights in Israel, Letter concerning the Proposed Law: Council for Higher Education (Amendment—Encouraging Access to Higher Education), 5777-2017, submitted to the Chairperson of the Ministerial Committee for Legislative Affairs and the Justice Minister, November 29, 2017, https://www.acri.org.il/en/wp-content/uploads/2017/12/Exclusion-of-Women.pdf.

Meanwhile, in Malaysia, the political sphere, at both the state and federal levels, has undergone substantial Islamization over the last four decades.[42] The Islamic *dakwah* ("religious revival") movement emerged in the mid-1970s.[43] The Pan-Malaysian Islamic Party (Parti Islam Se-Malaysia, PAS) has been gaining political support and clout since the 1980s.[44] In the hotly contested 2013 general elections, a coalition of PAS and its allies (the Pakatan Rakyat coalition, PKR), received the majority of the popular vote. Nonetheless, as a result of Malaysia's rather peculiar electoral system, the mainstream Barisan Nasional (BN) coalition has still managed to secure the majority of seats in the Parliament. The rise of political Islam has affected the mainstream moderate establishment. Even politicians affiliated with the BN must now resort to "religious talk" in their appeal to the Islamic vote. The former prime minister of Malaysia, Mahathir bin Mohammad, speaking as a representative of United Malays National Organisation (UMNO) (the largest political party in Malaysia, and a pillar of the BN coalition), declared in 2001 that the country was an Islamic State *(negara Islam),* not merely a country that had endorsed Islam as its official religion.[45]

The effect of the Islamization of political discourse on the sphere of Malaysia's constitutional jurisprudence has been profound. To provide but one example, a Catholic newspaper in Malaysia used the word "Allah" to refer to God in its Malay-language edition. A controversy arose regarding who may use the word "Allah": whether it is an exclusively Muslim word (as some Muslim leaders in Malaysia suggest) or a neutral term referring to One God that may be used by all regardless of religion, as the newspaper argued. A law was enacted in the 1980s to ban the use of the term in reference to God by non-Muslims, but had seldom been enforced prior to 2007. In 2009, the High Court in Kuala Lumpur ruled that the ban on non-Muslims using the word "Allah" to refer to God was unconstitutional as it infringed on freedom of expression and freedom of religion principles. The court went on to state that the word "Allah" is the correct word for "God" in various Malay translations of the Bible, and that it has been used for centuries by Christians and Muslims alike in Arabic-speaking countries. This ruling was viewed by radical Islamists as a legitimization of insidious attempts to convert Muslims to Christianity. Riots and

---

[42] Joseph Chinyong Liow, *Piety and Politics: Islamism in Contemporary Malaysia* (Oxford: Oxford University Press, 2009).

[43] Ahmad F. Yousif, "Islamic Revivalism in Malaysia: An Islamic Response to Non-Muslim Concerns," *American Journal of Islamic Social Sciences* 21 (2004): 30–56.

[44] For a discussion of the historical development and rise of PAS, see Farish A. Noor, "Blood, Sweat and Jihad: The Radicalization of the Political Discourse of the Pan-Malaysian Islamic Party (PAS) from 1982 Onwards," *Contemporary Southeast Asia* 25 (2003): 200–232.

[45] The impact on popular culture in Malaysia is evident. In 2017, Malaysia's film board censored the Disney film *Beauty and the Beast* for including a short homosexual scene. In 2008, to pick another anecdote, the National Fatwa Council, Malaysia's top clerical Islamic body, issued a decree according to which the practice of yoga could corrupt Muslims because it involves not just physical exercise but also Hindu spiritual elements, chanting, and worship.

church burning followed. The government appealed the High Court ruling (lest we forget: this is the government of a country that purports to be a polity of all of its members). In October 2013, Malaysia's Court of Appeal (in a three-judge, all-Muslim bench) reinstated the ban on the use of the term "Allah" in reference to God by non-Muslims. Supporting the government's position, the judges stated that the usage of the name "Allah," "is not an integral part of the faith and practice of Christianity. From such finding, we find no reason why the respondent [the Catholic newspaper] is so adamant to use the name 'Allah' in their weekly publication. Such usage, if allowed, will inevitably cause confusion." The newspaper appealed. But in June 2014, the Federal Court of Malaysia made the final call on the matter. It drew on technical judicial review grounds to uphold (4:3) the ban on the use of "Allah" when referring to God by non-Muslims.[46] And so, in a multiethnic polity where "Islam is the religion of the Federation; but other religions may be practiced in peace and harmony in any part of the Federation" (Article 3), where "every person has the right to profess and practice his religion and to propagate it" (Article 11.1), and where "every religious group has the right to manage its own religious affairs" (Article 11.3), the word "Allah" in reference to God may only be invoked by Muslims.

While "religious talk" may propel populist leaders to secure votes and power, inflaming the affinity between religion and collective identity is a dangerous strategy, since, even if initially promoted by the political establishment, it may easily get out of hand. Consider the constitutional implications of the rise of political Islam in Egypt. Article 2 of the Egyptian Constitution, to pick one example, was amended in 1980 so as to establish principles of Islamic jurisprudence (sharia) as the only primary (rather than one possible) source of legislation in Egypt. This significant change was preceded, however, by state patronage of religion, including nationalization of *waqf* assets and later of al-Azhar University, the great institution of higher Islamic learning in Cairo, and the imposition of state-control over al-Azhar's curriculum and faculty positions, including the appointment of Shaykh al-Azhar (head of al-Azhar University)—a major spiritual leader and sharia interpretive authority. Meanwhile, the Egyptian Supreme Constitutional Court (whose members are appointed by the government) developed an innovative interpretive matrix of religious directives—the first of its kind by a nonreligious tribunal—so as to interpret the aforementioned Article 2 in a moderate way, all while political power-holders repeatedly outlawed the increasingly popular Muslim Brotherhood movement.[47]

As often happens, religion's appeal cannot be fully tamed by government control, constitutional or otherwise. The Egyptian revolution of 2012 (also known as the January 25 revolution) followed. The constitution introduced in December 2012 by then-president Mohamed Morsi (of the Freedom and Justice Party founded by the Muslim Brotherhood)

---

[46] *Titular Roman Catholic Archbishop of Kuala Lumpur v. Menteri Dalam Negeri* [2014] 6 C.L.J. 541 [Malaysia].

[47] In 2007, for example, then-president Hosni Mubarak introduced a set of constitutional amendments (approved in a referendum) that imposed a ban on the establishment of religious parties (a blatant anti–Muslim Brotherhood move), and loosened controls over security forces in its "war on terror."

not only reproduced Article 2 (stating that principles of Islamic sharia are "the" source of legislation), but also introduced Article 219, which uses technical terms from the Islamic legal tradition to define what is actually meant by "the principles of the Islamic Shari'a" as stated in Article 2. That constitution also guaranteed (Article 4) that al-Ahzar would be consulted on matters of Islamic law, Article 11 stated that the state is to "protect ethics and morality and public order," and Article 44 prohibited the defamation of prophets and religious messengers, such that it may be interpreted as prohibiting blasphemy. This new constitution clearly veered to the side of religion at the expense of dissolving the previous balance of power between state and mosque. In a volatile political environment, where constitution-drafting and redrafting become a symbol and instrument of expressing different conceptions of the relation between law and religion, virtually all these pro-religion changes were eliminated by the 2014 counterrevolution and its new constitution, which essentially returned Egypt's constitutional recognition of religion to its pre-2012. Egypt's recent turmoil offers a cautionary tale of the deep risks associated with setting fire to the identity-religiosity flame in the constitutional context.

Turning our gaze back to continental Europe, we witness the rise of the "anti"-politics: anti-immigrant, anti-Muslim, anti-globalization, and anti-supranational courts (in particular, the European Court of Human Rights). These are just a few of the components that far-right populist parties have deployed in asserting their political message. This "anti"-politics is augmented by and infused with coded understandings of us/them that depict a threatened and vulnerable Europe, whose cultural and identitarian roots are described as Christian, or in some narratives, Judeo-Christian.[48] That "pristine" Europe is being changed from within, so goes the argument, by the entry of uncontrolled waves of refugees, immigrants, and other uninvited foreigners, who resist Europe's traditions and wish to "Islamize" it. This far-right discourse relies on the Huntingtonian-like clash of civilization image, according to which Europe's identity stands in "fundamental conflict with Islam, understood as a separate and alien civilization."[49]

We saw earlier that "religious talk" does not rely on strict adherence to religious scripture or practice. Rather, it functions as a marker of identity that is mobilized to draw us/them distinctions. Similarly, the "civilizational" discourse remains rather vague about

---

[48] In the public debate leading to the adoption of the Lisbon Treaty (2009) and the emerging European constitution, several notable scholars and prominent politicians argued that the preamble of a new European constitution should contain a reference to Europe's "Judeo-Christian tradition" so as to avoid an artificial "Christian deficit" that would in turn hinder efforts to create an authentically European political community. In Catholic Europe, the continued prevalence of religious morality and heritage sends Poland and Ireland to frequent rendezvous with the European Court of Human Rights (ECtHR). In 2009, Prime Minister Silvio Berlusconi of Italy reacted to the ECtHR ruling in *Lautsi v. Italy* (overturned by the ECtHR Grand Chamber in 2011) that called for crucifixes to be removed from Italian public-school classrooms by describing it as a "nonsensical attempt to deny Europe's Christian roots" and thus "unacceptable for us Italians."

[49] See Rogers Brubaker, "The New Language of European Populism: Why 'Civilization' Is Replacing the Nation," *Foreign Affairs*, December 6, 2017.

what precise content is given to the term, allowing political actors in different European settings to drum up fear and to draw upon their respective national or local histories to best deploy for their ballot boxes' success the sense of alienation and "left behind" expressed by many of their supporters. Combined with the anti-politics, this is a powerful and dangerous cocktail that poses risk to established liberal democratic constitutional principles and institutions.

Conclusion

Religion, as Charles Taylor reminds us, has never really departed public life. Unlike the conventional binary image of a "clash of civilizations," there is actually a strong echo of religion in each and all constitutional models in existence. In fact, all constitutions—every single one, from France to Iran and anywhere in between—address the issue of religion head-on. Some constitutions despise it, others embrace or even defer to it, and yet others are agnostic but willing to accommodate certain aspects of it. But not a single constitution abstains, overlooks, or remains otherwise silent with respect to religion. With the exception of the concrete organizing principles and prerogatives of a polity's governing institutions, the only substantive domain addressed by all modern constitutions is religion. What could be a more telling illustration of religion's omnipresence in today's world, or a stronger testament to constitutionalism's entanglement with, if not existential fear of, religion?

The source of this deep trepidation is manyfold, and reflects ideational differences, contestation between powerful belief systems, and elements of localism and universalism embedded in the two domains. Either way, the constitutional domain is now a main sphere through which high-profile clashes over the legitimate scope and limits of the influence of religion in public life are waged. Our analysis in this chapter has emphasized another vital intersection of religion and constitutionalism: the rise of exclusionary religion-infused rhetoric at the basis of populist-nationalist policies aimed at redrawing boundaries of membership and belonging. As we have shown, this trend runs against the liberal constitutional project, and in some instances undermines the very notion of constitutional democracy by threatening to change the terms of belonging to a polity and the accompanying rights and protections enjoyed by those who, under the current populist-nationalist revival, are seen as unfit for membership in the neo-tribal state.

30 Economic Inequality and Constitutional Democracy
Ganesh Sitaraman

DOES THE CONTEMPORARY crisis of constitutional democracy have anything to do with economic inequality? In popular commentary and scholarly discourse, the answers vary wildly. Many argue that the vote for Brexit in 2016, the election of Donald Trump as president of the United States, and even the popularity of socialist senator Bernie Sanders are a function, directly or indirectly, of widening economic inequality. Others contend that racism and nativism are the central issues. Some think that some basic constitutional structures are outdated and need to be reformed. But others hold that constitutional democracy isn't in *crisis* at all.

For hundreds of years, many political theorists, statesmen, and constitutional thinkers would have been surprised that the question even needed to be asked. "An imbalance between rich and poor," Plutarch once wrote, "is the oldest and most fatal ailment of all republics." The central concern was that economically divided societies would lead to class warfare between rich and poor, and ultimately to revolution. Either the rich would triumph and establish an oligarchy, or the poor's champion, a demagogue, would wrest control from the wealthy, only to become a tyrant. Economic inequality inevitably meant the end of republican government.

While the intellectual history of this idea is largely forgotten, scholars and commentators have recognized the basic claim and its relevance today. Debates on campaign spending, lobbyist influence, revolving door corruption, and the corporate capture of regulators and judges, for example, are all motivated by a fear that economic power translates into political power—and that this undermines constitutional democracy.

But in spite of popular fears along these lines, systematic answers to some basic questions have remained elusive: Why exactly is economic inequality a problem for constitutional democracy? And how might constitutions or constitutional provisions mitigate the problem? After briefly outlining some drivers of contemporary economic inequality, this chapter offers one set of answers to these important questions.

A Global Gilded Age

For many, the financial crash of 2008 exposed a severe weakness in the economies of advanced constitutional democracies around the world: a generation-long trend in widening economic inequality. Thomas Piketty's *Capitalism in the Twenty-First Century* captured public attention with its data showing that economic inequality widened considerably in the United States, France, Germany, and the United Kingdom over the latter decades of the twentieth century.[1] In the United States, for example, the top 1 percent of people in 1976 took home about 8.5 percent of the national income. By 2014, they were taking home more than 20 percent of the national income.[2] In Britain, the top 1 percent took home more than 14 percent of the national income—more than double the amount they captured in the late 1970s. In Australia, the top 1 percent took home only about 5 percent of national income, only to climb up to 10 percent by the late 2000s.[3] Journalists and commentators have filled in the picture with vivid accounts of the harrowing lives of the working class—books such as *$2.00 a Day* and *Evicted*— while other works with titles *Plutocrats* and *Superclass* describe the lavish lives of wealthy global elites.[4]

The causes of the staggering increase in economic inequality are many. Globalization and technology get much of the attention, but tax, labor, financial, and competition policies are as, if not more, important. Globalization—and liberalized trade, in particular— promises to increase the wealth of all societies. But one of the central challenges of globalization is that the gains from trade have not been distributed evenly within countries. In developed Western economies such as the United States, for example, the

---

[1] Thomas Piketty, *Capital in the Twenty-First Century* (Cambridge, MA: Harvard University Press, 2013).

[2] Data from Emmanuel Saez, table A3, col. P99-100, 2014; http://eml.berkeley.edu/~saez/TabFig2014prel.xls.

[3] Piketty, *Capital*, 316.

[4] Kathryn J. Edin and H. Luke Shaefer, *$2.00 a Day: Living on Almost Nothing in America* (New York: Houghton Mifflin, 2015); Matthew Desmond, *Evicted: Poverty and Profit in the American City* (New York: Crown, 2016); Chrystia Freeland, *Plutocrats: The Rise of the New Global Super-Rich and the Fall of Everyone Else* (New York: Penguin, 2012); David Rothkopf, *Superclass: The Global Power Elite and the World They Are Making* (New York: Farrar, Strauss, and Giroux, 2008).

industrial Midwest suffered from the downsides of trade liberalization over the last two generations.[5] Under economic theory, the gains from trade should exceed the downsides, thereby allowing the winners to compensate the losers. But in political reality, such compensation rarely happens—and when it does, it is limited and largely ineffectual.[6] Technological change is similar. As automation reduces the need for human labor, workers are displaced, left jobless, or forced to downgrade to lower wage work.[7] Here too, retraining programs have not been effective at mitigating the downsides of economic change.

Tax policy is a culprit as well. Within countries such as the United States, taxation has increasingly been lifted from the wealthiest people. After World War II, the top marginal income tax rate on individuals in the United States was 90 percent, and it remained at 70 percent through the 1970s. By the early twenty-first century, the rate had been cut to below 40 percent. Piketty, Saez, and Stancheva have shown that top marginal tax rates correlate with the share of income going to the top 1 percent. Where rates are low, such as in the United States and United Kingdom, the share going to the top 1 percent is relatively high. In contrast, in countries such as Sweden and Denmark, high marginal tax rates correlate with significantly lower shares of the income going to the top 1 percent.[8] In addition, some countries have set up tax havens for elites and multinational corporations. According to economist Gabriel Zucman, 8 percent of global wealth—or about $200 billion—is held in tax havens. The consequence, Zucman argues, is to "steal the revenue of foreign nations," which shifts the revenue burden within countries from the wealthy to the middle class.[9]

Over the last generation, one of the defining features of the global economy has been the rise of the financial industry. "Financialization" is the process by which the economy becomes increasingly dependent on the financial sector, rather than the real economy, for growth. In 1950, for example, the financial sector represented 2.8 percent of US GDP. By 2012, that number was 6.6 percent. Financialization has important downsides: it makes an economy more volatile and more susceptible to economic crashes, and it misallocates resources (both capital and talent) away from long-term productive uses and toward shorter-term financial gains. The increasing wages in the

---

[5] For an early history of these changes, see Jefferson Cowie, *Capital Moves: RCA's Seventy-Year Quest for Cheap Labor* (Ithaca, NY: Cornell University Press, 1999).

[6] Timothy Meyer, "Saving the Political Consensus in Favor of Free Trade," *Vanderbilt Law Review* 70 (2017): 1009–1010.

[7] Erik Brynjolfsson and Andrew McAfee, *The Second Machine Age: Work, Progress, and Prosperity in a Time of Brilliant Technologies* (New York: W.W. Norton, 2014).

[8] Thomas Piketty, Emanuel Saez, and Stefanie Stancheva, "Optimal Taxation of Top Labor Incomes: A Tale of Three Elasticities," *American Economics Journal: Economic Policy*, 6 (2014): 253.

[9] Gabriel Zucman, *The Hidden Wealth of Nations: The Scourge of Tax Havens* (Chicago: University of Chicago Press, 2015).

financial sector in the United States, some estimate, are responsible for 15–25 percent of inequality since 1980.[10]

Shifts in antitrust policy have also contributed to widening inequality. As industrial sectors become more and more concentrated, oligopolistic or monopolistic pricing squeezes consumers. The monopolist, however, benefits in the form of increased "capital gains, dividends, and executive compensation."[11] In a wide variety of highly consolidated sectors—hospitals, pharmaceuticals, telecommunications, airlines—this phenomenon appears to be at work.

One of the only significant countervailing forces against the economic and political power of the wealthy and of corporations is labor unions. But over the last generation, labor unions have been deliberately attacked and, as a result, their membership has shrunk significantly. The consequences are significant for inequality. In 2015, an International Monetary Fund (IMF) study looked at unionization rates in twenty advanced economies. It found that the decline in unionization was responsible for about half the rise in inequality between 1980 and 2010. Why do unions have such great capacity to counteract inequality? When workers have some power over corporate decisions—through bargaining and influence more broadly—corporations are responsive to worker needs. But with worker power waning, corporate managers can decide to pursue policies that distribute the wealth of the corporation upward—to managers and shareholders—rather than to everyone in the corporation.[12]

The result of all these developments is that rising economic inequality has been with us for a generation—and, in the absence of significant policy changes at a domestic and global level, is only likely to get worse.

The Importance of Economic Equality for Constitutional Democracy

What does economic inequality have to do with constitutional democracy? After all, most constitutions say nothing specifically about "economic inequality" or "economic equality" or the "middle class." Indeed, the debate about economic inequality is largely a policy debate, with economists, not constitutional lawyers, in the drivers' seat. When it veers from policy, it takes on a moral valence, in which philosophers debate the finer points of the moral differences between equality of conditions and equality of opportunity.[13]

---

[10] Gautam Mukunda, "The Price of Wall Street's Power," *Harvard Business Review*, June 2014, https://hbr.org/2014/06/the-price-of-wall-streets-power; Thomas Phillippon and Ariell Reshef, "Wages and Human Capital in the U.S. Finance Industry, 1909–2006," *Quarterly Journal of Economics* 127 (2012): 1551.

[11] Lina Khan and Sandeep Vaheesan, "Market Power and Inequality: The Antitrust Revolution and Its Discontents," *Harvard Law and Policy Review* 11 (2017): 235–294.

[12] Florence Jaumotte and Carolina Osorio Buitron, "Inequality and Labor Market Institutions," *IMF Staff Discussion Note*, July 17, 2015, 25.

[13] See, e.g., Harry G. Frankfurt, *On Inequality* (Princeton, NJ: Princeton University Press, 2015).

But for much of the history of Western political and constitutional theory, statesmen and political theorists understood that relative economic equality was essential to constitutional democracy. Aristotle declared that "the best political community is formed by citizens of the middle class." James Harrington, the seventeenth-century English political theorist, noted that "equality of estates causeth equality of power." Noah Webster, eighteenth-century author of the first American dictionary, thought that "[a]n equality of property . . . is the very soul of a republic." "There can be no real political democracy," Theodore Roosevelt wrote in the early twentieth century, "unless there is something approaching an economic democracy."

What these and others recognized was that an economically unequal society was fundamentally incompatible with a republican form of government. There were three interlocking reasons for this fear. First is private oppression. In a severely unequal society, the wealthy are able to exert considerable power over ordinary people. At one extreme is slavery, but feudalism and peonage are other examples of extreme situations in which those with economic power are able to control the lives of ordinary citizens. Modern examples of this phenomenon are now legion. At a direct level, many companies now control their employees' clothing, political speech online, recreation, and diet.[14] They also require employees to sign noncompete agreements that effective restrict their ability to get jobs in the future.[15] For many supporters of republican self-government, private oppression was a form of tyrannical government. Individuals were effectively *governed* in so much of their private life by economic elites that they were stripped of basic freedoms and self-government. Such economic arrangements are incompatible with constitutional democracy.[16]

The second reason is that in an unequal society, the wealthy will use their wealth to shape public policies in order to preserve and expand their wealth and power, even at the expense of others. The result, of course, is to concentrate wealth further, increase the wealthy's ability to further shape policy, and restart the cycle. One commentator calls this the "doom loop of oligarchy."[17] Studies of oligarchies throughout history identify some of the tactics the wealthy use to entrench their wealth and power absent popular support. Economically, they pursue "property defense" and "income defense" policies to ensure they can maintain their existing wealth and continue to grow their wealth.[18] Politically, wealthy elites attempt to keep the general public divided; as long as the general public cannot organize

---

[14] Elizabeth Anderson, *Private Government: How Employers Rule Our Lives (and Why We Don't Talk about It)* (Princeton, NJ: Princeton University Press, 2017).

[15] Orly Lobel, *Talent Wants to Be Free: Why We Should Learn to Love Leaks, Raids, and Free Riding* (New Haven, CT: Yale University Press, 2013).

[16] Anderson, *Private Government*; K. Sabeel Rahman, *Democracy against Domination* (New York: Oxford University Press, 2017).

[17] Ezra Klein, "The Doom Loop of Oligarchy," *Vox*, April 11, 2014, https://www.vox.com/2014/4/11/5581272/doom-loop-oligarchy.

[18] Jeffrey A. Winters, *Oligarchy* (New York: Cambridge University Press, 2011).

collectively against the elites, the elites will be likely to preserve their political power.[19] Notably, a government pervasively captured by wealthy elites is not a constitutional democracy or a republic. It is better described as an oligarchy or plutocracy.

Another way to think of this problem is that societies with severe economic inequality can suffer from declining policy representativeness. Political scientists have shown that elected officials are more responsive to the policy preferences of wealthy elites than of ordinary people, and that the wealthy enjoy considerably greater access to politicians as well.[20] Neoliberalism at the global level might also contribute to declining policy responsiveness. As David Schneiderman argues in this volume, the rise of global economic law has meant a reduction in the ability of states to regulate a variety of economic policy issues. This in turn means that citizens have less control over basic economic policies that affect them, which not only increases the likelihood that such policies will not be responsive to citizen preferences, but also alienates citizens who feel disempowered.[21] Evidence from OECD countries suggests this mechanism might be at work: studies show that with economic integration comes declining political participation.[22]

The third fear that accompanied economic inequality was that backlash to an oligarchic system would lead to demagoguery, revolution, and ultimately tyranny. In an unequal society, the people writ large might be so dejected or oppressed by the wealthy elites that they fall prey to a demagogue who presses for a populist revolution, only to establish a tyranny once in power. As Alexander Hamilton wrote in the first of the *Federalist Papers*, "of those men who have overturned the liberties of republics, the greatest number have begun their career by paying an obsequious court to the people; commencing demagogues, and ending tyrants."

It is worth noting here the relationship between economic inequality and racial animus. While there has been considerable public debate over whether recent political moments—Brexit, the election of Donald Trump—were driven by economic anxiety or racial animus, the two categories are likely related. In times of economic insecurity and anxiety, people might be more susceptible to anti-immigrant, anti-refugee, and racial animus—even if the underlying facts show that immigrants and other minorities are not

---

[19] Matthew Simonton, *Classical Greek Oligarchy: A Political History* (Princeton, NJ: Princeton University Press, 2017).

[20] Larry M. Bartels, *Unequal Democracy: The Political Economy of the New Gilded Age* (Princeton, NJ: Princeton University Press, 2008); Martin Gilens, *Affluence and Influence: Economic Inequality and Political Power in America* (Princeton, NJ: Princeton University Press, 2012); Kay Lehman Schlozman, Sidney Verba, and Henry E. Brady, *The Unheavenly Chorus: Unequal Political Voice and the Broken Promise of American Democracy* (Princeton, NJ: Princeton University Press, 2012); Nicholas Carnes, *White Collar Government: The Hidden Role of Class in Economic Policy Making* (Chicago: University of Chicago Press, 2013). In this volume Desmond King and Rogers Smith make this point. See Desmond King and Rogers M. Smith, "Populism, Racism, and the Rule of Law in Constitutional Democracy Today," in *Constitutional Democracy in Crisis?*, ed. Mark A. Graber, Sanford Levinson, and Mark Tushnet (Oxford University Press: New York, 2018).

[21] David Schneiderman, "Disabling Constitutional Capacity: Global Economic Law and Democratic Decline," in *Constitutional Democracy in Crisis?*, eds. Mark A. Graber, Sanford Levinson, and Mark Tushnet (Oxford University Press: New York, 2018).

[22] See ibid.

responsible for those conditions (and indeed, might even be contributing to economic growth and success).[23] The rise of anti-immigrant nationalist parties throughout Europe and the populist backlash to welcoming refugees, for example, might therefore be a function of both identity and economics, rather than one or the other.

By contrast, economically equal societies might be less susceptible to populist mobilization. Aristotle, David Hume, and others recognized that members of the middle class have roughly the same economic interests and therefore they are able to govern each other in turn without skewing policy in favor of one group or another. Relative equality also suggested a shared ethical, cultural, and social worldview, making it less likely that the polity would break into polarized factions. In a society with a middle class that is larger than either the poor or rich, the middle class would never consistently decide in favor of either the upper or lower class, thus keeping policy in relative stasis and keeping policy responsive to most of the people. As a consequence, populist mobilization that relies on racial animus or ethnic identity might also be less likely, as the mass of the public does not have grievances in search of scapegoats. Indeed, some scholars have held up economically and ethnically homogeneous societies such as Sweden and Japan as models for egalitarianism.[24] While these countries have experienced political shifts in recent years, they hardly seem to be at the edge of "constitutional crisis," likely in part because of their economic and ethnic homogeneity.

Thus far, the analysis has largely been focused on static economic conditions and the impact on the political regime. Under conditions of economic equality, democracy should be relatively stable; under conditions of economic inequality, oligarchy or mob rule are severe risks. But economic conditions themselves are not static, and as they change, they might impact the constitutional system. Scholars in political science and comparative constitutional law often emphasize that the stability of constitutional systems is dependent on whether the regime can adapt to changes in the political bargains that created the regime.[25] In other words, when the political equilibrium that created the constitution no longer exists, the constitution risks change or failure. But it is important to note that changes in political coalitions and conditions might *themselves* be a function of underlying changes in social and economic conditions. For example, if the distribution of wealth in a country changes significantly, new political coalitions might emerge based on economic interests. The resilience of a political bargain is therefore dependent on a

---

[23] Alexander Alienkoff essay in this volume gestures at some points along these lines. T. Alexander Aleinikoff, "Inherent Instability: Immigration and Constitutional Democracies," in *Constitutional Democracy in Crisis?*, ed. Mark A. Graber, Sanford Levinson and Mark Tushnet (Oxford University Press: New York, 2018).

[24] Max Haller, in collaboration with Anja Eder, *Ethnic Stratification and Economic Inequality around the World* (London: Routledge, 2016), 163–187.

[25] See Zachary Elkins, Tom Ginsburg, and James Melton, *The Endurance of National Constitutions* (New York: Cambridge University Press, 2009), for an example of this approach applied to explaining the longevity of constitutional regimes.

variety of social, cultural, and economic conditions.[26] As these underlying conditions change, the resulting political effects can threaten the constitutional system as a whole.

In the mid- to late-twentieth century, many leading scholars in comparative politics and sociology focused on this question, with an emphasis on how economic development shaped political order. In *The Social Origins of Dictatorship and Democracy*, sociologist Barrington Moore famously declared "no bourgeois, no democracy." For Moore, the transformation of the agricultural sector into one defined by commercial interactions was the key for defining political change toward dictatorship or democracy. When the bourgeois allied with existing leaders, the result was top-down rule; when they opposed the inherited rulers, the result was democratic reform. It was the rising bourgeois, with new economic strength, that pushed for political change, leading to reforms and revolutions around the world. The political scientist Samuel Huntington showed in *Political Order in Changing Societies* that economic development theorists had gotten it wrong when they assumed that all good things in international development—economic growth, stability, democratization—went together. In fact, a rising middle class created greater *instability* in autocratic states, Huntington argued, because members of the middle class pushed for constitutional reforms. Political stability was a function of the regime's ability to respond to changing constituencies and conditions. Others disagreed, arguing that while democracies are more likely to persist when there is a developed economy, economic growth by itself does not lead to the emergence of democracy.[27]

The emphasis on a rising middle class and economic growth made sense in the mid- to late-twentieth century, when those were defining features of the prior decades. But given that extreme political and economic inequality have defined the early twenty-first century, the more relevant question is: What happens when the middle classes collapses? In recent years, Francis Fukuyama has emphasized this question. Like Huntington, Fukuyama notes that the key question is whether political systems can be responsive to changing economic conditions.[28] But he also notes that political institutions decay over time, and that the decaying institutions are unlikely to be up to the challenges of reform.

Constitutional theorists have argued that republican forms of government are particularly susceptible to this kind of "constitutional rot."[29] The hollowing out of constitutional underpinnings (such as economic equality) leaves the shell of a constitutional democracy intact but without the substance needed to sustain it. In other words, when there is a

[26] Rahman, *Democracy against Domination*; see also Daryl J. Levinson, "Foreword: Looking for Power in Public Law," *Harvard Law Review* 130 (2016): 31–143.

[27] Adam Przeworski, *Democracy and Development: Political Institutions and Well-Being in the World, 1950–1990* (New York: Cambridge University Press, 2000).

[28] Francis Fukuyama, *Political Order and Political Decay* (New York: Farrar, Straus, and Giroux, 2014); Francis Fukuyama, "The Future of History: Can Liberal Democracy Survive the Decline of the Middle Class?," *Foreign Affairs*, January/February 2012, 53.

[29] See Jack Balkin, "Constitutional Rot," in *Can it Happen Here? Authoritarianism in America*, ed. Cass R. Sunstein (New York: Harper Collins, 2018).

mismatch between a constitutional structure designed for conditions of economic equality and the reality of a severely unequal distribution of wealth, the polity will formally remain a constitutional democracy but functionally transform into an oligarchy.[30] This kind of zombie constitutional democracy has all the features of traditional oligarchies (private oppression and government capture) and the attendant risks of backlash, mob rule, and tyranny.

Constitutional Design and Economic Inequality: Four Types

Constitutional democracy depends on a relatively egalitarian distribution of wealth in society. But the distribution of wealth can change over time, potentially undermining constitutional democracy. One important question, then, is whether constitutional design can play a role in trying to preserve the underlying economic conditions needed to sustain a constitutional democracy.

Constitutions writ large, or specific constitutional provisions, can take four basic approaches to grappling with the risks that attend an unequal distribution of wealth in society: class warfare, anti-poverty, anti-oligarchy, and middle class. While constitutional democracies could incorporate elements from any (or all) of these approaches, it is helpful to consider each approach separately for analytic clarity.

TYPE 1: CLASS WARFARE CONSTITUTIONS. For most of the history of the West, statesmen and philosophers thought that economic inequality was inevitable in society. The great threat to regime stability was that the rich would oppress the poor, leading to an oligarchy or aristocracy, or that the poor would seek to confiscate the wealth of the rich, leading to mob rule. The solution to this problem was to domesticate class conflict by channeling it into the political process. These kinds of constitutions can be called class warfare constitutions, though they are more conventionally (and somewhat misleadingly) referred to as "mixed government." Thus, in ancient Rome, the Senate represented the Patrician class, while the Tribunate represented the Plebeians. The gothic constitution in England was similar, with a House of Lords and a House of Commons. Aristotle explained that in these regimes, rich and poor alike had a share and stake in government; Polybius thought the important feature was that each class had a check on the other. On either approach, the goal was to prevent class inequality from spilling over into political instability and violence.

As a matter of design, class warfare constitutions suffer from important problems. First, it is not obvious why the rich won't use their wealth to bribe or otherwise influence members of the lower house. Indeed, this was a problem in the later stages of the Roman

---

[30] Ganesh Sitaraman, *The Crisis of the Middle-Class Constitution: Why Economic Inequality Threatens Our Republic* (New York: Knopf, 2017).

Republic. Later constitutional theorists and the Renaissance city-states tried to solve this problem by having exceedingly short terms of office for the commoners, and in some cases, by selecting those representatives through a lottery. But this creates a new problem: a severe informational and skill asymmetry between repeat-player elites and neophyte commoners. The second problem with class warfare constitutions is that it is not clear that they will have any greater longevity than other regime types. Polybius's history of the Roman Republic was designed to show how Rome conquered the Mediterranean world in less than a century. But within the next century, the Republic had descended into a decades-long civil war that would bring an end to the Republic altogether. The causes were both military conquest, which brought spoils and territory without sufficient attention to their distribution across the population, and lack of enforcement of the Republic's agrarian laws, which had been designed to ensure a relatively equitable distribution of lands. As economic conditions shifted, politics became more and more unstable, and the structural checks in the system failed.

TYPE 2: ANTI-POVERTY CONSTITUTIONS. Many modern constitutional democracies are best described as having anti-poverty features. During the middle part of the twentieth century, an era of economic growth and an expanding middle class across the West overlapped with the ideological dominance of liberalism, which places a strong emphasis on individual rights. The result was advocacy for and then the creation of constitutional provisions that established minimal social and economic rights that were justiciable in court. The Constitution of South Africa, for example, has rights to housing, healthcare, and education written directly into the document itself. Given the limited resources of the government, these rights are to be progressively realized over time. Many other constitutions around the world also have economic and social rights included in their text, though the specific rights vary country to country, as does the degree to which the rights are justiciable or aspirational.[31]

The emphasis on social and economic rights has a variety of limitations. First, the liberal-rights model has historically been individualized and tied to courts. Much therefore depends on whether the rights are justiciable or aspirational, and whether their "progressive realization" is practically possible or whether it functionally collapses otherwise justiciable rights into hortatory aspirations. Second, and relatedly, even when court decisions do encourage politicians to act, social and economic rights largely focus on a "minimum core." It is in this sense that these constitutions are appropriately considered "anti-poverty constitutions." Their emphasis is not on ensuring every individual a place in

---

[31] Cass R. Sunstein, "Social and Economic Rights? Lessons from South Africa," *Constitutional Forum* 11 (2000–2001): 123–132; Katharine G. Young, "The Minimum Core of Economic and Social Rights: A Concept in Search of Content," *Yale Journal of International Law* 33 (2008): 113–176; Courtney Jung, Ran Hirschl, and Evan Rosevear, "Economic and Social Rights in National Constitutions," *American Journal of Comparative Law* 62 (2014): 1043–1094.

the middle class, but rather just alleviating the greatest material or dignitary deprivations. While this minimalistic approach is both consistent with liberalism's negative rights approach and with the mid- to late-twentieth century's emphasis on alleviating poverty in the midst of relative plenty, the central flaw of this approach is that it does not address *inequality*, only poverty. The social and economic rights approach seeks only to lift up those at the very bottom; it provides no remedy to the problem of accumulation of great wealth at the very top, and it does not aspire to ensure relative equality as a societal goal.

More broadly, the anti-poverty approach, which focuses on rights, does little to change the basic power structures of the constitutional system itself. This means that policymaking remains in the hands of the powerful, even despite the granting of limited rights. In the Latin American context, for example, Roberto Gargarella has argued that constitutional reformers in the nineteenth century recognized that "because they cared about rights," they had to "modify[] the distribution of powers."[32] In contrast, recent Latin American constitutional reforms have focused heavily on declaring rights without accompanying reforms to the distribution of powers—to the detriment of the rights-holders. Both Bolivia and Ecuador, for example, adopted a variety of constitutional provisions to protect the rights of indigenous peoples, including recognizing the plural nature of the country, establishing the right of indigenous people to use their own language, and rights to preservation of the environment and cultural heritage, among other things.[33] But in reality, Gargarella argues, disputes over natural resources extraction, for example, persisted. When there were trade-offs, and even when there was litigation, the government opposed the position of the indigenous peoples.[34]

TYPE 3: ANTI-OLIGARCHY CONSTITUTIONS. In contrast to anti-poverty constitutions' focus on lifting up the very poor, constitutions may also focus on preventing the accumulation of wealth and political power among the very rich—that is, preventing oligarchy. Historically, the most prominent anti-oligarchy strategies were either structural (e.g., restricting the wealth to one branch or house of government so as to quarantine them) or selection-based (e.g., the use of lotteries to select representatives, which would ensure a standard distribution of the population serving in government). Some scholars have argued that the American Constitution was frequently interpreted with an anti-oligarchy gloss in the nineteenth and early twentieth centuries.[35] Others suggest that late eighteenth century laws abolishing the entail and primogeniture were understood at the time as small "c" constitutional provisions, essential to preserving republican government

---

[32] Roberto Gargarella, *Latin American Constitutionalism, 1810–2010: The Engine Room of the Constitution* (New York: Oxford University Press, 2013), 205.

[33] Gargarella, *Latin American Constitutionalism*, 182–183.

[34] Ibid., 183–184.

[35] Joseph Fishkin and William E. Forbath, "The Anti-Oligarchy Constitution," *Boston University Law Review* 94 (2014): 669–696.

and preventing the emergence of an aristocracy. Explicitly anti-oligarchy provisions are rare in contemporary constitutions, but the American constitutional provision prohibiting titles of nobility provides one example. Under the anti-oligarchy approach, there is a strong argument for polities to constitutionalize policies on campaign finance restrictions, estate taxes, and wealth taxes.

The central problem with anti-oligarchy constitutions (or even stray provisions with these effects) is that they are rare. One possible explanation is that many contemporary constitutions were designed with a rising middle class as the economic backdrop (or at least the aspiration), so the fear of an emerging oligarchy might have been limited. A more plausible explanation, however, is that relatively wealthy and powerful people dominate the political process in most societies and, as a result, they are unlikely to adopt policies that would severely restrict their wealth or power. Indeed, structural provisions (such as the tribune of the Plebs) were hard-fought concessions, and other provisions (such as estate taxes) are constantly under threat of abolition.

A second problem is what is called the "hydraulic effect" in the literature on campaign finance regulation. Money, the theory goes, is like water, and it will find a way through any regulatory cracks that might exist. Anti-oligarchy provisions, as a result, might lead to a whack-a-mole problem in which money flows to another place in the political process. This is why campaign finance restrictions are insufficient to address economic inequality. Great Britain, for example, has far more restrictive election laws and practices than the United States. And yet, moneyed influence still operates, just through other channels. British commentators decry the revolving door between regulators at the Financial Services Authority and tax authorities and London's biggest banks and accounting firms: "Corporate and financial power have merged into the state."[36] They note that corporations try to shape the media environment, and even go so far as to create think thanks so that their preferred policies look independent and technocratic.[37] Truly anti-oligarchy provisions therefore have to go further than just limiting the influence of money on elections or the legislative process: they have to think about who has power and how it is exercised.

TYPE 4: MIDDLE-CLASS CONSTITUTIONS. Middle-class constitutions come in two types, both of which recognize that relative economic equality is critical to constitutional democracy. The first type, *passive* middle-class constitutions, simply assume that a society has and will continue to have relative economic equality. The American

[36] Seumus Milne, "Corporate Power Has Turned Britain into a Corrupt State, *The Guardian*, June 4, 2013, https://www.theguardian.com/commentisfree/2013/jun/04/corporate-britain-corrupt-lobbying-revolving-door.

[37] Tamasin Cave and Andy Rowell, "The Truth about Lobbying: 10 Ways Big Business Controls Government," *The Guardian*, March 12, 2014, https://www.theguardian.com/politics/2014/mar/12/lobbying-10-ways-corprations-influence-government.

constitution, and many constitutions around the world, are of this type. The defining feature of these constitutions is that they include no provisions to preserve a large middle class, and no anti-oligarchy or class warfare provisions to prevent the ills that accompany inequality. Passive middle-class constitutions are the most susceptible to the mismatch problem: when economic conditions change and the distribution of wealth shifts away from a broad middle class, the constitutional design will be out of sync with the economic conditions in society. As a result, constitutional democracy may be unable to withstand threats either from would-be oligarchs or from populist backlash.

The second type, *active* middle-class constitutions, contain provisions designed to maintain the middle class over time. In other words, they include precommitment strategies to prevent the mismatch problem that emerges when economic conditions change. For much of history, the most commonly discussed provisions of this type were agrarian laws. Agrarian laws not only ensured minimum lands available to citizens but also prohibited land ownership over a certain acreage. Looking back at the Roman experience, for example, both Machiavelli and Montesquieu stressed the vital importance of agrarian laws for maintaining republican government. The failure of Rome's agrarian laws, each noted, led to widening inequality and ultimately the downfall of the Republic. In modern times, some commentators have suggested that constitutions could include provisions by which taxes and redistributional measures are triggered when inequality reaches certain levels. Like anti-oligarchy constitutions, however, active middle-class constitutions may be unlikely to be adopted. If political leaders are drawn from the wealthy and expect that they and their descendants will remain wealthy, it is not clear why we should expect them to adopt constitutional provisions that would restrict their future wealth or power.

The Mismatch Problem and the Future of Constitutional Democracy

Around the world today, most constitutional democracies have type 2 (anti-poverty) or type 4 (passive middle-class) constitutions. These constitutions have no built-in checks against oligarchy, no structural checks to domesticate class conflict into ordinary politics, and no active provisions to ensure relative economic equality or a large middle class. As a result, the mismatch problem is of paramount concern. When economic conditions change and the distribution of wealth becomes skewed toward the wealthy, these systems may be particularly susceptible to becoming a functional oligarchy or suffering from populist backlash.

The mismatch problem is not unique to economic change. A mismatch between background social conditions and constitutional assumptions can occur across a wide variety of sectors. In the context of the United States, for example, the background conditions for the Constitution (adopted in 1787) were a country with a relatively small population, territory on the western side of the Atlantic Ocean, and relative weakness in international geopolitics. More than two centuries later, none of these conditions remain. The United States has the third largest population of any country (after China and India), spans the North American continent, and is the preeminent military power globally. It is no surprise, as a result, that American constitutional law has developed in ways that, for example, give far more leeway to the president and the national government than the framers of that document anticipated when it comes to foreign affairs and national security issues.[38]

There are three standard ways to address the mismatch problem. First, a society could change the constitution so that it adapts to the new conditions. In some contexts, this might be normatively desirable. For example, the United States amended its constitution to abolish slavery and establish equal rights, as social conditions changed after the Civil War. The American Supreme Court's jurisprudence expanding deference to the national government on foreign affairs issues in the mid-to late-twentieth century is another example. In the context of widening economic inequality, however, adapting a constitution to new economic conditions might fundamentally change the nature of constitutional democracy. Constitutional democracies, on this approach, would have to formalize their status as oligarchies—a solution that seems both implausible and undesirable.

The second option is to reform the background social conditions so that they align with the constitutional system. On this theory, the solution to the current economic crisis of constitutional democracy is to adopt new economic policies that will counteract widening inequality. A number of policy solutions might plausibly help: higher marginal tax rates, wealth taxes, antitrust and antimonopoly policies, labor policies, higher minimum wages, regulation of the financial sector, and universal public programs. Shifts along these lines should, over time, re-establish the economic preconditions for constitutional democracy. It is worth noting that these are not constitutional changes; they are policy changes that have implications for the social conditions that are essential to constitutional democracy.

The third option combines the first two, and can be termed the Economic Ulysses. On this approach, constitutions could be amended or reinterpreted so that they help society manage the mismatch problem. For example, a polity could adopt anti-poverty, anti-oligarchy, and active middle-class constitutional provisions. The result would be to simultaneously help resolve the economic inequality problem in the short run and ensure that social and economic changes are less likely to threaten the regime in the long run. As with traditional precommitment theory, the Economic Ulysses approach seeks to entrench constitutional provisions at time one that would be self-correcting at time two, thereby preventing the emergence of mismatch problems in the future.

---

[38] Ganesh Sitaraman and Ingrid Wuerth, "The Normalization of Foreign Relations Law," *Harvard Law Review* 128 (2015): 1897–1979.

Consider, as an example, a constitutional provision that triggers extremely high wealth taxes or campaign finance restrictions when the concentration of wealth reaches a pre-determined level (for example the top 1 percent of people capturing 15 percent of the national income). Such a provision automatically kicks in when the triggering condition is satisfied, thereby absolving the polity of making a policy choice at time two, when the wealthy are likely to have significant power over the policy process.

Some countries have instituted structural provisions that help reduce the mismatch problem. Australia, for example, has a system of compulsory voting. Australians are required by law to vote, with modest fines imposed on those who choose not to. Rosalind Dixon and Anika Gauja argue that this insulates Australian politics from the rise of illiberal populists because a small number of highly-mobilized voters can't capture power in a low-turnout election.[39] But it also makes Australian public policy more responsive to the electorate at large. Dixon and Gauja note that both major Australian political parties have taken a more restrictive approach to migration policy—and that these policies have been very popular with the general public. Greater responsiveness means a lower likelihood of populist backlash. Indeed, some studies have also shown that mandatory voting results in a country adopting more egalitarian economic policies.[40] This finding is intuitive: when everyone votes, rather than a limited-population shifted toward the wealthy, elected officials have to be more responsive to middle- and lower-income citizens.

This kind of provision stands in contrast to constitutional provisions that are not self-correcting. During the Progressive Era, for example, the United States adopted a constitutional amendment to enable an income tax. Senator William Borah explained the amendment: the drafters of the Constitution did not want the burden of taxes to fall "upon the backs of those who toil" while "the great accumulated wealth of the Nation" pay nothing. "It was never so intended," he said. "[I]t was a republic they were building, where all men were to be equal and bear equally the burdens of government, and not an oligarchy, for that must a government be, in the end, which exempts property and wealth from all taxes." The income tax amendment, however, *permitted* (rather than *mandated*) progressive income taxation, and it had no self-correcting mechanism to change rates as conditions change. While it provides an example of constitutionalizing a policy choice that could reduce inequality, it does not include a precommitment mechanism that is self-correcting.

Another example of a constitutional reform comes from David Schneiderman's account of the Ecuadorian response to economic globalization. Prior to the election of

---

[39] See Rosalind Dixon and Anika Gauja, "Australia's Non-populist Democracy? The Role of Structure and Policy," in *Constitutional Democracy in Crisis?*, ed. Mark A. Graber, Sanford Levinson, and Mark Tushnet (Oxford University Press: New York, 2018).

[40] Alberto Chong and Mauricio Olivera, "Does Compulsory Voting Help Equalize Incomes?," *Economics and Politics* 20 (2008): 391–415. See also Anthony Fowler, "Electoral and Policy Consequences of Voter Turn-Out: Evidence from Compulsory Voting in Australia," *Quarterly Journal of Political Science* 8 (2013): 159–182.

President Rafael Correa, Ecuador had signed onto twenty-five bilateral investment treaties, which gave foreign multinational companies the ability to sue the state. Ecuador not only withdrew from consenting to international jurisdiction over investment disputes but also drafted a new constitution that included a provision stating that the country would not give jurisdiction to any international arbitration in commercial or contract issues. This provision reserves power to Ecuador's political and legal system over these disputes, thereby making it more likely decisions made on investment issues will be more amenable to the people of Ecuador (albeit indirectly).[41]

It is important to notice the contrast between both the Australian voting system and the Ecuadorian reservation of power over investor dispute resolution and anti-poverty constitutional provisions, such as housing, education, and welfare rights, that have become conventional since the late-twentieth century. In his book *Latin American Constitutionalism*, Roberto Gargarella distinguishes between minimum rights provisions and the "engine room of the constitution," the structural allocation of power within the government.[42] While the line between rights and structure is a blurry one,[43] the basic insight is important. The Australian and Ecuadorian provisions give power to the people (and political institutions) to shape policies, processes, and structures. Instead of trying to reach a particular outcome (as rights provisions do), the structural or "engine room" approach enables greater policy responsiveness over time. Of course, this is not to say that there is no place for constitutional rights, but only that increasing policy responsiveness through structural mechanisms akin to Australia's system of compulsory voting might increase the stability of the constitutional system.

Conclusion

Economic inequality is a problem for constitutional democracy. Constitutional democracies require a relative degree of economic equality to persist. Without it, freedom is at risk from private tyranny, public policy can become oligarchic due to capture, and the populist backlash to oligarchy can yield public tyranny. Constitutional design thus has much to do with the crisis of constitutional democracy in the early twenty-first century. Most constitutions today have few, if any, provisions that seek to foster relative equality or restrict the undue influence of wealthy elites. The result is that constitutional democracies might today be slipping into becoming functional oligarchies.

In the short run, the answers are not easy. Policy changes could bring the economic preconditions for republicanism back in line with democratic constitutions, and constitutional provisions could help entrench those policies. But with economic and political

---

[41] See Schneiderman, "Disabling Constitutional Capacity," 562–64.

[42] Gargarella, *Latin American Constitutionalism*.

[43] Daryl J. Levinson, "Rights and Votes," *Yale Law Journal* 121 (2012): 1286–1363.

power increasingly concentrated in the hands of a smaller and smaller group of people, it is unclear whether there will be enough public energy to reclaim government and re-establish the foundations of constitutional democracy. In much of the world today, the dilemma is one that US Supreme Court justice Louis Brandeis identified a century ago: "We may have democracy, or we may have wealth concentrated in the hands of a few, but we cannot have both."

31 Disabling Constitutional Capacity
Global Economic Law and Democratic Decline
David Schneiderman*

CITIZENS APPEAR TO be losing interest in democratic politics. Participation rates in democratic elections have been on the decline almost thirty years running. While numerous explanations can be offered for this malaise, one contributing factor might be the incapacity of citizens to direct national and local economic affairs. State ability to regulate over a variety of economic subjects has been diminished as a consequence of new global economic law. Trade rules enforced by the World Trade Organization, intellectual property rights guaranteed by TRIPs, and investment treaties that remove policy options from host states contribute to the sometimes perceived but oftentimes real inability of citizens to effect economic change in key sectors. If it appears to citizens that participating in electoral processes makes less of a difference, then democratic legitimacy is undermined. One response may be simply to disengage.[1]

This chapter argues that democratic decline in democracies may be explained, in part, by the narrowing of policy space available to citizens as a consequence of the rules and institutions of economic globalization. Principally post-1989 legal formations, they

* I am grateful to Ladan Merhanvar for translation help, Ahmed Alsisi, Mohammad Fadel, Vivien Gabriel, Marco Velásquez-Ruiz, Jimena Sierra, and Frederico Suarez for explaining developments on the ground, and Nicolás Perrone and Mark Tushnet for advice.
[1] Fritz W. Scharpf, "Monetary Union, Fiscal Crisis, and the Disabling of Democratic Accountability," in *Politics in the Age of Austerity*, ed. Armin Schäfer and Wolfgang W. Streeck (Cambridge: Polity Press, 2013), 108–143, 110.

operationalize what may simply be called a neoliberal policy agenda. If neoliberalism is both ubiquitous and productively vague, we should understand neoliberal law as comprising rules and institutions designed to insulate markets from ordinary politics.[2] The relationship between disabling state capacity and democratic decline admittedly is complex. So while I hypothesize that neoliberal legality contributes to democratic decline, it can also help give rise to backlash, precipitating movement to recover ceded policy space.[3]

Neoliberal legality is premised on the idea that citizens and states are incapable of managing markets, in which case, they should be mostly discouraged from intervening in economic affairs. If governments are "overloaded" by demands from citizens and by pressure from well-organized interests, resulting in an "excess of democracy," the best strategy is simply to disable states from being able to respond.[4] Economic subjects, if not managed via constitutional edict, are removed from state levers and jurisdiction allocated to regime-specific global legal orders. Such legal orders are treated as "global" to the extent that they purport to enforce universal norms worthy of respect everywhere.[5] They also happen to advance the interests of networks of powerful actors who have been able to influence the content of international rules so that the rules work to their benefit. In this way, democracy is not so much suppressed as managed.[6]

I should not be taken to be saying that states have been free, in the past, to pursue any economic path whatsoever. Constraints on state sovereignty have long been in place.[7] These constraints often have been the product of the coercive power of economically powerful states aiming to influence, if not control, political processes within host states. The difference today is that power is now exercised via legally binding constraints on a global scale. There is no better example of a global legal order advancing the interests of parochial vested interests, and the consequent narrowing of policy space, than the legal regime for the protection of foreign investment.

---

[2] This is an old project. Insulating economics from politics has been a "central aspiration of American legal thinkers," observes Morton J. Horowitz in *The Transformation of American Law, 1870–1960: The Crisis of Legal Orthodoxy* (New York: Oxford University Press, 1992), 9.

[3] On repoliticization, see Paul Fawcett and David Marsh, "Depoliticisation, Governance and Political Participation," *Policy & Politics* 42 (2014): 171–188 and Bob Jessop, "Repoliticising Depoliticisation: Theoretical Preliminaries on Some Responses to the American Fiscal and Eurozone Debt Crises," *Policy & Politics* 42 (2014): 207–223.

[4] Michel J. Crozier, Samuel P. Huntington, and Joji Watanuki, *The Crisis of Democracy: Report on the Governability of Democracies to the Trilateral Commission* (New York: New York University Press, 1975), 113 and analysis by Colin Hay, *Why We Hate Politics* (Cambridge: Polity Press, 2007), ch. 3.

[5] See Neil Walker, *Intimations of Global Law* (Cambridge: Cambridge University Press, 2015), 18ff.

[6] Sheldon S. Wolin, *Democracy Inc.: Managed Democracy and the Specter of Inverted Totalitarianism* (Princeton, NJ: Princeton University Press, 2008), 47.

[7] Stephen D. Krasner, *Sovereignty: Organized Hypocrisy* (Princeton, NJ: Princeton University Press, 1999), 220.

In the next part, I advance the claim that the rules and institutions of global economic law likely dampen democratic enthusiasm. I then turn to international investment law as an exemplar of the legal constraints taken up by states that are contributing to this malaise. This regime is, at present, a flashpoint for debates over law and globalization. States in various locales around the world, responding to national constitutional imperatives, have sought to cabin these constraints. This is a minority position, however. Most others willingly accept these limits at the urging of powerful capital-exporting states, despite ongoing constitutional tensions. For some, they are even welcome, as they serve not only to check state action but also to dampen citizen expectations. I take up examples of both responses, in a series of capsule country case studies. Some of these countries do not score so well on democratic indices. For this reason, the discussion is meant to illustrate the dampening effects on state capacity. They are not meant to display any correlation between investment law's constitution-like limits and democratic decline. Finally, in the Conclusion I consider the prospect of rolling back the regime, an event unlikely to occur without the complicity of powerful capital-exporting states. It turns out that the Trump presidency might have the effect of loosening the binds of investment treaty restraints insofar as his administration is advancing a position that will render such restraints optional, not mandatory. This is despite the fact that successive US administrations, under the control of both parties, have been ardent proponents of the regime since it took off in the mid-1980s.

Chastened States

Could it be that retreat in democratic practice can be attributed, in part, to the decline of state capacity in economic matters? It may be no coincidence that the steady decline in turnout rates for general elections in Western parliamentary democracies began in the 1970s just as neoliberal policy prescriptions were in the ascendance. By the 2000s, voter turnout was significantly lower than in the 1970s, reduced on average by ten to twenty points.[8] There is no evidence that this falling off will reverse any time soon. If political participation rates have improved in a few locales in 2016 (e.g., sub-Saharan Africa), they continue to decrease elsewhere. That voter turnout has declined so precipitously since the 1970s reveals the perversity of the "overload" thesis of the mid-1970s, described above. Democracy was not failing because of an overload of demands from constituents. Rather, democracy's foundations were weakening by virtue of a number of factors, including shrinking state capacity.[9]

---

[8] Armin Schäfer and Wolfgang W. Streeck, "Introduction: Politics in the Age of Austerity," in *Politics in the Age of Austerity*, ed. Armin Schäfer and Wolfgang W. Streeck (Cambridge: Polity Press, 2013), 11.

[9] Wolfgang Streeck, "The Politics of Public Debt: Neoliberalism, Capitalist Development and the Restructuring of the State," *German Economic Review* 15 (2013): 143–165, 146.

There are recent exceptions to falling participation rates. Turnout rates for the Brexit vote in the United Kingdom attracted record-setting participation—the highest since 2001.[10] Ecuador saw high participation rates in recent presidential elections, rising from one of Latin America's lowest levels to one of its highest, ever since the arrival of President Correa on the national scene.[11] It is noteworthy that Correa emerged victorious on a platform proclaiming the end of the "long and sad night of neoliberalism." Could these turnout rates be attributed to the fact that the legal fetters associated with economic globalization, made manifest by membership in the European Union (EU) and by embrace of neoliberal strictures in Ecuador, respectively, were on the table?

I want to suggest that some of the decline in vote turnout can be attributed to the cramped policy space accorded to states following the ascendance of neoliberal policy prescriptions.[12] If it is correct to attribute this malaise partly to the rise of neoliberal legality, the effect will have been exacerbated by austerity measures embraced following the 2008–2009 global financial crisis. Diminution in democratic capacity is compounded by states falling deeper into debt, resulting in budgetary priorities being directed toward debt financing. The budgetary space available to serve other interests, in particular less powerful ones, necessarily shrinks.[13] States become, in Streeck's provocative words, "debt-collecting agencies on behalf of the global oligarchy of investors."[14] One expected outcome, though certainly not the only one, is to dampen citizen expectations about what states can do.

Recent empirical work, premised upon a rational choice model, underscores this relationship. First, there is considerable evidence to support the proposition that citizens in developed democracies are aware of the constraining effects of economic globalization on domestic policy space and adjust their expectations accordingly.[15] Second, numerous studies support the hypothesis that voter turnout has been negatively affected by economic globalization. In one study of parliamentary elections in twenty-three OECD

[10] The Economist Intelligence Unit, *Democracy Index 2016*, 4–5, accessed February 26, 2018, http://www.eiu.com/Handlers/WhitepaperHandler.ashx?fi=Democracy-Index-2016.pdf&mode=wp&campaignid=DemocracyIndex2016 and International IDEA, *Voter Turnout Database*, accessed February 26, 2018, https://www.idea.int/data-tools/data/voter-turnout.

[11] "Half of Democracy Is Showing Up," *The Economist*, November 18–24, 2017, 425: 31.

[12] Decline in participation rates have also been attributed to generational shifts and to "sheer boredom." Mair finds these explanations, however, unconvincing in Peter Mair, *Ruling the Void: The Hollowing of Western Democracy* (London: Verso, 2013).

[13] Wolfgang Streeck and Daniel Mertens, "Public Finance and the Decline of State Capacity in Democratic Capitalism," in *Politics in the Age of Austerity*, ed. Armin Schäfer and Wolfgang W. Streeck (Cambridge: Polity Press, 2013), 29.

[14] Wolfgang Streeck, "The Crises of Democratic Capitalism," *New Left Review* 71 (2011): 5, 28.

[15] John Marshall and Stephen D. Fisher, "Compensation or Constraint? How Different Dimensions of Economic Globalization Affect Government Spending and Electoral Turnout," *British Journal of Political Science* 45 (2014): 353–389, 381; Timothy Hellwig, "Balancing Demands: The World Economy and the Composition of Policy Preferences," *Journal of Politics* 76 (2014): 1–4, 12.

countries between 1965 and 2006, Steiner concludes that "economic integration" has played a "major role in the general turnout decline within developed democracies over the last 40 years."[16] Marshall and Fisher, using OECD data from 1970 to 2007, find "robust evidence" showing a correlation between increased foreign ownership and a decline in voter turnout.[17] This influence is borne out not just at the macro level but also at level of the individual. A study of voter behavior during the 2001 British election reveals that those believing government has more of an influence on the economy were more likely to have reported turning out to vote.[18] These findings strongly support the hypothesis that economic globalization dampens electoral participation rates.

The phenomenon I am describing is familiar to those writing about "depoliticization." This literature seeks to analyze why some subjects move from the center of political life to a place beyond which ordinary politics can reach.[19] Neoliberal legality exhibits an unusual combination of the features Stone associates with depoliticization. There is, first, "institutional" depoliticization amounting to the delegation of authority to bodies far removed from local political control. Second, "rule-based" regimes are branded as "neutral and universal" and preferred over faulty domestic political processes. Third, "preference-shaping" and "agenda-setting" forms of depoliticization are directed at internalizing norms that constrain domestic policy agendas. Finally, "scientization" results in deference to a body of experts deemed better suited to make policy determinations.[20] Taken together, they amount to multiple pressure points that move matters beyond day-to-day democratic control.

It is no wonder that many citizens feel disempowered and choose to disengage or redirect their energies elsewhere. Investment in new social policy becomes impossible without raising taxes. According to the common sense dominating contemporary political culture, this is treated as a bridge too far. For those tossed about by prevailing economic winds, they are classified as "victims" or labeled as "losers." Economic inequality is reaching heights not seen since the Gilded Age,[21] giving rise to a constitutional "mismatch" between structures of accountability designed for citizens of roughly equal economic standing and rising inequality of wealth within states.[22] Nor are political parties likely to

---

[16] Nils D. Steiner, "Economic Globalization and Voter Turnout in Established Democracies," *Electoral Studies* 29 (2010): 444–459, 456.

[17] Marshall and Fisher, "Compensation or Constraint?," 359.

[18] Nils D. Steiner, "Economic Globalisation, the Perceived Room to Manoeuvre of National Governments, and Electoral Participation: Evidence from the 2001 British General Election," *Electoral Studies* 41 (2016): 118–128, 127.

[19] Hay, *Why We Hate Politics*, 80.

[20] Diane Stone, "Global Governance Depoliticized: Knowledge Networks, Scientization, and Anti-policy," in *Anti-Politics, Depoliticization, and Governance*, ed. Paul Fawcett, Matthew Flinders, Colin Hay, and Matthew Wood (Oxford, UK: Oxford University Press, 2017), 91–111, 93–95.

[21] Thomas Piketty, *Capital in the Twenty-First Century* (Cambridge, MA: Harvard University Press, 2014).

[22] See the discussion in Ganesh Sitaraman, "Economic Inequality and Constitutional Democracy," in *Constitutional Democracy in Crisis?*, ed. Mark A. Graber, Sanford Levinson, and Mark Tushnet (New York: Oxford University Press, 2018).

generate much more enthusiasm. With diminished political capacity, citizens are offered tepid party platforms shaped by the very same forces that constrain states.[23] In circumstances where citizens are expected to moderate their claims, they might simply choose to check out. [24]

In this way neoliberal legality is productive—it creates the conditions both for its success and its demise. If one response to this productivity is withdrawal from politics, on rare occasions it can precipitate taking to the streets, as occurred in Greece during the debt crisis or in Occupy Wall Street protests.[25] Practical disenfranchisement might not result, then, in quiescence. It can lead to redirection of political efforts into other channels and locales. For instance, Suzana Sawyer's study of Indigenous resistance in Ecuador reveals that an adherence to the neoliberal program promoted by multinational oil and adopted by the government "backfired." While reforms "undermined the very conditions that lent legitimacy and authority to the state's political system," she observed, it gave rise to new "transgressive political subjects" who "disrupted the confines and exposed the hypocrisy of the neoliberal dream."[26]

Nevertheless, there will be limits to what can be achieved. To the extent that neoliberalism succeeds in shrinking the horizon of expectations, measures for societal self-protection can be expected to go no further than to rectify market failures. As the response of states in the aftermath of the financial crises of 2008–2009 reveals, restoration of economic order, to the extent desired by market forces, will be permitted. But not much more will be allowed. The dampening of the possibility for countermovement helps to explain much of what has been happening in the global scene post-recession: the ascendance of demagogic populism in the United States and anti-immigrant sentiment driving Brexit.

Marshall famously traced the trajectory of citizenship rights beginning with civil rights, political rights, and, in the twentieth century, social rights. This latter category elevated citizens to the status of rough equality as a consequence of compressed incomes and equality of opportunity generated by the spread of public education. What mattered

---

[23] Nils D. Steiner and Christian W. Martin, "Economic Integration, Party Polarisation and Electoral Turnout," *West European Politics* 35 (2012): 238–265, 259 and Mair, *Ruling the Void*, ch. 2. On the unresponsiveness of the US Congress to those in the bottom third of income distribution, see Larry M. Bartels, *Unequal Democracy: The Political Economy of the New Gilded Age* (Princeton, NJ: Princeton University Press, 2008).

[24] For more on the linkages between depoliticization and inequality, see David Schneiderman and Nicolás M. Perrone, "Critical International Economic Law: Depoliticization, Inequality, Precarity," in *Research Handbook on Critical Legal Theory*, ed. Emilios Christodoulidis, Ruth Dukes, and Marco Goldoni (forthcoming Edward Elgar).

[25] Economic crises, such as the global financial crisis of 2008–2009, may also have "depressed turnout in countries with high levels of economic integration." See Jeffrey A. Karp and Caitlin Milazzo, "Globalization and Voter Turnout in Times of Crisis," in *Globalization and Domestic Politics: Parties, Elections, and Public Opinion*, ed. Jack Vowles and Georgios Xezonakis (Oxford: Oxford University Press, 2016), 190–206.

[26] Suzana Sawyer, *Crude Chronicles: Indigenous Politics, Multinational Oil, and Neoliberalism in Ecuador* (Durham, NC: Duke University Press, 2004), 15.

to citizens were not the specific claims to entitlement but citizens' "superstructure of legitimate expectations." These expectations, Marshall wrote, "were details in a design for community living."[27] With the ascendance of neoliberal values, this idea of a shared community of fate has been lost in favor of a drive to privatize everything. Losses no longer are shared collectively but privately, unless one is "too big to fail." Rather than being compressed, income divides are widening. It is the legitimate expectations of powerful economic actors that now matter most. It turns out that the legal regime for the protection of foreign investors delivers well on this promise.

The Ties That Bind

In this Section, I turn to a discussion of international investment law as the model of a binding global legal order that constrains state capacity. The rise of investment law is associated with the decline of the Soviet Union in 1989 and the stark choice facing states seeking out new foreign capital to finance public improvements and economic development. Pushed onto the international agenda by a network of powerful actors, in coordination with international financial institutions, states all over the world rushed into the embrace of the investment treaty regime. The regime is premised on the idea that mobile capital, once fixed within the boundaries of states, is vulnerable to changes in state policy that diminish value. So as order to forestall the diminution in value associated with political risk, investment law enables investors to sue, or just threaten to sue, for treaty violations in order to recoup losses.

At present, there are more than 3,000 bilateral investment treaties (BITs) in force in addition to numerous trade and investment agreements having their own investment treaty chapters. Though there will be some variety in their features, many of their limitations are borrowed from national legal systems that purport to represent "universal" standards of justice. For example, disciplines promote property and contract rights via norms of non-discrimination, prohibitions on expropriation, and guarantees of due process, all of which have their counterparts in the constitutions of capital-exporting states.[28] These rights are enforceable before investment tribunals that have authority to issue damage awards against host states. This is the system of investor-state dispute settlement (ISDS) that has been generating much heat in debates around economic globalization. Though there is some ambiguity in the data, taking into accounts settlements as well as win rates, investors probably win, on average, more often than do states.[29]

---

27 T.H. Marshall, "Citizenship and Social Class," in *Class, Citizenship and Social Development: Essays by T.H. Marshall* (Garden City, NY: Anchor Books, 1965) 71, 114–115.

28 See David Schneiderman, "Global Constitutionalism and International Economic Law: The Case of International Investment Law," *2016 European Yearbook of International Economic Law*, eds. Marc Bungenberg et al. (Springer International Publishing, 2016), 23–43.

29 Rachel L. Wellhausen, "Recent Trends in Investor-State Dispute Settlement," *Journal of International Dispute Settlement* 7 (2016): 117, 129 (possibly up to 62 percent of the time). Offering a different methodology is

During debates over granting to President Obama trade promotion authority to complete the Transpacific Partnership Agreement (TPP), the United States Trade Representative claimed that investment treaty obligations mirrored those under the US Constitution. This was why the United States had not yet lost a single investment arbitration as a respondent state, claimed US secretary of commerce, Penny Pritzker.[30] This is not the only explanation, however. While a number of claims against the United States have been without merit, others cannot be explained but by arbitrators narrowly construing investment treaty disciplines or departing from past arbitral practice. In at least one instance, the US State Department communicated worries to its tribunal appointee about congressional blowback if the United States were to lose the arbitration, putting the whole investment treaty system in peril.[31] One reasonably can surmise that this influenced at least one tribunal member's vote. On this occasion, the tribunal unanimously found the investor was treated unfairly—"what clearer case than the present could there be for the ideals of NAFTA to be given some teeth?" the tribunal asked—but offered no relief. Instead, the tribunal bucked arbitral practice and relied upon a stale procedural rule, not included in the NAFTA text, so as to deprive itself of jurisdiction to resolve the claim.[32]

Many states have not been as successful as the United States in defending claims. The consequence is that, by virtue of the trend lines in the jurisprudence generated in these other cases, the regulatory capacity of states everywhere is diminished. These disciplines have "bite," the United Nations Conference on Trade and Development (UNCTAD) declared, because they limit regulatory space. "Broad and vague formulation of [treaty] provisions has allowed investors to challenge core domestic policy decisions, for instance in the area of environmental, energy and health policies," UNCTAD acknowledged.[33] The Argentine government, for instance, was penalized for having responded to its 2001 economic crisis in ways that upset the "legitimate expectations" of foreign investors. Those investors were entitled to be compensated for having been promised returns that Argentinians were incapable of delivering on when faced with an economic crisis likened to the Great Depression of 1929. In another dispute, the government of Canada

Krysztof J. Pelc, "What Explains the Low Success Rate of Investor-State Disputes?," *International Organization* 71 (2017) 559–583 (finding indirect expropriation claims less likely to succeed than direct expropriation claims).

[30] United States Trade Representative, "The Facts on Investor-State Dispute Settlement," *Tradewinds: The Official Blog of the United States Trade Representative* (March 2014), https://ustr.gov/about-us/policy-offices/press-office/blog/2014/March/Facts-Investor-State%20Dispute-Settlement-Safeguarding-Public-Interest-Protecting-Investors; Penny Pritzker, U.S. Secretary of Commerce, interviewed by Al Hunt on *Charlie Rose* (airing on PBS May 11, 2015), http://www.charlierose.com/watch/60560245.

[31] David Schneiderman, "Judicial Politics and International Investment Arbitration: Seeking an Explanation for Conflicting Outcomes," *Northwestern Journal of International Law & Business* 30 (2010): 383–416.

[32] Loewen Group Inc and Loewen v United States, Award, ICSID Case No ARB(AF)/98/3 (2003), para. 241.

[33] United Nations Conference on Trade and Development, *World Investment Report 2015: Reforming International Investment Governance* (New York and Geneva: United Nations, 2015), 125.

was penalized for having followed the advice of an independent environmental assessment panel that recommended a US investor not be granted permission to construct a rock quarry and ferry terminal on sensitive Nova Scotia shoreline. The environmental review panel concluded that the proposed investment would substantially harm marine, land, and human environments. The investor successfully sued for damages, convincing the investment tribunal that the panel failed to respect its statutory authority. This, the majority of tribunal members concluded, was a failure that gave rise to an international treaty violation, requiring the payment of damages.

It is this disabling of state capacity that led a UN Commission of Experts to observe that enshrining limits, in BITs in addition to other international agreements, makes it difficult to "change the regulatory structure in ways which support financial stability, economic growth, and the welfare of vulnerable consumers and investors."[34] Many of the measures that states might be tempted to take up to help those left behind by the openness of the trade and investment regimes are vulnerable to legal attack. For instance, measures associated with "positive discrimination"—measures that target youth, women, or small to medium enterprises—that are intended to improve the economic situation of the most vulnerable are likely to run afoul of investment treaty standards. Measures directed at improving specific sectors of the economy, such as mandating the employment of local labor or service providers, are as likely to give rise to an investment dispute. Such measures are not merely in tension with investment law norms: they are in legal discord. In other words, these are not merely discursive or soft law constraints. They are, instead, the precisely intended legal consequences. It is no wonder that citizens in constitutional democracies perceive their legislatures as being able to do less.

As states become aware of the constraining effects of investment treaty obligations, some have sought to restore policy space. This might particularly be the case where the constitution commits the state to protect, preserve, or deliver on certain promises to its citizens. But these states are in the minority. The response more typically heard from states around the world is to continue to tolerate, even welcome, these constraints while continuing to tweak investment treaty texts. By seeking out new treaty partners, they turn out to be complicit in the spread of global legal orthodoxy. I turn to a discussion of both kinds of state responses in the next Section.

Capsule Country Studies

The countries canvassed in this Section are either resisting or promoting the binding regime of investment disciplines. These are deliberately brief discussions intended to

---

[34] United Nations, *Report of the Commission of Experts of the President of the United Nations General Assembly on Reforms of the International Monetary and Financial System* (September 21, 2009), 21, http://www.un.org/ga/econcrisissummit/docs/FinalReport_CoE.pdf.

highlight the ways in which investment rules can legally inhibit measures otherwise compliant with, and sometimes mandated by, local constitutional texts. The capsule country studies reveal differing responses to the constitutional tensions that arise—either resistance or compliance. In either instance, what is revealed is a set of enforceable legal limits that cover a vast range of government action. While a much deeper dive is warranted in each case study, given space limitations, the choice has been made to cover a number of countries across regions rather than an in-depth review of any single one.

It bears repeating that these case studies do not attend to the relationship between cabining political futures and democratic decline. Though there is good empirical support for suggesting such a linkage, there are multiple causes at work rendering that relationship more complex than the data suggests. For this reason, the discussion here is meant only to illustrate varying state responses, in light of constitutional commitments, to diminished state capacity. Nor do I mean to suggest that these are the only proper responses to address diminished state capacity.[35] As for election turnout rates, the data indicate that these six countries fall between the high and low ends of participation rates.[36] At least one of these countries, Egypt, scores poorly on most democratic indices. Rather than emphasizing declining participation rates, the discussion in this part gathers up state responses to the debilitating effects of investment rules.

RESISTANCE

Brazil

The tenuous relationship between signing investment treaties and attracting new inward investment is laid bare by the fact that Brazil was a principal magnet for investment in the late 1990s through to the mid-2000s. Yet, Brazil has not ratified a single investment treaty. The executive branch negotiated fourteen of them, but none successfully made its way through the Brazilian Congress. Congressional committees worried that these treaties ran afoul of provisions of the Brazilian Constitution and so were never approved.

In particular, there was concern that provisions on expropriation requiring payment of fair market value, in immediately convertible and transferable currency (associated with the formula devised by US secretary of state Cordell Hull), were inconsistent with Brazilian property guarantees. The Constitution contemplated a less stringent compensation requirement that departed from the Hull formula. Also, provisions for ISDS bypassed the Brazilian judiciary, running afoul of constitutional provisions preserving the authority of the judicial branch. Finally, the treaties discriminated against

---

[35] For example, see Nicolás M. Perrone, "The International Investment Regime and Local Populations: Are the Weakest Voices Unheard?" *Transnational Legal Theory* 7 (2016): 383–405.

[36] Economist Intelligence Unit, *Democracy Index 2016*, and International IDEA, *Voter Turnout Database*.

national economic actors in favor of foreign investors, contrary to constitutional equality provisions.[37]

Unconvinced that committing to violations of the constitution was defensible, Brazil instead developed, in conjunction with peak private sector interests, a new model for investment dispute resolution. It is one centered on an ombudsman-type official who fields investor concerns and that, failing conciliation, can give rise to state-state arbitration, the traditional mode of resolving international disputes.[38] Brazil has signed agreements with Latin American partner states and with Angola, Malawi, and Mozambique, none of which are yet in force. Whether this new model will catch on depends largely upon whether Brazil can find new treaty partners beyond those situated in the periphery. This may prove to be an insurmountable difficulty.

South Africa

Evidence that investment treaties have little effect in attracting new foreign direct investment prompted the South African government to rethink its investment treaty policy. Under the leadership of Nelson Mandela, South Africa hastily entered into investment treaties with a number of states in Europe, Africa, and Latin America using a UK model treaty as a prototype. Many of these commitments were undertaken at the very same time that South Africans were finalizing their new constitution. It took some time to realize that constitutional commitments around the promotion of equality and land reform were inconsistent with investment treaty obligations. It was, in particular, the flawed program for redistributing wealth, Black Economic Empowerment, aimed at increasing the hiring and promotion of disadvantaged South Africans and requiring the mandatory divestiture of ownership shares to well-connected ANC activists,[39] which appeared to run directly into investment treaty obligations, namely, those of non-discrimination and non-imposition of performance requirements. The government

---

[37] In addition, concerns were expressed over provisions guaranteeing the free transfer of capital. All of this is documented in Vivian Daniele Rocha Gabriel, "A Proteção Jurídica Dos Investimentos Brasileiros No Exterior," Dissertação de Mestrado, Universidade De São Paulo, Faculdade De Direito (2015), 46–85. Daniela Campello and Leany Lemos, "The Non-ratification of Bilateral Investment Treaties in Brazil: A Story of Conflict in a Land of Cooperation," *Review of International Political Economy* 22 (2015): 1055–1086 is helpful but mistakenly claims that protections were secured for investors by other means. For example, BIT disciplines concerning expropriation and fair and equitable treatment (including legitimate expectations) were not addressed via domestic measures.

[38] Vivian Gabriel, "The New Brazilian Cooperation and Facilitation Investment Agreement: An Analysis of the Conflict Resolution Mechanism in Light of the Theory of the Shadow of the Law," *Conflict Resolution Quarterly* 34 (2016): 141–161.

[39] On government corruption in post-apartheid South Africa, see Heinz Klug, "State Capture or Institutional Resilience: Is There a Crisis of Constitutional Democracy in South Africa?" in *Constitutional Democracy in Crisis?*

slowly began amending treaty text with developing states in the early 2000s in order to respond to these concerns.[40]

The South African Department of Trade and Industry (DTI) finally undertook a review of investment treaty policy in 2009. In an extraordinary admission, the DTI discussion paper acknowledged that "inexperienced" officials, having a "lack of knowledge" of investment law, negotiated these commitments. Because these treaties extended 'far into developed countries' policy space" it was time to reconsider investor obligations. Only after thinking through some of the constitutional linkages was South African leadership convinced to abandon the investment treaty regime entirely.[41]

Since then, South Africans have quietly denounced their BITs, preferring to rely instead on constitutional commitments to equality and to property. Rather than expecting binding commitments that limit unused constitutional capacity to attract new foreign investment, the government has been seeking out investors using a variety of techniques, such as sectoral charters and a new national investment law. All of this, the government says, will achieve the ends sought by investment treaties while recapturing constitutional space inadvertently given up.[42]

Ecuador

I have already mentioned that the election of President Correa signaled a change in the direction of investment policy. What is significant about the Ecuadorean case is that resistance to neoliberal legality took the form of judicial review and constitutional amendment. Ecuador ratified some twenty-five BITs, enabling investors to challenge a variety of measures, posing a real threat to the public fisc. Investor claims gave rise to questionable awards, with significant sums granted to large multinational companies, including an eye-popping $US 2.3 billion to Houston-based Occidental Petroleum (subsequently reduced to $US 1.06 billion).[43]

Upon assuming office, Correa immediately turned his attention to investment treaty policy. The president halted US-Ecuador negotiations leading to a new Free Trade Agreement. He also insisted upon an increased share in windfall profits accruing to multinationals generated by oil and gas revenues. Ecuador subsequently withdrew consent

---

[40] David Schneiderman, "Promoting Equality, Black Economic Empowerment, and the Future of Investment Rules," *South African Journal on Human Rights* 25 (2009): 246–279.

[41] South Africa, Department of Trade & Industry, "Bilateral Investment Treaty Policy Framework Review: Government Position Paper," June 25, 2009, 11, http://www.thedti.gov.za/ads/bi-lateral_policy.pdf.

[42] Xavier Carim, "International Investment Agreements and Africa's Structural Transformation: A Perspective from South Africa," in *Rethinking Bilateral Investment Treaties: Critical Issues and Policy Choices*, ed. Kavalit Singh and Burghard Ilge (The Netherlands: Both Ends/Madhyam/Somo, 2016), 51–67.

[43] Occidental Petroleum Corporation and Occidental Exploration and Production Company v. The Republic of Ecuador, ICSID Case No. ARB/06/11 (October 5, 2012), https://www.italaw.com/sites/default/files/case-documents/italaw1094.pdf.

to having investment disputes over oil and gas exploitation lodged under the auspices of the International Centre for the Settlement of Investment Disputes, housed in the World Bank. A constitutional assembly also was convened and a new Ecuadorean Constitution approved by national referendum in 2008. Included among its commitments was mandatory consultation of Indigenous communities in respect of mining ventures affecting their collective rights and, in a direct strike at global economic law, a declaration that no jurisdiction would be ceded to international arbitration concerning commercial and contractual disputes (Art. 422). The Constitutional Court of Ecuador declared that this provision encompasses investment treaty arbitration.[44]

Ecuador also began to denounce treaties. Encouraged by a Constitutional Court opinion that BITs contravened Article 422, a committee of the Ecuadorean Assembly recommended terminating treaties with developing states that had not attracted new inward investment. Nine investment treaties were then denounced. Subsequently, a special citizen's commission (CAITISA) was established and tasked with auditing the impact of Ecuadorean investment treaties.[45] CAITISA detailed noncompliance, and in some instances bare compliance, with constitutional provisions that required legislative approval of international treaties. In a single legislative session, seven treaties were approved at once and without debate, rendering them constitutionally problematic. Of particular concern to CAITISA were treaty obligations that contradicted constitutional provisions regarding expropriations (the Constitution does not acknowledge a doctrine of regulatory takings) and equality (preferential treatment for foreign investors giving rise to discrimination against locals). Finally, investment treaty commitments undermined the priority accorded to economic development in the new Constitution, which includes participatory planning, food sovereignty, and authority in the state to regulate strategic sectors in accordance with the precautionary principle and environmental sustainability. Compelled by the logic of Article 422, CAITISA recommended the termination of a further sixteen investment treaties, including those with capital-exporting states such as the United States, Canada, and China.

Yet resistance has been difficult to sustain. President Correa continued to court foreign investment in resource development over the objections of Indigenous communities and social movements.[46] Even while CAITISA was at work, Ecuador completed a new agreement with the EU, prompting the chair of the commission, Carlos Gaviria Díaz, to

---

[44] E.g. Constitutional Court of Ecuador, Caso No. 0008-10-Ti, Dictamen No. 020-10-DTI-CC (June 24, 2010) 13–26, https://www.italaw.com/sites/default/files/case-documents/ita0942.pdf.

[45] Comisión para la Auditoría Integral Ciudadana de los Tratados de Protección Recíproca de Inversiones y del Sistema de Arbitraje Internacional en Materia de Inversiones (CAITISA), "Auditoría integral ciudadana de los tratados de protección recíproca de inversions y del sistema de arbitraje en material de inversiones en Ecuador," May 8, 2017, http://caitisa.org/index.php/home/enlaces-de-interes.

[46] David Schneiderman, *Resisting Economic Globalization: Critical Theory and International Investment Law* (Basingstoke: Palgrave Macmillan, 2015), ch. 6.

resign.[47] Now the Moreno Government, elected in May 2017, has indicated that its priority is to revise its model BIT and renegotiate treaties with these same sixteen states.[48]

COMPLIANCE

Canada

Though Canadians have long been preoccupied with high rates of foreign ownership, particularly by firms domiciled in the United States, Canada has been energetically signing investment treaties since 1994, the year the North American Free Trade Agreement (NAFTA) came into force. It is noteworthy that the Canadian government built upon the template that the United States successfully promoted in NAFTA. Several modifications to the template were necessary to complete a BIT with China. This required substantially watering down commitments on transparency and giving up reciprocity as between Canadian and Chinese investors. Canadians continue to be subject to restraints within China that are not applicable to Chinese state-owned enterprises. Such concessions were warranted, Canadian officials asserted (without much publicly available evidence in support), because investor protections were a key strategy with which to attract new Chinese inward investment.[49]

For these reasons, the Canadian government remains a rule taker and not a rule-maker. Yet Canada could have made an independent contribution to the construction of global economic law. It is a successful G7 state that does not provide constitutional guarantees for property rights. Yet Canada simply follows the US lead by incorporating, for instance, Penn Central's multifactor analysis in the case of regulatory takings, into its model treaty text.[50] In the context of negotiations for a free trade and investment agreement with the European Union, the government succumbed, without any public consultation, to a European Commission proposal for an "investment court." This proposal is not about courts staffed by independent and impartial judges. Instead, it offers modest improvements to the current system of investment arbitration as a means of assuaging European critics of ISDS. Canadians are now promoting the Canadian-EU agreement (CETA) as

[47] Federico Suárez Ricaurte, "'Actuando bajo la ética de la convicción,' Ecuador" *Instituto de Estudios Constitucionales Carlos Restrepo Piedrahita, Universidad Externado de Columbia,* ed. Carlos Gaviria Díaz en CAITISA (April 18, 2015), http://icrp.uexternado.edu.co/federico-suarez-ricaurte/2015/04/18/actuando-bajo-la-etica-de-la-conviccion-carlos-gaviria-diaz-en-caitisa-ecuador/.

[48] Jacopo Dettoni, "Ecuador Foreign Trade Minister Looks to Mend Friendships," *FDI Intelligence,* December 10, 2017, https://www.fdiintelligence.com/Locations/Americas/Ecuador/Ecuador-foreign-trade-minister-looks-to-mend-friendships.

[49] Gus Van Harten, *Sold Down the Yangtze: Canada's Lopsided Investment Deal with China* (Toronto: Lorimer, 2015), 30.

[50] This calls for "a case-by-case, fact-based inquiry" that considers the "economic impact" of the measure, the extent to which it interferes with "distinct, reasonable investment-backed expectations," and the "character of the government action." See Penn Central Transportation Co. v. New York City, 438 U.S. 104, 124 (1977).

a "progressive" agreement so as to allay Canadian concerns that it merely empowers the already powerful. This amounts to a "stretching of the neoliberal policy repertoire" so as to render it more acceptable to a weary electorate.[51]

There has been a severe democratic deficit—contributing to democratic malaise— regarding Canada's continuing commitment to the regimes of global economic law.[52] This is compounded by the fact that foreign policy remains the sole purview of the executive branch. Canada's parliamentary system of government concentrates authority in the prime minister and his or her cabinet. This prerogative power has not been dispersed more widely. So long as Parliament remains under the control of the prime minister and his or her majority party, this is unlikely to change any time soon.[53]

Nor has the Canadian government undertaken, or made public, any study regarding the relationship between BITs and attracting new inward investment. One suspects this is because no such correlation actually exists. For the most part, the government seems more interested in providing consolation to Canadian investors abroad, mostly those in the mining industry with offices in the metropolises of Toronto and Vancouver. Yet Canada has been the subject of over twelve NAFTA claims, almost half of which Canada has lost to investors. In some cases, a dispute merely was threatened, resulting in the abandonment of proposed measures for plain packaging of tobacco products in 1994.[54] Nevertheless, the Canadian government and Canadian courts continue to treat the regime as constitutionally benign. Yet it has the effect of incorporating new standards of protection and contract not otherwise available under Canadian constitutional law or legislation. While attention has been drawn to Canada's rigid constitutional amending formula, it turns out that citizen expectations are being transformed without the necessity of formal amendment.

Colombia

The Colombian investment treaty program got off to a limping start when, in 1995, the Colombian Constitutional Court declared that agreements with the United Kingdom and others partly offended the 1991 Constitution. The Constitution represented a new beginning for Colombia as most rebel groups were prepared to lay down the arms. It also incorporated a host of new rights for Colombian Indigenous peoples, including rights

---

[51] Jamie Peck and Adam Tickell, "Neoliberalizing Space," *Antipode* 34 (2002): 380–404, 390.

[52] This is in contrast to the rosy picture drawn by Richard Albert and Michael Pal, "The Democratic Resilience of the Canadian Constitution," in *Constitutional Democracy in Crisis?*

[53] On the concentration of power in the Canadian executive branch, see David Schneiderman, *Red, White and Kind of Blue? The Conservatives and the Americanization of Canadian Constitutional Culture* (Toronto: University of Toronto Press, 2015).

[54] On this measure and others abandoned by Canadian governments, see David Schneiderman, *Constitutionalizing Economic Globalization: Investment Rules and Democracy's Promise* (Cambridge: Cambridge University Press, 2008).

to self-government and to participation in decisions around natural resource exploitation.[55] The UK BIT ran into trouble because it was inconsistent with provisions of the Colombian constitution regarding expropriation, which did not mandate the payment of compensation unless required by equity. Also, the treaty offended equality provisions by granting to citizens of British nationality preferential treatment in respect of property rights, treatment that was not available to Colombian nationals.[56]

In order to assuage foreign investors and continue with its investment treaty program, the Congress repealed two paragraphs of constitutional text in August 1999. The constitutional property clause would no longer permit expropriation without the payment of compensation, solving both equality and property law concerns. Colombia relaunched its program and, by 2016, concluded a further twelve treaties, of which seven are currently in force. The government's objective appears to have been to create a new El Dorado, where almost one-third of the country would be reserved for mining activities.[57]

The government has done little to preserve policy space for Colombian authorities. Newer treaties do include some preambular language, as in the 2010 Colombia-Korea BIT, which directs that the treaty's contents be interpreted "in a manner consistent with the protection of health, safety, and the environment and the promotion of consumer protection and internationally recognized labour rights." Qualifying language has also been added to the expropriations clause, along the lines of the US Supreme Court's *Penn Central* criteria. Little else has been done to curb investor rights.

Colombia now faces at least six investment claims. These include disputes arising out of Colombian Constitutional Court proceedings declaring certain mining concessions as running afoul of constitutional protections accorded to Indigenous communities or inconsistent with the lawful designation of national parks and areas of ecological significance. This has prompted Canadian and US-based companies to launch investment disputes, seeking damages for the "taking" of their investments.[58]

Egypt

Egypt was persuaded to sign onto the investment treaty regime and did so with gusto. The state signed some 111 treaties between the years 1997 and 2010, many of them without public consultation, 72 of which are currently in force. Eager to attract foreign investors, Egypt followed European templates. Egyptian negotiators, for instance, welcomed

[55] Subsoil rights, however, remain exclusively the property of the state (Art. 332).

[56] See the discussion of this episode in Schneiderman, *Constitutionalizing Economic Globalization*, 164–171.

[57] Ximena Sierra-Camargo, "Law, Mining and (Neo)colonialism: The Large-Scale Gold Mining Legal Policy in Colombia within a 'Coloniality Global' Context," unpublished draft PhD dissertation, Faculty of Law, Universidad del Rosario, Bogotá, Colombia, 2017.

[58] Marco Velásquez-Ruiz, "¿Qué pensará Canadá sobre el impacto de sus empresas extractivas en Colombia?" *El Tiempo Blog*, March 6, 2017, http://blogs.eltiempo.com/desmarcado/2017/03/06/que-pensara-canada-sobre-demandas/.

the opportunity to negotiate a new regional trade and investment pact with the United States because it would constrain Egyptian political capacity moving forward. It would prevent "anybody in the future from going backwards," explained the Egyptian finance minister.[59] The military plays an oversized role in the economy, controlling and deriving revenue from a variety of state-owned but military-controlled enterprises (estimates are that it controls up to 30 percent of Egyptian GDP). It is a constituent part of Egypt's "deep state" that includes the security service, bureaucracy, and political elites. The military's economic power is increasingly tied to foreign capital via public-private partnerships, in which investors are granted the type of physical security and political stability that they crave elsewhere.[60] Not much concern was paid to the reduction in policy space that flowed from these commitments. This might have been a problem, insofar as the Egyptian constitution of 1971 promised to deliver health and education and was committed to an economy in which the "people control all means of production" and "workers hav[e] a share in . . . profits." These constitutional commitments remained mostly "theoretical."[61]

The Constitution of 2014 was drafted by a committee of fifty and ratified via popular referendum (with a turnout rate of 38 percent) under the auspices of the Supreme Council for the Armed Forces led by Commander-in-Chief al-Sisi (later president). The Constitution specifies percentages of the national budget that are required to be dedicated to delivering constitutionally-mandated health services and education. The new Constitution also solidifies the military's role in directing the country's political and economic affairs.[62] The deep state, it turns out, never really left.[63]

A number of investment disputes arose during the interregnum between President Mubarak's ouster in 2011 and the brief tenure of President Morsi and the Muslim Brotherhood. Egyptian administrative courts, during this period, cancelled contracts and commitments that were marred by cronyism and corruption. This precipitated twenty investment disputes by foreign investors whose sweetheart deals under the Mubarak regime had soured with the rise of Morsi.[64]

---

[59] Edward Alden, "US Faces Tough Talks with Egypt in Its Push for Regional Trade Accords," *Financial Times*, September 29, 2005.

[60] Shana Marshall and Joshua Stacher, "Egypt's Generals and Transnational Capital," *Middle East Report* 262 (Spring 2012): 12–18.

[61] Zaid Al-Ali, "Egypt's Third Constitution in Three Years: A Critical Analysis," in *Egypt's Revolutions: Politics, Religion and Social Movements*, ed. Bernard Rougier and Stéphane Lacroix, trans. Cynthia Schoch (Basingstoke: Palgrave Macmillan, 2016), 123–137, 128–129.

[62] See, e.g., Articles 203 and 234.

[63] Mohammed Nosseir, "The Ugly Truth: Egypt's Deep State," *Egypt Daily News*, November 16, 2013, https://dailynewsegypt.com/2013/11/16/the-ugly-truth-egypts-deep-state/.

[64] See "Disputes with Investors: Government Attempts to Turn a New Leaf," *Daily News Egypt*, March 13, 2015, https://dailynewsegypt.com/2015/03/13/disputes-with-investors-government-attempts-to-turn-a-new-leaf/.

For example, the Red Sea development envisaged by Hussain Sajwani, a Dubai billionaire and one of President Trump's business partners, was enabled by the sale of valuable real estate under Mubarak's rule at significantly less than fair market value.[65] Sajwani subsequently was prosecuted, along with Egypt's tourism minister, for corruption. Sajwani was found guilty in absentia, ordered to return the land, and directed to pay a hefty fine and serve a five-year prison term. This was circumvented by an investment claim against Egypt that, once discontinued, resulted in the payment of a fine of about US$15 million and suspension of proceedings against Sajwani.[66]

Other claims arose as a consequence of Egyptian courts reversing the sale of state assets to friends of the Mubarak regime. Indorama launched an investment dispute in response to a court order renationalizing the company's textile factory. Because the Morsi government paid compensation equivalent to the sum paid by the investor, rather than the property's fair market value, Indorama sought to recoup the difference. The claim was settled upon payment of $US 54 million. In order to forestall any further third-party actions in Egyptian courts interfering with investor expectations, the al-Sisi government in 2014 enacted Law 32 to restrict their ability to challenge commercial contracts awarded by the government. This would have the effect of putting a halt to the rush of lawsuits challenging Mubarak-era deals.[67]

While the current government has made great efforts at settling these disputes, one outstanding claim concerns fulfillment of a waste management and street cleaning contract in the city of Alexandria. The French investor, Veolia, claims that damages were suffered as a consequence of a failure to modify contract terms to keep pace with inflation and wage increases due to new Egyptian labor laws. The company seeks to recoup damages of more than US $100 million.[68] As the dispute is being conducted under a cloak of secrecy, one surmises that the investor will claim that legitimate expectations were upset. The expectation is that Egyptian employees are not entitled to wage increases and, if they are, these wages cannot be paid without first compensating foreign investors.

---

[65] Kevin Sullivan, "Trump's Foreign Network: The President-Elect's Unorthodox Overseas Business Partners," *Washington Post*, January 13, 2017.

[66] Hussain Sajwani, Damac Park Avenue for Real Estate Development S.A.E., and Damac Gamsha Bay for Development S.A.E. v. Arab Republic of Egypt (ICSID Case No. ARB/11/16). The case was discontinued on September 10, 2014.

[67] See Jonathan Bonnitcha, "Investment Treaties and Transition from Authoritarian Rule," *Journal of World Investment & Trade* 15 (2014): 96–1011, 983 and James MacDonald and Dyfan Owen, "The Effects on Arbitration of the Arab Spring," *Global Arbitration Review*, April 20, 2016.

[68] Luke Eric Peterson, "French Company, Veolia, Launches Claim against Egypt over Terminated Waste Contract and Labor Wage Stabilization Promises," *Investment Arbitration Reporter*, June 27, 2012.

Conclusion

While global economic law has had some success in disabling constitutional capacity, this is not an achievement that will forever be secure. If neoliberal legality emerged triumphant after the fall of the Soviet Union, it has since been experiencing a series of calamities, often self-inflicted, undermining the very regimes that it seeks to preserve and enlarge. Nevertheless, there is reason to think that the investment rules regime will survive any legitimacy crisis it is now experiencing. Investment law is not yet destined for the dustbin of history. Commitments to investors, after all, are intended to last far into the future. Even when agreements are denounced by states, they continue to protect investments established during the life of the agreement from ten to twenty-five years, on average. Established investors will continue for some time to be able to launch investment disputes when states behave in ways that run afoul of the regime's open-textured constitution-like commitments.

This does not mean that investment law and other regimes of global economic law are irreversible. To the contrary, as discussed in the previous section, states in some locales are taking steps to loosen these constraints, even doing away with them entirely. Yet these are states situated at the periphery of global economic life. The question is whether powerful states at the center, rather than at the periphery, will consent to the rollback of the rules and institutions of global economic law. The EU faced this prospect when its founding Member States, Germany and France, threatened to drop investor rights from texts under negotiation with the United States and Canada. The EU response, mentioned above, was to propose procedural cures, namely an "investment court" modeled partly upon World Trade Organization dispute settlement bodies. Even then, there remains some residual resistance to taking on new investor obligations within EU Member States. No resistance is likely to be found coming from China, the leading source of new outward investment. China has altered its model investment treaty text so that its provisions look like those promoted by every other capital-exporting state, even as it pretends to be more developmentally friendly than its Western competitors.[69]

It turns out that the Trump presidency may be doing the most to upset the regimes of global economic law. Trump declared NAFTA to be a "disaster," even though the United States, as the dominant negotiating partner, determined most of its content. In the midst of NAFTA renegotiations, the Trump administration proposed that ISDS be made optional. The Trump negotiating strategy, it appears, is to undermine investment in Mexico and Canada and return it to the United States. The three economies, however, are already tightly integrated. It is hard to believe that elimination of this legal process will make much of a difference moving forward.

---

[69] Tyler Cohen and David Schneiderman, "The Political Economy of Chinese Bilateral Investment Treaty Policy," *Chinese Journal of Comparative Law* 5 (2017) 110–128.

This is a bargaining position that might yet change. It is anomalous, after all, for the Trump administration to take a position that is not potentially beneficial to Trump enterprises abroad. Consider the vulnerability of Trump foreign properties were the United States to take a position unpopular in some part of the world. Imagine if a foreign government were to target a Trump hotel, or fail to provide full protection and security to that property, unless the US government provided concessions of some sort. One would think that President Trump, who has not divested himself of profits in the Trump Organization, would prefer to have available to him the sorts of protections available in BITs. There is a likelihood, then, that President Trump will reconsider and make these obligations mandatory, even if only with non-NAFTA states. If this were to occur, the regime would continue to be sheltered from the peripheral storms that disturb it.

Yet, so long as constitutional capacities remain hindered, we should not expect disturbances initiated by disgruntled citizens to abate any time soon. Even if citizen expectations are dampened, expressions of indignation can be expected to periodically erupt. If not undoing the regimes of neoliberal legality, they are likely to render them contestable and, thereby, perpetually unstable.

32 Will Democracy Die in Darkness?
Calling Autocracy by Its Name
Sujit Choudhry*

The *Washington Post*'s New Slogan

Last year, the *Washington Post* adopted a new slogan: "Democracy Dies in Darkness." But what does this phrase precisely mean? It clearly speaks to the role of the media in a democracy. The press sheds light on exercises of public power, especially those decisions that governments would prefer to remain hidden in the shadows. The power of the public to hold governments accountable, through elections, in legislatures, and in the court of public opinion, requires transparency and information. But the phrase goes further, by linking darkness to the *death* of democracy. The spotlight of the press is not merely integral to the proper functioning and health of democracy; rather, it is essential to its very survival. How?

"Democracy Dies in Darkness" gestures toward a deeper theory of the relationship among political action, constitutions, and democratic stability. There is a widely held view in the United States that its institutions are resilient enough to protect constitutional democracy from a would-be autocrat. This mindset is not just an American one; across the world the fate of democracy is increasingly entrusted to constitutional design. But Steve Levitsky and Daniel Ziblatt argue in *How Democracies Die*, that even the most thoughtfully drafted constitutions cannot check the slide into autocracy if they are not underpinned by a set of

* An earlier version of this paper was presented at the GlobCon Colloquium at the WZB Berlin Social Science Center. I wish to thank Sumit Bisarya, Sam Issacharaoff, Mattias Kumm, Dilek Kurbam, Michael Meyer, Kai Möller, Ulrich Preuss, Mark Tushnet and Fred Felix Zaumseil for helpful questions and comments.

unwritten norms. They term these norms mutual toleration (the acceptance of the legitimacy of the political opposition)—and forbearance (the refusal to exercise power to its full legal limits to disable or destroy the opposition).[1] As Sam Issacharoff attests to in his contribution to this volume, these norms are under historically unprecedented strain in the United States. For example, he notes that the idea that presidents would use their executive power to prosecute political opponents was once unthinkable. Yet now, chants of "lock her up" take center stage at rallies of the Republican Party, urged on by President Trump himself.[2]

As I have argued elsewhere, the common mission of constitutional democracies across the world is to create a framework for bounded partisan pluralist contestation that is nested within the underlying political economy, within which the major social groups engage in political conflict and compete for power according to the rules and under the institutions of a constitutional order, because it is in their mutual advantage to do so.[3] On Levitsky and Ziblatt's account, what the norms of mutual toleration and forbearance do is to ensure that the institutions and rules of constitutional democracy are exercised in a manner that serves this intended purpose, to allow for collective decision-making under conditions of, and to preserve, political pluralism. Without those norms, those very same institutions and rules could be perversely "weaponized"—in contemporary jargon—to undermine the constitutional democracy and political pluralism they are designed to defend. Unwritten norms are fundamentally matters of a shared constitutional culture, not constitutional design. In the Commonwealth constitutional tradition, we would term them constitutional conventions. Mistakenly identified with the United Kingdom's so-called "unwritten constitution," unwritten norms are essential to the proper functioning of even the most detailed written constitutional texts.

The dependence of rules and institutions on unwritten norms raises perhaps the greatest challenge for scholars and practitioners of constitutional design. Contemporary authoritarians have come to understand that they can subvert democracy as readily by undermining conventions and norms as they can by changing laws and constitutions. Yet, this raises important questions about the extent to which constitutional design and implementation can thwart the rise of authoritarianism. In the midst of the great crisis facing contemporary democracy, in America and globally, is there nothing that the law can do? In this chapter, I suggest that the distinction between unwritten and written norms is not always as sharp as some suggest. Norms that are unwritten in some constitutional orders are written in others. Moreover, if a basic mission of *any* self-described constitutional democracy is to create an enduring framework for bounded, partisan, pluralist contestation, that unwritten norm can be interpreted as a central purpose underlying the written constitutional text, and therefore as a hard legal constraint on exercises of public power pursuant to that

[1] Steven Levitsky and Daniel Ziblatt, *How Democracies Die* (New York: Crown, 2018).
[2] Samuel Issacharoff, "Populism versus Democratic Governance," in *Constitutional Democracy in Crisis?*, ed. Mark A. Graber, Sanford Levinson, and Mark Tushnet (New York: Oxford University Press, 2018).
[3] Sujit Choudhry, "Resisting Democratic Backsliding: An Essay on Weimar, Self-Enforcing Constitutions, and the Frankfurt School," *Global Constitutionalism* 7 (2018): 54–74.

text, enforceable by the courts. Courts can therefore fuel political support for the same unwritten norms that make the courts effective at all—making the causal arrow run in both directions. To do so, courts must fearlessly call autocracy by its name.

Eric Holder's Tweet

Eric Holder—the former attorney general under President Obama—tweeted to his followers in December 2017:

> ABSOLUTE RED LINE: the firing of Bob Mueller or crippling the special counsel's office. If removed or meaningfully tampered with, there must be mass, popular, peaceful support of both. The American people must be seen and heard - they will ultimately be determinative.[4]

Holder's call to action is built around two concepts. Red lines are clear, uncontroversial boundaries; if officials traverse them, they are extremely likely to have abused their authority. Holder relies on the idea of a boundary that is basic or fundamental to American democracy—that is, a constitutional boundary. As well, Holder supposes that the American people ought to assess if a particular decision crosses a constitutional red line, and that if such a transgression occurs, they must publicly respond ("be seen and heard") because how they react will ultimately determine how the issue is resolved ("be determinative")—that is, whether the crossing of the red line stands or is reversed.

Holder's tweet presupposes a theory of constitutional self-enforcement, built around the concept of a focal point. As Barry Weingast has argued, constitutions coordinate the expectations of officials and citizens regarding the appropriate boundaries of public authority.[5] They do so by creating focal points—constitutional rules—that provide reasons for official behavior, benchmarks for assessing official conduct, and grounds to criticize actions that violate these rules. Constitutions are self-enforcing, in the sense that elites and masses can police the boundaries of official conduct without the need for a court to first rule that the constitution has been violated. Indeed, it is striking that Holder, once the nation's chief law enforcement official, does not mention a legal challenge to attempts to obliterate Mueller's authority, even in a supporting role.

The classic example of a focal point is a presidential term limit. Across the world, as in the United States, the norm in presidential and semi-presidential systems is to limit an individual to a total of two terms as president. A classic move in the autocrat's handbook is a blatant attempt to stay in office beyond a term limit—for example, by declaring a state

---

[4] Eric Holder. Twitter Post. Dec. 17, 2017, 11:49 AM. https://twitter.com/EricHolder/status/942481938165747712.
[5] Barry R. Weingast, "The Political Foundations of Democracy and the Rule of Law," *American Political Science Review* 91 (1997): 245–263.

of emergency, dissolving the legislature, and/or suspending elections. It is clear when this is happening, and more often than not, attempts to do so will lead political opponents to mobilize against such attempts, and bring citizens into the streets. Courts may get involved in checking attempts to change term limits (as has occurred in many countries), but they are not the only, or even the principal, line of defense.

Disregarding term limits is one example of a more general category termed the self-coup or *autogolpe*, which is an attempt by directly elected executives to extend their power once elected, invoking a democratic mandate from the people. A second category is the coup d'état, the unconstitutional seizure of power without any electoral legitimacy—for example, by the military. A third is blatant electoral fraud by incumbents to maintain the façade of democratic legitimacy. A fourth category is the closing of electoral space, through the outright prohibition of political parties, and crackdowns on freedom of assembly, association, and the press. During the Cold War, the relative clarity of these four phenomena made it relatively uncontroversial to identify, assess, and criticize them—even if they could not be reversed.

LA SUITE POLONAISE

But the character of threats to democracy has undergone a profound shift since the end of the Cold War. To understand how, consider the last few years of legal developments in Poland under the rule of the Law and Justice Party (better known by its Polish initials, PiS).[6] The PiS is nationalist, populist, and right-wing. It won a legislative majority in the 2015 elections to Poland's parliament, the Sejm. Since then, the Polish government has undertaken a systematic effort to undermine the framework of constitutional democracy, in order to remove impediments to its rule, and to entrench itself in power through future electoral cycles. The PiS's initial focus has been on the Constitutional Tribunal (Poland's Constitutional Court), although it has more recently targeted the ordinary courts and the electoral machinery. I collectively term these measures "La Suite Polonaise" to capture that they are a series of distinct initiatives that nonetheless are components of a coherent strategy with thematic unity.

The details are complex, but they matter. Appointments to the Constitutional Tribunal are governed by the Constitutional Tribunal Act, which requires the nomination and election of candidates by the Sejm, followed by a swearing-in by the president of Poland. Just before the 2015 elections, the outgoing Sejm (not under PiS control) nominated and elected new judges to fill vacancies (as well as some constitutionally suspect nominations for future vacancies). Immediately after the election, President Duda refused to swear in three of these justices, effectively blocking those appointments; in parallel, the

---

[6] For a comprehensive analysis of Polish developments, see Wojciech Sadurski, "Constitutional Crisis in Poland," *Constitutional Democracy in Crisis?*

Sejm amended the Constitutional Tribunal Act in November 2015, setting the stage for appointment of five judges aligned with the PiS. In early December 2015, four judges were nominated and elected by the Sejm, and three of them were sworn in by President Duda to take the place of the judges whose appointment he had blocked. Moreover, President Duda did so *before* the Tribunal handed down its decision in a constitutional challenge to the appointment of the judges by the old Sejm, in which it held that it was not necessary for the president of Poland to swear-in the judges for them to take office; rather, nomination and election by the Sejm sufficed. The effect of this ruling, along with President Duda's actions, meant there were two sets of judges who could lay claim to the vacancies on the Constitutional Tribunal.

The Sejm's next move was to adopt legislation, in mid-December 2015, requiring the Tribunal to sit *en banc* in all cases (as opposed to its past practice of also sitting in panels of three or five judges), and to require a two-thirds majority for it to declare laws unconstitutional—which in combination gave the newly appointed PiS justices a blocking veto that would prevent the Tribunal from striking down PiS legislation. In addition, the Tribunal was given the power *en banc* to reopen any decisions decided by a chamber, which was designed to allow the Tribunal to eventually overrule its own judgment validating the nomination and election of the judges by the Sejm. For several months, there was a stalemate on the Tribunal, with the president of the Constitutional Tribunal refusing to allow PiS-supported judges to participate in cases because they had been appointed, in his view, when there was no vacancy on the Tribunal. In November 2016, the Sejm adopted yet another law, which obliged the president of the Tribunal to assign cases to all judges sworn in, thereby forcing the PiS judges onto the Tribunal.

The conflict then shifted to the Tribunal's General Assembly, which consists of all its judges. The principal role played by the General Assembly is in the process of appointing the president of the Constitutional Tribunal, by sending a short list of current Constitutional Tribunal members to the president of Poland. The Sejm's November 2016 law created a new position, interim president of the Constitutional Tribunal, who would lead the court once its president had stepped down, and assigned it on the basis of a seniority rule gerrymandered to give it to a PiS-backed judge. One role for the interim president was to chair the General Assembly, which bypassed giving this responsibility to the Tribunal's vice president, as had been the normal procedure. Shortly before the retirement of the president of the Constitutional Tribunal, the General Assembly sent a short list to the president of Poland, which he rejected, on the basis that the General Assembly lacked a quorum because it included judges whom the president had not sworn in, and because of a boycott by the PiS judges. Immediately after the interim president took office, she reconvened the General Assembly, which now had a quorum because of the participation of the PiS-appointed judges, and which nominated her as the single candidate for president of the Tribunal, a position to which the president of Poland appointed her. She also included the PiS-appointed judges on the bench and assigned them to cases.

Let's stand back from this story and unpack the different dimensions of the PiS capture of the Constitutional Tribunal: its *democratic legitimacy, legal basis, pace, scope*, and *substantive character*.

The PiS commanded a parliamentary majority, secured in an election free of force or fraud. Likewise, President Duda was properly elected and commanded a democratic mandate. Both the Sejm and President Duda possessed democratic legitimacy when they acted; moreover, both were elected on the PiS platform in separate elections in 2015, suggesting broad public support for the PiS.

The Polish Constitution creates the Constitutional Tribunal, and sets out its basic institutional framework. But rather than deploying a constitutional amendment to capture the Tribunal in one fell swoop—for example, one that would have purged the Tribunal's judges and replaced them with an entire bench of PiS supporters—the PiS has instead captured the Constitutional Tribunal through a series of ordinary statutes, and exercises of statutory discretion and inherent powers by the president of Poland. Constitutional amendments require supermajority support, and in some cases, a referendum. The use of a special legislative procedure that departs from the normal rule of a simple majority, and a referendum that would include a campaign, are much more visible than legislation or presidential decisions. Moreover, we can think of visibility along two dimensions: domestically to the Polish public, and internationally to the international community, and, in the Polish context, the European Union. The greater visibility of constitutional amendments is deliberate, because as a general matter, constitutional amendments concern matters of greater consequence than ordinary law or exercises of presidentialial discretion; the visibility of constitutional amendments can catalyze domestic debate and trigger EU institutions to examine whether those amendments have any bearing on EU law. Because decisions of the president of Poland have less visibility than ordinary law, this creates the incentive for the Sejm to shift decisions to the president via grants of statutory discretion. In addition, the interim president of the Constitutional Tribunal and the judges appointed by the PiS played an important role within the Tribunal's General Assembly, in a manner that perhaps is the least visible of all.

Unlike a single, comprehensive constitutional amendment, the capture of the Constitutional Tribunal took place over a period of slightly over a year, at an uneven pace, with periods of intense activity followed by months of apparent inactivity. The PiS also acted incrementally, through a number of discrete decisions spread out over time. Moreover, those decisions involved different institutions and actors: the president of Poland, the Sejm, the interim president of the Tribunal, and the PiS-appointed judges within the General Assembly. The pace and scope and institutionally-fragmented nature of the PiS measures made the thread hard to follow, probably deliberately.

Finally, many of the changes were of a highly technical or procedural nature, which obscured their substantive impact. The new rules governing the constitution of panels, voting, the assignment of judges to cases, and the creation of the interim president of the Tribunal did not, in and of themselves, suggest the ulterior motive that underpinned them. Indeed, they seemed like housekeeping matters to increase institutional efficiency or promote legal certainty that fell within the scope of legitimate constitutional design and reasonable disagreement far from the shoals of constitutional capture. And the objections to these changes were also highly technical: for example, the apparent circumvention of the vice president of the Tribunal by creating a new position of interim president.

The End of History?

The capture of the Constitutional Tribunal by the PiS is part of a broader global story.[7] As Nancy Bermeo has observed, the prevalence of coup d'états and *autogolpes* declined steeply with the end of the Cold War.[8] What has partially replaced them is democratic backsliding, whereby a democratically elected government or president uses legal means to manipulate rules and institutions to remain in power in future electoral cycles, inter alia with respect to electoral system design, election administration, political party regulation, presidential term limits, civil and political liberties, independent institutions such as constitutional courts and agencies, and media regulation. The classic case lurking in the background of all contemporary discussions is the fall of Weimar Germany, which was captured from within. Democratic backsliding is sometimes termed "authoritarian backsliding" when the democratic regime under threat replaced a prior authoritarian regime to which it may revert, as in Poland.

The causes for this shift are major changes in the international environment. The widespread presupposition is now that democracy is "the only game in town." States must now presumptively present themselves to the world as constitutional democracies, because of strong international disincentives for governments to be transparently undemocratic. Thus, the PiS—and governing parties in Hungary, Turkey, and elsewhere—adopt the forms and rituals of constitutional democracy, such as written constitutions with bills of rights and the separation of powers; a commitment to the rule of law, constitutional courts, and an ordinary judiciary; and regular and periodic elections free of the widespread use of force or fraud.

---

[7] For other discussions of this point, see Sumit Bisarya and Sujit Choudhry, "Regional Organizations and Threats to Constitutional Democracy from Within: Self-Coups and Authoritarian Backsliding," in *The Rule of Law and Constitution Building: The Role of Regional Organizations*, ed. Raul Cordenillo and Kristin Sample (International IDEA, 2014) 183–202, http://www.idea.int/publications/rule-of-law-and-constitution-building/upload/rule_of_law_chapter_8.pdf); Sujit Choudhry, "Transnational Constitutionalism and a Limited Doctrine of Unconstitutional Constitutional Amendment: A Reply to Rosalind Dixon and David Landau," *International Journal of Constitutional Law* 15 (2017): 826–832; and Catalina Uribe Burcher and Sumit Bisarya, "Threats from Within: Democracy's Resilience to Backsliding," in *The Global State of Democracy: Exploring Democracy's Resilience* (2017: International IDEA), 70–94, https://www.idea.int/gsod/files/IDEA-GSOD-2017-REPORT-EN.pdf.

[8] Nancy Bermeo, "On Democratic Backsliding," *Journal of Democracy* 27 (2016): 5–19.

But the rules and institutions of constitutional democracy also provide the means whereby constitutional democracy undermines itself, and the political language to respond to critics. Fukuyama's "End of History" thesis was right, in the sense that democracy is now the near-universal basis of political legitimation, even if used rhetorically to give cover to undemocratic regimes.[9]

Instead of the collapse of democracy, we have its "degradation" (Larry Diamond)[10] or "retrogression" (Tom Ginsburg and Aziz Huq).[11] There is no binary, either-or distinction between democracies and autocracies with a bright line between them. Rather, we have a spectrum of regimes along a continuum with democracy and absolute dictatorship at its poles. This reality has generated a cottage industry of new terminology, such as "illiberal democracies" (Fareed Zakaria),[12] "competitive authoritarian regimes" (Steve Levitsky and Lucan Way),[13] "defective democracy" and "electoral authoritarianism" (Matthijs Bogaards)[14]—rooted in a shared project of describing shades of gray.

Bermeo has argued that the "vexing ambiguity" of democratic backsliding has important implications for political science.[15] In her view, democratic backsliding requires that we recognize that "democracy is 'a collage' of institutions" that is "put together piece by piece, and can be taken apart the same way."[16] This poses a great challenge for scholars of democratization, who have "focused on clear cases of democratic collapse," which contain "the bright spark that ignites an effective call to action" as opposed to "slow slides toward authoritarianism."[17] Political scientists must come to grips with this reality "or risk their own slide into irrelevance."[18] Less of a focus "on economic and institutional correlates" and more attention to "choices and choosers" is vital, because the latter "may be more amenable to direct influence and rapid intervention."[19]

There is a parallel challenge for constitutional law. In December 2017, colleagues and I convened a small workshop of constitutional experts in Berlin, to examine the prospects and pathways for recovering from authoritarian constitutionalism in Hungary and Poland. One of the participants was Marcin Matczak, a leading Polish constitutional academic and lawyer who has argued a number of constitutional challenges to PiS initiatives.

---

[9] Francis Fukuyama, *The End of History and the Last Man* (New York: Free Press, 1992).

[10] Larry Diamond, "Facing Up to the Democratic Recession," *Journal of Democracy* 26 (2015): 141–155.

[11] Tom Ginsburg and Aziz Huq, "How to Lose a Constitutional Democracy," *UCLA Law Review* 65 (2018): 78–169.

[12] Fareed Zakaria, *The Future of Freedom: Illiberal Democracy at Home and Abroad* (New York: W.W. Norton, 2007).

[13] Steven Levitsky and Lucan Way, *Competitive Authoritarianism: Hybrid Regimes after the Cold War* (New York: Cambridge University Press, 2010).

[14] Matthijs Bogaards, "How to Classify Hybrid Regimes? Defective Democracy and Electoral Authoritarianism," *Democratization* 16 (2009): 399–423.

[15] Bermeo, "On Democratic Backsliding," 15.

[16] Ibid., 14.

[17] Ibid.

[18] Ibid.

[19] Ibid., 5.

Matczak's view is that the PiS made very weak legal arguments in these cases. The opponents of the regime made stronger arguments, but the PiS-aligned Constitutional Tribunal rejected them. What was truly worrisome and troubling for Matczak was the failure of the opposition to persuade the public in the court of public opinion. Good legal arguments, rooted in the idea that the PiS had violated the "spirit" of the constitution by abusing its rules and institutions to undermine its very purpose, were insufficiently strong to overcome the public support for the regime.

What would Holder make of the failure of constitutional democrats in Poland to persuade their fellow citizens? For Holder, the crossing of red lines mobilizes regime opponents to resist anti-constitutional conduct, and hopefully translates into electoral victory. But Poland may be teaching us, in real time, that the we need to rethink the very idea of the red line. A red line implies a constitutional threshold that is clear and uncontroversial, that sounds in the language of principle, that is highly visible—perhaps because it is constitutionally entrenched—and that is traversed quickly and comprehensively. But the campaign of the PiS to subvert Polish democracy from within is none of those things.

Indeed, while firing Mueller might cross a red line, how about crippling him, as Holder put it? Persuading the public that something less-than-dismissal, which may fatally undermine Mueller, would nonetheless cross a red line, could be a tall order. This is true even in the United States, where the constitution serves the common reference point for political life, and constitutional argument is part of the grammar of politics, perhaps more than anywhere else in the world. While the great American contribution to constitutional thought is the anti-positivist idea that even the most basic, seemingly uncontroverted constitutional claims are interpretative, in Ronald Dworkin's famous formulation,[20] that noble idea has been taken up by conservatives and liberals alike to turn the legal system into a terrain of elemental, total ideological struggle where there are no longer few, if any, right or wrong answers at all. As a distinguished American colleague once explained to me before I moved to the United States, to my fascination and horror, "it's politics all the way down."

Presidential Impeachment through the Comparative Looking Glass

Can we reinterpret and resurrect Holder's red lines? I want to suggest how, through the question of presidential impeachment. Although not yet a live issue in the United States, this has been a central question in South Africa for the past couple of years. The unusual interventions of the South African Constitutional Court offer the outlines of a potential approach to renovating the relationship among courts, constitutions, and political mobilization.

---

[20] Ronald Dworkin, *Law's Empire* (Cambridge, MA: Harvard University Press, 1986).

The South African impeachment saga arises out of President Jacob Zuma's self-enrichment at public expense, through expensive renovations at his country home. These were initially defended as necessary for security upgrades, but South Africa's Public Protector—a law enforcement official created by South Africa's constitution with broad powers to investigate and remedy official wrongdoing—concluded that the upgrades included non-security measures such as building a swimming pool, and that the president had breached his constitutional obligations to comply with an ethics code and to not use his position to enrich himself. She ordered the president to repay some of the renovation expenses and to report to the National Assembly within fourteen days, and sent the report to the National Assembly.

The African National Congress (ANC) government used the transmission of the report to the National Assembly, where it commands an absolute majority, as a diversion strategy. The government created an ad hoc legislative committee that commissioned an alternative report from the minister of police, a member of Zuma's cabinet. That report exonerated the president; the National Assembly then passed a resolution endorsing that report and absolving Zuma of all liability.

Opposition political parties turned to the Constitutional Court, which held in *Economic Freedom Fighters 1* that the National Assembly had acted unconstitutionally by usurping the authority of the Public Protector, a fairly traditional separation-of-powers argument.[21] But the Court went further. The South African Constitution codifies the duties of the National Assembly to scrutinize, oversee, and hold the executive accountable, matters that are left to unwritten constitutional convention elsewhere. The Court held that the National Assembly had breached these duties by setting aside the Public Protector's report without even considering it. Indeed, the Court strongly hinted that the combination of the unconstitutional refusal to examine the Public Protector's report, and commissioning and substituting a manifestly unconstitutional alternative, amounted to acting for an unconstitutional motive: to shield for partisan ends the president from legal accountability.

The Court also affirmed the Public Protector's finding that the president had acted unconstitutionally, which emboldened the opposition parties to attempt to impeach Zuma on the basis that he had committed a "serious violation" of the Constitution. That vote unsurprisingly failed, given strong ANC party discipline. But the opposition parties went back to the Constitutional Court, which held in *Economic Freedom Fighters 2* that the failure of the National Assembly to put in place special procedures to regulate the impeachment process was unconstitutional.[22] The Court ruled that there has to be a special committee of the National Assembly to conduct "preliminary inquiry" into the meaning of the grounds for impeachment listed in the constitution, and whether the impugned

---

[21] *Economic Freedom Fighters v Speaker of the National Assembly and Others; Democratic Alliance v Speaker of the National Assembly and Others* [2016] ZACC 11.

[22] *Economic Freedom Fighters and Others v Speaker of the National Assembly and Another* [2017] ZACC 47.

conduct fell into that category. The Court also held that such a procedure would be unconstitutional if party representation on the committee mirrors representation in the National Assembly, because "members of the majority party . . . may prevent an impeachment process from proceeding . . . to shield a President who is their party leader."[23] What party composition *would* be constitutional the Court did not say. A plausible reading of the judgment is that a committee controlled by the majority party would be unconstitutional, with the implication being that the committee must be opposition controlled.

The Court's latest judgment continues an effort to square the circle between the partisan nature of the National Assembly and its constitutional duties to check the executive. But what practical goal would be served by an impeachment process that would ultimately fail in the Assembly, where the president is supported by the majority party? An answer comes not from the Court's opinion, but from news reports of the hearing before the Court, where the opposition parties stated that a special committee on impeachment would force Zuma to answer questions that he had thus not answered, presumably under oath.[24] Coupled with the requirement that the committee not be under ANC control, the hearings and resulting report—framed in terms of whether Zuma had violated the Constitution—would catalyze public debate and set the terms of the political agenda. Indeed, the Court looked ahead toward the eventual National Assembly debate on impeachment, by admonishing the Speaker (an ANC member) on the need to act impartially, and lecturing ANC National Assembly members that voting against impeachment for partisan reasons would be acting for an unconstitutional motive (italics mine):

> members may not frustrate the realization of ensuring a government by the people if its attainment would harm their political party. If they were to do so, they would be using the institutional power of the Assembly *for a purpose other than the one for which the power was conferred.* This would be inconsistent with the Constitution.

In short, the Court demanded that on the question of impeachment, legislators—including those from the ANC—put the country before party.

Zuma resigned as president of South Africa on February 15, 2018—about eight weeks after the judgment in *Economic Freedom Fighters 2.* He did so under the threat of a vote of no-confidence, an alternative to impeachment that also had been tried unsuccessfully against Zuma that had generated its own constitutional litigation over whether a secret ballot was required.[25] The ANC decided that it would join the opposition parties to vote against him. A number of factors led the ANC to this decision, including the election of a new president of the ANC in December 2017, Cyril Ramaphosa, who was opposed by ANC elites allied with Zuma. Ramaphosa's election set the path for a transition, both

---

[23] Ibid., para. 192.

[24] "Nkandla Returns to Haunt Zuma," *Legal Brief,* January 1, 2018.

[25] *United Democratic Movement v Speaker of the National v Assembly and Others* [2017] ZACC 21.

through its rejection of Zuma and providing a successor at hand. Another factor, though, was the prospect of Zuma testifying under oath before a committee of the National Assembly as a consequence of *Economic Freedom Fighters 2*, which would have been damaging to the electoral prospects of the ANC.

Back to America

To be sure, the terrain of South African constitutional jurisprudence differs markedly from that of American constitutional doctrine. An American court confronted with a parallel constitutional challenge would have viewed the questions of internal legislative procedure as raising non-justiciable political questions, and being vulnerable to near-fatal objections on the basis of ripeness and standing. Nonetheless, there are lessons for American public law to be gleaned from peering through the comparative looking glass.

There is something neo-Bickelian in the Constitutional Court of South Africa's decision. The core argument of *The Least Dangerous Branch* is that the federal courts should use techniques of decisional avoidance to remand difficult constitutional issues to the political branches, especially state legislatures and Congress.[26] Bickel's hope was that the political branches would openly and squarely debate difficult constitutional questions prior to the courts doing so. And Bickel hoped that these hard constitutional issues would, for the most part, be settled in politics, with public opinion serving as the ultimate guarantor of the constitution.

The Constitutional Court of South Africa likewise remanded a difficult constitutional issue to politics, by imposing on the National Assembly the duty to create a new procedure that would ensure that the impeachment of President Zuma would be debated once again, in a multiparty committee not controlled by the ANC, where Zuma would be forced to answer questions under oath. Moreover, it established constitutional parameters for that debate, including the specification of what would count as unconstitutional motives for members of the Assembly, by reference to the constitutional text. Ultimately, whether to impeach Zuma was a decision for the National Assembly, not subject to judicial second-guessing. It fell to the South African public to ensure that public power was used—to paraphrase the Constitutional Court—for the purpose for which that power was conferred.

Abstracting away from the South African case, we can recast the idea of red line as a combination of (1) judicial agenda-setting by forcing institutional deliberation on an issue, and (2) judicial delineation of unconstitutional motives that circumscribe the discursive boundaries of that deliberation, in a context where (3) the judiciary has not been captured, (4) the political opposition and perhaps elements of the governing party would take this opportunity to challenge the original decision on the issue as being rooted in

---

[26] Alexander Bickel, *The Least Dangerous Branch: The Supreme Court at the Bar of Politics*, 2nd ed. (New Haven, CT: Yale University Press, 1986).

unconstitutional motives, and (5) that kind of argument would resonate in the broader political culture among the public.

This conception of a red line can be adapted to the challenge of stemming the slide into autocracy. To be sure, the South African impeachment cases are about executive impunity for self-enrichment at the state's expense—that is, institutionalized corruption. But it is not hard to imagine a different case. A basic mission of any constitutional democracy is to allow for bounded, partisan, pluralist contestation. We might even call this mission an element of every constitution's "basic structure," to adopt a term from Indian constitutional law. And a basic principle of public law is that all grants of public power are inherently limited and can only be exercised for the purposes that the power has been granted. To be sure, these purposes may be extremely broad. However, they are not unlimited. Pulling these threads together yields the following legal principle: that executives and legislatures act for an unconstitutional motive if they exercise public power to erode or eliminate bounded, partisan, pluralist contestation. This purpose is core to the very idea of a constitutional democracy. It is simultaneously an unwritten norm that is part of constitutional culture, *and* a legal principle implicit in the design of any constitution that describes itself as one of a constitutional democracy.

As Jack Balkin and Sandy Levinson might put it, any government decision pursued in the name of "partisan entrenchment" is manifestly unconstitutional.[27] When governments act in this way, the courts must call autocracy by its name—to make it more likely that the people will do so as well. If the people make themselves "be seen and heard," as Holder puts it, his hope is that this "will ultimately be determinative." To be sure, adjudicating questions of legislative motive is to be approached cautiously by the courts. Motive is sometimes difficult to ascertain, and the charge is a serious one, because it is an accusation of bad faith. But following Larry Sager, those considerations should lead us to underenforce that norm, but to nonetheless accept that it is legally valid to its full conceptual limits.[28]

Firing or crippling Mueller would clearly fall into this category. At the center of his investigation is whether Russia interfered in the American political process, potentially "in collusion" with the Trump campaign. The goal of Russian interference would have been to shape the results of the 2016 presidential election to favor candidate Trump through a variety of means—WikiLeaks, Russian bots operating on social media, and perhaps other techniques that have yet to come into public view. There has been a great deal of discussion about the circumstances under which the fact of Russian assistance might constitute a crime under federal law, if it was "solicited." But on the argument I have offered here, whether such conduct actually constitutes a crime is merely evidence—albeit compelling

---

[27] Jack Balkin and Sanford Levinson, "Understanding the Constitutional Revolution," *Virginia Law Review* 87 (2001): 1045–1104.

[28] Lawrence Sager, "Fair Measure: The Legal Status of Underenforced Constitutional Norms," *Harvard Law Review* 91 (1978): 1212–1264.

evidence—of an unconstitutional motive, because the goal of the conduct would be to interfere with the election to favor one political party over another. Firing or crippling Mueller to prevent him from uncovering these unconstitutional motives would be an extension of the original, illegitimate conduct, aimed at undermining bounded, partisan, pluralist contestation.

In earlier scholarship on democratic backsliding, Sam Issacharoff and I trusted the courts to play the initial role in forestalling backsliding.[29] But neither of us had fully reckoned with backsliding supported by populist mobilization. That is precisely the scenario that confronts us now. In this situation, the question is whether the courts can withstand the populist surge and retain their credibility. It is indeed worrying that in Poland, one of the very first targets of the PiS was the Constitutional Tribunal, which has now been captured. As well, as Matczak has attested to, the broader constitutional culture in Poland is so degraded that even if the Tribunal had called autocracy by its name, it might have been too late. Although Zuma has effectively controlled appointments to the Constitutional Court of South Africa for many years, that court has demonstrated a great deal of independence from him; yet the sharp divisions in *Economic Freedom Fighters 2*, where there were vigorous dissents, suggests that the limits of the Court's involvement may have been reached. But its intervention, in combination with the contingent facts of a recent ANC leadership succession, a mobilized political opposition, and an institutional focus for the reconsideration of Zuma's conduct, was likely a contributing factor to his resignation.

It may then be fortuitous that President Trump has not yet had the opportunity to make many federal judicial appointments, and that there is Senate opposition—some of it bipartisan—to many of his judicial nominees. The contingent fact that he is on a collision course with Mueller so early into his first term after a two-term Democratic president might be what allows the federal courts to call autocracy by its name.

---

[29] Samuel Issacharoff, *Fragile Democracies: Contested Power in the Era of Constitutional Courts* (New York: Cambridge University Press, 2015); Sujit Choudhry, "'He Had a Mandate': The South African Constitutional Court and the African National Congress in a Dominant Party Democracy," *Constitutional Court Review* 2 (2009): 1–86.

Nothing is more permanent than the temporary.[1]

33 The Normal Exception
Oren Gross

Introduction

On October 18, 2017, the newly appointed United Nations Special Rapporteur on Promotion and Protection of Human Rights and Fundamental Freedoms while Countering Terrorism, Prof. Fionnuala Ní Aoláin, presented her first report to the Third Committee of the General Assembly.[2] In her report and subsequent remarks, Ní Aoláin identified four key issues that would be the focus of her mandate's work. The first substantive issue was be the "proliferation of permanent states of emergency and the normalization of exceptional national security powers within ordinary legal systems of states."[3]

In constitutional democracies, emergency powers are structured around an assumption of separation, defined by the belief in our ability to separate emergencies and crises from normalcy, and counterterrorism measures from ordinary legal rules and

---

[1] A proverb claimed by some to be Greek and by others to be Russian.

[2] UN Doc. A/72/43280.

[3] "Fionnuala Ní Aoláin (Special Rapporteur) on promotion and protection of human rights at the Third Committee, 23rd meeting—General Assembly, 72nd session," *U.N. Web TV*, October 18, 2017, http:// webtv.un.org/watch/fionnuala-n%C3%AD-aoláin-special-rapporteur-on-promotion-and-protection-of-human-rights-at-the-third-committee-23rd-meeting-general-assembly-72nd-session/5613073854001/?term#. WegYLUgrJow.facebook.

norms, confining the application of extraordinary measures to extraordinary times, and insulating periods of normalcy from the encroachment of vast emergency powers. However, if, as Ní Aoláin and I argue elsewhere,[4] bright-line distinctions between normalcy and emergency are frequently untenable, with the exception merging with the rule and emergency government becoming the norm, then fashioning legal tools to respond to emergencies in the belief that separation will serve as a firewall that protects human rights, civil liberties, and the normal legal system as a whole may be inadequate and misguided.

Emergencies are conceptualized in terms of a dichotomized dialectic. The term "emergency" connotes a sudden, urgent, usually unforeseen event or situation that requires immediate action, often without sufficient time for reflection and consideration. The notion of "emergency" is inherently linked to the concept of "normalcy" in the sense that the former is considered to be outside the ordinary course of events or anticipated actions. To recognize an emergency, we must have the background of normalcy. The concept of emergency is informed by notions of temporal duration and exceptional danger. For normalcy to be "normal," it has to be the general rule, the ordinary state of affairs. Emergency must constitute no more than an exception to that rule—it must last only a relatively short time and yield no substantial permanent effects. The belief that a clear line can be drawn between normal times and times of exceptional threats to the nation underlies all models of emergency powers. Application of emergency powers is designed to be of a temporary nature, to serve as a bridge between pre-crisis and post-crisis normalcy.[5]

The modern realities of global terrorism and the attendant counterterrorism measures present a major challenge to the traditional separation between the norm and the exception. Terrorist threats increase in magnitude; even nuclear attacks carried out by nonstate actors are now deemed plausible. In addition, the proliferation of global networks of terrorism result in a greater frequency of terrorist attacks. The increased frequency of terrorist attacks (or of threats thereof) and the vulnerability of nationals of most constitutional democracies to threats of terrorism, mean that governments have to contend on a more regular basis with the specter of terrorism. Such contraction of time and space, brought about by technological innovation, the communications revolution, and advances in transportation, increasingly challenges any capacity to keep emergency and normalcy separated, bringing new threats to states while significantly reducing the state's available time for response.

Rather than remaining exceptional, emergencies become entrenched and prolonged. Faced with the continuous threat, or fear, of terrorism, emergency regimes tend to perpetuate themselves, regardless of the intentions of those who originally invoked them. Once brought to life, they are not so easily terminable. Temporary emergency powers become the norm, the ordinary state of affairs. Time-bound emergency legislation is

---

[4] Oren Gross and Fionnuala Ní Aoláin, *Law in Times of Crisis: Emergency Powers in Theory and Practice* (Cambridge: Cambridge University Press, 2006), 171–243.

[5] Gross and Ní Aoláin, *Law in Times of Crisis*, 172–174.

often the subject of future extensions and renewals, despite Lord Devlin's caution that "It would be very unfortunate if the public were to receive the impression that the continuance of the state of emergency had become a sort of statutory fiction which was used as a means of prolonging legislation initiated under different circumstances and for different purposes."[6] It is commonplace to find on the statute books legislative acts that had originally been enacted as temporary emergency or counterterrorism measures, but subsequently transformed into permanent legislation. Sunset clauses and renewal requirements become nothing but mere bumps on the otherwise smooth road to the normalization of the exception. Consider the following two examples.

When originally enacted by the British Parliament, the Civil Authorities (Special Powers) Act (Northern Ireland) of 1922, which created an emergency regime in Northern Ireland, was meant to last for no more than one year. Its radical nature was best reflected in section 2(4), which provided that "If any person does any act of such nature as to be calculated to be prejudicial to the preservation of the peace or maintenance of order in Northern Ireland and not specifically provided for in the regulations, he shall be guilty of an offence against those regulations."[7] The Act was renewed annually until 1928, when it was extended for a five-year period. Subsequently, the Act was made permanent. The story of the series of Prevention of Terrorism (Temporary Provisions) Acts (PTA) was much the same. Originally introduced in Parliament in 1974, it was amended in 1975 and 1983, and re-enacted in 1984. In 1989, the PTA became a permanent part of the statute books of the United Kingdom. In 2000, the PTA of 1989 and the Northern Ireland (Emergency Provisions) Act of 1996 were replaced by the Terrorism Act of 2000. Since the terrorist attacks of September 11, the British parliament has enacted no fewer than thirteen Terrorism Acts dealing with the threat of terrorism to the whole of the United Kingdom rather than merely pertaining to Northern Ireland.

The Uniting and Strengthening America by Providing Appropriate Tools Required to Intercept and Obstruct Terrorism Act of 2001 (USA PATRIOT), passed merely a month and a half after the traumatic events of September 11, 2001, greatly expanded the surveillance and investigative powers of law enforcement agencies in the United States both in the context of collection of "foreign intelligence" information when there is probable cause that the target of surveillance is a foreign power or an agent of a foreign power, and access to communications in ordinary criminal investigations.[8] To alleviate concerns, a sunset provision was incorporated into the Act. This provision was scheduled

---

[6] Willcock v. Muckle, 2 K.B. 844 at 853–854 (1951) (Devlin, J.).

[7] Indeed, the South African minister of justice was quoted at the time to say, referring to section 2(4), that he "would be willing to exchange all the [South African] legislation of that sort for one clause in the Northern Ireland Special Powers Act." Committee on the Administration of Justice, *No Emergency, No Emergency Law: Emergency Legislation Related to Northern Ireland: The Case for Repeal* (Belfast: CAJ, 1993), 6.

[8] Uniting and Strengthening America by Providing Appropriate Tools Required to Intercept and Obstruct Terrorism (USA PATRIOT) Act, Pub. L. No. 107-56, 115 Stat. 272 (2001).

to terminate on December 31, 2005 several of the Act's sections that enhanced search and electronic surveillance powers of law enforcement agencies. The idea was that such a provision would enable legislators to review carefully, removed from the pressures of the moment, whether the expanded powers were needed and how well they had been used (or abused) as well as to assess their effectiveness, and to give incentives to the administration to cooperate with legislative oversight efforts.[9]

In its final report, the 9/11 Commission recommended that the burden of proof for showing that Congress should renew USA PATRIOT Act powers subject to sunset should be on the president, who must show that each power actually materially enhances security and that there is adequate supervision of the use of such powers to ensure that civil liberties are protected.[10] If the power is granted, the Commission emphasized, there must be adequate guidelines and oversight to properly confine its use. The Commission further stated: "Because of concerns regarding the shifting balance of power to the government, we think that a full and informed debate on the Patriot Act would be healthy."[11]

Once again, the pattern of temporary provisions becoming permanent was repeated. On July 21, 2005, the same day as the second round of terrorist attacks on London's transportation system, the United States House of Representatives voted by a wide margin to extend indefinitely and make permanent practically all the provisions of the USA PATRIOT Act that have been subject to the sunset provision.[12] On July 29, 2005, the Senate voted unanimously to make permanent virtually all the main provisions of the Act. This was made possible after several proposed changes to the Act—which would have expanded further the FBI powers under it to include the authority to demand records in terror investigations through administrative subpoenas, without a judge's order, and to have sole discretion in deciding whether to monitor the mail of terror suspects—had been withdrawn. While the renewed legislation included certain new restrictions on the government's powers, there were already at the time clear indications that the USA PATRIOT Act was becoming the new normality and benchmark for further legislation with the intelligence community taking its expanded powers and authorities under the Act as the new norm and seeking to expand them further.[13]

The entrenchment of states of emergency and the attendant emergency powers is facilitated further by the inability to define, ex ante, what an "emergency" may be. The very concept of "emergency" is an elastic one, and as such its invocation is often left in

[9] Section 224 of the USA PATRIOT Act; Robert O'Harrow, Jr., "Six Weeks in Autumn," *Washington Post*, October 27, 2002.
[10] *Final Report of the National Commission on Terrorist Attacks upon the United States* (The 9/11 Commission Report) (Washington: US GPO, 2004), 394–395, https://www.9-11commission.gov/report/911Report.pdf.
[11] *9/11 Report*, 394.
[12] Glen Johnson, "House Votes to Extend Patriot Act, Democrats Voice Civil Liberties Concerns," *AP DataStream*, July 22, 2005.
[13] Eric Lichtblau, "Senate Makes Permanent Nearly All Provisions of Patriot Act, With a Few Restrictions," *New York Times*, July 29, 2005.

the hands of the government or the executive branch. Even where Parliament plays a role in declaring or renewing a state of emergency, it is often no more than a mere rubber stamp to the executive wishes. Few situations can solidify broad national consensus behind the government. Times of crisis and emergency can and do.[14] Moved by perceptions of substantial physical threat, motivated by growing personal fear of being the next victim and by hatred toward the terrorists, and frustrated by the continuance of terrorist activities, the public, and its elected representatives, may "rally 'round the flag"[15] by supporting and calling on the government to employ more radical measures. Consensus may result in group polarization on both the level of the public at large and of any distinct groups of experts. This further stifles robust debate about the responses to the crisis and helps explain not only such phenomena as rushed legislation but also, more generally, the general acquiescence, indeed support, for the expansion, extension, and enhancement of governmental powers in times of crisis. As Harold Koh noted in a related context, the American president almost always wins in matters of foreign affairs due to the combination of executive initiative, congressional acquiescence, and judicial tolerance.[16]

Furthermore, to the extent that states of emergency require a careful balancing between security and liberty, such balancing is likely to result in a systematic undervaluation of one interest (liberty) and overvaluation of another (security) so that the ensuing balance would be tilted in favor of security concerns at the expense of individual rights and liberties. To give but one example,[17] states of emergency are likely to be extended in the face of terrorist threats even when such threats have a low-likelihood to materialize. Individuals tend to give excessive weight to low-probability results when the stakes are high enough and the outcomes are particularly bad.[18] In cases of high-magnitude, low-probability risks, attention is directed almost exclusively to outcomes rather than to the likelihood of such outcomes materializing. Individuals perceive risks as more "serious," the more "dreaded" and "unknown" they are, and "as risks become increasingly dreaded

---

[14] Oren Gross, "Chaos and Rules: Should Responses to Violent Crises Always Be Constitutional?," *Yale Law Journal* 112 (2003): 1011, 1035–1036.

[15] Bruce Russett, *Controlling the Sword: The Democratic Governance of National Security* (Cambridge, MA: Harvard University Press, 1990), 34 (describing the "rally 'round the flag effect" as the phenomenon by which "a short, low-cost military measure to repel an attack . . . is almost invariably popular at least at its inception. So too are many other kinds of assertive action or speech in foreign policy.").

[16] Harold H. Koh, "Why the President (Almost) Always Wins in Foreign Affairs: Lessons of the Iran-Contra Affair," *Yale Law Journal* 97 (1988): 1255; Harold Hongju Koh, *The National Security Constitution: Sharing Power after the Iran-Contra Affair* (New Haven, CT: Yale University Press, 1990), 117–149.

[17] For an elaboration of the problematics involved in balancing security and liberty in times of crisis and emergency see Oren Gross, "Security vs. Liberty: on Emotions and Cognition," in *The Long Decade: How 9/11 Has Changed the Law*, ed. David Jenkins, Amanda Jacobsen, and Anders Henriksen (Oxford: Oxford University Press, 2014), 45.

[18] Daniel Kahneman and Amos Tversky, "Prospect Theory: An Analysis of Decision under Risk," in *Choices, Values, and Frames*, ed. Daniel Kahneman and Amos Tversky (Cambridge: Cambridge University Press, 2001), 17.

and unknown, people demand that something be done about them regardless of the probability of their occurrence, the costs of avoiding the risk, or the benefits of declining to avoid the risk."[19] A risk is "dreaded" if people perceive it to be involuntary and potentially catastrophic, and one over which they lack control. It is "unknown" if it is new and not well understood, among other things. Terrorist attacks are "dreaded" risks and as such are considered to be of an especially serious nature.[20] At the same time, the range of "modern" terrorist threats creates what Kai Erikson calls a "new species of trouble" that makes analytical risk assessment extremely difficult and increases our reliance on affective assessment.[21] This leads to a focus on the worst-case scenario. Driven by a "powerful sense of cultural pessimism about society's ability to manage high-consequence risks to its security" we move away from thinking about risks in terms of probabilities toward a more "possibilistic" assessment of risks and threats.[22] Such possibilistic thinking routinizes the expectation of worst possible outcomes, leading to the "occasional demand for a restrained and low-key response to the risk of terrorism [to be] overwhelmed by the alarmist narratives of worst-case scenario."[23] The sense that we may lack the information to calculate the likelihood of future (major) terrorist attacks leads to a worst-case analysis that, in turn, reinforces the narratives of fear of terrorism.[24] This has been famously captured by former vice president Dick Cheney's statement: "If there's a one percent chance that Pakistani scientists are helping Al Qaeda build or develop a nuclear weapon, we have to treat it as a certainty in terms of our response."[25]

Over the past few years, several constitutional democracies have been targets of terrorist attacks and have responded to those by passing new legislation increasing, invariably, the scope of powers granted to the national governments. Before going further it is worth noting, as the UN special rapporteur Ní Aoláin does in her most recent report to the UN Human Rights Council, that "where counter-terrorism laws directly and substantially impinge on the full and equal enjoyment of human rights premised on

---

[19] Christina E. Wells, "Questioning Deference," *Missouri Law Review* 69 (2004): 903, 925.

[20] Paul Slovic, *The Perception of Risk* (London: Earthscan, 2000), 220–231; Paul Slovic, "What's Fear Got to Do with It? It's Affect We Need to Worry About," *Missouri Law Review* 69 (2004): 971, 985–986.

[21] Kai Erikson, *A New Species of Trouble: Explorations in Disaster, Trauma, and Community* (New York: Norton, 1994).

[22] Frank Furedi, "Fear and Security: A Vulnerability-Led Policy Response," *Social Policy and Administration* 42 (2008) 645, 653–654.

[23] Ibid., 654.

[24] Ronnie D. Lipschultz, "Terror in the Suites: Narratives of Fear and the Political Economy of Danger," *Global Society* 13 (1999): 4, 17; W. Kip Viscusi and Richard J. Zeckhauser, "Sacrificing Civil Liberties to Reduce Terrorism Risk," *Journal of Risk and Uncertainty* 26 (2003): 99, 101. As Masur observes, individuals "react most strongly to threats that have been much discussed within the press but that are sufficiently complex or 'scientific' that the average layperson cannot comprehend them." Jonathan S. Masur, "Probability Thresholds," *Iowa Law Review* 92 (2007): 1293, 1341–1342.

[25] Quoted in Ron Suskind, *The One Percent Doctrine: Deep Inside America's Pursuit of Its Enemies since 9/11* (New York: Simon and Schuster, 2006), 61–62.

the experience or threat of terrorist acts or actors, then both restrictions on rights and emergency law is implicated. In this context, *counter-terrorism law and practice should be understood as a particular sub-species of emergency regulation* and subject to heightened oversight."[26]

Thus, for example, as already noted above, since 2001 the United Kingdom passed a series of Terrorism Acts. Notable among those is the Prevention of Terrorism Act of 2005 that came as a response to the July 7 attacks on London's underground and bus system resulting in fifty-two deaths and around seven hundred injured. These Terrorism Acts have been described by Amnesty International as "among the most draconian in the EU," noting that the "longstanding laws and measures akin to an emergency regime, albeit adopted outside of a formally declared state of emergency, contain vague and overly broad formulations. Taken together with special counter-terrorism legislation, these provisions are open to abuse."[27] However, following a spate of attacks in 2017 (e.g., the Westminster attack,[28] the Manchester Arena bombing,[29] and the London Bridge attack),[30] the British prime minister, Theresa May, unveiled a four-point "enough is enough" plan to tackle extremism in the UK.[31] In presenting the new plan, May announced that "If human rights get in the way of doing these things, we will change those laws to make sure we can do them," suggesting that existing laws and regulations were, once again, insufficient to combat terrorism. However, even under the existing legal formulas, UK police were able to arrest 379 individuals on suspicion of involvement in terror-related offenses in the twelve months prior to May's speech, a rise of 68 percent in the number of those arrested.[32] One feature of the proposed plan, which already went into effect, is the addition of terror-related offenses to the unduly lenient sentencing scheme, which gives anyone the right to ask the attorney general to review a sentence for being unduly lenient.[33] Similarly to the United Kingdom, the German government proposed a new range of measures to fight terrorism[34] in the aftermath of the December 19, 2016, attack in a Christmas market

---

[26] UN Doc. A/HRC/37/52 (Jan. 15, 2018), para. 4 (emphasis added).

[27] Amnesty International, *Dangerously Disproportionate: The Ever-Expanding National Security State in Europe*, January 17, 2017, https://www.amnesty.org/en/documents/eur01/5342/2017/en/.

[28] "Westminster Terror Attack," *BBC News*, accessed February 26, 2018, http://www.bbc.com/news/uk-39365569.

[29] "Manchester Attack: What We Know So Far," *BBC News*, accessed February 26, 2018, http://www.bbc.com/news/uk-england-manchester-40008389.

[30] Harriet Alexander, "London Bridge Attack—Everything We Know," *The Telegraph*, June 6, 2017.

[31] Alan Travis, "What's in Theresa May's New Anti-terror Package?," *The Guardian*, June 7, 2017; Press Association, "UK Terrorism Law Expert Warns Government over Plans for New Legislation," *The Guardian*, October 24, 2017.

[32] Alan Travis, "UK Terror Arrests Rise 68% to Record Level during Year of Attacks," *The Guardian*, September 14, 2017; Alan Travis, "Number of UK Terrorism Arrests Hits Record High," *The Guardian*, December 7, 2017.

[33] Patrick Greenfield, "More Terror Offences to Be Covered by Rules on Unduly Lenient Sentences," *The Guardian*, December 28, 2017; Owen Bowcott, "Law to Be Changed So Terror Offenders' Jail Terms Can Be Lengthened," *The Guardian*, July 14, 2017.

[34] Alison Smale, "Germany Proposes Tougher Measures to Combat Terrorism," *New York Times*, August 11, 2016.

in Berlin leaving twelve dead and fifty-six injured,[35] the fifth terrorist attack on German soil in 2016. The UN special rapporteur, Ní Aoláin, has thus recently warned that "the challenge for human rights protection has been the absorption of emergency statutes into the ordinary legal framework, including counter-terrorism legislation, essentially normalizing the exception."[36]

It is also worth noting that the oxymoronic phenomenon of permanent emergencies has relatives in other types of emergencies, namely de facto, complex, and covert emergencies. Like the permanent emergency, so too these other types deviate from the model emergency notion under which emergency is merely an exception to an otherwise normal state of affairs. De facto emergencies arise in situations when restrictive governmental powers are exercised without formal acknowledgment of the existence of an emergency; complex emergencies are characterized by "[a] great number of parallel or simultaneous emergency rules whose complexity is increased by the 'piling up' of provisions designed to 'regularise' the immediately preceding situation and therefore embodying retroactive rules and transitional regimes."[37] The "piling up" effect is often one of the practices that facilitate the creation of a legal and political culture that supports an extended emergency regime. The system becomes self-defined and reliant upon the legislative support structures created by the emergency, and "normal" supports are lost in the process, thus making the return to normality more difficult. Complex states of emergency also sustain the enactment of repressive laws assuming the features of ordinary law. Thus, the complex emergency is facilitative of both hidden and permanent emergencies. Finally, covert emergencies may be recognized when parliaments and courts acquiesce to "[t]he minimal interpretations of certain [human] rights that stripped [the rights] of much of their content. This tactic has the effect of, at worst, seeking to create effective covert derogations and, at best, of redefining the rights so that they emerge only in a diluted form of practice."[38]

In recent years, no country in Western Europe has seen more terrorist attacks leading to more casualties than France. Thus, the next Section of this chapter examines recent patterns of normalization of the exception in that country, the cradle of civil liberties. After looking at the legal background for the exercise of emergency powers under French law, the analysis focuses on the state of emergency that was declared by President Hollande on November 13, 2015, and its long-term implications. The struggles to strike a balance between security and liberty in France, as well as the story of the transformation of emergency powers from the exceptional periphery to the normal mainstream, are interesting

---

[35] "Berlin Christmas Market Attack," *The Guardian*, January 2018, https://www.theguardian.com/world/berlin-christmas-market-attack.

[36] UN Doc. A/HRC/37/52 (January 15, 2018), para. 16.

[37] Nicole Questiaux, "Study of the Implications for Human Rights of Recent Developments concerning Situations Known as States of Siege or Emergency," UN ESCOR, 35th Sess., UN Doc. E/CN.4/Sub.2/1982/15 (1982), para. 118.

[38] Helen Fenwick and Gavin Phillipson, "Covert Derogations and Judicial Deference: Redefining Liberty and Due Process Rights in Counterterrorism Law and Beyond," *McGill Law Journal* 56 (2011): 863, 867.

not only because similar stories can be told about numerous other jurisdictions, but also because of the speed in which that transformation took place.

France

LEGAL BACKGROUND FOR THE EXERCISE OF EMERGENCY POWERS UNDER FRENCH LAW

The French legal system incorporates three legal sources for conferring emergency powers on the government. Two of these sources are found in the French Constitution of 1958, and one has a statutory basis in a law passed on May 3, 1955. President Hollande invoked that statutory source when he declared a nationwide state of emergency throughout the Republic on November 13, 2015, which went into effect at midnight on November 14.

Origins: The State of Siege (*État de Siege*)

The state of siege was originally imagined in terms of full governmental powers being conferred upon the military commander of a besieged fortress.[39] After the French Revolution, the state of siege came to be applicable not only to an area actually besieged by foreign invaders, but also to areas endangered by internal rebellion and disquiet. The rules were fairly straightforward. A state of siege could only be declared by law and only in the event of imminent danger resulting from a foreign war or an armed insurrection. An état de siege was reserved for the most exceptional circumstances.

When a state of siege was properly declared (by Parliament) all powers concerning the "maintenance of order" transferred, in their entirety, to the military. The main legal effect of a declaration of a state of siege was to transfer police and other powers relevant to the maintenance of peace and order from civilian to military authorities. In practice this meant, among other things, that military courts could assume jurisdiction over any offense pertaining to the safety of the Republic, against the Constitution, and against public peace and order, whether committed by military personnel or civilians. In addition, the military enjoyed powers to conduct searches in private premises, to deport certain persons from areas put under a state-of-siege regime, and to prohibit publications and assemblies that it judged to be of a nature to incite or sustain disorder.

On August 2, 1914, when parliament was in recess and a general mobilization for war was underway, a presidential decree imposed a state of siege on all of France to maintain public order. The decree was followed three days later by a law declaring that the state of siege would be in effect "for the duration of the war." The authority to declare a state of siege was not exercised again in the period between the two World Wars. Instead, the French government turned to another legal mechanism—the enabling act and broad

---

[39] Gross and Ní Aoláin, *Law in Times of Crisis*, 26–30.

delegations of power from the French Parliament—as the major source for emergency powers and accompanying executive lawmaking. The epitome of administrative emergency power usage came with the Daladier administration, which, from April 1938 until the final days of the Third Republic, governed France through executive decrees based on four enabling acts. These acts included the enabling act of March 19, 1939, which authorized the government to issue decrees with respect to "all measures necessary for the defense of the country," and the act of December 8, 1939, which made executive decree a permanent emergency institution for the duration of hostilities—making the existence of hostilities a sufficient condition for executive lawmaking without further legislative authorization.

The State of Emergency (*État D'urgence*)

By the end of the 1950s, France had lost most of its assets abroad, forced to relinquish Vietnam in 1954 and Tunisia and Morocco the next year, and its (at least self-perceived) status as a leading global power. The war in Algeria, waged from 1954 to 1962, put much more at stake than physical territory.[40] Algeria was regarded as protecting the southern flank of France against Islamist threats extending from the Middle East. More important, most French people—on both the right and the left sides of the political map—considered Algeria to be an inseparable part of the Republic. Indeed, under French law Algeria was an integral part of metropolitan France. "The Mediterranean," Pierre Mendès-France declared, "runs through France like the Seine through Paris."

Dealing with a violent confrontation in Algeria against the FLN (the National Liberation Front), the French government had largely symbolic reasons for refraining from declaring a state of siege. The legal solution was provided by the passage on May 3, 1955, of Public Law 55-385 authorizing the government to declare a state of emergency (état d'urgence). The law conferred broad police powers on the government, including the imposition of curfews and traffic bans, controlling of public movements, conducting of warrantless searches and house arrests day and night, prohibiting public gatherings and assembly, and closing down public meeting places. The law also raised the possibility (provided additional, specific decrees to that extent were issued) of "controlling the press" and authorizing military jurisdiction over criminal offenses and crimes. At the same time, under a declared state of emergency such broad powers were conferred on the civilian authorities rather than on the military, making it politically more acceptable when the powers are exercised domestically.

The law of 1955 was invoked twice in Algeria, in 1955 and 1958. In 1955 it was applied to curb the FLN. In 1958 it was invoked to deal with fears of an imminent military coup against the French government. When the government of Pierre Pflimlin took office on May 13, 1958, a riot broke out in Algiers, staged by French pieds noirs[41] assisted by

---

[40] Ibid., 190–195.
[41] The term "pieds noirs" refers to Europeans, mostly French, who lived in Algeria during the period of French rule in that country.

military commanders. The riot led the top commanders of the French forces in Algeria, Generals Massu and Salan, to form a Committee of Public Safety. This unchallenged revolt was soon followed by the establishment of similar local Committees throughout mainland France. Invasion of the mainland by paratroopers seemed likely within a matter of days. Though the invasion did not occur, the fear of insurrection was substantial though short-lived.

The State of Emergency Comes to France

Despite the declaration of a state of emergency, threats of extreme violence and instability persisted. On June 1, 1958, General Charles de Gaulle became France's president and was given emergency powers (including the power to prepare the new constitution for the Fifth Republic) for a period of six months.

The concentration of power in the Office of the President was substantial and raised many concerns about undue power being given to one individual. Nowhere is this clearer than in the context of article 16 of the Constitution of the Fifth Republic.[42] Article 16 invests sweeping emergency powers in the president of the Republic. The president is empowered to take "any measures required" in the event that the "institutions of the Republic, the independence of the nation, the integrity of its territory or the fulfillment of its international commitments are gravely and immediately threatened and the regular functioning of the constitutional public authorities is interrupted."

In an attempt to mitigate the extreme nature of article 16, several conditions for its exercise were introduced: First, resort to the expansive presidential powers under article 16 was to be made only in abnormal situations, and in order to invoke his or her powers under article 16, the president must identify serious and immediate threats to the nation and act to overcome them. However, the decisions as to what constitutes such a threat and what measures ought to be taken in any given case are left to the president's sole discretion, making this limitation of presidential power theoretical at best. Moreover, the president's actions, it would seem, are not reviewable by any of the judicial authorities. Second, the functioning of the constitutional institutions is interrupted. Third, article 16 provides that measures used under it "must stem from the desire to provide the constitutional public authorities, in the shortest possible time, with the means to carry out their duties." However, the decision of when to terminate the resort to article 16 is, again, left to the president's sole discretion. Fourth, article 16 imposes on the president a duty of consultation with the prime minister, the presidents of the assemblies, and the Constitutional Council. Article 16 allows the president to attain broad powers similar to those that she would have under a regime of a state of siege, while bypassing the procedural and substantive requirements of that regime.

---

[42] Gross and Ní Aoláin, *Law in Times of Crisis*, 197–200.

Article 16 was invoked only once[43]—on April 23, 1961, as a means to contain a military coup in Algeria after a referendum on independence for Algeria received overwhelming support by the French public. The goal was to prevent the coup from spreading to the mainland. Exercising the special emergency powers, the president established special military tribunals; instituted censorship; granted expanded powers of search, seizure, and arrest to the French police; modified parts of the criminal procedure; suspended the life-tenure appointment of judges; and dismissed thousands of military and police officers and personnel. Significantly, President de Gaulle prohibited the Parliament from voting on a motion of censure or legislating altogether. In line with their general attitude of deference to the political branches on such matters, both the Conseil d'État and the Constitutional Council refused to review on their merits the powers employed by the president, proclaiming those questions to be outside their scope of jurisdiction. This "rally around the flag" phenomenon is consistent with the response of the French Parliament to the decision to extend emergency powers in the aftermath of the recent Paris attacks.

Back to the Future: November 2005

For forty-four years, no state of emergency was declared in France itself.[44] On October 27, 2005, the City of Paris witnessed the eruption of ethnic riots following the accidental death of two French youths of Malian and Tunisian descent in an electrical substation in the Parisian suburb of Clichy-sous-Bois as they were fleeing the police. The riots soon spread to nearly three hundred cities and towns across France. Over the next three weeks, the rioters torched some 9,000 cars and scores of buildings causing damage estimated at €200 million. Nearly 2,900 rioters were arrested by the police. On November 8, two days after the worst night of rioting, which left more than 1,400 burnt cars across France, the French cabinet used the law of 1955 to declare a state of emergency, empowering departmental prefects to impose curfews, and allowing the police to set up roadblocks, conduct house searches, prohibit public assembly, and put people under house arrest.[45] Curfew breakers were liable to up to two months' imprisonment. On November 14, less than one week after the introduction of the state of emergency, the French cabinet decided to seek legislative approval for the extension of the emergency police powers for an additional period of three months. Both the National Assembly (on November 15) and the Senate (two

---

[43] The French constitution also retains a provision—incorporated into article 36—dealing with a state of siege. That provision has never been invoked.

[44] One declaration was made in January 1985 when a state of emergency was declared in New Caledonia, a French territory in the South Pacific, in response to violence led by the island's independence movement. It lasted until the end of June that year. Another declaration was made on October 29, 1987, in the Islands of Wallis and Futuna, a French overseas territory, to deal with a "dispute with traditional chiefs on Wallis Island" that resulted in "a minor ruckus." The state of emergency lasted for one day.

[45] Gross and Ní Aoláin, *Law in Times of Crisis*, 200–202.

days later) swiftly passed the necessary legislation. It is worth noting that despite the fact that some thirty municipalities were placed under nightly curfews for unaccompanied children under sixteen, and temporary orders banning public gatherings were imposed in Paris and Lyon, most prefects had chosen not to exercise the emergency powers. That state of emergency terminated on January 4, 2006.

THE EXCEPTION

Over the past three years, France has been the target of a series of terrorist attacks. Between December 2014 and December 2017 no fewer than twenty-seven terrorist attacks took place on French soil leaving over 240 people dead and 866 injured. Notable among those attacks were the January 7, 2015 attack on the offices of the satirical magazine *Charlie Hebdo* carried out by two terrorists identifying themselves as affiliated with al-Qaeda in Yemen, and the attack, two days later, on the Hypercacher kosher supermarket in Paris, carried out by a terrorist affiliating himself with ISIS; the November 13, 2015 terrorist attacks in Paris that left 130 dead, most of them in the Bataclan concert hall, which were the single deadliest terrorist attack in French history; and the Bastille Day 2016 terrorist attack in Nice, when a terrorist drove a cargo truck into a celebrating crowd in the city's promenade.

Within a few hours of the November 13, 2015 terrorist attacks on Paris that left 130 dead and 350 injured, President François Hollande declared a nationwide state of emergency, only the second time that a nationwide state of emergency was declared since the end of World War II. The state of emergency, which went into effect at midnight on November 14, granted broad police powers to the French government and to the prefectures. These powers—granted for up to twelve days—included the power to impose curfews and traffic bans, to control public movements, to prohibit assembly and public gatherings, to conduct warrantless searches and house arrests (day or night), to close theaters and other meeting places, and to limit where certain individuals, against whom an assigned residence order has been issued, may live or travel to, as well as require that they report to police stations several times each day.

Pursuant to the declaration of a state of emergency, in the first five days after the terrorist attacks, the French police and military conducted 793 raids—most notably a house raid in the Paris suburb of Saint-Denis that led to the killing of the person believed to have orchestrated the attacks, Abdelhamid Abaaoud. The government also detained 90 individuals and placed 164 under house arrest, charged 124 individuals with offenses, and seized 174 different weapons, including 18 described as "military-style firearms," 84 rifles, and 68 handguns (a notable fact, given France's stringent firearms laws).[46]

---

[46] Fionnuala Ní Aoláin and Oren Gross, "Liberté, Égalité, Fraternité . . . Sécurité," *Just Security*, November 25, 2015, https://www.justsecurity.org/27812/emergency-powers-accumulate/.

THE NORMALIZATION OF THE EXCEPTION

Periodic Renewals of the State of Emergency

A week after the initial declaration of a state of emergency, the French Parliament approved Law no. 2015-1501 extending the state of emergency for an additional period of three months. It did so by wide margins and with little debate and discussion (the lower house approved the extension by a 551-6 margin on November 19, and the French Senate voted to approve the extension on November 20).[47] The passage of the new Law reflects two interrelated phenomena pertaining to emergency powers: the (initial) consensus around such measures and the rush to legislate in the face of crisis and emergency.

We have already noted above the role of consensus in states of emergency. Such consensus is further bolstered and cemented when the perceived threats come from "others" who are well defined and clearly separable from more powerful parts of the community. The clearer the distinction between "us" and "them" and the greater the threat "they" pose to "us," the greater in scope the powers assumed by government and tolerated by the public become.[48] We note, of course, that in contemporary France the "us"/"them" phenomenon is a complicated proposition as it directly affects the rights and duties of citizens, rather than enemies conveniently located in a territory outside the state.

Emergencies also tend to bring about a rush to legislate, reminding one of the observation by the Athenian of Plato's *The Laws* that "no man ever legislates at all. Accidents and calamities occur in a thousand different ways, and it is they that are the universal legislators of the world."[49] The prevailing belief may be that if new offenses are added to the criminal code and the scope of existing offenses broadened, and if the arsenal of law enforcement agencies is enhanced by putting at their disposal more sweeping powers to search and seize, to eavesdrop, to interrogate, to detain without trial, and to deport, the country will be more secure and better able to face the emergency.[50] It is often easier to pass new legislation than to examine why existing legislation and the powers granted under it to government and its agencies were insufficient. By permitting the government to claim that the preexisting legal infrastructure was somehow deficient and forestalled effective actions against, and responses to, the threats, adding new legislation may result in the accumulation of legislative measures into a complex state of emergency characterized by "the great number of parallel or simultaneous emergency rules whose complexity is increased by the 'piling up' of provisions designed to 'regularize' the immediately

---

[47] Sam Schechner and William Horobin, "France Expands Government's Security Powers in Wake of Paris Attacks," *Wall Street Journal*, November 19, 2015; "French Senate Votes to Extend State of Emergency for 3 Months," *Associated Press*, November 20, 2015.

[48] Gross and Ní Aoláin, *Law in Times of Crisis*, 220–227.

[49] Plato, *The Laws*, trans. Trevor J. Saunders (London: Penguin Books, 1970), 164.

[50] Kent Roach, "The Dangers of a Charter-Proof and Crime-Based Response to Terrorism," in *The Security of Freedom: Essays on Canada's Antiterrorism Bill*, ed. Ronald J. Daniels, Patrick Macklem, and Kent Roach (Toronto: University of Toronto Press, 2001), 131, 138–142.

preceding situation and therefore embodying retroactive rules and transitional regimes."[51] The passage of new legislation allows government, in turn, to demonstrate that it is doing something against the dangers facing the nation rather than sitting idly. As Justice Robert Jackson noted: "fear and anxiety create public demands for greater assurance which may not be justified by necessity but which any popular government finds irresistible."[52] This is exacerbated further by the problem of legislative myopia. Legislatures tend to provide legislative tools necessary (or deemed necessary) to fight or stop the last war or the most recent threat.[53] The unpredictability of threats and their changing nature, coupled with the need for rapid counter-response, are almost guaranteed to ensure that the legislative branch will suffer from the "red queen effect," that is, it would take all the legislative running it can do in order to keep in the same place.[54]

Beyond merely extending the time frame of the state of emergency, Law no. 2015-1501 also amended the underlying 1955 law, expanding the scope of the government's emergency powers. The new Law of November 20, 2015, allowed the police to order warrantless house arrests of individuals when there are "serious reasons to believe that their behavior is a threat to public safety and order." In addition, under article 6 of the Law, an individual may be confined to a specific area or town or to a place of residence determined by the minister of the interior, and to report to a police station up to three times a day. Article 11 of the Law authorizes the police to conduct house searches both during daytime and at night, as well as to seize computer files during such searches. Police may also block websites and social media accounts that incite or condone terrorism. The Law invests authority to prohibit public demonstrations "of a nature that may provoke or sustain disorder" in the ministry of the interior (for prohibitions applicable nationwide) or prefects (for bans pertaining to a specific *département*). Finally, the Council of Ministers may dissolve by decree any associations and assemblies that "participate in the commission of acts that can seriously disturb public order or whose activities facilitate or incite commission of such acts." The Law also contains two important limitations on governmental powers: abolishing the power that government had under the original law to "control the press" and to engage in broad censorship, and prohibiting the police from carrying out warrantless searches in the homes or offices of lawmakers, lawyers, and journalists.[55]

[51] "Study of the Implications for Human Rights of Recent Developments concerning Situations Known as States of Siege or Emergency," UN Commission on Human Rights, 35th Sess., Agenda Item 10, at 29, UN Doc. E/CN.4/Sub.2/1982/15 (1982).

[52] Robert H. Jackson, "Wartime Security and Liberty under Law," *Buffalo Law Review* 1 (1951): 103, 107.

[53] Harold H. Koh, *The National Security Constitution: Sharing Power after the Iran-Contra Affair* (New Haven, CT Yale University Press, 1990), 123–126.

[54] Lewis Carroll, *Through the Looking Glass and What Alice Found There*, in *The Annotated Alice: Alice's Adventures in Wonderland and through the Looking Glass* (New York: Bramhall House, 1960), 145, 196–197.

[55] In addition to these measures, on November 16, 2015, President Hollande convened the two houses of the French Parliament and announced his intention to seek constitutional amendments to introduce a new category of emergency regime—a "state of security"—into French law and to authorize the stripping of

Since November 2015, the initial state of emergency has been extended six times, with concomitant derogations entered by France from several of its obligations under the European Convention on Human Rights and the International Covenant on Civil and Political Rights.[56] Such extensions and derogations had been made despite calls from five former United Nations special rapporteurs that the French government not extend the application of its emergency powers;[57] they noted that "[w]hile exceptional measures may be required under exceptional circumstances, this does not relieve the authorities from demonstrating that these are applied solely for the purposes for which they were prescribed, and are directly related to the specific objective that inspired them."

The extensions of the state of emergency have also been challenged by human rights and civil liberties groups claiming that the emergency powers exercised and made available under the state of emergency that existed in France since November 14, 2015, have not improved public safety and have been applied in a discriminatory manner against France's large Muslim population.[58] Of 670 judicial proceedings opened as a result of the emergency search measures before December 2016, only sixty-one were for terrorism-related offenses. The remaining 609 relate to non-terrorism-related offenses,[59] suggesting not only the disproportionality of the measures applied but also the use of emergency measures for nonemergency-related purposes. It has been suggested that "most of the searches [provided for under the state of emergency] were carried out by members of the [police] drug squad, especially in the Paris region," meaning that such searches "were used in relation to investigations unrelated to terrorism."[60]

Indeed, once emergency powers are introduced and invoked, government and its agents grow accustomed to the convenience that such powers offer. Once they experience the ability to operate with fewer restraints and limitations they are unlikely to be willing to give up such freedom. "So it always happens that whenever a wrong principle of conduct, political or personal, is adopted on a plea of necessity, it will be afterwards

---

French citizenship from dual nationals convicted of terrorism. Alfonso Serrano, "France's Hollande: Change Constitution to Tighten Security Powers," *AlJazeera*, November 17, 2015, http://america.aljazeera.com/articles/2015/11/17/call-to-arms-hollande-urges-constitutional-changes.html. Unable to secure the requisite majority for such constitutional amendments, President Hollande abandoned his suggestions on point.

[56] Fionnuala Ní Aoláin, "France: The Dangers of Permanent Emergency Legislation," *Just Security*, September 27, 2017, https://www.justsecurity.org/45263/france-dangers-permanent-emergency-legislation/.

[57] UNHCR, "UN Rights Experts Urge France to Protect Fundamental Freedoms while Countering Terrorism," January 19, 2016, http://www.ohchr.org/EN/NewsEvents/Pages/DisplayNews.aspx?NewsID=16966&amp%3BLangID=E.

[58] Deborah Acosta, "French Police Make 2,700 Raids in Month, Raising Tension with Muslims," *New York Times*, December 23, 2015.

[59] Erika Asgeirsson, "French Anti-terror Bill Threatens to Extend State of Emergency Abuses," *Just Security*, August 2, 2017, https://www.justsecurity.org/43771/french-anti-terror-bill-threatens-normalize-state-emergency/.

[60] International Federation for Human Measures & Human Rights: When the Exception Becomes the Norm Rights (FIDH), France: Counter-Terrorism (Paris, June 2016), 19–20.

followed on a plea of convenience."[61] This may also lead, in turn, to the use of emergency and counterterrorism legislation for purposes other than those for which it was originally promulgated.[62]

Moreover, compared to the 61 terrorism-related judicial proceedings from the emergency measures, 169 terrorism-related judicial proceedings were opened during the same period using regular criminal procedures—indicating that France's ordinary legal framework continues to work for preventing and prosecuting terrorism. Others have noted that in the first two years of the state of emergency, "French law enforcement have conducted over four thousand warrantless searches and raids, placed over seven hundred people under house arrest, and closed approximately two dozen mosques and other Muslim prayer spaces." Of the 4,000 raids, "only six have led to terrorism-related investigations, and these warrantless searches have only led to 20 indictments on terrorism charges, compared to the 150 terrorism indictments obtained without warrantless searches."[63] The "disproportionate impact" of France's state of emergency has similarly been documented.[64]

Despite such concerns, on November 15, 2016, President Hollande announced that the state of emergency would be extended until the 2017 presidential elections, declaring that such extension would be necessary to protect rallies and other events during the electoral campaign.[65] On May 24, 2017, in the aftermath of the Manchester Arena bombing in the United Kingdom, the new president, Emmanuel Macron, announced that he would ask Parliament to extend the state of emergency until November 2017.[66] Parliament granted a sixth extension to the declared state of emergency on July 6, 2017, with the state of emergency scheduled to expire on November 1, 2017.

---

[61] Julliard v. Greenman, 110 U.S. 421, 458 (1884) (Field, J., dissenting).

[62] Gross and Ní Aoláin, *Law in Times of Crisis*, 230.

[63] Human Rights First, "Issues Facing the Next President of France: Will Disruption Further Divide?," May 5, 2017, https://www.humanrightsfirst.org/resource/issues-facing-next-president-france-will-disruption-further-divide; Rapport fait au nom de la Commision d'Enquête, *relative aux moyens mis en œuvre par l'État pour lutter contre le terrorisme depuis le 7 janvier 2015* (July 5, 2016), http://www.assemblee-nationale.fr/14/rap-enq/r3922-t1.asp.

[64] Amnesty International, "France: Upturned Lives: The Disproportionate Impact of France's State of Emergency," February 4, 2016, https://www.amnesty.org/en/documents/eur21/3364/2016/en/; Human Rights Watch, "France: Abuses under State of Emergency," February 3, 2016, https://www.hrw.org/news/2016/02/03/france-abuses-under-state-emergency; Amnesty International, "France: A Right Not a Threat: Disproportionate Restrictions on Demonstrations under the State of Emergency in France," May 31, 2017, https://www.amnesty.org/en/documents/eur21/6104/2017/en/.

[65] Agence France-Presse, "François Hollande Seeks Extension of State of Emergency In France," *The Guardian*, November 15, 2016; Agence France-Presse, "French Parliament Votes to Extend State of Emergency until after 2017 Elections," *The Guardian*, December 13, 2016.

[66] France 24, "France's Macron Seeks to Extend State of Emergency to November," May 24, 2017, http://www.france24.com/en/20170524-france-president-macron-seeks-extend-state-emergency-manchester.

The Exception Becomes the New Legal Norm

Rather than seek further extensions of the state of emergency, the French government decided to change course. The government ended the declared state of emergency formally, while bringing several of the powers granted to it under the state of emergency into ordinary criminal and administrative law,[67] moving "a significant step closer to making permanent some of the emergency measures put in place after the terrorist attacks of 2015." [68] The new law has been attacked by some as too weak, and as a "sub-state of emergency,"[69] while others have decried the normalization of emergency powers.[70]

On July 18, 2017 and on October, 3, 2017,[71] the French Senate and the National Assembly, respectively, voted to approve a new antiterrorism law entitled *Loi renforçant la sécurité intérieure et la lutte contre le terrorisme* (Law to Strengthen Internal Security and the Fight against Terrorism).[72] The bill was signed into law by President Macron on October 30.[73]

The new law entrenches in French ordinary law several of the emergency powers that were made available to the government under the 2015 state of emergency, while providing vague definitions of terrorism and threats to national security (exacerbating concerns that the powers may be used in an arbitrary manner).[74] The law grants broadly enhanced powers to local and police authorities while limiting the ability of the judiciary to intervene. A variety of ordinary civil liberties are subject to restriction, including potential closure of places of worship for up to six months. Moreover, the minister of the interior is authorized to place suspected radical Islamists under strict surveillance and limited freedom of movement whenever the minister alleges, without judicial oversight, "serious reasons to believe" that the person in question "constitutes

---

[67] Samuel Osborne, "France Declares End to State of Emergency Almost Two Years after Paris Terror Attacks," *Independent*, October 31, 2017; Anne-Sylvaine Chassany, "France: The Permanent State of Emergency," *Financial Times*, October 2, 2017.

[68] Alissa J. Rubin and Elian Peltier, "French Parliament Advances a Sweeping Counterterrorism Bill," *New York Times*, October 3, 2017.

[69] Ludovic Galtier, "Loi antiterroriste: ce que propose Marine Le Pen," *RTL*, October 3, 2017, http://www.rtl.fr/actu/politique/loi-antiterroriste-ce-que-propose-marine-le-pen-7790346436 (quoting Marine Le Pen opining that the new law was "un sous-état d'urgence").

[70] See, e.g., Kartik Raj, "France's Counterterrorism Bill Normalizes Emergency Practices," *Human Rights Watch*, September 25, 2017, https://www.hrw.org/news/2017/09/25/frances-counterterrorism-bill-normalizes-emergency-practices.

[71] BBC, "France Approves Tough New Anti-terror laws," October 4, 2017, http://www.bbc.com/news/world-europe-41493707.

[72] http://www2.assemblee-nationale.fr/documents/notice/15/ta/ta0025/(index)/ta.

[73] Agence France-Presse, "Emmanuel Macron signe la loi antiterroriste," *Le Point*, October 30, 2017, http://www.lepoint.fr/politique/etat-d-urgence-emmanuel-macron-signe-la-loi-antiterroriste-30-10-2017-2168680_20.php.

[74] Letter from Fionnuala Ni Aolain to the French Government (September 22, 2017).

a particularly serious threat to public security and public order." Among other things, the law:

(1) grants increased powers to prefects in almost every French department to designate public spaces or sporting or cultural events as security zones, limiting who may enter and leave them; to limit the movement of people considered a national security threat; to close places of worship for up to six months if preachers are deemed to express "ideas or theories" that "incite violence, hatred or discrimination, provoke the commission of acts of terrorism or express praise for such acts"; and to search private property;

(2) limits the judicial overview of the exercise of the increased prefect's powers;

(3) authorizes the minister of the interior, the minister of defense, and the minister of transportation to collect data pertaining to telephone and email communications of suspicious individuals "for the prevention, detection, investigation and prosecution of terrorist offenses and serious crimes";

(4) introduces restrictions called "individualized administrative control and surveillance measures." The law allows the minister of the interior to place suspected radical Islamists who are not accused of a specific crime, but about whom there are "serious reasons to believe that his or her conduct constitutes a particularly serious threat to public security and public order," under a house arrest for up to one year, without the prior approval of a judge. While under the state of emergency, the individual was confined to his or her home, under the new surveillance measure, which can last up to a year, the individual may go beyond her front door but must remain within the boundaries of her town or city. If she wants to go further, she has to wear an electronic bracelet. In addition, she will be required to report once a day to a local police station;

(5) gives the police expanded powers to carry out warrantless stop-and-search operations not only in border areas, airports, seaports, and train stations, but also in the surrounding areas up to a radius of 20 kilometers. These "surrounding areas" encompass 28.6 percent of French territory and 67 percent of the French population;[75]

(6) a local police chief or prefect can ask a judge for a warrant to search the homes of people suspected of posing a threat to public security. The person whose home is searched can be held for up to four hours, during which documents, data, and objects can be seized. Under the state of emergency, the police have had the power to raid homes without a judge's pre-approval; and

---

[75] Jean-Baptiste Jacquin, "Le gouvernement prépare une extension massive des contrôles d'identité 'aux frontières,'" *Le Monde*, December 9, 2017.

(7) authorizes the transfer or dismissal of a civil servant working in fields related to national security or defense if she is found to hold beliefs that are "incompatible with the exercise of his or her duties." Soldiers are subject to discharge for similar reasons.

In all, the antiterrorism law continues the pattern established in previous emergency measures of sidelining ordinary court judges (as distinguished from administrative court judges), and authorizing measures such as search and seizure and house arrests without judicial review. However, whereas in the past, such measures were deemed exceptional, the new law brings them squarely into ordinary law that applies outside the context of a declared state of emergency. Whereas the initial declaration of the state of emergency, and its various extensions, were premised on the notion that exceptional powers are granted to the government in light of the exceptional, and temporally limited, nature of the threat, the new law represents a paradigm shift. As the French interior minister, Gérard Collomb, stated, the new legislation was "a lasting response to a lasting threat."[76]

It is also important to note that the 2017 antiterrorism law is not the only piece of legislation with an "emergency" justification underlying it. On July 24, 2015, Parliament approved, almost unanimously, the Intelligence Act.[77] The law, which was presented to Parliament as part of the government's response to the January 2015 attacks on Charlie Hebdo and Hypercacher, was pushed through the National Assembly using an emergency procedure that only allowed one round of debates. In essence, the law allows French intelligence agencies to collect telephone data of all individuals present in a particular area or location and to carry out extrajudicial surveillance. While such infringement of privacy was justified formally on a counterterrorism basis, the law is broad enough to include within its ambit not only situations of terrorism and similar violent emergencies but also, for example, the prevention of the commission of criminal offenses and organized crime.

Conclusion

France is under the largest risk of terrorist attacks of all countries in western Europe according to the Global Terrorism Index, published by the Institute for Economics and Peace.[78] According to reports, French police and intelligence services are surveilling around 15,000 jihadists living on French soil. Of these, some 4,000 are at "the top of

---

[76] Rubin and Peltier, "Sweeping Counterterrorism Bill."

[77] Loi n° 2015-912 du 24 juillet 2015 relative au renseignement, https://www.legifrance.gouv.fr/affichCode.do; jsessionid=BF72E2C1162C7C49D52DE78D65BEF5B4.tpdila07v_2?idSectionTA=LEGISCTA000030934 655&cidTexte=LEGITEXT000025503132&dateTexte=20160309.

[78] Oliver Smith, "Mapped: The Countries Where a Terrorist Attack Is Most (And Least) Likely," *The Telegraph*, November 15, 2017.

the spectrum" and most likely to carry out an attack.[79] More than two years after the November 13, 2015 terrorist attacks that struck the heart of Paris, French officials maintain that there remains an unprecedented level of "internal" threat. With the Islamic State losing ground in Iraq and Syria, hundreds of French citizens are expected to attempt to return to France, posing a major threat.[80] The French secret services estimate that about 690 French nationals are currently in Iraq and Syria.[81] Attacks may still be orchestrated by large terrorist cells on French soil, but are increasingly likely to be carried out by lone wolves using "low-cost" methods such as cars or knives.[82] At the same time, while one cannot independently verify the number of foiled terrorist attacks, according to the interior minister, extraordinary measures have helped intelligence agencies thwart more than thirty attacks in the last two years.[83] The French government's own assessment of terrorist threats against France is also shared by other governments. Thus, for example, the United Kingdom's travel advisory (as it stands at the time of writing) indicates that, "[t]errorists are very likely to try to carry out attacks in France."[84]

There is little doubt that the terrorist threats against France are real. The specter of terrorist attacks brings into sharp relief the "tragic dimensions" of the tension between democratic values and responses to violent emergencies.[85] Democratic nations faced with serious crisis by way of terrorist threats must maintain and protect not only the life of their citizens but also the democratic values and individual liberties that are necessary for the nation to remain truly democratic. Yet, emergencies directly challenge the most fundamental concepts of constitutional democracy.[86] The pernicious effect of such challenges may be somewhat mitigated when the state of emergency is, in fact, exceptional and temporally limited. However, the transformation of the exception into the norm, of the temporary into the permanent, suggests that the full thrust of the challenges that terrorism presents to constitutional democracies ought to be recognized for what it is. Constitutional and legal and political responses to terrorism that may be constructed around the belief that the threats are temporary and that emergency powers are given to government on a temporary basis may thus be misguided and ill-devised. The compression of space and time also suggests that the crises of constitutional democracies that have been identified in this chapter are here to stay.

---

[79] Soeren Kern, "France: New Anti-terrorism Law Takes Effect," October 31, 2017, https://www.gatestoneinstitute. org/11258/france-terrorism-law.

[80] Reuters, "Terrorist Threat in France Unprecedented, Officials Say," *Irish Times*, November 12, 2017; "Terrorist Attack Potential 'Very High' as 271 ISIS Jihadists Return to France—Interior Minister," *RT*, August 6, 2017, https://www.rt.com/news/398755-france-terrorism-high-chance-collomb/.

[81] Reuters, "Terrorist Threat."

[82] Ibid.

[83] Ibid.

[84] U.K. Government, "Foreign Travel Advice: France," accessed February 26, 2018, https://www.gov.uk/foreign-travel-advice/france.

[85] Pnina Lahav, "A Barrel without Hoops: The Impact of Counterterrorism on Israel's Legal Culture," *Cardozo Law Review* 10 (1988): 529, 531.

[86] Gross and Ní Aoláin, *Law in Times of Crisis*, 7–9.

34 The Climate Crisis and Constitutional Democracies
Robert V. Percival*

AFTER DECADES OF warnings from scientists, the horrifying consequences of global warming and climate change are becoming apparent more quickly than previously forecast. Record temperatures, droughts, coastal flooding, wildfires, and superstorms now occur with alarming frequency.[1] These and other consequences of the climate crisis are contributing to the displacement of record numbers of people, exacerbating a global refugee crisis and creating tensions that are polarizing the public in many constitutional democracies.[2]

---

* Robert F. Stanton Professor of Law and Director, Environmental Law Program, University of Maryland Carey School of Law.

[1] The five hottest years on record all have occurred since 2010, and seventeen of the eighteen hottest years have occurred since 2000. NASA, "Long-Term Warming Trend Continued in 2017," January 18, 2018, https://www.nasa.gov/press-release/long-term-warming-trend-continued-in-2017-nasa-noaa. In 2017 extreme weather events caused $306 billion in damage in the United States, an all-time record. NOAA National Centers for Environmental Information (NCEI), "Billon-Dollar Weather and Climate Disasters: Overview" (2018), https://www.ncdc.noaa.gov/billions/. NASA reports that "the past decade has been the hottest ever recorded since global temperature records began 150 years ago." NASA, "Global Climate Change: Vital Signs of the Planet," https://climate.nasa.gov/climate_resources/42/ (accessed February 21, 2018). The scientific consensus is that the planet's climate is warming.

[2] Anouch Missirian and Wolfram Schlenker, "Asylum Applications Respond to Temperature Fluctuations," *Science* 358 (2017): 1610–1614; Somini Sengupta, "Warming, Water Crisis, Then Unrest: How Iran Fits an Alarming Pattern," *New York Times*, January 18, 2018, https://www.nytimes.com/2018/01/18/climate/water-iran.html.

After a quarter century of negotiations, the nations of the world reached agreement in December 2015 on a global strategy for combating climate change. While clearly inadequate by itself to prevent the climate crisis, the Paris Agreement represents an important step that has been endorsed by every country of the world. President Obama enthusiastically supported the Paris Agreement, but in June 2017 President Trump announced his intention to withdraw the United States from it,[3] an action that cannot become effective until November 4, 2020, four years after the Agreement entered into force.

Are constitutional democracies capable of dealing effectively with the climate crisis? This chapter explores the relationship between the climate crisis and the design of constitutional democracies. It begins by exploring the difficult political challenges environmental protection measures face because they often impose immediate, concentrated costs on powerful entities in return for diffuse benefits accruing over extended periods of time. It examines why climate change magnifies these challenges because of the planetary scale of its sources and impacts. It then discusses how the judiciary is helping to overcome these challenges in countries where it has the power and independence to influence executive and legislative action. The chapter then discusses how subnational governments are shaping climate policy in countries with constitutions that give them substantial sovereign authority. It concludes by considering the long struggle to overcome a planetary "tragedy of the commons" by including developing countries in global efforts to control greenhouse gases (GHGs). The recent transformation in the climate policies of China—by far the world's leading source of GHG emissions—suggests that authoritarian regimes can more easily shift gears to implement stringent environmental regulations, but robust democracies also can do so if climate policies are designed to last.

The Political Challenge of the Climate Crisis

"It is much easier to understand why environmental laws are needed than it is to comprehend how they came to be adopted."[4] The reasons the free markets will not provide public goods such as clean air and clean water without government intervention are well understood. But despite wide agreement that collective action to protect the environment is in society's best interests, it is difficult to redress these problems through a political process that itself is prone to problems of free-riders and factional influence.

In his classic work *The Logic of Collective Action* the late economist Mancur Olson identified political barriers to taking collective action on behalf of diffuse public interests.[5]

---

[3] Statement by President Trump on the Paris Climate Accord, June 1, 2017, https://www.whitehouse.gov/briefings-statements/statement-president-trump-paris-climate-accord/.

[4] Robert V. Percival, "Environmental Legislation and the Problem of Collective Action," *Duke Environmental Law and Policy Forum* 9 (1998): 9–28.

[5] Mancur Olson, *The Logic of Collective Action: Public Goods and the Theory of Groups* (Cambridge, MA: Harvard University Press, 1965).

Olson's work questions the political feasibility of regulatory legislation that provides diffuse environmental benefits to the general public while imposing concentrated costs on well-organized industry groups. Climate change has been described as a "super wicked" problem because it is a global phenomenon that no nation can effectively redress on its own.[6] No other environmental problem has such global scale. The "actors who are best positioned to address climate change are those who are primarily responsible for causing it—and who lack incentives to take action."[7] The problem is affected by both sources and sinks of GHGs. There is no global institution that has the jurisdiction and authority to deal with the problem in its global scale. It makes no difference where GHG emissions originate because they all contribute to this truly global problem. Thus, to avoid a global "tragedy of the commons"[8] it is necessary that all nations try to coordinate their efforts to mitigate and adapt to climate change, something that the Paris Agreement promised for the first time, albeit in a voluntary and inadequate manner.

A study of climate policies around the world found that as of October 2017, there were 1,700 legislative and executive actions in various countries. Most of these (53 percent) were executive, rather than legislative actions (44 percent) and only one-quarter were climate-specific.[9] This represents a huge increase from the sixty official actions that had been taken when the Kyoto Protocol was signed in 1997. In developed G20 nations almost two-thirds of these 1,700 actions were legislative in nature while in least developed countries less than one-quarter were.[10] Strong, unitary governments were better able to pass climate legislation, which generally received bipartisan support except in the United States, Australia, and Canada.

A study of the factors driving the adoption of climate change legislation found that in most countries there was broad agreement concerning climate policies. As a result, there generally is no significant difference in climate legislation between conservative and liberal governments.[11] Climate skepticism seems to be confined to politicians in the United States, Australia, and Canada, particularly those who received support from fossil fuel interests. A study of ninety-four countries over twenty-four years (1990–2014) found that political orientation had no effect on a government's propensity to enact climate legislation. While business cycles also had no effect on enactment of climate legislation,

[6] Richard J. Lazarus, "Super Wicked Problems and Climate Change: Restraining the Present to Liberate the Future," *Cornell Law Review* 94 (2009): 1153–1234.

[7] United Nations Environment Programme, *The Status of Climate Change Litigation: A Global Review* (Nairobi: UN Environment Programme, 2017), 7, http://wedocs.unep.org/bitstream/handle/20.500.11822/20767/climate-change-litigation.pdf.

[8] Garrett Hardin, "The Tragedy of the Commons," *Science* 162 (1968): 1243–1248.

[9] A. Averchenkova, S. FankHauser, and M. Nachmany, eds., *Trends in Climate Change Legislation* (Northampton, MA: Edward Elgar, 2017), 4.

[10] Ibid., 5.

[11] Abbie Clare, Sam Fankhauser, and Caterina Gennaioli, "The National and International Drivers of Climate Change Legislation," in *Trends in Climate Change Legislation* (Northampton, MA: Edward Elgar, 2017) 19.

fewer climate laws were passed close to an election.[12] This effect (that electoral cycles matter) appeared most pronounced in well-developed democratic systems.

History shows that collective action problems can be overcome when environmental conditions get bad enough to demand public attention. In the United States. this occurred during the late 1960s and early 1970s when rivers caught fire. As presidential historian Theodore White notes, by 1970 "the environment[al] cause had swollen into the favorite sacred issue of all politicians, all TV networks, all goodwilled people of any party."[13] This produced what Dan Farber has described as remarkable "republican moments" when events such as Earth Day, Love Canal, Three Mile Island, the Exxon Valdez oil spill, and the Bhopal tragedy made environmental issues particularly salient politically.[14]

In China the current decade has featured repeated, highly visible "airpocalypses" with pollution reaching levels that have caused schools, roads, and airports to close. This spurred the Communist Party leadership to declare "war on pollution" in 2014[15] and eventually to adopt stringent measures to reduce the use of fossil fuels. China's leaders used their government's Five Year Plans to initiate policies to control GHG emissions, rather than by adopting climate legislation. After decades of insisting that it was too poor to afford to control its GHG emissions, China abruptly shifted gears in large part because it realized the economic opportunities posed by a shift to renewable energy sources.[16]

Brazil, Mexico, and the UK have adopted legislation to address the climate crisis, while the United States, Indonesia, and Russia have relied on executive action and Germany and South Africa on strategic policy documents.[17] But in some constitutional democracies it has been difficult to sustain aggressive climate policies.

Canada initially ratified the 1992 UN Framework Convention on Climate Change and its 1997 Kyoto Protocol that required a 6 percent reduction in the country's emissions of GHG during the period 2008–2012. However, soon after Conservative Party leader Stephen Harper became prime minister in February 2006 he announced that Canada could not and would not meet its Kyoto commitment. Harper feared that a strong policy

---

[12] Clare, Fankhauser, and Gennaioli, "The National and International Drivers," 21–22.

[13] Theodore White, *The Making of the President 1972* (New York: Atheneum Publishers, 1973), 45. William Rodgers Jr. astutely cautions that environmental laws may be less effective at overcoming the interests of the regulated community than is commonly thought. He observes that legislators can gain public support by voting for stringent-sounding laws that actually contain loopholes that regulatory targets can exploit. William H. Rodgers Jr., "The Lesson of the Owl and the Crows: The Role of Deception in the Evolution of the Environmental Statutes," *Journal of Land Use and Environmental Law* 4 (1989): 377, 378.

[14] Daniel A. Farber, "Politics and Procedure in Environmental Law," *Journal of Law, Economics and Organization* 8 (1992): 59, 66–67.

[15] Reuters, "China to 'Declare War' on Pollution, Premier Says," March 4, 2014, https://www.reuters.com/article/us-china-parliament-pollution/china-to-declare-war-on-pollution-premier-says-idUSBREA2405W20140305.

[16] Isabella Neuweg and Alina Averchenkova, "Climate Legislation in China, the European Union and the United States," in *Trends in Climate Change Legislation* (Northampton, MA: Edward Elgar, 2017), 37.

[17] Alina Averchenkova, Sam Fankhauser, and Michal Nachmany, "Introduction," in *Trends in Climate Change Legislation* (Northampton, MA: Edward Elgar, 2017).

to restrict the use of fossil fuels could handicap Canada's energy industry. In Canada's 2008 federal election the Liberal Party ran on a platform that relied heavily on a carbon tax to reduce GHG emissions, but they were defeated and Harper's Conservative Party retained power. After the Canadian government "deferred, denied, and dabbled" with the issue of climate change without taking significant action to combat the problem, in 2012 the Canadian Parliament repealed the country's Kyoto Implementation Act.[18]

The only two developed countries who initially failed to ratify the Kyoto Protocol were Australia and the United States. While his promise to ratify the Kyoto Protocol helped Labor leader Kevin Rudd become the Australian prime minister in December 2007, eventually a nationwide carbon reduction program was the undoing of Labor prime minister Julia Gillard. Decrying the Clean Energy Act of 2011 as imposing a "carbon tax," opposition leader Tony Abbott rose to power by pledging to repeal it. Abbott became prime minister in September 2013 and won repeal of the national GHG reduction program on July 17, 2014. This experience illustrates the difficulty of implementing climate measures that impose immediate costs on consumers in return for diffuse future benefits.

The Member States of the European Union have made climate policy an EU matter. This has enabled the adoption of stringent EU-wide limits on carbon emissions and targets for increasing renewable energy and energy efficiency. The EU's insistence on applying its emissions trading scheme to aviation, and its refusal to back down in the face of pressure from foreign governments, ultimately spawned a global program for controlling aviation emissions negotiated through the International Civil Aviation Organization (ICAO). In 2008 the United Kingdom adopted an ambitious Climate Change Act that set a long-term target to reduce GHG emissions by 80 percent by 2050. The Act was passed with nearly unanimous support from all political parties including the Conservative opposition. However, when Conservative leader Theresa May became prime minister in 2016 she abolished the Department for Energy and Climate Change, transferring its duties to the Department for Energy, Business & Industrial Strategy.

Least-developed countries, who are among the greatest victims of global warming and climate change, have enacted fewer policies to control their GHG emissions because of the small size of their emissions and their countries' more limited financial capacity.[19] In November 2015 Mexico took a bold move by announcing its willingness to cut its GHG emissions by 22 percent if it received financial assistance to help it increase the development of renewable energy sources.[20] Mexico subsequently adopted a General Law on Climate Change.

---

[18] Robert C. Paehlke, *Some Like It Cold: The Politics of Climate Change in Canada* (Toronto: Between the Lines, 2008), 56, 115.

[19] Michal Nachmany, Achala Abeysinghe, and Subhi Barakat, "Climate Change Legislation in the Least Developing Countries," in *Trends in Climate Change Legislation* (Northampton, MA: Edward Elgar, 2017), 59.

[20] Lisa Friedman, "Mexico Makes Landmark Pledge to Cut Greenhouse Gas Pollution," *E&E News*, March 30, 2015, https://www.scientificamerican.com/article/mexico-makes-landmark-pledge-to-cut-greenhouse-gas-pollution/.

It is easier to overcome collective action problems when pollution becomes horrendously visible, but it is much more difficult to generate political will to combat climate change. In 1987 EPA asked its scientists systematically to evaluate thirty-one types of environmental risk to develop a rank ordering of them in four categories: cancer risks, non-cancer health effects, ecological risks, and risks to public welfare. It then compared the rankings of EPA experts with the public's rank ordering of risks and the agency's actual priorities. The agency found that "EPA's priorities appear more closely aligned with public opinion than with estimated risks."[21] Of the risks identified by EPA's experts, global warming ranked relatively high, but it was at the bottom of the risks that concerned the public.[22]

Support for US action to address climate change has grown even as the US Congress is now controlled by climate deniers. In March 2017 the *New York Times* reported that a majority of adults in every congressional district in the country supported limits on GHG emissions from existing coal-fired power plants.[23] Altogether 69 percent of adults supported such controls. An even a larger majority—75 percent—supported regulating carbon dioxide as a pollutant, which the Supreme Court ruled the Clean Air Act authorized in *Massachusetts v. EPA*.[24] However, the same poll found that although most Americans believe that climate change will harm their fellow Americans, they do not think that it will harm them.

US climate policy has been subject to abrupt change with changes in presidential leadership. President George W. Bush rescinded his pledge to back legislation to control emissions of carbon dioxide less than two months after assuming office.[25] President Barack Obama failed to win enactment of comprehensive climate legislation despite his party controlling both houses of Congress from 2009 to 2010. He subsequently pursued aggressive regulatory action to reduce GHG emissions, but this is now being systematically dismantled by President Donald Trump.

---

[21] U.S. Environmental Protection Agency, *Unfinished Business: A Comparative Assessment of Environmental Problems* (Washington, DC: Environmental Protection Agency, 1987), 96.

[22] Ibid., 97.

[23] Nadia Popovich, John Schwartz, and Tatiana Schlossberg, "How Americans Think about Climate Change, in Six Maps" *New York Times*, March 21, 2017, https://www.nytimes.com/interactive/2017/03/21/climate/how-americans-think-about-climate-change-in-six-maps.html.

[24] 549 U.S. 497 (2007).

[25] During the 2000 presidential election campaign, candidate George W. Bush declared that climate change was a serious problem. In a speech in Michigan on September 29, 2000, Bush promised that, if elected president, he would seek new legislation to control emissions of carbon dioxide, the most ubiquitous GHG. However, less than two months after taking office, President Bush formally repudiated his campaign promise, arguing that it would damage the economy to regulate GHG emissions when China and India were not required to control theirs. Letter from the President to Senators Hagel, Helms, Craig, and Roberts, March 13, 2001, https://georgewbush-whitehouse.archives.gov/news/releases/2001/03/20010314.html.

Constitutions, the Judiciary, and the Climate Crisis

Courts increasingly are being called upon to address issues of climate change, and in nations with strong, independent judiciaries they occasionally are making a difference.[26] Considerable climate litigation seeks judicial action to force governments and/or large sources of GHGs to take action to reduce emissions. A study of climate litigation by the United Nations Environment Programme found that by March 2017 a total of 884 cases had been filed in twenty-four countries.[27] Most cases (654) had been filed in US courts; 80 had been filed in Australia, 49 had been filed in the United Kingdom, and 40 in the European Court of Justice. In nearly all of these cases, governments have been the defendants, though recently there have been several lawsuits filed by subnational levels of government against large sources of GHG emissions. The climate lawsuits that have been filed fall into five general categories: "holding governments to their legislative and policy commitments; linking the impacts of resource extraction to climate change and resilience; establishing that particular emissions are the proximate cause of particular adverse climate change impacts; establishing liability for failures (or efforts) to adapt to climate change; and applying the public trust doctrine to climate change."[28]

While many courts have rejected these challenges, in a few notable cases courts have ordered executive officials to take stronger action to address the climate crisis. Ruling on a petition from a farmer affected by climate change, the Lahore High Court Green Bench in Pakistan declared in September 2015:

> Climate Change is a defining challenge of our time and has led to dramatic alterations in our planet's climate system. For Pakistan, these climatic variations have primarily resulted in heavy floods and droughts, raising serious concerns regarding water and food security. On a legal and constitutional plane this is [a] clarion call for the protection of fundamental rights of the citizens of Pakistan, in particular, the vulnerable and weak segments of the society who are unable to approach this Court.[29]

The court found that the Pakistani government's failure to implement the National Climate Change Policy of 2012 and the Framework for Implementation of Climate Change Policy "offends the fundamental rights of the citizens which need to be safeguarded." Invoking the right to life and the right to dignity in Pakistan's Constitution, the court ordered government ministries and departments to prepare a list of adaptation

---

[26] Joana Setzer and Mook Bangalore, "Regulating Climate Change in the Courts," in *Trends in Climate Change Legislation* (Northampton, MA: Edward Elgar, 2017), 175.

[27] United Nations Environment Programme, *Status of Climate Change Litigation*, 10.

[28] Ibid., 14.

[29] Ashgar Legari v. Federation of Pakistan, W.P. No. 25501/2015.

measures and to implement Pakistan's National Climate Change Policy. It established a Climate Change Commission to help it monitor their progress.

The Urgenda Foundation, a Dutch environmental group, joined by nine hundred Dutch citizens, sued the government of the Netherlands for its adoption of GHG reduction goals that allegedly violated the government's constitutional duty of care to protect them. In June 2015 a Dutch district court in The Hague cited the European Convention on Human Rights and tort law theories to order the Dutch government to take stronger measures to respond to climate change.[30] The court mandated that the Dutch government reduce emissions of GHGs by 25 percent below 1990 levels by 2020.[31] The court concluded that the government's previous 17 percent reduction goal was inadequate to meet the nation's fair share of the emissions reductions required to protect its citizens.

Two Norwegian environmental NGOs, Greenpeace Nordic and Nature and Youth, sued the government of Norway for violating the constitutional right to a healthy and safe environment for future generations.[32] The groups claimed that the government's decision to lease new areas of the Barents Sea for oil drilling violated the Paris Agreement and the constitution. After a trial in November 2017, the Oslo District Court ruled in January 2018 that the government had acted lawfully. Although the court recognized that the government has a constitutional duty to safeguard the environment for future generations, it concluded that "[w]hether Norway is doing enough for the environment and climate, and if it was sensible to open fields so far north and east" are questions "better assessed through political processes."

Other lawsuits to force more aggressive government action to control GHG emissions have been filed in Austria, Switzerland, and Sweden.[33]

In the United States a particularly creative climate change lawsuit is being brought in federal district court in Oregon against the president and top US officials for failing to protect future generations against the impacts of climate change. In November 2016 a federal magistrate judge rejected the government's argument that the case raises a non-justiciable political question.[34] The plaintiffs, who include twenty-one people between the ages of eight and nineteen when the lawsuit was filed, allege that the federal government knew about the dangers of climate change for more than fifty years, but failed to take action to protect them. The children argue that this violated their substantive due process rights to life, liberty, and property as well as the government's obligation to hold natural resources in trust for future generations. The plaintiffs seek a declaration that their rights have been violated and an order requiring federal officials to develop a plan to control emissions of GHGs.

---

[30] Urgenda Foundation v. Kingdom of the Netherlands (2015).

[31] The decision is being appealed by the Dutch government.

[32] Article 112 of the Constitution of Norway grants every person "the right to an environment that is conducive to health and to a natural environment whose productivity and diversity are maintained," and it requires that natural resources be managed "to safeguard this right for future generations as well."

[33] UN Environment Programme, *Status of Climate Change Litigation*, 15.

[34] Juliana v. United States, 217 F. Supp. 3d 1224 (D. Ore. 2016).

Nearly every country that has enacted a new constitution or substantially revised an existing one since World War II has adopted constitutional provisions addressing environmental protection. More than one hundred countries now have constitutional provisions that declare a public right to a healthy environment and/or a duty for government to protect the environment.[35] To date these provisions have been largely symbolic, though some have relaxed restrictive standing requirements. Many countries have established specialized environmental courts; there are now more than 1,200 such courts throughout the world.[36]

The United States Constitution, the oldest written constitution in the world, is silent when it comes to the environment, although twenty-two state constitutions have provisions that expressly address environmental concerns.[37] Remarkably, this has not proven to be a significant obstacle to the erection of a robust federal regulatory infrastructure to protect the environment.[38] And the federal judiciary has used these environmental laws to spur executive action to protect the environment.

Relying on the Clean Air Act, the Supreme Court in *Massachusetts v. EPA* held that EPA has the authority to regulate emissions of GHGs under the Clean Air Act (CAA), and that EPA's decision not to do so during the George W. Bush administration was arbitrary and capricious.[39] The Court did not need to develop any new theory of constitutional law to reach this result; it simply held that the CAA required the government to protect the public against any pollutants that endanger public health or welfare. Writing in dissent, Chief Justice Roberts declared that "Global warming may be a 'crisis,' even 'the most pressing environmental problem of our time.' Indeed, it may ultimately affect nearly everyone on the planet in some potentially adverse way, and it may be that governments have done too little to address it."[40] Yet the chief justice and three other justices declared

---

[35] James R. May and Erin Daly, *Global Environmental Constitutionalism* (Cambridge: Cambridge University Press, 2014).

[36] Robert V. Percival, "The Greening of the Global Judiciary," *Journal of Land Use and Environmental Law* 32 (2017): 333–358.

[37] James R. May and William Romanowicz, "Environmental Rights in State Constitutions," in *Principles of Constitutional Environmental Law*, ed. James R. May (Chicago: American Bar Association, 2011), 305, 306, 315–321. The states with environmental provisions in their constitutions are: Alabama, California, Colorado, Florida, Hawaii, Idaho, Illinois, Louisiana, Massachusetts, Michigan, Minnesota, Missouri, Montana, New Mexico, New York, North Carolina, Ohio, Oregon, Pennsylvania, Rhode Island, Utah, and Virginia. Occasionally these provisions have been used by state courts to address environmental concerns. See Robinson Township v. Commonwealth of Pennsylvania, 83 A.3d 901 (Pa. 2013) (holding a law banning local regulation of hydraulic fracturing to violate the state constitution).

[38] Robert V. Percival, "'Greening' the Constitution—Harmonizing Environmental and Constitutional Values," *Environmental Law* 32 (2002): 809–872. The federal environmental laws consistently have been upheld as well within the congressional power to regulate interstate commerce. See, e.g., People for the Ethical Treatment of Property Owners v. U.S. Fish and Wildlife Service, 852 F.3d 990 (10th Cir. 2017), *cert. denied*, 2018 WL 311835 (2018).

[39] Massachusetts v. EPA, 549 U.S. 497 (2007)

[40] Ibid., 535 (Roberts, C.J., dissenting).

that the judiciary should leave such issues to the legislative and executive branches of government. But five other justices concluded not only that EPA had the authority to regulate GHG emissions under the CAA, but also that the agency's rationale for not doing so was arbitrary and capricious because it was not based on statutorily-relevant factors.

Although the Bush administration failed to decide before leaving office whether GHG emissions endanger public health or welfare, after taking office in January 2009 President Barack Obama moved quickly to reverse federal climate policy. The new president asked Congress to adopt legislation creating a national cap-and-trade program to reduce GHG emissions. He warned that if Congress failed to act, he would use the CAA to regulate GHG emissions. After Congress failed to do so, on December 7, 2009, EPA made a formal "endangerment finding" for GHGs, permitting their regulation under the CAA.[41]

State and local governments also are turning to the courts to seek redress for climate change through tort litigation. In July 2004 eight states and the City of New York filed a common law nuisance action against US electric utilities whose power plants contribute 10 percent of US emissions of carbon dioxide (CO_2).[42] They asked the court to hold defendants jointly and severally liable for contributing to climate change and an injunction ordering the companies to reduce their emissions of CO_2. In *American Electric Power v. Connecticut* the US Supreme Court dismissed the lawsuit by holding that the federal CAA displaced the federal common law of nuisance by assigning the task of regulating GHG emissions to EPA.[43] The Court reserved the question of whether the CAA preempted *state* nuisance actions.

States now are pursuing such actions against major sources of GHG emissions. On January 10, 2018, New York City sued five major oil companies, arguing that their products contributed 11 percent of all GHGs and that the climate crisis will require the city to spend billions to build a protective seawall around Manhattan. Several California cities have filed similar lawsuits.[44]

Subnational Governments and the Climate Crisis

In countries with robust federal systems that respect state sovereignty subnational levels of government are taking the lead in adopting programs to control GHG emissions.[45]

---

[41] Endangerment and Cause or Contribute Findings for Greenhouse Gases Under Section 202(a) of the Clean Air Act, 74 Fed. Reg. 66,496 (Dec. 15, 2009).

[42] Connecticut v. American Electric Power Co., 406 F. Supp. 2d 265, 267–68 (S.D.N.Y. 2005), *affirmed on other grounds*, 564 U.S. 410 (2011).

[43] American Electric Power Co. v. Connecticut, 564 U.S. 410 (2011).

[44] Chris Mooney and Dino Grandoni, "New York City Sues Shell, ExxonMobil and Other Oil Companies over Climate Change," *Washington Post*, January 10, 2018, https://www.washingtonpost.com/news/energy-environment/wp/2018/01/10/new-york-city-sues-shell-exxonmobil-and-other-oil-majors-over-climate-change/?utm_term=.76f10e3a3cc6.

[45] Ibon Galarrage, Elisa Sainz de Murieta, and Joan Franca, "Climate Policy at the Sub-National Level," in *Trends in Climate Change Legislation* (Northampton, MA: Edward Elgar, 2017), 143.

When national leadership on climate issues falters, state and local governments have developed creative partnerships to reduce their carbon footprints. In the United States, these include the Regional Greenhouse Gas Initiative (RGGI) of ten northeast and mid-Atlantic states who have been working together for a decade to reduce GHG emissions from the power sector.[46] Subnational governments in other countries such as Brazil also have played a leadership role on climate issues.[47]

The CAA allows states to adopt more stringent protections on air quality than required by EPA, except in one significant respect. States may not regulate emissions from motor vehicles in a manner different from the federal standard unless they adopt California's vehicle emission standards.[48] Congress allowed California with EPA approval to adopt more stringent motor vehicle emission standards than EPA[49] because it already had established such standards when the CAA was enacted in 1970, and because its motor vehicle market was large enough to enable automakers to produce a separate set of vehicles for that market.

In 2002 California enacted regulations to control GHG emissions from motor vehicles; these regulations were adopted by thirteen other states. In 2006 the California Legislature enacted the Global Warming Solutions Act (AB32) requiring that statewide GHG emissions be reduced to 1990 levels by 2020, a 29 percent reduction from 600 million metric tons to 426 million.[50] A California ballot proposition to repeal AB32, funded largely by fossil fuel interests, was decisively rejected by a 61–39 percent margin by California voters in November 2010. In 2016 the California legislature strengthened the state's cap-and-trade program to control GHG emissions by requiring a 40 percent reduction from 1990 levels by 2030.

Following the announcement by President Donald Trump of his intent to withdraw the United States from the Paris Agreement, the governors of California, New York, and Washington formed the United States Climate Alliance. This is a bipartisan coalition of states committed to upholding the objectives of the Paris Agreement within their borders by honoring the US pledge to reduce GHG emissions by 26–28 percent from 2005 levels by 2025 and by meeting targets set by the Obama administration's Clean Power Plan. The Alliance includes sixteen states and Puerto Rico, which account for more than 40 percent of the US population and nearly half (nearly $9 trillion) of the US gross domestic product.[51] Three of the states—Maryland, Massachusetts, and Vermont—have Republican governors. Representatives of the Alliance attended the 23rd Conference of the Parties to the

---

[46] "The Regional Greenhouse Gas Initiative," accessed February 21, 2018, http://www.rggi.org/program-overview-and-design/elements.

[47] Joana Setzer, "How Subnational Governments Are Rescaling Environmental Governance: The Case of the Brazilian State of Sao Paulo," *Journal of Environmental Policy and Planning* 19 (2014): 503–519.

[48] Clean Air Act § 209(a), 42 U.S.C. 7543(a) (1970).

[49] Clean Air Act § 209(b), 42 U.S.C. 7543(b) (1970).

[50] Assembly Bill 32, Division 25.5 California Health & Safety Code § 38500ff (2006)

[51] United States Climate Alliance, accessed May 12, 2018, https://www.usclimatealliance.org.

UN Framework Convention on Climate Change in Germany in November 2016 to reassure world leaders that their states will continue to honor the Paris Agreement. The governors of nine other states and the mayor of the District of Columbia also have pledged their support for the Paris Agreement even though they have not joined the Alliance. Thus, leaders of states with a majority of the US population have made it clear to the world that they continue to support the Paris Agreement.

The leaders of more than 7,700 cities worldwide with more than 723 million people have adopted the Global Covenant of Mayors for Climate & Energy pledging to support actions to reduce GHG emissions.[52] These and other non-federal actions suggest that the Trump administration's climate denial will not stop global efforts to reduce GHG emissions.

Some may view actions by states to reduce their carbon footprints as examples of "uncooperative federalism"[53]—state dissent from, and even defiance of federal policy. But given that federal environmental law always has been designed to enable states to do more to protect the environment if they so choose, state actions to address the climate crisis do not fit the uncooperative model. Although the Trump administration has emphasized giving states greater responsibility for environmental policy, it has hinted that it may try to preempt state laws that control GHG emissions more stringently than federal law.

Efforts to Overcome a Global "Tragedy of the Commons"

As noted in the introduction, climate change represents a classic "tragedy of the commons" where common pool resources—the planet's atmosphere—are degraded because no individual nation has a sufficient incentive on its own to reduce its GHG emissions. Because emissions anywhere in the world contribute to the problem, only collective action on a global scale can help mitigate the harm caused by climate change.

For more than a quarter century the nations of the world have tried to formulate an effective, collective response to the climate change problem. In June 1992, the UN Framework Convention on Climate Change (UNFCC) was signed by the nations of the world at the Rio Earth Summit. The UNFCC set up a negotiating process to develop a collective response to climate change. US president George H.W. Bush signed the UNFCC in Rio in June 1992. He submitted it to the US Senate, which ratified it unanimously in October 1992.

In December 1997 the nations of the world adopted the Kyoto Protocol to the UNFCCC. Because emissions of GHGs from developed countries had caused the climate crisis, the Kyoto Protocol provided that developed countries would take the first

---

[52] Global Covenant of Mayors for Climate & Energy, accessed May 12, 2018, https://www.globalcovenantof-mayors.org.

[53] Jessica Bulmen-Pozen and Heather K. Gerken, "Uncooperative Federalism," *Yale Law Journal* 118 (2009): 1256–1311.

steps to reduce their GHG emissions. It did not require developing countries to reduce their emissions, but it was well understood that eventually they would have to agree to do so if the climate crisis were to be avoided. President Clinton never submitted the Protocol to the Senate for ratification because four months prior to the Kyoto conference the Senate had adopted a resolution stating that the United States should not agree to any treaty that did not also require emissions reductions from rapidly developing countries such as China and India.[54]

The Kyoto Protocol required thirty-eight developed countries to reduce their aggregate, annual average GHG emissions by 5 percent (or 1 gigatonne of CO_2) below 1990 levels during the period from 2008 to 2012. It did not include any mechanism for enforcing this requirement other than the realization that rapidly developing countries would likely be unwilling later to control their emissions if the developed world failed to meet its initial commitments. In 2007 China's soaring emissions of GHGs exceeded those of the United States for the first time, making it the source of the most emissions of GHGs in the world. But with a population four times larger than the United States, China's emissions were far less in per capita terms than those of the United States. Together China and the United States accounted for nearly half of all global GHG emissions.

With China's emissions soaring, overall global emissions of GHGs increased during the 2008–2012 period, but emissions from the thirty-eight developed countries were 2 gigatonnes (2 $GtCO_2$) per year lower than in 1990 during the 2008–2012 period.[55] Although nine of the thirty-six developed countries that ratified Kyoto (Austria, Denmark, Iceland, Japan, Lichtenstein, Luxembourg, Norway, Spain, and Switzerland) emitted greater levels of GHG emissions than they promised, these countries missed by only a small amount (1 percent on average), and they actually complied with the Protocol on paper by using its flexibility mechanisms to acquire carbon credits.[56]

The Copenhagen Conference in December 2009 represented a turning point in global efforts to fashion a common response to the climate crisis. With the 2008–2012 commitment period of the Kyoto Protocol set to expire, developed countries hoped to expand the Protocol to require developing countries to control their rapidly growing emissions. China and other developing countries refused to agree to this, citing the UNFCCC's recognition of their "common but differentiated responsibilities."[57] Faced with this rejection, the leaders of the developed world shifted to a new, bottom-up approach, reflected

---

[54] S. Res. 98, A Resolution Expressing the Sense of the Senate Regarding the Conditions for the United States Becoming a Signatory to any International Agreement on Greenhouse Gas Emissions under the United Nations Framework Convention on Climate Change, Approved 95-0 on July 25, 1997.

[55] Michael Le Page, "Was Kyoto Climate Deal a Success? Figures Reveal Mixed Results," *New Scientist*, June 14, 2016, https://www.newscientist.com/article/2093579-was-kyoto-climate-deal-a-success-figures-reveal-mixed-results/.

[56] Igor Shishlov, Romain Morel, and Valentin Bellassen, "Compliance of the Parties to the Kyoto Protocol in the First Commitment Period," *Climate Policy* 16 (2016): 768–782.

[57] UN Framework Convention on Climate Change, Art. 3, paragraph 1 & Article 4, paragraph 1.

in the Copenhagen Accord. Each nation was asked to submit its own voluntary commitment reflecting what it planned to do to control its GHG emissions. While China and India refused to agree to cap their emissions, they submitted pledges to improve the energy efficiency of their economies by 40 and 20 percent respectively from 2005 levels by 2020.

At COP-17 in Durban, South Africa, in December 2011, developing countries agreed that they would join a new global climate regime to be finalized by COP-21 in Paris in December 2015. Stunned by the harsh criticism they received in Copenhagen and realizing that a transition to green energy would create economic opportunities for Chinese solar, wind, and electric car technology, Chinese officials agreed to this. With horrendously visible air pollution periodically shutting down Chinese schools, highways, and airports, in March 2014 Chinese premier Li Keqiang announced that the government was declaring "war on pollution."[58]

The prospects for a new global agreement were enhanced in November 2014 when President Obama and Chinese president Xi Jinping stunned the world by issuing a "Joint Announcement on Climate Change." In the announcement China pledged for the first time to halt the increase in its GHG emissions by 2030, if not earlier.[59] Both countries also pledged to work together on a broad array of projects to share and develop improved technology for green energy production and carbon capture and storage. In March 2015 Mexico surprised the world by announcing a detailed plan to cap its emissions by 2026 and to reduce them by 22 percent by 2030, contingent on substantial foreign assistance. In June 2015, the Vatican released a papal encyclical, *Laudato Si: On Care for Our Common Home*,[60] in which Pope Francis urged the nations of the world to adopt a strong new global agreement to respond to climate change.

The 21st Conference of the Parties to the UN Framework Convention on Climate Change (COP-21) was held in Paris from November 30 to December 12, 2015. Prior to the conference 184 countries submitted intended nationally determined contribution (NDC) pledges outlining what they would do to control their emissions of GHGs from 2020 onwards. On December 12, 2015, 195 nations endorsed a new global climate agreement. Although the agreement had been widely anticipated, it was a historic achievement because it commits virtually every country in the world for the first time to take action to control emissions of GHGs. Although it is well recognized that the NDCs each country submitted will not, taken together, be sufficient to meet the global target of keeping the rise in global temperatures well below 2 degrees Celsius, countries intend to

---

[58] Lucy Hornby, China declares war on pollution, *Financial Times*, March 5, 2014, https://www.ft.com/content/5c9b4d18-a437-11e3-b915-00144feab7de.

[59] U.S.-China Joint Announcement on Climate Change, November 12, 2014, https://obamawhitehouse.archives.gov/the-press-office/2014/11/11/us-china-joint-announcement-climate-change.

[60] Pope Francis, *Laudato Si'*, May 24, 2015, http://w2.vatican.va/content/francesco/en/encyclicals/documents/papa-francesco_20150524_enciclica-laudato-si.html.

strengthen their commitments every five years, and a robust system of transparency and monitoring will be established to measure progress.

With opponents of climate action in control of the US Congress, the negotiators from other countries knew that the Obama administration could not make any commitment that would require Senate ratification of a treaty. Thus, the Paris Agreement was carefully crafted so that the United States could accede to it as an executive agreement without seeking any new legislation from Congress. The only legally binding portions of the agreement are the transparency provisions that do not require new legislation for the United States to comply. The NDC pledge by the United States to reduce its GHG emissions, like the emission pledges of other countries, is purely voluntary.

On September 3, 2016, the United States and China both deposited their instruments of acceptance of the Paris Agreement with the UN. Pursuant to Article 21, the Paris Agreement entered into force on November 4, 2016, thirty days after the date on which fifty-five Parties to the UNFCCC accounting for at least 55 percent of global GHG emissions deposited their instruments of ratification, acceptance, approval, or accession. As of May 2018, 176 of the 195 signatories have ratified the Paris Agreement.[61]

There is no enforcement mechanism for the NDCs in the Paris Agreement, which relies on peer pressure to encourage countries to meet their commitments. Even if all countries meet their NDCs, it will not be sufficient to reach the goal of keeping global temperature rise to 2 degrees Celsius, much less the 1.5 degree ambition.[62]

President Trump may have thought that a US pullout from the Paris Agreement would spawn further defections, but the opposite has occurred. As noted above, many subnational units of government have responded by redoubling their own efforts to control GHG emissions. China, the world's largest emitter of GHGs, has responded by insisting that it will not waver in its commitment to reduce emissions or to relax the aggressive measures it is employing to "green" its economy."[63]

Since its signing of the Paris Agreement, China has taken extraordinary measures to reduce air pollution and GHG emissions. China has long struggled to enforce its environmental laws. One chronic problem has been the highly decentralized nature of its bureaucracy—China's Ministry of Environmental Protection has only a few hundred

---

[61] United Nations, "Paris Agreement—Status of Ratification," accessed May 12, 2018, http://unfccc.int/paris_agreement/items/9444.php.

[62] J.M. Rogelj et al., "Paris Agreement Climate Proposals Need a Boost to Keep Warming Well below 2 Degrees Celsius," *Nature* 534 (2016): 631–639 (estimating that a further 25 percent reduction would be required just to reach 2 degrees).

[63] Qi Ye, dean of the Tsinghua University School of Public Policy, states that "China sees the U.S. withdrawal from Paris as an unfortunate development." But he notes that China has "reiterated its intention to honor the commitments made under the Paris Agreement. Qi Ye, "China's Perspective on the U.S. Withdrawal from the Paris Agreement," *Brookings Unpacked*, June 29, 2017, https://www.brookings.edu/blog/unpacked/2017/06/29/chinas-perspective-on-the-us-withdrawal-from-the-paris-agreement/.

staff compared to the U.S. EPA's 15,000.[64] The real power in China's environmental bureaucracy has been at the local environmental protection boards. In 2017 the Chinese government assembled 5,600 employees from various departments to become environmental inspectors who forced tens of thousands of factories to reduce their emissions or to shut down. They also shut down residential use of coal-fired heating, shifting residents to natural gas. As a result of these and other measures, the number of "heavy pollution days" in Beijing fell to twenty-three in 2017 from fifty-eight in 2013. Greenpeace estimates that average PM2.5 levels in seventy-four cities in China fell by 35 percent during the last four years. "Steel production has been halved in the major coal cities, coal banned in China's coal capital, factories closed down for failing to meet environmental targets."[65] These measures appear to be working.[66] Beijing's mayor had promised the central government in 2014 that he would reduce concentrations of tiny, but deadly particulates (PM2.5) from 90 micrograms per cubic meter to 60, a goal he failed to achieve, leading to his firing. In 2017 average concentrations of PM2.5 fell by more than 20 percent in Beijing, its most significant improvement in air quality ever.[67]

China also is dramatically expanding its investment in renewable energy. It is estimated that in 2017 China installed 54 gigawatts of new solar photovoltaic capacity, a world record for new capacity. The Chinese government has announced plans to phase out gasoline-powered motor vehicles and China is expected to account for 40 percent of all global investments in electric vehicles through the year 2040. China also has launched a national cap-and-trade system to control carbon emissions.

Conclusion

As this volume documents, the apparent trend toward the spread of constitutional democracies now appears to have been reversed. Perhaps this should not be a surprise. The late evolutionary biologist Steven Jay Gould argued that progress is not the inevitable consequence of evolution.[68] Progress is no more inexorably the product of political evolution

---

[64] See Zhao Huiyu and Robert V. Percival, "Comparative Environmental Federalism: Subsidiarity and Central Regulation in the United States and China," *Transnational Environmental Law* 6 (2017): 531–549.

[65] Kristie Needham, "In China the War on Coal Just Got Serious," *Sydney Morning Herald*, October 13, 2017, http://www.smh.com.au/world/in-china-the-war-on-coal-just-got-serious-20171011-gyyvi6.html.

[66] Steven Lee Myers, "Sign of Beijing Progress on Pollution: A Blue Sky," *New York Times*, January 12, 2008.

[67] Simon Denyer, "Beijing Wins Battle for Blue Skies—But the Poor Are Paying a Price," *Washington Post*, January 13, 2018, https://www.washingtonpost.com/world/asia_pacific/beijing-wins-battle-for-blue-skies--but-the-poor-are-paying-a-price/2018/01/12/52f04468-f6f3-11e7-91af-31ac729add94_story.html?utm_term=.bc69e227caf5.

[68] Stephen Jay Gould, *Full House: The Spread of Excellence from Plato to Darwin* (Cambridge, MA: Harvard University Press, 1996).

than it is of biological evolution, as illustrated by the demise of Francis Fukuyama's "end of history" theory that briefly was popular after the collapse of the Soviet Union.[69]

The United States has become the global outlier on climate change because of the election of a president who lost the popular vote by more than 2.8 million votes, but who champions fossil fuel interests. The Trump administration has sharply reversed federal policy on climate change. In its National Security Strategy the Obama administration had considered climate change one of the major threats facing the United States and it made achieving global consensus on the need to contain climate change a national security priority. However, when President Trump released his National Security Strategy on December 18, 2017, it contained no mention of climate change.[70] President Trump's rejection of the Paris Agreement, from which the United States cannot formally withdraw until November 4, 2020 (the day after the next presidential election), has completely isolated the United States' position on global climate policy.

Some may conclude that the dramatic measures China is now employing to reduce pollution and GHG emissions demonstrate that authoritarian governments can respond more effectively to environmental problems than constitutional democracies. But China's regime is taking these measures largely because its environmental problems have become so visible that its regime fears they may spur civil unrest. Donald Trump tweeted on November 6, 2012, that "[t]he concept of global warming was created by and for the Chinese in order to make U.S. manufacturing non-competitive." Ironically, when I toured China in 2009 lecturing about climate change for the U.S. State Department's Office of Public Diplomacy, I occasionally heard prominent Chinese intellectuals claiming that climate change was a Western plot to limit the growth of the Chinese economy.

The structure of governments does influence how well climate and other environmental policies work. China's highly decentralized government that concentrates power in local environmental protection boards (EPBs) has made it hard to enforce central government policies because local EPBs are more subject to corruption and political pressure from local polluters. U.S. environmental laws have been easier to enforce than China's because they are the product of fierce debate and compromises with regulated industries during the legislative process, while China's are handed down from on high after being rubber-stamped by the National People's Congress.

---

[69] Ishaan Tharoor, "The Man Who Declared the 'End of History' Fears for Democracy's Future," *Washington Post*, February 8, 2007, https://www.washingtonpost.com/news/worldviews/wp/2017/02/09/the-man-who-declared-the-end-of-history-fears-for-democracys-future/?utm_term=.6a24b5db99ab.

[70] Not all Trump administration officials supported the president's decision to withdraw from the Paris Agreement. Secretary of State Rex Tillerson and Secretary of Defense Jim Mattis reportedly favored staying in the Paris Agreement. In response to written questions submitted to him during his confirmation process in January 2017, U.S. secretary of defense Jim Mattis stated that "climate change is impacting stability in areas of the world where our troops are operating today." Julian Borger, "Trump Drops Climate Change from U.S. National Security Strategy," *Guardian* (UK), December 18, 2017, https://www.theguardian.com/us-news/2017/dec/18/trump-drop-climate-change-national-security-strategy.

Episodes of official climate denial, as occurred during the administration of President George W. Bush, do not last forever, but they can have severe, long-term consequences by deferring climate action until a new president takes office. But coping with the climate crisis has become such a global imperative that market forces are now driving investment in green energy on a worldwide scale that cannot be undone by any single government,[71] as illustrated by the global response to Trump's announcement that he intends to withdraw the United States from the Paris Agreement.

India, a robust democracy, also is making remarkable progress toward greening its economy, despite its leaders' long-time resistance to shifting away from fossil fuels. Indian leaders long believed that cheap coal-fired power was key to rapid development. But India now has installed 12 gigawatts of solar power capacity and it has a national goal of increasing this to 100 GW by 2022. Investments in solar and wind energy have persuaded several Indian states to abandon plans to build new coal-fired power plants, and several states are adopting energy efficiency standards for new buildings. Weeks-long episodes of toxic smog in December 2017 have increased public support for anti-pollution measures.

Review of the history of environmental law indicates that when pollution problems become public health crises, governments are forced to act. As the horrendous consequences of the climate crisis become more visible, law and policy are evolving in creative and innovative ways to respond to the problem at subnational levels of government in the U.S. federal system and throughout the world, even in legal systems with very different structures, histories, and traditions. The precise language of constitutional provisions addressing environmental protection do not seem nearly as important in shaping climate policy as the views of the leader of the executive branch. But even with a climate denier as president of the United States, the checks and balances included in the U.S. constitutional framework will limit the president's ability to roll back climate policy.

President Trump's irrational withdrawal from the Paris Agreement has isolated the United States, but it has not tempered global zeal to respond to the climate crisis. The Paris Agreement is only the start, and it is expected that countries will strengthen their NDCs after the "stocktake" that will occur beginning in 2023 and every five years thereafter. The Agreement allows any country to revise its NDC at any time "with a view to enhancing its level of ambition."[72] It is open to debate whether this "review and ratchet" approach is a one-way ratchet to strengthen commitments, or whether it can be used to relax previous NDCs. The NDCs are not legally binding, and some argue that revisions

---

[71] Even companies who have long promoted climate denial are now realizing that the tide has changed. In May 2017, 62 percent of ExxonMobil shareholders defied company management to vote in favor of a shareholders' climate resolution. The resolution asks the company to report on the financial risks the company faces as nations slash fossil fuel use in response to the Paris Agreement. Shareholders of Occidental Petroleum and PPL, Pennsylvania's largest electric utility, approved similar resolutions. Marianne Lavelle, "Exxon Shareholders Approve Climate Resolution: 62% Vote for Disclosure," *Inside Climate News*, May 31, 2017, https://insideclimatenews.org/news/31052017/exxon-shareholder-climate-change-disclosure-resolution-approved.

[72] Paris Agreement, Article 4.1.

in either direction should be permitted to avoid deterring countries from making ambitious initial commitments. Article 4.3 provides that a "Party's successive nationally determined contribution will represent a progression beyond the Party's then current nationally determined contribution and reflect its highest possible ambition." The non-regression principle that is emerging in global environmental law would support the one-way ratchet approach.[73]

Political theory explains the difficulty of organizing collective action to combat environmental problems. These difficulties are magnified by the global scope of the climate crisis. Thus, we can expect that the climate crisis will continue to challenge constitutional democracies, and the responses of these governments may continue to be belated and inadequate, particularly when a climate denier is unexpectedly elected to run the executive branch. However, the Paris Agreement, while far from perfect, and the world's reaction to President Trump's announced intention to make the United States the only country in the world to reject it, demonstrate that progress is being, and will continue, to be made, despite the climate denial of the current U.S. president.

---

[73] Michel Prieur, "Non-regression in Environmental Law," *Sapiens* 5 (2012): 53–56, http://journals.openedition.org/sapiens/1405.

IV Observations

35 The Crumbling of European Democracy
J.H.H. Weiler

The New Democratic Deficit

Talking about a "Democracy Deficit" in and of Europe went out of fashion sometime in the mid-2000s. Historically, such talk was principally linked to the gap between the rapidly increasing spheres of competences and governance powers of the European Union and a concomitant lack of powers of what was perceived as its principal democratizing institution—the European Parliament. That gap constituted the "Deficit." But, the powers of the European Parliament were progressively enhanced in successive revisions of the Treaties constituting the European Union, not least in the last such revision, the Treaty of Lisbon, which itself was but the famous European Constitution repackaged differently. Now that the Parliament (representing the "peoples") had become a veritable co-legislator alongside the Council of Ministers (representing the Member States) the gap was deemed closed. Any continued talk of a European "Democracy Deficit" could be dismissed as anachronistic at best, or as hypocritical demagoguery of the extreme anti-European Left or Right. For, in the last of the Golden Years leading up to the 2008 crisis, the comfort zone of the centrist European *classe politique* conflated European Integration with liberal democracy. To believe in one was to believe in the other. To reject one was to reject the other.

It was, indeed, a comfortable comfort zone. For Europe did deliver prosperity and material deserts. There is nothing like prosperity and material deserts to legitimate any political status quo and thus, willfully or otherwise, a blind eye was turned by this *classe politique* to the hollowness of the democratic structures of the European Union and to long-term processes that were gnawing at the foundations of the political order of the Member States.

Some tell-tale signs did appear on the wall even prior to the present crisis, notably the rejection through referenda by the peoples of France and the Netherlands of the European Constitution in 2005, and prior popular rejections by the peoples of Denmark and Ireland of earlier Treaty revisions. These contretemps were dismissed with that well-tried Marxist notion of "false consciousness": Those people simply "didn't understand." So although, constitutionally speaking, these No votes were meant to tank the projects voted upon, the Danish and the Irish were unceremoniously asked to vote again (or else …), which they duly did, apparently having seen the light. And the French and the Dutch (and with them the rest of Europe) were served the same constitutional dish albeit differently garnished (a la Lisbon) though this time round making sure there were no referenda.

Another early sign that something was not how it should be in the House that Monnet et al. built was the declining voter turnout in elections to the European Parliament. This was really puzzling since the early disappointing figures (compared to turnout in Member State elections) were usually explained by the lack of power of the European Parliament. As the Parliament gained powers it was expected that voter turnout would follow suit. But the opposite happened so that in 2014 post-Lisbon elections, voter turnout was at a historical low. This time, too, the European ostrich stuck its head in the sand and grumbled about the need better to explain. But suddenly those little leaks in the liberal democracy/European Integration dike have cracked, and the leaks have become gushing torrents.

There is, thus, something tragicomic in the recent eruptions and cries of woe about democracy in Europe prompted by the emergence into the mainstream of powerful irredentist forces, democratically elected, whose rejection of liberal democracy is wrapped with a profound Euroscepticism. And it is not possible to dismiss such as the "as yet politically immature" Eastern Europeans (in explaining, say Poland and Hungary) when facing the phenomena of Wilders and Le Pen and AfD, and Kurtz, and Salvini and 5 Stelle all present, kicking and wildly popular in the heart of Old Europe.

The institutional reaction to a veritable crisis that can no longer be solved by pretending it is not there or explained away by false consciousness is most interesting in that it affirms the nexus between crises of democracy (most notable at the Member State level) and the fortunes of the European construct. The strategy, the only strategy, of addressing the crisis is a myriad of reform proposals of the European Union. Within the Member States the principal strategy has been more or less explicit triangulation toward the policy of the "populist" forces. The gist of these proposed reforms is to equip the Union with better tools to address the present (and future) economic crisis. The implicit assumption is that popular (typically characterized as "populist") discontent is material in nature and that equipping the Union with better tools to return to and consolidate prosperity is all that is needed.

There is far less willingness at the state level to do some soul-searching that will seek answers in processes that antedate the 2008 economic meltdown and the more recent "immigration crisis." And at the European level there is an equal reluctance to critically examine some of the foundations of European governance. Instead there is a flight to the safe zone of legitimation through "outputs" and "results" (the modern equivalent of the Roman "bread and circus").

It is obvious that I believe that the very real present crisis of democracy in and of Europe is but an eruption of long-term processes and that the present circumstances (economy, migration) merely acted as catalysts. I first suggest some long-term processes that in different ways lead to the present condition. I do not claim that this is the only way to describe and understand the current circumstance but I hope to persuade the reader that it offers some insight that the purely economic or even political prism lack. Then I will explain the depletion of legitimacy resources of Europe and the Union that aggravate the challenge of leadership in addressing the crises.

The Hollowing of European Democracy

Three processes began as reactions to the Second World War and have progressed over the last decades, which help explain the current circumstances.

The First Process: for reasons that are quite understandable, the very word "patriotism" became "unprintable" after World War II, notably in Western Europe. Fascist regimes (among others), by abusing the word and the concept, had "burned" it from our collective consciousness. And in many ways this has been a positive thing. But we also pay a high price for having banished this word—and the sentiment it expresses—from our psychopolitical vocabulary. Patriotism also has a noble side: the discipline of love, the duty to take care of one's homeland and people, of accepting our civic responsibility toward the collective. In reality, true patriotism is the opposite of fascism: "We do not belong to the State, it is the State that belongs to us." This kind of patriotism is an integral part of the republican form of democracy.

Today, we may call ourselves the Italian or French "Republic," but our democracies are no longer truly republican. There's the state, there's the government, and then there's "us." The Republican form of democracy has become Schumpeterian. Ours have become democracies who are as remote as are shareholders of a large enterprise. If the directorate of this enterprise called "the Republic" does not produce political and material dividends, we change managers with a vote during a meeting of shareholders called "elections." If there is anything that does not work in our society, we go to the "directors"—as we do, for example, when our internet connection isn't working: "We paid (our taxes), and look at the terrible service they're giving us . . ." The state is always the one responsible. Never us. It's a clientelistic democracy that not only takes away our own responsibility toward our society, toward our country, but also undermines the very notion of individual political responsibility from our understanding of the human condition. It does more: there is not only no responsibility—there is no control in this non-republican form of democracy. The possibility of replacing the government in elections is indispensable for democracy, but it is a minimal form of control over one's destiny and that of one's family and neighbors. Changing the gardener is a far cry from tending one's garden. Schumpeter famously extoled this form of material "democracy." Normatively I find it deplorable. But democracy in this context is not just a system of governance. It is a foundational *heimat* of the post-World War II generations. When our democracy becomes "hollowed out" in the accurate and damning term used by the late Peter Mair, the loss of faith in democratic institutions and democratic processes is fast to follow, and with it that security that democracy as mental and spiritual *heimat* promise shatters. Deep fear sets in, exploitable by even worse forms of "democracy" such as the oxymoronic "illiberal" democracy.

The Second Process came, once again, as a reaction to the War, and is paradoxical. We've accepted, both at the national and international levels, a serious and irreversible obligation rooted in our constitutions to protect the fundamental rights of individuals, even against the political tyranny of the majority. At a more general level, our political-juridical vocabulary has become a discourse of rights. The rights of an Italian citizen are protected by Italian courts, and, above all, by the Constitutional Court. But also by the Court of Justice of the EU in Luxembourg, and—again—by the European Court of Human Rights in Strasbourg. And in different variants this is so in just about in all our Member States. It's enough to make your head spin.

Just think about how common it has become, in the political discourse of today, to speak more and more about "rights." It's enormously important. I would never want to live in a country in which fundamental rights are not effectively defended. And we lawyers in particular celebrate such as the crowning achievement of our legal systems and legal culture. We are the Rights Generation. But here too—as with the banishment of patriotism—we pay a dear price.

First and foremost, the noble culture of rights does as we proudly proclaim put the individual at the center, but little by little, almost without realizing it, it turns him or her into a self-centered individual. It is always a discourse of entitlement, rarely of civic duties. It is always what we deserve, the deserts owed us, rarely, if you discount taxes, what we civically owe.

There is, however, a second effect to this "culture of rights"—which is a framework all Europeans have in common—a kind of flattening of political and cultural specificity, of one's own unique national identity. To explain this I need to digress and present my understanding of the most fundamental of all rights, the one that features first and foremost in so many of our constitutional documents—human dignity.

The notion of human dignity—the fact that we have been created in the image of God (or the secular equivalent)—contains, at one and the same time, two facets. On the one hand, it means that we are all equal in our fundamental human dignity: men and women, rich and poor, Italians and Germans, Muslims, Christians and Jews. On the other hand, recognizing human dignity means accepting that each of us is an entire universe, distinct and different from any other person. We are not fungible. Our uniqueness is, on this understanding, as essential to our dignity as our equality. When either of these elements of diversity is diminished or derided, we rebel. It is easy to understand the rebellion when our equality is violated. But the failure or refusal to recognize and respect our uniqueness is, normatively, equally offensive and psychologically equally humiliating. It offends our dignity. The uniqueness facet of our dignity plays an important role to our very sense of existential meaning, which, I believe, we are hardwired desperately to seek. We all ask, explicitly or otherwise, what is the meaning of our being, of our existence. Of course, it is up to each of us through our actions and emotions to give meanings to our lives. But if we lose our uniqueness, that meaning is diminished. Does it make a difference to a flock of birds if there is one more or less? It makes all the difference to the universe we occupy if there is one or more less. That is, indeed, why we privilege human dignity above all.

As humans we are social beings. The social is the context in which we live our lives be it family, tribe, or the modern liberal (nonracial, multicultural) nation. The two facets of dignity play out also in the context of the social, which brings us back to the culture of rights. The culture of rights—universal, pan-European—are the values we share, across family, tribe, nation, and state. At the same time, the ubiquity and celebration of such cannot but help flatten the uniqueness of collective identities, a flattening that is aggravated because normatively, let us admit it, the only form of patriotism permitted is "constitutional patriotism"—everything else is suspect for the reasons I outlined above. Let me somewhat polemically argue that the only thing we may unashamedly take pride in our state and nation is our football team. The essential balance of dignity—the universal and the unique—in our social context has been seriously skewed—and if I am right about the metaphysical significance of dignity (personal and collective) this is not a trivial loss. Here is another disorienting lost *heimat* grist to the mill of atavists and crypto-fascists.

The Third Process: secularization. Let me be clear: this observation is not an evangelical rebuke. I do not judge a person based on his or her faith or lack thereof. And even though, for me, it's impossible to imagine the world without the Lord—The Holy Blessed Be He—I also know many religious people who are morally odious, and many atheists of the highest moral character.

The social and political importance of secularism is in the fact that a voice that was at one time universal and ubiquitous, a voice in which the emphasis was on duty and not only rights, on personal responsibility in the face of what happens to us, our neighbors, our society, and not the instinctive appeal to public institutions, has all but disappeared from social praxis.

This process also began with World War II. Who among us, after having seen the mountains of shoes from millions of assassinated children at Auschwitz, didn't ask the question: God, where were you?

It has taken decades for these three processes to mature and produce now their "sour grapes" (Is. 5:2). We see the impact everywhere in Western Europe, not least in matters regarding the European Union.

Three Legitimacy Crises

What, then of Europe? We have seen that the challenges to liberal democracy are typically connected to some profound form of Euroscepticism. It seems as if instead of shoring the democracy up, European integration is pulling it down. The explanation is, I think, in the collapse of legitimacy of European Governance.

I would like to suggest the three most important types or forms of legitimacy that have been central to the discussion of European integration. Process (or input/throughput) Legitimacy—in the current circumstance can be, with some simplification, be synonymized with democracy. It is easier put in the negative: to the extent that the European mode of governance departs from the habits and practices of democracy as understood in the Member States, its legitimacy will be compromised. Result (or output) Legitimacy—again simplifying somewhat, would be that modern versions of bread and circus. As long as the Union delivers "the goods"—prosperity, stability, security—it will enjoy a legitimacy that derives from a subtle combination of success per se, of success in realizing its objectives, and of contentment with those results. There is no better way to legitimate a war than win it. This is compared to Telos Legitimacy or Political Messianism, whereby legitimacy is gained neither by process nor output but by promise, the promise of an attractive Promised Land. I illustrate the collapse of all three forms of legitimacy in the current European circumstance.

PROCESS LEGITIMACY. As regards process legitimacy, there is the persistent, chronic, troubling Democracy Deficit, which cannot be talked away.

First, despite twenty-five years or more of European citizenship, no veritable European demos, a primordial condition for democracy, has emerged. This became clear in the hard years of the financial crisis. Germans and Dutch and Finns were not saying: "A bailout is the wrong policy." Many of them were saying, why should we, Germans, or Dutch, or Finns, help those lazy Italians or Portuguese or Greeks who in the shameful words of one Euro leader were busy spending their money on women and wine: a visible manifestation of the No-Demos thesis of Europe's democracy crisis.

Second, there are failures of democracy that simply make it difficult to speak of governance by and of the people. The manifestations of the so-called democracy deficit are persistent, and no endless repetition of the powers of the European Parliament will remove them. In essence it is the inability of the Union to develop structures and processes that adequately replicate or "translate" at the Union level even the imperfect habits of governmental control, parliamentary accountability, and administrative responsibility that are practiced with different modalities in the various Member States. Make no mistake: it is perfectly understood that the Union is not a state. But it is in the business of governance and has taken over extensive areas previously in the hands of the Member States. In some critical areas, such as the interface of the Union with the international trading system, the competences of the Union are exclusive. In others they are dominant. Democracy is not about states. Democracy is about the exercise of public power—and the Union exercises a huge amount of public power. We live by the credo that any exercise of public power has to be legitimated democratically, and it is exactly here that process legitimacy fails.

In essence, the two primordial features of any functioning democracy are missing—the grand principles of accountability and representation.

As regards accountability, even the basic condition of representative democracy that at election time the citizens "can throw the scoundrels out"—that is replace the government—does not operate in Europe. The form of European governance, governance without government, is, and will remain for considerable time, perhaps forever such that there is no "government" to throw out. Dismissing the Commission by Parliament (or approving the appointment of the Commission President) is not quite the same, not even remotely so. And the hostility with which the Spitzenkandidaten exercise was met by the Member States does not auger well from that quarter.

Likewise, at the most primitive level of democracy, there is simply no moment in the civic calendar of Europe where the citizen can influence directly the outcome of any policy choice facing the Community and Union in the way that citizens can when choosing between parties that offer sharply distinct programs at the national level. The political color of the European Parliament only very weakly gets translated into the legislative and administrative output of the Union.

The Political Deficit, to use the felicitous phrase of Renaud Dehousse, is at the core of the Democracy Deficit. The Commission, by its self-understanding linked to its very ontology, cannot be "partisan" in a right-left sense, neither can the Council, by virtue of the haphazard political nature of its composition. This of course does not mean that the Commission is politically "neutral." Such neutrality is impossible. So any decision is obviously ideologically laden. But it is always below the surface. It is not openly and accountably a policy at the service of an ideological commitment. Democracy normally must have some meaningful mechanism for expression of voter preference predicated on choice among options, typically informed by stronger or weaker ideological orientation. That is an indispensable component of politics. Democracy without politics is an oxymoron. And yet that is not only Europe, but it is a feature of Europe—the "nonpartisan" nature of the Commission—which is celebrated. The stock phrase found in endless student textbooks and the like, that the Supranational Commission vindicates the European interest, whereas the intergovernmental Council is a clearing house for Member State interest, is, at best, naïve. Does the "European interest" not necessarily involve political and ideological choices? At times explicit, but always implicit?

Thus the two most primordial norms of democracy, the principle of accountability and the principle of representation, are compromised in the very structure and process of the

Union. It often serves governments (the executive branch) to play the game of European ideological neutrality, thus getting "cover" from Brussels for politics that would be unacceptable in national politics.

Two deeper and longer-term trends give expression to the above. The first is the extraordinary decline in voter participation in elections for the European Parliament. In Europe as a whole the rate of participation is below 45 percent, with several countries, notably in the east, with a rate below 30 percent. The correct comparison is, of course, with political elections to national parliaments where the numbers are considerably higher. What is striking about these figures is, as noted above, that the decline coincides with a continuous shift in powers to the European Parliament, which today is a veritable co-legislator with the Council. The more powers the European Parliament, supposedly the vox populi, has gained, the greater popular indifference to it seems to have developed.

RESULT LEGITIMACY. In analyzing the legitimacy (and mobilizing force) of the European Union, in particular against the background of its persistent democracy deficit, political and social science has indeed long used the distinction between process legitimacy and outcome legitimacy. The legitimacy of the Union more generally and the Commission more specifically, even if suffering from deficiencies in the state democratic sense, are said to rest on the results achieved—in the economic, social, and, ultimately, political realms. The idea hearkens back to the most classic functionalist and neo-functionalist theories.

I do not want to take issue with the implied normativity of this position—a latter day panem et circenses approach to democracy, which at some level at least could be considered quite troubling. It is with its empirical reality that I want to take some issue. I do not think that outcome legitimacy explains all or perhaps even most of the mobilizing force of the European construct. But whatever role it played it is dependent on the panem. Rightly or wrongly, the economic woes of Europe, which are manifest in the Euro crisis are attributed to the European construct. So when there suddenly is no bread, and certainly no cake, we are treated to a different kind of circus whereby the citizens' growing indifference is turning to hostility, and the ability of Europe to act as a political mobilizing force seems not only spent, but even reversed. The worst way to legitimate a war is to lose it, and Europe is suddenly seen not as an icon of success but as an emblem of austerity, thus in terms of its promise of prosperity, failure. If success breeds legitimacy, failure, even if wrongly allocated, leads to the opposite.

Thus, not surprisingly there is a seemingly contagious spread of "Anti-Europeanism" in national politics. What was once in the province of fringe parties on the far Right and Left has inched its way to more central political forces. The "Question of Europe" as a central issue in political discourse was for long regarded as an "English disease." There is a growing contagion in Member States in north and south, east and west, where political capital is to be made among non-fringe parties by anti-European advocacy. The spillover effect of this phenomenon is the shift of mainstream parties in this direction as a way of countering the gains at their flanks. If we are surprised by this it is only because we seem to have airbrushed out of our historical consciousness the rejection of the so-called European Constitution, an understandable amnesia since it represented a defeat of the collective political class in Europe by the vox populi, albeit not speaking through, but instead giving a slap in the face to, the European institutions.

At some level the same could have been said ten and even twenty years ago. The Democracy Deficit is not new—it is enduring. And how did Europe legitimate itself before it scored its great successes of the first decades?

MESSIANIC LEGITIMACY. As I hinted above, at the conceptual level there is a third type of legitimation, which, in my view, played for a long time a much larger role than is currently acknowledged. In fact, I believe, it has been decisive to the legitimacy of Europe and to the positive response of both the political class and citizens at large. I also argue that it is a key to a crucial element in the Union's political culture. It is a legitimacy rooted in the "*politically messianic.*"

In political "messianism," the justification for action and its mobilizing force, derive not from process, as in classical democracy, or from result and success, but from the ideal pursued, the destiny to be achieved, the "Promised Land" waiting at the end of the road. Indeed, in messianic visions the end always trumps the means.

Mark Mazower, in *The Dark Continent*, his brilliant and original history and historiography of twentieth-century Europe, insightfully shows how the Europe of monarchs and emperors that entered World War I was often rooted in a political messianic narrative in various states (in Germany, and Italy, and Russia, and even Britain and France). It then oscillated after the War toward new democratic orders, that is to process legitimacy, which then oscillated back into new forms of political messianism in fascism and communism. As the tale is usually told, after World War II Europe of the west was said to oscillate back to democracy and process legitimacy. It is here that I want to point to an interesting quirk, not often noted.

On the one hand, the western states, which were later to become the Member States of the European Union, became resolutely democratic, their patriotism rooted in their new constitutional values, narratives of glory abandoned and even ridiculed, and messianic notions of the state losing all appeal. Famously, former empires, once defended with repression and blood, were now abandoned with zeal.

And yet, their common venture, European integration, was in my reading a political messianic venture par excellence, the messianic becoming a central feature of its original and enduring political culture. The mobilizing force and principle legitimating feature was the vision offered, the dream dreamt, the promise of a better future. Unlike output democracy, which is measured by concrete results, messianism is built on a dream, and one often couched in metaphysical goods rather than material ones. The messianic vision found its expression in the Schumann Declaration, which offered a compelling dream of peace, prosperity, and a different form of relationships among peoples and states particularly potent in the aftermath of World War II. The functionalist messianic vision produced a culture of praxis, achievement, ever-expanding agendas and justification of such even if not corresponding to the habits of democracy of and within the Member States.

But part of the very phenomenology of political messianism is that it always collapses as a mechanism for mobilization and legitimation. It obviously collapses when the messianic project fails, when the revolution does not come. But interestingly, and more germane to the narrative of European integration, even when successful it sows its seeds of collapse. At one level the collapse is inevitable, part of the very phenomenology of messianic project. Reality is always more complicated, challenging, banal, and ultimately less satisfying than the dream that preceded it. The result is not only absence of mobilization and legitimation, but actual rancor. When, as we saw, output and input legitimacy are in shreds too, the collapse is a veritable *debelatio*.

Democracy was not part of the original DNA of European integration. It still feels like a foreign implant. With the collapse of its original political messianism, the alienation we are now witnessing is only to be expected. And thus, when failure hits as in the euro crisis, when the panem is gone, all sources of legitimacy suddenly, simultaneously collapse.

So, thus, not in the immediate—financial crisis/immigration—are we to look for the roots of the current challenges to, and disappointment with, our cherished forms of liberal democracy, but in the long term the hollowing processes both pan-European and within the Union governance itself into which the so-called populist forces were able to enter. Populist because popular, and popular because corresponding to the real needs that people feel and republican democracy require—needs to which we, the bien pensants of the comfortable center, were happy to shut our eyes.

36 Comparing Right-Wing and Left-Wing Populism
Mark Tushnet*

THAT MOST ACADEMIC writing on the apparent recent upsurge in "populism" is critical of the development is perhaps unsurprising. Academics attentive to such developments tend to be liberal cosmopolitans to a greater or lesser degree, and populisms are movements that set their faces against both liberalism and cosmopolitanism. Yet, the movements are, in my view, not all the same. Specifically, there seem to be what I will label, with some inaccuracy for purposes of exposition, left-wing and right-wing versions of populism currently under discussion. (In saying "currently under discussion," I mean to indicate that I adopt a nominalist definition rather than a conceptual definition of populism—"populism" is for me a list of those political movements most scholars describe as populist.) Most academic writing has focused on the right-wing versions. That writing generates critiques of what the authors describe as generic populism, critiques that the authors then apply to left-wing populism. It seems to me, though, that the critiques are mostly concerned with the "right-wing-ness" of the object of study, but present themselves in politically neutral terms—presumably because direct political criticism would seem unscholarly. Bring the left-wing versions directly into view, though, and we might see matters more clearly. Both right-wing and left-wing populist movements are

* I thank Bojan Bugarič for comments on a draft of this essay, which also draws upon conversations with a larger number of people than can be profitably listed here.

anti-liberal and anti-cosmopolitan, with right-wing movements more comprehensive in their anti-cosmopolitanism than some left-wing movements. The movements share these attributes because the attributes flow from roughly the same sorts of reasons.[1] Yet, left-wing populism shows that neither anti-liberalism nor anti-cosmopolitanism are politically problematic in themselves. Rather, the manifestations of one or the other (mostly, from my point of view, the right-wing versions) are open essentially *only* to direct political criticism.[2]

One preliminary problem with discussions of contemporary populisms is that it is not entirely clear what their staying power is. That is, many, though not all, appear to be the vehicles for charismatic politicians to achieve political power, perhaps merely for the sake of exercising that power (and obtaining the benefits, legitimate and corrupt, accruing to office). We cannot know whether or the extent to which a populism strongly associated with a charismatic leader will persist after he or she leaves the scene. Venezuela probably provides the strongest example so far, and the case is at best equivocal: the charismatic Hugo Chávez's successor Nicolás Maduro has attempted to sustain an authoritarian version of populism, but it is not yet clear that he will succeed. Perhaps we are observing not much more than the ordinary ebb and flow of politics, with populisms representing "long tails" on the left and right, but not located on some other dimension of politics. If so, contemporary populisms may have no implications for democracy in the long term.

Populisms might have staying power through the elements of their programs that involve constitutional change. One might think that such changes are likelier to be more "sticky" than populisms' policy agendas. Here too, though, one must be cautious. Stickiness depends on the amendment rule and, sometimes, on informal norms about the occasions when amendments are appropriate.[3] Whether populist-promoted amendments are sticky will therefore depend on the extent to which populism is repudiated. And, notably, a sufficiently determined repudiation can ignore the amendment rule altogether, invoking strong but well-established versions of the idea of constituent power. Again, we do not have enough experience to know whether these amendments will in fact be sticky.

---

[1] The left-wing populist movements that are not comprehensively anti-cosmopolitan have modernized the idea of international proletarian solidarity, seeing themselves as linked across national boundaries with, for example, Indigenous people or workers everywhere, but all still opposed to cosmopolitan elites.

[2] Although evaluation of economic programs lies beyond my competence, I feel compelled to note my belief that, though the programs of neither left-wing nor right-wing populism are likely to satisfy the voters who support those programs, the chance that right-wing populism will do is slightly lower than the chance that left-wing populism will. The weakness of right-wing populism lies in the difficulties of delivering on the promise of a robust social safety net supported by redistributive taxation; the obstacle for left-wing populism is its weakness in the face of its commitment to an internationalized economy.

[3] Populist-promoted constitutional amendments are likely to have already breached, and perhaps thereby changed, those norms. If so, only the amendment rule would matter.

Developing Criteria for Evaluating Whether Populism Is Anti-liberal

I begin with a brief description of the "liberalism" that plays a large part in what follows, deferring a discussion of cosmopolitanism. Or, more precisely, I begin by insisting that there is a range of different but reasonable specifications or institutional instantiations of liberalism (which I refer to throughout as the "range of specifications"). In all specifications, though, laws must be supported by popular consent elicited through reasonably reliable methods (of which reasonably free and fair elections are the core but not only method); the people must have the opportunity, both in form as protected by law and in practice, to express their views on matters of public concern; civil society organizations, including religious organizations, must have reasonable opportunities to sustain "spaces" within which opinions can be shaped independent of public direction; the courts administering the laws must have reasonable guarantees of independence from direct political control, again both formally and in practice (no "telephone justice" as occurs in the People's Republic of China) and from influences that strongly incline judges to rule in ways favored by governing elites. There may be other requirements, but these examples are sufficient for present purposes.

Many institutions can instantiate these elements of liberalism. Elections or referenda, or even formal consultative processes, might be used to elicit popular consent; judges might be chosen by judicial nominating commissions or by more openly political processes; once chosen they must have guarantees of tenure such as fixed terms and processes for removing them only for unprofessional conduct administered with no more than a modicum of direct political involvement (sometimes constrained as much by norms as by institutional arrangements). In this sense liberalism's institutional requirements are not terribly stringent. All that is required is that the institutions fall within the range of reasonable alternative specifications.

The foregoing description of the range of specifications suggests that "liberalism" does not impose stringent requirements for institutional arrangements. Yet, the requirements are in another sense quite stringent, to the extent that they require more than merely formal opportunities to express views, formal protections of judicial independence, and the like. Seen from the latter perspective even core examples of actually existing liberal states fall short of the ideal. For that reason we cannot demand complete satisfaction of institutional requirements for a political regime to count as liberal. We must use a metric allowing for shortfalls. Populist anti-liberalism occurs when a populist regime falls outside the range of specifications or falls too far short of liberal ideals to qualify as liberal. We might say that some contemporary left-wing populists are opposed to the liberalism of the elites governing their nations but not opposed to liberalism as such; that is true as well of some but not all right-wing populists.

An Important Objection

One objection to the relaxed view of the range of specifications is illustrated by concerns sometimes expressed about certain amendments to Latin American constitutions. Those amendments shift from a rule that presidents can serve only one term to the rule prevailing elsewhere in the world in presidentialist constitutions, that presidents can serve two terms. On their face, two-term provisions fall well within the range of specifications; indeed, one might plausibly contend that a one-term limit presses against the boundaries of reasonableness. Those seeing such amendments as a threat to liberalism suggest, though, that Latin American constitutions and, perhaps more important, Latin American political traditions concentrate power over lawmaking (through decrees) in the executive. The one-term limitation compensates for the concentration of power; critics suggest that in such systems a president's ability to reshape the law over the course of two terms poses a real threat to liberalism's stability.

Comparing the mechanisms for choosing Supreme Court justices in Canada and the United States provides another illustration. The formal rule in Canada is that the prime minister has complete discretion in making appointments subject only to the requirement that three of the Court's nine justices must be from Quebec. That formal system, though, is supplemented by extremely strong norms of deference to professional judgments about potential appointees' ability. The prime minister would act inappropriately, and suffer politically, by departing from those norms. Were the United States to adopt the Canadian system of complete executive discretion, we can readily imagine that disaster would follow, because there is little reason to think that, at least in the short to medium run, informal norms would constrain the president's choices.

The objection can be generalized: Consider two institutional specifications for judicial independence, eliciting consent, or supporting civil society, instantiated in different polities. The institutions might be supported in the first polity by a set of informal norms and traditions that might not transfer readily were the polity to adopt the institutions in the second—even though both institutional specifications fall within the range of reasonableness. I suggest that discussions of constitutional changes that replace one institution ordinarily within the range of specifications with another such institution should focus on whether, and the degree to which, the old institutions are supported by non-institutional factors such as norms and traditions that are unlikely to carry over to support the new institution.

The Origins of Contemporary Populism

Contemporary populism originated in the political economy of the early twenty-first century, and in the party structures associated with that political economy. Governing elites offered citizens a social and economic program after 1945 in Western Europe, 1989 in central and eastern Europe, and the 1990s in Latin America: The political system would produce what I will call international social welfare constitutionalism. The social welfare component had several elements: regularly increasing material well-being spread across all economic levels, with only occasional and temporary setbacks; a reasonably thick social safety net to help people weather those setbacks; a rough equality of sacrifice through taxes and burden-sharing in the ordinary course and when extraordinary events disrupted social functioning; and a weaker commitment to an even rougher sense of equality of benefit, constraining grossly disproportionate allocation of gains from economic growth. The international component was the increasing integration of national economies into a global economy that could provide the resources to support the social welfare component. The constitutional component was a system of political organization that had the capacity to deliver these elements of social welfare. Party systems were organized around the elite consensus, with the main political parties offering different versions of international social welfare constitutionalism.

Populism emerged when—and because—political elites failed to implement this promised program. On the constitutional level, domestic politics froze into patterns that made it impossible to respond with the flexibility needed to fulfill the promises of social welfare in dynamic economic conditions. (The US term for the phenomenon is "gridlock.") Political elites became corrupt, both in the ordinary venal sense that they used their power to enhance their personal wealth and in the political sense that they used political power to entrench themselves. In a relatively early contribution framed in terms of communication rather than constitutional theory Manuel Castells showed how the need to finance campaigns and political parties under modern conditions conduced to the latter form of corruption.[4] As political elites became increasingly cosmopolitan, self-reproducing, insulated from economic stress, and self-satisfied, they became increasingly indifferent to fulfilling the social welfare promises they had made. Not only did inequality increase, but the promised increase in material well-being for ordinary citizens did not occur. Elites dealt with the disruptions occasioned by globalization either by doing nothing because of gridlock or by adopting austerity programs that left more and more gaps in the social safety net. The range of policy options offered by the main political parties narrowed significantly.

Political entrepreneurs on the Left and the Right—outsiders to the political elites—noted an opportunity and moved to exploit it by offering populist programs, sometimes by forming new political parties, sometimes by asserting themselves within the existing parties by offering programs substantially outside the range of the elite consensus. What is common to populism is an attack, in my view largely justified, on failed and corrupt political elites. For the attacks to succeed—from either direction—the failed political elites have to be uprooted from their positions. Often this requires constitutional change. To put the point in its most general form, often constitutions must be changed

---

[4] For a recent summary of Castells's analysis, see Manuel Castells, *Communication Power* (New York: Oxford University Press, 2013), 240–264.

to eliminate some of the veto points that the failed elites have exploited. Sometimes this might mean creating a unicameral legislature by eliminating the body's upper house. Sometimes it might mean concentrating power in the executive. And, because courts are often one of those veto points, sometimes it might mean altering the composition of the courts, the mechanisms by which judges are selected, and their jurisdiction. Courts tend to be dominated by people drawn from the political class, and they are designed to make institutional transformation slow. Seeking to transform the courts, while not an inevitable component of efforts to displace failed political elites, may well be a sensible strategy.

The implication is straightforward: treating efforts to transform the courts as a strong point—"assaults on judicial independence"—against populism is a defense of the failed status quo, not a politically neutral defense of a central component of every good constitution. (In its best form, the argument against institutional transformation is something like this: the costs of transformation, such as a reduction in judicial independence, are so great that the failed status quo is preferable. I think it not unreasonable for populists to disagree, given their—again, often accurate—understanding of the costs of persisting with the status quo.)

Right-Wing and Left-Wing Populism Compared

As I have noted, the populist attack takes the form of anti-liberalism and anti-cosmopolitanism, but the right-wing and left-wing versions of the attack differ in important ways. Extracting positions on political economy from the statements of ambitious and entrepreneurial politicians is of course difficult. No one would contend, for example, that Viktor Orbán, much less Donald Trump, has a systematic account of political economy from which they derive their policies. So, it is not so much Orbán's famous statement that he rejects liberalism that matters, but rather the concrete policies his government has put in place. Similar points could be made about other populist leaders and their programs. It is hard to know, for example, what Senator Bernie Sanders means when he says that he is a socialist.

With that qualification, I believe we can characterize right-wing populism, as many have, as a movement of democracy against all versions of liberalism considered as a political theory premised upon ideas about the inherent equality of all people. Right-wing populist programs include sharply restricting the ordinary operations of civil society organizations, limiting judicial independence, and (having displaced the previous political elite) entrenching the populist party in every institution of government. As David Landau and Rosalind Dixon and Kim Lane Scheppele have pointed out, almost every element in these programs has its analogues in institutions in liberal polities.[5] For example,

---

[5] David Landau and Rosalind Dixon, "Competitive Democracy and the Constitutional Minimum Core," in *Assessing Constitutional Performance*, ed. Tom Ginsburg and Aziz Huq (New York: Cambridge University Press, 2016), 268–292; Kim L. Scheppele, "The Rule of Law and the Frankenstate: Why Governance Checklists Do Not Work," *Governance* 26, no. 4 (2013): 559–62.

rules against foreign support of domestic civil society organizations, if not common, are not unknown in core liberal democracies—and Russian interference in US elections has led to calls for strengthening those rules. Right-wing populist programs, though, accumulate these and similar regulations in ways that take them outside the range of reasonable specifications. The economic programs of right-wing populists, though, are often entirely compatible with the free-market commitments associated with classical economic liberals. For them, if domestic political economy went off the rails, it was because it extended social welfare guarantees "too broadly," meaning, once again roughly, to those who were not truly part of the nation's organically defined people.

Again with the qualification that left-wing populist leaders are not systematic political theorists, I believe that left-wing populism is different. Its program is, in my view, to realize one specification of liberalism—the social-welfare constitutionalism that political elites promised. They reject classical economic liberalism as a means for realizing the social-welfare components of that promise, but generally accept political liberalism's commitment to equality. Left-wing populists understand (or believe) that the institutional arrangements they inherited are one important reason that social-welfare constitutionalism has failed. In one sense, that understanding has deep roots, in the conservative critique of the social-welfare state mounted by Carl Schmitt and Friedrich Hayek. Schmitt and Hayek argued correctly that realizing the promises of social-welfare constitutions would necessarily interfere with classical liberal rights. As wealth distributions altered in response to changes in markets and in individual preferences, they argued, the social-welfare state would have to regularly intervene to deprive people of property they had accumulated and to disrupt their reasonable expectations; the latter, in particular, was, they thought, incompatible with basic ideas about the rule of law.

As left-wing populists see things, economic elites overlap with the political elites and, when they do not overlap economic elites are in a position to corruptly buy off opposition. Here too the political implications are clear. Realizing social-welfare constitutionalism requires limiting the effective political power of economic elites not merely in theory but in practice—it is the practice of liberalism by their national elites against which left-wing populists rail. Put in more traditional terms, realizing second-generation social and economic rights requires altering existing understandings about the content of first-generation political rights. Most obviously, regulations of campaign finance might be required—as might sharp limits on the contribution of nondomestic sources to domestic political parties. Expansive notions of corruption might be needed. And, where those understandings are embedded in judicially enforced doctrines, realizing second-generation rights may require changing the courts.

The question then arises: Are the constitutional changes required to implement the left-wing populist program within the range of reasonable specifications? The standard way contemporary constitutionalists address that question is by asking whether the changes are "proportionate." As suggested earlier, taken one by one many of the changes would be found proportionate by a court honestly applying existing doctrine.

Defenders of left-wing populism claim that, in contrast to right-wing populist programs, those changes even when taken in the aggregate remain within the range of reasonable specifications. For example, perhaps restrictions on political activities and the seeming entrenchment of the governing party do not interact in ways that are troubling from the perspective of liberalism.

Take, for example, the assertion that the left-wing Ecuadorean populist Rafael Correa sought to move that nation outside the range of reasonable specifications. He proposed a restructuring of the judiciary, with the effect of allowing him to appoint many new judges. He also supported formal and informal actions against media outlets that opposed him. One important piece of evidence for that assertion is that Correa sought constitutional changes that would have allowed him to remain in office indefinitely. Yet, despite Correa's seeming continuing popularity, this failed, and Correa accepted the result. The presidential candidate of Correa's party did win the ensuing election, though with a margin smaller than Correa's (and, observers suspected, smaller than Correa would have obtained). And, importantly, he repudiated some of Correa's constitutional innovations—showing that such innovations are not necessarily sticky. Coming to an overall judgment is difficult, but at least at present it seems as if the Ecuadorean political system remains within the range of reasonable specifications, with shortfalls of a sort not unknown in less complex cases.

Two difficulties attend any attempt to determine whether the changes implemented in populist regimes bring them outside the range of reasonable specifications. First, as noted already, proportionality doctrine is not well-suited to evaluating a set of changes and their interactions. Second, because changing the composition of the courts is a frequent component of the populist program, we cannot be confident that the transformed courts will actually apply proportionality doctrine honestly. Faced with a holding by a domestic court that some change or changes are proportionate, how can critics support a contrary judgment? Landau and Dixon suggest one source—comparison with constitutions elsewhere.[6] That source will not be available when each change is, by itself, within the range of reasonable specifications. Sometimes critics find solace in what they characterize as "strong" dissents against the domestic court's decisions, but such dissents clearly lack legal authority. In the end, then, it seems that the judgment that a package of constitutional changes moves a regime outside the range of reasonable specifications will have to be directly political.

A Note on the Role of Political Leaders

The origins of contemporary populism, I have argued, lie in the failure of existing political elites and the parties they lead to deliver on their promises. This provides an opening

---

[6] Landau and Dixon, "Competitive Democracy."

for political entrepreneurs either to hijack an existing party as occurred to some extent in the United States (Donald Trump and the Republican Party) and the United Kingdom (Brexit and the Conservative Party), or to create a new party. Sometimes those entrepreneurs are simply opportunists noticing a political "niche" they can fill; Viktor Orbán may be an example. Or, the entrepreneurs may have a principled commitment to their populist programs; in my admittedly controversial view Chávez (though not Maduro) was probably in this category. Whether a populist leader is opportunistic or principled is independent of whether the leader's program is right-wing or left-wing.

In a presidential system, entrenchment means ensuring that the political leader himself or herself will retain power, and that might seem an indicator of opportunism. That indicator is not available in parliamentary systems, where the leaders of dominant political parties can hold office for as long as they retain the support of their party. But, even more, as populists see things, they must reconstruct the failed political order, a project that might take more "political time" than the political calendar of the failed order allows.[7] Even principled populist leaders might want to entrench their power so that they can place the project on a path to success.

Populist Anti-cosmopolitanism

So far I have addressed how populism responds to the failure of political elites to deliver on the promises of social-welfare constitutionalism. Those promises were either backed up by or simply accompanied by an account of how a globalized economy would make it easier to realize social-welfare constitutionalism both domestically and throughout the world. Cosmopolitanism consists in part of attending to worldwide social welfare, and the reduction in the extent of desperate poverty around the world may perhaps vindicate cosmopolitanism. Populisms, though, are domestic political movements fueled by the failures of domestic social-welfare constitutionalism. From the populist perspective, cosmopolitans have ignored those failures.

The traditional theory of international trade acknowledges that such trade's benefits cause significant disruptions: Capital movement from the center to the periphery increases income in the periphery and lowers prices in the center, but throws some workers in the center out of jobs; international migration increases the income of immigrants (and, through remittances, of those who do not move) and lowers prices, but similarly reduces employment opportunities previously available to workers in nations receiving immigrants. In principle the political elites against whom populists react could have addressed their concerns. Job retraining programs and similar trade adjustment policies, as they are known in the United States, can allow workers adversely affected by international trade to obtain their share of trade's benefits. Political elites, though, did very

---

[7] I draw the notion of "political time" from the literature on American political development.

little in the way of adopting such policies, with the effect that they and their elite allies obtained the benefits of globalized trade (as did workers from the periphery), and displaced workers bore the burdens—again, contrary to the promise of equality in sharing the benefits *and* burdens of globalized social-welfare constitutionalism.

Here left-wing populisms differ from right-wing ones. Left-wing populist programs support restrictions on capital movement away from their nations, and so once again run up against the protections first-generation rights give to private property. They also support strong programs of redistribution of wealth within the nation, to move in the direction of equalizing benefits and burdens. And, as before, enacting these programs often requires weakening the political power of elites through constitutional revisions of prior understandings of political rights such as freedom of expression. To the extent that they divide the world into a preferred "we" and a disfavored "they," left-wing populisms define the categories with reference to something like economic classes rather than with reference to ethnonationalism.

Right-wing populist programs in contrast combine faith in purely domestic market processes with restrictions on the movement of people rather than capital. The "we-they" categories they use are ethnonationalist. In principle it is difficult to see how the restrictions on the movement of people can do much to promote even purely domestic social-welfare constitutionalism. The discussions about Brexit make clear the difficulties of programs that address only one of the aspects of the failure of international social-welfare constitutionalism—immigration—without addressing capital disinvestment. Immigrants, though, are a convenient target for populist organizing. Immigration does disrupt domestic employment, after all, and populist leaders can readily tie anti-immigrant sentiment to historic forms of ethnonationalism. Further, the rhetoric of ethnonationalistic anti-cosmopolitanism historically has offered a target for concern about the capital side of the problem, in the form of anti-Semitism, Jews being seen as controlling large amounts of capital. Anti-Semitism is in some sense a side effect of right-wing anti-cosmopolitanism, though occasionally one finds hints of anti-Semitism in left-wing populist rhetoric.

"Deconstructing the Administrative State"

In a widely noted speech Donald Trump's then-adviser Stephen Bannon spoke of deconstructing the administrative state. The adjective is distinctive to the US context, but the idea of deconstructing the state is intrinsic to right-wing and left-wing populism. Here too, their programs differ.

Right-wing populism focuses on the state's intrusiveness into ordinary life through prescriptive regulations of business and, in the form of the "nanny state," of everyone's typical daily activities. Deconstructing that state means eliminating intrusive regulations as comprehensively as possible. In the United States, for example, the Trump administration has committed itself to a rather mindless program in which adopting one new regulation requires the elimination of two older ones whose costs equal that of the new one.

Yet, some nontrivial portion of the targeted regulations are important components of social-welfare constitutionalism: occupational health and safety regulations, for example, and many environmental regulations. Administered sensibly, the "one in, two out" policy can improve regulatory policy, but there is little reason to believe that it will be administered sensibly: The Trump administration's version focuses on the costs of compliance, for example, without taking into account the benefits of the regulations to be eliminated. Were right-wing populist political leaders to deconstruct the state, they would come to stand in the shoes of the political elites whose failure gave rise to populism—a new group of political leaders but the same betrayal of political promises.

Left-wing policies aimed at deconstructing the state focus on the processes by which regulations are generated and seek to make them more participatory. The state is deconstructed in the sense that existing regulatory institutions are dismantled, but then they are—in theory—rebuilt. This form of deconstruction takes many forms. The most well established is probably participatory budgeting.[8] The South African Constitutional Court and the Interamerican Court of Human Rights have developed "consultative remedies," which require government agencies to engage in what the South African Court calls "meaningful" consultations with communities likely to be adversely affected by proposed government actions.[9] Left-wing populists in Latin America have used some experimentalist techniques. The verdict is not yet in on whether they are deeply committed to them as part of a general deconstruction of the state, or on whether the techniques actually achieve the desired combination of participation and substantive outcomes.

Charles Sabel and his colleagues have developed a general theorization of post-deconstruction regulatory mechanisms, which they call democratic experimentalism.[10] Notably, in this theorization an important trigger of the search for experimentalist solutions is a widespread sense that all the methods theretofore used to address an acknowledged problem have failed to come up with solutions—a trigger similar to that which sets populist movements going as well. Right-wing deconstruction of the state seems unlikely to satisfy the demand that elicited the program; left-wing deconstruction might do so.

---

[8] Archon Fung and Erik Olin Wright, "Deepening Democracy: Innovations in Empowered Participatory Governance," *Politics & Society* 29 (2001): 5–41, describes several examples in addition to participatory budgeting.

[9] For South Africa, see Occupiers of 51 Olivia Road v. City of Johannesburg, 2008 (3) SA 208 (CC) (19 February 2008).

[10] Michael C. Dorf and Charles F. Sabel, "A Constitution of Democratic Experimentalism," *Columbia Law Review* 98 (1998): 267–473.

Conclusion

Contemporary discussions of populism tend to use the term as a pejorative. Though populisms come in different forms, they are generally reactions to real failures by political elites. Their programs include constitutional changes that often respond to the causes of those failures. Perhaps, whatever their flaws and however much they have contributed to policy failures, existing constitutions cannot be improved without running excessive risks of different kinds of failures—authoritarianism, in particular. But, in light of the failures that generated the resurgence of populism we ought to be open to considering institutional innovations and constitutional changes on their merits. Some might be valuable, others too risky. That the innovations are promoted by populists is not in itself a reason to dismiss them.

37 The Continuing Specter of Popular Sovereignty and National Self-Determination in an Age of Political Uncertainty
Sanford Levinson

Introduction

The various essays collected together in this book present a variety of causes for present discontents throughout the world. Many of the analyses can be described, broadly speaking, as "materialist" in their search for such causes. Some focus on aspects of international economic development (i.e., "globalization"); some on the increasing inequality within given countries, whether caused by globalization or other developments; others on the impact of what appears to be ever-expanding immigration, whether provoked by desires for a brighter economic future or by refugees fleeing the ravages of war, especially the particular brutalities attached to civil wars. Finally, there is the simple sclerosis of existing political institutions, which I have identified in earlier works as an important reason for the particular malaise within the United States, where people of all political persuasions find it increasingly difficult, if not impossible, to perceive the national government as capable of effectively confronting the ongoing challenges to the social and political orders.[1]

---

[1] See Sanford Levinson, *Our Undemocratic Constitution: Where the Constitution Goes Wrong (And How We the People Can Correct It)* (New York: Oxford University Press, 2008); Sanford Levinson, *Framed: America's 51 Constitutions and the Crisis of Governance* (New York: Oxford University Press, 2012); Sanford Levinson and

In this chapter, however, I want to become more "idealistic," as it were, by emphasizing the importance of an idea, particularly the ideology of "popular sovereignty" and, more particularly, "national self-determination." My title is obviously drawn from the famous opening of *The Communist Manifesto*, in which Marx and Engels wrote that "[a] specter is haunting" Europe. Today, though, the specter is no longer communism, and Europe is not the only relevant venue. Instead, it is "self-determination," an idea that is almost literally limitless in its capacity both to inspire and to create perhaps endless mischief not only in Europe, but extending to the entire world. If there are still those discomforted by any affirmative citations to Karl Marx, then perhaps we should simply cite John Maynard Keynes instead. "It is ideas, not vested interests," he famously wrote, "which are dangerous for good or evil." He cautioned "practical men," often disdainful of the power of abstract ideas, to be aware of the extent to which they are "usually the slaves of some defunct economist. Madmen in authority, who hear voices in the air, are distilling their frenzy from some academic scribbler of a few years back." In this case the "scribblers" are not only academics, though there are surely many, going back at least to Thomas Hobbes, who have taken seriously the implications of popular rule when earlier notions of traditional authority, including the divine right of kings, broke down. Instead, the most important architects of the way "we" tend to think in the twenty-first century, across the world, include Thomas Jefferson and Woodrow Wilson. No doubt this emphasis reflects my own background as an American, and there are many others, particularly Europeans of the nineteenth century, who might be cited. Think only of Garibaldi and Kossuth, for starters, and theorists such as Herder. But one need not agree on the particular priority that I am giving Jefferson and Wilson to agree that any history of the concept (and political importance) of self-determination must include them. One must take seriously the ideas they presented and the impact they have had on those who, like Jefferson and Wilson themselves, determined to make their mark on the world well beyond the academy. Only such an understanding will allow us fully to understand many of the country-oriented essays in this collection.

Consider only Erin Delaney's chapter on the United Kingdom and Victor Ferreres's ruminations on contemporary Spain (and Catalonia). The first involves British secession from the European Union (and the causes thereof). Although that is legally legitimate under the terms of Article 50 of the basic treaty that constitutes the present EU, it is also obvious that Brexit is proving to be a significantly disruption of lives in both the UK and the rest of Europe. It also calls into question the nature of the constitutional project underlying the notion of a European Union (the subject of Joseph Weiler's essay). Moreover, lurking beneath Brexit is the possibility of Scottish secession from the United Kingdom, itself the product of the 1709 Treaty of Union. Approximately 45 percent of the voting electorate in Scotland voted in 2014 to leave the United Kingdom.

Cynthia Levinson, *Fault Lines in the Constitution: The Framers, Their Fights, and the Flaws That Affect Us Today* (Atlanta: Peachtree Publishers, 2017).

Subsequently, the Scottish National Party came to power in Scotland and continues to support a second referendum and secession. In the case of Catalonia, there is no constitutional provision allowing Catalonia to leave Spain, and the Spanish Constitutional Court, as Ferreres demonstrates, has been uniformly hostile to the proposition that Catalonia can hold a legitimate referendum by which the alleged people of Catalonia can declare their independence from Spain. But, to paraphrase Galileo's alleged statement, even after his recantation of the proposition that the earth revolves around the sun, "still it moves," one might well say, with regard to Catalonian secessionism, "still it continues," regardless of attempts by the official Spanish legal system to suppress it. If one purpose of constitutionalism is to provide political mechanisms that will resolve all significant disputes and maintain what the Preamble to the US Constitution calls "domestic tranquility," then one might well doubt the potential success of the Spanish constitution in this regard—and it is not alone. If secessionism is an extreme case of political and social disruption, generating obvious conflicts over what counts as authoritative constitutional propositions, the tensions provoked by multinationalism are often scarcely less important.

"We the People" as the Singular Source of Legitimacy

Late in her career, the formidably erudite Judith Shklar turned her attention to American political thought.[2] Inevitably, that meant paying attention to the American constitutional tradition. She thus wrote of the "momentous novelty" of the Constitution's opening words, "We the People."[3] For Shklar, that simple phrase manifested "a declaration of independence from the entire European past ... a declaration of popular sovereignty which makes the consent of the citizens the *sole legitimate ground* of government" (emphasis added). "America had discovered the future." One could obviously link this as well to the radicalism of the Declaration of Independence. Although Americans, for a number of reasons, prefer to emphasize the "inalienable rights" that are set out for "all men," the most radical implication of the Declaration, as David Armitage has well established,[4] was in the very first sentence, which audaciously claimed the right of "one people" to separate themselves from the existing government—in that case the British Empire—and in effect to secede from it in order to engage in self-government designed to achieve

---

[2] I have benefitted greatly from a yet-unpublished essay by Giacomo Gambino, "Our End Was in Our Beginning," Judith Shklar and the American Founding. In addition, many of the themes of this chapter found their initial articulation in Jack M. Balkin and Sanford Levinson, "To Alter or Abolish," *Southern California Law Review* 89 (2016): 399–426.

[3] See "A New Constitution for a New Nation," in Judith N. Shklar, *Redeeming American Political Thought* 165 (Chicago: University of Chicago Press, 1998).

[4] See David Armitage, *The Declaration of Independence: A Global History* (Cambridge, MA: Harvard University Press, 2008).

certain ends. Although the immediate occasion of the Declaration was to defend the particular acts of those engaging in the secession, its arguments, of course, took a far more universalistic form:

> [All] Governments are instituted among Men, deriving their just powers from the consent of the governed,—... [W]henever any Form of Government becomes destructive of these ends, it is the Right of the People to alter or to abolish it, and to institute new Government, laying its foundation on such principles and organizing its powers in such form, as to them shall seem most likely to effect their Safety and Happiness.

There is, as many people have recognized, a tension between the Declaration's later emphasis on the "long train of abuses" claimed to be "destructive" of certain universalistic rights, which ostensibly justified secession—and consequent violence—and the declaration that "the People" have a right "to alter or to abolish" *any* governments that are deemed insufficient to establishing "their Safety and Happiness." Such happiness may, perhaps, be linked to the particular expressions of group identity that constitute a "people" as something more than a collection of atomistic individuals. One might want place names and public monuments to honor one's own heroes and not those of some other hegemonic group, even if the hegemon is relatively benevolent and not fully "oppressive." Or some might view the state's refusal to pay sufficient honor to its own language as itself the kind of oppression that justifies the "creative destruction" of political status quos.

To be sure, the authors of the Declaration proclaimed as well that "Prudence, indeed, will dictate that Governments long established should not be changed for light and transient causes," but, perhaps like "terrorists and freedom fighters," one person's "prudence" is another's shameful capitulation to illegitimate oppression. The Declaration has served to invite any and all purportedly oppressed peoples to do something about it, including the destabilization of their existing political communities.

To get to the modern world—and the direct relevance of this particular chapter to the overall topic of this volume—we must supplement the Declaration and the Preamble with the thought of the American President Woodrow Wilson (1913–1921). As it happens, we are publishing this collection on the one hundredth anniversary of the conclusion of World War I, which we can increasingly recognize as simply the opening episode of the catastrophic long (and worldwide) war that characterized almost the entirety of the twentieth century. For Wilson, what justified the controversial entry of the United States in 1917 into what was widely perceived as a war simply among European powers was making "the world safe for democracy." A century later, we might ask also about how to make democracy—especially Wilson's version of it—safe for the world.

Anyone familiar with the biography of Wilson knows that he was in fact a partisan of the "lost cause" and the rationale for the creation of the Confederate States of America as a protest against the ostensibly overreaching and ever-more-hostile national government following the election of Abraham Lincoln (with less than 40 percent of the popular vote) in 1860. He was also, not to put too fine a point on it, a white supremacist, one of whose major acts as president was to resegregate the federal civil service and to try to maintain African Americans in their accustomed place of subordination. In any event, there is a direct link between the Declaration of Independence's right to alter and abolish existing governments, the rationale for Confederate secession in 1860–1861, and then Wilson's declaration in 1918 of the transcendent importance of "self-determination."

"Peoples are not to be handed about from one sovereignty to another by an international conference or an understanding between rivals and antagonists," Wilson proclaimed. Instead, "[n]ational aspirations must be respected; peoples may now be dominated and governed only by their own consent." No longer should "[s]elf-determination" be treated as "a mere phrase. *It is an imperative principle of actions which statesmen will henceforth ignore at their peril.*"[5] Indeed, for Wilson the "roots" of the Great War lay "in the disregard of the rights of small nations and of nationalities which lacked the union and the force to make good their claim to determine their own allegiances and their own forms of political life. . . ." Presumably, recognition of such claims would give some meaning to the slaughter that occurred between 1914 and 1918 and prevent future such wars.

Thus, he famously asserted that "every territorial settlement involved in this war must be made in the interest and for the benefit of the populations concerned," in contrast to the claims of traditional "rival states" in effect competing for traditional imperialist hegemony. This entailed, according to Wilson, that "*all* well defined national aspirations shall be accorded the utmost satisfaction that can be accorded them without introducing new or perpetuating old elements of discord and antagonism that would be likely in time to break the peace of Europe and consequently of the world." (emphasis added). One can ask, of course, whether the condition placed on the end of the sentence, with regard to the actual recognition of "national aspirations," ends up negating the glorious promise of the "all" at its beginning. A child being told that he or she will in fact be taken to Disneyland for a vacation might not pay attention to the caveats offered by a cautious parent and be bitterly disappointed if what was taken as a solemn promise is broken. Depending perhaps on the particular countries one wishes to focus upon, one can view the negotiations at Versailles as providing satisfaction to some of the parties or, instead, as a venue of bitter disappointment over broken promises with regard to other groups seeking the grail of self-determination.

What *did* justify Wilson's receiving the Nobel Peace Prize in 1919? The answer seems to lie in his efforts to create a League of Nations. That institution, of course, turned out to be a hollow hope, and the jury is still out on the full impact of its successor, the United Nations. But there can be little doubt that Wilson's ideas about self-determination have triumphed to an astonishing degree. They might well be said to be more powerful today than even when he enunciated them a century ago.

It is only a slight exaggeration to say that much of the present disorder especially in what is deemed the Middle East represents the unravelling of a variety of decidedly

---

[5] Address of Woodrow Wilson to Congress, on February 11, 1918 (emphasis added).

unWilsonian "settlements" during the War. The British and French, for example, simply drew arbitrary boundary lines to define the country we call Iraq; there are also the continuing consequences of the Balfour Declaration in which Great Britain promised the Jewish people a "homeland" in Palestine, while at the same time reneging on promises that T. E. Lawrence especially had made to those he viewed as Arab allies regarding their own self-determination in the aftermath of dissolving the Ottoman Empire.[6] And the imperial colonization of Africa would not begin its termination until well after World War II, in countries whose borders, drawn by the imperialists and not by the colonized themselves, would create their own problems with regard to the actual persons and groups contained within them.

To put it mildly, Wilson's "principles" raise many questions. Karl Meyer in a *New York Times* column some quarter-century ago wrote of "Woodrow Wilson's Dynamite."[7] There was nothing academic in his analysis. Meyer accurately described Wilson as "the man of the hour in post-Communist Europe" inasmuch as "[f]rom the Baltics to the Adriatic, from the Ukraine to the Balkans, oppressed millions have given new life to his imperative—and often troublesome—principle. Indeed, if results are the measure, Wilson has proved a more successful revolutionary than Lenin." Lenin was perceptibly in decline even in 1991; one may well believe today that, even more so than Elvis, Lenin has left the building, which is why one can say that the "specter of communism" is weak indeed, even perhaps in China.

Yet the language of popular sovereignty and self-determination is almost ubiquitous. Preambles to contemporary national constitutions regularly speak in the name of the people and their right to form a government, whatever potential problems might appear even on their surface. Thus the Preamble to the Constitution of the Islamic Republic of Pakistan emphasizes that "sovereignty over the entire Universe belongs to Almighty Allah alone, and the authority to be exercised by the people of Pakistan within the limits prescribed by Him is a sacred trust." Yet it also emphasizes the importance of honoring "the will of the people of Pakistan to establish an order Wherein the State shall exercise its powers and authority through the chosen representatives of the people," who will in turn honor "the principles of democracy, freedom, equality, tolerance and social justice, as enunciated by Islam."

The late historian Edmund S. Morgan began his important book *Inventing the People: The Rise of Popular Sovereignty in England and America* by quoting David Hume's laconic comment that those "who consider human affairs with a philosophical eye" are often surprised "to see the easiness with which the many are governed by the few."[8] Yet

---

[6] See, e.g., Scott Anderson, *Lawrence In Arabia: War, Deceit, Imperial Folly and the Making of the Modern Middle East* (New York: Anchor Books, 2013).

[7] Karl E. Meyer, "Editorial Notebook: Woodrow Wilson's Dynamite," *New York Times*, August 14, 1991, http://www.nytimes.com/1991/08/14/opinion/editorial-notebook-woodrow-wilson-s-dynamite.html.

[8] Edmund Morgan, *The Rise of Popular Sovereignty in England and America* (New York: W.W. Norton, 1988), 13.

rule almost everywhere is based on its purported link to a far wider "people." Morgan goes on to describe "popular sovereignty" as a "fiction," a just-so story that in fact serves to legitimize rule by the relatively few. But ideological "fictions" work only so long as those who are ruled accept them, whether they see the hand of God or of an evanescent "people" having chosen a particular ruler. They are always subject to critique, with sometimes literally revolutionary consequences should "the people" or, more to the point, those speaking in their name—sometimes referred to as "populists, another major theme of several essays in this book, including Mark Tushnet's—"rise up" (in the language of Lin-Manuel Miranda's version of Alexander Hamilton and American secessionist/revolutionaries) to displace those now subject to dismissal as out-of-touch elites.

Wilson's exuberant language did not go unchallenged even within his own administration. His secretary of state, Robert Lansing, described the magic slogan of "self-determination" as "simply loaded with dynamite." Meyer quotes a confidential memorandum written in December 1918, in which Lansing asked a number of prescient questions:

> What effect will it have on the Irish, the Indians, the Egyptians, and the nationalists among the Boers? Will it not breed discontent, disorder, and rebellion? Will not the Mohammadans of Syria and Palestine and possibly of Morocco and Tripoli rely on it? How can it be harmonized with Zionism, to which the President is practically committed?

Meyer noted that "the phrase was trumpeted by dictators as well as democrats. Lenin's Bolsheviks championed self-determination—for those not under Soviet control. Hitler claimed the right for those Herrenvolk who were outside Germany, while subjugating whole nations without pity or scruple." Perhaps we might agree with Meyer that "Lansing's initial misgivings were prudent" even if we ultimately believe, perhaps evoking Ecclesiastes, that the times for prudence might be overcome by times of engaged and revolutionary action.

Lansing's most probing question involved the nature of the "unit" Wilson was referring to. Was "self-determination" attached to groups defined by race, ethnicity, or, perhaps religion? Or was occupation of an existing geographical territory by quite disparate groups sufficient, at least if there was enough dissatisfaction with the government being provided by a likely foreign hegemon? Or could one simply suggest an inchoate sense of national community, perhaps one that was basically called into existence by organizing against the existing government? This possibility is what has made Benedict Anderson's *Imagined Communities: Reflections on the Origin and Spread of Nationalism*[9] a book of enduring significance. Lansing cautioned that "[w]ithout a definite unit which is

---

[9] New York: Verso, 1983.

practical, application of this principle is dangerous to peace and stability." After all, "Few states are tidily homogeneous; frontiers are often disputed." Still, as Meyer well recognizes, "qualifying a principle is very different from rejecting it." Do we really want to join Lansing in declaring that Wilson's vision was simply "the dream of an idealist who failed to realize the danger until too late. . . . What a calamity that the phrase was ever uttered!" Meyer responds that we should "[t]ry telling that to a billion people whose liberation has been speeded by a doctrine enshrined in the first article of the United Nations Charter." That article announces that one of the "purposes of the United Nations" is "to develop friendly relations among nations based on respect for the principle of equal rights and self-determination of peoples . . . " Wilson would have been proud!

Shklar certainly agreed with Lansing's theoretical caveat. She had described as especially "vexing" the determination of who exactly counted as part of the relevant "people" (and, necessarily, who was therefore excluded).[10] Perhaps one can sidestep this question if one adopts a truly universalistic theory of individual rights, which is one possible reading of at least part of the Declaration, and then declares that it is the purpose of any and all political institutions to realize this set of rights. We could identify any deviant states or other political entities—such as American Indian tribes dedicated to the preservation of certain traditional norms—as barely, if at all, legitimate. But the ideal world would be one in which there is no genuine "boundary" problem, as it is referred to by contemporary political theorists,[11] because *everyone* is part of the relevant demos, and everyone, therefore, should presumably be entitled to participate in fundamental political decision-making. This way, of course, lies either madness or world government.

In any event, that is not the world we inhabit, which continues to be divided into separate and would-be "sovereign" countries, 193 of whom (!) currently comprise the so-called United Nations. Given that there were only 51 states in the original UN in 1945, it is obviously true that most of the array of contemporary countries are remarkably young and predicate their legitimacy on one or another version of Wilsonian "self-determination," often manifested by the overthrowing of a colonialist legacy, though sometimes by secession from an existing country that can only with difficulty be described as colonialist (such as Bengaladesh's breakaway from Pakistan).

If one rejects universalism, for whatever reason, in favor of more particularistic understandings of politics (and therefore of "self-determination"), then we must face the crucial question as to precisely "who counts" as part of the relevant group. Jefferson might have adopted universalistic language, but we should also be aware of the decidedly more parochial approach taken by John Jay, writing as Publius, in *Federalist* 2 in support of

[10] I have explored a variety of such questions in "'Who Counts?' 'Sez Who?'," *University of St. Louis Law Journal* 58 (2014): 937–988.

[11] See, e.g., Shmuel Nili, "Democratic Theory, the Boundary Problem, and Global Reform," *Review of Politics* 79 (2017): 99–123; Arash Abizadeh, "On the Demos and Its Kin: Nationalism, Democracy, and the Boundary Problem," *American Political Science Review* 106 (2012): 867–882.

the new Constitution drafted in Philadelphia. Publius describes himself as having "often taken notice that Providence has been pleased to give this one connected country [by rivers and the like] to one united people—a people descended from the same ancestors, speaking the same language, professing the same religion, attached to the same principles of government, very similar in their manners and customs, and who, by their joint counsels, arms, and efforts, fighting side by side throughout a long and bloody war, have nobly established general liberty and independence." As I have written elsewhere,[12] this set of assertions was preposterous even at the moment of its writing in suggesting a cultural homogeneity that simply did not exist. What is important, though, is not the accuracy of Jay's assertion, but, rather, its felt utility with regard to establishing the nature of the "people" authorized to ordain the new Constitution. "We" were not organized around our commitment to the universalistic abstractions of the Declaration; instead, one must look to the alleged commonalities involving "ancestors," language," and "manners and customs." All of these are vital complements to whatever "attach[ment[to the same principles of government" might also unite us. Publius establishes the basis for constant anxiety should one perceive threats to his particular version of "one united people." It is altogether fitting, for example, that Samuel P. Huntington, in his final book, *Who Are We? The Challenges to America's National Identity* (2005) cited *Federalist* 2 and repudiated as Enlightenment idealism the view that any political system could be organized simply around commitments to universal rights or abstract principles of government. It is no coincidence that Huntington is probably best remembered for his prediction that the future would feature a "clash of civilizations," sparked largely by an Islamic resurgence.

Once we recognize the empirical importance of groups, we must confront the all-important question as to how membership in them is to be determined. Do we genuinely accept "self-identification," or can the group itself, through some kind of organizational procedure, specify who is "in fact" part of the group? Such questions arise with regard to *all* groups, but they obviously take on special import when considering polities and states. The issues arise in a variety of very different contexts, ranging from the assignment of initial citizenship—will *jus soli* suffice or will *jus sanguinis* instead be necessary to establish birthright citizenship?—to procedures of naturalization. But one may also need to confront the possibility of involuntary "denaturalization," the equivalent of "excommunication." Liberals are often uncomfortable with the very concept of "group rights," but it is clear that one cannot escape that question whenever we refer to the powers of those particular groups called states, especially if in turn we view states as in some ways the expression of "nations" living within them.

All of us have become all too familiar with the idea of "ethnic cleansing," whereby members of given groups are defined as Others who will not be allowed to imagine themselves

---

[12] See Sanford Levinson, *An Argument Open to All: Reading the Federalist in the 21st Century* (New Haven, CT: Yale University Press, 2015).

as part of the "nation-state" that is defined by homogeneity. There is, of course, nothing new about the practice. Think only of the expulsion of non-Christians by Spain in 1492, the transfer of Greeks from Turkey after World War I, or, indeed, the genocide committed against Armenians by Turks in 1915. It is all too easy to find additional examples on all of the inhabited continents. Or, perhaps, we want to think instead of the topic of immigration, the subject of Alex Aleinikoff's chapter in this volume, with its challenge to a receiving state of accepting the reality—and the desirability—of multiculturalism and multinationalism to replace an earlier understanding of a singular peoplehood.

As suggested at the outset, it is doubtful that many, if any, of the various "country essays" in this book can be understood without paying sufficient attention to the desires of local "nationalists" to preserve their own vision of what is entailed by "national self-determination" against those they perceive as invaders. This is most obvious with regard, say, to Hungary and Poland, two notable "backsliders" from the hopes they had generated at the end of the twentieth century with regard to developing a stable and, in fact, inspiring, model of democratic pluralism. The Preamble to the 1990 Polish Constitution was notable, among other things, for its scrupulous presenting of both a religious and secular underpinning for the new post-Communist constitutional order. "We the Polish Nation" was defined in terms of "all citizens of the Republic, Both those who believe in God as the source of truth, justice, good and beauty, As well as those not sharing such faith but respecting those universal values as arising from other sources, Equal in rights and obligations towards the common good—Poland." To be sure, all Poles should feel "Beholden to our ancestors for their labours [and] their struggle for independence achieved at great sacrifice for our culture rooted in the Christian heritage of the Nation and in universal human values." The effort to meld both the religious and the secular into one common Polish nation is palpable. And one might recall in this context as well that one of the greatest conflicts over the proposed Draft Constitution for the European Union early in this century involved its failure, in its own extensive Preamble, to pay what some regarded as due heed to the Christian heritage of Europe. But, obviously, what some considered a bug was for others an admirable feature of the new, basically secularized, understanding of the European project.

So consider a December 2017 statement by Poland's prime minister-designate, Mateusz Morawiecki, "My dream is to re-Christianize the EU," he said. To put it mildly, there are many who are not reassured by such a comment, especially when it entails highly controversial (and many would say bigoted) migration policies adopted by his party and generating tensions with the rest of the EU.[13] Quite obviously, one cannot understand contemporary Turkey without becoming aware of the Islamic thrust of the Erdoğan government and the patent hostility to the demand of the original Ataturk Constitution that

[13] Dorota Bartyzel and Marek Strzelecki, "Poland's Incoming Prime Minister: 'My Dream Is to ReChristianize the EU,'" *Bloomberg*, December 8, 2017, https://www.bloomberg.com/news/articles/2017-12-08/poland-approves-court-revamp-bill-scuppering-eu-reboot-chances.

Turkey as a constitutional polity be relentlessly secular. Nor can one understand contemporary India without paying sufficient attention to the attempts by the Modi government to "Hinduize" the official Indian self-understanding, whatever the reality of the fact that there are literally well over one hundred million Moslems living in that country. And, of course, one cannot possibly comprehend the realities of Israeli constitutionalism—and the threats posed to its liberal aspirations—without paying due heed to the demands of Jewish nationalists to privilege Israel's being a "Jewish state" over its being a "democratic one" should the latter threaten the former. One could, I suspect, march through all of the states currently viewed as presenting "problems" with regard to their commitment to liberal constitutionalism and find similar tensions. All of these can be read as Publius-like in terms of the importance of maintaining a "common religion" as the basis of the nation.

Similarly, though there are many underlying causes to contemporary unhappiness in France, one of them is the conflict especially between Muslim immigrants or, indeed, French citizens who are Muslim, and the radical republican idea of laïcité, which leads some of its adherents to support not only the banning of certain forms of Islamic dress, but also the refusal to offer alternatives to pork in meals served in the public schools. That would require actually taking the religious identity of French students into account, a violation of the most common definition of laïcité. One might wish to describe the radical secularism underlying laïcité as itself a form of "civil religion" that the state zealously seeks to maintain against the threat of pluralism.

As we move to the United States, it is equally impossible to understand contemporary discontents without acknowledging the monumental importance not only of the Voting Rights Act of 1965, which transformed the American political system particularly in the South, but also of the ideologically-related 1965 legislation that repealed the Immigration and Naturalization Act of 1924 in favor of adopting a remarkably more inclusive vision of who was eligible to join the American community. To an extent only scarcely appreciated at the time, this was complemented by the Simpson-Mazzoli Act of 1985 that notably gave amnesty to many so-called "illegal aliens" and furthered the demographic transformation of the United States. Donald Trump's election, and his actions thereafter as president, can easily be interpreted as an attempt, as much as possible, to restore the vision of the 1924 Act and, for that matter, the 1890 Chinese Exclusion Act whose vision is captured in its title. They both attempted to define the United States, as much as possible, as a white person's and "Nordic" country. There is a reason that Trump chose to focus on Norway as the model source of contemporary American immigrants (even though, as a matter of fact, very few Norwegians, who live in a country described as having the "happiest" citizens in the contemporary world, appear to wish to emigrate to the United States). His animus is not simply directed to "illegal" or "undocumented" aliens; it is felt as well by those who dare attempt to join the United States from such counties as Mexico or El Salvador, though, interestingly enough, undocumented aliens from Ireland living in Boston are apparently being caught up in the Trumpian nightmare.

Perhaps Lenin's most enduring question is his always timely "What is to be done?" Were there enough land to house every group that might plausibly wrap itself in the mantle of "popular self-determination," then perhaps one could be more enthusiastic about any and all such claims, though, obviously, one might still refrain from endorsing the dreams of at least some such groups. After all, what space will remain for those who reject a particular version of the "national project" and wish to create alternatives? What of those Poles, for example, who have no desire at all to see (or experience) a "re-Christianized" Poland, let alone Europe? In her book *Liberal Nationalism,* the Israeli political theorist Yael Tamir, though highly sympathetic to many of the claims of Israeli Arabs and Palestinians to varieties of cultural autonomy, ultimately declares that, like any other minorities in a multicultural country, they simply have to accept that another culture will in fact be dominant. "Tolerance" is inevitably limited in its scope. It is different from the genuine self-government that might be said to be promised by the Declaration of Independence. "Members of minority groups will *unavoidably feel alienated* to some extent" from the dominant culture; they will always, presumably, retain some sense of being guests in someone else's national home.[14] Does it suffice to remind those who feel alienated that, as a practical matter, alienation is better than brute suppression (or worse)? Affected groups can presumably flourish to at least some degree even if from their own perspective they are living in a less-than-ideal condition of political subordination to a dominant (albeit tolerant) majority. Is that enough?

Is there any reason to believe that *any* particular approach to the reality of multiculturalism or multinationalism within a given country will necessarily provide stability, especially, one might additionally wonder, if that country is facing a variety of economic or "national security" problems? I have already suggested that, practically speaking, there is no escaping this reality unless one is willing, as I am not, to endorse brutal measures, including those being carried out by the Trump administration, that can only be described as attempts at ethnic cleansing. Perhaps Iceland, with roughly half the population even of Vermont, and a few other even more microstates can continue to aspire to being a "true" nation-state, that is a polity with a demos that is identical to an *ethnoi*. Today, though, that is almost literally a reactionary (or worse) fantasy. None of the countries that are the subject of essays in this collection, whether the United States, Israel, Hungary, India, or Australia, can possibly believe that such a fantasy could be actualized in the absence of great injustice—and probably violence.

There are some eminent political theorists and political scientists who argue, quite cogently, that we should simply eliminate the term "sovereignty" from our working

---

[14] Yael Tamir, *Liberal Nationalism* (Princeton, NJ: Princeton University Press, 1993), 163 (emphasis added). See also Sanford Levinson, "Is Liberal Nationalism an Oxymoron? An Essay for Judith Shklar," *Ethics* 105 (1995): 626–645 (review of Tamir), reprinted in Levinson, *Wrestling with Diversity* (Durham, NC: Duke University Press, 2003), 256.

vocabulary.[15] Or, at the very last, there may be sympathy for Thomas Hobbes's notion of "the sleeping sovereign," who manifests itself only once, when "ordaining a constitution," for example, and thereafter lapses into permanent slumber.[16] But the reality, of course, is that would-be "sovereigns" can always awaken and make demands, which often strike at least some onlookers as just. For better or worse, one cannot escape the reality of the term "sovereignty"—and the belief that it refers to something both understandable and worthwhile—in ordinary political speech and then actions triggered by such speech. Can we have conceptions of constitutional government that do not rely on one version or another of "popular sovereignty" or "national self-determination," fictions though they may surely be? Or do the resolutions of at least some of the problems outlined in this book require a kind of collective therapy designed to limit the appeal of the Wilsonian dream by comparing it to many other fantasies that must be rejected by mature adults?

---

[15] See, e.g., Hent Kalmo and Quentin Skinner, eds., *Sovereignty in Fragments: The Past, Present and Future of a Contested Concept* (New York: Cambridge University Press, 2014); Stephen D. Krasner, *Sovereignty: Organized Hypocrisy* (Princeton, NJ: Princeton University Press, 1999).

[16] See Richard Tuck, *The Sleeping Sovereign: The Invention of Modern Democracy* (New York: Cambridge University Press, 2016).

38 What's in Crisis? The Postwar Constitutional Paradigm, Transformative Constitutionalism, and the Fate of Constitutional Democracy
Mark A. Graber

CONSTITUTIONAL DEMOCRACY EVOLVED during the twentieth century from a system committed to the rule of law that guarantees a limited set of negative rights to a system that promotes human dignity. Lorraine Weinrib describes a "postwar constitutional paradigm" that "would not merely define and stabilize the exercise of state power through majoritarian machinery but would give legal priority to equal citizenship and respect for inherent human dignity."[1] Inspired by the South African example, Karl Klare coined the phrase "transformative constitutionalism" to describe "a long term project of constitutional enactment, interpretation, and enforcement committed . . . to transforming a country's political and social institutions and power relationships in a democratic, participatory, and egalitarian direction."[2] New national constitutions, constitutional courts, and prominent constitutional thinkers committed to some version of the postwar constitutional paradigm or transformative constitutionalism[3] announced an expanded

---

[1] Lorraine E. Weinrib, "The Postwar Paradigm and American Exceptionalism," in *The Migration of Constitutional Ideas*, ed. Sujit Choudhry (New York: Cambridge University Press, 2006), 89.

[2] Karl Klare, "Legal Culture and Transformative Constitutionalism," *South African Journal on Human Rights* 14 (1998): 146–188, 157.

[3] The main difference between transformative constitutionalism and other versions of the postwar constitutional paradigm appears to be whether the commitments below were conceptualized as transformative or reform measures.

set of principles and rights that would or should be honored by all constitutional democracies. These commitments included:

1. Robust political freedoms in the form of far broader speech and voting rights than democratic citizens enjoyed during the nineteenth century;
2. Broadly shared commercial prosperity in the form of constitutional commitments to the provision of such basic goods as food, water, education, housing, and healthcare;
3. Inclusiveness in the form of strong prohibitions on discrimination based on race, ethnicity, religion, and sexual orientation;
4. Secularism in the form of a sharp separation between church and state and an abandonment of traditional notions of gender and sexuality;
5. Independent courts that facilitate and maintain these constitutional commitments.

With the fall of the Berlin Wall, the end of colonialism, and the collapse of apartheid, many commentators announced that this thickened constitutional democracy had triumphed over other forms of governance.[4] Such extralegal threats as military coups and foreign invasions remained, but constitutional democracies seemed immune to subversion from within the political system. Governing classes and general publics committed to robust political freedoms, broadly shared commercial prosperity, inclusiveness, secularism, and independent courts, conventional wisdom assumed, would maintain constitutional democracy and play by the constitutional rules. Crises of particular democratic constitutions might occur, as citizens learned that some constitutional arrangements were poor means for achieving the revised ends of constitutional democracy. Nevertheless, these crises of particular constitutional democracies and particular democratic constitutions did not threaten the postwar constitutional paradigm or transformative constitutionalism. Political leaders could be trusted to correct constitutional flaws through better constitutional interpretations, better constitutional provisions, or, if needed, better national constitutions.

The essays in the volume belie the optimistic view in the first decade of the twentieth-first century that constitutional democracy was a machine that "would go of itself."[5] Tom Ginsburg and Aziz Huq note how political freedoms are weakening globally. Ganesh Sitaraman and David Schneiderman detail how constitutional democracies are failing to produce general commercial prosperity, often adopting policies that enable a global elite to reap the lion's share of the benefits from economic upturns while distributing the burdens of economic downturns disproportionately to less well-off residents. The

---

[4] See Francis Fukuyama, *The End of History and the Last Man* (New York: Avon Books, 1992).
[5] Michael Kammen: *A Machine That Would Go of Itself: The Constitution in American Culture* (New York: Alfred A. Knopf, 1986).

chapters by Ran Hirschl and Ayelet Shachar and by Desmond King and Rogers Smith point out that substantial segments of democratic populations reject secularism and inclusiveness, insisting on more religious and ascriptive political identities. Samuel Issacharoff and other authors document right-wing populist hostility to the independent courts that were designed to protect and promote democratic, secular, and inclusive values.

The essays on specific countries and regions almost uniformly conclude that constitutional democracies throughout the world are being assaulted from within rather than from without.[6] Political leaders who reject crucial features of contemporary constitutional democracy have gained power according to established constitutional procedures, even if, as is the case with the Electoral College in the United States, established constitutional procedures may empower candidates with fewer popular votes than their main rival. Recep Tayyip Erdoğan's Justice and Development Party in Turkey and Jaroslaw Kaczyński's Law and Justice Party in Poland played by formal constitutional rules, including the rules for making constitutional modifications, when making the political and constitutional reforms necessary to entrench party rule. Benjamin Netanyahu[7] and Viktor Orbán, enjoy sizeable support among their general publics; they are at least as popular as any other political figure in their countries. Constitutional democracies in the twenty-first century are rarely challenged by military coups or foreign invasions. Recent coups in Turkey and Egypt were as much efforts to restore as to overthrow constitutional democracy. "The secular and democratic rule of law has been virtually eliminated," members of the Turkish army complained, when justifying their attempt to overthrow the Erdoğan government.[8]

The essays in this volume detail the political problems experienced over the past generation by regimes committed to some version of the postwar constitutional paradigm or transformative constitutionalism. That particular version of constitutional democracy under attack is a political project championed by late twentieth century constitutionalists, not the liberal republican project championed by the late eighteenth century elites responsible for the Constitution of the United States, which has largely been superseded in contemporary constitutional democracies.[9] The contemporary challenges to constitutional democracy the contributors discuss are typically directed at such texts as the Constitution of South Africa, the vision of such tribunals as the Supreme Court of Israel under Aharon Barak or the Supreme Court of Hungary during the first years of that nation's constitutional democracy, the universalistic philosophy ascribed to John Rawls

---

[6] Sandy Levinson and Mark Tushnet note Russian efforts to destabilize democracy in the United States and elsewhere through propaganda on social media. Unlike a military coup or a foreign invasion, however, such efforts are successful only to the extent that domestic voters are persuaded by the speech in question.

[7] At least when this sentence was written in the middle of May 2018.

[8] Ozan O. Varol, "Stealth Authoritarianism in Turkey," in *Constitutional Democracy in Crisis?*, ed. Mark A. Graber, Sanford Levinson, and Mark Tushnet (New York: Oxford University Press, 2018), 351.

[9] See David S. Law and Mila Versteeg, "The Declining Influence of the United States Constitution," 87 *New York University Law Review* 87 (2012): 762–858.

or Jürgen Habermas, and the cosmopolitanism associated with Martha Nussbaum. King and Smith point out that right-wing populist movements are better understood as "reactions against the dominant ideology revealed in the spate of drafting of new constitutions that occurred around the world in the last quarter century than as a rejection of previous understandings of constitutionalism."[10] Nelson Mandela's legacy is in far more jeopardy than that of James Madison.

As a whole, the chapters in this volume suggest four general observations.[11] (1) Constitutional democracy has thickened into a system that promotes human dignity through commitments to robust political freedoms, shared commercial prosperity, inclusiveness, secularism, and independent courts. (2) Conservative political entrepreneurs in the wake of the Great Recession have been far more successful activating right-wing populist identities than progressive political entrepreneurs have been in activating left-wing populist identities. (3) "Stealth authoritarianism," "abusive constitutionalism," and "constitutional hardball" are the tools of choice for undermining constitutional democracy, replacing military coups as the modal threat to that form of governance. (4) "Constitutional dictatorship" is replacing "democratic deficits" or, in the United States, the "counter-majoritarian difficulty," as the central institutional problem of constitutional democracy.

The contemporary constitutional politics documented in this volume suggest that persons committed to various versions of the postwar constitutional paradigm or transformative constitutionalism need a better product and need to sell that product more effectively. Globalization is an obvious place to begin. Some version of globalization is here to stay, but economies need to be managed so that both the benefits of economic upturns and the burdens of economic downturns are more broadly shared than at present. Jennifer Hochschild's essay is a cautionary tale about the political habits of communities that the global economy leaves behind. Robust political freedoms, broadly shared commercial prosperity, secularism, inclusiveness, and independent courts must rest on broader political foundations than judicial decisions or executive orders. Legislatures were the institution of choice for the progressive populists of the past in part because legislatures delivered progressive policies better than other governing institutions, and in part because broad-based and ongoing legislative campaigns did far more to activate progressive populist identities than litigation campaigns or the occasional election of a national executive. Constitutional theory and practice should refocus on effective governance as much as fundamental rights. Such challenges to contemporary constitutional democracy as climate change, the war on terror, threats to public health, and managing a globalized economy require governing forms that bring expertise to bear on vital social

---

[10] Desmond King and Rogers M. Smith, "Populism, Racism and the Rule of Law in Constitutional Democracies Today," in *Constitutional Democracy in Crisis?*, 463.

[11] These observations are mine and not those of my co-editors. Readers will draw their independent conclusions.

questions and an active public committed to what might be called "experienced-based politics" as least as much as parchment declarations of fundamental rights and principles.

The Thickening of Constitutional Democracy

Constitutional democracy thickened during the late twentieth century. The persons responsible for the Constitution of the United States thought constitutions were frameworks for governance that had no need for a specific enumeration of rights. Alexander Hamilton, when claiming that textual limits on government were unnecessary, insisted that "all observations founded upon the danger of usurpation ought to be referred to the composition and structure of the government, not to the nature or extent of its power."[12] Contemporary constitutions demand more of constitutional democracy. The national constitutions framed at the turn of the twenty-first century contain lengthy lists of both individual and community rights that government must refrain from violating and actively contribute to maintaining. The Constitution of Ecuador, a prominent transformative constitution, includes "social welfare rights to education, food, water, health, social security (meaning income supports for those not able to work), and employment for workers." The text prohibits "discrimination on the basis of ethnicity, place of birth, age, sex, gender, culture, civil status, language, religion, ideology, political affiliation, legal record, socioeconomic condition, migratory status, sexual orientation, health status, HIV carrier, disability or physical difference." That constitution mandates "affirmative action policies to address many forms of unjust inequality," requires that women be represented "equally with men," "makes international human rights directly enforceable in Ecuadorean courts," and "guarantees rights for nature herself."[13] Article 2 of the Lisbon Treaty, an instance of the postwar constitutional paradigm that provides the contemporary foundations for the European Union declares: "The Union is founded on the values of respect for human dignity, freedom, democracy, equality, the rule of law and respect for human rights, including the rights of persons belonging to minorities. These values are common to the member states in a society in which pluralism, non-discrimination, tolerance, justice, solidarity, and equality between men and women prevail."[14]

Transformative constitutions and their postwar European relatives protect and promote robust political freedoms, broadly shared economic prosperity, secularism, and inclusiveness in all phases of public life, commitments enforced by an independent judiciary. Liberal constitutional democracies, Ginsburg and Huq detail, must

[12] Alexander Hamilton, James Madison, and John Jay, *The Federalist Papers*, ed. Clinton Rossiter (New York: New American Library, 1961), 196.
[13] King and Smith, "Populism, Racism and the Rule of Law" (paraphrasing the Constitution of Ecuador), 464.
[14] Damian Chalmes, Gareth Davies, and Giorgio Monti, *European Union Law: Cases and Materials*, ed. Damial Chalmes, Gareth Davies, and Girogio Monti, 2nd ed. (Cambridge: Cambridge University Press, 2010), 43.

constitutionally guarantee "a democratic electoral system," "rights to speech and association," and "the rule of law sufficient to allow democratic engagement without fear or coercion."[15] Sitaraman treats as conventional wisdom among constitutional democrats that "Constitutional democracies require a relative degree of economic equality to persist."[16] Hirschl and Shachar speak of "constitutional democratic orders that are committed to fundamental rights, human dignity, the protection of minorities, and the values of pluralism and equality."[17] King and Smith discuss how "new 'transformative' constitutions ... promised a greatly expanded set of rights—social and economic rights, racial, ethnic, and religious minority rights, indigenous rights (and) environment rights."[18] Roberto Gargarella writes about the "New Latin American Constitutionalism" or social constitutionalism that includes "long lists of human rights, indigenous rights, and the rights of minority groups."[19] Manoj Mate and Ozan Varol detail how India and Turkey, respectively, were committed to particularly aggressive strains of secularism, but most constitutional democracies and constitutional judiciaries maintained an almost as sharp separation between church and state.

The postwar constitutional paradigm and transformative constitutionalism combine thickened notions of constitutional commitments with thinner notions of constitutional citizenship. Hochschild observes that cosmopolitans "define national identity as adherence to a set of values."[20] Constitutional citizens, in this common view, are persons committed to the ideals of constitutional democracy, not persons defined by race, ethnicity, religion, or other ascriptive characteristics.[21] Gábor Halmai writes, "The core of this kind of constitutional patriotism is a constitutional culture centered on universalist liberal-democratic norms and values, refracted and interpreted through particular historical experiences."[22] J.H.H. Weiler hopes that Europeans would develop political identities based on the Schumann Declaration, which called for "a wider and deeper community between countries long opposed to one another by sanguinary divisions."[23]

---

[15] Tom Ginsburg and Aziz Z. Huq, "Defining and Tracking the Trajectory of Liberal Constitutional Democracy," in *Constitutional Democracy in Crisis?*, 36.

[16] Ganesh Sitaraman, "Economic Inequality and Constitutional Democracy," in *Constitutional Democracy in Crisis?*, 548.

[17] Ran Hirschl and Ayelet Shachar, "'Religious Talk' in Narratives of Membership," in *Constitutional Democracy in Crisis?*, 516.

[18] King and Smith, "Populism, Racism and the Rule of Law," 459.

[19] Roberto Gargarella, "Latin America: Constitutions in Trouble," in *Constitutional Democracy in Crisis?*, 181.

[20] Jennifer Hochschild, "What's New? What's Next? Threats to the American Constitutional Order," in *Constitutional Democracy in Crisis?*, 94.

[21] For a discussion of liberal, republican, and ascriptive conceptions of citizenship, see Rogers M. Smith, *Civic Ideals: Conflicting Visions of Citizenship in U.S. History* (New Haven, CT: Yale University Press, 1997).

[22] Gábor Halmai, "A Coup against Constitutional Democracy: The Case of Hungary," in *Constitutional Democracy in Crisis?*, 248.

[23] Robert Schuman, "Declaration," *Building European Union: A Documentary History and Analysis*, ed. Trevor Salmon and Sir William Nicol (Manchester, UK: Manchester University Press, 1997), 45.

Leading constitutional commentators at the turn of the twenty-first century identify constitutional democracy with some version of the postwar constitutional paradigm or the transformative constitutional project in ways that blur, if not obliterate, previous distinctions between constitutionalism and democracy. Walter Murphy declared, "Constitutionalism demand[s] adherence ... to principles that center on respect for human dignity and the obligations that flow from those principles." In his view, no system that lacks protection for certain fundamental human rights is a constitutional democracy.[24] Weiler maintains that "human dignity" is "the most fundamental of all rights, the one that features first and foremost in so many of our constitutional documents."[25] Ronald Dworkin spoke of a "constitutional conception of democracy" that requires "political decisions that affect the distribution of wealth, benefits, and burdens" to "be consistent with equal concern for all," and respects an "individual's own responsibility to decide for himself what life to live."[26] Regimes not committed to secularism and inclusiveness are not, by definition, constitutional democracies. When Hirschl writes about regimes committed to advancing the one true religion, he describes them as constitutional theocracies rather than as theocratic constitutional democracies, even when the regime committed to the one true religion regularly holds elections and regime leaders are committed to the rule of law.[27]

The publication of and response to John Hart Ely's *Democracy and Distrust*[28] highlights how constitutional democracy has been thickened, even in the United States, whose constitutional framers pioneered a far thinner notion of constitutionalism. Ely advanced a "representative-reinforcing" theory of judicial review. The Supreme Court of the United States, he argued, should police the political arena to ensure basic democratic processes were respected and prevent discrimination against the politically powerless, but not interfere with substantive policies that did not discriminate on forbidden grounds. Ely's understanding of the political freedoms mandated by democracy was far more robust than that championed by most constitutional democrats before World War II. *Democracy and Distrust* defended on democratic grounds Warren Court decisions mandating one person/one vote, protecting false criticisms of public figures, ordering the immediate integration of public schools, prohibiting teaching creationism in public schools, and requiring extensive due process rights for persons suspected of criminal offenses. Ely did insist that representative-reinforcing courts should not overturn

---

[24] Walter F. Murphy, in *Constitutional Democracy: Creating and Maintaining a Just Political Order* (Baltimore, MD: Johns Hopkins University Press, 2007), 15–16.

[25] J.H.H. Weiker, "The Crumbling of European Democracy," in *Constitutional Democracy in Crisis?*, ed. Mark A. Graber, Sanford Levinson, and Mark Tushnet (New York: Oxford University Press, 2018), 632.

[26] Ronald Dworkin, *Freedom's Law: The Moral Reading of the American Constitution* (New York: Oxford University Press, 1996), 25–26.

[27] Ran Hirschl, *Constitutional Theocracy* (Cambridge, MA: Harvard University Press, 2010), 2–3.

[28] John Hart Ely, *Democracy and Distrust: A Theory of Judicial Review* (Cambridge, MA: Harvard University Press, 1980).

legislative judgments on such matters as abortion, but critics quickly demonstrated that his understanding of constitutional democracy could justify such decisions as *Roe v. Wade*.[29] Ruth Bader Ginsburg, Guido Calabresi, and many others noted how bans on abortion reflect the relative powerlessness of women, and that abortion rights are necessary for women to participate fully in political life.[30] When some of those Ely critics claimed that government provision of basic necessities is a better example of a good policy that is not judicially enforceable or an element of constitutional democracy,[31] their critics pointed out that impoverished persons cannot participate as equals in political processes and are often subjects of political discrimination.[32] If, following Sitaraman, constitutional democracies require a strong dose of economic equality, then government policies that secure broadly shared economic prosperity are as central to constitutional democracy as free speech. These responses to Ely, progressive constitutional scholarship,[33] and the most recent Democratic Party platform[34] illustrate how many Americans who identify with the political Left interpret the Constitution of the United States as protecting some variation of the rights protected by the transformative Constitution of Ecuador, with debates largely confined to details and disputes over which rights are judicially enforceable. Americans who identify with the political right are as committed to providing broadly shared commercial prosperity, even as they insist positive rights and redistribution are ineffective and illegitimate means for achieving that consensual end. No contemporary president could emulate Grover Cleveland, who insisted that alleviating the distress caused by the Panic of 1893 was not the business of the national government.

Constitutional politics in Israel illustrate the clash between contemporary and older constitutional visions. Yaniv Roznai details how the Netanyahu government is concentrating power in the executive branch of the government, weakening judicial authority to declare laws unconstitutional, passing laws restricting the freedom of speech and association, and vigorously championing Orthodox Jewish values in the public sphere. Roznai in his chapter and former chief justice Aharon Barak insist these measures violate

---

[29] 410 U.S. 113 (1973).

[30] See Ruth Bader Ginsburg, "Some Thoughts on Autonomy and Equality in Relation to *Roe v. Wade*," *North Carolina Law Review* 63 (1985): 375–386; Guido Calabresi, "Foreword: Antidiscrimination and Constitutional Accountability (What the Bork-Brennan Debate Ignores)," *Harvard Law Review* 105 (1991): 80–151.

[31] See Mark A. Graber, "The Clintonification of American Law: Abortion, Welfare and Liberal Constitutional Theory," *Ohio State Law Journal* 58 (1997): 731, 734–736.

[32] See, e.g., Frank I. Michelman, "Welfare Rights in a Constitutional Democracy," *Washington University Law Quarterly* 1979 (1979): 659, 675–678; Graber, "Clintonification," 755–756.

[33] See, e.g., Robin L. West, *Progressive Constitutionalism: Reconstructing the Fourteenth Amendment* (Durham, NC: Duke University Press, 1994); James E. Fleming and Linda C. McClain, *Ordered Liberty: Rights, Responsibilities and Virtues* (Cambridge, MA: Harvard University Press, 2013).

[34] See 2016 Democratic Party Platform, *American Presidency Project*, July 21, 2016, http://www.presidency.ucsb.edu/ws/index.php?pid=117717.

basic tenets of constitutional democracy, which they understand as committed to robust political freedoms, broadly shared commercial prosperity, secularism, and inclusiveness, enforced by an independent judiciary. Barak states, "[J]ust as there is no democracy without the rule of the majority, so too is there no democracy without the rule of values at the center of which are human rights."[35] Israeli government officials, pointing out that the present government was elected in fair elections, insist that they are the bearers of democracy in Israel. "Every day at the Justice Ministry," Justice Minister Ayelet Shaked declared in response to Barak, "I take another step in creating a democratic alternative to the constitutional revolution."[36]

The Right-Wing Populist Surge

Ayelet Shaked is one of many governing officials riding a right-wing populist surge taking place across the globe. Right-wing populists now govern in Turkey, Poland, Hungary, India, South Africa, Israel, and the United States. They are gaining ground in almost every European nation outside of Scandinavia, most notably in Germany, France, the United Kingdom, Italy, the Netherlands, and Austria. Right-wing populists are weakening the European Union. Even Australia has not been immune to the siren call of a more ethnic and religious nationalism. Rosalind Dixon and Anika Gauja note how mainstream Australian political parties are retaining their share of the vote in part by preempting right-wing populist demands for stricter immigration policies, reducing efforts to combat climate change, and providing fewer rights for indigenous persons.

Constitutional democracy seems stalled and in retreat even where right-wing populists are not empowered. Victor Ferreres Comella discusses the populist roots of the Catalonian secession movement challenging constitutional democracy in Spain, even if that movement is not a strain of right-wing populism. James Gathii details failures to launch throughout much of sub-Saharan Africa. Heinz Klug documents how transformative constitutional democracy in South Africa has been bogged down in corruption. Ana Michaela Alterio and Roberto Niembro discuss chronic problems of constitutional democracy in Mexico. Gargarella's essay documents chronic problems of constitutional democracy throughout Latin America.

Right-wing populists in power weaken democratic rights and democratic processes. Varol notes how Erdoğan in Turkey uses libel laws to limit political dissent. The Israeli government is cracking down on anyone affiliated with the Boycott, Divest and Sanction

---

[35] Tova Tzimuki and Amira Lam, "Aharon's Laws," *Yediot*, January 31, 2018, https://www.yediot.co.il/articles/0,7340,L-5078841,00.html [Heb.].

[36] "Justice Minister to Radical Former Chief Justice: Your Path Leads to the Tyranny of the Minority," *The Jewish Press*, February 4, 2018, http://www.jewishpress.com/news/politics/justice-minister-to-radical-former-chief-justice-your-path-leads-to-the-tyranny-of-the-minority/2018/02/04/.

(BDS) movement. Polish authorities pass laws preventing protests during government rallies and prohibiting claims about Polish participation in the Holocaust. Venezuela and Hungary are among the many countries that are passing laws and constitutional amendments entrenching the rule of populist leaders. The Republican Party in the United States retains control of the House of Representatives largely through gerrymandering and laws that in practice limit voting by poorer people. Members of the majority party in the United States, Poland, Catalonia, and other jurisdictions are adopting measures that exclude minority parties from practical participation in legislative debates.

Right-wing populists in power are actively undermining constitutional commitments to secularism. Eastern European countries are increasing public support for Christianity. Israel is increasing public support for Orthodox Judaism. Mate details how under the banner of Hindutva, India is increasing public support for Hinduism. Muslim majority countries are increasing support for Islam. The Erdoğan administration is abandoning the historic Turkish constitutional commitment to aggressive secularism. This new sectarianism consists not only in public support for religious teachings and practices, but also in government efforts to enforce by law traditional gender roles and sexual practices. The Trump administration, for example, is providing religious conservatives with numerous exceptions from state laws and appointing justices to the federal courts committed to permitting states to once again restrict same-sex marriage and ban abortion.

Right-wing populists are fostering more ethnic, less cosmopolitan national identities. T. Alexander Aleinikoff and Michaela Hailbronner describe how the recent refugee crisis is prompting a resurgence of ethnic, racial, and religious forms of national identity. Anti-immigration appeals, Aleinikoff writes, "play into an overall narrative of anxiety and of a loss of control—of the nation's borders (and respect for its laws), of the characteristics of the nation's people, of the scope and shape of the national labor market and the welfare state."[37] Political leaders throughout the globe are increasingly prone to define citizenship by race, ethnicity, and religion. Trump speaks for a great many populists when he welcomes immigrants from white, Christian Norway, while scorning persons of color seeking to immigrate from the Caribbean or Africa. Comella's essay on the Catalonian secession illustrates how populist rebellions against nationalist identities take the form of ethnically based subnational identities rather than universally based cosmopolitan identities.

Independent courts are falling prey to this right-wing populist surge. Wojceich Sadurski's essay on Poland details how the PiS first paralyzed political opponents in the judiciary and then staged a takeover of that governing institution. Similar efforts to manipulate jurisdiction and staffing practices are taking place in countries as diverse as the United States, Venezuela, Israel, and Hungary. Unsurprisingly, allied courts support

---

[37] T. Alexander Aleinikoff, "Inherent Instability: Immigration and Constitutional Democracies," in *Constitutional Democracy in Crisis?*, 490.

right-wing efforts to weaken democratic freedoms and processes, facilitate sectarianism, and promote more ascriptive political identities.

The right-wing-populist record on broadly shared commercial prosperity is more ambiguous. Sadurski notes how the PiS in Poland maintains power in part through a generous provision of family support. Such support, however, tends to be limited by race and ethnicity. The chapters by King and Smith and by Mark Tushnet note that right-wing populists are hostile to welfare and other government programs that they perceive distribute benefits primarily to ethnic and racial minorities.

Economics is one obvious cause of the right-wing populist surge and the weakening of constitutional democracy across the globe. Sitaraman asserts, "In times of economic insecurity and anxiety, people might be more susceptible to anti-immigrant, anti-refugee, and racial animus."[38] "Populism," Issacharoff writes, "responds to the perceived failure of democratic regimes to protect the laboring classes from economic distortion. The combination of the economic downturn after 2008 and the impact of globalized trade on wages in the advanced industrial countries tarnished the legitimacy of democratic regimes as an insider's game, a means of institutionalizing elite prerogatives."[39] Numerous essays on particular regimes agree that populist appeals gain currency during economic hard times and are particularly powerful in the most economically depressed regions. Eric Posner and Jennifer Hochschild detail how economic concerns fuel right-wing populism in the United States. Hochschild observes that Trump supporters come from those parts of the United States experiencing high rates of addiction, high mortality rates, and low prospects of economic improvement. Hailbronner points to the economic foundations of ethnocultural political identities when asserting, "The European debt crisis management also marked the moment when many Europeans fell out of love with the idea of Europe as a post-national community of solidarity."[40] These demographics of the right-wing populist surge support David Law and Chien-Chih Lin's suggestion that constitutional democracy is an acquired taste of people whose bellies are full. Constitutional democracy is not gaining a foothold in China, Singapore, Hong Kong, and Japan, they claim, because regimes committed to bureaucratic authoritarianism are stable when they deliver a high degree of economic prosperity or, at least, economic growth.

Economics standing alone does not explain why hard times privilege efforts to activate *right-wing* populist identities. Tushnet points out that populism comes in right-wing and left-wing flavors. Religion offered foundations for the cosmopolitan view of citizenship championed by liberal constitutional democrats as well as the more ethnocentric world

---

[38] Sitaraman, "Economic Inequality and Constitutional Democracy," 538.

[39] Samuel Issacharoff, "Populism versus Democratic Governance," in *Constitutional Democracy in Crisis?*, 447

[40] Michaela Hailbronner, "Beyond Legitimacy: Europe's Crisis of Constitutional Democracy," in *Constitutional Democracy in Crisis?*, 277.

view underlying right-wing populism. Hirschl and Shachar speak of the "transnational nature of religious solidarity and advocacy."[41] Weiler reminds us that all that major religions teach that every person is made in the image of the Diety. Their chapters suggest other drivers of right-wing populist identities than mere economic downturns.

Several chapters support Robert Dahl's concern that constitutional democracies function best in homogenous societies[42] by suggesting that cosmopolitan identities based on commitments to universal human rights are too thin for most citizens. Sandy Levinson notes that Wilsonian self-determination, often seen as foundational for constitutional democracy, implies a people united by racial, religious, ethnic, or cultural norms. Most democratic citizens, Kim Lane Scheppele maintains, are localists who "see their neighbors and their nation as the horizon of politics."[43] Halmai claims that members of fragile democracies are particularly vulnerable to appeals based on race, religion, and ethnicity. He thinks the success of right-wing populism in Hungary is partly explained by persons in nations that lack strong democratic traditions being far more likely to have ethnonationalist identities than cosmopolitan identities. Ethnic divisions explain much electoral violence in sub-Saharan Africa and the problems launching democratic constitutionalism in that region. Members of long-established democracies are as vulnerable to these ethnonational appeals. Right-wing political entrepreneurs in the United States have historically used racial and ethnic fears to mobilize populists for some very anti-populist causes.

The relationships between globalization and contemporary constitutional projects may underlie right-wing populist surges. Globalization, the postwar constitutional paradigm, and transformative constitutionalism share commitments to cosmopolitan identities. The same global elites who sponsor neoliberal economic policies celebrate independent courts, often champion secularization, and favor formally inclusive policies, particularly when doing so rejects traditional gender and sexuality norms. Globalism in practice, however, has more often undermined than buttressed constitutional commitments to robust political freedoms and broadly shared commercial prosperity. These failures empower right-wing political entrepreneurs who by highlighting the political and normative affinities among globalization, the postwar constitutional paradigm, and transformative constitutionalism successfully channel opposition to the first into movements against the second and third.

Many persons who champion robust political freedoms, broadly shared commercial prosperity, secularism, inclusiveness, and independent courts as enthusiastically champion globalization. Globalization, the postwar constitutional paradigm, and transformative constitutionalism all emphasize cosmopolitan outlooks in which traditional national boundaries and identities matter less and universal values and practices matter more. Free

---

[41] Hirschl and Shachar, " 'Religious Talk' in Narratives of Membership," 520.

[42] Robert A. Dahl, *Democracy and Its Critics* (New Haven, CT: Yale University Press, 1989), 255–256.

[43] Kim Lane Scheppele, "The Party's Over," in *Constitutional Democracy in Crisis?*, 496.

markets are secular. They are formally indifferent to the race, gender, religion, ethnicity, and sexual orientation of buyers and sellers. Global markets might help achieve the ends of constitutional democracy. Tushnet speaks of "international social welfare constitutionalism" as the post-World War II liberal project, a project committed to "the increasing integration of national economies into a global economy" as a means for providing "the resources to support the social welfare component" of constitutional democracy.[44] Most transformative constitutions recognize the sovereignty of international law, including the international law that regulates globalized markets.

The relationship between globalization and contemporary constitutional developments has a much darker side. Many cosmopolitans are far more committed to globalization, independent courts, and secularism than robust political freedoms, broadly shared commercial prosperity, and more robust conceptions of inclusivity. Different cosmopolitan visions are easy to confuse, particularly when prominent political elites have incentives to sow confusion. In his acclaimed *Towards Juristocracy*, Hirschl asserts that a neoliberal commitment to transnational open markets was the central concern of those who inaugurated what was mistakenly labelled transformative constitutionalism. Proponents of the new constitutionalism were engaging in "hegemonic preservation" rather than social democracy or social transformation. Politically weakened global elites responding to the stirrings of populist politics, Hirschl claims, retreated into the judiciary in order to preserve existing commitments to a secular neoliberal economic order.[45] Alterio and Niembro provide a variation on this theme when discussing how the Mexican elites who championed transformative constitutionalism in practice proved far more interested in preserving a favorable climate for foreign investment than promoting broadly shared commercial prosperity. Schneiderman and Scheppele offer related accounts of global constitutional developments during the past twenty years. Schneiderman details how such regimes as Ecuador, Columbia, and South Africa simultaneously adopted a transformative constitution and signed neoliberal trade agreements, either because political leaders thought the two consistent or simply because they needed the foreign investment. Over time, the neoliberal trade agreements proved stronger, directly limiting national power to achieve transformative ends when those ends conflicted with foreign investors and indirectly limiting national power through debt practices that severely constrained domestic spending. Scheppele discusses how politics throughout the world increasingly pits "educated, urban and cosmopolitan elites against less-educated, rural and localist masses."[46] Globalization, in her view, is a project of both traditional left and right elites, who, concerned to attract and protect foreign investment, when faced with substantial

---

[44] Mark Tushnet, "Comparing Right-Wing and Left-Wing Populism," in *Constitutional Democracy in Crisis?*, 643.

[45] Hirschl, *Toward Juristocracy* (Cambridge, MA: Harvard University Press, 2004).

[46] Scheppele, "The Party's Over," 507.

foreign debts abandon commitments to broadly shared economic prosperity by adopting austerity budgets.

The resulting ambivalent and ambiguous relationship between the cosmopolitan commitments inherent in the postwar constitutional paradigm and transformative constitutionalism and the cosmopolitan commitments inherent in globalization facilitate right-wing ethnonational appeals while complicating the task of left-wing political entrepreneurs. All right-wing populist leaders must do is mobilize citizens against cosmopolitans and cosmopolitanism.[47] Political entrepreneurs on the left must mobilize citizens against some cosmopolitans but not others, and some versions of cosmopolitanism but not others. Conservative elites enjoy the relatively simple task of persuading less fortunate citizens that the same persons and principles responsible for the company leaving town are responsible for immigrants taking what few jobs remain and uprooting long-established cultural norms. If the problem is foreign influence, then foreigners should be prohibited from entering the country, and long-standing national practices, including traditional religious practices, should be restored. If the problem is cosmopolitan elites, then given the strong practical and theoretical connections between elite commitments to globalization, secularism, and inclusiveness, ordinary people when rejecting globalization should reject related commitments to secularism and inclusiveness. Or so the argument easily goes. More progressive political entrepreneurs have a more daunting task. They must first distinguish conservative and progressive versions of globalization that may not be obviously distinguishable for many persons. They must then distinguish the not-to-be-trusted cosmopolitan proponents of neoliberalism from the trusted cosmopolitan proponents of broadly shared commercial prosperity, secularism, and inclusively, even though those two camps are hardly mutually exclusive. Given the importance of quick soundbites in contemporary democratic politics, persons mobilizing ethnocentric political identities clearly have an easier task at present than those mobilizing cosmopolitan identities.

The Hollowing of Constitutional Democracy

Right-wing populists are succeeding by using legal forms. Vote totals for right-wing populists are increasing sharply, even in such countries as France and Australia, where they have not yet gained power. When right-wing populists gain power with only a minority of total votes cast, as in the United States, Hungary, Poland, and Catalonia, they do so playing by existing constitutional rules such as the Electoral College in the United States, which under certain conditions empower minority coalitions. When in power, right-wing populists largely follow the existing rules when passing new laws that restrict speech, entrench their power, restrict rival institutions, and discriminate against national

---

[47] While obscuring their complicity in globalized markets.

minorities, at least as those rules are interpreted by judiciaries staffed with right-wing populist allies. When right-wing coalitions do not have the power necessary to pass new laws under the existing constitution, they modify constitutional rules, including the constitutional rules for amending the national constitution. In Venezuela, both Hugo Chavez and Nicolas Maduro successfully called for constitutional conventions that provided legal foundations for their rule. Mexican elites repeatedly pass constitutional amendments without much public notice that undercut transformative provisions in the national constitution.

The substitution of legal form for military coup as a means for weakening constitutional democracy is spawning a new vocabulary. David Landau coined the phrase "abusive constitutionalism" to describe how "leaders can use legal devices normally associated with democratic constitutionalism to destroy a democratic constitutional order."[48] Varol speaks of "stealth authoritarianism" when discussing how political leaders in Turkey and elsewhere "use the law to entrench the status quo, insulate the incumbents from meaningful democratic challenges, and pave the way for the creation of a dominant-party or one-party state."[49] Manoj Mate speaks of "constitutional erosion" when discussing how "the increased resort to and use of religiosity in elections and governance [is] continuing to weaken and undermine secularism as a constitutional and governing principle."[50] "Constitutional hardball," a term Tushnet coined, occurs when politicians violate long-standing conventions about constitutional practice, even when they stay within the letter of the law.[51] Jack Balkin suggests that one consequence of constitutional hardball is "constitutional rot," "a degradation of constitutional norms that may operate over long periods of time."[52] Scheppele speaks of the "Frankenstate," "an abusive form of rule, created by combining perfectly reasonable democratic institutions in monstrous ways."[53] The end result of these practices is "authoritarian constitutionalism," "a system of government that combines reasonably free and fair elections with a moderate degree of repressive control of expression and limits on personal freedom,"[54] and "illiberal democracy," "an elected government (that) fails to respect the substantive elements of democracy."[55]

---

[48] David E. Landau, "Constitution-Making and Authoritarianism in Venezuela: The First Time as Tragedy, the Second as Farce," in *Constitutional Democracy in Crisis?*, 174.

[49] Ozan O. Varol, "Stealth Authoritarianism," *Iowa Law Review* 100 (2015): 1673, 1678–1679.

[50] Manoj Mate, "Constitutional Erosion and the Challenge to Secular Democracy in India," in *Constitutional Democracy in Crisis?*, 380.

[51] Mark Tushnet, "Constitutional Hardball," *John Marshall Law Review* 37 (2004): 523–554.

[52] Jack M. Balkin, "Constitutional Crisis and Constitutional Rot," in *Constitutional Democracy in Crisis?*, 17.

[53] Kim Lane Scheppele, "Not Your Father's Authoritarianism: The Creation of the 'Frankenstate,'" *American Political Science Association European Political Sociology News*, Winter 2003, 5.

[54] Mark Tushnet, "Authoritarian Constitutionalism," *Cornell Law Review* 100 (2015): 391, 391.

[55] Jean d'Asoremont, "Legitimacy of Governments in the Age of Democracy," *New York University Journal of International Law and Policy* 38 (2006): 877, 879.

What unites all these practices, Sujit Choudhry notes, is that they challenge the constitutional norms that constrain how constitutional powers are exercised rather than plainly violate the constitutional text. Regimes, he points out, experience democratic backsliding when "a democratically elected government or president uses legal means to manipulate rules and institutions" in ways not sanctioned by past practice "to remain in power in future electoral cycles, *inter alia* with respect to electoral system design, election administration, political party regulation, presidential term limits, civil and political liberties, independent institutions such as constitutional courts and agencies, and media regulation."[56] Unlike a coup d'état, democratic backsliding does not occur overnight. Rather, democratic institutions are weakened by a series of apparently constitutional moves, often made with little publicity, each of which may seem technical, innocuous, and even progressive in isolation.

Constitutional and legal barriers provide some defense against these efforts to weaken constitutional democracy. Dixon and Gauja point to mandatory voting laws and electoral rules limiting representation of minority parties as reducing the power of right-wing populists in Australia. Putative nonvoters, they observe, are likely to be moderates less prone to support extremist parties than their more politically engaged neighbors. Richard Albert and Michael Pal celebrate the hard-to-amend Constitution of Canada and the maintenance of the bipartisan Canadian Electoral Commission for preventing partisan forces from subverting Canadian democracy. Scheppele looks to the constitutional restrictions on extremist parties ratified in Germany. Klug and Choudhry note how independent courts prevented ANC factions from keeping Jacob Zuma in power.

Whether law can hold back strong populist surges is nevertheless doubtful. A constitutional democracy that rests on forcing apathetic citizens to vote is unlikely to provide the goods promised by either the postwar constitutional paradigm or transformative constitutionalism. Institutional protections that rest on constitutional norms and conventions can be circumvented or abandoned. Sadurski notes how the PiS in Poland undermined the nonpartisan election commission that is such a democratic bulwark in Canada. Nonpartisan commissions are ineffective in Africa and most of Latin America. The same constitutional provisions that inhibit right-wing populist efforts to gain power help lock in right-wing populists in power. While Albert and Pal praise the hard-to-amend Constitution of Canada as a bulwark against right-wing populism, Posner regards the hard-to-amend Constitution of the United States as one cause of the constitutional ills in that regime. The behavior of Erdoğan's Justice and Development Party illustrates how factions may not show their true authoritarian colors until they have the political power that immunizes them from constitutional bans on undemocratic coalitions. Courts are

---

[56] Sujit Choudhry, "Will Democracy Die in Darkness? Calling Autocracy by Its Name," in *Constitutional Democracy in Crisis?*, 577.

bulwarks only until they are captured by political forces, which as many essays suggest, happens sooner rather than later during right-wing populist surges.

The history of constitutional democracy suggests that parchment constitutional barriers do not hold against strong political forces. More progressive constitutionalists are as likely as right-wing populists to engage in political hardball and change the rules of the game when doing so will best achieve their political vision. The tactics the Republican Party used to pass the post-Civil War Amendments freeing slaves and granting fundamental rights to persons of color included refusing to seat southern delegations in Congress and ignoring state decisions rescinding earlier ratifications of those constitutional amendments. Former Confederates and Democrats bitterly complained about these maneuvers, which would be considered the paradigmatic example of abusive constitutionalism had the cause of racial equality not triumphed. The cause of social democracy and transformative constitutionalism during the 1990s was advanced by new constitutions and new laws that sharply shifted power from legislators to courts. Social conservatives in good faith describe such liberal constitutional decisions as *Roe v. Wade* as being as outrageous an interpretation of the national constitution as progressives in good faith describe many constitutional decisions presently being handed down by tribunals packed with persons sympathetic to right-wing populist causes. Constitutional rules and forms inhibit the formation of strong political movements and delay their success,[57] but the history of constitutional democracy indicates that strong political movements that gain and retain power for any significant period of time find ways to overcome existing constitutional barriers.

A substantial number of citizens in constitutional democracies are rejecting the postwar constitutional paradigm and transformative constitutionalism. Political entrepreneurs promising a more sectarian regime that will privilege persons on the basis of their ancestry, race, and religion, and will enforce more traditional gender and sexuality norms, are gaining an increased share of the vote across the globe. Right-wing populists in office who curtail democratic liberties and undermine independent courts remain electorally popular, in part because these measures are often directed at minorities and in part because right-wing populists reshape the electoral universe to privilege their re-election. Still, even without electoral manipulation, the number of voters supporting the Trumps, Orbans, and Netanyahus of the world will exercise substantial influence on governmental practices in a constitutional democracy, no matter what the particular constitutional rules. The real challenge for the persons committed to robust political freedoms, broadly shared commercial prosperity, secularism, inclusiveness, and independent courts is finding political ways to reduce the number of right-wing populists, not finding legal ways to reduce their present influence.

---

[57] Jeffrey K. Tulis and Nicole Mellow, *Legacies of Losing in American Politics* (Chicago: University of Chicago Press, 2018).

Executive Power

Many chapters in this volume document a sharp rise in executive power. Regimes in which right-wing populists are ruling have transferred considerable authority to presidents and prime ministers. Chief executives in Turkey, Venezuela, Hungary, Mexico, South Africa, and the United States gained substantial formal and informal powers during the twenty-first century. Law and Lin discuss the rise of bureaucratic authoritarianism in such East Asian regimes as China, Singapore, Hong Kong, and Japan. The chapters on France and Canada detail how executive power is increasing in regimes where right-wing populism has been held at bay. Roussellier notes that the French now elect the national legislature immediately after electing the president, a practice that substantially augments executive power by practically guaranteeing more supportive representatives. Gargarella observes that hyper-presidentialism in Latin America "puts into question, if not directly undermines, the very logic of the system of check and balances."[58] Weiler and Hailbronner point to ongoing transfers of power from legislatures to executives in the European Union. Executives dominate constitutional politics in sub-Saharan Africa. Constitutional crises in that region are over the transfer of executive power. The factions Gathii discusses spend little energy fighting over control of the national legislature.

Legislative power is weakening even where executive power is not increasing. "The dysfunctionality of the legislative branches," Issacharoff asserts, "is a plague upon almost all houses of democracy."[59] Erin Delaney observes that matters the United Kingdom once resolved in Parliament are now being resolved by national referenda. "Referendum politics," she writes, "have introduced the possibility of shifting from a system of parliamentary sovereignty to one of popular sovereignty."[60] Klug documents the enfeebled capacity of the South African Parliament to investigate and punish executive corruption.

These changes in the actual institutional allocation of constitutional authority suggest that "constitutional dictatorship" should replace "democratic deficits" and the American obsession with the "counter-majoritarian difficulty" as the central concern of constitutional theory. Clinton Rossiter coined the phrase "constitutional dictatorship" in 1948 when discussing the need during a crisis to concentrate power in an executive, expand government authority, and narrow individual rights.[61] What Rossiter thought a temporary form of government is becoming permanent. Ellen Kennedy points out how contemporary efforts to shift powers to executives bear a disturbing resemblance to analogous events in Weimar Germany, both in their practice and justification. Enhanced executive

---

[58] Gargarella, "Latin America: Constitutions in Trouble," 185.

[59] Issacharoff, "Populism versus Democratic Governance," 450.

[60] Erin F. Delaney, "Brexit Optimism and British Constitutional Renewal," in *Constitutional Democracy in Crisis?*, 193.

[61] Clinton L. Rossiter, *Constitutional Dictatorship: Crisis Government in Modern Democracies* (Westport, CT: Greenwood Press, 1948).

power has become central to the principles and exercise of governance in both populist and non-populist regimes. Right-wing populists celebrate executive power because they believe a united people should be represented by a single executive (and a single party). Legislatures, prone to factionalism, are poorer vehicles for representing anti-pluralist sentiments. Non-populists appreciate how presidential power is often a means for effective governance. Robert Percival observes that nations with unified governments are far more likely to adopt strong environmental policies than governments in which power is divided. The presidency may also be the institution of choice for transformative constitutionalists given Stephen Skowronek's observation that the presidency is the most disruptive institution established by a national constitution.[62]

Constitutional dictatorship is also a consequence of "ordinary" politics at the turn of the twenty-first century. What Rossiter thought were temporary conditions are now permanent. Oren Gross details how "the proliferation of permanent states of emergency and the normalization of exceptional national security powers within ordinary legal systems of states" has sharply expanded executive power in France, the United Kingdom, and the United States.[63] The drug war, a different kind of emergency, is the vehicle by which executive power is expanding in Mexico. Executives have been the beneficiary of the increased place of foreign policy on political agendas. Harold Koh's observation that "the American president almost always wins in matters of foreign affairs due to the combination of executive initiative, congressional acquiescence and judicial tolerance" seems true of all constitutional democracies.[64] Transnational and international organizations privilege national executives. Hailbronner, Weiler, and Schneiderman document how the European Union and such organizations as the International Monetary Fund operate in ways that increase executive power at the expense of legislators, who are often confined to ratifying (some) agreements made by the president or prime minister.

"Democratic deficits" that are independent of concerns with constitutional dictatorship and the "counter-majoritarian difficulty" are becoming less pressing constitutional problems in light of the new judicial functions in an increasing number of regimes. Fewer and fewer judiciaries across the globe are playing a counter-majoritarian role, defending constitutional rights against elected officials, or a hegemonic preservation role, buttressing the power of weakened political coalitions. *Bush v. Gore*,[65] the case in which the Republican judicial appointees on the Supreme Court of the United States declared the Republican candidate to have won the 2000 national election, is replacing *Brown*

---

[62] Stephen Skowronek, *The Politics President Make: Leadership from John Adams to Bill Clinton*, revised ed. (Cambridge, MA: Harvard University Press, 1997).

[63] Oren Gross, "The Normal Exception," in *Constitutional Democracy in Crisis?*, 585.

[64] Harold H. Koh, "Why the President (Almost) Always Wins in Foreign Affairs: Lessons of the Iran-Contra Affair, *Yale Law Journal* 97 (1988): 1255–1342.

[65] 531 U.S. 98 (2000).

v. Board of Education[66] as the paradigmatic instance of judicial power. Courts staffed by right-wing populists serve as arms of executive power. Landau discusses how the Supreme Tribunal of Justice in Venezuela "has become a reliable partner of the regime in tilting the playing field."[67] Sadurski details how the Constitutional Tribunal in Poland was first paralyzed and then converted into a reliable supporter of PiS constitutional ambitions. Similar patterns appear in India, France, Turkey, and the United States. Gathii details how courts in sub-Saharan Africa tend to support executives seeking to circumvent constitutionally mandated term limits. South Africa is the rare exception of a regime in which courts remained sufficiently independent to frustrate and eventually help defeat a corrupt leader's attempt to retain power, perhaps because the ANC was internally divided on the Zuma presidency.

Constitution dictatorship is problematic, not simply a problem. Transformative constitutional projects both need and fear strong executive power. The New Deal in the United States illustrates how national policy made in large part by a single executive may be the best vehicle for promoting effective governance and transformative reforms. Roussellier celebrates the strengthening of the French executive precisely because strong executives deliver goods that weak executives cannot. Subnational units are poor providers of healthcare when they are subject to races to the bottom.[68] The more clashing the interests that participate in the making of laws on water rights, they more likely the resulting laws will be an incoherent log roll rather than a coherent effort to provide persons with a basic necessity. National policy made in large part by a single executive is also likely to violate the commitment to human dignity that underlies both the postwar constitutional paradigm and transformative constitutionalism. The energetic federal government that won World War II also removed Japanese-Americans from the West Coast and consigned them to camps that were little better than prisons. The Obama administration when fighting the war against terrorism maintained many policies that liberals complained violated fundamental human rights when adopted by the Bush II administration.[69] Precedents for strong executive power created by good presidents are obviously more than capable of being abused by bad presidents.

Fractionated power is a form of constitutional insurance.[70] Separating executive and legislative functions, bicameralism, judicial review, federalism, and broad-based political parties are means for curbing transformative political projects from the Left and the

---

[66] 347 U.S. 483 (1954).

[67] Landau, "Constitution-Making and Authoritarianism in Venezuela," 166.

[68] See David Brian Robertson, "The Bias of American Federalism: The Limits of Welfare-State Development in the Progressive Era," *Journal of Policy History* 1 (1989): 261–291.

[69] See Jack Goldsmith, *Power and Constraint: The Accountable Presidency after 9/11* (New York: W.W. Norton, 2012).

[70] See Tom Ginsburg, *Judicial Review in New Democracies: Constitutional Courts in Asian Cases* (New York: Cambridge University Press, 2003).

Right. Courts in regimes where power is fractionated have a good record on secularism, often making decisions that undermine traditional gender and sexual norms. With important exceptions, however, courts and other governing institutions where power is fractionated do not promote the redistributional projects necessary for broadly shared prosperity and greater participation by ordinary citizens in democratic governance.[71] National majorities bent on changing the status quo in a society where power is not centralized confront numerous veto gates that slow down and sometimes thwart their projects. Legislatures refuse to fund new presidential initiatives. Courts declare sectarian provisions unconstitutional. Localities pass environmental regulations being abandoned at the national level. Incrementalism is the name of the game in such regimes where changing the status quo can be done only with extraordinary difficulty and extraordinary majorities.

Proponents of robust political freedoms, broadly shared commercial prosperity, secularism, inclusiveness, and independent courts rarely regard the status quo in their regime to be a normatively reasonable state of affairs that should be adjusted only incrementally. The persons who inaugurated transformative constitutional projects in South Africa, Ecuador, Hungary, and throughout the world hoped to reform substantially national constitutional practices. Doing so requires strong united government. Jim Crow was abolished in the United States only when assaulted by all three branches of the national government willing to weaken the governing capacity of subnational units substantially. Social democracy is also best implemented by a strong unified state whose different institutions share common commitments rather than divided governments where institutions controlled by one faction attempt to interfere with policies made by institutions controlled by a different faction. Consider Sven Steinmo's observation that the American welfare state would have been vastly improved "if Presidents Franklin Roosevelt, Harry Truman, John Kennedy, and Lyndon Johnson could have called the Democratic party leadership together, and with this small group of elites, could have designed and implemented social welfare policies . . . without needing to tailor these programs to the demands or objections of particular members of Congress and the interest groups they represented."[72] The Goldilocks division of power that is just right is hardly obvious. Given their shared reformist or transformative ambitions, proponents of the postwar constitutional paradigm or transformative constitutionalism may be closer to right-wing populists on the precise allocation of constitutional power than prominent persons on all sides suspect.

---

[71] See Ran Hirschl, "Constitutionalism, Judicial Review, and Progressive Change: A Rejoinder to McClain and Fleming," *Texas Law Review* 84 (2005): 471–507.

[72] Sven H. Steinmo, "American Exceptionalism Reconsidered: Culture or Institutions?," in *The Dynamics of American Politics: Approaches and Interpretations*, ed. Lawrence C. Dodd and Calvin Jillson (Boulder, CO: Westview Press, 1994), 127.

More Politics, Less Law

The constitutional projects discussed in this volume depend too much on constitutional law and too little on constitutional politics. Proponents of robust political freedoms, broadly shared commercial prosperity, secularism, inclusiveness, and independent courts ratified strong constitutional provisions, crafted powerful judicial decisions, and produced ingenious constitutional theories, but paid less attention to the political foundations necessary for maintaining a regime with those commitments. Establishing those political foundations requires more attention to ordinary politics, legislatures, and governance than given by leading champions of the postwar constitutional paradigm and transformative constitutionalism. What might awkwardly be described as thickened progressive cosmopolitan constitutionalism must be sold politically, not defended legally. The postwar constitutional paradigm and transformative constitutionalism are legislative projects that can be aided by supportive courts rather than judicial projects in which elected officials play minor roles. The central problems of these democratic constitutionalisms more often concern the governing arrangements that best produce and maintain robust political freedoms, broadly shared commercial prosperity, secularism, inclusiveness, and independent courts than the precise legal expression of these commitments.

Persons committed to some version of thickened progressive cosmopolitan constitutionalism must find ways to shape the political identities that foster society-wide commitments to robust political freedoms, broadly shared commercial prosperity, secularism, and inclusiveness. Populist identity is fluid. Tushnet distinguishes between left-wing and right-wing populisms, but as sharp distinctions do not characterize the persons prone to left-wing and right-wing populist appeals. Many people appear to have general populist sensibilities that under different political conditions and inspired by different political entrepreneurs may be mobilized for either more liberal or more conservative projects. The same person may be induced to support different causes if mobilized into politics as a union member or as a Christian conservative. More than a few Americans in 2016 supported Bernie Sanders in the Democratic Party primary and then considered supporting Donald Trump in the national presidential election. Former Communists in France, Roussellier notes, are supporting Marine Le Pen.

Political entrepreneurs promoting left-wing populist identities should avoid several traps. Debating whether challenges to right-wing populism should mobilize racial minorities or the white working class plays into conservative efforts to activate ethnocentric political identities by structuring politics so that conflicts are perceived as being between different groups of less fortunate persons.[73] The challenge for progressive political actors is finding commonalities among different groups of less affluent citizens so

---

[73] See Ira Katznelson, *City Trenches: Urban Politics and the Patterning of Class in the United States* (Chicago: University of Chicago Press, 1982).

that they may be mobilized against those who possess a disproportionate share of social goods. Progressive campaigns against globalization are not the cure for what ails the Left. Globalization is here to stay. Proponents of broadly shared commercial prosperity must find ways to dispense better the benefits of international trade rather than pretend that their regime can successfully become an economic island. Constitutional commitments to secularism should not rule out efforts to foster certain religious identities. Roger Williams, James Madison, and other early champions of constitutional secularism promoted a sharp separation of state and church to prevent politics from corrupting religion. Religious commitments to the equal humanity of all persons and the obligation to share resources fit well within the postwar constitutional paradigm and the transformative constitutional project. The success of Martin Luther King and Desmond Tutu suggests that reformist and transformative constitutionalism fares best when partly identified with prominent religious figures.

The judiciary is the least promising branch for promoting thickened progressive cosmopolitan constitutionalisms. Courts support liberal or progressive constitutional causes only when electoral politics is largely controlled by liberals or progressives,[74] or when politics is divided between two non-ideological parties, both of whose elite wings are committed to liberal or progressive constitutional projects.[75] Neither is true in the vast majority of constitutional democracies at the moment. When politics is as polarized as in the United States and most other constitutional democracies, political movements must first gain control of the political system by election before gaining control over national judiciaries through appointments. Judiciaries have important limitations as reformist and transformative actors, particularly when asked to perform solo. Institutional capacity is one concern. Justices are far better at inhibiting than promoting government action. National judiciaries have more success when forbidding bans on abortion than when distributing water rights. Institutional staffing is a second concern. The elites who become judges are more sympathetic to the secular and inclusive commitments of the postwar constitutional paradigm and transformative constitutionalism than to the redistributive commitments. Justices in some countries have successfully nudged elected officials to make policies that help provide people with basic necessities, but courts are likely to do little to secure broadly shared commercial prosperity and the full conditions of political inclusivity in the absence of supportive legislation.[76]

Legislatures that control the power of the purse must take primary responsibility for ensuring broadly shared commercial prosperity. Social democracies and transformative constitutional orders require the intelligent allocation of resources that in turn requires

---

[74] See Lucas A. Powe, *The Warren Court and American Politics* (Cambridge, MA: Harvard University Press, 2000).

[75] See Mark A. Graber, "Judicial Supremacy and the Structure of Partisan Conflict," *Indiana Law Review* 50 (2016): 141–180.

[76] See Mark Tushnet, *Weak Courts, Strong Rights: Judicial Review and Social Welfare Rights in Comparative Constitutional Law* (Princeton, NJ: Princeton University Press, 2007).

a committed, active legislature with the power of the purse and the knowledge of local conditions. Courts may declare rights to resources and forbid discrimination against women, but elected officials must develop the plans that provide people with food, clothing, shelter, and education, and overcome the barriers that inhibit full gender equality in their regimes. An enfeebled legislative politics fosters an enfeebled constitutional regime. Transformative constitutionalism, Alterio and Niembro insist, must be rooted in strong political parties and the sort of deliberative participation that enables citizens to develop the identities and establish the skills necessary for constitutional democracy. This is a constitutional politics that privileges legislation and elections rather than one that privileges litigation campaigns.

Overreliance on judiciaries may weaken the political foundations of the postwar constitutional paradigm and transformative constitutionalism. Halmai writes, "legalistic constitutionalism falls short, reducing the Constitution to an elite instrument, especially in countries with weak civil societies and weak political party systems that undermine a robust constitutional democracy based on the idea of civic self-government." The combination of exceptionally active courts and "the rules and institutions of economic globalization," Schneiderman points out, substantially "narrows the policy space available to citizens."[77] A too thickened progressive cosmopolitan constitutional democracy, enforced by independent courts interpreting both national constitutions and international law, risks leaving citizens with too little to vote on.

The crucial role broadly shared commercial prosperity plays in contemporary constitutional projects places governance at the heart of constitutional politics. Constitutional commitments are not self-enforcing, particularly those concerned with political economy that require governing officials have particular skills as well as the relevant commitments. Issuing marriage certificates to same-sex couples is far easier than determining the tax rate that best promotes shared commercial prosperity or addressing the broader social issues that limit the capacity of women to participate as equals in public life. Some governance questions concern constitutional design. Gargarella points out that government institutions designed in the nineteenth century are not particularly effective at securing the positive rights established during the late twentieth century. Other governance questions concern the broader culture. A culture that disdains expertise and political experience is likely at best to generate such inexperienced political leaders as Emmanuel Macron, whose capacity for campaigning may exceed his capacity for governing, and at worse to generate such political leaders as Donald Trump, who displays no interest in or regard for an evidence-based domestic or foreign policy. Both design and culture questions go to what Sitaraman calls mismatch, a set of constitutional practices unlikely to generate the

---

[77] David Schneiderman, "Disabling Constitutional Capacity: Global Economic Law and Democratic Decline," in *Constitutional Democracy in Crisis?*, 551.

shared economic prosperity that is both a background condition for and an element of constitutional democracy.

Woodrow Wilson's Constitutional Democracy Revisited

Whether a global crisis of constitutional democracy exists in 2018 depends on the state of constitutional democracy in 1918, when Woodrow Wilson announced a constitutional commitment to making "the world safe for democracy." Wilson's democracy was characterized by severe restrictions on political dissent, sharp limits on the franchise, racial segregation, and few, if any protections, for most rights enumerated in contemporary constitutions.[78] Constitutional identity, Levinson points out, was rooted in race, ethnicity, and religion (as well as in gender and sexual orientation). During the past ten years many constitutional democracies have drifted or aggressively moved from the constitutional projects articulated by the Constitution of South Africa, the decisions of the Supreme Court of Hungary, and much contemporary constitutional theory to Woodrow Wilson's constitutional vision. Democratic rights are being curtailed, although not abandoned. Racial, ethnic, and gender barriers to full citizenship are being resurrected, even as no regime is returning to the Jim Crow American South. Social democracies and transformative projects are being discarded in favor of a narrower set of rights enjoyed by a narrower set of persons. Many right-wing populists celebrate these developments as restoring fundamental democratic and constitutional principles. If, however, the postwar constitutional paradigm and transformative constitutionalism are superior forms of democratic constitutionalism, then movements toward Wilsonian democracy mark what Balkin calls "constitutional rot," and other commentators describe as "democratic decline," constitutional retrogression" and the like. If Wilsonian regimes are not constitutional democracies at all by contemporary standards, then this ongoing movement toward Wilsonianism presents a global crisis of constitutional democracy.

Balkin and other contributors maintain, "A constitutional crisis occurs when there is a serious danger that a constitution is about to fail at its central task."[79] The central task of thickened progressive cosmopolitan constitutions was to reform or transform "a country's political and social institutions and power relationships in a democratic, participatory, and egalitarian direction." These projects failings may not produce the "anarchy, violence or civil war" that Balkin fears,[80] but simply different kinds of constitutional orders, whether they resemble the right-wing populist regimes of Eastern Europe or the bureaucratic authoritarian regimes that are taking root in East Asia. The weakening commitments across the globe to robust political freedoms, broadly shared commercial prosperity, secularism, inclusiveness, and independent courts provide strong evidence that the

---

[78] Hochschild's essay warns us to beware of "false nostalgia" for an imagined democratic past. Hochschild, "What's New? What's Next?" 100.

[79] Balkin, "Constitutional Crisis and Constitutional Rot," 14.

[80] Ibid.

postwar constitutional paradigm and transformative constitutionalism are in crisis, even as the failure of people to riot in the street suggests that no particular constitutional order is failing in a more narrow sense.

The year 1918 is a good reference point for thinking about a related global crisis of constitutional democracy. World War I resulted from a failure of governance. Barbara Tuchman famously detailed the series of diplomatic blunders that embroiled most European nations in brutal military combat for four years.[81] Contemporary constitutional democracies seem vulnerable to similar tragedies with higher stakes. The right-wing populist movements gaining traction in numerous constitutional democracies are often led by persons with limited political experience, limited interest in policy, limited global knowledge, and limited commitments to the self-restraint necessary to secure good relationships among nations. The president of the United States, a nation that exercises grossly disproportionate influence on almost all matters of global policy, brags about nuclear weapons, denies climate change, and regularly insults other world leaders. Percival's observation that constitutional democracies respond to crises better than they anticipate crises is frightening, given the possible scope of future environmental, nuclear, and public health disasters. The failures of governance responsible for World War I cost approximately 11 million lives. The costs of an environmental cataclysm, nuclear war, or public health catastrophe brought on by contemporary problems of constitutional governance are likely to be geometrically higher.

---

[81] Barbara Tuchman, *The Guns of August* (New York: MacMillan, 1962).

List of Contributors

Richard Albert is a professor of law at the University of Texas Law School

T. Alexander Aleinikoff is University Professor and director of the Zolberg Institute on Migration and Mobility at The New School, New York

Ana Micaela Alterio is an associate professor at the ITAM (Instituto Tecnológico Autónomo de México)

Jack M. Balkin is the Knight Professor of Constitutional Law and the First Amendment at Yale Law School

Sujit Choudhry is the I. Michael Heyman Professor of Law at the University of California, Berkeley, School of Law and the Director of the Center for Constitutional Transitions

Victor Ferreres Comella is a professor of constitutional law at Pompeu Fabra University, Barcelona

Erin F. Delaney is a professor of law at Northwestern University Pritzker School of Law

Rosalind Dixon is a professor of law at UNSW Sydney

Zachary Elkins is an associate professor in the Department of Government at the University of Texas at Austin

Roberto Gargarella is a professor of law at Universidad Torcuato di Tella, Buenos Aires and at the Universidad de Buenos Aires (UBA)

James Thuo Gathii is the Wing-Tat Lee Chair of International Law at Loyola University Chicago School of Law

Anika Gauja is an associate professor of politics at the University of Sydney

Tom Ginsburg is the Leo Spitz Professor of International Law and a professor of political science at the University of Chicago

Mark A. Graber is University System of Maryland Regents Professor at the University of Maryland Francis King Carey School of Law

Oren Gross is the Irving Younger Professor of Law at the University of Minnesota Law School

Michaela Hailbronner is a postdoctoral fellow at the University of Münster

Gábor Halmai is a professor and chair of comparative constitutional law at the European University Institute, Florence

Ran Hirschl is a professor of political science and law at the University of Toronto and the Alexander von Humboldt Professor of Comparative Constitutionalism at the University of Göttingen

Jennifer Hochschild is the H.L. Jayne Professor of Government and a professor of African and African American studies at Harvard University

Aziz Z. Huq is the Frank and Bernice J. Greenberg Professor of Law at the University of Chicago Law School

Samuel Issacharoff is the Bonnie and Richard Reiss Professor of Constitutional Law at New York University School of Law

Ellen Kennedy is an emerita professor of political science at the University of Pennsylvania

Desmond King is the Andrew W. Mellon Professor of American Government at the University of Oxford and Fellow, Nuffield College, Oxford

Heinz Klug is the Evjue-Bascom Professor in Law at the University of Wisconsin Law School, Madison and Visiting Professor at the University of the Witwatersrand School of Law.

David Landau is the Mason Ladd Professor at Florida State University College of Law

David S. Law is the Charles Nagel Chair of Constitutional Law and Political Science at Washington University in St. Louis and the Sir Y.K. Pao Chair in Public Law at the University of Hong Kong

Sanford Levinson is the W. St. John Garwood and W. St. John Garwood Jr. Centennial Chair in Law at the University of Texas Law School and professor of government at the University of Texas at Austin

Chien-Chih Lin is an assistant research professor at the Institutum Iurisprudentiae of Academia Sinica, Taipei

Manoj Mate is a visiting scholar at Harvard Law School's East Asian Legal Studies Program

Roberto Niembro is a professor of constitutional law at ITAM (Instituto Tecnológico Autónomo de México)

Michael Pal is an associate professor of law at the University of Ottawa Faculty of Common Law

Robert V. Percival is the Robert F. Stanton Professor of Law and director of the Environmental Law Program at the University of Maryland Carey School of Law

Eric A. Posner is the Kirkland & Ellis Distinguished Service Professor of Law and Arthur and Esther Kane Research Chair at the University of Chicago Law School

Nicolas Roussellier is an assistant professor of political history at Sciences Po, Paris

Yaniv Roznai is a senior lecturer at the Radzyner Law School of the Interdisciplinary Center (IDC), Herzliya

Wojciech Sadurski is the Challis Professor of Jurisprudence at the University of Sydney School of Law and a professor at the Centre for Europe of the University of Warsaw

Kim Lane Scheppele is the Laurance S. Rockefeller Professor of Sociology and International Affairs in the Woodrow Wilson School and the University Center for Human Values at Princeton University

David Schneiderman is a professor of law and political science at the University of Toronto

Ayelet Shachar is the director of the Max Planck Institute for Religious and Ethnic Diversity, Göttingen, and a professor of law and political science at the University of Toronto

Ganesh Sitaraman is a professor of law at Vanderbilt Law School

Rogers M. Smith is the Christopher H. Browne Distinguished Professor of Political Science at the University of Pennsylvania

Mark Tushnet is the William Nelson Cromwell Professor of Law at Harvard Law School

Ozan O. Varol is a professor of law at Lewis & Clark Law School, Portland

J.H.H. Weiler is University Professor at the New York University School of Law

Acknowledgments

The American baseball player Yogi Berra on "Yogi Berra Night" profusely thanked the sponsors for "making this night necessary." We as profusely thank and acknowledge the many people who thought this book necessary. The authors of the individual chapters made every deadline within reasonable parameters so that we could produce a timely volume. Our editor, Jamie Berezin, associate editor David Lipp, and the other members of Oxford University Press, most notably John Louth, gave us sound advice and dedicated themselves to the publication of this volume. Sue McCarty and the University of Maryland Carey Law School library staff did a fabulous job standardizing the footnotes. Balamurugan Rajendran deftly managed the production of this volume. Brooke Smith was a superb copyeditor. Our spouses and families tolerated our constant refrain that this latest project we are working on is really necessary.

Index

Figures, notes, and tables are indicated by f, n, and t following the page numbers.